RUSSIAN LITERATURE

This is the essential new guide to Russian literature, combining authority and innovation in coverage ranging from medieval manuscripts to the internet and social media. With contributions from thirty-four world-leading scholars, it offers a fresh approach to literary history, not as one integral narrative but as multiple parallel histories. Each of its four strands tells a story of Russian literature according to a defined criterion: Movements, Mechanisms, Forms, and Heroes. At the same time, six clusters of shorter themed essays suggest additional perspectives and criteria for further study and research. In dialogue, these histories invite a multiplicity of readings, both within and across the narrative strands. In an age of shifting perspectives on Russia, and on national literatures more widely, this open but easily navigable volume enables readers to engage with both traditional literary concerns and radical reconceptualisations of Russian history and culture.

SIMON FRANKLIN is Emeritus Professor of Slavonic Studies at the University of Cambridge. His recent books include *The Russian Graphosphere, 1450–1850* (Cambridge University Press, 2019), winner of the ASEEES/USC Prize for an outstanding monograph in literary and cultural studies, and *Information and Empire: Mechanisms of Communication in Russia, 1600–1850* (co-edited with Katherine Bowers, 2017).

REBECCA REICH is Associate Professor of Russian Literature and Culture at the University of Cambridge. She is the author of *State of Madness: Psychiatry, Literature, and Dissent after Stalin* (2018). She is also Consultant Editor for Russia, East-Central Europe, and Eurasia at the *Times Literary Supplement*.

EMMA WIDDIS is Professor of Slavonic Studies at the University of Cambridge. Her publications include *Socialist Senses: Film, Feeling and the Soviet Subject* (2017), *National Identity in Russian Culture: An Introduction* (co-edited with Simon Franklin, Cambridge University Press, 2004), and *Visions of a New Land: Soviet Film from the Revolution to the Second World War* (2012).

THE NEW
CAMBRIDGE HISTORY
OF RUSSIAN LITERATURE

*

Edited by

SIMON FRANKLIN

University of Cambridge

REBECCA REICH

University of Cambridge

EMMA WIDDIS

University of Cambridge

CAMBRIDGE
UNIVERSITY PRESS

CAMBRIDGE
UNIVERSITY PRESS

Shaftesbury Road, Cambridge CB2 8EA, United Kingdom

One Liberty Plaza, 20th Floor, New York, NY 10006, USA

477 Williamstown Road, Port Melbourne, VIC 3207, Australia

314–321, 3rd Floor, Plot 3, Splendor Forum, Jasola District Centre,
New Delhi – 110025, India

103 Penang Road, #05–06/07, Visioncrest Commercial, Singapore 238467

Cambridge University Press is part of Cambridge University Press & Assessment,
a department of the University of Cambridge.

We share the University's mission to contribute to society through the pursuit of
education, learning and research at the highest international levels of excellence.

www.cambridge.org
Information on this title: www.cambridge.org/9781108493482

DOI: 10.1017/9781108655620

First published 2024

Printed in the United Kingdom by CPI Group Ltd, Croydon CR0 4YY

A catalogue record for this publication is available from the British Library

Library of Congress Cataloging-in-Publication Data
NAMES: Franklin, Simon, editor. | Reich, Rebecca, editor. | Widdis, Emma, editor.
TITLE: The new Cambridge history of Russian literature / edited by Simon Franklin, Rebecca
Reich, Emma Widdis.
DESCRIPTION: New York : Cambridge University Press, 2024. | Includes index.
IDENTIFIERS: LCCN 2023053600 | ISBN 9781108493482 (hardback) | ISBN 9781108737104
(paperback) | ISBN 9781108655620 (ebook)
SUBJECTS: LCSH: Russian literature – History and criticism.
CLASSIFICATION: LCC PG2951 N49 2024 | DDC 891.709–dc23/eng/20240105
LC record available at https://lccn.loc.gov/2023053600

ISBN 978-1-108-49348-2 Hardback

Contents

Contents

HISTORY 2
MECHANISMS

Contents

Contents

Figures

Contributors

ANNA A. BERMAN is Assistant Professor of Slavonic Studies at the University of Cambridge. She is the author of *The Family Novel in Russia and England, 1800–1880* (2022) and *Siblings in Tolstoy and Dostoevsky: The Path to Universal Brotherhood* (2015), and the editor of *Tolstoy in Context* (2022).

EVGENII BERSHTEIN is Professor of Russian at Reed College. His recent publications include the book chapters 'Sokurov contra Eisenstein: The Balance of Gender', 'The Discourse of Sexual Psychopathy in Russian Modernism', 'Eisenstein's Letter to Magnus Hirschfeld: Text and Context', and 'The Notion of Universal Bisexuality in Russian Religious Philosophy'. He edited the English edition of Iurii Lotman's *Non-Memoirs* (2014), and he is working on a book on Sergei Eisenstein's theories of sexuality.

MARIJETA BOZOVIC is Associate Professor of Slavic Languages and Literatures, affiliated with Film and Media Studies and with Women's, Gender, and Sexuality Studies, at Yale University. She is the author of *Avant-Garde Post–: Radical Poetics after the Soviet Union* (2023) and *Nabokov's Canon: From Onegin to Ada* (2016), and a co-editor of *Watersheds: Poetics and Politics of the Danube River* (2016) and *Nabokov Upside Down* (2017). She is currently working on *Imagining Russian Hackers: Myths of Men and Machines*, co-authored with Benjamin Peters.

VITALY CHERNETSKY is Professor of Slavic Languages and Literatures at the University of Kansas. He is the author of *Mapping Postcommunist Cultures: Russia and Ukraine in the Context of Globalization* (2007) and of articles on Slavic literatures and cultures where he seeks to highlight cross-regional and cross-disciplinary contexts.

YURI CORRIGAN is Associate Professor of Russian and Comparative Literature at Boston University. He studies nineteenth-century Russian and European literature with interests in philosophy, religion, and psychology. He is the author of *Dostoevsky and the Riddle of the Self* (2017) and the editor of *Chekhov in Context* (2023).

JULIE CURTIS was Professor of Russian Literature at the University of Oxford until her retirement in 2021. She has written extensively on Mikhail Bulgakov and Evgenii Zamiatin. A recent research project resulted in her edited volume, *New Drama in Russian: Performance, Politics and Protest in Russia, Ukraine and Belarus* (2020).

List of Contributors

CONNOR DOAK is Senior Lecturer in Russian at the University of Bristol. He works primarily on Russian literature and culture from the nineteenth century to the present, with a special interest in gender and sexuality in the Russian context. He is currently working on a monograph on masculinity in Vladimir Maiakovskii's poetry.

EVGENY DOBRENKO is Professor of Russian Literature and Culture at Ca' Foscari University of Venice. He is the author, editor, and co-editor of thirty books, including *State Laughter: Stalinism, Populism, and Origins of Soviet Culture* (2022), *Late Stalinism: The Aesthetics of Politics* (2020), *Museum of the Revolution: Stalinist Cinema and the Production of History* (2008), and *Political Economy of Socialist Realism* (2007).

ALEXEI EVSTRATOV is Associate Professor of Slavic Languages and Cultures at the Université Grenoble Alpes. His published books include *Les Spectacles francophones à la cour de Saint-Pétersbourg (1743–1796)* (2016), *L'invention d'une société* (2016), and *The Creation of a Europeanized Elite in Russia, 1762–1825: Public Role and Subjective Self* (co-edited with Andrei Zorin and Andreas Schönle, 2016).

SIMON FRANKLIN is Emeritus Professor of Slavonic Studies at the University of Cambridge. His most recent books are *The Russian Graphosphere, 1450–1850* (2019) and *Information and Empire: Mechanisms of Communication in Russia, 1600–1850* (co-edited with Katherine Bowers, 2017). He is currently writing a cultural history of the Russian language.

BRADLEY A. GORSKI is Assistant Professor of Slavic Languages at Georgetown University and a specialist in post-Soviet literature and culture. His book *Cultural Capitalism: Literature and the Market after Socialism* will be published in 2025.

SERGEY A. IVANOV is Visiting Professor of Byzantine Studies at Northwestern University. He specialises in Byzantine culture and Byzantino-Slavic cultural relations. His books include *In Search of Constantinople* (2022), *Pearls before Swine: Missionary Work in Byzantium* (2015,) and *Holy Fools in Byzantium and Beyond* (2006).

POLLY JONES is Professor of Russian and Schrecker-Barbour Fellow in Slavonic Studies at University College, Oxford. Her books include *Revolution Rekindled: The Writers and Readers of Late Soviet Biography* (2019) and *Myth, Memory, Trauma: Rethinking the Stalinist Past in the Soviet Union, 1953–70* (2013). She is currently writing a short history of Gulag fiction.

KONSTANTINE KLIOUTCHKINE is Associate Professor of Russian at Pomona College. His research focuses on the cultural economy of nineteenth-century Russia and the history of media technologies, especially the press. He has published on Fedor Dostoevskii, Nikolai Nekrasov, Nikolai Chernyshevskii, Nikolai Dobroliubov, Anton Chekhov, and Vasilii Rozanov, and on the prominence of women's prose in Russian thick journals during the nineteenth century.

ILYA KUKULIN taught at the Higher School of Economics in Moscow until March 2022, when he emigrated for political reasons. Currently, he is a lecturer at Stanford University.

He is the author of a volume of essays entitled *Breakthrough to an Impossible Connection* (2019; in Russian), *Machines of Noisy Time: How Soviet Montage Became a Method of Unofficial Culture* (2015; in Russian), and, with Mark Lipovetsky, *A Guerilla Logos: The Project of Dmitry Aleksandrovich Prigov* (2022; in Russian).

MICHAEL KUNICHIKA teaches at Amherst College, where he is Professor of Russian and Film and Media Studies and the director of the Amherst Center for Russian Culture. He has published *'Our Native Antiquity': Archaeology in the Culture of Russian Modernism* (2015).

MARCUS C. LEVITT is Professor Emeritus in the Department of Slavic Languages and Literatures, University of Southern California. He has written on a broad spectrum of Russian topics from the eighteenth to twentieth centuries. His books include *The Visual Dominant in Eighteenth-Century Russia* (2011), *Early Modern Russian Letters: Selected Articles* (2009), and *Russian Literary Politics and the Pushkin Celebration of 1880* (1989).

STEPHEN LOVELL is Professor of Modern History at King's College London. His books include *How Russia Learned to Talk: A History of Public Speaking in the Stenographic Age, 1860–1930* (2020).

JESSICA MERRILL is Assistant Professor of Slavic Languages at Columbia University. She is the author of *The Origins of Russian Literary Theory: Folklore, Philology, Form* (2022) and has published articles on aspects of Russian and Czech modernism and literary theory.

ISOBEL PALMER is Assistant Professor of Russian at the University of Birmingham. She is the author of *Revolutions in Verse: The Medium of Russian Modernism* (2024). Her current project is *Poetry in Public: The Social Life of Russian Verse*, funded by the British Academy.

LYUDMILA PARTS is Professor of Russian at McGill University. Her books include *In Search of the True Russia: The Provinces in Contemporary Nationalist Discourse* (2018), *The Russian 20th-Century Short Story: A Critical Companion* (2009), and *The Chekhovian Intertext: Dialogue with a Classic* (2008). She has published on post-Soviet culture, nationalism, genre theory, and travelogue.

CATHY POPKIN is Jesse and George Siegel Professor Emerita in the Humanities at Columbia University. She is the author of *The Pragmatics of Insignificance: Chekhov, Zoshchenko, Gogol* (1993); the editor of *Anton Chekhov's Selected Stories* (2014) and *Essays on Anton P. Chekhov: Close Readings*, by Robert Louis Jackson (2023); and a co-editor of *Teaching Nineteenth-Century Russian Literature: Essays in Honor of Robert L. Belknap* (2014).

REBECCA REICH is Associate Professor of Russian Literature and Culture at the University of Cambridge. She is the author of *State of Madness: Psychiatry, Literature, and Dissent After Stalin* (2018) and the Consultant Editor for Russia, East-Central Europe, and Eurasia at the *Times Literary Supplement*.

ELLEN RUTTEN is Professor of Literature, chair of the Modern Languages Department at the University of Amsterdam, and editor-in-chief of *Russian Literature* (from 2024

onwards, *Slavic Literatures*). Among other publications, she is the author of *Sincerity after Communism* (2017) and a co-editor of *Imperfections* (2022).

TATIANA SMOLIAROVA is Associate Professor of Russian Literature at the University of Toronto. Her main areas of interest are the Age of the Enlightenment and its legacies in Russia and Europe. Her published books include *Three Metaphors for Life: Derzhavin's Late Poetry* (2018), *Lyrics Made Visible: Derzhavin* (2011; in Russian), and *Paris 1928: Ode Returns to Theatre* (1999; in Russian).

WILLIAM MILLS TODD III is Harry Tuchman Levin Professor of Literature and Professor of Comparative Literature, Emeritus, at Harvard University. Educated at Dartmouth College, Oxford, and Columbia University, he has published books and articles on literary history, literary theory, and sociology of literature. He is completing a book on serialisation.

EMILY VAN BUSKIRK is Associate Professor of Russian and East European Languages and Literatures at Rutgers University. Her published books include *Lydia Ginzburg's Prose: Reality in Search of Literature* (2016), and two Ginzburg-related volumes co-edited with Andrei Zorin. She is currently researching documentary prose on the Soviet experience of the camps.

ALEXEY VDOVIN is Associate Professor in the School of Philological Studies at the Higher School of Economics in Moscow. His published books include *The Enigma of the Narod-Sphynx: Tales about Peasants and Their Sociocultural Functions in the Russian Empire before the Emancipation* (2024; in Russian), *Ladies without Camellias: Private Correspondence between Sex Workers and Nikolai Dobroliubov and Nikolai Chernyshevskii* (2022; in Russian) and *Dobroliubov: A Raznochinets between the Spirit and the Flesh* (2017; in Russian).

ILYA VINITSKY is Professor of Russian literature in the Department of Slavic Languages at Princeton University. His main fields of expertise are Russian Romanticism and Realism, the history of emotions, and nineteenth-century intellectual and spiritual history. His books include *Transfers: Literary Translation as Interpretation and Provocation* (2022; in Russian), *Vasily Zhukovsky's Romanticism and the Emotional History of Russia* (2015), *Ghostly Paradoxes: Modern Spiritualism and Russian Culture in the Age of Realism* (2009), and *Russian Literature* (with Andrew Baruch Wachtel, 2009).

JOSEPHINE VON ZITZEWITZ has held research and teaching positions at the universities of Oxford, Bristol, Cambridge and The Arctic University of Norway. She is the author of two academic monographs on late Soviet samizdat literature – *The Culture of Samizdat: Literature and Underground Networks in the Late Soviet Union* (2020) and *Poetry and the Leningrad Religious-Philosophical Seminar 1976–1980: Music for a Deaf Age* (2016) – and numerous articles on late-twentieth-century and contemporary Russian poetry.

MICHAEL WACHTEL is a professor in the Department of Slavic Languages and Literatures at Princeton University. He is the author of several books on Russian poetry and poetics, including *The Cambridge Introduction to Russian Poetry* (2004).

Lisa Ryoko Wakamiya is Associate Professor of Slavic and Courtesy Associate Professor of English at Florida State University. Her publications include studies of transnational literary migration, post-Soviet literature and film, translation, and the intersections between narrative and material culture.

Emma Widdis is Professor of Slavonic Studies at the University of Cambridge. Her most recent book is *Socialist Senses: Film, Feeling and the Soviet Subject* (2017). She is currently working on a study of theories of spectatorship in Soviet culture.

Kirill Zubkov is Postdoctoral Researcher at the University of Bologna. His research interests are in the social institutions that informed the development of literature in the Russian Empire. His published books include *To Enlighten and to Chastise: The Functions of Censorship in the Russian Empire* (2023; in Russian) and *Scenarios of Change: The Uvarov Award and the Evolution of Russian Drama in the Age of Alexander II* (2021; in Russian).

Acknowledgements

Many, many colleagues provided valuable insights and feedback at each stage in the emergence of this book. We would particularly like to thank the anonymous readers who commented on the original proposal to the publisher, and the members of our Advisory Panel – Eric Naiman, Ellen Rutten, William Mills Todd III, Alexey Vdovin, and Ilya Vinitsky – who responded promptly and constructively to all our requests for their counsel. We are also grateful for the support of Caryl Emerson. Stefan Lacny, Delphi Mayther, Katerina Pavlidi, and Angus Russell translated into English those chapters and Boxes that were originally written in Russian. Katerina Pavlidi kept an essential record of the series of online workshops for contributors, at which the initial drafts of chapters were discussed. Puck Fletcher read the entire manuscript, checking meticulously for consistency and clarity. The detailed editorial process was supported by a Cambridge Humanities Research Grant, with additional contributions from Trinity College, Cambridge, and from the University of Cambridge's Faculty of Modern and Medieval Languages and Linguistics. Work on Chapter 1.9 was supported by an Emergency Fellowship grant from the Central European University. Work on Chapter 2.9 was funded by a Leverhulme Early Career Fellowship and subsequently by the European Union's Horizon 2020 Research and Innovation Programme. We are grateful to our colleagues and friends at the University of Cambridge for their practical support, and their insights, which have been indispensable to this project over its duration.

On Transliteration, Names, and Dates

In a book of this genre and scope, and with a multiplicity of audiences, transliteration can rarely be both entirely consistent and entirely satisfactory.

Where transliterations expressly represent the Russian language – that is, in bibliographical references, or in conveying the original forms of individual words and expressions – we use a version of the modified Library of Congress system that is common to most modern library catalogues and information resources.

Where transliterated names of people and places occur as part of the running text, we normally use the same system but without the superscript (') sometimes used to represent the Cyrillic soft sign. Technically, this indicates that the preceding consonant is palatalised, but this means little or nothing to most non-specialist readers. A feature of the modified Library of Congress system is that surnames end in *-ii, -oi, -aia*, etc., rather than *-y, -oy, -aya*.

Some names, however, have been anglicised, following strongly established English convention:

(i) emperors and empresses (hence Catherine, Paul, and Nicholas rather than Ekaterina, Pavel, or Nikolai)

(ii) a very small number of place names including St Petersburg (rather than Sankt-Peterburg), or indeed the name of Russia itself (rather than Rossiia)

(iii) originally Russophone writers who became established writers in other languages (e.g. Joseph Brodsky rather than Iosif Brodskii), and a very few cultural figures whose names in foreign convention are too well established to be comfortably rendered through our standard system (e.g. Eisenstein, and in a combination of transliteration practices, Tchaikovskii).

In bibliographical references and quotations, names retain the form given in the work cited.

Apart from the anglicised exceptions, geographical names are generally given in their current standard forms. This relates especially to places formerly within the Russian Empire: so Kyiv, Belarus, or Lviv rather than Kiev, Belorussia, or Lvov.

Dates for all writers are given on first mention in each chapter, as are the regnal dates of rulers of Muscovy and the Russian Empire.

Dates of literary works are more problematic. A reasonable case can be made for giving several different dates: the period of composition, the date of completion, the period of serialisation, the date of first publication as a book, the date of the definitive authorial version (that may not be the first printed edition), and so on. The default practice is: for books, we give the date of first separate publication *unless* a specific point is being made about, for example, composition (using the abbreviation 'comp.') or serialisation ('serial.'). In the case of short poems, we normally give the date of composition. In the case of periodicals, we give the full run dates. In the case both of pre-modern manuscript culture, and of contemporary internet culture, such dating criteria are often inapplicable or inappropriate.

Introduction

SIMON FRANKLIN, REBECCA REICH, AND EMMA WIDDIS

A new history of Russian literature cannot simply bring its story up to date. The story itself needs to be conceived and shaped differently. The last *Cambridge History of Russian Literature* was published in 1989 (two years before the collapse of the Soviet Union), and its narrative stopped in 1980.[1] Over the next three decades, it became clear that the study of Russian literature would have to change in fundamental ways to account for a wider range of voices and experiences, as well as for fundamental shifts in technologies. Efforts to push back against literary canons well beyond the Russian sphere highlighted the complexities of writing the 'history' of any literature. New theoretical frameworks transformed the critical lens through which scholars approached questions of gender, sexuality, and the colonial and postcolonial space. Electronic media generated new forms of expression and demanded reconsideration of literary works and practices. Over this period, studies of Russian literature have reflected and contributed to the wider debates. The field has become rich in diverse and destabilising analysis. We have shaped the *New Cambridge History of Russian Literature* to reflect this diversity, and to offer a new model of literary history writing.

Ideas of Russian literature, and of Russian culture more widely, have evolved with, and become integral elements of, ideas of Russia itself. As such, Russian literature has been a central component in the emergence and sustenance of a sense of distinctive community, of social and cultural belonging. At the same time, it has served both as a mechanism of cultural assimilation and domination within the empire, and as Russia's most successful and effective cultural export, profoundly influencing perceptions of Russia and Russianness far beyond the borders of empire. The imperial legacies of Russian literature were instrumentalised most evidently during Russia's

---

1 Charles A. Moser (ed.), *The Cambridge History of Russian Literature* (Cambridge: Cambridge University Press, 1989).

incursions into Ukraine from 2014 onwards, and in particular its full-scale invasion in February 2022, which were officially underpinned by an extreme version of an exceptionalist Russian cultural master-narrative. The problems and questions raised by such a narrative were not new, but they became especially acute when transferred to the battlefield. For generations accustomed to assuming that history had entered a more stable post-imperial age, especially in Europe, the resurgence of Russia's colonial ambitions came as a shock. This volume was not designed to address explicitly the war and its impact on the field. Nevertheless, we believe that its conception and structure model a flexible approach that can contribute to some of these urgent debates.

The expression 'Russian literature' implies that the object of study is one thing, in the singular. This is unavoidable, but also misleading. Here we start from the premise that Russian literature is not a given, not an immutable canon, but a contested space with shifting boundaries and definitions. It is precisely because this space remains contested that Russian literature has functioned, and continues to function, as a concept with cultural valence and semiotic power. It has its own institutions and practices, its own codes of behaviour and understanding, its own constellation of ideas and key preoccupations. It alters and renews these ideas over time, while retaining certain themes and frameworks. No history of Russian literature can take its object of study for granted. However, it is the responsibility of such a history to engage with Russian literature as a lived and ever-evolving idea: to historicise it, to examine its mechanisms and meanings, to trace its modes of production, dissemination, and reception.

A second premise of this volume is that there should be many Histories of Russian Literature, because Russian literature has many histories. The range and diversity of any literature require that it be approached from multiple, complementary angles. The book therefore unfolds through four distinct strands: histories constructed according to different criteria. The first strand, Movements, follows the sequence of and tensions among the dominant '-isms' of literary fashion and production, from what we call the 'devotional age' of pre-modernity through to contemporary movements in the electronic age. This was the framework for the previous *Cambridge History of Russian Literature*, albeit minus the electronic and the postmodern. The second strand, Mechanisms, tells a history of Russian literature through its institutions and primary media of production. Such mechanisms include spatially located institutions such as monasteries, the imperial court, and literary salons or circles; media such as print journals, publishers, and the internet;

and structures of regulation and demand such as censorship and markets; or, more pervasively, empire itself. The third strand highlights the history of literary Forms such as verse, novels, or digital platforms. The fourth is dedicated to Heroes, in the sense of emblematic character types (positive or otherwise), as they have evolved across a chronological range, from saints to madmen.

In order to convey a sense of historical continuity as well as change, our contributors have been asked to do two things: to provide a brief overview that indicates the fuller scope of a topic across time; and to focus on a historical period in which expressions of that topic became particularly pronounced. The sequencing of these temporal centres of gravity situates each chapter within its own history's chronological progression, while the inclusion of a longue durée narrative highlights the synchronicities and persistent frameworks that link the chapters and, indeed, the histories as a whole. We therefore invite our readers to navigate the book laterally as well as chronologically – and we indicate where they might do so in parenthetical references to parallel chapters.

In addition to the histories, and cutting across their boundaries, are thirty much briefer essays that we have called Boxes. The Boxes are arranged within six thematic clusters, each consisting of five essays. Since they are formed thematically, these clusters can be regarded as fragments of further, parallel historical strands. One cluster gives close readings of paradigmatic texts (for instance, a micro-story or an internet form); a second focuses on exemplary genres (e.g. satire or children's literature); a third deals with literary locations, such as St Petersburg, the village, or the apartment; a fourth highlights different kinds of narrative voice (e.g. the omniscient narrator or the unreliable narrator); a fifth introduces influential Russian critical framers of literature such as Vissarion Belinskii or Mikhail Bakhtin; and a sixth looks at 'literature beyond literature', whether in mythologies (for instance, of Aleksandr Pushkin) or in dialogue with other cultural forms (film, music, art). This combination of synchronic and diachronic narratives, and the resulting multiplication of conceptual frames, offers a new approach to the field of study that is Russian literature and goes some way towards capturing its shifting forms and definitions. Some of our histories (Movements, Forms) may appear conventional; others (Mechanisms, Heroes) will seem less so. Our aim in refusing to privilege one set of disciplinary questions over another is to make available a more multifaceted picture of any given historical moment or phenomenon.

We draw particular attention here to the history of Mechanisms. The chapters in this strand seek to understand the social, physical, and discursive

structures and categories that generated and shaped Russian literature and its communities of production and reception. The role played by these mechanisms may have been limiting as well as enabling, as will be clearest in chapters on 'The Monastery' and 'The Censor'. Readers may find it more unexpected to think about 'Empire', 'Queerness', or 'The Voice' as mechanisms that have constrained or facilitated particular literary modes or forms, but all have functioned as such in Russian literature. For example, in practical terms, the formation of empire prompted the travel that stimulated the narratives of Romantic prose and verse, and it created frameworks through which Russian (and non-Russian) writers encountered the diverse peoples contained within the constantly changing borders of imperial space. Here, on a more conceptual and pervasive level, the chapter on 'Empire' explores 'imperiality' as a constructive mechanism in generating literature. Likewise, thinking about queerness as a mechanism facilitates an analysis of how sexuality, and in particular resistance to heteronormativity, has prompted distinct modes of literary production. Heteronormativity is itself a mechanism, but it may be taken for granted unless confronted with challenges to its naturalisation, and its constructive power in shaping Russian literature emerges most clearly through an examination of counter-mechanisms of resistance.

In offering these diverse perspectives on Russian literature, we neither consistently affirm nor consistently revise a literary canon, because literary canonicity – that is, the affirmation of great writers and great works – is not a structural principle of the volume. Thus, although the forty-three chapters and thirty Boxes include discussions of several hundred writers and works, we have invited contributors to determine the hierarchy of individual coverage according to the demands of their particular chapters. As a result, some writers and works inevitably receive less – or more – attention than readers may reckon is their due. Nor do we divide up writers according to any social, ideological, or personal characteristics. Our contributors address questions of sexuality and ethnicity as they shape particular works of literature, rather than as biographical elements that categorise writers within particular groups. Thus, for example, we have no single chapter on 'women writers', as our contributors have considered texts by female writers within the bounds of their relevant chapters. This approach does not entirely address what remains an imbalance in Russian literary studies, but for several periods it more adequately reflects a diversity of literary production and immediate reception, which has often been distorted in subsequent canon formation.

Just as 'history' and 'Russian' are complex terms, so the category of 'literature' defies firm delineation. In this volume, our resistance to

conventional canons expands to a consideration of varied forms under the broad heading of 'literature'. We have not been prescriptive in setting limits to what can be considered literary production, and our contributors address a wide variety of forms (including memes, self-writing, artist's books), as mediated by changing technologies of production.

The conceptual framework of this volume is not claimed as definitive or exhaustive. We offer four parallel histories. More are possible, even desirable, just as each of the histories could itself be augmented with additional chapters. Our histories mainly explore how literature has come into being, what it has looked like, what it has said or meant in relation to the culture of its times. We pay less attention to how it has been received and used. There is no sustained work here on readership, for example, whether as a chapter within the history of Mechanisms or as an independent strand.[2] Similarly, while such themes are of necessity raised, we do not systematically address a topic that could be developed into an important additional history: literature's instrumentalisation as an agent of imperial assimilation, of social integration through education, or indeed of opposition and protest.

Our histories, in their dialogues with each other and with other established narratives, offer a composite description of the multifaceted thing we call Russian literature. But what is that 'thing'? What are the parameters of the object of study? What is, and is not, included within this volume's understanding of Russian literature? We stated above, as a general premise of this volume, that Russian literature is not a given, but a contested space with shifting boundaries and definitions. What are the main contestable and shifting elements, and how do we approach them?

Language

According to one criterion, Russian literature might be defined as literature written in the Russian language. Yet the Russian language is a language of empire, and it is also a global language. There are well-established distinctions between, for example, English and other Anglophone literatures, French and Francophone, Portuguese and Lusophone, Spanish and Hispanic. By analogy it might initially seem reasonable to distinguish Russian literature from broader Russophone literature or literatures.

---

2 See, however, the monumental study: Damiano Rebecchini and Raffaella Vassena (eds.), *Reading Russia: A History of Reading in Modern Russia*, 3 vols. (Milan: Di/Segni, 2020).

Analogies, however, are rarely precise. English, French, Portuguese, and Spanish are now the dominant national and/or administrative languages in many countries separate from the imperial homelands from which they were exported. The international Russophone presence is less transparently anchored. Russian has been the dominant national or official language only within the Russian Empire, the Soviet Union, and most markedly, the Russian Federation. In former imperial or Soviet territories, it often co-exists with other national languages in a diverse set of relationships. The global Russophone presence, for long periods concentrated in a few traditional centres of emigration, has expanded hugely since the fall of the Soviet Union. Current Russian state ideology posits a 'Russian world' to which all Russophone culture can or should belong. In international scholarship there is a fairly strong consensus that global Russophone literature should not automatically be appropriated in this way: that not all literature written in Russian should be counted as Russian literature. The parallel with Anglophone/English, or Francophone/French, makes this ostensible paradox straightforward in principle. American literature or the Anglophone literature of India are routinely differentiated from English literature, even though all are in English (and may even be taught alongside each other in faculties of English). This may be lexically inconsistent, but in practice it is not confusing, and the concepts have become habitual.

The previous *Cambridge History of Russian Literature* declared that one of its objectives was to 'promote the healing of the division' caused by emigration.[3] By contrast, at the outset our policy was that the present volume should *not* attempt systematically to incorporate or appropriate émigré or wider Russophone and diasporic literature. However, the geographies and identities of global Russophone writing are in flux, Russophone studies are at an early stage of development, and conventions for differentiation are still emerging.[4] Some kinds of guideline seem reasonably clear: for example, that modern Russophone writing in Ukraine should not be claimed for a history of Russian literature on grounds of language alone. More broadly, however, we have not imposed fixed boundaries or definitions, especially where the theme of a chapter demands a wider field of vision. For example, in the Heroes history, the chapter on 'The Émigré' traces the representation of

---

3 Moser (ed.), *The Cambridge History of Russian Literature*, p. viii.
4 See the survey by Marco Puleri, 'Russophonia as an epistemic challenge', *Ab Imperio* 1 (2023), 76–98; also Kevin M. F. Platt (ed.), *Global Russian Cultures* (Madison: University of Wisconsin Press, 2019); Andy Byford, Connor Doak, and Stephen Hutchings (eds.), *Transnational Russian Studies* (Liverpool: Liverpool University Press, 2020).

its protagonist across Russophone writing by non-Russian as well as Russian authors, some of whom have also produced works on the theme in other languages. While the chapter excludes diaspora authors who have written exclusively in languages other than Russian, it does make reference to non-Russian language works by authors who have also explored the theme in Russian. In such cases, bilingualism may be seen as a generative framework for the Russian-language works.

An equivalent issue of boundaries and definition arises with respect to literature rendered *into* Russian from other languages. It is not enough to say that Russian literature has been profoundly influenced by translations; at times, translations and adaptations can (arguably) be reckoned integral components of Russian literature. Through most of the pre-modern centuries, when much high-prestige writing was anonymous, texts that were translated and what we would call 'original' – that is, initially produced in a form of the Russian language – mingled freely in the manuscripts without consistent differentiation of provenance or status. Moreover, in manuscript transmission the texts of translations could be and were recast in ways that might be reckoned to convert them into original works. In post-medieval times, too, the line between translation and creative adaptation could be blurred. Literary translation has often been regarded as a high-prestige creative activity, and some translations and adaptations have come to be treated as significant works of Russian literature. Thus, versions of the Horatian *Exegi monumentum* by Gavriil Derzhavin (1795) and Aleksandr Pushkin (1836) are routinely included among their authorial works. In the twentieth century, generations of Soviet children enjoyed the verses of Samuil Marshak, which were inspired by but only very loosely adapted from the English originals that they ostensibly translate.

Like the distinction between Russian and Russophone, so the distinction between translated and original is both obvious and obscure, both necessary and resistant to definition.

Language is a prerequisite for determining Russian literature, but it is a highly problematic marker that cannot be applied automatically.

Place

For the present purposes of outlining the field of Russian literature, writing in Russian is a minimum requirement. It is not, however, a sufficient one. No less problematic is the question of place. Any attempt to draw an apparently straightforward distinction between literature written in Russia and literature

written outside Russia founders on at least three obstacles: the mutations of political geography; the variety of authorial biographies; and, particularly in contemporary culture, the dislocations that are enabled by technologies.

Where is Russia, over time? State borders have expanded and contracted dramatically over the centuries: from the compact Muscovite principality of the fourteenth and fifteenth centuries to the massive multilingual, multi-ethnic empire that eventually stretched from the Carpathians to the Pacific (and on to Alaska), from the Arctic Circle to the borders of Iran, and east across Central Asia. In one sense, little of that imperial space can properly be designated Russia or Russian. The Russian language, unlike English, in principle (though inconsistently) distinguishes the geopolitical (*rossiiskii*) from the ethno-cultural and linguistic (*russkii*). That is, it has separate words to denote that which relates to Russia, and that which relates to the Russian language itself. This lexical differentiation is convenient, but it does not solve the problem of how the two spheres of meaning should map onto each other in the case of literature. The implosion of imperial space with the collapse of the Soviet Union in 1991 left very substantial Russophone com-munities outside geopolitical Russia and created culturally and ethnically mixed populations of many freshly independent states. Many of these people do not consider themselves to be part of any imagined space of Russian letters.

The movement of borders is just one of the mechanisms that may dislocate literary production. Another is the movement of peoples, whether by emi-gration, exile, or simply travel. For instance, the apparently 'classic' Russian writer Ivan Turgenev drafted his most famous novel, *Fathers and Children*, while in England and France. The poet Fedor Tiutchev spent much of his life in Germany and Italy. The upheavals of the twentieth and twenty-first centuries have produced further waves of dislocation, including by authors who continued to produce literature in the Russian language while tempor-arily abroad. Such peregrinations are biographically interesting but are not seen as putting the works themselves in a special category. These are Russian writers writing works of Russian literature while they happen to be out of the country.

A thornier set of questions arises when it comes to emigration, exile, and the post-imperial space. Some histories of Russian literature have pointed to a distinction between literature produced in Russia (usually meaning the Empire and, in particular, the Soviet Union) and literature produced outside it (meaning, in particular, 'émigré' literature of the twentieth century). Since the break-up of the Soviet Union, and hence of large segments of the former

Russian Empire, émigré literature has become only a small subset of the linguistically fluid space of global Russophone and diasporic literatures.[5] The (in)significance of location is further complicated or undermined by the impact of electronic media, through which words can be produced and distributed anywhere instantly. To what extent does it matter whether those words happen to be entered into a device in Omsk or in Oregon?

A writer's own sense of identity and belonging cannot always be retrieved in retrospect. It may be hybrid, and not necessarily linked to place, or to just one place. The received canon of nineteenth-century Russian literature is almost inconceivable without the works of Nikolai Gogol, who was born and educated in rural Ukraine and moved to St Petersburg in 1828. His first collection of stories is set in Ukraine and written in a Russian language inflected with Ukrainian phrasing and folklore. His later tales, set in the imperial capital, crystallised one of the central tropes of Russian literature: the image of St Petersburg itself. Accounts of Ukrainian literature justifiably feature Mykola Hohol, yet his work is reducible to neither culture. Gogol was both a subject and a citizen of the Russian Empire, formed within the spaces of Ukrainian and Russian letters, and shaping both in turn. Or, in a later period, take the writer Chingiz Aitmatov. Until 1966 Aitmatov published simultaneously in Kyrgyz and in Russian, but subsequently almost exclusively in Russian. The supra-national, imperial identity was Soviet and the linguistic medium became fully Russian, yet Aitmatov is also treated as a major figure in the literary history of Kyrgyzstan.

In this volume, we understand Russian literature as an imagined community of letters, a set of practices and affiliations, contested and debated. According to this framework, language and place need not necessarily coincide. Instead, the focus shifts towards whether and how a writer writes *within* that imagined community. This may not be a question of conscious affiliation; indeed, it may be a case of coercion, or rejection, or of how the writer's work is received. All of those practices play out within what might be broadly construed as Russian literature, a discursive space which is emphatically not coterminous with the fixed and normative 'Russian world' that is instrumentalised by the Russian state. We do not claim to be comprehensive, whether with respect to any (putative) entirety of Russian literature, or with respect to a (putative) plurality of Russian literatures. Rather, we deliberately diminish some conventional assumptions about the subject, signalling Russian

---

5 On diaspora as a field of investigation, see Maria Rubins (ed.), *Redefining Russian Literary Diaspora, 1920–2020* (London: UCL Press, 2021).

literature as a contested space, refuting its claims of totalising inclusivity, while also recognising how it has encouraged and imposed categories of belonging.

Time

A third structuring question relates to chronology. What is the timespan of Russian literature as represented in this volume? The endpoint is arbitrary, for purely practical reasons: this is a history of Russian literature up to approximately 2021, when the drafts of most of the chapters were completed, though with sporadic reference to material up to early 2023. In the final stages of editing, contributors were given the opportunity to reflect on the possible implications, for their respective chapters, of any shifts of perspective prompted by the Russian invasion of Ukraine. But more reflexive, retrospective assimilation of currently unfolding events will be a matter for future histories of Russian literature.

The period of early Rus – from the turn of the eleventh century until roughly the Mongol conquest of the mid-thirteenth century – is the shared prehistory of the three modern East Slavic languages and cultures: Russian, Ukrainian, and Belarusian. It belongs to none and all of them. Historically, this is straightforward. Ideologically and lexically, it is not. It is complicated or contaminated by the fact that, in the Russian political and cultural tradition, there is a deeply embedded story of exclusive succession from early Rus to Russia. This is a myth of identity and can lead to a claim to retrospective ownership of the past, as has been the case with Vladimir Putin's assertions of the historical unity of Russia and Ukraine. The heritage of early Rus is not exclusive to Russia, or indeed to Ukraine, or Belarus.

One might reasonably choose to ignore early Rus and start with the literature of the principality of Moscow in, say, the fourteenth or fifteenth centuries. This solves one problem but creates others. In the first place, by an equivalent logic early Rus could be omitted from *any* national literary history, including Ukrainian or Belarusian. This would be a pity. Second, and perhaps more pertinent for the history of culture, the continuities of East Slav textual or artistic culture cannot be reduced to Russo-centric political teleology. Almost all the high-prestige writings of early Rus have reached us in later – Muscovite and Russian – manuscripts, through the culture of mutable textuality that typifies what we have called the 'age of devotion'. It would be misleading to exclude discussion of texts across that span, including, in some instances, their early Rus versions. While in this volume the temporal

focus of the pre-modern chapters is mostly in the Muscovite period, we do not abandon important textual continuities from the earlier period. However, by contrast with most histories of Russian literature, we do not tell a continuous story from the eleventh century.

Just as the beginnings of Russia as a geopolitical entity are vague, so too are the temporal beginnings of Russian as a language. The modern language, Contemporary Standard Russian – or, as it tends to be labelled in Russian textbooks, the 'Russian Literary Language' – emerged as a set of codified norms over the eighteenth and early nineteenth centuries. If the history of Russian literature is the history of literature in modern Russian, then there would be a case for starting in the eighteenth century, or at best in the late seventeenth century. The language of cultural prestige in Muscovy, as in early Rus, drew heavily on Church Slavonic, interacting in varying degrees with East Slav vernaculars. Though recognisably related, this is not the modern vernacular. On linguistic grounds it is justifiable to start with pre-modern texts, but one should be aware that today, even in editions aimed at native speakers, most such texts are printed along with translations into Contemporary Standard Russian.

***

Moments of separation can spur contact and exchange. When we began this project in 2017, our intention was to discuss the drafts with contributors at a single workshop in Cambridge. The Covid pandemic derailed that plan; instead, we held a series of online workshops dedicated to each of the histories. Drafts of all chapters were circulated to contributors, who attended and participated in higher numbers than would likely have been possible had we met in person. These virtual discussions not only provided valuable feedback as the authors prepared the next versions of their own chapters but also gave everyone a clearer sense of the volume as a whole, of the genre, of parallel chapters in other histories, of what fitted and what did not, and of what was still lacking. In short, the New Cambridge History of Russian Literature is more than a collage of separately written chapters. It may properly be said to be a work of collective authorship.

The connectedness that our community of contributors achieved despite the pandemic faces a different kind of challenge today. The Russian invasion of Ukraine has sharpened awareness of urgent questions about what the Russian literary tradition consists of, what it represents, and what it means to study it. The debates that have opened up in our field are difficult, but they are also essential. It is premature at a time of war to determine a decolonised

vision of Russian literature. But it is essential that such a vision be discussed; and this discussion begins by acknowledging the many ways of narrating Russian literary history. In its organisation, this volume contests the idea that a history of literature can be told in one way. It invites a multiplicity of readings, both within and across its chapters, and in the juxtaposing of its separate strands. It mobilises connections but also underscores debate. It reveals the rich and complex field of Russian literature without seeking to resolve it. We do not claim, then, that the *New Cambridge History of Russian Literature* is a definitive account. Rather, it seeks to frame the subject in ways that will engage and provoke still other framings by the communities that constitute our field.

Further Reading

Cornwell, Neil (ed.), *Reference Guide to Russian Literature* (London, Chicago: Fitzroy Dearborn, 1998).

Cornwell, Neil (ed.), *The Routledge Companion to Russian Literature* (London: Routledge, 2001).

Emerson, Caryl, *The Cambridge Introduction to Russian Literature* (Cambridge: Cambridge University Press, 2008).

Kahn, Andrew, Mark Lipovetsky, Irina Reyfman, and Stephanie Sandler, *A History of Russian Literature* (Oxford: Oxford University Press, 2018).

Kelly, Catriona, *Russian Literature: A Very Short Introduction* (Oxford: Oxford University Press, 2001).

Moser, Charles A. (ed.), *The Cambridge History of Russian Literature* (Cambridge: Cambridge University Press, 1989).

Terras, Victor, *A History of Russian Literature* (New Haven, London: Yale University Press, 1991).

Terras, Victor (ed.), *Handbook of Russian Literature* (New Haven, London: Yale University Press, 1985).

Wachtel, Andrew Baruch, and Ilya Vinitsky, *Russian Literature* (Cambridge: Polity, 2009).

HISTORY I

*

MOVEMENTS

The Age of Devotion

SIMON FRANKLIN

The age of devotion does not sit entirely comfortably in a history of literary movements. First is the problem of timescale. Most of the movements last no more than a generation or two. The age of devotion spans half a millennium, give or take a couple of centuries depending on the definition. Then there is the very idea of a 'movement'. Except, perhaps, at its inception, the age of devotion was not a programme, a project. And there is a deeper paradox in applying a word such as 'movement' in the context of a culture ostensibly dedicated to implying, in much of its production, precisely the opposite: a lack of movement, an aesthetic of reverential replication. Exponents of more recent literary movements tend to declare their newness; medieval writers tended to deny theirs. Moreover, the phrase itself, 'age of devotion', is not a standard label for a period in the history of Russian literature. It is not one of the familiar '-isms' that populate this strand of the *New Cambridge History*. It is merely an attempt to provide a succinctly descriptive alternative to the baldly chronological label 'medieval'. Since it is a new phrase, both of its principal components need unpacking: what are the boundaries of the 'age'? And what is meant by 'devotion'? Furthermore, what, in this context, should be reckoned 'literature'?

First, the age. The end is straightforward: for present purposes, the second half of the seventeenth century. The beginning is problematic. Most histories of Russian literature begin in the eleventh century. A problem with this is that in the eleventh century there was no such thing as Russia. Early Rus – the lands of the East Slavs up to the mid-thirteenth century – was a common ancestor for Russia, Ukraine, and Belarus, but the sole property of none. So, should one properly begin the age of devotion at a point when Russia itself came into being? Not so simple, for there is no such point. On geopolitical grounds one could construct a case for any period from the late thirteenth

century to the early sixteenth century. But a periodisation that makes sense in geopolitical terms does not necessarily make sense in literary terms. To complicate matters further, as we shall see, the processes of medieval text creation often differ fundamentally from a more familiar model based on the idea of an individual author's creation of an identifiable work. Text creation and text mutation can be continual, even over many centuries. This requires a somewhat different kind of history. Many of the general observations in this chapter will be as applicable to the literature of early Rus as to the literature of the Muscovite state. However, the main narrative will run from the fourteenth to the early seventeenth centuries,[1] while the temporal focus will be on the late fourteenth and fifteenth centuries.

Second: why 'devotion'? Because an overwhelming majority of literary texts – almost by whatever definition of literariness one chooses – were produced and consumed for Christian devotional purposes. Some were explicitly functional, for use in formal acts of devotion (church services). Others served to reinforce and explain the faith, to interpret the world and exemplify life according to the faith. Literate education came through the church. Most writers were churchmen or monks, though in the latter part of the period they were joined by increasing numbers of laymen trained in writing to meet the needs of an expanding state administration. The 'devotional' label does not mean that there was no room for aesthetic pleasure, nor does it mean that every text focused on expressly religious themes or was set in expressly religious terms. Indeed, some texts can be read as secular entertainment. Uniformity over several centuries would be odd, even in a conservative culture in which overt innovation was viewed negatively. However, 'devotional' is adequate as a generalisation.

That leaves 'literature'. There is no directly equivalent term in the language of the age. How does the familiar word map retrospectively onto unfamiliar phenomena? In order to qualify as literature, does a text need a literary *function*? Or should it display *formal* devices that signify literariness? Or should it be part of a literary *system* that may involve both form and function? Is literary status a product of authorial intention, or of readers' critical responses? In practice the label tends to have been applied to writings which seem to have been in some way – whether through forms, functions,

---

1 For a concise study of its precursor in the eleventh to thirteenth centuries, see Simon Franklin, 'East Slavonic', in Mark Chinca and Christopher Young (eds.), *Literary Beginnings in the European Middle Ages* (Cambridge: Cambridge University Press, 2022), pp. 276–98.

or devices – affective rather than baldly informative or directive. So, sermons may count, law codes and census lists do not. This is crude. A very great deal of time could be spent on attempting to reach closer definitions, but it is not clear that the outcome would be better.

Other chapters in the present volume will consider literary form and repertoire in more detail (see Chapters 2.1, 3.1). This chapter will focus on overall approaches, on ways of framing and characterising the literature of the age of devotion as a whole, as if it were a movement that can be circumscribed. The specific examples are illustrative, but too few to be adequately representative.

There are, broadly speaking, three complementary ways of representing the period: synchronic, diachronic, and dynamic. The synchronic description introduces general features of the literature of the age as a whole, the diachronic section outlines ways in which it has been constructed as changing over time, and the dynamic approach focuses on aspects of medieval textuality which complicate a linear chronological narrative of literary history.

Synchronic Approaches: Language, Style, Author, Text

Shifts in dominant literary movements – the swings from one '-ism' to the next – often involve cross-cultural contact, an interplay of internal requirement and external stimulus. By contrast, the literary culture of the age of devotion was, across most of its centuries, relatively self-contained. The primary encounter with external stimuli occurred early. In early Rus the external stimulus had been Christianity itself, following the official conversion in the late tenth century. The Rus assimilation of Christianity involved fundamental change across written and visual culture (writing itself came with Christianity), the applied arts, the built environment, public ritual, and aspects of social organisation – not to mention ethical standards, systems of belief, even articulations of identity. No further comparable shifts in the cultural paradigm occurred at least until the late seventeenth century. This is not to say that post-Rus Muscovite textual culture was entirely isolated. It was linked to the wider textual community of Orthodox Slavonic Christianity, within which texts and text producers migrated across geopolitical boundaries, sometimes with notable local consequences. Nor was it at all times hermetically sealed against any response to 'Latin' Christianity. Overall, however, the literature of the age of devotion has the appearance

of far more sustained stability than literatures of the equivalent centuries in western Europe.

The language of culture was Slavonic. Initially Slavonic had been a bridge to the assimilation of Christianity, but it was also a barrier to wider cultural dialogue. Unlike medieval western Europe, elite education was not based on Latin. There were no universities. Very, very few writers from Rus or Muscovy before the mid-seventeenth century would have read any Latin, or Greek, or indeed any vernacular language of western Europe. The western literary Renaissance had minimal resonance. The seventeenth-century shift in literary paradigms was closely linked to a shift in educational paradigms and to the influx of Latin- and Greek-educated bookmen (see Chapter 1.2).

Slavonic in Russia was not a uniform register. In the opinion of some scholars, it was not even a single language. At one end of a spectrum was Church Slavonic; and at the other end, East Slavonic. Church Slavonic was the written language that had been devised and developed expressly for the purpose of translating scriptural and liturgical texts. Anchored thus in the most authoritative writings of the faith, it retained an aura of dignity and solemnity even when appropriated into writings beyond the strictly devotional sphere. Church Slavonic had never been the everyday spoken language of the East Slavs. It was *a* vernacular but not *the* vernacular. Over the centuries it underwent contradictory developments. On the one hand, as a sacred register, it became ossified and remote; but at the same time, it continually interacted with the language of speech. Mutual contamination is a feature of literary history. One can debate theoretically as to whether Muscovite literary culture was bilingual, or diglossic, or flexible across a range of registers, or (on occasion) mildly chaotic.[2] The underlying point is the same: by drawing on the resources both of Church Slavonic and of East Slavonic, Muscovite writers possessed distinctive linguistic tools to enhance the range, flexibility, and nuance of expression.

From language to medium: the culture of elite writing in the age of devotion was almost exclusively a culture of manuscripts. The printing press was introduced to western Europe in the 1450s. Muscovite printing began in the 1550s, but its repertoire was very narrow indeed: before the accession of Tsar Aleksei Mikhailovich (r. 1645–76), every book printed in Moscow, with the exception of a few flimsy primers for the study of basic

2 See, for example, M. E. Remneva, *Puti razvitiia russkogo literaturnogo iazyka XI–XVII vv.* [Pathways in the development of the Russian literary language of the eleventh to seventeenth centuries] (Moscow: Izdatel'stvo Moskovskogo universiteta, 2003), pp. 165–303.

literacy, contained texts for church services. However, while the overwhelming predominance of manuscript for all texts other than the narrowly liturgical does mean that literature relied on the quintessentially medieval mode of production right through until the eighteenth century, manuscript culture could be enabling as well as restrictive. Crucial features of Muscovite textuality were made possible only because the medium of text creation and re-creation was the manuscript.

Mention of textuality leads to the question of authors and works. Literature of the age of devotion should not be imagined as a sequence of definitively established works created by known and named authors. Both author and work were on a spectrum from canonical fixity to irrelevance. At one end of the spectrum were works in what has been called a closed tradition.[3] Nobody disputed that King David was the author of the psalms, or that Matthew, Mark, Luke, and John wrote the four Gospels, or that St John Chrysostom was the author of very large numbers of homilies and works of exegesis (even if far more works were attributed to him than he actually wrote). However, the further one moves from scripture and liturgy, the more open the tradition becomes; the less fixed the text, the weaker its association with any named author.

Authorship was an ethical problem – or at any rate the kind of authorship that implies individuality and creativity and innovation. As in visual representation (iconography), in verbal representation the dominant aesthetic was imitative. Emulation of authoritative models cannot be reduced to an aesthetic preference. It was a moral imperative. The job of a writer was to illustrate and reinforce truths, not to challenge truisms. Standards had been set, exemplars had been established; the main purpose of visual and prestigious verbal representation was to affirm these exemplars. Most literary texts, like most icons, were anonymous. And where we happen to have a personal attribution, or where the first-person singular happens to play a role, the stress is on the *lack* of individuality. The individual merely borrows from the words of others, or sets down what he (writers were almost always male) has been told, or bears witness to what he has seen (see Box 4.1: The Medieval First-Person Singular). He is a vessel, or – at most – a craftsman, but not a creator. Innovation risks blasphemy, and individuality is pride.

Yet texts were created – and re-created. Paradoxically, the avoidance of explicit authorship also frees the text from the shackles of original intention.

---

3 William R. Veder, 'Texts of closed tradition: The key to the manuscript heritage of Old Rus'', *Harvard Ukrainian Studies* 12–13 (1988/9), 314–23.

The living text takes precedence over the Urtext. Truth was always traditional, but its representation left scope for re-presentation. In this respect the manuscript culture of the age of devotion could be analogous to oral tradition. Each teller may tell the tale in his own way, but none is its creator. There is no greater authenticity or authority in some notional 'original' version, even where such a thing can be identified. This was a culture of mutable textuality, not of the privileging of unique authors and their individualised works. If we are not overly preoccupied with a hierarchy that accords special status to the moment of authorial composition but look instead at the multiple textualities of a given period, then the literature of the age of devotion becomes a far more complex (and interesting) cultural phenomenon.

If there is no invention, there can be no fiction – or little that presents itself as such. Of course, there is a great deal in the literature of the age of devotion that may now seem implausible as documentary. A monk traps a demon who has emerged from his washbasin and compels it to carry him on an overnight round trip to the holy places in Jerusalem.[4] A holy man enters a church at night and, as he begins to chant, 'suddenly the walls parted, and, behold, the Devil entered, visible to the eye, with a multitude of his diabolical host [. . .] and they were dressed in the clothing and in the pointed hats of Lithuanians'.[5] A powerful king, who has defected to the Latin faith, sets a merchant of the Greek faith three riddles; if he fails to solve them, he must die. The merchant's young son solves them himself, becomes king, and frees the people to embrace the true faith.[6] In this literature there is much that is wondrous. One of its aims is to open people's eyes and minds to wonders. But there can be no invention. Everything is true. Parables are acceptable, as are visions and dreams (including visions of hell and the afterlife), but there is no place for Canterbury tales or divine comedies.

Mention of Chaucer and Dante highlights another absence: verse. There was plenty of scope for expressive and acoustic devices that can broadly be described as poetic. Church Slavonic can be densely metaphorical, and its rhetoric can be rhythmic and assonantal. Since it is a heavily inflected language, parallel syntactic structures can produce parallel patterns of

4 From a cycle of tales about Archbishop Ioann of Novgorod, in *Biblioteka literatury Drevnei Rusi* [Library of early Rus literature], 20 vols. (St Petersburg: Nauka, 1997–2020), vol. VI, pp. 450–8. This collection is hereafter cited as *BLDR*.
5 *Zhitie Sergiia Radonezhskogo* [Life of Sergii of Radonezh], in *BLDR*, vol. VI, p. 300.
6 *Povest' o Basarge i o syne ego Borzomysle* [The tale of Basarga and his son Borzomysl], in *BLDR*, vol. VII, pp. 472–82.

rhythm and sound reminiscent of rhyme. Substantial chunks of the literature are aimed at the ear rather than the eye, whether in general for reciting aloud or, more specifically, for musical chanting. Scriptural and Byzantine Greek poetry was transmitted in Slavonic prose, but an awareness of its poetic origins could remain. Psalms, for example, are routinely labelled as songs. Yet in translation and in native writings, there is no tradition of verse as a formal category. A few of the very earliest surviving Church Slavonic works were written in Byzantine-style syllabic verse, but there is no evidence that the practice, or even the understanding of the practice, migrated to Rus.[7]

Several of the above comments highlight absences: imaginative narrative but without the category of fiction; poetic expression but without verse; and, one could add, a great deal that was performative but with no theatre as such. What, then, *were* the dominant modes of the literature of the age of devotion? Here there is a paradox, or a distortion, in conventional literary history. The verbal art most integral and meaningful in the lives of its most focused and committed adherents was, almost certainly, biblical and liturgical. That is to say, the most prestigious written texts were devotional in the narrow sense. Their language set the standard, and their expressions permeated and lent authority to texts that were devotional in the broader sense.

Although in some respects restricted in form, the literature of the age of devotion reached across the boundaries of medium. Its words were often closely linked to pictures; verbal representation was in dialogue with visual representation. The links ran in both directions. Icons inspired narratives of their origins and of miracles associated with them, and episodes from saints' lives were translated into pictorial sequences of scenes surrounding the image of the saint in an icon. Icons always need textual justification, but a feature of the development of Russian iconography over the sixteenth and seventeenth centuries is an increase in narrative complexity, often accompanied by increasingly verbose verbal captions that can shade into continuous narratives.

When described in terms of its general characteristics, the literature of the age of devotion can sound not merely pious (which, at core, it was) but uniform and tedious, which it was not. It could be solemn and hypnotic, but it could also be lively, sharp, direct, subtle, dynamic, delightful, or shocking. A small sample of closer readings can help to provide a more nuanced sense of the range that lies behind the generalisations.

---

7 A. M. Panchenko, 'Perspektivy issledovaniia istorii drevnerusskogo stikhotvorstva' [Prospects for the study of early Russian versification], *Trudy Otdela drevnerusskoi literatury* [Proceedings of the early Russian literature section] 20 (1964), 256–73.

The spectrum of resources from Church Slavonic to current vernaculars provided, in theory, a lot of scope for flexibility of register and style. This relationship remained a key element in the development of literary expression right through to the emergence of modern standard Russian in the first half of the nineteenth century. The choices can be viewed on four levels. At its simplest, the difference was morphological, that is, to do with the forms of words. The Church Slavonic form, transmitted through scripture, liturgy, and exegesis, tended to have an aura of dignity and solemnity. The next level was lexical. Broadly speaking, Church Slavonic was richer in abstract vocabulary, while the lexicon of East Slavonic tended to be more concrete. Indeed, in many cases differences that had originally been morphological had become lexical-ised, such that the form derived from Church Slavonic retained an abstract meaning, while the cognate East Slavonic retained a concrete meaning (e.g., Church Slavonic *glava* – 'chapter', 'chief', but East Slavonic *golova* – 'head'). The third level is syntactic, relating to the structure of sentences. Complex sentences with multiple subordinate clauses or participial constructions tend to be a feature of Church Slavonic. Finally, there is rhetoric. The Church Slavonic tradition provided copious models of elaborate rhetorical figures, while ver-nacular expression tended to be more consistently direct. The description is binary; the practice was more subtle. Some texts are predominantly, even ostentatiously Church Slavonic; others are more consistently vernacular, but many are mixed. Moreover, hybrid texts can switch linguistic register depend-ing on the narrative focus, as when terse vernacular formulae of battle might be followed by a solemn eulogy to the victor in Church Slavonic.

Eulogy was a favourite display case for high rhetoric. For example, a eulogy to a mid-fifteenth-century prince, Boris Aleksandrovich of Tver (r. 1426–61), includes a particularly extensive version of the 'to what can I can compare you . . .?' topos: should I compare you to King Solomon? Or to the emperor Tiberius? Or to Leo the Wise? Or to Augustus? Or to Ptolemy Philadelphus, founder of the great library in Alexandria? Or to the emperor Constantine, or Justinian, or Theodosius? Or to Moses? Or to Joseph, whom God made lord over Egypt? In each case the eulogist adds a sentence to show why the comparison is inadequate, until he eventually gives up because Boris Aleksandrovich of Tver is simply incomparable: 'I have sought among the books of wisdom and among the kingdoms, but I have not found a tsar among tsars nor a prince among princes such as this great prince Boris Aleksandrovich.'[8] Thus the inordinately

---

8 *Smirennogo inoka Fomy slovo pokhval'noe o blagovernom velikom knaze Borise Aleksandroviche* [A panegyric by the humble monk Foma to the pious grand prince Boris Aleksandrovich], in *BLDR*, vol. VII, pp. 82–6.

loquacious eulogist confesses he is at a loss for words. To a modern reader the passage looks bizarrely disproportionate in almost any context, let alone in an address to a fifteenth-century prince of Tver. But in this kind of Church Slavonic rhetoric, plenitude was the norm: amplification beyond measure. In some ages the familiarity of a rhetorical convention provides a form of reassurance; in other times it marks the convention as inert and hence redundant. In the late fourteenth and early fifteenth centuries, the response was to cultivate a kind of aesthetic of rhetorical excess. One could almost (with caveats) call such flourishes Baroque. The conventional phrase is 'word weaving' (*pletenie sloves*).[9] The technique was to take any rhetorical figure – anaphoric, etymological, declamatory – and stretch it beyond familiar boundaries. Paradoxically, this can be seen as a means of 'making strange' (see Box 5.2: Viktor Shklovskii) while remaining ostentatiously ultra-traditional, a display of virtuosity without breaching etiquette.

Very rarely does the composer of any text in the age of devotion reflect on his own practices, or on how they might be perceived. We have to feed on the scraps, one of which is to be found in the *Life of Sergii of Radonezh* (*Zhitie Sergiia Radonezhskogo*), whose earliest version was put together in the late 1410s, but which (as is usual) survives only in later reworkings. The *Life of Sergii of Radonezh* is among the most verbose of all Muscovite hagiographies. The preface alone, declaring the hagiographer's unworthiness to perform his task, takes four pages in a quite densely printed modern edition. Then, towards the end of an equally expansive account of the saint's childhood, the hagiographer pauses: 'Is it really fitting to speak yet more, and with such prolixity of locution to make weary the ear of the listener? For density and prolixity of locution is the enemy of the ear, just as an overabundance and superfluity of food is the enemy of the body.'[10] This is a rhetorical non-apology: the hagiographer resumes his narrative with undiminished verbosity. Nevertheless, the aside on rhetorical plenitude, even though uncharacteristically brief, is a valuable reflection on the experience of consumption rather than the production of such literature. It is also notable for being phrased entirely in terms of reception by the ear, not the eye.

Church Slavonic markers of literariness are most blatant when displayed through the poetics of excess, but they do not have to be so demonstrative. For example, one of the most detailed narratives of the mid-fifteenth century is an account of the fall of Constantinople to the Ottoman Turks in 1453. This

---

9 See, for example, Faith C. M. Wigzell, *The Literary Style of Epifanij Premudryj: 'Pletenie sloves'* (Munich: Otto Sagner, 1976).

10 *Zhitie Sergiia Radonezhskogo*, in *BLDR*, vol. VI, pp. 272–4.

was taken as a hugely significant event not just in geopolitics but in sacred history. The city that had been the head and heart of the thousand-year empire of eastern Christianity was seen as having fallen to the infidel. The *Tale of the Taking of Tsargrad* [the Imperial City] *by the Turks in 1453 (Povest' o vziatii Tsar'grada turkami v 1453 godu)* is a day-by-day, occasionally hour-by hour and blow-by-blow report of actual events, a valuable resource for historians. It is also written in a literary register that goes well beyond routine chronicle cliché. For example, the description of one of the Turkish assaults on the walls begins with a standard military formula that can be found many times in any chronicle: 'And there was a great and fearsome battle.' But the text expands. Here the narrator is particularly concerned with sounds: the Turkish artillery, the church bells, the shouting, the clash of weapons, the screams and cries, such that 'it was impossible for one person to hear what another was saying', and 'everything conjoined into a single roar, like loud thunder'.[11] The agglomerative description is reinforced by alliterative and assonantal phrases. In English, the battle was 'most fearsome: from the banging of the cannons and the mortars and the pealing of the bells'. In the original (with alliteration in bold and assonance underlined): '*secha preuzhasna: ot pushechnogo bo i pishchalnogo stuku, i ot zuku zvonnogo*'. This is in the context of a text that does not strive for pristine-sounding Church Slavonic. The language here is characteristically hybrid: a productive assimilation of Church Slavonic devices in a hybrid linguistic register adapted to its contemporary purpose.

In the *Tale of the Taking of Tsargrad*, dramatic and acoustic devices resonate with the drama of events, but one can also find a seemingly opposite combination when the extremity of events is foregrounded precisely through the incongruously undemonstrative, almost deadpan manner of their telling. Another narrative from the late fifteenth century opens as follows:

> In the Wallachian land there lived a ruler, a Christian of the Greek faith, named in the Wallachian language Drakula, and in our language Devil. He was so cruel and so clever: as was his name, thus was his life. Once there came to him envoys from the Turkish sultan. And they entered into his presence and bowed down to him according to their custom, without removing their hats. And he asked them: 'Why do you do this? You enter into the presence of a great lord and show me such disrespect.' They answered: 'Such, lord, is our custom and the custom of our land.' And he said to them: 'And I wish to affirm your law, that you may hold fast to it.'

---

11 *Povest' o vziatii Tsar'grada turkami v 1453 godu* [Tale of the taking of Tsargrad by the Turks in 1453], in *BLDR*, vol. VII, p. 34.

And he ordered that their hats be nailed to their skulls with small iron tacks, and he let them go, saying: 'Go and say to your lord: he may be accustomed to enduring such disrespect from you, but we are not. Let him not send his own custom to other rulers who do not want it. Let him keep his custom to himself.'[12]

Thus opens the *Tale of Drakula* (*Skazanie o Drakule*), a Muscovite variant (not, it seems, a translation) of stories that also circulated in western Europe, inspired by the Moldavian ruler Vlad Tepeš (1431–76/7), also known as Vlad 'the Impaler' on account of his favourite mode of punishment. Some of the scenes are still more lurid. Drakula dines surrounded by stakes with the impaled and rotting corpses of those he has punished. When a servant is incautious enough to flinch at the stench, his punishment – of course – is likewise impalement. Yet let it not be thought that Drakula was randomly sadistic. In his way, he was just, and the severity of his rule kept his people honest. When he left a golden goblet by a well, nobody dared to steal it. Sixteenth-century redactions of the tale, in the age of Ivan IV ('the Terrible', r. 1533–84), articulate more extensive lessons about the wisdom of cruelty in a ruler; but, so far as we can tell, the earliest version narrates without embellishment and allows the contradictions to stand for themselves – a rare and early specimen of a text that can be read almost as tabloid entertainment.

In the *Tale of Drakula* restraint is a device, in this case to emphasise – through contrast rather than through amplification – the extremity of content. To this extent the *Tale* still fits the strand of tradition whereby protagonists tend to be represented with minimal nuance, as types more than as individuals, whether positive or negative. In search of immediacy it is counterintuitive to look at a life of a saint, who by definition must ultimately be presented as an exemplar, but here too there is a spectrum. Also from the 1470s, almost exactly contemporary with the earliest version of the *Tale of Drakula*, is an account of the death, in 1477, of Pafnutii of Borovsk, founder of what was to become one of Muscovy's major monasteries. The last week of Pafnutii's life is chronicled by his disciple, the monk Innokentii. This account, which has come to be known as the *Tale of the Death of Pafnutii of Borovsk* (*Rasskaz o smerti Pafnutiia Borovskogo*) is an intriguingly un-hagiographic fragment of putative hagiography, in which the self-effacing Innokentii depicts his hero as grumpy and querulous. Pafnutii scolds Innokentii for even suggesting he might receive any of the dignitaries who have come to see him: 'What were

---

12 *Skazanie o Drakule* [Tale of Drakula], in *BLDR*, vol. VII, p. 460.

you thinking of?' Pafnutii has spent sixty years being attentive to princes, boyars, and other laymen, 'and I don't know to what purpose'. Finally, he has realised: there is no point.[13] Through all the revered elder's grumblings, as a kind of surreal sideshow his novice (with whom he shares a cell) is fast asleep. Here too, of course, Pafnutii is exemplary – in his rejection of the world and of the cares of the worldly. But there is a rather rare representation of individuality in the relationship between the irritable holy man and his timid and fretful disciple.

Diachronic Approaches: Histories

What happens when these general characteristics are stretched onto a framework of time? The problem of constructing a history is reflected in the wide variety of shaping devices employed by those who have tried to do so. Crudely speaking, histories of the literature of the age of devotion apply one or more of four sets of criteria: chronological sequence, geopolitical context, dominant style, and epistemological progression.

An extreme example of the chronological approach is a textbook which simply allocates a chapter to each century, with no pretence that a century is a coherent unit by literary criteria.[14] A similarly pragmatic approach is taken by the main handbooks and anthologies, which similarly divide the age into sequential chunks of time (not necessarily century by century).[15]

The most widespread geopolitical periodisation divides literature into pre-Mongol (eleventh to early thirteenth century), literature of the period of Mongol domination (mid-thirteenth to late fifteenth centuries), and literature of the Muscovite state (sixteenth to seventeenth centuries).[16] This approach is not literary as such, but it does provide an explanatory framework for several of the empirical observations that are common ground among most historians of the subject. For example, literary production and focus before the late fifteenth century was more diffuse than

---

13 *Rasskaz o smerti Pafnutiia Borovskogo* [Tale of the death of Pafnutii of Borovsk], in *BLDR*, vol. VII, p. 276.

14 A. V. Arkhangel'skaia and A. A. Pautin, *Russkaia literatura XI–XVII vv.* [Russian literature of the eleventh to seventeenth centuries] (Moscow: Izdatel'stvo Moskovskogo universiteta, 2003).

15 Thus, in the twenty-volume *BLDR*; or the four-volume (in nine) *Slovar' knizhnikov i knizhnosti Drevnei Rusi* [Dictionary of bookmen and book culture of early Rus] (Leningrad: Nauka, 1987–9; St Petersburg: Dmitrii Bulanin, 1992–2017).

16 Among many examples see, for example, John Fennell and Antony Stokes, *Early Russian Literature* (London: Faber and Faber, 1974); Andrei Karavashkin, *Literaturnyi obychai Drevnei Rusi* [Literary custom in early Rus] (Moscow: ROSSPEN, 2011).

subsequently. Often it reflected regional interests: tales of locally venerated holy men, praise for local rulers. Specimens include the eulogy to Prince Boris Aleksandrovich of Tver, or the cycle of tales comprising the Life of Ioann, archbishop of Novgorod (d. 1186), cited above. The growth and eventual domination of the Muscovite state had a significant impact on literary production. It affected themes, prominent among which was the rise and God-given status of Moscow itself. It affected a process of canon formation, since among the major sponsored projects were vast and putatively definitive compilations both of historical narratives and of cycles of approved saints' lives. The rise of the Muscovite state could also affect the adaptation of existing texts (see Chapter 3.1).

This kind of scheme links literary change to external change. Histories based on stylistic or epistemological criteria seek evidence for change within literature itself. A particularly influential scheme based on a succession of 'styles of the age' was elaborated by Dmitrii Likhachev, who proposed a sequence of three dominant styles. The first period in his sequence, spanning the eleventh to thirteenth centuries (early Rus rather than Russia as such), was characterised by its 'monumental historicism'. This was the age of what came to be treated as the foundational texts in subsequent East Slav (Ukrainian, Russian, Belarusian) historical memory and identity: texts such as the *Primary Chronicle* (*Povest' vremennykh let*, compiled in the early twelfth century) and the *Sermon on Law and Grace* (*Slovo o zakone i blagodati*, mid-eleventh century) of Metropolitan Ilarion, which articulated a place for Rus in universal and sacred history. Next came the 'rhetorical-panegyric' style that typified what Likhachev called the 'Pre-Renaissance' of the fourteenth and fifteenth centuries, and then a 'second monumentalism' of the sixteenth century.[17] The most theoretically intricate scheme is devised by A. N. Uzhankov, who has constructed a multi-layered structure involving five stages of epistemological development and three stages in the development of consciousness, underpinning three stages of 'literary formation'.[18]

---

17 D. S. Likhachev, *Razvitie russkoi literatury X–XVII vekov. Epokhi i stili* [The development of Russian literature of the tenth to seventeenth centuries. Epochs and styles] (Leningrad: Nauka, 1973); cf. the less consistent 'stylistic' history by Dmitrij Čiževskij, *History of Russian Literature: From the Eleventh Century to the End of the Baroque* (The Hague: Mouton, 1971).

18 A. N. Uzhankov, *O spetsifike razvitiia russkoi literatury XI–pervoi treti XVIII veka. Stadii i formatsii* [The particular characteristics of the development of Russian literature from the eleventh to the first third of the eighteenth centuries. Stages and formations] (Moscow: Iazyki slavianskoi kul'tury, 2009).

A Dynamic Approach: Mutating Textualities

We open a printed edition, read the *text*, and believe that we have read the *work*. Of course, text editing in any age has its complications and its arcane disciplinary conventions. For printed literature of the modern era, an editor may have to deal with imperfect relationships between authorial drafts and printed texts, or between various printed editions that may reflect either the interventions of editors or changes in authorial intention. More remotely, in editions of the literature of the ancient world, where manuscript can also be separated from author by many centuries, the traditional aim of textual scholarship has been to restore the closest possible approximation of an authorial text, even if many readings are unavoidably hypothetical. Intellectually we know that the identification of the visible text with the underlying work may be an illusion, but for most practical purposes we can ignore that knowledge without significant loss.

In Russian literature of the age of devotion, the problem of text and work can be very different, and the illusion of their identity can be correspondingly more damaging. Back to the printed edition: turning to the apparatus, we are likely to see small-print references to the real texts from which the printed work is an extrapolation. There may be references to variant readings such as are normal and more or less unavoidable in manuscript transmission. Often, however, there will be references to more fundamental variations, in Russian editions usually labelled redactions: the long redaction, the short redaction, the chronographic redaction, the hagiographic redaction, the hybrid redaction, and so on. There may be elaborate graphic representations (stemmata, like interlocking geneal-ogies) of the relations of the redactions to each other, and, in turn, to their own various realisations in actual manuscripts. A given text is only one realisation of a notional work, and a given manuscript is only one realisation of a given text or redaction. There can be many, many different such realisations of the work. In such cases one can argue that the work, as a singular thing, does not exist. It is an abstract notion variously projected onto, or obliquely reflected in, a range of real texts. Moreover, textual genealogies create a further illusion: linear chronology. In one respect this is fair: they indicate sequences of textual dependency and change that can be mapped over time. However, unlike real family histories, in the life of texts the earlier generations do not necessarily die. On the contrary, versions that are born in sequence can live in parallel (and even cross-fertilise) for centuries.

In classic versions of textual history, one can fairly easily, if not always precisely, separate the work from its reception. The work is produced by its author, and reception is its subsequent cultural history. In the age of devotion, such a split between work and reception is far more problematic. The work is the totality of its sequential and co-existing realisations in time. It is a field of variously actualised possibilities and mutations.

Textual mutability can be regarded as particularly challenging when it applies to that very small group of materials that tend to be identified as strongly literary in a modern sense. Here the temptation to look for the canonical version is perhaps strongest. The battle of Kulikovo Field in 1380, when Prince Dmitrii Ivanovich (r. 1359–89) inflicted Moscow's first major defeat on a Mongol army, has become one of the standard landmarks in stories of the rise of Muscovy, and accounts of the battle have a special status in literary as well as historical mythology. There are extensive chronicle narratives, but in purely literary terms the most celebrated is known as the *Zadonshchina* (The events beyond the Don). The *Zadonshchina*, which probably originated in the 1380s, is an evocation more than a narrative: epic in its magnification of events and historical sweep, lyrical in its manner. It is thickly packed with metaphors, ostentatiously echoing a previous and still more lyrically saturated text in an equivalent mode: the *Tale of Igor's Campaign* (*Slovo o polku Igoreve*; see Box 6.1). A modern editor of the *Zadonshchina* bemoans the fact that (if we disregard a late-fifteenth-century abbreviation) it survives in five manuscripts of the sixteenth and seventeenth centuries, all of which contain texts that have been 'seriously distorted by copyists'.[19] Editors admit that even the hypothetical 'protograph' of the existing manuscripts was already only an approximation of the late-fourteenth-century original work.[20] Such caveats do little to inhibit modern readers from treating the modern editions as if they were indeed that original work.

The second example is more extreme in the disconnect of existing texts both from each other and from their remote and hypothetical original. Three manuscripts of the late seventeenth and eighteenth centuries include selections of episodes, combining elements of epic and of romance, about the origins and adventures of the warrior Devgenii. Devgenii's father was King Amir of the land of the Saracens. His mother was a fabled beauty, of the

19 L. A. Dmitriev, in *BLDR*, vol. VI, p. 532.
20 L. A. Dmitriev and O. P. Likhacheva (eds.), *Skazaniia i povesti o Kulikovskoi bitve* [Narratives and tales of the battle of Kulikovo] (Leningrad: Nauka, 1982), pp. 369–71. See also pp. 25–127 for the multiple redactions of another narrative of the same event, the *Skazanie o Mamaevom poboishche* [Tale of the battle against Mamai].

Greek faith, whom Amir had kidnapped. Yet Amir kept her in honour and dignity and made her his wife after being defeated by her three brothers and promising to abandon his faith and become Christian. Devgenii's own adventures include abducting the daughter of a general and killing a dragon. Devgenii's literary ancestor was Greek. The cycle of stories was derived from a set of Greek verse tales of Digenis ('of double birth') Akritas, which made their way into Slavonic in (according to the various conjectures) the twelfth, thirteenth, or fourteenth century. We therefore know that the tales of Devgenii lived through centuries of East Slav tradition, perhaps as much as half a millennium, despite the fact that no properly medieval manuscript survives. None of the configurations of episodes and readings in any of the Russian manuscripts corresponds precisely either to any of the other Russian manuscripts or to any of the Greek manuscripts (which themselves vary widely). Perhaps because of the subject matter and style, it is relatively easy to accept that such texts live and mutate, that questions of authorship and canonicity are not relevant to status and cultural history, that here there is no meaningful binary categorisation of translated versus native or 'original' versus copy or adaptation. The plainest analogy is with oral tradition, with which the stories of Digenis/Devgenii have obvious affinities. Each retelling belongs to the teller, even while situated in a tradition of the tale.

The final example is in a minor key, but it is in some ways more indicative in its complexity. It also begins with a battle, a date, and known protagonists. In 1170, forces sent by the prince of Suzdal attempted unsuccessfully to take the city of Novgorod. As an episode in late-twelfth-century politics, the Suzdalian campaign of 1170 was significant but not exceptional. The chronicles of the age are full of such episodes; indeed, we have narratives of this one from the perspective of both sides, in Novgorodian and Suzdalian chronicles. But that was far from the end of it. The battle of the Novgorodians and the Suzdalians resonated across texts and contexts for about six centuries. We do not know how the story changed in retelling by word of mouth over the first few generations, but by around the mid-fourteenth century it was no longer just a military tale. It had become a miracle tale. Novgorod was saved by an icon of the Mother of God. Archbishop Ioann heard a voice telling him that the icon would save the city. The icon initially refused to be taken by those who were sent to fetch it, but after appropriate prayer it consented to move. Carried to the ramparts, it faced the city and wept. God heard the entreaties of His mother and sowed confusion in the ranks of the Suzdalians.

The tale became popular. It was copied and re-copied, edited and re-edited, expanded and contracted, retold and restyled in several versions through to the late seventeenth century.[21] It came to be combined with a wide range of different texts, both in chronicles and in hagiography, where it formed part of the Life of Archbishop Ioann. It became a multimedia narrative, crossing from words to pictures and inspiring new versions of the iconography of miracles of the Mother of God. In its multiple changes it illustrates some of the key features of textuality in the age of devotion.

First, there is the matter of text and author. It makes no sense to speak of *the* author or of *the* text. As we saw above, the various versions are not corruptions of a notional original, nor do they constitute merely a history of reception. No embodiment is definitive; the story exists only in its mutations. The work is not a fixed thing but a field of variously realised possibilities that can continually reshape and recontextualise themselves over an extraordinarily long timespan. As for author: in a few cases we happen to know who shaped or copied a particular version, but in most cases we do not. There is no named author. In this mode of manuscript culture, every time a scribe sits down with a quill there is the possibility of fresh text generation.

Secondly, this text can stand for many others in the way it was transformed from a military narrative into a devotional narrative, from a story of a particular attempted invasion into an exemplary miracle tale of the Mother of God as protectress. Another popular example is the *Tale of Temir-Aksak (Povest' o Temir Aksake)*. Here the underlying battle narrative recounts how the fearsome Mongol tsar Temir, known more widely in western tradition as Tamerlane, appeared unexpectedly with his forces on the southern borders of Muscovy. Prince Vasilii Dmitrievich of Moscow (Basil I, r. 1389–1425) sent for the ancient icon of the Mother of God from the former capital of Vladimir, and Temir miraculously retreated.[22] Like the *Tale of the Battle of the Novgorodians and the Suzdalians*, the *Tale of Temir-Aksak* mutated over the centuries and spawned fresh episodes and new versions. It survives in over two hundred manuscripts. It migrated in and out of chronicles, and it became a component of collections of tales about the icon's miracles.

The third aspect of medieval textuality exemplified in the story of the Novgorodian miracle is that it crossed the boundaries of media. It was

---

21 L. A. Dmitriev, *Zhitiinye povesti russkogo severa kak pamiatniki literatury XIII–XVII vv.* [Hagiographic tales of the Russian north as works of literature of the thirteenth to seventeenth centuries] (Leningrad: Nauka, 1973), pp. 95–148. See p. 135 for the stemma of some of the versions.

22 *Povest' o Temir Aksake* [Tale of Temir-Aksak], in *BLDR*, vol. VI, pp. 230–40.

re-envisioned in iconography. Already in the fifteenth century we find the first examples of the composition. Two hundred years later it was still popular, and by no means just as a story of Novgorod. As late as the 1740s it appeared, for example, in the lush frescoes of a church in Iaroslavl.

This kind of dynamic is not conducive to a narrative history of literature structured around who wrote which works when, around the notion of definitive texts written in distinctive ways. However, when thus paraphrased, it is still linear, even if multi-directional. A particular complication is that, as we saw, fresh texts by no means always supersede older versions. They co-exist as parallel strands. Thus, out of nearly two hundred manuscripts listed in one study of various texts related to the life of Ioann of Novgorod, there is little obvious correlation between the dates of the manuscripts and the presumed date of origin of the versions that they convey.[23] We summarise a story of change, but here again a linear history misrepresents the dynamics of textualities.

The problems of text, work, and author are only three elements in the nexus of relationships which make the age of devotion so challenging to post-medieval (if not postmodern) assumptions about categories and processes of literary culture. Other dimensions are considered in the chapter that deals with medieval institutions of production (see Chapter 2.1). However, one should also be wary of excessive exoticisation. Summary simplifies, and dominant features are not universal rules. Despite the generalisations about mutability and fluidity, it would be wrong to imply that *no* texts adequately represent real and identifiable 'works', or that *no* works can be attributed to real and identifiable authors. Nevertheless, clear movement towards reconciling the three, as a trend, as part of an identifiable 'movement', is a feature of the latter part of the period, and then, in a more focused way, of the Baroque.

Further Reading

Biblioteka literatury Drevnei Rusi [Library of early Rus literature], 20 vols. (St Petersburg: Nauka, 1997–2020).

Čiževskij, Dmitrij, *History of Russian Literature: From the Eleventh Century to the End of the Baroque* (The Hague: Mouton, 1971).

Fennell, John, and Antony Stokes, *Early Russian Literature* (London: Faber and Faber, 1974).

23 Dmitriev, *Zhitiinye povesti*, pp. 281–9.

Karavashkin, Andrei, *Literaturnyi obychai Drevnei Rusi* [Literary custom in early Rus] (Moscow: ROSSPEN, 2011).

Likhachev, D. S., *Razvitie russkoi literatury X–XVII vekov. Epokhi i stili* [The development of Russian literature of the tenth to seventeenth centuries. Epochs and styles] (Leningrad: Nauka, 1973).

Likhachev, S. S., *The Poetics of Early Russian Literature*, trans. Christopher M. Arden-Close (Plymouth: Lexington Books, 2014).

Zenkovsky, Serge, *Medieval Russia's Epics, Chronicles and Tales*, rev. and enl. edn (New York: Meridian, 1974).

The Baroque Age

SIMON FRANKLIN

The label 'Baroque' in Russian culture refers to a period stretching roughly from the mid-seventeenth century to the early eighteenth century. The term is applied in retrospect. Like any such label, it is imperfect and occasionally contentious. Its appropriateness in a Russian context has been broadly accepted only since the last quarter of the twentieth century. Its purpose is clear: to signal that aspects of Russian culture can be regarded as analogous to, and in some areas stimulated by, features of Baroque culture elsewhere. It is not an exact term, and the Baroque is not a single or clearly circumscribed phenomenon even in its limited Russian versions, let alone across the rest of Europe. Comparative studies emphasise difference as much as similarity.[1] Nevertheless, the acceptance of the term does point to a significant shift in Russian culture, and part of that shift was an unprecedentedly sustained and multidimensional engagement with a range of western European cultural styles and practices. There had been earlier episodes. In the late fifteenth century, for example, Moscow's main cathedrals, and even the monumental walls of the Kremlin itself, had been built through the employment of Italian architects. The Baroque age was different. It was not a product merely of the temporary employment of foreigners (though this, too, occurred on a fairly large scale). It reflects an active cultural encounter: stimulated in some respects from outside, assimilated and adapted locally, and embedded in practice and eventually in education. In such respects the cultural dynamic of the Baroque age, unlike the prolonged age of devotion (see Chapter 1.1), is comparable to the processes that gave rise to the succession of '-isms' that

---

[1] On the fundamental functional differences between the western Baroque and the Russian Baroque, see Viktor Zhivov, 'Towards a typology of the Baroque in Russian literature of the XVII–early XVIII centuries', trans. Marcus C. Levitt, *Vivliothika: E-Journal of Eighteenth-Century Russian Studies* 9 (2021), 128–46.

followed. In written culture, the Baroque age can reasonably be reckoned to encompass Russia's first modern literary 'movement'.

Baroque fashion in Russia was not limited to literature. The literary movement was part of a wider cultural shift, which extended to architecture, to painting, to the applied arts, to performance. Sometimes the seventeenth century is called Russia's age of transition. The implied transition is, crudely speaking, from medievalism to modernisation, from the devotional to the secular, from self-absorption to curiosity, from Byzantinism to westernism, from golden-domed Moscow to pastel-palaced St Petersburg, and so on. Such binaries reflect the idea of a fundamental divide in Russian history and culture, with Peter I (r. 1682–1725) as the pivotal figure. In this scheme, the age of transition prepares the way for the Petrine reforms. The problem here is twofold. First, the label 'age of transition' characterises the culture of the mid- to late seventeenth century with reference to what it was not, rather than what it was. By contrast, the term 'Baroque' focuses attention on the thing itself. Second, the binaries are excessively schematic. The Baroque age was the cultural environment in which Peter I grew up, and in several respects Petrine culture was not a radical rejection of Peter's own past but an extension of it and from it. The 'Baroque' label stresses a kind of Petrine continuity, a counterbalance to the notion of a Petrine divide or a Petrine revolution. Rather than a fundamentally new beginning, the culture of the early eighteenth century becomes simply a new phase – the St Petersburg phase – of the Russian Baroque.[2]

The Baroque in Russia does not have a precise chronology; it did not manifest itself across all cultural media simultaneously, nor was it uniform. In architecture there is a considerable distance – in time, in influence, in style – between the Moscow or 'Naryshkin' Baroque of the late seventeenth century, with its affinities with central and eastern Europe, and the more Italianate Baroque of the mid-eighteenth century (sometimes called Elizabethan through its association with the reign of the empress Elizabeth from 1741 to 1762). In literature there is no moment of transition from the age of devotion to early Baroque, nor is there a clear boundary (and perhaps no clear distinction) between late Baroque and Classicism (see Chapter 1.3). By the very broadest definitions, features of it in literature can be traced across more than a hundred years, from the early seventeenth century up to

---

[2] See A. M. Panchenko, 'Dva etapa russkogo barokko' [Two stages of the Russian Baroque], *Trudy Otdela drevnerusskoi literatury* [Proceedings of the early Russian literature section] 32 (1977), 100–6. Cf. Kirill Rogov, 'Tri epokhi russkogo barokko' [Three ages of the Russian Baroque], *Tynianovskii sbornik* [Tynianov miscellany] 12 (2006), 9–101.

the second quarter of the eighteenth century. This chapter briefly surveys aspects of this long Baroque, before focusing on key figures of what might be called the high Moscow Baroque from the 1660s onwards.

Of the many processes in the emergence of the early modern Muscovite state over the sixteenth and seventeenth centuries, one can highlight four as being especially relevant to innovation in literature: the growth of bureaucracy, geopolitical developments that facilitated an enhanced engagement with 'Latin' (i.e. central and western European) culture, the establishment of printing, and the emergence of the court as a focus of innovative cultural patronage.

Over the sixteenth and seventeenth centuries, Muscovite governance was conducted through an ever-expanding system of chanceries (*prikazy*). Chanceries needed to be staffed. The proliferation of chanceries therefore led directly to the emergence of a new (for Russia) and substantial set of people whose job it was to write, to compose, to copy, to correct, and sometimes to translate. The new contexts for writing produced a new corps of writers, a non-ecclesiastical literate elite owing preferment to the state rather than to the church. Not in all cases were the limits of their cultural horizons set by their bureaucratic obligations. Some, at least, extended their interests into literature.

Engagement with 'Latin' culture (as western European culture tended to be designated) was, paradoxically, enhanced by periods of state weakness as well as strength. At its most vulnerable, during the Time of Troubles at the start of the seventeenth century, Moscow was twice subjected to Polish occupation, not without a degree of local support. This brought unprecedentedly direct contact with western and central Europe, side-effects of which can be traced in written culture. By extreme contrast, the mid-seventeenth century was a period of Muscovy's rapid and dynamic expansion both eastwards and westwards. If we were concerned mainly with scale, or indeed with the origins of Russia as a multi-ethnic and multicultural state, then we would probably focus on the Russian expansion to the east. This began a century earlier with the capture of the mosque-adorned city of Kazan by the troops of Ivan IV (r. 1533–84) in 1552 and continued with the appropriation of huge areas of Siberia in the seventeenth century. However, for the history of Russian literature and culture in themselves, the most significant expansion was to the west: not Peter I's founding of St Petersburg in 1703, but the annexation, in the mid-seventeenth century, of large swathes of what is sometimes termed Ruthenia – the traditionally Orthodox East Slav lands within the Polish-Lithuanian commonwealth. Broadly speaking, this equates

to modern Ukraine as far as and including Kyiv, plus Belarus. As political domination spread westwards, cultural appropriation and assimilation flowed back in the opposite direction to Moscow from its newly encompassed periphery. It brought within the Muscovite state a new kind of educated elite: men who, for the most part, professed Orthodoxy, but who had received a Latin-based education along Jesuit lines. Many of the shapers of Muscovite learning and writing in the latter half of the seventeenth century and the early eighteenth century were recruited from Ruthenia. Visually, verbally, and architecturally, the Muscovite Baroque drew on, and was in important respects shaped by, engagement with equivalents in the culture first of the Polish-Lithuanian commonwealth, then of the newly annexed Ukrainian lands.

The third kind of context is technological. Printing came to Moscow late and spread slowly. The first Moscow-printed books were produced in the 1550s. For over half a century they appeared sporadically, and for a further hundred years there was, most of the time, just one printing house in Moscow (the Moscow Print Yard). Printing in Moscow was not a catalyst for the kinds of cultural, economic, and social transformations that have been associated with its rise in western Europe. Throughout the seventeenth century, Muscovite printing served almost exclusively the agendas of the church. It was an instrument of change in one respect, as the means to standardise and disseminate the liturgical reforms instigated by Patriarch Nikon in the 1650s, the reaction to which triggered a major schism in the Russian church, but its contents and concerns were overwhelmingly devotional. However, and perhaps surprisingly, the influence of the Moscow Print Yard on Muscovite letters extended beyond its direct production of printed books. The Moscow Print Yard had a substantial library, and its directors and senior employees included some of the best-known scholars, educators, and writers of the age.

Finally, the fourth context to which attention should particularly be drawn is the court. Although Russian court culture tends to be associated especially with the eighteenth century (see Chapter 2.2), it was in the second half of the seventeenth century, under Tsar Aleksei Mikhailovich (r. 1645–76) and his son Fedor (r. 1676–82), that the palace rather than the church began to become a focus of cultural activity: not just as a source of patronage for ecclesiastical institutions but for its own amusement, interest, edification, and glorification. It is not customary to regard pre-Petrine Russian rulers as catalysts for cultural innovation, but court taste and court patronage supported and

stimulated the modern trends, whether in literature, in visual culture, or in performance.

Within these contexts, one can identify broad features characteristic of the literature of this period, which distinguish it from the literature of the devotional age that preceded it. The culture of Russia's early modernity allowed for a sharpening of focus on the individual. This is most simply seen in relation to production and attribution. A culture of anonymity turned into a culture of named authorship: not all at once and not universally, but substantially and significantly. Painters began to name themselves, both inconspicuously on the reverse of panel icons and prominently on the walls alongside their frescoes. The originators of texts – that is, authors, not just scribes – began to declare their authorship. For some, literary authorship became not just a fact but an aspect of identity. For a very few, in the latter part of the century, it even became, in effect, a profession.

Alongside the emerging individuality of the producer was an expanding scope for individuality in what was produced. Iconographers looked beyond conventional modes of representation and started to make extensive use of what were acknowledged to be the more 'life-like' styles found in western European engravings. Painters began to take commissions in an area that conventionally would have been reckoned at best frivolous, at worst blasphemous: individual portraits of living subjects. Gradually, beyond and even within the scope of the formalised religious image, Russian painting found room for the observational and the imaginary. Literature displayed increasingly individualised features of characterisation, of speech, of setting. Among the most notable literary products of the late seventeenth century is Russia's first substantial autobiography.

Parallel and in some respects linked to such shifts in the representations of author and subject, there were changes in literary form and function. With respect to form, Baroque fashion distanced the literary artefact, held it up for inspection in fresh ways, and created new meanings through focusing attention on aspects of verbal craft. In the devotional age there had of course been skilled rhetoricians, golden-tongued masters of mellifluous and affective rhetoric. Nevertheless, there is a fine but adequately clear distinction between, on the one hand, rhetoric that served conventional expectation and, on the other hand, displays of verbal virtuosity that focused attention on themselves. In Russian Baroque literature, form was foregrounded. It was schooled and studied, demonstrated and displayed, renewed and explored. With respect to function, literature in the Baroque age was less reticent about entertainment. Again, this is a matter of emphasis. On the one hand,

devotional literature could be engaging, lively, affective; on the other hand, Baroque literature rarely abandoned a sense of underlying serious purpose. Nevertheless, in Baroque fashion the balance of presentation tipped towards performance and entertainment. Literature could be entertainingly moral, or morally entertaining, but the manner drew attention to enjoyment in the artefact. The foregrounding of performative function is linked to the foregrounding of performative form.

As illustration, we can look more closely at two areas of literary production which at first glance seem almost unrelated and rooted in distinct traditions but which nevertheless both reflect the cultural shifts of the seventeenth century: parody and satire; and poetry.

Parody and Satire

Seventeenth-century parodies and satires were in many respects rooted in medieval conventions of written culture. They were almost all anonymous. They are hard to date. Several of them survive in dozens of manuscript copies and in a range of versions. They were not fixed authorial compositions but mutable modes in which each scribe could be a co-creator. At the same time, in their pointed distancing of form and in their highlighted displays of verbal dexterity, the parodies and satires are compatible with elite trends in the age of the Baroque. Parody relies on distortion: of style, perspective, situation, structure, characters, values, and so on. Like caricature, parody assumes that its reader has some sense of its undistorted prototype. Parody highlights its own dependence on the intertext. Russian seventeenth-century parodies play on a strikingly diverse range of implied source genres: transcripts of court proceedings; petitions; a dowry agreement; a book of medical remedies; an alphabetic acrostic common in primers; liturgies of various kinds. Most of them are quite brief, taking up just a few pages in modern editions. They are concentrated, intense performances of their respective techniques, not extensive compositions.

The Tale of Ruff Ruffson (*Povest' o Ershe Ershoviche*) purports to record litigation between fish (a ruff and a bream, with an array of other piscine witnesses, officials, and judges) in a dispute over ownership of the Rostov lake.[3] Originating probably in the mid-seventeenth century, the anonymous story mutated into variant versions, even changing the social status and

---

[3] *Povest' o Ershe Ershoviche* [The tale of Ruff Ruffson], in *Biblioteka literatury Drevnei Rusi* [Library of early Rus literature], 20 vols. (St Petersburg: Nauka, 1997–2020), vol. XVI, pp. 396–400. This collection is hereafter cited as *BLDR*.

character of the 'hero', but without altering the parodic device at the core. An abbreviated version migrated into popular prints.

Liturgy to a Tavern (*Sluzhba kabaku*) is perhaps the most extensive and complex of such works.[4] Written as if in the form of a service for vespers, parodying hymnographic and biblical texts as well as the overall structure and rhythms of the service, it is a sustained mockery of inebriation. Part of the parody is visual. *Liturgy to a Tavern* is structured around the subheadings that were standard in hymnographic manuscripts, indicating the tone and mode, the solo introduction, the verse for the choir, and so on. These are strong indicators of literate esoteric humour, of knowing winks to those who know.

The *Koliazin Petition* (*Koliazinskaia chelobitnaia*) represents itself as a formal complaint sent in 1677 from the clergy to Simon, bishop of Tver and Kashin, about the dictatorial and scandalous conduct of Gavriil, archimandrite of the Kaliazin monastery: the archimandrite's scrupulous insistence on monastic disciplines disgracefully keeps the petitioners from their beer and wine.[5] The *Kaliazin Petition* likewise exists in variant versions that were copied over the course of several decades. One variant, for example, reflects Petrine legislation of the mid-1720s.

The *Alphabet about a Naked and Destitute Man* (*Azbuka o golom i nebogatom cheloveke*) parodies the genre of alphabetic acrostic that was common in primers elementary textbooks for learning to read).[6] So, for example, beginning with the first letter of the alphabet – *az*, which is both the name of the letter and the first-person singular personal pronoun – where a version in printed primers begins, 'I am a light for all the world', the parody commences, 'I am naked; naked and barefoot; hungry and cold.'

Other brief compositions parody, for example, a book of medicinal remedies *Cures for Foreigners* (*Lechebnik na inozemtsev*) and a dowry contract (*Rospis' o pridanom*).[7] *The Tale of the Priest Sava* (*Skazanie o pope Save*) savages the villainy of a priest in the persona of one of his duped and exploited trainees. It ends with a mock-liturgical hymn to his vices and misdeeds.[8]

Comedy is notoriously tricky to interpret at a distance. It is collusive. Parody appears to undermine its prototype, but the balance between playful mockery and seriously pointed criticism – between the ludic and the caustic – can

4 *Sluzhba kabaku* [Liturgy to a tavern], in *BLDR*, vol. XVI, pp. 374–88.
5 *Koliazinskaia chelobitnaia* [Koliazin petition], in *BLDR*, vol. XVI, pp. 389–92.
6 *Azbuka o golom i nebogatom cheloveke* [Alphabet about a naked and destitute man], in *BLDR*, vol. XVI, pp. 405–6.
7 *Lechebnik na inozemtsev* [Cures for foreigners], and *Rospis' o pridanom* [Dowry contract], in *BLDR*, vol. XVI, pp. 423–4, 425–6.
8 *Skazanie o pope Save* [The tale of the priest Sava], in *BLDR*, vol. XVI, pp. 412–14.

depend on irretrievably lost but mutually understood contemporary nuances and inflections. In mid-twentieth-century Soviet scholarship, these and similar works were grouped under the designation 'democratic satire'.[9] The label has been influential, though as usual the classification reflects the agenda of the classifier: the idea of a 'democratic' trend in literature was important to mid- to late Soviet cultural historians.

However, such works have multiple roots and affinities. Parody and satire as such were not new to the seventeenth century. At one end of the scale, they can be linked to traditions widespread in medieval Christian literatures. Also in the medieval mode, they tended to be anonymous, and several of them mutated into multiple versions in manuscript transmission. At the other end of the scale, they are compatible with and to varying degrees adapted to literary trends of the seventeenth century. The parodied proto-types – mainly ecclesiastical, bureaucratic, or pedagogic – reflect the environ-ments of the principal groups of men of letters in the church and the chanceries. Possibly some of them were read as being subversive, but they are also semi-playful manifestations of the literature of moral entertainment, foregrounding form and manipulating the language of the parodied proto-type while undermining it through combinations of inappropriate situational and stylistic devices. To locate either the milieu or the message as 'demo-cratic' is both hazardous and anachronistic. These are bookish works which most likely emerged from, and which assume readers' familiarity with, the lettered pursuits of church and chancery. The lively folksiness of some of their rhythms and idioms is a sign of the parodist's virtuosity, not necessarily of social origin or attitude.

Most of the seventeenth-century parodies are written in prose. A few are in verse. The verse parodies seem to be clustered around variants of a particular form: the epistle. Moreover, some are preserved in manuscripts containing collections of model epistles (*pis'movniki*),[10] which again suggests that they fascinated as much for their parodic form – as exercises in composition (typically using the brisk intra-lineal rhyme of the folk form termed *raeshnyi stikh*) – as for their satirical content. They provide a bridge to the second

[9] See the anthology V. P. Adrianova-Peretts (ed.), *Russkaia demokraticheskaia satira XVII veka* [Russian democratic satire of the seventeenth century], 2nd edn (Moscow: Nauka, 1977). For an attempt at a more comprehensive anthology of satire, see V. K. Bylinin and V. A. Grikhin (eds.), *Satira XI–XVII vekov* [Satire of the eleventh to seventeenth centuries] (Moscow: Sovetskaia Rossiia, 1986), though here, too, the predominance of the seventeenth century is plain.
[10] *BLDR*, vol. XVI, pp. 393–5, 407–8, 435–6, 446–7.

characteristic phenomenon of the seventeenth century in general, and of the Baroque in particular: experiments in and with verse.

Verse and Poetry

Verse only became a regular feature of Russian literary culture over the course of the seventeenth century (see Chapter 3.3). In devotional written culture there was much that was, in a broad sense, poetic, whether in the figurative use of language, or in rhythmic and assonantal rhetoric, or in liturgical chant. However – leaving aside speculation about forms of oral recitation – there was no tradition of written verse in a strict sense: nothing that was subject to consistent formal conventions of versification. Greek verse was rendered regularly into Church Slavonic prose, even if it retained its label as verse (*stikh* – the word still in use today, of Greek origin). Early formal verse in Russia (*virshi*) was probably stimulated, at least in part, by Polish conventions of syllabic poetry, though it could also build on local rhythmic and assonantal habits. Among such habits was the use of the natural shape and rhyme that can be produced in an inflected language when using parallel syntactic structures: the rhythm comes from the repeated structure of phrase, the rhyme frequently from the parallel placing of verbs with the same or similar endings. In the seventeenth century, Russian verse (mainly in Church Slavonic) was based on such rhyming couplets. In the early part of the century, the line lengths often varied. Subsequently, poets tended to use lines with regular numbers of syllables.

The earliest of these versifiers wrote during the first quarter of the seventeenth century. The range was quite broad. At one extreme, a certain Evstratii, introducing a primer (c. 1621), gave thanks to God in the form of twenty-two lines of 'serpentine' verse, in which the lines of each couplet weave in and out of a sequence of shared elements.[11] At another extreme, Prince Ivan Khvorostinin (d. 1625) wrote an anti-heretical tract of some 1,300 lines (that is, around 650 couplets) adapted into Russian from a Ukrainian prototype but with many added formally marked elements such as acrostics.[12] By the mid-1630s, versifiers were numerous enough and coherent enough to be regarded in modern scholarship as a 'school'. Many of them worked in the Muscovite chanceries, knew each other, and even wrote verse epistles to each other. They have been labelled the Chancery School of

[11] Evstratii, *Predislovie k azbukovniku* [Preface to a primer], in *BLDR*, vol. XVIII, pp. 19–20.
[12] Ivan Khvorostinin, *Izlozhenie na eretiki-zlokhul'niki* [Disquisition on the heretical slanderers], in *BLDR*, vol. XVIII, pp. 21–30.

poetry,[13] arguably Russia's first literary group or movement (see Chapter 2.3), using literary discourse as a device and sign for mutual recognition and support in an autonomous context separate both from the church and from the direct patronage of the court. Nevertheless, the definitive period of Russian Baroque syllabic verse was not embodied in or heralded by the Chancery School, whose themes were mostly pious, if not directly devotional, and whose repertoire of forms was somewhat limited. These were notable beginnings, but in range, depth, cultural scope, and resonance it was not comparable to the high Baroque literature from the latter decades of the century and beyond.

A particular feature of Russian verse of the Baroque age was its close links with objects and pictures. The Baroque aesthetic spanned and mixed different media. This is apparent on two levels. In the first place, a lot of verse was inscriptional: physically and thematically linked to an object or image. And secondly, some writers experimented with ways of presenting verse *as* visual object, both through care for design and through the creation of word pictures.

Inscriptional verse was both miniature and monumental. The site most saturated with monumental inscriptional verse was probably the New Jerusalem monastery (also known as the Monastery of the Resurrection or the Voskresenskii monastery), established by Patriarch Nikon at Istra, to the northwest of Moscow, in 1656. Over the second half of the seventeenth century, verse inscriptions proliferated to form a kind of verse guide to the monastery – its history, its holy and notable places.[14] On a smaller scale were the diverse verse captions to illustrations in books: heraldic verses addressed to the armorial device of a printer's patron (common in Ruthenian printing, and first encountered in Moscow in 1663 in the earliest Muscovite printed Bible).[15] Where devotional iconography required written labels for the images and scenes, Baroque fashion provided verse mottoes decoding symbolic emblems (the emblem was a particularly characteristic Baroque form). Fedor Polikarpov's (c. 1670–1731) trilingual (Slavonic, Greek, Latin) primer of

---

[13] A. M. Panchenko, *Russkaia stikhotvornaia kul'tura XVII veka* [Russian verse culture of the seventeenth century] (Leningrad: Nauka, 1973), pp. 34–77.

[14] A. G. Avdeev, *Starorusskaia epigrafika i knizhnost': Novo-ierusalimskaia shkola epigraficheskoi poezii* [Old Russian epigraphy and book culture: The New Jerusalem school of epigraphic poetry] (Moscow: PSTGU, 2006).

[15] Simon Franklin, 'Printing Moscow: Significances of the frontispiece to the 1663 Bible', *Slavonic and East European Review* 88.1–2 (2010), 73–95.

1701 included eleven engravings, each of which was accompanied by verses.[16] The poets Mardarii Khonykov (fl. late seventeenth century) and Simeon Polotskii (1629–1680) both wrote cycles of verse captions to the images in imported albums of biblical engravings.[17] Captions sound like a minor genre, but these could be major works. Khonykov's cycle runs to 3,800 lines, and it was prefaced by a verse acrostic whose initial letters revealed his own authorship. The objects or images which prompted verses did not even have to be real. Inscription was a genre, a conceit of writing. An object or image could prompt a verse, but a verse could equally well conjure an imaginary object or image. The inscriptional imagination was a deeply embedded feature of the Baroque aesthetic in Russia.[18]

In this way, verse accompanied or evoked visual culture; verse *became* visual culture. Word play involved not just the display of verbal dexterity but the creation of visually signalled forms: word-pictures, serpentine verse, word squares, and cryptographic puzzles. Muscovite printing was not equipped to deal with such sophistication. The medium for Muscovite Baroque display was, in the first place, the luxury manuscript, and then the engraving. Among the most celebrated examples was the primer (*bukvar'*) of Karion Istomin (c. 1650–1722). Each page is devoted to one letter of the alphabet and includes multiple examples of how that letter may be written, illustrations of objects whose names begin with the letter, and a set of verses. The primer was first produced in manuscript as a gift for the royal children, then as a block-book engraved by Leontii Bunin.[19]

For all its panache, its delight in display, in Muscovy such Baroque production was almost inevitably esoteric. It was for a very select audience, and distribution was minimal. Most Muscovite Baroque literature was

---

[16] In full in D. N. Ramazanova and Iu. E. Shustova, *Kirillicheskie bukvari iz sobraniia Nauchno-issledovatel'skogo otdela redkikh knig Rossiiskoi gosudarstvennoi biblioteki: Opisanie izdanii i ekzempliarov* [Cyrillic primers in the collection of the Rare Books Research Department of the Russian State Library: a description of editions and copies] (Moscow: Pashkov dom, 2018), pp. 289–313.

[17] O. A. Belobrova, 'Virshi Mardariia Khonykova k graviuram Biblii Piskatora' [Mardarii Khonykov's verses for the engravings in the Piscator Bible], *Trudy Otdela drevnerusskoi literatury* 46 (1993), 345–435; O. A. Belobrova, 'Drevnerusskie virshi k graviuram Mattiasa Meriana' [Early Russian verses on the engravings of Matthias Merian], *Trudy Otdela drevnerusskoi literatury* 44 (1990), 440–79.

[18] L. I. Sazonova, *Literaturnaia kul'tura Rossii. Rannee Novoe vremia* [Russian literary culture. The early modern period] (Moscow: Iazyki slavianskikh kul'tur, 2006), pp. 320–31.

[19] Gary Marker, 'A world of visual splendor: The illustrated texts of Karion Istomin', in Michael S. Flier, Valerie Kivelson, Erika Monahan, and Daniel Rowland (eds.), *Seeing Muscovy Anew: Politics – Institutions – Culture; Essays in Honor of Nancy Shields Kollmann* (Bloomington, IN: Slavica, 2017), pp. 173–88.

confined to manuscripts. The shift towards a more deliberately outward form of Baroque multimedia display involving words, representations, and objects came slightly later – most dramatically in the triumphal arches erected and decorated for Peter I's victory parades.[20]

High Muscovite Baroque: Simeon Polotskii

The high period of Muscovite Baroque literature was the final third of the seventeenth century, and the key figure – for his energy, innovation, diversity, influence, and (not least) his talent – was Simeon Polotskii (see Chapter 3.3). Born Samuel Piotrowski-Sitnianowicz, educated in Kyiv and Vilnius, and steeped in Latin and Polish learning, Simeon (his monastic name) first impressed Aleksei Mikhailovich with a greeting in verse when the tsar visited Polotsk (Polatsk, now in Belarus) in 1656. In 1664, Simeon settled in Moscow, where he was known as – and sometimes signed his own work as – Simeon Polotskii. Accommodation was provided at the Zaikonospasskii monastery close to the Kremlin, where he was employed, in effect, as Aleksei Mikhailovich's court writer. Arguably, Simeon Polotskii was Russia's first literary professional.

Literature was not the only area in which Simeon was useful. For example, in 1667 he was commissioned to write a detailed refutation of the schismatics condemned at a recent church council and now known as the Old Believers or Old Ritualists. But his distinctive talent was for verse. Some of his poetry was formed through a creative engagement with traditional edificatory and devotional literature. He wrote a metrical and rhymed version of the Psalter (*Psaltir' rifmotvornaia*), for example, as well as a voluminous compendium of moral advice and aphorisms adapted into verse from a Latin prose prototype. The former was printed in 1680 and can reasonably be reckoned the first book of verse to be printed in Russia. The latter, entitled the *Garden of Many Flowers* (*Vertograd mnogotsvetnyi*, 1676–80), remained in manuscript until its first full publication was completed at the start of the twenty-first century.[21] These were translations in a loose sense, based on existing texts and traditional in content, though also formally innovative in Russia. However, Simeon's most original compositions – and his most enjoyably browsable today – were his works for the court, and the most magisterially flamboyant of these is *The*

---

[20] Simon Franklin, *The Russian Graphosphere, 1450–1850* (Cambridge: Cambridge University Press, 2019), pp. 149–52.

[21] Simeon Polockij, *Vertograd mnogocvetnyj* [Garden of many flowers], ed. Anthony Hippisley and Lydia I. Sazonova, 3 vols. (Cologne: Böhlau Verlag, 1996–2000).

Russian Eagle (Orel rossiiskii), written in 1667 to mark the proclamation of the tsar's son as heir.[22] It is a fairly substantial work: the text in the presentation manuscript is written on 53 folia (i.e., 106 pages), mainly in verse (of which there are some 1,500 lines) but also including prose and pictures. The eagle is the symbol both of the Muscovite state and of its tsar. The work was thus an emblematic and heraldic composition, as well as a sustained panegyric. Generically it is hard to define. Simeon called it one of his 'booklets'. It is a kind of cycle of cycles, put together from thematically linked but compositionally distinct elements. After two dedications (to the tsar and his son) and a prose panegyric and verse address to the eagle, it includes a cycle of ten poems on the Russian eagle, as if composed by Apollo and each of the nine Muses, and – its longest section – a cycle of twelve poems on the qualities of the heir to the throne, each linked to a sign of the zodiac. As a cycle of cycles, *The Russian Eagle* seems to have an affinity with the forms of the age of devotion, in the relationship between composite forms (which may contain several distinct and separable works) and their constituent forms (see Chapter 3.1). But Baroque fashion cannot let a convention rest at conventionality, and Simeon created multiple layers in which composite forms themselves became constituents. He was his own most assiduous anthologiser, and this and other cycles of cycles themselves became elements of his much larger collection entitled *Rifmologion (Rifmologion*, 1678).[23]

The Russian Eagle was a display of erudition and verbal virtuosity. One can represent Simeon's formal display on four levels: vocabulary and cultural reference; versification; visually enhanced word play; and word-pictures.

On the level of vocabulary and cultural reference, Simeon flaunts his familiarity with Greek. Besides Apollo and the Muses, each section has a Greek-derived subheading, and the work teems with mythological references and unfamiliar Graecisms. On the level of formal versification, Simeon revels in the demonstration of his dexterity. Thus, in the 'Apollo and the Muses' cycle, his Terpomene and Thalia use couplets of eight-syllable verse; the lines of Erato are of ten syllables; Terpsichore, Polyhymnia, and Apollo write in an eleven-syllable line; Euterpe prefers twelve syllables; Calliope's couplets are composed of thirteen-syllable lines; and Urania and Clio

---

[22] For a facsimile edition, see Simeon Polotskii, *Orel rossiiskii* [The Russian eagle], ed. L. I. Sazonova (Moscow: Indrik, 2015).

[23] Simeon Polockij, *Rifmologion. Eine Sammlung höfisch-zeremonieller Gedichte*, ed. Anthony Hippisley, Hans Rothe, and Lydia I. Sazonova, 2 vols. (Vienna: Böhlau Verlag, 2013–17).

compose in a form of quatrain consisting of three eleven-syllable lines followed by a five-syllable overhanging fourth line that rhymes with the third.

The third level is visually enhanced word play. In *The Russian Eagle*, Simeon runs through the repertoire of Baroque rhetorical games in the manipulation of words on a page. There are *versus concordantes*, where one column of words both completes a phrase begun in the previous column and begins a phrase completed in the following column. There are echo verses (with the echo words picked out in red), acrostics, and a series of anagrammatic poems playing with various arrangements of the letters in the tsar's patronymic. Simeon closes with a cryptographic representation of his own name, while at the same time explaining how it is to be deciphered. He aimed to delight and impress, not to bamboozle or confuse, and at every stage he showed just how the trick was done.

Finally, there are the word-pictures. The two most widely reproduced images from the presentation manuscript of *The Russian Eagle* are the illustrations of the double-headed eagle itself and the heart of verse. The eagle is depicted with three crowns, a sword, and a sceptre, and with the emblematic representation of the dragon-slaying equestrian tsar on its breast. This was normal for the time. Uniquely, however, Simeon placed the eagle in the centre of a representation of the sun, which consisted of forty-eight spiked or wavy rays, and in each ray – a word. The words are the names of virtues that shine forth from the eagle-tsar. It would be hard to find a plainer image of a sun-king. The second image is a heart created entirely from words: not just an outline but a continuous ribbon that starts at the centre and winds back on itself and around itself several times, so as to create a picture with volume and amplitude. The ribbon of words, when read as it twists its way to the heart's eventual completion, forms a forty-line poem in eleven-syllable rhyming couplets.

Not everybody among Moscow's elites found Simeon Polotskii's kind of culture delightful. For some it was downright dangerous: anti-devotional, steeped in Latin affectation and error, heretical. Simeon was well protected through the patronage first of Tsar Aleksei Mikhailovich, then of his son Fedor. Simeon's amanuensis, literary executor, and successor as court poet, Silvestr Medvedev (b. 1641), was less fortunate. Caught in a perfect storm of dynastic and theological rivalries, in February 1691 he was publicly beheaded on Red Square.

Despite such occasional dramatic conflicts, including not only Medvedev's execution but also some later condemnation of the memory of Simeon

Polotskii himself, the culture of the age was broader than any faction, and elite literature continued in much the same mode. The presentation manuscript of the playfully Baroque primer of Karion Istomin (a relative of Medvedev, as it happens) was gifted to the royal children in 1692, the year after Medvedev's execution. At the elite level, early Petrine literature was late Baroque, as practised by Simeon's younger contemporaries and successors – men like Istomin, and later Iosif Turoboiskii (dates unknown; active 1701–10) and Fedor Polikarpov, often with an equivalent educational background in Ukraine and in several cases also associated with the Moscow Print Yard. One of the reasons why this quite substantial body of Baroque verse has often been under-recognised in accounts of the emergence of Russian literature is that a very substantial proportion of it remained in manuscript – not merely in its own time (when manuscript was still the norm) but for most of the next three hundred years. Simeon Polotskii's two huge compendia of his own verses (the *Garden of Many Flowers* and the *Rifmologion*) were not printed in full until the twenty-first century. A collection of about 250 pages of occasional verses by Istomin, marking celebrations such as royal births, birthdays, and anniversaries, was first printed only in 2012.[24]

Old Believer Baroque?

High Baroque literature was a pastime for the elite. However, just as the Baroque emerged as part of a wider cultural shift, so its echoes can be detected more widely. Some features of the literature of the Baroque age seeped even into works by those who might be expected to be fundamentally opposed to any such thing: the Old Believers. The schism in the Russian church in the mid-seventeenth century, which continues to this day, was in part provoked by official attempts to reform and standardise devotional texts and devotional practices. The reforms were not intended to be innovative. On the contrary, they were meant to restore accuracy and authenticity through research into early Greek and Slavonic texts. The argument was thus between two kinds of conservatism: one based on top-down educated textual investigation and publication (the reformed texts were printed), the other based on bottom-up tradition. In this context one could well imagine the schismatics to be opposed to anything that reeked of merely modish

---

[24] A. P. Bogdanov, *Stikh torzhestva: Rozhdenie russkoi ody, posledniaia chetvert' XVII–nachalo XVIII veka* [Triumphal verse: The birth of the Russian ode in the final quarter of the seventeenth century and the start of the eighteenth century], 2 vols. (Moscow: Institut rossiiskoi istorii RAN, 2012). Istomin's 'archive' is in the second volume.

bookishness, or of individuality or originality, and especially of anything with a whiff of Latin (in all senses) culture.

One of the first-generation leaders of the schism, Avvakum Petrov (1620–1682), was an almost exact contemporary of Simeon Polotskii, but on the face of it could hardly have been more different. Simeon was the highly paid court poet,[25] crafter of ostentatiously mannered literary diversions and fulsome panegyrics to his patron. Avvakum was an implacable dissenter, exiled first to eastern Siberia for a decade, then – after a brief interlude in Moscow when the tsar tried in vain to soften his opposition – to Pustozersk in the far north, where, for his seditious writing, he was sentenced to death by burning. Avvakum was ostensibly anti-literary. He served truth, not form. And yet Avvakum was perhaps the most original writer of his age. In his many polemical works, but above all in his account of his own life,[26] which he wrote and revised (at least twice) in Pustozersk, Avvakum was as free with the conventions of the age of devotion as he was contemptuous of the affectations of the elite bookmen of his day. The work overflows generic definition. Part travelogue, part religious polemic, part sermon or confession, part autobiography or even a kind of auto-hagiography (see Chapter 3.10), it switches between styles – from florid Church Slavonic rhetoric to direct colloquialism – sometimes within a sentence. Written by an arch-traditionalist, it is strikingly original not as a bookish exercise in Baroque manner but as perhaps the quintessential expression of the seventeenth-century turn towards the individual. Despite the ambitions and pretensions of the scholar-bookmen, Avvakum's life of himself is the only work of the age that has consistently maintained its status in a Russian literary canon: a work bypassing eighteenth-century artifice, it is heralded as anticipating literary and linguistic developments of the modern age.

Avvakum's writing was exceptional even among Old Believers. The closest one gets to an Old Believer 'school' of writing developed in the next generation, especially in the community founded in the far northwest of Russia, on the river Vyg, by Andrei Denisov (1674–1730) and his younger

[25] On his wealth, see Aleksandr Lavrent'ev and Anastasiia Preobrazhenskaia, 'Simeon Polotskii: "finansovyi portret"' [Simeon Polotskii: a 'financial portrait'], *Slavia orientalis* 69.4 (2020), 747–65.

[26] *Zhitie protopopa Avvakuma, im samim napisannoe*, in *BLDR*, vol. XVII, pp. 64–118; English translation: Archpriest Avvakum, *The Life, Written by Himself*, trans. Kenneth N. Brostrom (New York: Columbia University Press, 2021).

brother Semen (1682–1740). The Denisov brothers left a substantial corpus of writings. The genres and the concerns are traditional: moral homilies and epistles, edifying tales of the lives of holy men, chronicles of the community, some epitaphs. Yet the means were of their own time and by no means always imitations of pre-schism equivalents. For example, one of the foundational narratives of the Vyg community was the *History of the Solovki Martyrs* (*Istoriia ob ottsakh i stradal'tsakh solovetskikh*), written in the 1710s by Semen Denisov. The Old Believer community on the Vyg traced its spiritual lineage to the monks of Solovki, who were repressed after an eight-year siege (1668–76) by the armies of the Muscovite state in support of the official church. Denisov begins his work with a classical rhetorical trope: if the heroes of the Trojan War merit such a literature of praise, then how worthy must be the noble martyrs of the siege of Solovki?[27] Tales of Troy were common in medieval literature and made their way to early Rus. However, Denisov here is not harking back to long-revered medieval manuscripts but to a new adaptation printed in Moscow in 1709. In a more striking example: recounting an episode when the tsar on his deathbed bids the patriarch (Ioakim) deal mercifully with the monks of Solovki, Denisov even breaks into syllabic verse.[28] Old Believer culture has a reputation for ultra-conservatism, for preserving medieval traditions even into the twentieth century,[29] and for a dogmatic insistence on pre-schism forms. However, not all Old Believer culture was aggressively stagnant or immune to its time. In visual culture the liveliness, even exuberance, of embellishment and illustration in Old Believer manuscripts is well established, and in verbal expression even the founders of Old Believer literature could find it useful to resort to the devices of the elite culture that in other respects they rejected. Semen Denisov's switch to syllabic verse is indicative not only of his own literary arsenal but also of his implied readership; and of the fact that, as is the case with other major literary movements, Baroque practices permeated beyond Baroque practitioners.

---

[27] Semen Denisov, *Istoriia ob ottsakh i stradal'tsakh solovetskikh* [History of the Solovki martyrs], in *BLDR*, vol. XIX, p. 178.

[28] Denisov, *Istoriia*, in *BLDR*, vol. XIX, pp. 197–8. On the Baroque in Old Believer rhetoric, see also O. D. Zhuravel', 'Iskusstvo propovedi Andreiia Denisova: Ritoricheskie strategii i priemy' [The art of Andrei Denisov's sermons: Rhetorical strategies and techniques], *Quaestio rossica* 10.4 (2022), 1377–93.

[29] See, for example, from the early twentieth century, Bishop Innokentii, *Sluzhba pustozerskim muchennikam* [A service to the martyrs of Pustozersk], in *BLDR*, vol. XX, pp. 249–60.

Further Reading

Brown, William Edward, *A History of Seventeenth-Century Russian Literature* (Ann Arbor, MI: Ardis, 1980).

Drage, Charles, *Russian Word-Play Poetry from Simeon Polotskii to Derzhavin* (London: School of Slavonic and East European Studies, 1993).

Hippisley, Anthony, *The Poetic Style of Simeon Polotsky* (Birmingham: University of Birmingham, 1985).

Lachmann, Renate (ed.), *Slavische Barockliteratur II* (Munich: Wilhelm Fink Verlag, 1983).

Morris, Marcia, *The Literature of Roguery in Seventeenth- and Eighteenth-Century Russia* (Evanston, IL: Northwestern University Press, 2000).

Panchenko, A. M., *Russkaia stikhotvornaia kul'tura XVII veka* [Russian verse culture of the seventeenth century] (Leningrad: Nauka, 1973).

Sazonova, L. I., *Literaturnaia kul'tura Rossii. Ranee Novoe vremia* [Russian literary culture. The early modern period] (Moscow: Iazyki slavianskikh kul'tur, 2006).

The Age of Classicism

MARCUS C. LEVITT

In the eighteenth century, modern Russian literature came into being and entered the western European cultural mainstream. The 'age of Classicism' witnessed the creation of a modern vernacular Russian literary language – the language for the business of state as well as secular culture, including belles-lettres – and it also saw the development of the basic features of a modern literature with its literary and institutional infrastructure. This included the creation of a standard grammar; dictionaries; a broad spectrum of literary genres in verse and prose; and institutions that fostered a spectrum of artistic, scientific, and scholarly pursuits: the Academy of Sciences, Moscow University, the Academy of Fine Arts, the Russian Academy, the Free Economic Society, Masonic lodges, the Smolnyi Institute for Noble Maidens, and a host of other educational and cultural establishments. It also witnessed the creation of literary journals and a Russian-language theatre, supported by an expanding cohort of writers and by institutional and private printing presses (especially under the Free Press Law of 1783–96, which allowed private individuals to publish without special government privilege). The eighteenth century witnessed the emergence of writing as a profession, although much literary production revolved around the court and was supported by court patronage (see Chapter 2.2). For most, writing served as an aristocratic pastime and, in some cases, as an aid to a career in state service.

In contrast to the age of the Baroque, a movement whose validity for Russia only became generally accepted in the later twentieth century, the term 'Classicism' came into use in the 1820s as a blanket category describing Russian literature of the previous century and was used in an almost exclusively pejorative sense. This was one of the results of the crisis of Russian identity in the post-Napoleonic period, which led to the pervasive conviction

that Russian culture had to start again from scratch. In the eyes of educated society, Classicism, as closely associated with the state and court-centred panegyric culture, suffered the same sharp decline in status as imperial, 'old regime' values. The entire eighteenth-century literary tradition was tarred with the same brush as monolithic, moribund, rule-bound, and hopelessly obsolete.

This patently myopic view of the Russian eighteenth century hardly corresponds to its complex, dynamic, and in fact rapidly changing literary and cultural character. During the age of Classicism, Russian letters decisively joined the modern European tradition and established itself as an independent literature. Pan-European Classicism defined the unchanging models of artistic beauty – the 'classics' – as those of ancient Greece; these were perfected by imperial Rome and revived at the court of Louis XIV, with its burst of literary genius. Russia joined this movement at a relatively late stage and compressed centuries of European development into decades as it strove to assimilate not only classical and modern trends but the entire European tradition. This presented the opportunity to adopt those aspects of European culture that were most amenable to indigenous needs and generated a motley and sometimes heterogeneous brand of Classicism.

In recent decades, scholars have been challenging the common and traditional view of the 'Petrine Revolution' as a total break with the past, the view that Peter I ('the Great', r. 1682–1725) imported European culture wholesale into Russia as if projected onto a *tabula rasa*. This narrative suggested the breathtaking possibilities for rapid, even radical, transformation and generated the allure of the Russian experiment for such Enlightenment thinkers as Voltaire. Recent scholarship has seriously undermined this Petrine myth, exploring the rich and complex indigenous cultural scene of the Petrine and Baroque eras which the later tradition almost completely ignored. This reassessment touches our understanding of both the cultural landscape of the late seventeenth and early eighteenth centuries and its covert and overt role as incubator for the eighteenth-century transformation. Some scholars even speak of 'Pre-Classicism' during the first decades of the eighteenth century, referring in particular to the works of Feofan Prokopovich (1681–1736), an architect of the Petrine reforms and important proponent of early Enlightenment ideology, and to those of Antiokh Kantemir (1708–1744), a Moldovan-born member of what Prokopovich referred to in a poem as his 'learned retinue' (*uchenaia druzhina*). Kantemir wrote nine verse satires, five of them before he left Russia in 1732 for the post of Russian ambassador

to London, and then Paris. The genre of verse satire not only gave Kantemir a platform to ridicule opponents of the Petrine reforms during a time of reaction but, together with his commentaries, also served to acquaint Russian readers with Enlightenment ideas and the rhetorical tradition of satire, from Juvenal and the entire classical tradition down through Nicolas Boileau (1636–1711), the most well-known proponent of French Classicism. Kantemir also translated several of Boileau's satires, but these and most of Kantemir's other works were unpublished until 1762, by which time they were already out of date, although the satires had long circulated in manuscript.

The New Literary Language

Peter I mandated the creation of a manifestly secular literary language in the Russian vernacular. Slavonic – the literary language that had been used throughout the medieval period – was now declared to be *Old Church Slavonic*, that is, both obsolete and the exclusive purview of the church. Peter helped design a new Latinate script whose aim was to visually distinguish the new language from the old and to make it more suitable for print. In typically autocratic fashion, he demanded a new literary language *ex nihilo*, ostensibly denying the earlier Slavonic literary and linguistic legacy. Vasilii Trediakovskii (1703–1768), in the introduction to his 1730 translation of Paul Tallement's *Voyage to the Island of Love* (1663), a popular work of French *précieux* salon literature, expressed the spirit of the Petrine linguistic programme as described in aesthetic terms:

> Do not, I humbly beg you, be angry with me, (even if you are still devotees of profoundly worded Slavonic pomposity (*glubokoslovnyia derzhites' slavensh-chizny*)), that I did not translate this book into Slavonic, but merely into the simplest Russian, that is, the kind we speak among ourselves. This I did for the following reasons. First, the Slavonic language is our church language, and this book is worldly. Second, in the present day the Slavonic language is very obscure (*temen*), and many of us are not able to understand it when reading. But this book is about *sweet love*, and so must be comprehensible to everyone. Third – which might seem the most frivolous to you, but which for me is the most serious – is that the Slavonic language now sounds harsh to my ears ...[1]

---

1 P. Tal'man [Paul Tallement], *Ezda v ostrov liubvi* [Voyage to the island of love], trans. Vasilii Trediakovskii ([St Petersburg: Akademiia nauk], 1730), foreword; V. K. Trediakovskii, *Sochineniia* [Works], 3 vols. (St Petersburg: A. Smirdin, 1849), vol. III, pp. 649–50.

The *Voyage*, to which Trediakovskii appended his own love poetry, has been dubbed the first Russian novel, insofar as 'a translator only differs from a creator in name ... If a creator has to be ingenious, a translator needs to be even more so', as Trediakovskii asserted in the introduction.[2] Indeed, during the period in which the new Russian literature came into being, translations played a key role, both in expanding the spectrum of themes and genres and in shaping the new literary language. However, despite Trediakovskii's assertion that his own work represented 'the simplest Russian, ... the kind we speak among ourselves', no such standard of educated linguistic practice existed in Russia (as opposed, for example, to that of Parisian salons). Hence those who would write in 'Russian' had no choice but to refer back to Russia's written, Slavonic, Baroque literary heritage, despite claims to the contrary.

In the eyes of contemporaries as well as many later scholars, the reform of Russian versification in the later 1730s marked the watershed break with the past (see Chapter 3.3). Since the first half of the seventeenth century, syllabic verse on the Polish model had been in use. This was the form of poetry systematised and refined by Simeon Polotskii (1629–1680), Prokopovich, and Kantemir, as well as the early Trediakovskii (as in his poetry accompanying the *Voyage*). The introduction of syllabo-tonic versification, based on metrical feet consisting of a regular number of syllables and a regular pattern of stress (or of potential stress), was initiated by Trediakovskii with his *New and Brief Method for Composing Russian Verse* (*Novyi i kratkii sposob k slozheniiu rossiiskikh stikhov*, 1735), which also included examples and analysis of classical and French Classicist poetic genres. The verse reform was made more systematic and complete by Mikhail Lomonosov (1711–1765) in his *Letter on the Rules of Russian Versification* (*Pis'mo o pravilakh rossiiskogo stikhotvorstva*, 1739). For its practitioners as well as for later scholars, the introduction of syllabo-tonic verse marked the starting point not only for Russian Classicism but for modern Russian poetry in general. The tradition of syllabic verse and its poetics were almost completely forgotten and remain poorly studied; Trediakovskii and Lomonosov's cohort believed that syllabo-tonic verse alone suited the particular rhythms of Russian, and they likened syllabic verse to bad prose. This seems unfair insofar as *any* poetic language by nature relies on understanding its conventions, which in this case have been lost.

Trediakovskii and Lomonosov pointed the way out of the problem of assimilating the Slavonic, Baroque literary heritage into the new Classicist

---

2 Trediakovskii, *Sochineniia*, vol. III, p. 649.

literary system. Trediakovskii modelled his 'Solemn Ode on the Surrender of the City of Gdansk' (*Oda o sdache goroda Gdanska*, 1734) on Boileau's experimental 'Ode on the Taking of Namur' (1693). Boileau's aim had been to create a high-style panegyric ode on the model of Pindar, in order, among other things, to validate the ancients in the then ongoing 'quarrel between ancients and moderns' (the modern camp rejected the idea that the classics represented the exclusive standard of literary value). While Boileau's experiment was considered unsuccessful in Europe, when 'translated' into Russia, it offered a way to legitimise the Baroque Slavonic linguistic heritage. Lomonosov's famous 'Ode to the Blessed Memory of the Empress Anna Ioannovna on the Victory over the Turks and Tatars and the Seizure of Khotin, 1739' (*Oda blazhennyia pamiati gosudaryne imperatritse Anne Ioannovne na pobedu nad turkami i tatarami i na vziatie Khotina 1739 goda*, pub. 1751), which accompanied his 'Letter on the Rules of Russian Versification', confirmed this development. Paradoxically, it established the place of the triumphal ode as the premier genre of Russian Classicism, despite its Baroque poetics and ample use of Slavonicisms. This paradox arguably represents the main tension (or even contradiction) within Russian Classicism, which, despite its professed adherence to French linguistic purism (i.e., commitment to the exclusive use of Russian vernacular), sanctioned assimilation of the Slavonic linguistic heritage. In terms of literary practice, the tension may be seen as between a 'strict' Classicism on the seventeenth-century French model and a more eclectic version that strove both to assert the value of the national past (in however anachronistic terms) and to embrace the multiplicity of European culture.

By the 1740s, while Russia's predominant literary orientation was to French Classicism (sometimes via German or other intermediary channels), there was simultaneously a turn away from the Petrine zero-sum opposition between Russian and Slavonic, which – as in Trediakovskii's foreword to the *Voyage* – had rejected the latter as exclusively ecclesiastical, obscure in meaning, and aesthetically unacceptable. The new cultural consciousness reflected what the scholar Viktor Zhivov labelled the 'Slaveno-Russian [*Slaveno-Rossiiskii*] cultural and linguistic synthesis',[3] which might be a more precise period designation than 'Russian Classicism'. As the term Slaveno-Russian suggests, Russian and Slavonic were now seen as 'of one nature', as one language, and Slavonicisms gained new prestige in Russian odes and high-style genres.

---

3 Victor Zhivov, *Language and Culture in Eighteenth-Century Russia*, trans. Marcus C. Levitt (Boston: Academic Studies Press, 2009), pp. 210–332.

This cultural synthesis had important ramifications. The subordination of church to state had been a central aspect of Peter's reform, as he put an end to the patriarchate and transferred control over the Russian Orthodox Church to what was labelled the Holy Synod: a body of bishops and lay bureaucrats under his authority. By mid-century, the conflict between secular and religious realms was no longer felt, and anti-clericalism (seen, for example, in Kantemir's satires as well as in much of French Enlightenment culture) played an insignificant role in the age of Russian Classicism. On the contrary, a new generation of Russian-born clerical leaders arose to replace those like Polotskii and Prokopovich who had come from Ukraine, and they took an active role in the new cultural scene. This group included Gedeon (Krinovskii, c. 1730–1763), Bishop of Pskov; Gavriil (Petrov, 1730–1801), Metropolitan of St Petersburg and Novgorod; Platon (Levshin, 1737–1812), Metropolitan of Moscow; Damaskin (D. E. Semenov-Rudnev, 1737–1795), Bishop of the Nizhegorod Region. They followed in the tradition of Prokopovich and professed what has been termed 'Enlightened Orthodoxy'.[4] This clerical cohort revived the sermon, now written and delivered in Slaveno-Russian, and was involved in contemporary literary life to an extent perhaps never seen before or since in Russia. Damaskin, for example, was a prolific writer, orator, translator, and editor. Among his translations were classical works from Latin and Greek into Slaveno-Russian, and his work as an editor included editions of Prokopovich and Platon as well as of Lomonosov. And when Princess Ekaterina Dashkova (1743–1810), founder of the Russian Academy, set out to create the six-volume *Dictionary of the Russian Academy* (*Slovar' Akademii Rossiiskoi*, 1789–94), one of Slaveno-Russian's greatest monuments, she gathered almost all of the major writers and literary figures of the day to work on it, and of the forty-seven of sixty Academy members who took part, nineteen (over 40 per cent) were clergymen. In sharp contrast, the French and German academies excluded clergymen altogether, and the Académie française even forbade *discussion* of theological issues.

Enlightened Orthodoxy has only recently begun to be explored, and in general the importance of religion both for the Enlightenment in Russia and

---

4 See Marcus C. Levitt, 'The rapprochement between "secular" and "religious" in mid to late eighteenth-century Russian culture', in *Early Modern Russian Letters: Texts and Contexts* (Boston: Academic Studies Press, 2009), pp. 269–93. Recently, Andrey V. Ivanov has described this as a 'spiritual revolution': *A Spiritual Revolution: The Impact of Reformation and Enlightenment in Orthodox Russia* (Madison: University of Wisconsin Press, 2020).

more widely has yet to be adequately appreciated. All of the major poets of
the age of Classicism – Lomonosov, Trediakovskii, Aleksandr Sumarokov
(1717–1777), Mikhail Kheraskov (1733–1807), Vasilii Kapnist (1758?–1823), Gavriil
Derzhavin (1743–1816) – wrote religious verse, including psalm paraphrases,
and Trediakovskii and Sumarokov translated the entire Psalter.[5] Yet apart
from a few well-known masterpieces – Lomonsov's 'Evening' (*Vechernee*,
1748) and 'Morning Meditations on God's Majesty . . .' (*Utrenee razmyshlenie,
o Bozhiem velichestve . . .*, 1751), and Derzhavin's ode 'God' (*Bog*, 1784) – the
majority of Russian Classicist spiritual poetry remains unstudied.

Sumarokov's *Two Epistles, The First Concerning the Russian Language and the
Second on Poetry* (*Dve epistoly, V pervoi predlagaetsia o russkom iazyke, a vo vtoroi
o stikhotvorstve*, 1747) attempted to outline a normative poetics and to promote the new literary language. Like Boileau's *The Art of Poetry* (1674), which
they emulated, Sumarokov's epistles have been called a manifesto of
Classicism; but where Boileau offered a codification and critique of an already
existing literary system, Sumarokov's epistle on poetry presented a blueprint
for the future. It laid out a system of genres – idyll, elegy, ode, epic, drama
(tragedy and comedy), satire, epigram, fable, mock-epic (high and low),
epistle, sonnet, rondeau, ballad, and song – which were a mixture of authentic classical and French Classicist genres. It not only presented the image of
a well-rounded literary system but also insisted on the centrality of genres
themselves:

> And if nature has endowed you with it,
> Strive to enhance your gift with art.
> In poetry know the difference in genres,
> And seek the proper words for what you undertake
> Without annoying the Muses with your poor success,
> With tears for Thalia and laughter for Melpomene.
> [. . .]
> Everything is laudable, whether drama, eclogue or ode;
> Compose that to which your nature draws you,
> Only let your mind be enlightened, writer;
> Our beautiful language is capable of anything.[6]

5 The important precedent for these was Simeon Polotskii's Psalter (*Psaltir' rifmotvornaia*,
   1680) (see Chapter 1.2).
6 A. P. Sumarokov, *Izbrannye proizvedeniia* [Selected works] (Leningrad: Sovetskii pisatel',
   1951), pp. 117 and 125 (my translation). For a complete prose version, see Harold B. Segel
   (ed. and trans.), *The Literature of Eighteenth-Century Russia: An Anthology*, 2 vols.
   (New York: Dutton, 1967), vol. I, pp. 221–38. This anthology contains many of the
   works discussed in this chapter.

In emulating Boileau and his focus on generic models, Sumarokov's epistles also exhibit Classicism's emphasis on *imitatio* (imitation) as contrasted with *inventio* (invention), based on the notion of imitating 'la belle Nature', an ideal of absolute, objective beauty as exemplified in the classics and embodied in genres. Contrary to the later stereotype that Classicism insisted pedantically on 'the rules', here it is art that gives poetic inspiration order and shape, embodied in various discrete genres. The contamination of genres – as in the confusion of Thalia and Melpomene, the Muses of comedy and tragedy – was proscribed.[7] Still, Sumarokov himself did not always follow the epistles' prescriptions and wrote in a great variety of genres, including those not part of the Classicist repertoire. Arguably, the two epistles themselves have a kind of generic duality, combining didactic epistle and satire, although the two complement each other as instructions on what to do and what *not* to do.

Perhaps inevitably, the notion of absolute, objective beauty could lead to sharp disagreements. Lomonosov, Trediakovskii, and Sumarokov, who came into conflict when the first two were assigned the role of censoring Sumarokov's early works at the Academy of Sciences, each claimed priority as the founder and arbiter of the new literature. Their notoriously harsh contention helped give Classicism its bad name in the later tradition; in part as a response, Sentimentalism, with its marked embrace of the subjective, generally rejected negative criticism (see Chapter 1.4). When Trediakovskii, mocked in Sumarokov's epistles, took their author to task for excessive imitation (i.e. plagiarism), Sumarokov countered:

> My epistle on poetry, says he [Trediakovskii], is all Boileau, while Boileau took everything from Horace [from his verse epistle 'Ars poetica', c. AD 19]. No, Boileau did not take everything from Horace, nor did I take everything from Boileau. Whoever cares to compare my epistle with Boileau's rules on poetry will clearly see that I took no more, perhaps, from Boileau than Boileau took from Horace; although I have never attempted to deny that something has been taken from Boileau.[8]

The problem of authority might be linked to the ideology of Russian political absolutism in its Petrine variant, as it informed the desire to create a new literature based on a hierarchy of established, enlightened norms. The

---

7 Sumarokov may have had in mind Prokopovich's tragi-comedy *Vladimir* (*Vladimir*, 1705), and he later railed against the mixed type of contemporary 'tearful' or 'bourgeois dramas' that challenged the primacy of Classicist tragedy.

8 A. P. Sumarokov, 'Otvet na kritiku' [An answer to criticism], in *Polnoe sobranie sochinenii v stikhakh i proze* [Complete works in verse and prose], ed. Nikolai Novikov, 2nd edn, 10 vols. (Moscow: N. Novikov, 1787), vol. X, p. 104.

Classicist striving for regularity and belief in objectively correct models accorded well with propagation of imperial culture, whose main prototype was ancient Rome. In the development of emerging national literatures in Europe, as well as in Russia, Rome was seen as the most successful example of cultural emulation, improving on Greek culture; it was not until the Romantic era that the demand for authenticity and original creation accorded Greece the place of honour (see Chapter 1.4).

A second landmark text that served as a manifesto of Classicism in Russia was Lomonosov's 'Foreword on the Use of Church Books in the Russian Language' (*Predislovie o pol'ze knig tserkovnykh v rossiiskom iazyke*, 1758), which prefaced a two-volume collection of his works. By this time, Lomonosov's powerful triumphal odes glorifying Empress Elizabeth (r. 1741–62) and the empire had made them the touchstone for the new poetry. As the title of the foreword suggests, it promoted Slaveno-Russian (without using the term, which was not used consistently), arguing that Russia's original literary language, Slavonic (created for the translation of the Bible and other church books from Greek), over time had assimilated that language's richness and abundance. Lomonosov put the writings of 'the great Christian teachers and writers' of the Eastern Orthodox Church – the church fathers who 'exalted ancient eloquence in their theological doctrines' and who created the magnificent poetry of the liturgy – on a level with the 'Homers, Pindars, and Demosthenes, and other heroes' who wrote in Greek.[9] This scheme allowed Lomonosov to claim the advantage of a continuous 700-year history for Russian literature, as opposed to Catholic lands, which had limited themselves to using Latin and which had only developed national literatures in recent times.

The second part of Lomonosov's foreword attempted to correlate Slaveno-Russian linguistic material, arranged in hierarchical order according to the classical scheme of 'three styles', with Classicist genres. Lomonosov argued that high-style genres – epic, ode, oratorical prose – should use Slaveno-Russian vocabulary, provided that the words in Slavonic were comprehensible and not overly archaic. Middle-style genres – encompassing theatrical works (unless particularly heroic or lofty), friendly epistles, satires, eclogues, elegies, and historical or scholarly prose – should be written primarily with Russian words, with an occasional admixture of high or low

9 M. V. Lomonosov, *Polnoe sobranie sochinenii* [Complete works], 11 vols. (Moscow, Leningrad: Akademiia nauk, 1950–83), vol. VII, p. 587.

lexicon. Genres in the low style – comedy, comic epigram, song, the familiar letter, and common descriptive prose – should avoid Slavonic vocabulary but may use some middle-style words as well as folk vocabulary, depending on need. Notably, Lomonosov included here prose genres that had been excluded by Boileau and Sumarokov in their programmatic epistles. In historical perspective, Russian drama as well as Sentimentalism developed from the middle linguistic zone.

Classicist Genres

About the time of his *Two Epistles*, Sumarokov published his first tragedies, *Khorev* (*Khorev*, 1747) and *Hamlet* (*Gamlet*, 1748), which established the genre's important position in Russian Classicism. His tragedies, written in iambic hexameter, the Russian syllabo-tonic equivalent of the French Alexandrine, employed a minimum of means – few characters, little action or plot, abstract settings (mostly labelled as ancient Russia), and no props except a dagger (traditional symbol of tragic theatre) – to maximum emotional effect. All share a classical (mostly five-act) structure and observe the three unities of space, time, and action. The crisis usually involves the struggle of two lovers between love and duty, on the one hand, and their conflict with the throne (a jealous, evil, or badly advised monarch), on the other. This was the scheme, broadly speaking, of all of Sumarokov's nine tragedies and was followed by the majority of other tragedians through the early nineteenth century. These included Aleksei Rzhevskii (1737–1803), Vasilii Maikov (1728–1778), Nikolai Nikolev (1758–1815), Iakov Kniazhnin (1740–1791), Petr Plavilshchikov (1760–1812), and Kheraskov, who also experimented with the repertoire by producing the first samples of bourgeois drama and Sentimental and Christian tragedy.

One of the main differences between the Russian Classicist tragedic tradition and the European was the absence of mythical and Greco-Roman plots, which were not part of the Russian cultural heritage. Instead, Russian tragedy predominantly showcased legendary, fictionalised events of what was imagined as Russian history, in many cases set in early Rus of the tenth to thirteenth centuries. In its consideration of the past and of older literary sources, Russian Classicism was inspired by such modern authorities as Voltaire, who – as in his epic the *Henriade* (1723) – acknowledged both the ancients (Homer, Virgil, Lucan) and the canonised moderns (Tasso, Camões,

and Milton); as W. Gareth Jones has written, adaptability to national contexts was very amenable to Classicism's stress on imitation.[10]

Sumarokov also wrote, in prose, the first Russian comedies. These were transparently satiric burlesques, closer to the old *intermedia* – comical interludes that came in between acts of Baroque school dramas – or to Russian folk farces (*igrishchi*), which Sumarokov theoretically repudiated, than to classical comedy. Much closer to Classicist prescriptions were the two prose comedies by Denis Fonvizin (1745–1792): *The Brigadier* (*Brigadir*, 1769) and *The Minor* (*Nedorosl'*, 1782). These witty though didactic comedies of manners, with clever dialogue and wonderful characterisation, are the only eighteenth-century works that have remained on the Russian stage. Kheraskov authored the first traditional Classicist comedy in verse, whose most celebrated example is the satirical *Chicanery* (*Iabeda*, 1798), by Kapnist.

The late 1750s and 1760s witnessed a new level of literary and intellectual engagement in Russia as well as a new generation of Russian poets and dramatists. Kheraskov, who had moved to Moscow to assist in the opening of Moscow University in 1755, worked there as press overseer and censor, and later as curator. He brought together a remarkable group of young literary men to publish a series of literary journals, the most successful of which was the weekly *Useful Entertainment* (*Poleznoe uveselenie*, 1761–2), which published some of the first poems by Ippolit Bogdanovich (1743–1803), Rzhevskii, Maikov, Fonvizin, and Elizaveta Kheraskova (1737–1809), among others. While many scholars, following G. A. Gukovskii, have described this group as the Sumarokov School, others have stressed its independence from strict Classicist prescriptions. C. L. Drage has described this group's 'great achievement' as introducing the belief 'that poetry should express every aspect of man and not only man as subject and citizen'.[11] Its members experimented with new metres and verse forms and greatly expanded the range of poetic subject matter. Among the most noteworthy works were Kheraskov's 'philosophical odes' (Horatian-Stoic rather than Pindaric), Rzhevskii's experimental sonnets, and Sumarokov's Anacreontic poems, which expressed far from the expected themes. Another young poet who emerged at this time, Vasilii Petrov (1736–1799), continued and developed the tradition of Lomonosov's celebratory odes. He caught the attention of Catherine II (r. 1762–96) with his

---

10 W. Gareth Jones, 'A Trojan Horse within the walls of Classicism: Russian Classicism and the national specific', in A. G. Cross (ed.), *Russian Literature in the Age of Catherine the Great: A Collection of Essays* (Oxford: Meeuws, 1976), pp. 95–120.

11 C. L. Drage, 'The Anacreontea and 18th-century Russian poetry', *Slavonic and East European Review* 41.96 (1962), 133.

first one – 'Ode to a Magnificent Carousel' (*Oda na velikolepnyi karusel'*, 1766), which described a pseudo-medieval celebration she had organised – and two years later he joined the empress's personal staff, becoming what she referred to as her 'pocket poet'. The empress's patronage, as well as the heavy style of his writing, earned Petrov the disapproval of many contemporary writers, although Andrei Zorin has shown that his odes helped express and shape Catherine's political and cultural ideology, especially relating to her so-called Greek project.[12]

The poems by Kheraskova in *Useful Entertainment* were among the first by a woman poet to appear in print and were close in theme and form to the moralising poems that her husband, Mikhail Kheraskov, published there. In this era, apart from home-schooling, there were almost no educational opportunities for women (Catherine II's Smolnyi Institute for Noble Maidens only opened its doors in 1764), and many of the first women poets – like Kheraskova – got their start through male relatives.[13] This was true for the poet and translator Mariia Sushkova (1752–1803), sister of the poet and diarist Aleksandr Khrapovitskii (1749–1801), who was Catherine's secretary, as well as for Kheraskov's cousin, Ekaterina Urusova (1747–after 1816). Urusova, a well-known poet in her day, authored the first book of poetry published by a Russian women writer, *Heroides Dedicated to the Muses* (*Iroidy, muzam posviashchennye*, 1777), in a genre created by Ovid that had been modernised and made popular by Alexander Pope in England and Charles-Pierre Colardeau in France. The tradition of Russian women's writing, only recently rediscovered by scholars, is one of the many lacunae in our understanding of eighteenth-century literature.[14] Women's writing in the Classicist tradition may seem surprising insofar as – as in Trediakovskii's *Voyage* – it was common to associate Slavonic writing (in higher genres like odes) with 'manliness' and 'tender' vernacular Russian (as expressed in lighter, middle-style poetic genres) with

12 Andrei Zorin, *By Fables Alone: Literature and State Ideology in Late-Eighteenth – Early-Nineteenth-Century Russia* (Boston: Academic Studies Press, 2014), pp. 24–60.

13 Sandra Shaw Bennett, '"Parnassian Sisters" of Derzhavin's acquaintance: Some observations on women's writing in eighteenth-century Russia', in Maria Di Salvo and Lindsey Hughes (eds.), *A Window on Russia: Proceedings of the V International Conference of the Study Group on Eighteenth-Century Russia* (Rome: La Fenice Edizioni, 1996), pp. 249–56; Wendy Rosslyn, 'Making their way into print: Poems by eighteenth-century Russian women', *Slavonic and East European Review* 78.3 (2000), 407–38.

14 Amanda Ewington (ed. and trans.), *Russian Women Poets of the Eighteenth and Early Nineteenth Centuries: A Bilingual Edition* (Toronto: Centre for Reformation and Renaissance Studies, 2014), helps remedy this deficiency.

women.[15] Classicism's claimed universalism, in both national and gender terms, acknowledged women writers, if only as part of the larger (implicitly male) hierarchy. This gender divide became much more clearly pronounced in Russian Sentimentalism, which spawned a long-lasting tradition of women's writing.

In 1767, Catherine convened the Commission for Creating a New Law Code, for which she wrote the famous *Instruction* (*Nakaz*). Based on the ideas of Montesquieu and Beccaria, this work displayed her attempt to establish liberal Enlightenment principles in Russia. She recruited a group of young men to keep records for the Commission which included Nikolai Novikov (1744–1818), Mikhail Popov (1742–c. 1790), Maikov, and Aleksandr Ablesimov (1742–1783), who were united by their interest in literature. After the Commission's suspension, Catherine continued to encourage and shape public opinion by publishing *All Sorts* (*Vsiakaia vsiachina*, 1769), a moral weekly that drew heavily on Addison and Steele's *Spectator* (see Chapter 2.2). Seven so-called satirical journals appeared between 1769 and 1772. Their writer-publishers included Mikhail Chulkov (1743?–1792), Fedor Emin (1735?–1770), Vasilii Ruban (1742–1795), and Novikov. Novikov produced four journals, the most famous of which was *The Drone* (*Truten'*, 1769–70), which took its cue from Sumarokov's *Diligent Bee* (*Trudoliubivaia pchela*, 1759), the first Russian literary journal, famous for its editor's sharply satirical essays.

Radical critics of the 1860s would later take Novikov's sparring with Catherine over the acceptable limits of satire in these journals as having been politically hostile to her, a view that Jones has shown to be mistaken, or at least greatly exaggerated. In part, this opinion anachronistically reflected the fact that Novikov, who became a leading figure in Russian publishing and philanthropy for the next two decades (see Chapter 2.5), was arrested and jailed by Catherine in 1792, ostensibly for his leading role in Russian Freemasonry.[16] Novikov's arrest, together with that of Aleksandr Radishchev (1749–1802) for his attack on serfdom two years earlier (in his *A Journey from St Petersburg to Moscow* (*Puteshestvie iz Peterburga v Moskvu*, 1790)), marked the final chapter in Catherine's 'Enlightened' absolutism,

---

15 Judith Vowles, 'The "feminization" of Russian literature: Women, language and literature in eighteenth-century Russia', in Toby W. Clyman and Diana Greene (eds.), *Women Writers in Russian Literature* (Westport, CT: Praeger, 1994), pp. 35–60.

16 W. Gareth Jones, *Nikolay Novikov, Enlightener of Russia* (Cambridge: Cambridge University Press, 1984).

which had been severely eroded by the Pugachev Rebellion (1773–5) and the French Revolution.

As noted, the Classicist generic hierarchy excluded prose genres with a few possible exceptions (as we saw with Lomonosov), yet Classicism's heyday in the 1750s–1770s coincided with a flood into Russia of translated European novels and romances, mainly French, a phenomenon that leading literary figures like Sumarokov, Lomonosov, and Novikov publicly decried. Except for a few works such as *Don Quixote* and François Fénelon's *The Adventures of Telemachus* (1699), the novel was not an approved Classicist genre, although several writers tried to create an acceptable example. The 1760s saw the first few original novels in Russian. The earliest were produced by Fedor Emin and represented several types, ranging from the novel of adventure and travel *Inconstant Fortune, or The Adventures of Miramond* (*Nepostoiannaia fortuna, ili Pokhozhdeniia Miramonda,* 1763) and *Constancy Rewarded, or the Adventures of Lizark and Sarmanda* (*Nagrazhdennaia postoiannost', ili Prikliucheniia Lizarka i Sarmandy,* 1764), to a philosophical-political novel entitled *The Adventures of Themistocles and Various . . . Conversations with His Son . . .* (*Prikliucheniia Femistokla i raznye . . . s synom svoim razgovory . . .,* 1763), to the epistolary novel *Letters of Ernest and Doravra* (*Pis'ma Ernesta i Doravry,* 1766) in emulation of Rousseau's *Julie, or the New Heloise* (1761). Emin admitted that he was writing for financial gain, and it has been suggested that with each successive type of novel he was testing the waters at the same time as helping to shape the Russian novel-reading public. Chulkov's fairy tale-chivalric adventure novel *The Mocker, or Slavic Fairytales* (*Peresmeshnik, ili Slavenskie skazki,* 1766–8) introduced a vogue for pseudo-historical and mock-mythological Slavic narratives that was taken up by Popov in his *Slavic Antiquities* (*Slavenskie drevnosti,* 1770–1, later renamed *Old-time Oddities* (*Starinnye dikovinki*)).

Of the above works, only Emin's *Adventures of Themistocles,* written in the manner of Fénelon's *Adventures of Telemachus,* could be considered an attempt at a Classicist novel. So too Kheraskov's first novel *Numa Pompilius, or Flourishing Rome* (*Numa Pompilii, ili Protsvetaiushchii Rim,* 1768), which clearly falls into the category of advice literature, instructing the monarch on how to achieve a utopian society. Kheraskov's later novels, *Cadmus and Harmonia* (*Kadm i Garmoniia,* 1789) and its sequel, *Polydorus, Son of Cadmus and Harmonia* (*Polydor, syn Kadma i Garmonii,* 1794), are sophisticated Masonic allegories that may also be considered attempts at Classicist novels.

To this brief survey, one should add Chulkov's masterpiece *The Comely Cook, or the Adventures of a Depraved Woman* (*Prigozhaia povarikha, ili Prikliucheniia razvratnoi zhenshchiny,* 1770). Earlier critics have primarily seen

in this work either a Russian echo of first-person western European narratives concerning distressed women, such as Daniel Defoe's *Moll Flanders* (1722), or a 'novel of everyday life and manners'.[17] However, more recent critics, following Alexander Levitsky, see *The Comely Cook* in far different terms as a brilliant, thorough-going *travesty* of serious Classicist literature.[18] *The Comely Cook* may thus be viewed as a 'mock novel', in accordance with accepted Classicist genres such as the mock-epic, practised by Chulkov himself. Sumarokov's 'Epistle on Poetry' had outlined two types of mock-epic ('comic heroic') poem: high and low. Whereas in Boileau's *Art of Poetry* low burlesque had been excluded, Sumarokov allowed for both the epic elevation of 'low' matter (as in Boileau's *The Lectern* or Pope's *The Rape of the Lock*) as well as travesty, in which high matter is stylistically lowered (as in Paul Scarron's *Virgil Travestied*). As Manfred Schruba and Angelina Vacheva have shown, in eighteenth-century Russian burlesque, high and low varieties were almost always mixed, producing a unique national variant.[19] Vasilii Maikov created the first attempt in this genre in 1763 (*The Ombre Player* (*Igrok lombera*)), although he had what is acknowledged to be his greatest success with *Elisei, or Bacchus Enraged* (*Elisei ili razdrazhennyi Vakh*, 1771). In this rollicking poem, a drunken peasant coachman is sent by Bacchus to punish the tax-farmers (*otkupshchiki*) for a rise in the price of vodka. The poem also parodies Vasilii Petrov's translation of the first book of the *Aeneid* that had come out the previous year.

These mock-epics derived part of their frisson from their association with the obscene burlesques of so-called Barkoviana, which were unprintable but widely circulated in manuscript. These works were collectively attributed to Lomonosov's pupil, the poet and translator Ivan Barkov (1732–1768), although many major literary figures – including Chulkov, Sumarokov, Lomonosov, and Fonvizin – also took part anonymously. The phenomenon of Barkoviana is remarkable for the fact that virtually all of the main genres of Russian Classicism were subjected to obscene burlesque; the degree of shock or

17 For example, V. S. Nechaeva, 'Russkii bytovoi roman XVIII veka. M. D. Chulkov' [The Russian eighteenth-century novel of everyday life. M. D. Chulkov], *Uchenye zapiski Instituta iazyka i literatury, RANION* [Proceedings of the Institute of language and literature of the Russian association of research institutes in the social sciences] 2 (1928), 5–41.

18 Alexander Levitsky, 'Mikhail Chulkov's *The Comely Cook*: The symmetry of a hoax', *Russian Literature Triquarterly* 21.2 (1988), 97–116.

19 Manfred Schruba, *Studien zu den burlesken Dichtungen V. I. Majkovs* (Wiesbaden: Harrassowitz Verlag, 1997); Angelina Vacheva, *Poema-burlesk v russkoi poezii XVIII veka* [The burlesque poem in Russian poetry of the eighteenth century] (Sofia: Karina M. Todorova, 1999).

humour – especially in the high genres – derived not only from the use of lewd vocabulary but from the disconnect between style and content. Since the fall of the Soviet Union, there has been significant scholarly attention to Barkoviana, first published in a critical edition by Andrei Zorin and Nikita Sapov in 1992.[20] As scholars have shown, it played a significant if mostly covert role in Russian literary development (see Chapter 2.6).

Like comedies, the genre of fable started out at the low end of the literary spectrum and rose progressively over the course of the century. Sumarokov's fables, among his most popular works during his lifetime, were full of coarse humour and were often directed at contemporary targets and literary foes. They were also among his most innovative works, written mostly in iambic lines of varied length (in emulation of La Fontaine's *vers libre*, but also with echoes of folk poetry) and capturing the dynamic intonations of popular speech. The variable iamb found use in other forms of poetry, most notably Bogdanovich's mildly erotic Rococo poem *Dushenka* (*Dushen'ka*, 1778), which took its cue from La Fontaine's 'Psyche' (inspired in its turn by Apuleius) and turned it into a stylised Russian folk tale.

The Final Ray of Classicism's Sunset

Just as the start of Russian Classicism is arguable, so too one could give various endpoints for this tradition. In terms of Classicism's centre of gravity, scholars often date the end of its leading position to about 1780 – about the time Kheraskov, arguably its last major representative, completed the first successful Russian epic, *The Rossiad* (*Rossiada*, 1771–8, pub. 1779), hailed at the time as a new classic. Poets including Kantemir and Lomonosov had tried their hand at this premier poetic genre of the Classicist hierarchy but had not got very far. Classicism began to lose its leading or exclusive role after the death of Sumarokov in 1777 and with the appearance of Derzhavin's genre-bending, playful ode 'Felitsa' (*Felitsa*, 1782; see Chapter 4.2).

Derzhavin is generally considered the greatest poet of the Russian eighteenth century, both as the culmination of Classicism and as the one who led the way to its dissolution. As Anna Lisa Crone has demonstrated, Derzhavin took the Classicist stylistic hierarchy and gave it a new twist, playing upon the contradiction between high-style language and morally low content and introducing heretofore impermissible elements into the ode, which since

20 A. Zorin and N. Sapov (eds.), *Devich'ia igrushka, ili Sochineniia gospodina Barkova* [A maiden's plaything, or The works of Mr Barkov] (Moscow: Ladomir, 1992).

Lomonosov had been the genre of highest prestige.[21] Like Radishchev's *Journey from St Petersburg to Moscow*, it both exposes high style that cloaks low, immoral reality and celebrates simple, vernacular language that expresses the truth.

In the 1780s and 1790s, Sentimentalism and pre-Romanticism – like Classicism, terms devised after the fact – challenged Classicism's hegemony. While the favoured Classicist genres were high style (ode, epic, oratory), Sentimental and pre-Romantic poets preferred the middle, 'feminine' registers that expressed a pastoral or more personal stance, even while the emphasis on the requirements of genre and on imitation remained strong. Scholars consider Kheraskov, who continued to write for almost thirty years after 1780, as a precursor of Sentimentalism.[22] This is an indication of the richness and complexity of the final decades of the century, when new literary and intellectual trends in Germany and England began to rival and overtake the French. At the same time, Classicism's influence continued to be felt through the 1820s, at least through Vladislav Ozerov (1769–1816), the most popular Russian dramatist of the early nineteenth century. Ozerov made his name with the play *Oedipus in Athens* (*Edip v Afinakh*, 1805), adapted from Sophocles via a French intermediary, and was considered even in his day to represent 'the final ray of tragedy's sunset' (in the memorable phrase of Osip Mandelshtam (1891–1938)).[23]

Alternatively, one might put the outer limit of the age of Classicism at the end of the long eighteenth century, that is at 1825, when the cultural and literary situation dramatically changed in the aftermath of the unsuccessful Decembrist revolt, when upon the death of Alexander I (r. 1801–25) a group of disaffected noblemen tried to stage a coup. This was the era when, as noted earlier, Classicism was branded with this then-pejorative label. During the final decades of the eighteenth century and first decades of the nineteenth, the Slaveno-Russian synthesis broke down as the quarrel

---

21 Anna Lisa Crone, *The Daring of Deržavin: The Moral and Aesthetic Independence of the Poet in Russia* (Bloomington, IN: Slavica, 2001).

22 G. N. Pospelov, 'U istokov russkogo sentimentalizma' [Sources of Russian Sentimentalism], *Vestnik Moskovskogo gos. Universiteta* [Herald of Moscow State University] 1 (1948), 3–27. See also Michael Green, 'Diderot and Kheraskov: Sentimentalism in its Classicist stage', in A. G. Cross (ed.), *Russia and the West in the Eighteenth Century* (Newtonville, MA: Oriental Research Partners, 1983), pp. 206–13.

23 This is the last line of Mandelshtam's poem 'There is an unshakeable core of values' (*Est' tsennostei nezyblemaia skala*, 1914).

between 'archaists' and 'innovators' (to use the well-known terms of Iurii Tynianov (1894–1943)) became central to literary life.[24] These were the advocates of Slaveno-Russian led by Aleksandr Shishkov (1754–1841), on the one hand, and the followers of Nikolai Karamzin (1766–1826), on the other. As the scholar Boris Uspenskii has noted, the Karamzinian linguistic programme, based on spoken educated Russian of the French salon type, harkened back to Trediakovskii's position in the foreword to the *Voyage*, the difference being that in the intervening years Russian letters had made great progress and educated salon society had by then indeed developed 'the kind [of language] we speak among ourselves' (see Chapter 2.3).[25] Scholarly consensus has it that it was the genius of Aleksandr Pushkin (1799–1835) that was able to create a new linguistic synthesis that overcame the clash between archaists and innovators and set the stage for the remarkable literary production of Russia's nineteenth century. From Pushkin on, literary conflicts took place *within* a unified literary language rather than between pro-Russian or pro-Slavonic linguistic parties. The single area in which Slaveno-Russian continued to be practised was among the clergy, which by the 1830s again became sharply differentiated from secular literary culture.

Further Reading

Drage, C. L., *Russian Literature in the Eighteenth Century: The Solemn Ode, the Epic, Other Poetic Genres, the Story, the Novel, Drama* (London: C. L. Drage, 1978).

Levitt, Marcus C. (ed.), *Early Modern Russian Writers, Late Seventeenth and Eighteenth Centuries*, Dictionary of Literary Biography 150 (Detroit: Gale Research, 1995).

Lotman, Iu. M., 'Ocherki po istorii russkoi kul'tury XVIII veka' [Essays on the history of eighteenth-century Russian culture], in *Iz istorii russkoi kul'tury* [From the history of Russian culture], 5 vols. (Moscow: Shkola Iazyki russkoi kul'tury, 1996–2002), vol. IV, pp. 13–346.

Marker, Gary, *Publishing, Printing, and the Origins of Intellectual Life in Russia, 1700–1800* (Princeton: Princeton University Press, 2016).

Ospovat, Kirill, *Terror and Pity: Aleksandr Sumarokov and the Theater of Power in Elizabethan Russia* (Boston: Academic Studies Press, 2016).

---

24 Iu. N. Tynianov, *Arkhaisty i novatory* [Archaists and innovators] (Leningrad: Priboi, 1929); Zhivov, *Language and Culture*, pp. 346–81.

25 B. A. Uspenskii, *Iz istorii russkogo literaturnogo iazyka XVIII–nachala XIX veka. Iazykovaia programma Karamzina i ee istoricheskie korni* [From the history of the Russian literary language of the eighteenth to early nineteenth centuries. Karamzin's language programme and its historical roots] (Moscow: Izdatel'stvo Moskovskogo universiteta, 1985).

Proskurina, Vera, *Creating the Empress: Politics and Poetry in the Age of Catherine II* (Boston: Academic Studies Press, 2011).

Ram, Harsha, *The Imperial Sublime: A Russian Poetics of Empire* (Madison: University of Wisconsin Press, 2003).

Wirtschafter, Elise Kimerling, *The Play of Ideas in Russian Enlightenment Theater* (DeKalb: Northern Illinois University Press, 2003).

1.4

Sentimentalism and Romanticism

ILYA VINITSKY

The present chapter covers a period of six decades (from the late 1780s through the late 1840s) and introduces two closely intertwined cultural movements, Russian Sentimentalism (also known as the age of sensibility) and Russian Romanticism (sometimes labelled the Golden Age of Russian poetry). Departing from century-long debates on the paradoxes of Russian Romanticism, I will consider the basic features (a kind of 'genetic code') of the movement through the prism of the oeuvre and literary impact of the father of Russian Romanticism, the poet Vasilii Zhukovskii (1783–1852).

Origins: The School of Melancholy

In his excellent and, to this day, methodologically relevant book on Zhukovskii, the literary historian Aleksandr Veselovskii argued that Russian Romanticism (at least in its classic form exemplified by the poetry of its founder) was nothing but a provincial version of western European Sentimentalism.[1] According to Veselovskii, the formative age of sensibility (the 1780s–90s) emerged as both a rejection and an adaptation of rationalist Neoclassicism (see Chapter 1.3). During the age of sensibility, an assortment of emotional modes were developed. Influential works such as *Studies of Nature* (1784), by the French Rousseauist Bernardin de Saint-Pierre, acted as handbooks of sensibility, regulating the expression of emotions in concrete situations.

One emotion emerged particularly strongly as part of this process. Reflective melancholy could be described as the dominant 'muse' of the

---

1 A. N. Veselovskii, *V. A. Zhukovskii: Poeziia chuvstva i 'serdechnogo voobrazheniia'* [V. A. Zhukovsky: The poetry of feeling and of 'the heart's imagination'] (St Petersburg: Tipografiia imperatorskoi akademii nauk, 1904).

71

period in Russian cultural history, which lasted for almost three decades, from the late 1780s to 1810s. The cult of melancholy was a sacralised fashion and bore all the hallmarks of (quasi-)religious ritual. Practitioners of Sentimentalism offered literary prayers to holy Melancholy, bowed before her images (allegorical portraits and sculptural representations as manifested in Nikolai Karamzin's (1766–1826) poem 'Melancholy' (Melankholiia, 1800)), and even built real shrines to her, where, withdrawing from earthly trifles, they could give themselves over to serious and virtuous thought.

The cult of melancholy had its own holy prophets. Many of them came from western Europe (e.g. Edward Young, Jean-Jacques Rousseau, and later Johann Wolfgang Goethe, the author of The Sorrows of Young Werther (1774)), but the Russian Karamzin, with his short story 'Poor Liza' (Bednaia Liza, 1792; see Chapter 4.4), also took his place in the pantheon. Not only the author of Russia's most formative Sentimental text, Karamzin provided for his readers a Russian encyclopedia of European emotional culture in his Letters of a Russian Traveller (Pis'ma russkogo puteshestvennika, 1791–2). In one of these literary letters, Karamzin tells the story of a French missionary who rendered Rousseau's essays into Arabic, beginning with a catechism: '"Who is the true prophet?" "Rousseau."'[2] In the Sentimentalist code of conduct, melancholy rituals included pilgrimages to places of sorrow, serious walks to cemeteries, and the contemplation of ruins. The Sentimental nobleman strove to surround himself with a melancholic setting appropriate to his convictions and artistic predilections: to create, in the midst of the large, unfeeling world, a reassuring artificial microcosm with a high aesthetic and spiritual status.

The melancholy literary school, founded by Karamzin, presented the canon (or cultural code) that the Sentimentalist followed in everyday life and that had a profound impact upon Russian literature. One of the distinguishing features of this canon was the cult of feelings, expressed in a peculiar focus on tears and public weeping. Thus, in the finale of 'Poor Liza', the narrator tells the reader about his frequent visits to the pond where the eponymous heroine, abandoned by her lover, had ended her days: 'They buried her next to the pond, under the sombre oak, and placed a wooden cross on her grave. I often sit here, lost in thoughtfulness, resting against the receptacle of Liza's dust; the pond stirs in my eyes, and the leaves rustle over

---

2 Nikolai Karamzin, Pis'ma russkogo puteshestvennika [Letters of a Russian traveller] (Leningrad: Nauka, 1984), p. 312.

my head.'[3] Here the odd preposition of 'in my eyes' (instead of 'in front of my eyes') shifts meaning from description to symbol: the pond becomes a teardrop. The latter acts as a mediator between nature and the imagination; it is a physical (or half-physical and half-psychological) object which connects and unites the narrator's inner and outer worlds. As such, the ending functions also to instruct the reader on how to perceive the text correctly: via shedding a tear. The latter is more than the calculated affect. It is essential physical proof of the reader's humanity and empathy, and it secures membership of the cult of feeling.

The Romantic Paradox

At the beginning of the nineteenth century, this Sentimental cult of tears was developed and modified by Zhukovskii in his seminal elegy 'A Country Cemetery' (*Sel'skoe kladbishche*) – a free translation of Thomas Gray's 'Elegy Written in a Country Churchyard' (1751) – published in Karamzin's journal *Messenger of Europe* (*Vestnik Evropy*, 1802–30) in 1802. The poem provided a complex of themes and motifs that would become the distinguishing features of Russian Romantic poetry: the celebration of the quiet life in the bosom of nature, far from cold civilisation; radiant melancholy; death as the entrance into another world; memory as the hope for a meeting in the world beyond; and the patient faith in resurrection. Finally, in its core image of the 'abject singer' (*pevets uedinennyi*) to whom the poem's epitaph is dedicated – a sensitive lover of nature and unknown poetic genius doomed to an early grave – Zhukovskii's elegy provided a model for the doomed hero of Romantic melancholy.

In Veselovskii's view, the Russian Romanticism shaped by Zhukovskii here lacked its western counterpart's passion for experimentation (that is, invention and originality). Originating, according to the traditional historical scheme, in the first decade of the nineteenth century, Russian Romanticism postdated its western European counterparts. And it could appear conceptually shallow. Russian Romantic writers showed, for example, almost no interest – at least until the 1830s – in metaphysics and grand mystical doctrines. Russian Romanticism also lacked influential independent ideological institutions and platforms (such as a major journal or university circle) to disseminate and promote Romantic agendas. It was imitative (sometimes

3 Nikolai Karamzin, 'Bednaia Liza' [Poor Liza], in *Moskovskoi zhurnal* [Moscow journal] 6 (1792), 277.

to the point of plagiarism), and in its early stages consisted almost entirely of translations – and translations of translations – or adaptations of (mostly second-rank) western Romantic works. It was provincial, politically conservative (with very few, yet notable, exceptions), and confusing in its uncritical and eclectic mixture of traditions (including Neoclassical poetry, the Enlightenment, Rousseauism, and German *Sturm und Drang*) and authors (Friedrich Schiller, Goethe, Germaine de Staël, Byron, and François-René Chateaubriand). Despite its obsessive zeal for translation, it did not notice the brothers August and Friedrich Schlegel, Novalis, William Blake, or William Wordsworth but considered Schiller and the anti-Romantic Goethe as supreme manifestations of Romanticism. The movement that we might call Russian Romanticism was also very modest in size. It consisted of a handful of very different writers – most notably the poets Zhukovskii, Konstantin Batiushkov (1787–1855), Evgenii Baratynskii (1800–1844), and Mikhail Lermontov (1814–1841), and the prose writers Aleksandr Bestuzhev-Marlinskii (1797–1837), Vladimir Odoevskii (1804–1869), and early Nikolai Gogol (1809–1852) – and a tiny readership, almost entirely belonging to the nobility and located mostly in the two capitals (St Petersburg and Moscow) with a few provincial oases.

Yet Russian Romanticism possessed a constant 'truth of mood' character-istic of the age of sensibility. And indeed, if one looks at the phenomenon of Russian Romanticism from within, it may seem even more Romantic – and certainly more significant – in its effect than its more celebrated western counterparts. The intensive and contradictory literary process of the Romantic age eventually led to the formation, almost (or seemingly) *ex nihilo*, of a complex cultural ecosystem with a sophisticated literary language; new genres; modes of emotional expression; a group of interrelated and formative works; a vibrant emancipated republic of letters, with its pantheon of master writers; and, last but not least, a powerful idea of the centrality of poetry (and literature in general) in the national culture-building and histor-ical destiny of Russia – an idea intensified by the Napoleonic Wars that culminated in the victorious campaign against the French in 1814.

In a word, while under-Romantic in comparison with its 'parental' German, French, and English traditions, Russian Romanticism is über-Romantic in its transformative outcomes. It also laid the foundation for the rapid development of Russian literature in consequent periods as an impetus for the novels of Aleksandr Herzen (1812–1870), Ivan Goncharov (1812–1891), Ivan Turgenev (1818–1883), Fedor Dostoevskii (1821–1881), and Lev Tolstoi (1828–1910) and, later on, for the aesthetic systems of the Modernist epoch. In

fact, Romantic ideas (the themes of ideal love, spiritual longing, universal brotherhood, beautiful nature, Gothic mysteries, fate, etc.) form an important undercurrent in major works of Russian literature of the nineteenth and twentieth centuries. Understanding the complex and generative process of assimilation and adaptation that was Russian Romanticism is therefore essential to our understanding of Russian literature.

Approaches and Interpretations

Historically speaking, the term 'romantic' was already used in Russian Sentimental journals in the late 1780s as a western-sounding characteristic of any 'miraculous' place: the romantic landscape or garden, the exotic country. In the late eighteenth century, it was applied to the so-called magic opera (as exemplified in Mozart's *The Magic Flute* (1791)). In the 1800s, Gavriil Kamenev (1772–1803) and Zhukovskii introduced German 'romantic' ballads as a new genre set in an enchanting and terrifying imaginary world with exotic settings, distinct national colour, strong passions, and extraordinary characters, including a host of supernatural creatures governed by a fateful power. French literary debates on the antithetical Romantic and Classical schools reached Russian journals in the late 1810s and culminated in polemics concerning Aleksandr Pushkin's (1799–1837) Byronic poems 'The Prisoner of the Caucasus' (*Kavkazskii plennik*, 1822) and 'The Fountain of Bakhchisarai' (*Bakhchisaraiskii fontan*, comp. 1823, pub. 1824) in the early 1820s. The first critical references to Russian Romanticism go back to the 1820s, in an 1824 essay by Petr Viazemskii (1792–1878) in Pushkin's defence, 'A Conversation between a Publisher and the Classic from the Vyborg Side or from Vasilevskii Island' (*Razgovor mezhdu izdatelem i klassikom s Vyborgskoi storony ili s Vasil'evskogo ostrova*). However, the concept of Russian Romanticism as a distinct cultural movement and period emerged only in the late 1830s in the critical essays of Nikolai Nadezhdin (1804–1856) and Vissarion Belinskii (1811–1848; see Box 5.1). In many cases, poets and critics of this period used the word with a slight ironic connotation, notably in Pushkin's *Eugene Onegin* (*Evgenii Onegin*, 1825–32) when he describes Vladimir Lenskii's style: 'Thus he wrote, vaguely and languidly – / Which is what we call Romanticism, / Although I don't see here anything Romantic whatsoever.'[4] By the end of the nineteenth century, Russian Romanticism

---

4 A. S. Pushkin, *Polnoe sobranie sochinenii v 17 tomakh* [Complete works in 17 volumes] (Moscow: Voskresen'e, 1995), vol. VI, p. 126.

had become an umbrella term that covered a number of authors, ranging from the poets Zhukovskii, Batiushkov, and Pushkin (during his 'Byronic' period) to the prose writers Bestuzhev-Marlinskii, Lermontov, and early Gogol.

Yet, as we have seen, despite its relative simplicity, Russian Romanticism is hard to define. Unsurprisingly, chapters on Romanticism in Russian literary dictionaries and textbooks often include a witty statement from Viazemskii's letter to the acknowledged legislator of the movement, Zhukovskii: 'Romanticism is like a domestic spirit [*domovoi*]; many people believe in it; there is a conviction that it exists – but where are its distinguishing features, how can you define it; how can you stick your fingers into it?'[5]

Since the 1820s, numerous attempts to capture and define this 'spirit' have been undertaken, but the elusive nature of the movement remains. The major problem is that Russian Romanticism is both vague and dynamic: various trends mix and evolve and do not correspond well to their western analogues. One can summarise the (overlapping) approaches to the history of Russian Romanticism as follows:

1. *The 'dictionary' method*: an introduction and brief survey of the major literary figures who represent the movement. The problem is that it is hard to find pure Romantics in Russian literature. The label largely depends on the scholar's beliefs. Is Pushkin a Romantic? Does he represent the 'completion' of the eighteenth-century libertine tradition? Is he a (proto-)Realist? Is Aleksandr Griboedov's (1795–1829) political comedy *Woe from Wit* (*Gore ot uma*, comp. 1824) Neoclassical or Romantic? When did Gogol stop being a Romantic writer? In fact, my own list of pure Russian Romantic authors of the 1800s–1840s includes only seven names: the dreamy poets Zhukovskii, Batiushkov, and Ivan Kozlov (1779–1840), the verbose fiction writer Bestuzhev-Marlinskii, the bombastic playwright Nestor Kukolnik (1809–1868), the pompous poet Vladimir Benediktov (1807–1873), and Aleksei Pugovoshnikov (1790s–1840s?) – an extremely minor poetaster from the lower strata of Russian society who painstakingly imitated the Romantic style in his metromaniac poetry about knights, devils, angels, chaste maidens, unhappy poets, and universal boredom.

2. *The 'genealogical' method*: a discussion of the Russian transformation of the major cultural sources of Russian Romanticism: its German idealistic

5 Cited in P. A. Viazemskii, *Estetika i literaturnaia kritika* [Aesthetics and literary criticism] (Moscow: Iskusstvo, 1984), p. 395.

(drawing on Schiller, Johann Gottlieb Fichte, the Schlegel brothers, Friedrich Schelling), Gothic (Ann Radcliffe), Byronic, or French (Rousseau, Madame de Staël) modus operandi. This approach integrates Russian Romanticism into the context of the western Romantic movement and invites us to discuss various mechanisms of cultural absorption and appropriation, but it also deprives Russian Romanticism of its distinctive cultural content.

3. *The 'Formalist' method*: a taxonomy of Romanticism focused on its major features and devices. In thematic terms, these are subjectivism; the cult of nature (and the denunciation of the city); the supernatural; a fascination with 'primordial' national history; folklorism; mythologism; extraordinary characters (the genius-artist, the villain, the angelic woman, the demonic seductress, the outcast, the noble savage, etc.); and exotic settings, often depending on colonising and military activities of the Russian Empire (from Ukraine and Finland interpreted as equivalents of the Romantic Scotland of Sir Walter Scott to the Caucasus and Siberia seen via Byronic lenses). In stylistic terms, we find fragmentariness, suggestiveness, irony, and the concept of 'the inexpressible'. Practitioners of this taxonomic approach survey the generic repertoire of Russian Romanticism: the horror ballad; the elegy; the Byronic oriental poem; the fantastic high society and chivalric tales (with their lofty style, women in distress, disillusioned men in despair, duels, and suicides); experimental forms, such as the novel in verse or narrative poem in prose; and, last but not least, a perpetual search for the national epic. This Formalist summary is undoubtedly the most traditional approach to the problem, yet it somehow reminds us of the method of Gogol's bride, who imagines an ideal husband as a combination of traits borrowed from different suitors: 'If the mouth of Nikanov Ivanovich could be placed under the fine nose of Ivan Kuzmich, and add to it the grace of Baltazar Baltazarovitch, and perhaps also a little of Ivan Pavlovich's good manners, then it would be easy to make my choice.'[6]

4. *The 'historical' approach*: based on a rigid chronological periodisation which usually presents Russian Romanticism as sandwiched between Karamzinian weeping Sentimentalism and the harsh realism of the Natural School (see Chapter 1.5). Such an approach sees Romanticism as passing through several stages, from the pre-Romanticism of the early

---

6 N. V. Gogol', *Sochineniia v chetyrekh tomakh* [Works in four volumes] (St Petersburg: Tipografiia A. Borodina, 1842), vol. IV, p. 284.

nineteenth century to the elegiac Romanticism of Zhukovskii and his followers to the Byronism of the 1820s as embodied in Pushkin's 'southern poems'. The next stage in this scheme would be the 'poetry of thought' exemplified in the works of Dmitrii Venevitinov (1805–1827) and the 'Moscow poets' of the 1830s, and thence via the metaphysical poetry of Fedor Tiutchev (1803–1873) and the aesthetic Schellingianism of Lermontov, the Hoffmannesque tradition of Russian fantastic tales of the 1830s (Bestuzhev-Marlinskii, Odoevskii, Gogol).

A problem in this approach is that these periods overlap, and also that other such historical schemes are available. For example, in one version the passage from schematic Neoclassicism to what would become known as Russian Realism focuses on Pushkin, seen as the major exponent of the Romantic trend in the early 1820s. Pushkin apparently overcame Romanticism's limitations (i.e. conventional Byronism) by the middle of the decade – already visible in one of his southern poems, 'The Gypsies' (*Tsygany*, 1824) – and created an original literary and ideological system as manifested in his novel in verse *Eugene Onegin* and his Shakespearian tragedy *Boris Godunov* (*Boris Godunov*, 1825). In this approach a similar metaphor of overcoming is applied to other writers: to Gogol, in his alleged movement from the fantastic Ukrainian tales of the 1830s to the 'romantic realism' of 'The Overcoat' (*Shinel'*, 1842) and *Dead Souls* (*Mertvye dushi*, 1842); and to Lermontov, who overcame his early ardent Byronism in his progression towards a more sober perspective on Byronic demonism, as exemplified in his unfinished parodic *Fairytale for Children* (*Skazka dlia detei*, 1841) and the novel *A Hero of Our Time* (*Geroi nashego vremeni*, 1840).

Or, in yet another historical schema, Russian Romanticism can also be constructed as a passage from naïve imitations of western trends towards the mature and complex Romanticism of Pushkin, Lermontov, Odoevskii, Gogol, and Tiutchev. From this perspective, Gogol's *Dead Souls* is certainly *more* Romantic than his early clichéd narrative poem *Hans Küchelgarten* (*Gants Kiukhel'garten*, 1829) and his Ukrainian tales such as *Evenings on a Farm near Dikanka* (*Vechera na khutore bliz Dikan'ki*, 1831–2). In this version, Pushkin's artistic development is no longer an overcoming of or an intentional distancing from Byron, but rather a movement towards a more real or human (in Pushkin's words) way of understanding of him.

Each of these approaches has its own pros and cons. In this chapter, I offer an alternative way of narrating the history of Russian Romanticism. I view it as a fluid and loose literary stream, rather than an organised self-reflective movement. In what follows, I will present Russian Romanticism in what might be called, stylistically, a Romantic fashion via a series of fragmentary snapshots which take as their point of departure foundational works by Vasilii Zhukovskii; I will use those snapshots to draw out essential unifying elements of the literature of the Romantic era as represented in concrete examples.[7]

The Atmosphere

The birth of Romanticism in Russia is usually associated with the publication in 1808 of 'Liudmila' (*Liudmila*), Zhukovskii's translation of 'Lenore' by the German *Sturm und Drang* poet Gottfried Bürger. The poem's atmosphere is Gothic and extremely dynamic (a sharp contrast to descriptive Neoclassical narrative poems): it features night, a skeleton, ghosts who accompany a girl and her dead fiancé, a cemetery, open graves. Characteristically, Zhukovskii transferred the setting of the German ballad to pre-Petrine Russia; changed the historical time of action to the Livonian Wars of the sixteenth century (clearly alluding to the 1808 Russian campaign against Sweden); changed the name of the heroine to the very Russian Liudmila, a name which has the further advantage of rhyming with the word *mogila* (grave); smoothed out the somewhat vulgar language of the original; and removed some images that might offend Sentimental taste (a gallows with a body hanging from it, for example). 'And that was the beginning of Romanticism in Russia!', as one of his friends would say years later.[8] Between 1808 and 1833, Zhukovskii would write (or more often translate) some forty ballads, whose central theme was generally that of crime and terrible punishment.

The power of 'Liudmila' derived from the way that Zhukovskii brought alive the world of the past – exotic, terrifying, and passionate – for the reader (the narrative begins by bringing the reader in *in medias res* and remains in the present tense throughout). The ballad became the prototype for the horror genre in Russian literature and affected the development of Russian Romantic prose

---

7 On the development of Zhukovskii's Romanticism and formation of his Romantic myth, see Ilya Vinitsky, *Vasily Zhukovsky's Romanticism and the Emotional History of Russia* (Evanston, IL: Northwestern University Press, 2015).

8 F. F. Vigel', *Zapiski* [Notes], 7 vols. (Moscow: Universitetskaia tipografiia, 1891–3), vol. III, p. 137.

more broadly, with the master theme of crime and punishment, the figure of the grief-stricken girl who cries for her beloved, and the image of the apocalyptic horse symbolising an inevitable death. Popular demonology became a legitimate theme of 'high-brow' literature, from Pushkin's 'Demons' (*Besy*, 1830) and *The Queen of Spades* (*Pikovaia dama*, 1833) to the Romantic tales of Antonii Pogorelskii (1787–1836) and Aleksandr Veltman (1800–1870) to Gogol's *Evenings on a Farm near Dikanka* and *Mirgorod* (*Mirgorod*, 1835).

Starting from 'Liudmila', Zhukovskii's chivalric and mystical ballads – most notably, 'Ritter Toggenburg' (*Rytsar' Togenburg*, 1816), 'The Forest King' (*Lesnoi tsar'*, 1818), and 'Castle Smalholm, or the Eve of Saint John' (*Zamok Smal'gol'm, ili Ivanov vecher*, 1824) – influenced the Romantic prose of Bestuzhev-Marlinskii, with its noble knights, sacrificial heroines, villains, unbridled passions, and supernatural creatures, as well as the Hoffmannesque fantastic tales written by Odoevskii in the 1830s and 1840s (a Schellingian, Odoevskii also drew from various occult and metaphysical sources). Finally, a group of 'classical' ballads (based on ancient Greek mythological plots) translated by Zhukovskii from Schiller introduced the important humanistic theme of the brotherhood of noble 'beautiful souls', which deeply affected Dostoevskii and resonated in his last novel, *The Brothers Karamazov* (*Brat'ia Karamazovy*, 1881).

Even from these beginnings, however, the Russian Romantics were engaged in complex and even ambivalent acts of adaptation and homage in relation to their literary antecedents. Zhukovskii and a number of his follow-ers adopted an ironic stance towards extreme balladic horrors and fantasies. In 1811–12, the poet revised the plot, imagery, and gloomy ideology of 'Lenore'/'Liudmila' in his ingenious Russian ballad 'Svetlana' (*Svetlana*). In this poem, the vision of a corpse turns out to be a nightmare brought on by a fortune-telling session, and the heroine marries her beloved who has returned safe and sound:

> Smile, my beauty,
> To my ballad;
> There are great miracles in it,
> Very little stock.
> Happy with your gaze
> I don't want fame either;
> Glory – we were taught – smoke;
> Light is a crafty judge.
> Here are my ballads:
> Our best friend in this life

> Faith in Providence
> The law of the builder is good
> Here misfortune is a false dream;
> Happiness is awakening.[9]

Zhukovskii's goal in this ballad was the creation of an ideal female character (see also Chapter 4.6), a literary embodiment of the Russian soul as he understood it. Distinct from the German prototype of the original Lenore's distinguishing features are the new Svetlana's purity, humility, submission to God, fidelity, tenderness, and radiant sadness. Dark forces are unable to harm such a pure soul, and the implacable judgement day characteristic of the western ballad gives way to the actions of wise providence. A few years later, Pushkin would employ this ideal image of Svetlana as the basis for his Tatiana in *Eugene Onegin*. Zhukovskii's ballad also served as a source of inspiration for Russian artists and composers of the Romantic age, for example Karl Briullov's (1799–1852) painting *Fortuneteller Svetlana* (1836) and Aleksandr Pleshcheev's (1778–1862) and Aleksandr Varlamov's (1801–1848) musical renderings of 'Svetlana' (1832 and 1834, respectively).

The Lover

The leading genre of early Romanticism was not the ballad but the 'dreamy' (*mechtatel'naia*) elegy, with its emphasis on sweet melancholy. This emotion was closely associated with the themes of (unrequited) love and recollection of a lost paradise. It was seen as proof of the dualism of human fate, as it revealed both a spiritual link to a better world and a physical imprisonment in mundane, carnal reality.

Prior to Zhukovskii, depictions of Romantic melancholy in Russian literature were strictly prescribed, featuring a limited range of themes and images and a singular scheme for the development of sentiment. The amorous melancholic hero was deserving of compassion from sentimental people. A victim of Eros, he would withdraw from the world, thinking only of his beloved. Karamzin, Zhukovskii's mentor in both literature and morality, had shown Romantic melancholy as a touching yet dangerous condition, one capable of driving the lover to suicide (as in the case of 'Poor Liza') or insanity (such as the incidents mentioned by Karamzin in the 'English' section of

---

9 V. A. Zhukovskii, *Polnoe sobranie sochinenii i pisem v dvadtsati tomakh* [Complete works and letters in twenty volumes] (Moscow: Iazyki slavianskikh kul'tur, 1999–), vol. III (2008), p. 38.

Letters of a Russian Traveller). In the understanding of most Neoclassical and Sentimental poets at the turn of the nineteenth century, Romantic melancholy held no joy and was viewed as a sickness. In Zhukovskii's interpretation, however, it became a spiritual messenger of a joy impossible in earthly life, a cure from despondency and boredom, and a proof of the human soul's immortality. This marked a fundamental shift from Sentimentalism to the Romantic mode.

Let us consider Zhukovskii's poem 'Hymn' (*Gimn*, 1809). This poem, written on the occasion of the name-day of the poet's beloved niece, Maria Protasova, can justly be called the *summa summarum* of his philosophy of love from 1805 to 1808 and one of the most exceptional works of Russian lyric poetry of the early nineteenth century. I take the Romantic liberty of quoting a literal translation of the poem in full here. I also italicise the keywords and key idioms of the Romantic lexicon introduced by Zhukovskii into Russian lyric poetry and prose:

> *My friend, my guardian angel,*
> O you who are without compare,
> I love you, *I breathe you,*
> But *how can I express my passion?*
> In all the beauties of nature
> I encounter your *dear image*;
> When I see [other] charming [women],
> I imagine only you in their features.
>
> I take a quill. I can trace with it
> Only [your] *unforgettable name*;
> I can praise you alone
> On my *enraptured lyre*:
> With you, [when] alone, close by, far away.
> To love you is my only joy.
> For me you are all that is good on earth.
> You [bring] life to my heart, [and] sweetness to [my] life.
>
> In the desert [or] in the roar of the city,
> I dream only of listening to you;
> When I fall asleep, *your image*
> *Melts together with my last thought*;
> The pleasant sound of your speaking
> Does not leave me in my dreams;
> *I awake, and there you are in my soul*
> Even before the day touches my eyes.

O! Am I to know separation from you?
You are my invisible companion everywhere;
When you say nothing, I understand your gaze
Which everyone else finds inexplicable.
I receive your voice in my heart;
I drink love in your breath . . .
Who can comprehend you, O raptures?
[Who can comprehend] you, [O] *enchantment of [my] soul?*

By you and for you alone
Do I live and find pleasure in life;
I feel myself through you,
In you am I astonished by nature.
And to what can I compare *my lot?*
What [else] to desire in such sweet fate?
Love is life to me – O! I would only wish
To love a hundred times more.[10]

This exultant manifesto of Platonic *Seelenliebe* (soul love) is the opening act in the history of Russian Romantic poetry, prefiguring lyrical works from Batiushkov, Pushkin, Tiutchev, Afanasii Fet (1820–1892), and Aleksandr Blok (1880–1921). The meaning of life itself is justified and determined by the lover's feeling for his beloved ('love is life to me'). In love, the poet finds his own individuality ('I feel myself through you') and the surrounding world becomes transformed into an enormous mirror in which every appearance is a reflection of his beloved's image. In a word, love presents itself as a new, life-affirming religion.

In the early 1820s, Zhukovskii's lyrical insights of the 1800s and 1810s were consolidated as the first Russian Romantic aesthetic theory of love in a cycle of poems and letters dedicated by the poet to his royal student, the grand duchess Aleksandra Feodorovna – 'The Mysterious Visitor' (*Tainstvennyi posetitel'*, 1824), 'Lalla Rookh' (*Lalla Ruk*, 1821), and 'The Appearance of Poetry in the Image of Lalla Rookh' (*Iavlenie poezii v vide Lalla Ruk*, 1821). In 1821 Zhukovskii wrote a lyrical essay about Raphael's *Sistine Madonna*, which became one of the most influential aesthetic manifestos of Russian Romanticism and, later, Symbolism (echoes of the central ideas of this article can be found in the work of Pushkin, Fet, Dostoevskii, Vladimir Solovev (1853–1900), and Blok). Zhukovskii describes Raphael's painting as a marvellous vision of the Mother of God, once revealed to the artist and

10 Zhukovskii, *Polnoe sobranie sochinenii i pisem,* vol. I, pp. 129–30; trans. Timothy Portice and Ilya Vinitsky.

accessible – in a moment of aesthetic revelation – to anyone who contemplates this picture, including the poet himself. This mystical philosophy of the 'genius of pure beauty' (*genii chistoi krasoty*) who appears on earth for a moment and leaves a memory as a harbinger of a better world is echoed in Pushkin's famous poem 'To *** [Anna Kern]' (*K *** [Anne Kern]*, 1825).

The lyrical apotheosis of Zhukovskii's chivalric doctrine of chaste love can be found in his ballad 'Vadim' (*Vadim*), a part of his Romantic tale *Twelve Sleeping Maidens* (*Dvenadtsat' spiashchikh dev*, 1817), which was written after the poet's beloved had married another man. The image of a pure youthful dreamer who entrusts his life to divine providence entered into the canon of Russian Romanticism. Forged by Zhukovskii, this type of character was received by readers in the 1810s as an ethical model ('the idol of chaste hearts')[11] and called forth a wave of imitations in literature and in life. Pushkin's Lenskii in *Eugene Onegin* is but one of the artistic reincarnations of this idealised type, as was, many decades after, the speaker in Aleksandr Blok's *Poems about a Beautiful Lady* (*Stikhi o prekrasnoi dame*, comp. 1901–2) (see Chapter 1.6).

Following Zhukovskii, the poets of the Romantic age created a specific poetic vocabulary and a set of affective modes that shaped the emotional outlook of at least two generations of writers (Vadim Vatsuro has called this group of authors the Russian Elegiac School).[12] Opposition to this increasingly conventional language was also present, as evidenced in a number of polemical attacks on the Romantic elegy and ballad, both from outside (as in the Neoclassical comedies of Aleksandr Shakhovskoi (1777–1846)) and from within the Romantic trend (in critical essays by Griboedov and Vilgelm Kiukhelbeker (1797–1846)). By the mid-1810s the trademark image of an 'ideal innocent youth' had frequently begun to take on a comic dimension and was often associated with the traditional Sentimental figure of the charming and virtuous woman. The result of this overlap was a parallel feminisation of Zhukovskii's public image. In 1815, Shakhovskoi mocked the poet by employing the image of an effeminate poet Fialkin (Mr Violet), an author of silly ballads addressed to 'sweet' maidens (indeed, Zhukovskii's implied audience was predominantly female, as characteristic of the emotional utopia of the age of sensibility). The response of Zhukovskii's supporters to this satirical attack was the formation of the parodic literary society

---

11 A. S. Pushkin, *Polnoe sobranie sochinenii v shesti tomakh* [Complete works in six volumes] (Moscow, Leningrad: Gosudarstvennoe izdatel'stvo khudozhestvennoi literatury, 1934), vol. IV, p. 227.

12 Vadim Vatsuro, *Lirika pushkinskoi pory: 'Elegicheskaia shkola'* [Lyric poetry in the age of Pushkin: The 'Elegaic school'] (St Petersburg: Nauka, 1994).

Arzamas, which united the 'knights of good taste' around their leader, who had been attacked by a 'barbarian'. It is revealing, however, that in the comic mythology of this literary order Zhukovskii received the female nickname Svetlana (after the heroine of his ballad) and was called 'the beautiful maiden'.

In fact, by the end of the decade even the appreciation of Zhukovskii's friends for his 'chaste' Romanticism became strained. Pushkin's literary strategy towards his mentor's ideal Romanticism was two-sided. On the one hand, he occasionally imitated Zhukovskii's 'beautiful and innocent' poetry; on the other, he also composed humorous, and openly erotic, reworkings of it. Zhukovskii's monastery of the twelve sleeping maidens becomes a filthy bordello in Pushkin's obscene ballad 'Barkov's Shade' (*Ten' Barkova*, 1814 or 1815; Ivan Barkov (1732–1768) was widely known as an author of hilarious pornographic verse), while in the fourth canto of *Ruslan and Liudmila* (*Ruslan i Liudmila*, 1820) it becomes an upper-class brothel. The sublime longing of Zhukovskii's lyrical ballads turns into open physical desire. Thus, the monk in Pushkin's 1819 lyric 'The Water Nymph' (*Rusalka*), which parodies Zhukovskii's 'Fisherman' (*Rybak*, 1818), is seduced by the water nymph mentioned in the older poet's ballad. This seduction of innocence was a literary metaphor: the older system of Platonic love must voluntarily surrender itself to a younger, more earthly version, focused on the liberation – rather than taming – of sexual desire and on unrestrained and corrupt imagination.

The comic peak of this literary theme of the seduction of the innocent muse can be found in Pushkin's openly sacrilegious poem the *Gabrieliad* (*Gavriliada*, 1823), which satirised Zhukovskii's increasing preoccupation with mystical ideas at the turn of the 1820s. In this poem, Pushkin merrily mixes motifs from a number of Zhukovskii's mystical ballads: the fight between the archangel Gabriel and Satan parodies the struggle between the devil and the saintly old man in Zhukovskii's *Twelve Sleeping Maidens*; the description of the dove that covers Mary's lap in Pushkin's story is a comic recasting of the dove that alights on Svetlana's breast. In the end, the pure, mystical poetry of Zhukovskii, exemplified in the image of Mary, freely gives itself up to its conqueror: Satan.

Pushkin's parodies of Zhukovskii consist of ironically revealing the poetic system of the older poet and then taking possession of it. This parodic act was an important moment in the history of Romantic love in Russian literature. It signalled the birth of a new earthly discourse of passion out of the spirit of the earlier Sentimental cult of chastity and

pristine brotherly feeling. The next stage in the literary history of the Russian domestication of Romantic love is associated with the transformation of the Byronic tradition in the works of Pushkin, Baratynskii, and Lermontov.

The Fallen Angel

Zhukovskii can be credited with introducing another formative topos into the history of Russian Romanticism: the demonic personality. In 1814, he translated a fragment about the demon Abbadona from Friedrich Klopstock's eighteenth-century Miltonic epic 'The Messiah' (1748–73):

> Why is the sweet entrance to the heavens closed off for Abbadona?
> O! Why can I not once more fly home,
> To the bright worlds of the Almighty, to forever quit
> This land of exile? [. . .]
> Today I stand, sombre, rejected, an orphaned exile,
> Saddened among the beauty of creation. O native sky,
> Seeing you, I tremble: there I lost bliss,
> There, turning from God, I became a sinner. O untouched world,
> My dear friend in the bright valley of tranquillity, where are you?
> In vain! The Judge has left me of bliss only a glimpse of heavenly glory,
> a pitiful remainder!
> Ach! Why do I not dare to proclaim to him 'My Creator'?
> Let the non-exiled in pure rapture proclaim the 'Father'.[13]

The cosmic sufferings of Klopstock's fallen angel introduced feelings of noble envy and mumblings of discontent at fate, reflecting a sense of tragic exclusion from an imagined paradise. These were reinforced by the Russian adaptations and revisions of Byronic poetry in the 1820s, centred around a sublime vengeful outcast, such as Pushkin's 'Demons' and 'The Gypsies' and Kiukhelbeker's mystical drama *Izhorskii* (*Izhorskii*, 1835). Such feelings also animated Lermontov's Romantic drama *Masquerade* (*Maskarad*, 1835) and his narrative oriental poem *The Demon* (*Demon*, 1839), which expresses what Vladimir Golstein calls the 'syndrome of vanishing bliss',[14] when the 'short dream of victory' becomes the Demon's curse and credo:

---

13 Zhukovskii, *Polnoe sobranie sochinenii i pisem*, vol. IV (2009), pp. 12–13; trans. Timothy Portice and Ilya Vinitsky.

14 Vladimir Golstein, *Lermontov's Narratives of Heroism* (Evanston, IL: Northwestern University Press, 1998), p. 37.

I swear by the first day of creation and by its last;
I swear by the shame of crime
and by the triumph of eternal truth
I swear by the bitter torment of fall,
and by the short dream of victory;
swear by our meeting
and by the separation which threatens us again.[15]

The figure of the fallen sublime being and vengeful outcast reappeared in an ironic and secularised form in the figure of Pechorin, protagonist of Lermontov's experimental psychological novel *A Hero of Our Time*. And, in another ironic mutation, the ghosts who swarmed Zhukovskii's 'Gothic' ballads morphed into the influential theme of 'petty demons' in Russian literature, found in Gogol's Ukrainian tales, Pushkin's poems, Dostoevskii's *Demons* (*Besy*, 1873), and in Symbolist novels (e.g. Fedor Sologub's (1863–1927) *The Petty Demon* (*Melkii bes*, 1905)) and poetry.

To paraphrase a dictum wrongly attributed to Dostoevskii, it would not be an exaggeration to say that the literary spectre of Russian Romanticism came out of the angelic robes of the lofty, melancholy, and chaste poet Zhukovskii, who playfully called himself 'poetic guardian [*diad'ka*] of the English and German devils and witches'.[16]

Further Reading

Brown, William Edward, *A History of Russian Literature of the Romantic Period*, 4 vols. (Ann Arbor, MI: Ardis, 1986).

Gasparov, Boris, 'Pushkin and Romanticism', in David M. Bethea (ed.), *The Pushkin Handbook* (Madison: University of Wisconsin Press, 2005), pp. 537–67.

Golburt, Luba, 'Alexander Pushkin as a Romantic', in Paul Hamilton (ed.), *The Oxford Handbook of European Romanticism* (Oxford: Oxford University Press, 2016).

Greenleaf, Monika, *Pushkin and Romantic Fashion: Fragment, Elegy, Orient, Irony* (Stanford: Stanford University Press, 1994).

Hammarberg, Gitta, *From the Idyll to the Novel: Karamzin's Sentimentalist Prose* (Cambridge: Cambridge University Press, 1991).

Karlinsky, Simon, *The Sexual Labyrinth of Nikolai Gogol* (Cambridge, MA: Harvard University Press, 1976).

Leighton, Lauren G., 'The great Soviet debate over Romanticism: 1957–1964', *Studies in Romanticism* 22.1 (1983), 41–64.

15 Mikhail Lermontov, *Polnoe sobranie sochinenii v 10 tomakh* [Complete works in 10 volumes] (Moscow: Voskresen'e, 2000–2), vol. IV (2000), p. 253.

16 Zhukovskii, letter to A. S. Sturdza, 10 March 1849, in *Polnoe sobranie sochinenii i pisem*, vol. VI (2010), p. 653.

Powelstock, David, *Becoming Mikhail Lermontov: The Ironies of Romantic Individualism in Nicholas I's Russia* (Evanston, IL: Northwestern University Press, 2005).

Ram, Harsha, *The Imperial Sublime: A Russian Poetics of Empire* (Madison: University of Wisconsin Press, 2003).

Vinitsky, Ilya, *Vasily Zhukovsky's Romanticism and the Emotional History of Russia* (Evanston, IL: Northwestern University Press, 2015).

The Natural School and Realism

ALEXEY VDOVIN

The term 'realism', like any other '-ism', is complex and multifaceted. It has been defined in many ways: in relation to authorial intention, for example, or to reader reception, or to particular techniques of depiction. In this chapter, Realism is understood as a specific historical movement, or the literary style that was dominant in Russia from 1845 to the 1880s. Of course, realism (with a lower-case 'r') as a technique for creating the 'reality effect' (as Roland Barthes labelled it), mimesis (as in Aristotle or Erich Auerbach), or 'fictional truth' (Michael Riffaterre) has existed in literature both before and since; from Homer to the present, verisimilitude and authenticity in depicting the world and emotions have remained important and sought-after attributes for texts in both Russian and world literature.[1] The Realism of the nineteenth century, however, according to literary historians and narratologists, appeared in various countries in Europe and in the USA between the 1830s and the 1860s as a result of a series of literary, cultural, and socioeconomic factors.

At the turn of the nineteenth century, the rise of Romanticism in literature and aesthetics led to the collapse of the hierarchical system of genres of the preceding centuries. If in the Neoclassical era there was a strict correlation between the object or subject being depicted and the language or literary form to be used (see, e.g., Chapter 1.3 on the link between the triumphal ode and linguistic Slavonicisms), with the rise of Sentimentalism and after it Romanticism this strict system began to erode and works were increasingly able to depict a wider spectrum of topics that lacked any link to a specific genre.[2] The novel moved to the centre of the European, and later Russian,

---

1 Roland Barthes, 'The reality effect', in *The Rustle of Language* (Berkeley: University of California Press, 1989), pp. 141–8; Erich Auerbach, *Mimesis: The Representation of Reality in Western Literature* (Princeton: Princeton University Press, 1955); Michael Riffaterre, *Fictional Truth* (Baltimore: Johns Hopkins University Press, 1990).
2 Jacques Rancière, *Mute Speech: Literature, Critical Theory, and Politics*, trans. J. Swenson (New York: Columbia University Press, 2011), p. 107.

literary market.[3] Novels satisfied the increasing demand among readers for depictions of individual human experience in its everyday dimensions. They contained descriptions of middle-class life, poverty, the world of urban crime, and – in the historical novel – specific details of the era. The novels of manners and historical novels of the late eighteenth and early nineteenth centuries, though not formally related to Realism, paved the way for the movement's development in Britain, France, and Russia.

Such explorations of the broader spectrum of society not only carried a democratising charge but were linked to developments in philosophy and science during the first half of the nineteenth century: in particular to the idea that it was possible to gain insight into the hidden essence of things and phenomena. This principle became a common cognitive platform for both the natural sciences and literature in the mid-nineteenth century. For this reason, Realism and its ideology should be regarded not only as a literary style but also as a discourse of understanding and interpreting reality. This explains the numerous comparisons of the Realist writer to a natural scientist who goes out into society in order to study it, aiming not to 'describe' it but to 'catalogue' it.[4]

As regards narrative theory (narratology), nineteenth-century Realism devised a series of special devices and techniques that helped to establish the illusion of reality: detailed descriptions of the material world, a simplification of literary style, and what Dorrit Cohn calls the 'transparent mind' technique. The latter shares that broader aim of gaining insight into hidden phenomena – in this case, into another person's thoughts and feelings, which would ordinarily be inaccessible but can be portrayed through omniscient narration.[5] It was in the era of Realism that this illusion of the accessibility of characters' thoughts and experiences became a key attribute of the novel genre.

A comprehensive history of the concept of Realism as a movement in Russia has not yet been written.[6] What is known for certain, though, is that its birth as a literary idea as well as a point of differentiation between its

---

3 Ian Watt, *The Rise of the Novel: Studies in Defoe, Richardson and Fielding* (Berkeley: University of California Press, 1957).

4 Vissarion G. Belinskii, introduction *(vstuplenie)* to *Fiziologiia Peterburga* [The physiology of Petersburg] (Moscow: Sovetskaia Rossiia, 1984), p. 40.

5 Dorrit Cohn, *Transparent Minds: Narrative Modes for Presenting Consciousness in Fiction* (Princeton: Princeton University Press, 1978).

6 Iurii S. Sorokin, 'K istorii termina "realizm" v russkoi kritike' [Towards a history of the term 'realism' in Russian criticism], *Izvestiia AN SSSR. Seriia Otdela literatury i iazyka* [Proceedings of the Academy of Sciences of the USSR. Department of literature and language] 16.3 (1957), 193–213. The German-language historiography of this term is much

meanings occurred in 1849, when the critic Pavel Annenkov (1813–1887) defined two types of realism among the authors of the then-popular Natural School: 'genuine' realism (exemplified by Ivan Turgenev (1818–1883), Ivan Goncharov (1812–1891), and Aleksandr Herzen (1812–1870)) and 'pseudo-realism' (found in the works of Fedor Dostoevskii (1821–1881) and his followers, Iakov Butkov (1821–1856) and his brother Mikhail Dostoevskii (1820–1864)). The critic condemned Fedor Dostoevskii's literary style as 'anti-artistry' (*protivokhudozhestvennost'*) for its depiction of the 'psychological history of insanity' among its protagonists and labelled it a 'fantastically sentimental kind of narration'.[7]

Why did Annenkov opt here for the word 'realism', which had not previously been employed in reference to literature in Russia? His statement formed part of a complex aesthetic and journalistic polemic between the main liberal journals of the era: *The Contemporary* (*Sovremennik*, 1836–66) and *Notes of the Fatherland* (*Otechestvennye zapiski*, 1839–84) (see Chapter 2.4). Annenkov, who sided with *The Contemporary*, aimed to show that the Natural School contained within it two fundamentally different trends: the realism of writers linked to *The Contemporary* and the pseudo-realism of those publishing in *Notes of the Fatherland*. In this way, Annenkov's use of the term 'realism' was a tactical act designed to demonstrate that there was no longer a single united Natural School. In this chapter I will show how the concept and practice that can be called Russian Realism evolved out of these debates that shaped the evolution of the Natural School in the 1840s.

Although the term 'realism' had scarcely been established as a literary concept in Russia by the time of Annenkov's article in 1849, the idea of a truthful representation of reality had circulated in Russian criticism since the early 1830s, at the twilight of the Romantic era. In 1830 the critic Ivan Kireevskii (1806–1856) wrote of the striving of poetry towards reality, while from the mid-1830s the leading literary critic of the era, Vissarion Belinskii (1811–1848; see Box 5.1), despite never using the word 'realism', promoted the idea of 'realistic poetry' (*real'naia poeziia*) or 'poetry of true reality' (*poeziia*

---

richer. See Wolfgang Klein, 'Realismus/Realistisch', in K. Barck, M. Fontius, F. Wolfzettel, and B. Steinwachs (eds.), *Ästhetische Grundbegriffe. Historisches Wörterbuch in sieben Bänden*, 7 vols. (Stuttgart: J. B. Metzler Verlag, 2000–5), vol. V, pp. 149–96. See also *The Cambridge History of Literary Criticism*, vol. VI: *The Nineteenth Century, c. 1830–1914*, ed. M. A. R. Habib (Cambridge: Cambridge University Press, 2013), which discusses the criticism and aesthetics of Realism.

7 Pavel V. Annenkov, 'Zametki o russkoi literature 1848 goda' [Notes on Russian literature in 1848], in *Kriticheskie ocherki* [Critical essays] (St Petersburg: Izdatel'stvo Russkogo Khristianskogo gumanitarnogo instituta, 2000), p. 31.

real'noi deistvitel'nosti).[8] Belinskii would later also categorise as texts of the newly emerging Russian Realism the prose of the late Romantics Nikolai Gogol (1809–1852) and Mikhail Lermontov (1814–1841): Gogol's comedy *Inspector General* (*Revizor*, 1836), his novel *Dead Souls* (*Mertvye dushi*, 1842), and his so-called Petersburg tales: 'The Diary of a Madman' (*Zapiski sumasshedshego*, 1835), 'The Nose' (*Nos*, 1836), and 'The Overcoat' (*Shinel'*, 1842), together with Lermontov's novel *A Hero of Our Time* (*Geroi nashego vremeni*, 1840).[9] Not all scholars would, in retrospect, agree with this. Nevertheless, it is beyond doubt that Gogol's urbanism, his exploration of the social side of the lives of functionaries and the petty bourgeoisie, and his keen interest in both the phenomenon of bureaucracy and human psychology had a profound influence on the style of such classic writers of Russian Realism as Fedor Dostoevskii, Mikhail Saltykov-Shchedrin (1826–1889), Aleksei Pisemskii (1821–1881), and Aleksandr Ostrovskii (1823–1886). Lermontov's subtle psychologism, in turn, became one of the sources of inspiration for the writings of Lev Tolstoi (1828–1910).

Belinskii's genealogy, then, identified the precursors of Realism in Russia. That Realism emerged, however, from a more immediate ancestor – the movement known as the Natural School, whose members shared a single aesthetic programme: to provide a truthful and socially accurate depiction of reality.

The Natural School

The Natural School was given its name by one of its irreconcilable enemies, the journalist, novelist, and publisher Faddei Bulgarin (1789–1859). In 1846, in his newspaper *The Northern Bee* (*Severnaia pchela*, 1825–59), Bulgarin pejoratively labelled the movement of the authors of the literary almanac *The Physiology of St Petersburg* (*Fiziologiia Peterburga*, 1845) 'natural': that is, primitively copying reality in all its 'dirty' manifestations.[10] Belinskii and others appropriated this label as the name of their approach to the literary depiction of reality. In fact, however, the authors, the ideology, and the aesthetics that

8 Vissarion G. Belinskii, 'O russkoi povesti i povestiakh gospodina Gogolia' [On the Russian tale and Mr Gogol's tales], in *Sobranie sochinenii v deviati tomakh* [Collected works in nine volumes] (Moscow: Khudozhestvennaia literatura, 1976), vol. I, pp. 144–5.

9 See Victor Terras, *Belinskij and Russian Literary Criticism: The Heritage of Organic Aesthetics* (Madison: University of Wisconsin Press, 1974), pp. 41–68; Rene Wellek, *Concepts of Criticism* (New Haven: Yale University Press, 1976), pp. 226–43.

10 Faddei Bulgarin, 'Zhurnal'naia vsiakaia vsiachina' [Journal miscellanea], *Severnaia pchela* [The northern bee], 26 Jan. 1846, 86.

made up the Natural School had already coalesced in the years 1842–5 and included the writers Ivan Panaev (1812–1862), Nikolai Nekrasov (1821–1878), Herzen, Turgenev, Evgenii Grebenka (Yevhen Hrebenka, 1812–1848; a Ukrainian bilingual writer), Dmitrii Grigorovich (1822–1899), Fedor Dostoevskii, and Vladimir Dal (1801–1871). They printed their works in the *Notes of the Fatherland* journal. The almanacs *The Physiology of St Petersburg* and *The Petersburg Miscellany* (*Peterburgskii sbornik*, 1846), both published by Nekrasov, became the flagships of the new movement; democratism and westernism became its ideologies; and social fiction became its aesthetic leitmotif. In his introduction to *The Physiology of St Petersburg*, Belinskii tied these ideas together to form a single consistent aesthetic and cultural programme. This programme emphasised the duty of literature to engage directly with social reality, exploring class and the geographical, ethnic, and cultural structure of Petersburg – and, by extension, of Russian society as a whole. For this goal, Belinskii proposed a genre that had been imported from France and Britain and was already widespread in Russian literature: the 'physiological sketch' (*fiziologicheskii ocherk* – referencing the French *physiologie*).

As a genre, the physiological sketch was rooted in the nineteenth century's particular combination of scientific conviction and social conscience. As Martina Lauster has shown, 'By translating scientific paradigms into modes of observation, and by observing the social body in action, sketches construct a moral grammar of modernity.'[11] For readers, this meant learning to read the signs of a big city and its marginalised groups (the poor, vagrants, sex workers, manual labourers, and so on) from a specific philanthropic-humanist viewpoint. This kind of critical-observational perspective emerged due to the close interaction of four factors: the popularity of almanacs (a special form of print media); the increasing availability of instruments of viewing (in particular dioramas and panoramas); Louis Daguerre's invention of the daguerreotype (a prototype of the photograph); and the popularisation of ideas of classifying types and species, influenced by botany and zoology.

If the main objects of description in Europe were the vast cities of Paris and London, in Russia it became St Petersburg. Belinskii included in *The Physiology of St Petersburg* a sketch entitled 'Petersburg and Moscow' (*Peterburg i Moskva*), which describes the major cultural, political, and social differences between life in the two largest cities of the empire. If Moscow

---

11 Martina Lauster, *Sketches of the Nineteenth Century: European Journalism and Its Physiologies, 1830–50* (New York: Palgrave MacMillan, 2007), p. 314.

embodied the old pre-Petrine Russia and the merchant class, the young Petersburg represented Russia's belonging to European civilisation; it was the realm of functionaries and bureaucracy.[12]

In physiological sketches, cities were mainly described by means of their most typical social 'types'. In the case of St Petersburg, these were organ-grinders (as in Grigorovich's sketch 'The Petersburg Organ-Grinders' (*Peterburgskie sharmanshchiki*)), feuilletonists (Panaev's 'The Petersburg Feuilletonist' (*Peterburgskii fel'etonist*)), and caretakers (Dal's 'The Petersburg Caretaker' (*Peterburgskii dvornik*)), as well as writers, speculators, fallen women, water carriers, coach drivers, and many others. The second most commonly depicted subject in *physiologies* was places: districts and even specific streets of Petersburg, the houses or meeting places of various social classes (as in Butkov's *Petersburg Summits* (*Peterburgskie vershiny*) collection, Belinskii's 'The Aleksandrinskii Theatre' (*Aleksandrinskii teatr*), Nekrasov's 'Petersburg Recesses' (*Peterburgskie ugly*), and Grebenka's 'The Petersburg Side' (*Peterburgskaia storona*)). In addition to social types and places, the sketches also portrayed traditional customs and rituals ('Tea in Moscow' (*Chai v Moskve*) and 'The Wedding in Moscow' (*Svad'ba v Moskve*) by Ivan Kokorev (1825–1853)).[13]

The Natural School was not limited in genre to the sketch. Between 1844 and 1847, representatives of the movement created short stories, novellas, novels, and even poetry, which adhered to their chosen ideology by exploring the correlation between human nature and its social environment. This artistic anthropology led to the creation of new models for the presentation of subjectivity: writers began to use personal narrative, *skaz* (see Chapter 2.8), free indirect speech, and 'dialogical conflict' (the equal presence in a text of two diametrically opposed ideological positions). In poetry, these techniques were practised by Nekrasov, who added elements of prose language to poetic speech and introduced characters from the common people and their voices into his works (such as the coachman's tale about his wife's fate in the 1845 poem 'On the Road' (*V doroge*)). Analogous subjects also began to appear in Russian painting of the same period.[14]

12 Nikolai Nekrasov (ed.), *Petersburg: The Physiology of a City*, trans. Thomas Gaiton Marullo (Evanston, IL: Northwestern University Press, 2009), p. 49.

13 See Iurii V. Mann, 'Filosofiia i poetika "Natural'noi shkoly"' [The philosophy and poetics of the 'Natural school'], in *Problemy tipologii russkogo realizma* [Problems in the typology of Russian realism] (Moscow: Nauka, 1969), pp. 272–3.

14 Molly Brunson, *Russian Realisms: Literature and Painting, 1840–1890* (DeKalb: Northern Illinois University Press, 2016), pp. 26–62.

In the second half of the 1840s, the Natural School split decisively into several prose movements and literary groups. This was partly linked to Belinskii's move from *Notes of the Fatherland* to *The Contemporary*, which was published by Nekrasov and Panaev from 1847. These two journals shared a similar direction but differed in their aesthetic programmes. Between 1847 and 1849, at least two trends within the Natural School were clearly visible, each representing distinct stylistic approaches in the strengthening Realist movement. The first trend designated as Realism by Annenkov was the prose of the authors from *The Contemporary*: Turgenev, Goncharov, Herzen, and Aleksandr Druzhinin (1824–1864), among others. The second was the 'sentimental naturalism' of the Dostoevskii brothers, Butkov, Aleksei Pleshcheev (1825–1893), Valerian Maikov (1823–1847), Saltykov-Shchedrin, and others. While the former writers modelled their works on the aesthetics of Belinskii, the latter sought to reach new horizons linked to the anthropology of Ludwig Feuerbach and French utopian socialism. For the critic Maikov, for instance, who was influenced by Feuerbach's philosophy, 'artistic forms were identical to the forms of reality'. From this perspective, writers had total freedom in depicting 'any reality' but on condition that they correctly 'guess' its 'sympathetic side'.[15] For this reason, Maikov – unlike Belinskii – highly rated Fedor Dostoevskii's second novel *The Double* (*Dvoinik*, 1846), despite its fantastical style, declaring it an exploration of the psychology of the modern man.

The aesthetic arguments of the late 1840s reveal the significant role of contemporary science in shaping Russian Realism. Realism established its own method and experimental reality, based on ideas from the social, physical, mathematical, psychological, biological, and physiological sciences. Writers who attentively followed the latest scientific discoveries gained new ideas about the connections between objects of reality that were invisible to the human eye, the reasons for the evolution of the human race, and the laws of the psyche. These ideas changed their methods of narration, shaping descriptions of the physical world and complicating and enriching representations of relationships and emotions. In this sense, the scientific and artistic spheres in the era of Realism in the mid-nineteenth century constituted a common system in which scientific ideas found literary form.

By the late 1840s, many literary observers felt that the Natural School had exhausted its means of describing reality. Both the mode of narration of the

---

15 Valerian N. Maikov, *Literaturnaia kritika* [Literary criticism] (Leningrad: Khudozhestvennaia literatura, 1985), pp. 100, 74, 110.

Natural School and the conceptual language that Belinskii had devised to legitimise it were called into question. Critics began to reflect on categories such as sketch, psychologism, Realism, and fiction. It is also worth remembering that many authors whose styles had been labelled sentimental naturalism simply stopped writing after 1849: Butkov almost never published again; in April 1849, Fedor Dostoevskii was arrested for involvement in the Petrashevskii Affair (a secret circle of Petersburg nobles and literati, headed by Mikhail Petrashevskii (1821–1866), who discussed socialist and utopian ideas as applied to Russia) and served four years of exile with hard labour in Siberia; Saltykov-Shchedrin was sent into exile for his involvement in the same incident; and Mikhail Dostoevskii did not publish prose after 1851.

The First Novels of Russian Realism

Before its demise, however, the Natural School provided Russian literature with its first three canonical Realist novels: Fedor Dostoevskii's *Poor Folk* (*Bednye liudi*, 1846), Herzen's *Who Is to Blame?* (*Kto vinovat?*, 1846), and Goncharov's *The Same Old Story* (*Obyknovennaia istoriia*, 1847). All of them carry traces of the *physiologies* (for instance, in their descriptions of life in Petersburg and the provinces and their biographical digressions into characters' pasts), but at the same time each novel moved beyond the limits of the Natural School and opened the door to the future of Russian Realism. All three novels are concerned with the fate of the 'ordinary' person: a functionary in the modern city attempting to fit into the social hierarchy and find their rightful place in it. In *Poor Folk*, that ordinary person is Makar Devushkin, a poor but intellectually and spiritually gifted Petersburg functionary who is helplessly in love with Varenka Dobroselova, a young woman forced by disastrous circumstances to marry the rich merchant Bykov while Makar is unable to help her. The main characters of *Who Is to Blame?* are Liubonka, the illegitimate daughter of a nobleman and a peasant woman, and her beloved Dmitrii Krutsiferskii, a poor intellectual who is forced to earn a living as a tutor in the house of the domineering general Negrov, Liubonka's real father. Krutsiferskii later attempts to support a growing family with Liubonka but is confronted with the infidelity of his wife with the aristocratic Beltov. The hero of *The Same Old Story* is Aleksandr Aduev, a man from the provinces who comes to Petersburg to seek his fortune and undergoes several changes of profession and world view in search of his place in the sun.

In terms of genre, each of the novels contains an innovative combination of western and Russian traditions. Dostoevskii adopted the form of the Sentimental European epistolary novel to tell his story of tragically separated lovers, while at the same time creatively developing motifs and situations from Gogol's prose. Herzen borrowed from the adultery and ideological novels of Jean-Jacques Rousseau (*Julie, or The New Heloise* (1761)) and George Sand (*Jacques* (1833) and *Horace* (1842)) but chose a different resolution: the love triangle between Liubonka, Krutsiferskii, and Beltov is ended by the latter's departure, but the family is broken and its future remains uncertain. In *The Same Old Story*, Goncharov became one of the first writers in Russian literature to produce a career novel in the style of Honoré de Balzac (*Lost Illusions*, ser. 1837–43); however, Aduev does not undergo either social failure or genuine spiritual development: at the end, he is appointed to a high rank and is about to marry a bride with a dowry of 300,000 roubles, though the narrator hints at his spiritual failure.

High Realism and Its Themes, 1855–1881

It is generally accepted that the main aesthetic manifesto of Russian Realism after the Natural School was a master's dissertation entitled *Aesthetic Relations of Art to Reality* (*Esteticheskie otnosheniia iskusstva k deistvitel'nosti*, comp. 1853, pub. 1855), written by Nikolai Chernyshevskii (1828–1889), a young critic from *The Contemporary*. This dissertation caused fierce controversy among writers, critics, and students, since in it Chernyshevskii proclaimed a new definition of beauty: 'beauty is life' and 'works of art are inferior to beauty (just as they are inferior to lofty ideals, tragedy and comedy) in reality and from an aesthetic perspective'.[16] Despite Chernyshevskii himself stating that he was influenced by the anthropology of Feuerbach, the primary hypotheses of his dissertation rely on the utilitarian philosophy of Rousseau and Denis Diderot.[17] Although Chernyshevskii's theory appeared absurd and even dangerous to many writers (including Turgenev and Tolstoi), it had a significant influence on the student population.

---

16 Nikolai G. Chernyshevskii, *Esteticheskie otnosheniia iskusstva k deistvitel'nosti* [The aesthetic relations of art to reality], in *Polnoe sobranie sochinenii v piatnadtsati tomakh* [Complete works in fifteen volumes] (Moscow: Goslitizdat, 1939–53), vol. II, pp. 90–1.

17 See Alexey Vdovin, 'Chernyshevskii vs. Feuerbach: (psevdo)istochniki dissertatsii "Esteticheskie otnosheniia iskusstva k deistvitel'nosti"' [Chernyshevskii vs Feuerbach: (pseudo-)sources of the dissertation 'Aesthetic relations of art to reality'], *Zeitschrift für Slavische Philologie* 68.1 (2011), 39–66.

Even before Chernyshevskii's manifesto, in the early 1850s new forms of Realism began to rise from the ashes of the Natural School, gaining huge popularity among readers for their realistic qualities. Aleksei Pisemskii, a young writer from Kostroma province, set a new standard for literature on social themes with his debut novel *The Simpleton (Tiufiak*, 1850), which offered a detailed depiction of country life, aiming for objective narration by neutralising the figure of the narrator and substituting secondary narrators from among the common people. Though he is almost unknown outside of Russia, Pisemskii has always held an important position in the Russian literary canon as the main Realist writer on social themes of the mid-nineteenth century.

Another writer publishing his first work in 1850 was the playwright Aleksandr Ostrovskii, whose comedy *It's a Family Affair – We'll Settle It Ourselves! (Svoi liudi – sochtemsia!*, 1850), and his many subsequent works, revealed to Russian audiences the lives first of the Moscow merchant class, and later of provincial merchant classes and the petty bourgeoisie. By the 1880s, Ostrovskii had become the most frequently performed Russian playwright and the creator of a Russian national theatre (see Chapter 3.4). His innovation lay in a skilful combination of high European comedy (such as the works of Molière) and Gogolian comedy based on the daily lives of merchants of varying degrees of wealth.

In the same year, Turgenev released *The Diary of a Superfluous Man (Dnevnik lishnego cheloveka*, 1850), a work whose title introduced the term 'superfluous person' into the Russian literary lexicon. The novella's protagonist, Chulkaturin, is dying and records the highlights of his short life in a diary. At every stage, he proves himself to have been superfluous in both a social and a metaphorical sense: superfluous in love (the object of his affections, Liza, had loved another man), in service, and in his family. The introspection and *ressentiment* shown by Chulkaturin anticipated the heightened self-awareness of the 'Underground Man', the central character of Dostoevskii's work *Notes from Underground (Zapiski iz podpol'ia*, 1864).

Finally, it would be remiss not to mention another debut author, Lev Tolstoi, whose first novel, *Childhood (Detstvo*, 1852), swiftly became one of the most popular works to depict the formation of a child's character and was included in many school anthologies from the 1860s onwards.

In the mid-1850s, the development of Realism was given further impetus by a series of era-defining social changes. The Crimean War (1853–6), the death of Nicholas I (r. 1825–55), and the liberal reform programme of the new emperor, Alexander II (r. 1855–81), resulted in a great expansion of the press,

print capitalism, population migration, railway construction, and other consequences of technological progress, all despite an economic crisis. Russia stood on the threshold of modernisation from above: the Great Reforms (the abolition of serfdom and reforms to the judiciary, military, and local government between 1861 and 1874) set in motion social processes and forces whose effects were too wide-ranging not to find reflection in literature. This period (1855–80) is conventionally considered the age of the greatest achievements of Russian Realist novels and drama. All the most celebrated novels and novellas of Turgenev, Dostoevskii, Tolstoi, Goncharov, Ostrovskii, Herzen, Saltykov-Shchedrin, Nikolai Leskov (1831–1895), and Pisemskii were written in these years (see Chapter 3.5).

What were the main themes and problems of Realist literature in this period? Firstly, since most authors of the era were of noble origin, they continued to explore the fate, opportunities, and role of the noble, educated elite and their kin under the new political and economic conditions of the Great Reforms. The most important and interesting works from this perspective were Turgenev's novels *Rudin* (*Rudin*, 1856), *A Nest of Gentlefolk* (*Dvorianskoe gnezdo*, 1859), and *Smoke* (*Dym*, 1867); Dostoevskii's *The Idiot* (*Idiot*, 1874), *Demons* (*Besy*, 1873), and *The Brothers Karamazov* (*Brat'ia Karamazovy*, 1881); Tolstoi's *A Morning of a Landed Proprietor* (*Utro pomeshchika*, 1856), *War and Peace* (*Voina i mir*, 1868–9), and *Anna Karenina* (*Anna Karenina*, 1878); Goncharov's *Oblomov* (*Oblomov*, 1859) and *The Precipice* (*Obryv*, 1869); Saltykov-Shchedrin's *The Golovlevs* (*Gospoda Golovlevy*, 1880); Pisemskii's *One Thousand Souls* (*Tysiacha dush*, 1858) and *Men of the Forties* (*Liudi sorokovykh godov*, 1869); Leskov's family chronicle *A Decayed Family* (*Zakhudalyi rod*, 1874); and Herzen's autobiography *My Past and Thoughts* (*Byloe i dumy*, 1852–68). All these novelists focused their attention on one or another aspect of noble life and presented it from a defined ideological viewpoint.

Turgenev's novels made sense of the strange combination of intellectual strength and low social activity among the gentry of the 1830s and 1840s, showing the collision between influential German philosophy and Russian reality. His eponymous hero Dmitrii Rudin is a brilliant orator capable of inspiring many of those around him, including the talented girl Natalia Lasunskaia, yet he lacks the courage to marry her in the face of her family's disapproval. In the novel's epilogue he is killed at the barricades of Paris during the 1848 revolution.

At the heart of Goncharov's *Oblomov* are two friends of opposite character types: the good-natured but idle Oblomov, who cannot get out of bed or stir himself into action, and Stoltz, a half-German who earns a fortune through

tireless hard work. In the figure of Oblomov, Goncharov encapsulated the Russian gentry's lifestyle and culture, reliant on serf labour, and created the concept of 'Oblomovism' (*oblomovshchina*), which became a symbol of everything archaic in Russian life. Expanding into allegory, the novel identifies the moment when Russia bids farewell to its 'Oblomovite' innocent futility in the face of the modernisation and technological change of the nineteenth century. It depicts a society on the brink of radical change.

Dostoevskii and Tolstoi both address the question of the future of the noble family in their great novels. But they do so in radically different ways. In Dostoevskii's novels, noble families are by no means always the central theme, but they do feature prominently in *The Idiot*, *Demons*, and *The Brothers Karamazov*. Dostoevskii transforms the theme of the noble family by exploring a more extended set of what might be called accidental families – networks of relations and connections – and picturing individuals who live from one day to the next, who struggle against impoverishment, and who fall into debauchery and perilous sexual relations. In *War and Peace* and *Anna Karenina*, by contrast, Tolstoi not only represents aspects of noble life and culture in a more positive light but also demonstrates that aristocrats such as Vronskii and Konstantin Levin could find a worthy use for themselves in the new post-reform reality. After his tragic affair with Anna, Vronskii sets off to fight in the Russo-Turkish War, while Levin applies himself to agriculture and attempts to improve both his own life and those of his hired peasants.

In his novel *The Golovlevs*, Saltykov-Shchedrin depicts the nobility's physical extinction, as several generations of a once-rich noble family degenerate, grow poor, bring ruin on each other, and finally die out. The greatest share of the blame lies with Porfirii Golovlev – known by the family nickname Little Judas (*Iudushka*) – whose cynicism, treachery, and greed lead to a string of deaths.

Secondly, and closely linked to the fate of the Russian nobility, writers of the period were also preoccupied with the issues of serfdom and the peasant question. In the 1850s the 'tale of peasant life' emerged as a genre within Realism, focusing on the daily lives of peasants, their traditions, and their distinctive thought (see Chapter 4.4).

Thirdly, one of the most contentious themes of Russian Realist literature was political radicalism and nihilism. Until 1905, Russia had no constitution, no parliament, and no developed public sphere in which to debate political questions. As a result, literature played a key role in hosting political discussions about whether to reform or maintain the status quo in all areas of social life. In novels, the representative of radical ideas was usually a young man or

woman who had come to believe in a new reformist ideology and tried to advocate it in word and deed (by the late nineteenth century, these figures had increasingly come to be called *intelligenty* (members of the intelligentsia); see Chapter 4.5). To bring these plots to life, authors often used the genre of the coming-of-age novel, or Bildungsroman. The first works of this subgenre were Nikolai Pomialovskii's (1835–1863) novellas *Bourgeois Happiness* (*Meshchanskoe schast'e*, 1861) and *Molotov* (*Molotov*, 1861), and Turgenev's novel *Fathers and Children* (*Ottsy i deti*, 1862), all of which feature an intellectual hero of common origin. This hero clashes with noble characters both ideologically and stylistically, and staunchly defends his means of understanding and transforming reality. Pomialovskii called his protagonist – Egor Molotov – a *homo novus* (new man), while Turgenev labelled his character Bazarov a nihilist. Unlike Molotov, who leads a successful and independent working life, Turgenev's Bazarov can defeat the noble Pavel Kirsanov only in debate. He suffers from failure: he is rejected by the woman of his affections, Odintsova, and at the end accidentally infects himself with typhus and dies.

A more positive, even utopian, version of the 'new person' biography appeared in one of the most notorious novels of Russian literature, Chernyshevskii's *What Is to Be Done?* (*Chto delat'?*, 1863; see also Chapter 4.7). This is a work that stretches the limits of Realism by being replete with dreams, the narrator's own journalistic arguments, unconventional language and style, and numerous biblical references. *What Is to Be Done?* is a female coming-of-age novel about Vera Pavlovna Rozalskaia, who escapes the oppression of her parents by means of a marriage of convenience to a doctor. Through her husband, she discovers a modern positivist world view, lives an independent life, and organises a sewing workshop based on collective principles, thereby gaining economic self-sufficiency. As Irina Paperno has shown, *What Is to Be Done?* served as an ethical life programme for all those who wanted to live progressively, presented in the form of quasi-religious texts and plot lines that were familiar to every Russian raised in the Orthodox faith (see Chapter 4.1).[18]

The impact of *Fathers and Sons* and *What Is to Be Done?* was so great that by 1865 an alternative novelistic subgenre had emerged in which the democratic/radical/nihilist agenda was refuted and discredited. The forerunners of this kind of narrative were Pisemskii's novel *Troubled Seas* (*Vzbalamuchennoe more*, 1863) and Leskov's novel *No Way Out* (*Nekuda*, 1864). These were followed by dozens more works in the 1870s and 1880s, the most significant

---

18 Irina Paperno, *Chernyshevsky and the Age of Realism: A Study in the Semiotics of Behavior* (Stanford: Stanford University Press, 1988).

of which were Dostoevskii's *Notes from Underground, Crime and Punishment* (*Prestuplenie i nakazanie*, 1867), and *Demons*; Goncharov's *The Precipice*; and Turgenev's *Virgin Soil* (*Nov'*, 1877). All these texts depict the behaviour of young people who have been corrupted by radical ideas and the fatal and tragic consequences of this for themselves and those around them. Hence, Raskolnikov in *Crime and Punishment* devises a theory that superior individuals have the right to commit murder for the good of the majority, and suffers a total moral collapse. In *Demons*, Petrusha Verkhovenskii, the son of an intellectual from the 1840s, runs an underground revolutionary organisation whose noble goals are used as a justification for murder. In *The Precipice*, Mark Volokhov, an exiled radical, seduces Vera, then abandons her, leaving her disgraced and disconsolate.

This political dimension of Russian Realism was tied to a fourth, related theme: the 'woman question' (*zhenskii vopros*) and female emancipation (see Chapter 4.6). Discussions of a new ethics of love and the problems of divorce, which had appeared in European literature from the 1830s (in the novels of George Sand, for instance), corresponded to more acute political questions in the Russian context, as the preservation of marriage was directly linked to the inheritance of property, the class system, and – consequently – support for the social status quo. Realist plots depicted transgression of these norms, such as breaking the accepted codes of marriage and attempts at a new sexual ethics, as political issues. The adultery novel and related forms allowed authors, including many women, to discuss pressing social problems, often using a first-person narrative and drawing on extensive documentary material. Works of this kind included *The Talnikov Family* (*Semeistvo Tal'nikovykh*, 1848, banned by the censors) and *A Woman's Lot* (*Zhenskaia dolia*, 1862) by Avdotia Panaeva (1820–1893); *The Boarding School Girl* (*Pansionerka*, 1861) and *Ursa Major* (*Bol'shaia Medveditsa*, 1871) by V. Krestovskii (pseudonym) (pen name for Nadezhda Khvoshchinskaia 1821–1889); Ostrovskii's plays *The Storm* (*Groza*, 1859) and *Without a Dowry* (*Bespridannitsa*, 1878); *Family Happiness* (*Semeinoe schast'e*, 1859), *Anna Karenina*, and 'The Kreutzer Sonata' (*Kreitserova sonata*, 1890) by Tolstoi; *On the Eve* (*Nakanune*, 1860) by Turgenev; and *Is She Guilty?* (*Vinovata li ona?*, 1855) and *In the Vortex* (*V vodovorote*, 1871) by Pisemskii.

Last but not least, an important theme of Russian Realism was bureaucracy and corruption in public administration. Owing to censorship, such themes were often represented indirectly, in the form of satires and comedies. The main author of bureaucratic satire was Mikhail Saltykov-Shchedrin, who penned dozens of satirical sketches that ridiculed the weaknesses of the political system in allegorical form. Sometimes the scope was broader, as with *The*

History of a Town (*Istoriia odnogo goroda*, 1870), a scathing parody of the history of the Russian state in the form of a chronicle of the various governors of the fictional town of Glupov (meaning 'Stupidville'; see Chapter 4.2). The novel offers a satirical depiction of the most firmly entrenched problems of the Russian state system: corruption, repressiveness, and abuse of power. In drama, Ostrovskii's comedies on the lives of functionaries and managers, such as *A Profitable Position* (*Dokhodnoe mesto*, 1856) and *Enough Stupidity in Every Wise Man* (*Na vsiakogo mudretsa dovol'no prostoty*, 1868), explored the moral dilemmas of young bureaucrats forced to adapt to the vertical structures of power. The distinctive high point of the functionary theme in Russian Realism was reached by two unusual plays by Aleksandr Sukhovo-Kobylin (1817–1903), *The Case* (*Delo*, 1861) and *The Death of Tarelkin* (*Smert' Tarelkina*, 1869), which were banned in Russia until the end of the nineteenth century for their grotesque depictions of rampant corruption in the Russian judicial system.

The Limits and Twilight of Realism

The five themes outlined above are not exhaustive. They are merely the mainstream. Besides these, in the years between 1860 and 1890, even the principal Realist writers produced works that went beyond the limits of Realism and examined themes that appeared marginal at the time but later became the new mainstream in the era of Modernism. Tolstoi's *The Death of Ivan Ilich* (*Smert' Ivana Il'icha*, 1886), for instance, which narrates the terminal illness of a mid-ranking judge, touches on existential and ethical issues that were clearly ahead of their time. Dostoevskii's story *The Dream of a Ridiculous Man* (*Son smeshnogo cheloveka*, 1877), in which the hero dreams of an alternative, unearthly perfect world that collapses through his own fault, in fact presents a kind of dystopia, a genre typical of Modernism. And Turgenev's late novella *Klara Milich* (*Klara Milich*, 1883), which tells the story of a mystical love between a modern Muscovite man and a young woman who has taken her own life and eventually leads him away after her, pointed more towards the future works of Russian Symbolism.

In the 1880s and 1890s, Realism in Russia was increasingly described by critics as a phenomenon of the past. Anton Chekhov (1860–1904) began his career in the late 1870s as a writer of humorous stories and sketches that were still undoubtedly within Realism. By the late 1880s, however, from the ashes of Realism, Chekhov had created the short novella, a genre in which Realist conventions were substantially transformed both thematically and

stylistically. Although Chekhov penned many purely Realist stories – 'The Death of a Government Clerk' (*Smert' chinovnika*, 1883), 'The Man in the Case' (*Chelovek v futliare*, 1898), 'Gooseberries' (*Kryzhovnik*, 1898), and 'Ionych' (*Ionych*, 1898), among others – his most significant works in prose and drama abandoned the strict social determinism typical of Realism. Instead, Chekhov explored the daily lives and experiences of people who belonged to a profession rather than a specific class (most commonly, doctors, teachers, petty functionaries, and journalists). In his plays, Chekhov moved even further away from established plots and rejected external social conflicts in favour of internal, psychological, and existential conflicts.[19]

Chekhov's innovative style and narrative techniques were taken up in the 1900s by many authors, including Ivan Bunin (1870–1953), Ivan Shmelev (1873–1953), Aleksei Nikolaevich Tolstoi (1883–1945), the young Evgenii Zamiatin (1884–1937), and Aleksandr Kuprin (1870–1938). These writers today are conventionally labelled 'Neorealists', though they themselves did not use this term and did not form a single group. In their prose, they rejected strict social and biological determinism and positivism, gravitated towards the symbolisation and psychologisation of narrative, and primarily wrote novellas and short stories.

Nineteenth-century Realism was later given a new reincarnation as Socialist Realism (see Chapter 1.8), which was proclaimed as the main style and movement of Soviet literature in the press and at the First Congress of Soviet Writers in 1934. Many of its aesthetic tenets, at least on the level of slogans, invoked the Russian classics of the nineteenth century, whose methods were termed 'Critical Realism' to distinguish this movement from its Socialist successor.

What Is Russian about Russian Realism?

This chapter has provided an account of the particular evolution of Russian Realism out of the Natural School and its determined engagement with sociopolitical reality. Is there anything, then, that fundamentally differentiated Russian Realism from Realism in other national literatures? A short and straightforward answer to this question was given in the late nineteenth century when the French diplomat and critic Eugène-Melchior de Vogüé, in his work *The Russian Novel* (1886), called on French naturalists to learn from

---

19 See Andrei Shcherbenok, '"Killing realism": Insight and meaning in Anton Chekhov', *Slavic and East European Journal* 54.2 (2010), 297–315.

Tolstoi, Turgenev, and Dostoevskii how to depict the microscopic movements of the human soul while maintaining a high religious and humanistic ideal.[20] In 1919, the Modernist Virginia Woolf wrote in praise of the prose of Chekhov and other Russian writers, suggesting that they had learned before the Europeans how to depict the fluctuations of human consciousness. By the early twentieth century, it had become commonplace to identify such distinct ideological and narrative features of Russian Realism. Modern scholarship, however, continues to seek more complex comparative frameworks: in particular through the comparative history of common themes (e.g. the novel of adultery, or the family novel).[21]

Besides questions of theme, one can explore the differences in the social imaginary between Russian and western European Realisms. It has been argued, for example, that authoritarianism and an absence of democratic institutions (as in Russia) may have lead to literature developing forms of writing that constitute 'national allegories', whereby seemingly domestic plots about characters' private lives can be read in a political sense and projected onto the life of the country and its society more generally.[22] Indeed, there are good grounds for reading Turgenev's novella *First Love* (*Pervaia liubov'*, 1860) not merely as the story of the unhappy first love of young Volodia and his rivalry with his own father for the heart of Zinaida Zasekina but also as an allegory of national life in Russia, where levels of violence were extremely high and even permeated sexual relationships. To generalise, a particular attribute of Russian Realism, compared to its European and American counterparts, was its frequent focus on the vertical relationships of power between people and the state, rather than the horizontal intrafamilial relationships between people and civil society.[23] Such features have made the Russian Realist movement distinctive, and attractive to readers and writers from other countries and continents; they have assured its legacy.

Translated by Stefan Lacny

---

20 Kristof Sharl', 'Frantsuzskoe literaturnoe pole i literaturnyi import: Rozhdenie litera-turnogo natsionalizma' [The French literary field and the literary import: The birth of literary nationalism], in *Intellektualy vo Frantsii* [Intellectuals in France] (Moscow: Novoe izdatel'stvo, 2005), pp. 109–33.

21 See Alison Sinclair, *The Deceived Husband: A Kleinian Approach to the Literature of Infidelity* (Oxford: Clarendon, 1993); Anna A. Berman, *The Family Novel in Russia and England, 1800–1880* (Oxford: Oxford University Press, 2022).

22 Fredric Jameson, 'Third-world literature in the era of multinational capitalism', *Social Text* 15 (1986), 65–88.

23 See Ilya Kliger, 'Scenarios of power in Turgenev's *First Love*: Russian Realism and the allegory of the state', *Comparative Literature* 70.1 (2018), 40.

Further Reading

Bogdanova, Olga A., 'Filosovskie i esteticheskie osnovy "natural'noi shkoly"' [The philosophical and aesthetic foundations of the 'natural school'], in *'Natural'naia shkola' i ee rol' v stanovlenii russkogo realizma* [The 'natural school' and its role in the development of Russian realism] (Moscow: Nasledie, 1997), pp. 9–36.

Bowers, Katherine, and Ani Kokobobo (eds.), *Russian Writers at the Fin de Siècle: The Twilight of Realism* (Cambridge: Cambridge University Press, 2015).

Ginzburg, Lidia, *On Psychological Prose* (Princeton: Princeton University Press, 1991).

Kliger, Ilya, 'Genre and actuality in Belinskii, Herzen, and Goncharov: Toward a genealogy of the tragic pattern in Russian Realism', *Slavic Review* 70.1 (2011), 45–66.

Knapp, Liza, 'Realism', in Deborah A. Martinsen and Olga Maiorova (eds.), *Dostoevsky in Context*, Literature in Context (Cambridge: Cambridge University Press, 2016), pp. 229–35.

Lounsbery, Anne, 'Russian families, accidental and other', in Dirk Göttsche, Rosa Mucignat, and Robert Weninger (eds.), *Landscapes of Realism: Rethinking Literary Realism in Comparative Perspectives*, vol. I, *Mapping Realism* (Amsterdam: John Benjamins, 2021), pp. 503–14.

Smirnov, Igor P., 'Realizm: Dikharonicheskii podkhod' [Realism: A diachronic approach], in *Megaistoriia. K istoricheskoi tipologii kul'tury* [Megahistory. Towards a historical typology of culture] (Moscow: Agraf, 2000), pp. 21–77.

Vaisman, Margarita, Alexey Vdovin, Ilya Kliger, and Kirill Ospovat (eds.), *Russkii realizm XIX veka: Obshchestvo, znanie, povestvovanie* [Russian realism of the nineteenth century: Society, knowledge, narrative] (Moscow: Novoe literaturnoe obozrenie, 2020).

1.6

Symbolism and the *Fin de Siècle*

YURI CORRIGAN

Russian literature, the poet Dmitrii Merezhkovskii (1865–1941) lamented in 1892, was a lonely occupation. Never, he observed, had Russia experienced a true Renaissance; never had there been that 'living, tolerant, conciliatory atmosphere, that cultural air in which opposing original temperaments' might 'strengthen and rouse each other to activity'. With the exception of some 'fleeting chance encounters in the desert' – that of Aleksandr Pushkin (1799–1837) and Nikolai Gogol (1809–1852), or those of the Belinskii circle (see Box 5.1: Vissarion Belinskii) – Russia's best writers had either fled from culture altogether or conceived of an 'invincible hatred' for each other. And now at the end of the nineteenth century, in the aftermath of a great literary moment, what Merezhkovskii saw was the yawning of a cultural void, an eerie silence, an atmosphere of tiredness and dispersion.[1]

Merezhkovskii was far from alone in describing the cultural age of Alexander III (r. 1881–94) in such terms. Among the intelligentsia, the common view of the era was one of decline: there was a confusing mixture of repressive politics and economic prosperity, the partial reversal of the Great Reforms of the 1860s, and the forcible relinquishing of Russia's progressive aspirations. What was distinctive about Merezhkovskii's 1892 essay in which he reviewed the 'Reasons for the Decline' of Russian literature was his diagnosis of Russia's cultural malaise as spiritual in nature. The problem, as he saw it, lay in the unchecked cultural supremacy of scientific materialism, a world view that over the course of the nineteenth century had become a 'Cyclopean dam' blocking out any recognition of the 'limitless and dark ocean' of the spirit. The walls of the dam were growing 'higher and higher', while the unheeded 'mystical demand of the nineteenth century' was only

---

1 D. S. Merezhkovskii, 'O prichinakh upadka i o novykh techeniiakh sovremennoi russkoi literatury' [Reasons for the decline and new currents in contemporary Russian literature], in *Polnoe sobranie sochinenii* [Complete works], 24 vols. (St Petersburg; Moscow: Izdanie T-va M.O. Vol'f, 1911–12), vol. XV, p. 216.

intensifying.[2] From out of this impasse, Merezhkovskii predicted an imminent Renaissance.

The Russian Symbolist movement, of which Merezhkovskii was a founding member, emerged at the turn of the century (roughly between 1894 and 1910) as a response to this 'mystical demand'. What united the two generations of poets who described themselves as Decadents or Symbolists was a fascination with 'other worlds' and the conviction that poetry and art were somehow uniquely capable of granting access to these mysteries. Though the epithets 'Decadent' and 'Symbolist' were borrowed from the French Modernists, the influence of European Symbolism was secondary. The poet Valerii Briusov (1873–1924), when cobbling together the movement's first anthologies, certainly borrowed his concept of Russian Symbolism from such figures as Paul Verlaine, Maurice Maeterlinck, and Stéphane Mallarmé. Yet the movement as a whole was distinctively home-grown. As the poet Zinaida Gippius (1869–1945) claimed, looking back on her role as a co-founder, 'I was never greatly interested in French poets in the 1890s and rarely read them. What I was interested in was not decadence but the problem of the individual and all the questions connected with it.'[3] Andrei Belyi (1880–1934), who would become the movement's leading novelist, was similarly definite on this point: 'Critics often derive Russian Symbolism from French Symbolism. This is wrong. Russian Symbolism is both deeper and more firmly grounded. Its most prominent representatives are connected by blood with Russian literature and poetry.'[4]

Russian Symbolism was built, as Belyi suggests, on the Russian literary tradition, but it was a tradition painstakingly reimagined as a metaphysical school, a reservoir of symbols and myths that could help a new generation of poets navigate the mystical terrain of the inner life. From Pushkin, the Symbolists drew – among many images – on the prophetic predicament of the poet whose heart had been ripped out by an angel and replaced with burning coal. Mikhail Lermontov (1814–1841) explained the insatiability of human longing through the image of the soul brought into the world by a singing angel and left behind to yearn in vain for its song. Gogol offered

---

2 Merezhkovskii, 'O prichinakh upadka', pp. 244–5.
3 Zinaida Gippius, 'Avtobiograficheskaia zametka' [Autobiographical note], in *Polnoe sobranie sochinenii* [Complete works], 15 vols. (Moscow: Russkaia kniga, 2001), vol. I, p. 526.
4 Andrei Belyi, 'Aleksandr Blok. Nechaiannaia radost'. Vtoroi sbornik stikhov' [Aleksandr Blok. Inadvertent joy. Second collection of poems], in *Aleksandr Blok: Pro et contra* [Aleksandr Blok: Pro et contra] (St Petersburg: Izdatel'stvo Russkogo Khristianskogo gumanitarnogo instituta, 2004), p. 51.

ways of imagining national concerns as personal ones in the images of Russia as a galloping troika or a sleeping maiden. Fedor Tiutchev (1803–1873) had described the vastness of the inner life and the powerlessness of words to plumb its mysteries. Afanasii Fet (1820–1892) had rendered the oppressively finite material world as a light-blue prison. Vladimir Solovev (1853–1900) had expressed his religious longing erotically, with regard to a divine Sophia, the feminine countenance of God and an embodiment of God's wisdom.

These predecessors helped illuminate mystical paths that pointed not away from reality, as was argued by Viacheslav Ivanov (1866–1949), poet and leading Symbolist theoretician, but towards deeper, more vital realities – or as Ivanov put it in his programmatic mantra, 'from the real to the more real'.[5] And it is perhaps this insistence on 'realism' that marks the greatest distinguishing (and possibly also the strangest) feature of the Russian Symbolists: namely their notion of mystical poetry as an ambitious form of real-world activism. Though sometimes perceived as otherworldly aesthetes, these poets were, on the whole, driven by a strong sense of political and historical awareness, having inherited yet another major legacy of the Russian literary tradition – its notion of activism as *inward* in nature. Fedor Dostoevskii (1821–1881) had advanced this idea in his 1880 speech on Pushkin, where he predicted that the Russian people would save the world by becoming a source of sustenance for others, but only if they could first discover something sacred and unshakeable within themselves.[6] Lev Tolstoi (1828–1910) had espoused a similar thought in his 1894 treatise *The Kingdom of God Is within You* (*Tsarstvo bozhie vnutri vas*), where he rejected the idea that society's fundamental problems (disunity, hypocrisy, cruelty, mass hypnosis) could be alleviated by changes in the 'external forms of life'.[7] All political progress, he argued, begins on the inward plane; only a transcendent truth, confronted inwardly, can unite and awaken people, turning the tide of history for the good.

As this chapter will suggest, the Symbolist movement was conceived as an alternative to the utilitarian-populist edifice of outward activism and social critique. This chapter will trace the growth of the movement's activist project over its two generations, beginning with the searching attempts of the first

---

5 Viacheslav Ivanov, 'Two elements in contemporary Symbolism', in Michael Wachtel (ed.), *Selected Essays*, trans. Robert Bird (Evanston, IL: Northwestern University Press, 2003), p. 28.

6 F. M. Dostoevsky, 'Pushkin (A sketch)', in *The Diary of a Writer*, trans. Boris Brasol (New York: Charles Scribner's Sons, 1949), pp. 967–80.

7 Leo Tolstoy, 'The Kingdom of God is within you', in *The Kingdom of God and Peace Essays*, trans. Aylmer Maude (London: Oxford University Press, 1951), p. 452.

generation of Symbolists – especially Merezhkovskii, Gippius, and Fedor Sologub (1863–1927) – to turn a fiercely secular culture in the direction of spirituality and religion. My particular focus will be on the explosive, influential, and wildly ambitious partnership of the second generation of Symbolists – Aleksandr Blok (1880–1921), Belyi, and Ivanov – who rose to prominence during the politically tumultuous age of the *fin de siècle* (the decade surrounding the revolution of 1905), an era galvanised by a pervasive sense of disorientation, groundlessness, experimentation, and apocalyptic presentiment. For these poets, in order to transform the world it was necessary first to find one's way into 'other worlds' and to draw on those worlds through the creative practice of theurgy – literally 'divine work' or 'the making of divine things'. As Blok put it, 'either those worlds exist or they do not. For those who say "they do not," then we are simply "run-of-the-mill decadents," the composers of singular sensations.'[8] On the other hand, if 'those worlds' did exist – as many of the Symbolists claimed to have experienced firsthand – then it was the poet who was their most finely attuned receptor, bearing the musical temperament to articulate the rhythms of history and the imaginative capacity to discover new myths and values that would reconcile and unite fractured nations. But where were these worlds? How could they be accessed? What kind of forces were these 'theurges' bringing into this world? How could they tell whether the intuitions that guided them were divine or infernal, or simply mistaken? The bitter arguments that surfaced over these questions grew into culture-shaping mythologies, yielding a larger-than-life pantheon of artists whose lives were altered by what they found in their poetic journeys 'beyond'.

First Generation: 'That Which Does Not Exist in the World . . .'

As a poet, Dmitrii Merezhkovskii was very much the product of the Russian tradition. At the age of fourteen, he was taken to see Dostoevskii, was asked to read one of his own poems, and was summarily rebuked for it. Dostoevskii's advice: 'in order to write well, one must suffer, suffer!'[9] During his adolescence, Merezhkovskii was mentored by such major writers of the liberal establishment as Ivan Goncharov (1812–1891), Apollon Maikov

---

8 Aleksandr Blok, 'O sovremennom sostoianii russkogo simvolizma' [On the current state of Russian Symbolism], in *Polnoe sobranie sochinenii* [Complete works], 20 vols. (Moscow: Nauka, 1997–2014), vol. VIII, p. 128.
9 Merezhkovskii, *Polnoe sobranie sochinenii*, vol. XXIV, p. 111.

(1821–1897), and the populist critics Nikolai Mikhailovskii (1842–1904) and Gleb Uspenskii (1843–1902), and he therefore spoke with authority when he rejected the populist ethos in his 1892 manifesto on the decline of Russian literature. The deadliest sins of the progressive literary establishment, he explained, lay not in its aims, which were generally noble, but in its banality and therefore in its ineffectiveness. Socially sentimental appeals, he argued, would never move people to any significant action; only the 'creative belief in something infinite and immortal' can 'burn the human soul', creating 'heroes, martyrs, and prophets'. And it was only the symbol, the poetic art of the non-discursive *image*, that could approach such mysteries, pointing the way towards 'new, as yet undiscovered worlds of experience'.[10]

A programmatic expression of the search for 'new, as yet undiscovered worlds' through the poetic symbol can be found in the 1893 poem 'Song' (*Pesnia*) by Gippius, who was by this time four years married to Merezhkovskii. Gippius's poem evokes the image of a 'window high above the earth', through which the 'sky promises miracles' but offers 'no compassion' to the seeker who mourns, strains, and weeps over these 'false promises'. The poem's final phrase would become seminal for the movement: 'I need that which does not exist in the world.'[11] Painfully frustrated otherworldly longing, the oppressive closeness of existence – these were the driving concerns of Gippius's writing, and together they led to her conception of evil as embodied in *poshlost'*: banality, vulgarity, cramped and stultifying blandness. Since *poshlost'* was the real Satan, Gippius, like the European Romantics before her, felt a revisionist's fondness for Lucifer as a 'misunderstood Teacher of great Beauty', an ally in the fight against inertia, and a co-sufferer in the ever-frustrated longing for the heavens.[12] *Poshlost'*, for Gippius, needed to be fought in both art and life, and her boldly stylised persona – sometimes virginal, sometimes devilish, sometimes androgynous – was one form of battle. Her unconventional marriage to Merezhkovskii could be seen as yet another. Apparently never consummated (possibly as a result of the couple's views on the spiritual importance of erotic longing), the marriage was robust enough to weather fifty-two years of constant companionship and even its expansion, for over a decade, to include a third member (see Chapter 2.6).

---

10 Merezhkovskii, 'O prichinakh upadka', pp. 303, 249.
11 Z. N. Gippius, 'Pesnia' [Song], in *Stikhotvoreniia* [Verses] (St Petersburg: Akademicheskii proekt, 1999), p. 75.
12 Gippius, 'Grizel'da' [Griselda], in *Stikhotvoreniia*, pp. 82–4.

To direct one's energies against finitude and *poshlost'*, it could be argued, presupposes a certain amount of economic stability. To hunger, as Gippius did, for 'that which does not exist in the world' suggests that one has enough actual food, and it bears mentioning that almost half a million Russians had died of famine between 1891 and 1892. It was in this context that Maksim Gorkii's (1868–1936) frustrated question – 'What is the social significance in any of this?' – could not be easily dismissed. Gorkii, whose real name was Aleksei Peshkov, would later rise to international celebrity as inheritor of the social-democratic Russian literary edifice and gravitational centre of the Realists, rival camp to the Symbolists. Is there not 'already enough of the incomprehensible and foggy in life', Gorkii asked in 1896, reviewing the work of the Decadents, without these 'nervous-ailing poems'?[13] The Symbolist poet Konstantin Balmont (1867–1942) had memorably declared his eagerness to fly 'beyond the borders of the bordered' into the 'abysses of bright Shorelessness'.[14] But if Balmont happened to get lost on his way, Gorkii taunted, 'would either life or art suffer any noticeable damage?'[15]

As far as the first generation of the movement was concerned, there were at least two ways of replying to Gorkii's question. The first was that of Sologub, the so-called Russian Schopenhauer, whose hopes for what art could accomplish were relatively modest. Sologub had arrived in Petersburg in 1892 after eight years as a schoolteacher in the provinces where he had ostensibly seen the evil of *poshlost'* up close, as depicted in his 1905 novel *The Petty Demon* (*Melkii bes*). Sologub's updated devil, Ardalen Peredonov, is a fearful civil servant and schoolteacher who crosses himself when he walks by a church to show respect for the authorities and who visits his students' parents to recommend that their children be beaten with birches. The demons that haunt the civil servant are not from the beyond. Like the 'scrofulous little demon with a runny nose' that characterises Dostoevskii's view of evil, Sologub's demons are without mystical content.[16] They mock and harass while feeding on the anxieties of the weak-minded. When Sologub proclaims in the opening line of his most famous poem that 'I am the God of a mysterious world' (*Ia – bog tainstvennogo mira*,

13 M. Gorkii, 'Beglye zametki' [Cursory notes], *Nizhegorodskii listok* [Nizhny Novgorod leaflet] 250 (10 Sept. 1896), 3.
14 K. D. Bal'mont, *Polnoe sobranie sochinenii* [Complete works], 7 vols. (Moscow: Knigovek, 2010), vol. I, pp. 126–7.
15 Gorkii, 'Beglye zametki', 3.
16 Fyodor Dostoevsky, *Demons*, trans. Richard Pevear and Larissa Volokhonsky (New York: Vintage, 1994), p. 293.

1896), it is primarily 'freedom' from such trivial aggravations that the poet seeks 'in the night, the peace, and the darkness' of the inner life.[17]

The Merezhkovskiis, by contrast, were activists. Their purpose was to forge a new, more robust religious consciousness for their society. By the turn of the century, Merezhkovskii was famous throughout Europe for his historical novels. In collaboration with Sergei Diaghilev (1872–1929), Gippius and Merezhkovskii had helped to foster the World of Art (*Mir iskusstva*) collective, which, beginning in 1898, had become a headquarters for Modernist art, literature, and philosophy. Their efforts helped to cross-fertilise the well-funded Moscow wing of Russian Symbolism with its Scorpion (*Skorpion*) publishing house, overseen by the prodigious energies and organisational acumen of Briusov. Yet for Gippius and Merezhkovskii, all this was still just talk. In the student and worker strikes that had been building in the final years of the century, in the proliferation of revolution-ary organisations, there was the sense of 'something breaking', as Gippius recalled later: 'something was being left behind; . . . where to? No one knew the answer, but already then, on the border of the centuries, *tragedy* could be felt in the air.'[18] A resolution to take action resulted in what was probably the most visible achievement of the Merezhkovskiis: the organisation of the Religious-Philosophical Meetings between 1901 and 1903, which brought together high-ranking members of the Russian Orthodox clergy with lead-ing representatives of the intelligentsia. As conceived by Gippius, this was a real-life, practical way of breaking open the dam that separated religion from high culture, an active step in the forging of a new religious consciousness.

Looking back two decades later, Blok would poke gentle fun at the proceedings. 'It was here', Blok recalls, 'that Merezhkovskii came to his decisive slogan: "It's time to stop talking – it's time to act." And then he started talking . . . And he's still talking, as we all are.'[19] For the next gener-ation of Symbolists, of which Blok was a part, it was poetry itself that would change the world, not social gatherings or political speeches. The high windows that taunted Gippius could be opened. This was what a symbol

---

17 F. Sologub, 'Ya – bog tainstvennogo mira . . .' [I am the god of a mysterious world . . .], in *Russkaia poeziia kontsa XIX–nachalo XX veka* [Russian poetry from the end of the nineteenth to the beginning of the twentieth century], ed. A. G. Sokolova (Moscow: Izdatel'stvo Moskovskogo universiteta, 1979), p. 252.

18 Gippius, *Polnoe sobranie sochinenii*, vol. XVI, p. xx.

19 A. Blok, 'O Merezhkovskom' [On Merezhkovskii], in *Sobranie sochinenii* [Collected works], 8 vols. (Moscow, Leningrad: Gosudarstvennoe izdatel'stvo khudozhestvennoi literatury, 1960–3), vol. VI, p. 394.

was – 'a window looking out into Eternity'[20] – and the practice of poetry, done right, could bring something into the world from beyond those windows that would be the decisive ingredient for historical change.

Heights vs Depths: The Three Theurges

Aleksandr Blok and Andrei Belyi both perceived a certain mythical quality in the fact of their simultaneous appearance on the literary scene. Long before they met, the two writers felt a mutual fascination, and when in 1903 they finally resolved to write to each other – both at the age of twenty-three – their letters crossed in the mail. Had they been fictional characters in a novel, it might have seemed somewhat contrived or overdone that the two writers – the leading novelist and leading poet of their age in Russia – would be born a month apart; that they would be from similar backgrounds (Belyi was from Moscow, Blok from Petersburg), from intertwined social circles, both the sons of prominent professors; that they would end up falling in love with the same woman (the daughter of the great scientist Dmitrii Mendeleev no less), at one point almost fighting a duel over her; and that they would think of themselves consciously as contrastive doubles, charting out their creative paths in relation to each other. Indeed, in Belyi's later attempts to 'save' Liubov Mendeleeva-Blok from her husband, it is tempting to compare them to the competing heroes of Dostoevskii's *The Idiot* (*Idiot*, 1874), Myshkin and Rogozhin. Andrei Belyi (the name translates as Andrew the White and was the pseudonym of Boris Bugaev) had some of Prince Myshkin's lightness; his peers described him as wildly charming, effervescent, his conversations incorporating elements of music and dance. Blok, by contrast, was often rendered in terms of a fixed gaze and a brooding, possibly dangerous depth.

When Blok first wrote to Belyi, it was in response to a perceived similarity in their view of poetry – a medium, as Belyi had argued in his 1902 essay 'The Forms of Art' (*Formy iskusstva*), uniquely poised between the here and the beyond, expressing both the invisible rhythms of music and the concrete images of the visual arts. Blok had conceived of his own poetry in similar terms, as a bridge between divine and human worlds. And it was this that Belyi responded to in his letter to Blok – the mystical intuition, poignantly expressed in Blok's cycle *Poems about a Beautiful Lady* (*Stikhi o prekrasnoi dame*, comp. 1901–2), that to behold beauty in the physical world was to experience

---

20 A. Belyi, 'Symbolism as a world view', in *Selected Essays of Andrey Belyi*, trans. Steven Cassedy (Berkeley: University of California Press, 1985), p. 82.

the divine directly with one's senses. This bedrock Platonic conviction had come to both poets partly through the writings of Vladimir Solovev, who had written, in both poetry and prose, of his visitations by the divine Sophia. The 'Thou' addressed in Blok's lyric poetry is both a feminine interlocutor and a heavenly being, not simply a poetic muse but something more closely akin to the Holy Spirit itself. The poet – as Blok expresses it in his 1902 poem 'Religion' (*Religio*) – resides 'here below, in the dust, in the squalor', but 'having glimpsed for a moment the immortal features', he establishes 'one Testament' for his 'whole life': 'the Testament of serving the Unattainable'.[21] Both Belyi and Blok conceived of themselves as knights in this service, and it was exhilarating – as Belyi put it in his letter to Blok – to affirm each other in this view, which was no longer 'the delirium of isolated eccentrics'.[22]

Encouraged by Blok, Merezhovskii, Gippius, Sologub, Briusov, and a growing community of like-minded artists, Belyi outlined a wildly ambitious programme in his theoretical writings from 1903 to 1905. Friedrich Nietzsche, he noted, had destroyed the old, dead values of European culture and had attempted a kind of theurgy – to create new eternal values that would guide and anchor the world. But while Nietzsche, an early aeronaut of the spirit, had crashed and burned, they – the Symbolists – would fly more surely for his example while also being wiser in their acknowledgement of divine realities outside of themselves. Like Solovev, the Symbolists perceived the divine Sophia in the heavens – the 'Beautiful Lady' of Blok's poems – and their work was to bring her into the world, through their poetry, in order to tame and integrate the chaos below. Belyi was aware that this was an impressive programme. In the world below, there was war, revolution, civil unrest, elements that actively resisted divinisation. 'As for now', he admitted in 1905, 'Her sign is still in heaven', but he believed that Blok's visionary poetry was an omen of greater things to come.[23]

One can imagine Belyi's dismay when Blok, in the full blush of their newly formed poetic brotherhood, began to change his mind. A decisive twist of the knife came in 1906 when Blok read his lyrical play *The Puppet Show* (*Balaganchik*) aloud at an evening gathering. In the play (which would be staged later that year, to cultural sensation, by Vsevolod Meierkhold

21 Blok, 'Religio' [Religion], in *Polnoe sobranie sochinenii*, vol. I, pp. 127–8.
22 Belyi, letter to Blok, 4 Jan. 1903, in *Andrei Belyi i Aleksandr Blok. Perepiska 1903–1919* [Andrei Belyi and Aleksandr Blok. Correspondence 1903–1919], ed. A. V. Lavrov (Moscow: Progress-pleiiada, 2001), p. 21.
23 Andrei Bely, 'Apocalypse in Russian poetry', in *Between Crisis and Catastrophe: Lyrical and Mystical Essays*, ed. and trans. Boris Jakim (Kettering, OH: Semantron Press, 2016), p. 100.

(1874–1940)), Belyi saw a mockery of everything he and his partner-in-theurgy had professed. Not only was the Eternal Feminine reduced to a piece of cardboard, a thin sign containing no substance, but Belyi was shown a version of himself as a harlequin, embracing his 'cardboard beauty' and rushing in mystical transport to leap into the 'beyond' through a window which turned out to be drawn on paper. The paper rips and the 'Harlequin flies head over heels into emptiness'.[24] Implied here were several intersecting statements: Blok was not only predicting Belyi's ultimately unsuccessful attempts to run off with Blok's wife, whom Belyi had come to see as the earthly incarnation of divine Sophia; he was also mocking Belyi's concept of Symbolism as a window to the heavens, not to mention rescinding his subscription to their knightly covenant.

Meanwhile the 'Beautiful Lady' of Blok's lyrical poetry was changing. In his landmark 1906 poem 'The Unknown Woman' (*Neznakomka*), she appears by the window of a bar on a 'putrid' sultry evening. Assuming now the degraded form of a prostitute, she remains the carrier of 'obscure mysteries' through whose 'dark veil' the drunken poet sees 'the enchanted distance'.[25] In Blok's subsequent experimentations, however, she would evolve into a different archetype altogether: no longer the embodiment of high celestial mysteries but an earthy, capricious, angry, chaotic, possibly destructive being who bears within herself the primordial memory of the Russian people. In the 1908 play *The Song of Fate* (*Pesnia sud'by*) – to select one representative work from a prolific period – Blok's hero leaves behind his lovely 'white house', where he lives with his 'white bride' in blissful ignorance of the world's chaos, to descend to the city in pursuit of a fallen woman, the singer Faina.[26] In the hero's pursuit of the mysterious woman, who mocks him and cuts his face with a whip, Blok examines his own agonised politics in the wake of the 1905 revolution, amid the strikes, uprisings, protests, and assassinations that were all calling painful attention to his own impotent detachment as an educated and westernised nobleman. The collective spirit that his hero discovers in the songs of Faina is not the ideal, aspirational communal soul that Belyi had described in his theoretical writings. Faina is a singer of the depths, the conduit of the collective soul of the Russian people, the bearer of ancient memories and violent barbaric energies that were both terrifying and enticing to the modern *intelligent*.

---

24 Blok, *Balaganchik* [The puppet show], in *Polnoe sobranie sochinenii*, vol. VI, pp. 19–20.
25 Blok, 'Neznakomka' [The unknown woman], in *Polnoe sobranie sochinenii*, vol. II, pp. 122–3.
26 Blok, *Pesnia sud'by* [The song of fate], in *Polnoe sobranie sochinenii*, vol. VI, p. 104.

Blok's preoccupation with an elemental chaos rising from the depths of the 'collective soul' of the people was by no means the fringe peculiarity of a poet-mystic. From among Gorkii's rival camp of Realists, the writer Leonid Andreev (1871–1919) had electrified Russian readers with his description – in the 1904 story 'The Red Laugh' (*Krasnyi smekh*) – of a 'Satanic roar', 'a cloud of madness', a 'vast, formless shadow', an 'avalanche' that would 'cleanse the whole world', making 'everything ... swirl and dance with fire'.[27] Andreev's story, which Blok admired, had captured a dominant fixture of the age, a widely shared *fin-de-siècle* mood of apocalyptic doom that coincided with Russia's crushing military losses to Japan in 1904–5 and with the first Russian revolution, which occurred in waves over the span of 1905. Belyi and Blok had walked the streets of Petersburg together in the hours and days after the Bloody Sunday massacre of January 1905. Both were stunned by the awareness that the world around them was changing irreversibly. But while Blok grew inclined to embrace the 'Satanic roar' as a transcendent gust of poetic inspiration, a vital spiritual storm rising from within the collective soul of the Russian people, Belyi recoiled from what he saw as a new, demonic form of Symbolism. Blok, he lamented in 1907, had become the purveyor of 'non-being, darkness, and emptiness'. He had betrayed his knightly vows to the heavens and succumbed to the volcanic chaos of the depths.[28]

Some part of the blame, or credit, for Blok's transformation could be placed at the feet of the third major Symbolist poet of the era, Viacheslav Ivanov, whose personality was equally a myth in the making. In 1905, recently returned from Europe, Ivanov and his wife – the writer Lidiia Zinoveva-Annibal (1866–1907) – moved into a spacious apartment in Petersburg with domed ceilings, semi-circular walls, and arresting views, which became known as the Tower, a place of meetings, discussions, revelries, and rites: the centre of Petersburg Symbolism (see Chapter 2.3). Ivanov's larger-than-life status was grounded in remarkable erudition. A classicist by training, he had written a doctoral dissertation in Latin on the topic of Roman tax farming under the guidance of Theodor Mommsen at the University of Berlin, had studied ancient Greek theatre and palaeography in Athens with the world's leading archaeologists, had studied Sanskrit in Geneva with Ferdinand de Saussure, and had been mentored in his poetry by Solovev. He could speak brilliantly on any topic, it seemed, in any language – French,

27 Leonid Andreyev, *The Red Laugh and the Abyss*, trans. Kirsten Lodge (Peterborough, ON: Broadview Press, 2021), pp. 23, 31, 44.
28 Belyi, 'Oblomki mirov' [The wreckage of worlds], in *Aleksandr Blok: Pro et contra*, pp. 96–9.

German, Italian, English, modern Greek – and by this time, at the age of thirty-nine, he was both a published poet of formally inventive but difficult esoteric poems and the author of a well-received study on Greek Dionysian religion. And yet for all his learning, he displayed no apparent haughtiness. On the contrary, he was radically hospitable, open to endless hours of conversation and revelry, and intent on mentoring and guiding the poets who were gathering around him.

Ivanov, unlike Belyi, was no lofty idealist. His god principle was an earthy one. From his study of Dionysian religion, he had concluded that 'the depths' were not to be feared or demonised. The energetic and orgiastic worship of Dionysius, he argued, *contra* Nietzsche, was a prefiguration of Christianity. The mystical intuition driving Ivanov's work was the joyous emancipation that arises, in his words, from the 'opening of the soul to the living streams that flow from the world's very depths', from the 'dark purple kingdom of the netherworld'. The work of the artist was to 'surrender his personality' in order to become 'the passive tool of the god that lives within him'.[29] Like Belyi and Blok, Ivanov saw the poet as a theurge, but he emphasised in his programmatic essays on Symbolism that the work of the theurge should be one of extreme 'receptivity'. Unlike the 'illusionism' of non-religious poetry – French Decadence, for example – which simply describes the phantasms of the poet's own subjective imagination, the work of the religious poet is to open oneself prayerfully, humbly, to the revelation of a symbol that comes not from one's own personal imagination but from a universally shared transcendent source. Only in this way can the poet discover a primordial myth that will speak not to the poet alone but to all people, thus reconciling and nurturing whole civilisations. For Ivanov, Symbolist art in this religious sense alone had a supreme political significance.

Ivanov's theory of Symbolism helped Blok conceive of an active and practical role for the poet in revolutionary times. Blok and Ivanov were united in the conviction that the Symbolist poet was no obtuse bystander but a prophet who journeys into the dark depths of the people's collective soul to bring something into the world from the elemental 'below'. There was, however, a crucial incompatibility in their world views. Ivanov's anarchism was inherently Christian. To give oneself up to the depths, for Ivanov, was to surrender oneself to a benevolent and loving God. For Blok, by contrast, mysticism had nothing to do with religion. The depths, for Blok, were hell. The energies to which he was attuning his artistic antennae were demonic,

---

29 Ivanov, 'The symbolics of aesthetic principles', in *Selected Essays*, pp. 10–12.

not divine, and there was something offensively facile, in Blok's view, about Ivanov's attitude to these inward abysses. There was nothing loving or forgiving or joyous in the collective spirit of the age. What Blok felt was terror – a terror that was creative and ecstatic but also destructive and apocalyptic. 'What if', he asks in 1907, Gogol's troika is 'racing straight at us?' What if when we, the intelligentsia, 'rush to the people, we are rushing to certain death under the hooves of a mad troika?'[30]

The mystical disagreement of the three theurges is among the most peculiar and yet most consequential in Russian literature. Blok, Belyi, and Ivanov agreed that poetry was theurgy, the creation of something drawn from other worlds, and yet all three held mutually incompatible views on the nature of this mystical 'beyond' – whether it was a height or a depth; a Platonic or a Dionysian mystery; or, yet again, whether poetic creation was a divine or an infernal task. Belyi, for his part, was no Dionysian, no demonist, and no anarchist. In 1907, he published an attack on the Petersburg mystics aimed at both Ivanov and Blok, among others, mocking their blasé attitude towards the 'boundless abyss' that stretched beneath their feet: 'The abyss is a necessary condition of comfort for Petersburg writers. There they visit their friends over the abyss, establish their careers over the abyss, put the samovar on over the abyss. Oh, what a nice abyss!'[31]

Belyi offers a more searching treatment of this problem in *The Silver Dove* (*Serebrianyi golub'*, 1909), the novel that marked his coming of age as a prose writer. Belyi's poet-protagonist Darialskii (recalling Blok's hero in *The Song of Fate*) forsakes his high-born fiancée to follow a mysterious woman into the world of the people and to become entangled in a mystical sect. Darialskii's rightful betrothed is a being of the heights, with eyes 'like the scraps of the blue night sky', while the peasant woman Matrena, by contrast, is a gateway to the depths, 'as though the deep blue sea were tossing behind her pock-marked face'.[32] Darialskii's predicament is that of Russia in microcosm, as belonging to but unable to unite or integrate the distinct worlds of the modern, Europeanised west and traditional, primordial east. Instead of illuminating the chaos that he finds 'below', Darialskii, somewhat like Blok himself, falls in love with it, descends powerlessly into a frenzied inferno, and

---

30 Blok, 'Narod i intelligentsia' [The people and the intelligentsia], in *Polnoe sobranie sochinenii*, vol. VIII, p. 76.
31 A. Belyi, 'Shtempelevannaia kalosha' [The stamped boot], in *Vesy* [Libra] 5 (1907), 49–50.
32 A. Belyi, *The Silver Dove*, trans. John Elsworth (Evanston, IL: Northwestern University Press, 2000), pp. 176, 170.

becomes ensnared in the murderous designs of his fellow sectarians.[33] In depicting the poet's failed attempt to transfigure and unite the world around him, the novel reflects the so-called crisis of Symbolism that, by the end of the decade, seemed to have splintered the movement irrevocably.

Though it is impossible to pinpoint the final moment of Russian Symbolism, and though many of the Symbolists continued to produce important (indeed some of their best) work in the second decade of the twentieth century, as a prominent and unified collective it did not survive beyond 1910. Much had happened by then in more than a decade of intense cultural activity. On the personal front, there was a long line of disputes, hurt feelings, nervous breakdowns, love triangles, misfired pistols, psychotic breaks, suicide attempts, miscarried duels, and untimely deaths, all of which lent substantial emotional weight to the movement's history. Ivanov himself had been widowed during this time, but not before having also lost some of his footing as guru amid the bold experimentations, sexual configurations, and apprenticeships that had characterised the manic life of the Tower (see Chapter 2.6). On the cultural front, a new generation of poets – including such writers as Mikhail Kuzmin (1872–1939) and Nikolai Gumilev (1886–1921), both fixtures of the Tower – had begun to question the supremacy of the movement. Among the Symbolists themselves, deep factions had consolidated. Merezhkovskii and Gippius were alienated both from Ivanov's Tower and from Briusov (leader of the Moscow Symbolists), who had, in turn, become a vocal critic not only of Ivanov's orgiastic brand of mysticism but of the entire theurgical enterprise. Though Briusov had initially advocated an unrestrainedly Romantic conception of poetry as prophecy, a series of polemics had gradually confirmed him in his position as a devotee of art for its own sake. Ivanov, ever the helpful guide, attempted in his 1910 essay 'The Testaments of Symbolism' (*Zavety simvolizma*) to make sense of all these fluctuations as part of a dialectical process. The optimistic mission to make the world divine had, in keeping with the unruliness of the time, yielded to an antithesis of confusion and despair, awaiting a synthesis that was yet to come.[34]

Blok's response to Ivanov – his 1910 speech, 'On the Current State of Russian Symbolism' (*O sovremennom sostoianii russkogo simvolizma*) – is remarkable in its attempt to give an up-close, step-by-step description of what it is like to be a theurge and to look back over the dangers, agonies,

---

33 Belyi, *Silver Dove*, p. 169.
34 Ivanov, 'The testaments of Symbolism', in *Selected Essays*, pp. 33–49.

and potential abuses of mystical poetry that had defined the movement. In impressionistic language, Blok describes the poet's contact with 'other worlds' through the image of a golden sword which pierces into both those 'purple-lilac worlds' beyond and directly into the 'heart of the theurge'. In the moment of being pierced, the poet hears a voice, but when the inspiration has passed, a blue-lilac gloom continues to pour into this world 'as if through a broken dam'. What does one do, Blok seems to be asking in bewilderment, with all these 'raging purple worlds'? He insists that there can be no question about the existence of these worlds, nor of his conviction that major events of recent history, including the 1905 revolution, had been born from their musical chaos. It is no surprise, Blok notes, that the Symbolists are burnt out and exhausted from their untutored and all too careless struggles with these very real mystical forces that 'pour in, mixing with this world, creating chaos, making art out of life'. As he puts it, memorably, 'it would be strange for us to be in a different state than we are now', when 'our faces are burnt and disfigured by the purple gloom'. The only way forward, he concludes, must be one of humility: 'the path of study, introspection, steadiness of gaze, and spiritual diet'.[35]

Raging Purple Worlds

Blok's speech is perhaps a fitting place to mark the end of Russian Symbolism as a coherent partnership. His emphasis on other worlds was itself indicative of what the emerging movement of Russian Acmeist poets – including Anna Akhmatova (1889–1966), Osip Mandelshtam (1891–1938), and Gumilev – would push back against, in, as Sergei Gorodetskii (1884–1967) put it, their 'struggle for this world, full of sound, colour, having shape, weight, and time, for our planet Earth'.[36] The golden swords and purple worlds of Blok's speech were symptomatic of the obscurities that Mandelshtam would later reject as Symbolic poetic excesses: 'Not a single clear word, only hints, things left unsaid. A rose nods at a girl, the girl nods at the rose.'[37] When Blok had finished speaking, Ivanov stood up and kissed him full on the lips, and, when the speech was published later that year, Belyi wrote to apologise and reconcile. Yet it would become clear for all three theurges that though they

---

35 Blok, 'O sovremennom sostoianii russkogo simvolizma', pp. 123–31.
36 S. Gorodetskii, 'Nekotorye techeniia v sovremennoi russkoi poezii' [Some currents in contemporary Russian poetry], *Apollon* 1 (1913), 48.
37 O. Mandel'shtam, 'O prirode slova' [On the nature of the word], in *O poezii. Sbornik statei* [On poetry. Collected articles] (Leningrad: Academia, 1928), p. 41.

might agree on the basic definitions of poetry and on the need for spiritual humility, the differences in their world views precluded a closely shared future programme.

Blok, still searchingly and uncertainly, had articulated his own path forward as a devotee of the 'purple gloom' that had 'burnt his face'. In his 1912 poem 'To the Muse' (*K muze*), he describes the 'fateful tidings of death' that the poet hears in the 'innermost songs' of his muse: 'For some you are the Muse and the miracle. / For me you are torment and hell.'[38] When read alongside his earnest hymns to the 'Beautiful Lady' from only a decade earlier, the poem marks the other end of what is possibly Russian literature's most accelerated authorial arc. In the last decade of his life, Blok would dedicate himself to the 'raging purple worlds'. That is, to the elemental chaos of the revolution, in the conviction that it would give birth to cosmos. The unsettling depiction of the revolutionary Red Guard as disciples of Jesus Christ in his major 1918 long poem, *The Twelve* (*Dvenadtsat'*), expresses some of Blok's anguish and ambivalence over the violently chaotic forces in which he had placed so many hopes.

Belyi too, in the years leading up to the Bolshevik Revolution, would turn his ear to descriptions of a rising, apocalyptic chaos. Unlike Blok, however, who encountered these elements gladly, Belyi was their unwilling diviner. Nowhere is this quandary more powerfully expressed than in his prose masterpiece *Petersburg* (*Peterburg*, 1913–14, 1922), where Blok's 'raging purple worlds' find an analogue in the presence of an emptiness that 'had been swelling from time eternal', an explosive chaos which emanates from within people and things, and which, in modern Petersburg, acquires the form of a ticking bomb.[39] Belyi's quasi-autobiographical protagonist does not wish to be the purveyor of these destructive potentialities, but he is. He has taken the bomb into his possession; he is aware of its ticking, unable to curb its energies, and is therefore responsible for the destruction it wreaks. With this image, Belyi's formerly idealistic programme of an all-divinising theurgy is transformed into a tortured and reluctant form of terrorism.

Merezhkovskii had dreamed of a Renaissance in which 'opposing original temperaments' would 'strengthen and rouse each other to activity', and it is a testament to the Symbolists' unprecedented realisation of this vision that, long after the apparent collapse of the movement, amid war and violent revolution, its practitioners continued to conceive of their work in

---

38 Blok, 'K muze' [To the muse], in *Polnoe sobranie sochinenii*, vol. III, p. 7.
39 A. Belyi, *Petersburg*, trans. Robert A. Maguire and John Malmstad (Bloomington: Indiana University Press, 1978), p. 226.

conversation with each other, through the myths and narrative patterns that they had discovered together. Nor did the poetic Renaissance end with the Symbolists. Indeed, Akhmatova, Velimir Khlebnikov (1885–1922), and Mandelshtam were only a few of those who read their early poems at the Tower and were nurtured by its atmosphere. Yet for all its fertility, the rich matrix of life, myth, and art that the Symbolists had conceived also placed inexorable demands on its adherents. The deaths of the three 'theurges' are three cases in point. Blok's myth as a lover of chaos seemed to necessitate an early demise, and while the circumstances surrounding his death in 1921 remain unclear, the myth preserved in the various reminiscences is that of a poet who, having dreamed of an all-renewing destruction, found silence and emptiness in its wake and died of an illness that was really a symptom of despair. As for Belyi, the unrepentant idealist who dreamed of clothing the world in the 'light of the sun' and who, as he put it in one poem, 'believed in the Golden brilliance, / And died from its solar arrows', would need, according to his myth, to die by heavenly edict. Belyi in fact died of a cerebral haemorrhage after a difficult decade of marginal obscurity in the Soviet Union, but the more apposite account, that he died from sunstroke, has become more or less canonical. Ivanov, for his part, so his myth required, would have to end his life in exile in Rome, close to the visible ruins of the ancient memories of the world. And yet, of course, it was not really exile, since the true homeland of the Symbolist, as Ivanov had often explained, was myth itself – the 'living, eternal memory, which does not die in those who partake of its initiations'.[40]

Further Reading

Bird, Robert, *The Russian Prospero: The Creative Universe of Viacheslav Ivanov* (Madison: University of Wisconsin Press, 2006).

Clowes, Edith W., *The Revolution of Moral Consciousness: Nietzsche in Russian Literature (1890–1914)* (DeKalb: Northern Illinois University Press, 1988).

Doherty, Justin, *The Acmeist Movement in Russian Poetry: Culture and the Word* (Oxford: Clarendon Press, 1995).

Grossman, Joan Delaney, *Valery Briusov and the Riddle of Russian Decadence* (Berkeley: University of California Press, 1985).

Matich, Olga, *Erotic Utopia: The Decadent Imagination in Russia's Fin de Siècle* (Madison: University of Wisconsin Press, 2005).

40 Viacheslav Ivanov and Mikhail Gershenzon, 'A correspondence between two corners', trans. Norbert Guterman, *Partisan Review* 9 (Sept. 1948), 965.

Paperno, Irina, and Joan Delaney Grossman (eds.), *Creating Life: The Aesthetic Utopia of Russian Modernism* (Stanford: Stanford University Press, 1994).

Presto, Jennifer, *Beyond the Flesh: Alexander Blok, Zinaida Gippius, and the Symbolist Sublimation of Sex* (Madison: University of Wisconsin Press, 2006).

Pyman, Avril, *A History of Russian Symbolism* (Cambridge: Cambridge University Press, 1994).

Wachtel, Michael, *Russian Symbolism and Literary Tradition: Goethe, Novalis, and the Poetics of Vyacheslav Ivanov* (Madison: University of Wisconsin Press, 1994).

Zlobin, Vladimir, *A Difficult Soul: Zinaida Gippius*, ed. Simon Karlinskii (Berkeley: University of California Press, 1980).

Modernism and the Avant-Garde

CONNOR DOAK

In a history of movements in Russian literature, the Modernist age – between 1890 and 1930, approximately – possesses an embarrassment of riches. This extraordinary period of artistic experimentation saw the emergence of competing groups – Symbolists, Futurists, and Acmeists, to name but a few – who had different visions of what art and literature should be. Many writers consciously perceived themselves to be part of a group or movement, sparring with their rivals. It is unsurprising, therefore, that the artistic manifesto emerged as one of the key genres of the age. The stakes were raised even higher after the Bolshevik Revolution in 1917. Literature became a tool for building socialism in the newly established Soviet Union, and writers had to nail their colours to the mast: some enthusiastically embraced the regime, seeking to establish themselves as the voice of the revolution, while others criticised the new regime, often privately or from a safe distance abroad. Still others were ambivalent about the Soviet project, which was often seen not simply as a political revolution but as a cultural transformation of apocalyptic proportions.

This chapter concentrates primarily on poetry, which saw a flowering of diverse schools in this period and the emergence of several major poets. While Russian verse had been dominated by Symbolism in the first decade of the century (see Chapter 1.6), by the early 1910s, rival groups such as the Futurists and Acmeists posed a challenge to the Symbolist world view and aesthetics. The avant-garde Futurists wanted nothing short of a radical overhaul of the Russian literary language, while the Acmeists called for a literature of restraint and craftsmanship. These 'post-Symbolist' movements saw the emergence of new major writers, many of whom have left an enduring legacy in Russian literature. The most prominent Futurists included Velimir Khlebnikov (1885–1922) and Vladimir Maiakovskii (1893–1930), while the Acmeists included Anna Akhmatova (1889–1966) and Osip Mandelshtam

(1891–1938). Some sat apart from any group or movement, notably Marina Tsvetaeva (1892–1941), whose work, while drawing on various Modernist currents, is highly distinctive in its formal and linguistic experimentation. Similarly, Boris Pasternak (1890–1960) soon moved away from his Futurist origins and developed an individual voice. The best Symbolists, such as Aleksandr Blok (1880–1921) and Andrei Belyi (1880–1934), absorbed and learnt from the challenges to Symbolism; both developed a wider range in their literary voice and a keen sense of self-irony. Belyi excelled as a writer of prose as well as poetry. His phantasmagoric novel *Petersburg* (*Peterburg*, 1913–14, 1922) ostensibly depicts a terrorist plot in Russia's northern capital, but the work transcends contemporary politics, engaging with mysticism, anthroposophy, and the occult and making use of the author's poetic skills.

For many avant-garde writers, the momentous events of the first decades of the century, and in particular the revolutions of February and October 1917, seemed like a political realisation of the great rupture foretold in their own art. Moreover, the newly created Soviet Union afforded great importance – and generous funding – to literature and the arts, and the writer was assigned a key role in the moral and ideological development of the 'new Soviet person' (*novyi sovetskii chelovek*; see Chapter 4.7). Indeed, the 1920s would prove one of the most fertile decades for experimentation, not least because of the efforts of Anatolii Lunacharskii (1875–1933), the Soviet Union's first commissar for enlightenment, who was generally sympathetic to the avant-garde. Lyric poetry now fell out of official favour – it was considered too individualistic – but narrative poetry grew in importance. Experimental prose attained a new significance in the hands of writers such as Isaak Babel (1894–1940), Iurii Olesha (1899–1960), Boris Pilniak (1894–1938), and Andrei Platonov (1899–1951). Theatre, too, saw significant innovation, with the director Vsevolod Meierkhold (1874–1940) challenging naturalism, developing his method of biomechanics, and founding his own theatre in Moscow.

The 1910s and 1920s also saw new methods emerge in literary theory and criticism. Viktor Shklovskii (1893–1984; see Box 5.2) pioneered the Formalist analysis of literary texts in works such as *The Resurrection of the Word* (*Voskreshenie slova*, 1914) and 'Art as Device' (*Iskusstvo kak priem*, 1917). Shklovskii's concept of defamiliarisation (*ostranenie*) sought to understand how art renews our perception of the familiar world. The Formalists were initially centred in the OPOIAZ group, founded in 1916; the name is a portmanteau of *Obshchestvo po izucheniiu poeticheskogo iazyka* (Society for the Study of Poetic Language). The group included Osip Brik (1888–1945), Boris Eikhenbaum (1886–1959), Roman Jakobson (1896–1982), Boris

Tomashevskii (1890–1957), and Iurii Tynianov (1894–1943). Formalism went on to have a remarkable influence on literary criticism worldwide. Shklovskii's essays are frequently anthologised in volumes of literary theory, while Jakobson would later make a major impact in structuralist linguistics. It should be remembered, however, that Formalism did not appear in a vacuum but emerged from a culture of literary experimentation in Russia. In particular, the Formalists' ideas about the power of literary language to remake the world owed much to the Futurists, and there was much cross-fertilisation of ideas between the two groups. The Formalists esteemed the avant-garde, and several created experimental literary works of their own.

For some writers, deeply opposed to the Bolsheviks, there was little point in remaining in Russia after the revolution (see Chapter 4.10). The poet and prose writer Ivan Bunin (1870–1953), a bard of the Russian countryside, quickly emigrated and took up the pen against the Soviets from abroad. The religious Symbolists Dmitrii Merezhkovskii (1865–1941) and Zinaida Gippius (1869–1945) also left, realising that their differences with Bolshevism were irreconcilable. Vladimir Nabokov (1899–1977) left Russia for Berlin in the mid-1920s, a city also home to the influential poet Vladislav Khodasevich (1886–1939).

Back in the Soviet Union, many of the opponents of the Bolshevik Revolution who chose to remain encountered persecution. Nikolai Gumilev (1886–1921), a leading Acmeist and one-time husband of Akhmatova, made no secret of his anti-Bolshevik views and was executed in 1922 for alleged involvement in a monarchist plot. Both Akhmatova and Mandelshtam found the cultural and political climate increasingly difficult; Mandelshtam was arrested and died en route to the Gulag in 1938. Even Evgenii Zamiatin (1884–1937), a one-time Bolshevik, found his dystopian novel *We* (*My*, comp. 1920) banned in the Soviet Union; he emigrated in 1931. Writers often trod a fine line during the 1920s: it was still possible – even encouraged – to satirise negative aspects of Soviet life, but not the revolution itself, nor the communist dream. The satirist Mikhail Zoshchenko (1894–1958) wrote biting, comic satires that proved enormously popular, but Mikhail Bulgakov (1891–1940) fell foul of the censor with his satirical science-fiction novella *Heart of a Dog* (*Sobach'e serdtse*, comp. 1925).

Even among supporters of the revolution, the 1920s was an era of great debate, with competing visions of what Soviet literature and culture would and should look like. Avant-garde writers argued forcefully that radical politics required radical poetics; formal experimentation was essential to achieving the Soviets' goal of remaking humankind. Representing this

wing, Maiakovskii and Brik co-edited *LEF*, the journal of the Left Front of the Arts (*Levyi front iskusstv*, 1923–5), and *New LEF* (*Novyi LEF*, 1927–9), which served as vehicles for avant-garde ideas and art. A new avant-garde collective, OBERIU (*Ob"edinenie real'nogo iskusstva*, Union of Real Art), founded in 1928 by Daniil Kharms (1905–1942) and Aleksandr Vvedenskii (1904–1941), caused controversy with provocative, non-representational theatre. Kharms and Vvedenskii also wrote poetry and prose, typically short, absurd pieces with black humour. As the 1930s progressed, they struggled to publish and took refuge in writing children's literature. Both were seen as politically dangerous and were arrested as the Stalinist Terror reached its height.

While this chapter focuses on verse, we should add here that prose also saw significant experimentation in the post-revolutionary period. Boris Pilniak represented the trend of ornamentalism, which shunned plot and character development in favour of stylised imagery and language. Pilniak's novel *The Naked Year* (*Golyi god*, 1922) depicts the revolution and civil war in strikingly metaphorical terms as a whirlwind or blizzard, a cleansing elemental force that sweeps away civilisation. Iurii Olesha took a different route in his experimentation in prose, satirising the creation of the new Soviet person in his comic novel *Envy* (*Zavist'*, 1927), which depicts the clash between the rational, healthy, productive new Soviet person and the unhealthy, unstable former people attached to the old order as well as the envy that the latter experience towards the former. The novel received a mixed reception, with critics pointing out that the strange dreams and jealous fantasies of the dropouts arguably captivate the reader more than the practical successes of the new Soviet people. Critics were divided about how to interpret *Red Cavalry* (*Konarmiia*, 1923–6), an outstanding cycle of short stories about the civil war by Isaak Babel. Babel's striking prose style told violent stories from the battlefield in an unsettling combination of documentary realism and poetic flourish, and critics still debate whether the cycle ultimately glorifies or mocks the revolutionaries.

However, by the late 1920s, such experiments were no longer possible. Opponents of the avant-garde had gained ground, arguing that experimental art and literature were unnecessarily obscure and championing instead more traditional forms, such as the Realist novel, which were to be endowed with revolutionary content. For example, Aleksandr Fadeev (1901–1956) argued that the Tolstoian psychological novel could be reimagined as a vehicle for Soviet ideas and demonstrated his vision with novels such as *The Rout* (*Razgrom*, 1927). By the end of the decade, it was obvious that the traditionalists had prevailed. The formation of the Union of Soviet Writers (*Soiuz*

sovetskikh pisatelei) in 1932 centralised control of literature, and the promulgation of Socialist Realism as the approved literary mode in 1934 (see Chapter 1.8) effectively ended the diversity and experimentation of the 1920s.

The Futurist Revolt

The word 'Futurism' might appear to imply an orientation towards modernity and technology, and a teleological world view that foresees a brighter future. Outside the Russian context, 'Futurism' refers most often to the Italian group around Filippo-Tommaso Marinetti (1876–1944), whose notorious 1909 Futurist Manifesto celebrated the machine and violence, and called for the destruction of museums and libraries. Across the Russian Empire, several rival artistic and literary groups adopted the name 'Futurists' in the early 1910s, the most important of which, in literature, was Hylaea (*Gileia*), a group that included Khlebnikov, Maiakovskii, David Burliuk (1882–1967), Nikolai Burliuk (1890–1920), Elena Guro (1877–1913), Benedikt Livshits (1886–1938), and Aleksei Kruchenykh (1886–1968). Their first collection, *A Slap in the Face of Public Taste* (*Poshchechina obshchestvennomu vkusu*, 1912), included a manifesto of the same title that declared war on the Russian literary establishment and which shows the influence of the Italian group. The Russian Futurists mocked the Symbolists and lambasted the classics, with a call to 'Throw Pushkin, Dostoevskii, Tolstoi, etc. etc. off the steamship of modernity'.[1] The Hylaea Futurists expressed a radical, iconoclastic attitude towards language, art, and society as a whole, although it should be emphasised that their early works were not explicitly politically or socially engaged in the manner of, say, the writing of Maksim Gorkii (1868–1936) or that of the nineteenth-century Realist novelists (see Chapter 1.5).

Like their Italian counterparts, the Futurists in Russia deliberately courted controversy, cultivating notoriety in order to shock. They held scandalous performances, often delivered in face-paint and outrageous clothing, during which they would hurl insults at the audience and the leading writers of the day. They gave readings at cabaret clubs such as the Stray Dog (*Brodiachaia sobaka*) café in St Petersburg, but their output also included plays, such as Maiakovskii's *Vladimir Maiakovskii: A Tragedy* (*Vladimir Maiakovskii: Tragediia*, 1913) and the opera *Victory over the Sun* (*Pobeda nad solntsem*, 1913). This opera, which narrated

---

1 D. Burliuk, Aleksandr Kruchenykh, V. Maiakovskii, and Viktor Khlebnikov, 'Poshchechina obshchestvennomu vkusu' [A slap in the face of public taste], in *Poshchechina obshchestvennomu vkusu. V zashchitu svobodnogo iskusstva. Stikhi, proza, stat'i* [A slap in the face of public taste. In defence of free art. Verse, prose, essays], ed. D. Burliuk et al. (Moscow: Izdanie G. L. Kuz'mina, 1912), p. 3.

nothing less than the capturing of the sun and the conquering of time, featured a libretto by Kruchenykh, a prologue by Khlebnikov, music by Mikhail Matiushin (1861–1934), and set design by Kazimir Malevich (1879–1935). This reveals the extent to which Futurism in the Russian Empire spanned multiple arts, including visual art, music, and fashion as well as literature. Several of the leading Futurists worked across multiple media, and graphic design and illustration were often as important in Futurist books as the text itself.

The Russian Futurists were less enthusiastic about modernity and technology than the Italians. One does not find the unabashed eroticism and violence of the Italian group among the Russians, nor the cult of the machine or skyscrapers. Rather, Maiakovskii's pre-1917 poetry often depicts the modern city as an alienating environment, while Khlebnikov and Kruchenykh had a strong primitivist bent, seen in their quest to recreate a primordial language. Indeed, Russian Futurism was arguably a linguistic project above all: one focused squarely on the possibilities of the word itself, its sonic properties, and experimentation with morphology. Such experiments can be seen as early as 1908–9 in poems by Khlebnikov such as 'Incantation by Laughter' (*Zakliatie smekhom*), 'Grasshopper' (*Kuznechik*), and 'Bo-beh-oh-bee sang the lips' (*Bobeóbi pelis' guby*). The last of these three poems offered a Modernist depiction of a face through sound patterning, some of which is onomatopoeic and some purely inventive:

> Bo-beh-*oh*-bee sang the lips,
> Veh-eh-*oh*-mee sang the glances,
> Pee-eh-*eh*-oh sang the brows,
> Li-eh-*ehy* sang the face,
> Gzee-gzee-gz*eh*-oh sang the chain.
> And so on the canvas of certain correspondences
> Beyond dimensions there lived a Face.

> (Bobeóbi pélis' gúby,
> Veeómi pélis' vzóry,
> Pieéo pélis' bróvi,
> Lieéei – pélsia óblik,
> Gzi-gzi-gzéo pélas' tsép'.
> Ták na kholsté kakíkh-to sootvétstvii
> Vne protiazhéniia zhílo Litsó.)[2]

2 Velimir Khlebnikov, 'Bobeóbi pelis' guby' [Bo-beh-*oh*-bee sang the lips], in *Sobranie sochinenii v shesti tomakh* [Complete works in six volumes] (Moscow: IMLI RAN, 'Nasledie', 2000–6), vol. I, p. 198.

The soundscape of the poem evokes what is being described: plosive conson-
ants /b/ and /p/ are used to depict the lips, while a fricative /z/ echoes the
sound of a chain. The poem uses the metaphor of a canvas, but the artistry
makes use of sounds, rather than colours, for effect.

Maiakovskii, too, used neologisms, but his greatest contributions were
perhaps in his experimental rhymes and his innovative imagery. In an early
programmatic poem, 'But Could You?' (*A vy mogli by?*, 1913), he threw down
the gauntlet to the reader, concluding with the lines:

> And you
> could you
> play a nocturne
> on a wastepipe flute?[3]

The promise to create poetry out of urban squalor – the unlikely source of the
drainpipe – typified not only Maiakovskii's ambition but also his sense of
humour and penchant for hyperbolic metaphors.

Kruchenykh was the most radical of the group, eschewing conventional
language altogether and creating what he called a new 'transrational language' or *zaum'*, which would recapture the newness of the world, soiled by
centuries of literary convention and cliché. Kruchenykh invented words that
supposedly had a primordial connection to the thing that they described: for
example, a lily would be *euy*, instead of the familiar Russian word *liliia*, which
had been 'soiled' and 'raped' by established use.[4] Kruchenykh wrote short
poems entirely in *zaum'*, such as 'Dyr bul shchyl' (*Dyr bul shchyl*, 1913). While
zaum' poetry had limited appeal, the Futurists' ideas of verbal experimentation, their innovations in rhythm and rhyme, and their challenge to representational art had an enormous impact on Russian literature.

Acmeist Restraint

'In view of the enormous emotional excitement connected with works of art
it is desirable that talk about art be distinguished by the greatest restraint.'[5]
Thus wrote Mandelshtam in 'The Morning of Acmeism' (*Utro akmeizma*,

---

3 V. V. Maiakovskii, 'A vy mogly by?' [But could you?], in *Polnoe sobranie sochinenii v
   trinadtsati tomakh* [Complete works in thirteen volumes] (Moscow: Gosudarstvennoe
   izdatel'stvo khudozhestvennoi literatury, 1955–61), vol. I, p. 40.
4 A. Kruchenykh, 'Declaration of the word as such', in Anna Lawton (ed.), *Russian
   Futurism through Its Manifestoes, 1912–1928* (Ithaca: Cornell University Press, 1988), p. 67.
5 Osip Mandelshtam, 'The morning of Acmeism', trans. Clarence Brown as
   'Mandelshtam's Acmeist manifesto', *Russian Review* 24.1 (1965), 47.

comp. 1913, pub. 1921), a manifesto of sorts for the Acmeist movement. Mandelshtam's remarks are a rejoinder to the scandal and hubbub around Futurism. Whereas Futurists dismissed heritage and tradition as irrelevant, the Acmeists saw themselves as the cosmopolitan heirs to a European tradition. Mandelshtam's manifesto draws inspiration from J. S. Bach's Baroque compositions and from the medieval Gothic cathedrals of Europe. Metaphors of construction and architecture are particularly prevalent in Mandelshtam's early poetry: his first collection was titled *Stone* (*Kamen'*, 1913) and included programmatic poems on 'Notre Dame' (*Notre Dame*) and 'Hagia Sophia' (*Aiia-Sofiia*). The latter extolled the Byzantine place of worship not so much as a religious site but as a great achievement of human civilisation and a demonstration of how culture endures throughout the ages:

> And this sagacious spherical building
> Will outlive the world's peoples and centuries,
> And the plangent weeping of seraphim
> Will not tarnish the dark gold surfaces.[6]

For the Acmeists, the Futurists had erred by concentrating merely on the formal properties of words, which were empty shells if deprived of what Mandelshtam called their 'conscious sense of the word': its 'Logos'.[7] The Symbolists, on the other hand, had erred by focusing exclusively on the transcendental realm rather than the phenomenal world; in Mandelshtam's memorable phrase, the Symbolists 'did not feel quite themselves in the cage of their own organisms'.[8] An alternative to Symbolism's de-emphasising of the body is seen as early as Mandelshtam's 1909 poem 'Breathing' (*Dykhanie*), which would later serve as the opening poem for *Stone*. The poem begins:

> I've been given a body – what will I do with it?
> So singular, so much my own.[9]

These lines reveal Acmeist poetry as a physiological poetry that insists on putting embodiment at the centre of human experience.

The Acmeists' keen sense of embodiment and physicality is similarly present in the poetry of Akhmatova, the other key figure in the movement. Yet Akhmatova's poetry also appears markedly personal. She created a compelling poetic persona, whom she placed in intimate and domestic

---

6 Osip Mandel'shtam, 'Aiia-Sofia' [Hagia Sofia], in *Kamen': Stikhi* [Stone: Poems] (St Petersburg: Akme, 1913), p. 30.
7 Mandelshtam, 'Mandelshtam's Acmeist manifesto', 48.
8 Mandelshtam, 'Mandelshtam's Acmeist manifesto', 49.
9 Mandel'shtam, 'Dykhanie' [Breathing], in *Kamen'*, p. 1.

situations. Though her persona was distinctively feminine, Akhmatova frequently challenged conventional representations of femininity. She also possessed a measure of self-irony. These features are exhibited in her 1912 collection *Evening* (*Vecher*), in poems such as 'I wrung my hands under my dark veil' (*Szhala ruki pod temnoi vual'iu* ..., 1911) and 'Song of the Last Meeting' (*Pesnia poslednei vstrechi*, 1911), both of which depict romantic separations. The latter poem contains the detail of the poet-speaker absent-mindedly putting her left glove on her right hand, a small physiological detail that expresses her psychological turmoil in a move that would become emblematic of Akhmatova's style. She frequently made excursions into the European literary canon, myth, and the Bible, reimagining familiar narratives from a wry woman's perspective. To give just two examples, Ophelia speaks back to Hamlet in 'Reading Hamlet' (*Chitaia Gamleta*, 1909), and 'Lot's Wife' (*Lotova zhena*, 1924) offers a sympathetic portrait of the biblical figure who defied God's command not to look back on her burning hometown. Akhmatova humanises Lot's wife, justifying her decision to look back as the impulse of a mother leaving her family home and its memories. Moreover, Akhmatova establishes her own role as a poet who speaks for the women who are excluded from the grand, epic narratives of history that are normally authored by men:

> Who will grieve for this woman?
> Does she not seem the smallest of losses?
> My heart alone will never forget
> The one who gave her own life for a single glance back.[10]

After 1917, Akhmatova decided not to leave Russia, and this decision became part of her poetic persona as she established herself as a spokeswoman for those who had chosen to stay behind – and their suffering. She fell out of favour: her personal brand of lyricism appeared inappropriate in the Soviet Union, which demanded an art of epic proportions. However, she produced the remarkable *Requiem* (*Rekviem*) in the 1930s, continuing to revise it into the 1960s. On one level, this poem addresses the Stalinist Terror from the autobiographical perspective of a mother who saw her son imprisoned. Yet on another, mythological, level, Akhmatova identifies with Mary, Mother of God, and with Mother Russia. Here, she further develops the idea of herself as the voice of oppressed women, projecting her critique of

---

10 Anna Akhmatova, 'Lotova zhena' [Lot's wife], in *Sobranie sochinenii v shesti tomakh* [Collected works in six volumes], vol. I, *Stikhotvoreniia 1904–1941* [Poems 1904–1941] (Moscow: Ellis Lak, 1998), p. 402.

Stalin's Terror onto a broader mythological canvas. The poem circulated orally in the 1930s, first appearing in print abroad in 1963 and in the Soviet Union only in 1987. Akhmatova's longest and most complex work, *Poem without a Hero* (*Poema bez geroia*, comp. 1940–62), is a polyphonic, metatextual meditation on the art and personalities of Russian Modernism, depicting the initial promise of the twentieth century; its descent into revolution, war, and terror; and her own unlikely survival when so many others fell.

Mandelshtam was one who did not survive; his attempts to reconcile Soviet socialism with his world view, based on a mixture of Judeo-Christian and cosmopolitan European heritages, ultimately failed. Mandelshtam's ambivalence towards the Soviet project resulted in some works praising the regime in the 1930s but a larger number questioning it, including the notorious Stalin epigram 'We live, not feeling the land beneath us' (*My zhivem, pod soboiu ne chuia strany*, comp. 1933), which expressed the climate of fear and contained a thinly veiled attack on Stalin himself (see Chapter 4.2). Mandelshtam, who had spent much of the decade in internal exile, was sentenced to five years in the Gulag in 1938 and died in transit to the camps.

Poetry in Revolution

While the Acmeists were not temperamentally or philosophically inclined to welcome the Bolsheviks, other Modernists viewed the revolution as the great transformation that they had long prophesied. Some Symbolists saw it as the cleansing apocalypse that would herald a new world, as seen in Belyi's poem 'Russia' (*Rossiia*), written in the summer of 1917, which exhorted Russia to rage with a purifying fire. Blok's long poem *The Twelve* (*Dvenadtsat'*, 1918), widely acknowledged as his masterpiece, mixes the sacred and the profane as it follows twelve revolutionaries through the streets of Petrograd. Though the poem was ostensibly written in praise of the revolution, it concludes with the unlikely appearance of Jesus Christ at the head of the gang of revolutionaries, hardly in keeping with Marxism-Leninism. Blok admitted his amazement at his own ending but also insisted on its inevitability: 'Unfortunately it has to be Christ.'[11] This uneasy fusion of revolutionary enthusiasm with mythological or philosophical world views apparently alien to socialism is common among Modernists in the revolutionary years and also marks the

---

11 Aleksandr Blok, *Sobranie sochinenii v vos'mi tomakh* [Collected works in eight volumes], vol. III, *Stikhotvoreniia i poemy 1907–1921* [Lyric and narrative poems 1907–1921] (Moscow: Gosudarstvennoe izdatel'stvo khudozhestvennoi literatury, 1960), p. 628.

work of some Futurists, particularly Khlebnikov. For example, his super-tale *Zangezi* (*Zangezi*, 1922) is a complex but fragmented experimental work that reflects his interest in transcribing birdsong, the Nietzschean usurpation of godhood, and the sense of freedom offered by linguistic experimentation – all of which appear distant from the task of building socialism.

Many in the Communist Party were nonplussed, even embarrassed, by their avant-garde supporters and their work. Vladimir Lenin dismissed Modernist experimentation as mere iconoclasm for its own sake, confessing, 'I cannot value the works of expressionism, futurism, cubism, and the other isms as the highest expression of artistic genius. I do not understand them.'[12] He preferred nineteenth-century Realism (see Chapter 1.5), particularly the work of Nikolai Chernyshevskii (1828–1889), and admitted to enjoying novels by Ivan Turgenev (1818–1883) and Lev Tolstoi (1828–1910), even if he did not share their politics.[13] While Lenin himself never developed a full-fledged theory of literature, the role of culture was a priority for the party in the post-revolutionary years as the Bolsheviks began the task of building social-ism throughout the Soviet Union. Literature, culture, and education became the preserve of the newly founded Narkompros, the People's Commissariat for Enlightenment. Lunacharskii, the first to lead this commissariat, was not only a dedicated revolutionary but a poet, playwright, and critic in his own right. More favourably disposed to experimental art and literature than Lenin, Lunacharskii patronised the Futurists as they sought to reinvent themselves as communists and supported experiments in theatre such as Meierkhold's biomechanics and Constructivist set design. Lunacharskii's promotion of the avant-garde frequently enervated Lenin, who wished to see more conventional Realist art serving the revolution. Correspondence from 1921 reveals Lenin's reaction to Lunacharskii ordering five thousand copies of Maiakovskii's narrative poem '150 000 000' (1921): Lenin called it 'rubbish' and 'pretentious nonsense' and called for 'no more than 1500 copies, for libraries and eccentrics'. 'And Lunacharskii should be whipped for his Futurism', Lenin added.[14]

Lunacharskii was also a leading figure in Proletkult, a cultural organisation founded just weeks before the revolution of October 1917. The organisation

---

12 Lenin's remarks appear in Clara Zetkin's *Reminiscences of Lenin* (New York: International Publishers, 1934), pp. 12–13.

13 See Stanley W. Page, 'Lenin, Turgenev, and the Russian landed gentry,' *Canadian Slavonic Papers* 18.4 (1976), 442–56.

14 V. I. Lenin and A. V. Lunacharskii, *Pis'ma. Doklady. Dokumenty*. [Letters. Speeches. Documents] (Moscow: Nauka, 1971), p. 281.

took its name from a portmanteau of the Russian words *proletarskaia kul'tura* (proletarian culture) and sought to give voice to the working class through a new, proletarian aesthetic. It began as an autonomous organisation, existing outside party control, but Lunacharskii used his position in Narkompros to support the organisation politically and financially. Representative of this movement is the following poem of Vasilii Kazin (1898–1981), one of the Smithy (*Kuznitsa*) poets that celebrated the sweat and labour of the working class:

> I plod homewards towards the Presnia
> My shoulders sore and warm with sweat,
> Still my worker's apron sings a red song
> Sings of bricks to the darkness.[15]

However, Lenin sought to curtail the autonomy of Proletkult, seeing alien influences in its ideological make-up, including the prominent role of Aleksandr Bogdanov (1873–1928), the revolutionary and intellectual who had once been a rival to Lenin in the Bolshevik party, before his expulsion in 1908. At the behest of Lenin, Proletkult was formally incorporated into Narkompros in late 1920, and the 'proletarian' label would later be claimed in the 1920s by writers fiercely opposed to the avant-garde. Nevertheless, the original organisation's promotion of a working-class aesthetic had a lasting influence on Soviet culture well into the 1920s.

The 'Peasant' Poets

Whereas the Futurist poets (at least in their post-revolutionary phase) and the Proletkult movement usually concentrated on urban environments – cities, factories, and proletarian workers – the post-revolutionary period also saw a flowering of 'peasant' poets whose work depicted the Russian countryside and the changes wrought by modernisation and the revolution. I place 'peasant' in inverted commas here because, although the movement's key poets depicted themselves as the champions of the Russian countryside, they were not working in the fields; rather, they were educated writers who were embedded in the literary circles of the two capitals.

The outstanding figure was Sergei Esenin (1895–1925), whose personal, and often melancholic work was accessible enough to grant him a celebrity status above and beyond the recognition normally afforded to poets. Like

---

15 Vasilii Kazin, 'Kamenshchik' [The bricklayer], in *Lirika* [Lyrics] (Moscow: Sovetskii pisatel', 1960), p. 6.

Maiakovskii and Akhmatova, Esenin was a figure whose poetic mythmaking extended beyond the page to encompass his entire life. In a programmatic poem, he proclaimed himself the 'last poet of the countryside', imagining his homeland destroyed by the forces of modernity:

> Soon, soon, the wooden clock,
> Will strike out my twelve in a rasp![16]

Esenin predicted his own demise and lived it out publicly. He was pursued by the secret police in the 1920s and suffered from alcoholism and fits of depression. He took his own life on 28 December 1925. Esenin's early death, his striking looks, and his emotional verse ensured an enduring popularity, and he remains one of the most widely read poets in Russia today.

Another prominent figure in the peasant movement was Nikolai Kliuev (1884–1937). Initially close to the Symbolists, Kliuev shared their spiritual interests, but for him, spirituality was found embodied in the Russian countryside, in its nature and its dwellers. His poem 'Youth' (*Iunost'*, 1927) celebrates youth, imagining his own body as part of nature's beauty. The central motif of the poet-speaker's red tie, which he compares to a carnation, symbolises both his loyalty to the communist cause and his relationship to nature. Kliuev thus attempt to reconcile Soviet symbolism with lyrical images of the Russian countryside and to thereby carve out a place for himself in the new Soviet Union. However, these attempts did not succeed. He was persecuted during the Great Terror – his religious views and his homosexuality did not fit well with Stalinism. In 1937 he was arrested for involvement in a monarchist conspiracy, and he was shot in late October of that year. There was no evidence such a conspiracy ever existed, and Kliuev was 'rehabilitated' during the period of reforms known as the Thaw that followed Stalin's death.

Homesickness: The Case of Marina Tsvetaeva

If the peasant poets lamented the mechanisation of the Russian countryside, then this sense of lament for a lost place and time is even stronger in Tsvetaeva's work. In one of Tsvetaeva's most famous poems, 'Missing my homeland' (*Toska po rodine*, 1934), written in emigration in Paris, the

---

16 S. A. Esenin, 'Ia poslednii poet dereveni' [I am the last poet of the countryside], in *Polnoe sobranie sochinenii v semi tomakh* [Complete works in seven volumes], vol. I, *Stikhotvoreniia* [Lyric poetry] (Moscow: Nauka, 1995–2005), p. 136.

poet-speaker contrasts herself with a man reading a newspaper, who is keeping up with the latest developments in the twentieth-century world:

> He belongs to the twentieth century,
> But, before any century, I am.[17]

Typically for Tsvetaeva, these lines represent not only a separation of space – she is physically detached from her homeland – but also of time. Her Russia has vanished, and, moreover, she imagines herself and her poetry belonging to a realm outside of space and time altogether.

This powerful sense of individuality, of loneliness, and of disconnection characterises much of Tsvetaeva's output. Her work has a candid, emotional intensity that can leave her readers overwhelmed, even embarrassed. Formally, this is achieved with a distinctive style that makes characteristic use of word play, particularly with the roots of Russian words, their derivations, and their associations. She makes frequent use of enjambment, exclamation, and ellipsis as well as of experimentation with rhythm and rhyme. Such formal innovation should make her a natural ally of the avant-garde and the Futurists, at least in terms of aesthetics, yet Tsvetaeva eschewed the membership of any movement or school. Moreover, she was unsympathetic to the revolution politically and produced a brilliant satire on the Bolsheviks, their ideology, and especially their language in her narrative poem *The Ratcatcher* (*Krysolov*, 1925–6), which retold the legend of the Pied Piper of Hamelin with the rats cast as the Bolsheviks. Tsvetaeva lived in emigration from 1922 to 1939 and died by suicide in 1941 shortly after her return to the Soviet Union.

Maiakovskii, Komfut, and the Left Front of the Arts

While Tsvetaeva fled the revolution and satirised it, many of Russia's avant-garde writers embraced it. Maiakovskii was perhaps the most successful in his attempt to marry the avant-garde aesthetics of Futurism with the social and political demands of the new regime. Poems such as '150 000 000' not only praised the revolution but aimed to provide a new language for revolutionary art, one based on Maiakovskii's characteristic use of colloquialisms, neologisms, extended metaphors, and unexpected rhymes. Moreover, Maiakovskii created a mythology of the artist as equally important to the revolution as the

---

17 M. I. Tsvetaeva, 'Toska po rodine! Davno . . .' [Missing my homeland! Long ago . . .], in *Stikhotvoreniia i poemy* [Lyric and narrative poems] (Leningrad: Sovetskii pisatel', 1990), p. 436.

manual worker or the soldier. This vision is central to poems such as 'The Poet-Worker' (*Poet rabochii*, 1918) and 'Order to the Army of Arts' (*Prikaz po armii iskusstv*, 1918).

Maiakovskii's penchant for exaggerated metaphors was now redeployed in service of socialism, as in 'The Poet-Worker' where he compares himself to a factory:

> Perhaps
> for us (poets)
> labour
> is more natural than any other activity.
> I too am a factory.
> And if I don't have chimneys,
> then, just maybe,
> that makes things harder for me.[18]

The poem places an equal value on physical labour and the craft of poetry: indeed, with typical hyperbole, Maiakovksii compares himself not just to a single labourer but to an entire factory. He remarks that he doesn't 'have chimneys', and yet the very shape of the poem – a thin, vertical column – evokes a smokestack, as if the poem is a physical product. Maiakovskii's stentorian bass and powerful reading of his poems also created the impression that poetry – or at least *his* poetry – was a physically demanding, masculine activity.

During the civil war years (1919–22), Maiakovskii also served the revolution by designing agitational propaganda (agitprop) posters to spread the messages of socialism to the masses. These satirical posters or 'windows' typically featured bright colours, cartoonish illustrations, and key messages from the Bolsheviks, often presented in rhyming form. This simple, bold aesthetic shows an effective fusion of the avant-garde and political messaging, an aesthetic which would prove influential in Soviet design for decades to come.

In 1919, a group of Futurists – including Maiakovskii, Brik, and the poet and critic Boris Kushner (1888–1937) – established a collective of Communist-Futurists, or Komfut. Komfut criticised the nascent Soviet institutions for not being sufficiently radical in their opposition to bourgeois art and culture. Their manifesto, laid out in their journal *Art of the Commune* (*Iskusstvo*

---

18 V. V. Maiakovskii, 'Poet rabochii' [The poet-worker], in *Polnoe sobranie sochinenii v trinadtsati tomakh* [Complete works in thirteen volumes] (Moscow: Gosudarstvennoe izdatel'stvo khudozhestvennoi literatury, 1956–61), vol. II, p. 18.

kommuny, 1918–19), stated that 'all forms of everyday life [*byt*], morality, philosophy and art' must be 're-created on a communist basis'.[19] Komfut proved short-lived, lasting only until 1921, but the name stuck throughout the 1920s as a label to refer to those who called for radical formal experimentation. Many members of Komfut later became members of the Left Front of the Arts (*Levyi front iskusstv*) group (known as LEF), which produced the journals *LEF* and *New LEF*. Maiakovskii, who served as general editor for both journals for the majority of their run, was considered the leader of the group. Like many projects of the Russian avant-garde, *LEF* brought together literature and visual art: several Constructivist artists and designers were involved, including Varvara Stepanova (1894–1958) and Aleksandr Rodchenko (1891–1956), the latter of whom designed the cover art for several issues of *LEF* and *New LEF*.

LEF's manifestoes reveal a desire among the Futurists to apologise for the clownish elements of their pre-revolutionary art. They emphasised how their pre-revolutionary art had challenged the bourgeoisie and admitted they had been politically naïve at times, but they claimed that they had been politically educated by the revolution. LEF took a strident, belligerent tone towards their rivals, such as those in the October (*Oktiabr'*) group, who called themselves 'proletarian writers' but who opposed formal experimentation and held strictly to the party line on matters such as the New Economic Policy (NEP), which granted limited permission to petty entrepreneurs in an attempt to address the economic crisis of the 1920s. The avant-garde, by contrast, criticised the NEP, satirising it famously in works such as Maiakovskii's 1929 play *The Bedbug* (*Klop*). Moreover, whereas LEF argued against formal conservatism, the October group warned against an emphasis on formal experimentation for its own sake. LEF believed that artistic activity itself was a form of life-construction (*zhiznestroenie*), a concept with echoes of the more individualistic and Romantic idea of life-creation (*zhiznetvorchestvo*) among the Symbolists (see Chapter 1.6). They defended their artistic work as politically agitational and rhetorically positioned themselves on the left of the debates about what kind of art should be produced in the Soviet Union. They renewed their attack against the classics and against contemporary opponents who proposed using traditional forms such as the Realist novel: 'with all our strength, we will fight against bringing the working methods of the dead into the art of today'.[20]

19 'Kommunisty-futuristy' [Communists-Futurists], *Iskusstvo kommuny* [Art of the commune] 8 (1919), 3.
20 LEF, 'V kogo vgryzaetsia LEF?' [Whom does LEF bite?], *LEF: Zhurnal levogo fronta iskusstv* [LEF: Journal of the Left Front of the Arts] 1 (March 1923), 8.

LEF versus RAPP

By the middle of the 1920s, firm battle lines had been drawn between the avant-garde, who defended formal experimentation as the *sine qua non* of revolutionary writing, and the self-professed 'proletarian' writers who emphasised the need for content to be ideologically correct. The party, itself beset by political factionalism, sought to respond to these diverging tendencies in June 1925 with a policy resolution on literature designed to clarify the official position. However, this resolution deliberately avoided granting official approval to any one tendency in literature, instead stating squarely that 'the party cannot support any one single faction in literature' and favouring 'the free competition of various groups and tendencies in this field'.[21] This resolution also called for tolerance towards the so-called fellow travellers (*poputchiki*), a term used to cover a wide array of writers who, while not opposed to the revolution, had not fully understood or embraced communism – at least in the view of the party. While the resolution called for the 'merciless' pursuit of 'antiproletarian' and 'counter-revolutionary' elements, it also emphasised the benefits of a diversity of approaches to proletarian literature and admitted that no definite answers had emerged on the question of artistic forms. This resolution bore the hallmarks of Lev Trotskii (1879–1940; see Box 5.3), who had taken a similarly tolerant position in his book *Literature and Revolution* (*Literatura i revoliutsiia*, 1923), insisting on the importance of literature to the revolution but refusing to commit to any particular tendency.

However, the resolution of 1925 served only to intensify the debates. The proletarian writers, now centred in a group known as the Russian Association of Proletarian Writers (*Rossiiskaia assotsiatsiia proletarskikh pisatelei*, or RAPP), launched increasingly vocal attacks on both the fellow travellers and the avant-garde. Under the leadership of Leopold Averbakh (1903–1937), RAPP openly called for Soviet writers to learn from the classics and praised the psychological novel as the best vehicle for proletarian culture. The ranks of RAPP included Dmitrii Furmanov (1891–1926), who had already published such a novel – *Chapaev* (*Chapaev*, 1923) – about the eponymous civil war hero, and Fadeev, whose 1927 novel *The Rout* brought Tolstoian Realism to the civil war. In response, LEF attacked RAPP in the pages of *New LEF*, mocking their

---

21 Postanovlenie Politbiuro TsK RKP(b) [Resolution of the Politburo of the Central Committee of the Bolshevik Party], 'O politike partii v oblasti khudozhestvennoi literatury' [On party policy in the field of literature] (18 June 1925), Lomonosov Moscow State University Faculty of History Electronic Resources Library, www.hist .msu.ru/ER/Etext/USSR/1925.htm, accessed 14 Feb. 2021.

quest for a 'red Tolstoi' and criticising the psychological novel as an exhausted art form.[22] Indeed, LEF had moved entirely away from fiction by the 1920s, calling instead for what they called a 'literature of fact', one based on genres such as newspapers, diaries, and memoirs rather than the novel with its focus on character and plot. Sergei Tretiakov (1892–1937) was a powerful voice in LEF defending this kind of documentary writing as the authentic literature of socialism and railing against the 'aesthetic-stupefying function' of belles-lettres.[23] LEF took as its exemplars works such as Shklovskii's *Third Factory* (*Tret'ia fabrika*, 1926), a hybrid text which is part autobiography, part manifesto, part satire, with an episodic structure and little discernible plot.

Yet this kind of formally innovative writing had limited popular appeal, and it was RAPP that gained the upper hand at the end of the decade. Maiakovskii, the stalwart defender of the avant-garde, resigned from LEF in 1928, and, after an abortive attempt to set up REF in 1929 – the Revolutionary Front of Art (*Revoliutsionnyi front iskusstva*) – joined RAPP in March 1930. Beset by both personal and professional anxieties, he took his own life one month later. The year 1930 is generally seen as the end date for Russian Futurism, and the following years saw the centralisation of literature and increased party control and censorship, with the establishment of the Writers' Union in 1932 and the adoption of Socialist Realism as the officially sanctioned mode of writing in 1934.

Conclusions

Histories of twentieth-century Russian literature have often told the story of a thriving, diverse, experimental literary scene in the 1910s and 1920s that is suddenly interrupted in the 1930s under the Stalinist dictatorship, with the emergence of Socialist Realism having a stultifying effect. According to this narrative, the line of Russian literature's development was artificially broken in the Soviet Union by a repressive regime, and Russian Modernism continued only among Russian writers in emigration or in secret among writers such as Akhmatova or Pasternak who wrote 'for the desk drawer', that is, without the expectation of publication. It is certainly true that the 1930s marked a threshold in Russian and Soviet literature, and one cannot deny

22 See S. Tret'iakov, 'Novyi Lev Tolstoi' [A new Lev Tolstoi], *LEF: Zhurnal levogo fronta iskusstv* 1 (1927), 34–8.
23 S. Tretyakov, 'Happy New Year! Happy *New Left!*', in Lawton (ed.), *Russian Futurism*, p. 267.

the real effects of state coercion on the development of literature. One cannot count the cost to literature – and the sheer human cost – of the deaths of writers such as Babel, Mandelshtam, or Pilniak, victims of state terror, or indeed the cost of the silence of authors such as Olesha, who largely stopped writing in the 1930s. The suicides of writers such as Esenin, Maiakovskii, and Tsvetaeva can also be attributed in part to the oppressive political climate of the 1930s and 1940s.

Yet it would be wrong to see the development of Russian literature in these years in black-and-white terms as a story of heroic, talented writers and artists, committed to freedom and struggling against a repressive state apparatus of hacks and toadies who sought to stifle all artistic independence and liberty. Such a narrative had an obvious appeal during the Cold War period in the west for ideological purposes and was also cultivated among dissident circles within the Soviet Union. However, this narrative is deficient for a number of reasons. First, it operates on an underlying – flawed – assumption that great literature must necessarily take a stance of political opposition against the current regime. A look at, say, Maiakovskii's ode to Lenin, *Vladimir Ilich Lenin* (*Vladimir Il'ich Lenin*, 1924) – a complex work that praises Lenin, the revolution, and the goal of communism, while questioning the emerging cult of Lenin at the time – provides evidence to challenge that assumption.

Second, the heroic narrative ignores the historical fact that writers were not faced with a binary choice between liberty and conformity but, rather, had to negotiate a complex set of circumstances if they wished to publish their work and – eventually – if they wished to survive. Even a writer such as Bulgakov, largely critical of the Soviet project, cultivated a working relationship with Stalin and wrote a flattering play about the leader's youth. His novel *The Master and Margarita* (*Master i Margarita*, comp. 1928–40, pub. 1966–7) should be read not simply as a satire of Stalinism and the Stalinist literary establishment but as a study of the writer's complicity (including his own) with state power. Historians now discuss the history of the early Soviet period not in terms of individuals who were for or against the regime, or in terms of citizens who believed or saw through the ideology. Rather, historians speak in terms of Soviet citizens' subjectivity and their ability to negotiate Soviet ideology and institutions.[24] The same is true of writers in this

24 For an overview of the literature on Soviet subjectivity, see Choi Chatterjee and Karen Petrone, 'Models of selfhood and subjectivity: The Soviet case in historical perspective', *Slavic Review* 67.4 (2008), 967–86.

period, with the caveat that some of the leading writers also had the ability to influence state power and ideology through their work.

Third, it is important to remember that many writers in this period, even those persecuted under the Soviet system, did not favour a liberal, western-style alternative to the Soviet project. The avant-garde writers associated with LEF, for example, were not calling for freedom of speech or the removal of censorship; rather, they envisaged greater formal experimentation precisely because they believed such experimentation led to writing that was *more* politically engaged. In this light, it is important to add that the emergence of Socialist Realism in the 1930s should not be seen simply as the victory of artistic traditionalism, as it arguably constitutes a kind of artistic experiment in itself. The best Socialist Realist novels, such as *Time, Forward!* (*Vremia, vpered!*, 1932) by Valentin Kataev (1897–1986), collapse time and space in a way obviously indebted to their Modernist predecessors. *Time, Forward!*, for example, charts a frantic attempt in one factory to break the record for concrete production. The critic Boris Groys (1947–) has made the intriguing argument that the Russian avant-garde planted the seeds for Socialist Realism (at least in the field of visual art), a perspective that challenges the view that Russian Modernism was artificially interrupted in the 1930s.[25] A rather different perspective is offered by Evgeny Dobrenko (see Chapter 1.8), who suggests that the so-called revolutionary avant-garde was nothing more than traditional pre-revolutionary art and that Socialist Realism was the only art *produced by* the Bolshevik revolution.

What is indisputable is the powerful legacy that Russian Modernism and the avant-garde have had on literature inside and outside Russia. Discounting, for a moment, Groys's hypothesis about Socialist Realism being a kind of avant-garde in its own right, the most immediate impact of Modernism on Russian literature may have arrived in the post-Stalin years of the 1950s and 1960s. This period saw a new generation of writers – including poets such as Evgenii Evtushenko (1932–2017) and Andrei Voznesenskii (1933–2010), and experimental prose writers such as Sasha Sokolov (1943–) or Iurii Mamleev (1931–2015) – who (re)discovered Modernism and formal experimentation as many suppressed works came into print and it became possible to challenge the dictates of Socialist Realism, at least up to a point. From the 1970s, nonconformist writers such as Dmitrii Prigov (1940–2007), Lev Rubinshtein (1947–2024), and Vladimir Sorokin (1955–) drew on Modernist inspiration; the way in which their writing often challenges the automatic

25 Boris Groys, *The Total Art of Stalinism* (Princeton: Princeton University Press, 1992).

perception and (Soviet) orthodoxies recalls Formalist ideas from early in the century.

The boomerang of Modernism returned again in the Glasnost era of the late 1980s, when key works such as Akhmatova's *Requiem* and Bulgakov's *Heart of a Dog* saw official publication for the first time in the Soviet Union; these works offered Russians access to a history and tradition that had been denied to them. Beyond Russia's borders, the Russian-American poet Joseph Brodsky (1940–1996) kept the flame of Russian Modernism alive in emigration: he was particularly indebted to Mandelshtam and Akhmatova, sharing their sense that the poet belongs to, and contributes to, world culture. The Northern Irish poet Seamus Heaney, a friend of Brodsky, was also drawn to Mandelshtam and his belief in the restorative power of poetry in the context of the Troubles, the conflict that dominated Northern Ireland in the second half of the twentieth century. Elsewhere, the more radical, politically charged poetry of Maiakovskii found imitators and admirers, particularly among the American Left: the declamatory political poetry of Allen Ginsberg was inspired by Maiakovskii, while the gay New York poet Frank O'Hara channelled the Russian's overblown style. The Futurists' influence has been felt as far afield as Brazil, where Augusto and Haroldo de Campos translated Khlebnikov and Maiakovskii, whose work provided inspiration for their concrete poetry.

Brodsky supposedly once quipped that the only thing that poetry and politics have in common is the fact that they both begin with the letters *p* and *o*.[26] But Brodsky, a poet deeply versed in Russian Modernism and the avant-garde, must have understood the profound, inextricable connection between the two. Reading Russian writers from this period alerts us to the enormous political potential of poetic language, as we see in the work of the Futurists and LEF, who aimed at nothing less than changing the world through their artistic experiments. Yet the Russian avant-garde also shows us the dangers of the limitations of such a belief, and their possible consequences, which are revealed to powerful effect in the later poetry of Blok as well as the work of Akhmatova and Tsvetaeva.

Further Reading

Balina, Marina, and Evgenii Dobrenko (eds.), *The Cambridge Companion to Twentieth-Century Russian Literature* (Cambridge: Cambridge University Press, 2011).

26 Joseph Brodsky, quoted in Lev Loseff, 'Politics/Poetics', in Brodsky, *Poetics and Aesthetics*, ed. Lev Loseff and Valentina Polukhina (Basingstoke: Macmillan, 1990), p. 34.

Erlich, Victor, *Modernism and Revolution: Russian Literature in Transition* (Cambridge, MA: Harvard University Press, 1994).

Forrester, Sibelan E. S., and Martha M. F. Kelly, *Russian Silver Age Poetry: Texts and Contexts* (Boston: Academic Studies Press, 2015).

Markov, Vladimir, *Russian Futurism: A History* (Berkeley: University of California Press, 1968).

Masing, Irene-Delic, *From Symbolism to Socialist Realism: A Reader* (Brighton, MA: Academic Studies Press, 2011).

Paperno, Irina, and Joan Delaney Grossman (eds.), *Creating Life: The Aesthetic Utopia of Russian Modernism* (Stanford: Stanford University Press, 1994).

I.8

Socialist Realism

EVGENY DOBRENKO

Socialist Realism was the (only) art officially sponsored in the Soviet Union after 1934. It emerged, developed, and faded away along with the Soviet regime. The uniqueness and specificity of Socialist Realism lies in the fact that it was the product of the activity of the state and bureaucracy. This gave Socialist Realism originality and novelty. However, the combination of the political servility, explicit propagandistic aims, and aesthetic inferiority of this populist art has made it largely unpopular among literary critics and scholars, who view Socialist Realism as lowbrow mass culture.

Nevertheless, discussions about the nature and genesis of Socialist Realism have proliferated since the mid-1950s when, after Stalin's death, Andrei Siniavskii (1925–1997, pseud. Abram Terts) published a pamphlet 'On Socialist Realism' (Chto takoe sotsialisticheskii realizm, 1957) in tamizdat (published outside the Soviet Union; see Chapter 2.9). Siniavskii argued that Socialist Realism had nothing to do with either socialism or realism. Rather, it should be seen as a modern version of Classicism.[1] Following Siniavskii, Socialist Realism has been analysed not only as a purely political phenomenon, as it was viewed by traditional Sovietology,[2] but variously as the Soviet version of the Bildungsroman;[3] a confirmation of the return of Soviet society to petty bourgeois ideals and values;[4] the realisation of a revolutionary aesthetic utopia;[5] a distorted version of the aesthetics of the

1 Abram Tertz, 'The Trial Begins' and 'On Socialist Realism', trans. Max Hayward and George Denis (New York: Vintage Books, 1960).
2 Max Eastman, Artists in Uniform (New York: A. A. Knopf, 1934); Herman Ermolaev, Soviet Literary Theories, 1917–1934: The Genesis of Socialist Realism (Berkeley: University of California Press, 1963); Ernest Simmons, Through the Glass of Soviet Literature (New York: Columbia University Press, 1953).
3 Katerina Clark, The Soviet Novel: History as Ritual (Chicago: University of Chicago Press, 1985).
4 Vera Dunham, In Stalin's Time: Middleclass Values in Soviet Fiction (Cambridge: Cambridge University Press, 1976).
5 Régine Robin, Socialist Realism: An Impossible Aesthetic, trans. Catherine Porter (Stanford: Stanford University Press, 1992).

Symbolist movement that preceded it;[6] and as the Soviet version of totalitarian kitsch.[7]

Despite all these differences, scholars are largely agreed that Socialist Realism replaced Modernism in Soviet Russia. This idea was clearly articulated by Igor Golomstock. Referring to material from Stalinist Russia, Nazi Germany, Fascist Italy, and communist China, Golomstock argued that 'totalitarian art' follows the same evolutionary trajectory under all anti-liberal regimes.[8] Vladimir Paperny formulated a more specific vision for Russia in his concept of 'Culture 1' (Modernism) and 'Culture 2' (Socialist Realism), arguing that versions of these cultures have replaced one another cyclically over the longue durée of Russian history.[9] Paperny's historicisation and normalisation of Socialist Realism was challenged by Boris Groys, however, who argued that Socialist Realism was not a refutation of avant-garde Modernism but rather its realisation: in Stalin's version of the historical avant-garde, the leader himself becomes an artist-demiurge.[10]

In this chapter we will touch on these and other approaches to Socialist Realism in an attempt to show that it was in fact a much more complex project, which depended not only on aesthetic doctrines and political considerations but on literary institutions, social formations (such as the creation of categories of 'new reader' and the professionalisation of 'new writers')[11], the degradation of Marxism in Russia, and a combination of other factors.

Populist Modernism: From Revolutionary Art to Stalinist Realästhetik

In chronological terms, Socialist Realism replaced the revolutionary art that had dominated the Russian literary and artistic scene in the 1910s and 1920s (see Chapters 1.6, 1.7). According to the prevailing view, early Soviet

6 Irina Gutkin, *The Cultural Origins of the Socialist Realist Aesthetic, 1890–1934* (Evanston, IL: Northwestern University Press, 1999).
7 Svetlana Boym, *Common Places: Mythologies of Everyday Life in Russia* (Cambridge, MA: Harvard University Press, 1994).
8 Igor Golomstock, *Totalitarian Art: In the Soviet Union, the Third Reich, Fascist Italy, and the People's Republic of China*, trans. Robert Chandler (London: Collins Harvill, 1990).
9 Vladimir Paperny, *Architecture in the Age of Stalin: Culture Two*, trans. John Hill and Roann Barris (New York: Cambridge University Press, 2002).
10 Boris Groys, *The Total Art of Stalinism: Avant-Garde, Aesthetic Dictatorship, and Beyond*, trans. Charles Rougle (Princeton: Princeton University Press, 1992).
11 Evgeny Dobrenko, *The Making of the State Reader: Social and Aesthetic Contexts of the Reception of Soviet Literature*, trans. Jesse Savage (Stanford: Stanford University Press, 1997); Evgeny Dobrenko, *The Making of the State Writer: Social and Aesthetic Origins of Soviet Literary Culture*, trans. Jesse Savage (Stanford: Stanford University Press, 2001).

revolutionary art was rooted in Modernism, utopianism, and radical avant-garde practices in its search for a new art to reflect a new world. Hence, all subsequent development in Soviet culture is seen through the prism of an implicit theory of decline, whereby the 1930s are marked by the suppression of avant-garde activity and the imposition of the official doctrine of Socialist Realism from above. This view sees Stalinist culture as monolithic and rigid, as characterised by excessive political control of art, and as destroying revolutionary art and visions of revolutionary utopia.

This view is rooted in an assumed convergence between the revolutionary visions of artists and ideologues in the first decade after 1917. And certainly, since avant-garde artists were anti-establishment, opposed to bourgeois tastes, and disposed towards destructive gestures, they had a predilection for 'revolution'. In practice, however, the utopian dreams of the avant-garde rapidly diverged from those of Bolshevik leaders. As soon as the dust of the civil war settled in the late 1920s, power firmly fell into Stalin's hands. Lenin's utopian slogans of 'international revolution' were replaced by Stalin's pragmatic policy of 'socialism in one country', and it became clear that the Bolshevik 'revolution' was merely a national modernisation project dressed up in Marxist rhetorical garments and that Soviet socialism was nothing more than the construction of state capitalism under socialist slogans. In other words, the Russian Revolution itself was not sufficiently socialist and was too Russian for avant-garde art to become the sanctioned art of the revolution.

I suggest, however, that what is usually called 'the art of the revolution' in Soviet Russia was in fact nothing more than traditional pre-revolutionary art developing in a Modernist direction. Futurism in poetry, abstract art in painting, montage in cinema, and nascent forms of so-called proletarian art had appeared in Russia *before* the revolution. The literary and artistic manifestos of numerous artistic and literary groups of the 1920s reveal that what they called 'revolutionary culture' was, in fact, pre-revolutionary culture – historically, politically, and aesthetically. This culture ranged widely, from LEF – the Left Front of the Arts (*Levyi front iskusstv*, 1922–9) – which was simply red-painted Futurism, to Proletkult, which grew from a pre-revolutionary proletarian literary movement and died with it as a result of the victory of the actual (so-called) proletarian revolution, not to mention the various 'fellow traveller' groups (see Chapter 1.7) that directly appealed to pre-revolutionary cultural traditions.

The 1920s was a time of rapid evolution and creativity in Russian culture. No matter what political views artists espoused, their art was under enormous and persistent political pressure. The clash between traditional culture

and the new regime was always dramatic and usually tragic, but it was also often very productive – as evidenced in the extraordinary works produced by a wide range of writers, from Mikhail Bulgakov (1891–1940) to Andrei Platonov (1899–1951), from Vladimir Maiakovskii (1893–1930) to Boris Pasternak (1890–1960), from Evgenii Zamiatin (1884–1937) to Iurii Olesha (1899–1960), from Isaak Babel (1894–1940) to Mikhail Zoshchenko (1894–1958), from Anna Akhmatova (1889–1966) to Osip Mandelshtam (1891–1938), from Vsevolod Meierkhold (1874–1940) to Dmitrii Shostakovich (1906–1975), from Sergei Eisenstein (1898–1948) to the Ukrainian Soviet Oleksandr Dovzhenko (1894–1956), and from Aleksandr Rodchenko (1891–1956) to Dziga Vertov (1896–1954). These works cannot, however, be seen as culture produced *by* the Bolshevik Revolution. Avant-garde artistic experiment may have continued through the 1920s, but so-called revolutionary culture flourished only as long as the Bolsheviks were preoccupied with the more pressing problems of survival during the first decades of power. Indeed, even during the 1920s, as soon as it became obvious that an independent avant-garde represented potential danger for the regime, that avant-garde was mercilessly crushed. As early as 1920, Lenin destroyed Proletkult. And when the Bolsheviks did turn to creating a new and distinctive culture, they turned first to the 'proletarianisation' of culture, sponsoring a range of 'proletarian' groups such as VAPP – the All-Russian Association of Proletarian Writers (*Vserossiiskaia assotsiatsiia proletarskikh pisatelei*, 1920–5) later RAPP, the Russian Association of Proletarian Writers (*Rossiiskaia assotsiatsiia proletarskikh pisatelei*, 1925–32) – in literature and its equivalents in other arts: RAPM, the Russian Association of Proletarian Musicians (*Rossiiskaia assotsiatsiia proletarskikh muzykantov*, 1923–32), in music; and AKhRR, the Association of Revolutionary Artists (*Assotsiatsiia khudozhnikov revoliutsionnoi Rossii*, 1922–32), in the visual arts. Subsequently they turned to the creation of Socialist Realism and the unequivocal destruction of the avant-garde.

Unlike the avant-garde, Socialist Realism *was* a product of the revolution; in fact, I suggest that it was *the* art of the revolution. It was the product of what we must understand as a populist degeneration of the avant-garde. This had its roots in the evolution of Soviet political structures. Before the October coup of 1917, the key political force of the Russian Revolution was the Socialist Revolution Party, which was traditional left-wing populist and nationalist, preaching an ideology of national agrarian socialism. The smaller Bolshevik Party was politically more opportunistic and managed to outmanoeuvre the Socialist-Revolutionaries to take power in the October

Revolution, but they could not outmanoeuvre the political reality of their largely peasant country.[12]

The Russian Revolution found its final resolution in Stalinism, which was a Russian national version of a universal phenomenon: the conservative reaction of a patriarchal society to processes of modernisation and liberalisation. As such, Stalinism was simultaneously the modernisation and transition of an agrarian society into an industrial one, and a form of resistance to this same process. Examples of such evolutions are found not only in the Soviet Union but also in Fascist Italy, Nazi Germany, and Franco's Spain. All these revolutions, and the regimes born out of them, were first and foremost national revolutions, and they all undertook a process of nation-building through culture.

So what form did Socialist Realism take in literature? It is common to define Socialist Realism following Andrei Zhdanov's (1896–1948) opening speech at the First Congress of Soviet Writers in 1934, when he called for literature that would exhibit ideological commitment (*ideinost'*), party-mindedness (*partiinost'*), and popular spirit (*narodnost'*). In fact, however, the main characteristic of Stalinist culture was its eclecticism. And the only definitive characteristics of Socialist Realism were not ideological commitment or party-mindedness but radical pragmatism (because it was an important element of Stalin's total aesthetic and political project), functionalism (because it had to appeal to the semi-literate peasants who were now being transformed into communist 'workers'), and opportunism (because the doctrine of Socialist Realism was nothing more than a set of vague and contradicting categories).

As the voice of the regime, then, Stalinist culture was more pragmatic and opportunistic than it was ideological. It rested with ease on ideological doctrines that were completely divergent and often even diametrically opposed to each other. But Socialist Realism was also – indeed primarily – a machine for decoding (and re-coding) the desires of the mass audience: its tastes, prejudices, sensitivities, and horizons of expectation. The masses required an appropriate language to be provided to them by the state. The state's project was still more ambitious, however: it was one of moulding the masses into new political subjects. This was a matter of survival.

The revolution changed not only literature but also its audience. The cultured reader of pre-revolutionary Russia was either eliminated during the years of civil

---

12 See Mikhail Agursky, *The Third Rome: National Bolshevism in the USSR* (London: Routledge, 1987); David Brandenberger, *National Bolshevism: Stalinist Mass Culture and the Formation of Modern Russian National Identity 1931–1956* (Cambridge, MA: Harvard University Press, 2002).

war or fled the country. In the 1930s, the new reader was yesterday's illiterate peasant, who had fled to the city from the horrors of the Stalinist collectivisation of the countryside and its associated famine and devastation. In the eyes of the Soviet leadership, this new mass readership – only recently literate (due to vast educational campaigns) – was unprepared to comprehend complex culture and did not perceive urban culture as its own. Hence there was a strong demand for cultural simplification. The new reader needed emotional support and the comfort of melodrama rather than complex literature. These readers did not enjoy Modernist experimentation and demanded verisimilitude. As a result, a total infantilisation of culture took place. Socialist Realist literature was a peculiar return to a primitive spiritual childhood with suitable stylistic and plot paradigms: noble heroes, infernal villains, deals of collectivism and comradeship, and so on.

We return, then, to the question of how to define and understand Socialist Realism. If, as Groys suggests, Stalinist culture realised the political and ideological project of the avant-garde, then it did so only through an alliance with mass culture. At the heart of this synthesis was a desire to cater to the aesthetic demands of the mass consumer. Socialist Realist aesthetics never recognised the thesis of the ontological elitism of art, which was central to avant-garde practice. Struggling against 'Formalism' (or, to put it bluntly, against elitism and Modernism), party ideologists insisted that the art of the avant-garde – be it atonal music, abstract painting, or trans-sense poetry – was unnatural and unhealthy in a literal sense. Zhdanov notoriously compared Modernist music to a dentist's drill or a noisy concrete mixer.[13] This quasi-physiological approach to art reveals a particular understanding of 'realism' on the part of the Soviet state. The 'realism' in literature, cinema, and music that Stalin and Zhdanov advocated was realistic not so much stylistically as functionally: it was a matter of extreme pragmatism, using aesthetics as a strategy of power. By analogy with 'realpolitik' it can be called 'realästhetik'.

The Aesthetic Arsenal: Socialist Realism as an Instrument

In his foundational essay 'On Socialist Realism', Siniavskii wrote that the chief peculiarity of Socialist Realism was its functionality and instrumentality: 'To capture motion towards a goal and facilitate reaching a goal by reworking the

---

13 *Soveshchanie deiatelei sovetskoi muzyki v TsK VKP(b)* [Conference of figures of Soviet music in the Central Committee of the All-Union Communist Party of Bolsheviks] (Moscow: Gospolitizdat, 1948), p. 143.

reader's consciousness in accordance with that goal is the goal of Socialist Realism, the most goal-oriented art of the present day.'[14] For Siniavskii, the ultimate goal of Socialist Realist literature was pedagogical: to create a new society and new human subjects. 'The goal is communism', Siniavskii writes. 'A poet does not simply write poems, but rather assists the building of communism with his poems. ... Like all our culture, all our society, our art is thoroughly teleological.'[15] Socialist Realist art fulfilled a range of political functions that were vital to the regime: it transformed a powerful ideological discourse into a language of images so that it could be interiorised by readers.

The period which we might call the 'Russian Revolution' (up to the death of Stalin) was one of enormous political, social, economic, and cultural disruption: three revolutions, one civil and two world wars, collectivisation, industrialisation, cultural revolution, and the Great Terror, not to mention lesser campaigns. These events impacted every family, causing unimaginable loss and suffering. The profoundly traumatised Soviet society needed therapy. Hence, it was appropriate to endow literature with a *normalising* function: by embedding trauma into the dominant narrative of power, Socialist Realist literature gave its readers the illusion of normalcy. It did this in a broad and eclectic range of literary styles.

To illustrate, let us consider the civil war theme. Among the novels retrospectively integrated into the Socialist Realist canon were Aleksandr Fadeev's (1901–1956) *The Rout* (*Razgrom*, 1927), written in the style of traditional psychologism; Aleksandr Serafimovich's (1863–1949) *The Iron Flood* (*Zheleznyi potok*, 1924), in the mode of the heroic epic; and Dmitrii Furmanov's (1891–1926) *Chapaev* (*Chapaev*, 1923), in a documentary style. Another was Nikolai Ostrovskii's (1904–1936) autobiographical novel *How the Steel Was Tempered* (*Kak zakalialas' stal'*, 1934), a story about individual sacrifices, widescale violence, and the defeat of Red Army soldiers, which was constructed around the author's own tragic and traumatic experience. For all their stylistic and generic differences, these civil war narratives shared a common aim: to serve as therapeutic texts for the mass reader. They controlled the civil war narrative while at the same time allowing the regime to confront – and fictionally resolve – conflicts between the individual and the state. They were real conflicts arising in families, in the collective, or in war.

---

14 Andrei Siniavskii, *Chto takoe sotsialisticheskii realism. Literaturnyi protsess v Rossii* [On Socialist Realism. The literary process in Russia] (Moscow: Rossiiskii gosudarstvennyi gumanitarnyi universitet, 2003), p. 140.
15 Siniavskii, *Chto takoe sotsialisticheskii realism*, p. 141.

They were caused by forced collectivisation, administrative deportations, arbitrary convictions, and repressions. It also allowed them to depict hunger, want, and poverty – and to address the themes of death (except heroic death), doubt, weakness, and the like.[16]

Such difficult subjects were also subject to taboos, of course, and to the sharp eye of state censorship. As such the next important function of Socialist Realism can be described as a *de-realisation* of Soviet reality, which was sterilised not only at the level of themes but also at that of language, style, and genre, as 'neutral' language was cultivated, no stylistic innovations at all were encouraged, and established genres and genre conventions – those of the so-called industrial novel, the collective farm poem, the patriotic play – were strictly adhered to. But the most striking characteristic of Socialist Realism was its purging from reality of everything that did not fit into the dominant political narrative.

However, the picture of the world created by Socialist Realism could not abide a vacuum. It was filled instead with images of a transformed Soviet reality: a new aesthetic of realised utopia. This revealed itself most clearly in the genre of the collective farm novel, which flourished in the 1930s and in particular after the Second World War. If the first volume of Mikhail Sholokhov's (1905–1984) *Virgin Soil Upturned* (*Podniataia tselina*, 1932) had described the process of collectivisation and the conflicts of that era, then the postwar collective farm novels by Galina Nikolaeva (1911–1965; *The Harvest* (*Zhatva*, 1950)), Elizar Maltsev (1916–2004; *Straight from the Heart* (*Ot vsego serdtsa*, 1948)), and Semen Babaevskii (1909–2000; *The Cavalier of the Golden Star* (*Kavaler Zolotoi zvezdy*, 1947–8)), which all received the Stalin Prize, exemplified what was called 'conflictless literature'. Babaevskii's novel, for example, tells of a hero returned from the war who achieves incredible success: he rebuilds the collective farm, constructs an electrical station, makes an astounding career for himself, and marries a beauty who gives him twin sons. This fantastic character – idealised, selfless, and capable of overcoming all obstacles – typified the hero of postwar Soviet literature. These were fairy-tale novels offering happy endings and the joyful resolution of all potential conflicts (such as that between industry and the countryside or between personal life and social duty).

While de-realising life, then, Soviet literature created a new 'socialist' life. Indeed, whatever Soviet reality was (and it was, above all, a system of personal power for Stalin as leader, to which collectivisation, modernisation,

16 See Efim Etkind, 'Sovetskie tabu' [Soviet taboo], *Sintaksis* 9 (1981), 8.

and terror were all ultimately subordinated), the purpose of Socialist Realist literature and art was to turn *that* reality into socialism. This *transformative* function was one of the fundamental purposes of Socialist Realism: not merely the production of certain symbols but the production of verbal and visual substitutes for reality. The industrial novel is an example of such a transformation of Soviet reality into socialism. In this genre, which arose in the 1920s, for example in Fedor Gladkov's (1883–1958) *Cement* (*Tsement*, 1925), and flowered in the early 1930s – e.g. Leonid Leonov's (1899–1994) *Sot* (*Sot'*, 1930), Marietta Shaginian's (1888–1982) *Hydrocentral* (*Gidrotsentral'*, 1931), Valentin Kataev's (1897–1986) *Time, Forward!* (*Vremia, vpered!*, 1932), and Ilia Erenburg's (1891–1967) *The Second Day* (*Den' vtoroi*, 1933) – the merciless exploitation and brutal conditions of labour and daily life were transformed into enthusiasm for labour, comradely assistance, and new industrial relations.

In this sense, Socialist Realism described a world to the existence of which it alone bore witness. If we try to imagine Soviet 'socialism' without Socialist Realism – without novels and poems about joyous labour, films about happy socialist life, songs and paintings about the wealth of the Soviet land, and so on – then we are left with nothing that can distinctively be called socialism. Grey workdays, routine daily labour, and an unsettled and oppressive every-day life are all that are left. And since a reality like this could be attributed to any other economic system, nothing of socialism would remain. The purpose of Socialist Realism, then, was to give material form to the symbolic values of socialism.

The core task of Socialist Realist literature, however, was the legitimisa-tion of the regime. This *legitimitising* function was accomplished through three key strategies: image, historicisation, and mobilisation.

Socialist Realist literature created and sustained two core images: 'the people' and 'state power'. As stated above, the image of the people (the masses) was created in industrial and collective farm novels, poems, and songs, where their life affirmed the rightness of party and state policy. This image of the people – the supreme legitimising authority – sanctified at its opposite extreme the images of Soviet leaders that Soviet literature began to create long before the proclamation of Socialist Realism. Through the Soviet period, a flood of poems, novels, plays, popular non-fiction, and children's literature about Lenin and Stalin created and sustained an image of power to correspond to the current political situation. Practically every Soviet poet left some poems about Lenin and/or Stalin. However, the cult of the leaders remained flexible. Thus, if in Stalin's time the image of Lenin was stylised

after Stalin as his 'faithful pupil', then in the era of the Khrushchev Thaw it was quite the opposite: Lenin was positioned as a counterweight to Stalin.

Images of leaders were part of Socialist Realism's historicising function, creating a legitimising narrative. This narrative was shaped for the most part by historical and historical-revolutionary novels, poems, films, and songs. The historical-revolutionary novel appeared in Soviet literature before the proclamation of Socialist Realism and was retrospectively incorporated into the Socialist Realist canon. The works of Fadeev, Serafimovich, Furmanov, and Ostrovskii mentioned above belonged to varying genres but were later all recreated as exemplars of the Socialist Realist historical-revolutionary novel. Superimposed onto the genre of the classic family novel (see Chapter 3.5), these novels told of the coming of (uneducated) workers into revolutionary consciousness and of their 'allies' in this process, drawn from both the peasantry and the intelligentsia. Among such later novels of this type are Aleksei Nikolaevich Tolstoi's (1883–1945) trilogy *The Road to Calvary* (*Khozhdenie po mukam*, 1921–41) and Konstantin Fedin's (1892–1977) *Early Joys* (*Pervye radosti*, 1945), *An Unusual Summer* (*Neobyknovennoe leto*, 1948), and *The Conflagration* (*Koster*, 1967). Such narratives gained historical resonance from historical-biographical novels about more remote eras and historical figures such as Aleksei Tolstoi's *Peter I* (*Petr I*, 1929–34) and Valentin Kostylev's (1884–1950) trilogy *Ivan the Terrible* (*Ivan Groznyi*, 1943–7), which, by transforming history in accordance with the current political agenda, created a useful past for the purposes of historical legitimisation of the regime.

It was not by chance that the flowering of Socialist Realist historical literature coincided with the prewar and wartime periods as well as with the early, most acute stage of the Cold War. This was when the *mobilisational* function of Socialist Realism was worked out: at times of duress, when reality might be giving a Soviet reader a sense of inferiority or anxiety, literary texts sought to give them a sense of superiority and confidence. This was particularly the case for so-called patriotic poetry, such as poems by Aleksei Surkov (1899–1983), Konstantin Simonov (1915–1979), and Nikolai Tikhonov (1896–1979), which exalted love for the party, faith in the progress of communism, and the greatness of the Soviet Union. This echoed the cultural rhetoric of the early Cold War. Similar civic virtues were celebrated in the voluminous and widely promoted wartime literature that propagandised the victory cult, such as Erenburg's novels *The Storm* (*Buria*, 1947) and *The Ninth Wave* (*Deviatyi val*, 1950), and Simonov's trilogy *The Living and the Dead* (*Zhivye i mertvye*, 1959–71).

Finally, the characteristic features of Socialist Realism – its propensity for verisimilitude, craving for melodrama, evenness of style, and linguistic and

structural conventionality – can be explained by their instrumentality: to interiorise the message of a Socialist Realist text, the reader had to empathise with its characters, find a sublimated image of reality in them, and identify with them. This process of *interiorisation* was Socialist Realism's ultimate aim, which its formal features aimed to facilitate.

These functions (normalisation, de-realisation, transformation, and interiorisation) enable us to understand the fuller definition – deliberately contradictory, extensible, and opaque – of Socialist Realism that was given in Zhdanov's speech in 1934 and incorporated almost word for word into the Charter of the Soviet Writers' Union adopted at this congress:

> Socialist Realism, which is the fundamental method of Soviet belles-lettres and literary criticism, requires of the artist a truthful, historically specific depiction of reality in its revolutionary development. At the same time, the truthfulness and historic specificity of the artistic depiction of reality must be combined with the aims of ideological transformation and education in the spirit of socialism.[17]

Here we see the familiar principles of the Socialist Realist doctrine: party-mindedness, ideological commitment, and popular spirit. We also see the functional elements that I have drawn out above: the transformation of reality, revolutionary romanticism, historicism, and historical optimism. And in each case, we can suggest that the characteristic may have a dual meaning: 'popular spirit' (*narodnost'*), for example, may ostensibly refer to the accessibility of literature for the mass reader, but it also describes literature's aim to *create* an officially sanctioned image of the 'popular', and to embed that in mass consciousness.

Beyond the Doctrine: Socialist Realism as an Institution

Socialist Realism was not so much the style it purported to be, nor the aesthetic doctrine that it allegedly was, nor even a corpus of canonical texts. It was, rather, a politically functional and socially sensitive system for producing, propagating, and consuming an aesthetic product. The interminable discussions about Socialist Realism that flooded the field of Soviet aesthetics from 1932 through 1990 aimed to conceal the main thing: just as Stalinism was not a theory but rather, first and foremost, a system of state

---

17 *Pervyi Vsesoiuznyi s"ezd sovetskikh pisatelei: Stenograficheskii otchet* [First All-Union Congress of Soviet Writers: Verbatim report] (Moscow: GIKhL, 1934), pp. 4–5.

violence, so Socialist Realism was not a theory but rather an institution. The theory was needed only to the extent that it created a discursive fog that legitimised and assured the uninterrupted and effective workings of the institutions of control, normalisation, and violence.

Russian literature can claim few firsts. Literature as defined today began to be imported from the west into Russia in the reign of Tsar Aleksei Mikhailovich (r. 1645–76) and, beginning in the era of Peter I (r. 1682–1725), this imported phenomenon became an important part of the modernisation of the country, alongside other European innovations, institutions, and practices (see Chapter 1.3). None of the fundamental trends in Russian literature in the modern era originated in Russia – neither Classicism, Romanticism, Realism, Symbolism, nor Futurism. Rather, they arrived from Europe in translation and then acquired Russian characteristics. Soviet Russia, however, can claim the dubious honour of being a pioneer in the instrumentalisation of literature for the needs of political propaganda and state terror, as well as in creating the mechanisms and institutions of totalitarian art. Socialist Realism arose before the Italian, German, Spanish, Chinese, and other national forms of a similar type. The All-Russian Association of Proletarian Writers, or VAPP – the first literary union, founded and directly governed by the party-state – was created in 1920, two years before the Novecento Italiano (1922); the creation of the Soviet Writers' Union began in 1932, a year and a half before Germany's Reichskulturkammer (Reich Chamber of Culture) was created in 1933.

It was not by chance that the politburo resolution of 23 April 1932, which changed the entire landscape of Soviet culture and introduced a single aesthetic canon in Soviet art, was entitled 'On the Restructuring of Literary and Artistic Organisations' and was markedly institutional. It announced the break-up of all existing literary groups and established the basic organisational parameters of the future Soviet Writers' Union (and other creative unions).

In twentieth-century dictatorships, Stalinism among them, culture was politically instrumentalised in a hitherto unheard-of way. Faced, on the one hand, with the unwillingness of Modernist art to take mass taste into account in its aesthetic practice and subordinate itself to party directives and, on the other hand, with the unpreparedness of the mass consumer of art to accept and comprehend the aesthetic products of Modernism, the Soviet party-state came to the necessity of 'restructuring' the 'literary and artistic organisations'.

Culture *mattered* for twentieth-century dictatorial regimes based on violence in a way that was fundamentally different from modern liberal-democratic regimes. It was understood to be a universal weapon of political power: as a way to reach, engage, or oppose political subjects; as a domain of

political imagery; and hence as a necessary object of centralised planning and coordination. Culture was the only instrument with which power could produce its own image. It was also an instrument for producing the image of 'the people' as the supreme legitimising subject for state power. This is why the culture of modern dictatorships, including that of Stalinism, was so central to the survival of these regimes. This was understood earlier in Soviet Russia than in other countries.

The production of Socialist Realism was undertaken by special agents (writers, musicians, visual artists, architects, and critics) who worked within the framework of institutions (the bureaucracy of creative unions, the editorship of literary and specialist journals, in selection committees and competition juries, committees awarding prizes, censorship bodies, and so forth). It was not the 'artistic products' (i.e. Socialist Realist texts) they made that produced Socialist Realist discourse. Socialist Realist production did not support the institutions; nor was it Socialist Realist doctrine that gave birth to censorship. Rather, it was exactly the opposite: censorship (which had existed long before then) gave birth to Socialist Realism and created the conditions for its functioning. In other words, Socialist Realism was above all the institutions that (re)produced agents (producers and consumers) who in turn ensured the production of Socialist Realist texts, their doctrinal formulation, stylistic peculiarities, and social functions.

Thus, the institutions of Socialist Realism were not by any means 'superstructures' external to an abstract aesthetic (or doctrine) of Socialist Realism. On the contrary, without the conditions for Socialist Realist production, this aesthetic could not have come to exist, functioned, been reproduced, or influenced consumers. In this respect, the Socialist Realist aesthetic was merely a derivative of Socialist Realism as an institution. In other words, without the Gulag, there would have been no censorship; without censorship, there would have been no Soviet Writers' Union; without the Soviet Writers' Union, there would have been no literary process, no Soviet writers producing texts; without Soviet schools, libraries, journals, and publishers, there would have been no Soviet readers consuming these texts; and so on. And for texts such as *The Cavalier of the Golden Star* – or for the towering skyscrapers of Stalin's Moscow – to evoke admiration and jubilation rather than horror and terror, for them not to ooze blood, they needed to be rationalised through theory and filled with the discursive syrup of lofty words. Hence, the important thing was not the discourse itself but its institutional functions.

Socialist Realism could not function outside its institutional framework. It was a totally institutional aesthetic, containing all the elements of production

and consumption of art within its institutional frameworks. The production of literature began with the production of writers who were professionalised through study in the Literary Institute and institutionalised through the Soviet Writers' Union. The Union was essentially a ministry of literature, centralised and subordinated to the party. All its upper-level bureaucrats were from the party and were subordinated to party organs at all levels, from the city and regional divisions of the union up to its republic-level unions. The Soviet Writers' Union (and through it, the party) in turn controlled the whole process of producing literature through the literary journals and publishers that belonged to it. All publications were subject to confirmation in the party echelons through preliminary censorship. There were no other paths to publication in the USSR (see Chapter 2.7).

The very nature of a writer's work underwent radical change: the creative process itself was re-envisaged. Writing turned from a means of self-expression into a process of fulfilling an assignment. As a reward, the social status of writers rose sharply. The writer became a trusted representative of power, a privileged party bureaucrat. Membership in the Soviet Writers' Union opened up access to the very same benefits that the party elites enjoyed, with luxury apartments, dachas (summer houses), sanatoriums, medical facilities, honoraria, cars, and special distributions of scarce goods (at a time when everything was scarce, from clothing and soap to bread and butter). In the course of two decades (the 1920s and 1930s), the new Soviet literature, almost completely reborn from its pre-revolutionary forebears, travelled the path from absolute revolutionary nihilism to just as absolute imperial servility, and it became fully controllable.

The consumption of literature was also controlled. The shaping of writing habits and the development of speech was fostered by the reading of selected literary exemplars in the school programme, where literature (both classic and Soviet) held a key position. The literary canon established in schools was maintained at the highest level by the celebration of anniversaries of the classics (both pre-revolutionary and Soviet) as state-level festivities. Literary studies and literary criticism guaranteed appropriate interpretations of both classic and contemporary literature. Contemporary literature was promoted to readers through reader conferences in workplaces and in libraries, which played a key role in the dissemination of this literature up to the end of the Soviet era.

Without these institutions, the functioning and consumption of Socialist Realist literature would have been impossible. Therefore, anyone who approaches Socialist Realism with purely aesthetic standards will find nothing

in it. Nonetheless, Socialist Realism was the only possible aesthetic for the cultural milieu to which it was addressed. It was extremely popular and allowed the vast majority of the population to identify with the images it produced. It was highly effective in fulfilling the aims for which it was created: legitimisation of the regime, indoctrination and mobilisation of the population, interiorisation of the values required for shaping the Soviet nation. Finally, for better or worse, it pioneered and tested a system of institutions, mechanisms, and practices for the control of the entire process of the production, functioning, and consumption of cultural products.

The Post-Stalin Afterlife of Socialist Realism

The golden age of Socialist Realism coincided with the Stalin era, when the monopoly of the party-state over political, ideological, and aesthetic activities was absolute. After Stalin's death, this monopoly, though preserving its previous political appearance, began to weaken – at first due to de-Stalinisation in the Khrushchev Thaw era, and then, in the Brezhnev era, with the rise of dissident activity and foreign and domestic underground literature (*tamizdat* and *samizdat*). As the institutions weakened, so too did the doctrine begin to lose its rigidity. The process of liberalisation that began with the death of Stalin was unstoppable.

Khrushchev's 'secret speech' triggered an unrelenting process of separation between literature and Socialist Realist discourse. In Stalin's time, Socialist Realism was an operational category that loyally served the critics, the censors, and the party managers of Soviet literature. After 1956, Socialist Realism moved increasingly into the sphere of theoretical discussions and counter-propaganda. Its institutional arrangements remained more or less secure, but they were deprived of their instrumental status; they increasingly had only symbolic value, losing their legitimising role. Literary debates of the early 1960s bore traces of attempts to restore a connection between the living literary process and the demands of Socialist Realism. For example, in the debates on new war prose at the beginning of the 1960s, orthodox critics still tried to appeal to the demands of Socialist Realism. But by the 1970s a complete break between Socialist Realist theory and living artistic practice occurred, with the former fully retreating into the sphere of the history and theory of literature. At about that time, literary criticism ceased to invoke Socialist Realism, and discussions of the new wave of war prose, Village Prose, lyric poetry, and city prose took place with no reference to Socialist Realism whatsoever. Participants in these debates now turned for support

not to Socialist Realist doctrine but to the national past and moral and social issues.

Socialist Realist texts continued to be produced in the 1970s and 1980s, mainly by literary and party functionaries, such as secretaries of the Writers' Union; it became known disparagingly as 'secretarial literature'. Indicative works include propaganda poems by Sergei Mikhalkov (1913–2009), Egor Isaev (1926–2013), Anatolii Sofronov (1911–1990), and Nikolai Gribachev (1910–1992), who rhymed party slogans, as well as huge (sometimes multi-volume) novels by Georgii Markov (1911–1991), Vadim Kozhevnikov (1909–1984), Anatolii Ivanov (1928–1999), and Sergei Sartakov (1908–2005), which retold the history of the revolution and establishment of the Soviet regime according to schemata which had changed little since Stalin's times. However, with huge print runs, this literature gathered dust on the shelves of bookstores, unable to compete with the literature that represented the critical trend. As soon as the institutions behind these authors collapsed, their works ceased to be published and disappeared from circulation.

By the beginning of Perestroika in the late 1980s, Socialist Realism had been firmly relegated to the history of literature, and even ritualistic incantations from the highest levels of power about loyalty to its ideals became quite rare. The death of Socialist Realism did not attract much attention; Socialist Realism simply failed to regain consciousness, drifting into non-being in an endless chain of academic debates. At a certain point, the comatose patient was, finally, disconnected from the life-support system.

In this sense, one could say that, after 1956, the marriage contract between literature and Socialist Realism, even though it was not officially dissolved, became completely void. The married partners started living separately, having lost all contact with each other, so that when Socialist Realism died, literature did not even notice. Literature had been living its own independent life for quite some time already, though perhaps keeping the family name, and with both partners sharing access to the same artistic centres, first-class apartments, and literary funds. The arrangement resulted in certain inconveniences but also guaranteed significant privileges for the literary officials who had been responsible for keeping 'the most advanced artistic method' in a state of suspended animation for decades. The comatose spouse, living for decades in the intensive-care unit, was dressed up and made presentable for anniversaries and special occasions, and then returned to the life-supporting environment of academic conferences and connected to the respiratory equipment supplied by collected volumes of academic articles on 'current problems of Socialist Realism'. Only the grandchildren of the heroes of

Socialist Realism – the Conceptualists and masters of Sots-art – remembered the once deadly weapon and were inspired by its aesthetics (see Chapter 1.9). The Postmodernists alone brought a wreath of irony to the gravestone of Socialist Realism.

Further Reading

Any, Carol, *The Soviet Writers' Union and Its Leaders: Identity and Authority under Stalin* (Evanston, IL: Northwestern University Press, 2020).

Clark, Katerina, *The Soviet Novel: History as Ritual* (Chicago: University of Chicago Press, 1985).

Dobrenko, Evgeny, *Political Economy of Socialist Realism* (New Haven: Yale University Press, 2007).

Dunham, Vera, *In Stalin's Time: Middleclass Values in Soviet Fiction* (Cambridge: Cambridge University Press, 1976).

Golomstock, Igor, *Totalitarian Art: In the Soviet Union, the Third Reich, Fascist Italy, and the People's Republic of China*, trans. Robert Chandler (London: Collins Harvill, 1990).

Groys, Boris, *The Total Art of Stalinism: Avant-Garde, Aesthetic Dictatorship, and Beyond*, trans. Charles Rougle (Princeton: Princeton University Press, 1992).

Gutkin, Irina, *The Cultural Origins of the Socialist Realist Aesthetic, 1890–1934* (Evanston, IL: Northwestern University Press, 1999).

Paperny, Vladimir, *Architecture in the Age of Stalin: Culture Two*, trans. John Hill and Roann Barris (New York: Cambridge University Press, 2002).

Robin, Régine, *Socialist Realism: An Impossible Aesthetic*, trans. Catherine Porter (Stanford: Stanford University Press, 1992).

Tertz, Abram, *'The Trial Begins' and 'On Socialist Realism'*, trans. Max Hayward and George Denis (New York: Vintage Books, 1960).

1.9

Postmodernism

ILYA KUKULIN

In 1991, the poet and critic Viktor Kulle (1962–) organised a conference entitled 'Postmodernism and Us' at the A. M. Gorkii Literature Institute in Moscow – an institution which had been training the Soviet literary establishment for decades. Despite the conference receiving almost no official support, the hall was packed for three full days and several newspapers covered the proceedings. It was a paradoxical event. For many of the attendees, it was the first they were hearing of a global cultural movement called 'Postmodernism', let alone of its existence within Russia itself. Yet almost all the presenters talked about Russian Postmodernism as if it had existed for a long time and been shaped by the particular conditions of Russian culture – specifically, by the uncensored space of late Soviet literature that could not be published and was distributed by hand through *samizdat* (see Chapter 2.9).

This story of a homegrown Russian Postmodernism dating back to the late Soviet period was not, however, the dominant one that emerged throughout the 1990s in journals in Russia and Slavic journals in the west. These journals regularly featured articles arguing that Postmodernism had resulted from a conscious or unconscious appropriation of western trends after the collapse of Soviet ideology and of the officially sanctioned artistic doctrine of Socialist Realism (see Chapter 1.8). Assuming that Russian Postmodernism was a post-Soviet phenomenon, their authors could argue that it had nothing in common with Soviet literature and its ideologisation.[1] They could also argue for a

---

1 See, for example, Viacheslav Kupriianov, 'Nechto nichto, ili snova o postmodernisme' [Something nothing, or once again on Postmodernism], *Novyi mir* [New world] 10 (1997), 237–41; Serafima Roll, *Postmodernisty o postkul'ture: Interv'iu s sovremennymi pisateliami i kritikami* [Postmodernists on post-culture: Interviews with contemporary writers and critics] (Moscow: R. Elinin, 1996); Serafima Roll, *Contextualizing Transition: Interviews with Contemporary Russian Writers and Critics* (New York: Peter Lang, 1998).

neat affinity between the morpheme 'post-' in 'post-Soviet' and 'postmodern'.[2] Favouring western theories of Postmodernism that were grounded in economic determinism, many scholars claimed that Postmodernism could not have existed previously in Russia because neither late Soviet nor early post-Soviet Russia had gone through what Fredric Jameson called 'late capitalism'.[3] This argument was reinforced by the fact that Modernist culture – which many western scholars viewed as the precursor to Postmodernist culture – had been stigmatised in the USSR since the mid-1930s.

Yet as the authors of unofficial publications argued already in the late 1970s and early 1980s, and as the conference 'Postmodernism and Us' confirmed, Russian Postmodernism in fact originated in underground culture long before the collapse of the USSR in 1991.[4] Literary works that anticipated the key aesthetics of Postmodernism – irony, irreverence, hybridity of genre, citationality – appeared as early as the 1940s. At the start of the 1950s, for example, the physiologist Vasilii Parin (1903–1971), the occultist and poet Daniil Andreev (1906–1959), the cultural historian Lev Rakov (1904–1970), and the playwright and historian Daniil Alshits (1919–2012) co-authored a parodic encyclopedia entitled *The Newest Plutarch* (*Noveishii Plutarkh*) while incarcerated in the Vladimir Central Prison on trumped-up political charges (they were later rehabilitated). This work displays characteristics of the genre of docufiction.[5] However, no one could or did interpret such early works as examples of a broader aesthetic trend.

This changed between 1969 and 1975 when a significant number of literary works of early Russian Postmodernism were distributed in the USSR, particularly within circles of uncensored culture in Moscow. Visual artists such as Ilia Kabakov (1933–2023), Erik Bulatov (1933–), Vitalii Komar (1943–), and Aleksandr Melamid (1945–) were among the first to learn about western Conceptualism and performance art and to create consonant works of their own. But Postmodernist strategies spread to literature as well. Between 1973

---

2 Here I rephrase the title of an article: Kwame Anthony Appiah, 'Is the post- in Postmodernism the post- in postcolonial?' *Critical Inquiry* 17.2 (1991), 336–57.
3 Fredric Jameson, *Postmodernism, or, The Cultural Logic of Late Capitalism* (Durham, NC: Duke University Press, 1991).
4 See, for example, Boris Groys, 'Moscow Romantic Conceptualism' (1979), in *History Becomes Form: Moscow Conceptualism* (Cambridge, MA: MIT Press, 2010), pp. 35–55.
5 Mark Lipovetskii, 'Rozhdenie postmodernizma vo Vladimirskom Tsentrale' [The birth of Postmodernism in the Vladimir Central Prison], in Julia Vaingurt and William Nickell (eds.), *Nestandart: Zabytye eksperimenty v sovetskoi kul'ture, 1934–1964 gody; sbornik statei* [Non-standard: Forgotten experiments in Soviet culture, 1934–1964; collected essays] (Moscow: Novoe literaturnoe obozrenie, 2021).

and 1974, Dmitrii Prigov (1940–2007) and Lev Rubinshtein (1947–2024) developed original poetic styles which by today's standards reflect Postmodernist aesthetics. It was in those years that the first Postmodernist manifestoes in Russian also appeared. These include Evgenii Saburov's (1946–2009) essay 'Utopia and Hope' (*Utopiia i nadezhda*, 1973), written under the pseudonym Pavel Zarnitsyn and published in the émigré journal *Messenger of the Russian Christian Movement* (*Vestnik RSKhD*, 1925–), and Zinovy Zinik's (1945–) manifesto 'Sots-Art' (*Sots-art*, 1974), published in 1979 in the émigré journal *Sintaksis* (*Sintaksis*, 1978–2001).[6]

Why did Postmodernist culture crystallise so quickly in Russia? In his influential study *The Condition of Postmodernity* (1991), David Harvey observes a similarly rapid transition to Postmodernist aesthetics within British and American art in the first half of the 1970s. He attributes this phenomenon to economic factors and, particularly, to the emergence of a new form of capitalism which in turn generated new ways of experiencing time and space in art.[7] Yet the economic factors that Harvey identifies do not apply to the USSR, and articles about Postmodernism which were published in the USSR during Perestroika and the early post-Soviet period mentioned neither Harvey nor Jameson, who proposed a related economic model for the emergence of Postmodernist culture under late capitalism.[8] Those articles drew directly or indirectly on the work of French theorists, especially that of Jean-François Lyotard.[9] In *The Postmodern Condition* (1979), Lyotard described Postmodernism as a culture that came into being as a result of a societal incredulity towards metanarratives.[10] Building on Lyotard, late Soviet and post-Soviet scholars described Russian Postmodernism as a movement that responded to a crisis of ideology, rather than resulting from economic factors. Given that the Soviet 1960s had witnessed a collapse of ideological metanarratives, the 1970s could be viewed as a post-utopian period of 'advanced socialism' characterised by the ritualisation of ideological formulae.

---

6 Il'ia Kukulin, 'Novaia logika: O perelome v razvitii russkoi kul'tury i obshchestvennoi mysli 1969–73 godov' [New logic: On the crisis in the development of Russian culture and social thought 1969–73], *Toronto Slavic Quarterly* 61 (2017); Pavel Zarnitsyn, 'Utopia i nadezhda' [Utopia and hope], *Vestnik RSKhD* 107.1 (1979), 143–59; Zinovii Zinik, 'Sots-art', *Sintaksis* 3 (1979), 74–102.

7 David Harvey, *The Condition of Postmodernity: An Enquiry into the Origins of Cultural Change* (Cambridge, MA: Wiley-Blackwell, 1991).

8 Jameson, *Postmodernism*.

9 See, for example, articles on Postmodernism by Viacheslav Kuritsyn and Il'ia Il'in.

10 Jean-François Lyotard, *The Postmodern Condition: A Report on Knowledge*, trans. Geoffrey Bennington and Brian Massumi (Minneapolis: University of Minnesota Press, 1984).

There is one further dimension to consider when analysing the specificity of Russian Postmodernism and its prehistories. According to the scholar Mark Lipovetsky, Russian Postmodernist movements of the twentieth century developed gradually and were grounded in a reflection on the relationship between culture and violence. Lipovetsky argues that in Modernism this relationship was perceived as inevitable, whereas in Postmodernism it is seen as a fundamental conflict concealed by contemporary culture. Yet because reflecting on the terror that the Bolsheviks induced was of utmost importance throughout uncensored culture, Postmodernist traits existed already in the Modernist Russian literature of the 1920s, such as the prose of Konstantin Vaginov (1899–1934) and Osip Mandelshtam (1891–1938).[11] Lipovetsky's analysis is among the most complex and accurate theories of Russian Postmodernism to have emerged to date, but it does not explain what makes Russian Postmodernism postmodernist in the sense in which the term is used in western Europe and North America: that is, within the frameworks set out by Harvey, Jameson, and Lyotard. This chapter outlines such a framework through a history of the emergence of Russian Postmodernist literature in the late 1960s and of the movement's development through the late Soviet period into contemporary forms and manifestations.

Ideology as a Form of Consciousness

In what follows, I propose my own view on Postmodernism, based partly on the ideas of Lyotard, Jameson, and Harvey and partly on those of Russian Postmodernist theorists such as Zinik and Mikhail Aizenberg (1948–).[12] Postmodernism may be described as a response to two interconnected phenomena: a crisis of belief in progress, on the one hand, and a reconceptualisation of history, on the other. In western countries, the crisis of belief in progress played out from the second half of the 1960s through the early 1970s as intellectuals lost faith in the welfare state and a younger generation began questioning the conformism and consumerism of its elders. A similar crisis arose in the USSR for different reasons. One key factor was the failure of Nikita Khrushchev's promises of reform and prosperity in the 1950s and early

---

11 Mark Lipovetskii, *Paralogii: Transformatsii (post)modernistskogo diskursa v russkoi kul'ture 1920–2000-kh godov* [Paralogies: Transformations of the (Post)modernist discourse in Russian culture of the 1920s–2000s] (Moscow: Novoe literaturnoe obozrenie, 2008).

12 Zinik, 'Sots-art'; Mikhail Aizenberg, 'Vozmozhnost' vyskazyvaniia' [The capacity to speak], in *Vzgliad na svobodnogo khudozhnika* [A view on the free artist] (Moscow: Gendalf, 1997), pp. 7–31.

1960s – a failure which led to the delegitimisation of the communist ideology he represented. Another factor was geopolitical: after the Yom Kippur War of 1973, a coalition of Arab states raised the price of oil. The rationale was to punish western countries for supporting Israel, but it was the Soviet Union that benefited primarily. With oil revenues high, the Soviet elite could de-prioritise the country's own scientific and technological development in favour of importing raw materials. This shift was accompanied by a gener-ational conflict in urban communities, where the industrial economy came to co-exist paradoxically with a post-industrial society that emphasised the leisure and service sectors over citizens' actual jobs and operated largely within the context of a shadow economy. Postmodernism could thrive in such a society. Yet it could only thrive in communities that embraced the critique of ideology as a form of consciousness while cultivating an estrange-ment from the rhetorical means that were used to shape ideology in the public sphere.

Alongside their rejection of the utopian belief in progress, Postmodernist artists and authors reconceptualise history by rejecting teleological narratives such as nationalist stories of origin. Instead, they see such narratives as compilations of symbols drawn from different eras and the human self as a product of propaganda, advertising, and other people's words and images, which can be made 'one's own' only through repeated personal effort and without achieving any finalised result. The postmodern consciousness emerges when artists realise that their social status does not render them privileged and that therefore they cannot distance themselves from a world that is characterised by an endless inflation of symbols.

This view of reality became increasingly widespread in Soviet underground culture in the 1970s and was articulated by Saburov in 'Utopia and Hope':

> the utopia of autonomous culture, the utopia of patriotism, the utopia of almighty science ('the mind will eventually figure everything out and offer solutions to everything') serve as evidence only for our ability to give in to illusions, when we find ourselves to be the stepchildren of history. The era of 'dying ideologies' in which we must live has dominated us to a much larger extent than we ever imagined. It doesn't matter that we don't believe in certain slogans; what matters is that we live in the space of their decompos-ition. The fact that we allow ourselves to distrust them and subject them to irony does not mean that we are not involved in the ideological crisis plaguing our time. For it also plagues us despite all our freedom of thought, our private wit and our 'outsider's viewpoint'.[13]

13 Zarnitsyn, 'Utopia i nadezhda'.

As Saburov's manifesto suggests, in the USSR the Postmodernist attitude towards culture and history became a tool for critiquing ideology not as an external force but as an element of the artist's own consciousness.

The Postmodernist critique of ideology as a form of consciousness is encapsulated in a song written by the dissident mathematician and poet Nikolai Viliams (1926–2006) in 1969:

> The Communists captured a young man
> They dragged him to their KGB:
> 'Tell us, who gave you the book,
> Was it the leadership of the underground struggle?
>
> Why did you commit crimes
> Slandering our Leninist order?'
> 'I wanted to shit on your Lenin',
> The young hero replied.
>
> 'Let it be my turn for the concentration camp
> I am not afraid of camps or prisons!
> Soon the herd of capitalism's sharks
> Will rip the Soviet Union apart.'[14]

Modelled on revolutionary ballads and frequently sung to the tune of 'La Marseillaise', Viliams's song shows how easily dissidents' lives could be re-coded as Bolshevik heroic narratives. Yet the hero of the song is fighting not for a free society but for the very sort of capitalism that was vilified in Soviet propaganda. During performances, Viliams would invite the audience to shout out ironic slogans such as 'Land to the landlords!' and 'Long live the 12-hour workday!' It is the ideological consciousness per se that Viliams's song critiques, and not the specifics of its given Soviet or dissident manifestation.

The problematisation of ideological modes of thinking was taboo in the Soviet Union. For this reason, the Postmodernist consciousness became possible, first and foremost, within the relatively free space of uncensored literature.

Time and Space

Jameson and Harvey maintain that the postmodern era is defined by a profound shift in the experience of time and space. Harvey identifies a 'time–space compression': the related feelings of the connectedness of

---

14 Nikolai Vil'iams, 'Kommunisty poimali mal'chishku' [The communists captured a boy], A-Pesni, http://a-pesni.org/dvor/kommpojmali.php, accessed 7 Oct. 2022.

space due to globalisation and of the non-linear link between different historical eras.[15] Jameson further maintains that in Postmodernist culture, space becomes much more important than time.[16] A similar effect in Russian culture was generated under different circumstances. During the 1970s, the Soviet leadership channelled its efforts into preserving the status quo and slowly spreading its influence across the globe. Within the realm of culture, this generated an experience of time as stagnant and of space as confining and claustrophobic.

These circumstances resulted in an interest among Soviet intellectuals in the culture of previous centuries and other civilisations. This 'culturosophy', or worship of culture as an atemporal space in which writers and artists of various eras could co-exist, was both escapist and emancipatory. In the 1970s, many intellectuals subscribed to the Library of World Literature (*Biblioteka vsemirnoi literatury*) book series, which consisted of 200 volumes and included works ranging from the *Epic of Gilgamesh* to twentieth-century texts approved by Soviet censorship. But such participation in an 'eternal' cultural existence was not sufficient for critically minded authors, and some of them began to seek alternative models of temporal organisation. Leonid Likhodeev's (1921–1994) novel *In the Beginning Was the Word* (*Snachala bylo slovo*, 1987) may be viewed in this context. Written before Perestroika, it is a biographical novel about the nineteenth-century revolutionary Petr Zaichnevskii (1842–1896). The chapters follow a reverse chronological order: the action begins with the death of Zaichnevskii and ends with the events of 1862, when as a young student he wrote a proclamation calling for the violent overthrow of the monarchy. This type of experiment was not uncommon even in sanctioned literature of the 1970s and 1980s, although it could be met with resistance by publishers and censors. Likhodeev managed to publish his novel in the liberal Fiery Revolutionaries (*Plamennye revoliutsionery*) book series only because it was dedicated to the life of a revolutionary. The processes of remembering and the co-existence of present and past in the literary hero's consciousness also feature in the late works of Iurii Trifonov (1925–1981), such as *The House on the Embankment* (*Dom na naberezhnoi*, 1976).

Alongside the compression of time, space was perceived as closed and isolated from the rest of the world. The self-sufficiency of this space was typical of Socialist Realism, but even as the doctrine eroded, the model persisted as a claustrophobic view of a world from which there could be no escape. The clearest allegory of this late Soviet view of space may be found in

---

15 Harvey, *Condition of Postmodernity.*   16 Jameson, *Postmodernism.*

The Inhabited Island (*Obitaemyi ostrov*, 1969), by the nonconformist science-fiction writers and brothers Arkadii (1925–1991) and Boris (1933–2012) Strugatskii. The novel is set on the imaginary planet Saraksh, where the atmosphere refracts light in such a way that the landscape resembles a giant basin. For this reason, the planet's denizens believe they are living not on the surface but *within* a closed sphere and, indeed, that no other planets exist. Here, the madman is the person who suggests that there might be many inhabited worlds.

The experience of time and space changed dramatically during Perestroika and especially in the first years after the collapse of the Soviet Union. The liberalisation of the regime, the abrupt easing of censorship, the rapid publication of books that had previously been banned, the opening of the borders and the possibility of emigration – all these factors served to intensify the experience of time–space compression, even as the claustrophobic imaginary space that had been characteristic of the late Soviet epoch began to expand. This essentially postmodern condition laid the groundwork for the increased production of Postmodernist art.

In the postmodern era all authors to some extent respond to changes in politics, economy, and interpersonal relationships. Yet only some develop a new aesthetic consciousness for conceptualising and articulating those changes. It is the art of these authors that we describe as Postmodernist.

Postmodernist Poetry

Unlike in some cultures – including countries outside Soviet Russia (and even some republics within the USSR) – the driving force of Russian Postmodernist literature in the 1970s was poetry, not prose. Communities of unsanctioned poets formed in Leningrad, Moscow, and other cities only to evolve in different ways. The poets in Moscow maintained close relations with painters and even – as with Prigov and Andrei Monastyrskii (1949–) – combined these capacities. Conceptualist ideas stemming from American visual art were quick to shape their work. In the 1950s and 1960s, a community called the Lianozovo group emerged in Moscow, with the poets Evgenii Kropivnitskii (1893–1979), Ian Satunovskii (1913–1982), and Vsevolod Nekrasov (1934–2009) among its members. Their poems explored the mechanisms by which Russian poetic thinking operates, specifically the cognitive effects of versification structures such as rhythm, syntax, and

intertextual references. This plays out in the following poem by Nekrasov
from 1966:

> I remember a wondrous moment
> The Neva's sovereign flow
> I love you, Peter's great Creation,
>
> Who wrote that poem
>
> I wrote the poem[17]

Cobbling together lines by Russia's national poet Aleksandr Pushkin
(1799–1837), the poem presents an ostensibly streamlined text that is
nevertheless semantically absurd. Against the backdrop of the Soviet
cult of the nineteenth-century classics, Postmodernist reflections upon
such rhetorical mechanisms acquired an anti-authoritarian and hence
political meaning.

The Conceptualist poets radicalised this approach by analysing the
discourses that shaped the consciousness of the Soviet person, specifically, and showing how the surrounding – that is, Soviet – world came to
be seen as *given*. Their analysis was grounded in the device that the
Formalist critic Viktor Shklovskii (1893–1984; see Box 5.2) called
'estrangement' (*ostranenie*), whereby artists renew the perception of phenomena by rendering them 'strange' and unfamiliar.[18] In Russophone
Conceptualism, estrangement is used to demonstrate how specifically
ideological texts or images are accepted uncritically or rejected wholesale. This effect, which is related to Edmund Husserl's idea of the 'phe-
nomenological reduction', is integral to the work of Lev Rubinshtein.[19] In
the early 1970s, Rubinshtein invented a new system of versification. He
would jot down fragments of poetry or prose on numbered index cards of
the kind used in library catalogues and then shuffle the cards during public
readings. This transformed the recitation of poetry into a performance.
From his very first poems on index cards, Rubinshtein explored how
Soviet intellectuals gave meaning to the world around them. In
'Testimony for M.Kh.S.R.K.S.Kh.M.K.R.' (*Svidetel'stvo o M.Kh.S.R.K.S.
Kh.M.K.R.*, 1974), among other works, he suggests that it is not ideology

---

17 Vsevolod Nekrasov, *Stikhi. 1956–1983* [Poems. 1956–1983], ed. Mikhail Sukhotin, Galina
   Zykova, and Elena Penskaia (Vologda: Poligraf-Kniga, 2012), p. 139.
18 Viktor Shklovsky, 'Art as device', in *Theory of Prose*, trans. Benjamin Sher (Champaign,
   IL: Dalkey Archive Press, 1990), pp. 1–14.
19 Edmund Husserl, *Ideas: General Introduction to Pure Phenomenology*, trans. W. R. Boyce
   Gibson (London: Routledge, 2012).

itself but the grammatical structures of that ideology that shape perceptions of phenomena:

25. Paths for new ways of relating to the material
26. The search for paths for new ways of relating to the material
27. Describing the search for paths for new ways of relating to the material
28. Ways of describing the search for paths for new ways of relating to the material[20]

The Soviet consciousness represented in this excerpt articulates itself through a cumbersome bureaucratic syntax that postpones meaning in an ever more neurotic and confusing way, and indeed ultimately refuses any meaning at all.

The most popular Conceptualist poet was Prigov, who depicted what he called the 'enlivening' (*ozhivanie*) of Soviet discourses to show how they inadvertently revealed their own meaninglessness and internal contradictions. Such is the case in a poem from 1976:

> The people are divided into those who are not the people,
> And the people in the literal sense
> Those who are not the people – it is not that they're deformed
> They're rather mongrels in the highest sense
>
> And those who are the people – it is not that they're the people
> They're rather an expression of the people
> So you can't point and say: there's the people
> But you can make the point: the people exists. Endpoint[21]

The subject of the poem seeks to make sense of the Soviet concept of 'the people', which in fact could not and was not meant to be defined, as it was a tool of manipulation. It designated an essential, cohesive social unit from which party officials, members of the security services, and propagandists could rhetorically exclude dissenters by describing them as 'enemies of the people'. Any attempt to concretely define this unit served to reveal that Soviet discourse had supplanted the political interpretation of the people as society with the ideological definition of the people as a moral ideal. These two conceptions of 'the people' were indistinguishable in public discourse, yet even as many people in the USSR were aware of this fact, they could not

---

20 Lev Rubinshtein, 'Svidetel'stvo o M.Kh.S.R.K.S.Kh.M.K.R.' [Testimony for M.Kh.S.R. K.S.Kh.M.K.R], *Chasy* [The clock] 34 (1981), 121–6.
21 Dmitrii Prigov, *Sobranie stikhov* [Collected poems], 5 vols. (Vienna: Wiener Slawistischer Almanach, 1996–2009), vol. II, p. 163.

say it out loud. The poem's 'naïve' attempt to explain such ideological concepts violates an unspoken taboo. Moreover, it transforms 'the people' from a pseudo-scientific term (as it was used in the Soviet press) into an openly mythologised subject. This estrangement of the mythological essence of Soviet language was, it would seem, what Prigov meant by the term 'enlivening'.

Elements of Postmodernist aesthetics took centre stage during the 1970s in the works of authors who made their debut in the 1950s and 1960s, such as the Leningrad poet Viktor Sosnora (1936–2019). In his early work, Sosnora followed the Russian Futurists in presenting a stylised view of medieval Rus, but with a heavy accent on violence and trauma that hinted in obvious ways at the imprint of state terror and the Second World War that had been left upon the consciousness of the people of the 1960s. However, the furious heroic romanticism of his early works changed in the 1970s and 1980s. In the long poem 'Anno Iva' (*Anno Iva*, 1983), the 'I' occupies multiple timeframes:

> There is one more resident in the apartment: a parrot
> He flies up the stairs, a green spirit.
> [...]
> ... Even Kant somehow loved him
> For his Romanesque mind and cruel temper.
> Caught by the squadron on pies, he was imprisoned
> And transferred to the USSR from the Americas
> Poor comrade, he flew and sang
> Waving his emerald wing through the night
> [...]
> And how the Russian ferocity sighed
> When they sent to Siberia
> All the bastards from the Supreme Soviet.[22]

In keeping with Harvey's idea of time–space compression but elaborated with reference to the cultural claustrophobia of late Soviet society, Sosnora's references to different historical periods within the bounds of a single poem serve to create a bricolage, to use Claude Lévi-Strauss's term.[23] Instead of reconstructing distinct historical eras, Sosnora's later works present an obvious historical fantasy.

Similarly, the Postmodernist features of Joseph Brodsky's (1940–1996) poetry increased sharply in the 1970s and especially in the 1980s, after the

---

22 Viktor Sosnora, *Stikhotvoreniia* [Poems] (St Petersburg: Amfora, 2011), pp. 732–3.
23 Claude Lévi-Strauss, *The Savage Mind* (London: Weidenfeld & Nicolson, 1966), pp. 24–5ff.

Leningrad-based poet left the USSR. This becomes especially evident in 'Vertumnus' (*Vertumn*, 1991):

> One Caravaggio equals two Bernini,
> turning either into a cashmere scarf
> or a night at the opera. Now these cited
> metamorphoses, left apparently unattended,
> continue by pure inertia. Other objects, however, harden
> in the condition you left them in,
> thanks to which, from now on, they can be afforded by,
> no one. Display of loyalty? Plain predilection for
> monumentality? Or is it simply the brazen future
> barging in through the doors, and a sellout-resistant soul
> acquires before our eyes the status
> of a classic, of solid mahogany, of a Fabergé
> egg?[24]

Here, Brodsky deploys the Postmodernist device of estrangement to depict the contemporary person who lives in the wake of the crisis of faith in progress. In that historical context, the person's consciousness becomes little more than a collection of ideological symbols, signs of 'high culture', and literary plots – a cabinet of curiosities from which it is possible to create only temporary versions of the self.

The 1970s also saw the emergence of a movement of unofficial poets with religious overtones. Leningrad poets who represent this strain of Postmodernism include Viktor Krivulin (1944–2001) and Elena Shvarts (1948–2010), but the Moscow-based poet Olga Sedakova (1949–) also developed an interest in religious themes. Apart from Moscow and Leningrad, few regional centres possessed the kind of unofficial cultural structures that were needed to shape a postmodern consciousness. Nonetheless, at least one regional community coalesced around the couple Ry Nikonova (pseud. of Anna Tarshis, 1942–2014) and Sergei Sigei (pseud. of Sergei Sigov, 1947–2014). Sigei and Nikonova lived in Sverdlovsk before moving to the town of Eisk, on the Azov Sea. There, they released the journal *Transponans* (*Transponans*, 1979–87), which published their own work alongside that of many unofficial authors from Moscow and Leningrad who employed devices used in Russian Futurism and German Dadaism in the 1910s–1920s and in French Lettrism and Situationism in the 1950s. The conscious compilation of this encyclopedia of avant-garde poetics constituted, in itself, an expression of the postmodern consciousness.

---

24 Joseph Brodsky, 'Vertumnus', trans. Joseph Brodsky, in *Selected Poems 1968–96*, ed. Ann Kjellberg (London: Penguin Books, 2020), p. 137.

Postmodernist Prose

Many different forms of artistic experimentation could be contained within this new postmodern consciousness. Furthermore, as in previous historical eras such as that of Mikhail Lomonosov (1711–1765) – whose art had mixed Baroque and Classicism (see Chapters 1.2, 1.3) – Russian Postmodernists combined elements of earlier styles, including Modernist ones. This was particularly the case with Postmodernist prose. The first truly Postmodernist works of prose include Andrei Bitov's (1937–2018) novel *Pushkin House* (*Pushkinskii dom*, comp. 1964–71), Sasha Sokolov's (1943–) novel *A School for Fools* (*Shkola dlia durakov*, 1973), and Venedikt Erofeev's (1939–1990) prose poem *Moscow–Petushki* (*Moskva–Petushki*, 1969–70). All these works touch on the impossibility – or difficulty – of distinguishing between that which is 'one's own' (*svoe*) in the author's or characters' consciousness and that which is 'foreign' (*chuzhoe*) to it. In *Moscow–Petushki*, there is no clear line between the events which actually happen to the hero and those which are the product of his imagination. *A School for Fools* depicts reality from the perspective of an intellectually impaired boy who suffers from a split personality disorder yet gains the reader's confidence by expressing himself in a clever and meaningful way.

Pushkin House narrates the life of Lev Odoevtsev, a philologist and man of aristocratic origin who lives in Leningrad. The novel's chapter titles reference Russian literary works such as Ivan Turgenev's (1818–1883) *Fathers and Children* (*Ottsy i deti*, 1862) or are hybrids of a number of such works. For example, the third section is called 'The Poor Horseman' and one of the novel's several epilogues is called 'Bronze Folk' – versions of the titles of Pushkin's poem *The Bronze Horseman* (*Mednyi vsadnik*, 1833) and Fedor Dostoevskii's (1821–1881) novel *Poor Folk* (*Bednye liudi*, 1846). Adding to this literary self-consciousness is the fact that one of Lev's main concerns is how to relate to figures such as his father (a philologist) and a character named Dmitrii Iuvashev, also known by the nickname Uncle Dickens, who has returned from imprisonment in the Gulag and whose name alludes to the real surname of the absurdist writer Daniil Kharms (1905–1942): Iuvachev. Lev's own consciousness is deeply textual: he finds that he cannot separate himself from the experiences of others, including his grandfather, whose diaries he reads. Moreover, the narrator engages in long, metatextual digressions that stress the fictionality of Lev's character. For Odoevtsev, to distinguish between that which is 'his own' and that which is 'foreign' would mean taking responsibility for society's traumatic past – something he does not

wish to do. The questions Bitov poses through Postmodernist form thus acquire a political meaning from the start of the novel.

The 1980s saw the emergence of several prose writers who became crucial to the evolution of Russian Postmodernist literature, in particular Vladimir Sharov (1952–2018), Viktor Pelevin (1962–), and Vladimir Sorokin (1955–). The novels of Sharov share features with alternate history. But Sharov complicates the genre: in his fantastical versions of the history of the Russian Revolution, Soviet history becomes the result of actions taken by religious sects of his own invention or is described from the perspective of strange and fantastical characters. Sharov wrote his first novels without intending to publish them. Indeed, the publication of his works in the post-Soviet era caused a scandal. When the literary journal *New World* (*Novyi mir*, 1925–) printed Sharov's novel *Before and During* (*Do i vo vremia*, 1987) in 1993, an open letter by critics protesting its publication appeared in the same issue. The plot of the novel is based on the biography of the French writer Germaine de Staël, but in Sharov's telling de Staël becomes a Russian aristocrat who gives birth to herself twice with the help of a mandrake root and subsequently becomes Stalin's mother. Sharov – or rather his heroes – thus offer an intentionally absurdist explanation for the origin of the dictator's pseudonym (Stalin's real surname was Dzhugashvili). Sharov's predilection for the grotesque transformation of real events shocked establishment critics who were used to discussing Stalinism only in the tragic mode of works such as those of Aleksandr Solzhenitsyn (1918–2008).

An abiding theme in Sharov's novels is the characters' attempts to find meaning in Soviet history, which otherwise appears to be a vicious circle of violence. However, these attempts result in a surrealist image of reality, and in this sense they cannot be considered a success. Sharov's novels frequently feature storyteller-witnesses who have participated in real or imaginary – yet always significant – historical events. These witnesses often seem mentally ill, and as a result we cannot rely on their narratives.[25] Sharov's novels mark an important turn: rather than offering explanations for twentieth-century Russian history – as many dissidents did – their plots centre on the very process of searching for explanations, and the consequences of that process.

Pelevin began publishing his works at the end of the 1980s. It was not long before he became famous: first among readers of science fiction, and then among a younger generation of readers. Pelevin has clearly been influenced

---

25 For the thought on the significance of unreliable narrators in Sharov's novels, I am grateful to Mark Beloziorov.

by the ideas of Zen Buddhism that had filtered into Europe through the New Age movement. His stories and novels present the reality that lies beyond human consciousness as incomprehensible or illusory and the consciousness itself as something that is formed by media and by the virtual reality that computers generate. These ideas recall the concept of simulacra developed by the French philosopher Jean Baudrillard.[26] However, in his rare interviews Pelevin has avoided discussing his philosophical influences. His best-known novel, *Generation 'P'* (*Generation 'P'*, 1999), represents the Russian elections and the political struggle of the 1990s as a simulacrum generated by PR manipulators. The novel appeared almost simultaneously with the film *The Matrix*, directed by the Wachowskis, and indeed Pelevin's portrayal of reality as staged resembles the portrayal of reality in the film. Pelevin and the Wachowskis came to their ideas independently, yet both responded to the same phenomenon: the mediatisation of society that had come with the spread of computers and the internet throughout the 1990s and a new stage of development of television in the same decade.

There are also noticeable differences between *Generation 'P'* and *The Matrix*. The mythology of *The Matrix* foretells a collective liberation led by the charismatic Neo. But Pelevin has long insisted that the liberation of consciousness must happen on an individual level, and that it inevitably results in the severance of social relations. Pelevin perceives all revolutionary or reformist movements through an ironic lens and represents them in ways that reflect their portrayal in Russian television propaganda of the 2000s–2010s. He was the first author in Russia to combine a Postmodernist aesthetic with the pessimistic and conservative world view that holds that the public sphere is always a mirage and the elite always lies to the people. This aesthetic did not make extensive inroads into Russian culture, and Pelevin's conservative individualism remains an isolated case. Instead, Russia saw the formation of a right-wing populist aesthetic that treats Postmodernism as a purely semiotic mechanism for mocking any attempt to discuss post-Soviet society and for predicting the phantasmatic resurrection of the USSR or those ancestral forms of collectivity that the German sociologist Ferdinand Tönnies called *Gemeinschaft*. Examples may be found in the work of the writer and singer Mikhail Elizarov (1973–).[27]

---

26 Jean Baudrillard, *Simulacra and Simulation*, trans. Sheila Faria Glaser (Ann Arbor: University of Michigan Press, 1994).

27 On the mechanisms of Elizarov's success, see, for example, Il'ia Kukulin, 'VRIO vmesto Klio: Obrazy istorii v dvukh literaturno-khudozhestvennyh polemikakh 2008 goda' [VRIO instead of Klio: Views of history in two literary polemics in 2008], *Pro et Contra* 13.1 (2009), 20–35.

Like Pelevin, Sorokin is known worldwide and his works are, without a doubt, Postmodernist. During the Soviet era, he belonged to the circle of Moscow Conceptualists and became the only visible writer of prose among the poets in this community. (To be sure, some Conceptualist poets turned to prose later on.) Sorokin's early stories play out the self-destruction of Soviet discourses: they begin as exemplary works of Socialist Realism, but then their heroes begin to behave strangely and end up performing cruel rituals or sexual acts that are described in a naturalistic way. Together, his early works expose the violent subconscious of Soviet discourses or present society as a purely discursive phenomenon. Sorokin's first novel, *The Queue* (*Ochered'*, 1985), thus consists entirely of the utterances of people who are standing in an endless queue to purchase a product that is in short supply:

> – I wanted to go look at the poster and find out what's on, but would you believe, I couldn't get past.
> – Why not?
> – 'Cos our queue stretches all the way up there. That's where the end is.
> – Right up at *Synthetics?*
> – Uh-huh.
> – Can't be.
> – It can.
> – That's quite something.
> – And new people are joining on, that's the thing.
> – Then of course it makes sense to stay.
> – That's what I thought.
> – And we're so near too.
> – You young people are pushing me right into the wall . . .
> – Sorry.[28]

As many critics have observed, the novel presents the queue as a discursive phenomenon: the reader cannot tell which product the characters wish to obtain; the narrative consists mostly of typical utterances that might be exchanged by people in a queue.

In the post-Soviet period, Sorokin wrote and published many novels, stories, and plays and even a libretto for Leonid Desiatnikov's (1955–) well-known opera *The Children of Rosenthal* (*Deti Rozentalia*, 2003); he also wrote screenplays for a number of films. For years, his novels provoked scandals with their brutal scenes of violence and sex as well as their parodies of an official cult of Russian classics and a local cult of unsanctioned literature

---

28 Vladimir Sorokin, *The Queue*, trans. Sally Laird (New York: New York Review Books, 2008), pp. 19–20.

among the critically minded intelligentsia. In the novel *Blue Lard* (*Goluboe salo*, 1999), Stalin and Khrushchev are portrayed as gay lovers, while famous poets such as Anna Akhmatova (1889–1966) and Vsevolod Nekrasov appear in a ridiculous, grotesque light. This novel depicts an anti-utopia where the dominant cultural power of the twenty-first century is now totalitarian China, and the heroes' language abounds in jargon derived from Chinese words. A similar Sinicisation of the future occurs in Sorokin's filmscript *Target* (*Mishen'*), which the director Aleksandr Zeldovich brought to the screen in 2010. The sex scenes that permeate Sorokin's novels, as well as the author's ironic stance towards the cult of Russian classics (which became a feature of civic religion in Russia under Vladimir Putin), provoked attacks by conservative youth organisations which were triggered and supported by Putin's administration as well as other cultural figures.

Sorokin and Pelevin are often compared, and their popularity is frequently perceived by conservative critics as a sign of the degradation of readers' tastes in post-Soviet Russia. Yet their political views differ. Sorokin has noted many times that what interests him is the discursive nature of society and literature. But works such as *Telluria* (*Telluriia*, 2013) – which consists of fifty novellas presenting the future fragmentation of Russia into separate states and communities – make it clear that his own approach to discourse is rooted in consistently anti-totalitarian and, ultimately, liberal views. Like Prigov, Sorokin is interested chiefly in the hegemonic languages of politics and mass culture, which theoretically can be resisted. In contrast to Pelevin, the finale of *Telluria* suggests that individual liberation does not offer a way out of the dead end; rather, it precipitates a civilisational crisis. In his collection of stories, *The Monoclone* (*Monoklon*, 2010), and to a certain extent in the novella *Day of the Oprichnik* (*Den' oprichnika*, 2006) and the collection *Sugar Kremlin* (*Sakharnyi kreml'*, 2008), Sorokin uses his signature methods to satirise the repressive Russian state in its Soviet as well as contemporary manifestations. Moreover, in 2022 he published several articles in the European press that sharply criticised Russia's invasion of Ukraine.

The Afterlives of Postmodernism?

During the 1990s, critics often complained that all of the Russian publishing houses and galleries had been 'hijacked' by Postmodernists, and that this spelled an end to Russian Realism, which is allegedly one of the most important pillars of Russian culture. In 1993, for instance, Solzhenitsyn received the Medal of Honour for Literature from the National Arts Club

in New York City and dedicated his acceptance speech to complaining about the 'grip' of Postmodernism. Any effort to test such claims produced a strange effect. The cultural historian Andrei Zorin (1956–) has described this effect in an essay recounting his chairmanship of the Russian Booker Prize jury in 1998, when he read several dozen novels published the previous year:

> Contemporary literary criticism had taught me to perceive contemporary literature as a battlefield between the traditionalists and the postmodernists. I cannot judge the extent to which my own assumptions were correct for our literature overall, but I did not find any postmodernists whatsoever. . . . The conservative-realist way of writing was represented by a few uninteresting works, while the vast majority of nominated texts belonged more to the styles of neo-decadence and neo-modernism. In 1997, the Russian novel had succumbed to an epidemic of sweet, languorous erotica, mystical symbols and belated experiments with stream of consciousness.[29]

Zorin's words illuminate an important paradox. During the 1990s two phenomena came to co-exist in public space: on the one hand, the emancipatory Postmodernism which had originated in the unsanctioned literature of the 1970s, and, on the other, a mass commercial style which combined traits of Modernism and Postmodernism and was grounded in the aesthetics of épatage: the representation of sexual scenes, cruelty, and transgression. It was precisely these sensationalist elements that post-Soviet critics labelled Postmodernist traits, even though they had appeared already in French Naturalism of the nineteenth century. They may have come to this conclusion because, in addition to offering such shocking descriptions, mass-market works of the 1990s also parodied the language of Soviet and post-Soviet media. After this wave of sensationalist mass culture was replaced by a nationalist version of mass culture, critics became convinced that Russian literature had 'overcome' Postmodernism. This was patently untrue. Instead, one can identify two distinct processes of transformation in Postmodernist culture since 2000.

The first of these processes has been the use of the Postmodernist critique of ideology to legitimise mass political cynicism as a new world view that Russian society must adopt in order to show solidarity with the authorities. Lipovetsky has termed this hybrid aesthetic 'pseudomorphosis', a productive use of the geological metaphor first introduced by Oswald

---

29 Andrei Zorin, 'Kak ia byl predsedatelem' [When I was chairman], in *Gde sidit fazan: Ocherki poslednikh let* [Where the pheasant sits: Essays of recent years] (Moscow: Novoe literaturnoe obozrenie, 2003), p. 53.

Spengler in his book *The Decline of the West*.[30] As Lipovetsky explained in 2018, 'postmodernism was replaced by outwardly similar but fundamentally different – if not contrasting – discursive components that neutralised the critical potential of postmodernism. This took place parallel to the development of a theoretical (rather, pseudotheoretical) pseudomorphosis that enabled the legitimisation of reactionary ideas in a trendy new outfit.'[31] Those who subscribe to this world view go so far as to call themselves Postmodernists, as is the case with the far-right radical political philosopher Aleksandr Dugin (1962–).

The second process that has reshaped Russian Postmodernist culture since 2000 is its development of a new aesthetic. In 2008, Lipovetsky hypothesised about the advent of 'late Postmodernism' by analogy with Jameson's idea of 'late capitalism'.[32] While I agree broadly with Lipovetsky, I disagree with the term itself. The concept of 'late capitalism' presupposes that capitalism will end in the foreseeable future. But I, unlike Jameson, am not a Marxist and so I cannot know whether capitalism will ever end. The same holds true for Postmodernism. I therefore propose terming the new phase of this style 'communicative Postmodernism' as a way of capturing how contemporary innovators in Russia and across the Global North seek to re-create 'communication protocols' among people. Since 2010, Postmodernist literature has shown how an understanding of the endless fluctuations between that which is 'one's own' and that which is 'foreign' within the consciousness of the contemporary person can facilitate a re-evaluation of the experiences of friendship, love, empathy, and solidarity. Works that stand out in this regard include those by Iulii Gugolev (1964–), Mariia Stepanova (1972–), Linor Goralik (1975–), Maria Boteva (1980–), Denis Osokin (1977–), Stanislav Lvovskii (1972–), Dmitrii Garichev (1987–), Dmitrii Gerchikov (1996–), Stanislava Mogileva (1983–), Oksana Vasiakina (1989–), Daria Serenko (1993–), and Galina Rymbu (1990–). It is the duty of future scholars to engage in serious analysis of this new stage of Russian Postmodernism.

Translated by Katerina Pavlidi

---

30 Oswald Spengler, *The Decline of the West*, vol. I, *Form and Actuality*, trans. Ch. F. Atkinson (London: George Allen & Unwin, 1929).

31 Mark Lipovetskii, 'Psevdomorfoza: Reaktsionnyi postmodernizm kak problema' [Pseudomorphosis: Reactionary Postmodernism as a problem], *Novoe literaturnoe obozrenie* [New literary review] 151 (2018), 223–45.

32 Lipovetskii, *Paralogii*.

Further Reading

Beumers, Birgit, and Mark Lipovetsky, *Performing Violence: Literary and Theatrical Experiments of New Russian Drama* (Bristol: Intellect, 2009).

Chernetsky, Vitaly, *Mapping Postcommunist Cultures: Russia and Ukraine in the Context of Globalization* (Montreal: McGill-Queen's University Press, 2007).

Dobrenko, Evgeny, and Mark Lipovetsky (eds.), *Russian Literature since 1991* (Cambridge: Cambridge University Press, 2015).

Epstein, Mikhail, Aleksandr Genis, and Slobodanka Vladiv-Glover (eds.), *Russian Postmodernism: New Perspectives on Post-Soviet Culture*, Studies in Slavic Literature, Culture, and Society 3 (Providence: Berghahn Books, 1999) and rev. edn (New York: Berghahn Books, 2016).

Lipovetsky, Mark, *Postmodern Crises: From Lolita to Pussy Riot*, Ars Rossica (Boston: Academic Studies Press, 2017).

Lipovetsky, Mark (ed.), 'Russian poetry in the 2000s–2010s', special issue, *Russian Studies in Literature* 54.1–3 (2018).

Noordenbos, Boris, *Post-Soviet Literature and the Search for a Russian Identity*, Studies in European Culture and History (New York: Palgrave Macmillan, 2016).

Sandler, Stephanie, 'Kirill Medvedev and Elena Fanailova: Poetry, ethics, politics, and philosophy', *Russian Literature* 87–9 (2017), 281–313.

Sandler, Stephanie, 'Mandelstam among contemporary poets: Zhdanov, Eremin, Glazova', in Julie Hansen, Karen Evans-Romaine, and Herbert Eagle (eds.), *Living through Literature: Essays in Memory of Omry Ronen* (Uppsala: Uppsala University's Acta Upsaliensis, 2019), 121–40.

Uffelmann, Dirk, *Vladimir Sorokin's Discourses: A Companion* (Boston: Academic Studies Press, 2020).

Contemporary Movements

MARIJETA BOZOVIC

In memory of Dmitrii Golynko

Introduction: End of the Ceasefire

While the first post-Soviet literary movements can be mapped in terms of their relationship to the marketplace, the decades that followed the 1990s marked the return of politics to Russian literature. Beginning early in the 2000s and building to a crescendo during the years of protest against Putin's rule in 2011–12, then again in response to the annexation of Crimea in 2014 – with demonstrations that braved Siberian winters and a global pandemic alike in 2020 – and reaching new heights with the shocking invasion of Ukraine in 2022, the cultural sphere in Russia is now characterised by political polarisation. If post-Soviet Russia dared to dream of joining the former west in the 'after history' fantasy of the 1990s – reflected in the arts by the flattened horizon of ever-expanding Postmodernism and economically in the worst privatisation-as-pillaging catastrophe across the former Second World – history returned to Russia with a vengeance in the twenty-first century.[1] I mark 1999 as a watershed moment: the year of Vladimir Putin's ascendance and, in the literary sphere, the publication of Viktor Pelevin's (1962–) prescient novel *Generation 'P'* (*Generation 'P'*). Many – most – cultural producers might not have fully realised it at the time, but what the poet Aleksandr Skidan (1965–) has called the political 'ceasefire' in culture was over.[2]

---

1 Marija Hlavajova and Simon Sheikh, *Former West: Art and the Contemporary after 1989* (Cambridge, MA: MIT Press, 2017); Francis Fukuyama, 'The end of history?', *National Interest* 16 (Summer 1989), 3–18; Stephen Crowley, 'Russia: The reemergence of class in the wake of the first "classless" society', *East European Politics & Societies* 29.3 (2015), 699.

2 My subheading is inspired by Aleksandr Skidan's prescient review of Kirill Medvedev. A. Skidan, 'Konets peremiriia: Zametki o poezii Kirilla Medvedeva' [The end of the ceasefire: Notes on the poetry of Kirill Medvedev], *Kriticheskaia massa* [Critical mass]

Over the course of Putin's many terms as de facto leader of Russia, an increasingly conservative and nationalist ideology has taken over much of the country. It has drawn energy from the far-right fringe movements as well as from centre-right elite institutions. Most of the opposition to the regime has come from what I will loosely term the liberal centre: a relatively popular liberalism with a steady base in the intelligentsia and strong connections abroad. However, as early as 2001 smaller movements daringly began to declare their opposition from the left.[3] The cultural sphere indeed remains the only space for left-orientated, or explicitly Marxist, critique in post-Soviet Russia, particularly in cheaper (less monitored, less funding-dependent) arts like poetry and performance. If earlier generations were shaped politically and aesthetically by the collective traumas of state socialist repression – and so rejected socialism as any possible basis for a new system – the generations that came to adulthood in the 1990s and after saw in late capitalism (disaster capitalism, cognitive capitalism, globalism) no viable alternative. In the words of feminist socialist poet Galina Rymbu (1990–):

> I'm sure no workers' children went hungry in the 1970s and 1980s. I grew up in a factory settlement in Omsk, in Siberia, and when I went to school, I often saw workers' children faint from hunger during class. I myself am the daughter of a worker and a schoolteacher, and they went years without receiving their salary.[4]

Over the past two decades, a small but growing number of Russian artists and writers (in particular as part of leftist, feminist, and queer activist movements) have based their practices on the premise that alternative social organisation is not only still imaginable but practicable, and that, as Alain Badiou puts it, 'all those who abandon this hypothesis immediately resign themselves to the market economy, to parliamentary democracy – the form of state suited to capitalism – and to the inevitable and "natural" character of the most monstrous inequalities'.[5] The question of whether Badiou's 'communist hypothesis' might have a cultural correlative in the shell-shocked former Second World seems

2006.1: https://magazines.gorky.media/km/2006/1/konecz-peremiriya.html, accessed 12 March 2023.

3 The landscape of the New Russian Left is sketched in Rossen Djagalov and Marijeta Bozovic, 'Post-Soviet aesthetics', in Colleen Lye and Christopher Nealon (eds.), *After Marx: Literature, Theory, and Value in the Twenty-First Century* (Cambridge: Cambridge University Press, 2022), pp. 143–60.

4 Joan Brooks, 'A conversation with Galina Rymbu', *Music & Literature* (4 Feb. 2016), www.musicandliterature.org/features/2016/1/31/a-conversation-with-galina-rymbu, accessed 3 Sept. 2021.

5 Alain Badiou, *The Communist Hypothesis* (London: Verso, 2010), p. 6.

increasingly pressing for Russian activist writers. Naturally gravitating towards collaboration and collective initiatives, these cultural producers have formed some of Russia's most arresting contemporary movements in literature.

As I revise this chapter in the spring of 2023, one of its subjects has tragically passed; another was recently in a bomb shelter; others fear arrest; and most are refugees.

From Foment to Fire

Literary production in the 1990s took place under the aegis of the new book market (see Chapter 2.10), or on its fringes, in the chaotic world of literature online (see Chapters 2.11, 3.11). As the authors of *A History of Russian Literature* describe it, 'Popular literature flourished: translated and pseudo-translated literature gave way to original and prolific new work. The sheer abundance of texts transformed the publishing industry.'[6] Against and alongside the boom of new strategies for marketing literary works as profitable commodities, dedicated alternative spaces also began to multiply, geared towards a different field of cultural production. Russia's biggest cities witnessed a boom and metamorphosis of once-underground cultural strategies and mechanisms: readings, events, and prizes were pulled into new, semi-public – if privately owned – spaces like literary cafés (such as Moscow's beloved club Project OGI). A decade or so later, such alternative venues became the breeding ground for avant-garde, leftist, feminist, and LGBTQ+ literary foment.

Before the 1990s, as Bradley A. Gorski notes, any critique of contemporary culture as over-commercialised would have been hard to imagine.[7] Two early exceptions to the rule, however, were the leftist poet and activist Kirill Medvedev (1975–) and the collective of artists who call themselves Chto Delat (What is to be done). Together they formed the vanguard of Russia's New Left. Although Medvedev did not publish his manifestos until after 2003 (when he criticised not just the commercialisation of culture but its imbrication with pseudo-fascism), there was explicit critique of the new bourgeoisie in his very first book of poetry, *Everything Is Bad* (*Vse plokho*), as early as 2001. The openly Marxist collective Chto Delat emerged in 2003 and quickly rose to international fame. In short, for the post-Soviet Russian avant-garde, the

---

6 Andrew Kahn, Mark Lipovetsky, Irina Reyfman, and Stephanie Sandler, *A History of Russian Literature* (Oxford: Oxford University Press, 2018), p. 766.

7 See Bradley A. Gorski, 'Authors of success: Cultural capitalism and literary evolution in contemporary Russia', unpublished PhD thesis, Columbia University (2018), p. 244.

'cynicism, commodification, and capitalization of culture' was evident within a few years of Putin's rise to power.[8]

Russia's anti-fascist left thus emerged seemingly overnight, nearly synchronously with their eponymous enemy. Indeed, Russia's right populist fringes grew from the same suffering and resentment that fuelled the return of a Russian left. Outlandish figures such as Eduard Limonov (1943–2020) and Aleksandr Dugin (1962–) emerged as the charismatic leaders of new right movements. As Fabrizio Fenghi notes, Limonov, Dugin, and other figureheads of the Russian right avant-garde embrace 'strongly anti-egalitarian and antidemocratic views' and 'appropriate totalitarian symbols and ideas'. At the same time, they articulate concerns that cut across the political spectrum, 'uncovering the risks connected with the widespread cultural and ideological conformism that took over after the fall of the Soviet Union'.[9] Medvedev, writing in the first decade of the twenty-first century, identified these same figures as having a near-monopoly on post-Soviet protest culture.[10] Populism was on the rise. It *had* to rise, Medvedev recognised, given the ballooning size of Russia's morbidly poor. If no one could offer a more inclusive, left-populist alternative to Dugin, trouble was on the way.

Spectrum Scan: Right to Left

The two dominant aesthetic styles in Russia since 2000 have been Postmodernism (see Chapter 1.9) and New Sincerity. I will argue here that these two styles have proven more similar than was immediately apparent, and that, ultimately, they have followed the same trajectory: practitioners who may have initially appeared progressive or cast themselves as apolitical largely moved politically to the right. Giants of the post-Soviet novel such as Pelevin and Vladimir Sorokin (1955–) continued to publish after 2000, but their works had a different energy. Those of Sorokin felt increasingly like declawed Conceptualism turned racy entertainment for middle-brow elites. The ranks of their stylistic heirs could be said to include the likes of Kremlin ideologist Vladislav Surkov (1964–) – the putative author of a number of Pelevin-like novels and stories under the pseudonym Natan Dubovitskii, such as the 2009 succès de scandale *Almost Zero* (*Okolonolia*). Peter Pomerantsev and other critics have gone so far as to accuse Surkov and his ilk of turning

---

8 Gorski, 'Authors of success', p. 244.
9 Fabrizio Fenghi, *It Will Be Fun and Terrifying: Nationalism and Protest in Post-Soviet Russia* (Madison: University of Wisconsin Press, 2020), p. 222.
10 Fenghi, *It Will Be Fun*, p. 222.

Russian politics into postmodern theatre.[11] The tactics and techniques of Poststructuralism turned out brilliantly suited to right-wing appropriation across the former Second World, but Russian culture and politics sped especially quickly towards what Hal Foster presciently termed reactionary Postmodernism as early as 1983.

In the introduction to *The Anti-Aesthetic: Essays on Postmodern Culture*, Foster describes the 'postmodernism of reaction' as a strategic repudiation of Modernism: 'neoconservatives sever the cultural from the social, then blame the practices of the one (modernism) for the ills of the other (modernization). With cause and effect thus confounded, "adversary" culture is denounced even as the economic and political status quo is affirmed.'[12] If we keep reactionary Postmodernism firmly in mind, we should be less surprised by its fluid merging with Russia's other key movement: New Sincerity. Indeed, the latter begins to look like reactionary Postmodernism's end game. Ellen Rutten traces the explosion of the term 'New Sincerity' in contemporary Russia: 'Bloggers, politicians, and cultural critics use the phrase to explain nostalgia for the Soviet era, Putin's media policy, and the Russian interventions in Ukraine' alike, while academics and intellectuals converge in terming '"sincerity" the prime aesthetic mode of "post-post-Communist" ... arts'.[13] Poets once linked to Moscow Conceptualism, like Timur Kibirov (1955–), have seemingly embraced concepts like sincerity, nostalgia, and authenticity – so thoroughly deconstructed decades before. Rutten identifies New Sincerity as linked to the 'paradigm to which it responds and whose lessons it incorporates: postmodernism'.[14] If I insist on specifying *reactionary* Postmodernism here, it is because I am keen to point out the implicit and explicit politics of New Sincerity, which I view as the aesthetic arm of twenty-first-century populism.

In their writing and politics, Limonov and his 'national bolshevik' followers (*natsboly*) straddle Postmodernism and New Sincerity, and it is their slide from the right avant-garde margin to defining, for a brief period perhaps, the political/cultural agenda of the Russian state that I select here as paradigmatic. Returning to Russia from exile in the 1990s, Limonov became an icon and role model to generations of Russian youth, who emulated his writing and also his

---

11 See, for example, Peter Pomerantsev, 'Putin's Rasputin', *London Review of Books* 33.20 (20 Oct. 2011), www.lrb.co.uk/the-paper/v33/n20/peter-pomerantsev/putin-s-raspu tin, accessed 3 Sept. 2021.

12 Hal Foster (ed.), *The Anti-Aesthetic: Essays on Postmodern Culture* (New York: New Press, 2002), pp. xii–xiii. First published 1983 by Bay Press (Seattle).

13 Ellen Rutten, *Sincerity after Communism: A Cultural History* (New Haven: Yale University Press, 2017), p. 2.

14 Rutten, *Sincerity after Communism*, p. 7.

personal style and politics. On paper and in person, Limonov overtly challenged the image and values of the classic Soviet and Russian *intelligent* (see Chapter 4.5). As Fenghi writes: 'The cult of marginality, heroism, and political violence; the play with gender and sexuality, often in the form of aggressive masculinity; and generally, the cult of beauty and physical strength, which the *natsboly* borrowed from Limonov's writing and public image – all of these elements represented a strong reaction against the traditional values of the Russian intelligentsia.' Fenghi suggests that Limonov's political art project 'attempted to create an alternative intellectual class oriented toward political and revolutionary action, a counter-intelligentsia'.[15]

The right margins share with left avant-gardes not only a longing for broader audiences (in Russia especially, given that their authors are typically denied access to state or liberal opposition platforms) but also for an aesthetics of and for a new political subject. While the artists of Russia's New Left try to locate that subject in pluralistic visions of 'the people', those on the right have found an easier focus in nationalism. Anti-elitist, anti-corruption themes have erupted organically all over Russian contemporary culture, but their tendency has been towards a populism 'of the Russian people'.[16] Seduced by the growing sense of opposition between 'the Russian people' and elite pro-western liberal intelligentsia, a number of cultural figures have made their way to the kind of populism so successfully co-opted by the state in recent years, and not only in Russia.[17] The writers Zakhar Prilepin (1975–) and Sergei Shargunov (1980–), for example, have moved from critique of Russia's socioeconomic realities and calls to revolt to full identification with Russian foreign policy and active participation in the wars in Ukraine.

A particularly Russian or post-Soviet element of what is, after all, a global phenomenon – the rise of populism and nationalism – is the role played by the intelligentsia. From its heights in the long nineteenth century to its complicated relationship with the Soviet state throughout the short twentieth century, the intelligentsia retained its peculiar collective identity as Russia's secular moral and aesthetic compass (see Chapter 4.5). From 'going to the people' (to educate and learn from the peasantry) to memorialising the Gulags, the intelligentsia – never entirely a class so much as an identity, defined by taste and education – fought, fed, and interbred with governing groups. And then things changed: the authors of *A History of*

---

15 Fenghi, *It Will Be Fun*, p. 13.
16 See for example Ernesto Laclau, *On Populist Reason* (London: Verso, 2005).
17 Benjamin McKean, 'Toward an inclusive populism? On the role of race and difference in Laclau's politics', *Political Theory* 44.6 (2016), 797–820.

Russian Literature suggest that 'internal divisions' led to a 'dramatic decline in the intelligentsia's social status' in the 1990s, in response to the economic and political pressures outlined above.[18] The divisive topics that they identify as driving Russia's intelligentsia apart include: 'Putin and his regime of power, the church, feminism and homophobia, anti-American and Russian nationalism, and as of 2014, the Maidan, the occupation of Crimea, and the "hybrid war" in Eastern Ukraine.'[19] Anne Applebaum's 2020 essay *Twilight of Democracy* illustrates a similar phenomenon in eastern Europe: Applebaum poses the question, seemingly without attendant self-doubt, why are so many of my friends now fascists?[20]

This narrative of a splintering intelligentsia might be reimagined as that of a centre increasingly unable to police its margins – in Russia, but also across much of the world. Russia's right and left alike 'attacked the Russian intelligentsia for its alleged passive acceptance of the status quo, for its hypocrisy, and for its ill-concealed elitism', as Fenghi writes of the *natsboly*.[21] While right-wing avant-gardes (such as Limonov) sought to conjure into being an anti-elite, openly nationalistic counter-intelligentsia based on rejecting a demonised west, left-wing avant-gardes longed instead for a globally oriented (not exclusively towards the former west) cross-class movement of emancipated intellectuals. This left the liberal centre, in some sense, without a coherent ideology or collective identity. While many of its institutions – the prestigious and productive *New Literary Review* (*Novoe literaturnoe obozrenie*, 1992–), independent publishing houses, numerous non-state prizes – have done relatively well, it is more difficult to speak of cultural or literary movements in this context, as much of the liberal intelligentsia's creative production is built on individual labour and recognition. To these ranks belong the names of celebrated writers such as Liudmila Ulitskaia (1943–) and Belarus's Nobel laureate Svetlana Aleksievich (1948–) – but we hardly speak of the Alexievich School or Ulitskaia movement. If we tell the story of contemporary Russian literature through its movements, what emerges is the story of a centre overshadowed by energies from both sides. I dedicate the rest of this chapter to the leftist activist writers.

---

18 Kahn et al., *History of Russian Literature*, p. 766.
19 Kahn et al., *History of Russian Literature*, p. 766.
20 Anne Applebaum, *Twilight of Democracy: The Seductive Lure of Authoritarianism* (New York: Doubleday, 2020); published in the UK as Applebaum, *Twilight of Democracy: The Failure of Politics and the Parting of Friends* (London: Allen Lane, 2020).
21 Fenghi, *It Will Be Fun*, p. 22.

For the Russian left, the twenty-first-century version of the Russian long-ing for 'world culture' meant (re)joining a global canon of Marxist thought and art. Since 2003, members of the Chto Delat collective have emerged as the most influential and internationally recognised representatives of Russian leftist art.[22] A group of artists and philosophers (including Dmitrii Vilenskii (1964–2023), Olga 'Tsaplia' Egerova (1968–), Nikolai Oleinikov (1976–), and Nina Gasteva; academically luminous names such as Oksana Timofeeva (1948–), Artem Magun (1974–), Alexei Penzin (1974–), and Ilia Budraitskis (1981–); and [Translit] poets Aleksandr Skidan (1965–) and Keti Chukhrov (1970–)), Chto Delat produces an international leftist newspaper and also performances, installations, videos, and philosophical texts, crossing histor-ical avant-gardes with contemporary art and critical theory from around the world. The group, which defines itself as a 'self-organized platform . . . intent on politicizing "knowledge production" through redefinitions of an engaged autonomy for cultural practice today', shares its name with Nikolai Chernyshevskii's (1828–1889) 1863 novel and Lenin's 1902 tract, both titled *What Is to Be Done?* (*Chto delat'?*).[23] Their manifesto proclaims:

> At this reactionary historical moment . . . We have to move away from the frustrations occasioned by the historical failures to advance leftist ideas and discover anew their emancipatory potential. . . . [W]e stand for a distribution of the wealth produced by human labor and all natural resources that is just and directed towards the welfare of everyone.
>
> We are internationalists: we demand the recognition of the equality of all people, no matter where they live or where they come from.
>
> We are feminists: we are against all forms of patriarchy, homophobia, and gender inequality.[24]

Nearly two decades after its formation, Chto Delat continues to find ways of producing challenging, politically relevant art, and their unofficial School of Engaged Art serves as a crucible for emerging artists across Russia year after year. In February 2022, members of Chto Delat were among the first Russia-based artists to openly voice their opposition to the invasion of Ukraine.

The closely related and also St Petersburg-based poetry journal [Translit] was founded one year after Chto Delat and brought together the poets of

---

22 Rossen Djagalov and I first wrote about Chto Delat as the pioneers of the New Russian Left in Djagalov and Bozovic, 'Post-Soviet aesthetics'.

23 Chto Delat website, https://chtodelat.org/b5-announcements/a-7/chto-delat/, accessed 12 Jan. 2023.

24 Chto Delat, 'A declaration on politics, knowledge, and art', Chto Delat website (Dec. 2008), https://chtodelat.org/b5-announcements/a-6/a-declaration-on-politics-k nowledge-and-art-4/, accessed 14 Nov. 2022.

Chto Delat and a younger generation who had studied closely with the Leningrad underground legend Arkadii Dragomoshchenko (1946–2012). I have written about the *[Translit]* collective elsewhere, and I highlight in particular the work of Aleksandr Skidan, Dmitrii Golynko (1969–2023), Keti Chukhrov, Kirill Medvedev, Roman Osminkin (1980–), Pavel Arsenev (1986–), and Galina Rymbu.[25] These poets are frequent collaborators, linked through the journal and varied independent publishing efforts as well as artistic and political events and actions in Russia and abroad. They are among the brightest stars in a broader contemporary constellation that shares an interest in the long history of the Russian avant-garde(s) and that conceives poetry as participating in a broader emancipatory project. These seven poets are united by their explicit Marxist political engagement: half are members or leaders of the oppositional Russian Socialist Movement political party.[26]

I argue that the return of a politically radical Russian poetic avant-garde began when Kirill Medvedev vowed to stop publishing poetry in the literary institutions and emerging neoliberal marketplace of Russia in the first decade of the twenty-first century. Initially hailed by Moscow literary society for his translations of the American writer Charles Bukowski into Russian and for his documentary tendencies and free verse form, Medvedev distanced himself through a series of refusals from a literary world that he saw as infected by reactionary politics and mercenary values. His refusal to publish and his transubstantiation of poetry into other forms and actions shaped an audacious and appealing new left poetics. When Medvedev began to publish again (primarily in platforms that he had started himself or had helped to build), his collection *March on City Hall* (*Pokhod na meriiu*, 2014) won the Andrei Belyi Prize for poetry, Russia's oldest and most prestigious non-state award. Medvedev connects both his poetic experiments and his political organising with the cause of independent Russian labour unions. Casting aside dichotomies between elite art and populist causes, he reimagines the avant-garde poet as, quite literally, the vanguard of tomorrow's citizenry. Since the late 2000s, he has been channelling his creative energies into supporting social movements, ranging from individual pickets and multiple arrests to his

25 Here I sum up my argument in Marijeta Bozovic, 'The voices of Keti Chukhrov: Radical poetics after the Soviet Union', *Modern Language Quarterly* 80.4 (2019), 453–78; and draw also from my monograph on the movement; see Marijeta Bozovic, *Avant-Garde Post-: Radical Poetics after the Soviet Union* (Cambridge, MA: Harvard University Press, 2023).

26 The Russian Socialist Movement (*Rossiskoe sotsialisticheskoe dvizheniie*, or RSD) is a left-wing political organisation in Russia that emerged out of several earlier organisations (including Vpered, or Forward) in 2011.

publishing house (Free Marxist Press (*Svobodnoe marksistskoe izdatel'stvo*)); video channel (Allende); and, most visibly, his protest rock band Arkady Kots (named after the Russian translator of the socialist hymn to the Internationale), by now a regular feature of anti-government rallies, union gatherings, and migrant solidarity events. As of March 2023, despite mass departures immediately around him, Medvedev has refused to leave Russia and is determined to remain a vocal and local opponent of the regime and war in Ukraine.[27]

In 2006, Pavel Arsenev joined with Roman Osminkin (whom he met in Arkadii Dragomoshchenko's underground poetry seminar, as if literalising a genealogical metaphor) to found a journal dedicated to their shared aesthetic and political convictions. Twenty print issues later, *[Translit]* (*[Translit]*, 2006–) has won numerous awards. Moving fluidly between print and online platforms, *[Translit]* has reimagined the avant-garde journal for the twenty-first century and offered a new and Marxian vision of world culture for contemporary Russia. Alongside its print publications and related public events, the *[Translit]* blog and social media pages see weekly, even daily updates and showcase unpublishable multimedia content, such as Arsenev's own video-poetry experiments. Arsenev's poetics cannot be understood outside the context of the collective endeavour: he is a curator and remediator of words across languages and media, best known nationally for his political slogans, which took centre stage in the protests of 2011–12. Arsenev's work with the Laboratory of Poetic Actionism and other new media experiments combine digital forms with the familiar features of the infinitely adaptable avant-garde journal as platform and medium. If Medvedev's poetics of refusal were the first to catch the public eye, locally and globally, Arsenev's efforts via *[Translit]* and related publications, discussions, festivals, and on- and offline outreach have done the most to forge the connective tissue binding the poets associated with the journal (each in turn a central hub in a growing network that includes many other artists, curators, activists, translators, and scholars) into a distinctive cultural phenomenon. Medvedev's gauntlet, thrown to the existing literary institutions of Putin's Russia, sparked a new left Russian poetry, but Arsenev made it a movement. Both Arsenev and Osminkin have since left the country but continue their literary activities from abroad.

---

27 I first wrote about Medvedev in Marijeta Bozovic, 'Poetry on the front line: Kirill Medvedev and a new Russian poetic avant-garde', *Zeitschrift für Slavische Philologie* 70.1 (2014), 89–118; repr. in Marc James Léger (ed.), *The Idea of the Avant-Garde and What It Means Today*, vol. II (Bristol: Intellect, 2019).

Second Sex after the Second World

Much of the most discussed recent Russophone political poetry comes from socialist feminist and radical queer communities. The notoriously difficult to characterise work of artist-philosopher Keti Chukhrov adds a transnational, decolonial lens. She is neither Russian nor entirely a poet: born Ketevan Chukhrukidze in Tbilisi, Soviet Georgia, Chukhrov moved to Moscow to study literature and philosophy. Her work slides between poetry, drama, contemporary art, political philosophy, and cultural criticism. Chukhrov's intellectual and political interests and extraordinary erudition are in evidence in her poetic works, which tend towards long dramatic verse forms and collect the voices of Moscow's various subalterns: migrant workers, sex workers, and precarious surplus populations. Chukhrov's work demands collectivity and remediation through form while conjuring post-Soviet political subjects in content. In a 2015 interview, Chukhrov explained that her dramatic forms were driven by dissatisfaction with other genres and their institutions: 'Contemporary art is too constrained by the gallery and by fixation on the art object, lyric poetry is too focused on the experience of the individual, and neither is an effective means for moving people to political insight or action.'[28] Gender themes are central to all of Chukhrov's works and interventions; likewise, Chukhrov's Russian texts are peppered with Caucasian actants and intrusions, which function as a disruptive outside to the European modernity project. Despite the many voices rumbling through her work, Chukhrov embeds her politics in institutional critique, lends her labour to collectives and collaborations, and refracts her poetic voice into multitudes. She uses her own vocal talents in some performances of her work but more frequently hands over her scripts to collaborative interpretations, stagings, and screenings by other politically and philosophically like-minded artists.

In 2014, amid the global tremors of Russia's unexpected annexation of Crimea and internal war against 'sexual deviants' and other so-declared undesirables with the legislative acts of 2013, Chukhrov debuted a piece that reads as painfully prescient today.[29] 'Not Even Dead', a half-Russian

---

28 Keti Chukhrov, roundtable interview by Marijeta Bozovic, Kevin Platt, and Stephanie Sandler, 2015, University of Pennsylvania. I develop this reading of Chukhrov's work and her significance to the larger *[Translit]* project in Bozovic, 'Voices of Keti Chukhrov'.

29 Chukhrov's piece, 'Not even dead', was performed at 'Reports to an Academy', a 'non-academic symposium' organised by Ekaterina Degot and David Riff, Akademie der Künste der Welt, in Cologne, 17–19 Oct. 2014.

and half-English verse drama, is set in a post-Soviet post-civil-war present that could be nearly anywhere (Ukraine; Armenia; Azerbaijan; Ossetia; Abkhazia; with a quick language change, Bosnia). Chukhrov locates us among those who supported 'the side of those that besieged the place', who have refused to relocate after losing, and who can expect only sporadic aid from Russia. These lingering 'post-' (post-Soviet, perhaps post-imperial, certainly post-apocalyptic) losers are the not-even-dead. The title refers therefore to the sorriest imagined incarnations of the post-Soviet subject. In the middle of the piece, however, a character suddenly shares an alternative potential origin for the title:

> If we now take the Georgian-Megrelian kvart-kvintaccord [this is a musical term referring to a chord] – this will be the key to cure and convalescence, it was even used to revive the dead, if the dead were children. Like in the song 'Sisa.' A mother steals the body of the baby, who is already in the coffin, and rushes into the forest to hide there and to sing this song to her son Bondo until he resurrects. Whether or not she succeeded nobody knows.[30]

The Georgian musical insertion into the endless grappling between two languages of empire appears linked to the theme of possible resurrection: the not-even-dead may well rise again.

Galina Rymbu in turn captured the imagination of Russian literary society in 2014–15 with poems such as the untitled 'the dream is over, Lesbia, now it's time for sorrow …' (*son proshel, Lesbiia, nastalo vremia pechali …*). Joan Brooks's English translation reads marvellously:

> the dream is over, Lesbia, now it's time for sorrow,
> time to throw off our rings and dresses at the bloody feast
> in honor of the memory of our sisters
> let's smash our glasses![31]

As the opening lines make clear, Rymbu makes allusions to Catullus and to Sappho; Eugene Ostashevsky also points out an echo of classical metres in her free verse.[32] However, the language she uses for her allusions is something else entirely, contemporary and elementally wild. She seizes on slang and

30 Keti Chukhrov, 'Keti Chukhrov v Tsentre vizual'noi kul'tury' [Keti Chukhrov at the Centre for Visual Culture] (2015), www.youtube.com/watch?v=eDE014uOsYg, accessed 20 March 2023. The English quoted here is as in the original.
31 Galina Rymbu, 'the dream is over, Lesbia, now it's time for sorrow …', trans. Joan Brooks, *Life in Space* (Brooklyn, NY: Ugly Duckling Press, 2020), p. 67.
32 Eugene Ostashevsky, 'Eugene Ostashevsky introduces three poems by Galina Rymbu', *Music & Literature* (2 Feb. 2016), www.musicandliterature.org/features/2016/1/31/eugene-ostashevsky-introduces-three-poems-by-galina-rymbu, accessed 4 March 2016.

political clichés, such as the 'Putinist slogan "Russia rises from her knees"', but renders them as literal, obscene, and shockingly living speech.[33]

Moving from youthful publications in local Omsk journals to leading Russian literary platforms in the space of a few years, Rymbu has been recognised by one cultural arbiter after another as the leading voice in Russian poetry of her generation. She has held that position and added an international readership stretching from Siberia to San Francisco. Her poems in English have appeared widely online over the past five years. In December of 2020 she was profiled in *Time* magazine, along with other founding members of the F-Letter (*F-pis'mo*) feminist writing collective; the *Los Angeles Review of Books* in the same month called Rymbu the voice of feminism.[34] Through classical references, sliding pronouns, oblique treatment of grammatical gender in Russian, and other formal play, Rymbu's work highlights gender and sexuality as central to understanding her region's histories and to contemporary possibilities for cultural and political change. Rymbu's gender politics inspire her doubled critique: of the neoliberal global present from its left margin; and of much of the left from feminist sidelines.

Rymbu left Russia for Ukraine to escape political persecution in 2018 and chose to remain in Lviv in 2022 despite the air raids and bombing. Rymbu's and Chukhrov's work reminds us that the literary and artistic practices of left feminism offer a vocal and compelling alternative to 'populism for the Russian people'. As the world polarises still more with the ongoing war in Ukraine, such writers challenge us to replace the term 'Russian' with 'Russian-language' or 'Russophone', or 'global Russian' across much of our scholarly work. What real and symbolic violence are we complicit in when we do otherwise? What purpose do literary histories serve – and how can we work to subvert, pluralise, and emancipate the genre?

Further Reading

Bozovic, Marijeta, 'The voices of Keti Chukhrov: Radical poetics after the Soviet Union', *Modern Language Quarterly* 80.4 (2019), 453–78.

Bozovic, Marijeta, *Avant-Garde Post-: Radical Poetics after the Soviet Union* (Cambridge, MA: Harvard University Press, 2023).

33 Ostashevsky, 'Three poems by Galina Rymbu'.
34 Suyin Haynes, 'How Russia's feminists are changing what it means to protest', *Time* (21 Dec. 2020), https://time.com/5908168/russia-feminist-poets-protest/; Francesca Abel, 'The voice of feminism: On "F-Letter: New Russian feminist poetry"', *Los Angeles Review of Books* (6 Dec. 2020), www.lareviewofbooks.org/article/the-voice-of-feminism-on-f-letter-new-russian-feminist-poetry/, accessed 8 Jan. 2021.

Brooks, Joan, 'A conversation with Galina Rymbu', *Music & Literature* (4 Feb. 2016), www.musicandliterature.org/features/2016/1/31/a-conversation-with-galina-rymbu.

Chto Delat, 'A declaration on politics, knowledge, and art' (Nov. 2008), https://chtodelat.org/b5-announcements/a-6/a-declaration-on-politics-knowledge-and-art-4/. Previously published as *When Artists Struggle Together* (St Petersburg: Chto delat', 2008).

Crowley, Stephen, 'Russia: The reemergence of class in the wake of the first "classless" society', *East European Politics & Societies* 29.3 (2015), 698–710.

Fenghi, Fabrizio, *It Will Be Fun and Terrifying: Nationalism and Protest in Post-Soviet Russia* (Madison: University of Wisconsin Press, 2020).

Foster, Hal (ed.), *The Anti-Aesthetic: Essays on Postmodern Culture* (New York: New Press, 2002).

Gorski, Bradley, 'Authors of success: Cultural capitalism and literary evolution in contemporary Russia', unpublished PhD thesis, Columbia University (2018).

Hlavajova, Marija, and Simon Sheikh, *Former West: Art and the Contemporary after 1989* (Cambridge, MA: MIT University Press, 2017).

Lye, Colleen, and Christopher Nealon (eds.), *After Marx: Literary Criticism and the Critique of Value* (Cambridge: Cambridge University Press, 2021).

Rutten, Ellen, *Sincerity after Communism: A Cultural History* (New Haven: Yale University Press, 2017).

Boxes 1
Close Readings

Box 1.1 Close Readings

Box 1.1 A Nineteenth-Century Verse Form: The Onegin Stanza

Aleksandr Pushkin (1799–1837) was a poet firmly embedded in tradition, not a radical innovator but always aware of his predecessors and alert to ways of adapting and improving the models they provided. The exception that proves the rule is the Onegin stanza, the only instance in all of Pushkin's oeuvre where he created his own stanzaic form. He did so for his unprecedented 'novel in verse' *Eugene Onegin* (*Evgenii Onegin*), widely considered the cornerstone of the Russian literary tradition. Composed from 1823 to 1831 and published serially between 1825 and 1832, the work is marked by sudden shifts in theme, character, setting, and mood.

The canonic text of *Onegin* consists of eight chapters, each of which contains about fifty stanzas. For a work of this length, it was essential that Pushkin devise a form that allowed both continuity and flexibility. Lacking prior associations, the Onegin stanza allowed him to convey the strange mix of tragic and comic that has intrigued readers for two centuries. It is the glue that holds together a consciously fragmentary plot, narrated at times with lengthy digressions, at times with striking omissions.

The Onegin stanza consists of fourteen lines of iambic tetrameter, broken down into three four-line units (quatrains) followed by a two-line unit. The first quatrain uses cross rhyme (a-b-a-b), the second adjacent rhyme (c-c-d-d), and the third ring rhyme (e-f-f-e). The stanza closes with a rhymed couplet (g-g). Following standard Russian practice, Pushkin alternates feminine rhymes (where stress falls on the penultimate syllable) with masculine rhymes (where it falls on the final syllable), so each stanza begins with a feminine rhyme and ends with a masculine rhyme.

> I vnóv' zadúmchivyi, unýlyi
> Pred míloi Ól'goiu svoéi,
> Vladímir ne iméet síly
> Vcheráshnii dén' napómnit' éi;
> On mýslit: 'búdu éi spasítel'.
> Ne poterpliú, chtob razvratítel'
> Ogném i vzdókhov i pokhvál
> Mladóe sérdtse iskushál;
> Chtob chérv' prezrénnyi, iadovítyi
> Tochíl liléi stebelék;
> Chtoby dvukhútrennii tsvetók

Uviál eshché poluraskrýtyi.'
Vse éto znáchilo, druz'iá:
S priiátelem streliáius' iá.

(Once more in solemn, rapt attention
Before his darling Olga's face,
Vladimir hasn't heart to mention
The night before and what took
   place;
'It's up to me', he thought, 'to
   save her.
I'll never let that foul depraver
Corrupt her youthful heart with lies,
With fiery praise . . . and heated
   sighs;
Nor see that noxious worm devour
My lovely lily, stalk and blade;
Nor watch this two-day blossom fade
When it has yet to fully flower.'
All this, dear readers, meant in fine:
I'm dueling with a friend of mine.)

(*Eugene Onegin*, chapter 6, stanza 17, with equimetrical
translation by James E. Falen)

Some scholars regard the Onegin stanza as a variation of the sonnet, since both have fourteen lines. However, biographical, literary-historical, and formal considerations all indicate that this was not its origin. If anything, Pushkin was expanding on the eighteenth-century Russian odic stanza, which employed two different quatrain rhyme schemes and a rhyming couplet.

In our exemplary stanza, the pauses suggested by the rhyme scheme coincide with the syntax. Strong logical breaks come after lines 4, 8, and 12. These quatrains are then followed by a pithy, grammatically independent two-line conclusion. Precisely because Pushkin invented the form, such pauses are by no means obligatory (as they would be in a Petrarchan sonnet, for example), and Pushkin often sets the syntax against the formal constraints. So why does Pushkin have them operate in concert here? The first four lines belong to the narrator and use a relatively uncomplicated and almost neutral style. Vladimir, an elegiac poet, is given appropriate – and unsurprising – elegiac epithets: 'pensive' and 'melancholy' (rendered by the translator as 'solemn' and 'rapt'). Similarly, his fiancée Olga is 'dear' ('darling'), an adjective that might have come directly from Vladimir's

Box 1.1 Close Readings

love poems. Lines 5–12 relay directly the thoughts that enter Vladimir's mind. They are expressed in a suitably 'poetic' register. Vladimir's former friend Onegin has suddenly become a seducer, causing Vladimir to cast himself in the heroic role of saviour. His thoughts become increasingly metaphorical: the seducer becomes a 'noxious worm' that attacks the beloved 'lily'. After this prolix display of indignity, the narrator returns in the final two lines: he translates – and lowers – Vladimir's eight-line flight of fancy, ultimately compressing it into a single prosaic line.

Pushkin's narrator constantly reacts to the language of his characters, and this interplay of 'voice zones' gives the novel its richness. When Vladimir later perishes in the very duel that he here imagines in such flowery terms, the narrator will use that same verb 'to fade' to describe his death. Whether this later usage should be read as ironic commentary or tragic lament – or both at once – is the kind of question that Pushkin leaves his readers to resolve.

The Onegin stanza left a mark on Russian literature as distinct as *Onegin* itself. So strong was its association with Pushkin's novel in verse that subsequent Russian poets wrote in Onegin stanzas only if they wanted their work to be understood in relationship to Pushkin, whether as a humorous variation or a nostalgic homage.

Michael Wachtel

> ## Box 1.2 A Nineteenth-Century Prose Form: *A Hero of Our Time*
>
> Russia's first great literary critic, Vissarion Belinskii, declared in 1847 that 'with us the personality is just beginning to peck its way out of its shell'. In the early nineteenth century, the word he used for personality, *lichnost'*, had its modern sense (a person's uniqueness) only as a secondary meaning. Its primary meaning was 'personal dignity'. This range of meanings haunts Russia's first psychological novel, *A Hero of Our Time* (*Geroi nashego vremeni*, first edition 1840) by Mikhail Lermontov (1814–1841).
>
> For his final version of the novel (1841), Lermontov assembled five stories, three of them already published, and added two pieces of front matter: an authorial preface to the entire volume, and the 'Preface to Pechorin's Journal', which explains and justifies the inclusion of the three stories narrated by the novel's hero, Pechorin. This second preface, interior to the plot of the novel, is provided by the travelling narrator of the first two stories. Ordered in this fashion, the novel has engaged its readers as a profoundly intricate study of Pechorin's struggle to understand himself in conflict with often hostile characters, challenging circumstances, and diverse social settings. It operates simultaneously on multiple levels not just on the fictional level as a psychological, social, and moral inquiry but on a fiction-making level as an exploration of the narrative, rhetorical, and generic resources which might make such an inquiry possible.
>
> At each step of the way, the novel reveals, complicates, and withholds details which might explain the causes and nature of Pechorin's personality, cloaking them in the genre conventions of the five stories: 'Bela' (travel notes by the eventual editor of Pechorin's journal and an exotic Romantic adventure tale told to him by an unsophisticated army captain), 'Maksim Maksimych' (*Maksim Maksimych*, physiological description of Pechorin), 'Taman' (*Taman'*, mock tale of supernatural dread), 'Princess Mary' (*Kniazhna Meri*, society tale), and 'The Fatalist' (*Fatalist, conte philosophique*). The two prefatory pieces offer ambiguous clues for interpretation: the author's introduction (added for the second and definitive edition in 1841) attacks Russian readers for their gullibility and misunderstanding of irony; the travelling narrator-editor's preface foregrounds the problem of Pechorin's history and character, beclouding the potential resolution with reference to treachery, duplicity, vanity, and – once again – irony, all the while withholding those parts of Pechorin's journal which do not concern his time in the Caucasus but which might have shown the development of his personality.

Box 1.2   Close Readings

This pattern of snares, equivocations, and acknowledgements of insolubility on the fiction-making level soon find replication and amplification on the fictional level, as Pechorin increasingly moves to centre stage in a series of encounters with the non-Russian peoples of the Caucasus ('Bela'), Russians of lesser cultural competence ('Bela' and 'Maksim Maksimych'), Cossack smugglers ('Taman'), Russian polite society ('Princess Mary'), and predestination ('The Fatalist'). The simple captain and the narrator-editor present Pechorin superficially, observing a series of contradictions in his behaviour and appearance. Pechorin speaks little, and in their narration his romantic confession to Maksim Maksimych also becomes superficial, if not trite. But to a culturally competent reader, Pechorin's illness and mad laughter ('Bela') and his pallor at the mention of Bela's name ('Maksim Maksimych') offer a promise of emotional life and conscience, as do the ten journals he has left with the captain and which pass to the narrator-editor for unintended posthumous publication.

Pechorin fulfils this promise most completely in the novel's longest section, 'Princess Mary', the part of his journal devoted to the social setting – westernised polite society – in which he was raised and whose conventions he has mastered. All of the novel's sections feature callousness and violence (the frequent juxtaposition of women and horses is a leitmotif), but polite society manifests them most subtly and Pechorin depicts himself as masterful at the prized social performances of seduction, humiliation, unmasking, and concealment. As 'hero' of his time, he embodies its vicious characteristics in superior measure, with greater self-consciousness, sensibility, and creativity than the other characters whom his first-person narrative presents, characters who serve as foils for his analytic ability (Dr Werner) and performative skills (Grushnitskii, Princess Mary). Engaged in the machinations which lead to his killing Grushnitskii in a duel and winning Mary's love, Pechorin's desires become mediated by those of his rivals, his actions become reactions, and conscience glimmers but faintly through the lines of his narrative. This moral awareness and the metaphysical daring he shows in the final chapter stake Pechorin's claim to 'personality' in the sense that Belinskii welcomed.

William Mills Todd III

Box 1.3 A Twentieth-Century Verse Form:
Maiakovskii's *lesenka*

Collaborating with visual artists to create handmade books and experimenting with typography, the Russian Futurists aimed to make poetry
tangible as *poetry* by challenging received ideas about the relationship
between the written text and its sounding counterpart. This often
amounted to nothing more than the use of bold fonts and other typographical gimmicks. In his poem 'From Street to Street' (*Iz ulitsy v ulitsu*,
1912), however, the Futurist Vladimir Maiakovskii (1893–1930) investigates
the interaction of sonic and graphic elements in verse in more depth:

Ú-
litsa.
Lítsa
U
dógov
godóv réz-
che. Ché-
rez
zheléznykh konéi
s ókon begúshchikh domóv
prýgnuli pérvye kúby.
('A / Street. / Mastiff / faces / sharp-/ er / than years. O-/ ver / iron horses / the
first cubes leapt / from the windows of running houses'; trans. Jenny Wade)

Written in the form of a *stolbik*, or 'little column', and published in an
obscure Moscow almanac in 1914, 'From Street to Street' inverts the usual
hierarchy between poetry's metrical and sonic elements and its visual form,
giving precedence to the latter. Rather than the exception, enjambment –
when a syntactical unit exceeds the visual limits of the single verse line – is
here the aggressive rule. This effect is further emphasised by the poem's
palindromic opening, pleasingly symmetrical to look at but awkward to
pronounce, lending the poem a halting quality that impedes metrical
scansion and may even prevent us from hearing the rhyme between *godóv*
and the later *domóv*. That the graphic arrangement of Maiakovskii's *stolbik*
conceals this rhyme from the eye further de-emphasises the sonic element.
In this manner, the *stolbik* highlights the tension between the look of the
poem and its sound, challenging us to move between, and so acknowledge,
poetry's multiple material strata.

The *lesenka* (stepladder) layout for which Maiakovskii later became famous
thus represents something of an about-face: while the look of these poems,

Box 1.3   Close Readings

with each metrical line split across several consecutive lines on the page, is certainly striking, this is a layout devised to facilitate oral recitation and to ease comprehension. As Maiakovskii writes in 'How to Make Verse' (*Kak delat' stikhi*, 1926), his most substantial discussion of poetics, this layout ensures that not only meaning and rhythm but also emotional tone is conveyed to the reader. Division into steps can transform the 'dispassionate' tone of a line such as 'Nádo výrvat' rádost' u griadúshchikh dnéi' ('One must tear happiness from days to come') into an impassioned 'shout':

> Lózung:
>> výrvi rádost' u griadúshchikh dnéi!

> (A slogan:
>> Tear happiness from days to come!)

Introducing a pause after the first word, the *lesenka* layout changes the rhythm of the line as well as its intonational profile; both effects are intensified by the shift to imperative mood, which heightens the emphasis placed on the verb and invites exclamatory rather than declarative intonation.

There is some debate as to whether the *lesenka* constitutes an independent poetic form, since it is not associated with any particular metre. In fact, the layout was devised in part to ensure that more complex metrical profiles remained legible for mass audiences: while appearing to detach graphic lineation from metrical organisation, the stepped lines help to mark the most important divisions in each line and to make Maiakovskii's innovative approach to rhyme more apparent, as in the following lines from 'Conversation with the Taxman about Poetry' (*Razgovor s fininspektorom o poezii*, 1926):

> Vám,
>> konéchno, izvéstno
>>> iavlénie 'rífmy'.
> Skázhem,
>> stróchka
>>> okónchilas' slóvom
>>>> 'ottsá',
> i togdá
>> chérez stróchku,
>>> slogá povtorív, my
> stávim
>> kakóe-nibud':
>>> *lamtsadritsa-tsá.*

```
(You are,
        of course, familiar
                with the phenomenon of 'rhyme'.
Let's say
        a line
                ends with the word 'ottsá' [father]
Then
        one line after,
                repeating the syllable, we
put
        some other word:
                lamtsadritsa-tsá.)
```

The lines make fun of the taxman, who, the poem goes on to remark, treats rhymes like a 'bill of exchange', satisfied when a rhyme word pays exactly what is owed even when the result is nonsensical (*ottsá* / *lamtsadritsa-tsá*). The intervening rhyme is less predictable in that it is compound or broken – that is, the rhyme is created across a word division (*rífmy* / *povtoгív, my*) – but it is similarly exact. The lines thus represent a commentary on the limitations of traditional rhyme more broadly, in which the final word of each line is all-important. By contrast, the *lesenka* layout renders all parts of the line potential participants in the rhyme scheme, including the first word of the next line (*ottsá* / *togdá*), the first words of alternate lines (*skázhem* / *stávim*), or adjacent words (*konéchno* / *izvéstno*). This array of inexact and approximate rhymes holds the poem together as much as any exact, line-end rhyme.

The *lesenka* also fulfils a number of other identifiable formal functions, such as dividing the line into phrasal groups. Together with the greater prominence of rhyme, this makes the lines accessible even for audiences unfamiliar with versification and established conventions. These techniques are used so regularly as to occasionally threaten to become mechanical, an effect that is compounded by the civic or didactic message contained in many of Maiakovskii's *lesenka* poems. However, such examples are the exception rather than the rule. Even when composing political verse, Maiakovskii's imaginative use of the form speaks to his commitment to transforming poetry into a medium for communication with the masses. This became its primary function during the Soviet era, as the prominence of the *lesenka* in officially sanctioned poetry indicates.

Isobel Palmer

Box 1.4 Close Readings

Box 1.4 A Micro-Story: 'Blue Notebook No. 10'

In 1937 Daniil Kharms (1905–1942) wrote down a text in a blue note-book, numbered it '10', and added an enigmatic comment in the margin: 'Against Kant'. In 1939 he incorporated the text into the cycle *Happenings* (*Sluchai*) – a handwritten book containing absurdist stories and short plays in verse and prose – and gave it the deliberately formal title: 'Blue Notebook No. 10' (*Golubaia tetrad' No. 10*). The story was unpublishable in the Soviet Union, and it remained so until Perestroika began in 1985.

'Blue Notebook No. 10' has no plot in the conventional sense. Or rather, its 'plot' lies in the gradual disappearance of its protagonist by means of language: 'There was once a redheaded man, who had no eyes or ears. He had no hair either, so people called him redheaded only in a manner of speaking. He couldn't speak, since he had no mouth. He also had no nose' (trans. Anthony Anemone and Peter Scotto). The story's narrator resembles a machine that is programmed to progressively destroy the narrative instead of developing it.

The marginal note 'Against Kant' suggests that, for Kharms, the text was not only an absurdist farce but also a philosophical paradox. Kharms was friends with the underground non-Marxist philosophers Iakov Druskin and Leonid Lipavskii, who themselves were well versed in the work of Immanuel Kant and the neo-Kantian German philosophers of the beginning of the twentieth century, who interpreted Kant in Modernist ways. Viewed from this perspective, Kharms's story polemicises with Kant's *Critique of Pure Reason*. According to Kant, individuals cannot experience reality directly, as their knowledge of reality is determined by structures that exist a priori in the mind. Kharms, however, demonstrates that reality is constructed not only within the mind but also through language. The same mechanisms that language uses to construct reality can also be used to destroy it: 'He couldn't speak, since he had no mouth. He also had no nose.'

'Blue Notebook No. 10' can also be read as a polemical parody of a fragment from the theoretical treatise of the artist and pioneer of abstraction Kazimir Malevich, *The World as Objectlessness* (*Suprematizm. Mir kak bespredmetnost' ili Vechnyi pokoi*, 1921–2), which Kharms may have come across in manuscript form. The treatise was partly incorporated into Malevich's published book *God Is Not Cast Down* (*Bog ne skinut*, 1922), which Malevich

himself gifted to Kharms in 1927. However, the following fragment was not published in Malevich's lifetime:

> The third student understood nothing. There was nothing about the teacher that could have been understood. The teacher was objectless; he had within him nothing of the world of objects. He had within him no reasons, no Art, no Perfection, no Culture, no power, no matter. . . . The teacher had no hands, no legs, no head, no tongue, he had nothing that could be used to sense or feel, to understand. And he had nothing that could become the object of analysis – the teacher was a liberated nothing. The student went nowhere. . . . He remained in objectlessness, that is in nothingness. He became like his teacher. No one could understand him, just as no one could understand his teacher.

It may well be that Kharms was using his story to investigate the common epistemological thread stretching from Kant to Malevich, which presupposes that the world of essences is incomprehensible, inaccessible to the mind, and alienated from the world of phenomena that individuals can perceive. It is possible that Malevich was referring to the Kantian tradition when he named the first part of his treatise 'Suprematism as Pure Knowledge'.

The aesthetic that Kharms developed in the second half of the 1930s clearly anticipated Postmodernism. One recurring theme is the limitation of linguistic expression. For Kharms, the only true existence is that which takes place within a transcendent reality; any attempt to depict the world through literature thus founders due to the rigidity of literary discourse. In order to demonstrate the limitations of literature itself, Kharms based at least two texts on the principle of consistently dismantling the worlds they depict. These texts are 'On Phenomena and Beings No. 2' (*O iavleniiakh i sushchestvovaniiakh No. 2*, 1934) and 'Blue Notebook No. 10'. In other stories, and in tales such as 'The Old Woman' (*Starukha*, 1939), he uses a range of devices to show that the reader's encounter with depictions of reality is always mediated through discourse. It would therefore appear that this comical micro-story carried for Kharms an utterly serious theoretical meaning.

Ilya Kukulin
Translated by Katerina Pavlidi

Box 1.5 Close Readings

Box 1.5 An Internet Form: The Meme

A meme, the social-media expert Limor Shifman writes in *Memes in Digital Culture*, is 'a piece of digital content that spreads quickly around the web in various iterations and becomes a shared cultural experience'. Memes, put differently, are easily shareable tools (often funny, sometimes corny, sometimes quite violent, racist, or sexist) for communication, information-sharing, commenting on news, and emotional expression.

Memes are by definition intertextual. They often make viewers laugh because they refer to widely known slogans, songs, images, or pop-cultural icons. In Russia, where Soviet leaders long instrumentalised new and older literary texts to win citizens' hearts and minds, memes also often hark back to Russia's much-mythologised literary classics. Aleksandr Pushkin, for instance, appears as the nation's first rapper in a series of so-called image-macro memes – memes that pair an (often edited) image with a witty text. Their makers portray the writer, whose great-grandfather had come to Russia from Africa, with reversed baseball cap or headphones, and – as the cultural historian Eliot Borenstein has analysed – other accessories that irreverently (and not always unproblematically) frame Russia's leading literary icon in African American 'ghetto' visuals (see fig. 1).

Following Russia's full-scale invasion of Ukraine on 24 February 2022, another classic of Russian literary history morphed into a meme. Two days after the invasion, the internet censor board Roskomnadzor sternly instructed web users to refer to the events in Ukraine not as a 'war',

Figure 1 'You when you've found a new rhyme and go for it', internet meme, 2010s.
http://1001mem.ru/p3902770.

'attack', or 'invasion' but as a 'special (military) operation'. The mandate jibed with the longer-term, gradual but unmistakable rebirth of double-speak in Vladimir Putin's Russia, but this particular propaganda slogan was so at odds with reality that it triggered a vivid stream of online jokes and puns. A widely shared example is the meme in Figure 2, which appeared within a day of the Roskomnadzor decree. Rather than adding new text to an existing image – as in the Pushkin image-macro

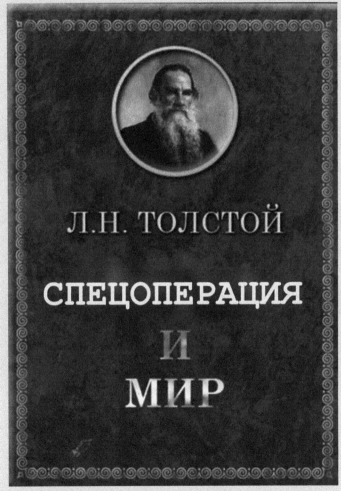

Figure 2 'L. N. Tolstoi, *Special Operation and Peace*', internet meme, 2022. https://newizv.ru/news/2022-02-27/mem-dnya-lev-tolstoy-spetsoperatsiya-i-mir-353249.

Box 1.5   Close Readings

memes – this meme builds on the popular online practice of replacing existing book titles with topical new titles. The image neatly mimics a classic edition of *War and Peace* (*Voina i mir*, 1868–9), Lev Tolstoi's world-famous novel about Russian aristocratic life before and during the French invasion of Russia. The cover – with its ornamental gold border, glossy capitalised serif fonts, and gold-rimmed fragment of a famous portrait by the painter Ilia Repin – oozes literary canonicity. But while the author's name is left untouched, the word 'War' in the title is replaced with 'Special Operation' (*spetsoperatsiia*), printed in a more modern and bureaucratic-looking font. The meme, in short, comments on the war in Ukraine by offering viewers an intentionally clumsy yet still official-looking version of what is perhaps Russian literature's most famous story of national history and military trauma.

The 'Special Operation and Peace' meme epitomises the vivid afterlives that Russia's literary classics can lead online. By 27 February, the newspaper *New News* (*Novye izvestiia*, 1997–) had labelled 'Special Operation and Peace' its meme of the day in an article featuring two variations on the meme (as well as the image in Figure 2, the report included another mock book cover in which the word 'War' was struck through and replaced with 'Special Operation' in red capitals). On the days that followed, these and similar images circulated online – invariably without image credits – in op-eds, blog posts, and across various social media, where they were actively liked, exchanged, and shared. By the summer of 2022, a Google search for the slogan was generating roughly 10,000 hits, including links to Ukrainian, Belarusian, and Japanese web domains. A Russia-based T-shirt company called DreamShirts even went so far as to monetise the meme: customers were offered shirts with the lettering 'Lev Tolstoi / *Special Operation and Peace*' in multiple colours and sizes.

Shifman rightly warns that 'the extent to which memes actually influence political processes such as legislation or regime change remains unclear'. This is no doubt true for the Tolstoi meme. Yet its online life does demonstrate something else: with its reliance on parody and provocation of laughter, the genre of the literary meme is ideally equipped for emotional expression and collective political commentary.

Ellen Rutten

Boxes 2

Genres

Box 2.1 Genres

Box 2.1 *Povest'*

Walking down an aisle of a Russian bookstore or library, one sees numerous books with the title *Rasskazy i povesti*. This common title for an author's collected works is difficult to translate: it could be 'short stories and short novels' or 'short and long stories'. As these awkward pairings show, the *povest'* occupies the space between the short story and the novel, both in length and in the scope of its engagement with its subject.

For most of the nineteenth century, in prose and in verse, writers used the word *povest'* in their titles and subtitles simply as a synonym for narrative, broadly understood, without generic specificity. Aleksandr Pushkin's *The Bronze Horseman* (*Mednyi vsadnik*, 1833), in verse, is subtitled 'A Petersburg Tale' (*Peterburgskaia povest'*); here the term is a space holder anchoring the adjective that carries the main information, as in such subtitles as 'An Eastern Tale' (*Vostochnaia povest'*, Mikhail Lermontov) and 'A Finnish Tale' (*Finliandskaia povest'*, Evgenii Baratynskii). Prose genre definitions were quite fluid: Nikolai Gogol titled one of the stories in his collection *Mirgorod* (*Mirgorod*, 1835) 'The Tale [*povest'*] of How Ivan Ivanovich Quarreled with Ivan Nikiforovich' (*Povest' o tom, kak possorilsia Ivan Ivanovich s Ivanom Nikiforovich*); Fedor Dostoevskii subtitled *Poor Folk* (*Bednyi liudi*, 1846) and *White Nights* (*Belye nochi*, 1848) as 'novels' but called *Notes from Underground* (*Zapiski iz podpol'ia*, 1864) a *povest'* and 'The Eternal Husband' (*Vechnyi muzh*, 1871) – a text longer than *Notes from Underground* – a 'short story'.

The *povest'* preceded the classic Russian novel and served as a stepping stone to it. Nineteenth-century romantic tales, adventure tales, society tales, and 'tales from the life of the people' (see Chapter 4.4) did not aspire to exhaustive treatment of their subject but still aimed to address it at considerable length. The *povest'* form allowed the writer to elaborate details of setting; it provided space for fuller descriptions of nature. Usually, the *povest'* had a single plot line, but unlike the short story (as it is understood today) the *povest'* was able to develop that plot line thoroughly and at leisure. A well-rounded timeline sets up a central event in the life of a character; the event compels the character – and the reader – to form a (moral) judgement. This focus on a single plot line and character kept the *povest'*'s concerns within the confines of the private sphere, rather than the national one that was to become the novel's domain.

Like the short story, the *povest'* achieved generic autonomy in the twentieth century. Several twentieth-century writers profited from the very in-betweenness of the *povest'*, which enabled them to sidestep the Soviet novel's

demand for a comprehensive ideological world view but did not limit them to the tight focus of the short story. The Soviet *povest'*, one might argue, was a self-consciously apolitical genre, used to explore in relative length concerns neglected – and even despised – by the Soviet novel: concerns of the private sphere. The *povest'*'s preferred hero is the ordinary person: an individual rather than a social type.

The Soviet war *povest'* is a genre of particular interest. Written by writers who became correspondents during the Second World War and worked under pressure to capture the individual and national experiences of the war, these tales often border on journalistic sketches and include personal observations alongside letters and newspaper reports. Distinct from the epic war novels that emerged in later Soviet literature, the *povest'* of the immediate postwar years has a limited scope: one soldier's fate or a group's heroic act. Viktor Nekrasov's 'In the Trenches of Stalingrad' (*V okopakh Stalingrada*, 1946), for example, is a young lieutenant's first-person account of the Stalingrad battle. With their focus on the everyday experience of war and lack of pathos, works by Nekrasov, Emmanuil Kazakevich, Vasil Bykau, Viktor Kurochkin, Boris Vasilev, and Iurii Bondarev set the narrative parameters of how to write about bloody battles, bravery, and heartbreak.

In the 1960s, a new generation of writers created what would become known as 'confessional' or 'youth prose'. Vasilii Aksenov's *povest'* 'Ticket to the Stars' (*Zvezdnyi bilet*, 1961) introduces its typical hero: a teen driven by youthful nihilism, deliberately defiant behaviour, and dreams of romantic adventure. In the 1970s, these writers – Andrei Bitov, Iurii Trifonov, Viacheslav Petsukh, Vladimir Makanin – turned to tales of family and career considerations. Trifonov, for example, offered detailed examinations (not glimpses as a short story would) of the minds of the generation that came of age after Stalin's rule, focusing on their conformism and heightened regard for the fragile privacy of their homes.

Women writers have often been drawn to the *povest'* as a genre that allows them a focus on women's lives and the struggles of the drab everyday. Works such as Natalia Baranskaia's *A Week Like Any Other* (*Nedelia kak nedelia*, 1969); Irina Grekova's tales about the life of a university department; and Galina Shcherbakova's 'Could One Imagine?' (*Vam i ne snilos'*, 1979), a story of Shakespearian passions unfolding in an unremarkable high school, avoid overt ideological engagement. In effect, however, they constitute (anti-)ideological statements.

Lyudmila Parts

Box 2.2 Genres

Box 2.2 Satire

Astolphe de Custine, an insightful and imaginative observer who visited Russia in 1839, wrote: 'If they [the Russians] ever succeed in bringing to full light their real genius, the world will see, not without some surprise, that it is a genius for caricature.' He believed that malicious accusatory laughter, a tendency to ridicule that is akin to mockery, was a product of the repressive nature of the Russian state.

From the early eighteenth century, when literature began to take shape in Russia as an institution, it developed under the specific conditions of tsarism, and then the dictatorship of the Bolsheviks. Because of the restrictions on direct expression of opinion, literature became almost the only platform from which it was possible to articulate, albeit indirectly, the current social, political, ethical, and philosophical agenda. Literature was able to develop in conditions of freedom, that is uncensored, only by the end of Mikhail Gorbachev's Perestroika.

Russian satire evolved within strictly permitted limits. Initially it took the form of a fable, a parody, a comedy, an epigram, usually based on ancient and Classicist examples. This Enlightenment satire was created by Antiokh Kantemir, Aleksandr Sumarokov, Denis Fonvizin, and Ivan Krylov. It ridiculed social and personal vices – laziness, greed, stupidity, ignorance – and rarely engaged with political issues, remaining mainly in the sphere of public mores.

A high point in Russian satire, even in the darkest conditions of censorship and the police state under Nicholas I, was reached by Nikolai Gogol. The strength, vividness, and artistic persuasiveness of the satirical types created by Gogol in his comedy *Inspector General* (*Revizor*, 1836), the 'poem' (as he called his novel) *Dead Souls* (*Mertvye dushi*, 1842), and other works brought an unprecedented variety of satirical characters to Russian literature. The main successor of this tradition was Mikhail Saltykov-Shchedrin, whose work fell in the era of the reforms of Alexander II. In much of his work, satire took on sharply grotesque and farcical features, to which contemporary critics responded negatively. But in his main works, such as *The History of a Town* (*Istoriia odnogo goroda*, 1870) and *The Golovlevs* (*Gospoda Golovlevy*, 1880), Saltykov-Shchedrin achieved more versatile satirical typification.

After the Bolshevik Revolution, at first there was no place for satire at all. The very phrase 'Soviet satire' was found by Marxist critics to be an oxymoron: satire directed against the Soviet regime was declared counter-revolutionary. However, it was in the 1920s that Russian literary satire

reached its apogee. Never before had so many brilliant authors in all genres – from poetry and drama to short stories and novels – worked in the satirical mode at the same time. There was Mikhail Bulgakov's grotesque surrealism; Vladimir Maiakovskii's sharp criticism of Soviet bureaucracy; Evgenii Zamiatin's gloomy, dystopian satire; the parabolic and densely quotidian satire of Iurii Olesha; the subversive transformations of language in Mikhail Zoshchenko's and Andrei Platonov's writings; the picaresque novels *The Twelve Chairs* (*Dvenadtsat' stul'ev*, 1928) and *The Golden Calf* (*Zolotoi telenok*, 1931) by Ilia Ilf and Evgenii Petrov, which enjoyed incredible popularity throughout the Soviet era; and the satirical dramaturgy of Nikolai Erdman.

Socialist Realism – established in the 1930s, with its positive heroes, historical optimism, and the depiction of life 'in its revolutionary development' – completely avoided satire. As a result, everything that depicted Soviet reality in a critical light was subjected to sharp criticism, as happened in 1946 when Stalin and his head of cultural policy, Andrei Zhdanov, attacked Zoshchenko, practically outlawing satire.

At the same time, however, the regime managed to appropriate satire and instrumentalise it. Official satire flourished in the USSR, aimed at bureaucracy, philistinism, and bourgeois mores, thus creating a special mode of criticism that simulated a 'struggle against deficiencies' and soothed social discontent. This satire was also used to prepare society for repressions against those categories of the population that were targeted by Stalin. Preparing a new campaign of purges in 1952, Stalin demanded the return of 'the Gogols and Shchedrins', who might 'burn all the shortcomings from Soviet life with the fire of satire'. This type of satire was to be completely loyalist. As Iurii Blagov wrote in 1953:

> We're for laughter! But we'd like
> Shchedrins of a kinder stripe
> And Gogols of the sort that don't
> Needle us, as was his wont.

The tradition of subversive satire did survive the Stalin period. The Brezhnev era saw a new flowering of satirical works by authors such as Vladimir Voinovich, Fazil Iskander, and Iuz Aleshkovskii, which appeared in the dissident and émigré milieu and revived the experience of Soviet satire of the 1920s.

Evgeny Dobrenko

Box 2.3 Genres

Box 2.3 Travelogue

Travel narratives are defined by a first-person narrator; a linear, itinerary-like progression; and a combination of factual and fictional elements. The genre effortlessly incorporates elements of the travel guide and treatises on history and art; philosophical, political, and ideological statements; and observations, impressions, and encounters that are pointedly personal, even intimate. The Russian travelogue, while clearly in this class, is also distinguished by its sociopolitical leanings: the ideological dimension often subsumes all others.

European travellers of the eighteenth and nineteenth centuries knew that they represented the norm against which foreign architecture, customs, art, cuisine, or climate were to be judged. By contrast, Russian literary accounts of western travels reveal the Russian traveller's acute awareness of being perceived by Europeans as 'other', or as representing a less developed, even exotic, civilisation. Denis Fonvizin, in his *Letters from the Second Journey Abroad* (Pis'ma iz vtorogo zagranichnogo puteshestviia, 1777–8), reacts to this perception by denigrating and ridiculing Europeans. Nikolai Karamzin, in his own *Letters of a Russian Traveller* (Pis'ma russkogo puteshestvennika, 1791–2), challenges it in turn by claiming European culture as the common ground for all educated people, including Russians.

Karamzin's *Letters* is a paradigmatic Russian travelogue: it established the archetype of the Russian traveller as a self-assured and sensitive individual who feels at home in Europe. This archetype would be imitated and contested by future Russian travelogues. Fedor Dostoevskii challenges it in *Winter Notes on Summer Impressions* (Zimnie zametki o letnikh vpechatleniiakh, 1863): his traveller directs his ire at the Russians' 'slavish kowtowing to European forms of civilization'. Dostoevskii refuses to hold up the west as a model and proceeds to denigrate it; only half in jest, he suggests that condemnation of the west is the Russian patriot's duty: 'to love one's country means to vilify foreigners' (in Richard Lee Renfield's translation).

While Russian narratives of travel to the west are occasions to ponder Russia's uneasy relationship with that part of the world, authors travelling to the Caucasus (the Russian Orient) and to the east assumed they were participants in the European colonising project and, therefore, on equal footing with European practitioners of orientalism. Aleksandr Pushkin's *A Journey to Arzrum* (Puteshestvie v Arzrum, 1829–36) is an ironic take on Russia's civilising mission in the Caucasus, but Ivan Goncharov in *The Frigate Pallada* (Fregat Pallada, 1858) indulges in condescension towards

other races as he travels through East Asia and the Pacific, thereby adopting a pose of superiority as a European explorer and would-be coloniser.

In the early twentieth century, the proletarian travellers Maksim Gorkii, Sergei Esenin, and Vladimir Maiakovskii described America as a terrifyingly mechanised and soulless society in accordance with the anti-capitalist ideology of the Soviet 'social order'. Gorkii's essay 'City of the Yellow Devil' (*Gorod zheltogo d'iavola*, 1906) renders New York almost entirely in terms of mechanical, frightening noise. The brief essay contains no human sounds, dialogue, or details of Gorkii's own movements and reception, only the cacophony that a voice cannot penetrate. Maiakovskii's *My Discovery of America* (*Moe otkrytie Ameriki*, 1926), too, is a propaganda piece trying to pass as a travelogue. In the first parts of his trip (in Cuba and Mexico), Maiakovskii hews closely to the travelogue genre: in addition to details of his movements and meetings, he provides historical data, political commentary, demographic information, and distances. But as he enters the United States, he begins recycling anti-capitalist and generally anti-western clichés. Ilia Ilf and Evgenii Petrov in their *One-Storied America* (*Odnoetazhnaia Amerika*, 1936), an account of their road trip across America during the Great Depression, avoid crossing the ideological line by rendering themselves silent observers and listeners and thereby safely forgoing personal interaction with the foreign.

Few people travelled abroad during the Cold War, and even fewer wrote about it, but those who did adhered to safe ideological frameworks. Viktor Nekrasov in his travel essay 'First Impressions' (*Pervoe znakomstvo*, 1960) emphasises his interaction with the Italians who fought the Nazis. Daniil Granin's travel sketch about Japan 'Rock Garden' (*Sad kamnei*, 1971) opens with the puzzling claim that the country has never been visited before, and indeed, Granin's narrator enters a country never visited by a Russian writer: Japan after the atomic bomb. Nekrasov and Granin, both war veterans in their own right, present Italy and Japan as if the Russian travelogue tradition had been burnt out by the war. They unite the Japanese, Italians, and Russians through the bonds of their common fight and shared victimhood: 'this bomb was dropped on us too'.

Like the Russian novel, the travelogue emerged in an intertextual dialogue with well-established western models. But more than any other genre, the travelogue remains to this day a means for reflecting on what it means to be Russian in contrast to various foreign Others.

Lyudmila Parts

Box 2.4 Genres

Box 2.4 Children's Literature

It was only in the early 1800s that imaginative literature specifically intended for children began to appear in Russia. The Romantic period provided fertile ground for children's literature to take root for several reasons: a new conception of childhood as a unique stage of life emerged, together with a fascination with the imagination and the fantastic and an interest in folklore. These elements came together in works such as *The Little Black Hen, or The Underground People* (*Chernaia kuritsa, ili Podzemnye zhiteli*, 1829) by Antonii Pogorelskii. The story concerns a boy's rescue of a favourite chicken destined for slaughter, which leads him to an enchanted underground world, where he is granted a wish that will later have disastrous consequences. This period also saw the appearance of fairy tales in verse by Aleksandr Pushkin. Pushkin drew not only on Russian folk culture but also on the works of the Brothers Grimm, Washington Irving, and others, reimagined for a Russian audience.

By the late nineteenth century, Russian children's literature had been professionalised, with a significant number of authors, journals, and publishing houses specialising in works for young people. Lev Tolstoi wrote extensively for children. Women writers now came to dominate, including Evgeniia Tur and, for younger children, Klavdiia Lukashevich. The prolific Lidiia Charskaia was by far the most popular author in this period, penning boarding-school stories and romanticised historical novels.

The revolution of October 1917 fundamentally altered the landscape of children's literature. The Soviets placed an enormous emphasis on children's ideological and moral development. The high profile of children's literature meant that even major writers such as Vladimir Maiakovskii and Iurii Olesha produced work for children in the 1920s. Contemporary debates around the direction of Soviet culture generally gained special significance in the realm of children's literature. Fairy tales and fantasy became an ideological battleground, with one camp arguing that they were irrelevant and dangerous, while others thought they could be transformed to serve revolutionary ends. Olesha's *Three Fat Men* (*Tri tolstiaka*, 1928) is a wonderful attempt to combine fantastic elements with a revolutionary message. The two leading writers of children's verse in the early Soviet period, Kornei Chukovskii and Samuil Marshak, had both spent time in England and were influenced by Lewis Carroll and the nonsense poet Edward Lear.

During the Stalin period, children's literature was expected to adhere to the demands of Socialist Realism. Tales of heroic deeds became popular, such

as *Timur and His Gang* (*Timur i ego komanda*, 1940) by Arkadii Gaidar. The book combines the traditional boys' adventure story with Soviet precepts of morality. The prolific children's author Agniia Barto produced patriotic poetry during the Second World War. Barto's realistic style eschewed flights of fancy and linguistic playfulness.

The Thaw meant that children's literature became less dogmatic in its interpretation of Socialist Realism. The possibilities widened for humour and protagonists who were less than perfect, and this period saw the emergence of some of the most enduringly popular heroes in Russian children's literature. A case in point from the 1950s and 1960s is the cycle *Dennis Stories* (*Deniskiny rasskazy*) by Viktor Dragunskii, featuring the amusing adventures of a boy growing up in Soviet Moscow. In children's verse, Boris Zakhoder rekindled the experimental spirit of the avant-garde. The space race gave a newfound popularity to science fiction, such as the long-running futuristic cycle *The Adventures of Alisa* (*Prikliucheniia Alisy*, 1965–2003) by Kir Bulychev, which feature a girl's interplanetary escapades. But perhaps the best-loved heroes from this period are Crocodile Gena and his companion Cheburashka, a cute monkey-like creature. They first appeared in the story *Gena and His Friends* (*Krokodil Gena i ego druz'ia*, 1966) by Eduard Uspenskii, but it was the stop-motion animated series that captured the hearts of a generation.

The fall of the Soviet Union led to a loss of state support for children's literature. But the early twenty-first century saw a strong recovery, with children's literature becoming increasingly sophisticated and daring in its themes. One example is *The Gray House* (*Dom v kotorom . . .*, 2009) by Mariam Petrosian, set in a boarding school for children with disabilities. The novel *Playing a Part* (*Shutovskoi kolpak*, 2013) by Daria Wilke offers a sensitive exploration of homosexuality and gender identity against the backdrop of a puppet theatre. Yet Russia's turn towards a repressive ideology of patriotism, and the passing of legislation that forbids the promotion of 'non-traditional' sexual relations, makes it unlikely that such diversity will be sustained in future years.

Connor Doak

Box 2.5   Genres

Box 2.5   Civic Poetry

The Russian term 'civic poetry' (*grazhdanskaia poeziia*) signifies, first and foremost, political satire and other poetry that alludes to politics. Throughout Russia's history the relationship between personal autonomy and the state has been problematic, and civic poetry has played an important role in asserting such autonomy.

The first civic poet in the sense that the term is understood today was Aleksandr Radishchev. In his ode 'Freedom' (*Vol'nost'*, 1781–3), he proclaims ideas about the sovereignty of the people and their right to execute or overthrow monarchs who do not fulfil their duties.

Civic poetry flourished during the nineteenth century and carved out a new role for itself by claiming to prioritise 'vivid civil sentiment' over 'art'. In the introduction to his long poem 'Voinarovskii' (*Voinarovskii*, 1824), Kondratii Ryleev – who was later hanged for his participation in the Decembrist revolt of 1825 – acknowledges the poem's 'artlessness', and in a famous couplet he asserts: 'Yet you will find living feelings, – / I am not a Poet, but a Citizen.' This rhetorical juxtaposition, along with an explicit contrast between the 'civic' and the 'artistic', became a popular theme in poetry. In 1855, Nikolai Nekrasov wrote the dialogue 'Poet and Citizen' (*Poet i grazhdanin*), echoing Ryleev: 'You do not have to be a poet, / But you must be a citizen.'

At the same time, poets understood the artifice of thus contrasting the unworldly poet with the artless but committed citizen. For example, in this poem which opens with the words 'I am not a poet' (*Ia ne poet*, 1859) Vasilii Kurochkin insists on the artlessness of his verse, yet does so through a complex interplay of line length and paradoxical rhyme, such that the poem's form refutes its content.

The twentieth century saw a rapid development of civic poetry. The years between 1905 and 1907 were characterised by the intense development of political satire ridiculing the rhetoric both of the monarchy and of rising Russian ultra-nationalism.

In the 1920s and 1930s, civic poetry in the USSR split into two types: staged and unsanctioned. Officially sanctioned 'staged' civic poetry zealously exposed those who were prosecuted in Joseph Stalin's show trials as well as foreign leaders, the bourgeoisie who allegedly obstructed progress, and others. From the 1930s until the mid-1950s, unsanctioned civic poetry existed only in the deep underground. Key works of unsanctioned civic poetry in the period before the Second World War include

Anna Akhmatova's *Requiem* (*Rekviem*, comp. 1934–62) and works by Olga Berggolts, Georgii Obolduev, and Vladimir Shchirovskii. The political poetry of Boris Slutskii is representative of the civic poetry of the second half of the twentieth century. Its main hero is a sceptic and existentialist who sees that – in the words of Slutskii's poem 'Thomas Speaking' (*Govorit Foma*, before 1961) – 'Everything is propaganda / All the world is propaganda', yet nonetheless continues his endeavours to distinguish good from evil, to recognise the paths to freedom and unfreedom.

From the 1960s to the 1980s, guitar singer-songwriters ('bards') and rock musicians assumed the role of civic poets. One of the most import-ant is Aleksandr Galich. His songs present Soviet life as a world of lies, which his fellow citizens have adopted and internalised. During the period of Perestroika, political songs written by rock musicians such as Iurii Shevchuk and his band DDT, Mikhail Borzykin and his band Televizor ('The Television Set'), and Egor Letov and his band Grazhdanskaia Oborona ('Civil Defence') were crucial for the develop-ment of civic poetry. In 1987 Borzykin wrote and performed a song titled 'Your Dad Is a Fascist' (*Tvoi papa – fashist*). This song extended the boundaries of freedom in public poetic expression:

> Don't tell me that he is kind
> Don't tell me that he loves freedom . . .
> I saw his eyes – it is hard to love them.
> [. . .]
> Your dad is a fascist!
> Don't look at me like that,
> I know it for sure – he is simply a fascist!

Throughout the 1990s, expressions of political views in verse were rare except in the civic poetry of ultra-nationalists or supporters of the former Soviet regime. However, in the early years of the twenty-first century there was a rapid re-politicisation of poetry. Poets developed new methods to make sense of the intensifying conflict between state and society. The second Chechen war (1999–2000), and wars against Georgia in 2008 and against Ukraine from 2014, resulted in a new wave of anti-war poetry. Initially, this wave was small-scale and included works such as Stanislav Lvovskii's verse beginning with the line 'In someone else's words' (*Chuzhimi slovami*, 2008), a documentary poem about Russia's war against Georgia, which consists of notes from social media, remarks by intellectuals in Russia and western Europe,

Box 2.5   Genres

and fragments from Georgian and even German poetry (Hölderlin). The regime's aggression against Ukraine in 2022 resulted in the huge growth of civic poetry, including by many authors who had previously avoided any explicit political expression.

Ilya Kukulin
Translated by Katerina Pavlidi

HISTORY 2

★

MECHANISMS

The Monastery

SIMON FRANKLIN

During the age of devotion, monasteries were the dominant institutions for the production, preservation, and consumption of books. They therefore had a profound influence on the nature and repertoire of book culture. Books were not a monastic monopoly, nor were monasteries dominant to the same degree throughout the centuries. Over the sixteenth and seventeenth centuries, the administration and the court became increasingly significant as focuses of production and patronage. Nevertheless, as the core institutions of devotion itself, monasteries were key to the shaping and sustaining of its written culture. The present chapter will touch on aspects of monastic book culture across the age of devotion as a whole, from the shared East Slav civilisation of early Rus through to the first decades of the seventeenth century (see Chapter 1.1), but the temporal focus will be on the period from the late fourteenth century to the end of the fifteenth century, the main age of monastic expansion.

Institutional Growth

A holy man goes out into the wilderness – deserts, mountains, caves, forests – to lead a solitary and contemplative life. Others hear of his feats of asceticism and are drawn towards him to observe, imitate, learn. They begin to cooperate with each other in day-to-day tasks, in acts of worship, in dealing with outsiders. Eventually they become a community, they build churches, adopt rules and a Rule (a kind of constitution, specifying the monastery's devotional, organisational, and disciplinary practices), establish a division of labour and a hierarchy of authority and responsibility. And thus, according to the classic pattern going back to the tales of early Christianity, there is formed that paradoxical, almost oxymoronic institution: the cenobitic monastery, the

community of solitude. In early Rus this was the pattern for the emergence of the most prestigious community, the Caves monastery in Kyiv, which was responsible for a significant proportion of the surviving narratives from the eleventh to the thirteenth centuries. In Muscovy, although monastic foundations proliferated right through to the early eighteenth century, the hundred years or so from the mid-fourteenth century are commonly regarded as the golden age of monastic expansion. Monasteries mushroomed, not just on the fringes of urban settlements, such as the Trinity monastery of St Sergii of Radonezh (1314–1392) northeast of Moscow, but in previously remote areas of the north such as the White Lake (the Kirillo-Belozerskii monastery) and eventually, by the 1430s, even on islands in the White Sea (the Solovetskii monastery).

This is sometimes even called an age of monastic 'colonisation'. The monasteries were not just centres of prayer and contemplation. Several of them became rich and powerful institutions.[1] They acquired lands and the income therefrom, they enjoyed significant tax exemptions, they could engage in trade, they built multiple churches and, in some cases, mighty walls, and their treasuries filled with precious objects. They attracted abundant patronage and could exercise significant political influence.[2] They also supplied the personnel for the higher offices of the church. In the Orthodox church, parish priests could marry but bishops were supposed to be celibate, and hence the path to high ecclesiastical rank passed through the monasteries.

Despite the emphasis on monasteries that grew mighty in remote places, one did not have to go on a distant pilgrimage in order to come across a large monastery. Urban and suburban enclosure likewise thrived. Anyone who has travelled around Russia's 'historic' pre-Petrine towns must have been struck by the prominence of monasteries. Indeed, apart from the citadel (the *kreml'*, hence 'kremlin'), monasteries are often the principal features that shape the urban landscape. Grand monasteries dominate the towns of the so-called

---

1 On monasteries in Russia, see Igor Smolitsch, *Russisches Mönchtum. Entstehung, Entwicklung und Wesen 988–1917* (Würzburg: Augustinus-Verlag, 1953); Ia. E. Vodarskii and E. G. Istomina, *Pravoslavnye monastyri i ikh rol' v razvitii kul'tury (XI–nachalo XX v.)* [Orthodox monasteries and their role in the development of culture (eleventh to early twentieth centuries)] (Tula: Grif i K., 2009). On particular monasteries see, for example, David B. Miller, *Saint Sergius of Radonezh, His Trinity Monastery, and the Formation of the Russian Identity* (DeKalb: Northern Illinois University Press, 2010); Roy R. Robson, *Solovki: The Story of Russia Told through Its Most Remarkable Islands* (New Haven: Yale University Press, 2004).
2 Miller, *Saint Sergius of Radonezh*, pp. 105–37.

Golden Ring to the northeast of Moscow: walled complexes such as the Spaso-Iakovlevskii monastery in Rostov (founded 1380), the Pokrovskii and Spaso-Evfimiev monasteries in Suzdal (founded 1352 and 1364), the Ipatiev monastery in Kostroma (first mentioned 1432), and the Spaso-Iaroslavskii monastery in Iaroslavl (originally a twelfth-century foundation), not to mention the grandest of them all, the Troitse-Sergiev monastery, founded in 1337. Closer still to the centre are the monasteries originally clustered around the Moscow suburbs, now absorbed into the city itself, such as the Andronikov monastery (1357), the Danilov monastery (late thirteenth century, re-endowed mid-sixteenth century), the Simonov monastery (1370s, almost totally destroyed in the Soviet era), the Novospasskii monastery (1480), and the Novodevichii monastery (1524). And right at the heart of the state, on the territory of the Kremlin itself, the Chudov monastery (1365, also destroyed in the Soviet era).

In the Orthodox church there were no monastic orders as such, no direct equivalent to Benedictines, Cistercians, Carthusians, and the like. In principle, monasteries were independent foundations, each with responsibility for its internal regulation under the authority of the abbot. In practice, however, there was a significant degree of mutual conformity at both formal and informal levels. In the ordering of their regimes of devotion, most tended to adopt or adapt versions of the same Rule. At the informal level many of the major monasteries were well networked with each other. For example, the Troitse-Sergiev monastery was founded by Sergii of Radonezh, and a monk of the Troitse-Sergiev monastery became the first abbot of the Andronikov monastery. The Simonov monastery was founded by Sergii's nephew and disciple Fedor (c. 1340–1394). Kirill (1337–1427), founder of the Kirillo-Belozerskii monastery, began his monastic life at the Simonov monastery under Fedor, where he also met Sergii of Radonezh. The first settlers at the Solovetskii monastery were monks from the Kirillo-Belozerskii monastery. Pafnutii (1394–1477), founder of one of the very largest monasteries – at Borovsk to the southwest of Moscow – had been a novice under a pupil of Sergii of Radonezh, and among Pafnutii's own disciples was Iosif Volotskii (1439–1515), founder of a major monastery to the west of Moscow at Volokolamsk. Despite the distances and the lack of formally coordinated regulation, the monasteries of the mid-fourteenth and fifteenth centuries can be seen as a community of communities, not least in the character of their book culture. Texts and people migrated between them, they shared core practices, and they were significant and interconnected centres of book

production and consumption; they were, in a sense, foundational foundations in the emergence of the book culture of Muscovy.

Book Culture

Although there is more than adequate evidence for practical urban literacy in Rus and Muscovy at least since the mid-eleventh century,[3] the culture of books was almost a monastic monopoly. There were no universities in Russia until the middle of the eighteenth century, no 'academies' until the late seventeenth century. Several texts refer to 'teachers', but it is difficult to find persuasive indications of the existence of formal institutions of education and learning. New demand for literate education developed with the growth of a state administration (and the consequent growth in bureaucratic procedures and paperwork) from the late fifteenth century onwards. Some of the chanceries (*prikazy*) required a fairly high level of specialist education: a knowledge of languages at the Ambassadorial Chancery (*Posol'skii prikaz*); a medical education in Latin at the Apothecary Chancery (*Aptekarskii prikaz*), which was almost entirely staffed by foreigners. Some state bureaucrats developed literate interests beyond the practical demands of their office and contributed to wider book culture. Already in the late fifteenth century, for example, a diplomat, Fedor Kuritsyn (?–after 1500), is posited as the creator of at least two very distinctive specimens of book culture: the quasi-cryptographic *Laodicaean Epistle* (*Laodikiiskoe poslanie*), and the macabre *Tale of Drakula* (*Skazanie o Drakule*; see Chapter 1.1).[4] From the early seventeenth century, it is even possible to identify what has been called the 'Chancery School' in a branch of literary culture that had no ancient monastic tradition in Russia: poetry (see Chapter 1.2). The court, too, could at times play a prominent role, notably in relation to some high-prestige, large-scale projects in the mid-sixteenth century. Nevertheless, there is a fundamental difference. Bureaucrats needed quill and paper for administrative purposes and could *choose* to pursue broader bookish interests according to taste. Monasteries had no choice. The role of the state bureaucracy as an institution of literary production cannot compare with that of the monasteries even in

---

3 Simon Franklin, *Writing, Society and Culture in Early Rus, c. 950–1300* (Cambridge: Cambridge University Press, 2002); Jos Schaeken, *Voices on Birchbark: Everyday Communication in Medieval Russia* (Leiden: Brill, 2018).

4 Ia. S. Lur'e and A. Iu. Grigorenko, 'Kuritsyn Fedor Vasil'evich', in *Slovar' knizhnikov i knizhnosti Drevnei Rusi* [Dictionary of bookmen and book culture of early Rus], 4 vols. in 9 parts (hereafter cited as *SKKDR*) (Leningrad–St Petersburg: Nauka, Dmitrii Bulanin, 1987–2017, vol. II, pt 1 (1988)), pp. 504–10.

the later Middle Ages, still less in the period which serves as the temporal focus of the present chapter: the mid-fourteenth to the end of the fifteenth centuries.

The contribution of monasteries does not rest merely on the fact that they were the main centres of learning and that bookmen therefore tended to be monks. This in itself is superficial. Nor does it rest on the fact that monasteries were closely involved in the physical processes of manuscript production. A significant proportion of scribes were monks, but the influence of monasteries on the extent and nature of book culture does not depend critically on how large or how small that proportion may have been at any given time or in any given locality.[5] To some extent the dominance of monastic culture in the surviving legacy of medieval Russian book culture is due to the fact that monasteries were the principal institutions of preservation. Monasteries had libraries and a degree of institutional stability which could help stave off dispersal. The overwhelming majority of medieval books that survived into the modern age did so because they were preserved for centuries in monasteries. Moreover, monastic libraries are also partly responsible for the fact that our knowledge extends beyond what happens to have survived physically. Monasteries made lists of their treasures, which included their books. From the Solovetskii monastery, for example, we have a sequence of five inventories between 1514 and 1597, which enables us to trace the development of the repertoire across eight decades.[6] The final inventory lists nearly 500 volumes. Just over seventy books from the Solovetskii inventories have been securely identified as surviving in modern libraries.

Monastic conservation is important as a source for our own reconstruction of book culture, but the key factor in establishing the monasteries' role as the dominant institutions of production was their role as the dominant institutions of *consumption*. Monasteries did not collect books primarily out of intellectual curiosity. They collected books because they had to. The bulk of their collections consisted of books that were necessary for the conduct of

---

5 For detail on scribal production in the sixteenth century, see A. S. Usachev, *Knigopisanie v Rossii XVI veka: Po materialam datirovannykh vykhodnykh zapisei* [The writing of books in sixteenth-century Russia: The evidence of dated colophons] (Moscow: Al'ians-Arkheo, 2018).

6 Z. V. Dmitrieva, E. V. Krushel'nitskaia, and M. I. Mil'chik (eds.), *Opisi Solovetskogo monastyria XVI veka* [Inventories of the Solovetskii monastery] (St Petersburg: Dmitrii Bulanin, 2003). Cf. for other monasteries, A. P. Balachenkova, 'Knizhnye inventari Kirillo-Belozerskogo monastyria XV–XVII vekov' [Book inventories of the Kirillo-Belozerskii monastery from the fifteenth to the seventeenth centuries], *Ferapontovskii sbornik* [Ferapontov studies] 5 (1999), 42–59; M. V. Kukushkina, *Monastyrskie biblioteki russkogo severa* [Monastic libraries of the Russian north] (Leningrad: Nauka, 1977).

monastic life. Monks might then choose to expand the repertoire, even according to individual taste, but the core was functional. Medieval Russian book culture was, in the first instance, shaped by the needs of the monasteries. In a sense this implies no more than the assertion that medieval Russian culture was predominantly associated with Christian devotion. The wider church, too, needed books. However, monasteries shaped the repertoire more thoroughly because of the sheer scale of monastic devotional practice, of the regular rhythms of liturgy and prayer and communal reading, especially in the larger cenobitic communities. Monastic book consumption – the main driver of monastic book production – can be described in terms of three different zones or locations.[7] The first zone is the church, in the performance of the liturgy and the books needed to support services every day of the year, often for many hours a day. The second zone can be represented by the refectory or other communal space, where the Rule advised or prescribed that, rather than engage in idle chatter, the brethren should listen to the reading of instructive and edifying texts. The third zone is the individual cell, the zone of texts for private reading. In content the books used in the three zones could overlap: saints' lives, psalms, prayers, or sayings of the church fathers could sound across any of them. They differed from each other in balance and emphasis, often in format, and in the degree of fixity or choice.

In the devotional life, the rhythms of church services imposed not only content but structure. The cycles of readings for every month, every week, every day were specified in the monastic Rule. The repertoire of texts copied and used in the age of devotion was to a significant extent set by the requirements of that Rule. This had implications for the units of production and storage: the manuscripts. If the patterns of consumption can be described spatially in terms of the three zones, the patterns of manuscript production can be to a large extent defined temporally. For devotional purposes there would have been little point in producing large quantities of separate small manuscripts for each bit of each service. Instead, manuscripts tended to contain cycles of readings, and the most common organising principle was calendrical. To complicate matters, there were two interlocking calendars: the moveable cycles of festivals and commemorations tied to the date of Easter; and the fixed cycles of festivals and commemorations tied to the days of the month through the year, particularly as marked by the calendar of saints' days. So, for example, a manuscript might contain readings and hymns

7 I. M. Gritsevskaia, *Chtenie i chet'i sborniki v russkikh monastyriakh XV–XVII vv.* [Reading and non-liturgical manuscript miscellanies in Russian monasteries from the fifteenth to the seventeenth centuries] (St Petersburg: Dmitrii Bulanin, 2012).

for the Sundays of the Easter cycle, or brief Lives of the saints for September through November (the fixed ecclesiastical calendar began in September, not in January). When a manuscript was organised according to any of the cycles, it was neither a 'work' to be read as a whole nor an anthology to be sampled, extrapolated, or reordered. Even the core scriptural texts were more commonly copied in calendrical cycles of readings rather than as continuous works: as Gospel lectionaries, for example, rather than manuscripts of the four Gospels (let alone of the full New Testament) as such. This emphasis on liturgy-based or calendar-based manuscript production has some surprising consequences. Although books *of* the Bible were, of course, central to the faith, and reading *from* the Bible was central to almost all devotional practices, no complete Bible *as a book* appeared in Slavonic until 1499, half a millennium after the adoption of Christianity in early Rus.

The second zone, that of communal but non-liturgical reading, was also shaped in some degree by the monastic Rule as well as by the calendar. Some of the collections for communal reading were stable in structure and content; others were more flexible. Several of the texts with relatively stable structures were interrelated. Thus, the *Zlatostrui* (golden stream), whose earliest manuscripts are from the twelfth and thirteenth centuries, consists of homilies by or attributed (often spuriously) to one of the most authoritative of the early Christian writers, John Chrysostom (347–407). Some texts from the *Zlatostrui* also found their way into collections that were structured calendrically rather than thematically, notably *Zlatoust* (the 'golden-mouthed', i.e. Chrysostom) and the *Torzhestvennik* (festive readings). The *Torzhestvennik* contained readings for major feast days. It was transmitted in two main versions, dependent on the two types of calendar: the 'menological' *Torzhestvennik*, according to the feasts of the fixed cycle (the Annunciation, Christmas, the Dormition of the Mother of God, etc.); and the 'triodic' *Torzhestvennik*, with readings for the cycles of commemorations dependent on the date of Easter.[8]

Individual text units were not necessarily tied to one type of manuscript. They could migrate from compilation to compilation as constituent forms in a range of different composite forms (see Chapter 3.1). Take, for example, a short apocryphal narrative known as the *Tale of Afroditian (Skazanie ob Afroditiane)*. This starts with a miracle in Persia. The statues of the classical gods begin to talk, and they tell of the virgin birth. The king therefore despatches the magi, who tell of their encounter with Mary and the infant

---

8 Summary by T. V. Chertoritskaia, 'Torzhestvennnik' [Festive readings], in *SKKDR*, vol. II, pt 2 (1989), pp. 433–5.

Christ. Originating probably in the fourth or fifth century, translated from Greek into Slavonic more than once, and periodically condemned as apocryphal and false, the *Tale of Afroditian* nevertheless migrated from manuscript to manuscript in Russia throughout the Middle Ages and even into the nineteenth century. According to its modern editor, it can be found in at least a dozen distinct genres of composite manuscript.[9]

In the third zone, manuscripts for cell reading tended to be less closely tied to calendrical cycles. They could reflect individual choice of whatever was felt to be particularly useful, edifying, or interesting. In general, the types of texts copied for private reading were not radically different from those prescribed for communal reading. Most of the contents of most of the 'cell miscellanies' (*keleinye sborniki*) are broadly equivalent to and taken from the communal repertoire. Thus, for example, a miscellany written out by Kirill Belozerskii (1337?–1427) himself in the early fifteenth century consists of 431 leaves, of which the first 150 contain extracts from canon law, followed by 20 leaves with various texts on heresies and 15 on calendrical calculation. Then comes a selection of somewhat disparate texts, long and short, simple and complex, theoretical and practical, presumably reflecting the tastes and concerns of the compiler: on anti-Jewish polemic; on the 'Latins'; on the earth, the oceans, and the mountains; on practical aspects of monastic devotion and discipline; on the interpretation of psalms; several liturgical chants; a list of 'false' books; some prayers; a twenty-leaf explanation of the Easter cycle; and tales of the early fathers. The only obviously East Slav material comes right at the end, with six leaves on the commemoration of saints Boris and Gleb.[10] Kirill's miscellany is unique and typical. It is unique in its precise contents, typical in the dominance of texts that reflect venerable and authoritative Orthodox tradition.

Not all cell miscellanies were so strictly encompassed by the communal repertoire. An emblematic figure in this respect is a monk of the same monastery, Efrosin, whose known scribal activities date roughly from the 1460s to the 1490s. Efrosin's hand has been detected in nearly three dozen surviving manuscripts, but he was the principal scribe of six fat volumes, four of which were apparently intended for cell reading. In a detailed modern

9 A. G. Bobrov, *Apokrificheskoe 'Skazanie Afroditiana' v literature i knizhnosti Drevnei Rusi* [The apocryphal *Tale of Afroditian* in the literature and book culture of early Rus] (St Petersburg: Nauka, 1994), p. 44.
10 *Entsiklopediia russkogo igumena XIV–XV vv. Sbornik Prepodobnogo Kirilla Belozerskogo* [The encyclopedia of a Russian abbot of the fourteenth to fifteenth century. The miscellany of Kirill Belozerskii], ed. G. M. Prokhorov (St Petersburg: Izdatel'stvo Olega Abashko, 2003).

description, the full list of 'works' included in Efrosin's miscellanies runs to more than 700 items, most of which are in the usual edificatory, pastoral, or disciplinary modes.[11] But at the fringes Efrosin chooses also to include some intriguing texts. Some are traditional apocrypha, such as a version of the story of Solomon and Kitovras ('Kitovras' is a distortion of the medieval Greek *Kentavros* – 'centaur'), or relative exotica such as the *Tale of the Indian Kingdom* (*Skazanie ob Indiiskom tsarstve*) and the *Tale of the Twelve Dreams of King Shakhaisha* (*Skazanie o dvenadtsati snakh Shakhaishi* – i.e. of 'Shahanshah', Shah of Shahs). The non-prescribed material can be near-contemporary, such as the *Tale of Drakula*, probably composed in the early or mid-1480s. Some of the juxtapositions seem quite random, as in the following sequence in one of the manuscripts: extracts from early Rus legislation for the church; some further extracts from canon law (on the age at which one should start confession, on giving communion to one who is terminally ill, on aspects of monastic clothing, etc.); a widely cited text on good and bad women, sometimes attributed to John Chrysostom; then, with no explanation or apparent logic, a version of the *Zadonshchina*, the tale of the victory of Prince Dmitrii Ivanovich of Moscow (r. 1359–89) over the Mongols in 1380 'beyond the Don'; and then a very extensive account of a pilgrimage to the Holy Land written by the abbot Daniil in the early twelfth century.[12] The same manuscript also includes a version of the translated story of Alexander the Great (the *Alexander Romance*).[13] Sometimes Efrosin returned to the same materials, though not always in the same versions. Thus in another of his manuscripts the *Tale of Drakula* is preceded by a far more extensive text of the *Alexander Romance* on nearly 200 leaves (i.e. nearly 400 pages); plus, again, the *Tale of the Indian Kingdom*; and after the Drakula story again Daniil's pilgrimage, but this time only in brief extracts.[14] Thus the cell miscellanies were a capacious and flexible medium in which traditional devotional and didactic texts mingled with diverse quasi-secular narratives in a way that forms and reflects a book culture of what might, albeit in a very limited sense, be termed a reading public.

Monastic book production and book culture was not fully self-contained. Books could flow in both directions, to the monastery from outside, to

---

11 M. D. Kagan, N. V. Ponyrko, and M. V. Rozhdestvenskaia, 'Opisanie sbornikov XV v. knigopistsa Efrosina' [Description of the fifteenth-century miscellanies of the scribe Efrosin], *Trudy Otdela drevnerusskoi literatury* [Journal of the Old Russian literature section] 35 (1980), 3–300.

12 Kagan, Ponyrko, and Rozhdestvenskaia, 'Opisanie', 118–21.

13 Kagan, Ponyrko, and Rozhdestvenskaia, 'Opisanie', 140.

14 Kagan, Ponyrko, and Rozhdestvenskaia, 'Opisanie', 174–6.

outside from the monastery. In the first place, as the inventories make clear, significant numbers of books in a monastic library might arrive through donation, not through production in situ. Second, not all scribes who worked in monasteries were necessarily monks. For example, for three decades at the start of the sixteenth century, a significant amount of book production at the Nikolskii monastery – just a couple of hundred metres northeast of Red Square in Moscow – was carried out by and under the supervision of a certain Mikhail Medovartsev, who was probably not himself a monk.[15] Third, monastic scribes and scriptoria could produce books not only for internal use but for outsiders, on commission or for the market. Besides being essential to monastic life, books could be useful to the monastic economy.[16]

Though originating in the monasteries and based on their repertoire, the practice of compiling personalised miscellanies also spread into wider devotional culture. Structurally they are analogous to the monastic versions. For example, a miscellany from the early seventeenth century that belonged to a village priest, Grigorii Grigorev, includes commentaries on the six days of Creation, on several parts of the liturgy, and on half a dozen psalms; visions of the afterlife taken from Byzantine hagiography; extracts from canon law (e.g. on clerical income, on marriage, on beards); a series of acrostics (on penitence, on refuting Jews); a tale of an encounter between St Makarios of Egypt and the devil; plus a small sprinkling of texts that originated in Rus and Muscovy: a couple of exegetic extracts from the works of Maksim Grek ('the Greek', 1470–1556) in the mid-sixteenth century, and – perhaps the most 'literary' fragment in this miscellany – a version of the aphoristic 'petition' ascribed to Daniil Zatochnik ('the Exile') and originating in the twelfth or thirteenth century.[17]

Thus far this survey has focused on books that were generated by the needs of monastic devotional practice, whether liturgical, communal, or personal. The range of such texts was dictated partly by prescription and partly by choice. However, monasteries also generated their own stories. If we are primarily interested in creation rather than in selection and recombination, then we should focus on the writings that monasteries produced about

15 N. V. Sinitsyna, 'Knizhnyi master Mikhail Medovartsev' [Mikhail Medovartsev, master bookman], in O. I. Podobedova and G. V. Popov (eds.), *Drevnerusskoe iskusstvo. Rukopisnaia kniga. Sbornik pervyi* [Old Russian art. The manuscript book. Collection I] (Moscow: Nauka, 1973), pp. 286–317.

16 On monasteries and markets, see Valerii Perkhavko, *Torgovyi mir srednevekovoi Rusi* [Commerce in medieval Rus] (Moscow: Academia, 2006), pp. 309–74.

17 V. V. Kuskov (ed.), *Krug chteniia drevnerusskogo knizhnika XVII veka* [The reading of an early Russian bookman of the seventeenth century] (Moscow: KRUG, 2013).

themselves. Monasteries were made and sustained by people trying to lead exemplary lives, or at any rate to follow the lead of those whose lives were reckoned exemplary. And in doing so, some monks also came to be revered as exemplars, often initially for their successors within their own monasteries, sometimes far more widely. Our main sources for stories about the formation of the principal monasteries of the period of expansion from the mid-fourteenth to the mid-fifteenth centuries are the hagiographies of their founders: the *Life of Sergii of Radonezh* (*Zhitie Sergiia Radonezhskogo*) by Epifanii Premudryi ('the Wise', d. c. 1420), which also includes stories of the foundation of new monasteries by his disciples; the *Life of Kirill Belozerskii* (*Zhitie Kirilla Belozerskogo*) by Pakhomii Logofet (d. after 1484); the *Life of Pafnutii Borovskii* (*Zhitie Pafnutiia Borovskogo*) by Vassian Sanin (d. 1515; brother of Iosif Volotskii); the *Lives of Zosima and Savvatii of the Solovetskii Monastery* (*Zhitiia Zosimy i Savvatiia Solovetskikh*) by Dosifei (Zosima's disciple and abbot of the monastery); and others.[18]

Beyond the individual Lives were the collections. As the calendars became more densely populated by local saints, so the calendar-based books for liturgical and communal reading included more locally generated texts. The *Prolog*, originally a translation of the Byzantine *Synaxarion* (brief summaries of saints' lives and miracles mainly for liturgical purposes), acquired an increasingly local Rus flavour, as did *minei* (menologia, more extensive monthly cycles of hagiographic narratives). Some monasteries compiled *pateriki*, tales of their own venerable fathers. Translated paterica, with anecdotes and sayings of the desert fathers of early Christianity, featured regularly in the repertoire of devotional reading.[19] In Rus the prestigious precedent for such a collection had been set in the monastery of the Caves in Kyiv. Some of the tales of the Caves monks (including an extensive Life of one its founders, Feodosii, d. 1074) existed before the end of the eleventh century, and the collection in the form of the Caves *paterik* was assembled in the first half of the thirteenth century.[20] Among the substantial late medieval collections of monastic deeds, visions, and miracles was the *Volokolamsk Paterik*, partly attributed to Iosif Volotskii and Pafnutii Borovskii.[21]

---

18 D. S. Likhachev et al. (eds.), *Biblioteka literatury Drevnei Rusi* [Library of early Rus literature], 20 vols. (St Petersburg: Nauka, 1997–2020), vol. VI, pp. 254–410; vol. VII, pp. 132–216; vol. XIII, pp. 36–152. (This collection is hereafter cited as *BLDR*.)
19 See the articles by N. I. Nikolaev in *SKKDR*, vol. I (1987), pp. 299–308, 313–24.
20 Muriel Heppell (trans.), *The 'Paterik' of the Kievan Caves Monastery* (Cambridge, MA: Harvard University Press, 1989).
21 *BLDR*, vol. XI, pp. 20–68; cf. also the narrative history of the Pskovo-Pecherskii monastery: *BLDR*, vol. XIII, pp. 476–532.

Monastic Book Culture and Russian Literature

The functions of monasteries in shaping book culture are reasonably clear. However, that still leaves open the answers to two somewhat more specific and contentious questions: first, on the relation between medieval book culture as a whole and the subset of it that we might wish to define as literature; and second, on the relation between this (literature) and the smaller subset that might be defined as *Russian* literature. Beyond the fact that it is almost entirely devotional, the most obvious feature of the repertoire of monastic book culture is that most of its constituent texts are derived from translations.

What, in this repertoire of books, should be the object of study in a history of literature? We cannot send a questionnaire into the monasteries of the past in order to gauge contemporary opinion, but in any case the question would probably have seemed puzzling. Readers could appreciate (and writers could occasionally flaunt) a mastery of words, but to separate a subset of monastic book culture and label it as literature is counter to the practice and the spirit of its production (see Chapter 1.1). An obvious solution is to avoid making distinctions and to treat the whole spectrum of monastic book culture as the object of study.[22] At the same time, we are of course free to pose our own questions and hence to superimpose our own criteria of literariness, so long as we recognise that in doing so we are creating a category rather than reflecting one.

The issue of Russianness is no less awkward and anachronistic. In the monastery a text was valued and copied on account of its function, not on account of its linguistic or national provenance. The relationship between a translated text and a native text was not a straightforward binary contrast but a spectrum. The general issue extends well beyond the Middle Ages: translations, adaptations, assimilations, and appropriations feature in Russian literary culture in subsequent centuries (see especially Chapters 1.3, 1.4, and the introduction). But the specific properties of medieval textuality make it particularly difficult, and often quite inappropriate, to draw sharp distinctions between the local and the imported components of monastic book culture.

There is no problem of definition at either end of the spectrum, but between the extremes is a zone of dynamic interaction. So, for example,

22 As in the fullest multi-volume reference work, *SKKDR*, which comprises four parts in nine volumes issued between 1987 and 2017, including multiple supplementary articles and bibliographies. See also the approach in the handbook of early Rus book culture by Gerhard Podskalsky, *Christentum und theologische Literatur in der Kiever Rus' (988–1237)* (Munich: C. H. Beck, 1982).

the biblical book of Psalms – the Psalter – is a work of remarkable literature by any measure, and it was absolutely central to monastic book culture. Monks had to learn it by heart, and its words permeate monastic compositions. Yet nobody would treat the Psalter itself as a product of early Rus or Russian literature – not, at any rate, until its metrical version by Simeon Polotskii (1629–1680), *Psaltir' rifmotvornaia*, published in 1680, which became the first printed book of verse in Russia (see Chapter 1.2). However, many translated texts were more mutable. They were not fixed like the Psalter or the Gospels, but they could be edited, extracted, combined, glossed, interpolated, and in other ways possessed, assimilated, or moulded to local contours. Pastoral advice, rules, and homilies could be configured to taste and need. Old and New Testament apocrypha could be integrated into fresh composite narratives or extracted individually and recombined with other texts in the manuscript miscellanies. A Byzantine world chronicle might be copied separately *as* a Byzantine world chronicle, or it could be combined with other translated texts, or spliced into local chronicles so as to create a new account of world history culminating in Russia.[23] Over the centuries some texts became so thoroughly altered that, although they were originally derived from translations, they can no longer be adequately classed as such (see Chapter 1.1). With such a spectrum of local input, there can be no hard boundary between the native and the non-native. And, as in the case of 'literature', Russian bookmen in the age of devotion themselves show little or no concern for such distinctions.

If we want to understand how and why monasteries functioned as mechanisms for the production of medieval book culture, then we should be cautious about manipulating the results according to criteria implied in a modern history of a national literature. The criteria are extraneous to the culture. There is an obvious danger of anachronistic cherry-picking, of selecting what happens to fit our own notions either of the national (in language, in location, in provenance) and/or of the literary. It is perhaps more proper to stick with the broad notion of monastic book culture rather than to disrupt its integrity through retrospective selection. Unless, that is, we regard the practice as having been implicitly legitimised by the monks themselves. For, in compiling their cell miscellanies, they not only gathered and transmitted surprisingly diverse and dynamically mutable assemblages of texts that spanned the liturgical and the historical, the instructional and the

---

23 O. V. Tvorogov, *Drevnerusskie khronografy* [Early Rus chronographic compilations] (Leningrad: Nauka, 1975).

entertaining, the ploddingly pious and the almost profane, but also exercised a kind of consumer choice; and that, in turn, albeit within tight institutional constraints, comes close to constituting the creation – or the faint prehistory of the creation – of an autonomous sphere of letters.

Further Reading

Gritsevskaia, I. M., *Chtenie i chet'i sborniki v russkikh monastyriakh XV–XVII vv.* [Reading and non-liturgical manuscript miscellanies in Russian monasteries from the fifteenth to the seventeenth centuries] (St Petersburg: Dmitrii Bulanin, 2012).

Knizhnye tsentry Drevnei Rusi. Knizhniki i rukopisi Kirillo-Belozerskogo monastyria [Centres of early Rus book culture. Bookmen and manuscripts of the Kirillo-Belozerskii monastery], ed. N. V. Ponyrko and S. A. Semiachko (St Petersburg: Pushkinskii dom, 2014).

Knizhnye tsentry Drevnei Rusi. Knizhniki i rukopisi Solovetskogo monastyria [Centres of early Rus book culture. Bookmen and manuscripts of the Solovetskii monastery], ed. S. A. Semiachko (St Petersburg: Dmitrii Bulanin, 2004).

Knizhnye tsentry Drevnei Rusi. Solovetskii monastyr' [Centres of early Rus book culture. The Solovetskii monastery], ed. S. A. Semiachko (St Petersburg: Dmitrii Bulanin, 2001).

Knizhnye tsentry Drevnei Rusi. Severnorusskie monastyri [Centres of early Rus book culture. North Russian monasteries], ed. S. A. Semiachko (St Petersburg: Dmitrii Bulanin, 2001).

Knizhnye tsentry Drevnei Rusi. Rostovo-iaroslavskaia zemlia [Centres of early Rus book culture. The Rostov-Iaroslavl land], ed. S. A. Semiachko (St Petersburg: Pushkinskii dom, 2022).

Miller, David B., *Saint Sergius of Radonezh, His Trinity Monastery, and the Formation of the Russian Identity* (DeKalb: Northern Illinois University Press, 2010).

Smolitsch, Igor, *Russisches Mönchtum. Entstehung, Entwicklung und Wesen 988–1917* (Würzburg: Augustinus-Verlag, 1953).

Vodarskii, Ia. E., and E. G. Istomina, *Pravoslavnye monastyri i ikh rol' v razvitii kul'tury (XI–nachalo XX v.)* [Orthodox monasteries and their role in the development of culture (eleventh to early twentieth centuries)] (Tula: Grif i K., 2009).

2.2

The Court

ALEXEI EVSTRATOV

Throughout the long eighteenth century, from the reigns of Peter I (r. 1682–1725) to Alexander I (r. 1801–25), the Russian court played a major role in defining the realm in which literary texts circulated and in shaping their cultural, social, and political mission. It is with good reason that the scholar Iurii Lotman (1922–1993; see Box 5.5) has called this period the noble (*dvorianskii*) age of Russian culture. Yet it was in the 1750s and 1760s specifically that the court became the dominant – and almost the exclusive – institution stimulating the production of literature. During that narrower span of years, as the scholar Grigorii Gukovskii has written, 'the palace was the primary sphere of application of the force of art and thought; it played the role of a political and cultural centre, of a club for grandees and nobles, of a temple of the monarchy, of a theatre, on which was staged a magnificent spectacle, whose meaning was to demonstrate the power, the grandeur and the unearthly character of the earthly authority'.[1] With some caveats, this description of the palace could be transposed to any period of imperial Russia, as literary texts and practices continued to maintain a connection with the palace until the revolution of 1917.

The court's hegemony over the arts, the sciences, and education manifested itself most intensely in the mid-eighteenth century. This was when the court constituted what social theory identifies as *dispositif*: a heterogeneous mechanism, composed of material, discursive, and non-discursive elements, whose primary aim is to model and to control a social body. Indeed, in Gukovskii's description, the palace appears as a kind of *Gesamtkunstwerk* – a total work of art – that embraces not only different

---

1 Grigorii A. Gukovskii, *Ocherki po istorii russkoi literatury XVIII veka. Dvorianskaia fronda v literature 1750–1760-kh godov* [Studies in Russian literature of the eighteenth century. Aristocratic opposition in the literature of the 1750s and 1760s] (Moscow, Leningrad: Izdatel'stvo Akademii nauk SSSR 13.

artistic media but also combines political and aesthetic functions. In the realm of literary production and reception, the court dominated various aspects, ranging from the topics of specific works to the codes of aesthetic perception. It defined what literature should be and had a clear vision of its raisons d'être.

By the end of the century, dissenting voices had begun to question the court's overwhelming authority (see Chapters 1.4, 2.3). Although various features of the initial *dispositif* survived across the centuries – court patronage, the position of the court at the apex of the social hierarchy, support for the imperial theatres, the court-sanctioned surveillance of some writers and policing of literary works, and so on – its central, dominant, and almost exclusive role as a mechanism for generating literature did not outlast the eighteenth century.

Images of the court, and courtly life, in literary works reflect shifting social and political frameworks. They also demonstrate the potent mythology of the eighteenth-century court – and Catherine II's reign (1762–96) in particular – which seems to have been the most perfect embodiment of the imperial Enlightenment. In one of the stories from *Evenings on a Farm near Dikanka* (*Vechera na khutore bliz Dikan'ki*, 1831–2) – the collection that made the young Nikolai Gogol (1809–1852) famous – a blacksmith named Vakula travels from a Ukrainian village to St Petersburg on the devil's back. His mission: to take the boots from the empress's feet so as to earn the hand of his beloved Oksana. Vakula succeeds in accessing the imperial palace with a delegation of Zaporozhian Cossacks. Amused by the young man's naïve and touching manners, the fictional Catherine II suggests that an unnamed writer present in her retinue take this original fellow as an object of inspiration:

> 'Here,' the empress went on, directing her eyes at a middle-aged man with a plump, but somewhat pale face, who was standing further off than the others and whose modest caftan with big mother-of-pearl buttons showed that he did not belong to the number of the courtiers, 'you have a subject worthy of your witty pen!'
>
> 'You are too gracious, Your Imperial Majesty. Here at least a La Fontaine is called for,' the man with the mother-of-pearl buttons replied, bowing.
>
> 'I tell you in all honesty, I still love your *Brigadier* to distraction. You read remarkably well!'[2]

---

2 Nikolai Gogol, *The Collected Tales*, trans. Richard Pevear and Larissa Volokhonsky (New York: Vintage, 1998), pp. 56–7.

In this dialogue one can easily recognise Denis Fonvizin (1745–1792, Fonvizin being the Russianised form of his family name of von Wiesen), the author of satirical comedies and one of the emblematic literary figures of the eighteenth century. Gogol demonstrates here that he is familiar with Fonvizin's confessional memoirs, first published in 1830, in which the author tells of the success of his comic play *The Brigadier* (*Brigadir*, 1769) at Catherine's court. More importantly for our purposes, the scene also illustrates a retrospective vision of the relations between the court and literature. According to Gogol's reconstitution of this model, each participant plays a part in a precisely staged ceremony. A perfectly literate Zaporozhian Cossack, for instance, switches to a popular idiom when he addresses himself to the empress. Amid this *mise en scène*, the monarch picks a topic and recommends it to a writer she had previously distinguished – which explains his presence in the palace in the first place. In response, the author humbly mentions someone better qualified to realise Catherine's idea, Louis XIV's court writer Jean de La Fontaine (1621–1695), thus both reinforcing the empress's intuition and subtly comparing St Petersburg to Versailles and, consequently, his own position to that of one of the classics of French court literature. The monarch's artistic authority is as a result endorsed by the canonical author's unattainable perfection, while the parallels with the past contribute towards emphasising a political and aesthetic continuity between the two imperial regimes.

Gogol's simultaneously nostalgic and ironic depiction of eighteenth-century literary mechanisms captures several interrelated phenomena that contributed to making the court's interconnections with the literary world particularly strong in the eighteenth century: a new ceremonial culture, the emergence of court society, and the practice of court patronage. At the same time, it shows how the eighteenth-century court came to function as the agent of its own cultural and sociopolitical mythology. The literary production approved by the court for its political and artistic value shaped a canon that was crystallised in the nineteenth century by writers such as Gogol and that has survived in literary studies to the present day.[3]

Literature and Court Ceremonial Culture

The court was an agent in literary processes throughout its history, but from the late seventeenth to the late eighteenth centuries it was the main sponsor

---

3 Luba Golburt, *The First Epoch: The Eighteenth Century and the Russian Cultural Imagination* (Madison: University of Wisconsin Press, 2014).

and judge of the new literary culture. The Russian court of the eighteenth century imported a new paradigm of literature from western Europe, adjusting its forms and practices to local circumstances but also challenging native customs and idioms. This process involved not only the translation and imitation of texts but the adoption – from European courts – of the very idea of state-supervised and supported secular belles-lettres. As Vissarion Belinskii (1811–1848; see Box 5.1) later wrote: 'The notion of poetry was ordered by post from Europe and shipped to Russia, where it emerged as an overseas innovation.'[4] Indeed, eighteenth-century Russian literary production is in many cases barely intelligible without a solid knowledge of its multilingual background. Scripture, the classical heritage, and works in European languages all came together to shape the canon of absolutist literature, with specific codes of representation tightly linked to the ceremonial cultures deployed at the imperial palace and beyond.

In 1721, Peter I proclaimed Russia an empire and the imperial court replaced the sovereign court (*gosudarev dvor*) that had been in place since the days of early Muscovy. During the rule of Peter's father, Tsar Aleksei Mikhailovich (r. 1645–76), the court had already become a platform for the implementation of a new ceremonial culture. Peter's endeavour thus contributed to the institutionalisation of new forms of public life and imperial performance among Russian elites. In the words of Gavriil Golovkin – chancellor under Peter – in a speech of 1721, Russia had emerged 'from the darkness of ignorance on to the stage of global renown'.[5] Golovkin's declaration also reflects a trend in the development of the public sphere in Russia: the court displayed its power before an audience that was constituted by the performance of power.

From the 1700s onwards, in order to cope with the demands of the early modern version of global capitalism as well as with domestic challenges, the Russian government sought alternative ways to enhance social cohesion, encouraging – or coercing – members of the noble elite into state service and creating social mobility. Literature and art were to serve this purpose. In Gukovskii's words: 'Literature and art were a part of a ritual of aesthetic

---

4 Vissarion Belinskii, 'Sochineniia Aleksandra Pushkina' [The works of Aleksandr Pushkin] (1843), cited in Andreas Schönle and Andrei Zorin, *On the Periphery of Europe 1762–1825: The Self-Invention of the Russian Elite* (DeKalb: Northern Illinois University Press, 2018), p. 146.

5 [Gavrill Golovkin], *Rech' kotoraia publichno v tserkvi ego tsarskomu presvetlomu velichestvu, ot Sinoda i Senata govorena* . . . [Speech, which was publicly delivered in the church to his sovereign illustrious majesty on behalf of the Synod and the Senate . . .] (St Petersburg, 1721), p. 1.

propaganda for the monarchy, affirming its immediate aims and intentions, at the same time legitimising its right to power.'[6] Although literary production had already reflected ceremonial codes and shaped the absolutist ideology of the court of Aleksei Mikhailovich, in the eighteenth century literature found itself at the core of state-building. It was to serve the court's aims by producing universally relevant representations that placed the imperial palace at the centre of the entire society and affirmed its position at the pinnacle of hierarchies of value.

The court's initiatives and sponsorship were essential to establishing sites for the production, circulation, and conservation of literary artefacts that reached beyond the imperial palace – such as the Academy of Sciences, educational institutions, libraries, and the public theatre. The Academy of Sciences, founded in 1725, was the first secular institutional environment providing qualified authors to satisfy the court's needs in the elaboration of what Richard Wortman calls 'scenarios of power', whereby the common theme of a given reign is evoked in a series of texts, artefacts, and public ceremonies. In the spirit of the eighteenth-century polymathy, 'literature' – then most often referred to as *poeziia* (poetry) or *slovesnost'* (humanities) – belonged both to the domain of the arts, as self-sufficient belles-lettres with no aims other than distraction and entertainment, and to *nauki*, literally 'sciences', where it constituted a domain of practical knowledge with links to several academic disciplines including history, rhetoric, and versification. In the new academy, writing was perceived as a craft necessary for courtly entertainment, alongside such things as firework displays. Indeed, the total spectacle of the imperial court usually required a wide collaboration of different craftsmen and engineers to stage mass festivities.[7]

To associate absolutely all literary production in Russia with the imperial court would be a stretch even for the eighteenth century, but the most emblematic literary practices were tightly linked to various features of the court. Occasional poetry and Neoclassical drama provide striking examples of court-generated forms that progressively gained broader social currency. Both genres were closely tied to the calendar of court ceremonies, a continuous series of celebrations and commemorations that combined Orthodox feasts with the anniversaries of the imperial family and other dates significant for the reign, such as the ascension to the throne or days

6 Gukovskii, *Ocherki*, p. 9.
7 See Simon Werrett, *Fireworks: Pyrotechnic Arts and Sciences in European History* (Chicago: University of Chicago Press, 2010).

marking dynastic orders or significant military events, victories, and peace treaties.[8]

Frequent topics of court poetry included the promise of a domestically and internationally peaceful reign, or – as in the case of the empresses Elizabeth (r. 1741–62) and Catherine II – the justification and glorification of the palace coup that had brought the ruler to power. In his famous 1747 ode celebrating six years of Elizabeth's rule, Mikhail Lomonosov (1711–1765) intertwines these two motifs:

> When she upon the throne ascended,
> As God on High gave her the crown,
> 'Twas she who brought you back Russia
> And put an end to further war.
> Embracing you she kissed you warmly
> And said: 'I have my fill of triumphs,
> For which a stream of blood has flown.
> The Russians' happiness delights me.
> Their peace I would not give in barter
> For all the West and all the East.'[9]

The 'you' in the poem is 'beloved tranquillity' (*vozliublennaia tishina*) – that is, peace – a notion that seems to be in contradiction with the reality of Russian imperial expansion throughout the century. This tension is inherent in the mode of representation typical of court culture: shifts from periods of violence to the status quo are celebrated across artistic media, as are shifts in the opposite direction.

In the sphere of drama, Neoclassical tragedy – imported to Russia in the 1740s by a French theatre company – had a similar function: painful and violent events from the past were represented so as to help the local noble audience reflect on the often traumatic histories of their own families, subjected to the whims of court politics. The French actors were of course hired by the imperial court. The first Russian theatre company was founded in 1756 under the supervision of Aleksandr Sumarokov (1717–1777; see Chapter 3.4). His tragedies, such as the much-celebrated *Semira* (*Semira*, 1751), depicted the actions of princes and didactically presented key episodes of Russian history. More generally, comedies aside, the Russian stage was initially resistant to non-court settings, such as those represented in English

---

8 See Richard Wortman, *Scenarios of Power: Myth and Ceremony in Russian Monarchy*, vol. I (Princeton: Princeton University Press, 1995).

9 Mikhail V. Lomonosov, 'Ode on the ascension of the Empress Elizabeth Petrovna, 1747', in Harold B. Segel (ed.), *The Literature of Eighteenth-Century Russia*, 2 vols. (New York: E. P. Dutton, 1967), vol. I, p. 194.

domestic tragedies or French *drame*. Its tragic repertoire was distinctively aristocratic, even if the court theatre sometimes opened its doors to a non-noble audience.

Foreign reactions to these representations were critical of the Russian court's cultural ascendancy. Often responding to the expansive territorial politics of the new empire, of which St Petersburg was the emblem, European authors described the Russian court as an imitative endeavour, a façade lacking any roots in local culture. Moreover, the very splendour of the St Petersburg palaces was perceived as the epitome of despotic rule. In the early days of the city's existence, the banks of the Neva – where the royal residence was transferred from Moscow in 1709 – featured more huts than stone houses. In travel accounts, such as William Richardson's *Anecdotes of the Russian Empire* (1784), impoverished locals are depicted as an army of slaves catering to the sovereign's wild ambitions to build a European civilisation amidst the 'oriental', despotic empire.[10] The most authoritative intellectual framework for understanding the phenomenon of the new empire was Montesquieu's theory of government, linking together the geography (and climate in particular) and political organisation of countries. From the perspective of this theory, Russia offered an odd example of a European power with a peculiar kind of despotic rule, one driven by and focused on change. According to Montesquieu, despotism is an appropriate form of government for Russia due to the spread of the country's territory, not its climate, for despotism is a feature of warm countries. Montesquieu's political theory also helped to popularise tropes about the northern climate that had circulated before his treatise appeared, such as the one employed in the letter of a French diplomat writing to his minister from St Petersburg in August 1762: 'I find this climate little suitable for the sciences and for the arts in general.'[11]

The production of a national, Russian court poetry, ostensibly equivalent to its European predecessors, was, in part, felt to be a necessary response to such perceptions. In his essay 'On Poetry' (*O stikhotvorstve*, 1762), Sergei Domashnev (1743–1795) listed poetry as among the primary indicators of the 'undying glory' of the empress Elizabeth.[12] Domashnev added that the

---

10 For a study of travel accounts, see Larry Wolff, *Inventing Eastern Europe: The Map of Civilization on the Mind of the Enlightenment* (Stanford: Stanford University Press, 1994).
11 *Sbornik Imperatorskago Russkago Istoricheskago Obshchestva* [Proceedings of the Imperial Russian Historical Society], vol. 140 (St Petersburg: Tipografiia V. F. Kirshbauma, 1912), p. 46.
12 Sergei Domashnev, 'O stikhotvorstve' [On poetry], in Pavel Efremov (ed.), *Materialy dlia istorii russkoi literatury* [Materials for the history of Russian literature] (St Petersburg: Tipografiia I. I. Glazunova, 1867), p. 191.

primary aim of poetry was to improve morals, thus linking literature to the disciplining project of Russian autocrats and the creation of a compliant public sphere. These autocrats were impatient to advertise the success of their cultural policies. Thus, some of Lomonosov's poetic works and Sumarokov's tragedies were translated into European languages, and accounts of literature native to Russia were published in European periodicals. The eagerness to demonstrate the nation's creative capacities occasionally led to curious results: some Russian works were first published as, say, German translations and only appeared in Russian years later. One striking example is *Satires* (*Satiry*) by Antiokh Kantemir (1708–1744), first published in French translation in 1749, then in German in 1752. It was only a decade later, in 1762, that the Russian original appeared.

Court Society

In the late seventeenth century, new forms of court culture had stimulated the emergence of literary production – panegyric and didactic poetry, rhetorical prose, and court theatre (see Chapters 1.2, 3.3).[13] In the 1730s, a series of endeavours to import prestigious foreign literary forms into Russia attracted the attention of the ruling class. These literary phenomena can be seen as symptoms of the emerging court society, a distinctive form of sociopolitical organisation.[14] Vasilii Trediakovskii's (1703–1768) *Voyage to the Island of Love* (*Ezda v ostrov liubvi*, 1730), for example, is an attempt to forge the idiom of genteel amorous commerce through the translation of a French Baroque novel (see Chapter 1.3).[15] Hence the idea of the transformative power of the new literary paradigm whose emergence coincided with the European Enlightenment. The state reinvented itself and, in this process, required new technologies.

The formation of European courts was a symptom of the domestication of noble elites. But the 'theoretically unlimited power of Russian autocracy' was, according to the historian David Ransel, in fact reliant on the 'familial and personal patronage networks that dominated the court and upper

---

13 Aleksei N. Robinson, *Bor'ba idei v russkoi literature XVII veka* [The struggle of ideas in seventeenth-century Russian literature] (Moscow: Nauka, 1974).

14 For a historical account of the Russian court in the eighteenth century, see Olga G. Ageeva, *Imperatorskii dvor Rossii, 1700–1796* [The imperial court of Russia, 1700–1796] (Moscow: Nauka, 2008).

15 For a recent study and a bibliography, see Igor Fedyukin, 'Lost in translation: Trediakovskii's *Journey to the Island of Love* and its courtly context', *Slavonic and East European Review* 97.4 (2019), 601–28.

administration'.[16] The court was therefore the place where the monarch could keep closer watch on the nobility and where court factions took social shape, sometimes provoking coups. The latter were particularly frequent in eighteenth-century Russia, up to and including 1801, when Catherine II's son and Alexander I's father, Paul I (r. 1796–1801), was assassinated.

On the administrative level, the Office of Her or His Imperial Majesty coordinated the court offices until 1826, when the Ministry of the Imperial Court and Principalities was instituted. In terms of social organisation, court ranks were included in the table of ranks, both a catalogue of grades and a system of service promotion instituted by Peter I in 1722 (see Chapter 4.3).[17] These ranks aimed at creating an elite class by way of moving up the ranks rather than relying on family background. Insofar as the 'enlightened' court was an agent of social engineering, literary texts and other rhetorical genres helped to reinforce the culture and its related social hierarchies.

Public literary debate began in the 1740s. In 1743, three leading authors – Trediakovskii, Lomonosov, and Sumarokov – took part in a literary competition, writing poetic renditions of a psalm using the kinds of versification they thought would be the most appropriate for the new Russian poetry. What used to be considered a purely literary dispute was now seen as a milestone in the process of the elaboration of a new discourse of power. Drawing on biblical concepts, lyricists of the imperial regime collectively reflected on the idiom of domination and submission suitable for a modern political theology. In the early 1750s, as Ivan Shuvalov (1727–1797) rose to the status of the official favourite of Empress Elizabeth, the first national literary canon – with Lomonosov and Sumarokov at its core – would become an object of state promotion, and Shuvalov's role in this was paramount. A new social role of public writer was thus established at the core of the Russian monarchy, with the court's direct support.

The prestige of literary occupations reached its peak when Catherine II began to apply herself to the publication of a review, *All Sorts* (*Vsiakaia vsiachina*, 1769), containing periodical essays that followed the model of Addison and Steele's *Spectator*. Catherine II was a prominent patron of the arts, notable for her support of both local talents and European celebrities (such as Denis Diderot, who visited her court in the early 1770s). What makes her stand out, not merely in the Russian but also in the European context,

---

16 David L. Ransel, *The Politics of Catherinian Russia: The Panin Party* (New Haven: Yale University Press, 1975), p. 1.

17 Irina Reyfman, *How Russia Learned to Write: Literature and the Imperial Table of Ranks* (Madison: University of Wisconsin Press, 2016).

however, is her own dedication to writing. The empress herself exemplifies the intimate connection between the court and literary production. She tried her hand at writing memoirs, comic plays (in Russian and in French), operas, short stories and literary folk tales, polemical treatises, letters in three languages, and even a dictionary.[18] She does not appear to have attempted to write verse, but according to Gavriil Derzhavin (1743–1816) in his poem 'Felitsa' (*Felitsa*, 1782; see Chapter 4.2), she did appreciate poetry.[19]

Catherine's own writings have little to do with the scenarios of deification of the monarch typical of the ceremonial strand of literary production and usually taking on the form of solemn odes or Baroque operas. Yet her mission was very close to what Sumarokov, in an ode to Peter I (*Oda na Gosudaria Imperatora Petra Velikogo*, 1755), had described in terms of Peter's radical social engineering: 'PETER . . . / Inserts new souls in us.'[20] In the words of Voltaire in one of his letters to Catherine II, she was born 'to instruct people just as much as to govern them. It will be difficult to instruct the populace; but all those who will have received only tolerable education will profit from the enlightenment you spread more and more.'[21] Catherine's own writings and literary works thus more generally pursued the double task of enlightening a part of society – first and foremost her own court – and of advertising the project of instruction itself, along with its results, to broader publics. It is not surprising, therefore, that her output included a range of comic plays, the modern versions of satire.

Catherine also continued Peter I's project of turning public theatre in Russia into what Elise Wirtschafter calls 'a tool of social and cultural transformation'.[22] Early in her reign, she encouraged a group of young authors serving under her private secretary Ivan Elagin (1725–1794) to compose comedies featuring Russian realities and targeting local

18 See Monika Greenleaf, 'Performing autobiography: The multiple memoirs of Catherine the Great (1756–96)', *Russian Review* 63.3 (2004), 407–26; Lurana Donnels O'Malley, *The Dramatic Works of Catherine the Great: Theatre and Politics in Eighteenth-Century Russia* (Aldershot: Ashgate, 2006).

19 See Elena Pogosian, 'Uroki imperatritsy: Ekaterina II i Derzhavin v 1782 godu' [The empress's lessons: Catherine II and Derzhavin in 1782], in L. O. Zaionts (ed.), '*Na mezhe mezh Golosom i Ekhom*'. *Sbornik v chest' Tat'iany Vladimirovny Tsyv'ian* ['On the line between Voice and Echo'. A collection in honour of Tatiana Vladimirovna Tsyv'ian] (Moscow: Novoe izdatel'stvo, 2007), pp. 241–68.

20 Sergei Nikolaev (ed.), *Petr I v russkoi literature XVIII veka. Teksty i kommentarii* [Peter I in eighteenth-century Russian literature. Texts and commentaries] (St Petersburg: Nauka, 2006), p. 189.

21 *Les œuvres complètes de Voltaire* [Complete works of Voltaire], 205 vols. (Oxford: Voltaire Foundation, 1968–2021), vol. 122 (1975), pp. 141–2.

22 Elise Kimerling Wirtschafter, *The Play of Ideas in Russian Enlightenment Theater* (DeKalb: Northern Illinois University Press, 2003), p. 4.

vices.[23] This encouraged the first dramatic works of Vladimir Lukin (1737–1794), Denis Fonvizin, and some lesser-known playwrights, but, as so often, the empress decided that nobody could interpret her own policies better than herself, so she wrote her first series of plays in 1771. In her very first comedy, *Oh These Times!* (*O vremia!*, 1772), Catherine II draws on both current events, such as the Moscow plague riots, and her experience of coming of age at the Russian court to produce a complex dramatic allegory, full of rational optimism. In this and other plays, such as *The Siberian Shaman* (*Shaman sibirskii*, 1786), she shows how the new society of the educated serving class of St Petersburg successfully challenges the old-world nobility with its obscurantism, superstition, and idleness. To some extent, Fonvizin's comedy *The Minor* (*Nedorosl'*, 1782) takes on the same task, but with superior literary craft.

In his study of the foundational moment of Russian imperial literature, Kirill Ospovat has described its social role in this way: 'Literature – secular writings, definable as *poetry* or *fiction* – acts as a medium in which the secular polity appropriates the regulatory and disciplinary competence of clerical literature and its control over the models of subjectivity.'[24] The close connection between literary occupation, moral authority, and social discipline was crystallised in the court status of successful authors. 'A poet is born into the world to converse with tsars', writes Vasilii Petrov (1736–1799) in an unpublished epistle to Catherine II.[25] In some cases, rulers decided to entrust to literary celebrities the education of their children and their spouses. In the early 1760s, Catherine II invited Jean d'Alembert to supervise the education of the future Paul I. The encyclopedist declined the invitation, and the grand duke was instead schooled by a local man of letters, Semen Poroshin (1741–1769), whose diary gives a clear idea of the importance of literary and dramatic texts in the princely education. Mikhail Muravev (1757–1807), an

---

23 See Vladimir Lukin, 'Predislovie k *Motu, liuboviiu ispravlennomu*' [Preface to *The Wastrel Cured by Love*], in *Sochineniia i perevody Vladimira Lukina* [Works and translations by Vladimir Lukin] (St Petersburg: Tipografiia Akademii nauk, 1765), pp. III–IV. On the aesthetics and politics of adaptation in court drama, see Alexei Evstratov, 'Drama translation in eighteenth-century Russia: Masters and servants on the court stage in the 1760s', in Leon Burnett and Emily Lygo (eds.), *Art as Accommodation: Literary Translation in Russia* (Oxford: Peter Lang, 2013), pp. 31–54.

24 Kirill Ospovat, *Pridvornaia slovesnost': Institut literatury i konstruktsiia absoliutizma v Rossii serediny XVIII veka* [Belles-lettres at court: The institution of literature and the construction of absolutism in mid-eighteenth-century Russia] (Moscow: Novoe literaturnoe obozrenie, 2020), p. 26.

25 Luba Golburt, 'Vasilii Petrov and the poetics of patronage', *Вивлиофика: E-Journal of Eighteenth-Century Russian Studies* 3 (2015), 47–69.

important author in the late eighteenth century, was a preceptor to Paul's sons, Aleksandr and Konstantin. Later, the poet Vasilii Zhukovskii (1783–1852) taught Russian to several members of the imperial family, including the future Alexander II (r. 1855–81).

It is not surprising, therefore, that some of the best-known authors had court titles or court ranks. The practice, common in the eighteenth century, was marginalised over the course of the nineteenth. Aleksandr Pushkin (1799–1837), for example, was dissatisfied with being granted the title of *kameriunker*, the lowest in the court hierarchy, in 1833.

Court Patronage

Peter I's policies led to the emergence of what can be seen as a secular cult of service duty. This transformed the status and mission of the author. As Aleksandr Panchenko has put it, 'a monk or a lay brother becomes a state servant; a writer, composing to fulfil a vow or out of inner conviction, is transmuted into a scribe who writes in response to a command or by decree'.[26] Kantemir, Trediakovskii, Lomonosov, Sumarokov, Fonvizin, Derzhavin – all of these celebrated authors, along with dozens of others of lesser renown, worked for the imperial court and benefited from its support.[27] The quasi-monopoly that governmental institutions maintained over the printing press also enhanced the central position of the court networks in the mediasphere. An anonymous late-eighteenth-century commentator on Christoph Hermann von Manstein's memoirs of mid-eighteenth-century Russia wrote: 'Without royal encouragement, the finest minds and the most exquisite natural gifts will wane, perish and lapse into obscurity.'[28] According to Gukovskii, virtually all literary endeavours in the 1750s and 1760s – a period crucial to the emergence of the local version of a literary sphere – were supported by the court. How can

26 Aleksandr M. Panchenko, 'O smene pisatel'skogo tipa v petrovskuiu epohu' [On the change in the type of writer during the Petrine era], in *Russkaia istoriia i kul'tura: Raboty raznyh let* [Russian history and culture: Studies from different years] (St Petersburg: Iuna, 1999), pp. 333–4.

27 See Kirill Ospovat, 'Mikhail Lomonosov writes to his patron: Professional ethos, literary rhetoric and social ambition', *Jahrbücher Für Geschichte Osteuropas* 59.2 (2011), 240–66.

28 'Zamechaniia na "Zapiski o Rossii generala Manshteina"' ['Remarks on "General Manshtein's notes on Russia"'], in *Perevoroty i voiny* [Revolutions and wars] (Moscow: Fond Sergeia Dubova, 1997), p. 444, quoted in Kirill Ospovat, *Terror and Pity: Aleksandr Sumarokov and the Theater of Power in Elizabethan Russia* (Boston: Academic Studies Press, 2016), p. viii.

one explain this hegemony of a governmental institution in the cultural domain?

One major cause is the relatively late emergence of a literary marketplace in Russia: even in the nineteenth century only one or two dozen very successful authors could sustain themselves by creative work alone. The court, on the other hand, was a major economic agent that managed its own land and serfs, which contributed to its income. In the eighteenth century, the court's expenditure could reach up to 20 to 25 per cent of the state budget. Unlike some European courts, however, the Russian courts did not maintain an official post of court poet. How exactly did the court implement its patronage, then? Several methods were employed in different periods. The method that is particularly emblematic of the eighteenth century was for the sovereign to present the author of a well-appreciated work with a gift such as an expensive snuffbox, a ring, and/or a significant sum of money. Another was to grant a pension either to the writer himself or to his family members. Catherine II went so far as to practise this kind of sponsorship with European celebrities, such as Voltaire and Diderot. The granting of a noble title was another way to confer distinction on a man of letters. Catherine's epistolary interlocutor the Swiss doctor Johann Zimmermann (1728–1795) became a knight of the Order of St Vladimir, thus acquiring nobility. Finally, literary talent – in conjunction with other qualities and useful connections – could lead to a service career at court. Favoured authors, such as Derzhavin and Petrov, held various positions such as reader (i.e. with the duty of reading aloud for the empress) and state secretary.

Patron–client relations were crystallised in panegyric verse. Starting with Kantemir's poetic addresses to his patron, Prince Nikita Trubetskoi, in his *Satires*, such verses grew ever more numerous through the century, with Vasillii Ruban (1742–1795) and Dmitrii Khvostov (1757–1835) emerging as prominent contributors. A frequent leitmotif is the support that the addressee granted to the arts: cultural philanthropy is represented as a necessary feature of a great man or woman.

The solemn ode is a quintessential genre of panegyric culture (see Chapters 1.3, 4.2) in which the poet's enthusiasm for the sovereign – who is both the main object of the text and the addressee of this work – serves to constitute a reading community. A famous early example is Lomonosov's 'Ode to the Blessed Memory of the Empress Anna Ioannovna on the Victory over the Turks and Tatars and the Seizure of Khotin, 1739' (*Oda blazhennyia pamiati gosudaryne imperatritse Anne Ioannovne na pobedu nad turkami i tatarami i na vziatie Khotina 1739 goda*), usually referred to as 'Ode on the Seizure of

Khotin'. Not for another thirty years did an ode writer address a nobleman rather than a member of the imperial family.[29] Petrov's ode to the empress's favourite, Grigorii Orlov – 'Ode to His Excellency Count Aleksei Grigorevich Orlov on His Arrival from the Archipelago in St Petersburg. 4 March 1771' (*Oda ego siiatel'stvu grafu Alekseiu Grigor'evichu Orlovu na pribytie ego iz Arkhipelaga v Sankt-Peterburg. 1771 marta 4 dnia*) – is one of the first examples of such a dedication. The solemn ode continued to exist as a genre well into the early nineteenth century, but this shift from the crowned addressee to a grandee seems to have taken something from the genre's aura. Close connections between writers and grandees are manifested in the dedications that sometimes preface printed works. An author had to secure permission from the court in order to publish their work with such a dedication. The latter used a variety of devices, literary and typographical, sometimes just stating the addressee, sometimes providing a paragraph or two explaining the relevance of the literary endeavour or making explicit the link between the author and the addressee.[30]

Beyond the imperial patronage of individual authors, the court took on the roles of sponsor of policies, laboratory for literary experiments, and model for imitation among the educated classes, for whom both the consumption and the production of literature progressively became respectable occupations.

In the late 1780s, several private initiatives in the sphere of publishing – those of the Moscow Freemasons and that of Aleksandr Radishchev (1749–1802) – revealed the limits of the cultural autonomy and the criticism that could be tolerated by the court. In the first case, Catherine II targeted a group of people that seemed to have gained too much autonomy, both intellectual (spiritual) and operational, from the government. Indeed, supervised by the writer and philanthropist Nikolai Novikov (1744–1818), several printing presses, including Moscow University Press, issued up to a quarter of the overall number of titles printed in the 1780s. The persecution of Novikov's activities, directed from St Petersburg, started with a series of censorship cases, went on to a large-scale examination of his printed production, and ended in arrest and imprisonment. Radishchev's case, provoked by his self-published book *A Journey from St Petersburg to Moscow* (*Puteshestvie iz*

---

29 Nadezhda Alekseeva, *Russkaia oda: Razvitie odicheskoi formy v XVII–XVIII vekakh* [The Russian ode: The development of the odic form in the seventeenth and eighteenth centuries] (St Petersburg: Nauka, 2005), p. 300.

30 Natal'ia D. Kochetkova, *Posviashcheniia v russkih izdaniiah XVIII veka: Issledovanie, teksty, bibliograficheskii ukazatel'* [Dedications in Russian editions of the eighteenth century: Study, texts, bibliography] (Moscow: Al'ians-Arheo, 2020).

Peterburga v Moskvu, 1790), was also contemporaneous with the French Revolution and, unlike books printed by Novikov, did contain a radical critique of the absolutist order. Like Novikov, Radishchev was first sentenced to death but then exiled to Siberia. These two cases illustrate the limits of the court-sponsored Enlightenment. Representatives of the new – educated – ruling class, whose career started during Catherine's reign, sought spaces for literary and social activity removed from the palace. Despite initial signs of encouragement, the empress and autocrat did not tolerate such emancipation.

These early signs of scepticism directed at the centrality of the court to creative processes resonated with the quest for authenticity initiated by the educated landed nobility in the second half of the century. New values were affirmed and explored – values linked to the nuclear family, domesticity, and privacy. The court life – and, more generally, a career in state service – began to be regarded as less desirable: at best a compromise necessary to fulfil social expectations, at worst a deprivation and a source of suffering. Upon leaving imperial service, sometimes prematurely, many authors – Andrei Bolotov (1738–1833), Ivan Bariatinskii (1772–1825), and Dmitrii Buturlin (1763–1829), to name just a few – engaged deeply with agricultural improvement, new pedagogical ideas, and creative writing. Although distanced from the court, these authors tended to fashion their subjectivity in relation to the narratives and topics associated with St Petersburg. Indeed, a commonplace in their writings is a critical depiction of the deceptive and futile world of high society. It is not surprising that their works were rarely published. However, some authors did break into print with paeans to sentimental friendship and domestic tenderness. The best-known such text (though by no means unique in this respect) is *Letters of a Russian Traveller* (*Pis'ma russkogo puteshestvennika*, 1791–2) by Nikolai Karamzin (1766–1826). The interest in individual sensibilities and private mythologies had the potential to clash with the didactic orientation of court literature and its ceremonial tendencies and bombastic rhetoric. However, the new, educated subject developed the capacity to navigate between the different spaces, and literary practices (reading, writing, theatre-going, etc.) played a central role in the reconciliation of conflicts of value.[31]

---

31 See, for example, Andrei Zorin, *Poiavlenie geroia. Iz istorii russkoi emotsional'noi kul'tury kontsa XVIII–nachala XIX vv.* [The rise of the hero. From the history of Russian emotional culture of the late eighteenth and early nineteenth centuries] (Moscow: Novoe literaturnoe obozrenie, 2016).

Interestingly enough, literature circulating at court actively drew on these two apparently critical themes: the hostility of court life and the attraction of a retired existence. While exploiting the dichotomy of St Petersburg (court residence, centre, European culture) vs Moscow (capital of idle nobility, periphery, Asian obscurity), Catherine II and other writers practised playful self-orientalisation. The commonplaces borrowed from the pastoral mode helped to represent the court and the city as a paradise on earth (Peter I's term for St Petersburg). It suffices to visit just one of the imperial residencies today to realise the extent to which depictions of angels, Eden, and pre-urban landscapes with peasants and shepherds dominated the representations in the palace. Literary texts reflected and complemented this reality.[32] The empress playfully featured herself as a landlady and kept away from her salon, the Hermitage, those courtiers and diplomats who could not put aside their social status for the duration of her exclusive soirées.

But regular and violent political vicissitudes disrupted the tranquillity, which then had to be restored – politically and discursively. In other words, although there were very few attempts to challenge the court's cultural hegemony, its literature demonstrates an awareness of the tensions that existed around representations. Literary texts and discussions, especially in the second half of the eighteenth century, document these tensions.

Further Reading

de Madariaga, Isabel, *Russia in the Age of Catherine the Great* (New Haven: Yale University Press, 1981).

Keenan, Paul, *St Petersburg and the Russian Court, 1703–1761* (Houndmills, Basingstoke: Palgrave Macmillan, 2013).

Klein, Joachim (ed.), '18th-century literature', special issue, *Russian Literature* 75 (2014).

Lotman, Iurii M., 'Ocherki po istorii russkoi kul'tury XVIII – nachala XIX veka' [Essays on the history of eighteenth-century and early nineteenth-century Russian culture], in Tatiana D. Kuzovkina and Vlada I. Gekhtman (eds.), *Iz istorii russkoi kul'tury* [From the history of Russian culture], 5 vols. (Moscow: Iazyki slavianskoi kul'tury, 1996–2002), vol. IV, pp. 11–346.

Proskurina, Vera, *Creating the Empress: Politics and Poetry in the Age of Catherine II* (Boston: Academic Studies Press, 2011).

Ram, Harsha, *The Imperial Sublime: A Russian Poetics of Empire* (Madison: University of Wisconsin Press, 2003).

Whittaker, Cynthia H., *Russian Monarchy: Eighteenth-Century Rulers and Writers in Political Dialogue* (DeKalb: Northern Illinois University Press, 2003).

32 See Stephen L. Baehr, *The Paradise Myth in Eighteenth-Century Russia: Utopian Patterns in Early Secular Russian Literature and Culture* (Stanford: Stanford University Press, 1991).

Zhivov, Viktor M., 'The myth of the state in the age of Enlightenment and its destruction in late eighteenth-century Russia', *Russian Studies in History* 48.3 (2009), 10–29.

Zhivov, Viktor M., 'Pervye russkie biografii kak sotsial'noe iavlenie: Trediakovskii, Lomonosov, Sumarokov' [The first Russian biographies as a social phenomenon: Trediakovskii, Lomonosov, Sumarakov], in *Razyskaniia v oblasti istorii i predystorii russkoi kul'tury* [Investigations into the history and prehistory of Russian culture] (Moscow: Iazyki slavianskoi kul'tury, 2002), pp. 557–637.

Zorin, Andrei, *By Fables Alone: Literature and State Ideology in Late Eighteenth- and Early Nineteenth-Century Russia* (Boston: Academic Studies Press, 2014).

2.3

The Salon and the Circle

ILYA VINITSKY

It would not be an exaggeration to say that the history of Russian literature as a cultural institution is one of numerous emerging, interacting, evolving, and splintering literary groups and writers' networks: professional and friendly circles, literary salons, *jour fixes* (literary presentations that happen on a fixed day every month), soirées, and codified literary societies, all associated with certain educational institutions, imperial and aristocratic elites, families, student communities, spaces, editorial boards, or political institutions. Most of these motley forms (or havens) of literary socialisation and domesticity (*literaturnyi byt*), which began to emerge in the eighteenth (if not the seventeenth) century, were borrowed from the west and adjusted to Russia's cultural conditions and social structures. They shaped the emergent model of Russian culture, generated new forms and modes of writing, and presented the literary process as constantly changing constellations of writers and their friends, rather than 'lonely' individual authors.

Some of these literary gatherings elaborated sophisticated rituals and agendas and produced their own programmatic periodicals (these groups are usually labelled as literary societies). Others were essentially friendly conversations about various aesthetic or ideological issues and did not pursue any publication beyond albums or infrequent almanacs. Some groups conveyed 'official' (i.e. state-approved) points of view in their activities. Others were in opposition to the government. There were groups with leaders, strict regulations, and even hierarchies. There were more loosely organised societies that cherished their internal, intimate freedom of expression and made fun of their more official peers. There were groups organised under the auspices of a certain wealthy or influential patron and those that functioned as a chivalric cult of a generous hostess. Some authors and readers attended different circles at the same time. All in all, these literary groups served as

social and emotional channels of expression to test the shared literary beliefs and tastes characteristic of a given epoch. In terms of Russian cultural history, they can be classified (with reservations) chronologically as Neoclassical, Enlightened, Sentimental, Romantic, Realist, Modernist, Soviet official, and Soviet dissident.

In their classic study of the subject, Mark Aronson and Solomon Reiser mention that there were at least four hundred circles, salons, and other forms of writers' communities from the 1730s to the 1860s.[1] Yet the book covers only thirty groups, carefully selected by its authors. Manfred Schruba's dictionary of literary associations from 1890 to 1917 introduces more than 350 literary associations, including circles and salons, operating in Moscow and St Petersburg in the designated period.[2] Numerous authors discuss major literary groups of the early Soviet period as well as Soviet dissident circles in Leningrad and Moscow. Although there are many scholarly works on individual provincial literary groups, no encyclopedic study on the subject has been written. Numerous groups remain unknown due to their fleeting nature and lack of information.

This chapter focuses on literary groups that fall under the category of circles (associations of friends who shared literary tastes and ideas) and salons (elite gatherings of authors at a house of an influential host or hostess) as they emerged in the seventeenth and eighteenth centuries and across their longer history, with the peak of influence being in the 1820s and 1830s. Unlike literary societies, these communities, with very few exceptions, did not have any formal membership, written rules, or programmatic documents that regulated their activities. Instead, they favoured friendly chats on various subjects, literary recitations, and discussions on certain days of the week, sometimes accompanied by musical performances. They also exemplified strong personal bonds and shared memories between their members, which outlived the physical existence of a given group. In most cases, the lifespan of a literary circle was quite short. Salons, with their socially influential patrons and fluid heterodox membership, tended to last longer. Some of these communities created their own circle languages with recurrent motifs, insider jokes, and domestic mythologies. The predominantly oral modus

---

1 Mark Aronson and Solomon Reiser, *Literaturnye kruzhki i salony* [Literary circles and salons] (Leningrad: Priboi, 1929).
2 Manfred Schruba, *Literaturnye ob"edineniia Moskvy i Peterburga 1890–1917 godov. Slovar'* [Literary associations of Moscow and Petersburg. A dictionary] (Moscow: Novoe literaturnoe obozrenie, 2004).

operandi of these circles precluded detailed documentation of what actually happened during their meetings. We can only try to reconstruct their activities by drawing on available printed and archival sources, such as ego-documents (letters, diaries, memoirs), literary works, and sometimes secret police reports. From this perspective, the history of literary circles and salons is the history of the vanished 'everyday life' of their participants – their improvisations, relationships, celebrations, losses, quarrels, reconciliations, and recollections.

Community Building: The Seventeenth and Eighteenth Centuries

One of the first known literary circles in Russian history was the pre-Petrine Chancery School in seventeenth-century Moscow (see Chapter 1.2). This small group consisted of educated officials (clerks and diplomats), monks, and some courtiers, connected through their professional and personal ties and their interest in versification. The members of this group exchanged syllabic epistles – a core genre in the history of literary groups – informed by Polish and Ukrainian Baroque poetry. Consider a typical fragment from corrector Savvatii's epistle to his friend and co-worker Vasilii Lvovich, which offers a symbolic glorification of the intimate group of literary friends and co-workers:

> Rays of sun illuminate the universe,
> And faithful friends perform many good things.
> It is frightful, truly frightful, to live without a friend and to spend one's
>   earthly life in poverty.
>
> The fragrance pleases your sense of smell.
> The friendly love provides reason with benevolent thoughts.[3]

One of the best scholars of eighteenth-century Russian culture, Grigorii Gukovskii, observed that in the first half of the century,

> the sphere where art and thought could be applied was first and foremost the court, which played the role of political and cultural center as well as that of an aristocratic club, a church of the monarchy and a theater, where the most grandiose spectacle was staged, the idea of which consisted in the

---

3 Savvatii, 'Poslanie d'iaku Vasiliiu L'vovichu' [Epistle to the clerk Vasilii Lvovich], in V. K. Bylinin and A. A. Iliushin (eds.), *Virshevaia poeziia: Pervaia polovina XVII veka* [Verse poetry: The first half the seventeenth century] (Moscow: Sovetskaia Rossiia, 1989), p. 188.

display of power, greatness, of the unearthly character of earthly power. The Academy of Sciences and the salons of the grandees existed as auxiliary institutions or branches of the court.[4]

Thus, the reforms of Peter I (r. 1682–1725) led to the creation of a new form of cultural socialisation associated with the so-called assemblies of modernised nobility. Foreigners (mostly of German and French origin) played an important role in these proto-salons. Thus, the courtier Willim Mons (the brother of Peter's mistress and, conceivably, the empress's lover, who was eventually beheaded for corruption) compiled and distributed among Russian ladies and other courtiers German Baroque love poems and songs, written in Russian but transliterated into Latin letters. In the early eighteenth century, Vasilii Trediakovskii (1703–1768) attempted to transpose a French salon culture into Russia by means of a textbook of chivalric behaviour, *Voyage to the Island of Love* (*Ezda v ostrov liubvi*, 1730) – a translation of Abbé Paul Tallement's 1663 novel *Voyage de l'île d'amour* (see Chapters 1.3, 2.2). The attempt failed. The translation was successful, but the love poems were considered scandalous, and the culture itself was too foreign to take root.

According to some scholars, the so-called Learned Cohort (*studiosa cohors*) – a grouping composed of the three main leaders of Peter's reforms, the theologian and writer Feofan Prokopovich (1681–1736), the historian Vasilii Tatishchev (1686–1750), and the diplomat and amateur poet Antiokh Kantemir (1708–1744) – was one of the first literary-philosophical associations in modern Russian history. Its goal was the dissemination of the ideas of the early Enlightenment and the lambasting of its critics. In the 1730s–50s, literary circles appeared within some of the professional military schools founded by Peter and his heirs. At the same time, a wealthy Russian courtier and Moscow University curator, Ivan Shuvalov (1727–1797), created a literary salon in which he amused himself and other guests by staging fierce disputes between two pillars of Russian Neoclassicism, Mikhail Lomonosov (1711–1765) and Aleksandr Sumarokov (1717–1777).

The political and social reforms of Catherine II (r. 1762–96) led to the relative emancipation of the Russian nobility and consequently to the formation of several private literary circles, which laid the foundation for Russian literary journalism. A number of oppositional circles, mostly of a moralistic and satirical nature, emerged in the 1760s and 1770s as branches of the

4 Grigorii Gukovskii, *Ocherki po istorii russkoi literatury XVIII veka: Dvorianskaia fronda v literature 1750-kh–1760-kh godov* [Essays on eighteenth-century Russian literature: Gentry Fronde in Russian literature of the 1750–1760s] (Leningrad: Academiia nauk, 1962), p. 13. See also Chapter 2.2.

international Masonic 'knightly' orders centred on Paris, Berlin, and Stockholm. Masons introduced and successfully promoted the mode of the brotherly association of seekers, based on their spiritual and emotional kinship and mutual apprenticeship rather than social and familial ties and hierarchies. They also developed and practised new literary and musical genres (integral parts of the elaborate Masonic ritual), from the friendly song (or toast) to the allegorical didactic speech and the solemn religious hymn – as exemplified in the magnificent song 'How Glorious Is Our Lord in Zion' (*Kol' slaven nash Gospod' v Sione*, 1794) by the composer Dmitrii Bortnianskii (1751–1825), with the verses of poet Mikhail Kheraskov (1733–1807):

> Oh God, let our voices
> Enter Thy dwelling,
> And let our tender sense
> Rise to Thee like morning dew!
> To Thee in our hearts we'll raise an altar,
> For Thee we sing and glorify![5]

All in all, the literary circles of Catherine's age played an important role in the formation of the Russian literary cultural environment – both ideological and emotional. Let us consider three examples. In the second half of the century, a group of writers and lovers of literature gathered in Moscow in the home of Fedor Karin (1739–1800), a wealthy nobleman, sybarite, and amateur author and translator. An ardent follower of Sumarokov ('the Russian Racine'), Karin wrote a programmatic 'Letter to N. P. Nikolev Concerning Transformers of the Russian Language' (*Pis'mo k Nikolaiu Petrovichu Nikolevu o preobraziteliakh rossiiskogo iazyka*, 1778), which was addressed primarily to his literary friends. According to Karin, Sumarokov modified Russian language and poetry by familiarising Russian readers with the genres of tragedy, fable, elegy, and pastoral. He argued that Sumarokov 'had reached the very core of beauty of poetry and simple speech and thus transformed it and given it a new power'.[6] In this epistolary tract, Karin focused on the polishing and further development of the Russian literary language (a core theme and goal

---

5 'Prelozhenie psalma 64' [Adaptation of psalm 64], in *Russkaia krestomatiia, ili, Otbornaia sochineniia russkikh pisatelei v proze i stikhakh* [Russian Reader, or selected works of Russian writers in prose and verse] (St Petersburg: Tipografiia Il'ii Glazonova, 1942), p. 706.
6 Vladimir Saitov, *Fedor Grigor'evich Karin. Odin iz maloizvestnykh pisatelei vtoroi poloviny XVIII v.* [Fedor Karin. One of the less-known writers of the second half of the eighteenth century] (St Petersburg: Izdanie redaktsii zhurnala 'Bibliograf', 1893), p. 18.

of eighteenth-century literary criticism): 'As a skilled gardener revives an old tree with a young graft, clearing away the dry vines on it and the thorns growing by its roots, so the great writers I mentioned here served in the transformation of our language, which was itself poor, but as counterfeit Slavic became downright hideous.'[7] Among the members of his friendly circle were the lofty blind poet and talented playwright Nikolai Nikolev (1758–1815), known as 'the Russian Milton'; the satirical poet Prince Dmitrii Gorchakov (1758–1824), who flooded Russian underground literature with political and bawdy poems; the author of the first translation of Homer's *Iliad* into Russian, Ermil Kostrov (1755–1796); the promising playwright and, later on, notorious poetaster Dmitrii Khvostov (1757–1835); and one of the founders of Russian Sentimentalism, Mikhail Muravev (1757–1807). The circle was actively involved in the major literary battles of the second half of the century. Its participants considered themselves defenders of true literary taste, exemplified by Sumarokov's poetry (another common motif in the history of literary circles), and cultivated such polemical genres as the friendly epistle (in verse and prose), satire, epigram, parody, comic opera, and comedy. The participants of this circle also created a number of fictional authors, or literary masks, who promoted their agenda in a playful, theatrical manner.

Another model of the late-eighteenth-century literary commune is Nikolai Karamzin's (1766–1826) salon at Znamenskoe, the gentry estate of the Pleshcheev family. This circle worshipped the hostess Anastasia in Sentimental epistles and gallant poems. It cultivated literary parlour games, improvisations, album poetry, and family theatrical performances. The aesthetic goal of the circle was the creation of a certain familial, Sentimental utopia – an emotional haven or paradise of pure loving hearts, happily beating far from the cold, corrupted civilisation of St Petersburg. By the early 1800s, similar oases of cultivated sensibility had mushroomed in the Russian provinces and prepared the soil for the further development of the Russian age of Sensibility (as in Vasilii Zhukovskii's (1783–1852) family circle in Tula) and Romanticism (as in the Bakunin family circle in Priamukhino).

The first pre-Romantic circle in Russian literary history emerged at the dawn of the nineteenth century among a group of students from Moscow University and the University Noble Pension: Andrei Turgenev (1781–1803), Vasilii Zhukovskii, Aleksandr Turgenev (1784–1845), Semen Rodzianko (1782–1808), Aleksei Merzliakov (1778–1830), and Aleksandr

---

7 Saitov, *Fedor Grigor'evich Karin*, p. 17.

Voeikov (1779–1839). These young enthusiasts, followers of Friedrich Schiller, Johann Wolfgang Goethe, and Jean-Jacques Rousseau, shared a cult belief in poetry as a transformative force (in this regard, they were forerunners of the future Romantic and Symbolist circles). Their views included a devotion to Rousseau's *Julie, or The New Heloise* (1761), a general orientation towards German literature of the pre-Romantic aesthetic movement known as *Sturm und Drang* (storm and stress), adoration of brotherhood and friendship (a secular version of the Masonic cult of learned and pious brothers), an ecstatic faith in humanitarianism, moral enthusiasm, and exalted patriotism. The unspoken hymn of the circle was Schiller's 1785 'Ode to Joy', which depicts the love of a woman, or of a friend, as 'the general principle' of the world, which transforms chaos into harmony, 'bringing disparate elements into a coherent unity, similar to the way the forces of gravity organize the universe'.[8] The members of the circle (which had close links with the Moscow Masonic circle) quickly began to perceive themselves as part of a spiritual family, a kind of fraternal union, called upon to carry out a vital mission in the coming century. By 1801, the group had evolved into the Literary Society of Friends (*Druzheskoe literaturnoe obshchestvo*), complete with rules and regulations and regular meetings. Merzliakov, the son of a provincial merchant and himself a future professor and dean of Moscow University, joined Zhukovskii and Andrei Turgenev in forming a triumvirate of poets at the head of the organisation. Already in 1800 the three friends had been planning to publish a literary almanac under the title 'M. Zh. T.' (the first letters of each of their last names), in which their works would be published with no indication of individual authorship: a collective poetic text of like-minded brothers. The members of the Literary Society of Friends presented speeches on literary, moral, and religious issues (on fatherland, on happiness, on misanthropy, etc.); recited poems and translations; and composed programmatic literary satires (one of these satires personally attacked Karamzin). The charismatic leader of the group, Andrei Turgenev (son of a prominent Russian Freemason), experimented in cultural self-fashioning based on the models offered in German literature of the *Sturm and Drang* period. When he died at the age of twenty-two, the literary theme of the dead young genius took on personal resonance for

---

8 Vadim Vatsuro, *Lirika Pushkinskoi pory: Elegicheskaia shkola* [The lyric poetry of Pushkin's time: The elegiac school] (St Petersburg: Nauka, 1994), p. 29.

the members of the group, who regarded his poetry as a prophetic gift. Zhukovskii presented the death of Andrei as a consolatory overflowing of earthly existence into the beyond (a kind of Elysium of poets), concluding with the final meeting of one's close friends and family in a fixed eternity:

> Forgive me! We are not to live forever! We shall see each other again;
> Fate has set for us a meeting in the grave!
> Hope is sweet! Anticipation [is] pleasant!
> With what happiness shall I die![9]

Republics of Letters: The Nineteenth Century

The Golden Age of Russian poetry (from 1800 to the 1820s) witnessed a proliferation of various literary communities and associations, ranging from court salons to university professors' and students' gatherings to gentry circles in Moscow, St Petersburg, and provincial towns and estates. The court continued to play a role in developing these communities (see Chapter 2.2). In her royal salon in the Pavlovsk summer imperial residence, the German-born dowager empress Maria Feodorovna (widow of Paul I (r. 1796–1801)) patronised home-grown musicians, artists, and literati and promoted German Romantic values, including orientation towards 'court Romanticism': a call for simplicity, naturalness, fidelity to national traditions and religious practices, the 'correction' of artistic tastes and mores through the imitation of classical models, and the adoration of nature, family values, and an exalted sentimentality. On the empress's request, Russian poets composed and recited works to glorify the happy life of her model family and her beautiful park with its pavilions, chalets, gazebos, isles, and river, its amusements, festivals, and sacred memories.

In 1817, Zhukovskii – a member of the empress's poetic circle – became the Russian-language tutor of the grand duchess Aleksandra Fedorovna, wife of the future emperor Nicholas I (r. 1825–55) and elder daughter of King Friedrich Wilhelm III and Queen Louise of Prussia. The princess had her own Romantic salon, and Zhukovskii became her personal poet. As her biographer August von Grimm noted, 'Instead of the stiff etiquette of the

---

9 Vasilii Zhukovskii, *Polnoe sobranie sochinenii i pisem: V dvadtsati tomakh* [Complete works and letters in twenty volumes] (Moscow: Iazyki russkoi kul'tury, 1999–2012), vol. I, p. 59, trans. Timothy Portice and Ilya Vinitsky.

Dowager empress, the most refined and easy demeanor prevailed here; the most serious conversations, as well as the most playful jests and innocent *jeux de société*, were carried on in the same good taste and made the evenings pass rapidly and pleasantly.'[10] Aleksandra Fedorovna would recall that 'in the evening our *petit cour* would gather in my study; we would read and play.'[11] For Zhukovskii – particularly in the first years of his service at court – this salon was the incarnation of the beautiful circle of kindred souls in which it was possible to make use of the amenities of the best society without losing one's own independence. In 1818, the poet published several issues of his courtly journal-almanac *For the Few* (*Für Wenige*), which was addressed to his royal student and a group of chosen readers and included his best translations, mostly from German poetry, along with the originals. The title referred the reader to Horace's Tenth Satire, which portrays the true poet as 'not desirous of the astonishment of the masses, but rather sustenance for the few'.[12] The bilingual composition of the almanac graphically signalled the process of transformation from the original into the translation, the path from the flourishing German Romantic tradition to the 'young' Russian poetry – and to a new family of soulmates.

In 1815, a group of followers of Karamzin's literary reform (see Chapter 1.4) and admirers of Zhukovskii's Romantic ballads organised a carnivalesque literary community called the Arzamas Society of Unknown People (*Arzamasskoe obshchestvo neizvestnykh liudei*). The group included Zhukovskii, Petr Viazemskii (1792–1878), Aleksandr Turgenev, Voeikov, Vasilii Pushkin (1766–1830), Dmitrii Dashkov (1788–1839), and Sergei Uvarov (1786–1855), among others. Arzamas took the form of a parodic Masonic lodge of knights of true literary taste and made fun of what it saw as the old-fashioned, state-sponsored literary society the Colloquy of Lovers of the Russian Word (*Beseda liubitelei russkogo slova*), which gathered in the home of Gavriil Derzhavin (1743–1816). Arzamas members created a sophisticated parodic ritual centred on comic funeral speeches in poetry and prose, dedicated to their impotent ('dead') literary opponents. The society played a significant role in the canonisation of one of the key literary forms of the period: the ironic friendly epistle in verse,

10 August Theodor von Grimm, *Alexandra Feodorowna, Empress of Russia*, trans. Lady Grace Wallace, 2 vols. (Edinburgh: Edmonston and Douglas, 1870), vol. I, p. 110.

11 Cited in von Grimm, *Alexandra Feodorowna, Empress of Russia*, p. 110.

12 Horace, 'Satira X', in *Horatii Flacci Poëmata: The Works of Horace, with explanatory notes, selected from the larger edition*, ed. Charles Anthon (London: T. Tegg and Sons, 1835), p. 358.

with its intimate tone, playful freethinking, thematic and emotional variety, deep rootedness in contemporary literary debates (hence its all-pervasive intertextuality), insider jokes, and a specific kind of 'white melancholy' (Thomas Gray's term) as a manifestation of the ultimate passage of their beautiful youth. The Arzamas Society fell apart in 1818, but the circle of its core participants, which had been joined by the young Aleksandr Pushkin (1799–1837), remained active through the 1830s. Zhukovskii's vision of the relationship between 'the few' and 'the masses' (*tolpa*) formed the basis for the Romantic understanding of the concept of poetic brotherhood mani-fested in Pushkin's epistle addressed to the author of *For the Few*:

> You're right, you sing for just the few
> And not for jealous connoisseurs
> Or all that wretched, carping crew
> Who love to parrot what they've heard,
> But only for the loyal friends
> Of sacred truth and talent's ends.
> Good fortune doesn't shine on all,
> Not all were born to wear a wreath;
> But blest who hears the subtle call
> Of lofty thought and poet's speech!
> Who took delight in beauty's spell
> When beauty hovered near
> And understood the joy you felt
> With joy as fierce and clear.[13]

The literary circles and societies that flourished in the 1810s–1830s were predominantly male and included the Society of Lovers of Russian Letters (*Obshchestvo liubitelei rossiisskoi slovesnosti*), Nikita Vsevolozhskii's (1799–1862) Green Lamp (*Zelenaia lampa*), Decembrist circles, the Lovers of Wisdom group, and the circle of Semen Raich (1792–1855). In contrast, literary (and musical) salons were usually hosted by women, as exemplified in the influ-ential salons of Ekaterina Karamzina (1780–1851), Karolina Pavlova (1807–1893), Evdokiia Rostopchina (1811–1858), Zinaida Volkonskaia (1789–1862), Sofia Ponomareva (1794–1824), and Avdotia Elagina (1789–1877). Some writers and literary critics organised their own salons which gathered on different days of the week: Vladimir Odoevskii's (1804–1869) Saturdays, Petr Pletnev's (1792–1865) Sundays, Nikolai Grech's (1787–1867) Thursdays, Zhukovskii's Fridays, etc.

---

13 Aleksandr Sergeevich Pushkin, *Selected Lyric Poetry*, trans. James E. Falen (Evanston, IL: Northwestern University Press, 2009), p. 24.

The speedy development and politicisation (sometimes radicalisation) of semi-formal and informal literary groups was perceived as conspicuous and dangerous by the imperial government. In the early 1820s, Masonic lodges, as well as any other secret societies, were banned in the Russian Empire. After the failed revolt on 14 December 1825, the government tried to closely monitor and control the literary activities of the educated class, including various forms of literary socialisation (one of the leaders of the Decembrists was the influential poet Kondratii Ryleev (1795–1826) who was famous for his political invectives in verse and advocacy for lofty republican moral values). The popular writer and journalist Faddei Bulgarin (1789–1859) in his report to the secret police expanded on the subversive nature of certain literary groups of the previous period and demonised some of those societies as foreign agents striving to corrupt national morals and destroy the empire's political order.[14] Yet new salons and circles continued to emerge, increasingly focusing on new ideological agendas: idealistic, all-embracing German philosophy; French politics and social utopianism; Catholicism and Greek Orthodoxy; mysteries of history and providence (a theme propelled into public consciousness by the transformations of Europe in the age of the Napoleonic Wars); the national character of Russian literature vis-à-vis its western counterparts; and the question of whether there might be a specific, and different, Russian model of cultural development. In the crucible of ideological debate in the Moscow salon of Avdotia Elagina, and in the circle of students of Nikolai Stankevich (1813–1840) – attended by the future literary critic Vissarion Belinskii (1811–1848; see Box 5.1), the political thinkers Mikhail Bakunin (1814–1876) and Mikhail Katkov (1818–1887), the historian Timofei Granovskii (1813–1855), the writer Konstantin Aksakov (1817–1860), and, later, Ivan Turgenev (1818–1883) – two leading trends of Russian nineteenth-century thought emerged: Slavophilism and Westernism.

It is important to emphasise that major literary circles not only formulated and disseminated their ideas but also created their own cultural mythologies centred on the figures of their charismatic leaders, especially those who died at a young age. In this context it is intriguing to note the similarities and differences between the image of Andrei Turgenev fostered by the first generation of Russian Romantic writers and that of Stankevich and his friends

14 Faddei Bulgarin, *Vidok Figliarin: Pis'ma i agenturnye zapiski F. V. Bulgarina v III otdelenie* [Vidok Figliarin: The letters and informant reports of F. V. Bulgarin in the third section] (Moscow: Novoe literaturnoe obozrenie, 1998), p. 105.

as presented in Aksakov's recollections, in which he resurrects the emotional atmosphere of the circle:

> In 1832 the best students gathered around Stankevich. These were all young people, still in the first season of their youth. Some of them did not even have the right to call themselves youths. Comradery, common interests, and mutual attraction tied together about ten students. If someone were to glance, in the evening, into the low, small rooms full of tobacco smoke, he would see a lively, motley picture: amid the smoke pianos rumbled, singing was heard, loud voices resounded; young, cheerful faces were seen from all sides; behind the pianos sat a young man of beautiful appearance; dark, almost black hair fell down his temples; beautiful, lively, intelligent eyes animated his physiognomy.[15]

As this memoir suggests, the patriotic and aesthetic zeal of the early Romantic circles, characterised by their desire to create a new national poetic tradition, was replaced by millenarian expectations and the enthusiastic political imagination of the early 1830s, which was more interested in political philosophy and socially oriented literary criticism. A new form of literary socialisation appeared in the 1830s – literary evenings run by publishers (such as Aleksandr Smirdin (1795–1857); see Chapter 2.5) and the editors of influential journals. These literary networks manifested a further level of professionalisation and social diversification. As the century progressed, they also became increasingly engaged in the sponsorship of Russian literature. In the 1850s, representatives of new social groups entered the literary communities – sons and daughters of priests; minor clerks; merchants; and, in a few cases, educated peasants. The topics debated were increasingly political. They included the pace of reforms in Russia, various social ills, the place of peasants and women in society, the role of the sciences and religion, relationships between literature (and art in general) and 'reality', and the social mission of literature and the writer. Literary issues were actively discussed as a means of propaganda in Russian political circles and societies, and later on they would become an important ingredient of various political platforms.

Ivory Towers: The Age of Modernism (1890–1917)

The Modernist movements originating in Russia in the late 1880s prompted a new awakening of literary circles. Schruba's dictionary of literary

---

15 Cited in *Poety kruzhka N. V. Stankevicha* [Poets of N. V. Stankevich's circle], ed. S. I. Mashinskii (Moscow, Leningrad: Sovetskii pisatel', 1964), pp. 12–13.

communities of this age distinguishes professional associations (comradeships, unions, charity organisations, guilds), literary circles, academies, salons, pseudo- and 'mock' associations, and creative associations (Acmeists, Cubo-Futurists, Symbolists, Ego-Futurists, etc.; see Chapter 1.7). It does not count provincial groups.

Perhaps the most characteristic and influential circle of this period was Viacheslav Ivanov's (1866–1949) Wednesdays (sredy), also known as the Tower (Bashnia). Poets and philosophers met in the flat of the hosts – Ivanov (a Symbolist poet and mystical thinker) and his wife, Lidiia Zinoveva-Annibal (1866–1907), a Symbolist writer as well – between 1905 and 1907 (see Chapter 2.6). These meetings, beginning late in the evening and often continuing almost until morning, took place in a corner room on the sixth floor of a Modernist building on Tavricheskaia Street in St Petersburg: an elegantly bohemian apartment with an unexpected street view from the strange, spacious Gothic mansard with a low ceiling, a large palm tree, and several bronze candelabras. These gatherings, which included philosophical debates (on mystical anarchism, beauty, love, sex, the transformative power of art, etc.) as well as poetic recitations, were considered a spiritual antidote to the cold official Petersburg. Resembling the meetings of mystical sects, they were envisaged as transformative rituals aimed at the creation of a new artistic world, populated by new artistic personas. Major participants of these gatherings included the philosopher Nikolai Berdiaev (1874–1948); the Symbolist poets Valerii Briusov (1873–1924), Fedor Sologub (1863–1927), Aleksandr Blok (1880–1921), and Andrei Belyi (1880–1934); and the younger Modernists Nikolai Gumilev (1886–1921), Sergei Gorodetskii (1884–1967), Osip Mandelshtam (1891–1938), Aleksei Remizov (1877–1957), Mikhail Kuzmin (1872–1936), and Velimir Khlebnikov (1885–1922). No formal membership in this literary academy was required. A contemporary wrote that 'almost the entire young poetry of Russia came out from Ivanov's "Tower"'.[16]

For a historian of Russian Modernism, the peculiar atmosphere of these ritualistic gatherings matters no less than the topics debated. Zinoveva-Annibal recalls that for the debate 'In what does the Beauty of Life consist?' they shoved a rug into the main hall between the armchairs and other chairs, and about forty participants sat down on the floor surrounded by 'a marvellous bouquet of large lilies, roses, carnations, hyacinths, absolutely enormous, like the type beloved actors get, as well as a bush of chamomile', so

---

16 Konstantin Makovskii, *Portrety sovremennikov* (New York: Izdatel'stvo imeni Chekhova, 1955), cited in Schruba, *Literaturnye ob"edineniia*, p. 62.

that the entire room turned into an enchanted forest. Later on, the guests climbed onto the roof for a poetry reading and continuation of debate on the issue of 'which beauty we are approaching: the beauty of tragic great feelings and catastrophes or of cold wisdom and refined epicureanism'. According to Zinoveva-Annibal, participants of the circle readdressed this question to her: 'We have a secret plan about which you shouldn't tell anyone: we will organize a Persian tavern à la Hafiz, very intimate, very daring, in costumes, on rugs; it will be philosophical, artistic and erotic.' After the debates, poems were read, including Ivanov's 'Sleeplessness' (*Bessonnitsa*, 1905) and Briusov's 'In the Bordello' (*V publichnom dome*, 1905). The gathering ended at 4 am. As the hostess of the salon concludes,

> We parted with such intimacy and warmth that there was not enough room on my hands for all the kisses, and I parted with the women with fervent kisses, even with some of the men, and there was an indubitable atmosphere of love and the dissolution of individual loneliness that evening. ... We continued to wander around on the roof, then I set up the samovar and we drank tea. We spoke in a strangely open fashion about love.[17]

The 'demonic paradise' of Ivanov and Zinoveva-Annibal's Tower was described in many memoirs and literary works of the first half of the twentieth century. It was not only a master meeting place of the major authors and artists of the Modernist age but also a testing ground for various literary forms and aesthetic manifestoes promoted by its participants.

From under the Rubble: The Soviet Period and Beyond

After the October Revolution, new forms of literary socialisation emerged, such as 'educational' poetic circles at factories; various unions of proletarian and peasant writers, patronised by different leaders of the new state (in the rapidly changing ideological climate of the early Soviet Union, these groups eventually became hostages of these political affiliations); and literary brotherhoods of avant-gardists (from the Futurist group 41° in Tiflis in Georgia, to the Absurdist OBERIU – an acronym for *Ob"edinenie real'nogo iskusstva*, the Association of Real Art) and 'fellow travellers' (such as the Serapion Brothers; see Chapter 1.7). Simultaneously, Russian émigré literary

---

17 Cited in Nikolai Bogomolov, 'Pervyi god Bashni' [The first year of the Tower], *Toronto Slavic Quarterly* 70 (Fall 2019), http://sites.utoronto.ca/tsq/24/bogomolov24.shtml, accessed 24 Jan. 2023. I thank Professor Michael Wachtel for the translation.

societies and circles emerged in Berlin, Paris, Prague, New York, and Harbin. In the 1920s, numerous literary and artistic circles operated in Moscow, Leningrad, and other cities and towns of the Soviet state.

These independent or semi-independent groups were often at odds with each other and were closely monitored and infiltrated by agents of the Soviet secret police. Consider, for example, a telling report by a secret agent of the NKVD (an acronym for the People's Commissariat for Internal Affairs) on Mikhail Bulgakov's (1891–1940) reading of his new anti-Bolshevik short novel *Heart of a Dog (Sobach'e serdtse*, 1925) at the influential literary salon run by the writer and publisher Evdoksiia Nikitina (1895–1973) in 1914–34:

> Bulgakov read his new novella . . . The whole thing was written in hostile tones that exuded infinite disdain for the Soviet system. . . . All this was heard to the accompaniment of the maliciously gleeful laughter of Nikitina's auditorium. Someone couldn't hold back and with spite exclaimed: 'Utopia.' . . . Bulgakov definitely hates and disdains the whole Soviet system, rejects all of its achievements. Moreover, the book is spangled with pornography, dressed in a businesslike, supposedly scientific guise.[18]

The agent emphasises the fact that the first part of this book was already read to an auditorium of forty-eight people, of whom 90 per cent were writers themselves. For this reason, 'it has already infected the writerly minds of the listeners and will sharpen their quills'. He concludes that such toxic counter-revolutionary works, read 'in the most luminous Moscow literary circle, are much more dangerous than the useless-harmless speeches of authors of the 101st sort at meetings of the "All-Russian Union of Poets"'.[19]

In 1932, the Central Committee of the Communist Party of the Soviet Union disbanded existing literary organisations and merged all professional Soviet writers' associations and groups into one large union ruled and totally controlled by the party (to be sure, by the leader of the party) and based on the literary method of Socialist Realism. The national branches of the Union appeared in all Soviet republics. Active members of different private literary societies were arrested, exiled, or executed. Informal literary and artistic circles still existed at universities (for example, the circle of poets at the Moscow Institute of History, Philosophy, and Literature (IFLI)), editorial boards, and intelligentsia apartments (such as the salon of the famous pianist Mariia Iudina (1899–1970)) and summer houses (*dachas*).

---

18 'Svodka sekretnogo otdela OGPU no 110' [Brief report of the secret division of OGPU no. 110], cited in Boris Sokolov, *Mikhail Bulgakov. Zagadky tvorchestva* [Mikhail Bulgakov. Enigmas of his art] (Moscow: Vagrius, 2008), p. 46.
19 'Svodka sekretnogo otdela OGPU no 110', p. 46.

Stalin's death in 1953, and the process of de-Stalinisation in the 1950s and early 1960s, led to the re-emergence of writers' networks, as manifested by the speedy development of the Literary Associations (LITOs) which functioned as islands of literary freethinking during the Thaw period, such as the Literary Association at the Technological Institute in Leningrad. Other literary circles operated at so-called Pioneer Palaces (spaces of organised leisure for young people), in domestic 'salons' of the 1950s and 1960s, and within the pages (and offices) of influential 'thick' journals (see Chapter 2.4). After the end of the Thaw and its relative cultural liberalism, however, independent literary life went underground. Popular forms of literary and artistic socialisation of this period included so-called apartment seminars, gatherings in cafés, and religious and dissident political circles. An incomplete list of prominent circles and salons of this period includes such diverse associations as the Lianozovo group (*Lianozovskaia shkola*), including Evgenii Kropivnitskii (1893–1979), Igor Kholin (1920–1999), Genrikh Sapgir (1928–1999), Ian Satunovskii (1913–1982), and Vsevolod Nekrasov (1934–2009); the Sexual Mystics (*Seksual'nye mistiki*), among whose members were Iurii Mamleev (1931–2015) and Vladimir Kovenatskii (1938–1986); the group of poets subsequently dubbed Akhmatova's Orphans (*Akhmatovskie siroty*), to which Evgenii Rein (1935–), Joseph Brodsky (1940–1996), Dmitrii Bobyshev (1936–), and Anatolii Naiman (1936–2022) belonged; Gleb Semenov's (1918–1982) LITO, SMOG, which included Leonid Gubanov (1946–1983), Iurii Kublanovskii (1947–), Vladimir Aleinikov (1946–), Arkadii Pakhomov (1944–2011), Vadim Delone (1947–1983), and Sasha Sokolov (1943–); the circles of David Dar (1910–1980) and Konstantin Kuzminskii (1940–2015); the Moscow Conceptualists, with Dmitrii Prigov (1940–2007), Lev Rubinshtein (1947–1924), Rimma Gerlovina (1951–), and Andrei Monastyrskii (1949–); the Meta-Meta circle, including Ivan Zhdanov (1948–), Aleksei Parshchikov (1954–2009), and Aleksandr Eremenko (1950–2021); and Club Poetry. Although Moscow and Leningrad were considered centres of informal culture, there were many circles and salons in other cities and national republics of the USSR.

The following description of one of the bohemian underground salons in Leningrad may serve as a vivid illustration of the intimate life of a late 1960s group. The account is presented in an encoded essay by an American visitor. One night he takes a cab to get to the apartment of his Russian friend. He enters a 'Dostoevskian kitchen' and finds there 'a frail young man hunched up on a bed, a shy girl with red hair by his side, a beautiful television actress . . ., a smartly dressed young scholar with a famous name, a bearded

intellectual who looks like a Circassian chieftain, a frail and nervous young boy of perhaps thirty, a husky young poet'. He also finds his American friend, 'and a homely woman who rises, kisses, greets in second-person familiar and gives welcome into this intimate world'. The flat is shabby and most guests are intoxicated, but the cultural atmosphere is enchanting:

> This is where one may request instant recitation of chapter and stanza from *Eugene Onegin*, and where a magic moment is easily recollected. Eliot is as welcome in this room as Pasternak, and Whitman reached some peaks of the Russian language in this room. ... This is where conversation shifts in cadence from [Efim] Etkind on translation to an analysis of John Donne's 'Navigator' to an impromptu defense of [Samuil] Marshak's [translations of Robert] Burns to an essay on the language of children to Eisenstein's monographs on Pushkin as a cinematographer to Norman Mailer as an existentialist pamphleteer to Nabokov's commentary on *Onegin* to the Catholicism of Flannery O'Connor to the colloquialisms of [Aleksandr Solzhenitsyn's] *Ivan Denisovich* to Bulgakov's Pontius Pilate [in *Master and Margarita*] to Lermontov's *Demon* to [Andrei Voznesenskii's] *Anti-Worlds* to a heated-up argument over the intricately rambling form of Dostoevskii's 'Winter Recollections of Summer Impressions' to a rumour of a new novel about Dante's circles [an allusion to Solzhenitsyn's novel *First Circle*].[20]

Guests freely enter and leave. The visitor calls this bohemian salon a fantastic mirror world akin to the eerie visions of St Petersburg that we find in Pushkin, Dostoevskii, Belyi, and Nabokov. 'It is an introspective, intellectually incestuous world', he comments:

> It is a self-enclosed and self-perpetuating world, a world unto itself, peculiarized, almost unreal in its tenacious temporaneity. It is not necessarily a nice world, for intimacy jars nerves and sometimes turns affection to spite. The people of this world, some of them, can take delight in hurting others, and there are casualties. But in its larger outlines this is a world of warmth and affection.[21]

The third awakening of Russian literary circles occurred during the period of Perestroika and flourished during the post-Soviet period as a legitimatisation and expansion of the late Soviet literary associations and as an experimentation with new forms: the literary cafés of the late

---

20 Larry Gregg [pseud. Lauren Leighton], 'Winter recollections of summer impressions of Leningrad', *Descant: The Texas Christian University Literary Journal* 16.2 (1972), 11.
21 Gregg, 'Winter recollections of summer impressions of Leningrad', 11.

1980s, carnivalesque groups, poetic festivals, internet poetic forums, and social media literary communities (ZhZh (LiveJournal), Vavilon, Facebook literary groups, online literary journals, and international workshops), etc. Thus, in many ways, the traditional elitist intimacy of Russian literary circles and salons has become democratised, globalised, digitised, and squeezed to the size of a laptop screen.

As a complex conglomerate of social networks and circles, literature can be compared to the symbolic globe which, in *War and Peace* (*Voina i mir*, 1868–9), Tolstoi's Pierre Bezukhov sees in his dream:

> This globe was alive – a vibrating ball without fixed dimensions. Its whole surface consisted of drops closely pressed together, and all these drops moved and changed places, sometimes several of them merging into one, sometimes one dividing into many. Each drop tried to spread out and occupy as much space as possible, but others striving to do the same compressed it, sometimes destroyed it, and sometimes merged with it.[22]

Literary circles, societies, and salons can be identified with these droplets which grow, merge, disappear from the surface, sink to the depths, re-emerge, and remain in cultural memory as reflections of historical and cultural projects and conflicts as well as major originators of new literary genres and forms of relationship between literature and society.

Further Reading

Bobrova, Alina, 'Literary societies in Russia of the first half of the 19th century: Problems of interdisciplinary description', *Russkaia literatura* 1 (2021), 293–313.

Brodskii, N. L. (ed.), *Literaturnye salony i kruzhki: Pervaia polovina XIX veka* [Literary salons and circles: The first half of the nineteenth century] (Moscow, Leningrad: Akademiia, 1930).

Dolinin, V. E., B. I. Ivanov, B. V. Ostanin, and D. Ya. Severiukhin (eds.), *Samizdat Leningrada, 1950-e–1980-e: Literaturnaia entsiklopediia* [Leningrad samizdat, 1950s–1980s: Literary encyclopedia] (Moscow: Novoe literaturnoe obozrenie, 2003).

Evstratov, Alexei G., 'Dramatic conflicts and social performance at the Russian court in the 1760s: A sociocultural perspective on marital infidelity', in Andreas Schönle, Andrei Zorin, and Alexei Evstratov (eds.), *The Europeanized Elite in Russia, 1762–1825: Public Role and Subjective Self* (DeKalb: Northern Illinois University Press, 2016), pp. 70–89.

Levitt, Marcus C., *Russian Literary Politics and the Pushkin Celebration of 1880* (Ithaca: Cornell University Press, 1989).

---

22 Leo Tolstoy, *War and Peace*, trans. Louise Maude and Aymer Maude, ed. George Gibian (New York: W. W. Norton, 1966), pp. 1181–2.

Lotman, Yu. M., *Andrei Sergeevich Kaisarov i literaturno-obshchestvennaia bor'ba ego vremeni* [Andrei Sergeevich Kaisarov and the literary and social struggle of his time] (Tartu: Uchenye zapiski Tartusskogo gosudarstvennogo universiteta, 1958).

Peschio, Joe, *The Poetics of Impudence and Intimacy in the Age of Pushkin* (Madison: University of Wisconsin Press, 2012).

Schruba, Manfred, *Literaturnye ob"edinenia Moskvy i Peterburga 1890–1917 godov: Slovar'* [Literary associations in Moscow and Petersburg, 1890–1917: A dictionary] (Moscow: Novoe literaturnoe obozrenie, 2004).

Todd, William Mills, III, *Fiction and Society in the Age of Pushkin: Ideology, Institutions, and Narrative* (Cambridge, MA: Harvard University Press, 1986).

Vatsuro, V. E., *S.D.P., Iz istorii literaturnogo byta pushkinskoi pory* [SDP: From the history of literary life in the age of Pushkin] (Moscow: Kniga, 1989).

Walker, Barbara, *Maximilian Voloshin and the Russian Literary Circle: Culture and Survival in Revolutionary Times* (Bloomington: Indiana University Press, 1984).

The Thick Journal

WILLIAM MILLS TODD III

At first glance, a Russian thick journal (*tolstyi zhurnal*) might not excite a modern reader's imagination: plain covers, no illustrations, advertisements only for itself (subscription information) or for other print materials by the same publisher. Both the thick journals of the mid-nineteenth century, which are the focus of this chapter, and the twentieth-century ones can now be difficult to read, as black print fades to brown and the paper – especially the newsprint-journal paper of the Soviet period – also turns brown. This unprepossessing appearance stands in marked contrast to the elegant small-format almanacs of the Pushkin period with their delicate vignettes, the glossy illustrated weeklies of the late nineteenth century, and the multicolour electronic journals of the twenty-first century.

This first glance would, however, be deceptive. The thick journal, from its inception in the 1800s to the present day, is at once an enduring cultural institution, an index of Russian intellectual life, and an important publishing mechanism which has shaped the best of Russian literature, especially prose fiction. Other national literatures developed important comprehensive journals, for example the *Revue des Deux Mondes* (1829–) in France, *Blackwood's Magazine* (1817–1980) in Great Britain, or *The Atlantic* (1857–) in the United States, and these enjoyed much larger subscription lists than did their Russian equivalents, sometimes by factors of hundreds. But Russia's much lower literacy rate during the nineteenth century, less-developed distribution networks, and virtual absence of inexpensive books gave the thick journal a central place in Russian culture and an institutional solidity that has maintained its importance, with ups and downs, to the present day. During their heyday in the mid-nineteenth century, the thick journals were not inexpensive, costing 20 rubles or so a year at a time when the landed gentry could be cash poor

and the average civil servant earned a salary of 600 rubles a year. To access them, readers had to subscribe or visit a public library, club, or reading room; individual issues were not for sale on newsstands.

In this chapter I will first discuss the importance of thick journals for the development of the Russian novel and then give a brief history of this crucial mechanism, from its origins in the early nineteenth century to its continuing vitality (often online) in the twenty-first.

Thick Journals and the Novel

From the 1840s to the 1880s, the thick journals published every subsequently canonical Russian novel except for Nikolai Gogol's (1809–1852) *Dead Souls* (*Mertvye dushi*, 1842), typically in serial format; Gogol feared that serialisation would lessen his novel's impact upon its readers, while other great novelists welcomed the prolonged process of interaction that serialisation afforded, to say nothing of the considerable honoraria that the journals provided, honoraria which far exceeded what they could earn from the sale of individual editions. Nineteenth-century thick journals were edited and guided by Russia's leading literary and social critics, among them the Sentimentalist Nikolai Karamzin (1766–1826); Russia's national poet, Aleksandr Pushkin (1799–1837); the first radical critic, Vissarion Belinskii (1811–1848; see Box 5.1); the novelist Fedor Dostoevskii (1821–1881); the conservative Nikolai Strakhov (1828–1896); the novelist Evgeniia Tur (1815–1892); the civic poet Nikolai Nekrasov (1821–1878); the nihilist Dmitrii Pisarev (1840–1868); the satirist Mikhail Saltykov-Shchedrin (1826–1889); and the materialist radical critics Nikolai Chernyshevskii (1828–1889) and Nikolai Dobroliubov (1836–1861). All of these also wrote either fiction or important critical analyses of fiction, sometimes both.

The thick journals made accessible to their readership not only fiction and (less frequently) verse and drama but also works of criticism, history, philosophy, the natural sciences, and the social sciences. The mixture of topics could vary from journal to journal and issue to issue. The journal would serialise some of these articles as well as the novels, creating an expanding galaxy of discourses, many of which would migrate into the thematics and styles of the fictions they surrounded. The historical, social, economic, and political concerns of Realist fiction found ready contextualisation in the thick journal. A representative table of contents from *The Russian Herald* (*Russkii vestnik*, 1856–1906) of January 1879 sandwiches the first instalment of Dostoevskii's *The Brothers Karamazov* (*Brat'ia Karamazovy*,

serialised 1879–80) in the middle of the issue between articles on forestry, abstract principles in philosophy (from Vladimir Solovev's (1853–1900) doctoral dissertation), the playwright Aleksandr Griboedov (1795–1829), student life in Germany, European politics, and regions for imperial expansion or conflict (the Caucasus, Bulgaria, the disintegrating Ottoman Empire). Book notices recognise new works by or about Petr Viazemskii (1792–1878), Shakespeare, and contemporary European authors (Berthold Auerbach, Thérèse Bentzon, and Friedrich Ritschl). A poem by Apollon Maikov (1821–1897) and a play by Dmitrii Averkiev (1836–1905) complete the issue. Readers of Dostoevskii's novel will recognise references to the topics of the articles in the pages of the novel, not because Dostoevskii would have seen the table of contents in advance or been governed by the journal's choices but because these were topics of interest as the novel was conceived and serialised, especially the fate of Russia's forests, its imperial boundaries (Bulgaria, the Caucasus, the east), European politics, and the rising star of Russian philosophy. Furthermore, two of the novel's characters, Ivan Karamazov and Mikhail Rakitin, contribute to the periodical press, and in a manically comic episode, the novel makes fun of a rival journalist and journal, Mikhail Saltykov-Shchedrin and *The Contemporary* (*Sovremennik*, 1836–66), that had been shut down by the government.

Several years before, in 1875–7, *The Russian Herald* had serialised Lev Tolstoi's (1828–1910) *Anna Karenina* (*Anna Karenina*). The January 1875 issue, in which Tolstoi's first instalment appeared, offered richer literary entries, including translations into Russian of Wilkie Collins's *The Woman in White* and, in a supplement, Edward Bulwer-Lytton's *Parisians*. But the issue not only indulged the Anglomania of the publisher, Mikhail Katkov (1818–1887), it continued to assert his imperialist and political concerns by placing these literary pieces among sketches from China, memoirs about the siege of Sevastopol, and politically charged pieces about the Russian universities and about a new biography of Belinskii by Aleksandr Pypin (1833–1904). Like other novelists, Tolstoi incorporated such topics in *Anna Karenina*, but not respectfully – sometimes as superficial dinner table chat, sometimes in ways that ran counter to the journal's adherence to the official nationalism of the Russian state, which celebrated 'Orthodoxy, autocracy, and national spirit'. Tolstoi's ungovernability finally led Katkov to reject the last part of the novel, in which the characters caustically debate Russia's unofficial participation in the Serbian uprising against the Ottoman Empire. The journal's readers had to be satisfied with a terse summary or else buy the concluding part in a separately published booklet. As these examples

illustrate, the publication of novels in thick journals could magnify their participation in ongoing cultural and political debates.

During much of the thick journals' history, Russian political life featured no competing political parties or contested elections to representative legislative bodies. This vacuum, perceived as such by comparison with western countries, was filled by the thick journals, which proved organs of an incipient public sphere, a space where issues of interest to the educated public could be raised and debated – always with an eye towards censorship – and where public opinion could, however tentatively, take shape. Literary criticism was almost always an important section in a thick journal, but it acquired additional weight when the state repressed political and social controversy and when literary critics became sociopolitical ones by criticising the representation of social issues in literary works. Critics across the ideological spectrum would regularly take issue with representations in works of fiction along political lines, sometimes rewriting the novel's plot and characterisations to suit their own polemical needs. Dostoevskii created for his own journal, *The Diary of a Writer* (*Dnevnik pisatelia*, 1876–7, 1880–1), a scene in which the male protagonist of *Anna Karenina*, Levin, is forced to witness a Turkish soldier torturing a Slavic child.[1] Katkov had refused to publish this eighth part of the novel; Dostoevskii devoted many pages to a refutation of the offending passage.

On the pages of the thick journal *The Russian Word* (*Russkoe slovo*, 1859–66), Pisarev provided perhaps the most famous and extensive instance of this polemical rewriting in his tersely entitled essay 'Bazarov' (*Bazarov*, 1862), a response to Ivan Turgenev's (1818–1883) *Fathers and Children* (*Ottsy i deti*, 1862). Turgenev, celebrated by Henry James as 'the novelist's novelist' and widely respected for his art in western Europe, is immediately stripped of that artistry by Pisarev, who declares the novel's plot, structure, interest, and idea unworthy of consideration.[2] Turgenev becomes the critic's research assistant, providing character types, episodes, and scenes for Pisarev's reconstruction of the novel's central character, the nihilist Bazarov. Pisarev expands Bazarov's biography and develops his interiority, using this reconstruction to provide lessons for the radical intelligentsia. En passant, Pisarev – capable of brilliant observations – does take notice of

---

1 Fyodor Dostoevsky, *A Writer's Diary: Volume 2, 1877–1881*, trans. Kenneth Lantz (Evanston, IL: Northwestern University Press, 1994), p. 1096.
2 Henry James, *The House of Fiction: Essays on the Novel* (London: R. Hart-Davis, 1957), p. 170.

structural patterns and parallels. But he makes it clear that this is not the purpose of his critical essay.[3]

The thick journal's particular mode of presenting imaginative literature has left deep traces in the Russian novel and in Russian theories of fiction. Even after the serialisation of novels was supplanted by publication in separate volumes as the primary mechanism for disseminating fiction in the twentieth century, the Russian novel has tended to preserve features of the serialised fiction facilitated by the thick journals of the earlier period: long length, variable modes of narration, a wealth of inserted genres, and close critical contact with the processes and controversies of contemporary life.

One specific Russian serialisation pattern had a particularly important impact on novelistic construction. A number of prominent Russian novelists – including Dostoevskii, Tolstoi, and Saltykov-Shchedrin – would begin serialisation of their novels before drafting them in their entirety. This could, and did, eventuate in substantial pauses as the novelists came up against impasses in plotting or needed to conduct further research before continuing. In theory the readers of a journal were promised an entire novel during the subscription year, but this was often a promise unfulfilled, sometimes spectacularly so. The serialisation of the ethnographic fictions *In the Woods* (*V lesakh*) and *In the Hills* (*Na gorakh*) by Pavel Melnikov-Pecherskii (1818–1883) spanned ten years, 1871–81, in part because *The Russian Herald* only used his instalments as filler when other novelists did not deliver their contributions in a timely fashion. Tolstoi dragged out the publication of *Anna Karenina* over two and a half years, suspending serialisation while he was in what he called his 'summer condition' (*letnee sostoianie*) and was concerned primarily with activities on his country estate.[4]

It took Saltykov-Shchedrin five years – from 1875 to 1880 – to complete the serialisation of his greatest novel, *The Golovlevs* (*Gospoda Golovlevy*) in the journal *Notes of the Fatherland* (*Otechestvennye zapiski*, 1839–84), but this was not due to indolence or lack of interest on the part of the busy editor and writer. In this case the future novel began with a series of four sketches in the midst of his well-received satirical series on varieties of contemporary

---

3 For an English translation of the essay, somewhat abridged, see Dmitry I. Pisarev, 'Bazarov', in Ivan Turgenev, *Fathers and Children*, trans. and ed. Michael R. Katz (New York: W. W. Norton, 2009), pp. 193–215. On Pisarev's critical practice, see Edward J. Brown, 'Pisarev and the transformation of two Russian novels', in William Mills Todd III (ed.), *Literature and Society in Imperial Russia 1800–1914* (Stanford: Stanford University Press, 1978), pp. 151–72.

4 L. N. Tolstoi, *Polnoe sobranie sochinenii* [Complete works], ed. V. G. Chertkov et al., 90 vols. (Moscow: Goslitizdat, 1928–59), vol. XX, p. 619.

hypocrisy, *Well-intended Speeches* (*Blagonamerennye rechi*). Publication of this series had been under way in the journal for three years when the thirteenth of these sketches, 'Family Court' (*Semeinyi sud*), appeared. It surpassed the previous ones in length, in the number and depth of its characters, in the range of its plot, and in the detail of its setting. Its focus on family dynamics played into the general novelistic concern with family themes in Russian novels of the 1870s. So, it should not be surprising to find a contemporary reviewer, A. M. Skabichevskii, singling it out from the other sketches in the series:

> Here to the fore is not that stinging salt of witty, well-targeted derision and exposé by caricature of the more absurd aspects of life, not, in short, those qualities of Mr. Shchedrin's satire to which we are accustomed; no, we have before us here a masterly sketch of types of the now bygone past, a profound, psychological analysis, and satire in the narrow sense has been replaced by a bitter humor which, by the end, is transformed into stunning tragedy of a very particular kind.[5]

Saltykov-Shchedrin devoted three more sketches to the Golovlev family before committing himself to gathering the first four, adding three additional ones, and publishing the ensemble as a novel. In this instance the liberties accorded to Russian serial novelists in thick journals helped inspire an intense and haunting work of fictional art.

Dostoevskii, perhaps the most professional of the great Russian novelists, drove himself to meet his deadlines and usually came close to succeeding, struggling against illness, poverty, fear of censorship, and interventions by nervous publishers. A former editor himself, he understood the importance of serial fictions to the success of a journal, and he could boast that his *Crime and Punishment* (*Prestuplenie i nakazanie*, serialised 1866) had won an additional 500 subscribers for *The Russian Herald* at a moment when Turgenev had no new fiction for the journal and when Tolstoi had decided not to continue serialising *War and Peace* after the section of the novel 'The Year 1805' (serialised 1865–6; the full novel appeared in book form in 1868–9).[6] But Dostoevskii, serialising *The Idiot* (*Idiot*) in *The Russian Herald* in 1868, encountered a problem that less professional writers would have solved merely by

5 A. M. Skabichevskii, 'Blagonamerennye rechi g. Shchedrina' [Well-intended speeches of Mr Shchedrin], *Sankt-Peterburgskie vedomosti* [St Petersburg news] 307 (1875), quoted in I. P. Foote (ed.), *Saltykov-Shchedrin's* The Golovlyovs: *A Critical Companion* (Evanston, IL: Northwestern University Press, 1997), p. 47.
6 Joseph Frank, *Dostoevsky: The Miraculous Years, 1865–1871* (Princeton: Princeton University Press, 1995), p. 46.

delaying the submission of their next instalments. Part I of the novel represents Dostoevskii's writing at its finest: tight plotting, intriguing characters, striking themes, and memorable scandalous scenes. The last of these scenes, in which Nastasia Filippovna hurls a bundle of banknotes into a fireplace, sends the characters scattering in all directions. But Dostoevskii concluded this part not knowing where to go next, and the flurry of 'plans' in his notebooks did not immediately solve his problem. He did not have an instalment for the March issue of the journal, and his plotting moves fitfully forward through the next two parts, with two of the novel's most intriguing and powerful characters – Rogozhin and Nastasia Filippovna – absent from these central sections and held present in the reader's mind largely through rumour and letters.

In his desperation to continue, Dostoevskii hit upon a mode of narration that he would develop further in *Demons* (*Besy*, serialised 1871–2) and in *The Brothers Karamazov*. Although the narrator occasionally has the power of omniscience, for the most part the story is told by a chronicler-narrator who follows closely upon the events, reporting them in terms of the characters' own understanding of them. He sometimes learns of events long after they happen, and he registers material that he does not analyse: rumours, visits, letters. His explanations, especially of the more psychologically intricate characters, become increasingly incompetent, until in Part IV he more or less gives up and limits himself to 'a plain exposition of the facts, as far as possible without particular explanations, and for a very simple reason: because we ourselves, in many instances, are hard put to it to explain what happened'.[7] Of the six months that elapse in the story between Part I and Part II, the reader learns of only a few events, often from brief comments dropped by the characters in their conversations. Readers are compelled to speculate, infer, and – increasingly – explain and piece together the novel for themselves. This mode of narration constitutes a daring risk on the author's part, but it is a brilliant solution to his problems with the plot, a way of getting his readers to share the burden of putting all of these characters and incidents together. It is no exaggeration to surmise that the conditions of Russian serial publication led Dostoevskii to invent the contingent plotting and unreliable narration which have come to characterise Modernist fiction.

Such Russian theories of the novel as Mikhail Bakhtin's (1895–1975; see Box 5.4), which stresses the openness of the novel to other discourses, its contact with everyday life, and its unfinalised characters, or Lidiia Ginzburg's

---

7 Fyodor Dostoevsky, *The Idiot*, trans. David McDuff (London: Penguin, 2004), p. 668.

(1902–1990; see Chapter 3.10), which sees the novel as a genre that models character and behaviour that in turn change over time and which can arise from philosophy or social thought as readily as from the traditions of imaginative literature, reflect the way the thick journals of the nineteenth century presented works by Tolstoi, Dostoevskii, Turgenev, Saltykov-Shchedrin, and other subsequently canonical novelists.[8]

The Thick Journal: An Institutional History

The memory of the thick journal's importance has kept the medium alive at times when it seemed threatened with extinction – as in 2018, when the print run of *New World* (*Novyi mir*, 1925–) dropped to 2,200 copies. In one such moment in 2001, the writer Viktor Nikitin called the thick journals 'islands of spirituality and education, ultimately of the historical memory of the nation'.[9]

During the period on which this chapter focuses, the 1800s to the 1880s, a monthly issue would be 100 to 300 pages in length, packed to the margins of the page with printed text, not visual material. Furthermore, the nineteenth-century thick journal was capacious not only in its number of pages but also in the number of topics it pursued, as we have seen. Thick journals are not merely literary journals but are encyclopedic in their range of inquiry. Robert Maguire – who has given the classic definition of the medium – argues, moreover, that the thick journal is not merely encyclopedic, it also has a guiding critical tendency or ideology and is associated with a prominent critic.[10]

Competing thick journals organised the debates at many crucial moments in Russian history. In the 1820s and 1830s, they discussed the commercialisation and professionalisation of the previously amateur or patronage-centred ways of Russian literary life. In the 1840s they brought to a head debates over the orientation of Russian culture, towards Europe (the Westernisers) or Russian tradition (the Slavophiles). In the 1850s and 1860s they discussed the

8 M. M. Bakhtin, 'Epos i roman' [Epic and novel], in *Voprosy literatury i estetiki* [Questions of literature and aesthetics] (Moscow: Khudozhestvennaia literatura, 1975), pp. 447–83; L. Ia. Ginzburg, *O psikhologicheskoi proze* [On psychological prose] (Leningrad: Sovetskii pisatel', 1977), pp. 3–34; Ginzburg, *O literaturnom geroe* [On the literary hero] (Leningrad: Sovetskii pisatel', 1979), pp. 5–149.
9 Viktor Nikitin, 'Zhurnalu "Pod"em" 70 let' [Seventy years of the journal *Ascent*], *Russkii pereplet* [Russian bookbinding], www.pereplet.ru/podiem/, accessed 7 July 2020.
10 Robert A. Maguire, *Red Virgin Soil: Soviet Literature in the 1920s* (Princeton: Princeton University Press, 1968), pp. 40–4.

utility of imaginative literature and its potential role in defining and transforming Russia. In the 1920s, born again after the upheavals of the revolution when the last of the old thick journals had been closed by the new Bolshevik government, they served as a site for generating a Marxist-Leninist approach to culture. In the 1980s, during the years of Glasnost and Perestroika when Soviet censorship relaxed, they debated social and cultural issues with what seemed breathtaking openness and their print runs soared – in the case of *New World* to 2.7 million copies in 1990, aided no doubt by its publishing of long-forbidden authors.

Certainly the thick journals which have best survived in Russian memory have been associated with a particular cast of mind, but – I would argue – the importance of such guiding ideas precedes the struggles of the mid-nineteenth century to include a few journals of the early nineteenth century, such as *Messenger of Europe* (*Vestnik Evropy*, 1802–30), founded by the writer Nikolai Karamzin and soon handed over to a succession of editors. Its subscription list grew from approximately 600 to a high of 1,200, and it published the leading Russian poets and essayists of its time. A monthly, it lived up to its name in publishing cultural, political, and economic news from Europe (an important role given Russia's virtual lack of private newspapers until mid-century) as well as programmatic pieces by Karamzin and the poet Vasilii Zhukovskii (1783–1852), who exemplified a gradualist approach to enlightenment through the amelioration of manners. Among the translated authors were Mme de Genlis, Thomas Gray – his famous 'Elegy Written in a Country Churchyard' in Zhukovskii's no less famous translation, 'A Country Cemetery' (*Sel'skoe kladbishche*, 1802) – Byron, Walter Scott, Washington Irving, and E. T. A. Hoffmann. The journal, at least initially, made a profit and a handsome income for Karamzin, although not for its contributors, who were not paid for their efforts. Karamzin's programmatic essay 'On the Book Trade and on the Love for Reading in Russia' (*O knizhnoi torgovle i liubvi ko chteniiu v Rossii*, 1802), published in the fourth issue, proclaimed the success of Russia's incipient commercial literature and defended popular demand for novels 'rich in all kinds of knowledge' and depicting 'people like us' and 'ordinary passions'.[11] Novels would become the centrepiece of the thick journals, but at the beginning of the century Karamzin could name few native ones to rival the foreign fictions which attracted Russian readers.

11 N. M. Karamzin, 'On the book trade and the love for reading in Russia', in Harold B. Segel (ed.), *The Literature of Eighteenth-Century Russia: A History and Anthology*, 2 vols. (New York: E. P. Dutton, 1967), vol. I, pp. 451–2.

Despite the relative success of *Messenger of Europe*, the thick journal was slow to take root in Russian literary life. To be sure, sixty journals appeared during the first decade of the century alone. But most were short-lived organs of literary circles and learned societies.[12] Petr Viazemskii, one of Russia's most trenchant essayists, could justly dismiss them as 'school archives of pupils' essays'.[13] Viazemskii himself, a wealthy aristocrat, joined in a socially improbable alliance with a lively young journalist of merchant origins, Nikolai Polevoi (1796–1846), to launch an important attempt at an encyclopedic journal of broad appeal to the amorphous middle ranks of Russian readers, which were slowly expanding in the first decades of the nineteenth century. This was a readership made up of civil servants and military officers, teachers, university students, literate merchants, descendants of the clergy who practised law and medicine, and members of the provincial gentry. Their journal, *The Moscow Telegraph* (*Moskovskii telegraf*, 1825–34), attracted at its peak an estimated 2,500 subscribers.[14] For two years the collaboration between Viazemskii and Polevoi worked well, and the journal covered a variety of topics, including science, technology, economics, and European politics, and even provided fashion plates. Furthermore, it could boast that it was the first Russian journal to give literary criticism a prominent, regular place. Both Viazemskii and Polevoi vigorously defended European and Russian Romanticism in debates with other periodicals, such as *Messenger of Europe*, edited at this point by M. T. Kachenovskii (1775–1842); Faddei Bulgarin's (1789–1859) newspaper, *The Northern Bee* (*Severnaia pchela*, 1825–59); and Nikolai Grech's (1787–1867) biweekly *Son of the Fatherland* (*Syn otechestva*, 1812–44, 1847–52). But Viazemskii left the journal after Polevoi criticised Karamzin's *History of the Russian State* (*Istoriia gosudarstva rossiiskogo*, 1818–29), and the polemics with other journals turned increasingly nasty as these periodicals contended for the ultimately small public able to afford subscriptions. Polevoi would come to brand his opponents self-entitled aristocrats, and they would in turn accuse him of Jacobinism. The imperial government, anxious to stifle any form of unrest, took advantage of the

---

12 V. E. Evgen'ev-Maksimov et al. (eds.), *Ocherki po istorii russkoi zhurnalistiki i kritiki* [Studies in the history of Russian journalism and criticism], 2 vols. (Leningrad: Izdatel'stvo Leningradskogo universiteta, 1950–65), vol. I, pp. 155–6.

13 Quoted in Iu. M. Lotman, 'P. A. Viazemskii i dvizhenie Dekabristov' [P. A. Viazemskii and the Decembrist movement], *Uchenye zapiski Tartuskogo gosudarstvennogo universiteta* [Scholarly transactions of Tartu State University] 98 (1960), 50.

14 Chester M. Rzadkiewicz, 'N. A. Polevoi's *Moscow Telegraph* and the journal wars of 1825–1834', in Deborah A. Martinsen (ed.), *Literary Journals in Imperial Russia* (Cambridge: Cambridge University Press, 1997), p. 65.

heated polemics to close down *The Moscow Telegraph* in 1834. Commerce in literary periodicals seemed to be a game played for small stakes.

Just six years later, the situation had changed significantly, and Belinskii, who would come to dominate Russian criticism and journalism, could declare: 'the journal has now swallowed up our entire literature – the public doesn't want books, it wants journals, and in the journals they publish entire plays and novels, and each issue of the journals weighs forty pounds'.[15] The difference was largely owed to the astonishing success of *Library for Reading* (*Biblioteka dlia chteniia*, 1834–64), the journal edited by Osip Senkovskii (1800–1858; Senkovskii being the Russified form of his originally Polish name, Sękowski). Its subscription list reached seven thousand, one of the highest for a nineteenth-century thick journal. Its publisher, Aleksandr Smirdin (1795–1857), paid Senkovskii a base salary of 15,000 rubles a year (roughly seven times the estimated minimal income for a writer with a family). It became the first journal to pay its contributors by the signature (i.e. printed sheet, cut and folded into two to thirty-two pages), which also contributed substantially to the professionalisation of Russian literature, a result sought not only by non-nobles such as Polevoi but also by such cash-poor 'aristocrats' as Pushkin himself. The persona Senkovskii assumed for the journal's criticism, Baron Brambeus – taken from the name of a subliterary fictional character – outraged high-minded contemporaries with a seeming lack of critical principles, reliance on his own seemingly capricious taste, and his mordant wit. Senkovskii was, in Lidiia Ginzburg's deft phrase, 'in principle unprincipled'.[16] His avoidance of critical polemics (an avoidance, to be fair, imposed on him by imperial censorship) and reliance on taste, not rules or critical principles, seemed to place him within the same ideological framework, the ideology of polite society, as had shaped Karamzin's journal. But Senkovskii published a greater variety of material (the subtitle of his journal was 'A Journal of Literature, The Sciences, The Arts, News, and Fashions'), and he found, despite the journal's expensive annual subscription rate, a readership undreamed of by earlier publishers and editors. However much his

15 V. G. Belinskii, letter to V. P. Botkin, 31 Oct. 1840, in *Sobranie sochinenii v deviati tomakh* [Collected works in nine volumes], ed. N. K. Gei et al. (Moscow: Khudozhestvennaia literatura, 1976–82), vol. IX, p. 411.
16 L. Ia. Ginzburg, '"Biblioteka dlia chteniia" v 1830-kh godakh. O. I. Senkovskii' ['The Library for Reading' in the 1830s. O. I. Senkovskii], in Evgen'ev-Maksimov, *Ocherki*, vol. I, p. 332. On the history of this journal, see Melissa Frazier, *Romantic Encounters: Writers, Readers, and the 'Library for Reading'* (Stanford: Stanford University Press, 2007). On the material conditions of writers in the imperial period, see S. S. Shashkov, 'Literaturnyi trud v Rossii (istoricheskii ocherk)' [Literary labour in Russia (a historical outline)], *Delo* [The cause] 8 (1876), 3–48.

competitors railed against him, he succeeded in attracting most of Russia's best writers and in publishing important translated works.

The history of the thick journal, as most Russians remember it, really begins with *Notes of the Fatherland* (1839–84; not to be confused with an earlier journal of the same title, published 1820–31). Its publisher, Andrei Kraevskii (1810–1889), planned from the outset a journal of unusual breadth, with eight permanent sections: Contemporary Chronicle of Russia; Science and Scholarship; Imaginative Literature; Domestic Management, Agriculture, and Industry in General; Criticism; Contemporary Bibliographical Chronicle; and Miscellany. Literature and criticism played the central role, however, and the journal's leading critic generally set the tone, the ideological tendency, and the aesthetics of the journal, as with other thick journals. In this case, Kraevskii scored a major coup for his young journal by enlisting Belinskii, a critic so influential that provincial booksellers were said to place their orders according to his reviews.[17] When Belinskii left to work for the rejuvenated *Contemporary* in 1846, Kraevskii managed to attract a distinguished list of successors, including Valerian Maikov (1823–1847), Nekrasov, Saltykov-Shchedrin, Nikolai Mikhailovskii (1842–1904), and the younger populists. The journal's literary offerings were no less distinguished, as it published Mikhail Lermontov (1814–1841), Turgenev, Aleksandr Herzen (1812–1870), Ivan Goncharov (1812–1891), Dostoevskii, and other prominent prose writers. Its circulation, which began at 1,200 copies, rose to 4,000 by 1847 and 8,000 by the 1870s, making it the most popular of the thick journals.[18] This popularity, in turn, made it a target for government censors and for commercial and ideological rivals, such as Katkov, who for decades lobbied to have the government close down Kraevskii's publications. In 1884, *Notes of the Fatherland* was suppressed for alleged connections with Russia's growing terrorist movements.

Notes of the Fatherland, unlike the earlier journals of Karamzin and Senkovskii, had a succession of serious competitors for the attention of what was, until the very end of the century, a minuscule Russian reading public. Dostoevskii estimated in 1863 that only one Russian in five hundred

---

17 For a concise account of Belinskii's influence, through the journals, on Russian criticism, see Victor Terras, 'Belinsky the journalist and Russian literature', in Martinsen (ed.), *Literary Journals in Imperial Russia*, pp. 117–28.

18 A. I. Reitblat, *Ot Bovy k Bal'montu i drugie raboty po istoricheskoi sotsiologii russkoi literatury* [From Bova to Balmont and other works on the historical sociology of Russian literature] (Moscow: Novoe literaturnoe obozrenie, 2009), p. 47.

(i.e. 2 per cent) could read this literature.[19] This public could support but a handful of journals at a time, but a number of them survive in historical memory, largely because of their differing tendencies and because of the memorable fiction and criticism they published. The most successful, in addition to the *Library for Reading*, *The Contemporary*, and *Notes of the Fatherland*, included Katkov's *The Russian Herald*, *The Russian Word*, *Time* (*Vremia*, 1861–3), *The Epoch* (*Epokha*, 1864–5), *Day* (*Den'*, 1861–5), *The Cause* (*Delo*, 1866–88), *Dawn* (*Zaria*, 1869–72), *Russian Wealth* (*Russkoe bogatstvo*, 1876–1918), *Rus* (*Rus'*, 1880–6), *Russian Thought* (*Russkaia mysl'*, 1880–1918), and *Messenger of Europe* (*Vestnik Evropy*, 1866–1918), a separate journal from the one with the same title that had been founded by Karamzin.

The coincidence of many closing dates with political events (the 1866 and 1881 attempts to assassinate the tsar, the Polish uprising of 1863–4, the Bolshevik Revolution of 1917) is not accidental. The imperial government held the thick journals in suspicion and subjected them to censorship of various kinds – at first prior censorship, later a warning system similar to that in France, whereby a periodical that repeatedly provoked government disapproval could be suspended for up to six months. It closed down some of the most successful ones, including *Time*, *The Contemporary*, and *Notes of the Fatherland*. For those which steered clear of confrontations with the government's repressive state apparatuses, economic difficulties could prove insurmountable. Dostoevskii, who was de facto editor of the successful *Time* and the failure *The Epoch*, estimated that a journal required a subscription list of 2,500 to survive, and many could not sustain this minimal level of popularity.[20] But for the handful of novelists and critics this system could support, the journals provided a respectable income, especially for the writers at the top of hierarchy, such as Tolstoi, who received 500 rubles a signature (sixteen printed pages) for *Anna Karenina*; Turgenev, who regularly received 400 rubles a signature; or Dostoevskii, Saltykov-Shchedrin, Goncharov, and V. Krestovskii (pseudonym) (pen name for Nadezhda Khvoshchinskaia, 1821–1889), who reached 300 rubles a signature.[21] The most successful of the journals in gathering top novelistic talent was *The Russian Herald*, which

---

19 F. M. Dostoevskii, 'Zimnie zametki o letnikh vpechatleniiakh' [Winter notes on summer impressions], in *Polnoe sobranie sochinenii v tridtsati tomakh* [Complete works in thirty volumes] (Leningrad: Nauka, 1972–90), vol. V, p. 51. Sales and circulation figures suggest the figure may have been one in a thousand.
20 Dostoevskii, letter to A. E. Vrangel', 31 March–14 April 1865, in *Polnoe sobranie sochinenii*, vol. XXVIII, book 2, pp. 118–19.
21 Reitblat, *Ot Bovy k Bal'montu*, chap. 5.

attracted readers with major fiction by Tolstoi, Turgenev, Dostoevskii, Nikolai Leskov (1831–1895), and Aleksei Pisemskii (1821–1881).

Within the limits imposed by government restrictions, the mid-century journals provided a wide range of opinion, from radical and socialist (*The Russian Word, The Cause, The Contemporary*) to populist (*Notes of the Fatherland* in its last years, *Russian Wealth*) to moderately liberal and westernising (*Notes of the Fatherland, Messenger of Europe*) to moderately nationalist (*Time*) to conservative and nationalist (*The Russian Herald, Dawn*). In general, novelists published with journals whose orientation they found sympathetic. When *The Russian Herald* could not meet Dostoevskii's terms for publishing his novel *The Adolescent* (*Podrostok*), he was willing to print it in *Notes of the Fatherland* in 1875 because that journal's tendency had turned from liberal to populist in the 1870s, an evolution that he found potentially promising. Occasionally, ideological disagreements between writers and editors or critics arose. Turgenev left *The Contemporary* when it began to review his novels negatively. Katkov, as we have seen, refused to publish the last part of *Anna Karenina* in *The Russian Herald* because the novel opposed Russia's military adventures in the Balkans, but rifts had already begun to appear; the journal's house critic had already reviewed it in less than complimentary terms.

The rise of newspapers in the later decades of the nineteenth century deprived the thick journals of their news-providing function, and the rise of weekly illustrated journals also took readers from them; both of these types of periodical far surpassed the thick journals in numbers of subscribers, reaching over 250,000 in the case of the most popular of the illustrated journals, *The Grainfield* (*Niva*, 1870–1917). They drew not just readers from the thick journals but also writers, such as Tolstoi, who in 1899 serialised his last novel, *Resurrection* (*Voskresenie*), in *The Grainfield*. By the end of the imperial period, the thick journals had ceased to be a pre-eminent cultural force, and the revolution of 1917 brought the few remaining ones to an end. But rapidly increasing literacy and the intellectual ferment of the 1920s gave them second life. In the difficult conditions following the civil war, when paper and working presses were in short supply, an official in the People's Commissariat of Education, Aleksandr Voronskii (1884–1937), with the support of Vladimir Lenin, his wife Nadezhda Krupskaia, and Maksim Gorkii (1868–1936), proposed the founding of a new thick journal, *Red Virgin Soil* (*Krasnaia nov'*, 1921–42). Until Voronskii was removed from the editorship for alleged allegiance to Lev Trotskii (1879–1940; see Box 5.3), the journal fulfilled many of the functions of a traditional thick journal: lively criticism, polemics, and the publication of talented young writers – including Vladimir

Maiakovskii (1893–1930), Leonid Leonov (1899–1994), Fedor Gladkov (1883–1958), Isaak Babel (1894–1940), Konstantin Fedin (1892–1977), Aleksandr Fadeev (1901–1956), and Boris Pasternak (1890–1960). But penalties for ideological incorrectness were generally more severe in the Soviet period than in imperial Russia, and Voronskii was ultimately arrested and died in prison.

During the remainder of the Soviet period, a number of journals aspired to work in the great tradition of their nineteenth-century precedents, among them *New World*, *October* (*Oktiabr'*, 1924–), *The Banner* (*Znamia*, 1931–), and *The Star* (*Zvezda*, 1924–). They served as organs of Soviet institutions, such as the Writer's Union and the Communist Party, and their range of ideological difference was considerably narrower than that of their predecessors. But differences did exist, and the journals occasionally surprised their readership with unexpected works, as when *New World* published Aleksandr Solzhenitsyn's (1918–2008) *One Day in the Life of Ivan Denisovich* (*Odin den' Ivana Denisovicha*) in 1962. Journals could serve as lightning rods for party campaigns, as when Joseph Stalin's henchman Andrei Zhdanov (1896–1948) in 1946 attacked the journals *Leningrad* (*Leningrad*, 1940–6, 2013–) and *The Star* for 'servility to everything foreign' and for publishing the allegedly anti-Soviet poet Anna Akhmatova (1889–1966) and the satirist Mikhail Zoshchenko (1894–1958).[22]

Exiled intellectuals carried the tradition of the thick journal abroad after the revolution. In Paris, the journal *Contemporary Notes* (*Sovremennye zapiski*, 1920–40) deliberately assembled its title from those of *The Contemporary* and *Notes of the Fatherland*. A quarterly, often 500 pages in length, it was certainly thick. It published prominent émigré(e) writers, including Ivan Bunin (1870–1953), Dmitrii Merezhkovskii (1865–1941), Aleksei Remizov (1877–1957), Aleksandr Kuprin (1870–1938), Mark Aldanov (1886–1957), Zinaida Gippius (1869–5), Vladislav Khodasevich (1886–1939), Marina Tsvetaeva (1892–1941), and Vladimir Nabokov (1899–1977). Just as Katkov had refused to publish part of *Anna Karenina* when it violated the direction of his journal, so *Contemporary Notes* refused to publish chapter 4 of *The Gift* (*Dar*, 1938), Nabokov's savagely hilarious biography of Chernyshevskii, the chief critic of the nineteenth-century *Contemporary* and the émigré journal's intellectual ancestor.

---

22 Postanovlenie orgbiuro TsK VKP(b), 'O zhurnalakh "Zvezda" i "Leningrad" [Decision of the Organisational Office of the Central Committee of the All-Union Communist Party (Bolshevik) 'About the journals "Star" and "Leningrad"'], *Vlast' i khodozhestvennaia intelligentsiia. Dokumenty TsK RKP(b)* [Power and the artistic intelligentsiia. Documents of the Central Committee of the Russian Communist Party (Bolshevik)], ed. A. Artizov and O. Naumov (Moscow: Mezhdunarodnyi fond 'Demokratiia', 1999), pp. 587–91.

Just as new media (newspapers, illustrated journals) threatened the hegemony of the thick journal at the end of the nineteenth century, so newly liberated newspapers, specialised periodicals, and television threatened the place of the thick journals in post-Soviet Russia. Subscriptions fell dramatically. *The Star*, for instance, went from a print run of 344,000 in 1990 to a mere 3,400 in 2006. Like other thick journals of the Soviet period, it has become independent of institutional affiliation. More oriented towards literature than the nineteenth-century thick journals, it – like other post-Soviet journals – has branched out in new directions with sections on philosophy and on the Caucasus and with special issues on specific authors or topics.

The internet, which might seem a rival to the journals with its online texts and news features, at the same time makes many of Russia's prominent journals accessible to the far reaches of the Russian-speaking world through the website Hall of Journals (*Zhurnal'nyi zal*, 1997–). This new mechanism, which captures the journals' content but not their spartan, dingy visual presentation, preserves the values and interests of the intelligentsia, including the impact that the older mechanism made not only on the structure of Russian literature but on ways of understanding and contextualising it.

Further Reading

Breininger-Umetayeva, Olga, 'A scholarly look at "thick journals" today: The crisis of the institution', *Russian Journal of Communication* 6.1 (2014), 20–31.

Evgen'ev-Maksimov, V. E. et al. (eds.), *Ocherki po istorii russkoi zhurnalistiki i kritiki* [Studies in the history of Russian journalism and criticism], 2 vols. (Leningrad: Izdatel'stvo Leningradskogo universiteta, 1950–65).

Frazier, Melissa, *Romantic Encounters: Writers, Readers, and the 'Library for Reading'* (Stanford: Stanford University Press, 2007).

Fusso, Suzanne, *Editing Turgenev, Dostoevsky, and Tolstoy: Mikhail Katkov and the Great Russian Novel* (DeKalb: Northern Illinois University Press, 2017).

Kozlov, Denis, *The Readers of Novyi Mir: Coming to Terms with the Stalinist Past* (Cambridge, MA: Harvard University Press, 2013).

Maguire, Robert A., *Red Virgin Soil: Soviet Literature in the 1920s* (Princeton: Princeton University Press, 1968).

Martinsen, Deborah A. (ed.), *Literary Journals in Imperial Russia* (Cambridge: Cambridge University Press, 1997).

Reitblat, A. I., *Ot Bovy k Bal'montu i drugie raboty po istoricheskoi sotsiologii russkoi literatury* [From Bova to Balmont and other works on the historical sociology of Russian literature] (Moscow: Novoe literaturnoe obozrenie, 2009).

2.5

The Publisher

WILLIAM MILLS TODD III

The rise of secular, non-governmental publishing in the eighteenth and nineteenth centuries made it possible for authors to become remunerated professionals and to become the entertainers, the tribunes, and the conscience of the nation. By the end of the imperial period, enterprising publishers had found ways to make this literature affordable and widely accessible to readers. Under the administrative-command economy of the Soviet Union, after a slow beginning, publishing expanded further still. The post-Soviet rebirth of print capitalism brought new writing, new media, and new challenges.

In this chapter I will discuss trends in the print publication of the imaginative literature treated in other chapters of this history. This will leave largely to the side Russia's rich manuscript and later typescript traditions as well as important and substantial print realms, such as the religious, the scholarly, the practical, the political, and the pedagogical. The tradition of the 'thick journal' (tolstyi zhurnal) is treated separately in Chapter 2.4. Focusing primarily on the 1820s–1890s, I will explore the interrelationship between pioneering publishers and the circumstances under which they worked as well as the ways in which this interrelationship shaped the literature that emerged. I will argue that only in the 1840s did educated publisher-intellectuals supplant the artisan-publishers and merchant-booksellers, becoming a force for shaping the imaginative literature that was produced, primarily through the thick journals. Until this time, authors and publishers failed to achieve the productive dialogue imagined by Aleksandr Pushkin (1799–1837) in his lyric 'Conversation of a Bookseller with a Poet' (Razgovor knigoprodavtsa s poetom, 1824), in which the two parties learn each other's language and the bookseller proposes topics to the poet. Even then, the publisher often remained a creaky mechanism for producing literature, with poorly fitting parts and thin financial lubrication.

Beginnings

The roles, services, and intellectual functions of modern publishing as an institution have developed over centuries and would have been, in their entirety, unimaginable to medieval Muscovy's first known printers, Ivan Fedorov and Petr Mstislavets, who printed a liturgical version of Acts and Epistles in 1564 at the Printing Office (*Pechatnyi Dvor*), established in 1553 at the order of Ivan IV (r. 1533–84), a century after Gutenberg had developed a press with moveable metal type. This establishment seems to have provoked a hostile reaction from local scribes and reputedly burned down. It was restored in fits and starts but only began more or less continuous operations from around 1615. It produced almost exclusively books for ecclesiastical purposes. In 1721 it was placed under the administration of the Holy Synod, which managed it until 1917.

For much of the eighteenth century, printing remained under the ownership of state establishments, initially the Academy of Sciences in St Petersburg and the Holy Synod in Moscow. Concerned primarily with providing practical manuals, state proclamations, alphabet primers, devotional books, and official newspapers, they paid little attention to Russian-language imaginative literature.

Moscow University, founded in 1755, established what was – for the time – a substantial printing facility, with eleven printing presses and seventy-eight full-time employees.[1] The Academy of Sciences' printing operation in St Petersburg grew by the 1770s to seventeen presses. Their production of prose fiction lagged well behind other European countries: no original novels before 1763 and only a total of twelve by 1775.[2] The books of these presses were sold and advertised primarily in the two capital cities, in print runs of 300 to 1,200 copies. They sold poorly, and the Academy depended on private and imperial sponsorship to cover the costs of printing.

With such rudimentary distribution networks, neglect of native literature, and unclear publication principles, it is clearly premature to speak of publishing as a literary mechanism in the eighteenth century. But new opportunities for private printing and publishing slowly began to emerge in the last quarter of the century: first for foreign-language printers; then for those able to rent the academic presses; and, finally, for all comers, as Catherine II (r. 1762–96) issued in 1783 an edict permitting private individuals

---

1 Gary Marker, *Publishing, Printing, and the Origins of Intellectual Life in Russia, 1770–1800* (Princeton: Princeton University Press, 1985), p. 83.
2 Marker, *Publishing*, p. 101.

to own or operate presses without special government permission. The life expectancy for these new enterprises was short, typically five to eight years. Labour and materials were expensive, print runs small, and modest economies of scale available only to publishers of textbooks and calendars.[3]

Among these enterprising publishers, the figure of Nikolai Novikov (1744–1818) stands out in bold relief. A graduate of Moscow University, army officer, secretary to Catherine's Commission on Laws, and editor of satirical journals, he most comprehensively represented the institution-building aspirations of the Russian Enlightenment. He was not the only member of the educated westernised nobility to take up publishing, but he was the most committed (he sold inherited estates to fund his activities), the most altruistic, and – at the same time – the most commercially aware. He sought to expand the reading public for serious writing by engaging the marketing services of provincial merchants and clergymen, by extending credit, and by offering discounts.[4] His younger contemporary Nikolai Karamzin (1766–1826) would write that Novikov had increased newspaper circulation from 600 to 4,000. He not only leased Russia's largest press, that of Moscow University, but also founded his own printing firm. He balanced the publication of serious moral and philosophical works with more profitable adventure novels and textbooks, and he was able to stay financially afloat by securing considerable investments and philanthropic contributions. Between 1784 and 1791, his company published 900 editions, or 28 per cent of the entire Russian book production during those years.[5] Novikov's concerns spread beyond the dissemination of literature to its production and consumption, and he founded two schools for poor children, seminars at Moscow University for teachers and translators, Russia's first children's magazine, a magazine about practical economics, and Russia's first student society. He also took a first step towards the institutionalisation of Russian literature by compiling *An Attempt at an Historical Dictionary of Russian Writers* (*Opyt istoricheskogo slovaria o rossiiskikh pisateliakh*, 1772).

3 Marker, *Publishing*, pp. 116–18.
4 T. Grits, V. Trenin, and M. Nikitin, *Slovesnost' i kommertsiia (knizhnaia lavka A. F. Smirdina)* [Literature and commerce (the bookshop of A. F. Smirdin)], ed. V. B. Shklovskii and V. M. Eikhenbaum (Moscow: Federatsiia, 1929), pp. 80, 86; M. N. Kufaev, *Istoriia russkoi knigi v XIX veke* [A history of the Russian book in the nineteenth century] (Leningrad: 'Nachatki znanii', 1927), p. 32.
5 G. P. Makogonenko, *Nikolai Novikov i russkoe prosveshchenie XVIII veka* [Nikolai Novikov and the Russian Enlightenment of the eighteenth century] (Moscow: Gosudarstvennoe izdatel'stvo khudozhestvennoi literatury, 1951), p. 507.

While Novikov's activities represent the best aspirations for a commercially viable, socially responsible publishing enterprise that would engage the interest and participation of people from a variety of social classes and regions, his fate shows that such an independent full-service public institution was not yet feasible in the Russian Empire. Novikov became financially overextended, and – even more catastrophic – his all-too-visible operations could not be tolerated by the 'enlightened monarch' Catherine II, who had become in the wake of the French Revolution increasingly fearful of the various strands of Enlightenment thought that Novikov published. Just as systematically as his project had engaged the entire literary process, the government dismantled it. It confiscated his publications, making booksellers reluctant to take them. It harassed him with special investigations, seized control over his schools, deprived him of the right to publish textbooks and religious works, and refused to renew his lease on the Moscow University press. Financial ruin followed. In secret proceedings, he was sentenced to fifteen years in the dread Shlisselburg Fortress. Released from prison at the beginning of Paul I's reign (r 1796–1801), he was not allowed to return to publishing and died in poverty.

The thoroughness of this punishment and the empress's vindictive desire to destroy her one-time journalistic rival explain why literature remained a matter of patronage and small familiar circles (see Chapter 2.3) and not the product of successful publishing enterprises and a modern profession of letters. Novikov had attempted to circumvent, even to confront, the autocratic government, and the government – unchecked by public opinion, an independent judiciary, a legal profession, or well-developed commerce – had demonstratively asserted its supreme power.

Throughout most of the nineteenth century, these conditions prevailed. Westernisation and secularisation had been imposed from above by Peter I (r. 1682–1725) and his successors, but they resisted such cultural forces when they arose from below and from outside state establishments. A century and a half after Peter, Alexander II (r. 1855–81) – one of the more liberal autocrats – would direct his commission on reforming press regulations to 'arm the administrative and judicial authority with the strength necessary to repel the dangers which are the result of the ungovernability and excesses of the printed word'.[6] A discussion of publishing during the imperial period cannot fail to take cognisance of the state's ambivalence. It may have sponsored secular printing, invited artisans from abroad to staff early printing

---

6 Charles A. Ruud, *Fighting Words: Imperial Censorship and the Russian Press, 1804–1906; With a New Introduction* (Toronto: University of Toronto Press, 2009), p. 186.

establishments, and called for an educated class of servitors who would become the producers and consumers of secular literature, but it stood poised over the publishing process, capable of interfering with any stage in that process at almost any time, thereby hindering the institutional viability of even a modestly independent press. The laws, such as they were, changed rapidly during the decades following the edict of 1783, especially before the end of the Crimean War and the ascension of Alexander II. Private presses were permitted, banned, and re-established. Once pre-publication censorship was clearly established in 1804, ambiguous passages in a text were interpreted in favour of authors, then held against them, then disregarded, and then – de facto – held against them again. Censorship agencies proliferated, supervising and often contradicting one another; there were no fewer than a dozen by the end of Nicholas I's reign (r. 1825–55). The relatively enlightened statute of 6 April 1865, which lifted preliminary censorship for books of over ten signatures in length and which replaced preliminary censorship with a system of warnings for periodicals, was frequently amended during the following decades – and not in favour of increased freedom of the press. But these rapid changes in the legal process were not, in themselves, the chief problem facing the publisher, the would-be professional writer, or the reading public. Laws, however rapidly they changed, could at least enable people to predict the consequences of their actions. Nor was censorship, in itself, necessarily a principal retarding force. Much of the censoring was performed by professor-litterateurs who shared the aspirations of publishers, writers, and the public, and a number of well-known writers – including Sergei Aksakov (1791–1859), Petr Viazemskii (1792–1878), Fedor Tiutchev (1803–1873), and Ivan Goncharov (1812–1891) – held positions in the censorship. Furthermore, the stated purpose of censorship to protect religious dogma, government, morals, and the personal honour of individuals remained constant once articulated in the 1804 Statute on Censorship. The central problem was the unpredictability, arbitrariness, and vindictiveness of the government, which could at times permit politically radical publications by writers such as Nikolai Chernyshevskii (1828–1889) while censoring works by cultural conservatives, such as Fedor Dostoevskii (1821–1881). Although for much of this period the censors examined works prior to publication, writers and publishers could be punished subsequent to publication – even when the laws ostensibly protected them – if the published work incurred the displeasure of someone in high places. The censors themselves were also vulnerable. A publication that displeased higher authorities could result in severe reprimands, loss of position, or brief jail sentences.

A second continuing problem for would-be Russian publishers was the lack of readership. Only in 1897 was mass literacy measured in the Russian Empire, at which time – after several decades of increased educational opportunities – the level of minimal literacy reached only 21 per cent, no better than a quarter of the percentage that facilitated profitable publishing in Europe, Japan, and the United States.[7] In the eighteenth and nineteenth centuries, not only was the literacy rate most likely far lower but the populace was not broadly committed to book purchasing or sufficiently educated to respond to sophisticated works. This situation could, and did, make publishing a precarious enterprise, with limited possibilities for writers and nasty Grub Street competition, especially between periodical publishers. Russia could support only a handful at a time of the thick journals that, rather than book publication, best satisfied the financial needs of leading authors. Writing in 1876 in the socialist journal *The Cause* (*Delo*, 1866–88), Serafim Shashkov could argue – with considerable evidence – that the material circumstances of Russian writers had not improved since the early nineteenth century.[8]

One type of publishing which could and did surmount these obstacles was the production of cheap broadside prints (*lubki*) and chapbooks. These relatively inexpensive illustrated pages with captions or texts, generally in crude vernacular, represented the only print material that most Russians encountered. This type of publishing thrived from the mid-eighteenth century to the 1917 revolution, when the new regime closed it down. Market stalls distributed these works to urban readers, and wandering pedlars (*ofeni*) took them to places and to a public that high literature rarely reached. Sometimes cheaply printed books were appropriated for this form of publication or distributed together with them, so that the adjective *lubochnaia* came to apply not just to primitive broadsheets but to mass literature, particularly adventure novels that were often 'translated' (i.e. freely adapted) from foreign models and produced for an indiscriminating audience. As we have seen with Novikov, more upmarket publishers would occasionally print such potboilers as a source of revenue, but generally they were provided by a different set of publishers. A successful title would go through many editions, while a subsequently canonical work might have only one or two. There is no more striking example than the now forgotten historical novel by

---

7 Boris N. Mironov, 'The development of literacy in Russia and the USSR from the tenth to the twentieth centuries', *History of Education Quarterly* 31.2 (1991), 244, 247.

8 S. S. Shashkov, 'Literaturnyi trud v Rossii (istoricheskii ocherk)' [Literary labour in Russia (an historical essay)], *Delo* 8 (1876), 37.

Ivan Zakharovich Krylov (1816–1869, not to be confused with the far better known fabulist Ivan Andreevich Krylov (1769–1844)), *The Legend of How a Soldier Saved Peter the Great from Death* (*Predanie o tom, kak soldat spas Petra Velikogo ot smerti*), which appeared in over a hundred separate editions as book and chapbook between 1843 and 1916.[9] By contrast, Lev Tolstoi's (1828–1910) *War and Peace* (*Voina i mir*, 1868–9) appeared as a separate complete edition only twice in the nineteenth century; after the two editions of 1868–9, it had to be purchased as part of Tolstoi's collected works. Likewise, *Anna Karenina* (*Anna Karenina*, 1878) appeared only twice as a separate edition. When novelist Ivan Turgenev (1818–1883) described Tolstoi in 1880 as the most popular Russian writer, he was – like most educated readers, scholars, and critics – ignoring the vast realm of *lubochnaia* literature.

The late eighteenth and early nineteenth centuries witnessed a very different sort of printing and publishing from this mass literature: the production of expensive editions for a public at the opposite end of the spectrum from those who purchased the broadsheets and pulp fiction. Beginning in the reigns of Catherine II and Paul I, printers, booksellers, editors, and publishers from a variety of non-gentry backgrounds entered the Russian book trade and began printing and selling more expensive books and periodicals for a more elite readership, primarily in the capital cities of Moscow and St Petersburg. A few of their enterprises survived well into the nineteenth century and even beyond.

The Age of Smirdin

After the introduction of private printing in 1783, artisans and merchants dominated the marketplace. Many were foreign born and had been invited to Russia to practise their skills, such as high-quality printing and bookbinding. They stayed to open bookstores with catalogues and sometimes reading rooms. Johann Weitbrecht, for example, started by managing the Academy of Sciences bookstore in St Petersburg, stocking it with French and German books, and then opened his own bookstore, which derived much of its income from compiling personal libraries for such wealthy patrons as Catherine II.

When Weitbrecht eventually went bankrupt, he was able to sell his considerable stock of books to Ivan Glazunov (1762–1831), one of three

9 Jeffrey Brooks, *The Firebird and the Fox: Russian Culture under Tsars and Bolsheviks* (Cambridge: Cambridge University Press, 2019), pp. 19–22.

brothers of merchant origin whose family firm looms large in the pre-revolutionary book trade. In 1782, the three brothers began selling books in Moscow; they then opened their own store in St Petersburg (1788) and founded a publishing house and press (1790). Under Ivan's son Ilia (1786–1849), the firm published the last lifetime edition of Aleksandr Pushkin's *Eugene Onegin* (*Evgenii Onegin*) in 1837, and a posthumous three-volume edition of Pushkin's collected works in 1841. The third generation continued to prosper, with bookstores in the capitals and publishing projects that included textbooks and works by major authors, such as Antiokh Kantemir (1708–1744), Denis Fonvizin (1745–1792), Mikhail Lermontov (1814–1841), Vasilii Zhukovskii (1783–1852), Ivan Turgenev, Ivan Goncharov, and Aleksandr Ostrovskii (1823–1886). Ilia's son Ivan (1826–1889) became mayor of St Petersburg and was granted hereditary nobility. The 1917 revolution brought an end to the firm's activities, but during its existence it published over a thousand titles of imaginative literature in 12 million copies.[10]

Few of these early firms, however, produced future press barons. Most were fortunate to last a few decades. Vasilii Plavilshchikov (1768–1823), of merchant origin, organised a publishing and bookselling operation in St Petersburg. His bookstore became the first public reading room in the city. By 1820, its catalogues listed 7,000 Russian titles – and the catalogues continued to appear after he willed his store, library, press, and considerable debts to his clerk, Aleksandr Smirdin (1795–1857), who would become the most famous and successful publisher of the 1830s and a major figure in making professional authorship possible in Russia.

Writing in 1834, Vissarion Belinskii (1811–1848; see Box 5.1), the most influential critic of the time, divided Russian literary history into five epochs: those of Mikhail Lomonosov (1711–1765), Nikolai Karamzin, Pushkin, national prose, and Smirdin. Belinskii ignored Smirdin's lack of literary gifts – Smirdin had received primary schooling from a Moscow deacon and was apprenticed at ten to a Moscow bookseller who specialised in *lubochnaia* literature – but other booksellers whom he outmanoeuvred, such as the Glazunovs, and gentleman-writers such as Pushkin, would comment on it, and the social barrier between Smirdin and the writers he published not infrequently eventuated in their exploiting his generosity. 'Smirdin, naturally, is no Novikov', as his author Faddei

10 'Literaturnye izdatel'stva (russkie)' [Russian literary publishing houses], in *Literaturnaia entsiklopediia* [Literary encyclopedia], 11 vols. (Moscow: Izdatel'stvo Kommunisticheskoi akademii, 1929–39) vol. VI (1932), pp. 453–4: http://feb-web.ru/feb/litenc/encyclop/le6/le6-4501.htm, accessed 30 Jan. 2023.

Bulgarin (1789–1859) ungraciously put it.[11] But Smirdin paid his authors and the editors of his periodicals unprecedented honoraria and salaries: Ivan Krylov received 40,000 rubles for the rights to his fables, and Osip Senkovskii (1800–1858) earned 15,000 rubles a year for editing the popular thick journal *Library for Reading* (*Biblioteka dlia chteniia*, 1834–64). Smirdin paid Pushkin by the line for his verse, and prose writers were paid by the signature. In all, he published over seventy Russian writers.

One of those writers was Faddei Bulgarin, whose picaresque novel *Ivan Vyzhigin* (*Ivan Vyzhigin*, 1829) became Smirdin's first publishing success: purchased from the author for 2,000 rubles, it sold an unprecedented 7,000 copies in two years, bringing Smirdin a handsome profit and making Bulgarin Pushkin's principal rival in popularity. It played an important part, hard to appreciate today, in making Russian prose fiction acceptable and even popular with upmarket readers. Translated within three years into eight European languages, it became the first Russian international literary success. Smirdin's further triumphs of the 1830s – a new bookstore at a fashionable St Petersburg address (1832); a lavish and successful almanac, *Housewarming* (*Novosel'e*, 1833–4), which celebrated this move; and the *Library for Reading*, which soon reached 7,000 subscribers – gave him, for a time, a near monopoly over Russian literature.

Smirdin's projects broadened the reach and appeal of Russian literature. His attempts to publish Russian literature in affordable editions were exemplary. They were also unrealistic. Overextended and undercapitalised, he fell into bankruptcy and was forced to sell his bookstore in 1847. He died in poverty a decade later, but in his heyday he had shown how an enterprising publisher could provide the mechanism for expanding the Russian literary public, while leaving it to his editors and authors – such as Bulgarin and Senkovskii – to dictate taste and, in Senkovskii's case, shape works (see Chapter 2.4).

Publisher-Intellectuals

The next generation of historically significant publishers followed Smirdin in realising the potential of the thick journals and literary miscellanies for reaching a broader audience. They also bridged the social and cultural gap that had separated early nineteenth-century publishers from their authors and readers. They not only published periodicals but at times also edited and contributed to them. Nikolai Nekrasov (1821–1878), Andrei Kraevskii (1810–1889), and Mikhail

---

11 *Severnaia pchela* [The northern bee], 1833, no. 300 (30 December), 1186.

Katkov (1818–1887) are three salient examples of the mid-century publisher-intellectual.

Nekrasov, who was born to a gentry family and audited courses at St Petersburg University, is now remembered primarily as a canonical poet, but he began publishing activities with collections in the mid-1840s: *The Physiology of St Petersburg* (*Fiziologiia Peterburga*, 1845) and *The Petersburg Miscellany* (*Peterburgskii sbornik*, 1846). These included early works of subsequently prominent writers such as Dmitrii Grigorovich (1822–1899), Dostoevskii, Turgenev, Aleksandr Herzen (1812–1870), and Apollon Maikov (1821–1897). From there Nekrasov went on to publish and edit two of the most influential thick journals of the time. In 1846, he leased a journal founded by Pushkin, *The Contemporary* (*Sovremennik*, 1836–66), and – before it was closed by the government in 1866 – it and his almanacs published the leading critics and fiction writers of the time, including Dostoevskii, Herzen, Tolstoi, Turgenev, Goncharov, Evgeniia Tur (1815–1892), Mikhail Saltykov-Shchedrin (1826–1889), Belinskii, Chernyshevskii, and Nikolai Dobroliubov (1836–1861). It became the principal radically oriented journal of its time, losing its less politically extreme contributors – such as Tolstoi and Turgenev – to Katkov's *The Russian Herald* (*Russkii vestnik*, 1856–1906) in the early 1860s. Nekrasov himself moved to the previously more moderate *Notes of the Fatherland* (*Otechestvennye zapiski*, 1839–84), which absorbed much of the staff of the closed *Contemporary*. He leased it from its owner, Kraevskii, and edited it together with Saltykov-Shchedrin for the rest of his life. Under close surveillance by the government, *Notes of the Fatherland* nevertheless became a haven for young Russian populists in the 1870s, publishing, among others, Gleb Uspenskii (1843–1902), Nikolai Mikhailovskii (1842–1904), and Fedor Reshetnikov (1841–1871) as well as Nekrasov's own poetry and Saltykov-Shchedrin's highly popular sketches and fiction.

Andrei Kraevskii did not have Nekrasov's literary talent, but he parlayed modest social beginnings, an education at Moscow University, and access to St Petersburg literary circles into a long and largely successful publishing career. He got a start in periodical publishing by helping Pushkin organise *The Contemporary*, then in 1839 he became the editor and publisher of *Notes of the Fatherland*, a title he had previously leased from its previous founder, Pavel Svinin (1787–1839). He soon made it a successful and respected competitor of the *Library for Reading*, scoring a major coup by publishing the component stories of his friend Lermontov's *A Hero of Our Time* (*Geroi nashego vremeni*) in 1839–40 (first book publication 1840) and by attracting Belinskii as the journal's principal critic. Other prominent or promising poets and prose writers – such as Vladimir Odoevskii (1803–1869), Evgenii Baratynskii (1800–1844), Zhukovskii,

Viazemskii, Nikolai Gogol (1809–1852), Herzen, Nekrasov, Dostoevskii, Turgenev, and Goncharov – had joined them by the end of the 1840s. It had a healthy subscription list that was in the four thousands during the 1840s, rising to 8,000 by 1870. But it did not enjoy smooth sailing. In 1846 it lost Belinskii to the revived *Contemporary* and, as a consequence, lost prestige with the liberal intelligentsia. The European rebellions of 1848 led the fearful Russian government to impose particularly harsh censorship between 1848 and 1855 (the death year of Nicholas I). This proved difficult for all periodicals. Kraevskii was called to testify before a commission on the thick journals and forced to admit that his journal had offended against all that censorship was supposed to protect: state, religion, individual dignity, and public morality. He escaped with a severe reprimand. A near decade of relative stagnation followed, until the closing of *The Contemporary* drove that journal's editors and contributors back to Kraevskii, who – with their participation – kept *Notes of the Fatherland* appearing until the government closed it in 1884 for publishing dangerous ideas and for harbouring contributors who belonged to secret societies.

Kraevskii was also an innovative newspaper publisher. In 1871, he founded the International Telegraph Agency with a twelve-year lease from the government; it brought news immediately to St Petersburg from the far reaches of the empire and beyond.[12] *The Voice* (*Golos*, 1863–83), which he founded when the government permitted newspapers to carry political news and advertising, became the most successful of the post-emancipation newspapers, eventually reaching a circulation of 25,000 copies. Moderately liberal in politics, gradualist with respect to reforms, and capitalist in economic policy, it appealed to a western-oriented urban readership. Under relentless attack from conservative rivals, such as Katkov's *Moscow News* (*Moskovskie vedomosti*, 1756–1917), it managed to publish a lively and balanced set of political, overseas, economic, scientific, and cultural articles and aimed for accurate reportage. It also earned multiple warnings and closures, and was banned from selling separate issues; in 1881 it was closed down again for six months. Finally, in 1883, having received three warnings in one year, it was subjected to preliminary censorship, which rendered impossible its mission to provide the news in a timely fashion, and it folded. Like the other newspapers discussed in this section, it carried regular reviews of literary works, helping to determine which works and authors would attract readers and, eventually, enter the canon of Russian literature. Authors and works

12 Louise McReynolds, *The News under Russia's Old Regime: The Development of a Mass-Circulation Press* (Princeton: Princeton University Press, 1991), p. 47.

ignored by the reviewers had little chance of attracting either contemporary attention or that of posterity.

The third of the prominent mid-century publisher-intellectuals, Mikhail Katkov, would become – in Tolstoi's estimation – 'a terrifying, all-powerful force', a scourge of rival publishers and of liberal or moderate government officials who were less than harsh in their treatment of rebellious nationalities and radical intellectuals.[13] Like Nekrasov and Kraevskii, Katkov had gentry origins and a university education. Starting in Moscow, from whose university he graduated, Katkov travelled in Europe and audited Friedrich Schelling's philosophy lectures in Berlin. He took part in the Stankevich Circle of young philosophers and writers, and helped introduce Belinskii to Hegel's thought, before eventually breaking ties with him. He then returned to Moscow University, where he taught philosophy until the government – fearing contagion from radical foreign thinking – closed the department in 1850.

Katkov's career in the publishing world began the following year, when he became editor of the venerable *Moscow News*, founded by Moscow University and once published by Novikov. Katkov would himself eventually lease and publish the newspaper (1863–87). At first it was somewhat liberal in its orientation, but by the mid-1860s it had turned conservative and nationalist, sometimes excessively so: in 1866 it ran afoul of the government and was closed for three months, until Katkov successfully played support from Alexander II against the emperor's own government.[14] In 1887 it received a warning for its extremely xenophobic criticism of allegedly western-oriented government officials. The wrath of Alexander III (r.1881–94) soon dissipated, and as usual Katkov could count on the support of the nobility, the imperial family, and influential members of the government. Katkov's thundering front-page fulminations against Russia's enemies and his ongoing crusades in favour of classical (as opposed to practical and scientific) education and in favour of conscripting rebellious university students usually found approval in these circles. Thanks to government support, *Moscow News* became the most widely circulated daily newspaper of the 1870s, highly profitable because it enjoyed the lucrative right to print official notices.[15]

Katkov published translations of such eminent Victorian novelists as Charles Dickens, William Makepeace Thackeray, Anthony Trollope, and Wilkie

13 G. A. Rusanov and A. G. Rusanov, *Vospominaniia o L. N. Tolstom, 1883–1901gg.* [Reminiscences about L. N. Tolstoi, 1883–1901] (Voronezh: Tsentral'no-Chernozemnoe knizhnoe izdatel'svto, 1972), p. 53.
14 Ruud, *Fighting Words*, pp. 156–7.
15 McReynolds, *News under Russia's Old Regime*, p. 35.

Collins, but his principal contribution to Russian literature was *The Russian Herald*, a thick journal he founded with a group of predominantly liberal Moscow intellectuals in 1856. At first a fortnightly, it published a broad spectrum of literary, historical, critical, scholarly, and philosophical articles – Russian and translated. Unlike most of the other thick journals, it included verse, with poems by Afanasii Fet (1820–1892), Fedor Tiutchev, Adam Mickiewicz (1798–1855), Apollon Maikov, and Karolina Pavlova (1807–1893). But soon disagreements among the founders led them to break up, leaving Katkov and Pavel Leontev in charge of the journal as well as owners of its printing press.

In 1861, the journal became a monthly, and Katkov took advantage of discord among leading contributors to *The Contemporary* to attract writers who would later become internationally canonised – among them Tolstoi, Turgenev, Dostoevskii, and Goncharov – to whom he paid handsome honoraria and occasionally substantial advance payments. In the journal's peak years, from the early 1860s to the early 1880s, readers could expect to find instalments of works by these heavyweights as well as by such popular and well-respected writers as Nikolai Leskov (1831–1895), Aleksandr Ostrovskii, Aleksei Pisemskii (1821–1881), and Pavel Melnikov-Pecherskii (1818–1883), and it attracted more than 6,000 subscribers. In the February 1866 issue, for instance, readers found instalments of both *Crime and Punishment* (*Prestuplenie i nakazanie*) and *War and Peace* as well as a translated excerpt from Wilkie Collins's recently published *Armadale*. Katkov's important contribution to the prospering of the Russian novel was not, however, matched by his ability to work harmoniously with his authors. He parted with Turgenev on ideological grounds, and Tolstoi did not complete the serialisation of either *War and Peace* or *Anna Karenina*, in the latter case because he refused to share Katkov's jingoistic enthusiasm for Russian military adventures in the Balkans. Katkov also locked horns with Dostoevskii over *Crime and Punishment*, when he objected to the scene in which the prostitute Sonia reads the Gospel to the murderer Raskolnikov, and over *Demons* (*Besy*) in 1872, when he refused to publish Stavrogin's confession to child rape. Dostoevskii was able to publish the blasphemous 'Grand Inquisitor' chapter of *The Brothers Karamazov* (*Brat'ia Karamazovy*, serialised 1879–80) in *The Russian Herald* only after composing brilliant letters on the rhetorical design of his novel and after enlisting the support of Konstantin Pobedonostsev, advisor to the emperor and ober-procurator of the Holy Synod. Katkov's publications survived his death in 1887, becoming organs of extreme antisemitic reaction. *The Russian Herald* folded in 1906, and *Moscow News* was shut down in 1917, two days after the October Revolution.

Thick journals such as *The Contemporary*, *Notes of the Fatherland*, and *The Russian Herald* provided a handsome income for the best-known novelists by serialising their works. The publication of individual works or of a writer's collected works was not yet equally profitable in mid-century Russia. The case of Dostoevskii is illuminating. Deep in debt after the failure of his brother's journal – *The Epoch* (*Epokha*, 1864–5) – and already under contract to Katkov to finish *Crime and Punishment* in 1866, Dostoevskii signed a contract with a Petersburg publisher, Fedor Stellovskii, that has become famous for its penalty clause: if Dostoevskii, notorious for not meeting deadlines, failed to deliver a substantial new novel by 1 November 1866, Stellovskii would have the right to publish, at no cost, all of Dostoevskii's works for the next nine years. The overburdened novelist found himself in a predicament as melodramatic as any Victorian novelist – himself included – ever created.

Fortunately for Dostoevskii, the melodrama's opening acts of potential tragedy were followed by the obligatory happy ending, as Dostoevskii agreed to work with Anna Snitkina, one of Russia's first professional stenographers. With her help he met Stellovskii's deadline, although not without a further novelistic adventure: Dostoevskii was forced to register the manuscript with the police at ten o'clock on the evening of 1 November, because Stellovskii had skipped town in hope that this would make it impossible for Dostoevskii to fulfil the contract. Personally and professionally, the ending proved even happier for Dostoevskii. He married the young stenographer, and she turned out to be a remarkable helper in producing his manuscripts, archiving his papers, and publishing his works. From their apartment in St Petersburg, she managed the publication of his one-person journal, *The Diary of a Writer* (*Dnevnik pisatelia*, 1876–7, 1880–1), and she eventually arranged for the publication of his collected works. The first posthumous edition (fourteen volumes for a price of 25 rubles) brought her a profit of 75,000 rubles (approximately a million US dollars in today's money).[16]

Large-Scale Publishing

The publishing world in which Anna Dostoevskaia came to operate was radically different from the one that she and her husband had first encountered, the one shaped by publisher-intellectuals and the monthly periodicals.

---

16 Andrew D. Kaufman, *The Gambler Wife: A True Story of Love, Risk, and the Woman Who Saved Dostoevsky* (New York: Riverhead Books, 2021), p. 285.

That she licensed the fifth edition of Dostoevskii's works to the publisher Adolf Marks (1838–1904, also spelled Marx or Marcks), one of a number of Russian publishers who took their business to a level of influence and prosperity previously unthinkable in Russia, symbolised the changing situation of the late nineteenth century. Technological innovation (steam power, rotary presses, linotype composition, polychrome printing, and cheap wood-pulp paper); a significant rise in basic literacy, especially among the urban population of the empire; and the virtual cessation of censorship in 1906 all facilitated a flourishing industry. Its products ranged from cheap newspapers and penny dreadfuls at one extreme to the elegant, if short lived, periodicals and artistic editions of Russia's vibrant avant-garde, which made Russian Modernism part of an international movement in the arts. In the middle stood classical Russian literature, whose works were canonised in school curricula, public criticism, and mass festivals, such as the hundredth anniversary of Pushkin's birth in 1899.

Three publishers of diverse origins and talents stand out in this upsurge of print activity in the last decades of the Russian Empire: Marks, Aleksei Suvorin (1834–1912), and Ivan Sytin (1851–1934). Marks, the son of a factory owner, was born in Stettin and received commercial schooling before moving to Russia, where he worked for a bookseller and began to publish books. His new career took flight when he began publishing Russia's first illustrated weekly, *The Grainfield* (*Niva*, 1870–1917), whose subscription list would expand from an initial 9,000 to 250,000 by the early twentieth century. Marks is famous for the free supplements he provided to his subscribers – at first calendars and reproductions of paintings, then the collected works of Russian writers on whose writings the copyright had expired, and later (as the business became more profitable) the works of writers to whom or to whose heirs he paid royalties. His most famous contract captured Tolstoi's *Resurrection* (*Voskresenie*), serialised in *The Grainfield* in 1899 for 21,915 rubles, which Tolstoi contributed to support the emigration to North America of the persecuted religious sect of the Dukhobors (Spirit Warriors).[17] His most infamous contract trapped Anton Chekhov (1860–1904), in need of ready cash, into giving Marks the right to publish all of his previous stories for 75,000 rubles – a large sum, certainly, but less than contemporaries thought them worth. The contract gave the author a share in the profits only on future stories, which proved ruinous for Chekhov – who died before he could

---

17 Anastasiia Tuliakova, 'Skol'ko zarabatyvali russkie pisateli' [How much did Russian writers earn], *Arzamas* (8 July 2016), http://arzamas.academy/mag/315-money, accessed 6 May 2021.

produce many of those stories – and highly profitable for Marks.[18] Marks established a substantial printing plant in St Petersburg and, after his death, the firm became a joint stock company. His numerous editions had helped establish the canon of Russian literature and had made it available to a broad readership.

Aleksei Suvorin, the son of a peasant who had risen to officer's rank during the Napoleonic Wars, received a military education but soon left the military to become a provincial teacher. Unlike Marks, he began his career in the world of letters by writing and translating, which brought him to Moscow. He compiled books for Russia's newly literate readers and published stories in *The Contemporary* and *Notes of the Fatherland* as well as in a journal, *Iasnaia Poliana (Iasnaia Poliana)*, that Tolstoi published in 1862 for peasant readers. He moved to St Petersburg and wrote articles for the liberal thick journal *Messenger of Europe (Vestnik Evropy*, 1866–1918) as well as a popular Sunday feuilleton for the *St Petersburg News (Sankt-Peterburgskie vedomosti*, 1703–) under the pseudonym 'Stranger' *(Neznakomets)*, in which he boldly attacked such conservative nationalists as Katkov. His obstreperousness earned him a readership among the intelligentsia but also a three-week jail term and the burning of his collected sketches.

In 1876, Suvorin was able to acquire his own newspaper, *New Times (Novoe vremia*, 1868–1917), which came out seven days a week, eventually in both morning and evening editions, with an illustrated weekly supplement from 1891. As the newspaper's political stance turned strategically to the populist right, it acquired a profitable circulation of 60,000 copies by 1900, together with the right to print official announcements and the right to sell individual copies in railway stations. It published a wealth of cultural and popular scientific news as well as literary works by such writers as Suvorin's friend and frequent correspondent Chekhov, but by the early twentieth century it was scorned by intellectuals for its antisemitism and pro-government stance. The newspaper format, much more limiting than that of the monthly thick journals, helped bring very short fiction (pointed, humorous, and anecdotal in its plotting) to the fore of Russian literature. Chekhov turned the form into high art with his variety of endings and tones and his play with reader expectations.

The newspaper represented but one part of Suvorin's multifaceted literary and publishing activity. He owned a successful printing plant, for which he

18 *The Letters of Anton Chekhov*, trans. Michael Henry Heim with Simon Karlinsky (New York: Harper and Row, 1973), pp. 340–3.

opened a school to train his workers, and he took pride in treating his authors and employees fairly. He was also an occasional novelist, a playwright, owner of the Petersburg Little Theatre (*Peterburgskii Malyi teatr*), and an important diarist. Suvorin devoted much of his considerable energy to publishing inexpensive editions – similar to Routledge's Railway Library in England and Reklam's Universal-Bibliotek in Germany – and his series, the Cheap Library (*Deshevaia Biblioteka*), had by 1895 sold 3.8 million copies of Russian and foreign works, primarily canonical ones, both ancient and contemporary.[19] At 25 kopecks a volume, they may have been too expensive for literate peasants, but they could reach urban readers and travellers, for Suvorin's editions enjoyed a monopoly over book sales at railway stations.[20] When he died, the emperor sent a wreath for his funeral.

Ivan Sytin's long-lived and prosperous publishing activity catered to readers less financially and culturally privileged than those of Marks and Suvorin. As the son of a literate peasant who became a canton clerk, his origins were more modest than theirs, and after a mere three years of schooling he began his rise to becoming Russia's most prolific publisher. Chekhov, who shared Sytin's peasant origins, would characterise him in 1899 as 'completely illiterate'.[21] He began his career in the book trade as a teenager in Nizhnii Novgorod, commissioning pedlars to distribute *lubok* broadsheets. He was soon able to purchase a French press to print by chromolithography and his own print shop. In 1877, he achieved his first major success by publishing a map of the Russo-Turkish War for newspaper readers. His business expanded rapidly. By 1909 he was publishing 37 per cent of all *lubki* in the Russian Empire and by 1914 a quarter of all books, eight newspapers, and fourteen journals.[22] Along the way, he acquired cultural prestige by collaborating with Tolstoi's closest associate, Vladimir Chertkov (1854–1936), to found the Intermediary (*Posrednik*) publishing house in 1884, which provided morally instructive works – including Tolstoi's – for newly literate peasant readers. His daily newspaper, *The Russian Word* (*Russkoe slovo*, 1895–1917), was among the least expensive in the empire and had a print run of

19 Jeffrey Brooks, *When Russia Learned to Read: Literacy and Popular Literature, 1861–1917* (Princeton: Princeton University Press, 1985), p. 341.

20 Hugh McLean, 'Suvorin', in Victor Terras (ed.), *Handbook of Russian Literature* (New Haven: Yale University Press, 1985), p. 456.

21 A. P. Chekhov, letter to I. Ia. Pavlovskii, 22 May 1899, in *Polnoe sobranie sochinenii pisem v tridtsati tomakh* [Complete works and letters in thirty volumes], vol. VIII: *Pis'ma* [Letters] (Moscow: Nauka, 1980), p. 190.

22 Brooks, *When Russia Learned to Read*, p. 99; 'Sytin, Ivan Dmitrievich', Wikipedia (Russian edition, last modified 13 Aug. 2022), https://ru.wikipedia.org/wiki/Сытин_Иван_Дмитриевич, accessed 28 Jan. 2023.

1.2 million copies in its last year. His broadsides and chapbooks were remarkable for their quality and for their low prices as well as for their profitability, which drove competitors out of business. Among his acquisitions in the 1910s were Marks's and Suvorin's companies. His tightfistedness was legendary: he paid his typesetters by the character but would not pay them for punctuation marks. During the revolution of 1905, his workers went on strike and burned one of his printing plants. Sytin survived this setback, the nationalisation of his enterprises in 1918, and two arrests (in 1918 and 1924). He continued to manage two printing plants in Moscow, but he was unable to re-establish his firm during the short-lived period of the New Economic Policy (NEP, 1821–8), during which the Soviet government permitted the establishment of private economic ventures, and he retired in 1928.

Publishing under the Administrative-Command Economy and Beyond

The October Revolution of 1917 brought an abrupt and sweeping end to the periodicals, *lubok* trade, and publishing houses discussed in this chapter. Civil war and the radically transformational policies of the new Soviet government contributed to a severe disruption of printing and distribution until the mid-1920s, especially distribution to the countryside. Printing machinery wore out and was not easily replaced, paper production fell to 10 per cent of prewar levels, many remaining pre-revolutionary book stocks were pulped, the postal system proved inadequate, and Soviet economic policy militated against continuing the old system of pedlars. The NEP brought no restoration of a smoothly functioning system: only half of the books produced between 1921 and 1925 found purchasers, and readers were provided no equivalent of the cheap *lubochnaia* literature of the pre-revolutionary period.[23] The printing of fiction fell to 15 per cent of pre-revolutionary levels by 1922, although it did rebound to double pre-revolutionary production by 1927.[24] Books and newspapers that did appear often featured political and scientific jargon that was incomprehensible to Russia's newly literate readers.

This clearing away of prewar institutions took at least a decade, and massive state publishing operations came to take their place during the

23 Jeffrey Brooks, 'The breakdown in production and distribution of printed material, 1917–1927', in Abbott Gleason, Peter Kenez, and Richard Stites (eds.), *Bolshevik Culture: Experiment and Order in the Russian Revolution* (Bloomington: Indiana University Press, 1985), pp. 151–74.
24 Brooks, 'Breakdown', p. 159.

ensuing decades. Leonid Brezhnev would come to boast that Soviets had become the 'readingest people' (*samyi chitaiushchii narod*), but this pride in the success of literacy campaigns concealed a persistent book hunger born of chronic paper shortages, miscalculation of reader interests (and deliberate inattentiveness to them), and the stop-and-go process of five-year plans. Information on reader preferences was not made publicly available until the rebirth of literary sociology in the 1960s, and studies of the Soviet reader did not track such phenomena as access to self-publishing (*samizdat*) or to publishing abroad (*tamizdat*) (see Chapter 2.9). During these decades, publishing houses were not indifferent to the sale and distribution of their products, and while print runs could seem inversely proportional to the demand for particular editions, a number of publishing projects undertaken by the Academy of Sciences and by the State Publishing House for Literature were of broad appeal and high quality, especially such multi-volume scholarly editions as the collected works of Dostoevskii (1972–90). The state did eventually provide an approximation of *lubochnaia* literature, the *Novel-Newspaper* (*Roman-gazeta*, 1927–), founded by Maksim Gorkii (1868–1936). By the 1960s it had reached a print run of half a million copies, and it still appears twice a month.[25]

Since the collapse of the planned economy, publishing has to a large extent returned to the commercial relationships of the pre-revolutionary period, although the first post-Soviet capitalist publishers could miscalculate reader demand no less egregiously than party bureaucrats. A literary return of the repressed brought previously forbidden literature (Russian and foreign Modernism, émigré literature) and popular genres (especially detective fiction) to readers eager for new literary experiences. New publishing phenomena (such as the 'bestseller') and new means of distribution (the internet) challenged the state's former top-down organisation of literary distribution.[26] Digitisation of previously published works and online publishing now make both serious academic editions and current literature broadly accessible. Bestsellers, as Bradley Gorski has argued (see Chapter 2.10), provide an index of a fluctuating market-driven literature, but there remain alongside them vestiges of older, state-sponsored ways of literary life (e.g. multi-volume academic editions and growing state control

25 *Book Publishing in the USSR: Reports of the Delegations of US Book Publishers Visiting the USSR October 21–November 4, 1970, August 20–September 17, 1962* (Cambridge, MA: Harvard University Press, 1971), p. 119.
26 Bradley A. Gorski, 'The bestseller, or the cultural logic of postsocialism', *Slavic Review* 79.3 (2020), 613–35.

over the internet).[27] Publishing remains at once a labour of love, a risk-laden business, and a potential wellspring of social ferment.

Further Reading

Barenbaum, I. E., *Knizhnyi Peterburg: Tri veka istorii. Ocherki izdatel'skogo dela i knizhnoi torgovli* [Book Petersburg: Three centuries of history. Sketches of the publishing business and of the book trade] (St Petersburg: Kul'tInformPress, 2003).

Book Publishing in the USSR: Reports of the Delegations of US Book Publishers Visiting the USSR October 21–November 4, 1970, August 20–September 17, 1962 (Cambridge, MA: Harvard University Press, 1971).

Brooks, Jeffrey, 'The breakdown in production and distribution of printed material, 1927–1921', in Abbott Gleason, Peter Kenez, and Richard Stites (eds.), *Bolshevik Culture: Experiment and Order in the Russian Revolution* (Bloomington: Indiana University Press, 1985), pp. 151–74.

Brooks, Jeffrey, *When Russia Learned to Read: Literacy and Popular Culture, 1891–1917* (Princeton: Princeton University Press, 1985).

Gorski, Bradley A., 'The bestseller, or the cultural logic of postsocialism', *Slavic Review* 79.3 (2020), 613–35.

Grits, T., V. Trenin, and M. Nikitin, *Slovesnost' i kommertsiia (knizhnaia lavka A. F. Smirdina)* [Literature and commerce (the bookshop of A. F. Smirdin)], ed. V. B. Shklovskii and V. M. Eikhenbaum (Moscow: Federatsiia, 1929).

Kufaev, M. N., *Istoriia russkoi knigi v XIX veke* [A history of the Russian book in the nineteenth century] (Leningrad: 'Nachatki znanii', 1927).

Marker, Gary, *Publishing, Printing, and the Origins of Intellectual Life in Russia, 1770–1800* (Princeton: Princeton University Press, 1985).

McReynolds, Louise, *The News under Russia's Old Regime: The Development of a Mass-Circulation Press* (Princeton: Princeton University Press, 1991).

Tatsumi, Yukiko, and Taro Tsurami (eds.), *Publishing in Tsarist Russia: A History of Print Media from Enlightenment to Revolution* (London: Bloomsbury Academic, 2020).

27 Adam Satariano and Paul Mozur, 'Russia is censoring the internet, with coercion and black boxes', *New York Times*, 22 Oct. 2021, www.nytimes.com/2021/10/22/technology/russia-internet-censorship-putin.html, accessed 10 Nov. 2021.

2.6

Queerness

EVGENII BERSHTEIN

Russia's queer literary tradition can be seen as comprising two types of works: texts that affirmatively explore non-heteronormative sexualities and non-normative genders, and texts that engage queer themes and reflect queer sensibilities in a transparent enough way but without making sexual and gender alterity their main focus. Queer – understood in today's analytical sense as gay, lesbian, bisexual, transgender, non-binary, and gender-nonconforming – literary perspectives gained particular prominence in Russian letters as part of the fin-de-siècle Modernist aesthetic movements of Decadence and Symbolism (see Chapter 1.6). However, literary explorations of queer themes significantly pre-date the wave of interest in alternative sexualities and new sexual openness that occurred at the turn of the twentieth century, just as diverse expressions of 'sexual and gender dissent' can be found in Russian literature since its very beginning.[1] In this chapter, queerness is approached as a mechanism producing literary discourses which have their own thematics, poetics, epistemology, and pragmatics. The methods of writing sexual and gender otherness that emerged in the early Modernist period had a lasting impact on modes of literary expression, remaining influential for both émigré and underground 'Soviet' literature as well as for an increasingly vocal post-Soviet queer literature. Accordingly, the chapter will provide an overview of the longue durée of Russian literature's engagement with non-heteronormative sexuality as well as a more

---

1 The term 'sexual and gender dissent' was applied to Russian gay and lesbian history by Dan Healey in his formidable *Homosexual Desire in Revolutionary Russia: The Regulation of Sexual and Gender Dissent* (Chicago: University of Chicago Press, 2001). Simon Karlinsky, who pioneered the study of Russian gay and lesbian literature, specifically insisted on its early roots in Russian medieval writing. Semen Karlinskii, "'Vvezen iz–za granitsy . . ."? Gomoseksualizm v russkoi kul'ture i literature' ['Imported from abroad . . .'? Homosexuality in Russian culture and literature], *Literaturnoe obozrenie* [Literary review] 11 (1991), 104–7; Simon Karlinsky, 'Introduction: Russia's gay literature and history', in Kevin Moss (ed.), *Out of the Blue: Russia's Hidden Gay Literature: An Anthology* (San Francisco: Gay Sunshine Press, 1997), pp. 15–18.

extended focus on the Modernist period as a time when queerness operated as a particularly generative cultural mechanism, stimulating new modes of literary production.

At various historical periods, the non-heteronormative presence in Russian letters manifested itself in assorted ways and by different literary means. During the Neoclassicist and Romantic periods of the late eighteenth and early nineteenth centuries (see Chapters 1.3, 1.4), this presence made itself known both in libertine sex-themed poetry and through poets' curiosity, often ethnographic and orientalist, about erotic lives deviating from the accepted norm. Both provided literary reflections of same-sex desire and practices in texts which, although largely unprintable, often circulated widely among the still rather small reading public. Some genres and modes of queer literary expression originated in the customs of – and opportunities afforded by – institutions of noble privilege, such as elite single-sex educational and military establishments. Additionally, the imperial court and high society served as important institutions of worldly tolerance towards covert and occasionally unconcealed sexual eccentricity and libertinism.

During the age of Realism in the mid- to late nineteenth century (see Chapter 1.5), a fairly large urban homosexual subculture formed in Russia; this subculture became reflected in psychological prose and, as before, in bawdy poetry. In addition, towards the end of the century, in both western Europe and Russia, the emerging medical field of sexual psychopathology made sexually nonconforming patients and their social networks an object of its investigation. Studies of 'sexual psychopathy' not only provided the nomenclature and detailed accounts of psychosexual 'pathologies' to their professional readership but also gave patients a platform to speak in their own voice: forensic and psychiatric accounts of non-normative sexuality and gender commonly featured their subjects' autobiographies. These narratives were often skilfully constructed, featuring intrigue and rich psychological and social detail. In the early twentieth century, such patient accounts proliferated still further, becoming common reading among the educated public and informing some works of fiction.[2]

It was at the crossroads of scientific, aesthetic, and philosophical discourses and in the hothouse atmosphere of early twentieth-century Modernism that the Russian queer literary canon was established and its paradigm-setting texts were written. The resulting queer literary tradition, which has endured through the Soviet and into the post-Soviet period, may strike today's reader

---

2 Evgenii Bershtein, 'The discourse of sexual psychopathy in Russian Modernism', in Irina Shevelenko (ed.), *Reframing Russian Modernism* (Madison: University of Wisconsin Press, 2018), pp. 143–71.

as more metaphysically minded than its western European and American counterparts and as lacking an equivalent focus on social reform. A good deal of its creative energy was and is devoted to the contemplation of queerness as an existential condition and to the development of literary poetics that adequately express the metaphysical meanings of this condition.

Philosophically and ideologically, Russian queer writing offers an epistemological perspective that differs from and complements its mainstream western counterpart in significant ways. Interestingly, many authors central to Russian queer writing – as discussed below – remain relatively unknown outside of Russia, in contrast to several queer figures in the Russian non-literary arts. Composer Petr Tchaikovskii (1840–1893); ballet, opera, and arts impresario Sergei Diaghilev (1872–1929); and film director Sergei Eisenstein (1898–1948) all achieved worldwide renown in their lifetimes and created works that continue to influence their respective artistic fields. But even for these giants, some crucial aspects of their creativity cannot be fully understood outside the broader context of the Russian queer literary, intellectual, and aesthetic environments which helped shape their artistic sensibilities, agendas, and methods.[3]

The Eighteenth and Nineteenth Centuries: Queerness in Libertinism and Orientalism, and Queerness as an Urban Phenomenon

A few texts of bawdy poetry on homosexual themes, written in the late eighteenth and the first half of the nineteenth century and published much later, offer a straightforward – if humorous – poetic apologia for sodomy. The earliest of such texts, the undated 'Conversation between Ass-Lover and Cunt-Lover' (*Razgovor Liubozhopa s Liubopizdom*), circulated as a part of the collection entitled *Maiden's Toy* (*Devich'ia igrushka*), which was attributed to the notoriously scabrous poet Ivan Barkov (1732–1768) but in fact comprised poems of varied authorship.[4] 'Conversation' boldly mixes a semi-parodic

---

3 Recent biographies illuminate the role of queerness in the creative worlds of Tchaikovskii, Diaghilev, and Eisenstein. See Alexander Poznansky, *Tchaikovsky: The Quest for the Inner Man* (Boston: Schirmer, 1991); Aleksandr Poznanskii, *Petr Chaikovskii. Biografiia* [Petr Tchaikovskii. A biography], 2 vols. (St Petersburg: Vita Nova, 2009); Sjeng Scheijen, *Diaghilev: A Life* (Oxford: Oxford University Press, 2009); Oksana Bulgakowa, *Sergei Eisenstein: A Biography* (San Francisco: Potemkin Press, 2001).
4 'Razgovor Liubozhopa s Liubopizdom' [Conversation between ass-lover and cunt-lover], in *Devich'ia igrushka, ili Sochineniia gospodina Barkova* [A girl's toy, or the writings of Mister Barkov], ed. A. L. Zorin and N. S. Sapov (Moscow: Ladomir, 1992), pp. 242–4.

philosophical dispute about free will and freedom of sexual choice with highly graphic physiological detail rendered in comically foul language. Along with the obscene, heterosexually themed poetry attributed to Barkov (so-called Barkoviana), 'Conversation' was copied by hand and apparently had a considerable adult, male, upper-class readership in the late eighteenth and early nineteenth centuries.

In contrast to 'Conversation', the humorously pornographic works by the great Romantic poet Mikhail Lermontov (1814–1841) feature no philosophical agenda but rather reflect the libertine spirit and sexually charged atmosphere of the elite St Petersburg cavalry cadet school, where he studied and boarded. Two of Lermontov's 1834 cadet poems (*Iunkerskie poemy*) – 'Ode to the John' (*Oda k nuzhniku*) and 'To Tisenhausen' (*K Tizengauzenu*) – address sexual relations among cadets playfully yet very explicitly.[5] Not counted among Lermontov's masterpieces, these poems bring together the Barkovian tradition of poetic obscenity and the Romantic poetic idiom, setting them in the milieu of the St Petersburg all-male schools and the regiments of the Imperial Guard. Lermontov's ribald poems were published for the first time in Geneva in 1879, in the uncensored collection *Russian Eros Not for Ladies* (*Russkii Erot ne dlia dam*), which presented erotic texts emanating from the St Petersburg educational institutions for boys and young men of noble birth: the introduction listed two elite military schools – including one attended by Lermontov – and the Imperial School of Jurisprudence as being notorious for homosexual relations among their students.[6] The anonymous publisher does not mention the Page Corps – another elite institution with a similar reputation – but the longest poetic text included in the collection is the narrative poem titled 'The Adventures of a Page' (*Pokhozhdeniia pazha*), attributed to Aleksandr Shenin (1803–1855), although the attribution has been questioned by scholars.[7] This long poem depicts a busy homosexual life among the Page Corps' cadets through the eyes of a sexually adventurous young page who begins with taking other pages as lovers, then conquers the heart of the corps' colonel, and finally adopts the female gender and enjoys great erotic success in St

---

5 Mikhail Lermontov, 'Two poems', trans. Vitaly Chernetsky, in Moss (ed.), *Out of the Blue*, pp. 36–7.

6 *Eros Russe. Russkii Erot ne dlia dam* [The Russian Eros. Russian Eros not for ladies] (Geneva: n.p., 1879), p. 1.

7 'Pokhozhdenie pazha' [The adventures of a page], in *Eros Russe*, pp. 15–44; A. Shenin, 'Pokhozhdeniia pazha', in V. N. Sazhin and M. Zolotonosov (eds.), *Zanaveshennye kartinki: Antologiia russkoi erotiki* [Curtained pictures: Anthology of Russian erotic writing] (St Petersburg: Amfora, 2006), pp. 155–92. On the attribution, see Lev Klein, *Drugaia liubov': Priroda cheloveka i gomoseksual'nost'* [The other love: Human nature and homosexuality] (St Petersburg: Folio Press, 2000), pp. 547–51.

Petersburg society. The poem features two quasi-ethnographic sections in which the first-person narrator paints a picture of Persia as a paradise of same-sex love and fantasises of a similarly rich erotic existence in Russia's imperial capital.

The homoerotic poetry of Aleksandr Pushkin (1799–1837) features both orientalist and Greek stylisation, resistant to translation and deployed with astonishing mastery. Owing to Pushkin's status as Russia's national poet, his homoerotic texts were not affected by the Soviet ban on printing any direct literary expression of same-sex eroticism. For generations of Russian and Soviet students, therefore, Pushkin's poems 'From Hafez' (*Iz Gafiza*, 1829), 'Imitation of the Arabic' (*Podrazhanie arabskomu*, 1835), and 'To the Statue of a *Svaika* Player' (*Na statuiu igraiushchego v svaiku*, 1836) marked their first encounters with the literary affirmation of same-sex desire.

In 'From Hafez', the lyrical subject articulates erotic admiration for a beautiful youth and appeals to him to stay away from a battlefield in order to preserve his 'tender and timid beauty' ('prelest' negi i styda').[8] 'Imitation of the Arabic' is organised around a simile comparing a loving union between a man and a 'sweet lad, tender lad' ('otrok mily, otrok nezhnyi') to 'the kernel of a double nut / In a single shell' ('dvoinoi oreshek / Pod edinoi skorlupoi').[9] The latter image, central in the poem, is borrowed from the thirteenth-century Persian poet Saadi Shirazi; rephrasing the original, Pushkin adds a statement of amatory triumph and an entreaty to the youth to not be ashamed of having given himself to a man, both phrased in an exalted Romantic fashion.[10]

'To the Statue of a *Svaika* Player' describes Aleksandr Loganovskii's Neoclassical sculpture of a Russian peasant youth playing the village game of *svaika* (in which the player is required to throw a very large, heavy-headed iron nail into a small ring lying on the ground).[11] While the sculptor links the player of *svaika* – a game known for its sexual symbolism – to the classical

---

8 A. S. Pushkin, 'Iz Gafiza' [From Hafez], in *Sobranie sochinenii v desiati tomakh* [Collected works in ten volumes] (Moscow: Gosudarstvennoe izdatel'stvo khudozhestvennoi literatury, 1959), vol. II, p. 250.

9 Alexander Pushkin, 'Podrazhanie arabskomu' [Imitation of the Arabic], in *Sobranie sochinenii*, vol. II, p. 450 (my translation). In English see 'Imitation of the Arabic', trans. Michael Green, in Moss, *Out of the Blue*, p. 29. See also Michael Green, 'A Pushkin puzzle', in Moss (ed.), *Out of the Blue*, pp. 30–5; Michael Wachtel, *A Commentary to Pushkin's Lyrical Poetry, 1826–1836* (Madison: University of Wisconsin Press, 2011), passim.

10 Pushkin, 'Podrazhanie arabskomu', p. 450.

11 Pushkin, 'Na statuiu igraiushchego v svaiku' [To the statue of a *svaika* player], in *Sobranie sochinenii*, vol. II, p. 469. See also Wachtel, *Commentary*, pp. 367–8.

Greek ideal of a youthful athletic body, Pushkin's poem goes further in exploring the 'Greek' (and thus unavoidably homoerotic) significance of this body's effortless power and beauty. This effect is achieved through both the poem's form and its theme: Pushkin uses the classical elegiac distich and ends the poem with a vision of the *svaika* player resting after the game in the friendly embrace of a discobolus (alluding to the famous Ancient Greek sculpture of the Discobolus by Myron).

Judging by Pushkin's many jocular comments in letters and informal epistolary poetry on the 'Socratic' tastes of his writer friends, such as Arkadii Rodzianko (1793–1846) and the notorious Filipp Vigel (1786–1856), the young Pushkin felt a kind of erotic solidarity with other aristocratic libertines, regardless of their sexuality. However, in his later, more conservative period, Pushkin did not hesitate to use the tainted sexual reputations of his rivals and enemies for satirical purposes, despite adopting – as we have seen – a homoerotic perspective in some of his own poems. Pushkin's shifting – now homophile, now homophobic – poetic attitude provides a striking and rare example of queerness as a purely artistic mechanism for generating poetic meanings.

Pushkin's ethnographic interest in Muslim sexualities reached its culmination in the travel and war memoir entitled *A Journey to Arzrum* (*Puteshestvie v Arzrum*, 1829–36), where the poet provides several detailed descriptions of the fully institutionalised and normalised pederasty he witnessed among Muslim warlords in the Caucasus and Anatolia, on both sides of the 1828–9 Russo-Turkish War. In the memoir, the author also visits a harem, interviews eunuchs, talks with a castrate about the latter's physiology, and examines a 'hermaphrodite' whose anatomy he describes in Latin. Boy-loving pashas and their beautiful companions have a prominent place in Pushkin's gallery of ethnographically fascinating phenomena, and they are described in a detached and non-judgemental tone.

The notion of same-sex love as the erotic custom of an imagined Orient entered not only the writerly imagination but also the common language: the 'oriental taste' in love was a standard nineteenth-century euphemism for male homosexual relations, more prevalent even than the references to 'Greek' love. Curiously, in a short story by the Slavophile political writer Konstantin Leontiev (1831–1891), 'Khamid and Manoli' (*Khamid i Manoli*, 1869), Greece and the Orient meet in the love affair between a Cretan Christian teenager, Manoli, and his Islamic Turkish admirer, Khamid. Ethnic riots and tensions in Turkish-ruled Crete serve as a background for this distinctly ethnographic narrative.[12]

---

12 Konstantin Leontiev, 'Khamid and Manoli', trans. Gerald McCausland, in Moss (ed.), *Out of the Blue*, pp. 49–66.

In the Romantic epoch, although there were few female authors and women's writing had not yet made room for the expression of sexual attraction between women, there emerged a notable gender-nonconforming writer: assigned female at birth and named Nadezhda Durova (1783–1866), she/he lived for nearly sixty years as a man named Aleksandr Aleksandrov. As a writer, Durova/Aleksandrov used both last names, feminine (Durova) and masculine (Aleksandrov), as well as both masculine and feminine pronouns, and became a literary and cultural celebrity thanks to the memoir *Notes of a Cavalry Maiden* (*Zapiski kavalerist-devitsy*, 1836), which describes the author's life as a Hussar officer.[13] The book tells a wondrous story of a young noblewoman who escapes the expectations and restrictions imposed on her gender by society by assuming a man's identity and fighting valiantly in the Napoleonic Wars. The patriotic 'Russian Amazon' attracted attention, and Alexander I (r. 1801–25) granted her permission for military service and a new masculine name and identity, under which Durova, now Aleksandrov, continued to live.[14] The success of the memoir led to a prolific four-year period of literary production, after which Aleksandrov lived a long life as a military retiree. To this day, Durova/Aleksandrov is celebrated in Russia, where both fictional and non-fictional books, a play, a film, a museum, and two equestrian monuments have been devoted to her/him.

The sexuality of the great Romantic writer Nikolai Gogol (1809–1852) has attracted attention and caused controversy among scholars, who have examined it both biographically and philologically. Gogol did not marry, did not have affairs with women, and developed – in some of his works – the theme of the harm brought to his sensually depicted male characters by female love. It has been argued, influentially, that Gogol's works reflect his own traumatically repressed homosexuality.[15] A short fragmentary piece of lyrical prose entitled 'Nights at the Villa' (*Nochi na ville*, 1839) has become central to this debate. Its autobiographical narrator uses the idiom of erotic intimacy to express his crushing love for a dying 22-year-old friend, Count Iosif Vielgorskii, a graduate of the Page Corps.[16] 'Nights at the Villa', only

---

13 Nadezhda Durova, *The Cavalry Maiden: Journals of a Russian Officer in the Napoleonic Wars*, trans. Mary Fleming Zirin (Bloomington: Indiana University Press, 1989).

14 The notion of the 'Russian Amazon' (*russkaia amazonka*) comes from one of the initial titles for *Notes of a Cavalry Maiden* that Durova/Aleksandrov suggested to Aleksandr Pushkin, her first publisher. See Pushkin, letter to Durova, c. 10 June 1836, in *Sobranie sochinenii*, vol. X, p. 297.

15 Simon Karlinsky, *The Sexual Labyrinth of Nikolai Gogol*, 2nd edn (Chicago: University of Chicago Press, 1992).

16 N. Gogol, 'Nights at the villa', trans. Simon Karlinsky, in Moss (ed.), *Out of the Blue*, pp. 38–40.

published long after Gogol's death, adds a piercing and morbid lyrical note to the satirical, grotesque, and absurdist treatment which erotic themes receive in Gogol's major works.

The age of Realism paralleled in literature and the arts the massive social and economic shifts, including rapid urbanisation, that followed the reforms of the 1860s. By the 1870s, an urban gay culture had taken shape in major Russian cities, including a male cruising and sex trade scene occurring under the surveillance of both the police and, increasingly, the public health authorities.[17] Queer themes and characters entered the prose of the epoch's leading writers Fedor Dostoevskii (1821–1881) and Lev Tolstoi (1828–1910). In Dostoevskii, a number of interpretatively intriguing minor characters are associated with homosexuality: Sirotkin, a 'pretty boy' prisoner in *Notes from the House of the Dead* (*Zapiski iz mertvogo doma*, 1862); Trishatov, a 'pretty' youth linked to the blackmailing gang in *The Adolescent* (*Podrostok*, 1876); and Kalganov in *The Brothers Karamazov* (*Brat'ia Karamazovy*, 1881).[18] For Tolstoi, the theme of same-sex love and desire was both personally consequential and artistically significant. *Anna Karenina* (*Anna Karenina*, 1878), Tolstoi's novel focusing on the social and moral accommodation of erotic desire, features not only flashes of homoerotic sentiment experienced by numerous characters but also a gay couple, a closeted homosexual, and a society lesbian. While Tolstoi clearly wanted to present the full spectrum of desire and its fluidity, his introduction of the first Russian homosexual couple into Russian print literature also served the compositional purposes of the novel. Placed within the Vronskii scenes, the two 'inseparable' officers are shunned by their peers even in the setting of the Imperial Guard barracks, which – as Tolstoi carefully shows – permits a good deal of homoerotic atmosphere and behaviour.[19] Soon, the adulterous heterosexual protagonists, Anna and Vronskii, are also punished

17 See V. V. Bersen'ev and A. R. Markov, 'Politsiia i gei: Epizod iz epokhi Aleksandra III' [Police and gays: An episode from the epoch of Alexander III], *Risk: Al'manakh* [Risk: An almanac] 3 (1998), 105–16.

18 F. M. Dostoevskii, *Zapiski iz mertvogo doma* [Notes from the house of the dead], in *Polnoe sobranie sochinenii v tridtsati tomakh* [Complete works in thirty volumes], vol. IV (Leningrad: Nauka, 1972), pp. 38–9; Dostoevskii, *Podrostok* [The adolescent], in *Polnoe sobranie sochinenii v tridtsati tomakh*, vol. XIII (Leningrad: Nauka, 1975), p. 350. See also Igor Volgin, 'V napravlenii Sodoma' [Towards Sodom], in *Propavshii zagovor. Dostoevskii i politicheskii protsess 1849 g.* [A conspiracy that has vanished. Dostoevskii and the 1849 political trial] (Moscow: Libereia, 2000), pp. 272–98; Susanne Fusso, *Discovering Sexuality in Dostoevsky* (Evanston, IL: Northwestern University Press, 2006), pp. 42–68; Eric Naiman, 'Kalganov', *Slavic and East European Journal* 58.3 (2014), 394–418.

19 L. N. Tolstoi, *Anna Karenina* [Anna Karenina], in *Sobranie sochinenii v dvadtsati tomakh* [Collected works in twenty volumes], vol. VIII (Moscow: Gosudarstvennoe izdatel'stvo khudozhestvennoi literatury, 1963), p. 209.

for not concealing their own affair in another sexually lenient milieu. However, Tolstoi also shows the stratospheric success – in the imperial capital – of some society figures who perform their queerness or adulterous exploits with a proper balance of secrecy and candour: queer characters such as the young general Prince Serpukhovskoi (Vronskii's former classmate at the Page Corps, currently his admirer, and a kisser of soldiers) and the socialite Sappho Stolz exemplify this kind of success.

The Fin de Siècle: Queer Visibility, Queer Mysticism, and the Queer Literary Milieu

A new, modern queer visibility appeared abruptly in Russian letters, over the course of roughly a dozen years running between 1895 and 1907. This fast-growing queer openness had two main mechanisms: first, the expansion of the disciplinary fields regulating sexual dissent (psychiatric, forensic, legal, and pedagogical writing on sexual and gender 'aberrations'); and second, the flourishing of Decadence and Symbolism – Modernist artistic movements which questioned and deconstructed the existing system of sexual norms and taboos. A number of significant literary texts and events marked the rapid change of the status of queerness in literature and its generative power.

In 1892–4, the philosopher and poet Vladimir Solovev (1853–1900) published a series of essays meant for the general public and entitled *The Meaning of Love (Smysl liubvi)*. In this work, which was to become influential, he ridiculed then present-day views of sexuality and especially the new branch of psychiatry dedicated to studying less common sexual phenomena. Solovev argued that the contemporary notion of 'the norm' in sexual relations was unjustifiable both morally and philosophically. The true philosophical meaning of sexual love lay in transcending all kinds of human separateness, including the separation of the sexes. Solovev welcomed the androgyne: 'the separation of the sexes . . ., separation of the male and female elements of the human being . . . is . . . the beginning of death . . . Only the human being in its entirety can be immortal.'[20]

In 1895, the three trials of the popular British author Oscar Wilde were reported by the Russian press in excruciatingly scandalous detail.[21] The final

---

20 Vladimir Solovyov, *The Meaning of Love*, trans. Jane Marshall, rev. Thomas R. Beyer, Jr (West Stockbridge, MA: Lindisfarne Press, 1985), p. 73.
21 Evgenii Bershtein, '"Next to Christ": Oscar Wilde in Russian Modernism', in Stefano Evangelista (ed.), *The Reception of Oscar Wilde in Europe* (London: Continuum, 2010), pp. 285–300.

trial found Wilde guilty of 'gross indecency' (a legal euphemism for homosexual acts) and sentenced him to hard labour. In Russia, the mass-circulation national daily *New Times* (*Novoe vremia*, 1868–1917) – published by Aleksei Suvorin (1834–1912) – reported the trials in eighteen articles, and the rest of the Russian press followed suit. *New Times* presented Wilde's legal proceedings as a serialised psychological narrative on sexual vice, dropping hints which pointed to similarly deplorable cases at home. The initiated knew that the hints targeted Vladimir Meshcherskii (1839–1914), publisher of the conservative newspaper *Citizen* (*Grazhdanin*, 1872–9, 1882–1914) and Suvorin's competitor for political influence. Because of this political fortuity, the name of Wilde became known to virtually every educated and semi-educated Russian, despite the fact that his major works had not yet been published in Russian. The sexuality which used to be euphemistically called 'oriental' or 'Greek' received the new name of 'Oscar Wilde's tastes' (*vkusy Oskara Uail'da*) and a distinctly western cultural flavour. At that moment, Wilde became the symbol of the modern queer; a few years later, many Russian Symbolists would see him as a martyr and some even as a saint.

In 1898, Zinaida Gippius (1869–1945) – a Decadent poet and critic – spent a month in Taormina, where she befriended Baron Wilhelm von Gloeden, the famous homoerotic photographer whose pictures attracted international gay tourists to this Sicilian town (Oscar Wilde and André Gide were among von Gloeden's visitors). In Taormina, Gippius developed two love interests, one a homosexual man and the other a masculine woman. The experiences of that spring – to which Gippius would keep returning in her poetry, prose, and diaries – confirmed her sense that she could not completely identify as either a woman or a man. The fluidity and non-binary nature of her gender became a central theme of Gippius's lyrical poetry and some of her prose.[22] As a prolific and influential critic, Gippius published under her own name and under many male pseudonyms (Anton Krainii – literally, Anton 'the Extreme' – was the most popular of them). In her critical writings, Gippius developed a theory of gender, according to which masculine and feminine elements were mixed – in different proportions – in every person, regardless of their biological sex. This theory was influenced by Otto Weininger's best-selling book *Sex and Character*

---

22 Olga Matich, *Erotic Utopia: The Decadent Imagination in Russia's Fin de Siècle* (Madison: University of Wisconsin Press, 2005), pp. 162–211; Matich, 'Zinaida Gippius v Taormine: Wil'gel'm fon Gleden, Elizaveta fon Overbek i drugie' [Zinaida Gippius in Taormina: Wilhelm von Gloeden, Elizabeth von Overbeck, and others], in Ol'ga Blinova (ed.), *Merezhkovskie i Evropa* [The Merezhkovskiis and Europe] (Moscow: IMLI RAN, 2023). See also Jenifer Presto, *Beyond the Flesh: Alexander Blok, Zinaida Gippius, and the Symbolist Sublimation of Sex* (Madison: University of Wisconsin Press, 2008).

(1903). Like Weininger, Gippius had a rather negative view of the so-called feminine element: it was too biological, too carnal, and too material. The co-existence of masculine and feminine aspects within the lyrical subject and lyrical object provided plots for some of Gippius's best poems, such as 'She' (*Ona*) and 'You' (*Ty*), both written in 1905. Structurally, both poems are built on a play with the gendered grammatical forms of the Russian language; the traumatic duality of the bi-gendered self is expressed by means of language itself.

In 1906, the leading literary journal of Russian Symbolism – *Libra* (*Vesy*, 1904–9) – published a poetic cycle entitled *Alexandrian Songs* (*Aleksandriiskie pesni*) by Mikhail Kuzmin (1872–1936), and later that year it dedicated an entire separate issue to his novel *Wings* (*Kryl'ia*). In 1907, *The Balance* featured Kuzmin's programmatic lyrical cycle *This Summer's Love* (*Liubov' etogo leta*). Because of the openly gay message of the novel and the intensely homoerotic atmosphere of Kuzmin's poetry, the press declared Kuzmin 'the Russian Oscar Wilde'. Although Wilde's tragic fate was dramatically at odds with Kuzmin's message of ecstatic happiness, retrospectively one indeed sees in Kuzmin a foundational figure for Russian gay culture, just as Wilde became for its western European counterpart.

In a powerful and original poetic voice, Kuzmin articulated his pro-gramme for a full, bright, and vibrant life, in which the delights of art met the delights of sensual love. Contemporaries were astonished by Kuzmin's absolute openness about the orientation of his love life, the poetic declaration of which was made without the Decadent embrace of sickness or Symbolism's obscure mysticism. Virtuosic and original, Kuzmin's early poems immediately made him a leading voice in Russian letters. Simultaneously, his novel *Wings* enjoyed a *succès de scandale* and made Kuzmin Russia's first openly gay celebrity.[23]

Wings marks the point when Russian male homosexual subculture began to enter the cultural mainstream. It is built around the coming-of-age story of Vania Smurov, a middle-class teenager who learns to accept his budding love for a mysterious Russian Englishman named Larion Shtrup. In his mini-Bildungsroman, Kuzmin advances a philosophical argument in favour of fully consummated loving unions between men and presents the ecstatically

---

23 Mikhail Kuzmin, *Wings*, trans. Hugh Aplin (London: Hesperus Press, 2007). See also Evgenii Bershtein, 'An Englishman in the Russian bathhouse: Mikhail Kuzmin's *Wings* and the Russian tradition of homoerotic writing', in Lada Panova and Sarah Pratt (eds.), *The Many Facets of Mikhail Kuzmin: A Miscellany* (Bloomington, IN: Slavica, 2011), pp. 75–87.

experienced, love- and art-filled homosexual life as an ideal rooted in classical Greece and the Italian Renaissance. Despite its symbolic connections to past cultures, Kuzmin affirms this erotic scenario as achievable for his forward-looking contemporaries and therefore as emphatically modern. Moreover, in *Wings*, a dreamy vision of a Hellenically coloured erotic utopia rises from the pictures of everyday life in St Petersburg and Russia, which include more than a few realistically rendered details of urban gay life. Whereas contemporaries were shocked by the novel's references to the gay sex trade occurring in public bathhouses and the novel's worldly acceptance of this and other realities of modern sexuality, these offending passages would seem perfectly decorous to most readers today. On the other hand, some of these same readers may well be troubled by the young age of the novel's protagonist: Vania Smurov is in his mid-teens when he decides to enter into a relationship with Shtrup.

Mikhail Kuzmin has remained a central figure in the Russian queer canon to the present day. Apart from his early lyrical poems and *Wings*, his late, nearly surrealist long poem 'The Trout Breaks the Ice' (*Forel' razbivaet led*, 1929) is particularly influential and widely considered a masterpiece.[24] After the revolution, Kuzmin gradually became a persona non grata in Soviet literature. His life partner, the writer Iurii Iurkun (1895–1938), outlived Kuzmin only to be arrested and executed during Stalin's purges. The multi-volume scholarly publication of Kuzmin's expansive and brilliant diary – another major work of his – began in 2000 and is still ongoing.[25]

In pointing towards classical antiquity and the Renaissance as sources of aesthetic and social ideals for the homosexual 'new people' (see Chapter 4.7) he imagined in *Wings*, Kuzmin was in league with other Modernists who sought archaic genealogies for their artistic movement and used them to shape aesthetic form. In the 1900s, the leading theoretical voice in this movement belonged to the Symbolist poet, philosopher, and classicist Viacheslav Ivanov (1866–1949). Developing the ideas of Nietzsche, Ivanov called for the revival of the orgiastic and elemental Dionysian element in contemporary culture. As a classical scholar, Ivanov investigated the ancient

---

24 Mikhail Kuzmin, 'The trout breaks the ice', in Michael Green and Stanislav Shvabrin (ed. and trans.), *Selected Writings* (Lewisburg, PA: Bucknell University Press, 2005), pp. 102–23.

25 Mikhail Kuzmin, *Dnevnik 1905–1907* [Diary 1905–1907], ed. N. A. Bogomolov and S. V. Shumikhin (St Petersburg: Izdatel'stvo Ivana Limbakha, 2000); Kuzmin, *Dnevnik 1908–1915* [Diary 1908–1915], ed. N. A. Bogomolov and S. V. Shumikhin (St Petersburg: Izdatel'stvo Ivana Limbakha, 2009); Kuzmin, *Dnevnik 1934* [Diary 1934], ed. G. A. Morev, 2nd edn (St Petersburg: Izdatel'stvo Ivana Limbakha, 2011).

cults of Dionysus and discovered in them a precursor for early Christianity. He interpreted the tragic figure of Oscar Wilde as a symbol of both the Dionysian 'unbridling of sexual passions' and Christian redemptive suffering; in Ivanov's eyes, Wilde stood 'next to Christ'.[26] Ivanov called for a revival of Dionysus that would be religious in nature but free from the restrictions of Christian moral doctrine. Chief among the restrictive social rules ripe for Dionysian destruction were those of normative gender and sexual propriety. Ivanov fused the Nietzschean vision of the Dionysian with the Russian philosophical concept of *vseedinstvo* (all-unity), as developed by Solovev. He followed Solovev in envisioning the androgynous fusion of the sexes as a necessary part of the process leading towards the future universal unity.

Russian Symbolists developed a theory and practice of 'creating life' (*zhiznetvorchestvo*) as if it were art. The breaking of gender boundaries and sexual barriers was often a part of this project. In the spirit of life-creation, both Ivanov and his wife Lidiia Zinoveva-Annibal (1866–1907) had same-sex romantic involvements: Ivanov's love for and courtship of the young poet Sergei Gorodetskii (1884–1967) was documented in both Ivanov's diary and his poetic cycle *Eros* (*Eros*, 1906). The same year, Zinoveva-Annibal authored Russia's first work of lesbian prose: the novella *33 Abominations* (*33 uroda*). Whereas Ivanov's poetry was complex, packed with classical allusions, and extremely high-brow, Zinoveva-Annibal's prose was received by some readers as part of the growing genre of popular erotic fiction, adding a queer angle and a Platonic philosophical ambition to it. Written in a titillating style, *33 Abominations* made its author the subject of a criminal prosecution for pornography.[27] The short-lived prosecution briefly delayed sales of the book but helped its publicity by further increasing the work's appeal for a readership increasingly fascinated by the 'sex question' (as the heated debate in the press of 1906–8 on the social aspects of sexuality was named). A few years later, *The Wrath of Dionysus* (*Gnev Dionisa*, 1910), the best-selling novel by Evdokiia Nagrodskaia (1866–1930), would also fictionalise a sexual theory, namely Otto Weininger's model of universal bisexuality. Sensationalist and schematic, Nagrodskaia's novel successfully realised the commercial potential of light, entertaining prose that treated modern themes

26 Viacheslav Ivanov, 'Nitsshe i Dionis' [Nietzsche and Dionysus], in *Po zvezdam. Borozdy i mezhi* [By the stars. Furrows and boundaries] (Moscow: Astrel', 2007), p. 32.

27 Lydia Zinovieva-Annibal, *Thirty-Three Abominations*, trans. Samuel D. Cioran, in Carl Proffer and Ellendea Proffer (eds.), *The Silver Age of Russian Culture* (Ann Arbor, MI: Ardis, 1975), pp. 325–48.

of androgyny, gender fluidity, and same-sex attraction.[28] Kuzmin, who was personally close to both Zinoveva-Annibal and Nagrodskaia, also produced many volumes of this type of mass-appeal fiction as a way to earn a living. His contemporary-themed light prose was far more refined than Nagrodskaia's, however, and – perhaps for this reason – it did not sell as well.

In 1905–6, Ivanov and Zinoveva-Annibal hosted Russian Modernism's most influential literary salon in their St Petersburg apartment, 'the Tower'. In 1906, they also assembled a more intimate homoerotic circle named the Hafez. Among the members were Kuzmin, Gorodetskii, the artists Konstantin Somov (1869–1939) and Leon Bakst (1866–1924), the critic Valter Nuvel (1871–1949). A few years later, the enterprising Nagrodskaia had her own salon with a homoerotic ambiance. The fiction and art works produced in the relaxed atmosphere of the St Petersburg bohemia testified to the dramatically increased visibility and acceptance of non-normative sexuality in this milieu.

A weightier and even more consequential interpretation of queer desire and lives was offered by a thinker who was connected to the Symbolist bohemia only tangentially. Vasilii Rozanov (1856–1919) – a brilliant and controversial journalist and prolific philosophical writer who was occasionally called 'the Russian Nietzsche' – translated his virtual obsession with the sex question into the treatise *People of the Moonlight: Metaphysics of Christianity* (*Liudi lunnogo sveta. Metafizika khristianstva*, 1911), in which he developed the theory of 'spiritual sodomy' and its cultural significance. By spiritual sodomy, Rozanov meant unrealised or repressed same-sex desire and a lack of sexual desire for the opposite sex. In this work, Rozanov claims that a small but extremely influential part of humanity – 'spiritual sodomites', 'people of the moonlight', or 'third sex' – experience (often unconsciously) predominantly same-sex desire. According to Rozanov, though largely failing to act on their desire, 'spiritual sodomites' feel the same aversion to the heterosexual act and procreation as the 'normal' person feels towards sodomy. Excluded from procreative living and its rewards and satisfaction, Rozanov's 'people of the moonlight' sublimate their inverted sexuality into spiritual, cultural, and political activities, making an enormous impact on these spheres. Rozanov credits them, for instance, with creating Christianity and the ascetic Christian civilisation. At the same time, he decries them for suppressing the expression of heterosexual desire; according to Rozanov, 'spiritual sodomites' fill the

---

28 Evdokia Nagrodskaia, *The Wrath of Dionysus: A Novel*, trans. Louise McReynolds (Bloomington: Indiana University Press, 1997).

ranks of monastic clergy and shape religious doctrine so as to limit and denigrate the heterosexual, reproductive core of being.

In Rozanov's view, this omnipresent and culturally prominent 'third sex' possesses a peculiar psychological and sometimes biological constitution. While the feminine and masculine elements co-exist in every person, the moonlight person is distinguished by the stronger presence of the opposite sex in his or her psyche and possibly his or her body as well. The moonlight person is not necessarily a strongly effeminate male or masculine female. According to Rozanov, between such extremes as the virile man and 'man-maiden' (*muzhedeva*) stands a continuum of men, in whom the degree of heterosexual desire progressively decreases and the degree of 'sodomitic' inclination progressively increases. Rozanov saw the duality and co-existence of genders not only as the most fundamental feature of human ontology but also as part and parcel of the divinity: 'there are two Gods – His *masculine* side and the *feminine* one'.[29]

Rozanov had a valuable interlocutor in Father Pavel Florenskii (1882–1937), a theologian and polymath who debated the metaphysics of homosexuality in his voluminous correspondence with Rozanov; contributed an anonymous afterword to the second edition of *People of the Moonlight*; and in his main theological work, *The Pillar and Ground of the Truth* (*Stolp i utverzhdenie istiny*, 1914), imagined an Orthodox community made up of chaste, loving male couples whose unions were blessed through the ancient Christian rite of *adelphopoiesis* (brother-making).[30] Written as a set of letters to a male friend, Florenskii's 'theodicy' stunned many contemporary readers by its tone of intense longing for same-sex attachment, heard distinctly amidst Florenskii's scholastically refined theologising.

Florenskii and Rozanov learned from each other; for the latter, the baring of his soul (and body) in fragmentary, confessional, contradictory, often sex-themed notes – intensely personal and metaphysical at the same time – became a trademark literary method. Rozanov included many reflections on queer sexuality in his books written this way – most notably *Solitaria* (*Uedinennoe*, 1912) and *Fallen Leaves* (*Opavshie list'ia*, 1913–15). The author's reflections on queerness were not as formative for these works as they were for *People of the Moonlight*, nor did they form a systematic argument. However, Rozanov's

29 Vasilii Rozanov, *Liudi lunnogo sveta. Metafizika khristianstva* [People of the moonlight. Metaphysics of Christianity], 2nd edn (St Petersburg: n.p., 1913), p. 31.
30 Pavel Florensky, *The Pillar and Ground of the Truth: An Essay in Orthodox Theodicy in Twelve Letters*, trans. Boris Jakim (Princeton: Princeton University Press, 1997), pp. 284–330.

genre of sundry notes – in which a complex, idiosyncratic, and tragic personality of the author transpires through the minutiae of his physical, emotional, and intellectual life – turned out to be enormously influential in Russian letters in general and Russian queer writing in particular.

Kuzmin's celebration of gay love as a bright path leading to a sensual and artistic bliss and Rozanov's dark ('moonlight') religious metaphysics of queer desire produced two main competing paradigms for Russian queer literature. These models opposed each other not only philosophically but also in their literary form. In *Wings*, Kuzmin built the narrative of coming out to suggest a social, aesthetic, and ethical accommodation of homosexuality; he ended the novel with a scene of sunny stasis. This model contrasts with Rozanov's vision of unending tragic struggle between the procreative element and the moonlight one, which became associated with his signature genre of metaphysically tinged fragmentary notes focused on sundry quotidian psychological, literary, and existential themes. It was precisely that latter prosaic genre, known as *rozanovshchina*, which generations of queer Russian writers – as discussed below – adopted and developed further, aware of the fact that it carried in itself the memory of Rozanov's philosophy of sex.

After the Silver Age

After the Silver Age giants Kuzmin and Ivanov, the later Modernist period saw the appearance of other important poets whose works thematised and occasionally problematised queer desire. In her poetic cycle *Girlfriend* (*Podruga*, 1914–15), Marina Tsvetaeva (1892–1941) addressed her then lover Sofiia Parnok (1885–1933) – a significant poet in her own right, known as 'Russia's Sappho'.[31] Later, in emigration, the bisexual Tsvetaeva discussed same-sex love in her French-language essay 'Letter to the Amazon' (*Lettre à l'Amazon*, 1932–4), directed to the celebrity lesbian writer and hostess Natalie Clifford Barney. In that essay, Tsvetaeva draws a picture of a lesbian relationship falling apart tragically because of the impossibility for two women to conceive a child together.[32] Tsvetaeva's final prose work – *The Tale of Sonechka* (*Povest' o Sonechke*, 1937), a memoir – reimagines the life of young Moscow bohemia in 1918–19, depicting the poet's Platonic love affair with

---

31 Diana Lewis Burgin, *Sophia Parnok: The Life and Work of Russia's Sappho* (New York: New York University Press, 1994).

32 Marina Tsvetaeva, '*Mon frère féminin*: Letter to the Amazon', trans. Gaëlle Cogan and A'Dora Phillips, *Kenyon Review*, n.s., 35.4 (2013), 118–36.

actress Sofia Gollidei, which occurred amidst the extreme privations and intense creativity of the civil war period.

Nikolai Kliuev (1884–1937), a prominent Silver Age poet, addressed same-sex eros in his characteristically stylised archaic diction of peasant poetry. In the 1930s, Kliuev's poetic cycle *What the Night Cedars Rustle About* (*O chem shumiat nochnye kedry*, 1930–2) uniquely combined homoerotic themes with praise for the revolution and new Soviet life.[33] Male homosexuality was legal in Soviet Russia from 1922 until 1933–4, when Stalin recriminalised it. Kliuev's openness about his personal life, his political status as a 'fellow traveller on the right' (*pravyi poputchik*), and his bold attempts to publish his love poetry led to his 1934 arrest (along with that of his young boyfriend), criminal prosecution, and exile.[34] Kliuev was re-arrested and shot during the Great Terror.

In Stalin's Soviet Union, queer literature could exist only underground, and in the late Soviet period, it could circulate only in *samizdat* (unofficial self-publication) or in illegally smuggled foreign editions (*tamizdat*) (see Chapter 2.9). Two important writers, Lidiia Ginzburg (1902–1990) and Evgenii Kharitonov (1941–1981), integrated the impossibility of publishing their writings into their very poetics, much influenced by Rozanov's genre of 'private' notes and his view of queer people possessing a dark and special ontological status. They developed Rozanov's private, fragmentary, proto-existentialist narrative in two somewhat different directions: where Ginzburg cultivated the genre of pseudo-impersonal analytical miniatures, written – for a long time – for the drawer, Kharitonov produced short prose texts, confessional and stylised at the same time, some of which were literally unprintable (hard, if not impossible, to typeset due to his creative use of the typewriter). Like their author, Kharitonov's unprintable texts were meant to exist only marginally.

Ginzburg, a literary scholar by profession, was private about her homosexuality. She wrote most of her non-scholarly texts as prose miniatures or fragments, calling them 'notes' (*zapisi*). While fitting the category of non-fiction, these are neither diaries nor memoirs. Rather, they form a new, experimental genre of psychological literature, in which testimony and psychological analysis – including the narrator's self-analysis – converge to portray a historically and socially shaped human reality. Ginzburg's influential *Notes of a Blockade Person* (*Zapiski blokadnogo cheloveka*, 1984) examines the experience of surviving the German siege of Leningrad during the Second

---

33 Gleb Morev, *Osip Mandel'shtam: Fragmenty literaturnoi biografii* [Osip Mandelshtam: Fragments of a literary biography] (Moscow: Novoe izdatel'stvo, 2022), p. 106.

34 Morev, *Osip Mandel'shtam*, pp. 96–119 (quotation on p. 104).

World War.[35] Working on this text for several decades, Ginzburg gradually excised the more transparently autobiographical material and created a generalised 'blockade person', a masculine subject of third-person narration (see Chapter 3.10). She used similar depersonalising narrative techniques in her 'Conversations about Love' (*Razgovory o liubvi*, 1930s–62). These overheard Socratic dialogues (conversations) address permutations of queer desire, but – as in *Notes of a Blockade Person* – the narrative alter ego uses the masculine grammatical gender and generalising analytical formulas: the alter ego is referred to as 'person' (*chelovek*), a grammatically masculine word in Russian.[36] In this way, Ginzburg's analysis of ever-doomed queer love reveals the fluidity of gender while concealing the author's lesbianism.

Whereas Ginzburg lived to old age and saw – late in her life – the crumbling of the oppressive Soviet institutions, the publication of her many works, and considerable public recognition, Kharitonov's life was short, and his lifetime renown was limited to the Moscow theatre and unofficial literary worlds. Most of his writings – produced in 1969–80 and in many genres – fit into one compact volume, *Under House Arrest* (*Pod domashnim arestom*, 1981), which Kharitonov collected shortly before his death.[37] Kharitonov's texts circulated in the unofficial network of *samizdat* and *tamizdat* in the 1980s but were picked up by the mass-circulation press in the early 1990s to a strong critical response. In these texts – largely first-person, fragmentary, vaguely autobiographical narratives – Kharitonov creates an intensely tragic picture of life in the Soviet gay underground and portrays gay desire as being as intense and refined as it is futile and dangerous. Kharitonov's texts are shockingly explicit, ideologically illiberal in the Rozanovian tradition (which rejects western notions of freedom and rights), inimitably original in tone, and piercingly emotional. A number of them – 'Oven' (*Dukhovka*, pub. 1979), 'Alesha Serezha' (*Alesha Serezha*, pub. 1985), 'The Leaflet' (*Listovka*, pub. 1985), and 'Tears on the Flowers' (*Slezy na tsvetakh*, pub. 1981) – were proclaimed 'gay classics' immediately upon their publication, although some post-Soviet critics objected to the label, fearing that

---

35 Lydia Ginzburg, *Notes from the Blockade*, trans. Alan Myers, rev. Emily Van Buskirk (London: Vintage Classics, 2016).

36 Lydia Ginzburg, 'Conversations about love', in Emily Van Buskirk and Andrei Zorin (eds.), *Lydia Ginzburg's Alternative Literary Identities: A Collection of Articles and New Translations* (Oxford: Peter Lang, 2012), pp. 343–52. See also Emily Van Buskirk, 'Marginality in the mainstream: Lesbian love in the third person', in *Lydia Ginzburg's Prose: Reality in Search of Literature* (Princeton: Princeton University Press, 2016), chap. 3.

37 Evgenii Kharitonov, *Pod domashnim arestom: Sobranie proizvedenii* [Under house arrest: Collected works], 2nd edn, ed. Gleb Morev (Moscow: Glagol, 2005); English translation in Yevgeny Kharitonov, *Under House Arrest*, trans. Arch Tait (London: Serpent's Tail, 1997).

it would undermine Kharitonov's standing in the national literary canon. Retrospectively, one could argue that their fear was justified and that the quick adoption of Kharitonov in the 1990s as a queer icon may have precluded his becoming a part of the national literary canon, despite the significance and impact of his works.

The late 1980s and early 1990s saw the appearance of institutions of queer literary publishing. Along with the anarchistic, rude, and scandalous *It's Me, Eddie* (*Eto ia – Edichka*, 1979, first published in Russia in 1991) by Eduard Limonov (1943–2020), Kharitonov's posthumous 1993 collection *Tears on the Flowers* (*Slezy na tsvetakh*) was among the very early books brought out by the new queer-oriented publisher Glagol, privately owned by poet Aleksandr Shatalov (1957–2018). For Shatalov and Iaroslav Mogutin (1974–), two writers involved in the production of Kharitonov's *Tears on the Flowers*, this signature project became a stepping stone towards significant careers in queer literature.

With male homosexuality quietly decriminalised in 1993, Russian culture seemed increasingly queer-friendly in the decades immediately following the collapse of the Soviet Union; the cultural mainstream appeared to be integrating LGBT writing. Notable among many widely accessible queer literary publications were the periodical almanac *Mitia's Journal* (*Mitin zhurnal*, 1985–2020) and books by the publisher Kolonna. Directed by the journalist Dmitrii Volchek (1964–), both *Mitia's Journal* and Kolonna published a stream of remarkable contemporary Russian queer-themed prose by such authors as Aleksandr Ilianen (1958–), Aleksandr Markin (1974–), Sergei Ukhanov (1975–), and Margarita Meklina (1972–).

In poetry, Lida Iusupova (1963–), Dmitrii Kuzmin (1968–), and Oksana Vasiakina (1989–) broke new ground by directly and effectively engaging the themes of contemporary sexual and gender politics. Vasiakina also authored the critically acclaimed novel *Wound* (*Rana*, 2021): having absorbed the Russian queer poetics of fragment, Vasiakina's autobiographical text takes the reader into the thematically new territory of working-class life in the remote corners of Putin's Russia. Vasiakina's mixing of the grimy social physiology of Russian life with direct descriptions of the physiology of sex and body stunned and impressed many critics.

At the start of the 2020s, Russian queer literature – including its growing politically active segment – was more widespread and vibrant than ever. However, as the Russian state has taken an increasingly sharp far-right political turn, queer authors have found themselves in an uncertain and potentially vulnerable situation. Direct queer expression is again under social

and political pressure in Russia. Still, there can be no doubt that both the thematic concerns of Russian queer literature (such as the metaphysics of sexuality and gender) and its creative methods (such as the poetics of existential fragment) maintain their high cultural and literary relevance, generating new texts and meanings.

Further Reading

Baer, Brian James, *Other Russias: Homosexuality and the Crisis of Post-Soviet Identity* (New York: Palgrave Macmillan, 2009).

Engelstein, Laura, *The Keys to Happiness: Sex and the Search for Modernity in Fin-de-Siècle Russia* (Ithaca: Cornell University Press, 1992).

Healey, Dan, *Homosexual Desire in Revolutionary Russia: The Regulation of Sexual and Gender Dissent* (Chicago: University of Chicago Press, 2001).

Matich, Olga, *Erotic Utopia: The Decadent Imagination in Russia's Fin de Siècle* (Madison: University of Wisconsin Press, 2005).

Moss, Kevin (ed.), *Out of the Blue: Russia's Hidden Gay Literature: An Anthology* (San Francisco: Gay Sunshine Press, 1997).

2.7

The Censor

POLLY JONES

In characterising the censor, it is perhaps easier to ask who did *not* participate in censorship of Russian and Soviet literature. For much of the imperial and Soviet eras, censorship was enshrined in law and entrusted, in theory, to a single state institution. In practice, however, censorship in both periods was enacted by a much broader range of institutions and individuals. In any analysis of censorship in the region, including this one, the censor therefore quickly becomes the censors, plural. What effects, then, did these many censors have on literature and the literary process? In many or indeed most cases, they inflicted collective, cumulative damage to texts. However, censorial authority could also be contested or dispersed precisely because so many different agents were de facto assigned censorial roles. Robert Darnton's comparative study of international censorship practices emphasises their ubiquitous 'network[s]' and 'negotiations' and their irreducibly 'human system'.[1] While not denying the aspiration to total control of publications, nor the profound asymmetry of power relations within Russian and Soviet literature, this chapter similarly analyses censorship as a dynamic human process embedded in a complex literary world.

The imperial era not only established censorship as a legitimate and enduring state practice but also embedded some of the institutional and interpersonal complexity that has characterised its operations ever since. Nonetheless, scholars largely concur that Soviet censorship was unprecedented in its scope and ambition and, consequently, in the huge range of institutional and individual actors that it came to encompass: it has even been termed an 'omnicensorship'.[2] In the Soviet era – the main

---

1 Robert Darnton, *Censors at Work: How States Shaped Literature* (New York: W. W. Norton, 2014), p. 233.
2 Marianna Tax Choldin, 'Closing and opening and closing: Reflections on the Russian media', in Miranda Remnek (ed.), *The Space of the Book: Print Culture in the Russian Social Imagination* (Toronto: University of Toronto Press, 2017), pp. 281–300.

focus of this chapter – the functionaries of Glavlit, or the Main Administration for Literary and Publishing Affairs (*Glavnoe upravlenie po delam literatury i izdatel'stv*), were the only formally designated censors. However, their functions were supplemented or duplicated by others with prerogatives to intervene in the publication process: editors; party departments and officials, including the party leader; creative unions; and non-literary institutions with a particular stake in a text, such as state ministries or academic institutions. Writers themselves also often engaged, willingly or under duress, in editing of their own texts that amounted to censorship. This astonishing and bewildering multiplicity of censorial agents has meant that Soviet censorship has often been conceptualised as a 'many-tiered' or 'pyramid' structure, through every stage of which texts were filtered, and progressively impoverished.[3] However, this vertical model does not fully capture the complexity of the system: each type of Soviet censor had a broadly distinct sphere and mode of activity, and most – apart from the party leader – could not claim total authority over a text. As such, Soviet censorship is an illuminating example of how the aspiration to total control can lead to the proliferation of different agents and modes of censorship, and produce unpredictable outcomes.[4]

This chapter will first distinguish among different censors and roles within the censorship process, and then examine the nature and effects of their interactions. Very often, these multifaceted interventions were destructive and distressing. However, censorship decisions were also characterised by a certain unpredictability, which not only stoked consistent criticism of censorship as arbitrary but also encouraged some writers and editors to keep playing the uncertain game of pushing texts past censors and through to publication. The distinctive forms of writing, of reading, and of texts themselves which resulted from these negotiations are examined in the final section of the chapter.

---

3 Arlen Blium, *A Self-Administered Poison: The System and Functions of Soviet Censorship* (Oxford: European Humanities Research Centre, 2003), pp. 2–3 and passim; cf. Arlen Blium, *Russkie pisateli o tsenzure i tsenzorakh: Ot Radishcheva do nashikh dnei, 1790–1990* [Russian writers on censorship and censors: From Radishchev to the present day, 1790–1990] (St Petersburg: Poligraf, 2011), pp. 424–30.

4 Cf. Michel Hockx, *Questions of Style: Literary Societies and Literary Journals in Modern China, 1911–1937* (Leiden: Brill, 2003).

Mechanisms and Institutions

Censorship in Russia was first institutionalised in the last years of the eighteenth century when Catherine II (r. 1762–96) ordered the closing of private printing presses and the opening of censors' offices in major cities of the Russian Empire. By 1804, when Alexander I (r. 1801–25) enacted the first statute on censorship, printed matter had been circulating for over two centuries. For the next century, all texts were subject to censors' post-publication scrutiny, and – especially in the era of Nicholas I (r. 1825–55) – to stringent pre-publication checks and cuts as well. While less bureaucratically complex (or muddled) than the multitude of Soviet censors examined below, tsarist censorship was hardly the work of a single institution or type of censor either (see Chapter 2.5).

The original censors' offices were staffed by representatives of church, academia, and court. The Holy Synod retained a distinct sphere of censorial authority over all texts considered religious, even after the establishment of the Chief Administration of Press in 1865, which encompassed all other censorship activity (though now, at this time, limited to post-publication checks). Criteria for non-ecclesiastical censorship varied in content and stringency but broadly sought to block any works that disrespected, or threatened to destabilise through sedition the tsarist system and its core values. As in the Soviet era, concerns about 'harmful tendencies' could be used to justify a wide range of censorship decisions, from the requirement for adherence to the official ideology of 'autocracy, orthodoxy, and nationality' in the 1820s and 1830s, to what Daniel Balmuth describes as an uneasy tolerance for some diversity of opinion in publications of the second half of the nineteenth century.[5]

By 1917, when the Bolsheviks overthrew this system, pre-print censorship had been de jure absent for over a decade (having been abolished in the wake of the 1905 revolution). Yet the Bolsheviks' promises of freedom of expression held for only a few days. The establishment of state control of all publishing on Soviet territory got under way very early in the civil war that followed the Bolshevik Revolution; indeed, this nationalisation of publishing and the simultaneous re-emergence of military and state censorship was initially couched as a wartime necessity. After the end of the civil war, the 1922 institutionalisation of the state censorship authority, Glavlit, reinforced the dawning sense that the Bolsheviks would create a more encompassing and

---

5 David Balmuth, *Censorship in Russia, 1865–1905* (Washington, DC: University Press of America, 1979).

repressive system of pre- and post-publication censorship than the tsarist system, staffed by a new breed of censors. Indeed, this system endured until 1991.

The codification of obligatory pre- and post-publication censorship proceeded apace in the 1920s, producing some major casualties even in this supposedly liberal era, including Mikhail Bulgakov's (1891–1940) *Heart of a Dog* (*Sobach'e serdtse*, comp. 1925) and Boris Pilniak's (1894–1938) *Tale of the Unextinguished Moon* (*Povest' o nepogashennoi lune*, 1926), both banned as political allegories – of the project of creating the new Soviet person (see Chapter 4.7) and of the suspicious death in 1925 of leading Bolshevik Mikhail Frunze, respectively. However, only a major reorganisation of Glavlit in 1930–1 fully institutionalised its role. From that point onwards, a Glavlit plenipotentiary was installed in every publishing institution in the country, effectively becoming its political editor. All works intended for publication needed to be brought to the secret office of the censor, and a stamp of approval or 'visa' had to be issued before printing could begin. Glavlit also had its own headquarters in central Moscow, which inter alia examined cases escalated from individual institutions and organised the implementation of Central Committee censorship directives. A growing network of republican and regional censorship authorities did the same locally.

These formally designated censors formed a huge network across the Soviet Union: by 1955, Glavlit boasted a staff of nearly 7,000. Employees were comparatively well-paid but bore a heavy workload of checks on all proposed publications as well as post-publication removals of works that had been deemed unacceptable from bookshops and libraries. In a typical year, Glavlit would identify potential problems in many thousands of unpublished and already published texts: over the course of the Second World War, for example, censors made 2.2 million interventions in texts submitted for their scrutiny, including prohibition of more than 80,000. Their reports to higher authorities expressed pride in the sheer volume of pages checked and a desire to overfulfil norms for efficient and effective censorial scrutiny.

The details of how this work should be implemented for each text were copiously (if confidentially) articulated in party-state guidelines and reinforced by continuous training. Censors were tasked, first and foremost, with combing texts for 'secret' information: that is, checking that nothing in the manuscript was listed in the 'Summary' (*Perechen'*), a list of forbidden references, encompassing sensitive geographical information, silenced historical data, and many other taboos, and widely referred to as the 'Talmud'. This list grew year on year: in 1930, for example, it expanded to include

references to the recent campaign of repression against rich peasants (kulaks), the activities of the Secret Police (OGPU), suicides, fires, and explosions.

However, Glavlit's pre- and post-publication checks also sought, more broadly, to verify that a text was not pornographic, liable to stoke religious or national fanaticism, or subversive of Soviet ideology. Herman Ermolaev categorises these tasks, broadly, as 'puritanical' and 'political' censorship.[6] The latter was the aspect of Glavlit's work that most resembled the aspirations of the tsarist censors. Unlike decisions on secrecy, there was no single bible to guide Glavlit's political assessments, though censors drew on authoritative texts such as the official party history textbook (which was the *Short Course of the History of the Communist Party* for much of the Stalin era) and party policies on literature and culture as well as consultations with top-tier institutions such as the Institute of Marx, Engels, Lenin, and Stalin (IMELS).

Certain aspects of these censorship decisions were non-negotiable. Glavlit censors always possessed clear prerogatives to ban a text or to send it back for reworking. As its informal name suggests, the 'Talmud' was the authoritative source on individual taboos, and only Glavlit employees had access to this highly sensitive document. As such, their decisions on violations of secrecy were not subject to question: any such information, once circled with the censor's red pencil, had to be cut as a condition of publication.

By contrast, Glavlit did not have exclusive authority to define a text's status vis-à-vis the broader Soviet censorial criteria of ideological benefit or harm and adherence to Socialist Realism, even though their 'remarks of a political-ideological character' about these transgressions were issued alongside the mandatory cuts to 'secrets', suggesting that both were equally obligatory for the editor to enforce. Glavlit's remarks targeted a wide range of alleged infractions. Texts would routinely be sent back or banned outright on the grounds that their central protagonists were not sufficiently positive or heroic, or that they even seemed immoral. Similarly, a depressing or pessimistic view of contemporary Soviet urban or rural life often doomed texts to a lengthy purgatory or prohibition, with censors citing relevant party policies to refute the author's apparent views. Meanwhile, Glavlit's remarks on non-contemporary subject matter would point out unacceptable discrepancies with the official historical narrative. Some infractions were clear: censors could confidently ban works praising tsarism or mourning its demise, for example. Other historical material demanded more detailed deliberation or

---

6 Herman Ermolaev, *Censorship in Soviet Literature, 1917–1991* (Lanham, MD: Rowman and Littlefield, 1997), pp. 15–47.

outside expertise, especially during flux in official historiography. Post-Stalinist authors who broke new ground in depicting Leninism and revolution, such as Mikhail Shatrov (1932–2010) or Emmanuil Kazakevich (1913–1962, a writer born in Ukraine who wrote in both Russian and Yiddish during his career), often found themselves mired in lengthy disputes with the censorship body and their advisors in IMELS. So, too, did writers such as the Belarusian war writer Vasil Bykau (1924–2003), who tried to stretch the boundaries of representation regarding World War II and in doing so involved the military censors in scrutiny of his novels, or those who attempted to broach the themes of the Stalinist Terror and the Gulag.

Glavlit censors thus loomed large as gatekeepers without whose permission no publication could proceed: the printing presses could not start until every printer's sheet of a publication had been stamped for approval. As we will see, this obligation to secure a text's 'visa' regularly generated delays, many disruptive to the schedules of journals and publishing houses, and some extraordinarily long. However, the very centrality of 'Talmudic' checking to Glavlit's day-to-day work and the lack of discussion about their assessments, especially with authors, undermined the credibility of their decisions. The party itself periodically reminded Glavlit that it should undertake deep analysis of texts, rather than just checking them against the 'Talmud', but the latter remained the censor's top priority and the task most associated with the state censor. Consequently, the spectre of the uneducated or uncultured censor haunted Glavlit.[7] There was some factual basis for this – in 1955, some 3 per cent of censors, or nearly 200 employees, possessed only high-school education. The state censorship functionary was also structurally rather lowly within the publishing ecosystem, and became increasingly so.

In fact, one of the key trends over nearly seven decades of Soviet censorship policy, especially in the post-Stalin era, was the delimiting of Glavlit's role and the exhortation of other, more expert, agents to play a correspondingly greater part in the publication process. The role of party authorities, creative unions, and editors gradually grew over the decades after Glavlit's creation. There was therefore some scope for Glavlit's assessments to be challenged, especially in the post-Stalinist, post-Terror publishing world.

---

7 These claims were common in Aleksandr Solzhenitsyn's 1967 letter to the Fourth Writers' Union Congress, and in other writers' letters of support for his protest against censorship: Leopold Labedz, *Solzhenitsyn: A Documentary Record* (London: Allen Lane, 1970), pp. 64–80.

The Central Committee of the Communist Party – especially the shifting constellation of departments in charge of propaganda, culture, and ideology – was always entitled to intervene in decision-making in any work. Some publishing houses and journals were obliged to send all proposed content direct to the Central Committee for checking, while other publications could be referred to them at any time, either by editors themselves or more usually by Glavlit censors. The party's rights both to maintain general oversight and to swoop in on any publication were periodically reinforced with reminders to Glavlit to escalate any particularly troublesome works or tendencies. In 1933, for example, the Central Committee issued 'new tasks for censorship organs', including mandatory reporting of major controversies to the Central Committee Secretariat and Department of Culture.[8] Glavlit often appeared relieved to foist responsibility upwards, especially during Stalinism: Denis Babichenko argues that they preferred to make decisions only on minor writers and increasingly invoked the weightier authority of the Central Committee to validate censorship of more prestigious authors.[9] The Central Committee was alert to this problem. In 1944, for example, they claimed that censors and editors were leaving too many decisions to them, some several hundred annually. Such admonitions did little to change the practice of upward verification; indeed, it became more entrenched during the postwar ideological and cultural crackdown. As Katerina Clark and Evgeny Dobrenko observe, 'censorship had turned into virtually a routine activity for Stalin and the Politburo'.[10]

Nonetheless, this 'routine' Central Committee activity still skewed towards controversial texts and worrying directions (in a journal, for instance), rather than systematic verification of every intended Soviet publication, as continued to be expected of Glavlit. Moreover, the Central Committee's assessment of texts focused above all on the broad ideological benefits or harms of publication, and its judgements on these political questions were more authoritative than those of Glavlit (though they could still be overridden by the party leader). During the Stalin era, the Central Committee's Department of Agitation and Propaganda (created in 1939, with a dedicated section for art and literature from 1943), the Central Committee

---

8 Tat'iana Goriaeva, *Istoriia sovetskoi politicheskoi tsenzury* [The history of Soviet political censorship] (Moscow: ROSSPEN, 1997), p. 299.

9 D. L. Babichenko, *Pisateli i tsenzory: Sovetskaia literatura 1940-kh godov pod politicheskim kontrolem TsK* [Writers and censors: Soviet literature of the 1940s under the political control of the Central Committee] (Moscow: Rossiia molodaia, 1994).

10 Katerina Clark and Evgeny Dobrenko, *Soviet Culture and Power: A History in Documents, 1917–1953* (New Haven: Yale University Press, 2007), p. 271.

Orgbiuro, Central Committee Secretariat, and the Politburo itself issued prohibitions, on political grounds, on works by dozens of authors, including Nikolai Erdman (1900–1970) – whose satirical drama *The Suicide* (*Samoubiitsa*, 1928) was banned by the Central Committee in 1932 – Bulgakov, Ilia Selvinskii (1899–1968), Leonid Leonov (1899–1994), and the Ukrainian writer Oleksandr Dovzhenko (1894–1956).

This reasonably regular scrutiny of individual cases also accumulated the evidence for the party's periodic campaigns against controversial journals or literary groupings, which represented the most extreme, and most public, means of addressing censorship crises. These included the late-1940s attacks by Culture Minister Andrei Zhdanov (1896–1948) on Leningrad journals and writers, including Anna Akhmatova (1889–1966) and Mikhail Zoshchenko (1894–1958), or the equivalent Central Committee officials' attempts to rein in the cultural reforms of Nikita Khrushchev's Thaw in the 1950s and 1960s. In fact, the latter, supposedly more liberal period saw a proliferation of party-state censorial institutions: the Central Committee created its own Ideological Commission in 1962, while the State Committee on the Press reinforced the authorities' surveillance of publications from 1963 onwards. Throughout the Stalin and post-Stalin eras, local party authorities also reinforced censorship criteria: local or regional bodies in charge of the area where particularly controversial works had been written or published had to conduct ideological campaigns aimed at preventing any further violations. In Leningrad, for example, the city and regional authorities held crisis meetings about the errors of local writers and journals throughout the Stalin and post-Stalin eras.

The Central Committee also issued frequent reminders of other agents' responsibilities. The Soviet Writers' Union (the main Soviet writers' organisation, which was created by edict in 1932 and held its first congress in 1934) was often instructed to take part in censorship decisions and to scold authors and editors who transgressed acceptable limits. The union never possessed executive authority over any work, but its leaders' opinions could influence the decisions of other bodies. This was true even before the Soviet Writers' Union was created. The most radical of its predecessor institutions, the Russian Association of Proletarian Writers (*Rossiiskaia assotsiatsiia proletars-kikh pisatelei*, or RAPP), persuaded censors and party leaders to ban works including Bulgakov's *Flight* (*Beg*, 1926–7), Pilniak's *Mahogany* (*Krasnoe derevo*, 1927), and Evgenii Zamiatin's (1884–1937) *Attila* (*Attila*, 1928) during the proletarian episode of the late 1920s and early 1930s when Stalin's cultural revolution empowered radical leftist writers' groups to persecute 'fellow

traveller' authors. ('fellow travellers' or *poputchiki* were writers not affiliated to the party, but thought by the party authorities to be gradually 'travelling towards' being more ideologically committed). The Soviet Writers' Union would occasionally equal RAPP's ferocity: after complaints from multiple writers and editors about his overly zealous criticisms of literature, the union's secretary Dmitrii Polikarpov (1905–1965) was sacked in 1946 and replaced by Aleksandr Fadeev (1901–1956) – who himself was not immune to censorship scandals, being forced to rewrite his popular novel *The Young Guard* (*Molodaia gvardiia*, 1946; revised edition 1951) after incurring Stalin's displeasure. Later, backlashes against daring publications – such as Aleksandr Solzhenitsyn's (1918–2008) short stories in the early 1960s – were often spearheaded by the conservative Writers' Union of the Russian Republic, another invention of the Khrushchev era. Around this time, the Soviet Writers' Union also came under pressure to resolve the crisis around the journal *New World* (*Novyi mir*, 1925–) and its project of rewriting the Soviet past (see Chapter 2.4); their interventions culminated in the re-staffing of the journal's editorial board with more obedient figures by the early 1970s. However, as the next section explores, the union could lobby *for* writers as well as against them.

The union's auxiliary function contrasts with the expansion of the editor's role in the policing of literature, which grew in rough parallel to the shrinking of Glavlit's authority. After a flurry of institutional reorganisations in the immediate aftermath of Stalin's death in 1953, a major Central Committee resolution of 1957 titled 'On the Work of Glavlit' criticised Glavlit's insensitive and dictatorial interventions in texts and urged editors at journals and publishing houses to do more censorial work themselves. This ongoing redistribution of powers, combined with a reduced fear of lethal punishment, meant that post-Stalinist, and especially late Soviet, editors had more agency than at any time since the installation of Glavlit plenipotentiaries. They still could not authorise works for publication though: Arlen Blium argues that, while editors substantially 'supplanted' censors in the post-Stalin period, Glavlit retained the authority to ban or delay works.[11] However, editors certainly came to bear greater personal responsibility for what was eventually published and did occasionally try to bypass Glavlit. By the Brezhnev era, editors were expected to do most – ideally all – of the checking and reworking of a text's ideological correctness *before* submission to Glavlit, leaving the latter to run only final checks. Crucial was the Central Committee resolution

---

11 Blium, *Self-Administered Poison*, p. 6.

of January 1969, issued in response to the Soviet crackdown in Prague, which enjoined editors to 'heighten their responsibility' for the 'ideological-political level' of their output.[12] This remained a key reference point throughout late socialism, with Glavlit often citing it in allegations of editorial laxity in the 1970s.

These enhanced censorial responsibilities for editors could cut both ways, making their role potentially, even inherently, Janus-faced. On the one hand, editors became ever closer to Glavlit agents: as the scholar Anthony Adamovich noted drolly in the 1970s, 'In the Soviet Union you have the editor fulfilling the functions of a censor, while the actual censor [is] himself an editor as well.'[13] Editors were expected to internalise official censorial criteria and then to communicate the requisite cuts to authors. As often noted, this pressure to present a virtually perfect text to Glavlit made the Brezhnev era the peak of editorial 'excessive caution' (*perestrakhovka*). However, on the other hand, Glavlit's reports of the time often accused editors of *failing* to enforce authorial cuts prior to censorship checks. Indeed, the intermediary role of editors embedded a close – though by no means always harmonious – relationship between editor and author during the stage before the censor's scrutiny. This could, as we will see, encourage connivance in concealing controversial elements.

These broad ranks of censorial agents expanded still further thanks to frequent, if unpredictable, instances of party leaders playing the role of 'censor in chief': Stalin and Khrushchev (though less so Brezhnev) periodically issued personal verdicts on authors and works, often in response to authorial petitions. Stalin received a steady stream of petitions from writers, including Pilniak, Zamiatin, Bulgakov, Zoshchenko, and Marietta Shaginian (1888–1982), exposing how figures lower in the literary hierarchy were blocking the authors' intended publications and ruining their literary careers. Khrushchev was also sometimes addressed in a similar fashion, as were other intended or actual 'patrons' in the Central Committee. Such petitions demonstrated the belief that the leader possessed the charismatic authority to override the irrational decisions of the censors below him, once informed about them. In fact, leaders were rarely ignorant of such matters by the time that they were raised in this fashion, but it is true that some works would not have seen the light of day if not for their personal interventions after

---

12 RGANI (Russian State Archive of Contemporary History), f. 4, op. 19, d. 131, ll. 2–6.
13 Anthony Adamovich, contribution to symposium discussion 'What is the Soviet Censorship?', in Martin Dewhirst and Robert Farrell (eds.), *The Soviet Censorship* (Metuchen, NJ: Scarecrow Press, 1973), p. 19.

receiving these petitions. Stalin's actions were decisive in breaking the logjam of the latter instalments of Mikhail Sholokhov's (1905–1984) politically and morally ambiguous *The Quiet Don* (*Tikhii Don*) in the 1930s, and Khrushchev personally authorised publication of daring works about Stalinism by Aleksandr Tvardovskii (1910–1971) – *Distance beyond Distance* (*Za dal'iu dal'*, 1954) and *Terkin in the Other World* (*Terkin na tom svete*, 1963) – and Solzhenitsyn (most notably, *One Day in the Life of Ivan Denisovich* (*Odin den' Ivana Denisovicha*, 1962)). However, the unfavourable decisions of leaders doomed many more authors to non-publication, or, especially in the Stalin era, even to arrest or death.

Finally, leaders' public interventions also possessed an outsize importance in setting (or resetting) the parameters for banning or approving texts. Stalin's public praise or awarding of the Stalin Prize (established 1941) rendered previously controversial works immune to criticism, at least for a while – as with Bulgakov's play *The Days of the Turbins* (*Dni Turbinykh*), which premiered in 1926, or Sholokhov's *The Quiet Don*, completed in 1940. Conversely, leaders' direct criticisms of texts or authors could spark volte-faces in censorial policy. For instance, a series of speeches by Khrushchev (and his ideological chief Leonid Ilichev) in 1963 sounded the death knell for the Thaw's brief exploration of Stalin's crimes. Glavlit, citing these and similar subsequent pronouncements to validate their decision-making, squeezed criticism of the 'cult of personality' out of Soviet publications by the late 1960s.

Practices

Soviet censorship was thus characterised by considerable institutional, inter-personal, and systemic complexity, raising the question of how these many elements worked together in practice and with what consequences for texts, writers, and readers. At the heart of this system were core principles and structures that aimed to channel its moving parts in the same direction. All censorial decision-making was supposed to be governed by the principles of ideological benefit (and harm), propriety, and adherence to Socialist Realism (see Chapter 1.8). Nevertheless, many accounts of censorship emphasise the messiness of its operations: its constituent parts, observes Blium, were 'curiously intermeshed', with no 'clear line' of authority.[14]

At the root of this messiness was the fact that not all censorial agents were obliged to issue decisions on all texts – which would have been an excessive duplication of effort even for a notoriously tangled state bureaucracy – but all

---

14 Blium, *Self-Administered Poison*, p. 9.

were entitled to give their views on any work. The heavy use of expert consultation, especially in disputes, broadened still further the range of inputs into publication decisions. Anatolii Kuznetsov (1929–1979), for example, recalled of his Holocaust novel *Babi Yar* (*Babii Iar*, 1966) that he 'counted seven or eight stages through which the manuscript . . . passed, and each one resulted in cuts and abridgements, and each time I had to back down'.[15] He derived 'no pleasure or joy, not the slightest, when they came out' in such eviscerated form.[16] This was an unusually, though not uniquely, large number of interventions; Babichenko observes that more typically 'only a few links in the long chain' were deployed.[17] However, there was no set pattern for which 'links' would participate in any given deliberation. The different permutations meant that editorial or censorial demands could be appealed to, or by, bodies not involved in the initial decision-making. Let us now turn to an example of how this censorial complexity worked in practice.

In the summer of 1949, Vasilii Grossman (1905–1964) submitted the manuscript of a Second World War novel – then entitled *Stalingrad* (*Stalingrad*) – to *New World* for consideration. Grossman was a celebrated war journalist and novelist, on whom hopes for a Soviet war epic (or 'Red Tolstoi') rested. At the same time, he was under pressure from the ramping-up of antisemitism, and this partly accounted for the lengthy vetting of the work, whose main character was a Jewish physicist, Viktor Shtrum. However, the saga of *Stalingrad*'s journey to publication was above all shaped by the complex interrelations of the multitude of Soviet censors, including the author himself.

Between mid-1949 and mid-1952, when the novel finally went to press, its manuscript was vetted by all the censors outlined above – and indeed a few more: Glavlit; *New World*'s editors (Konstantin Simonov (1915–1979), then Aleksandr Tvardovskii) and its editorial board (which fatefully included rival war novelist Mikhail Bubennov (1909–1983)); the Soviet Writers' Union; the Central Committee; the military censorship body and army leadership; and IMELS.[18] The manuscript's journey through these multiple institutions was neither linear nor logical: at many points, various combinations of censors were scrutinising the manuscript simultaneously and suggesting different changes to push it through to publication, or even intimating that it might

---

15 Anatoly Kuznetsov, contribution to symposium discussion 'The unofficial censorship', in Dewhirst and Farrell (eds.), *Soviet Censorship*, pp. 88–9.
16 Kuznetsov, 'Unofficial censorship', p. 93.   17 Babichenko, *Pisateli i tsenzory*, p. 148.
18 This summary draws on Grossman's diary of the journey to publication: RGALI (Russian State Archive of Literature and Art), f. 1710, op. 2, d. 1, ll. 1–30.

never be publishable. This is not to deny the existence of a hierarchy of opinion: indeed, many of the most prolonged – and most stressful – delays to the manuscript happened when the editors and Soviet Writers' Union heads were waiting for state or party authorities to issue their verdicts, a clear example of *perestrakhovka*. The strain of awaiting decisions manifested in the growing frustrations that Grossman confided to his diary and in the frequent disappearances and drinking binges by Tvardovskii and the Soviet Writers' Union head Fadeev.

Exacerbating these delays and anxieties, though, was the fact that the Central Committee was not under a formal obligation to issue such verdicts, and it – along with Stalin himself (who may or may not have read the manuscript) – seemed reluctant to issue a view *in toto*, even though it mandated a great many changes. These included a title change from *Stalingrad* to *For a Just Cause* (*Za pravoe delo*) and the substantial downgrading of the role of the Jewish character Shtrum. Grossman made the cuts that he found bearable from the lists issued by various institutions, though he refused to remove Shtrum altogether. However, what really prolonged the fate of the novel was not these revisions, which Grossman generally made quickly, but rather the absence of clear overall directives that might have resolved matters much earlier. As time went on, more and more institutions vetted the manuscript, but still 'no one would say yes, but no one would also say no'.[19] Ultimately, the novel proceeded to publication in the summer of 1952 because none of those institutions objected decisively to its substantially revised version and Glavlit could therefore finally give it the nod. However, a Central Committee and Soviet Writers' Union backlash followed within a few months of publication (spurred partly by renewed antisemitism and further machinations by Bubennov). Hopes for the book edition could only be revived after the death of Stalin.

The saga of *Stalingrad* was unusually complex and lengthy, and it cemented Grossman's 'categorical disagree[ment]' with the view 'that novels and poems can be created collaboratively with editors. Communism has nothing to do with this. Just as communism has nothing to do with childbirth.'[20] Nonetheless, he would embark on another saga within a few years for the novel's sequel, *Life and Fate* (*Zhizn' i sud'ba*, completed 1959). It, too, came to involve a wide range of censorial bodies: journal editors (of *The Banner* (*Znamia*, 1931–), a more conservative journal than *New World*); Glavlit;

19 RGALI, f. 1710, op. 2, d. 1, l. 16.
20 Quoted in Alexandra Popoff, *Vasily Grossman and the Soviet Century* (New Haven: Yale University Press, 2019), p. 205.

the Soviet Writers' Union; the Central Committee and Khrushchev; and the KGB, or security police. This time, though, despite Grossman's appeals direct to Khrushchev, all of these censors swiftly concurred on the need for total censorship, and indeed destruction, of the manuscript (years after the KGB's confiscation, a hidden copy was microfilmed and smuggled out of the country, allowing publication in Switzerland in 1980). This decisive and speedy consensus of multiple censors on prohibition, based above all on the taboo comparison of Nazi and Stalinist totalitarianism, was far from unique. *New World*, though it would push the boundaries of Soviet literature in the 1950s and 1960s, was similarly unambiguous in its 1956 rejection of Boris Pasternak's (1890–1960) *Doctor Zhivago* (*Doktor Zhivago*), describing it as imbued with 'the spirit of non-acceptance of the socialist revolution'.[21] With Soviet publication rendered immediately impossible, it instead came out in Milan in 1957, becoming one of the first and most scandalous texts smuggled abroad for publication in *tamizdat* after Stalin's death (see Chapter 2.9).

A further possible outcome, beyond these torturously long approvals and rapid rejections, was prolonged negotiation between multiple censors which ultimately ended in prohibition. Such lengthy rejection processes were common when the party line was in flux, as during the gradual end to de-Stalinisation in the early Brezhnev era. Protracted sagas unfolded around Solzhenitsyn's *Cancer Ward* (*Rakovyi korpus*, completed 1966), Konstantin Simonov's war diaries, and Aleksandr Bek's (1903–1972) *The New Appointment* (*Novoe naznachenie*, completed 1964). All three works probed, in very different ways, the baleful effects of Stalinism on Soviet history and the Soviet people. *New World* nearly went to press with Bek's novel several times in the late 1960s and 1970s, supported by the Moscow branch of the Soviet Writers' Union. However, on each occasion it was stopped just before printing. While Glavlit was formally responsible for each ban, its decisions were informed by the objections of several other actors, including industry officials – insulted at the depiction of Stalinist metallurgy – and Brezhnev himself. The novel came out only during Glasnost, in 1987. For all these works, the involvement of multiple censors ultimately tipped the balance towards prohibition, especially in an environment of intensifying ideological vigilance, where excessive caution was safer than too little.

---

21 '"Doctor Zhivago": Letter to Boris Pasternak from the editors of "Novyi Mir"', *Daedalus* 89.3 (1960), 648–68.

Soviet authors and editors became grimly accustomed to such labyrinthine and lengthy decision-making – and to the fact that it could just as easily (if not more so) end in prohibition rather than permission. However, they did not accept the principle or the process unprotestingly. Even before the creation of Glavlit, writers had branded the 'arbitrary' actions of state censors 'a paroxysm of censorial disease',[22] while a 1934 collective petition claimed that 'the country has been in a condition absolutely precluding any possibility of free expression for 17 years already'.[23] Late Soviet polemics, sharpened by disillusionment at the end of the Thaw, accused censorship of 'banning, destroying, tearing, burning, arrests and killing', and of epitomising the 'festering' disease of the Soviet system.[24] The tentacular and enervating processes of censorship provoked similar outrage. The émigré writer Roman Gul (1896–1986) sketched in 1937 four 'echelons' of censorship (from Glavlit up to Stalin himself), any of which could halt or derail a publication.[25] In 1968, Lidiia Chukovskaia (1907–1996), a vocal critic of the curtailment of de-Stalinisation, contrasted tsarist censorship to the 'less visible, but all-penetrating' Soviet censorship, which 'has at its disposal dozens of means to bury an unsuitable manuscript without resorting to the red pencil'.[26] More pragmatically, editors also protested to the authorities that such disruption to schedules harmed their publications' reputations and readership. Tvardovskii regularly appealed in such terms against censorial delays to *New World* in the 1960s, but so too did Stalin-era editors. Anatolii Tarasenkov (1909–1956), deputy editor of *The Banner*, wrote to Zhdanov in 1945, saying that it was his 'party duty' to protest the 'never-ending excessive caution [*perestrakhovka*]' and 'crisscrossing controls', including by Glavlit, the Soviet Writers' Union, ministries, and the Central Committee, 'which so slow down the work of our journal'.[27]

However, aside from such protests, writers and readers developed other, more productive strategies of coping with censorship. Lev Loseff's 1984 study of the 'beneficence of censorship' was the first substantial challenge to the scholarly consensus on censors' unilateral impoverishment of the text.[28]

22 Goriaeva, *Istoriia sovetskoi politicheskoi tsenzury*, p. 425.

23 Blium, *Russkie pisateli*, pp. 458–9.

24 Blium, *Russkie pisateli*, p. 540 (Arkadii Belinkov); Labedz, *Solzhenitsyn*, p. 161 (Solzhenitsyn).

25 Blium, *Russkie pisateli*, pp. 468–86.   26 Blium, *Russkie pisateli*, p. 563.

27 D. L. Babichenko and D. Bairau, 'Literaturnyi front': *Istoriia politicheskoi tsenzury, 1932–1946 gg.: sbornik dokumentov* ['The literary front': The history of political censorship, 1932–46; collected documents] (Moscow: Entsiklopediia rossiiskikh dereven', 1994), pp. 153–5, quoting RGASPI (Russian State Archive of Socio-Political History), f. 17, op. 125, d. 366, ll. 20–5.

28 Lev Loseff, *On the Beneficence of Censorship: Aesopian Language in Modern Russian Literature* (Munich: O Sagner in kommission, 1984).

Censorship's principal benefit, he argued, lay in the development of sophisti-cated strategies of authorial concealment and reader decipherment that aimed to enable texts to get through all the many checks before publication. Such 'Aesopian language' was not a Soviet invention; indeed, the term was coined by the satirist Mikhail Saltykov-Shchedrin (1826–1889) in the 1880s. Even before that, awareness of harsh censorial constraints could predispose readers to read sensitively, even suspiciously, for meanings beneath the text's surface: to perceive an allegory of the anti-tsarist Decembrist move-ment and the repressive regime of Nicholas I within Aleksandr Pushkin's (1799–1837) *The Bronze Horseman* (*Mednyi vsadnik*, 1833), for example. Such suspicion also came to surround Soviet texts that may not have intended such double meanings, such as Kornei Chukovskii's (1882–1969) *The Monster Cockroach* (*Tarakanishche*, 1921), often read as an allusion to Stalin.

However, allusion and allegory were by no means a sure shield as censors and editors strove ever more zealously to 'abolish ambiguity', in the words of Jan Plamper.[29] The use of animal symbolism, a quintessentially Aesopian device, in Mikhail Zoshchenko's *Adventures of a Monkey* (*Prikliucheniia obe-z'iany*, 1946) and Evgenii Shvarts's (1896–1958) *Dragon* (*Drakon*, 1944) gener-ated accusations of political subversion. Shvarts's play was quickly banned, and an ideological campaign was unleashed against Zoshchenko, whose satirical prose had remained remarkably unscathed up to that point. The more beleaguered Bulgakov, whose novel *The White Guard* (*Belaia gvardiia*, 1925) and play *Flight* had already fallen foul of the censors for misrepresenting the civil war, found that more distant historical eras were not immune either. His play *The Cabal of Hypocrites* (*Kabala sviatosh*), about Molière's relationship with the court of Louis XIV, was banned in 1936 as an alleged allegory of Stalin, the NKVD, or security police, and the tragic fate of the Soviet writer.

Such Aesopian fiction thrived more fully after Stalin's death and especially after the crackdown on the Thaw: science fiction and historical fiction became popular across the late socialist Eastern bloc as spatially and tempor-ally indirect means to tackle sensitive questions. The Brezhnev era was the heyday of texts that, to use Loseff's terms, 'screened' their potentially subversive content while 'masking' it with superficial conformity to official requirements.[30] Such sleight of hand often entailed the connivance of editors, though it was sometimes implemented to bypass their censorial zeal. A notable example of the former was the Fiery Revolutionaries (*Plamennye*

---

29 Jan Plamper, 'Abolishing ambiguity: Soviet censorship practices in the 1930s', *Russian Review* 60.4 (2001), 526–44.

30 Loseff, *On the Beneficence of Censorship*, p. 51.

revoliutsionery) biographical series, published by the conservative publisher Politizdat from 1968 to 1990. Many historical novels in the series managed to seem to fulfil the commission of praising revolutionary heroes, while hinting towards ambivalence (about violence or fanaticism) or allegory (of contemporary phenomena such as the dissident movement or political 'Stagnation'). This was a gesture often described by writers and readers as a covert flicking of a v-sign (*kukish v karmane*). For example, Iurii Trifonov's (1925–1981) *Impatience* (*Neterpenie*, 1973), about the People's Will anti-tsarist terrorist movement, placed a marker of the text's contemporary relevance in its chronologically vague first sentence: 'By the end of the '70s', it opened, 'it was clear to contemporaries that Russia was sick.'[31]

If the dense encryption of some Aesopian writing has become more inscrutable to subsequent generations of readers, the effects of the different phases of censorship on the text itself remain all too visible. At one end of the spectrum are texts that were written 'for the desk drawer', where the early realisation of the impossibility of publication meant that writers continued to revise their work in private, producing texts akin to palimpsests. Bulgakov worked on *The Master and Margarita* (*Master i Margarita*) from 1928 up to his death in 1940, arguably leaving it unfinished. Soviet publication of a heavily edited version in 1966–7, a full Soviet edition in 1973, and subsequent foreign editions further multiplied variants of the text. Anna Akhmatova's multi-part poems *Poem without a Hero* (*Poema bez geroia*, comp. 1940–62) and *Requiem* (*Rekviem*, comp. 1934–62) were continually revised from the 1930s to the 1960s, even as versions started to circulate among friends, unofficial networks, and – later – readers outside the Soviet Union. These multiple versions underscored both texts' representations of the layering of memories and identities over time and their challenge to the didactic, anti-Formalist discourse of Socialist Realism.

At the other end of this spectrum are works that were censored for the sake of Soviet publication. Their original manuscripts were often lost or destroyed by the time that 'uncensored' versions were permitted – especially for victims of state persecution or authors who had subsequently emigrated, often scattering their archive across several locations. For many years there were two extant versions of Solzhenitsyn's *First Circle* (*V kruge pervom*, first pub. in New York, 1968): one with eighty-seven chapters, and a more politically daring text of ninety-six chapters. A definitive version was only confirmed in 2006, two years after Solzhenitsyn's death. For works that *were* published in

31 Iurii Trifonov, *Neterpenie* [Impatience] (Moscow: Politizdat, 1973), p. 1.

Soviet outlets, manuscripts could also proliferate during pre-publication scrutiny and redrafting. Robert and Elizabeth Chandler's 2019 translation of Grossman's *Stalingrad* – whose pre-publication saga was examined above – spliced together over ten such manuscripts, both enriching and destabilising the originally published version.[32] This hybrid of more- and less-censored texts highlighted how much bolder Grossman's original plans were than the Soviet published edition (1952), helping to revive interest in a work previously dismissed as conformist relative to his uncensored sequel *Life and Fate*.

A Soviet text's evolution *after* it had passed through censorship and into publication could multiply its extant versions too. Typical is the extensive rewriting by Fedor Gladkov (1883–1958) of his factory novel *Cement* (*Tsement*), reissued repeatedly over three decades after its first publication in 1925. Each edition – rewritten by the author in line with the instructions of editors and censors – produced a different version of the novel, though it broadly progressed towards more sanitised language and ideologically orthodox treatment of the key themes of family and identity. While offering a fascinating case study of evolving censorship requirements, these multiple versions complicate the status of the definitive text. Sholokhov's *The Quiet Don* – despite (and partly because of) its equally 'classic' status – was also redrafted over multiple editions, again targeting aspects of style and content that had become troubling in the light of the evolving party line. In this way, both censorship's absence and its oppressive presence could generate unstable or unfinalised texts.

However, the main consequence of censorship was an incalculable loss to twentieth-century readers. Thousands of works never appeared until the very final years of Soviet power when Glasnost radically rethought the canon, and readers were overwhelmed by belated publications, some of which did not receive the attention that they might have had in a less hectic environment. Many key twentieth-century authors received only posthumous recognition, sometimes several generations later. For Osip Mandelshtam (1891–1938), Andrei Platonov (1899–1951), Marina Tsvetaeva (1892–1941), Bulgakov, and Akhmatova – among others – there was a yawning gap between their very limited publications in the Lenin, Stalin, and even post-Stalin eras and a far larger corpus of censored texts appearing only in the 1980s or later. In the post-Stalin period, the unofficial textual network of *samizdat* shortened this lag somewhat: by the end of the 1960s,

---

32 Vasily Grossman, *Stalingrad*, trans. Robert Chandler and Elizabeth Chandler (New York: NYRB Classics, 2019).

recently banned works including Vladimir Voinovich's (1932–2018) *The Life and Extraordinary Adventures of Private Ivan Chonkin* (*Zhizn' i neobychainye prikliucheniia soldata Ivana Chonkina*, comp. 1963–9) and Georgii Vladimov's (1931–2003) *Faithful Ruslan* (*Vernyi Ruslan*, completed 1964) were already part of the samizdat canon. So, too, were works that refused even to enter the institutional maze of censorship and were thus 'born *samizdat*', such as Venedikt Erofeev's (1939–1990) *Moscow–Petushki* (*Moskva–Petushki*, 1969–70). However, it remained easier for western audiences to read contemporary authors through large print-run editions published abroad (*tamizdat*) than it was for Soviet readers to access the same texts – for example, Vladimov's *Faithful Ruslan* first reached a wide international readership through its English-language translation and publication in 1975. Soviet samizdat networks, unlike more institutionalised unofficial publishing in other parts of the socialist bloc including Poland, remained limited, fragile, and skewed towards the intelligentsia (see Chapter 2.9).

Glavlit was dismantled in 1991, and it has no direct post-Soviet equivalent, despite the creation of an agency for the protection of state secrets in the same year. However, as in the Soviet era, multiple forces wield editorial and censorial authority over post-Soviet culture – and increasingly so in the course of Vladimir Putin's presidency. Indicative are the arrest in 2017 of the director Kirill Serebrennikov (1969–) and the long delays to his Bolshoi production of a ballet about Rudolf Nureyev (1938–1993). Such bursts of censorial activity have issued from a range of institutions and officials, including the Culture Ministry; conservative Duma, or parliament, deputies; the state media watchdog, Roskomnadzor; and Vladimir Putin himself. Although censorship itself was not enshrined in law, these decisions were often justified by reference to legislation such as the Law on Extremism (2006–7) and the so-called Gay Propaganda law (2013), whose strictures against the 'promotion of non-traditional sexual relations' were further strengthened in revisions passed in June 2022. In March 2022, following the Russian invasion of Ukraine, another set of laws was passed, prohibiting the expression and dissemination of anti-war sentiment (which includes terming the conflict a 'war' rather than using the official term, 'special operation'). Violations are punishable by substantial prison terms. These various laws do not amount to a reinstatement of total pre-publication censorship, but they clearly signal a more draconian and destructive mode of censorship than anything preceding it in the post-Soviet era. An almost immediate consequence of the legislation was that many non-state media outlets – including the last remaining TV channel, Rain (*Dozhd'*), and the Echo of Moscow (*Ekho*

Moskvy) radio station – shut down altogether or began to self-censor to an unprecedented degree. *New Newspaper* (*Novaia gazeta*, 1993–) suspended print publication. Some of its last Russian editions pointedly printed blank pages.

These very recent developments reinforce the idea that the proliferation and overlapping of censorial forces, despite some unpredictable outcomes, tend to be more conducive to a repressive publishing environment, especially when there is a clear government line on taboos. More broadly, the post-Soviet era's overlapping censorial agencies, and the elastic criteria used to assess harm to state and society, suggest the continuing influence of Soviet and even tsarist practices. Yet institutional and discursive messiness is also a persistent feature of censorship internationally, suggesting that it could be a central, even essential, element of censorial operations anywhere.

Further Reading

Balmuth, David, *Censorship in Russia, 1865–1905* (Washington, DC: University Press of America, 1979).

Blium, Arlen, *A Self-Administered Poison: The System and Functions of Soviet Censorship* (Oxford: European Humanities Research Centre, 2003).

Darnton, Robert, *Censors at Work: How States Shaped Literature* (New York: W. W. Norton, 2014).

Dewhirst, Martin, and Robert Farrell (eds.), *The Soviet Censorship* (Metuchen, NJ: Scarecrow Press, 1973).

Ermolaev, Herman, *Censorship in Soviet Literature, 1917–1991* (Lanham, MD: Rowman and Littlefield, 1997).

Ermolaev, Herman, and Marianna Tax Choldin (eds.), *The Red Pencil: Artists, Scholars and Censors in the USSR* (Boston: Unwin Hyman, 1989).

Loseff, Lev, *On the Beneficence of Censorship: Aesopian Language in Modern Russian Literature* (Munich: O Sagner in kommission, 1984).

Ruud, Charles, *Fighting Words: Imperial Censorship and the Russian Press, 1804–1906* (Toronto: University of Toronto Press, 1982).

Sherry, Samantha, *Discourses of Regulation and Resistance: Censoring Translation in the Stalin and Khrushchev Era Soviet Union* (Edinburgh: Edinburgh University Press, 2015).

2.8

The Voice

STEPHEN LOVELL

The subject of this chapter requires more introduction than others discussed in this section, as the voice is a mechanism less clearly defined than a publishing house or a censorship apparatus. The voice is not just a metaphor: it is a technology with ancient pedigree. The relationship between manuscript and print has rightly drawn a great deal of scholarly attention in literary histories of Russia. But if we take a long-range view, the relationship between speech and writing has been no less important for determining the boundaries, nature, and purpose of Russian literature.

To some extent, this reflects a pan-European logic of literary history. For the ancient Greeks, after all, poetry was oral and performative. It was only after many centuries, towards the middle of the second millennium, that rhetoric largely shed its original purpose as the art of oral persuasion and became instead the art of written (usually prose) composition.[1] In this form it served as the incubator for a modern secular literature. At the same time, oral performativity remained an important cultural resource for literature. On occasion, voice took 'real', acoustic form, as in literary readings in salons or assembly rooms. More often, as in the works of certain Modernist poets, it was to be understood metaphorically as a rhetorical mode or a means of projecting the authorial self.

Russian literature broadly follows this European trajectory but with at least three important qualifications. The first is the matter of timing. Russia's acquaintance with western rhetoric was relatively late, relying on seventeenth-century Ukrainian churchmen as a conduit of Polish learning. The practice of panegyrics and formal speeches then played a full part in court life

---

1 See, for example, Ben McCorkle, *Rhetorical Delivery as Technological Discourse: A Cross-Historical Study* (Carbondale: Southern Illinois University Press, 2012).

and propaganda of the late Muscovite and Petrine eras: Dmitrii of Rostov (1651–1709), Stefan Iavorskii (1658–1722), and Feofan Prokopovich (1681–1736) – leading lights of Russia's Baroque – delivered hundreds of sermons among them. There was a rather short distance from this body of work, largely a product of the subjection of church to absolutist state, to the beginnings of a more autonomous secular literature in the second half of the eighteenth century.[2] Similarly, Russia's Modernism coincided with the colossal social upheavals of 1905 and 1917, which confronted elite aestheticians with demotic language in full force.

The second salient feature of modern Russian literature is the restrictions on publication under which it operated. To be sure, every continental European country in the first half of the nineteenth century had censorship that we would find overbearing, but the fact remains that Russia was an extreme case and, unlike other places, it showed few signs of liberalisation in the post-1870 era (see Chapters 2.5, 2.7, 2.9). This meant that, for Russian literature, 'voice' had a very particular ring of authenticity: it was possible to say things in front of a face-to-face audience that one never could have written. It also helped that the literary elite, for much of modern Russian history, was tiny and close-knit: it really was possible for some Russian writers in the 1830s or the 1890s (or even the 1960s) to imagine that they were addressing their entire audience when declaiming poetry across the dinner table. Conversely, when speakers were able to address a larger audience, 'voice' served as a powerful metaphor and symbol: it was to do not only with speaking but also with articulation and projection, sometimes in conditions of adversity or in defiance of authority. *Glasnost'*, the term that denotes Russia's two great liberalising campaigns of the 1860s and the 1980s, has the word 'voice' (*golos*) embedded within it.

Russia's third distinctive feature is the existence of huge cultural chasms that could only be bridged by direct address via the spoken word. Even in the early twentieth century, this was a society with a tiny educated elite and a vast unlettered majority. It was also an enormous, dispersed, and multilingual empire. Even if we restrict ourselves to Russian, it did not have a stable literary language until the nineteenth century, and the boundaries between

2 P. E. Bukharkin, 'Torzhestvennoe krasnorechie petrovskoi epokhi: Barochnoe slovo mezhdu Tserkov'iu i Imperiei' [The ceremonial eloquence of the Petrine era: Baroque discourse between Church and Empire], in Petr Bukharkin, Ulrike Jekutsch, and Natal'ia Kochetkova (eds.), *Okkazional'naia literatura v kontekste prazdnichnoi kul'tury Rossii XVIII veka* [Occasional literature in the context of the festive culture of Russia in the eighteenth century] (St Petersburg: Filologicheskii fakul'tet Sankt-Peterburgskogo gosudarstvennogo universiteta, 2010), pp. 19–32.

literary and popular language remained both fluid and controversial even after that. Above all, the educated elite became increasingly concerned both to speak to the wider population and to render adequately how 'the people' actually spoke. Ethnographers were prominent participants in this quest, but writers were just as important. A more or less stylised popular voice was heard ever more frequently in Russian literature from the 1840s onwards and would give rise to one of Russia's main contributions to modern literary theory: *skaz*, or a narrative voice that sounds like oral speech (see Box 4.3).

As Eric Griffiths has observed, all modern printed poetry (and, perhaps, literature *tout court*) is haunted by a sense of 'lost community': the awareness that the printed page is always rendering a voice, but without the clues (such as intonation) that the spoken word provides.[3] Russian literature, it might be said, is franker than its western counterparts in acknowledging this disjuncture but also takes stronger measures to attempt to transcend it. The divide between voice and print can never entirely be bridged. But Russian literature provides many nice illustrations of Griffiths's follow-up argument: if there remains a gap between the voice as rendered in print and the voice as imagined or 'heard' by the reader, this opens up new scope for literary creativity and for active reader participation. Even when Russian works stop short of *skaz*, their narrative voices rarely affect Olympian detachment. And the famously sprawling Russian psychological novel often has the effect of destabilising the author-narrator, putting him (almost never her) in competition with other voices, whether articulated in interior monologues, in embedded documents such as letters or diaries, or in dialogue and direct speech. This idea was potently developed in Mikhail Bakhtin's (1895–1975) study of Fedor Dostoevskii's (1821–1881) 'dialogism' (see Box 5.4), according to which each character's consciousness is 'turned outward' and always addressing an implied other. Bakhtin's choice of author was, however, quite arbitrary: even that supposedly most 'monologic' of authors, Lev Tolstoi (1828–1910), has his characters engage in outwardly directed interior monologues as well as placing them in implicit dialogue with each other.[4]

The rest of this chapter is divided into three parts. The central section focuses on the period 1941–70, which may be seen as the Golden Age of the literary voice in Russia. The Second World War and the Thaw of the 1950s brought a renewed emphasis on the sincerity and authenticity of the writer as well as providing the lyrical subject or the civic tribune with powerful media

---

3 Eric Griffiths, *The Printed Voice of Victorian Poetry* (Oxford: Clarendon Press, 1989), p. 61.
4 Mikhail Bakhtin, *Problems of Dostoevsky's Poetics*, ed. and trans. Caryl Emerson (Manchester: Manchester University Press, 1984), chap. 5 (quotation on p. 251).

through which to convey that authenticity (radio broadcasts, mass poetry readings, tape recordings). The concluding section contains some reflections on the Russian literary voice in the new technological and political conditions of the late-twentieth and early twenty-first centuries. First, however, we need to survey the earlier phases of modern Russian literature and investigate the ramifications of voice in the worlds of court, salon, assembly room, and manuscript as well as in a burgeoning print culture.

Voice as Literary Mechanism and Rhetorical Tool: Russia's Path from the Baroque to the Modern Age

A natural point of departure for the story of literature and speech in Russia is the ode. This was Russia's pre-eminent genre in the eighteenth century, and it also had a strong performative dimension: the ode became the 'sovereign lyric genre' at the courts of Anna Ioannovna (r. 1730–40) and Elizabeth Petrovna (r. 1741–62), and its implied (though not necessarily actual) mode of delivery was recitation at court ceremonies (see Chapters 2.2, 3.3, 4.2). After the mid-1750s the odic environment was weakening: Catherine II (r. 1762–96) recast the ceremonial culture of the court, making space for satire as well as for lower linguistic registers. Literary activity moved to new circles and journals, which in turn implied new forms, new audiences, and new ways of engaging those audiences. The imagined addressee of literature was the reader rather than the listener – or, if a listener, a participant in a literary circle rather than the empress or an attendee at a court function (see Chapters 2.3, 2.4).[5]

Nonetheless, literature continued to have a life beyond the page. The new literary language promoted by the writer and historian Nikolai Karamzin (1766–1826) in the late eighteenth century took as its model the polite conversation of the educated, westernised gentry. Moreover, literature not only reflected the imagined norms of polite society but developed out of specific interactions within that society. New works were read out in the salons of the first third of the nineteenth century and were often revised in response to the 'friendly' criticism they received. Some of the genres of salon literature – bouts-rimés, epigrams, letters, elegies – were by definition collaborative or at least implied specific addressees or interlocutors (see Chapter 2.3).[6] Literature also gained oral presence from its close association with music in the first third of

---

5 James von Geldern, 'The ode as performative genre', *Slavic Review* 50.4 (1991), 927–39 (quotation on p. 927).
6 William Mills Todd III, *Fiction and Society in the Age of Pushkin: Ideology, Institutions, and Narrative* (Cambridge, MA: Harvard University Press, 1986), esp. pp. 55–72.

the nineteenth century: in Russian Romanticism, as elsewhere, music enjoyed high prestige as a vehicle of the ineffable, and the boundaries between literary and musical composition were not as strictly drawn as they would be subsequently. The result was that the genres of literary romance and art-song developed in close collaboration; they were even known by the same word – *romans*.[7]

Aleksandr Pushkin (1799–1837) had little patience with the conventions of salon literature, but he also depended on his first listeners as a sounding board. He was a poet embedded in a typical close-knit Romantic milieu and is often depicted or imagined reading his work to intimates in small gatherings: he can thus be seen to have been speaking not just for all times but also for a very particular group of people in his own time. But Pushkin's performativity was not just the spontaneous and 'authentic' self-invention of the Romantic poet (see Chapter 1.4). The most famous image of Pushkin as reader of his own work is Ilia Repin's (1844–1930) painting of 1911, which shows him declaiming his poetry at the graduation ceremony of the Tsarskoe Selo Lyceum in 1815. This, of course, was a far from spontaneous occasion. As Pushkin's academic pedigree at the Lyceum suggests, he did not emerge *ex nihilo* but owed a great deal to the eighteenth-century rhetorical tradition that would soon be castigated as 'scholastic' by the radical critic Vissarion Belinskii (1811–1848; see Box 5.1) and others. Undoubtedly, literary production in the age of Pushkin drew a great deal of energy from the interaction between manuscript and oral performance in the intellectual circles (*kruzhki*) of the time. But the voice of Pushkin and his associates was still more that of classical rhetoric than of gritty ethnographic realism.[8]

A *locus classicus* is 'The Prophet' (*Prorok*, 1826), Pushkin's canonical assertion of the truth-telling voice of the poet, where a 'six-winged seraph' tears out the poet's 'sinful, idle and cunning tongue', replacing it with a 'snake's sting'. The poem ends with a divine exhortation in Old Testament style:

> Arise, and let My voice be heard,
> Charged with My Will go forth and span
> The land and sea, and let My Word
> Lay waste with fire the heart of man.[9]

7 Thomas P. Hodge, *A Double Garland: Poetry and Art-Song in Early-Nineteenth-Century Russia* (Evanston, IL: Northwestern University Press, 2000).
8 A. B. Rogachevskii, *Ritoricheskie traditsii v tvorchestve A. S. Pushkina* [Rhetorical traditions in the work of A. S. Pushkin] (Moscow: Institut mirovoi literatury, 1994).
9 A. Pushkin and Maurice Baring (trans.), 'The Prophet', *Slavonic and East European Review* 12.34 (1933), 1–2.

Nonetheless, Pushkin also paved the way for a more ethnographic approach in Russian literature of the mid-century. When confined to his Mikhailovskoe estate in the mid-1820s due to political indiscretions, Pushkin whiled away the time listening to folk tales from his nanny, Arina Rodionovna. This much-mythologised relationship established for posterity Pushkin's credentials as a 'popular' poet. It also made him an early participant in the quest to render in literature the 'popular voice'. The quest was taken up with greater purpose in the 1840s when the Slavophile–Westerniser controversy – a debate among Russian intellectuals about whether their country was sui generis or bound to follow a common European historical path – posed with new urgency the question of how to speak in the people's name. The most powerful and influential early attempt to 'hear' the Russian people came from that quint-essential Westerniser Ivan Turgenev (1818–1883) in his *Notes of a Hunter* (*Zapiski okhotnika*, 1852), which presents a series of brief encounters between the nobleman narrator and peasants he meets on his hunting expeditions. Here the peasant's voice, even if ventriloquised by the highly educated narrator, is more direct and less stylised than ever before in Russian literature.

The following decade brought an even more pronounced emphasis on the voice, understood both literally and metaphorically. The main catalyst was the reform era of Alexander II (r. 1855–81), one of whose watchwords was *glasnost'*. Usually translated as 'openness' or 'publicity', the term can be understood more literally. The late 1850s and early 1860s saw a surge of spoken-word events. Literary readings attracted large audiences and featured such celebrity writers as Aleksandr Ostrovskii (1823–1886), Aleksei Pisemskii (1821–1881), and Fedor Dostoevskii (only recently returned from prison and exile). By all accounts these writers were gifted performers, but they did even more to project a voice in their written work. Both Ostrovskii and Dostoevskii adopted quasi-ethnographic methods in rendering non-standard speech. Ostrovskii was himself of merchant stock but was also renowned for constantly replenishing his store of characteristic turns of phrase from Moscow's petty bourgeoisie. Dostoevskii, less by choice, had conducted extensive fieldwork among the lower classes in his years in Siberia: his prison quasi-memoir, *Notes from the House of the Dead* (*Zapiski iz mertvogo doma*, 1862), could lay claim to greater ethnographic authenticity than any other contemporary work.

This heightened attention to the varieties of voice gave rise to one of the much-attested distinctive characteristics of Russian literature: the unreliable (or downright repellent) narrator (see Box 4.2). Russia's major writers forced their readers to listen in to the stream of consciousness of a morbidly insecure

sociopath (Dostoevskii's novella *Notes from Underground* (*Zapiski iz podpol'ia*, 1864)), a wife-batterer (Dostoevskii's short story 'The Meek One' (*Krotkaia*, 1876)), and a wife-murderer (Tolstoi's novella *The Kreutzer Sonata* (*Kreitserova sonata*, 1890)). Along with the unreliable narrator came the unreliable or unreceptive listener: the narrator of *The Kreutzer Sonata* is also a listener, who is trapped in a noisy train carriage and forced to hear the murderer's lengthy self-rationalisation and argument for universal celibacy. In Anton Chekhov's (1860–1904) story 'The Drama' (*Drama*, 1887) the protagonist brings a paper-weight down on the head of an aspiring writer who is driving him to distraction by reading out to him her new play.[10]

A further surge of literary interest in the voice came at the turn of the twentieth century. Partly, this was a response to the possibilities of new technology: Silver Age poets were among the first to have their voices recorded by the gramophone, and the author's voice became another attribute of celebrity at the fin de siècle. The cult of the poet Aleksandr Blok (1880–1921), for example, was sustained not only by his published verse but also by his readings.[11] And even if Modernist works were designed for the printed page, they were inclined to sound effects: Andrei Belyi's (1880–1934) novel *Petersburg* (*Peterburg*, 1913–14, 1922), Russian Modernism's greatest literary tribute to the cacophony of modernity, has been dubbed the 'first Russian acoustic novel'.[12] The Modernist move from syllabo-tonic to tonic verse – which implied a less regular relationship between stressed and unstressed syllables, making rhythm a more dynamic factor – also brought a renewed attention to the sound of poetry (see Chapter 3.8). But above all, the voiced word became a renewed preoccupation in the early twentieth century as a means of recovering the magical, transcendent qualities of language in a modern world that had become thoroughly disenchanted.

The revolution in 1917 gave this mission even greater urgency. A group of politically engaged Russian Modernists considered the spoken word as a way of finally breaking down the barriers between the elite and the 'masses'. For Vladimir Maiakovskii (1893–1930), poetry was performance, and words could not be kept to the artificial confines of the printed page. Maiakovskii's famous semaphoric punctuation and typography, with its abundant dashes and single

---

10 For these and other examples, see Gabriella Safran, 'The troubled frame narrative: Bad listening in late imperial Russia', *Russian Review* 72.4 (2013), 556–72.
11 For example, his reading of his famous essay on the intelligentsia at the Literary Society in November 1908. See Avril Pyman, *The Life of Alexander Blok*, vol. II, *The Release of Harmony, 1908–1921* (Oxford: Oxford University Press, 1980), pp. 28–9.
12 Oksana Bulgakova, *Golos kak kul'turnyi fenomen* [The voice as a cultural phenomenon] (Moscow: Novoe literaturnoe obozrenie, 2015), p. 149.

sentences chopped into short bursts of words spread over several lines, was a constant reminder that the real life of the poem lay with the declamatory persona of the poet himself – a persona that was most fully realised in the act of public performance (see Box 1.3). Maiakovskii had launched his performance career before the First World War as a young Futurist out to shock, and in the revolutionary period he threw himself into the Bolshevik cause.

The unpleasant irony for Maiakovskii and his brethren was that the leading Bolsheviks had little time for the extravagant schemes of the Futurists. Vladimir Lenin was dismissive of Maiakovskii's '150 000 000' (1921), an attempt at a revolutionary folk epic.[13] Maiakovskii's most obvious reference to the 'voice' of poetry – his extended poem *At the Top of My Voice* (*Vo ves' golos*, 1929–30) – was an appeal to posterity rather than an expression of aesthetic victory in the present. Nonetheless, Modernist experimentation with the printed boundaries of the literary work left significant traces in early Soviet culture. In the 1920s, for example, the actor Vladimir Iakhontov (1899–1945) created a new type of spoken word event, splicing together poetry, political works, and newspaper texts. In one of these compositions, he broke up the Communist Manifesto into rhythmic lines; he also provided a declamatory setting of Lenin's pamphlet *What Is to Be Done?* (*Chto delat'?*, 1902).[14]

In due course, the spoken literary word was able to benefit from a new medium: radio. The early 1930s saw a lengthy debate on the extent to which radio literature represented a new art form: writing designed for oral performance, with the possibility of new sound effects. As a result of the anti-Formalist campaign, which in the mid-1930s railed against western-inspired Modernist excesses, the debate was resolved in favour of the conservative position – in other words, that the role of radio was to reproduce and disseminate existing literature, not to generate new art forms. But even this was a boon to writers in the 1930s: it raised their profile and gave them a new source of income. It also meant that many of them spent time in the studio, where they could not fail to recognise the importance of the 'speakability' of their texts. The existence of radio did not, however, change the fact that prewar Soviet culture was increasingly scriptural. Stalinist radio censorship reached new extremes of vigilance, and radio delivery was widely bemoaned as ponderous and deadening.

13 Edward J. Brown, *Mayakovsky: A Poet in Revolution* (Princeton: Princeton University Press, 1973), p. 205.
14 V. Iakhontov, *Teatr odnogo aktera* [The theatre of a single actor] (Moscow: Iskusstvo, 1958).

From War to Thaw: The Heyday of the Literary Voice in Russia

All this changed to a significant extent with the Second World War, which once again put the onus on performativity. Wartime radio was a vehicle for a heartfelt intimacy quite at odds with the norms of late-1930s Stalinism. Nowhere did broadcasts have greater resonance than in besieged Leningrad, where wired radio provided nothing less than reassurance that the city was still alive. The most compelling voice of Leningrad radio was the poet Olga Berggolts (1910–1975), who had lived through a series of personal tragedies in the preceding years: her older daughter had died, her first husband had been arrested and executed, and Berggolts herself had been arrested in 1938. Her wartime poetry acknowledged the suffering that had become the common lot of the Soviet people; it drew official criticism for its melancholy and lack of conventional patriotism but made her a trusted and valued voice for Soviet readers and listeners.[15] Berggolts also took inspiration from the voices of ordinary Soviet people, who during the war were allowed to the microphone with far fewer restraints than in the 1930s. As she recalled in a memoir published just after the war (see Chapter 3.10), as early as 19 September 1941 a woman stormed into the studio to give a heart-rending account of how her two children had been killed an hour before in a bombing raid: 'the whole of Leningrad, and the fighters in the immediate outskirts of the city . . . listened to her breathing, the breathing of grief itself, and of courage, and they committed it all to memory'. Berggolts summed up her wartime aesthetic credo thus:

> art mounted this unprecedented tribune in front of the whole city not just to hold rallies, to agitate, to call to action. No, apart from this it conversed with its fellow citizens – speaking softly, in the true sense of the phrase 'heart to heart', it reflected aloud on the most urgent questions of life, it gave advice, it consoled, it grieved and rejoiced along with those who heard it, penetrating their souls in the way that only art knows.[16]

Even if there was also plenty of agitation and patriotic uplift on wartime Soviet radio, this was still a remarkable injection of intimacy into the militarised Soviet public sphere.

---

15 Katharine Hodgson, *Voicing the Soviet Experience: The Poetry of Ol'ga Berggol'ts* (Oxford: Oxford University Press, 2003).

16 O. Berggol'ts, *'Govorit Leningrad'* ['This is Leningrad speaking'] (Leningrad: Lenizdat, 1946), p. 8.

The young postwar generation of the intelligentsia was proudly Soviet. Yet it drew from the war not only patriotism but also a cult of literature and idealistic inclinations. Poetry – including writers as far out of the Soviet mainstream as Anna Akhmatova (1889–1966) and Boris Pasternak (1890–1960) – became an intellectual currency of the time.[17] In the constrained conditions of late Stalinism, much of this enthusiasm remained confined to friendship groups (*kompanii*). But the early Khrushchev years, when incipient de-Stalinisation was combined with a more solicitous official attitude to the cultural intelligentsia, brought a loosening of the norms of public expression and a promotion of the values of sincerity, authenticity, and spontaneity. This period also brought practical and institutional support: after Stalin's death in 1953, recruiting new literary talent to the field of poetry became the official policy of the Writers' Union. By the early 1960s, there were reckoned to be more than 6,000 practising poets in Leningrad alone.[18]

The new spirit of the years after Stalin's death made possible the publication of works that pushed the boundaries of Stalinist expression: they took aim at heartless and despotic state functionaries and put forward alternative values of moral integrity and emotional authenticity. The emotional turn of the Thaw placed a premium on civic-lyrical intensity and brought young poets who embodied this value the kind of celebrity that in contemporary western cultures was accorded only to rock stars. Evgenii Evtushenko (1932–2017), Bella Akhmadulina (1937–2010), Robert Rozhdestvenskii (1932–1994), and Andrei Voznesenskii (1933–2010) were famous not just for their published verse but also for poetry readings that were held in theatres, concert halls, and even stadiums. One such occasion is recorded in the quintessential Thaw film *The Gate of Ilich* (*Zastava Il'icha*, dir. Marlen Khutsiev (1925–2019), 1962). At least until the early 1960s, the ethos of the Thaw poets was in accord with the public values of Soviet culture: following the institution of a nationwide Poetry Day in 1955, writers were given every opportunity to cultivate a popular following – by signing autographs in bookshops, answering readers' questions, and (especially) giving public readings at venues such as the Palace of Sport in Moscow.[19] For Evtushenko, the public reach of poetry was explicitly part of its appeal: 'a poem takes much less time to write than

---

17 Vladislav Zubok, *Zhivago's Children: The Last Soviet Intelligentsia* (Cambridge, MA: Harvard University Press, 2009), p. 30.

18 Emily Lygo, *Leningrad Poetry 1953–1975: The Thaw Generation* (Oxford: Peter Lang, 2010), p. 14.

19 Gerald Stanton Smith, *Songs to Seven Strings: Russian Guitar Poetry and Soviet 'Mass Song'* (Bloomington: Indiana University Press, 1984), p. 44.

a novel, and it can be read in public even before appearing in print. So I chose the public platform as the battlefield on which to defend my views.'[20] Or, as he wrote in a poem that may be regarded as a jaunty Thaw-era equivalent of Pushkin's 'The Prophet':

> It doesn't matter
>> whether anyone is studying you,
> what matters
>> is whether anyone is following you.
> What value do our words have,
>> if they're not
> primed with the desire to awaken,
> endowed with the seed of the future –
> the sacred possibility of continuation?!'[21]

In the 1950s, Russian literature also reinitiated its productive relationship with other media and art forms, some of them with an oral dimension. Radio plays, proscribed since the late 1930s, became once more a legitimate field of endeavour, and the rigid norms of public expression on the broadcast media loosened somewhat in the early 1960s. Theatre (and theatre-going) experienced a revival (see Chapter 3.7). But the Thaw era's greatest claim to literary originality lay in the distinctive Soviet phenomenon of 'guitar poetry'. The habit of singing to seven-string accompaniment had gained immense popularity during the war; this was perhaps the main form of folklore generated by the frontline experience. A decade later, with the new quest for emotional authenticity in the mid-1950s, this mode of folklore was taken up by a number of skilled and charismatic poet-performers. The resonance of their work was guaranteed by the happy coincidence that affordable and portable tape recorders were starting to reach the Soviet consumer in the late 1950s. The pioneer among these Soviet 'bards' was Bulat Okudzhava (1924–1997), son of a Georgian Bolshevik shot in the Stalinist Terror, who embarked on a literary career in the 1950s after war service and work as a schoolteacher in provincial obscurity. Okudzhava was never a dissident, joining the Writers' Union in 1961 and seeking the usual channels to publish his work, but he was increasingly treated with suspicion by the authorities, losing his party membership in 1972. He was a versatile operator, producing historical novels as well as poetry. But his reputation rests largely on the corpus of about 200 songs that

20 Yevgeny Yevtushenko, *A Precocious Autobiography*, trans. Andrew R. MacAndrew (New York: E. P. Dutton, 1963), p. 96.
21 Evgenii Evtushenko, *Vzmakh ruki: Stikhi* [A wave of the hand: poems] (Moscow: Molodaia gvardiia, 1962), p. 77.

he began to write and perform in the 1950s. His first public performance was in Leningrad in January 1960, and national celebrity soon followed. The private production and circulation of tape recordings – *magnitizdat* – amply compensated for the limitations placed on Okudzhava's access to television and the recording industry.

Okudzhava was perhaps the leading creator of a new hybrid genre that blended music and text, folklore and high art. His distinctive, faintly exotic voice – untrained, understated, but intensely lyrical – was an essential part of the moral-aesthetic package he offered. As one of his early supporters put it, 'The poetry is not exceptional, the music is not professional, the singing is nothing special, but everything together is genius.' Sections of the literary establishment might have cast aspersions – for some members of the older generation, Okudzhava's songs were trivial and the guitar an irredeemably vulgar instrument – but there was no question that he was in the vanguard of a new cultural form that managed to be both of the intelligentsia and of the people.[22] Guitar poetry, in combination with the phenomenon of *magnitizdat*, created an entirely symbiotic relationship between text and voice: these works lost the greater part of their force and meaning when they were read silently rather than performed. Moreover, the only performance that was truly adequate was the author's own – and preferably not in studio conditions but in a low-quality tape recording made at a small-scale gathering of intimates.[23]

The spoken word remained an important vehicle of Soviet culture, and literature in particular. The memorisation of text, especially poetry, was a core pedagogical practice in Soviet schools from the 1930s onwards: what better way to demonstrate patriotism and 'culturedness' (*kul'tur-nost'*) than to know Pushkin by heart? But the oral performance and circulation of poetry also had special significance as a means of building familiar networks of trust and of circumventing draconian censorship. In the 1930s when the poet Osip Mandelshtam (1891–1938) composed a devastating sixteen-line portrait of Stalin as a 'Kremlin highlander' endowed with worm-like fingers and cockroach moustache, he did not risk committing the poem to paper (see Chapter 4.2). But its oral transmission was so effective that even Genrikh Iagoda, the head of the NKVD, or security police, knew it by heart; the impermanence of orality did not in fact save Mandelshtam from arrest and exile. Pushkin, similarly, was sent into southern exile in the 1820s because his scurrilous

22 Dmitrii Bykov, *Bulat Okudzhava* [Bulat Okudzhava] (Moscow: Molodaia gvardiia, 2011), pp. 292–6, 354 (quotation), 406–8.
23 Smith, *Songs to Seven Strings*, pp. 219–20.

verse proved so memorable to its first listeners.[24] In the Thaw era, poets set out to be not just memorable but also memorisable: as he was limbering up for his poetic career, Evtushenko pored over a dictionary and filled a notebook with 10,000 new rhymes.[25]

The spoken word, then, always existed both in the public sphere and in familiar circles, and for that reason it had an unstable quality: civic pathos could give way to a far more equivocal diction. In the 1950s–60s, voice was an important way of conveying the core Thaw values of sincerity and authenticity, a cause that could be pursued in the most public venues imaginable – mass poetry readings, new radio rubrics, landmark films. But the resolutely upbeat mood of early Evtushenko was counterposed by instances of communication failure and painful silence even on the Soviet big screen. Away from the public domain, Soviet life had various cultural substrata where the spoken word took no heed of decorum or the literary canon. One of the most deeply buried was the oral storytelling that took place in the labour camps. As described by Varlam Shalamov (1907–1982), the pre-eminent prisoner-writer of Russia's twentieth century, a *roman* (stressed on the first, not the second syllable) was a yarn spun on the basis of an existing story from literature or popular culture; quite often the raconteur was an educated prisoner keen to enter the good graces of the hardened criminals, or *blatari*, and secure an extra food ration. The *blatari* deplored reading but were avid consumers of loose retellings (without attribution) of crime and adventure narratives, usually from a nineteenth-century repertoire that included anything from Russian potboilers to Alexandre Dumas's *The Count of Monte Cristo* and Tolstoi's *Anna Karenina* (*Anna Karenina*, 1878). Here was a modern *Thousand and One Nights*, set within the Soviet penal system.[26]

The Late Soviet and Post-Soviet Afterlife of the Literary Voice

Shalamov's example was certainly extreme, but there was no doubt that the public pathos of the spoken word was waning by the 1970s. Soviet political discourse in the Brezhnev era was notoriously deadening, and the authorities

---

24 Mikhail Gronas, *Cognitive Poetics and Cultural Memory: Russian Literary Mnemonics* (New York: Routledge, 2011), esp. pp. 7–8, 84–5.
25 Yevtushenko, *A Precocious Autobiography*, p. 37.
26 V. T. Shalamov, 'Kak "tiskaiut rómany"' [How 'yarns are spun'] (1959), in *Sobranie sochinenii v chetyrekh tomakh* [Collected works in four volumes] (Moscow: Khudozhestvennaia literatura; Vagrius, 1998), vol. II, pp. 92–100.

kept a close watch on all forms of public assembly. By now there was less scope for youthful poets to galvanise the Soviet public through stadium recitals, and the mood of the literary intelligentsia was inclined more to gloomy introspection than to inspirational oratory. But the 'Stagnation' label often applied to the late Soviet period is misleading, not least because the turn of the 1960s was the dawn of a new audiovisual era that brought new creative possibilities to all Soviet cultural actors, including its writers. The years around 1970 brought the advent of television as a true national medium and the golden age of Soviet cinema as measured by the diversity of its output and the size of its audiences. The Soviet film industry continued to produce occasional masterpieces, some of them drawing attention to the voice as a means of emotionally authentic expression. The most striking example is Ilia Averbakh's (1934–1986) *The Voice* (*Golos*, 1982), where the lead actress dies in the difficult final stages of a film's production, leaving behind a disembodied trace in the voice-overs she has completed.

Outside the official public sphere, guitar poetry continued to flourish. By now its most charismatic exponent was Vladimir Vysotskii (1938–1980), whose rasping voice and astringent manner formed a stark contrast with the understated Okudzhava. Vysotskii's celebrity was further boosted by his status as a leading theatre and film actor. In one of his early movies, *Brief Encounters* (*Korotkie vstrechi*, dir. Kira Muratova (1934–2018), 1967), he plays a geologist whose own guitar song contrasts favourably with the speech-making of the woman in his life, a local official. But it was *magnitizdat* that provided Vysotskii's most powerful vehicle, as only part of his work could be accommodated in Soviet canons. He kept up a frenetic pace of composition and performance, operating in many different genres and registers. His oeuvre contained ballads, parodies, lyrics, and bravura comedy, and he adopted personae including a camp-hardened criminal, a sportsman, a war veteran, and a Soviet everyman. His best work made virtuosic use of rhyme and rhythm, features that were accentuated by his oral delivery: there was no other poet for whom tempo (often breakneck) played such a part in the affective charge of a voiced text.[27]

The Gorbachev period fundamentally changed the conditions of public and semi-public speech of all kinds. Although Okudzhava was now granted more public prominence as a writer, becoming part of the Perestroika-era literary establishment, his style of performance was losing currency: like other members of his generation, Okudzhava railed at the inexorable rise

27 See Smith, *Songs to Seven Strings*, pp. 145–79.

of the pop song (*estradnaia pesnia*).[28] 'Kitchen talk' (the beloved conversational genre of the Soviet intelligentsia) and guitar poetry seemed much less compelling when it was possible to talk politics (and literature) on national television. The prestige of the voice further waned when the always talkative Mikhail Gorbachev lost his early charisma and came to be resented as an ineffectual yet overbearing chatterbox.

The post-Soviet era produced a sense of crisis in writers even more than in other sections of the cultural establishment, as state publishing subsidies were withdrawn and 'high' literature had so many sources of competition from the new mass culture. An even more fundamental problem was how writers were to retain intellectual and moral authority in a raucously commercialised society where cynicism, by the 2000s, was practically de rigueur – and how to do so, moreover, in a rapidly changing media environment where audiences were fickle and inattentive. But, as at previous moments of political and technological flux such as the early twentieth century, writers showed they could be resourceful rather than despondent in the face of wrenching changes. Just as Modernist poets once explored the gramophone and the radio, so some writers of the early twenty-first century found that the internet could give them new modes of expression. Literary bloggers playfully transgressed literary norms, self-consciously adopting an 'aesthetics of imperfection' as a mark of authenticity in the digital age.[29] Writers also tapped the new orality of the internet. One telling example came in 2011 when the prolific writer, critic, and commentator Dmitrii Bykov (1967–) composed a series of poems that alluded to the Russian literary tradition but took satirical aim at very contemporary political themes. Initially called 'Poet and Citizen' (*Poet i grazhdanin*) in a direct quotation from the nineteenth-century civic poet Nikolai Nekrasov (1821–1878), the series became known as 'Citizen Poet' (*Grazhdanin poet*) when it migrated to the internet. Performed by the actor Mikhail Efremov (1963–) and offering affectionate pastiches of the work of writers ranging from Pushkin and Nekrasov to Evtushenko and Okudzhava, this series of sixty or so poems showed that the literary voice could still hold the attention of an audience, even in the crowded audiosphere of the early twenty-first century.

---

28 G. S. Smith, 'Okudzhava marches on', *Slavonic and East European Review* 66.4 (1988), 558–9.

29 Ellen Rutten, '(Russian) writer-bloggers: Digital perfection and the aesthetics of imperfection', *Journal of Computer-Mediated Communication* 19.4 (2014), 744–62.

Further Reading

Brang, Peter, *Zvuchashchee slovo: Zametki po teorii i istorii deklamatsionnogo iskusstva v Rossii* [The sounding word: Notes on the theory and history of the art of declamation in Russia] (Moscow: Iazyki slavianskoi kul'tury, 2010).

Bulgakova, Oksana, *Golos kak kul'turnyi fenomen* [The voice as a cultural phenomenon] (Moscow: Novoe literaturnoe obozrenie, 2015).

Gorham, Michael S., *Speaking in Soviet Tongues: Language Culture and the Politics of Voice in Revolutionary Russia* (DeKalb: Northern Illinois University Press, 2003).

Lygo, Emily, *Leningrad Poetry 1953–1975: The Thaw Generation* (Oxford: Peter Lang, 2010).

Smith, Gerald Stanton, *Songs to Seven Strings: Russian Guitar Poetry and Soviet 'Mass Song'* (Bloomington: Indiana University Press, 1984).

Stites, Richard (ed.), *Culture and Entertainment in Wartime Russia* (Bloomington: Indiana University Press, 1995).

2.9

The Self-Publisher

JOSEPHINE VON ZITZEWITZ

Self-publishing – making texts available without the involvement of a formal publisher or any official entity – has a long tradition in Russia. In this sense, monks in medieval monasteries copying out religious texts by hand engaged in self-publishing. This chapter, however, conceptualises self-publishing mainly as a reaction to state censorship and examines self-published secular literature only. While ecclesiastical censorship had existed since the mid-sixteenth century, secular printing began only in the early eighteenth century, and the emperor or empress themselves acted as censor. The institution of the censor's office was established during the reign of Catherine II (r. 1762–96) (see Chapter 2.7). By the early nineteenth century, many writers were distributing manuscript copies of texts that did not pass the censor: Aleksandr Griboedov's (1795–1829) comedy *Woe from Wit* (*Gore ot uma*, comp. 1824) circulated widely from the mid-1820s onwards while the censor's office was still deliberating whether to allow its print publication; the play was published in full only in 1862.[1] Aleksandr Pushkin (1799–1837) disseminated many of his political poems and epigrams in handwritten form.[2] Mikhail Lermontov's (1814–1841) passionate response to Pushkin's violent death in 1837 – 'On the Death of a Poet' (*Na smert' poeta*), which he penned and distributed shortly after the event – earned Lermontov a spell of military service in the Caucasus and was only published after his own death, and even then not in Russia. In 1856, Aleksandr Herzen (1812–1870) included the poem in his London-based almanac *The Polar Star* (*Poliarnaia zvezda*, 1855–69).[3] But of course not all self-publishing is

---

1 See Simon Franklin, 'Mapping the graphosphere: Cultures of writing in early 19th-century Russia (and before)', *Kritika* 12.3 (2011), 554.
2 See D. Blagoi, *Tsenzura i Pushkin. Putevoditel' po Pushkinu* [Censorship and Pushkin. A guide to Pushkin] (Moscow: Gosudarstvennoe izdatel'stvo khudozhestvennoi literatury, 1931), pp. 368–72.
3 Mikhail Lermontov, 'Na smert' poeta' [On the death of a poet], *Poliarnaia zvezda* [The polar star] 2 (1856), 31–2.

a response to censorship. The Futurists – avant-garde poets of the 1910s – created some of their collections by hand, using non-standard media (including wallpaper) and richly decorating them with visual images to underline the materiality of their art; these collections were not intended for copying or mass production. Today, an ever-larger number of writers circumvent editorial oversight and challenge established institutions, using social media to introduce new texts to a wide readership, which they curate themselves.

The focus of this chapter is a phenomenon that was central to Russian literature in the second half of the twentieth century and which created a universally recognised acronym: *samizdat*. Samizdat shares traits with earlier and later forms of self-publishing. It entailed a process of making by hand, using whatever materials were available; it emerged in response to censorship; and it reached a large number of readers throughout the Soviet Union because texts proliferated through networks beyond the author's own circle of acquaintances. Yet it was the combination of all three factors that made samizdat so particular, and it is perhaps the unusual censorship model of the Soviet Union – in place until its demise – that explains the success of samizdat.

When Socialist Realism was proclaimed the only permissible style in art in 1934, the state not only stipulated what was not permissible (private publishing houses were closed and independent literary groups disbanded), but also prescribed what writers should write about and how they should write (see Chapter 1.8). Yet while a limited number of texts circulated among close acquaintances even during high Stalinism (mostly poetry with no political content that was nevertheless unpublishable for formal reasons or because the author had fallen into disgrace), self-publishing on a large scale proliferated only after Stalin's death. This chapter will examine samizdat in a roughly chronological manner, first as a mode of literary production that provided an outlet for texts rejected or suppressed by the official means of publication, and then as a mode of sociocultural organisation that had a decisive influence on the intellectual climate during the final decades of the Soviet Union. Each mode will be explained with the help of a detailed case study.

The Birth of Samizdat

The term *samizdat* now triggers associations with barely legible typescript on onion-skin paper, which was used by samizdat typists to maximise the

number of copies that could be produced using carbon paper during a single typing session. The term pre-dates the phenomenon itself and is commonly attributed to Nikolai Glazkov (1919–1979), who self-published in the Soviet Union in the 1940s. He would mark self-bound typescripts of prose miniatures with the word *samsebiaizdat* (self-publishing house) and give them to his friends. *Samsebiaizdat*, later shortened to *samizdat*, is a pun on the acronyms of Soviet publishing houses, such as Litizdat (*Literaturnoe izdatel'stvo*, Literary Publishing House) or Gosizdat (*Gosudarstvennoe izdatel'stvo*, State Publishing House).[4] The high time of samizdat was the long 1970s: the years sometimes described as Stagnation (*zastoi*), between the Soviet invasion of Czechoslovakia in 1968 and the onset of Perestroika in 1985. But the seeds were planted much earlier, during the resurgence of cultural activity during the period of reforms known as the Thaw (*ottepel'*) that followed Stalin's death in 1953 and the Twentieth Party Congress in 1956. In particular, samizdat as a mass phenomenon had its roots in the poetry boom of the late 1950s that saw emerging writers such as Evgenii Evtushenko (1932–2017), whose texts contained elements of formal experimentation and an exciting breadth of topics and moods, fill entire stadiums in public poetry readings. A newfound enthusiasm for lyric poetry inspired citizens to organise cultural events, such as the weekly gatherings on Maiakovskii Square in Moscow from 1958 onwards where young people would read poetry out loud.[5] In the centrally organised Soviet cultural sphere, such spontaneous initiatives were a novelty, and the forces they unleashed proved impossible to suppress.

It was not just contemporary poets who captured the attention of the Soviet audience. Much of the poetry of the Silver Age – as the period of pre-revolution Russian Modernism is commonly known – had not been repub-lished under early Soviet rule, but it re-emerged slowly during the late 1950s and 1960s. New official editions notwithstanding – and such editions were always selective – Silver Age poets were not widely published in the Soviet Union, even after Stalin's death.[6] As a result, readers who owned such texts,

---

4 See Aleksandr Daniel', 'Istoki i smysl sovetskogo samizdata' [The sources and meaning of samizdat], in V. Igrunov, M. Barbakadze, and E. Shvarts (eds.), *Antologiia samizdata: Nepodtsenzurnaia literatura v SSSR 1950-e–1980-e* [An anthology of samizdat: Uncensored literature in the USSR in the 1950s–1980s], 3 vols. (Moscow: Mezhdunarodnyi institut gumanitarno-politicheskikh issledovanii, 2005), vol. I, p. 18.
5 See Liudmila Polikovskaia, *'My predchuvstvie, predtecha ...'. Ploshchad' Maiakovskogo 1958–1965* ['We are a premonition, a harbinger ...' Maiakovskii Square 1958–1965] (Moscow: Zvenia, 1996).
6 An early example is the first (re)publication of forty-two poems by Marina Tsvetaeva in a literary miscellany: *Tarusskie stranitsy* [Pages from Tarusa] (Kaluga: Kaluzhskoe knizhnoe izdatel'stvo, 1961). The first substantial post-Stalin edition of Osip Mandelshtam

including pre-revolutionary editions, began to copy them out and share them. Hand- or typewritten copies of Silver Age poems remained a mainstay of literary samizdat up into the 1980s, the final decade of the Soviet Union. This sustained demand for literature that was emphatically non-contemporary was another factor distinguishing late Soviet samizdat from earlier forms of self-publication. But increasingly, literary samizdat was shaped by contemporary writers who could not – or did not try to – publish in the official press.

From the mid-1960s, samizdat began to include a wider range of material: not just literature but anything proscribed by official culture, from erotica such as the *Kama Sutra* to material relating to history, religion, politics, public affairs, and other topics. At the same time, samizdat acquired an international reputation due to texts generated by members of the growing human rights movement who became known as 'dissidents' (see Chapter 4.9). The human rights movement had close ties to literature from the start: an early action was the so-called rally for openness (*miting glasnosti*) in December 1965, held in support of the writers Andrei Siniavskii (1925–1997) and Iulii Daniel (1925–1988), who had been charged with anti-Soviet agitation and propaganda for publishing prose and essays abroad (under the pseudonyms Abram Terts and Nikolai Arzhak, respectively).[7] Some writers, such as the novelists Vladimir Maksimov (1930–1995) and Aleksandr Solzhenitsyn (1918–2008) and the poet Natalia Gorbanevskaia (1936–2013), became figureheads of the human rights movement. But for the most part, the dissidents produced protest letters and news items such as appeared in the bulletin *Chronicle of Current Events* (*Khronika tekushchikh sobytii*, 1968–83). The *Chronicle*, which was compiled in great secrecy, documented human rights abuses, arrests, and information from prison camps.[8] Western radio stations – such as the BBC, Voice of America, Deutsche Welle, and the purposely founded Radio Liberty/Radio Free Europe – broadcast samizdat texts back to the Soviet Union, hugely increasing their audience. Yet the vast majority of unofficially reproduced and circulated texts were not political and many related to everyday life or leisure interests, such as yoga manuals and recipe books. The poet Lev Loseff

only appeared in 1973: Mandel'shtam, *Stikhotvoreniia* [Poems] (Moscow: Sovetskii pisatel', 1973).

7 See Leopold Labedz and Max Hayward (eds.), *On Trial: The Case of Sinyavsky (Tertz) and Daniel (Arzhak)* (London: Collins and Harvill Press, 1967).

8 The *Chronicle* was also smuggled out to the west. The first eleven issues were published in one volume: Peter Reddaway (ed. and trans.), *Uncensored Russia: The Human Rights Movement in the Soviet Union* (London: Jonathan Cape, 1972). In 1971, Amnesty International began publishing individual issues in English translation.

(1937–2009) identified six categories: literary, political, religious and philo-sophical, mystical and occult, erotica, and instructions.[9] Loseff categorised all texts circulating unofficially as samizdat, while many bestowed this distinc-tion only on 'serious' texts pertaining to the first three categories.[10] Many of the most recognised Russian writers of the late twentieth century first disseminated their key texts via samizdat.

By the late 1960s, samizdat had acquired a new facet: texts were smuggled abroad, printed in Russian, and smuggled back into the Soviet Union – a practice known as *tamizdat* (literally, 'published over there'). Tamizdat was mostly realised through émigré publishing houses, which revived a nineteenth-century tradition: back then, émigré intellectuals had founded publishing houses to promote texts unpublishable in Russia. For example, Herzen's Free Russian Press (*Vol'naia russkaia knigopechatnia*) published periodicals such as *The Polar Star*, *The Bell* (*Kolokol*, 1857–67), and *Voices from Russia* (*Golosa iz Rossii*, 1856–60), all featuring poetry by Russia's great poets alongside political texts. After the 1917 revolution, successive waves of émigrés promoted literature in Russian abroad. The YMCA Press, which published many seminal works in the 1970s, was originally an Orthodox Christian publisher and transferred from Russia to Paris in 1925, and the openly anti-Soviet publishing house Posev was founded in Germany in 1945.[11] But the exponential growth in tamizdat was driven by the so-called third wave of emigration in the 1970s–1980s (see Chapter 4.10). Siniavskii, who emigrated to Paris in 1973, founded the almanac *Sintaksis* (*Sintaksis*, 1978–2001). Vladimir Maramzin (1934–2021), another émigré to Paris, co-founded and co-edited the literary journal *Echo* (*Ekho*, 1978–86) and founded a Russian-language publishing house, also called *Echo*. The human rights activist Valerii Chalidze (1938–2018), who emigrated to the United States in 1972, set up two publishing houses: Khronika Press and Chalidze Publications. And Tatiana Goricheva (1947–) – editor of several samizdat periodicals – settled in Paris in 1980 where she founded the publishing house Beseda, which produced a journal of the same name (1983–93) as well as monographs. However, it was not only Russian émigrés that promoted unpublishable Russian texts. Ardis Publishers was founded in 1971 by Americans Carl and Ellendea Proffer

9 Lev Losev, 'Samizdat i samogon' [Samizdat and moonshine], in *Zakrytyi raspredelitel'* [Closed supply channel] (Ann Arbor, MI: Hermitage, 1984), pp. 170–4.
10 Josephine von Zitzewitz, *The Culture of Samizdat: Literature and Underground Networks in the Late Soviet Union* (London: Bloomsbury, 2020), chap. 2.
11 For an account of the YMCA Press's early years, see Matthew Lee Miller, *The American YMCA and Russian Culture: The Preservation and Expansion of Orthodox Christianity, 1900–1940* (Lanham, MD: Lexington Books, 2012).

in Ann Arbor, Michigan, initially catering to scholars. Over the course of the 1970s, Ardis became a major producer of tamizdat destined for the USSR.[12]

By the mid-1970s, tamizdat had become a major driver of samizdat and the most important source of longer works of uncensored literature.[13] Tamizdat copies would turn into blueprints for subsequent hand-made reproductions, returning an authoritative version of the self-published text to samizdat circulation. The tamizdat editions of many iconic texts inadmissible for publication in the USSR pre-dated the first Soviet or Russian editions by decades.[14] These works were inadmissible on a variety of grounds, including the world view expressed (political or religious) and aesthetic reasons. Texts such as Boris Pasternak's (1890–1960) *Doctor Zhivago* (*Doktor Zhivago*, pub. in Milan, 1957) and Solzhenitsyn's novels *Cancer Ward* (*Rakovyi korpus*, pub. in Frankfurt, 1968) and *First Circle* (*V kruge pervom*, pub. in New York, 1968), not to mention the latter's non-fiction work *The Gulag Archipelago* (*Arkhipelag GULAG*, comp. 1968, pub. in Paris, 1973), undoubtedly belong to the first category. By contrast, Joseph Brodsky's (1940–1996) poetry – brought together in the collections *Poems* (*Stikhotvoreniia i poemy*, pub. in Washington DC and New York, 1965) and *A Stop in the Desert* (*Ostanovka v pustyne*, pub. in New York, 1970) – live in an aesthetic space utterly alien to Soviet (literary) reality and defined by poetic dialogue with the great poets of the western and Russian tradition (Virgil, Anna Akhmatova (1889–1966), W. H. Auden, Robert Frost, and others). Maksimov's novels *Seven Days of Creation* (*Sem' dnei tvoreniia*, pub. in Frankfurt, 1971) and *Quarantine* (*Karantin*, pub. in Frankfurt, 1973) are written in a style shaped by Socialist Realism, exhibiting epic scope and a clear teleology. However, both novels are essentially religious works, that is, moral tales based on biblical allegories – a clear violation of Socialist Realist dogma. Vladimir Voinovich's (1938–1980) novel *The Life and Extraordinary Adventures of Private Ivan Chonkin* (*Zhizn' i neobychainye prikliucheniia soldata Ivana Chonkina*, comp. 1963–9, pub. in Paris, 1979) takes satirical aim at the Second World War. Venedikt Erofeev's (1939–1990) cult classic *Moscow–Petushki* (*Moskva–Petushki*, comp. 1969–70, pub. in Israel, 1973, and Paris, 1977), a complicated prose poem

---

12 For the history of Ardis, see Ann Komaromi, 'Ardis facsimile and reprint editions: Giving back Russian literature', in Friederike Kind-Kovacs and Jessie Labov (eds.), *Samizdat, Tamizdat and Beyond: Transnational Media during and after Socialism* (New York: Berghahn, 2013), pp. 27–50. For a list of titles published, see pp. 333–8.

13 See Daniel', 'Istoki i smysl sovetskogo samizdata'.

14 For a case study, see Gleb Struve, 'Kak byl vpervye izdan "Rekviem"' [How 'Requiem' was first published], in Anna Akhmatova, *Rekviem. 1935–1940* [Requiem. 1935–1940], 2nd edn (New York: Tovarishchestvo zarubezhnykh pisatelei, 1969), pp. 22–4.

replete with literary references, revels in the religious visions of its alcoholic hero, Venichka (read as a holy fool by various researchers), who dies a pointless, violent death described in gruesome detail (see Chapter 4.9). Vasilii Grossman's (1905–1964) monumental war epic *Life and Fate* (*Zhizn' i sud'ba*, comp. 1950–9, pub. in Lausanne, 1980) comes to the devastating conclusion that the Soviet regime exhibits some of the same characteristics as Nazi Germany, essentially agreeing with Hannah Arendt's thesis that the totalitarian systems are similar. Iurii Dombrovskii's (1909–1978) *The Faculty of Useless Knowledge* (*Fakul'tet nenuzhnykh veshchei*, comp. 1964–75, pub. in Paris, 1978) describes the confrontation between eternal human values and the Soviet Terror in the late 1930s – experienced firsthand by Dombrovskii, who spent more than twenty years in camps and in exile – through the experience of a museum curator arrested on false charges.

Tamizdat also supplied the first print editions of older works suppressed at the time of writing, such as Andrei Platonov's (1899–1951) novels *The Foundation Pit* (*Kotlovan*), which was written in 1930 but first published in print in Ann Arbor only in 1973, and *Chevengur* (*Chevengur*), which was completed in 1929 and published in Paris in 1972. These novels are highly original attempts at capturing a situation where the abstract linguistic concepts (i.e. Soviet bureaucratese) that are supposed to shape a new world collide with existing reality, which turns out to be as unyielding as the soil of the eponymous foundation pit that turns the projected 'proletarian home' into a grave. Evgenii Zamiatin's (1884–1937) dystopia *We* (*My*, comp. 1920) was first published in English in New York in 1924, and published in Russian in full for the first time in New York only in 1952. Mikhail Bulgakov's (1891–1940) previously unpublished *The Master and Margarita* (*Master i Margarita*, comp. 1928–40) became hugely popular after the Soviet journal *Moscow* (*Moskva*, 1957–) serialised a heavily censored version in 1966–7, but it was the YMCA Press in Paris that first published an unabridged version in 1967. The salvaged oeuvres of Aleksandr Vvedenskii (1904–1941) and Daniil Kharms (1905–1942) – the most outstanding members of the 1920s Absurdist group OBERIU (*Ob"edinenie real'nogo iskusstva*, Union of Real Art), whose style was condemned as 'Formalism' in the sense of ideologically vacant experiments in form – also first appeared abroad, in Ann Arbor and Bremen, respectively.

Case Study 1: *The Gulag Archipelago*

Aleksandr Solzhenitsyn's *The Gulag Archipelago* is monumental in more than one sense. Consisting of seven parts in three volumes and running to well

over a thousand pages, it constitutes the epitome of what many people think samizdat is: a work produced in secret, advancing a devastating indictment of the Soviet state, leaving a mark on public opinion, arguing that mass repression was an integral part of the Soviet project. After the suicide of his typist, Elizaveta Voronianskaia, following her apprehension by the KGB,[15] Solzhenitsyn authorised publication abroad; the YMCA Press published the first volume in Paris in 1973. *The Gulag Archipelago* provided substantial information about the scale of Soviet state terror to an international audience as well as to those in the Soviet Union who could access illicit copies. The publicity Solzhenitsyn afforded the Terror contributed to the decision of state authorities to strip him of his Soviet citizenship and deport him in 1974. Now an arch-enemy of the regime, Solzhenitsyn became a hero in the Soviet dissident community and in the west, thus embodying a Cold War dichotomy according to which people, opinions, and texts that opposed Soviet policy were by default considered to be supportive of western ideas and policies. It was of little importance to his admirers that Solzhenitsyn's own stance as an advocate of a Russian national state based on Orthodox Christian tradition did not affirm their world view. *The Gulag Archipelago* is a prime example of 'truth-telling' samizdat / tamizdat literature: the Gulag remained largely taboo in official Soviet culture, and texts on this topic were suppressed systematically. Samizdat's reputation for being a reliable source of information was founded on works such as *The Gulag Archipelago* and the idea that if a work was banned, it must concern some truth the government did not want readers to access.

How Samizdat Was Made

While print runs in Soviet official literature were dictated from above, in an 'ordinary' book economy with a market element a text must be endorsed by a large enough number of readers to remain accessible / in print. In this respect samizdat was no exception. The hunger for a greater variety of reading matter and information dwarfed other driving forces of samizdat, such as the need of writers for publication platforms or any political motivation. However, the specifics of textual production and distribution differed significantly from those that concerned printed texts or even manuscripts.

15 See A. V. Korotkov, S. A. Mel'chin, and A. S. Stepanov (eds.), *Kremlevskii samosud. Sekretnye dokumenty Politburo o pisatele A. Solzhenitsyne* [Mob law in the Kremlin. The Politburo's secret documents on the writer A. Solzhenitsyn] (Moscow: Rodina, 1994), pp. 250–1.

Liudmila Alekseeva (1927–2018) – the veteran dissident and chairwoman of the Moscow Helsinki Group, a prominent human rights organisation – remembers:

> The mechanism of samizdat was like this: the author would print their text in the way that was most accessible to a private individual under Soviet conditions – i.e. on the typewriter, in a few copies – and give these copies to his acquaintances. If one of them considered the text interesting, they would make copies from the copy they had got and give them to their acquaintances, and so on. The more successful a work the more quickly and widely it would be disseminated.[16]

Here Alekseeva identifies a key component in the success of samizdat, namely multiplication at one remove from the author's own circle.

Samizdat was a variant of print culture rather than a separate phenomenon altogether – a hybrid in technological, organisational, and material terms.[17] Technologically, the iconic samizdat instrument, the typewriter, was fit for private use, unlike a professional printing press, but could produce (using carbon paper) a limited number of absolutely identical copies. In organisational terms, samizdat was often hybrid too, especially in its highly structured forms such as the periodicals of the 1970s: unofficial writers and journal makers used the familiar models of official publications to present texts that were unfit for publication in those same official journals. Materially, samizdat was a hybrid because a significant proportion of the circulating texts existed in print but were also reproduced by hand because no new editions were available. This happened, for example, with pre-revolutionary literature and contemporary texts produced in very small print runs, such as the novels of Arkadii (1925–1991) and Boris (1933–2012) Strugatskii, a hugely popular duo of science fiction writers.

The circulation of print is ordinarily influenced by a balanced matrix of intellectual and/or aesthetic, socioeconomic, and political factors.[18] In the

---

16 Liudmila Alekseeva, *Istoriia inakomysliia v SSSR* [A history of dissent in the USSR], new edn (Moscow: RITs Zatsepa, 2001), p. 112.
17 Franklin uses the term 'hybrid' to describe a writing culture situated between manuscript and print in 'Mapping the graphosphere'. See also Boris Belenkin, '"Rukopisnoe" ili "pechatnoe"? ... "Pechatnoe" kak "rukopisnoe"? ... Malotirazhnye izdaniia v kontekste sovremennogo kul'turnogo protsessa' ['Manuscript' or 'print'? ... 'Print' as 'manuscript'? ... Small print-run publications in the context of the cultural process today], *Acta Samizdatica/Zapiski o samizdate* [Acta Samizdatica/Notes on samizdat] (Moscow: GPIB Rossii – Mezhdunarodnyi Memorial – 'Zvenia', 2012), pp. 14–23.
18 Robert Darnton's 'The communications circuit' is a helpful tool for visualising these forces. See Robert Darnton, 'What *is* the *history of books?*', *Daedalus* 111.3 (1982), 68, figure 1.

case of samizdat, these factors were distorted and unbalanced: market pressures had little bearing as commercial literary samizdat remained very rare (although tamizdat books were sold on the black market), and censorship blew political criteria out of proportion. This, in turn, had an impact on intellectual and/or aesthetic considerations, as readers might have been more benevolently inclined towards a text on the sole grounds that it was 'forbidden'. However, samizdat's greatest distortion of the mechanisms we know from the book industry concerned the roles of intermediaries that determined the path of a printed text from author to reader: publishers, printers, distributors, booksellers, and librarians. In the overwhelming majority of cases, all these functions – from the decision to publish (i.e. to circulate the text) to printing (or typing or hand-copying), distributing, binding, stocking, and preserving for posterity – were carried out by readers without the involvement of any middlemen. In the case of new literature (as opposed to out-of-print works), to set the cycle in motion the original author had to circulate the manuscript/typescript to the initial reader or group of readers, effectively fulfilling the role of publisher. The typewriter as a method of production and the absence of an editorial process meant that the threshold for becoming a 'published' author was low. However, a samizdat text could only become successful – i.e. be read by many people – if subsequent readers spontaneously decided to produce more 'print runs'.[19]

Reading samizdat was the opposite of leisurely private reading: copies had to be passed on quickly to the next person because demand was high and copies were few; there is much anecdotal evidence about typescripts being loaned for a night only and of people gathering to read forbidden literature together.[20] At the same time, if a typewriter, carbon paper, and a person with typing skills were available, it was possible to 'acquire' one's own copy while simultaneously running off further copies for circulation; one 'set' – a group of copies produced in a single typing session – usually consisted of four to seven copies, in some cases over ten. The author lost control over their own text the moment he or she 'published' it; this was the price of it reaching the reader. Samizdat thus challenged the Gutenberg model that was established when print made it possible to widely reproduce identical physical copies of a text. This paradigm presupposes that the text has been created by one or several individually known authors; that the printed text is final; and that it is

---

19 F. J. M. Feldbrugge has described this phenomenon where the reader, rather than the publisher or author, controls circulation as 'snowballing'. Feldbrugge, *Samizdat and Political Dissent in the Soviet Union* (Leiden: A. W. Sijthoff, 1975), p. 7.

20 For data and analysis, see von Zitzewitz, *Culture of Samizdat*, chap. 2.

the author or authors, together with the editors and publishers, who have ultimate responsibility for the text.[21]

While the production of printed books is generally tailored to changing reader interest, which is expressed in economic terms, the reach of samizdat texts was limited by basic material and temporal constraints as well as by the risk of persecution for owning, producing, or copying those texts. Secondary copies were produced in great haste. The consumables needed for making texts – paper, typewriter ribbon, and carbon paper – needed to be purchased (if resources permitted) or else purloined (for example, from the workplace). Typewriters were expensive and at times hard to come by. Contrary to a common myth, typewriters were not registered by the KGB, but the secret police did sometimes identify the origin of confiscated texts by comparing the typeface with that of other such texts; hence, typists who produced politically sensitive material texts avoided using a typewriter that could be traced back to them. It was the selfless work of countless women – typist (*mashinistka*) was a female profession, and many girls learned to type in school – that made samizdat a success. Typing large amounts of text on a mechanical typewriter required physical strength, considerable skill, the willingness to remain nameless, and the ability to invest a lot of time – and only a minority of samizdat typists were remunerated for their work.

Naturally, the production method had a major impact on the state of the text as a physical object. Different copies of the same text often display an astonishing degree of variation beyond typos or accidental omissions. Typescripts were corrected by hand, and words in Latin script and footnotes were added by hand, too, as the typewriter could not produce them. This practice introduced differences even between copies pertaining to the same set. Moreover, the informality of reproduction changed the attitude towards the text as an inviolable whole. Readers and translators took liberties and made decisions that were normally the prerogative of authors or editors. Sometimes they reproduced only part of a text or collection to save time or highlight what they considered most important. Once circulated, such copies led to new versions becoming established. The prolific translator Natalia Trauberg (1928–2009) would leave out large sections of religious and

---

21 On the topic of authorial control, see Valentina Parisi, 'The dispersed author: The problem of literary authority in samizdat textual production', in Parisi (ed.), *Samizdat: Between Practices and Representations; Lecture Series at Open Society Archives, Budapest, February–June 2013* (Budapest: IAS Publications, 2015), pp. 63–72. Printing as a means of standardisation is discussed by Elizabeth Eisenstein, *The Printing Press as an Agent of Change: Communication and Cultural Transformations in Early Modern Europe* (Cambridge: Cambridge University Press, 1979).

philosophical texts because she had decided that her readers lacked the knowledge necessary to appreciate them.[22] For authors and reproducers alike, the unreliability of samizdat texts was an accidental consequence of their material reality rather than anything engineered deliberately. On the contrary, those involved in producing samizdat strove for more durable formats to make the process less labour-intensive and ensure wider circulation. Tamizdat was one such format, and the increasing availability of complete print editions to copy from may have provided an additional impulse for improving production methods. Two mechanical copying technologies were popular: photocopying (*kserokopiia*, derived from the brand name Xerox) and photography (*fotokopiia*). While photocopiers were often tied to the workplace, photography equipment was available to private individuals. Printing from negatives, while resulting in a bulky end product, made possible a theoretically infinite number of prints on demand. One well-documented circle that favoured this technique was the samizdat 'library' run in Odesa by a group of samizdat collectors around Viacheslav Igrunov (1948–) between 1967 and 1982.[23] Like all samizdat libraries, it was not a building with repositories and reading rooms but a network of people. Rather than passing on the texts they reproduced, Igrunov's team would lend them to pre-approved readers; the texts ultimately returned to their erstwhile keeper. The purpose of this practice was to increase the public's exposure to texts the collectors considered important. A side-effect of the emergence of authoritative versions and mechanical reproduction was the loss of the individual samizdat script as a unique artefact. Conversely, the material artefact of the samizdat text – barely legible letters on translucent onion-skin paper – became the trademark sign of unofficial culture and textual 'authenticity', indicating that a text had been produced in adverse conditions because it contained elements that were unacceptable to the authorities.

Case Study 2: Literary Periodicals in Leningrad

In the 1970s, intellectuals in Leningrad – many of them poets – began producing typewritten periodicals in order to circulate their own texts and

---

22 Natalia Trauberg, 'Vsegda li pobezhdaet pobezhdennyi?' [Does the vanquished always win?], in *Sama zhizn'* [Life itself] (St Petersburg: Izdatel'stvo Ivana Limbakha, 2008), pp. 411–12.

23 For a descriptive analysis, see Elena Strukova, 'Delo ob odesskoi biblioteke samizdata' [The case of the Odesa samizdat library], *Bibliografiia* [Bibliography] 2 (2012), 50–9. For a conceptual analysis of samizdat libraries, see von Zitzewitz, *Culture of Samizdat*, chap. 4.

other writings that were of interest to them. While the earliest titles – *37* (*37*, 1976–81; edited by Goricheva, Viktor Krivulin (1944–2001), and others; twenty-one issues) and *The Clock* (*Chasy*, 1976–90; edited by Boris Ivanov (1928–2015), Boris Ostanin (1946–2023), and others; eighty issues) – published new literature alongside philosophical and theological material and translations of foreign classics of twentieth-century intellectual history, later journals were more specifically focused on literature and literary criticism. These included *Bypass Canal* (*Obvodnyi kanal*, 1981–93; edited by Sergei Stratanovskii (1944–) and Kirill Butyrin (1940–2016); nineteen issues) and *The Northern Post* (*Severnaia pochta*, 1979–81; edited by Sergei Dediulin (1950–) and Krivulin; eight issues).[24]

Literary journals were a symptom of mature samizdat, signalling that what had started as a spontaneous phenomenon was becoming an increasingly professionalised literary process. As periodical publications, they depended on a more or less stable group of individuals who conceived, compiled, produced, and distributed them; they nurtured the emergence of literary currents as opposed to individual voices. In the 1970s, Leningrad was the undisputed capital of poetry, represented by the so-called Leningrad School of Krivulin, Stratanovskii, Aleksandr Mironov (1948–2010), Elena Shvarts (1948–2010), Vasilii Fillipov (1955–2013), Oleg Okhapkin (1944–2008), and others. At the same time, the journal editors were attentive readers: when Moscow Conceptualism – a postmodern movement in fine art, performance, and literature – gained traction in the early 1980s, the works of poets such as Dmitrii Prigov (1940–2007) and Lev Rubinshtein (1947–2024) began to feature in the journals. As the journals published not only texts but also sections announcing, chronicling, and analysing unofficial events, they contributed to the impression of a well-organised, organic scene. Today, they constitute important repositories of information about unofficial culture.

The makers and authors of the Leningrad periodicals exemplified a stance typical of the 1970s.[25] Unlike earlier writers who had sought to expose the shortcomings of the Soviet system, they endeavoured to live their creative

---

24 These periodicals are described closely in Dmitrii Severiukhin, Viacheslav Dolinin, Boris Ivanov, and Boris Ostanin (eds.), *Samizdat Leningrada 1950e–1980e: Literaturnaia entsiklopediia* [Leningrad samizdat in the 1950s–1980s: A literary encyclopedia] (Moscow: Novoe literaturnoe obozrenie, 2003). For a list of more than 300 titles, see Ann Komaromi and Gennadii Kuzovkin (eds.), *Katalog periodiki samizdata* [Catalogue of samizdat periodicals] (Moscow: Mezhdunarodnyi Memorial, 2018).

25 For an analysis of the distinction between the decades, see Boris Ostanin and Alexander Kobak, 'Molniia i raduga: Puti kul'tury 60–80-kh godov' [Lightning and rainbow: The paths of culture in the 1960–1980s], in *Molniia i raduga: Literaturno-kriticheskie*

lives as if the prescriptions and proscriptions of official culture did not exist – an apolitical stance that was nevertheless deeply political. To complicate the picture, the literary journals copied certain elements of official literature, such as editorial committees, literary prizes (the Andrei Belyi Prize was inaugurated by the editors of *The Clock* in 1978), poetry readings in people's flats, and subscription schemes (to cover typing fees). This illustrates the uneasy co-existence of official and unofficial literature that marked the twilight years of the Soviet regime and resists easy dichotomies. The milieu that arose around the journals and the possibility to publish, albeit to a limited audience consisting mostly of other writers and acquaintances, arguably encouraged literary and cultural activity that might not have happened otherwise. It made a very significant contribution to Russian Postmodernism, specifically to the branch that sought to re-establish continuity with the pre-revolutionary Modernist tradition, forcibly interrupted by the 1917 revolution.[26] Interestingly, while individual representatives of this subculture did publish in tamizdat, this happened comparatively late, in the 1980s.[27] However, the cultural ferment which brought forth this poetry was not reflected in tamizdat publications.

Soviet Samizdat as a Network Phenomenon

For nearly three decades, there were two Russian literatures (or even three, if we distinguish between samizdat and tamizdat): works printed in the official press, and works that bypassed these channels. As a 'network of networks', samizdat was a symptom of societal development. During the final decades of the Soviet Union, semi-legal networks proliferated and increasingly replaced official institutions. The functions they fulfilled ranged from the procurement of deficit foodstuffs to favours at work – and the procurement of alternative reading material. Samizdat enabled a significant minority to circumvent a literature-centric society's prescriptive print culture. Whether a person was able to read samizdat at all, which texts they read, and how many

---

stat'i 1980-kh godov [Lightning and rainbow: Literary critical articles from the 1980s] (St Petersburg: Izdatel'stvo imeni N. I. Novikova, 2003).

26 See Mikhail Epshtein, *Postmodernizm v Rossii* [Postmodernism in Russia] (Moscow: Azbuka, 2019).

27 E.g. Viktor Krivulin, *Stikhi* [Poems] (Paris: Ritm, 1981); Krivulin, *Stikhi* [Poems], 2 vols. (Paris, Leningrad: Beseda, 1988); Elena Shvarts, *Tantsuiushchii David: Stikhi raznykh let* [Dancing David: Poems from various years] (New York: Russica Publishers, 1985); Shvarts, *Stikhi* [Poems] (Leningrad, Paris, and Munich: Beseda, 1987); Oleg Okhapkin, *Stikhi* [Poems] (Leningrad, Paris: Beseda, 1989).

depended on the people they knew. But samizdat was not just a new currency in certain social networks. Samizdat was the backbone of a cultural reality that gradually emancipated itself from official supplies and dictates not just in the area of reading. According to Alekseeva, 'These groups ... often replaced non-existent or for various reasons inaccessible institutions – publishing houses, lecture halls, exhibitions, notice boards, confessionals, concert halls, libraries, museums, legal consultations, knitting circles ... as well as seminars on literature, history, philosophy and linguistics.'[28]

Samizdat networks were heterogeneous groups with fluid membership driven by acquaintance and mutual trust. As they continued to be effectively illegal, they remained outside official Soviet culture but were nevertheless part of cultural reality. Outside observers, especially those who identify samizdat with dissidence, might assume that people involved in samizdat were actively opposed to the Soviet regime, following the example laid out by Solzhenitsyn in his samizdat article 'Live Not by Lies' (Zhit' ne po lzhi, 1974). The reality for the overwhelming majority of those who read samizdat was more complicated. They did not follow the famous dissident's exhortation to cease all participation in Soviet life. On the contrary, being 'inside-yet-outside',[29] that is, able to move in different circles simultaneously, characterised the lifestyle of a large proportion of the late Soviet intelligentsia.[30] These circles exhibited different degrees of closeness to official culture: a person might read or even reproduce samizdat at the same time as earning their living working for a Soviet cultural institution. The attitude of many samizdat readers was one of passive rejection; while people were willing to read forbidden literature and engage in lengthy debates in friends' kitchens, for the majority of them this represented an internal attitude rather than a call to action. The overlap between official and unofficial life has been explored by numerous researchers during the 2010s. Samizdat has been conceptualised as one of many informal networks that supplied goods which the state could not or would not supply, and as a form of grassroots organisation that provided a space for people to connect outside their usual circles and learn skills that enabled them to oppose

---

28 Liudmila Alekseeva and Paul Goldberg, Pokolenie ottepeli [The Thaw generation] (Moscow: Zakharov, 2006), p. 91.
29 To use a term coined by Alexei Yurchak, theorised in Yurchak, Everything Was Forever, until It Was No More: The Last Soviet Generation (Princeton: Princeton University Press, 2005).
30 On different types of engagement, see Laurent Thevenot, 'The plurality of cognitive formats and engagements: Moving between the familiar and the public', European Journal of Social Theory 10.3 (2007), 409–23.

the Soviet system, however tacitly.[31] The significant overlap between some unofficial and official literary groupings during the very early and very late phases of samizdat can also be explained with the help of these paradigms. A particularly salient example is the literary association Club-81 (*Klub 81*), founded in 1981 by Leningrad samizdat writers as part of a deal with the KGB concerning a space for uncensored literature; the organisation was co-curated by a functionary from the Soviet Writers' Union.[32] While those who wrote and circulated texts that contradicted political or aesthetic proscriptions were no longer in mortal danger after Stalin's death, many if not most self-publishers endured persecution at some point. Pasternak faced a hate campaign and had to renounce the Nobel Prize when *Doctor Zhivago* was published in Italy, and Siniavskii and Daniel received labour camp sentences because the words of their fictional protagonists were interpreted as anti-Soviet propaganda. Many writers whose work circulated unofficially were strongly encouraged or forced by the authorities to leave the Soviet Union on a one-way ticket; others were arrested and imprisoned – a formidable brain drain. Among them was Brodsky, whose samizdat activity had already earned him a five-year term of internal exile to the Arkhangelsk region and who emigrated to the USA in 1972. Maksimov was excluded from the Soviet Writers' Union in 1973 and emigrated to France in 1974. Voinovich left the Soviet Union in 1980. Two writers widely published during the Thaw, Anatolii Gladilin (1935–2018) and Vasilii Aksenov (1932–2009), emigrated in 1976 and 1980, respectively. Scholars and supporters also suffered persecution: the philologist Efim Etkind (1918–1999), who compiled – together with Maramzin – a five-volume samizdat collection of Brodsky's poetry (1972–3) and concealed a typescript copy of *The Gulag Archipelago*, was exiled and emigrated to France in 1974, where Maramzin ended up also. Another philologist, Mikhail Meilakh (1945–) – one of the men responsible for resurrecting the work of Kharms and Vvedenskii – was arrested and sentenced in 1983 for circulating anti-Soviet literature. Editors of samizdat periodicals were not exempt. Goricheva and Dediulin were exiled in 1980 and 1981, respectively. While some of those active in the unofficial cultural sphere managed to maintain 'regular' careers, many more retreated into a form of internal emigration and worked in menial jobs – either by necessity, because

31 Ilya Kukulin, 'Prodistsiplinarnye i antidistsiplinarnye seti v pozdnesovetskom obshchestve' [Prodisciplinary and antidisciplinary networks in late Soviet society], *Sotsiologicheskoe obozrenie* [Sociological review] 16.3 (2017), 136–74. Ann Komaromi describes samizdat groups with the help of Nancy Fraser's concept of 'counterpublic' in 'Samizdat and Soviet dissident publics', *Slavic Review* 71.1 (2012), 70–90.

32 See Boris Ivanov, *Istoriia Kluba-81* [The history of Club 81] (St Petersburg: Izdatel'stvo Ivana Limbakha, 2015).

nothing else was available to them, or by choice. The result was an impoverished bohemia, the members of which romanticised their own marginal lifestyle, which was the price for living within Soviet reality while disregarding its ideological premises and limitations.[33] In this context, the 'samizdat' provenance of a text became a marker of authenticity: anything rejected by official culture, the tropes of which were no longer taken seriously by many members of the educated public, must be worth reading by default. Samizdat writers, on the other hand, were separated from the usual elements of the literary process, in particular the critical eye of editors and a market where readers choose their reading matter based on literary quality, entertainment value, or topicality alone. Deprived of a general readership, relying exclusively on each other for professional affirmation, and surrounded by admirers, samizdat writers – in particular the unofficial poets who produced their own periodicals – led a life in which literature occupied centre stage. They appeared to be the true heirs to the great Russian literary tradition – a literary myth in its own right.[34]

The End of Samizdat

Russian literature, which had existed in an unnaturally fragmented way for decades, began a process of rapid consolidation when censorship was gradually relaxed following the proclamation of Mikhail Gorbachev's policy of Glasnost in 1986. Official and unofficial literature began to merge. Texts which were known to the samizdat-reading public through self-made copies flooded the pages of Soviet thick journals: excerpts from *The Gulag Archipelago* and *The Faculty of Useless Knowledge* were serialised in the journal *New World* (*Novyi mir*, 1925–) in 1988; *Life and Fate* was published by the journal *October* (*Oktiabr'*, 1924–) in 1988. Other important texts that became available to a mass readership for the first time were Evgeniia Ginzburg's (1904–1977) account of her time in the Gulag, *Into the Whirlwind* (*Krutoi marshrut*; first Soviet edition in 1990), and Nadezhda Mandelshtam's (1899–1980) multivolume memoirs of the 1930s, *Hope against Hope* and *Hope Abandoned* (*Vospominaniia* and *Vtoraia kniga*, first published in the Soviet Union in 1990). Another huge success of the Perestroika years was the 1987 serialisation of the first volume of Anatolii Rybakov's (1911–1998) trilogy *The*

---

33 This is the topic of the song 'Pokolenie dvornikov i storozhei' [A generation of caretakers and nightwatchmen] (1988), by the cult band Akvarium.

34 Stanislav Savitskii, *Andegraund. Istoriia i mify leningradskoi neofitsial'noi literatury* [Underground. The history and myths of Leningrad unofficial literature] (Moscow: Novoe literaturnoe obozrenie, 2002).

Children of the Arbat (*Deti Arbata*, 1982–94). First composed in the 1960s, this fictional account of the early years of the Soviet Union and the destruction of the Stalin years was unabashed in its criticism of the Soviet system. The return of such long-awaited 'truth-telling' texts was an important cultural event of Perestroika, and the significance of experimental contemporary writing paled by comparison. As private printing was no longer outlawed, samizdat journals ceased to be illegal; at the same time, the number of new grassroots periodicals exploded.[35] Most of them were even more highly specialised and short-lived, exemplifying the variety of writing and reading tastes that had been fostered by unofficial culture and could now be expressed in the climate of relaxing censorship. This process culminated in the adoption of the Law on Printing in 1990, which abolished censorship altogether.[36]

It has become popular to compare samizdat to the internet and to social media in particular (see Chapter 2.11).[37] Samizdat preceded the internet's challenge to the Gutenberg model of print, and both phenomena are based on informal network structures, allow for the spontaneous generation of texts at grassroots level, and are largely free of commercial interests. However, while research into samizdat can supply concepts that are useful for the study of internet literature, a direct comparison is of little use for this chapter because the chapter posits samizdat as a specific response to both prescription and censorship. Samizdat texts, laboriously reproduced, were a scarce commodity, and this scarcity might have acted as a quality-control mechanism: most social media posts would not warrant the effort required to turn them into physical documents. Most importantly perhaps, while the samizdat process concealed the links between a text and its reader, the internet renders the reading and distribution of texts visible in the literal sense of the word.

35 O. N. Ansberg and A. D. Margolis (eds.), *Obshchestvennaia zhizn' Leningrada v gody perestroiki. Sbornik materialov* [Civic life in Leningrad during the Perestroika years. A Collection of materials] (St Petersburg: Serebriannyi vek, 2009); Komaromi and Kuzovkin (eds.), *Katalog periodiki samizdata*.

36 For a timeline, see 'Putevoditel' po vystavke "Ot tsenzury i samizdata k svobode pechati. 1917–1990"' [Guide to the exhibition 'From censorship and samizdat towards freedom of print, 1917–1990], in *Acta Samizdatica/Zapiski o samizdate* [Acta Samizdatica/ Notes on samizdat] (Moscow: GPIB Rossii and Mezhdunarodnyi Memorial, 2016), pp. 221–39.

37 Eugene Gorny has researched samizdat as a metaphor to describe the Russian internet in *A Creative History of the Russian Internet* (Düsseldorf: VDM Verlag, 2009), p. 189.

Further Reading

Alexeyeva, Ludmilla, *Soviet Dissent: Contemporary Movements for National, Religious, and Human Rights*, trans. Carol Pearce and John Glad (Middletown, CT: Wesleyan University Press, 1985).

Epstein, Mikhail, *After the Future: The Paradoxes of Postmodernism and Contemporary Russian Culture*, trans. Anesa Miller-Pogacar (Amherst: University of Massachusetts Press, 1995).

Kind-Kovacs, Friederike, and Jessie Labov (eds.), *Samizdat, Tamizdat and Beyond: Transnational Media during and after Socialism* (New York: Berghahn, 2013).

Komaromi, Ann, *Uncensored: Samizdat Novels and the Quest for Autonomy in Soviet Dissidence* (Evanston, IL: Northwestern University Press, 2015).

Komaromi, Ann, *Soviet Samizdat* (Ithaca: Cornell University Press, 2022).

Lygo, Emily, *Leningrad Poetry 1953–1975: The Thaw Generation* (Bern: Peter Lang, 2010).

Yurchak, Alexei, *Everything Was Forever, until It Was No More: The Last Soviet Generation* (Princeton: Princeton University Press, 2005).

von Zitzewitz, Josephine, *Poetry and the Leningrad Religious-Philosophical Seminar 1976–1980: Music for a Deaf Age* (Oxford: Legenda / Modern Humanities Research Association (MHRA) and Routledge, 2016).

von Zitzewitz, Josephine, *The Culture of Samizdat: Literature and Underground Networks in the Late Soviet Union* (London: Bloomsbury, 2020).

The Market

BRADLEY A. GORSKI

Russian literature became modern, one might argue, only when it formed a relationship with a market beyond the tsarist court. Aleksandr Pushkin's (1799–1837) transformation of the Russian language into a modern literary instrument capable of creating not only paeans to monarchical power but also encyclopedias of Russian life hinged on his appeal to a commercial audience. Indeed, literature's very claim to autonomy from power – an autonomy gained through agonistic struggle during Pushkin's own lifetime and recorded in many of his canonical poems – relies on the ability to reach a broad-based consumer public. The professionalisation of the writer, as Irina Reyfman has demonstrated, undergirds not only the Golden Age of Russian poetry but also the late-nineteenth-century age of the Realist novel, when serialised fiction became a major subscription generator for Russian periodicals (see Chapter 2.4).[1] The interactions between writer and commercialised audience were perhaps nowhere more direct in this era than in Fedor Dostoevskii's (1821–1881) *The Diary of a Writer* (*Dnevnik pisatelia*, 1876–7, 1880–1), a periodical written entirely by Dostoevskii and published and sold by his wife, Anna Snitkina-Dostoevskaia, all for material compensation. Economic pressures and direct engagement with his audience pushed Dostoevskii to hone many of the traits that would be associated with market-facing literature in years to come: sensationalism, seriality, and an endless stream of new content.

As literacy grew in the late imperial period, the book market grew alongside it, investing the mass reader with a power that Jeffrey Brooks calls 'a genuine manifestation of consumer sovereignty'.[2] For the first time in Russian literary publishing, in Brooks's view, consumption drove

---

1 Irina Reyfman, *How Russia Learned to Write: Literature and the Imperial Table of Ranks* (Madison: University of Wisconsin Press, 2016).
2 Jeffrey Brooks, *When Russia Learned to Read: Literacy and Popular Literature, 1861–1917* (Princeton: Princeton University Press, 1985), p. xvii.

production and not the other way around. Newly literate consumers bought the wood-print booklets known as *lubok* literature alongside serialised novels, and publishers sought more of the same, creating Russia's first wave of mass literature (see Chapter 2.5). After the 1905 revolution and the attendant weakening of censorship, the burgeoning readership began to show an unmistakable preference for imported genre literature, often with western heroes and settings. The 1917 revolution brought an end to tsarist censorship and, in the following decade, the introduction of relatively free trade, while early Soviet literacy campaigns transformed reading into a truly mass pastime. As more workers learned to read, however, the new Soviet state became concerned that they spent their leisure time not with edifying literature but with commercialised entertainment from the decadent west, and several solutions were proposed. Recalling that 'Marx, as is generally known, read crime novels with great enthusiasm', Bolshevik leader Nikolai Bukharin, for instance, suggested producing socialist analogues of genre fiction. An interesting plot, he argued, could be filled with any ideological content. 'The bourgeoisie knows and understands this. . . . We do not yet have this, and this must be overcome.'[3]

Though a rash of so-called red Pinkertons answered Bukharin's call, another solution ultimately won out: the state-sponsored aesthetic doctrine of Socialist Realism (see Chapter 1.8). In its attempt to 'produce a literature that would be internationally acclaimed as literature yet remain accessible to the masses', the socialist cultural authorities turned to the masses themselves.[4] Library patrons, book buyers, and newly literate citizens expressed their reading preferences in a series of surveys that, as Evgeny Dobrenko has shown, contributed directly to the formulation of Socialist Realism and its topoi. Readers, it seemed, wanted plot-based realistic fiction with a positive central hero – traits that were borrowed from imported mass fiction.[5] Thus, somewhat unexpectedly, the early twentieth century's market forces directly informed the socialist aesthetic that would dominate literature for the rest of the Soviet era.

3 Nikolai Bukharin, 'Kommunisticheskoe vospitanie molodezhi v usloviiakh Nep'a' [Communist education under the conditions of NEP], *Pravda*, 14 Oct. 1922, 2, quoted in Boris Dralyuk, *Western Crime Fiction Goes East: The Russian Pinkerton Craze 1907–1934* (Boston: Brill, 2012), p. 26.
4 Katerina Clark, *The Soviet Novel: History as Ritual*, 3rd edn (Bloomington: Indiana University Press, 2000), p. 42.
5 Evgeny Dobrenko, *The Making of the State Reader: Social and Aesthetic Contexts of the Reception of Soviet Literature* (Palo Alto, CA: Stanford University Press, 1997).

Indeed, the state never fully stamped out market forces and, in the waning years of the Soviet Union, market ingresses appeared from all edges of Soviet literature. Work published abroad – *tamizdat* – had been subject to (and beneficiary of) international markets since at least November 1958 when an English translation of Boris Pasternak's (1890–1960) *Doctor Zhivago* (first pub. in Milan, 1957) knocked Vladimir Nabokov's (1899–1977) *Lolita* (1955) from atop the *New York Times* Best Seller list. At home, Soviet publications dedicated to foreign literature had to contend not only with Soviet censors but, starting in 1973, also with international copyrights and royalties (see Chapter 2.7). By the late 1980s, the new imperatives of Glasnost and Perestroika allowed for the publication of long-suppressed authors, both foreign and domestic, and the circulations of Soviet thick journals rose to dizzying heights. Though the millions of copies of the journal *New World* (*Novyi mir*, 1925–) circulated ostensibly outside the market, even within the Soviet system the pressures of consumer demand had become clear.

Nor were they resisted. Though the unmistakable dominance of the market would come only after Perestroika – and that era is the focus of this chapter – something very close to market-based popularity began to surface through new voices and even new genres before the 1980s had even come to a close. Liudmila Petrushevskaia (1938–), for instance, was counted among the 'discoveries' of the last Soviet years. Though she had been a relatively well-known figure on the fringes of Moscow's literary world – several of her plays had been performed in official theatres and she co-wrote the animated film *Tale of Tales* (*Skazka skazok*, 1979) – her own prose was published only in the late 1980s. Petrushevskaia's uncompromising vision of everyday (and especially family) life became emblematic of the new genre known as *chernukha*, a pessimistic realism characterised by 'often sadistic violence . . . against a backdrop of poverty, broken families, and unrelenting cynicism'.[6] In Petrushevskaia's story 'Revenge' (*Mest'*, 1990), for instance, a woman tries to kill her neighbour's baby out of unmotivated spite; the neighbour, in turn, fakes her own baby's death in order to drive the original aggressor to suicide. Though not overtly political, such works flew in the face of state-mandated optimism. Not only was *chernukha* allowed to appear in the last Soviet years, its popularity clearly showed that consumer demand – and not official priorities – was already shaping literary innovation.

---

6 Eliot Borenstein, *Overkill: Sex and Violence in Contemporary Russian Popular Culture* (Ithaca: Cornell University Press, 2008), p. 11.

Paper

Just as Glasnost was easing censorship on new genres like *chernukha*, market reasoning made a separate foray into the publishing industry through its material substrate: paper. Despite the world's largest timber reserves, Russia had struggled with paper production not only throughout the Soviet period but much earlier as well. Before the eighteenth century, all Russian paper had to be imported. While domestic paper mills began to emerge under Peter I (r. 1682–1725), it wasn't until the late nineteenth century that cheap wood-pulp paper would make print material a viable market commodity. But even then the problem was not solved, and throughout the Soviet era paper shortages continued to dog the state. In the last years of Perestroika, a long-simmering question was finally posed: just because there was not enough paper for what the state wanted to publish, did that necessarily mean there was not enough for what people wanted to read? One attempt to answer this question came in a 1990 article by Tatiana Zhuchkova that appeared in the major publishing industry weekly *The Book Review* (*Knizhnoe obozrenie*) under the title 'Not enough paper, or ... Print runs and demand' (*Ne khvataet bumagi ili ... Tirazh i spros*). It used statistics gathered from library patrons to show that state publishing priorities did not at all correspond with reader preferences. Unpopular authors like Nikolai Garin-Mikhailovskii (1852–1906) and Dmitrii Mamin-Sibiriak (1852–1912) were published in millions of copies, while writers in high demand, such as Aleksandr Solzhenitsyn (1918–2008) and Vladimir Voinovich (1932–2018), appeared in mere thousands of copies. Most concerningly for the article's author, 'No paper has yet been found for an edition of the poetry of the long-suffering Nobel laureate Joseph Brodsky.'[7] A better alignment between print runs and demand (a transparent proxy for the market laws of supply and demand), the article implied, could improve late Soviet publishing, suggesting a market cure for an ailing socialist culture.

That same year, the Soviet government adopted the Law on Printing (*Zakon o pechati*, 12 June 1990), which not only finally lifted the last censorship restrictions but also allowed for the creation and registration of private publishing collectives without prior approval from the state. Unlike Soviet legacy publishers, the new collectives were not guaranteed paper from state producers but had to buy on the newly created *birzha*, or wholesale market.

---

7 T. Zhuchkova, 'Ne khvataet bumagi ili ... Tirazh i spros. Mnenie spetsialista' [Not enough paper or ... print runs and demand. The opinion of a specialist], *Knizhnoe obozrenie* [The book review], 2 March 1990, 5–6.

Consequently, for the new collectives, sales had to fund the purchase of new paper – a point which may seem obvious in retrospect but was far from the norm in late Soviet publishing. The need to buy paper, in turn, pushed new publishers to print what customers would actually buy (rather than what they wanted to print), introducing capitalist thinking into the publishing world before the end of the Soviet era. Soon, even state publishers were drawn into the capitalist logic of 'print runs and demand', and by the second half of 1991, Soviet-era stockpiles were brought to market and long-time paper shortages showed signs of easing. Prices tumbled, and by January 1992, *The Book Review* reported: 'the groans of "there's not enough paper" have somehow disappeared . . . There is enough paper. . . . Paper turns up when it's needed and where it's needed.'[8]

Publishers and Places

If the proliferation of new publishers helped release hoarded paper, it also unleashed a kind of chaos. Between 1991 and 1992, 456 licenses were granted to new publishers, and by 1994, more than 6,500 publishers were registered and working. Spurred by profits and often piracy, the astonishing growth of private publishing acted quickly to fill the lingering demand for previously censored and other difficult-to-acquire books and soon set about creating and exploiting new market niches. Those publishers who proved adept, like the St Petersburg house Severo-Zapad, often cultivated semi-legal and certainly informal structures for the acquisition of raw materials and distribution of final products. In the absence of reliable distribution outside the city, one editor recalled, the press loaded trucks with thousands of copies of the latest pulp fiction and sent them out to the provinces, where workers would sell them for cash at open-air markets until the inventory was exhausted, at which point they would drive back to St Petersburg to repeat the process.

While such informal networks and local distributors managed to supply readers in and around the capitals to a certain extent, they failed to reach much farther than 100 kilometres outside of any major publishing centre. Stavropol, for instance, a city in the north Caucasus 1,500 kilometres from Moscow, found itself all but cut off in the 1990s. Though its half a million residents had been served by a Dom Knigi (House of Books) state bookshop in the late Soviet years, by the end of the 1990s, the building had been

8 Tat'iana Ivanova, 'Sekret dvukh protsentov. Vstrecha s vitse-prezidentom kontserna "Bumaga"' [The secret of the two per cent. A meeting with the vice-president of the 'Paper' conglomerate], *Knizhnoe obozrenie*, 17 Jan. 1992, 5.

repurposed as a makeshift emporium for everything from cosmetics and cell phones to internet plans, cactuses, washing machines, and children's clothes. 'The formerly spacious rooms, now divided up by the pedlars' kiosks', according to one local observer, 'leave the impression of a communal apartment in an old gentry home'. Meanwhile, those in the know bought their books under a staircase in the local university from a man named Kolya Tuzu, 'the only person in the city who brings in anything you could call books'.[9] Tuzu, and unlicensed merchants like him elsewhere, would drive to large cities, buy books at markets, and resell them in the provinces, creating vital but tenuous bibliographic connections between publishers and publics outside the capitals.

Even within the capitals, the new situation presented challenges. Huge markets, the biggest forming at Moscow's Olympic Stadium in 1993, served as chaotic distribution centres for the new popular literature. Print runs in the hundreds of thousands would sell out to retail firms – both newsstands and bookstores – within half an hour. The same market, however, also sold directly to consumers, with four levels of book stalls doing rapid business throughout the week, even as the corridors filled with discarded packing material from wholesale deliveries.

Without reliable distribution networks or exclusive access to inventory, bookstores had to compete with book stalls on street corners and with the wholesale markets themselves. Many closed, and those few that survived were forced to innovate. The former Knizhnyi Mir (Book World) in Moscow, for instance, changed its name to Biblio-Globus in 1992 and introduced a 'new philosophy', with expanded offerings including office supplies, music, films, and even jewellery, echoing the transformation of Stavropol's Dom Knigi. More presciently, it promised a computerised catalogue of its holdings and opened a 'cultural centre' – a first-of-its-kind performance space within a Soviet legacy bookstore – to host poetry readings, book presentations, round tables, and other events. Within the next year, another store – Moskva (Moscow) – introduced self-service shopping and soon added book signings and readings of its own. Such changes suggested that the successful post-Soviet bookstore would need to become more than a retail outlet where one could acquire books by asking for a title. It would need to be a new kind of space, one that hosted events inviting readers into the book world along with technologies and services to help them navigate its dizzying offerings.

9 Denis Iatsutko, 'Chtivo: Stavropol'. Zapiski iz kel'i' [Pulp: Stavropol. Notes from the monastery], *Topos. Literaturno-filosofskii zhurnal* [Topos. A literary-philosophical journal], 22 Feb. 2002, www.topos.ru/article/151, accessed 15 July 2021.

The Bestseller

The dizzying offerings meant that the industry as a whole – not only readers but publishers and booksellers as well – needed a whole new epistemology, a new way of knowing the book world for the capitalist era. In the first post-Soviet years, *The Book Review* began to publish a new, nearly weekly 'operational glossary' filled with terms like *privatizatsiia* (privatisation), *reiting* (rating), and *konversiia* (conversion), terms necessary for articulating and absorbing the new market realities pervading publishing. In this context, no term was more influential than 'bestseller'.

Simply transliterated into Cyrillic, the term *bestseller* became a powerful focaliser for the market dreams of the book industry as it aspired to modernise Russian publishing and bring it into closer alignment with its western counterparts. 'Defining the bestseller in our country is a difficult task, almost hopeless', ran an editorial comment in *The Book Review*. 'For in other countries the most bought, the most read, the most printed book, and the book most desired for reading, all of these are one and the same concept: the BESTSELLER. With us, all too often one thing is desired for reading, another is read, a third is published, and as for what people buy, well . . .'[10] According to this logic, the bestseller – an apparently transparent indicator of reader demand – was invested with the power to bring supply in line with demand and to transform post-Soviet publishing into a mature market for culture.

Over the ensuing years, the bestseller pursued precisely this goal. In weekly lists published between 1993 and 1998, *The Book Review* undertook Russian publishing's most sustained attempt to measure and publicly represent reader demand, unmatched before or since. The bestseller lists, which began as small notices in the bottom corner of page two or three of a given issue, soon blossomed into full-page features splashed across the newspaper's centrefold. As the printed lists grew in size, they revealed unexpected truths about consumption habits. Though publishers often expected high-brow literature to sell as well as it had during the heady days of Glasnost and Perestroika, by the post-Soviet era readers had already shifted preferences. It was not newly uncensored literature but previously unavailable genre fiction, self-help, and celebrity biographies that topped bestseller lists in the early 1990s.

Just as in the early twentieth century, readers in the 1990s showed strong preferences specifically for *imported* mass literature. But instead of turning

---

10 G. Nezhurin, 'Superbestseller-90' [Superbestseller-90], *Knizhnoe obozrenie*, 11 Jan. 1991, 16. Capitalisation in original.

away from the foreign sources of the bestseller, as the Soviet government had done in the 1920s, post-Soviet publishers embraced them. Several launched series of new and old translations with titles like World Bestsellers (*Mirovoi bestseller*), Bestsellers of Bygone Days (*Bestseller bylykh vremen*), and World Library of the Bestseller (*Vsemirnaia biblioteka bestsellera*), variations on mid-century 'great books' collections or Maksim Gorkii's (1868–1936) World Literature series (*Vsemirnaia literatura*, 1919–24, which printed the best works of the eighteenth through twentieth centuries from across the globe) but reimagined for the market age. *The Book Review* encouraged this kind of international thinking, printing bestseller lists from abroad opposite its own rankings in order to hint at what publishers might pursue next. Soon, however, translation was not enough, and Russian publishers and writers looked for ways to create a domestic bestseller. A flurry of articles with titles like 'What Is a Bestseller?', 'Anatomy of a Bestseller', and 'The Magic of the Bestseller' attempted to demystify the power of the category, while an ongoing feature, 'The Formula for Success', offered strategies for creating bestsellers from scratch.

By the mid-1990s, several Russian authors had adopted genre conventions from best-selling imports and transformed them into domestic sensations that successfully blended foreign plotting with Russian realia. The first wave of homegrown bestsellers brought western crime fiction into contact with post-Soviet urban decay and supercharged the genre with testosterone-inflected plot lines that Helena Goscilo distils as 'bedding women and pulverizing men'.[11] Though centred on crime, bestsellers along these lines – like the Mad Dog (*Beshenyi*) series by Viktor Dotsenko (1946–) – borrowed more from Rambo than from Sherlock Holmes and revealed an implicit preference for the most violent forms of aspirational justice.

Perhaps in response to this hyper-masculine vision of law and order, a new genre emerged that would come to dominate bestseller lists over the next years: the 'women's detective' (*zhenskii detektiv*).[12] These mystery novels – whose protagonist, author, and intended audience were all women – plunged into the grittiest depths of the Russian nineties with a pluck and determination that upended the bestseller's regressive gender norms. The protagonist

---

11 H. Goscilo, 'Big-buck books: Pulp fiction in post-Soviet Russia', *Harriman Review* 12.2–3 (1999), 9.

12 See Mariia Cherniak, 'Zhenskii detektiv: Tvorchestvo A. Marininoi i vektory razvitiia zhanra' [The women's detective: The work of A. Marinina and the vectors of the genre's development], in *Massovaia literatura XX veka. Uchebnoe posobie* [Mass literature of the twentieth century. A textbook] (Moscow: Flinta, 2009).

of Aleksandra Marinina's (1957–) blockbuster novels, Anastasiia Kamenskaia, for instance, combines a lack of concern for her own sexuality (unless necessary for her work) with a tenacious work ethic, incisive logic, and crackerjack computer skills to unspool vast conspiracies. Though Kamenskaia, who works for the police, invariably solves each novel's mystery, she is often powerless to stop the criminal mastermind at its centre, and many of Marinina's novels end not with violent confrontations but with philosophical acceptance of lawlessness and the weakness of state power. Marinina (and others, such as Daria Dontsova (1952–) and Polina Dashkova (1960–)) proved even more popular than Dotsenko and his ilk, shifting the terms of the genre from action to psychology and the mode of confronting injustice from violence to intellect.

Instead of waiting for a talented author to adapt the bestseller, some Russian publishers attempted fabrication. Certain features of the bestseller, as one 'Formula for Success' article (written by the British scholar Donald Rayfield) suggested, are 'easier to predict than the internal strength of an author. They can even be artificially created.' A certain 'mysterious character' of the author was recommended, alongside international settings and characters, sensationalism, and seriality.[13] Russian publishers soon took up the challenge, assembling author collectives to write market-oriented mass fiction that would be published under foreign-sounding pseudonyms. When the popular Mexican soap *Simply Maria* (*Prosto Mariia*) ended its run on Russian television in 1994, for instance, one such collective produced a continuation 'translated' from the Spanish called *Forgive Me, Maria!* (*Prosti, Mariia!*), which spent several weeks on the bestseller lists that year. On the heels of *Gone with the Wind*'s popularity, a Minsk-based collective published a series of (unauthorised) sequels with titles like *Scarlett's Last Love* (*Posledniaia liubov' Skarlett*, 1994) and *Rhett Butler's Son* (*Syn Retta Batlera*, 1995), all bestsellers appearing under the pseudonym Dzhuliia Khilpatrik.

Such curiosities should not simply be relegated to the *Kunstkamera* of literary history: the strategies developed through these imitative bestsellers – pseudonymous authorship, borrowed genre tropes, and international flair – not only characterised short-lived bestsellers but also pervaded the literary mainstream through authors like Leonid Iuzefovich (1947–). When a new literary prize was introduced in 2001, it chose for its first winner Iuzefovich's *The Prince of the Wind* (*Kniaz' vetra*, 2000), the third book in

---

13 D. Reifil'd, 'Chto-takoe bestseller?' [What is the bestseller?], *Knizhnoe obozrenie*, 16 May 1995, 6, 12.

a series of mystery novels that bore all the traces of the bestseller's influence. This particular prize, called the National Bestseller and introduced with a logo that was simply a bar code, sought to bring market logic into the realm of high literary fiction. The National Bestseller's explicit commercial orientation, however, only revealed the market logic that subtended prize culture throughout the 1990s. The decade's most prestigious prize – the Russian Booker – was launched, according to its own publicity materials, 'to support serious literature in the conditions of the contemporary market, to help it become competitive in store windows that are filled with glossy covers, and to once again open a path to readers'.[14] By attempting to counteract the draw of glossy bestsellers, such literary prizes in fact adopted their market logic. The Russian Booker, the National Bestseller, and other prizes promised expanded print runs, media exposure, and ultimately sales, suggesting that (market-based) success – and not some extra-market promotion of literary quality – was the end goal of the prize process. In this way, the consumer-orientation that characterised the bestseller spread even to the 'serious literature' that these prizes intended to support. This pervasive orientation towards the market not only affected literary commerce, but also made markets, commodification, and success into major thematic concerns in post-Soviet literature.

Success

In one of the decade's most scandalous novels, Vladimir Sorokin's (1955–) *Blue Lard* (*Goluboe salo*, 1999), classical Russian literature is at once commodified and violently deformed. At a genetic laboratory in the Far East (and near future), clones of Lev Tolstoi (1828–1910), Dostoevskii, and several other classic authors are chained to desks and made to write. The torturous 'script-process' deforms their bodies but produces a substance called blue lard with supernatural properties. As this valuable commodity – produced by but immediately dissociated from literature itself – circulates through the novel's world, it traces a path through the genres that defined the 1990s bestseller: romance, thriller, occult and alternative history, even erotica. As literary worlds in each of these genres are created and immediately discarded, the narrative follows only the lard, and the reader is caught in a para-literary

---

14 *Russkii Buker. Literaturnaia premiia. 1992* [The Russian Booker. A literary prize. 1992], Buklet [Pamphlet] (Moscow, 1992).

system that prizes the exchange value of the commodity while rejecting any artistic creation along the way.

But if Sorokin's invocation of canonical literature mounts a critique of the post-Soviet commodification of literature, a countervailing tendency simultaneously worked to make market-based success acceptable, and even respected, in mainstream literature. No author did more to foster success culture among the literary establishment than Grigorii Chkhartishvili (1956–), the co-editor of the prestigious journal *Foreign Literature* (*Inostrannaia literatura*, 1955–). Under the pseudonym Boris Akunin, Chkhartishvili wrote a series of wildly popular mystery novels set against a pastiche of late imperial Russia with plenty of clever references to Russian history and the literary canon. From mass fiction, Chkhartishvili borrowed not only plot devices but also pseudonymous authorship, seriality, and exotic locales (all enumerated as essential to the bestseller's 'formula for success'). His ability to marry all these components with an elegant prose style and erudite allusions made the Akunin novels into what one critic called the first genre fiction that was not 'embarrassing for an intelligent person to hold in his hands'.[15] Just as in Sorokin's *Blue Lard*, here too the literary heritage acts as a playful backdrop. But instead of mounting a critique, Akunin's work made mass fiction acceptable to the elite. As Chkhartishvili himself asserted, his success meant that 'it is no longer considered shameful to write detective stories'.[16] No longer literature's dirty word, success – popular, market-based success – became an acceptable and even a prominent vector of authorial aspirations.

Chkhartishvili's promotion of success goes beyond his use of genre tropes to achieve popularity. Success characterises the very universe of his novels. Chkhartishvili's first (and still most popular) novels feature the detective-protagonist Erast Petrovich Fandorin who, through a combination of wit, doggedness, and charm (and in conformity with genre expectations), unfailingly unfurls the criminal plot at the centre of each novel. Like Marinina's protagonist Kamenskaia, Fandorin works for an ultimately impotent state and the criminals often slip away. But Fandorin is rewarded throughout the series with the external markers of success. A one-time penniless orphan, he rises through the imperial table of ranks (see Chapter 4.3) from the lowly fourteenth rank in the first book to the fifth rank by book six. In other words,

---

15 Konstatin Bocharov, 'Orkestr v kustakh' [An orchestra in the shrubs], *Knizhnoe obozrenie*, 3 April 2000, 16.
16 Vanora Bennett, 'Akuninization: *The Winter Queen* by Boris Akunin', *Times Literary Supplement*, 16 May 2003, 32.

Chkhartishvili places Fandorin in a reliable meritocracy, a system designed to recognise good work and reward it with success.

Chkhartishvili's vision of benevolent meritocracy and uncomplicated success struck a chord with a reading public already deeply invested in success culture at the time. By the late 1990s, according to the sociologist Boris Dubin, a straightforward vision of success had become a central trope of Russian culture. Arguing that the 'American success story' had emerged especially from television commercials, Dubin writes that this new master plot presents scenes which 'follow one after another according to a single model of "action-reward"', suggesting a 'utopia of social order' in which positive actions are always rewarded and in which one can 'in a very simple manner bring order into life, and control it with elementary and generally understood . . . methods'.[17] Such a social utopia is at the heart of the mystery genre as exemplified in Akunin's novels and others. Not incidentally, it also formed the very foundation of capitalism's post-Soviet promise.

In reality, post-Soviet Russia witnessed, at best, a perverted version of this capitalist dream. Alongside the social decay, chaos, and crime that characterised the 1990s (and provided the backdrop for its gritty crime fiction), capitalism also held out the promise of extreme social mobility – previously inconceivable success for those with the wherewithal to make their own fate. Such upward mobility became the central theme of a new genre that appeared in the 2000s, so-called glamour prose (*glamurnaia proza*): stories that glorified social climbing, the concerns of the rich, and the glossy exterior of high-end materiality. Most prominently represented by novels such as Oksana Robski's (1968–) *About Loff/on* (*Pro Liuboff/on*, 2006) and Sergei Minaev's (1975–) *Soulless* (*Dukhless*, 2006) – both titles are written half in Russian and half in English and are hence bilingual wordplays – glamour prose took the 'American success story' to its post-Soviet extreme and, in many cases, began to critique its inner emptiness.

But perhaps the novel that captures the market age better than any other is Viktor Pelevin's (1962–) *Generation 'P'* (*Generation 'P'*, 1999). The novel charts the astronomic rise of its protagonist Vavilen Tatarskii through the advertising industry. The master genre of the market age, advertising proves to be a proleptic mode of writing that has the power to change the world, to make itself come true. A product presented as desirable generates desire; representing success creates success; and Tatarskii, who at first only pretends to be an

17 Boris Dubin, 'Novaia russkaia mechta i ee geroi' [The new Russian dream and its heroes], in *Slovo–pis'mo–literatura* [Word–writing–literature] (Moscow: Novoe literaturnoe obozrenie, 2001), pp. 200–11.

advertising guru, becomes one. His preternatural insight into the workings of advertising leads him to see the entire world as a simulacrum created by television. If people used to believe that reality was the material world, he reasons, now they believe 'that reality is the material world as it is shown on television'.[18] 'Our mind and our world are the same thing', he concludes, and so the world itself – and not only free-market capitalism – is infinitely manipulable through advertising.[19] Not only does Tatarskii quickly rise from post-Soviet poverty to society's upper echelons, he even reaches the heights of political power. By the end of the novel, Pelevin shows that not only consumption but politics and even mystical higher powers are manipulated by the simulacra accessible through the secrets of advertising.

It is no accident that it is precisely advertising and consumer capitalism that lead Pelevin (and his protagonist) to these classically postmodern insights, insights that echo the theories of Jean Baudrillard and Fredric Jameson at least as much as they do those of the advertising experts Pelevin quotes. If earlier iterations of Russian Postmodernism – from Venedikt Erofeev's (1939–1990) *Moscow–Petushki* (*Moskva–Petushki*, 1969–70) to Andrei Bitov's (1937–2018) *Pushkin House* (*Pushkinskii dom*, comp. 1964–71) to Pelevin's own earlier work – played on the Russian literary canon and Soviet traditions of pervasive propaganda, logocentrism, and the instability of the historical record (see Chapter 1.9), then a more popular (and populist) postmodern novel was born of the capitalist transition. The postmodernism of the market age, in other words, was exemplified, if not inaugurated, by Pelevin's generation-defining novel, in which previously unthinkable success in the new capitalist environment provides not only material riches but also great power and deep insight into the true workings of the world.

Authorship

Pelevin's exemplary novel of the market age begins not with greed or material need but, perhaps unexpectedly, with the protagonist's literary aspirations. Still in the late Soviet era, Tatarskii dreams of becoming the next Pasternak. He enrols in the Literary Institute and is well on his way to devoting 'his creative labours to eternity', when the Soviet Union suddenly disintegrates.[20] It is not so much the political end of the USSR, however, but a metaphysical crisis that destroys his literary dreams: he finds that the

---

18 Victor Pelevin, *Homo Zapiens*, trans. Andrew Bromfield (New York: Penguin, 2002), p. 81.
19 Pelevin, *Homo Zapiens*, p. 33.   20 Pelevin, *Homo Zapiens*, p. 3.

eternity he wanted to address in his work began to 'curl back in on itself and disappear'.[21] Eternity turns out to be nothing more than a product of collective belief, and, what is more, that belief 'could only exist on state subsidies, or else – which is just the same thing – as something forbidden by the state'.[22] The novel's opening chapter ends with a judgement on Tatarskii's poems, but one that could be extended to 'literary labours' more broadly: 'with the collapse of the Soviet Union, they had simply lost their meaning and value'.[23]

The crisis of authorship that Pelevin diagnoses affected all corners of Russian literature. State subsidies disappeared. The Writers' Union lost all power. Circulations of Soviet-era periodicals collapsed. Writers who had found 'official' success in the Soviet Union were no longer guaranteed an outlet to readers. Just as destabilising, the state's repressive apparatus disappeared, and those who had published in *tamizdat* or *samizdat* were faced with both new opportunities and new challenges as they sought to publish domestically under market conditions (see Chapter 2.9). Even the practices of 'writing for the desk drawer' or defiantly *not* writing lost all meaning when they were no longer positioned against the state. To repurpose the Formalist critic Boris Eikhenbaum's (1886–1959) observation of 1927, the question of 'how to write' was once again eclipsed in the 1990s by the question of 'how to be a writer'.[24] The modes of writing and publishing engendered by the bestseller provided one possible answer, but those writers whose work – for reasons of genre, sensibility, or difficulty – did not easily fill available market niches had to find different pathways to readers. Consequently, authorship itself changed. From a (largely imagined) solitary creator of texts, the author became an active, online, multimedia, and often celebrity phenomenon. Even the highly pedigreed writer, beloved of the older generation, Tatiana Tolstaia (1951–) found renown not only through her prose but at least as effectively through her literary talk show, *School for Scandal* (*Shkola zlosloviia*). Sorokin has worked in every genre imaginable, including visual and performance art; created a pavilion at the Venice Biennale; and has even written librettos commissioned by the Bolshoi Theatre. Liudmila Ulitskaia (1943–) mobilised her literary celebrity to launch a series of children's books on tolerance. Petrushevskaia sings cabaret. And one of the most indefatigable

---

21 Pelevin, *Homo Zapiens*, p. 4. 22 Pelevin, *Homo Zapiens*, p. 5.
23 Pelevin, *Homo Zapiens*, p. 5.
24 Boris Eikhenbaum, 'Literaturnyi byt' [The literary environment] (1927), in *Moi vremennik: Slovesnost', nauka, kritika, smes'* [My chronicle: Words, science, criticism, miscellany] (Leningrad: Izdatel'stvo pisatelei Leningrada, 1929).

forces in post-Soviet letters, Dmitrii Bykov (1967–), is not simply an author – though he has written award-winning novels, biographies, essays, and poetry; he has been something closer to an impresario of literature and literary performance. He has hosted television and radio broadcasts, written rhyming op-ed columns, befriended and supported up-and-coming authors and poets, cast opinions on everything from politics to prose, and marshalled his fame to mould Russian literature past and present. For Bykov, writing has been anything but a solitary task; it has been one part of active cultural engagement that omnivorously consumes all available media, modes, and genres.

Though Bykov's energy has been unparalleled, his approach is not unique. Many of those he has championed have taken up several of his strategies of multimedia audience engagement. Perhaps one of the most interesting cases of this new authorial mode is Aleksei Ivanov (1969–), a Ural writer who burst onto the literary scene with a series of best-selling historical novels in the early 2000s (championed by Bykov, among others). Like many writers, Ivanov has brought his novels to the screen, writing adaptations and even starting his own production company. But beyond that, Ivanov conceived his work *Gold of the Rebellion* (*Zoloto bunta*, 2005) as a multimedia project from the beginning, creating the novel, a screenplay, and a video-game scenario simultaneously. For several years Ivanov hosted a festival of medieval reconstruction in the northern Urals based on another of his novels, *The Heart of the Parma* (*Serdtse parmy*, 2003), and he has lobbied government tourism boards throughout the region to feature aspects of his works as local attractions. The ambition of Ivanov's entire project, which he calls a 'corporation called Aleksei Ivanov', approaches a *Gesamtkunstwerk*. Ivanov's 'corporation', however, aspires to a diffuse totalisation, not meant to overwhelm all the senses at once but instead to encourage sustained and repeated audience engagement in various modes and at different times and places.

Audience engagement is a key component to authorship in the market age, and no format is better equipped to facilitate continuous interaction than the internet and social media. By the 2000s, no post-Soviet author could survive without a personal website, and many of the decade's most interesting new writers first found audiences digitally. Though online literature, especially poetry, proliferated throughout the 1990s as internet access spread, it was not until the advent of social media, and specifically LiveJournal, that the internet proved capable of bringing new voices to the surface on a significant scale (see Chapters 2.11, 3.11). Among the first authors to emerge from LiveJournal fame was Evgenii Grishkovets (1967–). An actor,

screenwriter, director, and musician as well as a writer, Grishkovets first gained national attention through a one-man show performed in his hometown of Kemerovo and posted online. Soon Grishkovets's LiveJournal page was filled with admirers of the recording who became avid readers of a quickly growing blog that not only delved deeper into the memories and personality at the heart of the original performance but also analysed the online medium and the modes of communication it encouraged. Furthermore, Grishkovets effectively translated the confessional style of his one-man show into online prose, pioneering a playfully sincere tone that made a viable mode of internet celebrity out of what Dmitrii Prigov (1940–2007) called the 'new sincerity', or a return to direct, emotional expression after the irony and play of postmodern experimentation. Grishkovets's internet presence was so successful that it led to stage and screenwriting invitations, film roles, and print publications, not only of novels and short stories but also of eight volumes (as of 2020) collected directly from his LiveJournal posts.

Russia's most popular contemporary poet, Vera Polozkova (1986–), also rose to prominence through LiveJournal, and her trajectory shows a mode of authorship that pushes audience engagement to another level. From Polozkova's earliest LiveJournal posts in 2003, she exploited not only the intimacy of the medium but also its social functionality. She tagged other users, often incorporating them into her poetry or prose, and asked them to respond in kind. Many of her followers posted creative responses, often in verse, to which she unfailingly responded with encouragement. Some followers gave her direct feedback, suggesting at times that a line was too obvious or clunky, while others contributed to the blog itself, which became a collaborative poetic space led by Polozkova. By 2008, her page had attracted more than 10,000 followers. Soon she was performing her poetry to sold-out crowds of thousands in Moscow and St Petersburg. When she finally printed her first bound collection of poems, it sold out its first two print runs within the year, instantly making her Russia's best-selling poet.

Polozkova's mode of audience engagement might be thought of alongside fan fiction as exemplary of 'prosumer' literature. Blurring consumption and production, 'prosumption' (a term coined by Alvin Toffler) is characteristic of online and social media such as YouTube and Facebook in which all users collaboratively consume *and* produce the site's content.[25] Dmitrii Vodennikov (1968–), who launched his LiveJournal in 2004, has cultivated his own online

25 Alvin Toffler, *The Third Wave* (New York: Bantam Books, 1980).

following through constant interaction with his readers, often creating new posts *about* recent comments, weaving his online text from the fabric of commenters' words. Linor Goralik (1975–), whose online presence has been prolific and multifaceted since the mid-1990s, has experimented with diverse literary personae, genres, and tonalities, all in interaction with her thousands of followers. The prosumer literature practised by these writers draws in audiences by recognising that they may not be content consuming literature from afar; rather, they wish to see themselves as poets in their own right. And in turn, the authorial persona cultivated online is that of an aspiring writer in constant dialogue with her audience, always in a state of becoming. The metatext of these authors' online personae become compelling Bildungsromans: portraits of the artist in the age of internet celebrity. They are stories of aspiration, hard work, and eventual recognition – that is, capitalist-era success stories – that encourage the mimetic desire of their audiences. As audience members both participate in those stories through their own comments and contributions and follow the stories through the digital traces they leave behind, their mimetic desire translates into market value, available once again for capitalisation through concert tickets, book sales, and media appearances.

Literature beyond the Market

The marketisation of literature and the power of the mass consumer has been the subject of critique from the very early post-Soviet years. The literary critic Natalia Ivanova lamented the demise of the great Russian novelist under market conditions in her elegiac essay 'Death of the Gods' (*Gibel' bogov*, 1991). In 1993, Moscow hosted an International Congress in Defence of the Book, which advocated (unsuccessfully) for market protections for 'publications with high social and cultural value'. Later in the decade, the sociologist Mikhail Berg bemoaned the disappearance of the Soviet underground and the avant-garde art developed there. Without a space free from the homogenising influence of the market, Berg argued, consumer-age literature effectively 'blocks the recognition of the value of innovative impulses'.[26] Under market conditions, anything too radical sells poorly and soon dies. Either government protections or an underground avant-garde might provide a space of autonomy from the market, where

26 Mikhail Berg, *Literaturokratiia. Problemy prisvoeniia i pereraspredeleniia vlasti v literature* [Literaturocracy. The problem of accumulation and distribution of power in literature] (Moscow: Novoe literaturnoe obozrenie, 2000), p. 26.

innovation could be fostered for its own sake, safe from the demands of the mass consumer. Like government intervention, however, the underground could not survive under post-Soviet conditions. It had positioned itself largely against the state, and once the Soviet Union no longer existed, it lost meaning and withered away. If a new space of literary autonomy was to be created, it would not position itself primarily against the state but against the market.

By the mid-2000s, several new models for literary creation did just that. In a 2004 manifesto, a collective of St Petersburg poets and artists called Chto Delat (What is to be done; see Chapter 1.10) described Russia's cultural landscape as dominated by 'consumers' conception of pleasure' and the 'cynicism of commodity-monetary relations, [which] pervade society from top to bottom'. In answer to the group's eponymous question, they proclaim, 'It's time to stop considering how best to correctly and effectively sell ourselves – we need to learn to simply give [ourselves] away.'[27] The same year, the poet Kirill Medvedev (1975–) publicly renounced copyright over his own texts. More recently, Pavel Arsenev (1986–) travelled Russia teaching audiences 'How to Not Write Poetry', turning Vladimir Maiakovskii's (1893–1930) post-revolutionary version ('How to Make Verses' (*Kak delat' stikhi*, 1926)) on its head. In 2012, when the leading arts and culture site OpenSpace.ru found itself badgered by a nexus of state power and capital, its editorial board – led by the poet Mariia Stepanova (1972–), who has spent her career finding ways *not* to rely on the market – started the first crowdfunded Russian media outlet, Colta.ru. Though less politically explicit, the aspirations of Colta's funding model are no less radical than those of the New Left. Indeed, when Russia invaded Ukraine in February 2022, Colta first suspended its operations and then found itself blocked by increasingly repressive censorship. The state, at least, seemed to see the extra-market arts and culture website as politically dangerous. All of these writers and activists have sought ways to exist outside of (and against) the capitalist paradigm of market-age literature. They have developed publishing and dissemination models that rely on donations, that create 'crafted' chapbook-style texts from cheap materials, and that bring together like-minded activists and artists to build distribution networks outside of the market. By setting loose such innovative energies, these extra-market efforts have not only begun to

---

27 Chto Delat, 'Chto delat'?' [What is to be done?], *Chto delat'? Gazeta novoi tvorcheskoi formy* [What is to be done? A newspaper of a new creative format] 1 (2004), 2, https://chtodelat.org/category/b8-newspapers/c1-1-what-is-to-be-done/, accessed 15 Aug. 2017.

carve out a place beyond the hegemony of capitalism in culture but have torn through the consumer imperative and opened a pathway into a new space where literature might be able to flourish beyond the market.

Further Reading

Barker, Adele Marie (ed.), *Consuming Russia: Popular Culture, Sex and Society since Gorbachev* (Durham, NC: Duke University Press, 1999).

Borenstein, Eliot, *Overkill: Sex and Violence in Contemporary Russian Culture* (Ithaca: Cornell University Press, 2008).

Brooks, Jeffrey, *When Russia Learned to Read: Literacy and Popular Literature, 1861–1917* (Princeton: Princeton University Press, 1985).

Dwyer, Jeremy, 'The *Knizhnoe obozrenie* bestseller lists, Russian reading habits, and the development of Russian literary culture, 1994–98', *Russian Review* 66.2 (2007), 295–315.

Gorski, Bradley A., *Cultural Capitalism: Literature and the Market after Socialism* (Ithaca: Cornell University Press, 2025).

Goscilo, Helena, 'Big-buck books: Pulp fiction in post-Soviet Russia', *Harriman Review* 2.2–3 (1999), 6–24.

Lovell, Stephen, *Russia's Reading Revolution: Print Culture in the Soviet and Post-Soviet Eras* (London: Routledge, 1999).

Menzel, Birgit, and Stephen Lovell (eds.), *Reading for Entertainment in Contemporary Russia: Post-Soviet Popular Literature in Historical Perspective* (Munich: Verlag Otto Sagner, 2005).

Olcott, Anthony, *Russian Pulp: The Detektiv and the Way of Crime* (Oxford: Rowan & Littlefield, 2001).

The Internet

MARIJETA BOZOVIC

The internet transformed our world: in thirty years, most of the globe has come to depend on computer networks for work, education, politics, religion, love, war, crime, play – and art of all kinds. This includes the production and dissemination of literature, the paradigmatic global art form of our imagined communities. The ways in which the internet mediates literature are both fundamentally transnational and, in cases like the Russian-language internet, distinctive from American-led trends. Problems of definition quickly proliferate when we try to speak of Russian literature and the internet. Scholars have devoted many pages to distinguishing between modes of online literary production: for example, separating digitised literature from that which is produced for the internet ('born digital'). Yet these efforts only scratch the surface of the study of a human cultural production so vast as to be self-evidently unmasterable.[1]

If we define our object of study narrowly – Russian literature of a born digital and experimental nature – we risk missing the forest for a few odd trees.[2] The vast majority of Russian literature online is digitised but of print origin: classical or technical (or translated) literature stored in so-called shadow libraries of various shades of legality or in equally massive transnational commercial sites. Even of the Russian literature born online (fan fiction, internet poetry, autobiographical blogs, quarantine diaries during the Covid-19 pandemic), the vast majority readily translates back and forth into print form, offering a new arena for self-publishing (or *samizdat*; see Chapter 2.9). How then do we make sense of the internet as a mechanism influencing the reading and writing of Russian literature? What, if anything, is

---

1 See the excellent summary by Henrike Schmidt, 'From samizdat to New Sincerity: Digital literature on the Russian-language internet', in Daria Gritsenko, Mariëlle Wijermars, and Mikhail Kopotev (eds.), *The Palgrave Handbook of Digital Russia Studies* (Cham: Palgrave Macmillan, 2021), pp. 255–75.
2 Pavel Arseniev, 'To see the forest behind the trees: Biological bias in literary criticism from Formalism to Moretti', *Russian Literature* 122–3 (May–July 2021), 67–83.

special about the Russian case and distinct from, say, German-language or Turkish-language literatures of the network age?

In what follows I reassess our understanding of the Russian-language internet (or Ru.net), focusing on the historical and political peculiarities that help to explain the global prominence of Russian shadow libraries, and the real and imagined links with the legacies of samizdat. I aim to sketch the key features of the literature of Russia's digital era, while highlighting the potential for online literary experimentation and varied multimedia forms.

From Cold War Net to Tinkering Nation: The Road to Ru.net

The internet was born of the Cold War. From the technological jockeying for supremacy to the fear of nuclear vulnerability through centralisation, the internet came into being in a world traumatised by the Second World War and shaped by the mutually fuelling rivalries between the United States and the Soviet Union. The world order could well have, and nearly did, go in the other direction. As Benjamin Peters asks, 'Given unprecedented Soviet investments and successes in mathematics, science, and some technology (such as nuclear power and rocketry), why did the Soviet Union not success-fully develop computer networks that were capable of benefiting a range of civilian, economic, political, social, and other human wants and needs?' Peters argues that, paradoxically, the socialists behaved like capitalists and the capitalists like socialists: the relative centralisation of the US military-industrial-academic complex and the era's extraordinary funding of basic science led the USA to accomplish what the bureaucratically dispersed and internally competitive Soviet regime failed to do.[3]

In the USSR, the state-led plan to create a connected computer network was complicated by competing interests. The military wanted nothing to do with civilian affairs; the economic ministries wanted to maintain the net-working project under their control and fought to the point of mutiny and sabotage to keep it that way; the administrating bureaucrats were afraid that new bureaucrats would rise to power if the networking plan succeeded; factory workers worried that an integrated information network would challenge the existing informal grey economy; and, perhaps most unexpect-edly, liberal economists resisted the implementation of networks, thinking

---

3 Benjamin Peters, *How Not to Network a Nation: The Uneasy History of the Soviet Internet* (Cambridge, MA: MIT Press, 2016), p. 2.

that they would prevent the market reforms that economists were trying to introduce in the last years of the Soviet Union.

Meanwhile, in the United States, the Advanced Research Projects Agency Network (ARPANET) flourished, thanks to funds from ARPA, an agency of the Department of Defense. According to Walter Isaacson, 'During and after WWII, three groups had been fused together into an iron triangle: the military industrial academic project.'[4] The Department of Defense and the National Science Foundation became prime funders of American science, combined with hybrid research centres such as the RAND Corporation and the Stanford Research Institute – all of which emerged as key in the US networking push. The engineer Paul Baran, who reputedly saw his life mission as preventing nuclear holocaust, came up with the innovation of breaking messages down into units with address headers describing where they should go.[5] Packets move through a network from node to node, without a main hub or even regional hubs to control switching and routing (unlike, for example, a standard telephone system). If the enemy took out a few regional hubs, a centralised system could be incapacitated. But if control were distributed – if every node had equal power to switch and route the flow of data – it would empower individuals and de-incentivise the use of nuclear bombs in a total communications war.

The Americans outstripped the Soviets in building their own network, but both sides flung themselves headlong into the cybernetics race. Cybernetics aspired to be the science of everything nonlinear and recursive; a 'theory of messages'; the study of the information systems that organise the cosmos, people, and machines. On the eastern front, the death of Stalin marked a turning point in Soviet science: a move from being powerful and celebrated after the Second World War to becoming even higher in status and (relative) autonomy.[6] In no time at all, American intelligence was panicking about the advanced state of Soviet science, and specifically cybernetics. 'The modernization of communication may have the paradoxical effects', one American visitor to the USSR presciently warned, 'of actually enhance[ing] totalitarian control by making a fully centralized network of administrative communications channels really feasible.'[7] The popular press on both sides wondered if computers might not be the machines of communism.

---

4 Walter Isaacson, *The Innovators: How a Group of Hackers, Geniuses, and Geeks Created the Digital Revolution* (New York: Simon & Schuster, 2014), p. 217.
5 Isaacson, *Innovators*, p. 238.
6 See Michael Gordin, 'The forgetting and rediscovery of Soviet machine translation', *Critical Inquiry* 46.4 (2020), 835–66.
7 Cited in Peters, *How Not to Network a Nation*, p. 44.

Far from it: computers seem to have been machines of capitalism instead. As the Soviet Union fell apart and market-based telecommunications industries took over, Russian computer networks came together. Relcom was the first to connect nationally, on 1 August 1990, at the Kurchatov Institute of Atomic Energy in Moscow. In March 1991, the National Science Foundation allowed Eastern Bloc countries to connect to the global TCP/IP network (the 'internet proper').[8] Already in the mid-1990s, computer networks were a part of life across post-Soviet states, which began forming their own nets (Ru.net, Kaz.net, Uz.net, and others). By 2011, Russia overtook Germany in the European market for highest numbers online; by 2013, Russian became the second most common language on the web.[9] By 2020, Ru.net (the term is used to refer to both the internet in Russia and the far more vast and diverse Russian-language internet) purportedly boasted more than 80 per cent of the country's population. Web 2.0 platforms (sites that emphasise user-generated content) are especially strong in Russia; social networks like Odnoklassniki.ru, VKontakte, and LiveJournal were popular very early on. Mobile broadband connectivity matches advanced global economies, mobile phone usage is among the highest in the world, and Russia leads in affordable broadband.[10] (A separate but fascinating article could and should be written about the underground wiring of one-sixth of the world by inconceivable kilometres of fibre-optic cable.) In short, internet use shot up from about 2 per cent of the Russian population in the 1990s to nearly the highest global levels by the early 2020s. During this time, crucially, the Russian internet also went from largely unregulated to adhering to international copyright regulations after Russia joined the World Trade Organization (WTO) in 2013.

Late Soviet culture and the creative, law-agnostic turmoil that followed it produced some of the best programmers, computer artists, pirates, and hackers worldwide and exported that knowledge across Latin America, China, India, and Africa.[11] The scholars Lev Manovich and Dennis Yi Tenen, among many

---

8 Anatolii Klesov, 'Dvadtsat' let spustia, ili kak nachinalsia Internet v Sovetskom Soiuze' [Twenty years later, or how the internet started in the Soviet Union], *Wayback Machine* (25 Sept. 2013), originally published in *Ogonek* 45 (2001), www.pseudology.org/web master/Klyesov_Internet.htm, accessed 11 Jan. 2021.

9 See, for example, Matthias Gelbmann, 'Russian is now the second most used language on the web', *W3Techs* (19 March 2013).

10 See Niall McCarthy, 'The most and least expensive countries for broadband', *Forbes* (22 Nov. 2017), www.forbes.com/sites/niallmccarthy/2017/11/22/the-most-and-least-exp ensive-countries-for-broadband-infographic/, accessed 10 Jan. 2021.

11 This argument is developed in a forthcoming monograph, Marijeta Bozovic and Benjamin Peters, *Imagining Russian Hackers: Myths of Men and Machines* (Chicago University Press, planned publication 2024).

others, attest to the tinkering culture and computer clubs that fuelled their childhood interests in literature and computers alike in the late Soviet years.[12] The same culture, funnelled through brain drain into Ronald Reagan's 1980s America, helped shape Silicon Valley as we know it today. Technologies which now dominate the global cyberspace – The Google algorithm, PayPal, various Web 2.0 platforms, and Pavel Durov's (1984–) freeware Telegram – were all created by Soviet- or post-Soviet-educated men and women and testify to the excellent mathematical education freely available in the Soviet Union, the high status of science during the Cold War, and the Second World DIY culture that combined so much talent and education with few commercially and legally available products for satisfying Soviet citizens' longing for tech and novelty. Fiction fed and reflected tinkering culture:

> The world of Soviet sci-fi is full of mad scientists. ... Shurik [the nerdy protagonist in a series of Soviet films beloved by generations] is a stereotypical technical intellectual, without whom Soviet reality is unimaginable. In the late 1950s, three times more engineers graduated from universities in the Soviet Union than in the United States. They may not have built time machines, but they turned their bathrooms into darkrooms and almost every young man in the Brezhnev era could make a radio out of improvised materials.[13]

It should be no surprise then that, from its inception, the Russian internet shone with unexpected flashes of brilliance, from the anarchic world of web poetry that flourished in literature-fetishising Russia to hacker spaces filled with young people learning the basics of code outside the law because none of the tools, games, films, and titles flashing before their eyes were locally affordable.[14]

If we imagine late- and post-Soviet Russia as a nation of technologically enthusiastic tinkerers, we find another argument for dismantling the popular cliché of 'two Russias', which posits a generational and cultural divide between urban and provincial populations that also imagines the audiences of internet and television at odds. Like any other model, this narrative

---

12 For interviews with Dennis Yi Tenen (30 Oct. 2020) and Lev Manovich (6 April 2021), by Marijeta Bozovic and Benjamin Peters, see the website for the Yale University project 'Imagining Russian hackers: Myths of men and machines', https://hackersinitiative .yale.edu/interviews, accessed 12 April 2021.

13 Daria Borisenko, 'Prometheus unbound', *InRussia* (2016–17), https://inrussia.studio/ prometheus-unbound, accessed 10 April 2021; the site has since been taken down.

14 See Jamie Bartlett, *The Dark Net: Inside the Digital Underworld* (Brooklyn: Melville House, 2016); also Eliot Borenstein, 'A song of orcs and trolls' (7 Oct. 2019), www.eliotborenstein .net/soviet-self-hatred/vjw0bb53g2ughmybqrwchtjfyr31vww, accessed 15 April 2021.

illuminates some truths at the expense of others, and not without ideological motivation. As Ilya Matveev argues, the 'two Russias' theory of cosmopolitan Moscow and St Petersburg versus a barely literate, wild east 'constructs a veritable "ontology" of Russian politics, naturalizing differences in ways of life, behaviors and tastes that otherwise could be critically explained by social and economic conditions ... into "primordial", eternal qualities, forcing their bearers into an ahistorical and unresolvable confrontation'.[15] So, too, the clichéd division of Russia into a cosmopolitan laptop-toting youth culture and a vast rural expanse of feral *babushki*.

Russian Literature Online and Russian Literature Online 2.0

The coincidence of regime and media change after the dissolution of the Soviet Union in 1991 felt profoundly interrelated to the reeling citizens of this brave new world. As Henrike Schmidt writes, cultural producers experienced the political and economic reorganisation of life as linked with the aesthetics of Postmodernism:

> the structural horizontality of the Internet was hailed as a technological embodiment of postmodernist concepts, including de-hierarchization and non-linearity (*ignoring the fact that the technology was actually developed as part of United States [US] military programs*). ... on a pragmatic level, the abolition of censorship put an end to the hunger for books of the late 1980s, an appetite that was immediately satisfied on the Internet – at least for those who could access it.[16]

Viktor Pelevin (1962–) provides perhaps still the most prescient and incisive satire of the emancipatory potential of imported Postmodernism in his novel *Generation 'P'* (*Generation 'P'*, 1999), which casts *homo-post-sovieticus* as the no longer recognisably human *homo zapiens*. Pelevin declares that the human condition itself has been hacked (not to mention the economy, politics, and media). Where there had once been individuals, there are now only hosts with oral and anal wow impulses to earn or spend: 'Comrades in the struggle! The position of modern man is not merely lamentable; one might even say there is no condition, because man hardly exists. ... HZ is simply the residual luminescence of a soul fallen asleep.'[17]

---

15 Ilya Matveev, 'The two Russias culture war: Constructions of the "people" during the 2011–2013 protests', *South Atlantic Quarterly* 113.1 (2014), 188.

16 Schmidt, 'From samizdat to New Sincerity', p. 260, emphasis mine.

17 Viktor Pelevin, *Homo Zapiens*, trans. Andrew Bromfield (New York: Viking, 2002), p. 82. See also Leila Guberina, 'Postmodernism in Pelevin's *Generation 'P'*: The New Society

The dream of universal access to all literature, meanwhile, proved extremely strong across the former Second World, sparking the wide, post-Soviet, IT-based alternative world of shadow libraries (very broadly defined as open databases of otherwise less accessible content). In the 1990s and early 2000s, research articles for scientists and doctors were as unaffordable in Russia (and much of the world) as Hollywood films and computer games. Lightly obfuscating his sources, Tenen explains the many motivations driving Russian 'prospectors' to work on collections such as the mega shadow library he calls Aleph. As Tenen notes, it would be 'remiss to describe *Aleph* merely in terms of book piracy, understood in conventional terms of financial gain, theft, or profiteering'. '*Aleph* answers the definition of peer production, resembling in many respects projects like *Linux*, *Wikipedia*, and *Project Gutenberg*. ... Yet, *Aleph* is also patently a library. Its work can and should be viewed in the broader context of Enlightenment ideals: access to literacy, universal education, and the democratization of knowledge.'[18] Online shadow libraries are in fact the way many cultural consumers worldwide access fiction, film, and theory, as well as technical and academic literature. A neo-operaist tract written in 2022 in Italian, for example, is likely to be translated into global English and disseminated via global Russian shadow libraries to eager readers in New Delhi years before an official English translation hits Amazon – if at all.[19]

Other projects have followed diverging trajectories that illustrate the interpenetrations among legal, illegal, and semi-legal ways of disseminating literature online. The no-longer-shadow Moshkov Library offers a fascinating case study that sketches the changing backdrop of Russian online literature. Programmer Maksim Moshkov (1966–) founded Lib.ru (known as the Moshkov Library) in 1994, built entirely on crowd-sourced digitised contributions scanned and processed by countless volunteers. The library flourished for a decade before Moshkov was sued for copyright violation in 2004, in what turned out to be a landmark case in Russia. Without much delay, the Moshkov Library regrouped and went legal, switching to only collecting work in the public domain, while Moshkov built a sister platform, Samizdat, where authors could share their own works freely as before. Moshkov has

(ORANUS) and the New Man (*homo sapiens*)', *Knjizevna Smotra* 44 (2012), 85–92; Sofya Khagi, 'The monstrous aggregate of the social: Toward biopolitics in Victor Pelevin's work', *Slavic and East European Journal* 55.3 (2011), 439–59.

18 Dennis Tenen and Maxwell Foxman, 'Book piracy as peer preservation', *Computational Culture* 4 (9 Nov. 2014), http://computationalculture.net/book-piracy-as-peer-preservation/, accessed 10 April 2021.

19 Ravi Sundarum, *Pirate Modernity: Delhi's Media Urbanism* (Abingdon: Routledge, 2009).

claimed to have received government support via grant money for his projects, and Samizdat has, in turn, prompted pay-to-print self-publication from authors, bringing it into the commercial realm. While large commercial sites for purchasing literature online (for e-readers and other formats) also exploded in the 2010s, at last estimate 'about half of all e-books were being downloaded illegally using torrents and social networks or being read free of charge from online libraries'.[20] Old habits, in short, die hard.

The burning question remains, how has the online dissemination of literature affected or inspired its production? Russian literature born online (web poetry, web prose, web diaries, fan fiction, text memes, blogs of infinite variety, experiments with hypertext of varied interest, etc.) resembles that of much of the world, but some genres and forms follow different trajectories due to the peculiarities of the early local Russian online scene, associations with regime change and political dissidence, the lasting cultural weight of samizdat in the Russian-language context, and the effects of late adherence to international copyright laws. Poetry and code met early and often: the first Russian web poetry was the domain of the same computer virtuosos who led the charge in accessing the online realm in the 1990s. In general, Russian-language poets proved early adapters to the World Wide Web and Web 2.0. Mark Lipovetsky and Evgeny Dobrenko have noted that authors' blogs, internet-based magazines, and online literary portals (e.g. the archive of contemporary poetry at Vavilon.ru, and cultural fora such as OpenSpace. ru) became 'venues for constant everyday interaction between writers and their readers, a place for publication of both the newest texts and critical reflection on them'.[21]

As internet usage became more and more widespread each year, the technically advanced pioneers of Ru.net were replaced by what Schmidt calls 'a mass of unsophisticated enthusiasts'.[22] Access rapidly democratised, making it easier to participate in the literary world online and leading to the proliferation of diverse and ambitious projects and archives; meanwhile online literature slowly drifted towards symbiosis with the nascent capitalist book market (see Chapter 2.10). While there were some relatively

---

20 Sergei Anur'ev, 'Rynok elektronnyh knig. Tendentsii razvitiia i predvaritel'nye rezul'-taty 2017 goda' [The ebook market. Trends in development and preliminary results from 2017] (n.d.), https://bookunion.ru/upload/iblock/f83/f833d535c0995e199fb6206 c056d03eb.pdf, quoted in Schmidt, 'From samizdat to New Sincerity', p. 263.

21 Evgeny Dobrenko and Mark Lipovetsky, 'The burden of freedom: Russian literature after communism', in Evgeny Dobrenko and Mark Lipovetsky (eds.), *Russian Literature after 1991* (Cambridge: Cambridge University Press, 2017), p. 11.

22 Schmidt, 'From samizdat to New Sincerity', p. 257.

independent new institutions, others reflected the second lives of familiar journals: the digital archives of the journal *New Literary Review* (*Novoe literaturnoe obozrenie*, 1992–), for example, form another important node in the contemporary Russian literary scene, as do platforms like Openspace.ru and Colta.ru, not to mention LiveJournal, Facebook, and VKontakte.[23] One of the most visible and celebrated curated online libraries of contemporary poetry was Vavilon.ru, an anthology that founder Dmitrii Kuzmin (1968–) developed into a web-based publication as early as 1997.[24] Its successor, LitKarta (New Literary Map of Russia), launched a decade later and has been going strong since 2007. Such sites, typically by fellow writers, aim to highlight the work of the best, or best-known, contemporary Russian-language writers with their participation and approval.

Far harder to describe in terms of aims and agency is the anarchic and politically polarised backdrop of author-posted web poetry and prose. Even in the early 2000s, the poet and political activist Kirill Medvedev (1975–) recognised web poetry as a 'concentrated portrait of the Russian uncon-scious, a collection of its most painful neuroses', which could manifest 'as an inert, conservative, and very aggressive mass'.[25] Some of this poetry resides in nationalistic platforms that rest on carefully chosen selections from the Russian literary classics situated alongside contemporary reading material responding with patriotic fervour to the annexation of Crimea, the Olympics, or – most recently – the invasion of Ukraine in 2022.[26] Stylistically, much of this online literary world is marked by the post-postmodern aesthetics of New Sincerity, the dominant aesthetic mode of contemporary populism (see Chapter 3.11) – and hence by nationalism, misogyny, and other symptoms of mass suffering.[27]

In schematic terms and in retrospect, it may be fair to say that the political unconscious of early Russian online poetry projects like Vavilon.ru and LitKarta reflected hope for a liberal public sphere. By contrast, much web poetry and

---

23 See Andrew Kahn, Mark Lipovetsky, Irina Reyfman, and Stephanie Sandler, *A History of Russian Literature* (Oxford: Oxford University Press, 2018), p. 766.

24 Kirill Medvedev comments that 'in this, as in so much else, [Kuzmin] was so far ahead of the rest of the literary field as to be playing in some different game entirely'. Kirill Medvedev, *It's No Good: Poems/Essays/Actions*, trans. Keith Gessen, with Mark Krotov, Cory Merrill, and Bela Shayevich (New York: n+1 with Ugly Duckling Presse, 2012), p. 184.

25 Medvedev, *It's No Good*, pp. 198–9.

26 See Jacob Lassin, 'Sacred sites: The Russian Orthodox Church and the literary canon online', PhD thesis, Yale University (2019).

27 See Ellen Rutten, *Sincerity after Communism: A Cultural History* (New Haven: Yale University Press, 2017). See also Jonathan Crary, *24/7: Late Capitalism and the Ends of Sleep* (London: Verso, 2013).

prose in the late 2010s and early 2020s has provided a place for celebrating right populism and policing borders – of Russianness, of gender and sexuality, of literary canon, language, and form. Against this grim backdrop, refreshing experimental practices on the political left (see Chapter 1.10) seek to draw attention to the media and online platforms themselves – and to the way that they shape us. Conscious of the politically fraught background of the Russian-language internet, small but compelling groups of critically minded writers, artists, and thinkers strive to create provocatively self-aware literary art online.

But how can experimental and politically engaged literature make use of tempting but complicit platforms, moving beyond utilitarian dissemination practices or the simplest forms of remediation?[28] While the embeddedness of social media within the apparatus of power and economic domination is old news, writers around the world continue to use any tools available – at times remarkably effectively. This is particularly true of the Russian-language literary internet, where a generation of cultural producers such as the leftist poet and editor Pavel Arsenev (1986–) from the *[Translit]* collective, and the feminist poet Galina Rymbu (1990–; editor of *F-Letter* (*F-pis'mo*), the first Russian-language public platform dedicated to queer writing, and now a resident of Ukraine) read as 'digital natives' yet nevertheless recognise Web 2.0 (like the Russian state, or neoliberal America) as enemy-controlled terrain. By the second decade of the twenty-first century, no one misses the ironies of using Facebook to organise anti-capitalist protest or of turning to Amazon to pre-order the latest radical Verso book. All the more reason for poets and artists to shape their own digital archives – something cultural producers such as Arsenev, Rymbu, and others do with speed and ingenuity. In their practices, contemporary Russian-language poetry merges with other forms, media, and languages through digital remedi-ation, collective translation, and immediate dissemination via social media and other online platforms. Moving fluidly between print and online platforms, literary journals, for example, are reimagined for the twenty-first century, allowing for weekly or even daily updates and featuring multimedia work such as video-poetry. Offline and online worlds interact with and necessitate one another: while books and journals appear in hard copy, most materials are readily found on journals' or poets' websites as well as on Facebook, VKontakte, YouTube, Vimeo, Telegram, and other platforms. Digital dissemination reflects the way we primarily read, share, and reference this material; hard copies

---

28 I follow Jay D. Bolter and Richard Grusin's use of the term in *Remediation: Understanding New Media* (Cambridge, MA: MIT Press, 2000).

meanwhile provide physical support, serving the purposes of collecting, fund-raising, and archiving, or signing, personalising, and gift giving.

Much contemporary political poetry insists on physical performance, on the presence of the poet's body at protests and other activist events, on physical and ethical risk, and on breaking down the walls between performer and spectator.[29] Readings, concerts, festivals, performances, actions, sit-ins, pro-tests, and encampments demand and build the 'strong ties' required for collective action, in Malcolm Gladwell's words.[30] Their remediated traces invite new participants to join in, prolong the lives of otherwise ephemeral collectivities, and infuse events with symbolic significance – sometimes long afterwards. Paolo Gerbaudo speaks of the 'symbolic construction of public space' on- and offline, witnessed during the organisation of various twenty-first-century global protest events. He suggests that 'social media use must be understood as complementing existing forms of face-to-face gatherings (rather than substituting for them), but also as a vehicle for the creation of new forms of proximity and face-to-face interaction'.[31] Remediations of political art online both represent and shape their histories; at their most self-aware, they also push against the limitations of digital technologies in creative and charged ways.

Coda: The Doorway

A compelling final example from the *[Translit]* constellation (see Chapter 1.10) shows us how the weapons of the enemy might be reprogrammed into word machines of the avant-garde, mobilising subversive potential. If, as Natalia Fedorova (founder of St Petersburg's annual Festival of Mediapoetry) puts it, media poetry is 'the translation of literature to the present time', then the newest avant-garde must throw that too from the rocket ship of twenty-first-century modernity.[32] *[Translit]* tries to use contemporary technologies in ways that resist and expose the fault lines behind the translation of literature

29 I write about Roman Osminkin's practice as paradigmatic in Marijeta Bozovic, 'Performing poetry and protest in the age of digital reproduction: Roman Osminkin', in Birgit Beumers, Alexander Etkind, Olga Gurova, and Sanna Turema (eds.), *Cultural Forms of Political Protest in Russia* (New York: Routledge, 2017); and Marijeta Bozovic, *Avant-Garde Post-: Radical Poetics after the Soviet Union* (Cambridge, MA: Harvard University Press, 2023).
30 Malcom Gladwell, 'Small change: Why the revolution will not be Tweeted', *The New Yorker* (4 Oct. 2010), www.immagic.com/eLibrary/ARCHIVES/GENERAL/NE WYKRUS/N101004G.pdf, accessed 10 April 2021.
31 Paolo Gerbaudo, *Tweets and the Streets: Social Media and Contemporary Activism* (London: Pluto, 2012), p. 13.
32 Natalia Fedorova, 'Art.Is.Natalia' (2018), http://artisyou.ru/, quoted in Jana Kostincova, 'Dora Vey lives and works in St Petersburg: Russian poetry written by people and

to the present or the digital. Such experiment or subversion must operate on more than the level of content: as Jana Kostincova writes, 'their works utilize new technology while exploring it and reflecting its influence on writing and reading. They do not perceive it as a tool or a means of producing and disseminating texts, but rather as a phenomenon which redefines contemporary literary discourse and simultaneously can help to interpret it.'[33]

[Translit] has a long history of exploring the limits of 'evil media', relatively overlooked compared to the journal's Marxist politics and critique of the Russian regime from the left. The journal's motto, printed on the cover of every early issue, borrows Robert Frost's line in English: 'The best way is always through.'[34] The allusive title, in turn, with its enigmatic bracketing, suggests translation and transliteration, but also quite specifically 'translit': informal romanisations of Cyrillic from earlier days of computing. For the journal's showrunner Arsenev, a self-described Noam Chomsky fanatic, that way 'through' always refers to language itself, which he holds at a seemingly permanent distance and discovers anew each time as a profoundly alien object. (Arsenev's chapbook *Colourless Green Ideas Furiously Sleep* (*Bestsvetnye zelenye idei iarostno spiat*, 2011) takes its title from Chomsky's *Syntactic Structures* (1957), where the phrase is offered as a textbook example of a sentence that is grammatically correct but semantically nonsensical.) Arsenev (born in Leningrad in 1986) has served as the backbone of *[Translit]* from its modest beginnings in 2006 to its broader legitimisation with the Belyi Prize in 2012 and its international presence today. Arsenev's mission, as Molly Blasing summarises in a review of his bilingual anthology *Reported Speech* (2018), appears to be 'to continue the legacy of the Russian avant-garde and factographic movements of the 1920s' while simultaneously 'working to fill a void left in the wake of the collapse of *samizdat* culture of the 1970s'.[35] The surprisingly tenacious and well-received journal *[Translit]* serves both goals, while Arsenev's own remediations, experiments, and provocations push the boundaries of Russian-language poetry to the edge of recognition.

algorithms', *Novaia rusistika* 13.1 (2020), 38–9. I am indebted to Kostincova's insightful article, which notes the references to Russian cosmism in Federova's work.

33 Kostincova, 'Dora Vey', 39.

34 Robert Frost, 'A servant to servants', in *North of Boston* (New York: Henry Holt, 1915). *[Translit]* omits the word 'out' from the original quotation, which reads: 'He says the best way out is always through.'

35 Molly Thomasy Blasing, 'Polyphonic transpositions: Pavel Arseniev's *Reported Speech*', *Reading in Translation* (21 June 2019), https://readingintranslation.com/2019/06/21, accessed 16 April 2021.

In the digital age, it is far from enough for contemporary leftist poetry to stop at experimental form or to subscribe to progressive political stances in its content. Instead, Arsenev argues that radical texts should be:

> built on what can be called the *pragmatic paradox*, which gives a poem the properties of a speech event, a self-fulfilling prophecy, or an archive that unpacks itself. . . . This requires *(self-)critique of the utterance's ability*, included in its very production. [. . . *Such* texts] rebel, as it were, against being read in traditional institutional circumstances. Only texts that invent anew each time a pragmatic frame for their realization . . . have the right to be called experimentally poetic.[36]

Arsenev looks to serial music, concrete poetry, and 1990s-era code for a continuation of Sergei Tretiakov's (1892–1937) 'literature of fact' (*literatura fakta*) and Dziga Vertov's (1896–1954) 'film truth' (*Kino-Pravda*). These great early Soviet contributions to world culture, he writes, aimed to apply dialectical montage to life itself by introducing 'accidental material into the work, like pierced holes in a representational system'.[37] So too now, the only practices that interest Arsenev are ones that fundamentally change – and challenge – the rules of the game. Moreover, they should be nearly impossible to appropriate or assimilate, even on the level of structure and form.

The poetic practices of *[Translit]* were inspired also by the work of left-leaning American poets, introduced into Russian verse through the efforts of the late Soviet poet Arkadii Dragomoshchenko (1946–2012) and his creative exchanges with the American Lyn Hejinian.[38] Arsenev and Roman Osminkin (1979–), founding editors of *[Translit]*, met in Dragomoshchenko's last home seminar in the 2000s – making them something like the literary grandchildren of the most generative love affair between the American 'Language School' poets (gathered around the 1970s journal L=A=N=G=U=A=G=E) and the Leningrad literary underground. We accordingly see elements of discourse poetry, found fragments of language, and other globally familiar poetic techniques reflected in their work. But often in their practice, this found and performed poetry can only be published in video format, as when, for

---

36 Pavel Arseniev, 'The pragmatic paradox as a means of innovation in contemporary poetic speech', in 'Pavel Arseniev: Poetry and prose', trans. the Cement Collective, 'Poetry after Language', Stanford University's ARCADE: A Digital Salon, http://arca de.stanford.edu/content/pavel-arseniev-poetry-and-prose.

37 Arseniev, 'Pragmatic paradox'.

38 See Stephanie Sandler, 'Arkadii Dragomoshchenko, Lyn Hejinian, and the persistence of Romanticism', *Contemporary Literature* 46.1 (2005), 18–45; and Aleksandr Skidan, 'Poznanie pyli', in *Summa poetiki* [Essentials of poetics] (Moscow: Novoe literaturnoe obozrenie, 2013), pp. 119–26.

example, embedded in the *[Translit]* blog. The added frame of digital remediation challenges our preconceived uses of the framing platform just as it does the manipulated content.

Ultimately, the poets of the *[Translit]* constellation maintain an active and creative presence online, even as they remain deeply sceptical of the neoliberal and surveillance potentialities inherent in Web 2.0 technologies. In Foucauldian terms, the location of resistance is the same as that of power: *[Translit]* frequently features essays critical of user-generated content platforms even as many in the group use the very same to push the boundaries of poetic remediation and online dissemination.[39] They expose ideology within and against poetry, within and against the digitised word; by doing so, they remind us of poetry's complicity with imaginaries of the individual genius, the liberal subject, and national identity – and of the dangerous potential of amplifying such imaginaries. Any cursory look at nationalist Russian-language poetry celebrating the invasion of Ukraine will suffice to illustrate. Rather than amplify such poetics, however, I will close here with a look at their subversion.

In 2017, in a brilliantly avant-garde gesture, Arsenev made the following nomination to the Dragomoshchenko Prize for poets under twenty-seven: 'Dora Vey is a poetry machine that uses the technology of spamdexing, based on Markov chain algorithms (doorway). . . . Dora Vey's poetry book is about to be published in the *kraft series. Dora lives and works in St. Petersburg.'[40] Dora's 'given name' echoes Freud's most (in)famous case study of female hysteria crossed with a reference to fellow *[Translit]* author and media theorist Mikhail Kurtov's (1983–) essay 'Doorways. Life and Work' (*Dorvei. Zhizn' i tvorchestvo*, 2014), published in the ninth issue of the journal. In it, Kurtov describes the strange poetics of so-called doorway web pages as follows:

> Doorways are texts automatically generated from random-texts and key words, designed exclusively to be read by search-engine robots. Ordinary users do not see them: when they click on the doorway in the search results, they are automatically directed to a new page, where they will be offered an appropriate product or service. . . . doorways are agents of pure machine communication.[41]

39 See also Matthew Fuller and Andrew Goffey, *Evil Media* (Cambridge, MA: MIT Press, 2012).
40 The project is a collaboration between Arsenev and *[Translit]* theorist Mikhail Kurtov. See Pavel Arsen'ev, 'Dora Vei', *Premiia Arkadiia Dragomoshchenko*, https://atd-premia .ru/2017/09/21/dora-vey/ (2017), accessed 14 April 2023. See Kostincova, 'Dora Vey'.
41 English translation in Kostincova, 'Dora Vey', 41; see also Mikhail Kurtov, 'Dorvei. Zhizn' i tvorchestvo' [Doorways. Life and work], *[Translit]* 9 (2014), 80.

In Kurtov's imaginative interpretation, reading 'doorway poetry', as he calls the random texts, actually becomes a subversive peek into a world never intended for our eyes but 'actually created to manipulate people, to influence their navigation on the Internet'.[42]

In the letter justifying his nomination of Dora Vey for the Dragomoshchenko Prize, Arsenev clearly battles against what he sees as a conservative, white-washing appropriation of the legacy of his beloved former mentor. (He also targets critics who have grumbled that [Translit]'s texts 'allegedly resemble the results of machine translation, "lack soul", etc.'[43]) And yet, the emancipatory potential Arsenev and Kurtov find in Dora Vey's work is also entirely serious. According to Kostincova:

> In 2017, Kurtov published a printed anthology of doorway poetry called *Gagarin's Lactate. Selected Works by Search Engine Spam.* ... He identifies the doorway as imagination outlaws, self-liberating generators, which offer new meanings every day through new word strings, explore the valency of words, and with their experiments broaden our ideas of what is possible. The name of the collection is obviously a product of doorway poetics. Kurtov explains his choice of words by playing with the theme of cosmos, the Soviet era, the 1960s, which he considers a period of machine naivety and innocence. The reference to the 1960s also refers to the development of computers, the expectations associated with them in contrast to today's state of sobering.[44]

The most interesting forms of online Russian-language literary experimentation thus return not only to the legacies of the avant-garde and samizdat but also to the early days of post-Soviet online tinkering with poetry and code – for another enticing road not (yet) taken to its end.

All literary subversion in the internet age must grapple in some way with the dominant mechanism mediating its production, dissemination, and reception. In the Russian-language literary context, those explorations include deep digs into speculative pre-histories and imagined refractions of an alternative modernity.

Further Reading

Bozovic, Marijeta, 'Performing poetry and protest in the age of digital reproduction: Roman Osminkin', in Birgit Beumers, Alexander Etkind, Olga Gurova, and Sanna Turema (eds,), *Cultural Forms of Political Protest in Russia* (New York: Routledge, 2017).

42 Kostincova, 'Dora Vey', 41.   43 Kostincova, 'Dora Vey', 40.
44 Kostincova, 'Dora Vey', 42.

Crary, Jonathan, *24/7: Late Capitalism and the Ends of Sleep* (London: Verso, 2013).

Gerbaudo, Paolo, *Tweets and the Streets: Social Media and Contemporary Activism* (London: Pluto, 2012).

Hayles, N. Katherine, *My Mother Was a Computer: Digital Subjects and Literary Texts* (Chicago: University of Chicago Press, 2005).

Isaacson, Walter, *The Innovators: How a Group of Hackers, Geniuses, and Geeks Created the Digital Revolution* (New York: Simon & Schuster, 2014).

Kostincova, Jana, 'Dora Vey lives and works in St Petersburg: Russian poetry written by people and algorithms', *Novaia rusistika* 13.1 (2020), 37–43.

Matveev, Ilya, 'The two Russias culture war: Constructions of the "people" during the 2011–2013 protests', *South Atlantic Quarterly* 113.1 (2014), 186–95.

Peters, Benjamin, *How Not to Network a Nation: The Uneasy History of the Soviet Internet* (Cambridge, MA: MIT Press, 2016).

Schmidt, Henrike, 'From samizdat to New Sincerity: Digital literature on the Russian-language internet', in Daria Gritsenko, Mariëlle Wijermars, and Mikhail Kopotev (eds.), *The Palgrave Handbook of Digital Russia Studies* (Cham: Palgrave Macmillan, 2021), pp. 255–75.

Tenen, Dennis, and Maxwell Foxman, 'Book piracy as peer preservation', *Computational Culture* 4 (9 Nov. 2014), http://computationalculture.net/book-piracy-as-peer-preservation/.

Empire

VITALY CHERNETSKY

In the Russian literary canon, few poets can rival the recognition enjoyed by Fedor Tiutchev (1803–1873): his love poems, philosophical poems, and nature poems are known by heart and quoted frequently. By contrast, his poetry on political themes has largely languished in obscurity. Yet politics and government service were central to Tiutchev's life, from his two-decade career as a diplomat to his later work as a censor of foreign editions in St Petersburg. Following the European revolutions of 1848, Tiutchev devoted his poetry to opposing revolutionary change. In the verse 'Russian Geography' (*Russkaia geografiia*, 1848–9), he proclaims:

> From the Nile to the Neva, from the Elbe to China
> From the Volga to the Euphrates, from the Ganges to the Danube
> Thus lies the Russian tsardom ... and it shall never pass away,
> As the Holy Spirit foresaw and as Daniel prophesied.[1]

While it would be reductive to claim that all of Tiutchev's poetry is equally determined by and grounded in Russian imperialism, 'Russian Geography' casts into sharp relief an 'imperiality' that spans the poet's work. From the emergence of its secular forms in the mid-seventeenth century, Russian literature has been profoundly impacted by imperiality as a matrix of power that operates through hegemony over the society at large and the individual subjectivities within it.

This notion of imperiality, as distinguished from imperialism, has been introduced by analogy to the decolonial theorist Anibal Quijano's notion of coloniality, as distinguished from colonialism. For Quijano, coloniality is a broader sociopolitical and cultural framework, indeed a cognitive model, underpinning the European constructions of modernity and rationality – one

---

1 Fedor Tiutchev, *Polnoe sobranie stikhotvorenii* [Complete poems] (Leningrad: Sovetskii pisatel', 1987), p. 152.

which has endured after the destruction of colonialism as an explicit political order.[2] For David Slater, imperiality designates 'the perceived right, privilege and sentiment of being imperial or of defending an imperial way of life' that is linked to imperial discourses and what he calls 'an imperial ethos of care'.[3] While some, like Revathi Krishnaswamy, use it in a narrower sense, tying it specifically to phenomena that are 'post-Communist, post-Cold War, post-modern, and, above all, postcolonial', for others, like Heinrich Kirschbaum, it is a category with broader implications that are manifested across an extended timescape.[4] It is this understanding of imperiality that underpins this examination of empire as a mechanism in the context of the history of Russian literature. But as Krishnaswamy suggests, some of imperiality's most telling manifestations emerged after the collapse of the Soviet Union. This chapter will provide an account of the evolution of imperiality as a mechanism across Russian and Soviet literature, and explore its ramifications in the post-Soviet and contemporary eras.

Imperial Foundations

The very beginnings of literature as an institution in the Muscovite state are inextricably tied to the rise of Muscovy as an imperial power. On 1 September 1667, Tsar Aleksei Mikhailovich (r. 1645–76) and his son Aleksei Alekseevich (1654–1670) were presented with a cycle of verses entitled *The Russian Eagle* (*Orel rossiiskii*), through which Russia's first professional writer, Simeon Polotskii (1629–1680), praised the ruler and suggested a grand vision for Russia's future (see Chapter 1.2). In the early eighteenth century, the archbishop and prolific rhetorician Feofan Prokopovich (1681–1736; see Chapter 4.2) wrote treatises on imperial power but also reflected and pro-jected it in literary works, such as his pioneering play *Vladimir* (*Vladimir*, 1705). Simeon had been brought to Moscow from Polatsk; Feofan was originally from Kyiv. Their careers demonstrate the empire's efficiency in absorbing and promoting talent from the populations it came to dominate

---

2 Anibal Quijano, 'Coloniality of power, Eurocentrism, and Latin America', *Nepantla* 1.3 (2000), 533–80; Quijano, 'Coloniality and modernity/rationality', *Cultural Studies* 21.2 (2007), 168–78.

3 David Slater, 'Questions of (in)justice and imperiality of power', *Colección de Estudios Internacionales* 13 (2013), 9.

4 Revathi Krishnaswamy, 'Postcolonial and globalization studies: Connections, conflicts, complicities', in Krishnaswamy and John C. Hawley (eds.), *Postcolonial and the Global* (Minneapolis: University of Minnesota Press, 2007), p. 13; Heinrich Kirschbaum, 'The verbatim drama of Lisbon: Stenography of (anti-)imperiality', *Zeitschrift für slavische Philologie* 72.1 (2016), 9–22.

through colonial expansion: Prokopovich's individual ambition found synergy with an imperial power on the rise. As the eighteenth century progressed, literature became a vocal amplifier of imperial aims. In 1739, for example, Mikhail Lomonosov (1711–1765) celebrated a victory over the Ottomans by writing his 'Ode to the Blessed Memory of the Empress Anna Ioannovna on the Victory over the Turks and Tatars and the Seizure of Khotin, 1739' (*Oda blazhennyia pamiati gosudaryne imperatritse Anne Ioannovne na pobedu nad turkami i tatarami i na vziatie Khotina 1739 goda*), which begins: 'Sudden rapture has captured the mind'.[5] As Harsha Ram has noted, the opening line presents poetic inspiration as the violent imposition of an external force, analogous to the political power that it describes.[6]

In the early nineteenth century, the Caucasus emerged as the key locus for articulating literary imperial visions,[7] but many other locales also figured. Thus, Valeria Sobol highlights the prominence of two other topoi in the Russian literary imagination during the first half of the nineteenth century: Finland and the broader Baltic 'north', on the one hand; and Ukraine and the broader 'south', on the other.[8] Russian-language writers were aware of, and responded to, literary texts from the minority or colonised literary traditions that criticised the Russian imperial project. For instance, the Polish poet Adam Mickiewicz (1798–1855) and the Ukrainian poet Taras Shevchenko (1814–1861) responded in direct ways to the Russian Empire as a mechanism impacting, and even generating, literary discourse – see especially Shevchenko's pioneering articulation of anti-colonial solidarity in his poem 'The Caucasus' (*Kavkaz*, 1845). Still, Mickiewicz and Shevchenko were the rare 'subaltern' interlocutors of imperial Russian literary discourse; overall, this discourse was, as Susan Layton notes, 'essentially a cultural monologue'.[9]

Alongside literary scholarship, historians have convincingly argued that imperiality was a defining feature of Russian nationalism in the nineteenth century, and that there was no contradiction between the two.[10] Within the literary sphere, especially in the period associated with Romanticism

---

5 M. V. Lomonosov, *Polnoe sobranie sochinenii* [Complete works], 11 vols. (Moscow, Leningrad: Akademiia nauk, 1950–83), vol. VIII, p. 16.
6 Harsha Ram, *The Imperial Sublime: A Russian Poetics of Empire* (Madison: University of Wisconsin Press, 2003), p. 5.
7 Susan Layton, *Russian Literature and Empire: Conquest of the Caucasus from Pushkin to Tolstoy* (Cambridge: Cambridge University Press, 2004).
8 Valeria Sobol, *Haunted Empire: Gothic and the Russian Imperial Uncanny* (Ithaca: Cornell University Press, 2020).
9 Layton, *Russian Literature and Empire*, p. 8.
10 Mark Bassin, *Imperial Visions: Nationalist Imagination and Geographical Expansion in the Russian Far East* (Cambridge: Cambridge University Press, 1999), pp. 12–13.

(see Chapters 1.4, 4.8), empire came to function as a driver and a condition of possibility. Thus, Aleksandr Pushkin's (1799–1837) southern exile and first-hand experience of the Caucasus resulted in his appropriation of the Byronic oriental tale in early narrative poems such as 'The Prisoner of the Caucasus' (*Kavkazskii plennik*, 1822) or 'The Fountain of Bakhchisarai' (*Bakhchisaraiskii fontan*, 1823). These poems in turn played a pivotal role in developing Russian orientalist discourse and in establishing the view of Pushkin's southern poems as 'national' for Russia.[11] Their popularity inscribed in readers' imaginations a very specific view of the empire's southern frontier – the Caucasus and (parts of) Ukraine and Moldova – while also contributing to the discursive construction of Russia itself and its own mission.[12] Yet imperiality runs throughout Pushkin's oeuvre, and not just in his 'southern' poems of the early 1820s. Engagement with empire past and present – praised, feared, and occasionally mocked – can be traced through to later works that are as different in theme and style as *The Bronze Horseman* (*Mednyi vsadnik*, 1833; see Chapter 4.2) and *A Journey to Arzrum* (*Puteshestvie v Arzrum*, 1829–36), even if one leaves aside the overtly imperialist texts from that period, such as 'To the Slanderers of Russia' (*Klevetnikam Rossii*, 1831).[13]

The writings of Mikhail Lermontov (1814–1841) and Nikolai Gogol (1809–1852) are no less imperially determined than those of Pushkin. Lermontov had a complex attitude towards Russia's imperial project, yet both his life circumstances, including two tours of military service in the Caucasus, and his literary efforts, from his teenage poetry to the mature works of the final years of his short life, are inextricably bound to it; even more than Pushkin, he was an inventor of the Caucasus as a Russian literary topos. While Lermontov's presentation of Russia's colonial wars is far from an endorsement, there is no consistent anti-colonial pathos either. In his early writings the Caucasus natives were presented primarily as 'noble savages' who served as 'an allegorical screen on which the Russian gentry writer could project, and deflect, his own political alienation', as Ram has argued.[14] Later, Lermontov went deeper in exploring the vision of the Caucasus during the colonial war as the paradoxical combination of a site of genocidal warfare and an Edenic space of creativity and spiritual renewal. Participation in the

---

11 Katya Hokanson, *Writing at Russia's Border* (Toronto: University of Toronto Press, 2008).
12 Monika Greenleaf, *Pushkin and Romantic Fashion: Fragment, Elegy, Orient, Irony* (Stanford: Stanford University Press, 1994), esp. pp. 108–55.
13 See Edyta Bojanowska, 'Pushkin's "To the Slanderers of Russia": The Slavic question, imperial anxieties, and geopolitics', *Pushkin Review* 21 (2019), 11–33.
14 Ram, *Imperial Sublime*, p. 208.

imperial project was thus conceptualised as a 'quest of sublime, restorative wilderness' for the Russian elites.[15]

In the case of Gogol, who was born and raised in rural Ukraine yet became a key literary presence in the Russian capital after his move to St Petersburg in 1828, the relation to imperiality is clearly manifested in the dual identity that emerges from his texts. Gogol's work presents the Ukrainian culture of his home as a precious legacy of the past yet combines it with an 'imperial patriotism' that embraces Russia as both the mysterious carrier of a great future and a site of dark grotesquery in the present. The author gained initial success as a purveyor of exoticised presentations of his native culture for consumption by the imperial centre and went on to offer harsh critiques of contemporary Russia as a national space in his so-called Petersburg tales, his play *Inspector General* (*Revizor*, 1836; see Chapter 3.4), and his novel *Dead Souls* (*Mertvye dushi*, 1842).[16]

While over the course of the nineteenth century the national focus gained increasing prominence in Russian literary discourse, the understanding of nationhood that developed within it was fundamentally underpinned by imperiality.[17] The defining role played by imperiality has been increasingly recognised by scholars of Russian literature in the age of Realism. Thus, Edyta Bojanowska has refocused attention on Ivan Goncharov's (1812–1891) travelogue *The Frigate Pallada* (*Fregat Pallada*, 1858) – notes and observations on a voyage from St Petersburg to Japan via Portsmouth, the Cape of Good Hope, and Java – as an articulation of Russian imperial consciousness in its rivalry with other empires.[18]

Within this broader context, Lev Tolstoi (1828–1910) constitutes a special case. Some of Tolstoi's earliest publications, such as the stories 'The Raid' (*Nabeg*, 1853) and 'The Wood-Felling' (*Rubka lesa*, 1855), focused on the war in the Caucasus, rebelling against the Romantic paradigm with an unsparingly Realist vision of its brutality. The posthumously published *Hadji Murat* (*Khadzhi-Murat*, 1904; see Chapter 4.2) has been recognised as a particularly

---

15 Layton, *Russian Literature and Empire*, pp. 230, 231.
16 On Gogol's identity dilemmas and his complex relationship to Russia's imperiality, see Edyta Bojanowska, *Nikolai Gogol: Between Ukrainian and Russian Nationalism* (Cambridge, MA: Harvard University Press, 2007). For a postcolonial take on Gogol's Ukrainian-themed texts, see Roman Koropeckyj and Robert Romanchuk, 'Ukraine in blackface: Performance and representation in Gogol''s *Dikan'ka Tales*, book 1', *Slavic Review* 62.3 (2003), 525–47.
17 Olga Maiorova, *From the Shadow of Empire: Defining the Russian Nation through Cultural Mythology, 1855–1870* (Madison: University of Wisconsin Press, 2010), pp. 6, 18.
18 Edyta Bojanowska, *A World of Empires: The Russian Voyage of the Frigate Pallada* (Cambridge, MA: Harvard University Press, 2018).

powerful reassessment and indictment of Russia's colonial violence. Yet while critiquing imperiality, *Hadji Murat* also reinforces it through its discursive stance: despite giving voice to its Caucasian protagonist, it nevertheless, as Layton notes, 'approached the tribesman as a culturally muzzled figure who needed a mediator to bring him into an authentic dialogue with the Russian readership'.[19] Imperiality is a key feature also in Tolstoi's most celebrated works, *Anna Karenina* (*Anna Karenina*, 1878) and *War and Peace* (*Voina i mir*, 1868–9). In *Anna Karenina*, it is in the background, most obviously in Aleksei Karenin's influential government position (Karenin's main prototype was the notorious minister Petr Valuev, responsible for the restrictions on the public use of Ukrainian imposed in 1863) and in the military career of Aleksei Vronskii. *War and Peace* has been described as a work that 'fulfilled the demand in Russia for an imperial epic'. In its presentation of Napoleon's invasion, *War and Peace* 'consolidated the myth of Russian imperial innocence' by way of contrast and elided the distinction between the Russian Empire and ethnic Russia.[20] Although imperialism is not directly thematised in the novel, it leaves its traces in the Bezukhov family's wealth, which depends on serf labour from estates acquired in territories annexed from the Polish–Lithuanian Commonwealth in 1793, less than two decades before Napoleon's invasion of Russia. The novel helped cement among its Russian readers the view of eastern and central Europe as a 'rightfully Russian' sphere of influence and consolidated a canonical view of Russian history which blurred its colonial practices with a compelling self-image of Russia as a magnificent and much-put-upon nation state.[21]

This very persistent background of imperiality would continue meaningfully through the oeuvre of many a Russian writer. In Anton Chekhov (1860–1904), for example, imperiality is perceptible not only in his travelogue *Sakhalin Island* (*Ostrov Sakhalin*, 1895), or in his complicated attitude to his Ukrainian roots, but also in what Bojanowska has dubbed his call 'to colonize responsibly' as articulated in his Caucasus-set novella *The Duel* (*Duel'*, 1891).[22] In Andrei Belyi's (1880–1934) *Petersburg* (*Peterburg*, 1913–14, 1922), imperiality constitutes one of the richest sources of both the novel's innovative aesthetics and its ideological critique of the Russian society of its era; it is crucial for the

---

19 Layton, *Russian Literature and Empire*, p. 264.
20 Ewa M. Thompson, *Imperial Knowledge: Russian Literature and Colonialism* (Westport, CT: Greenwood, 2000), pp. 86, 87–88.
21 Thompson, *Imperial Knowledge*, p. 106.
22 Edyta Bojanowska, 'Chekhov's *The Duel*, or how to colonize responsibly', in Angela Brintlinger and Carol Apollonio (eds.), *Chekhov for the 21st Century* (Bloomington: Slavica, 2012), pp. 31–48.

novel's construction of space, for its presentation of its characters and their thought processes, and for its vision of modernity that precipitates the empire's crisis.

Soviet-Era Transformations

Imperiality is also the key tool for grasping how the institution of Soviet literature functioned. The Soviet-era term 'literature of the peoples of the USSR' (*literatura narodov SSSR*) has two distinct meanings. On the one hand, this term was used to refer to the entire history of national literatures of the nations that were part of the Soviet Union; on the other, it referred specifically to literature written on Soviet territory in all the languages of the Soviet Union since 1917. Just as the Russians were an unmarked dominant nation in the USSR, so too did the term 'nationalities' often mean 'all the nationalities except Russian'. By extension, the term 'literature of the peoples of the USSR' usually stood for all the national literatures of the USSR except Russian.

In the immediate aftermath of the establishment of Soviet rule, however, the imperiality of Russian literature temporarily retreated, yielding to a utopian vision of world revolution. It did not completely disappear but was greatly diminished in visibility. The Soviet Union was among the world's most ethnically and linguistically diverse states. Some of the nations comprising it (such as the Armenians) could boast a literary tradition going back almost 2,000 years; others had no writing system of their own. The 1920s saw the emergence of an ambitious programme of 'nativisation' (*korenizatsiia*), which promoted the republics' distinct languages and cultures in public life and education, and in the promotion of local people to administrative roles. At first, literary production in the languages of the Soviet Union was largely left to its own devices. This changed in around 1929, when a consistent policy was initiated to bring all the distinct national literatures and cultures of the USSR into one orbit. A new imperial paradigm was constructed and asserted in keeping with the hierarchical system of a 'friendship of peoples' (*druzhba narodov*), within which Russia assumed the role of older brother. The proclamation of Socialist Realism (see Chapter 1.8) as the only official Soviet style grouped all the diverse national literatures and cultures under the formula 'socialist in content, and national in form', referring to the unified delivery of the same content enlivened by each nationality's culturally specific, 'picturesque' form. National cultures were showcased through specially designed festivals and through an ambitious programme for publishing translations. This vision of unity was also projected onto the past as national canons of

'progressive' literature were engineered on a cookie-cutter basis (in many cases writers from the past, for instance from Turkic-language cultures, were assigned modern national affiliations based on loose and contradictory criteria). The literary journal *Friendship of Peoples* (*Druzhba narodov*, 1939–) was launched in order to showcase the development of the national literatures of the USSR.

As critical voices were silenced during the Great Terror of the mid- to late 1930s, nativisation policies were abandoned and large-scale purges of non-Russian intelligentsias wiped out or scared into conformity their leading literary talents. By the end of the 1930s, there was depressing uniformity in literary production, characterised by vacuous propagandistic content and ritualised decorative form. The Soviet-era imperial mechanism of culture thus differed in an important way from its nineteenth-century predecessor: collectively, Soviet national literatures formed, to use the apt formulation of Marko Pavlyshyn, not a dynamic canon but a rigidly structured iconostasis.[23] That is, each of the national literatures was represented by a few deified figures of writers past and present, who were officially admired but usually not read by the wider public. This iconostasis was strictly hierarchical, with the position of highest privilege being reserved for Russian literature.

Familiar pre-Soviet imperial paradigms, however, soon returned. Their force was felt palpably in the 1940s, both in the mobilisation of Russian imperial history for the motivational support of the war effort in fighting the Nazi invasion and also in later war-related novels, perhaps most notoriously in Vasilii Azhaev's (1915–1968) *Far from Moscow* (*Daleko ot Moskvy*, 1948), a production novel set in the Far East in the early months of the war. This book deliberately fictionalises an actual project built by Gulag convict labour, reinventing it as a heroic and voluntary construction project. At the same time, it contrasts the main characters – all of them transplants from Moscow and the European part of the USSR – with a reductively exoticised indigenous population.[24]

As an imperial system, multinational Soviet literature had a strict classificatory grid imposed on it by the official Soviet literary scholarship. Individual national peculiarities were often glossed over: each of the national literatures was supposed to have followed the evolution of the Soviet literary canon, from the revolutionary romanticism of the 1920s to the so-called workers'

23 Marko Pavlyshyn, 'Aspects of the literary process in the USSR: The politics of recanonization in Ukraine after 1985', *Southern Review* (Adelaide) 24.1 (1991).

24 See Thomas Lahusen, *How Life Writes the Book: Real Socialism and Socialist Realism in Stalin's Russia* (Ithaca: Cornell University Press, 1997).

enthusiasm of the 1930s, before solidifying in the historical novels that characterised the postwar period (see Chapter 3.9). Even during the period of reforms known as the Thaw, following Joseph Stalin's death in 1953, unique local styles, such as the Ukrainian chimeric novel (an indigenous form of magic realism), were explained away. On the all-Union level, attention was primarily granted to iconic writers from numerically small ethnic groups (for instance, Rasul Gamzatov (1923–2003), an Avar, or Iurii Rytkheu (1930–2008), a Chukchi); to writers who self-translated their work into Russian (such as Chingiz Aitmatov (1928–2008), a Kyrgyz; or Vasil Bykau (1924–2003), a Belarusian); or to those who entirely switched to writing in Russian (such as Fazil Iskander (1929–2016), an Abkhaz). Most non-Russian writers, however, wrote primarily for audiences in their own languages and were preoccupied with the preservation and development of their national cultures.

Even dissident texts, such as Aleksandr Solzhenitsyn's (1918–2008) novel *Cancer Ward* (*Rakovyi korpus*, 1966, pub. in Frankfurt, 1968), can serve to illustrate the enduring power of imperiality in Soviet contexts. *Cancer Ward* is particularly striking in its imperial framing. Although set in Tashkent, the novel unfolds in a space dominated by the imperial culture and its values; local histories and indigenous cultures are all but invisible. *Cancer Ward*, as Ewa Thompson notes, 'leaves an impression of Tashkent as largely populated by Russians or Russified Uzbeks, for whom Russian rule presents no problems (other than the common problem of Soviet oppression, which touched Russians and non-Russians alike)'.[25] Russian characters are vividly and movingly depicted, but when indigenous characters do appear they remain flat and colourless: they are depicted as naïve, simple-minded, and yearning for Russian instruction. The specificity of local tragedies of Turkestan as colonised by Russia and divided and managed by Soviet rule is never acknowledged.

Reflecting (on) Imperiality

The prodigious development of public discourse during the late 1980s and early 1990s, the years associated with the policies of Glasnost and Perestroika, did not at first prioritise questions of empire. Rather, in works ranging from Realist narratives to parables, the primary focus was the oppressive authoritarian qualities of the past. But as shedding light on Stalin-era criminal persecutions meant airing topics directly related to imperial policies,

25 Thompson, *Imperial Knowledge*, p. 111.

reflections on Soviet imperiality became unavoidable. Thus, Anatolii Pristavkin's (1931–2008) novella *A Golden Cloud Spent the Night* (*Nochevala tuchka zolotaia*, 1987) builds upon the author's firsthand witness experience, as a teenage orphan, of the North Caucasus immediately after the deportations of the Chechens and the Ingush in 1944, presenting a trenchant critique of the imperial oppression of indigenous peoples.

A discourse of what I will call 'critical imperiality' increased considerably in the early 1990s, in texts that were written shortly before or soon after the collapse of the Soviet Union. Liudmila Ulitskaia's (1943–) novels reflect on Soviet imperiality by exploring the ethical and moral issues experienced by characters caught in the turmoil of history. Ulitskaia has been championed as a writer engaged in a 'steadfast promotion of difference, manifest in the hybridity of characters who combine varying backgrounds and beliefs', whose work 'affirms diversity and rejects monolithic forms of thought while avoiding superficial plurality'.[26] Some critics have found some of the depictions and underlying messages of her texts problematic, as at times they reify prejudicial stereotypes even if they call for sympathy or compassion for people associated with those stereotypes (notably in the case of gay characters). Nevertheless, Ulitskaia's foregrounding of ethical questions makes her work a crucial example of a critical reassessment of Russian imperiality. Ulitskaia's oeuvre does not ultimately transcend or reject this imperiality; instead, it imagines alternative positive versions of it.

Ulitskaia's early story 'The Daughter of Bokhara' (*Doch' Bukhary*, 1994) is set in Moscow immediately after the Second World War. It presents two encounters with otherness: first, residents of an old Moscow residential courtyard meet a Central Asian woman, the new daughter-in-law of its highest-respected resident, an elderly doctor; later, we follow the story of Milia, this woman's child, who has Down's syndrome. While the encounter with the daughter's disability and the neighbours' own evolution from fear and hostility to a grudging acceptance of difference are related with nuance and tact, the depiction of the mother's exoticised colonial otherness remains problematic. In its critique of Soviet attitudes to disability, the text uses the mother's difference as a mechanism to advance the story's central message, and its narrative focalisation remains that of the initially prejudiced gaze of the neighbours.

---

26 Elizabeth Skomp and Benjamin Sutcliffe, *Ludmila Ulitskaya and the Art of Tolerance* (Madison: University of Wisconsin Press, 2015), p. 3.

'The Daughter of Bokhara' is set in one of the 'backstreet spaces of the capital' that, for Edith Clowes, constitutes one of the pathways by which Ulitskaia's characters seek to escape the 'ideological and social dysfunction' of Russia's imperial centre. Among other such potential pathways are emigration, the focus of the novel *The Funeral Party* (*Veselye pokhorony*, 1997), and especially the ways in which 'characters resist Moscow by exploring the geographical edges of the empire and experiencing their palpably different cultures and historical narratives'.[27] This paradigm is clearly manifested in the novel *Medea and Her Children* (*Medeia i ee deti*, 1996). Structured as a family chronicle, this novel is set in Crimea, with flashbacks from the 1970s to earlier in the century and an epilogue in the 1990s. It centres on Medea Sinoply Mendes, a Pontic Greek woman who does not have biological children of her own but who comes to serve as a maternal figure not only for members of her extended family but also to a Crimean Tatar named Ravil, a descendant of an old acquaintance who comes to visit her from Central Asian exile and to whom she eventually wills her house. Crimea in this text is not a superficially portrayed Soviet riviera but a place of profound cultural hybridity that Soviet rule mostly destroyed, including by the multiple Stalin-era deportations of 'undesired' ethnicities (among them, both Crimean Tatars and the local Greeks). The novel's Crimea is simultaneously a palimpsest of traumas and a life-affirming idyll thanks to its natural beauty and the dignity and stoicism of characters like Medea. Most importantly, it is a symbolic imperial borderland that is positively valued in opposition to the dominating centre. Ulitskaia's Crimea becomes an imagined alternative space of a better, more just version of the empire; but to her it is inseparable from imperiality.

Written immediately after *Medea and Her Children*, *The Funeral Party* represents another defamiliarising reckoning with Russo-Soviet imperiality. Set in August 1991 in the New York loft apartment of Alik, an émigré artist dying of an autoimmune disease, the novel turns that space into a microcosm of rethought identities created by modern Russian and Soviet history. Alik's death symbolically coincides with the death of the Soviet Union, and his quest for his death, and his last days, to be accompanied not by despair but by reconciliation and love proposes a utopian vision of (post-)imperial reconciliation. The accidental family gathered in Alik's loft invites a rethinking of the relationships between a person's innate qualities and the social construction of identities, of affinities, and of what makes a family. With its tolerant

27 Edith Clowes, *Russia on the Edge: Imagined Geographies and Post-Soviet Identity* (Ithaca: Cornell University Press, 2011), p. 123.

acceptance of ethnic, religious, cultural, and bodily diversity, Alik's accidental family becomes a vision of a Soviet Union that never was.

Within post-Soviet critical reflections on imperiality, a unique and important place belongs to Andrei Volos (1955–), whose short stories began to be published in the late 1980s. The writer later organised fourteen of these stories as 'a novel in facets' titled *Hurramabad* (*Khurramabad*, 2000); of these, thirteen are set in Tajikistan and one (the final one) in Russia. Born into a family of Russian geologists working in Tajikistan, Volos provides clear insight into the conflicted feelings and traumas of what we could call Soviet 'pieds-noirs'. The protagonists of his stories are the Russophone and culturally Russian members of the colonial elite of managers and experts crucial to Soviet industrialisation projects, as well as their children and grandchildren, born in those colonised locales, often (as in the case of Volos himself) deeply knowledgeable about local culture and history but with a complex and contradictory relationship to empire and its impacts. Tajikistan suffered through a bloody civil war from 1992 to 1997, and Volos, like his protagonists, was among the many Russians who left Tajikistan for Russia. *Hurramabad* builds a mosaic of individual experiences, following characters with diverse backgrounds and differing degrees of attachment to and identification with the land where they have lived. He shows characters unmoored by the rapid collapse of imperial structures and puzzled by their (non-)belonging.

Critical engagements with Russo-Soviet imperiality from the final years of Soviet rule and the early post-Soviet era were by no means limited to the new types of realist writing. Late Soviet and post-Soviet Postmodernist art (both verbal and visual; see Chapter 1.9) approached official Soviet culture as a semiotic system with its own hierarchical relationships, taboos, and myths and proceeded to deconstruct it from within.

The writings of Dmitrii Prigov (1940–2007), a leading figure of Conceptualism in Russian literature and visual art, point to the imperial underpinnings of the Soviet 'empire of signs'.[28] In his poetic cycle *Moscow and the Muscovites* (*Moskva i moskvichi*, 1982), Prigov constructs a new, deliberately over-the-top myth as envisioned by an imaginary ecstatic imperial poet. The work starts with a parodic allegory depicting a personified ancient Moscow reading the dreams of the Assyrian king Ashurbanipal about a battle between an eagle and a snow leopard. In other poems in the cycle, Moscow becomes an object of obsession for all of its enraptured visitors, whom it

---

28 See Roland Barthes, *Empire of Signs*, trans. Richard Howard (New York: Hill and Wang, 1982).

either paralyses or converts into Muscovites. Moscow is also depicted as the cradle of all nations, ancient and modern, from the Assyrians and the Chinese to the Georgians and the Jews. In one poem, Moscow is directly linked to ancient Rome, with Muscovites wearing togas to the senate and the proud hearts of Muscovites becoming the envy of the whole world. Ultimately, Moscow grows and expands further, reaching Warsaw, Prague, Paris, and New York – 'Moscow is everywhere', 'where Moscow is not, there is emptiness'.[29] Imperial greed is thus pushed to its limit, giving us the mythic image of a monster swallowing the entire world.

In the early post-Soviet era, powerful literary critiques of Russian imperiality were mounted by representatives of the formerly colonised nations, such as the Ukrainian poets and prose writers Iurii Andrukhovych (1960–) and Oksana Zabuzhko (1960–). However, insightful investigations of Soviet imperiality can also be found in the works of two leading contemporary Russian writers, Viktor Pelevin (1962–) and Vladimir Sorokin (1955–).

Pelevin's texts are constructed as heterotopias: each one creates a world that is very much like ours, but slightly askew.[30] From his first collection of short stories, *The Blue Lantern* (*Sinii fonar'*, 1991), to his celebrated novel *Generation 'P'* (*Generation 'P'*, 1999), Pelevin has explored the breakdown of the Soviet empire as a breakdown of stable identities. It is thus not politics that fascinates the author but the characters' attempts to find their place within a realm of shifting meanings. As such, Pelevin's early writing presents an exploration of individually experienced worlds. His first novel, *Omon Ra* (*Omon Ra*, 1992), the story of a boy who wants to become a cosmonaut, takes the reader to an absurd world that is shockingly close to the reality of the late Soviet period. Here, Soviet civilisation's propensity for the mass production of empty ideological signs makes it impossible to be certain where the real ends and the make-believe begins. By the end of the novel, it turns out that instead of the actual space flight that he had been promised, the protagonist has been subject to mind games: the Soviet space programme is a deception, and all flights are nothing but imitations staged in secret tunnels underneath

29 Dmitrii Aleksandrovich Prigov, 'Moskva i moskvichi' [Moscow and the Muscovites], in *Sovetskie teksty* [Soviet texts] (St Petersburg: Izdatel'stvo Ivana Limbakha, 1997), pp. 177–91 (quotation on p. 184).

30 Brian McHale, *Postmodernist Fiction* (London: Routledge, 1989), pp. 43, 45. I expand McHale's term to describe textual organisation, seeing heterotopia as a condition when multiple textual regimes come into contact to create a new symbiotic entity, a chronotope of co-existence that is simultaneously asserted and ironically subverted. See Vitaly Chernetsky, *Mapping Postcommunist Cultures: Russia and Ukraine in the Context of Globalization* (Montreal: McGill-Queen's University Press, 2007), pp. 88–113.

Moscow. The Meresev Flying School, which the protagonist joins to fulfil his lifelong dream, presents a particularly biting caricature of Soviet imperial hierarchies. Each of the stages of the multi-stage rocket in which the protagonist is supposed to be launched to the Moon is manned by a flight school graduate. The protagonist, the main cosmonaut, is Russian, while the roles of 'rocket stages' are distributed among representatives of Soviet nationalities, including a Ukrainian and a Latvian, depicted according to Socialist Realist stereotypes. When this elaborate charade collapses and the protagonist finds himself ejected into a Moscow subway tunnel, the fictional world of the novel collapses as well. The reader thus cathartically relives the experience of deception and self-deception as it was lived by the Soviet subject – an experience that ultimately led to the breakdown of the Soviet system itself. Pelevin turns the textual condition of a heterotopia, balancing on the very edge of the familiar (Soviet) existence, into an exquisite mechanism for subverting the Soviet empire's authoritarian mindset.

In this way, Pelevin's hyperrealistic heterotopic texts offer a devastating critique of the decaying Soviet empire. The drama that plays out in his early texts is that of the awakening of the mind of the 'little person' (see Chapter 4.3) from their zombie-like stupor of routine existence to a critical awareness of the world that surrounds them – and to an awareness of the fact that these worlds are ultimately as numerous as our individual minds. Yet while these texts problematise the post-Soviet condition, they also partake of this diseased and absurd 'reality' by using it as building blocks in textual constructions that – it can be argued – preach escapism as the ultimate solution. Pelevin reached the end of his early period of writing with *Generation 'P'*, a biting satire on Russia's chaotic transformation in the 1990s, which is underpinned by a mixture of influences from the theoretical writings of the philosopher Jean Baudrillard to Assyro-Babylonian mythology. After a pause of several years, he returned to publication in 2003, and since then he has been publishing a steady stream of works that provide ironic commentary on contemporary Russian culture and politics while continuing to play with his earlier approaches. These novels and scattered short-story collections have been commercially successful in Russia, but they have not generated either the critical acclaim or the international recognition enjoyed by his earlier works. Some have speculated that 'Pelevin' himself has become a commercial brand that employs the help of ghostwriters.[31]

31 See the blog post by Mikhail Malyshev, 'Taina Viktora Pelevina: Kul'tovyi pisatel' kak kooperativ' [The mystery of Viktor Pelevin: Cult writer as cooperative], LiveJournal (16 Sept. 2015), https://mimal.livejournal.com/1327558.html, accessed 11 June 2023.

Like that of Pelevin, Sorokin's writing can be divided into two distinct periods. Most of Sorokin's later texts, starting with *Blue Lard* (*Goluboe salo*, 1999), are also structured as heterotopias; however, his earlier work offers a unique model of Conceptualist practice in Russian prose fiction and thus a critique of the Soviet 'empire of signs'. Sorokin's novel *The Queue* (*Ochered'*, 1985) consists entirely of remarks uttered by people waiting in a long queue for unknown goods; however, it was not conceived as an exposé of the shortages of consumer goods during the Brezhnev era. Sorokin's stated intention was to render the queue not 'as a socialist phenomenon, but as a carrier of a specific speech practice, as an extra-literary polyphonic monster'.[32] The novel is a tour-de-force performance of speech genres of *lingua Sovietica*, where the workings of Soviet empire as a discursive mechanism are made evident on multiple levels. In *The Queue*, as in the many other works he produced from the late 1970s through to the publication of his novel *Four Stout Hearts* (*Serdtsa chetyrekh*) in 1991, Sorokin presents skilful simulacra of conventional literary styles, most often of Socialist Realist narratives, only to reveal the violence underpinning the 'empire of signs' through sudden intrusions of transgressive acts or vocabulary; frequently, such puncturing leads to the total disintegration of the text.[33]

The collapse of the Soviet Union in 1991 precipitated a crisis in Sorokin's career, and in the following years he appeared to be searching for a new discursive paradigm, culminating in the publication of his novel *Blue Lard* in 1999. This book heralded the arrival of a new, 'reinvented' Sorokin whose critique of imperiality would go on to be realised most vividly in the short novel *Day of the Oprichnik* (*Den' oprichnika*, 2006). The novel's central premise is that, in the near future, Russia is ruled by an oppressive autocrat whose control over the country is managed by the *oprichniki*, the now-revived secret police of the time of Ivan IV ('the Terrible', r. 1533–84). The novel's title references a classical text connoting resistance to tyranny, Solzhenitsyn's novella *One Day in the Life of Ivan Denisovich* (*Odin den' Ivana Denisovicha*, 1962; see Chapter 2.7). Another intertextual engagement is with the dystopian tradition, most notably Evgenii Zamiatin's (1884–1937) novel *We* (*My*, comp. 1920–1; see Chapter 4.7).

Day of the Oprichnik is set in the year 2028, in a neo-imperial Russia that has moved beyond the Red and White Troubles of the Soviet and

---

32 V. Sorokin, 'Tekst kak narkotik' [Text as a narcotic], in *Sbornik rasskazov* [A collection of stories] (Moscow: RUSSLIT, 1992), p. 121.

33 For more on Sorokin's early writing, see Chernetsky, *Mapping Postcommunist Cultures*, pp. 75–87.

immediate post-Soviet past. The country is now surrounded by a Great Wall that separates it from both Europe and China, and it is ruled by a Sovereign who can be compared to Zamiatin's Benefactor. Like the Benefactor's guardians in *We*, the Sovereign's oprichniki uphold the monarchy by ruthlessly persecuting any sedition. As in *We*, there is a first-person narrator, the highly placed oprichnik Andrei Komiaga. Yet there are key differences between the two novels. Whereas Zamiatin's dystopian OneState was ruled as a scientifically rational society guaranteeing 'mathematically infallible happiness',[34] Sorokin's oprichniki regard themselves as being above the rest of the nation in their patriotic fervour; they themselves are the pillar of the monarch's rule. The world of the novel is a fusion of sixteenth-century Muscovy, elements of modern technology (such as cars and mobile phones), and some futuristic details. Within it, Soviet and old Muscovite mentalities persist and overlap. Individuals have no rights; they are not bound to society by any moral or collective bonds; each of them is alone at the mercy of the state. Russia is thus posited as essentially outside history as dynamic development. As the historian Stephen Kotkin has noted in a review of the novel, Sorokin's oprichniki resemble Putin's *siloviki*, or security forces, who keep the rich few on a short leash while solidifying their own control over various aspects of the state (including the most profitable branches of the economy). 'Sorokin's imaginative diagnosis of Putinism further grasps that the officials' looting is driven not by profiteering alone, but by their conviction that they are defending Russian interests', Kotkin writes. 'Everything Sorokin's oprichniks do is a transaction, but their love of country runs deep.'[35] In *Day of the Oprichnik*, the Russia of the future is both a fortress and a prison. It is the apotheosis of repressive imperiality.

While in general the twenty-first century has witnessed the rise of a revanchist neo-imperial culture in Russia, and the domestic cultural sphere offers numerous disturbing instances of warmongering and xenophobia, there is also a significant corpus of both literature and art of political protest, as well as literary texts that critically investigate Russian imperiality. Among the practitioners of the latter trend, I would highlight the Russophone Daghestani novelist Alisa Ganieva (1985–) and the Moscow native Sergei Lebedev (1981–). Ganieva offers a remarkable example of postcolonial (or

---

34 Yevgeny Zamyatin, *We*, trans. Clarence Brown (London: Penguin Books, 1993), p. 3.
35 Stephen Kotkin, 'A dystopian tale of Russia's future', *New York Times*, 11 March 2011, www.nytimes.com/2011/03/13/books/review/book-review-day-of-the-oprichnik-by-vladimir-sorokin.html, accessed 14 May 2023.

here, rather, anti-colonial) literature that 'writes back to the centre',[36] offering deep insights into the complex hybridity of contemporary Daghestani culture; thus her novel *Festive Mountain* (*Prazdnichnaia gora*, 2012) imagines a near future where the Russian authorities decide to build a wall separating the North Caucasus from the rest of Russia and ethnic and religious tensions mount. Half dystopia, half work of magic realism, the book portrays empire as a mechanism whose power can be asserted with ominous effectiveness even when not resorting to outright violent repression. Similarly, Lebedev's debut novel, *Oblivion* (*Predel zabveniia*, 2010), is structured as a journey by a young Russian who has learned that the man he considers his grandfather, and who saved his life when he was a child, was in fact a Gulag executioner. The book becomes a melancholy meditation on the persistence of Stalinism and on the ravages of Soviet civilisation on both its citizens and the natural environment. It is an incisive, if sad, affirmation of the persistent power of empire as a mechanism defining Russian culture, even when this mechanism is rusted and its joints are falling apart.

Russia's full-scale invasion of Ukraine in 2022 marks the start of a new chapter in the country's history, including its cultural history. So far, with very few exceptions, literary voices appear to be stumped by the challenge of critically reflecting on the catastrophe precipitated by neo-imperial revanchism. Some first tentative attempts at grasping this new reality have begun to appear, such as in the anthology *The Doomsday Poetry. Chronicles* (*Poeziia poslednego vremeni. Khronika*, 2022), compiled by the US-based scholar Yuri Leving and published in Russia.[37] In this well-intended but highly uneven volume of anti-war poems, we can see glimpses of new discourses that are emerging – and some of them give one hope. However, we can be certain that the process of exorcising imperiality from Russian literature and culture more broadly will be lengthy and extraordinarily difficult.

Further Reading

Bojanowska, Edyta, *A World of Empires: The Russian Voyage of the Frigate Pallada* (Cambridge, MA: Harvard University Press, 2018).

Clowes, Edith, *Russia on the Edge: Imagined Geographies and Post-Soviet Identity* (Ithaca: Cornell University Press, 2011).

36 See Salman Rushdie, 'The Empire writes back with a vengeance', *The Times*, 3 July 1982, p. 8.
37 Iurii Leving (ed.), *Poeziia poslednego vremeni. Khronika* [The doomsday poetry. Chronicles] (St Petersburg: Izdatel'stvo Ivana Limbakha, 2022).

Hokanson, Katya, *Writing at Russia's Border* (Toronto: University of Toronto Press, 2008).

Layton, Susan, *Russian Literature and Empire: Conquest of the Caucasus from Pushkin to Tolstoy* (Cambridge: Cambridge University Press, 2004).

Maiorova, Olga, *From the Shadow of Empire: Defining the Russian Nation through Cultural Mythology, 1855–1870* (Madison: University of Wisconsin Press, 2010).

Ram, Harsha, *The Imperial Sublime: A Russian Poetics of Empire* (Madison: University of Wisconsin Press, 2003).

Shkandrij, Myroslav, *Russia and Ukraine: Literature and the Discourse of Empire from Napoleonic to Postcolonial Times* (Montreal: McGill-Queen's University Press, 2001).

Sobol, Valeria, *Haunted Empire: Gothic and the Russian Imperial Uncanny* (Ithaca: Cornell University Press, 2020).

Thompson, Ewa M., *Imperial Knowledge: Russian Literature and Colonialism* (Westport, CT: Greenwood, 2000).

Boxes 3
Places

Box 3.1 The Camp

Labour camps, known for most of their seven decades by the acronym GULag (Main Administration of Camps), were a defining feature of the Soviet system, and one of its most baleful legacies. Concentrated in peripheral, hostile environments, they showed disregard for human life and health and resulted in mass death and disability. The release of millions from the camps, especially in the amnesties of the early post-Stalin years (1953–6), created a vast network of survivors, with many seeking to testify to their experiences.

The resulting corpus of Gulag memoirs dwarfs that of Gulag fiction, though the boundaries between them are fluid. A handful of returnees have dominated the canon, but key works were also authored by those who had never been in the camps, including twenty-first-century authors reworking the theme at several generations' remove. These narratives betray the influence of pre-revolutionary prison literature, such as the emphasis on spiritual redemption in Fedor Dostoevskii's *Notes from the House of the Dead* (*Zapiski iz mertvogo doma*, 1862) and the bleakness of Anton Chekhov's investigation of tsarism's most remote and brutal carceral settlement in *Sakhalin Island* (*Ostrov Sakhalin*, 1895). However, they also seek out new forms: as Tomas Venclova observes, 'the age-old topoi betrayed their falseness and weakness when applied to the modern standardized mass prison'.

The early Soviet camps were not a taboo topic. The most famous was Solovki, in the Solovetskii Islands, which produced its own newspapers and journals and hosted writers' visits, such as that recorded in Maksim Gorkii's celebratory essay 'Solovki' (*Solovki*, 1929). Nor did the shift to the more industrialised and repressive Stalinist model of forced labour at the end of the 1920s immediately silence the theme. The White Sea Canal construction project of the early 1930s produced Soviet literature's most strident celebration of the camps' 'reforging' mission, in the co-authored volume *The White Sea Canal* (*Belomorsko-Baltiiskii kanal imeni Stalina*, 1934).

Such propaganda disappeared in the second half of the 1930s with the Great Terror. However, the brief reappearance of the Gulag in Soviet publications of the early 1960s broadly aligned with the official rhetoric of de-Stalinisation. If Georgii Shelest's 'The Nugget' (*Samorodok*, 1962), the first Gulag story after nearly three decades of silence, no longer claimed that prisoners had been reforged, it did show that prisoners had not lost their communist faith. Aleksandr Solzhenitsyn's *One Day in the Life of Ivan*

Box 3.1 Places

Denisovich (*Odin den' Ivana Denisovicha*, 1962) was a crucial exception in its focus on a peasant with no interest in ideology who revealingly considers his day of hunger, cold, and hard work to have been 'rather happy'.

Given these tight controls, it is no surprise that the vast majority of camp literature did not appear in Soviet publications, but rather in *samizdat*, *tamizdat*, and émigré publishing. This was a corpus shaped by the urge to polemicise against official silences and euphemisms. Solzhenitsyn's *The Gulag Archipelago* (*Arkhipelag GULAG*, 1973), a seven-volume, 2,000-page 'artistic investigation' of the hidden camp network, relentlessly exposes its barbarism and vast human costs. Varlam Shalamov's multi-volume *Kolyma Tales* (*Kolymskie rasskazy*, first published in *tamizdat* in the 1970s though circulated in *samizdat* earlier) demolishes not only the Soviet myth of meaningful labour but also the humanism of Solzhenitsyn's Gulag writing. In Shalamov's stories, hunger, cold, and brutality reduce inmates to a barely sentient state. Vasilii Grossman, never himself imprisoned, dared in *Life and Fate* (*Zhizn' i sud'ba*, completed 1959, first published abroad, 1980) and *Everything Flows* (*Vse techet*, completed 1964; first published abroad, 1970) to trace the Gulag's Leninist roots and the similarities with Nazi camps. Other camp fiction experimented with alternative perspectives: Georgii Vladimov's *Faithful Ruslan* (*Vernyi Ruslan*, completed 1964; first published abroad, 1975) and Sergei Dovlatov's *The Zone* (*Zona*, completed 1968; published abroad, 1982) employ the fantastic and the absurd to explore the mindset of Gulag guards.

Glasnost and the early post-Soviet years saw the publication of formerly prohibited literature, including works by Grossman and Solzhenitsyn as well as Georgii Demidov's previously confiscated short stories. Some works, including Solzhenitsyn's *Ivan Denisovich* and *Gulag Archipelago*, even appeared on the national curriculum. Contemporary Gulag literature has made use of generational distance to produce surreal representations of the camps' haunting of post-Soviet society, as in Sergei Lebedev's *Oblivion* (*Predel zabveniia*, 2011) and Evgenii Vodolazkin's *Aviator* (*Aviator*, 2016). Where recent works have deployed more traditionally epic and humanist narratives – in Zakhar Prilepin's best-selling *Abode* (*Obitel'*, 2014), Guzel Iakhina's *Zuleikha Opens Her Eyes* (*Zuleikha otkryvaet glaza*, 2015), and Viktor Remizov's *Permafrost* (*Vechnaia merzlota*, 2021) – it has been to show the camps as sites of moral and psychological transformation, both negative and positive.

Polly Jones

Box 3.2 The Front

More than an event or a tragic social phenomenon, war is a paradigm that structures perceptions both in the public sphere and in the domestic realm, even outside wartime. Armed conflicts, whether contemporary or historical, have provided texture for epic narratives, both in poetry (especially between the 1740s and the 1830s) and in prose. Thus, Mikhail Lomonosov's first experiences in ode writing glorified military achievements in the war against the Ottoman Empire ('Ode to the Blessed Memory of the Empress Anna Ioannovna on the Victory over the Turks and Tatars and the Seizure of Khotin, 1739' (*Oda blazhennyia pamiati gosudaryne imperatritse Anne Ioannovne na pobedu nad turkami i tatarami i na vziatie Khotina 1739 goda*, 1739)); the first Neoclassical dramas written by Aleksandr Sumarokov addressed the internecine conflicts of the country's medieval history; and military actions on various borders of the constantly expansionist Russian state provided settings for works by Aleksandr Pushkin, Mikhail Lermontov, and Nikolai Gogol. The fact that a military career was a central obligation for male members of the ruling class from the early eighteenth to the late nineteenth centuries, and that the nobility dominated the literary sphere during this time, helped to perpetuate the centrality of war in the cultural sphere. The experience of the Napoleonic Wars (1803–15) made war important not only politically and socially but also existentially and spiritually.

Russia's major writers have addressed the theme of warfare in recognition of its importance but without necessarily glorifying the country's armed forces or war itself. Some narratives are at least ambivalent; some are explicitly critical of hostilities. Lev Tolstoi's *Sebastopol Sketches* (*Sevastopol'skie rasskazy*, 1855) are a demystifying depiction of the battlefield, pictured as both heroic and anti-heroic. Drawing on his personal experience of military service during the Crimean War (1853–6), the author multiplies points of view, reproducing the chaos inherent to any situation of mass violence. Tolstoi further developed this paradigm in *War and Peace* (*Voina i mir*, 1868–9): in that novel warfare is pictured as a form of work, rather than heroic action. Later writings drew on Tolstoi's model, with medical personnel appearing as exemplary protagonists of this vision of warfare-as-labour. Mikhail Bulgakov, a medical doctor by profession, places the characters of his novel *The White Guard* (*Belaia gvardiia*, 1925) in the centre of Kyiv, a besieged city seized by different armies during the civil war. Boris Pasternak's Iurii Zhivago serves as a doctor on several sides of different wars.

Box 3.2 Places

The Tolstoian epic style remained an authoritative paradigm for military scenes in the realist novel of the twentieth century. Vasilii Grossman's *Life and Fate* (*Zhizn' i sud'ba*, 1959) makes this legacy explicit: in one scene, two military commanders argue about Tolstoi's involvement in the Patriotic War of 1812. However, in Soviet-era depictions of war, Tolstoi's vision of the battlefield as a moral and practical community was reimagined as an institutional network determined by the intersection of various levels of the military hierarchy. Viktor Nekrasov's novel *In the Trenches of Stalingrad* (*V okopakh Stalingrada*, 1946), for example, pictures the front in terms of practical details and multiple social worlds. Nekrasov and other representatives of so-called lieutenants' prose (such as Iurii Bondarev or the Belarusian writer Vasil Bykau) focus on day-to-day military operations, showing little interest in the epic narrative.

Several important Soviet writers, such as Emmanuil Kazakevich and Aleksandr Tvardovskii, worked as war correspondents for national or military newspapers, communicating between the front and the broader public. Tvardovskii's poem *Vasilii Terkin* (*Vasilii Terkin*, 1942–5) was published in the official newspaper of the western front. This optimistic, pseudo-folkloric, poetic narrative – focused on the ordinary soldier Terkin – proved to be an efficient tool for mass mnemonics. However, texts such as this, approved for publication through complex processes of censorship, could not do justice to the numberless and divergent direct experiences of war. This role fell in part to unofficial poetry, sometimes written by approved Soviet authors. Boris Slutskii's poem 'Vanka the Platoon' (*Van'ka-vzvodnyi*, 1989) evokes a battle that leaves only one person alive and questions the notion of truth and fact so central to the tradition of war writing.

Indeed, tensions between truth and fact are a key feature of literary depictions of more recent wars. The novels of Vladimir Makanin (*Asan* (*Asan*, 2008)) and Zakhar Prilepin (*The Pathologies* (*Patalogii*, 2005)) are indicative in this respect. Svetlana Aleksievich, a Russian-language author of Belarusian and Ukrainian descent, turns to documentary prose, interviewing witnesses and participants of the Soviet wars. The controversial public response to her *Boys in Zinc* (*Tsinkovye mal'chiki*, 1989–91), about the Soviet war in Afghanistan (1979–89), reveals the polarising effects of that war and its memory within the Soviet and post-Soviet societies. It remains to be seen how Russian-language literature will grapple with the full-scale invasion of Ukraine that began in 2022.

Alexei Evstratov

Box 3.3 St Petersburg

Founded officially by Peter I (r. 1682–1725) in 1703 on the site of a former Swedish fortress in the hostile, swampy estuary of the Neva River and prone to floods and even sinking, St Petersburg came to symbolise the idea of a rational utopia located uneasily on the edge of a bottomless abyss. Many of the apocalyptic overtones of its literary image result from the story of its genesis. In keeping with the city's image as – in the words of Fedor Dostoevskii's iconic Underground Man from *Notes from Underground* (*Zapiski iz podpol'ia*, 1864) – 'the most imaginary city' in the world, the myth of St Petersburg originates not in any real event but in literature alone; it is a creative fiction.

The new capital city, conceived to be as unlike Moscow as possible, was part of Peter's plan to modernise the Russian state and turn it into an empire according to western European models, with a modern army, robust administration, and a church subject to state power. Peter's detractors accused him of having brought about the downfall of 'Holy Russia', the old order that was dominated by Orthodox Christianity. Consequently, St Petersburg came to embody dichotomies that continue to resonate even today: first and foremost, the question of whether Russia should orientate itself towards Europe or not – an issue that lies at the centre of the religious polemic in Dostoevskii's major novels of the 1860s. This was raised by Aleksandr Blok in his poem 'The Scythians' (*Skify*, 1918) and came to a head repeatedly in political events of the twentieth and twenty-first centuries.

The duality and tension inherent in the history of St Petersburg – simultaneously Peter I's vaunted *paradiz* and a version of the netherworld – gave rise to a peculiar cultural symbolism. This duality was first given literary form by Aleksandr Pushkin in his narrative poem *The Bronze Horseman* (*Mednyi vsadnik*, 1833). The 'horseman' is the equine monument to Peter by Étienne Falconet, unveiled in 1782. It is impossible to establish with certainty whether the poet, pitting his hero – the 'little man' Evgenii – against the towering equine statue of Peter I that tries to crush him, has found an ingenious way of portraying state power as oppressive or whether we are observing the hero during a bout of madness. Madness and manifestations of the fantastic – phenomena situated at the threshold between reality and imagination – would evolve to become common occurrences in texts set in St Petersburg. The motif of the statue of the Bronze Horseman come to life reappears in Andrei Belyi's Symbolist novel *Petersburg* (*Peterburg*, 1913–14, 1922) as an unambiguous harbinger of destruction with distinct echoes of the biblical horsemen of the Apocalypse.

Box 3.3 Places

While for Pushkin, the tension surfacing in St Petersburg was sociopolitical in nature, Nikolai Gogol's Petersburg tales – 'Nevsky Prospect' (*Nevskii Prospekt*, 1835), 'The Nose' (*Nos*, 1836), 'The Portrait' (*Portret*, 1835), and 'The Overcoat' (*Shinel'*, 1842) – reflect the response of nineteenth-century consciousness to modern urban life. Gogol portrays the capital city with its shifting ground and wafting fog as a place where demonic forces are allowed to run free. Dostoevskii inherited this image of St Petersburg as a city of miserable backstreets rather than a symbol of imperial might. Dostoevskii, however, largely dispensed with the grotesque and otherworldly elements of Gogol's vision. The evil that seems begotten by the suffocating tenements of St Petersburg – such as the temptation that drives Raskolnikov, the hero of *Crime and Punishment* (*Prestuplenie i nakazanie*, 1867), to overstep moral and social law in the name of a pseudo-scientific thought experiment – assumes metaphysical traits: ultimately, it probes the relationship between man and God.

Scholars defining a coherent set of traits for what some call the 'Petersburg text' usually locate it in the nineteenth century, though recognisable elements persisted into the age of Modernism. We find them, for example, in Blok's poems exploring the city's nightlife in the early 1900s, in Fedor Sologub's Decadent novel *The Petty Demon* (*Melkii bes*, 1905), or in Belyi's *Petersburg*. However, even in the 1970s and 1980s Elena Shvarts produced many poems featuring a Leningrad/St Petersburg that makes ample reference to the time-honoured myth. In her *Black Easter* (*Chernaia Paskha*, 1974), a thin veneer of (European) civilisation, symbolised by the city's then-ruined Baroque façades, forms a precarious barrier against a seething current of sinister forces. Shvarts identifies these forces as belonging to an unreformed, chaotic 'Russia' – symbolised by the ancient city of Moscow which Peter I disliked so much.

Josephine von Zitzewitz

Box 3.4 The Village

The village was the most common type of peasant settlement and population centre in the Russian Empire and Soviet Russia from the beginning of the seventeenth century until the end of the 1920s. It should therefore come as no surprise that so many works of Russian literature of that period take place in the village. The contemporary Russian word for 'village' is *derevnia*, the meaning of which has evolved since the seventeenth century to correspond most closely to that of the English word 'hamlet': a peasant farming community and settlement. During the eighteenth and nineteenth centuries, the word *derevnia* acquired another important meaning: that of the aristocratic estate, at the centre of which was a manor house surrounded by a garden and adjacent fields, with peasant huts visible in the distance. It is precisely in this sense that Aleksandr Pushkin uses the word *derevnia* in his novel in verse *Eugene Onegin* (*Evgenii Onegin*, 1825–32), rendered as 'country place' in James E. Falen's translation: 'The country place where Eugene suffered / Was a delightful little spot.'

In the Russian cultural and literary imagination, the village – whether as a peasant settlement or as an aristocratic estate – stands in opposition to the cityscape of the district town, provincial city, or capital. The plot of many classic works of literature is built around the movement of its heroes from the village space to the city space, or vice versa. Such works include Aleksandr Radishchev's *A Journey from St Petersburg to Moscow* (*Puteshestvie iz Peterburga v Moskvu*, 1790), Pushkin's *Eugene Onegin*, Nikolai Gogol's *Dead Souls* (*Mertvye dushi*, 1842), Ivan Goncharov's *The Same Old Story* (*Obyknovennaia istoriia*, 1847), Lev Tolstoi's *Anna Karenina* (*Anna Karenina*, 1878), Anton Chekhov's 'Peasants' (*Muzhiki*, 1897), and many more.

As is the case with any socially and culturally meaningful space, the Russian village gradually made its way into literature. The pastoral was the first and most common mode of village representation to appear in Russian literature. It became dominant in the eighteenth century in eclogues, idylls, and comic operas, where the village featured as a natural space in contrast with the depravity of the city – space which awakened a desire to work hard and improve oneself. The forced labour of peasants held as serfs and the abuse of power by landowners were beyond the scope of such idyllic depictions. Rather, landowners and peasants were depicted as existing in a symbiotic relationship and as an organic whole: a patriarchal world of caring 'father' noblemen and their 'child' peasants. This tradition is evident in the eclogues written by Aleksandr Sumarokov, in Aleksandr Ablesimov's

Box 3.4 Places

The Miller Who Was a Wizard, a Cheat, and a Matchmaker (*Mel'nik-koldun, obmanshchik i svat*, 1779), and in idylls written by poets of the 1810s and 1820s. Idyllic depictions continue to resound in Ivan Turgenev's *Notes of a Hunter* (*Zapiski okhotnika*, 1852), Goncharov's *Oblomov* (*Oblomov*, 1859), Tolstoi's *War and Peace* (*Voina i mir*, 1868–9), and other works.

The end of the eighteenth century brought a backlash to the pastoral mode with the rise of a polemical literary tradition rooted in republicanism. This new mode depicted the village first and foremost as a place where the nobility exploited the peasants. Beginning with Radishchev and with the young Pushkin's political invective 'The Countryside' (*Derevnia*, 1819), the village gradually acquired a second resonance. It became synonymous with a critique of the current regime as an entity grounded in slavery and in the absence of political freedoms. Such texts usually circulated in manuscript form because censorship made it difficult to publish them. But writers managed to find a compromise through forms that allowed them to express at least their empathy with the suffering peasantry. In this tradition, the village was presented as a place of hard peasant – and later factory – labour, constant deprivation, death, conscription of peasant children, hunger, and forced marriage. These themes populate Nikolai Nekrasov's poems and Dmitrii Grigorovich's short stories, and – after the abolition of serfdom in 1861 – the prose of Fedor Reshetnikov, Gleb Uspenskii, Chekhov, Ivan Bunin, and Semen Podiachev.

After the 1917 revolution, the village became the topos of a battle between the new communist and old individualistic forces. Although there were several sceptical voices, such as Andrei Platonov, the 1930s and 1940s were characterised by optimistic representations of the successful collective farm (*kolkhoz*). After Joseph Stalin's death, this Socialist Realist mode gave way to a nostalgic one among writers of Village Prose (*derevenshchiki*). Here, in the work of Aleksandr Solzhenitsyn, Fedor Abramov, Vasilii Belov, and Valentin Rasputin, the village appeared as a place of lost paradise and a preserve of Russian spirit and wisdom.

Alexey Vdovin
Translated by Katerina Pavlidi

Box 3.5 The Apartment

Place makes itself felt in most works of literature, and this is perhaps especially true in the literature of the modern city. Streets, squares, cafés, theatres, and many other urban locations made possible the varieties of human encounter and display that formed the consuming interests of the nineteenth-century novelist. One of the most distinctive and intensively used urban spaces of nineteenth- and twentieth-century Europe was the apartment building, and it is no surprise that Russia – with its vigorous but often jarring entry into modernity – has produced some memorable, even canonical, literary accounts of apartment life.

Russia has also provided one of the most influential attempts to theorise space in the novel. In his long essay 'The Forms of Time and the Chronotope in the Novel' (*Formy vremeni i khronotopa v romane*, 1937–8), Mikhail Bakhtin argues that European literature has distinct space–time parameters. In his conclusions he briefly suggests what these might be for nineteenth-century Russian literature: the temporal circularity of the provincial town, the immediacy of the threshold, the unhurried biographical time of the country estate. In his discussion of other European fiction, Bakhtin also mentions the 'sitting room/salon' chronotope of Stendhal and Honoré de Balzac, with its distinctive blending of the public and private.

The French salon was largely a function of the imposing new apartment buildings of Paris in the Restoration and July Monarchy periods. But Russia's cities were also moving from a low-rise to a high-rise model in the nineteenth century, especially in the era after the emancipation of the serfs, and this left traces almost everywhere in literature. The 'threshold' that Bakhtin associated with Fedor Dostoevskii was in part an existential state of liminality and indeterminacy, but it also required physical spaces – and these were most often the corridors, staircases, and hallways of apartment buildings. Lev Tolstoi, according to Bakhtin, was least of all a writer of the threshold: his beloved setting was the country estate, and his preferred pace was slow. But Tolstoi also provides perhaps the most famous ever literary depiction of disruptive encounters in the urban household – in the opening pages of *Anna Karenina* (*Anna Karenina*, 1878). The Moscow and St Petersburg houses of the Oblonskiis and the Karenins might be far grander than the apartments in Dostoevskii's St Petersburg tenements, but here, too, the partitioned spaces of domestic life form a counterpoint to the psychological drama. Oblonskii's journey from the couch in his study through dining and drawing rooms to Dolly's

Box 3.5 Places

bedroom provides a guide to their marriage in a few short steps; the very same drawing room will later provide the setting for the decisive act of Levin's courtship of Kitty.

In the twentieth century, domestic space took on even greater significance in Russian culture. The scarcity of housing in post-revolutionary Moscow and Leningrad made apartments an object of acute longing and even more acute contestation. As a character in Mikhail Bulgakov's *The Master and Margarita* (*Master i Margarita*, comp. 1928–40) famously observes, the Muscovites of the 1930s were much like their predecessors, except that 'the apartment question has spoiled them'. The apartment also took on significance as a symbol and guarantor of the private sphere: Bolshevik Russia was no place for a salon-style embrace of the public in the private. The same Bulgakov left a loving and hilarious portrait of the bourgeois apartment in the Bolshevik city: in *Heart of a Dog* (*Sobach'e serdtse*, 1925), the old-world Professor Preobrazhenskii lives defiantly in a seven-room apartment, facing down the indignant proletarians from the residents' committee. Much more typical of the Soviet urban experience was the communal flat, where an apartment such as Preobrazhenskii's would be shared by several families. This *kommunalka*, too, has left a rich literary legacy – most memorably in the early Soviet short stories of Mikhail Zoshchenko.

But squalor and overcrowding in Russia's cities did not date only from the Soviet era. These themes had been common in nineteenth-century literature, as migrants poured into the central districts of Moscow and St Petersburg. The relative absence of social segregation – the fact that rich and poor, aristocrats and recently emancipated peasants could inhabit the same streets – gives the apartment chronotope of Russian literature a particular edge. The locus classicus of the apartment theme remains Dostoevskii's *Crime and Punishment* (*Prestuplenie i nakazanie*, 1867), where a number of crucial encounters take place in the haunting and claustrophobic corridors and stairwells of apartment buildings crammed into the Haymarket district of St Petersburg. Raskolnikov's route to murder begins with an anxious descent from his cage-like room at the top of a five-storey building and ends with his fateful passage up the staircase to the pawnbroker's fourth floor. Every step of the way, his psychological state is shadowed by the urban environment.

Stephen Lovell

Boxes 4

Narrative Voices

Box 4.1 Narrative Voices

Box 4.1 The Medieval First-Person Singular

It is a truism to say that medieval literature was largely anonymous. Chronicles accumulated over the centuries without indication of author or compiler. Scores of saints' lives were composed, expanded, redacted, and paraphrased by unnamed writers and editors. It can be surprising, therefore, to find that the use of the first-person singular is not as uncommon as the truism might imply. Who is he (the first-person singular is almost invariably male), and what are his roles and functions?

His most common guise is the reluctant text creator apologising for his unworthiness: the scribe who asks for indulgence towards his errors in copying; the compiler who insists that he is merely putting together the words of others and adding nothing from himself. These are versions of the very widespread device known as the modesty topos, sustained by formulae of self-effacement such as 'I, a sinner ... ', 'I, unworthy ... ', 'coarse and uneducated though I am ... ', and the like.

A more constructive function of the first-person singular, in narrative texts, is as a witness. Here, by contrast with the modesty topos, the text creator does accept responsibility for the content as well as its transmission. Again, however, there is explicit denial of invention. As the scribe and the compiler merely copy or combine the words of others, so the witness merely copies down the deeds of others.

The witness records events that are still relatively fresh. At a greater remove in time, the first-person text creator combats the fading of events into oblivion. He justifies resorting to the written word as a bulwark against the failings of collective memory. In the mid-thirteenth century, the monk Polikarp – one of the compilers of the *Paterik* of the Kyivan Caves monastery – writes to his archimandrite Akindin: 'If I keep silent, they [the deeds of the monks of former times] will be completely forgotten, not even their names will be remembered, as was the case up to this day.' Twenty-six years after the death of Sergii of Radonezh in 1392, his hagiographer is vexed that no life has been written, so he undertakes the task, fearful lest the deeds of the holy man be 'cast into the abyss of oblivion'.

Having established the role of witness, the first-person text creator can choose to what extent he himself is present in his text. Witnesses mostly recede into the background once they have established their credentials *as* witnesses. It is not unknown, however, for the text creators to write themselves more integrally into their discourse. They become, in a sense, witnesses also to themselves, and the first-person singular is transformed into

a constituent of the narrative, a character in the story. For example, the monk Innokentii, who chronicles the last week in the life of St Pafnutii of Borovsk at the end of April 1477, conveys almost as much about himself as about his subject in his fretful solicitousness as he tries to placate the apparently capricious demands of the saintly hero who struggles to dissociate himself from the onerous and odious demands of the world.

Very occasionally self-witness extends into focused self-writing, so that the narrative becomes overtly autobiographical. In travel writing, indeed, this is to some degree unavoidable. Visitors to the sacred sites of Constantinople and the Holy Land structure their narratives according to their own itineraries – though here the emphasis is still on the places, not the witness as such. A notable exception is the Tverian merchant Afanasii Nikitin, who tells of his adventures and (mostly) misadventures on a journey 'beyond three seas' to India in 1468–75. His focus is on himself. He chronicles something close to a spiritual path: his physical tribulations, the pains of separation from Orthodoxy, and over time even his assimilation of some of the devotional practices of his Indian surroundings. The earliest full-scale autobiography (or auto-hagiography) is that of the schismatic archpriest Avvakum Petrov in the late seventeenth century.

Very rarely the mask of first-person authenticity slips to reveal itself more or less explicitly as a fictive device. Daniil Zatochnik ('the Exile') is ostensibly the author of an aphoristic petition to a prince. He showcases his wit and ingenuity in a plea for favour, contrasting his poor but clever self with the rich dullards of the prince's entourage. There have been many attempts to locate Daniil in time, place, and society. An 'original' Daniil may or may not have existed, but in manuscript the texts that ostensibly speak in his voice vary widely over the centuries. Perhaps he was once a person, but in effect he became a literary persona. In the age of devotion this is about as close as one gets to a tradition of fiction.

Simon Franklin

Box 4.2 Narrative Voices

Box 4.2 The Unreliable Narrator

In *S/Z* in 1970, Roland Barthes posed the question, 'What is the value of a narrative?', in order to suggest that narratives can be regarded as transactions in which a text is offered to the reader, who then decides whether to 'buy' the story. The notion of a contractual negotiation fruitfully captures the hesitancy of readers as they are drawn into a text and put into a position where they must eventually evaluate what they have been told.

How is trust established between narrator and reader? Can I believe your story? Is an apparently objective third-person narrator any more reliable than an explicitly subjective first-person voice? Does Aleksandr Pushkin render his narrative voice more – or less – authoritative when he suggests that he somehow belongs in his own invented universe, claiming that he was formerly a friend of his fictional character Evgenii Onegin?

In the early days of prose writing in Russian, Pushkin and Nikolai Gogol simultaneously produced cycles of stories which problematised this issue of narration. The prefatory notes to Pushkin's *The Tales of Belkin* (*Povesti Belkina*, 1831) and Gogol's *Evenings on a Farm near Dikanka* (*Vechera na khutore bliz Dikan'ki*, 1831–2) both provide comically elaborate obfuscations of the stories' origins. The improbably pompous 'Publisher's Note' introducing *The Tales of Belkin* is signed by 'A.P.', who claims that a certain Belkin has simply written down all these stories told to him by storytellers of varying social standing. In Gogol's Dikanka tales, the 'Preface' is provided by the beekeeper Rudyi Panko, who describes the merry winter evenings when the locals gather to tell stories in his house. Like Pushkin, he attributes the stories to a range of different narrators, such as the deacon, Foma Grigorevich. The very blatancy of the device of denying authorship allows us to appreciate the exhibitionist nature of the author's performance. But do these individual tales actually feel as though they are told by differentiated voices, or do they discreetly slide back into being narrated by a recognisably authorial Gogolian or Pushkinian voice?

Paradoxically, in Gogol's story 'The Diary of a Madman' (*Zapiski sumasshedshego*, 1835) an apparently very unreliable narrative voice – one which traces the diarist's collapse into extreme mental disturbance, reflected in the increasing incoherence of his language – provides an entirely accurate, reliable account of his growing delusions. The petty clerk claims that he has become the king of Spain, yet we readers know better. But how is our 'superior' understanding constructed, even from within the text itself?

A similar diary format allows Evgenii Zamiatin in his novel *We* (*My*, comp. 1920) to construct a narrative lacking any external, 'objective' authorial perspective, and here too a form of madness allows the diary to reveal to readers the truth of the situation. The engineer D-503 is describing his world for the inhabitants of other planets. As a loyal citizen he unquestioningly starts by copying down official propaganda. But as sexual infatuation leads him towards political subversiveness, his increasingly metaphorical and colourful language reflects his emotional turmoil and confusion. He desperately clings to his former beliefs, but we readers once again know better: he has irrevocably lost his faith in state ideology as he has lost his confidence in the certainties of mathematics. Gogol's and Zamiatin's unreliable narrators thus both somehow provide readers with the tools for drawing correct conclusions.

Lev Tolstoi is a renowned Realist. In *War and Peace* (*Voina i mir*, 1868–9), we trust him completely when he captures mannerisms which reveal character, or when he describes Pierre Bezukhov's bewilderment on the battlefield, or Natasha Rostova's joy at her first dance. And yet his apparently reliable, omniscient prose can also feel manipulative at times: he blatantly exaggerates the virtues and vices of the poor man and the rich man in *Master and Man* (*Khoziain i rabotnik*, 1895), and we may perhaps mistrust his maliciously misogynistic portrayal of Natasha's foolish mother in the closing pages of *War and Peace*. Tolstoi's 'objective' narrations are sometimes reliable, sometimes unconvincing.

Can an author truly recreate and inhabit the voice of another through narrative devices? Aleksandr Solzhenitsyn's *One Day in the Life of Ivan Denisovich* (*Odin den' Ivana Denisovicha*, 1962) conjures the voice, idiom, and limited understanding of an ill-educated peasant. Does it matter if a narrative voice differs from that of the author, whether in class, education, or gender? Free indirect discourse is also used here, but nowhere can we 'hear' the voice of its highly educated author. The world has certainly read Solzhenitsyn's novel as an accurate, authentic account of living in the Gulag. In truth, the merits of an unreliable narrator may be just as effective as a reliable one in getting us to buy the story.

Julie Curtis

Box 4.3 Narrative Voices

Box 4.3 *Skaz*

The word *skaz* can be used to mean 'a tale', or it can refer to a kind of narrative voice, for example, a *skaz* narrator. In the first meaning, *skaz* is used to evoke associations with oral narration or folkloric discourse. As a term in literary theory, *skaz* refers to a narrative technique, and an association with oral narration remains central to its theoretical definition. Boris Eikhenbaum was the first to use *skaz* as a term in literary theory. In his essay 'Leskov and Contemporary Prose' (*Leskov i sovremennaia proza,* 1927), he writes:

> By *skaz* I mean that form of narrative prose which in its lexicon, syntax, and selection of intonations reveals an orientation toward the oral speech of a narrator, [...] a form which fundamentally departs from written discourse and makes the narrator as such a real personage.

Eikhenbaum's formulation of *skaz* has been much debated. One outcome of this has been the recognition that *skaz* as a technique overlaps with several other concepts in literary studies: embedded narration, free indirect discourse, and heteroglossia (the juxtaposition of diverse linguistic-ideological discourses within a single work).

The study of *skaz* narration has focused on acknowledged masters of the technique in the Russophone literary tradition, including Nikolai Gogol, Nikolai Leskov, Mikhail Zoshchenko, Aleksei Remizov, and Isaak Babel. Analysing works by these authors and others, theorists have routinely divided *skaz* narrators into two types: characterising and ornamental.

Characterising *skaz* is what Eikhenbaum refers to when he writes that *skaz* 'makes the narrator as such a real personage'. This kind of narrator is a persona that is created by sharply differentiating the narrator's voice from that of the implied author of the text. This allows the reader to form a separate psychological portrait of the narrator. Characterising *skaz* is often used for the voice of a frame narrator (the narrator who introduces a set of stories).

The frame narrator of Gogol's *Evenings on a Farm near Dikanka* (*Vechera na khutore bliz Dikan'ki,* 1831–2), Rudyi Panko, illustrates features considered exemplary of characterising *skaz*. Panko addresses the reader directly and as if spontaneously, using colloquial language evocative of an oral storyteller:

> At home, dear readers – no offense meant (you may be annoyed at a beekeeper like me addressing you so plainly, as though I were speaking to some old friend or crony) – at home in the village it has always been the peasants' habit, as soon as work in the fields is over, to climb up on the stove and rest there all winter ... As soon as evening comes on, laughter and singing

are heard in the distance, there is the twang of the balalaika and at times of the
fiddle, talk and noise . . . Those are our *evening parties!* As you see, they are like
your balls, though not altogether so, I must say.

(Constance Garnett's revised translation)

The stress we see here on the cultural and class differences between Panko
(a Ukrainian beekeeper) and the implied reader (of the Russian upper
classes) is also typical of characterising *skaz* narration.

Eikhenbaum wrote that *skaz* signals the 'liberation' of writing 'from the
traditions connected with the culture of the printed word'; *skaz*, in other
words, allows increased stylistic freedom. *Skaz* narrators can use non-literary
syntax, regionalisms, slang, and dialectal spellings. In characterising *skaz*,
these features are motivated by the goal of convincingly portraying social
types. Leskov remarked on his own efforts to have 'my priests talk like priests,
my nihilists like nihilists, my peasants like peasants, upstarts from their
ranks . . . talk a deformed jargon and so on'.

Ornamental *skaz* may employ features typical of characterising *skaz* but
does not produce a portrait of a narrating persona. Rather, its effect is
described as narration through a series of verbal masks. Using Leskov's
categories, in ornamental *skaz* the narrator might speak as one persona
(e.g. the nihilist) at one moment, but as another persona (e.g. the peasant)
at another. This can further accentuate what Eikhenbaum called the 'shift of
gravity' from *what* happens (the 'facts' of the story) to *how* it is told.

However, the distinction between characterising and ornamental *skaz* is
not absolute. The disorienting potential of ornamental *skaz* is also present in
the apparently stable persona of a narrator-character. Even as Rudyi Panko
appears to invite the reader for a pleasurable evening of entertainment, the
question of how the reader is positioned in relation to the narrator (in class,
gender, or national terms) is insistently foregrounded. Readers are not
ultimately prompted to simply immerse themselves in a good tale but to
consider their own judgements as to who is speaking and why it might
matter. *Skaz* narrators point to the mediating role of social discourses in
narrative communication.

Jessica Merrill

Box 4.4 Narrative Voices

Box 4.4 The Omniscient Narrator

Omniscience is a privilege assumed by the author-scribes of sacred texts, who derive their authority from divine inspiration, and by writers of fictional narratives. A novelistic omniscient narrator, typically telling the story in the third person and in the past tense, knows more than the characters and readers of the unfolding fiction. This excess knowledge can have multiple aspects. Temporally omniscient narrators can flash backwards or forwards, reminding the reader of events that have already taken place or revealing events which only they – not readers or characters – can know. Spatially omniscient narrators can range across the fiction's entire story setting, indicating actions taking place simultaneously in several locations. Conceptually omniscient narrators may provide the moral values, articulate the social conventions, and suggest the psychological notions by which a reader can understand the world of the novel. No doubt the most striking manifestation of omniscience, however, is that which gives readers access to characters' minds.

Modern narratologists, drawing on distinctions between showing (mimesis) and telling (diegesis) that go back to Plato and Aristotle, have coined many terms to chart the ways in which fictional narrators present their stories, terms which provide useful grids of possibility for charting a work's narratorial presentation but which can hardly exhaust the specific achievements of outstanding novels in all of their subtlety. Narrators differ considerably in their degree of intervention in their accounts, from being dramatised participants in the story at one extreme, to being impersonal, barely perceptible reporters external to the story at the other. In Russian literature, Fedor Dostoevskii's narrator-chroniclers represent the former; Anton Chekhov frequently employs the latter to assert varying degrees of omniscience. Narrators differ in their degree of artistic self-consciousness, with the author-narrator of Aleksandr Pushkin's *Eugene Onegin* (*Evgenii Onegin*, 1825–32) making the process of creating the novel one of its two major plot lines, while the increasingly impersonal omniscient narrators of later nineteenth-century novels tend to forgo such literary metacommentary.

In narrating the inner workings of their characters' minds, Russian novelists deploy their omniscient narration through a variety of devices that range from summarising thoughts in an orderly fashion or commenting knowingly on their characters' self-deception, to showing the twists and turns of consciousness in delirium, despair, ecstasy, mental breakdown, dreaming, and what Nikolai Chernyshevskii – writing about interior

monologue in Lev Tolstoi's early fiction – called 'the dialectic of the psyche'. Such passages of omniscient narration, unmotivated by any account of how the narrator came to know them, are among the most memorable in Russian fiction: Tatiana's dream in *Eugene Onegin*, Chichikov's creative ruminations about his newly purchased dead serfs in Nikolai Gogol's *Dead Souls* (*Mertvye dushi*, 1842), Raskolnikov's anguish and defiance in Dostoevskii's *Crime and Punishment* (*Prestuplenie i nakazanie*, 1867), the contrast between Levin's movement from epiphany to analysis and Anna's relentlessly accelerating despair in Tolstoi's *Anna Karenina* (*Anna Karenina*, 1878), and the cognitive dissolution of the characters' minds in Mikhail Saltykov-Shchedrin's *The Golovlevs* (*Gospoda Golovlevy*, 1880).

The canonical nineteenth-century Russian novels, beginning with *Eugene Onegin* and *Dead Souls*, are remarkable for their lack of consistency in narration, as they use various combinations of impersonal, dramatised, and self-conscious narration, employing omniscience selectively to a variety of ends. The refusal to reveal the inside of a character's mind, for instance, can suggest psychological depth and complexity or its opposite: utter vacuousness. At the same time, inner views can turn flat, minor characters into rounded ones. Such a multiplicity of techniques at times drew the disapproval of such western masters as Gustave Flaubert, who objected to Tolstoi's 'preaching', or Henry James, whose tidy experiments in precise focalisation ran counter to the polymorphic narrative presentation of Dostoevskii and Tolstoi.

The evolving narration of Dostoevskii's *Idiot* (*Idiot*, 1874) illustrates such complexity in full measure, as the omniscient narrator of Part I confidently presents dysfunctional families and scandalous scenes from multiple points of view and in the voices of explosively hostile characters, recording the thoughts of some but relying mostly on dialogue and description. As the novel unfolds, however, the narrator gradually loses control of the situation and becomes as puzzled by the behaviour and even whereabouts of the central characters as are the remaining characters. The intricate, excruciating narration of the central character's epileptic seizure, presented from within his mind, reverberates with other manifestations of fragmentation and violence. By the final part of the novel, the narrator has self-consciously ceased to explain the unfolding disasters, surrendering that role to minimally comprehending secondary characters and providing a 'simple exposition of the facts', leaving – as has become common in modern fiction – the reader to make sense of what the increasingly unreliable, increasingly non-omniscient narrator cannot.

William Mills Todd III

Box 4.5 Narrative Voices

Box 4.5 The Collective Voice

Collective creativity defined folk culture from its beginnings. At least, so argued the literary theorists Roman Jakobson and Petr Bogatyrev in 1929. Literary history, on the other hand, had traced a trajectory of individualisation which reached its zenith in the nineteenth century with the idealised individual of Romanticism and the supra-individual narrative voice of high Realism. Though much in Modernism revived the Romantic vision of the individual, Jakobson and Bogatyrev pointed to a different tendency, one that blurred the border between 'so-called high art [and] the so-called primitive' and that had been enjoying something of a resurgence in the modern era.

In the Russian context, the latter tendency was associated with the avant-garde and perhaps found no better expression than in the poetry of the Futurists. In collaborative works like *Worldbackwards* (*Mirskontsa*, 1914), Aleksei Kruchenykh worked together with Velimir Khlebnikov and several visual artists to create a primitive folk aesthetic that implicitly voiced a nameless semi-literate collectivity. After the 1917 revolution, fellow Futurist Vladimir Maiakovskii dedicated his epic poem '150 000 000' (1921) to all the citizens of the Soviet Union and even made the collective into the author of the poem itself. The epic's first line reads, '150 000 000 is the name of the craftsman of this poem.' Other members of the Soviet avant-garde, meanwhile, realised collective authorship more literally in such works as *Great Fires* (*Bol'shie pozhary*, 1927), a 'novel of twenty-five writers' dreamed up by Mikhail Koltsov, with chapters by the likes of Isaak Babel, Aleksei Nikolaevich Tolstoi, and Vera Inber, all united by a single plot.

This strategy of collective authorship was taken up directly by the Stalinist state in such works as a lavishly illustrated volume on the Belomor Canal (1934) – the first great construction project of Soviet prison labour – which included contributions from several who had participated in *Great Fires*, alongside Maksim Gorkii, Viktor Shklovskii, and Mikhail Zoshchenko. Through such undertakings, a collective voice emerged that came to define Stalinist culture. A unified people spoke of the aspirations and achievements of the new society. The collective voice of Stalinism found perhaps its most widespread and memorable expression in song, usually performed in chorus. The 'Aviator's March' (*Aviamarsh*, 1923), for instance, a popular song throughout the 1930s, begins with a collective self-definition: 'We were born to make fairy tales reality.'

Opposing the enforced optimism and obsequiousness of this official collective voice, Anna Akhmatova's *Requiem* (*Rekviem*, comp. 1934–62) begins with a counter-collective rendered voiceless by the state. Hundreds wait in the freezing cold for some word of imprisoned loved ones. A woman turns to the poet and asks, 'Can you describe this?' 'I can', she responds. And in the ensuing verses, Akhmatova's lyrical 'I' channels the muffled scream of a 'hundred million people' into a poetic voice rescued from silent suffering.

In a similar way, Aleksandr Solzhenitsyn's monumental *The Gulag Archipelago* (*Arkhipelag GULAG*, comp. 1968, pub. in Paris, 1973) gathers the millions of voiceless incarcerated Soviets into a huge communal narrative that undermines the image of collectivity in official culture. In these projects the writer's voice becomes a conduit for a voiceless counter-collective, presenting an alternative to Stalinist culture that emerges through the singular, courageous voice of the individual writer.

As many late Soviet dissidents turned inward, others – especially those associated with Moscow Conceptualism – experimented with the collective discourses of the Soviet era, repurposing the verbal stamps of the socialist world. Vladimir Sorokin's early novel *The Queue* (*Ochered'*, 1985), for instance, is constructed from nothing but quotations of nameless Soviet individuals waiting in an endless line. The novel's voices, culled from generic Soviet speech, mix together into a collective late Soviet babel that reveals both the surprising poetry of the era and the distance between language and reality. Lev Rubinshtein's celebrated notecard poems likewise comprise snippets of everyday speech, official rhetoric, and lyrical insights, each typed on a separate notecard, to be shuffled and read by the poet in the course of a performance.

Performance became intertwined with the collective voice in the late- and post-Soviet eras in venues such as the 1990s Club of Literary Performance, hosted by Nikolai Baitov and Svetlana Litvak, or the 2010s Society of Anonymous Artists at Moscow's Teatr.doc. Such gatherings concentrated not on readings by well-known poets but on the collective anonymous creativity that would join poets and public as co-authors of an ephemeral text-performance each evening. Simultaneously, the rise of the internet gave poets and writers a new medium through which to co-create collaborative texts with their audiences. Online forums gave the collective voice new life while also connecting it back to its roots in the anonymous creativity that Jakobson and Bogatyrev had discerned in folk culture.

Bradley A. Gorski

HISTORY 3

✦

FORMS

3.1

Forms before Genres

SIMON FRANKLIN

Composite Form and Constituent Form

Literatures tend to operate through frameworks of expectation and variation. Writers and readers know the norms and the forms. At any level, from the work as a whole to every phrase within it, writers may choose to reinforce expectation or to frustrate it or, in various ways, to play with it. In some periods, established formal norms are systematised as genres. With regard to Russian literature of the age of devotion (see Chapter 1.1), the notion of genre is controversial. Some scholars have described this literature in terms of a 'genre system'.[1] Others have argued that genres as such did not exist.[2] How can one account for such radically differing assessments? Since the object of study is the same, there are two main variables: on the one hand, the applicability or otherwise of modern concepts of genre; and on the other hand, medieval categories themselves.

How broad or transferrable is the notion of literary genre? The word has become too widely used to be semantically consistent, and problems of definition are not limited to discussion of the medieval period. Can genre be a rather vague synonym, in a literary context, for type or category, or should it be used as a precise term honed through theory? Do forms exist within genre, or vice versa? Is the novel a genre, of which, say, the detective novel and the science fiction novel are forms? Or is the novel an overarching form, within which the detective novel and the science fiction novel are genres? Is genre principally determined by subject – or by context or by

1 D. S. Likhachev, *The Poetics of Early Russian Literature*, ed. and trans. Christopher M. Arden-Close (Lanham, MD: Lexington Books, 2014), pp. 61–85.
2 See Gail Lenhoff, 'Towards a theory of proto-genres in medieval Russian letters', *Russian Review* 43.1 (1984), 31–54; and the subsequent debate in *Slavic and East European Journal* 31.2 (1987): Norman W. Ingham, 'Genre-theory and Old Russian literature', 234–45; Klaus-Dieter Seemann and Norman W. Ingham, 'Genres and alterity in Old Russian literature', 246–58; Gail Lenhoff, 'Categories of early Russian writing', 259–71.

function – irrespective of form? Or is form itself a determinant or a sign of genre? Any or all of the above can be argued, individually and in combination.

These are problems of genre in general. However, with regard to the age of devotion discussions of genre are further complicated by two key features of medieval form. A broad assumption in much post-medieval discussion of literary form is that the *work* and its *text* are, for the most part, the same thing. This is not to trivialise the problems of establishing the (or a) text from authorial manuscripts or from variants in early editions and so on. But in the age of devotion the question of the relationship of text to work can be fundamentally different not only in complexity but in nature. This is partly because of the culture of mutable textuality, the extent to which, in manuscript transmission over the centuries, texts could mutate, both by accumulated accident and by radical design, such that a notional 'work' can be embodied in a multiplicity of widely differing real text (see Chapter 1.1). Perhaps even more important, however, is a key feature of form. Several types of large-scale medieval text were formed by compilation. Writers often represent composition primarily as compilation. Modern editions of individual early literary works can be misleading, in that they present as independent works texts that do not exist as such in the sources but have been extrapolated from larger entities. Form, in early Russian literature, needs to be understood simultaneously on at least two levels, through distinguishing what we might term *composite* forms and *constituent* forms. Such a distinction is not unique to Russia. After all, the Bible itself is a composite form with its constituent, independent books. Some constituents of a composite form may themselves be composites, such as the New Testament, or – more homogeneous but still anthologies – the Psalter or the book of Proverbs. Yet, while by no means limited to Russia, the interplay of composite and constituent forms is particularly characteristic of Russian literature in the age of devotion.

Some composite forms were relatively stable. The most regular determinant of composite form was the calendar (see Chapter 2.1). So, manuscripts of liturgical chants or prayers or readings, such as the *oktoikh* or *chasoslov* or varieties of Gospel lectionary (*aprakos*), arranged according to calendrical cycles, may vary in their textual details but are quite consistent in their structures. They can be regarded as forms or genres themselves. Or, equally, they can be regarded as assemblages of individual constituent works that were quite possibly composed by different original authors in different times and places and were intended for reading or recitation on separate defined

occasions. Non-calendrical composite forms, too, could be structurally consistent, even if more open and variable in their contents. A thematic anthology of wise quotations is a thematic anthology of wise quotations, however much its selection is edited or changed. The translated Byzantine florilegium known as *The Bee* (*Pchela* in Slavonic, *Melissa* in Greek) provided a common metaphor of author-as-anthologist, as the bee gathering the sweetness of words. Other composite forms were more open, especially those intended for individual reading (see Chapter 2.1).[3] The more open the composite form, the less fixed was its correlation with any particular set of constituent forms, which could migrate promiscuously from collection to collection.[4] The relationship of composite and constituent forms lies behind the notion that there was a 'hierarchy' of genres.[5]

How were forms or categories labelled in the sources themselves? Both at the level of composite texts and at the level of constituents, medieval terminology is problematic. If we are wary of modern retrospective systematisation, we might hope to take refuge in the authentic vocabulary of the age. Unfortunately, the labels turn out to be notably inconsistent. Names of manuscript books can appear at the start of the text, or in the colophon of the individual scribe, or in ownership inscriptions, or in the lists of books in monastic inventories. Although there are some broad patterns of nomenclature, it is not so unusual to find, for example, manuscripts with the same contents but different labels, or manuscripts with different contents but the same labels.[6] As for the constituent forms, around a hundred ostensibly generic names have been identified, which at times seem to have been used interchangeably and in various combinations.[7] Modern scholarship invents new generic categories for the purpose of textual analysis

---

3 On cycles and miscellanies as forms, see also A. S. Demin, *Istoricheskaia semantika sredstv i form drevnerusskoi literatury. Istochnikovedcheskie ocherki* [The historical semantics of devices and forms of early Rus literature. Essays on sources], 2nd edn (Moscow: Iazyki slavianskikh kul'tur, 2019), pp. 343–480.

4 On the 'portability' of what we are here calling constituent forms as an argument 'for the existence of works, and hence of literature', see Norman W. Ingham, 'Early East Slavic literature as sociocultural fact', in Michael S. Flier and Daniel Rowland (eds.), *Medieval Russian Culture*, vol. II (Berkeley: University of California Press, 1994), esp. pp. 12–13.

5 Likhachev, *Poetics*, 65–7. Cf. Demin, *Istoricheskaia semantika sredstv i form*.

6 See the very thorough study by M. S. Krutova, *Kniga glagolemaia. Semantika, struktura i var'irovanie nazvanii russkikh rukopisnykh knig XI–XIX vv.* [A book called . . . The semantics, structure, and variability of names of Russian manuscript books of the eleventh to nineteenth centuries] (Moscow: Pashkov dom, 2010).

7 Likhachev, *Poetics*, esp. pp. 61–5.

('military tales', 'princely lives', etc.); it then produces anthologies that group together the texts thus artificially defined.[8]

This chapter does not attempt to re-impose a consistent taxonomy of form where none exists in the sources, nor does it aim to characterise the full range in the manner of a handbook. There will be no discussion of sermons, for example, or of the forms and devices of liturgical chant. The question of verse form (or the lack of it) is treated elsewhere (see Chapter 1.1). Here the focus is on narrative: on hagiography and on chronicles, represented mainly through their principal composite forms, which range across the spectrum from the relatively stable to the relatively open. The focus on narrative form reinforces the coverage of 'heroes' in the present volume, since the principal human subjects of hagiography and chronicle are, respectively, saints and rulers (sometimes in the same person). Chronologically this chapter deals mainly with texts from fifteenth- and sixteenth-century Muscovy. However, as will become clear, in some cases this is only one stage in a long history of textual creation and mutation that began centuries earlier, in pre-Mongol Rus or even in Byzantium.

Hagiography

Hagiography is not by any reasonable definition either a genre or a form. The word denotes the subject – writing about saints. Apart from biblical and parabiblical stories, saints were by far the most common narrative subjects. What else was there to write about? In the absence of society novels, psychological novels, adventure novels, romantic novels, etc., hagiography was the most widespread, most popular, and most flexible written medium for illustrating human virtue and frailty, conflict and resolution, temptation and illusion, cruelty and empathy, drama and serenity.

Saints measured time, and they helped to make time meaningful. In the everyday, they opened channels beyond the quotidian. '14 February' and '8 July' are abstractions, but they resonate with meaning when one remembers that every 14 February one celebrates and commemorates Cyril 'the Philosopher', who brought Christian writing to the Slavs; or that every 8 July

---

8 E.g. V. P. Adrianova-Peretts (ed.), *Voinskie povesti Drevnei Rusi* [Military tales of early Rus] (Moscow, Leningrad: Akademiia nauk SSSR, 1949); John Fennell and Antony Stokes, *Early Russian Literature* (London: Faber and Faber, 1974), pp. 80–107; V. V. Kuskov (ed.), *Drevnerusskie kniazheskie zhitiia* [Early Rus Lives of princes] (Moscow: KRUG, 2001); cf. N. I. Prokof'ev and L. I. Alekhina (eds.), *Drevnerusskaia pritcha* [Early Rus parables] (Moscow: Sovetskaia Rossiia, 1991).

is a prompt for reflection about the wonder-working holy fool Prokopii, who arrived in Novgorod as a merchant from the 'German' lands (in this instance Lübeck) in the mid-thirteenth century, saw the truth, entered a monastery, and eventually lived in ragged poverty in Ustiug. Saints were everyday companions, models of piety in living or dying, intercessors, healers, protectors. They were also very numerous and very varied and were often – to those who imagine piety to be bland – surprisingly lively. Saints' lives and Lives could be ritualistic and formulaic, but they could also be dramatic, individual, affective, shocking, and dense with episode and adventure. Convention is to some degree necessary to the recognition of sanctity, and sanctity is not arbitrary. A saint is an imitator of Christ, so hagiographical writing will often include conventional verbal and compositional pointers that indicate the relevant type of *imitatio*.[9] Sometimes these dominate to the extent that the representation can look rather like a box-ticking exercise. But there was almost endless scope for variation on the themes, and indeed in the forms, of writing about saints.

Saints were evoked though word, sight, and sound, and even through physical presence of a kind. Scenes from the stories of the life were displayed in cycles framing the depiction of the saint's iconic likeness, saints were venerated in prayer and chant, and they were revered through the preservation of miracle-working fragments of their bones. Narrative was only one way of bridging the gap from this life to the other, from our time to sacred time, every day of the year. Because the company of saints, between them, marked out time, it is not surprising that the two principal composite forms of hagiography (of which the individual saint's story is a constituent form) were calendrical.[10] They were arranged not by the type of saint or by location, or whether the text was originally in Greek or in Slavonic, nor even in any hierarchy of popularity or preference or significance, but simply by sequence of day through each month of the year (which, in the Orthodox calendar, ran from September to August). Both types of composite form were derived from Byzantine equivalents, and both developed and were adapted over the centuries in Rus and Muscovy. One was initially for liturgical use; the other was for reading. One tended to

---

9 See, for example, T. R. Rudi, 'Topika russkikh zhitii (voprosy tipologii)' [Thematic formulae in Russian saints' Lives], in S. A. Semiachko and T. R. Rudi (eds.), *Russkaia agiografiia. Issledovaniia. Publikatsii. Polemika* [Russian hagiography. Studies. Publications. Polemics] (St Petersburg: Dmitrii Bulanin, 2005), pp. 59–101.

10 On the non-calendrical composite form of *paterik* (in the East Slav tradition, tales of the holy men of a particular monastery), see Chapter 2.1.

be functionally brief; the other could be expanded at will and eventually became quite elephantine.

The liturgical composite form was known as the *Prolog* (the stress is on the first syllable). The earliest *Prolog* was simply a translation from a Greek *Synaxarion*[11] – a collection of brief summaries of the most relevant aspects of saints' lives or deaths or miracles for use in church on the relevant days. Hagiographic texts in the *Prolog* are brief, generally from a few lines to a few paragraphs. Many are quite formulaic, though there was also scope for terse anecdote. A typical example:

> 1 April: Commemoration of the venerable Mary of Egypt. Mary was from Egypt. She lived in fornication. Having lived thirty-one years in fornication, she then devoted herself to strict abstinence and virtue, and she became so elevated in her dispassionateness that she would cross impassable rivers and would hover in the air when she prayed. Crossing the Jordan, she spent more than forty-seven years in the wilderness, in feats of piety, with no dwelling or shelter, naked, seeing nobody, and she transcended her human nature. Later, by Divine providence, she appeared to the holy elder Zosima, who came into the depths of the wilderness, and she conversed with him and told him about herself. Some while later she again crossed the Jordan, and received communion, and then returned to the place where she had met Zosima, and she died. After a while Zosima came and discovered that her remains had been buried by a lion, which dug her grave with its front paws, by Divine providence.[12]

Two points of form, in particular, are worth noting here. First, the *Prolog* narrative (or this *Prolog* narrative) is allusive, as if a reminder of a fuller form. And second, despite its paraliturgical packaging, there is nothing ritualistic in the summary. On the contrary, the point here is to highlight as succinctly as possible the distinctive, individual features of a given saint. Over time the East Slav *Prolog* grew with local accretions: not only summaries of local

---

11 *Slaviano-russkii Prolog po drevneishim spiskam. Sinaksar' (zhitiinaia chast' Prologa kratkoi redaktsii za sentiabr'-fevral')* [The Slavono-Rus *Prolog* according to the earliest manuscripts. The *Synaxarion* (the hagiographic part of the short redaction of the *Prolog* from September to February)], 2 vols. (Moscow: Azbukovnik, 2010).

12 D. S. Likhachev et al. (eds.), *Biblioteka literatury Drevnei Rusi* [Library of the literature of early Rus], 20 vols. (St Petersburg: Nauka, 1997–2020), vol. II, p. 402. (This collection is hereafter cited as *BLDR*.) See also the selected extracts in O. A. Derzhavina, *Drevniaia Rus' v russkoi literature XIX veka. Prolog. Izbrannye teksty* [Early Rus in nineteenth-century Russian literature. The *Prolog*. Selected texts] (Moscow: Akademiia nauk SSSR, Inst. mirovoi literatury, 1990).

saints,[13] but extensive additional edifying readings.[14] It became a treasury of accessible and often vivid vignettes, widely circulated beyond its liturgical origins.

The other major composite form of hagiography was the *mineia* (menaion, menologion). The terminology can be confusing since the same label is applied to two distinct types of book. One type of *mineia* is again liturgical, containing the offices (propers) for saints month by month through the year ('menaion' derives from the Greek word for a month). This is sometimes known as a 'service' menaion (*mineia sluzhebnaia*). The other variant is a 'menaion for reading' (*mineia chet'ia*). A 'menaion for reading' was devotional in the broad sense, in that it served the veneration of saints, but not in the narrow sense of having a function during church services. Unconstrained by a performative context, the texts in a 'menaion for reading' tended to be more expansive: less frequently limited to the summary of salient features and more often veering into substantial, multi-character, multi-episodic stories of a saint's life, deeds, death, and miracles.

Like the *Prolog*, a 'menaion for reading', though fixed in its overall composite form, could acquire any number of constituent forms by accretion over time. The grandest embodiment of the form is the *Great Menaion for Reading*, assembled over a quarter of a century by Metropolitan Makarii (1481/2–1563). Its fullest manuscript, completed in 1552, consists of twelve volumes (one per month), each of which contains between 1,500 and 2,000 leaves, so that the whole work comes to some 20,000 leaves or 40,000 pages.[15] This allowed a great deal more flexibility in the form of the constituent texts. Some of them are not so different from their *Prolog* equivalents, a few paragraphs indicating the salient points. But Makarii also included very substantial narratives, such as the *Life of Stefan of Perm*, written by Epifanii Premudryi ('the Wise', d. c. 1420) in the late fourteenth or early fifteenth century, which fills around a hundred closely packed pages of modern print.[16]

---

13 O. V. Loseva, *Zhitiia russkikh sviatykh v sostave drevnerusskikh Prologov XII–pervoi treti XV vekov* [Lives of Rus saints included in early Rus *Prologs* from the twelfth to the first third of the fifteenth century] (Moscow: Rukopisnye pamiatniki Drevnei Rusi, 2009).

14 See the list of nearly 700 such texts assembled by S. A. Davydova, 'Vspomogatel'nyi ukazatel': Intsipity didakticheskikh chtenii Prologa (po spiskam XIII–XV vv.)' [Supplementary index: Incipits of the didactic readings in the *Prolog* (from manuscripts of the eleventh to fourteenth centuries)], in D. M. Bulanin (ed.), *Katalog pamiatnikov drevnerusskoi pis'mennosti XI–XIV vv. (rukopisnye knigi)* [A catalogue of monuments of early Rus written culture of the eleventh to fourteenth centuries (manuscript books)] (St Petersburg: Dmitrii Bulanin, 2014), pp. 876–914.

15 For extracts, see *BLDR*, vol. XII, pp. 12–318. Not surprisingly, the entire work has never been printed in full, let alone translated.

16 *BLDR*, vol. XII, pp. 144–230.

Makarii's purposes extended beyond hagiography. The *Great Menaion for Reading* is encyclopedic in its ambition. As Makarii says in his introduction: 'In these menaia for reading all the holy books have been assembled and written down'; he lists, among others, books of the Bible, patristic sayings and sermons, and six different *paterica* (tales of holy monks and ascetics) as well as 'the lives of all the holy fathers, and the torments of the holy martyred men and women'.[17] Like the *Prolog*, therefore, a 'menaion for reading' was an open form not restricted to its initial hagiographic function. Nevertheless, it is indicative that Makarii chose to shape his devotional encyclopedia around the core of the composite hagiographic form: not as a thematic or indexed anthology but as readings for the days of the year. Saints structured not only time but the consumption of knowledge.

Just as the hagiographically based composite forms of *Prolog* and *mineia* could extend beyond hagiography, so the constituent forms (narratives of individual saints) could migrate beyond the explicitly hagiographic composites. They appear, for example, in many of the collections of texts for communal or private reading and can figure extensively in some chronicles.

The depiction of wholly positive heroes can raise questions of plausibility. In the age of Realism, a standard path to plausibility was psychological, through character flaws and inner complexity. The critic Nikolai Dobroliubov (1836–1861) criticised Ivan Turgenev's (1818–1883) depiction of Insarov, a committed revolutionary in his novel *On the Eve* (*Nakanune*, 1860), on the grounds that he lacked flaws and self-doubt ('the qualities for which anybody with pretensions to decency should bitterly reproach themselves').[18] In the world of Marvel Comics and superheroes the solution is honest fantasy. For the hagiographer, too, plausibility could pose a problem of form. One should not imagine that medieval readers and listeners were universally more gullible than their modern equivalents, such that for them no credibility gap existed. Realism's psychological complexity was not available to the medieval hagiographer. There could be inner struggles against temptation, or a path from error to truth (as in the case of Mary of Egypt); but the choices tended to be binary. In the lives of some types of saint, complexity can lie in the semiotics of outward behaviour, whereby essential virtue is

---

17 *BLDR*, vol. XII, pp. 10, 12.
18 N. A. Dobroliubov, 'Kogda zhe pridet nastoiashchii den'?' [When will the real day come?], in *Sobranie sochinenii v deviati tomakh* [Collected works in nine volumes], ed. B. I. Bursov et al. (Moscow: Khudozhestvennaia literatura, 1961–4), vol. VI, p. 116. More generally: John Givens, *The Image of Christ in Russian Literature: Dostoevsky, Tolstoy, Bulgakov, Pasternak* (Ithaca: Cornell University Press, 2018).

wrapped in the appearance of its opposite. A classic example is the sixteenth-century Muscovite 'holy fool' Vasilii the Blessed, who, among other ostensibly impious eccentricities, smashed an icon of the Mother of God because he (and nobody else) knew that under the sacred image there was a depiction of the devil (see Chapter 4.1). But even this semblance of ambiguity is sanitised by its hagiographical context, by the fact that the protagonist is known to be, or is being proposed as, a saint.

For the hagiographer, solutions to the problem of plausibility lay in form. Once a saint's cult was established, tick-box conventionality could be adequate to affirm it. But, especially in its early stages or when making the case for recognition as a saint (see Chapter 4.1), hagiographers often resorted to formal devices to enhance a sense of authenticity and reliability, such as firsthand authorial recollection (e.g. the author was a disciple or amanuensis of the saint), or reference to eye-witnesses or to a chain of transmission from eye-witnesses to author via intermediaries. Ultimately the plausibility – the proof – lay not in facts or recollections about the living saint; it was posthumous, in the signs that the deceased truly continued to act as an intercessor. Hence the agglomeration of attested miracles as a frequent component of hagiographical forms. The force of such 'documentary' devices could be amplified through recourse to a florid rhetorical wrapping.

Thus, the posthumous life cycle of a saint could generate many forms of Life, whether because the same material was reworked in different ways – in Formalist terminology, variations of *siuzhet* (particular narrative) for the same *fabula* (underlying theme) – or because new hagiographers decided to start again. The range of literary projections of a life could reflect adaptations to the functional specifics of the composite forms; changing local, institutional, or temporal agendas; or simply variations of taste and fashion.[19]

Chronicles

In the literature of the age of devotion, chronicles are both exceptional and typical. They are exceptional because their production and consumption were, for the most part, not tied to regular occasion, function, or location (such as refectory or liturgical reading, or a particular day of the year), nor were the composite forms arranged in cycles. Chronicles could be composed or maintained regularly – or very irregularly – at the behest of abbots,

---

19 See, for example, the detailed study by Gail Lenhoff, *Early Russian Hagiography: The Lives of Prince Fedor the Black* (Wiesbaden: Harassowitz Verlag, 1997).

bishops, or princes. Chronicles were not even devotional in any narrow sense, except to the extent that they can be said to demonstrate the operations of divine providence in human affairs. Yet chronicles also have to be regarded as typical. They were compiled and maintained throughout the medieval period; they are large and composite in form; and they contain a substantial proportion of extant native narrative texts in general, and in particular (second only to hagiographical collections) of the narrative texts that tend to be regarded as in some sense literary. Chronicles are studied partly for their relationships with things outside the texts (i.e. as sources for events) and partly for their properties *as* texts. With regard to literary form, chronicle texts tend to be approached from two seemingly contrasting perspectives: from a distance, surveying the composite chronicle form as a whole; and in close-up, focusing on constituent narratives that are often treated as separable. In order to understand the latter, we need first to look at the former. What are the general features of composite chronicle form, and how did the form develop over time?

Crudely speaking, medieval European history writing follows one of two structural principles: the thematic and the annalistic. Thematic narratives (sometimes simply 'histories') tend to deal with self-contained episodes or periods: a ruler's reign, a war or sequence of wars. Annals are shaped by regular divisions of measured time, recording events year by year. Annals *can* be crafted so that the year-breaks are barely noticeable as narrative breaks, but the form is more naturally conducive to the accumulation of separable and often disparate episodes and bulletins. While thematic histories can ostensibly follow and explain the logic of events, annals – through dividing complex sequences into artificial chunks according to what happened in each year – can seem to be more concerned with record than with explanation. There is not an easy fit between the annalistic and the analytical. The dominant composite form of chronicle before the sixteenth century was annalistic. In the sixteenth century there was a very notable shift towards the thematic, towards the production of large-scale, themed histories.

The annalistic form is implicitly open, both horizontally (in the entries for each year) and vertically (in the overall sequence of years). On the horizontal plane, chroniclers could, of course, have their own particular concerns and priorities, which are reflected in the choice of events that they included or omitted. However, because of the relative lack of an overarching thematic structure, narratives could be added, removed, or adapted to suit the concerns and prejudices of subsequent scribes and editors. Some manuscripts are direct copies of their predecessors, but the study of chronicle texts over

several centuries shows frequent revisions, redactions, and mutations, all meticulously collated in modern scholarship and arranged into diagrams of dependency and variation according to an elaborate vocabulary of classification. Where classical textual criticism has often sought to use comparison and conjecture in order to get as close as possible to an original authorial text, Russian chronicle 'textology' has been more concerned with textual genealogies that reflect mutations across centuries, with the branches and sub-branches of the diagrammatic family tree – the *stemma* – illustrating how the manuscripts and versions, real and hypothetical, are related to one another.[20]

On the vertical plane, although some chronicles culminate in an event of particular significance to their scribes, there is no necessary end to the sequence of years except at the end of time itself. Nor is there a necessary beginning except Creation or some other formative moment of sacred history. When determining where to start, chroniclers tended not to reinvent the sequence before the years of their own narratives. Instead, they either copied or paraphrased previous chronicles, of which their own annals became continuations. The result is that most major chronicles are in fact a mixture of composition and compilation, in which compilation may constitute the bulk of the text.

These are abstract assertions that need illustration. We can consider two of the most intensely studied manuscripts of chronicles: the Laurentian codex (*lavrent'evskii spisok*) and the Hypatian (*Ipat'evskii spisok*). The Laurentian codex gets its name from its scribe, Lavrentii, who wrote it out in 1377. It is a fairly straightforward copy of an earlier lost codex. We assume this because its narrative ends in 1305, long before the scribe's own time. The Hypatian codex is somewhat later. It has no precisely dated colophon, but it was probably written around the 1420s. It, too, is a copy of an earlier text, ending its narrative in 1292. Both of these codices are compilations. Their components are, for the most part, not intermixed like a kind of anthology but are put together in a sequence of lengthy chunks. What makes these two codices so celebrated is the main text that they share. From an account of the division of lands among the sons of Noah after the Flood, through to the narratives of the second decade of the twelfth century, the Hypatian and Laurentian manuscripts more or less coincide; of course, there are variant readings, but it is clear that their source (or the source of their source) was once a distinct chronicle. Headed *Tales of the Years of Time* or *A Tale of Bygone Years*

---

20 D. S. Likhachev, *Tekstologiia. Na materiale russkoi literatury X–XVII* [Textology. On the basis of Russian literature from the tenth to seventeenth centuries], 2nd edn (Leningrad: Nauka, 1983).

(*Povest' vremennykh let*; both the exact form of the original and its proper translation are disputed), this is the text commonly designated in English the *Primary Chronicle*.[21] The *Primary Chronicle* does not exist as a separate text except in modern editions that have extracted it from the later compilations, though it is reasonably reckoned an early Rus work in its own right, later incorporated into Muscovite compilations and manuscripts. This was the textual process through which, in Russian tradition, Muscovy came to be represented as a (or, more contentiously, *the*) linear successor to early ('Kyivan' in some modern designations) Rus (see also Chapter 1.1).

After the text of the *Primary Chronicle*, the Laurentian and Hypatian manuscripts diverge. The Laurentian continues with narratives and notices focused on southern Rus up to the early 1160s, before switching (after a couple of 'blank' years) to a text focused on Suzdal in the northeast. By contrast the Hypatian manuscript sticks to the south, with a detailed Kyivan chronicle for the twelfth century, followed by a chronicle of Galich in southwestern Rus. It is notable that the Galician chronicle appears originally to have been thematic rather than annalistic, but the Hypatian codex contains a version adapted to the dominant annalistic form.

So, the surviving manuscripts are compilations from which one can extract originally separate chunks of chronicle. But that is only the start of chronicle textology. The consecutive chunks are themselves rarely integral compositions. They tend to reflect cumulative or periodic records in their respective locations, updated and revised from time to time. Manuscripts such as the Laurentian or the Hypatian therefore contain not just compilations but compilations of compilations. It is impossible to say exactly how many hands may have contributed to the emergence of the composite chronicles in their surviving forms over the centuries. Each scribe or editor may have had his own agenda, but the mode of production was intrinsically collective.

What was the impact of all this on the way that chronicles were written, on style and manner? There were conventions and regularities, and certainly it is possible to identify elements of a 'normal' chronicle manner of narrating. Some chroniclers could be quite expansive, but the default was terse: plain statements of action; narratives dense with names and places; and regular formulae such as 'there was a fierce battle, and X prevailed', or 'X sat upon the throne of his father and grandfather'. However, conventions did not have to be flat. Normal chronicle narrative records exchanges between protagonists

<hr />

21 For a view of the textual transmission, see Donald Ostrowski (ed.), *The 'Povĕst' vremennykh lĕt': An Interlinear Collation and Paradosis*, 3 vols. (Cambridge, MA: Harvard University Press, 2003), vol. I, pp. xvii–lxxiii.

as direct speech, which can create a sense of immediacy, even liveliness. More important, however, is the fact that the normal, conventional mode of narration is far from the only mode. It was treated as a default, not as an obligation. Compilers and copiers of the annalistic chronicles were rarely engaged in consistent style-editing of the components. Perhaps because the entry for each year was structurally separate, so that the form was naturally episodic, there was little concern to create an impression of unified composition. Alongside the standard stories, there was scope for heterogeneous collage, and the constituent forms of annalistic chronicles might include segments that varied widely in style, focus, structure, and language, such as diplomatic documents and treaties, extensive citations of translated Byzantine texts, eye-witness reports, legal codes, stories of monastic piety, eulogies, testaments, prayers, and letters – even (in the case of the Laurentian manuscript) an autobiographical dossier from a prince with advice on how to rule and a summary of his own deeds. It is not surprising, therefore, that chronicle has been treated both as an overall literary form and as a repository of different forms. The literary study of chronicles has involved both the textology of the chronicle form as a whole and the disaggregation of its constituents, the extraction of texts for analysis and publication as separate, individual, non-chronicle works, even if no medieval manuscript has preserved them as such.

Annalistic chronicles continued to be compiled and maintained throughout the medieval period. However, the balance of forms in large-scale historical narrative shifted significantly over the course of the sixteenth century in the direction of the thematic. The first large-scale thematic composition is known as the *Russian Chronograph* (*Russkii khronograf*), probably dating from 1512, or perhaps slightly later. The earliest and standard version of the *Russian Chronograph* – there were many later versions and adaptations – ran from the Creation to the fall of Constantinople to the Turks in 1453. There had been previous compilations of translated sources for world history. They were drawn mainly from biblical and pseudepigraphal accounts and from Byzantine chronicles, although they had also included substantial thematic narratives – notably *The Jewish War* by the first-century historian Flavius Josephus, and the so-called *Alexander Romance*, a narrative about Alexander the Great that circulated widely in many languages throughout medieval Europe and beyond. The *Russian Chronograph* was different in two principal ways. First, it combined world history with native history in order to craft a single integrated narrative subdivided not by year or by source but by topic. Second, rather than cutting and pasting from its multiple sources, it

moved quite a long way in the direction of stylistic harmonisation. This had paradoxical implications for its literariness. On the one hand, the *Russian Chronograph* has been described as an 'outstanding literary monument' for the way it represents an authorial (though anonymous) vision and imposes an authorial style on a vast and complex narrative.[22] On the other hand, for the same reason, precisely because it muffles somewhat the formal and stylistic autonomy and diversity of its sources, it no longer serves as a repository of distinct and legitimately separable texts that may be of literary interest in themselves. One should not overemphasise the harmonisation, however. Even here there are still segments that have been read as generically distinctive insertions.[23]

Ambitious, bulky, and tendentiously rhetorical, history writing reached a new level from the middle of the century, in works that seem like products of a state project to magnify and justify the Muscovite state under Ivan IV (r. 1533–84).[24] The culmination of the early sixteenth-century *Russian Chronograph* had been the fall of Constantinople, which (in Muscovite ideology) left Moscow as the principal earthly vessel for the true faith. In the mid-sixteenth century the transformative moment was the conquest of Kazan in October 1552: Moscow's first major incursion east of the Urals and its first subjugation and annexation of a significant Muslim population, and hence, arguably, de facto (if not yet in official terminology) a key moment in the formation of an empire. Two huge narratives capture and embody this moment: with regard to Muscovite history, the *Book of Degrees of Royal Genealogy* (*Stepennaia kniga tsarskogo rodosloviia*); and, with regard to Kazan itself, the *Kazan History* (*Kazanskaia istoriia*).

The *Book of Degrees* is the first full-scale non-annalistic history of the Muscovite state and its precursors; or rather, of the polities that Moscow claimed as its precursors (the various principalities of early Rus), for this is history as ideology rather than history as disinterested investigation.[25] It fills

22 O. V. Tvorogov, 'Khronograf russkii' [Russian chronograph], in *Slovar' knizhnikov i knizhnosti Drevnei Rusi. Vtoraia polovina XIV–XVI v. Chast' 2. L–IA* [Dictionary of bookmen and books of early Rus. From the late fourteenth to the sixteenth century. Part 2. L–Ia] (Leningrad: Nauka, 1989), p. 501.

23 See the analysis of a 'chorus of genres' in the *Russian Chronograph* in Demin, *Istoricheskaia semantika sredstv i form*, pp. 287–332.

24 Not that sixteenth-century thematic history was limited to the official: cf. Prince Andrei Kurbskii, *Istoriia o delakh velikogo kniazia moskovskogo* [A history of the deeds of the Grand Prince of Moscow], ed. K. Iu. Erusalimskii (Moscow: Nauka, 2015); English translation of one version in J. L. I. Fennell (ed. and trans.), *Kurbsky's History of Ivan IV* (Cambridge: Cambridge University Press, 1965).

25 See the essays in Gail Lenhoff and Ann Kleimola (eds.), *'The Book of Royal Degrees' and the Genesis of Russian Historical Consciousness* (Bloomington, IN: Slavica, 2011).

700 pages in its modern printed edition.[26] Prefaced by an extensive life of the tenth-century Princess Olga as the forerunner of the Christian rulers of early Rus, it is organised into seventeen 'degrees' according to a dynastic principle: each is devoted to a generation of the family, from Vladimir (Volodymyr) of Kyiv (d. 1015) to Ivan IV. It is further divided into some 350 chapters, all of which are indicated in its detailed list of contents,[27] a sign of compositional design unthinkable in the standard annalistic form. Some of the chapters are split into headed subsections (*titly*). Ideologically controlled, and often rhetorically expansive, the *Book of Degrees* nevertheless retains elements of the chronicle's thematic and literary diversity. At one extreme, for example, the prefatory life of Olga fills nearly fifty pages with solemn grandiloquence. At another extreme, the tenth chapter of the seventeenth degree – devoted to the conquest of Kazan, which is represented almost entirely in religious rather than military terms – starts with a sequence of very brief anecdotal *titly* about omens in Kazan itself, foreshadowing the momentous event: a Tatar holy fool (*iurodivyi*) outrages the inhabitants of Kazan by loudly proclaiming, 'Tatars will not live here; Russian people will'; a cow gives birth to a human child, witnessed by many; and the child is suddenly transformed into an armed man who urges onlookers to submit to the ruler of Moscow or perish. Fishermen from Kazan snare in their nets an old man who likewise warns them to submit to the merciful ruler of Moscow; and black-robed monks mysteriously appear at the royal palace and at the city walls yet melt away as soon as anybody tries to grab hold of them.[28] These vignettes capture in miniature the spirit of the whole; the political story is sacralised. The *Book of Degrees* is a prolonged demonstration of the divine favour manifested in Rus and Moscow through its ruling house.

The *Kazan History* – or, to give it its full title, the *Brief Narrative from the Beginning of the Kazan Kingdom and on the Battles and the Victories of the Grand Princes of Moscow over the Kings of Kazan, and on the Recent Taking of Kazan* (*Skazanie vkrattse ot nachala tsarstva kazanskago i o branekh, i o pobedakh velikikh kniazei moskovskikh so tsari kazanskimi, i o vziatie Kazani, ezhe novo byst'*)[29] – is perhaps the most innovative and enigmatic of the new major sixteenth-century thematic histories. It covers the period from the origins of the

26 N. N. Pokrovskii and Gail D. Lenhoff (eds.), *Stepennaia kniga tsarskogo rodosloviia po drevneishim spiskam: Teksty i kommentarii* [The book of degrees of royal genealogy according to the earliest manuscripts: Texts and commentaries], 3 vols. (Moscow: Iazyki slavianskikh kul'tur, 2007–12).

27 Pokrovskii and Lenhoff (eds.), *Stepennaia kniga*, vol. I, pp. 197–217.

28 Pokrovskii and Lenhoff (eds.), *Stepennaia kniga*, vol. II, pp. 359–61.

29 *BLDR*, vol. X, pp. 262–508.

Kazan khanate in the thirteenth century to its conquest by Ivan IV in 1552. Its anonymous author presents himself as having lived in Kazan for twenty years as a captive, though highly favoured by its rulers. He stresses that all captives had to convert to Islam if they were to avoid being sold into slavery; he converted back to Christianity after the Muscovite conquest. The work was written in the mid-1560s and was immensely popular, surviving in hundreds of manuscripts and dozens of variant versions.

The *Kazan History* is clear in its ideological thrust, variegated in its literary inspirations, and unprecedented in its type of subject matter. It draws on military tales from earlier chronicles, chancery documents, diplomatic correspondence, and Tatar legends of the origins of Kazan. Its devices range from solemn panegyric to what are assumed to be folk motifs and idioms. The narrator stresses that the khan 'loved me greatly, and his magnates cherished me beyond measure',[30] yet he is conventionally extreme in his demonisation of his benevolent captors. They subjected unconverted adult prisoners to the most gruesome forms of torture, which he describes in graphic detail; and as for children, 'when innocent infants, laughing and playing, reached out to them in love, as if to their own fathers, then these accursed bloodsuckers grabbed them by the throat and throttled them, and took them by the feet and smashed them against a rock or a wall, and impaled them on spears and held them aloft'.[31] But when the defenders of Kazan finally saw that they were to be defeated, they froze in silence; and when they woke from their terrified stupor, they were 'confused, as if drunk; and all their wisdom and all their capabilities were devoured by Christ's grace, and their laughter turned to lament, and instead of merriment and music and dancing, they clung to each other and wept and sobbed inconsolably'.[32]

Conclusion

The composite narrative forms of hagiography and historiography illustrate why it can be problematic to develop a consistent terminology of genre for the literature of the age of devotion. Chronicles can, without too much strain, be treated as a genre, with annalistic and thematic histories as variants or subgenres. Hagiography cannot be characterised so neatly. At best, composite forms such as the *Prolog* and the *Menaion for Reading* can be reckoned types of books. And categorisation of the composite forms, whether hagiographic or historiographic, is only of limited help in surveying their many and varied constituent forms.

---

30 *BLDR*, vol. X, p. 254.   31 *BLDR*, vol. X, p. 316.   32 *BLDR*, vol. X, p. 460.

Further Reading

Čiževskij, Dmitrij, *History of Russian Literature: From the Eleventh Century to the End of the Baroque* ('S-Gravenhage: Mouton & Co., 1971).

Demin, A. S., *Istoricheskaia semantika sredstv i form drevnerusskoi literarury* [Historical semantics of devices and forms of early Rus literature], 2nd edn (Moscow: Iazyki slavianskikh kul'tur, 2019).

Ingham, Norman W., 'Genre-theory and Old Russian literature', *Slavic and East European Journal* 31.2 (1987), 234–45.

Krutova, M. S., *Kniga glagolemaia. Semantika, struktura i var'irovanie nazvanii russkikh rukopisnykh knig XI–XIX vv.* [A book called … The semantics, structure, and variability of names of Russian manuscript books of the eleventh to nineteenth centuries] (Moscow: Pashkov dom, 2010).

Lenhoff, Gail, 'Towards a theory of proto-genres in medieval Russian letters', *Russian Review* 43.1 (1984), 31–54.

Likhachev, D. S., *The Poetics of Early Russian Literature*, ed. and trans. Christopher M. Arden-Close (Lanham, MD: Lexington Books, 2014).

Seemann, Klaus-Dieter, and Norman W. Ingham, 'Genres and alterity in Old Russian literature', *Slavic and East European Journal* 31.2 (1987), 246–58.

3.2

Folk Genres

JESSICA MERRILL

This chapter provides an overview of some of the primary genres of folk narrative that were productive in the nineteenth and early twentieth centuries. This is the period when a canon of folklore genres was established as a result of decades of collecting, classifying, and publishing folklore in print collections. These publications, such as *Songs Collected by P. V. Kireevskii* (*Pesni, sobrannye P. V. Kireevskim*, 1860–74) or Aleksandr Afanasev's (1826–1871) *Russian Folk Tales* (*Narodnye russkie skazki*, 1855–63), provided readers, including literary authors, with collections of exemplary texts. These were typically transcriptions of oral, performative speech. When they were published in print, these texts were grouped into genres according to their themes and formal features. (By formal, I am referring primarily to recurring features such as metrical patterns, clichéd phrases, or typical organisational structures.) In order to understand how these folkloric genres, as collections of texts, came to have the shape that they do, this chapter begins with a brief history of folklore study in Russia.

The History of Folklore Collection

The scholarly transcription and collection of creative oral speech as 'folklore' was initiated by the German philosopher Johann Herder. He was the first to make systematic use of the term 'folk song' and the first, in the 1770s, to collect and publish folk songs as such.[1] The rationale for the study of folk songs and other genres of oral culture was that these were remnants of a much older, prehistoric culture. Herder defines folk songs as songs remarkable for their ancientness and longevity, their oral transmission and popularity, and their aesthetic properties. In Herder's words, folk song is 'easy',

---

1 Johann Gottfried Herder, *Song Loves the Masses: Herder on Music and Nationalism*, trans. and ed. Philip Bohlman (Berkeley: University of California Press, 2017), pp. 5, 71.

'pleasurable to the ear', 'gentle', and close to 'nature'.[2] In creating his collections, Herder especially privileged narrative songs (ballads, romances, and epic songs) and songs which illustrate the diversity and commonalities of world culture. His work inspired scholars of vernacular languages in central and eastern Europe to collect and study folk songs and other genres.

Folklore collection continued on an increasingly wide scale with the formation of societies of folklorists in the early 1800s. Quantity was important for folklorists, as they saw that the connection between the contemporary folklore they collected and the distant past could be better established by more examples. The invariant (shared) properties found in many texts were thought to indicate the more ancient features of a tradition. Jacob and Wilhelm Grimm were particularly influential in promoting the scholarly collection and study of folklore. In 1815 Jacob Grimm sent a letter on folklore collection to more than 400 addressees, in which he informed them that 'a society has been formed . . . and it has as its goal to salvage and collect all that there is in the way of song and legend from the common German country-people. Our fatherland still abounds everywhere with this treasure that our forefathers have transmitted to us.'[3] He lists in boldface the following genres, which are to be sought out and accurately recorded: folk songs and rhymes, legends (*Sagen*) in prose, children's tales, local legends, and animal fables. The Grimms' famous collection *Children's and Household Tales* (*Kinder- und Hausmärchen*) was first published in two volumes in 1812 and 1815, respectively. These were followed by two volumes of magical and historical legends, and in 1835 Jacob Grimm published his encyclopedic *Germanic Mythology* (*Deutsche Mythologie*). The Grimms prized narrative folk genres, such as tales and legends, as evidence for a prehistorical, mythological system of thought, which Jacob in particular sought to reconstruct using the comparative historical method he was pioneering in the analysis of the history of word forms. This mythological system was what gave contemporary folklore its deeper meaning. For the Grimms, the tales were fragments of a vast and integral ancient mythical conception of the world, evidencing its gradual disintegration.

In Russia, scholarly collection of folklore began in the 1830s. A surge of interest in folklore at this time was driven in part by literary authors. In 1831 the poets Aleksandr Pushkin (1799–1837) and Vasilii Zhukovskii (1783–1852) competed with each other in writing fairy tales in verse, resulting in works

---

2 Herder, *Song Loves the Masses*, pp. 51–2.
3 Jacob Grimm, 'Circular concerning the collecting of folk poetry', in Alan Dundes (ed.), *International Folkloristics: Classic Contributions by the Founders of Folklore* (Oxford: Rowman & Littlefield, 1999), p. 5.

such as Pushkin's 'The Tale of Tsar Saltan' (*Skazka o tsare Saltane*, 1831) and Zhukovskii's 'The Sleeping Tsarevna' (*Spiashchaia tsarevna*, 1832). Also in these years Nikolai Gogol (1809–1852) published a collection of stories referencing Ukrainian folk legends, *Evenings on a Farm near Dikanka* (*Vechera na khutore bliz Dikan'ki*, 1831–2). Although such folkloristic literary works were often inspired by published European sources, authors were also amateur collectors of folk tales and songs and contributed to emerging archives of Slavic folklore. I return to the relationship between literature and folklore in the conclusion of this chapter.

The most important early Russian folklore collection project was led by Petr Kireevskii (1808–1856), who was the centre of a circle of collectors. Owing to their combined efforts, Kireevskii's collection amounted to several thousand items by the 1840s.[4] Kireevskii himself only published one collection of folklore, his *Russian Folk Songs* (*Russkie narodnye pesni*, 1848) – a collection of spiritual songs. The posthumous publication of the rest of his collection in the 1860s and 1870s resulted in ten volumes of epic and historical songs. These genres are discussed in detail in the next section. Kireevskii, like the Grimms, understood folklore as the legacy of distant forefathers. He identified peasants, particularly those isolated from urban life, as the best sources of folklore. Like Herder, Kireevskii also defined authentic folklore in aesthetic terms. As Kireevskii writes, 'everywhere that village life has been touched by urban fashions the character of songs is disfigured: in place of former beauty and depth of feeling one finds the ugliness of moral corruption, expressed in a meaningless combination of words, in part confusedly taken from an old song, in part newly and discordantly invented.'[5]

This conception of folklore informed the way transcribed texts were treated. In 1837–8, Kireevskii composed a 'Song Announcement' (*pesennaia proklamatsiia*) in which he stressed the importance of recording songs 'word for word'. Like Grimm, he tells folklore enthusiasts that every song, no matter how fragmentary it might seem, should be copied down. He explains that 'sometimes the singer mixes parts of several songs into one, and the real song only emerges from comparing many transcriptions made in different places'.[6] Here Kireevskii makes a distinction between the 'real' song and the songs that

---

4 Mark Azadovskii, *Istoriia russkoi fol'kloristiki* [The history of Russian folkloristics], 2 vols. (Moscow: Gosudarstvennoe uchebno-pedagogicheskoe izdatel'stvo, 1958–63), vol. I, p. 337.

5 Petr Kireevskii, *Russkie narodnye pesni* [Russian folk songs] (Moscow: Izdanie Imperatorskogo obshchestva istorii i drevnostei rossiiskikh, 1848), p. 3.

6 Cited in Azadovskii, *Istoriia russkoi fol'kloristiki*, vol. I, pp. 335–6.

a contemporary singer might perform. In his editing work, Kireevskii created songs from different versions, using the one he considered best as its core. He would add features (epithets, images, plot elements) taken from other songs, remove features, or swap lines of verse from one song to another.[7] The license to edit texts this way came from the view that the real object of folklore study was not in fact the verbal culture of the nineteenth-century Russian peasantry but an ideal proto-text.

The Russian folklorist Aleksandr Afanasev dedicated much of his career to the reconstruction of a Slavic mythological system. Following the Grimms' model, Afanasev published a canonical collection of tales (*Russian Folk Tales*), accompanied by a separate collection of legends (1855). He also assembled a collection of 'tales not for print' – with erotic and anti-clerical content – which were published anonymously in Geneva as *Russian Secret Tales* (*Russkie zavetnye skazki*, 1872). The culmination of Afanasev's work on folklore was a three-volume, encyclopedic monograph on mythology.[8] Afanasev collected folklore himself, but most of the material that he used to create his collections came from Vladimir Dal (1801–1871) and from the archives of the Russian Geographical Society. For the *Russian Folk Tales* his work was primarily that of an editor. Afanasev used the style of some tales as a model and edited others to match. He was particularly guided by the style of tales transcribed by the peasant folklorist Aleksandr Zyrianov (1830–1884) of the Perm region.[9] A comparison of the published tales with the few extant archival sources reveals that, as an editor, Afanasev consistently removed foreign words and language that gave texts a literary or clerical style. He both added and removed regionalisms and added features deemed typical of a folksy style, such as the use of paired synonyms – for example, *zhil-prozhival* (he lived-he resided). Some details deemed morally objectionable were also removed.[10]

Afanasev's changes have been interpreted as aimed at making folk tales suitable for a wider readership, including children. His editing work can be compared to the changes the Grimms made to their collections. Jack Zipes describes the Grimms as not so much mere collectors of 'pure' folk tales but rather 'artists'. Their major accomplishment was to '*create* an ideal type for

---

7 Azadovskii, *Istoriia russkoii fol'kloristiki*, vol. I, p. 339.
8 Aleksandr Afanas'ev, *Poeticheskie vozzreniia slavian na prirodu* [The poetic views of the Slavs on nature], 3 vols. (Moscow: Izdanie K. Soldatenkova, 1865–9).
9 Azadovskii, *Istoriia russkoii fol'kloristiki*, vol. II, p. 75.
10 Tristan Landry, 'Words tell the tale: The motivation behind A. N. Afanas'ev's editing of sources from the archives of the Russian Geographical Society for his "Narodnye Russkie Skazki"', *Revue des études slaves* 85.1 (2014), 35.

the *literary* fairy tale', which sought to be 'as close to the oral tradition as possible, while incorporating stylistic, formal, and substantial thematic changes to appeal to a growing middle-class audience'.[11] The collective project of transcribing, selecting, editing, and arranging oral tales as print collections was an act of unification and homogenisation often undertaken in national terms. Kireevskii and Afanasev explicitly strove to include material from all parts of European Russia. These collections thus fulfilled a goal ascribed to Herder's folk-song anthologies: they were 'a way of transforming the differences of oral tradition into the commonalities of written tradition'.[12] The result was a canon of published collections that were themselves a product of aesthetically informed editing practices, which in turn served as sources of inspiration for literary authors.

In the later nineteenth century, folklore study became increasingly positivist and historicist as well as (sometimes) increasingly concerned with the individual rights of informants. By the 1920s, the definition of folklore had been reformulated: it was no longer thought to be the poetic remnants of a lost mythological system of thought but rather the oral culture of subaltern groups – primarily of the Russian peasantry but also the working class and colonised peoples. Scholars such as Boris and Iurii Sokolov and Mark Azadovskii called attention to the impact of a performer's personality and biography on his or her repertoire. Folklorists began to collect a wider range of material, which was often organised according to district, or even by performer, rather than by genre. Substantive editorial interventions in folkloric texts were no longer considered a legitimate practice, and linguistically trained scholars transcribed oral speech according to dialectological standards. The resulting publications were not popular editions such as the collections aimed at a general readership by Kireevskii or Afanasev. Today, contemporary folkloristics takes an even more all-encompassing approach and has turned increasingly to ethnographic research methods. Russian folklorists in the twenty-first century often study urban folklore, which is sometimes referred to as 'post-folklore'. This research can focus on genres, such as contemporary jokes or urban songs, but more frequently studies a wide range of folk groups and subcultures, for instance the folklore of hitchhikers, tourists, computer programmers, students, prisoners, or hospital staff.[13]

---

11 Jack Zipes, *The Brothers Grimm: From Enchanted Forests to the Modern World* (New York: Palgrave Macmillan, 2002), p. 31; italics in original.
12 Herder, *Song Loves the Masses*, p. 23.
13 For example, A. F. Belousov, I. S. Veselova, and S. Iu. Nekliudov (eds.), *Sovremennyi gorodskoi fol'klor* [Contemporary urban folklore] (Moscow: Rossiiskii gosudarstvennyi gumanitarnyi universitet, 2003).

Genres of Russian Folklore

The central genres of Russian folklore collected in the nineteenth and early twentieth centuries fall into the following four categories:

1. Versified narratives (e.g. epic songs, historical songs, religious verses)
2. Prose narratives (e.g. fairy tales, legends, mythological stories)
3. Lyric songs (e.g. calendar songs, laments)
4. Small genres (e.g. riddles, proverbs, charms)

The primary oppositions used to create this system of genres are: narrative vs. lyric; versified vs. prosaic; sung vs. spoken; fictional vs. non-fictional; religious vs. secular; and long vs. short, in terms of length of performance. In addition, particularly for categories (3) and (4), ritual and social contexts of performance are used to define genre and subgenre categories. In what follows, I will focus only on genres of folk narrative, that is, the first two categories. My descriptions will refer to generic features of a *formal* nature, observations regarding typical *thematic* content, and considerations of *stance* (the prevailing attitude regarding the utterance, such as whether it is understood to be fiction or non-fiction).

In the nineteenth century, genres of versified narrative were given pride of place; they were the object of the most extensive scholarly research and debate. Scholars divided versified narrative into the following categories: the epic, the historical song (*istoricheskaia pesnia*), and spiritual songs (*dukhovnye stikhi*). Among these, the epic was the first genre to be studied in detail by folklore scholars in the nineteenth century. The oral epic is referred to using the term *bylina* (plural *byliny*), a term invented by a Russian folklorist in the 1830s. Performers of the genre referred to them as old tales (*stariny*). An importantly early collection (published in 1804) is the twenty-five *bylina* texts recorded by Kirsha Danilov, a servant of the Demidov family and a performer of the genre. The bulk of collecting for this genre occurred later, in the second half of the nineteenth and the early twentieth centuries. Collection was done primarily in the Russian north – in the Arkhangelsk, Olonetsk, and Onega regions and parts of Siberia – where the active transmission of these songs was studied and recorded.

Scholars have divided the epics into martial and non-martial novella-like narratives or into cycles. These cycles are further split into three categories, typically described as the mythological *byliny*, the Kyivan, and the Novgorod cycles. The first category is understood to be the oldest in its origins. Mythological epics feature mysterious heroes, primarily Volkh Vseslavevich

and Sviatogor. The first is a sorcerer-like figure of supernatural origins who can take the shape of different animals. The second is a giant whose name means 'holy mountain' and who lives in the mountains because the earth cannot hold his weight. Epics about Sviatogor revolve around his fated death. The Kyivan cycle is the largest group of epics. These are centred on the court of Prince Vladimir, whose character may incorporate various historical rulers of early Rus. Some of the prominent themes and personae in this cycle are thought to have originated in the tenth through fourteenth centuries. Prince Vladimir organises great feasts in his palace in Kyiv and assigns tasks to the heroes (*bogatyri*) of the epics. These heroes, extraordinary humans, are the primary actors. Their tasks typically include fighting foreign invaders, brigands, and dragon-like monsters. The most popular character in this genre is Ilia Muromets, who is described as a 'defender of orphans, widows, and the poor ... [he is] free from avarice, from the desire for personal enrichment; the ideal figure of a man who has dedicated himself to the general good'.[14] Some of the most popular stories about him, each recorded in around a hundred versions, are *Ilia Muromets and Nightingale the Robber* (*Il'ia Muromets i Solovei-razboinik*), *Ilia Muromets and Falconer* (*Il'ia Muromets i Sokol'nik*), and *Ilia Muromets and Kalin Tsar* (*Il'ia Muromets i Kalin-tsar'*). Dobrynia Nikitich is second after Ilia in the hierarchy of 'Kyivan' heroes. He is sometimes the uncle of Prince Vladimir and is described as the diplomat of his society. He is well spoken, a musician and chess-player, and is differentiated by his polite behaviour, education, and age. Another central character is Alyosha Popovich (his last name indicates that he is the son of a priest), who is sometimes depicted as a jealous, greedy, or boastful character. He defeats enemies through trickery rather than strength. The themes of the Novgorod cycle are tied to the culture of this commercial city associated with the Hanseatic League. The epic songs in this cycle feature two primary heroes: Sadko, a merchant and harp (*gusli*) player who travels to an undersea kingdom, and Vasilii Buslaev, a native of the city who fights against the people of Novgorod.

The genre of the *bylina* is also defined by its poetic form and performance style. When these songs were transcribed in the late nineteenth and early twentieth centuries, they were performed by single singers without instrumental accompaniment. Songs were sung to a melody, with each singer typically having one to three melodies which they would use for different

---

14 Yuri Sokolov, *Russian Folklore*, trans. Catherine Smith (New York: Macmillan, 1950), p. 323.

songs. These melodies could be tranquil, stately, or swift and merry.[15] The *byliny* typically consist of a single episode and contain 300 to 500 lines.[16] The length of each line is elastic, ranging from approximately nine to seventeen syllables. Scholars have identified several different kinds of metres used in the *byliny*. One prominent form is three-stress tonic verse, with a set number of main stresses per line but with a varying number of unstressed syllables between them. There is no regular system of rhyming, although assonance and rhyme are common. The structure and verbal style of the *bylina* has been referred to as epic 'ceremonialism'. The epic can open with an introductory verse unrelated to the themes of the song. This is followed by a beginning which sets the scene (Vladimir's court, for example), a central narrative action, and a proverb-like ending. *Byliny* rely heavily on the use of commonplaces or *loci communes* – formulaic descriptions of recurring situations. In addition to Vladimir's banquets, these include the hero's entrance into the hall, his galloping horse, the killing of the enemy, and descriptions of nature. Repetition is prominent at the level of words and phrases, in the repetition (possibly verbatim) of entire episodes, and in forms of parallelism. A typical stylistic feature is negative parallelism, for example:

> A bright falcon didn't swoop down on the geese, on the swans,
> And on the small migratory gray ducks –
> A Holy Russian *bogatyr*
> Swooped down on the Tatar army.[17]

Other notable features of the language of the *bylina* are fixed or stock epithets. For example, the horse is always 'good'; the steppe, the road, and the yard are always 'broad'; the day and the tent are always 'white'. In these cases the adjective loses its specific meaning, conveying instead the idea of a road or a tent in general. Another stylistic feature is hyperbole, especially regarding the speed of events, number of enemies, or weight of a hero's weapons.[18]

The genre of *bylina* is typically juxtaposed with the historical song as a neighbouring generic category. The definitive features of this category are less distinct as this is a grouping that describes a diverse range of songs that have some, but not all, of the characteristics definitive of the classic *bylina*. In the period when folklorists were recording the oral epics, they found that the same performers combined both genres in their repertoires

---

15 Sokolov, *Russian Folklore*, p. 311.
16 James Bailey and Tatyana Ivanova, 'The Russian oral epic tradition: An introduction', in *An Anthology of Russian Folk Epics* (Armonk, NY: M. E. Sharpe, 1998), p. xxviii.
17 Bailey and Ivanova, 'Russian oral epic', p. xxv.   18 Sokolov, *Russian Folklore*, pp. 306–7.

and referred to both as *stariny*.[19] Folklorists initially saw historical songs as a more recent stage in the development of the *byliny*. In the ten-volume collection of songs collected by Kireevskii, mentioned above, volumes one through five are dedicated to the *byliny* and six through ten to historical songs, which are organised chronologically according to the events to which they refer. However, subsequent researchers have argued that the two genres existed simultaneously and can be distinguished by differing historical stances and formal features.[20] In the narration of an epic, the singer is more concerned with the depiction of a mood and a poetic image. The events are of a very distant past. For historical songs historical plausibility is more import-ant and there is less exaggeration.[21] Historical songs can be performed in the same metrical form as the *byliny*, but they generally lack the features described above as epic ceremonialism. They are, as a result, shorter (many are under fifty lines) and more succinct.

Iurii Sokolov compares a rare 1618 recording of a historical song about the recent poisoning (in 1610) of the Russian prince Mikhail Skopin-Shuiskii with nineteenth-century recordings of songs about Skopin-Shuiskii's death. In Sokolov's view, the comparison reveals how narratives 'gradually lose the features of the concrete historical facts and are transformed into typical *byliny* (within inclusion in the Kyiv cycle and with reference to the time of Prince Vladimir, with typical motifs of boasting at the feast . . .)'. Not only is the subject matter changed but 'the whole of its poetics: the historical song, as a genre, in these instances, was transformed into a *bylina*' – it is 'overgrown' with the devices of epic ceremonialism.[22]

The broad category of historical songs is typically divided according to the historical events and figures to which they refer. Some of the most prominent groups are songs about the political and private life of sixteenth-century ruler of Muscovy Ivan IV ('Ivan the Terrible'); 'Cossack songs' about the sixteenth-century Cossack leader Ermak Timofeevich; and songs about the Cossack heroes Stenka Razin and Emilian Pugachev, who led popular uprisings against the Russian nobility in the seventeenth and eighteenth centuries. Another group, 'soldier's songs', refers to military campaigns of the eight-eenth and nineteenth centuries. Other narrative songs which do not fit into

19 Sokolov, *Russian Folklore*, p. 342.
20 Boris Putilov, *Russkii istoriko-pesennyi fol'klor XIII–XVI vekov* [Russian historical-song-like folklore of the thirteenth to sixteenth centuries] (Moscow: Izdatel'stvo Akademii nauk SSSR, 1960).
21 Mikhail Speranskii, *Russkaia ustnaia slovesnost'* [Russian oral folklore], Slavistic Printings and Reprintings (The Hague: Mouton, 1969 [1917]), p. 330.
22 Sokolov, *Russian Folklore*, p. 353.

the above groupings have been referred to as 'ballads'; these are songs about love, family conspiracies, and intrigue.[23]

The third major category of versified narrative folklore is the spiritual songs (*dukhovnye stikhi*). This category is also often juxtaposed with the *byliny* and like the category of historical songs it also contains a diversity of poetic forms. Scholars have distinguished between epic and lyric spiritual songs. In the nineteenth century, the former were recorded primarily in northern and central Russia, and the latter were recorded in Ukraine and Belarus. Kireevskii, who devoted his attention to this genre, notes that in Russia performers of these songs refer to them simply as verses (*stikhi*). The lyric religious songs performed to the south and west of Russia are referred to as *psalmy* or *kanty*; unlike the epic-type songs, these are composed in a syllabic metre and are rhymed.

All of the spiritual songs, it is generalised, were originally derived from literary sources. The epic, narrative-type spiritual songs are based on hagiography and apocryphal writings and often focus on warrior- or martyr-type saints such as Egor the Brave (St George), who is tortured by the tsar Deklianishche (the emperor Diocletian) before escaping from a deep cellar and travelling through Rus proclaiming the holy faith. In other songs Egor rescues a maiden from a snake. Other heroes include Fedor Tiron (St Theodore Tiro), Anika the Warrior (Digenes Akritas), and Dmitrii Solunskii (St Demetrius of Thessalonica). The latter is depicted defeating the Tatar Mamai, rather than Tsar Kaloyan of Bulgaria, his opponent in the original Life. While these songs can share many of the poetic features of the *byliny*, scholars have stressed that they are distinguished by their stance; they express 'a moralizing or didactic goal, a desire to satisfy the religious sentiment of the composer or the listener'.[24] Other famous spiritual songs include the 'Book of Profound Wisdom' (*Golubinaia kniga*), a popular cosmogony in the form of questions and answers on the creation of the world; 'Aleksei, the Man of God' (*Aleksii, chelovek Bozhii*); the 'Lament of Adam' (*Adamov plach*); and songs about the Last Judgement. The history of this genre is traced to medieval religious pilgrimage and to later societies of wandering pilgrims who were blind or disabled (*kaliki perekhozhie*). Spiritual songs are also particularly well represented in the folklore of Old Believers and of other Eastern Orthodox sectarian communities.

23 Vladimir Propp, 'Generic structures in Russian folklore', trans. Maria Zagorska Brooks, ed. Dan Ben-Amos and Philip Tilney, *Genre* 4.3 (1971), 222–6.
24 Speranskii, *Russkaia ustnaia slovesnost'*, p. 359.

The three categories of versified narrative, described above, are contrasted with three primary genre categories of *prose* narrative: fictional tales (*skazka*, plural *skazki*); religious legends; and mythological stories. The organisation of fictional tales in Afanasev's *Russian Folk Tales* largely corresponds with the genre subcategories acknowledged by folklorists.[25] Tales are divided into fairy tales (*volshebnye skazki*), animal tales, cumulative tales, realistic or novella-like tales, and anecdotes. The fairy tale anchors the system of prose narrative genres in a manner analogous to the *bylina* for versified narrative. It is the most precisely described genre, against which other categories are differentiated. The pre-eminent scholar of the genre, Vladimir Propp, writes that these tales are 'distinguishable by their very nature', while other prose genres are 'isolated by structural characteristics not coinciding with the structure of the fairy tale'.[26] Surveying the corpus of Russian oral tales in the early twentieth century, Sokolov estimated that 20 per cent were fairy tales.[27] He further noted that the great majority of the subjects of Russian fairy tales are shared in common with the tale traditions of western Europe.

The hero of the fairy tale is often a king's son (Ivan, Vasilii), who is so indescribably handsome 'you cannot take your eyes from him'; or, in contrast, the hero is Ivanushka the Fool who 'sits on the stove, winding his snot into a ball'.[28] Heroines are beauties saved by the heroes (Elena the Fair, Vasilisa the Wise), although they are sometimes described as warrior-like themselves – as *bogatyr*-maidens, valiant princesses, or powerful enchantresses. Suffering heroines, often step-daughters, are Zolushka (Cinderella), the Ice Maiden, or little sister Alenushka. They are typically described as kind and virtuous. All of these primary characters receive aid from magical helpers, whose abilities are often indicated by their names. The Great Eater (*Obedalo*) can eat great quantities; the Great Drinker (*Opivalo*) drinks forty barrels of wine; and Big Whiskers (*Usynia*) blocks up a river with his moustaches, catching all the fish in his mouth. Animals – horses, fish, pigs, mice, and birds, among others – are also typical helpers. Magical objects are often inexhaustible or have agency: tablecloths spread themselves with food, horns produce drink, carpets fly, hatchets chop. The enemies of the heroes include, most prominently, the witch Baba Iaga, who lives in a hut on chicken legs at the edge of the forest. She is often depicted as barely fitting into her hut, with her nose (sometimes made of iron or bone) pressed to the ceiling. The other primary villain is Kashchei the Immortal, whose death resides in

---

25 Azadovskii, *Istoriia russkoii fol'kloristiki*, vol. II, p. 75.
26 Propp, 'Generic structures in Russian folklore', 214.   27 Sokolov, *Russian Folklore*, p. 419.
28 Sokolov, *Russian Folklore*, p. 423.

an egg and who can take on the appearance of a dragon with three, six, nine, twelve, or more heads.

Regarding the structure of the fairy tale, Propp has famously argued that tales in this genre all follow the same sequence of plot events (which he calls functions), beginning with an act of villainy or state of lack and ending with the punishment of the villain and/or a marriage.[29] In its formal style, the fairy tale can open and end with typical formulae. It may begin with an opening (*priskazka*) which is not thematically connected to the content of the narrative (like the opening verse of the *bylina*). This part 'is usually spoken in a dashing manner, and ... is customarily humorous in content'. Other opening formulae include versions of 'In a certain kingdom, in a certain realm, there once lived (*zhil byl*) a prince, a tsar, a merchant, etc.' The tale is often concluded with a distinct ending, which is 'usually rhythmic, is spoken with a rapid "tongue-twisting", and sometimes has rhyme'.[30] The language of the tale itself is also marked by *loci communes* for the description of characters – a hero's beauty or a wedding, for instance.

A second subcategory of fictional tales are stories in which the main characters are animals. The chief heroes are the fox, described as crafty and beautiful, with oily lips and 'a beautiful talker'. The wolf, in contrast, is the 'stupid old wolf', the 'grey fool' upon whom the fox plays her tricks. The bear, 'Mikhailo Ivanich', is clumsy and sluggish; he is 'the forest crusher'.[31] Jack Haney remarks that 'the narrative structure of the animal tale tends to revolve around some form of deception'; the animals 'mostly ... argue and outwit and defraud each other'.[32] Many animal tales are constructed on the motif of a meeting, where a variety of animals are brought together and engage in a dialogue. Each animal's speech is often marked by the use of onomatopoeic phrases. The dog's speech, for instance, always begins with 'Tiaf, tiaf, tiaf'.[33] These dialogues can be spoken in prose or sung as poetry. By the twentieth century, animal tales were usually quite short and were primarily for children. Some tales with animals as main characters follow a particular structure described as that of the 'cumulative' tale and which folklorists consider a separate category. These are relatively few in number and have a particular rhyme and rhythm. These stories, such as 'The Little

---

29 Vladimir Propp, *Morphology of the Folktale*, trans. Laurence Scott (Austin: University of Texas Press, 1968).
30 Sokolov, *Russian Folklore*, pp. 430, 431.   31 Sokolov, *Russian Folklore*, p. 435.
32 Jack Haney, *An Introduction to the Russian Folktale*, The Complete Russian Folktale 1 (Armonk, NY: M. E. Sharpe, 1999), pp. 90–1.
33 Sokolov, *Russian Folklore*, p. 438.

Turnip' (*Repka*), 'The Small Round Loaf' (*Kolobok*), or the 'Tower-Chamber of the Fly' (*Terem mukhi*), are based on the repetition of actions and dialogue, resulting in a piling up of characters who all end up living together or forming a chain.

The largest category of *skazki*, which Sokolov estimated at 60 per cent of Russian oral tales, are defined negatively: these are tales *not* about magic or featuring animals as main characters. These are described as tales about 'real people' or dealing with 'everyday life', thus 'realistic tales'. Their events are located in the world of the narrators (rather than 'once upon a time'). Their stock characters are smart guessers, wise counsellors, clever thieves, robbers, bad wives, hosts and farmhands, priests, fools, and others. Sokolov summarises that the basic themes of these stories are built around contrasts: between wealth and poverty, personal independence and fate, good and ill fortune, cleverness and stupidity, and fidelity in marriage versus deceit. One of the most popular tales in this category is the story of the husband who, following his wife's advice, sells her wares for three pieces of counsel (e.g. 'finish what you have begun'). With the help of this counsel, he becomes rich. Another popular plot relates the improbable chain of events whereby a poor man who is foretold to become a rich man's heir realises this prophesy. Haney views these tales as, overall, harsher than the fairy tale: 'there is more brutality than beauty, more vice than virtue, and a good amount of vulgarity. The humor is indelicate, even coarse and cruel.' He further comments on 'the frequency with which the villain is a female and often a relative of the hero. ... The unfaithful wife, the stubborn wife, the profligate wife, the lazy wife – all the types are here in abundance.'[34] Folklorists often consider the genre of anecdote (*anekdot*) adjacent to tales of everyday life, as thematically they have much in common. The anecdote is, however, structured more like a narrative joke: it is 'characterized by its brevity and condensation, it has greater humorous or satirical acuteness, and the whole center of attention is carried over to the climax of the action, which is to be found at the very end of the narration, where also the denouement of the whole situation occurs'.[35]

Folklorists have opposed these (five) types of the fictional *skazka* to tales about non-fictitious, historical, religious, or eye-witnessed events. This broad category is more difficult to systematise and is often referred to as non-*skazka* prose (*neskazochnaia proza*). I will mention two of the more clearly defined genres within this field: the legend and the mythological story. The only genre of non-fictional folkloric prose narrative to be systematically collected

34 Haney, *Introduction to the Russian Folktale*, p. 109.   35 Sokolov, *Russian Folklore*, p. 449.

in the nineteenth century was the legend. Afanasev's collection *Russian Folk Legends* (*Narodnye russkie legendy*, 1855) was devoted largely to tales on religious subjects. The thematic core of the Russian religious legend is similar to that of the spiritual songs. The themes of both the prose and the versified narratives can be traced to literary and oral legends (*skazanie*), apocrypha, or lives of the saints. The characters in the legends are often Jesus Christ, his disciples, and the devil. A favourite theme is the appearance of Christ as a wandering beggar. In one tale, Christ, disguised as a beggar, asks a miller for alms, but the miller refuses him. A poor peasant then offers the beggar some of his small store of rye. As he pours out the rye, it turns out that there is a never-ending supply.[36] Legends also frequently describe the punishments meted out by Christ, God, or one of the saints (in the guise of beggar) to those inhospitable to guests.[37] Also common are stories about children sold to or carried off by the devil. According to Sokolov, at the beginning of the twentieth century the most popular Russian legend was 'The Little Brother of Christ' (*Khristov bratets*), a story about a man who is permitted to see what awaits him and others in the afterlife and then returns to earth to relate what he has seen.[38]

The last genre I will mention is the mythological story (*bylichka*). This is a firsthand account of an extraordinary, often supernatural, experience. Folklorists have traditionally organised these according to the mythological personae that they feature.[39] The most common are nature spirits: the guardians of the forest (*leshii*), of ponds and rivers (*vodianoi*), and of the field (*polevoi*), as well as a kind of naiad (*rusalka*). Another prominent figure is the guardian of the home (*domovoi*). Personal narratives referring to these entities vary; for instance, the forest spirit may be evoked to explain why someone got lost in the woods, or the house spirit to explain finding one's hair tangled on waking up in the morning. Narratives referencing these figures have generally been transcribed as evidence of folk belief rather than for their formal or performative features.

Folklore and Literature

When describing the relationship between literature and folklore, literary scholars have historically stressed that Russian authors drew inspiration from the oral culture of the peasantry. Pushkin, in particular, was hailed as having

---

36 Haney, *Introduction to the Russian Folktale*, p. 107.   37 Sokolov, *Russian Folklore*, p. 454.
38 Sokolov, *Russian Folklore*, p. 455.
39 E. V. Pomerantseva, *Mifologicheskie personazhi v russkom fol'klore* [Mythological figures in Russian folklore] (Moscow: Nauka, 1975).

'penetrated the spirit of Russian folk poetry' and credited with having 'initi-ated an era of rapprochement between literature and folklore' by virtue of his ability to 'assimilate the riches of popular verbal art'.[40] However, folklorists who have studied the relationship between oral and print culture stress that this relationship was bidirectional; not only was Pushkin inspired by folklore but folklore was often inspired by Pushkin. In his study of the sources of Pushkin's poem 'The Hussar' (*Gusar*, 1833) – in which a hussar comically recounts how he ended up at a witches' Sabbath – Petr Bogatyrev concludes that Pushkin's immediate source of inspiration was a short story by Orest Somov (1793–1833) and that recorded oral folklore (*skazki* and folk drama) with similar themes reflects the assimilation of Pushkin's poem into vernacu-lar traditions.[41] This is not an isolated case. Sokolov notes that the fifth most frequently recorded oral tale by the 1900s was the 'Tale of Tsar Saltan'.[42] This is the title of Pushkin's tale in verse, which is loosely based on a fairy-tale plot widespread in both Russian and European folklore.[43] Pushkin's poem is particularly close to a tale included in Antoine Galand's French translation of *A Thousand and One Nights*. Azadovskii argues that the reason that there are so many richly detailed variants of this story in Russian oral tradition is because of the 'reverse influence' of Pushkin's work.[44]

Careful study of the reciprocal exchange of plots between print and oral culture has allowed folklorists to formulate an understanding of the relation-ship between folklore and literature as one between two modes of creativity.[45] These modes exist at two ends of a spectrum. At one end, folkloric creativity is popular, shared knowledge manifest in many different versions. It is epitomised by oral culture. At the other end, literary creativity is the acknowledged original work of a (professional) author, epitomised by

---

40 A. A. Gorelov, F. Ia. Priima, and A. D. Soimonov (eds.), *Russkaia literatura i fol'klor: Pervaia polovina XIX v.* [Russian literature and folklore: The first half of the nineteenth century] (Leningrad: Nauka, 1976), p. 143.

41 Petr Bogatyrev, 'Stikhotvorenie Pushkina "Gusar": Ego istochniki i ego vliianie na narodnuiu slovesnost'' [Pushkin's poem 'The Hussar': Its sources and its influence on folklore], in *Ocherki po poetike Pushkina* [Studies in Pushkin's poetics], Slavistic Printings and Reprintings (The Hague: Mouton, 1969 [1923]), pp. 147–95.

42 Sokolov, *Russian Folklore*, p. 421.

43 This is a tale type classified as ATU 555 'The Fisherman and His Wife' in the Aarne–Thompson–Uther Index.

44 Mark Azadovsky, 'The sources of Pushkin's fairy tales' [1936], trans. James McGavran, *Pushkin Review* 20 (2018), 28–9. For a thorough reconsideration of this subject, see Michael Wachtel, 'Pushkin's turn to folklore', *Pushkin Review/Pushkinskii vestnik* 21 (2019), 107–54.

45 Petr Bogatyrev and Roman Jakobson, 'Folklore as a special form of creativity', trans. Manfred Jacobson, in Peter Steiner (ed.), *The Prague School: Selected Writings, 1929–1946* (Austin: University of Texas Press, 1982), pp. 32–46.

print culture. The example of Pushkin's 'Tsar Saltan' suggests that the relationship between literature and folklore need not be conceived as the assimilation of some popular Russian 'spirit' into literary form but may rather be understood in terms of an endless multidirectional translation between cultures, languages, and media.

Further Reading

Afanas'ev, Alexander, *Russian Fairy Tales*, trans. Norbert Guterman (New York: Random House, 1973).

Bailey, James, and Tatyana Ivanova (eds.), *An Anthology of Russian Folk Epics* (Armonk, NY: M. E. Sharpe, 1998).

Haney, Jack, *An Anthology of Russian Folktales* (London: Routledge, 2015).

Ivanits, Linda, *Russian Folk Belief* (New York: M. E. Sharpe, 1989).

Kononenko, Natalie, *Slavic Folklore: A Handbook* (Westport, CT: Greenwood Press, 2007).

Panchenko, Alexander, 'Russia', in Regina F. Bendix and Galit Hasan-Rokem (eds.), *A Companion to Folklore* (Chichester: Blackwell, 2012).

Propp, Vladimir, *Morphology of the Folktale*, trans. Laurence Scott (Austin: University of Texas Press, 1968).

Reeder, Roberta, *Russian Folk Lyrics* (Bloomington: Indiana University Press, 1993).

Sokolov, Yuri, *Russian Folklore*, trans. Catherine Smith (New York: Macmillan, 1950).

Warner, Elizabeth, *Russian Myths* (Austin: University of Texas Press, 2002).

Verse I

MICHAEL WACHTEL

Written and Oral Poetry

It is helpful to conceive of the history of Russian poetry as two independent traditions that have rarely intersected. The first, a folkloric (oral) tradition, flourished almost entirely unobserved or ignored by outsiders until the eighteenth century, when literate enthusiasts set down on paper a small number of poems. In the nineteenth century, ethnographers took up this work and transcriptions became more frequent and accurate. This vibrant oral tradition gradually came to an end in the twentieth century, a victim of modernisation, cultural homogenisation, and the spread of literacy. Russian written poetry represents a much shorter tradition. It began only in the seventeenth century, more or less coinciding with the westernisation of Russia and the establishment of the modern Russian language. Narrow at its origin but becoming increasingly broad with the passing of each decade, this tradition continues unabated to the present day. There are several significant observations to be made about this dual poetic tradition. Firstly, the inception of written poetry occurred independently of the prior oral tradition. Secondly, even when the literary tradition was firmly established, poets rarely looked back to folklore. Finally, and perhaps most surprisingly, even when Russian poets did turn to folklore for inspiration, they rarely incorporated their indigenous tradition.

In formal terms, Russian folklore uses three different types of versification: syllabic, tonic, and syllabo-tonic. Although no examples survive, the principles of the earliest Russian folkloric poetry have been established through comparison with similar poetry from other Slavic languages. This verse was syllabic, which is to say that each line contained an identical number of syllables. The lines did not rhyme, but the line ending (cadence) was marked by a fixed stress pattern. This easily recognisable cadence usually had a stress three syllables from the end of the line (called the 'antepenultima'), which

was followed by two unstressed syllables. As the tradition evolved, some poems developed a different cadence: the final stress of each line fell on the penultimate syllable rather than the antepenultima. Within a single poem, however, the cadence was invariant. Such regularity presumably served as a mnemonic device for the performer, who was of course reciting from memory; it also satisfied the listener's need for structural predictability.

At some point, this syllabic verse ceased to exist, probably as a result of profound phonetic changes in the Russian language. (In some Slavic traditions, where these phonetic changes did not occur, the syllabic line persisted not only in folklore but also in literary versification.) In place of Russian syllabic folk verse (see Chapter 3.2), two different systems of versification arose: syllabo-tonic and tonic verse. Which of these two systems preceded the other is disputed and, for present purposes, not essential. What deserves emphasis is that the systems co-existed. Moreover, the type of versification used was usually determined by the genre. Syllabo-tonic verse, defined by the regular alternation of stressed and unstressed syllables throughout the line and, indeed, throughout the entire poem, was common in shorter, lyric genres. Though syllabo-tonic verse had a wide range of possibilities, including binary (iambic and trochaic) and ternary (dactylic, amphibrachic, and anapaestic) metres, Russian folklore generally limited itself to a single type: the trochaic.

> Ákh! talán li moi, talán takóv,
> Ili úchast' moia gór'kaia,
> Na rodú li mné napísano,
> Na delú li mné dostálosia [. . .][1]

> (Oh! Is it my good fortune, such fortune,
> Or is it my sad fate,
> Whether determined from birth,
> Whether determined by lot [. . .])

Trochaic verse is defined by the absence of stress on the even-numbered syllables and the potential for stress on the odd-numbered syllables. In the example above, each line has nine syllables, with a strong stress on the third and seventh and an absent or weaker stress on the first and fifth. The stress on the seventh syllable, the antepenultima, is obligatory. The two syllables that follow it are either unstressed or (like the final syllable of the first line)

---

1 *Sobranie raznykh pesen M. D. Chulkova.* [M. D. Chulkov's collection of various songs] (St Petersburg: Imperatorskaia akademiia nauk, [1913]), p. 192.

reduced in stress, so that the dactylic line ending sounds clearly. Such insistent rhythmic patterning, combined with strong syntactic parallelism and word repetition, is typical of Russian folkloric verse. Literary poetry, while also relying on repetitions, rarely uses them to this extent.

The epic genres of Russian folklore usually feature tonic versification, in which each line has the same number of stresses but where the number of unstressed syllables between them varies. In the heroic tale (*bylina*), the line usually has three stresses, separated by intervals of one, two, or three unstressed syllables. A brief excerpt from a *bylina* about Ilia Muromets, a courageous if foolhardy hero, gives a sense of the tonic verse of folklore:

> Mne naprávo idtí – bogátu byt',
> Mne nalévo idtí – zhenátu byt',
> Mne napriámo idtí – ubítu byt'.
> Mne bogátstvo stáromu ne nádobno,
> Zhenít'sia stáromu ne khóchetsia, –
> Ia poidú staryi priámo-nápriamo [. . .]²

> (If I go right I'll be rich,
> If I go left I'll get married,
> If I go straight I'll be killed.
> This old man doesn't need wealth,
> This old man doesn't want to marry, –
> I, old man, will go straight ahead.)

Like the syllabic poetry that preceded it and the trochaic example above, the line concludes with an unrhymed dactylic cadence, that is, a stress on the antepenultima followed by two unstressed syllables. As in the trochaic passage, these lines feature insistent repetitions on the lexical, syntactic, and rhythmic levels. Unlike the trochaic passage, they are not isosyllabic; five lines have ten syllables, but the fourth has eleven. Most importantly, the rhythm is not predictable. In the first three lines, stresses fall on syllables 3, 6, and 8; in the fourth line on 3, 5, and 9; in the fifth on 2, 4, and 8; and in the sixth on 3, 6, and 8. (The potential stress on *stáryi* in the final line is omitted both because consecutive stresses tend to be avoided in Russian poetry and because it would add a fourth stress to the line.) Though the first two lines rhyme, this is simply a coincidence arising from the emphatic repetition of the same grammatical construction. What stands out at the end of all the lines is not rhyme but the dactylic cadence.

2 F. Selivanov (ed.), *Byliny* [Heroic tales] (Moscow: Sovetskaia Rossiia, 1989), p. 204.

Syllabic Verse

Russian written poetry emerged in the seventeenth century, much later than in the rest of Europe. Several factors contributed to this delay, among them widespread illiteracy, the distrust of neighbouring countries, and the resulting limited cultural intercourse with them. The flowering of poetry and philosophy that took place in western Europe during the Renaissance went no further east than Poland and Ukraine. The clergy, the only people who might have created a Russian poetic culture, were for centuries discouraged and at times expressly forbidden from doing so.

The emergence of 'learned' (written) poetry in Russia can be traced to the early seventeenth century and to Polish influence. In terms of quantity and range of output, the outstanding figure was Simeon of Polotsk (now Polatsk) or Simeon Polotskii (1629–1680; see also Chapter 1.2). Born in what is now Belarus (then part of the Polish-Lithuanian Commonwealth), he studied at the Kyiv Academy, an institution that had been influenced by western educational practices and included poetry in the curriculum. Upon finishing his studies, Simeon returned home to Polotsk, where he served as a monk and taught at a school. When visiting this newly conquered territory in 1656, the Russian tsar Aleksei Mikhailovich (r. 1645–76) was greeted by Simeon, who recited an original poem in his honour. Aleksei Mikhailovich, who did not share his predecessors' hostility to western influence, was flattered. He eventually brought Simeon to Moscow, where he served as court poet, court preacher, and tutor to the tsar's children. Over more than two decades in Russia, Simeon wrote an enormous quantity of poetry. This poetry was written in an archaic and artificial language somewhere between Russian and Church Slavonic. After all, Russian was not Simeon's native language; he was more comfortable with Belarusian, Ukrainian, and (probably) Polish. When it came to poetics, it was natural for him to apply the syllabic system of versification familiar from those 'western' languages and literary traditions.

The precise realisation of Simeon's syllabics shows that he was imposing on the Russian language principles that had been established a century earlier in Polish poetry by Jan Kochanowski. This is particularly clear in the rhymes. Since the Polish language has a fixed stress on the penultimate syllable, it favoured feminine rhymes, that is, rhymes where the stress falls on the penultimate syllable. The Russian language does not have fixed stress, so there would be nothing precluding masculine rhymes (where the stress falls on the final syllable) or dactylic rhymes (where the stress falls on the ante-penultima). As we have seen, Russian folklore strongly favoured dactylic

cadences. Later Russian poetry would take advantage of all three possibilities, but to Simeon, accustomed as he was to Polish versification, masculine and dactylic rhymes sounded wrong.

Simeon's poems are read today only as historical and linguistic curiosities. The typically moralistic proverb 'Wakefulness' (*Bdenie*, date unknown), consisting of only two lines, serves as a concise example:

> Polézno vynu bdéti, ne mnógo zhe spáti,
> Ibo sílen són délom zlým píshchy daiáti.[3]

> (It is useful always to be wakeful, not to sleep a lot,
> because sleep has the power to nourish evil deeds.)

Both lines contain thirteen syllables, and they are linked by a grammatical rhyme (in this case two infinitives). In keeping with the Polish model, the rhyme words are stressed on the penultimate syllable. In addition to the syllable count and the rhyme, there is one other invariant found in Simeon's thirteen-syllable lines: a word break (caesura) comes after the seventh syllable. In this particular example, there is also a caesura after the fifth syllable, but that is not a requirement of the form and should be regarded as a coincidence. In terms of the rhythmic organisation of Simeon's lines, the only expectation is that the twelfth syllable of each line must be stressed and the thirteenth must not. In all other positions it does not matter where the stresses fall.

Most of Simeon's poetry remained in manuscript. However, a few works – such as his rhymed translation of the Psalter (*Psaltir' rifmotvornaia*, 1680) – were printed and widely disseminated. His application of the syllabic system of versification influenced the nascent Russian poetic tradition and was used exclusively in Russia for approximately eighty years. Many of these subsequent 'Russian' poets were, like Simeon himself, not native speakers of Russian. Often they were Ukrainian theologians who were invited to Moscow (and later, to Petersburg) to occupy high positions in the Russian church. Their familiarity with Polish, Belarusian, and Ukrainian traditions, when combined with Simeon's powerful precedent, predetermined their choice of syllabic verse for Russian poetry.

For example, Feofan Prokopovich (1681–1736), the erudite advisor and assistant of Peter I (r. 1682–1725), studied in Kyiv and Rome before being

---

3 A. M. Panchenko (ed.), *Russkaia sillabicheskaia poeziia XVII–XVIII vv.* [Russian syllabic poetry of the seventeenth and eighteenth centuries] (Leningrad: Sovetskii pisatel', 1970), p. 118.

called to serve in Petersburg. In addition to legal documents, he wrote theological treatises, sermons, and poetry (see Chapter 4.2). As regards stanzaic forms, he greatly enriched Russian poetry. The first stanza of his poem 'To the Author of Satires' (*K sochiniteliu satir*, 1729–30) shows his resourcefulness. The poem is addressed to Antiokh Kantemir (1708–1744), whose satires had been disseminated anonymously in handwritten copies.

> Ne znáiu, któ tí, proróche rogátii,
> znáiu, kólikoi dostóin ti slávy.
> Da pochtó zh býlo ímia ukriváti?
> Znát', tebé stráshny síl'nykh gluptsóv nrávy.
> Pliún' na ikh grózy! Tí blazhén trikráti.
> Blágo, chto dál Bóg úm tebé tol zdrávii.
> Púst' ves' mír búdet na tebé gnevlívyi,
> Tí i bez shchást'ia dovól'no shchaslívii.[4]

> (I don't know who you are, o horned prophet;
> I know what great glory you are worthy of;
> But why do you hide your name?
> Truly, you fear the dispositions of powerful idiots.
> Spit on their threats! You are blessed thrice.
> It is great that God gave you such a healthy mind.
> Let the whole world be angry at you,
> You are happy enough even without that happiness.)

Simeon had relied exclusively on rhyming couplets (A-A-B-B), but Feofan varied his rhyme schemes. In this poem he introduced the Italian octave, a virtuoso stanza consisting of three pairs of alternating rhymes followed by a couplet (A-B-A-B-A-B-C-C). While Simeon had relied on grammatical rhyme (rhymes based on morphological endings, usually verbs, which in a language like Russian demand little ingenuity from the poet), Feofan added non-grammatical rhymes, in which different parts of speech are used. This creates a less predictable and semantically more interesting line ending. In the present poem, the 'A' rhymes are *rogatii* (an adjective), *ukryvati* (a verb), and *trikrati* (an adverb). The fact that the word *trikrati* – meaning 'thrice' – appears as the third rhyme is an expressive touch, showing a poet who is thinking about using the formal requirements of verse to enhance the semantic effect.

However, all the rhymes in this poem (and the vast majority in Feofan's verse overall) are feminine, a 'Polish' inheritance from Simeon's practice.

---

4 Panchenko, *Russkaia sillabicheskaia poeziia*, p. 276.

In the context of stresses that otherwise fall unpredictably, these line endings provide the only rhythmic constant. In addition to the syllable count and the cadence, Feofan, like Simeon, applies a third ordering principle in the form of a caesura. In the octave cited above, each line has eleven syllables, with a mandatory word break coming after the fifth. It might be noted that the choices of both the thirteen-syllable line (the text cited above by Simeon) and the eleven-syllable line (the Feofan excerpt) betray foreign influence, since these were the canonic line lengths of Polish poetry. In the case of Feofan's octaves, the eleven-syllable line may also reflect the influence of the *endeca-sillabo*, the standard line of Italian poetry from the time of Dante, which is likewise syllabic and relies on feminine line endings.

The Emergence of Syllabo-tonic Verse

The most significant change in Russian syllabic poetry occurred at the very end of its eighty years of dominance. Vasilii Trediakovskii (1703–1768), a scholar and poet who had spent five years abroad (three in Paris), returned to Russia in 1730. In translations and adaptations from French, he introduced a number of genres – such as the solemn ode and the love poem – that would have an enormous influence on subsequent Russian poetry. French poetry was of course itself syllabic, but it had an additional structural feature that Trediakovskii decided to apply to Russian verse: a stressed syllable before the caesura. Up until this point, Russian poets had not concerned themselves with the cadence before the caesura. Once Trediakovskii introduced this additional fixed stress, the line became much more rhythmically organised. Recognising the value of such rhythmic structure, Trediakovskii went still further. In long lines (i.e. those of eleven or more syllables), he believed that a regular rhythmic pulse should be felt throughout. The ideal metre, he decided, should be trochaic, which would (in lines of eleven or thirteen syllables, which were by far the most common) place a stress on the syllable before the caesura and also accommodate the stress on the penultimate syllable of the line, as had always been favoured in Russian syllabic verse. Interestingly, Trediakovskii supported his argument for the trochaic – as against the iambic – by noting that this was the traditional metre of Russian folklore and was, as it were, sanctioned by the very nature of the Russian language.

Trediakovskii proposed these innovations in a treatise of 1735 as a means of reconciling the syllabic poetry of the past eight decades with the syllabo-tonic principle that he postulated was inherent to Russian verse. He ignored the need for such rhythmic patterning in lines of less than eleven syllables, since he

considered syllable count and feminine endings sufficient to mark these shorter lines as poetry. His ideas were only beginning to take hold when, in 1739, a still more radical suggestion for the revision of Russian versification occurred. Mikhail Lomonosov (1711–1765), a Russian polymath studying in Germany, sent to the Russian Academy of Sciences an ode together with a 'Letter on the Rules of Russian Versification' (*Pis'mo o pravilakh rossiiskogo stikhotvorstva*) in prose, in order to introduce his own programme for Russian poetry. Lomonosov was acquainted with Trediakovskii's treatise, but he disagreed with most of the assumptions and conclusions. Because he was living in Germany, Lomonosov had become familiar with the poetry being written there. Just as Trediakovskii's innovations had been spurred by the French poetry that he admired, so Lomonosov took his inspiration from German models. The essential difference stemmed from the nature of the respective languages. In the German language word stress is essential, while in French phrasal stress is far more important. As a result, French poetry was syllabic, organised around the one phrasal stress per line segment (that is to say: one stress before the caesura and one after it). In the German language, the insistent word stress had led to the adoption and canonisation of syllabo-tonic versification. Because iambs tended to dominate German poetry, Lomonosov wrote his own ode in iambs. Lomonosov dismissed Trediakovskii's argument that trochees were more appropriate because they were found in Russian folk verse. As far as he was concerned, poetry was supposed to speak about elevated subjects, and the further away it was from folklore, the better. Russian poetry was only beginning, he argued, and what had been haphazardly imported from Poland was no better than the indigenous folklore of illiterates. Among his innovations was the regular alternation of masculine and feminine rhymes. This meant that lines with masculine rhymes would be one syllable shorter than lines with feminine rhymes – a rejection of the fundamental principle of syllabic verse. If Trediakovskii advocated the evolution of Russian verse, Lomonosov opted instead for a revolution.[5]

The ensuing polemics were strident and nasty, but in the end Lomonosov's argumentation won the day. Within a few years syllabic poetry was written only in places so provincial that the poetic practitioners were simply unaware of the radical changes that had unfolded in the capital. For all practical purposes, syllabo-tonic poetry quickly rendered syllabic poetry

---

5 M. L. Gasparov, *Ocherk istorii russkogo stikha* [Studies in the history of Russian verse] (Moscow: Fortuna, 2000), pp. 21–42.

obsolete, and even Trediakovskii would rewrite his syllabic poems in accordance with the new principles.

Lomonosov's very first ode gives a good sense of the new syllabo-tonic poetry. In many respects, it sets the model for the solemn (or 'Pindaric') ode as it would be practised in Russia for the next half-century. In terms of versification, it introduced the iamb, which has dominated Russian versification ever since. The following stanza, the fourth of twenty-eight, is part of a lengthy battle description.

> Krepít otéchestva liubóv'
> Synóv rossíiskikh dúkh i rúku;
> Zheláet vsiák prolít' vsiu króv',
> Ot gróznogo bodrítsia zvúku.
> Kak síl'nyi lév stadá volkóv,
> Chto kázhut óstrykh iád zubóv,
> Ochéi goriáshchikh gónit strákhom,
> Ot révu lés i brég drozhít,
> I khvóst pesók i pýl' mutít,
> Razít izvívshis' síl'nym mákhom.[6] (1739)

> (The love of the fatherland strengthens
> The soul and arm of the sons of Russia;
> Everyone wants to spill all his blood,
> Everyone gains courage from the threatening sound.
> As a powerful lion chases away packs of wolves
> That bare the poison of their sharp teeth,
> By means of the fear of its burning eyes,
> The forest and shore shake from its roar,
> And its tail stirs up the sand and dust,
> After winding itself up, it strikes with a sudden powerful blow.)

Trediakovskii had already pioneered the ode in Russia. Using the French Neoclassicist Nicolas Boileau (1636–1711) as his model, he had introduced the odic stanza, a ten-line construction with rhyme scheme A-B-A-B-C-C-D-E-E-D. That same rhyme scheme can be found in Lomonosov's poem. However, whereas Trediakovskii had used lines of nine syllables with exclusively feminine rhymes, Lomonosov, taking his cue from a German ode by Johann Christian Günther (1695–1723), used lines of either eight or nine syllables. True to Günther's model, the eight-syllable lines end with masculine rhymes, the nine-syllable lines with

---

6 M. V. Lomonosov, *Izbrannye proizvedeniia* [Selected works] (Leningrad: Sovetskii pisatel', 1986), p. 62.

feminine rhymes. These rhyme types alternate, producing a scheme of a-B-a-B-c-c-D-e-e-D (with masculine rhymes designated by lowercase letters and feminine rhymes by capital letters). Hence each stanza begins with a masculine rhyme and concludes with a feminine rhyme, preparing the alternating masculine rhyme that starts the next stanza. In the vast majority of subsequent ten-line odes in Russian, the sequence of masculine and feminine rhymes is reversed, A-b-A-b-C-C-d-E-E-d, so that the masculine ending at the end of each stanza becomes firmly associated with closure.

The excerpt cited above shows that Lomonosov made considerable effort to put a word stress on every even-numbered syllable. This is not easy to do. Unlike English, the Russian language has no secondary stress, so that words longer than two syllables – unless they are stressed on the second syllable – disrupt the flow of fully stressed iambs. The word *otechestvo* (fatherland, Latin *patria*) is essential to the genre of the ode, but the fact that it has four syllables means that it interrupts the iambs, producing one iambic foot and one 'pyrrhic' foot (a foot consisting of two unstressed syllables). Lomonosov initially tried to avoid pyrrhics because he wanted the metrical pattern to sound with maximal clarity. Within a few years, however, when iambs became familiar, he relaxed his stance and accepted pyrrhics as a necessary evil. It has been suggested that the four-syllable name of his patron the empress Elizabeth (r. 1741–62) forced him to recognise the necessity of pyrrhic feet.[7] In any case, later poets were untroubled by pyrrhics. In Aleksandr Pushkin's (1799–1837) iambic tetrameters, they become the rule rather than the exception. Andrei Belyi (1880–1934), the first to study this phenomenon systematically, tried to create as many pyrrhics as possible in his own verse, insisting that these missing stresses lent Russian poetry its distinctiveness and rhythmic richness.[8]

Given the prominence that Lomonosov's poem achieved in the history of Russian poetry, it is worth commenting on more than simply its innovative versification. In terms of genre, the poem is a 'solemn ode', which is to say, a poem on a subject of national significance. As such, it relies on the high style, which is achieved not simply by older, Slavonic word forms (e.g., *breg* as against *bereg*) but also by elevated rhetoric. The above-cited stanza features a wealth of tropes: hyperbole (exaggeration: each person wants to spill *all* his blood), zeugma (the yoking of a single verb with a literal and figurative object: love of the fatherland strengthens *the arm and the soul* of the Russians),

7 M. I. Shapir, *Universum Versus. Iazyk – Stikh – Smysl v russkoi poezii XVIII–XX vekov* [Universum Versus. Language – Verse – Meaning in Russian poetry of the eighteenth to twentieth centuries] (Moscow: Iazyki russkoi kul'tury, 2000), p. 166.
8 Andrei Belyi, *Simvolizm* [Symbolism] (Moscow: Musaget, 1910), pp. 259–81.

hendiadys (two subjects with a singular verb: 'the forest and the shore shakes' (rather than 'shake')). Of course, the most striking trope is the extended (epic) simile, which is presented as a hysteron proteron (the second thing coming before the first: the lion chases the wolves away and then strikes them, whereas logically the lion would strike them and then chase them away). Lomonosov's knowledge of lions presumably came from heraldic depictions rather than observation, so one can excuse his assumption that it attacks with its tail. However, he certainly was aware that wolves do not have poisonous teeth. The point to be made here is that Lomonosov was aiming not for a realistic but rather for a symbolic depiction. His battle of the lion against the wolves is allegorical, to be understood as a battle between the inherently noble and fearsome Russian army and the hordes of ignominious Turks. Lomonosov's complicated, Latinate syntax is difficult to read not simply because it is so far removed from today's Russian. Even to contemporaries, this poetic style was obscure and challenging. And that was very much part of Lomonosov's programme. He intended poetic language to be maximally removed from anything familiar. It was meant to express elevated subject matter, to remove – or raise up – readers (or listeners) from their everyday world to an inspired state of being. His vocabulary was explicitly modelled on scripture, which likewise sought to rise above everyday concerns.

In Russia, the solemn ode achieved a prominence and status far greater than in the French and German traditions that were its source. It stood atop the hierarchy of genres throughout the eighteenth century, not only in Lomonosov's era but for decades after his death. This is not to say, however, that other types of poetry did not thrive. Russian eighteenth-century poetry is remarkable for its generic range. This included several other 'high' genres – such as so-called spiritual odes (translations of the Psalms), verse tragedies, and epics – as well as 'lower genres' such as Anacreontic odes (both translations and imitations of the popular Anacreontic corpus of poems that praised the fleeting pleasures of life) and fables. What is remarkable in eighteenth-century poetics is the intimate connection of form and genre. For example, Russian tragedies were written in rhymed iambic hexameter couplets. This was the Russian equivalent of the French Alexandrine, which had been standard practice in Racine's plays, and which served as the model for the Russians. The versification of Anacreontic odes was likewise based on western European adaptations of an ancient Greek form. In antiquity these poems were written in a metre that had seven syllables, which Russians, guided by recent western European practice, rendered either as iambic trimeter (which had six or seven syllables, depending on the cadence) or trochaic tetrameter

(which had either seven or eight syllables). Since the poetry of antiquity did not rhyme, Russian Anacreontics were generally unrhymed – very unusual for poetry of the period. Fables were written in a mix of iambic metres, including very short lines (monometer and dimeter). In these poems, the rhyme was insistent and essential, though the rhyme scheme was unpredictable. While fables were an ancient genre, Russians took their cue not directly from antiquity but from the highly influential French versions by La Fontaine, which depended on rhyme for their effect.

Among the major poets and innovators of the eighteenth century, Aleksandr Sumarokov (1717–1777) and Gavriil Derzhavin (1743–1816) stand out. Sumarokov was probably best known as a tragedian, but his lyric poetry reflects a mind constantly alert to new formal possibilities. He used a wide range of stanzas, and some of his experiments (for example, with caesura) would not be attempted again for more than a century. Derzhavin was an innovator not so much in versification as in poetic language. He saw himself as the poet who introduced the 'amusing style' into Russian poetry and who 'with a smile' could tell the truth to tsars.[9] Though capable of writing serious odes in the vein of Lomonosov, he also authored works of satire and humour more broadly. This playful quality can be seen in a passage from his ode 'Felitsa' (*Felitsa*, 1782), in which he praises the monarch's appreciation of poetry (see also Chapter 4.2):

> Sniskhódish' tý na lírnyi lad;
> Poéziia tebé liubézna,
> Priiátna, sládostna, polézna,
> Kak létom vkúsnyi limonád.[10]

> (You are indulgent to the lyre's harmony;
> You consider poetry dear,
> Pleasant, sweet, useful,
> Like tasty lemonade in the summer.)

These are the final lines of an odic stanza which shares the iambic tetrameter as well as the rhyme scheme with the odes of Lomonosov. However, the tone is worlds apart, marked most strikingly by the familiar and almost comic rhyme of *lad* / *limonad* (harmony / lemonade).

---

9 From the poem 'Monument' (*Pamiatnik*, 1796), a rewriting of Horace's famous *Exegi monumentum*: G. R. Derzhavin, *Sochineniia* [Works] (St Petersburg: Akademicheskii proekt, 2002), p. 224.
10 Derzhavin, *Sochineniia*, p. 77.

The 'Golden Age' of Russian Poetry

In the early nineteenth century, a distinctly new type of poetry emerged. The precursor and spiritual father of this movement was the poet and prose writer Nikolai Karamzin (1766–1826), who himself had ceased to write creative literature in the first years of the nineteenth century in order to concentrate all of his energies on his monumental *History of the Russian State* (*Istoriia gosudarstva Rossiiskogo*, 1818–29). As a poet, Karamzin had developed a fluid style that contrasted sharply with the bombastic and consciously archaic language of the eighteenth-century ode. Karamzin's heirs – foremost among them Konstantin Batiushkov (1787–1855), Vasilii Zhukovskii (1783–1852), Petr Viazemskii (1792–1878), and their younger contemporary Aleksandr Pushkin – formed a literary association in Petersburg called Arzamas (after a provincial city). The purpose of the society was to defend the urbane and intimate Karamzinian innovations against a group of 'archaists', who formed their own association known as Beseda (meaning 'conversation', 'colloquy') and who championed the high style. The leading poet of the Beseda group was the aged Derzhavin, who in spite of his lexical experiments considered the solemn ode the quintessential Russian genre.

The Arzamas poets favoured the elegy. If the solemn ode was intended to commemorate glorious events of national significance, the elegy was consciously small-scale, focused on the feelings of the individual. These were poems of love and loss, often modelled on recent western poetry. They featured a refined elegance, achieved through a limited lexicon and relatively uncomplicated syntax. Thomas Gray's 'Elegy Written in a Country Churchyard' (1751) was a significant influence, as were numerous poems by a host of now forgotten French poets (Évariste de Parny and Charles Millevoye, for example). In the early nineteenth century, the solemn ode went into decline, not simply because it sounded so convoluted but also because social conditions changed. In the eighteenth century, the patronage system was the main source of income for poets. A poem was considered an appropriate accompaniment to court festivities, and the tsar and his courtiers were prepared to pay to have an event memorialised poetically. In the nineteenth century, the central venue for poetry moved from the court to the salon (see Chapter 2.3). Poets were members of the gentry, not salaried servants. They wrote poetry for one another, and they sought to entertain rather than to curry favour with the authorities. Pushkin was the first poet of his age to attempt to make a living through his writing, a difficult task in a country that lacked copyright laws.

Still more difficult was the task of the woman poet, whose gender prevented her from participating as an equal in circles where poetry was cultivated. Until the twentieth century, women's poetry was viewed as a curiosity rather than an organic part of the Russian tradition, and this hostile attitude made it difficult for women to contribute to literary life and impossible for them to achieve widespread recognition. Karolina Pavlova (1807–1893) and Evdokiia Rostopchina (1811–1858), both gifted nineteenth-century poets, endured condescension and resistance from their male counterparts. Pavlova wrote a novel that combined poetry and prose, a daring formal innovation that was overlooked for more than a century.

In a speech of 1816, Batiushkov defended the elegy against the epic (and odic) genres. In the latter, he remarked, readers are so moved by the poet's passionate outpourings that they do not notice stylistic imperfections.[11] In more intimate genres like the elegy, however, there can be no roughness of style. The poet seeks the utmost purity in expression. It was this refined style that the young Pushkin inherited. While Pushkin soon moved beyond the elegy – and even mocked it in the character of Vladimir Lenskii in *Eugene Onegin* (*Evgenii Onegin*, 1825–32; see Box 1.1) – he never completely renounced it, and one finds elegiac elements even in his very last poems.

Pushkin

Pushkin was indisputably the greatest Russian poet of his age. He learned his craft at the Lyceum, a school for children of the nobility, where he enrolled at age twelve. It was located in the environs of St Petersburg in the 'tsar's village' (Tsarskoe Selo), which housed, among other things, the imperial summer palace. The education at the Lyceum was intended to create cultured high-level civil servants, hence considerable effort was expended on what would today be called the humanities. Russian poetry of the eighteenth century as well as modern European literature were essential parts of the curriculum. The students were also encouraged to write poetry, and Pushkin was quickly recognised as the most talented, though two other major poets – Anton Delvig (1798–1831) and Vilgelm Kiukhelbeker (1797–1846) – emerged from his class of a mere thirty students. As the winner of a competition, Pushkin recited one of his first major works in front of the aged Derzhavin, a year or two before literary polemics would situate them in

11 K. N. Batiushkov, *Opyty v stikhakh i proze* [Essays in prose and verse] (Moscow: Nauka, 1977), p. 11.

opposing camps. That poem, 'Memories in Tsarskoe Selo' (*Vospominaniia v Tsarskom sele*, 1814), betrayed a detailed knowledge of both eighteenth-century odic conventions and the more recent elegiac writing.

The rapidity of Pushkin's poetic development is remarkable. He never repeated himself but was constantly seeking out new possibilities and new means of expression. Pushkin had what Iurii Lotman (1922–1993) has compared to a 'Midas touch', an ability to transform all life experience, whether good or bad, into brilliant poetry.[12] Whatever the genre – elegy, epigram, nature poem, love poem, meditation, friendly epistle, occasional poem, religious poem – Pushkin turned it to poetic gold. In addition to his lyric poetry, he created unsurpassed large-scale poetic works – tragedies; narrative poems (verse tales and epics); and his novel in verse, *Eugene Onegin*.

Formally speaking, Pushkin was conservative. While he experimented with a wide range of set forms – the sonnet, the octave, *terza rima*, the 'Burns stanza', the elegiac distich of antiquity, blank verse – much of his work was written in metrically unremarkable iambic tetrameter, either freely rhymed or in rhymed quatrains.

Pushkin's verse is always in conversation with the poetry of his predecessors and contemporaries. These include the Russian eighteenth-century poets, the English Romantics (especially Byron and Barry Cornwall), Shakespeare, French poets (Musset, Chénier, Parny), and the poets of antiquity. Since French was a second native language for Pushkin, and since he was otherwise a poor student of languages, most of his knowledge of western culture – ancient and modern – came through French translations. Very often his sources are minor poets, but he had an extraordinary ability to recognise unexplored possibilities or to develop what had earlier been inexpertly deployed.

Though a poet of the Romantic period, Pushkin was not himself a Romantic. He was curious about recent developments, but everything he read was refracted through his own Classicist sensibility. Byron's fragmentariness, expressed as lack of structure, becomes in Pushkin a series of carefully constructed fragments. Everywhere in Pushkin there reigns a sense of balance and proportion. His poetry is remarkable for its restraint, with a relatively simple lexicon and straightforward syntax. He avoids the most marked poetic devices (figurative language), relying instead on grammatical tropes (parallelism, chiasmus). As Roman Jakobson (1896–1982) has

12 Iu. M. Lotman, *Pushkin. Biografiia pisatelia. Stat'i i zametki, 1960–1990. 'Evgenii Onegin'. Kommentarii* [Pushkin. Biography of a writer. Articles and notes, 1960–1990. *Eugene Onegin*. Commentaries] (St Petersburg: Iskusstvo-SPb, 1995), p. 388.

demonstrated, grammatical categories function as poetic devices in Pushkin's poetry.[13] The profundity of expression is sometimes hidden beneath the easily readable façade.

Pushkin's experiments with folklore are instructive. With the advent of Romanticism in Europe came an interest in folklore and folk poetry. In Germany, this led to various collecting projects (e.g. those of the brothers Grimm or Achim von Arnim and Clemens Brentano) as well as the creation of literary ballads in the spirit of folklore. Until this time, Russian interest in folk poetry had been rare, but it became central in the work of Zhukovskii. However, Zhukovskii was essentially a conduit for western European Romanticism (see Chapter 1.4). A translator of genius, his versions of Friedrich Schiller, Johann Wolfgang Goethe, and Gottfried August Bürger became celebrated in their own right, committed to memory and recited as if they were original Russian poems. Zhukovskii's success as a translator depended on a generous degree of poetic licence. He did not hesitate to depart from the original in order to make his translations more compelling. Formally speaking, this had significant consequences. German folk songs and folk ballads were often written in a tonic metre. Each line had a constant number of stressed syllables separated by intervals of either one or two unstressed syllables. Zhukovskii, accustomed to the syllabo-tonic poetry that had dominated Russian poetry since Lomonosov, felt uncomfortable introducing a form that ran contrary to it. His solution was to make these 'irregular' rhythms distinctive yet predictable. One way he did so was by replacing the German tonic verse with ternary metres. Ternary metres (dactyls, amphibrachs, anapaests) had been in the reper-toire of Russian poets since Lomonosov, but they were far less common than binary metres (iambs and trochees). When Zhukovskii started to apply them with regularity, they attained for the Russian ear a folkloric colour-ation, though such an association lacked a historical basis in both Germany and Russia.

Whereas Zhukovskii's folklore was formally at a remove from both German and Russian sources, Pushkin showed an unusual interest in actual Russian folkloric form. This work was based less on ethnographic experience than on careful study of the work of the brilliant philologist Aleksandr Vostokov (1781–1864). In a treatise on Russian poetry published in 1804, Vostokov had established the principles of what he called 'the

---

13 Roman Jakobson, 'Poetry of grammar and grammar of poetry', in *Language in Literature* (Cambridge, MA: Harvard University Press, 1987), pp. 121–44.

Russian metre'.[14] This was the oral tradition of the *bylina*, which predated Lomonosov's syllabo-tonic revolution (see Chapter 3.2). A few of these poems had recently been published in a volume of folklore collected in the eighteenth century by the otherwise obscure Kirsha Danilov. With remarkable acuity, Vostokov had determined the tonic principles that governed this form. He himself wrote original poems in this metre and encouraged others to do so. In his view, it was *genuinely* Russian, as against the syllabo-tonic verse that Lomonosov had made synonymous with Russian poetry. When Pushkin sought to stylise Russian (or Slavic) folklore, he opted for this non-canonical form. Thus, two of his three songs about the famous Russian bandit Sten'ka Razin were written in Vostokov's Russian metre as well as many of his folkloric stylisations in *Songs of the Western Slavs* (*Pesni zapadnykh slavian*, 1834) and his beloved 'Fairy Tale about the Fisherman and the Fish' ('*Skazka o rybake i rybke*', 1833–4).

Pushkin is often credited with a 'democratisation' of Russian poetry.[15] Insofar as this is understood as the introduction of a less ornate lexicon and simpler syntax, it has a certain validity. Pushkin's poetry is unquestionably closer to vernacular Russian than Lomonosov's was, but it would be naïve to assume that it reflects the language as it was actually spoken. While Pushkin's lexicon includes certain words that would have been considered inappropriate by earlier poets, he never used substandard language in his verse or even in his prose – at least not in works intended for publication. He also did not hesitate to apply the high lexical register of the eighteenth century when the context demanded it. To create the appropriate 'biblical' colouration for his celebrated poem 'The Prophet' (*Prorok*, 1826), Pushkin used numerous archaic words and grammatical forms. In religious lyrics of his last years, he turned to iambic hexameter, a form mainly associated with eighteenth-century tragedy. For readers of his age, this would have sounded remote, which was precisely the effect he was seeking.

Poetry after Pushkin

After Pushkin's death, two major Russian poets emerged, each representing a different strain of Romanticism. Mikhail Lermontov (1814–1841), a poet in the Byronic mould, invariably portrays a troubled lyric persona searching for an ever-elusive calm.

---

14 A. Kh. Vostokov, *Opyt o russkom stikhoslozhenii* [A study of Russian versification] (Kazan': Nasledie, 2002), pp. 142–67.

15 V. V. Vinogradov, *The History of the Russian Literary Language from the Seventeenth Century to the Nineteenth*, adapt. Lawrence L. Thomas (Madison: University of Wisconsin Press, 1969), pp. 127–57.

Vykhozhú odín ia na dorógu;
Skvoz' tumán kremnístyi pút' blestít.
Nóch' tikhá. Pustýnia vnémlet Bógu,
I zvezdá s zvezdóiu govorít.

V nebesákh torzhéstvenno i chúdno!
Spít zemliá v siián'i golubóm . . .
Chtó zhe mné tak ból'no i tak trúdno?
Zhdú l' chegó? Zhaléiu li o chëm?[16] *(1841)*

(Alone I step out onto the path;
Through the fog the flinty path glistens.
The night is quiet. The wilderness perceives God,
And star speaks with star.

In the heavens it is solemn and wondrous!
The earth sleeps in the moon's glow . . .
So why am I feeling pain and difficulty?
Am I waiting for something? Do I regret something?)

This passage, the first two stanzas of a five-stanza poem, can serve as the quintessential picture of Lermontov's paradoxical protagonist, whose inner disharmony stands in stark contrast to the complete harmony of nature. The form that Lermontov used here – quatrains of trochaic pentameter – was unprecedented in Russian poetry. For numerous subsequent poets this combination of form and theme proved irresistible. To express their own profound sense of alienation in an unsympathetic world, Fedor Tiutchev (1803–1873), Aleksandr Blok (1880–1921), Ivan Bunin (1870–1953), Vladimir Nabokov (1899–1977), and others turned to precisely this combination of metre and rhyme scheme, often repeating the same key words (e.g. the path, night) and motifs (wandering).

Tiutchev, whose earliest poetry appeared in a journal that Pushkin edited, is much closer to German *Naturphilosophie* than to Byronic Romanticism. This type of poetry is characterised by an attempt to understand the self through its relationship to the world beyond (nature in the broadest sense). Tiutchev's nature poems tend to feature a poetic 'we' rather than an 'I', and they sometimes eschew a first-person pronoun altogether. This poetry is metaphysical and mystical, situating the human in a mysterious cosmos that is at once alluring and forbidding. At the same time, Tiutchev was a forerunner of the Slavophiles, writing fervent poems about Russia in

16 M. Iu. Lermontov, *Polnoe sobranie stikhotvorenii v dvukh tomakh* [Complete verse in two volumes] (Leningrad: Sovetskii pisatel', 1989), vol. II, p. 83.

which he lauded its simplicity, faith, and humility as a rejection of the soulless rationality of its haughty western neighbours.

In formal terms, Tiutchev returned to the elevated diction and, at times, to the complicated syntax of the eighteenth century, especially in moments of high pathos. The poem 'A Vision' (*Videnie*, 1829) is cited here in its entirety:

> Est' nékii chás, v nochí, vsemírnogo molchán'ia,
>   I v ónyi chás iavlénii i chudés
>   Zhiváia kolesnítsa mirozdán'ia
> Otkrýto kátitsia v sviatílishche nebes.

> Togdá gustéet nóch', kak kháos na vodákh,
>   Bespámiatstvo, kak Átlas, davit súshu . . .
>   Lish' múzy dévstvennuiu dúshu
>   V prorócheskikh trevózhat bógi snákh![17]

> (At night there is a certain hour of universal silence,
> And at that hour of epiphanies and miracles
> The living chariot of the universe
> Rushes openly into the sanctuary of the heavens.

> Then night thickens, like chaos on the waters,
> Oblivion, like Atlas, presses on the earth . . .
> It is only the virginal soul of the muse
> That the gods disturb in prophetic dreams.)

The poem is written in iambic quatrains with a rhyme scheme that varies from stanza to stanza and in line lengths that shift unpredictably between tetrameter and hexameter. The lexicon is distinctly high, and the references to mythology remove us from the Judeo-Christian world to pagan antiquity. As the title suggests, the poem is devoted to a visionary moment, but the vision is imprecise and curiously impersonal. The poem concludes, as it were, at the epiphany. When the muse appears in the penultimate line, the syntax becomes especially complicated. Initially, one might think that *muzy* is the subject (muses, nominative plural) and that the muses agitate the virginal soul of the poet. However, when one reaches the penultimate word in the poem, it is unambiguous that the gods agitate the virginal soul *of the muse* (genitive singular) and that the poet is never mentioned. In the final exclamatory line, the prepositional phrase 'in prophetic dreams' (*v prorocheskikh . . . snakh*) is interrupted by the subject and verb of the sentence. Such

---

17 F. I. Tiutchev, *Polnoe sobranie stikhotvorenii* [Complete verses] (Leningrad: Sovetskii pisatel', 1970), p. 79.

a construction, recalling the unidiomatic predilections of the eighteenth-century ode writers, was foreign to the poetics of Pushkin and Lermontov.

After the deaths of Pushkin and Lermontov, both killed at a young age in duels, prose began to take centre stage in Russian literary culture. Tiutchev, a professional diplomat who spent much of his adult life abroad, continued to write excellent poetry but had an extremely casual attitude towards publishing it. The only poet prominent in literary life for several decades after 1840 was Nikolai Nekrasov (1821–1878). Nekrasov developed a distinct style, creating a poetry that was socially engaged and sometimes satirical. The characters of his poems are generally outcasts, religious fanatics, or hypocritical aristocrats. Though the strong narrative component of his verse brings it close to the Realist prose of his day, Nekrasov is very much a part of the Russian poetic tradition. His innovations are thematic, stylistic, and formal. He often makes familiar metres sound unfamiliar by imparting a low lexical register. The ternary metres which Zhukovskii had canonised in the ballad, a fantastic genre set in a far-off place and time, become in Nekrasov's work a way to depict quotidian reality. In the poem 'The Railroad' (*Zheleznaia doroga*, 1864), for example, Nekrasov shows the nasty underside of techno-logical progress by contrasting the benefits to the wealthy with the suffering of the labourers who actually built it. This particular stanza, one of forty, is spoken by those anonymous masses:

> Mý nadryvális' pod znóem, pod khólodom,
> S véchno sognútoi spinói,
> Zhíli v zemliánkakh, borólisia s gólodom,
> Mërzli i mókli, boléli tsingói.[18]

> (We busted our guts in the heat, in the cold,
> Our backs were eternally bent,
> We lived in dugouts, fought with hunger,
> Froze and got soaked, suffered from scurvy.)

The poem is written in dactylic tetrameter (with occasional trimeter lines) and alternating rhymes, the odd-numbered lines ending in either dactylic or feminine rhymes, the even-numbered lines always masculine. Though dactylic metre has no folkloric provenance, dactylic rhymes do. Commonly found in the line cadences of the *bylina*, this stress pattern imparts a folkloric colouration to what is otherwise unmistakably literary verse.

---

18 N. A. Nekrasov, *Polnoe sobranie stikhotvorenii v trekh tomakh* [Complete verse in three volumes] (Leningrad: Sovetskii pisatel', 1967), vol. II, p. 160.

Nekrasov's vocabulary is decidedly prosaic: the final word of this stanza ('scurvy') would have been unthinkable to prior poets; the verb *nadryvat'sia* (meaning 'to bust one's guts') would be more appropriate to a novel by Fedor Dostoevskii (1821–1881).

At the same time that Nekrasov was writing his socially engaged poetry to great acclaim, Afanasii Fet (1820–1892) was producing brilliant 'art-for-art's-sake' poetry that was of little interest to most contemporaries. Fet used a wide range of poetic forms, but his subjects were the 'eternal' themes of poetry: love, beauty, nature.

> Siiála nóch'. Lunói byl pólon sád. Lezháli
> Luchí u náshikh nóg v gostínoi bez ognéi.
> Roiál' byl vés' raskrýt, i strúny v něm drozháli,
> Kak i serdtsá u nás za pésniiu tvoéi.[19] *(1877)*

> (The night glistened. The garden was full of moonlight. The rays
> Lay at our feet in the sitting room without lights.
> The grand piano was wide open, and the strings in it shuddered,
> Like our hearts in response to your song.)

This stanza, the first of four, sets the scene for a love poem, or rather, for a poem dedicated to the memory of a lost love. In the age of the Realist novel, its combination of moonlight, music, and tender emotion could be read as nostalgic, anachronistic, or even trite. Indeed, the themes of the poem (a musical performance of a love poem that in itself recalls a different temporal plane) is reminiscent of Pushkin's 'Don't sing in my presence, o beauty' (*Ne poi, krasavitsa, pri mne*, 1828). However, Fet's formal decisions are strikingly original. This poem is in iambic hexameter, a form that had its heyday in the eighteenth century and which Pushkin in his last years had radically repurposed for religious lyrics. To use it in a love poem is unexpected, yet Fet does something still more remarkable. Russian iambic hexameter invariably has a caesura in the middle of the line, and Fet retains this convention. In the first line, however, he inserts two logical breaks (marked by periods), neither of which coincides with the caesura, which occurs after the word *lunoi*. Moreover, that same first line concludes with an enjambment, a highly unusual feature in iambic hexameter. The syntax is played off against the semantics, producing a disquieting effect that sets an appropriately eerie tone for the poem that follows.

---

19 A. A. Fet, *Stikhotvoreniia i poemy* [Verses and poems] (Leningrad: Sovetskii pisatel', 1986), p. 166.

When the Symbolists ushered in a renaissance of Russian poetry in the 1890s, they did so in large part by developing congenial elements of the poetics of all of their nineteenth-century predecessors. According to their syncretic ideal, Nekrasov and Fet could both be celebrated, joining Pushkin, Lermontov, and especially Tiutchev as essential precursors. Historians of literature have traditionally labelled this flowering of Russian poetry from the 1890s to the 1920s the 'Silver Age', thus drawing a direct parallel to the 'Golden Age' of Pushkin and his contemporaries.

Further Reading

Bailey, James, *Three Russian Lyric Folk Song Meters* (Columbus, OH: Slavica, 1993).

Gasparov, M. L., *A History of European Versification*, trans. G. S. Smith and Marina Tarlinskaja, ed. G. S. Smith with Leofranc Holford-Strevens (Oxford: Clarendon Press, 1996).

Kahn, Andrew (ed.), *The Cambridge Companion to Pushkin* (Cambridge: Cambridge University Press, 2006).

Kelly, Catriona, *A History of Russian Women's Writing, 1820–1992* (Oxford: Clarendon Press, 1994).

Khitrova, Daria, *Lyric Complicity: Poetry and Readers in the Golden Age of Russian Literature* (Madison: University of Wisconsin Press, 2019).

Levitt, Marcus C., *Early Modern Russian Letters: Texts and Contexts* (Boston: Academic Studies Press, 2009).

Pratt, Sarah, *Russian Metaphysical Romanticism: The Poetry of Tiutchev and Boratynskii* (Stanford: Stanford University Press, 1984).

Reyfman, Irina, *Vasilii Trediakovsky: The Fool of the 'New' Russian Literature* (Stanford: Stanford University Press, 1990).

Scherr, Barry P., *Russian Poetry: Meter, Rhythm, and Rhyme* (Berkeley: University of California Press, 1986).

Silbajoris, Rimvydas, *Russian Versification: The Theories of Trediakovskij, Lomonosov, and Kantemir* (New York: Columbia University Press, 1968).

Zhivov, Victor, *Language and Culture in Eighteenth Century Russia*, trans. Marcus C. Levitt (Boston: Academic Studies Press, 2009).

3 · 4

Drama I

KIRILL ZUBKOV

Drama occupies a unique place among literary forms: it is unthinkable in isolation from performance. Performance entails the participation of both actors and an audience; the dramatic text is perceived in the act of listening. But any play can also be published and be read as a literary work. The form taken by a dramatic work hence speaks to two distinct audiences – one that watches the performance, another that reads the text. The development of Russian drama is barely comprehensible without appreciating the interplay between theatre and literature more broadly – or, for that matter, the interplay between state and society, both actively involved in the evolution of Russian theatre. Its history from the seventeenth to the nineteenth centuries illustrates the shifting interactions between state, society, and the individual as well as how writers sought to position themselves among them. The evolution of the vision of the audience changed radically from the 1670s to 1870s, from plays destined for the court theatre to those aimed at a wider audience. From excluded observer to passive recipient of a play's educational message, the audience gradually emerged as a co-creative participant in the life of a play.

From Court Theatre to Public Theatre: The Seventeenth and Eighteenth Centuries

It is difficult to pinpoint a single moment that marked the beginning of Russian drama. Russian theatre appears to have emerged out of several western European prototypes that attracted increasing interest in the latter half of the seventeenth century. The first plays to appear were either translations or direct imitations of foreign works. At this stage, Russian drama as a specific entity can only be loosely separated from theatre

produced in other Slavonic languages; both geographically and linguistically, its development was closely linked to Polish and Ukrainian culture.

Seemingly, the first theatrical productions in Russia were 'ballets' performed for Tsar Aleksei Mikhailovich (r. 1645–76) and his inner circle in February and May 1672, before there were any purpose-built theatres or professional actors. Often, however, a slightly later court production is given as the starting point: *The Play of Artaxerxes* (*Artakserksovo deistvo*), staged on 17 October 1672 by the German pastor Johann Gottfried Gregory (1631–1675). Alongside several collaborators and translators, Gregory not only wrote the text and organised its staging but also established his own school of actors. The plays written by Gregory and his collaborators were most likely grounded in German drama, while possibly also taking influence from Italian *commedia dell'arte*.

Aleksei Mikhailovich's court theatre continued for several more years. Its repertoire primarily consisted of plays translated from German or based on the Bible, saints' lives, or – more rarely – history and mythology. The main figure at the court theatre was the tsar himself, who presumably attended all of its performances. Members of the court were also obliged to attend performances, which could sometimes last up to ten hours. In large part, the peculiarities of drama in this period were rooted in this focus on the tsar's court. This is reflected in the attention paid to the ruler's portrayal and in allusions to contemporary political events. For instance, *The Play of Temir-Aksak: A Short Comedy about Bayazet and Tamerlane* (*Temir-Aksakovo deistvo: Malaia komediia o Baiazete i Tamerlane*, 1675) – based on the French bishop Jean du Bec's *History of Tamerlane the Great* (1595) – revolves around the confrontation between two rulers: the wise and God-fearing Timur (Tamerlane) and the hubristic Ottoman sultan Bayezid I, whose reign culminates in catastrophic military defeat and his own suicide. The unexpectedly positive depiction of Timur was precipitated by the ongoing conflict between Russia and the Ottomans, which would continue until 1681; the Ottomans' enemy could only be viewed positively at the Russian court.

In parallel with court theatre, the seventeenth century also witnessed the development of 'school drama' (*shkol'naia drama*). Its emergence owed much to Ukrainian culture, the genre having flourished at the Kyiv-Mohyla Academy. Among the academy's graduates was Simeon Polotskii (1629–1680; see Chapters 1.2, 3.3). One of the most significant centres of school drama was the Slavonic-Greek-Latin Academy in Moscow, established in 1687. School drama was based on the Roman comedies of Terence and Plautus and replicated the structure of classical Greek theatre, with an

anti-prologue, prologue, and epilogue interspersed with choruses and with dances set to music. Plots were taken from religious and political history and featured an abundance of mythological and allegorical images, alongside magnificently opulent staging.[1] Muscovite school drama also reflected contemporary political events, especially during the reign of Peter I ('the Great', r. 1682–1725).

In the first half of the eighteenth century, court theatres in St Petersburg and Moscow continually appeared and disappeared. When operating, they would stage Italian, French, and German plays, mostly in their original languages. To overcome the language barrier, audiences were provided with a plot summary. While Russian theatre remained oriented primarily around the court, performances at the theatre established by Peter I's sister, Princess Natalia Alekseevna, were made accessible to a broader audience. Whereas under Aleksei Mikhailovich actors were often coerced into performing, the first half of the eighteenth century saw the rise of the so-called hunters (*okhotniki*), who sought to become actors of their own volition (this, rather than hunting, is what is expressed in the archaic use of the term *okhota*). These hunters rarely came from the highest strata of society, although interest in the theatre did also grow among the privileged youth of St Petersburg and Moscow, for whom participation in productions offered direct access to the monarch.

A turning point came with the plays of Aleksandr Sumarokov (1717–1777). Sumarokov had studied in St Petersburg at the Land Forces Cadet School, an elite institution for aristocrats. From the school's students he had found the actors for his tragedy *Khorev* (*Khorev*, 1747), performed at the court of the empress Elizabeth (r. 1741–62). *Khorev* was the first of Sumarokov's nine tragedies, which would form the core repertoire of Russian theatres until the 1780s.

In terms of composition, plot structure, and form, Sumarokov looked above all to French drama of the seventeenth and eighteenth centuries.[2] He directly invoked Voltaire, translated a scene into Russian from his tragedy *Zaïre* (*Zaïre*, 1732), and even engaged in correspondence with the French

---

1 Iu. K. Begunov, 'Ranniaia russkaia dramaturgiia (konets XVII–pervaia polovina XVIII v.)' [Early Russian drama from the late seventeenth to mid-eighteenth centuries], in L. M. Lotman (ed.), *Istoriia russkoi dramaturgii: XVII–pervaia polovina XIX veka* [A History of Russian dramaturgy from the seventeenth to the first half of the nineteenth century] (Leningrad: Nauka, 1982), p. 34.

2 Unlike the purely syllabic form of earlier Russian plays, Sumarokov wrote in iambic hexameter.

writer.[3] Sumarokov considered tragedy's primary task to lie in depicting violent passions: 'hearts are most sensitive to tragedy, and it entrusts itself to such artists whom thought can lead into the passions of others and who can feel the woes and misfortunes of others'.[4] While his tragedies reflect the prevailing court culture of Elizabeth's reign, they also betray a distinctive agenda: to emotionally educate a new and Europeanised type of aristocrat. Sumarokov offered his audiences models of behaviour and experience from Russian history, prompting them to reflect on their feelings and obligations towards their family and country as well as towards forms of authority both just and unjust. Sumarokov's tragedies were notably popular with audiences, including the empress herself, who decreed that other Russian writers should also compose tragedies. Consequently, Sumarokov's main literary rivals turned their hand to the genre, and 1750 saw the appearance of *Deidamia* (*Deidamiia*) by Vasilii Trediakovskii (1703–1768), and *Tamira and Salim* (*Tamira i Salim*) by Mikhail Lomonosov (1711–1765).

Sumarokov is also considered the author of the first Russian comedy. Earlier plays that had been defined as comedies (*komediia, komidiia*) hardly adhere to modern notions of the genre. Sumarokov's comedies fulfilled a new cultural function by engaging with contemporary literary debates. *Tresotinius* (*Tresotinius*, 1750), for instance, lampoons Trediakovskii, depicting him as a farcical pedant – a role most likely influenced by Molière's comedy *The Learned Ladies* (1672). Trediakovskii responded in kind. Continuing Sumarokov's comedy with a scene of his own, entitled 'Arkhisotolash' (*Arkhisotolash*, 1750), he portrayed Sumarokov as a rude, uncouth dandy with pretensions to cultural influence.

By the latter half of the eighteenth century, Russian theatre – with a repertoire now bolstered by Sumarokov and his acolytes – was no longer limited to court circles, a shift illustrated by the career of Fedor Volkov (1729–1763). Volkov came from a merchant family and had spent time in St Petersburg and Moscow, where he was introduced to both school drama and court theatre; he subsequently founded his own theatre in Yaroslavl, where he played tragic roles. Volkov – usually considered the forefather of publicly accessible theatre in Russia – would later lead the actors' company at the first state-run public theatre, established in 1756 with Sumarokov as

---

3 Sumarokov's letter has not survived. For Voltaire's flattering reply, see Amanda Ewington, *A Voltaire for Russia: A. P. Sumarokov's Journey from Poet-Critic to Russian Philosophe* (Evanston, IL: Northwestern University Press, 2010), pp. 157–8.

4 Aleksandr P. Sumarokov, 'Two epistles: Epistle II', in Harold B. Segel (ed. and trans.), *The Literature of Eighteenth-Century Russia*, 2 vols. (New York: E. P. Dutton, 1967), vol. I, p. 238.

director. Scholars have suggested that Volkov's familiarity with anti-absolutist plays of the time led him to take an active role in the palace coup of 1762, when Peter III was deposed and replaced by Catherine II ('the Great', r. 1762–96).

Catherine's reign saw the rapid development of theatre: state- and privately run theatres proliferated not only in St Petersburg and Moscow but also in provincial Russia. Among especially wealthy and influential nobles, it became fashionable to establish estate theatres, with actors drawn from the ranks of both the local nobility and serfs, the latter often by coercion. These theatres became sufficiently influential that they gave rise to 'folk drama' (narodnaia drama), a genre that nonetheless remained strongly influenced by 'literary' plays. In performances of plays such as Tsar Maksimilian (Tsar' Maksimilian) and The Boat (Lodka), which took place in market squares and during festivities, the principles of traditional folklore and the influence of modern theatrical culture came together in complex ways. For example, the subjects of these plays reflected both historical events (such as the murder of Prince Aleksei by Tsar Peter I) and grassroots social conflicts.

The need to provide theatres with an adequate repertoire prompted a swift growth in the number of both original dramatic works and translations. Russian drama of this period, in particular comedy, was largely aimed at entertainment, though the state authorities and many among the elite considered theatre's core function to lie in shaping the audience's behaviour, emotions, and political beliefs. This was the view of Catherine II herself, who wrote several satirical comedies including Oh These Times! (O vremia!, 1772), which ridiculed those who blindly imitated French society, and The Siberian Shaman (Shaman sibirskii, 1786), which took aim at Freemasonry.

The most significant development of the later eighteenth century was the appearance of two prose comedies by Denis Fonvizin (1745–1792): The Brigadier (Brigadir, 1769) and The Minor (Nedorosl', 1782), the latter of which is still regularly performed in Russia and features on the secondary school curriculum. Both of Fonvizin's comedies satirise the morals of a nobility that, in the absence of any genuine enlightenment, is incapable of fulfilling its social and moral obligations to the state. The theme of enlightenment and its absence is especially pronounced in The Minor. The provincial noblewoman Madame Prostakova's inability to either manage her affairs or properly raise her son, Mitrofan, leads to catastrophic results: for cruelly treating their serfs, Prostakova and her husband are forbidden from selling their property and

lose control of their household entirely. Mitrofan rudely spurns his mother when he realises that she cannot bring him any material gain. Fonvizin's notion of educating an ideal member of the nobility within a modernising monarchy is underlined when Prostakova refers to a recent decree of Catherine II:

SKOTININ   Do you mean to tell me that a gentleman hasn't got the right to clout a servant when he wants to?

PRAVDIN   When he wants to? But what a thing to want! A real Beast, you are. No, Madam [Prostakova], nobody is free to act the tyrant.

PROSTAKOVA Not free! A gentleman not free to flog the servants when he wants to! What was the point, then, of giving us the Decree of the Freedom of the Gentry![5]

The most significant authorial mouthpiece of the play, in the mould of Molière's *raisonneurs*, is the evocatively named Starodum – an amalgamation of *staryi* (old) and *dumat'* (to think). Starodum sharply criticises contemporary morals, contrasting them with the social order of Peter I's Russia: 'my father brought me up in the style of his day, and I have never found any need to re-educate myself. He served Peter the Great.'[6]

Fonvizin's works were enormously successful. He conducted multiple readings of *The Brigadier*, including to the empress herself, who offered her 'most gracious congratulations on [his] reading'.[7] When *The Minor* was staged at Karl Knipper's privately run theatre in 1782, it enjoyed similar success: by some accounts, the adoring audience threw purses full of money onto the stage.

Satirical Comedy and Russian Society: Griboedov's *Woe from Wit*

The turn of the nineteenth century witnessed the state's desire to exercise ever greater control over the theatre, especially in St Petersburg and Moscow. By this time, theatres across Russia were being attended by a wider range of audiences than 'serious' literature attracted, ranging from

---

5 Denis Fonvizin, *The Minor*, in Joshua Cooper (trans.), *Four Russian Plays* (Harmondsworth: Penguin, 1972), p. 117. Skotinin's name is derived from *skot* (livestock).
6 Fonvizin, *The Minor*, p. 73.
7 D. I. Fonvizin, *Sobranie sochinenii v dvukh tomakh* [Collected works in two volumes] (Moscow: Gosudarstvennoe izdatel'stvo khudozhestvennoi literatury, 1959), vol. II, p. 97.

the aristocracy to the peasants working in the towns. The situation sufficiently concerned the authorities that they implemented particularly strict controls – not least as privately run theatres were now competing with those run by the state. To this end, the so-called theatre monopoly was introduced, banning privately run theatres from operating in St Petersburg and Moscow. Censorship of drama also grew progressively stricter: from 1825, staging a play meant obtaining personal authorisation from the head of the political police. Such measures led to the emergence of a unique working environment for playwrights. Compared to other authors, they were required to write for a generally less educated audience, to submit to strict censorship rules, and to cultivate relationships with the bureaucrats who oversaw performances – all while producing works in the enormous quantities demanded by theatres.

As a result, a specific form of writing for the stage developed. Its authors rarely held out any hope of achieving critical success, and they often failed to publish their work at all. The critic Vissarion Belinskii (1811–1848; see Box 5.1) remarked that 'drama in this country forms a kind of discrete sphere, lying outside of Russian literature'.[8] Literary historians have tended to gloss over such writers for the stage, despite their enormous success and influence. One such playwright was Aleksandr Shakhovskoi (1777–1846), who wrote more than one hundred plays for the stage while also serving as an official in the Imperial Theatres Directorate. Shakhovskoi sought to create Russia's own form of national comedy, grounded in both Romantic tendencies and the plays of Molière.

Aleksandr Griboedov's (1795–1829) comedy Woe from Wit (Gore ot uma, comp. 1824) marked a watershed in Russian drama. The literary scholar Iurii Tynianov (1894–1943) suggested in the early twentieth century that the play was primarily written for success on the stage, rather than to be read.[9] More recent scholars have, however, shown convincingly how Woe from Wit owed much both to the poetics of high comedy at the turn of the nineteenth century and to the French dramatic tradition: it was to France that Griboedov, in Tynianov's terms an 'archaist', turned in search of an alternative to Romanticism. At first glance, Woe from Wit is an entirely conventional play. Not only is it written in iambic verse of varying line lengths but the

8 V. G. Belinskii, 'Russkaia literatura v 1842 godu' [Russian literature in 1842], in *Sobranie sochnienii v deviati tomakh* [Collected works in nine volumes] (Moscow: Khudozhestvennaia literatura, 1976–82), vol. V, p. 215.

9 Iu. N. Tynianov, *Pushkin i ego sovremenniki* [Pushkin and his contemporaries] (Moscow: Nauka, 1968), p. 146.

action takes place across a single day in a single house – the mansion of the wealthy and high-ranking bureaucrat Famusov. The premise of the play is also entirely conventional. Several suitors vie for the attention of Famusov's daughter, Sofia: the career-minded colonel Skalozub; Famusov's meek and impoverished secretary, Molchalin; and Chatskii, a childhood acquaintance of Sofia's and the play's protagonist. Chatskii assumes the role of comic eccentric, delivering lengthy monologues on a range of subjects while failing to realise that those around him are unable, and do not want, to understand him. Although Sofia had once admired Chatskii's wit, she no longer approves of his bitterly ironic world view – and in any case she is not in love with him but with Molchalin.

Nonetheless, Griboedov by and large avoids conventional comic strategies. Whereas a verse comedy is meant to have five acts, *Woe from Wit* only has four. Griboedov's play also neglects the standard comic finale: a wedding. *Woe from Wit* ends with Famusov and his guests mistakenly believing that Sofia is at a secret rendezvous with Chatskii. Her reputation destroyed in the eyes of Muscovite society, Sofia is sent away by her incandescent father to live on her aunt's provincial estate. Meanwhile, Molchalin turns out to be both a fraud – it becomes clear almost immediately that he prefers Sofia's servant Liza – and a victim of Sofia, whose elevated social position allows her to ruin his career at any moment. Most significant, however, is the protagonist's own transformation. It is Chatskii who often acts as the play's *raisonneur*, delivering lengthy monologues on prevailing Muscovite mores – pronouncements largely borne out by the other characters' behaviour. He is sharply contrasted with Muscovite society, failing to find any common ground with those around him; Sofia, hence, has little difficulty convincing them that he is simply mad. In Fonvizin's plays the truth of the protagonist's world view can at least be confirmed with reference to a higher political authority. In *Woe from Wit*, Griboedov instead emphasises how Chatskii is incapable of getting along not only with the Muscovite elite but also with bureaucrats in St Petersburg:

> We heard the story
> from Tatiana Iurevna on her return
> from Petersburg. It seems the minister
> in favour, did an unexpected turnaround [against Chatskii].[10]

---

10 Alexander Griboedov, *Woe from Wit*, trans. Betsy Hulick (New York: Columbia University Press, 2020), p. 80.

Within the confines of the play, the sole guarantee of Chatskii's judgement is his self-confidence. In this vein, his disappointment in Sofia and his desire to flee his 'native Moscow' – to which he has only just returned – are in many ways closer to the motif of the Romantic hero, fleeing in search of the fundamentally unattainable. A similar process of disappointment also afflicts Sofia, who realises that Molchalin has never loved her and was merely pretending in fear of her influence. As Chatskii remarks:

> Farewell to Moscow, to its days and nights!
> I'm off to search the wide world round
> for somewhere I can go to ground
> and set insulted sense to rights.
> My carriage! Bring my carriage round![11]

By depicting both Muscovite society and a protagonist opposed to it, Griboedov assumes the existence of an external source of authority, capable of independently judging the events of the play. At the very least, it is difficult to describe *Woe from Wit* as a Romantic play: Chatskii 'is both a Romantic hero and a parody of one whose truest home is the road'.[12] The play presents a sweeping panorama of Muscovite life, a peculiarly self-contained world inhabited by memorable characters understood at the time both as witty caricatures of specific people and as contemporary social types. Yet Griboedov also repeatedly emphasises the profound immorality of that society. It was hardly a coincidence that this social aspect of *Woe from Wit* appealed to Russian writers in the second half of the nineteenth century, the age of Realism.

It was for the audience to adjudicate on the conflict depicted in *Woe from Wit*. On one level, they were called upon to sympathise with Chatskii; on another, to appreciate the funny side of his situation. While a single character can hardly withstand the massed ranks of Griboedov's Moscow, the community formed by the audience may be more willing. During Griboedov's life, however, no audience ever saw the play: while one version was staged in 1831, the censors banned the full text from being published until 1833, and then only with excisions. Faced with this censorship, *Woe from Wit* was instead extensively distributed in handwritten manuscripts.

---

11 Griboedov, *Woe from Wit*, p. 152.
12 Ingrid Kleespies, '"What good is all this cleverness and travel?" The woe of the road in Griboedov's *Woe from Wit*', *Slavic and Eastern European Journal* 63.4 (2019), 539.

Satirical Comedy and Russian Society: Gogol's
The Government Inspector

Comedy that addressed social and political issues remained the prevailing genre even after Griboedov, retaining its success both in literary circles and on the stage. Intriguingly, it was never a genre that Aleksandr Pushkin (1799–1837) turned to during his experiments with drama in the late 1820s and early 1830s. His cycle of so-called little tragedies published in 1830 – *The Miserly Knight* (*Skupoi rytsar'*), *Mozart and Salieri* (*Motsart i Sal'eri*), *The Stone Guest* (*Kamennyi gost'*), and *A Feast during the Plague* (*Pir vo vremia chumy*) – bear little relation to the overall development of Russian drama. His play *Boris Godunov* (*Boris Godunov*, 1825), meanwhile, formally replicated Shakespeare's histories and was based on the Time of Troubles at the turn of the seventeenth century. It, too, was hardly written with the stage in mind. The main direction taken by Russian drama, however, is associated not with Pushkin but with Nikolai Gogol (1809–1852). Gogol paid close attention to his comedies' staging, to the point of giving detailed instructions to the actors. His most famous play, *Inspector General* (*Revizor*, 1836), fundamentally reshaped the comedic form. To the surprise of contemporary audiences, there is barely any love story in the play, which instead focuses on social and political issues; Gogol himself was a great admirer of Aristophanes and evidently sought to update ancient Greek political comedy for a nineteenth-century audience. The action focuses on the corrupt and ignorant bureaucrats of an anonymous town in the depths of Russia, from whence 'you could gallop for three years without reaching a foreign country'.[13] A high-ranking inspector is due to arrive from St Petersburg, but a wild misunderstanding leads the bureaucrats to believe that the inspector is Khlestakov, a low-grade official living off credit at the local hotel. After giving Khlestakov a vast sum of money and deferentially escorting him from the town, the bureaucrats relax – only for a gendarme to appear at the end of the play, announcing the arrival of the real inspector.

The notion of the mirror image, both identical and diametrically opposed to reality, plays a vital role in *Inspector General*. The normal functioning of town life is flipped on its head. The bureaucrats do not merely commit crimes but are convinced that they are supposed to. For instance, the head of the local police rebukes a police constable not for taking bribes but because he is

---

13 Nikolai Gogol, *Plays and Petersburg Tales*, trans. Christopher English (Oxford: Oxford University Press, 2008), p. 250.

pocketing too much: 'you're taking more than your rank permits'.[14] In the so-called lying scene, meanwhile, Khlestakov attempts to behave as the local bureaucrats expect him to, reflecting their preconceptions about the capital. He ever more animatedly describes himself as an extraordinarily influential figure in Petersburg society. Declaring that 'even the State Council is scared stiff of me', Khlestakov upends the bureaucratic hierarchy.[15] As the audience already knows, he occupies the lowest possible rank in that hierarchy – collegiate registrar – while this last claim makes him almost tsar-like. At the end of the play, the motif of the mirror returns in a different guise: its reflection is held up to the audience itself. Stunned by the sudden arrival of the gendarme, all the bureaucrats freeze, petrified in front of the audience. Gogol himself insisted that this 'mute scene' should last several minutes. The difficulty, and the challenge, to both audience and actors, of this demand makes better sense in light of the play's proverbial epigraph: 'it's no use blaming the mirror if your face is askew'.[16] By all accounts, the frozen characters were meant to be understood as a kind of mirror image of the auditorium: Gogol intended that the audience should recognise themselves in the characters. Such an interpretation is suggested by the mayor's words to his fellow bureaucrats – words that are of course also to the audience:

> I shall be the laughing stock of the country. And as if that weren't sufficient, some hack, some penny-a-liner will come along and stick us all in a comedy. That's the worst of it! They'll spare nothing! They'll take no notice of rank, or reputation; anything to raise a few cheap laughs and to make the rabble clap. What are you laughing at? You're laughing at yourselves, that's what![17]

The range of interpretations of Gogol's play is remarkably broad. On the one hand, it has been understood as an accurate depiction of daily life in provincial Russia, a 'mirror' to the morally lamentable state of Russian society. It was this interpretation that found favour with Belinskii, who believed that Gogol sought to contrast the characters' false consciousness with the reality invoked by the genuine inspector. On the other hand, in his later writings Gogol insisted on a religiously allegorical reading of the play: 'the inspector is our conscience, now awoken, forcing us to suddenly look at ourselves with our eyes wide open. Nothing can escape this inspector, for he

---

14 Gogol, *Plays and Petersburg Tales*, p. 261. 15 Gogol, *Plays and Petersburg Tales*, p. 288.
16 Gogol, *Plays and Petersburg Tales*, p. 245. 17 Gogol, *Plays and Petersburg Tales*, p. 334.

is sent by His Own Highest Command, and his coming will be announced when there is no chance of retreat.'[18]

Either way, Gogol's play aimed to reveal to the audience its own inner self – whether socially or metaphysically – and encourage its moral transformation. While laughing at Gogol's characters, the audience was meant to recoil in horror at this reflection of their world and to renounce their own vices. In a famous commentary on his own work, Gogol lamented, 'I'm sorry nobody noticed the honest face in my play. . . . That honest, noble face was *laughter.*'[19]

Drama in an Age of Reform: The Case of Ostrovskii

The mid- to late nineteenth century was marked by rapid developments in Russian theatre. While the theatre monopoly continued to apply in St Petersburg and Moscow, there was a boom in the number of theatres in provincial Russia. In cities such as Nizhny Novgorod and Kazan, privately owned theatres appeared for the first time. Such high-risk ventures frequently failed but eventually became more financially secure. Throughout Russia, theatres needed more and more plays. While the stage had been dominated in the 1830s and 1840s by patriotic historical plays and vaudevilles, in the two decades following 1850 its repertoire became rapidly politicised. Especially successful were plays that tackled contemporary issues: bribe-taking bureaucrats, as in the trilogy *Pictures of the Past* (*Kartiny proshlogo*, 1854–69) by Aleksandr Sukhovo-Kobylin (1817–1903); nihilism; and the collapse of the traditional social order. However, most popular playwrights – figures such as Nikolai Polevoi (1796–1846), Petr Karatygin (1805–1879), and, later, Nikolai Lvov (1821–1872) and Viktor Diachenko (1818–1876) – were not seen as notable writers and reviews were disparaging.

The most successful synthesis of 'serious' literature with writing for the stage was achieved by Aleksandr Ostrovskii (1823–1886). On the one hand, Ostrovskii's works aimed to update the theatre repertoire (of his roughly fifty plays, nearly half are still performed in Russia). On the other, his plays were also published in the so-called thick journals (see Chapter 2.4) and discussed

18 N. V. Gogol', 'Razviazka Revizora' [The denouement of *Inspector General*], in *Polnoe sobranie sochinenii v 14 tomakh* [Complete works in 14 volumes] (Moscow: Izdatel'stvo Akademii nauk SSSR, 1937–52), vol. IV, p. 130.

19 N. V. Gogol', 'Teatral'nyi raz"ezd posle predstavleniia novoi komedii' [Leaving the theatre after the performance of a new comedy], in *Polnoe sobranie sochinenii*, vol. V, p. 169.

by critics. Like Gogol before him, Ostrovskii wrote with a wide spectrum of audiences in mind – from the well-educated to the illiterate, and from wealthy nobles to the urban poor. This helps explain several overarching features across his plays. The influential critic Nikolai Dobroliubov (1836–1861) defined Ostrovskii's works as 'slice-of-life plays' (*p'esy zhizni*); in other words he rejected dramatic and literary conventions to instead reflect social reality. In fact, Ostrovskii seems to have seen no contradiction between these two goals. His plays include patently conventional characters alongside allusions and references to a variety of authors and periods. He was very familiar with European drama and had even translated Shakespeare, Cervantes, Goldoni, and others into Russian. Yet Ostrovskii equally sought to reflect social questions, and his plays touched on serfdom, the emancipation of women, the development of capitalism, and other contemporary issues. He was convinced that the audience should be able to laugh – he considered most of his plays to be comedies – while also being immersed in the plot, empathising with the characters, and encountering dramatic influences from abroad. All this was intended to enable the development of a modern audience, capable of learning something from the play.

Ostrovskii's first play, which brought him enormous literary success as well as the personal animosity of Nicholas I (r. 1825–55), was the comedy *It's a Family Affair – We'll Settle It Ourselves! (Svoi liudi – sochtemsia!*, 1850). As in *Inspector General*, its plot is built around the conventional motif of a crook who ends up deceived. A rich Muscovite merchant, Samson Silych Bolshov, declares himself bankrupt. To deceive his creditors, he transfers all his property to his clerk, Lazar Podkhaliuzin. At the same time, Bolshov marries off his daughter, Olimpiada, to Podkhaliuzin. By the end of the play, however, neither Bolshov's daughter nor his son-in-law are in any hurry to pay for his release from the debtors' prison he has ended up in. Ostrovskii's contemporaries were quick to draw the parallel between Bolshov, beseeching his daughter to save him, and King Lear – as if Shakespeare's protagonist had reappeared in Moscow merchant society.

It's a Family Affair also depicts the gradual disintegration of a coherent merchant community. On learning in the newspapers about an epidemic of fake bankruptcies, Bolshov initially counts on his personal connections in the merchant community: 'he [one of Bolshov's creditors will] pay me back in full, out of friendliness'.[20] Eventually convinced of other merchants' untrustworthiness, however, Bolshov instead relies on members of his extended

---

20 Alexander Ostrovsky, *Five Plays*, trans. Eugene K. Bristow (New York: Pegasus, 1969), p. 57.

family – his daughter and her husband. By contrast, Podkhaliuzin, part of the next generation of Moscow merchants, trusts only his very closest relatives: while he is happy to trick Bolshov, he genuinely does fulfil the promises he has made to his wife. In a world of newspapers, financial machinations, and business deals, any patriarchal sense of social identity is no longer possible, and so this disintegrating community of Moscow merchants gives way to another, more modern form of social organisation. At the end of the play, one of Podkhaliuzin's victims finally finds a figure of authority he can turn to: the audience.

RISPOLOZHENSKII   You think nobody will believe me, do you? Won't believe me, is it? Well, let them say what they want to me. I will ... Here's what I'll do. [...] Oh, most respectable public![21]

And a few lines later:

RISPOLOZHENSKII   Hold on a bit, will you! Oh, most respectable public! [...]

PODKHALIUZIN   He's lying about everything, ladies and gentlemen. A very shallow person, ladies and gentlemen. That's enough, you, stop it.[22]

The audience, hence, serves as a model of contemporary society. While earlier playwrights had explicitly highlighted the role of the state, Ostrovskii believed the aesthetic and moral arbiter to be the audience itself. At the time, the state's absence in *It's a Family Affair* was sufficiently unexpected that the censor banned its staging for ten years. When it was finally permitted, Ostrovskii was required to introduce a standard 'police' ending, with Podkhaliuzin punished not in the court of public opinion but at a criminal trial.

Ostrovskii took a different direction in his most famous play, *The Storm* (*Groza*, 1859). Set in the (fictional) town of Kalinov, on the banks of the Volga, the play focuses on the fate of Katerina, the wife of a merchant she does not love. After being unfaithful to her husband, Katerina tries to atone with a public show of repentance, only to succeed in attracting the ire of her traditionalist mother-in-law, the despotic Kabanikha (her name is a nickname and describes her as a 'boar'). Unable to reconcile with herself or those

---

21 Ostrovsky, *Five Plays*, p. 107.   22 Ostrovsky, *Five Plays*, pp. 107–8.

around her, Katerina commits suicide. The other characters hold not only Katerina herself responsible for the tragedy but also the wider inertia of provincial life. Shortly before her death, Katerina's husband, Tikhon, physically assaults her – not out of rage at her betrayal but on the orders of his mother. In the final scene of the play, he finally blames his mother for Katerina's death: 'Mama, you have killed her! You, you, you . . .'.[23] Elsewhere, an entire monologue on the social order of provincial Russia is delivered by Kuligin, a self-taught mechanic who naïvely enlightens the audience:

> long before dusk, [the rich people of the town have] bolted their gates and untied their dogs. I suppose you'd think they were hard at work or repeating their prayers. No, sir, that's not it at all. And they haven't locked their doors because of thieves, either. It's simply they don't want people to see the way they browbeat their servants. Yes, and the way they ride roughshod over their own family. And the tears that are shed behind those locked doors – tears that no one sees, cries that no one hears.[24]

Nearly all Ostrovskii's contemporaries read *The Storm* as a critique of *narodnost'*, a key issue in Russian literature leading up to the emancipation of the serfs in 1861. Derived from *narod* (people), the term defies easy translation, and critics at the time defined *narodnost'* differently: the radically minded Dobroliubov believed that the *narod* constituted victims of social and political inequality; Apollon Grigorev (1822–1864), an adherent of the 'return to the soil' movement (*pochvennichestvo*), defined *narodnost'* as the expression of a mysterious national spirit; and the moderate liberal Pavel Annenkov (1813–1887) perceived *narodnost'* as a unique form of culture that had escaped Europeanising influences.[25]

In any event, what critics could agree on was that Katerina was destined to elicit sympathy from any audience. She certainly finds sympathy with all the other characters, from her European-educated lover, Boris, to the ordinary inhabitants of Kalinov. Ostrovskii's emphasis on the inevitability of her

23 Ostrovsky, *Five Plays*, p. 276.   24 Ostrovsky, *Five Plays*, p. 248.

25 N. A. Dobroliubov, 'Luch sveta v temnom tsarstve' [A ray of light in a dark kingdom], in *Sobranie sochinenii v deviati tomakh* [Collected works in nine volumes] (Moscow: Gosudarstvennoe izdatel'stvo khudozhestvennoi literatury, 1961–4), vol. VI, pp. 289–363; A. A. Grigor'ev, 'Posle "Grozy" Ostrovskogo' [After Ostrovskii's *The Storm*], in *Sochineniia v dvukh tomakh* [Works in two volumes] (Moscow: Khudozhestvennaia literatura, 1990), vol. II, pp. 212–45; P. V. Annenkov, '"Groza" Ostrovskogo i kriticheskaia buria' [Ostrovskii's *The Storm* and a critical storm], in *Kriticheskie ocherki* [Critical essays] (St Petersburg: Izdatel'stvo Khristianskogo gumanitarnogo instituta, 2000), pp. 233–57.

downfall – during her first appearance on stage, Katerina abruptly announces that she will soon die – has been identified by many scholars as bringing the play closer to classical tragedy as described by Aristotle. Deeply devout, Katerina considers her betrayal a grave sin and must commit suicide to absolve her guilt. Read in this way, *The Storm* – much like *It's a Family Affair* – is designed to unite the audience. In this case, however, the overriding emotional response is not outrage at the protagonist's crimes but compassion for a victim of historical processes that are eroding the traditional social order.

By the 1870s and 1880s, the number of privately owned theatres in provincial Russia was growing sharply, but their character was changing: no longer semi-amateur ventures, they were increasingly successful, able to attract successful actors and generate significant profit. In these circumstances, the theatre monopoly grew ever less relevant and was eventually abolished. This growth in the number of theatres led to increasing differentiation. 'Popular' theatres, aimed at illiterate and semi-literate peasants and workers, became increasingly divorced from those catering to 'respectable' audiences. In these circumstances, the earlier division between 'literary' theatre, on the one hand, and plays written for the stage, on the other, gave way to new tensions: between plays (*p'esy*), which were aimed at the 'cultured' classes, and performances produced for a mass audience, which continued to attract strict censorship. Certainly, the major Russian playwrights of earlier decades continued to write, and in this period Ostrovskii produced one of his masterpieces, *Without a Dowry* (*Bespridannitsa*, 1878). But the most notable dramatic achievements of the era are associated with new authors responding to new issues (see Chapter 3.7).

Conclusion

At the risk of oversimplifying the picture, three main phases can hence be discerned in Russian drama up to the 1870s. While dramatic works in the earliest phase were destined to be shown exclusively to the tsar and the court – or in the case of school drama, written strictly for didactic purposes – the most successful theatre of the second phase, from the mid-eighteenth to early nineteenth centuries, was related to efforts to educate a wider audience in a manner beneficial to the state and/or certain elements of the elite. The mid-nineteenth-century dramatists of the third phase, especially Gogol and Ostrovskii, sought to affect the audience on a different level, to create a unique type of community in the theatre: one united by an increasingly

strong imperative to pass judgement – on the state, on Russian society, and on themselves. It was this focus on the audience that was to define the next stage of Russian experimentation in theatre (see Chapter 3.7).

Translated by Angus Russell

Further Reading

Frame, Murray, *School for Citizens: Theatre and Civil Society in Imperial Russia* (New Haven: Yale University Press, 2006).

Golden, Robert Justin (ed.), *The Frightful Stage: Political Censorship of the Theater in Nineteenth-Century Europe* (New York: Berghahn Books, 2009).

Kholodov, E. G. et al. (eds.), *Istoriia russkogo dramaticheskogo teatra* [A history of Russian dramatic theatre], 7 vols. (Moscow: Iskusstvo, 1977–87).

Ospovat, Kirill, *Terror and Pity: Aleksandr Sumarokov and the Theater of Power in Elizabethan Russia* (Brighton, MA: Academic Studies Press, 2016).

Petrovskaia, I. F., *Teatr i zritel' provintsial'noi Rossii. Vtoraia polovina XIX veka* [The theatre and the spectator in provincial Russia in the second half of the nineteenth century] (Leningrad: Iskusstvo, 1979).

Schuler, Catherine A., *Theatre and Identity in Imperial Russia* (Iowa City: University of Iowa Press, 2009).

Sofronova, L. A., *Poetika slavianskogo teatra XVII–pervoi poloviny XVIII veka: Pol'sha, Ukraina, Rossiia* [The poetics of the Slavic theatre from the seventeenth to the first half of the eighteenth century: Poland, Ukraine, Russia] (Moscow: Nauka, 1971).

Starikova, L. M., *Teatr i zrelishcha rossiiskikh stolits v XVIII veke. Istoriko-dokumentirovannye ocherki* [Theatre and spectatorship in the Russian capital in the eighteenth century. Historical and documentary sketches (Moscow: GTsTM im. A. A. Bakhrushina, 2018).

Swift, E. Anthony, *Popular Theater and Society in Tsarist Russia* (Berkeley: University of California Press, 2002).

Wirtschafter, Elise Kimerling, *The Play of Ideas in Russian Enlightenment Theater* (DeKalb: Northern Illinois University Press, 2003).

3.5

The Novel I

ANNA A. BERMAN

The Russian novel rose to prominence in defiance of the genre. From its inception as a vital new tradition in the nineteenth century, the Russian novel has always been celebrated by both foreigners and Russian authors alike for *not* following the rules but instead offering something fresh and new. Astute critics like Eugène-Melchior de Vogüé, Henry James, and Virginia Woolf have attempted to characterise the difference, focusing on the formal peculiarities, the penetrating psychological depth, and what they described as the spiritual aura of these novels. Woolf claimed the Russians 'seemed to possess an entirely new conception of the novel and one that was larger, saner, and much more profound than ours. It was one that allowed human life in all its width and depth, with every shade of feeling and subtlety of thought, to flow into their pages. . . . Life was too serious to be juggled with. It was too important to be manipulated.'[1] For many critics abroad, Russian novels felt like a jolt of new life into a genre that was becoming too rigidly set in its ways. Russian authors saw this somewhat differently. Many who wrote the canonical works that shaped the nine-teenth-century tradition claimed they were *not* writing novels, describing their works as, for example, a 'novel in verse' with a 'devil of a difference' from the standard prose novel (*Eugene Onegin* (*Evgenii Onegin*, 1825–32) by Aleksandr Pushkin (1799–1837)); a collection of first- and third-person fragments (*A Hero of Our Time* (*Geroi nashego vremeni*, 1840) by Mikhail Lermontov (1814–1841)); a 'narrative poem', or *poema* (*Dead Souls* (*Mertvye dushi*, 1842) by Nikolai Gogol (1809–1852)); a sketch (*A Double Life* (*Dvoinaia zhizn'*, 1848) by Karolina Pavlova (1807–1893)); and an indefinable profusion of words that mixed fiction, history, and philosophical essays (*War and Peace* (*Voina i mir*, 1868–9) by Lev Tolstoi (1828–1910)). With these non-novels

---

1 Virginia Woolf, 'On rereading Meredith', in *Granite and Rainbow: Essays by Virginia Woolf* (London: Hogarth Press, 1958), p. 49.

as its basis, the Russian tradition has operated within less restrictive conventions.

At the same time, many novelists in the Russian Empire *were* writing more traditional novels. These, however, were not considered as great and did not come to define the canon. This is not just a matter of later scholars' tastes but also that of critics at the time who were carefully curating the nascent tradition. The pioneering literary critic Vissarion Belinskii (1811–1848; see Box 5.1), with his unfailing eye, picked out Pushkin, Lermontov, Gogol, and the young Fedor Dostoevskii (1821–1881) as exemplars of what Russian literature was and as beacons for the path the tradition should follow. Although Gogol was born and raised in Ukraine, he belongs in this list because he wrote in Russian, lived for a time in St Petersburg, positioned himself as a member of the Russian literary elite, and was a crucial inspiration and point of reference for the Russian writers who followed him. A combination of experimental initiators and deliberate, self-reflexive shaping of the tradition led the Russian novel to gain and maintain its reputation for pushing the boundaries and redefining the genre, despite the mass of more traditional works also produced. Thus, our understanding of 'the Russian novel' today is based primarily on exceptions – as well as on omissions. One misbelief that must finally be discarded is that the Russian nineteenth-century novel was an exclusively male tradition.[2] Nineteenth-century Russians would have been quite surprised by this idea, as the 'thick journals' in which most novels appeared (see Chapter 2.4) both published and reviewed many female authors alongside their male counterparts. Indeed, some of these women were considered among the best writers of their day, though, for a variety of reasons, they have subsequently dropped from view. Restoring them to their rightful place provides a more balanced picture of the novel's key features and scope in nineteenth-century Russia.

This chapter begins by considering the origins of the Russian novelistic tradition, acknowledging the eighteenth-century texts that helped develop Russian print culture but did not blaze a trail that later authors would follow. It then finds its centre of gravity in the true rise of the Russian novel in the mid- to late nineteenth century, with innovative originators such as Pushkin, Lermontov, and Gogol and powerful critics such as Belinskii. The remainder

---

2 We find this belief in standard reference works like *The Cambridge Companion to the Classic Russian Novel*, where Malcolm Jones claims, 'There have been no outstanding women prose writers in Russia until very recently.' Editor's preface to *The Cambridge Companion to the Classic Russian Novel*, ed. Malcolm V. Jones and Robin Feuer Miller (Cambridge: Cambridge University Press, 1998), p. 15.

of the chapter considers the defining characteristics of the great nineteenth-century Russian novels, focusing first on their formal traits and then on their content: their engagement with contemporary debates, their philosophical and psychological depth, and the important role played by Russia and national identity. Indeed, the form was defined in many ways by the breadth and depth of the material the novel was made to encompass: from the illusion of capturing everyday life through non-linear, multi-plot structures, to the penetration into the psyche that shaped narrative perspective. Therefore, the chapter will treat the content of these novels as an element that helped to define their form.

The Rise of the Russian Novel

Russia was a latecomer to writing novels and therefore, by necessity, built on European models. While some eighteenth-century Russian novels did help prepare the soil for the tradition's nineteenth-century flowering, these were mostly derivative of their western cousins, as, for example, Pavel Lvov's (1770–1825) *Russian Pamela* (*Rossiiskaia Pamela ili istoriia Marii, dobrodetel'noi poselianki*, 1789), which explicitly references its Richardsonian model in the title. New novels produced in Russia ranged from the politico-philosophical, to sentimental epistolary works, to the picaresque. Some scholars give credit to authors like Fedor Emin (1735?–1770), Mikhail Chulkov (1743?–1792), and Matvei Komarov (1730–1812) for going beyond blind imitation and note the way they parodied conventions, but their works – however original – did not launch a new national tradition.[3] Indeed, they quickly disappeared from print, as a result of which few people had the opportunity to read them, vastly diminishing their impact. However, these eighteenth-century writers played an essential role in laying the groundwork for a flourishing print culture in the nineteenth century.

The true rise of the Russian novel came in the second third of the nineteenth century under conditions that challenge western theories about what is required for a nation to embrace novel writing. According to Ian Watt's foundational (but much contested) *The Rise of the Novel* (1957), three factors contributed to the novel's ascent in England in the eighteenth century: capitalism, with its strong individualist ethic and the rise of the bourgeoisie; Protestantism, with its emphasis on personal spiritual quest; and

---

3 On the vindication of the eighteenth-century Russian novel, see David Wayne Gasperetti, *The Rise of the Russian Novel: Carnival, Stylization, and Mockery of the West* (DeKalb: Northern Illinois University Press, 1998), p. 5.

marriage practices that gave greater freedom to women, making possible the 'marriage plot' that is central to the European novel.[4] Russia, of course, had none of these things. Its tradition arose in a country with almost no bourgeoisie but instead a landed gentry and *raznochintsy* (literally, 'people of various ranks') who shared an intellectual milieu. Russian Orthodox, or Eastern, Christianity was infused with a communal spirit – Slavophiles emphasised *sobornost'* (togetherness, or spiritual unity) and *obshchina* (community) as central tenets – rather than the Protestant individualism touted by Watt.[5] And Russia had not inherited the courtly love tradition of the west that could be combined with a marriage tradition of free choice, making it poor soil for European-style courtship plots. Given these factors, it should be obvious that the novel would take a different form in Russia.

When Pushkin, Gogol, and Lermontov took up the pen, they were acutely aware of creating a new national tradition for the lands of Russia's growing empire. Andrew Kahn writes of a 'discontinuity principle', pointing to the way writers of the 1820s and 1830s saw themselves as initiators, a stance Belinskii reinforced in his essays.[6] Literary development in imperial Russia is notable for its belatedness and rapidity. While in the west scholars often write of a literary genealogy – Harold Bloom's famous 'anxiety of influence' – where sons must overthrow their 'poetic fathers', the relations between Russian authors were more fraternal; they wished to join, not overthrow, their elders. Pushkin and Tolstoi were born less than thirty years apart (with Gogol, Ivan Goncharov (1812–1891), Lermontov, Ivan Turgenev (1818–1883), Dostoevskii, and Mikhail Saltykov-Shchedrin (1826–1889) all born in the interval). Between the completion of *Eugene Onegin* in 1832 and *The Brothers Karamazov* (*Brat'ia Karamazovy*) in 1880, less than half a century had elapsed. Given these authors' concern for creating a national tradition for the Russian Empire, there was a sense of camaraderie in this shared endeavour.

Yet even as these trailblazers strove for originality, they were still deeply indebted to European models. Dostoevskii would call this a strength, framing

---

4 Ian Watt, *The Rise of the Novel: Studies in Defoe, Richardson and Fielding* (London: Pimlico, 2000), esp. pp. 60–1, 74–5, 84–5, 138.

5 *Sobornost'* was in fact a Romantic-era Slavophile invention, but this does not change the fact that Russians believed it was central to their faith. See Vasily V. Zenkovsky, 'The spirit of Russian Orthodoxy', *Russian Review* 22.1 (1963), 38–55, esp. 44.

6 Andrew Kahn, 'The rise of the Russian novel and the problem of romance', in Jenny Mandler (ed.), *Remapping the Rise of the European Novel* (Oxford: Voltaire Foundation, 2007), p. 186.

the Russians as the great inheritors and synthesisers of all European literature:

> every European poet, thinker, and humanitarian is more clearly and more intimately understood and received in Russia than he is in any other country in the world save his own. . . . And if this quality is truly our distinctively Russian national trait, then surely no oversensitive patriotism or chauvinism could have the right to object to it and not desire, on the contrary, to regard it primarily as a most promising and prophetic fact to be kept in mind as we speculate about our future.[7]

The Russians borrowed structures, tropes, and scenes from both French and English literature. Lermontov attempted to dramatise Denis Diderot's ideas about fatalism, while Dostoevskii – inspired by Honoré de Balzac – added the spiritual dimension he felt to be missing from the French novel.[8] Multiple authors wrote novels that were acknowledged re-envisionings of George Sand's *Jacques* (1833).[9] Writing after Sand's death, Dostoevskii claimed that she had 'become a Russian poet' and that in her influence on Russian thought she had 'become almost a Russian force'.[10] Dostoevskii, Tolstoi, and many others drew heavily on Charles Dickens, reworking characters, themes, and whole scenes from his novels. But this was not simple imitation. Dostoevskii's *The Insulted and the Injured* (*Unizhennye i oskorblennye*, 1861) may feature a Nellie who is based on Dickens's heroine from *The Old Curiosity Shop* (1840), but Dostoevskii's Nellie displays her author's unique psychological concern with pride, and her fate follows its own Dostoevskian course.

Form: Novels that Are Not Novels

Russian authors claimed they were not writing novels. Pushkin's *Eugene Onegin* is often the topic of 'chapter one' in studies of the Russian novel, yet as Pushkin wrote to Petr Viazemskii (1792–1878) after beginning composition, 'I am writing now – not a novel – but a novel in verse, a devil of

---

7 Fedor Dostoevskii, *Polnoe sobranie sochinenii v tridtsati tomakh* [Complete collected works in thirty volumes] (Leningrad: Izdatel'stvo Nauka, 1972–90), vol. XXIII, p. 31; English in Fyodor Dostoevsky, *A Writer's Diary: Volume 1, 1873–1876*, trans. Kenneth Lantz (Evanston, IL: Northwestern University Press, 1994), pp. 506–7.

8 On the Russians' responses to French literature, see Priscilla Meyer, *How the Russians Read the French: Lermontov, Dostoevsky, Tolstoy* (Madison: University of Wisconsin Press, 2008).

9 See Aleksandr Druzhinin's *Polinka Saks* (*Polinka Saks*, 1847) and Mikhail Avdeev's *Underwater Stone* (*Podvodnyi Kamen'*, 1860).

10 Dostoevskii, *Polnoe sobranie sochinenii*, vol. XXIII, p. 32; Dostoevsky, *Writer's Diary: Volume 1*, p. 507.

a difference (*une diable de différence*).[11] He created a unique fourteen-line stanza form in which to convey a traditional novelistic plot (see Box 1.1). *Onegin* merges the form and concerns of poetry with those of the novel, making Russia's transition to a prose-based tradition one of its central themes. The work is novelistic in its plotting of unhappy love and the character portraits it sketches. The heroine, Tatiana, has read the novels of Samuel Richardson, Jean-Jacques Rousseau, and Madame de Staël, and they shape her romantic imagination as she encounters Onegin. But the dominant narrator, with his lyrical digressions and reflections on his poetic muse, roots the work in the verse tradition. There is indeed a 'devil of a difference'.

This tantalising hybrid set a precedent for Russian novels to defy easy generic classification. Playing on the interaction of poetry and prose in a very different manner from Pushkin (and likely drawing on German models), Karolina Pavlova brought the two together in *A Double Life*. Each chapter moves between a society tale that is narrated in prose and the heroine Cecile's dreams, which appear in verse. The blended form demonstrates the two realms of Cecile's life: her prosaic everyday existence, in which her consciousness has been 'corseted' by the restrictive education society girls receive, versus her stifled inner life, which is poetic and emerges in sleep. Pavlova called the work not a novel but a 'sketch' (*ocherk*).[12]

Gogol's *Dead Souls* is a prose work that has the outward appearance of a novel, yet he labelled it a *poema*. This classification hints at its epic pretensions as the first part of what was meant to be a trilogy, leading readers from the inferno, to purgatory, to paradise. Many Russian novels blurred the boundaries between genres by incorporating poetry, essays, or even an 'ethnographic sketch of daily life in Petersburg prisons', as we find in *Petersburg Slums* (*Peterburgskie trushchoby*, 1864–6) of Vsevolod Krestovskii (1840–1895).[13] By the time the novel reached its heyday between the 1860s and 1880, such flexibility was an accepted feature.

---

11 Letter to Viazemskii, 4 Nov. 1823, in A. S. Pushkin, *Sobranie sochinenii v desiati tomakh* [Collected works in ten volumes] (Moscow: Gosudarstvennoe izdatel'stvo khudozhest-vennoi literatury, 1959–62), vol. IX, p. 77. A classic study that follows this model of beginning with *Onegin* is Richard Freeborn's *Rise of the Russian Novel: Studies in the Russian Novel from Eugene Onegin to War and Peace* (Cambridge: Cambridge University Press, 1973), which is typical in its range of coverage. After dealing with the eighteenth century very briefly, Freeborn has chapters on *Onegin*, *A Hero of Our Time*, *Dead Souls*, the period from the 1840s to the 1860s, the novels of Goncharov, *Crime and Punishment*, and finally *War and Peace*.

12 Karolina Pavlova, *A Double Life*, trans. Barbara Heldt (New York: Columbia University Press, 2019), p. 29.

13 A footnote at the start of Part IV of *Petersburg Slums* informs readers that the first eleven chapters of this part not only provide novelistic interest but also an ethnographic

Tolstoi's *War and Peace* is now considered one of the greatest novels of all time; however, Tolstoi claimed it was not a novel but 'what the author wanted and was able to express, in the form in which it is expressed'.[14] The work mixes genres, bringing together fictional heroes (the novel), an account of the war against Napoleon (history), and essays discussing the forces that move history and the relationship between freedom and necessity (philosophy). The original reviewers were baffled by this generic fluidity, complaining that the work lacked unity and a clearly defined plot.[15] They failed to see that this was deliberate on Tolstoi's part. He was polemicising with the genre of the novel, trying to show that a clear linear plot cannot be true to life, where we cannot know which details, incidents, or people will ultimately prove important. The fictional heroes' experiences act as a model in microcosm for Tolstoi's thesis in the philosophical essays about the individual's role in history. Each experiences the illusion of freedom in the present, unable to see the innumerable forces that constrain their actions; only from a distanced historical vantage point do these become clear. There is unity to *War and Peace*, but not traditional novelistic unity.

Authors like Tolstoi and Gogol who refused to call their works novels were not just being contrarian. While that might seem to be the case when measured against our twenty-first-century definitions of the genre, their resistance to the 'novel' label responded to more rigid mid-nineteenth-century generic expectations. Many nineteenth-century critics expected novels to create order from the messiness of life. Henry James argued that novelists must create a 'geometry' that confines relations to a clean circle, simplifying life.[16] Russian geometry, by contrast, was often about expansion. In the Russian novel, interest spreads laterally, focusing on characters' moral, social, and spiritual state in the present as they wrestle with the 'eternal questions', rather than being channelled towards a future marriage, death, or birth. Readers were baffled by such lateral spread. The French critic de Vogüé proclaimed in his foundational study *The Russian Novel* (1886), 'As we enter into their works we are disoriented by the lack of composition and apparent

sketch of the locale. They are replete with copious footnotes to explain the terminology and prison customs that appear in the sketch.

14 'A few words apropos of the book *War and Peace*' (1868), in Leo Tolstoy, *War and Peace*, trans. Richard Pevear and Larissa Volokhonsky (New York: Alfred A. Knopf, 2007), pp. 1217–24 (quotation on p. 1217).

15 See Gary Saul Morson, *Hidden in Plain View: Narrative and Creative Potentials in 'War and Peace'* (Stanford: Stanford University Press, 1987), pp. 49–52.

16 Henry James, 'Preface to Roderick Hudson', in *The Art of the Novel: Critical Prefaces, with an Introduction by R. P. Blackmur* (New York: Charles Scribner's Sons, 1937), p. 5.

action ...; they create on too large a scale and bring in too extraneous material for our taste'.[17] The Russian novel developed a reputation for formlessness, with James famously calling *War and Peace* a 'loose, baggy monster'.[18] Early European readers were more comfortable with Turgenev and his more traditionally structured narratives.

The looser approach to structure and composition of many Russian authors, however, was by design. As Anton Chekhov (1860–1904) later explained: 'There is no need for any plots. Life doesn't have plots; in life, everything is mixed together – the profound with the shallow, the great with the trivial, the tragic with the ludicrous.'[19] Such a flexible conception of plotting also had ideological implications; it created the illusion that the novels captured 'life' not 'art'. Russian authors were sceptical about traditional novel plots that led to prede- termined endings. Avoiding the determinism of such plots contributed to another distinctive feature of many Russian novels: their lack of narrative closure. Russian writers fought against what D. A. Miller calls 'the tyranny of a narrative so thoroughly predestined that it does nothing but produce spuri- ous problems for a solution already in place'.[20] When Jane Austen opens *Pride and Prejudice* (1813) with the claim, 'It is a truth universally acknowledged, that a single man in possession of a good fortune, must be in want of a wife', we already know that the novel will conclude with a marriage. Looser plots lack a clear denouement that could provide such closure.

Often Russian novels stop, rather than end. V. Krestovskii (pseudonym) (pen name for Nadezhda Khvoshchinskaia, 1821–1889) finishes *Ursa Major* (*Bol'shaia medveditsa*, 1871) with her unwed heroine looking up at the stars and hearing her former beloved call her name: 'No one was visible. / It was late! And tomorrow she had a lot to do.'[21] There is more that could be narrated. Dostoevskii explains in the closing lines of the epilogue of *Crime and Punishment* (*Prestuplenie i nakazanie*, 1867):

> But here begins a new account, the account of a man's gradual renewal, the account of his gradual regeneration, his gradual transition from one world to

17 E.-M. De Vogüé, preface to *Le Roman russe* [The Russian novel] (1866), excerpted as 'On Russian and French Realism', in George Joseph Becker (ed.), *Documents of Modern Literary Realism* (Princeton: Princeton University Press, 2015), p. 337.

18 Henry James. *The Tragic Muse: In Two Volumes* (London: MacMillan and Co., Limited, 1921), vol. I, p. xi.

19 As recorded in A. I. Bunin, *O Chekhove* [About Chekhov] (New York: Izdatel'stvo imeni Chekhova, 1955), p. 212.

20 D. A. Miller, *Narrative and Its Discontents: Problems of Closure in the Traditional Novel* (Princeton: Princeton University Press, 1981), p. xiii.

21 V. Krestovskii, *Polnoe sobranie sochinenii* [Complete collected works], 6 vols. (St Petersburg: A. A. Kaspari, 1913), vol. VI, p. 731.

another, his acquaintance with a new, hitherto completely unknown reality. It might make the subject of a new story – but our present story is ended.[22]

The stopping point is not the end of the story; life goes on.

Content: Ideological and Philosophical Weight

Russian novels are known for their philosophical heft and intense intellectual debates. Given the tight censorship in Russia and the lack of viable forums for public discourse, much of the social critique and commentary that in Europe would have had other outlets found its way into novels and literary criticism. The radical critic Dmitrii Pisarev (1840–1868) wrote in 1861:

> [Russian realist novels] have for us not only an aesthetic but also a social interest. The English have Dickens, Thackeray, and Eliot, but they also have John Stuart Mill; the French have journalists and socialists as well as novelists. But in Russia the whole sum of ideas about society, about the human personality, about social and family relations, is concentrated in *belles lettres* and in the criticism of *belles lettres*; we do not have an independent moral philosophy, we do not have a social science, and so we must look for all of this in literary works.[23]

This heightened role helps account for the seriousness with which the Russians treated the genre and for some of the expansiveness of its form. There was much to accommodate. *Anna Karenina (Anna Karenina*, 1878) is not a straightforward adultery novel like Flaubert's *Madame Bovary* (1856); Tolstoi is also seriously concerned about the role of the peasant in agriculture, new aesthetic movements, and advances in science. Scenes like Levin's dissatisfaction with a concert of programme music or his discussions of farming practices may not move the plot forwards in any essential way, but the novel was not motivated by a linear plot. Similarly, many of the most famous scenes in Dostoevskii's novels are heated intellectual exchanges that do not produce or resolve action but supply the novel with its core philosophy and meaning. Ivan's 'rebellion' and his legend of the Grand Inquisitor are the philosophical heart of *The Brothers Karamazov*, anchoring its plot.

---

22 Dostoevskii, *Polnoe sobranie sochinenii*, vol. VI, p. 422; English in Fyodor Dostoevsky, *Crime and Punishment: A Novel in Six Parts with Epilogue*, trans. Richard Pevear and Larissa Volokhonsky (London: Vintage Books, 2007), p. 551.
23 Dmitrii Pisarev, *Sochineniia v chetyrekh tomakh* [Works in four volumes] (Moscow: Gosudarstvennoe izdatel'stvo khudozhestvennoi literatury, 1955–6), vol. I, p. 192, quoted in translation in E. J. Brown, 'Pisarev and the transformation of two Russian novels', in William Mills Todd III (ed.), *Literature and Society in Imperial Russia 1800–1914* (Stanford: Stanford University Press, 1978), p. 155.

Big, existential questions play an oversized role in the Russian novel, but so too do topical social concerns. Small talk is often markedly big; questions about women's education or family law are valid topics of discussion around the Russian novelistic dinner table. Russian women writers were sometimes criticised for their emphasis on society gossip, but their novels in particular show just how crucial what went on in drawing rooms and parlours was to the position of women, in terms of social connections, marriage prospects, and opportunities for family advancement. This engagement with social and political questions was also echoed in the formal frames of the novels' publication. With serial publication in journals, most novels appeared in the company of articles on social and political themes, often the same themes with which the novels themselves engaged. Furthermore, many characters author their own articles on these themes within the novels. For example, Raskolnikov writes an article about the psychological state of the criminal while committing a crime; Levin is writing about the role of the worker in Russian agriculture while rethinking his farming practices; and Ivan Karamazov is introduced to the reader through his article on the ecclesiastical courts and their scope. The world of ideas within the novels cannot be separated from the world outside the novel; each intervened in the other.

Female novelists were not at the margins in this process of literary social critique. Krestovskii (pseud.) – who wrote scathingly about urban elites, provincial corruption, and oppressive family structures – was the third-highest-paid author by Russian journals in the 1870s, following only Turgenev and Tolstoi (and ahead of Dostoevskii).[24] Dostoevskii admired her writing in his *Diary of a Writer* (*Dnevnik pisatelia*, 1876–7, 1880–1). In 1871, the Russia correspondent for the London-based *Athenaeum* praised Krestovskii's *Ursa Major* as 'the one good novel of the year' to come from Russia and placed Krestovskii 'but little below Tolstoi and Tourguénief'.[25] Evgeniia Tur (pen name for Elizaveta Vasilevna Salias de Tournemire, *née* Sukhovo-Kobylina, 1815–1892) also enjoyed very high regard for her novels, which often portrayed women's difficult lot. Chekhov praised the writing of the two women, referring to 'that same something, solid and noble in spirit' found in the works of both.[26] Turgenev was publicly critical of Tur as well as

---

24 See Jehanne Gheith, *Finding the Middle Ground: Krestovskii, Tur, and the Power of Ambivalence in Nineteenth-Century Russian Women's Prose* (Evanston, IL: Northwestern University Press, 2004), pp. 17–18.

25 E. Schuyler, *The Athenaeum* 2305 (30 Dec. 1871), 879.

26 Anton Chekhov, *Polnoe sobranie sochinenii i pisem v tridtsati tomakh* [Complete collected works and letters in thirty volumes] (Moscow: Izdatel'stvo Nauka, 1977), vol. V, p. 32.

laudatory, but his own fiction shows an unacknowledged debt to her.[27] When we factor these women back into our understanding of the Russian novel – along with others like Avdotia Panaeva (1820–1893); Sofia Khvoshchinskaia (1828–1865, sister of Krestovskii); Marko Vovchok (pseud. of Mariia Vilinska, 1833–1907, a Ukrainian writer of Russian descent who wrote in both Ukrainian and Russian); and Sofia Smirnova (1852–1921) – we see continuity with our male-centric conception of the Russian novel but also some noteworthy differences. Their social critiques place greater emphasis on the trapped position of women (breaking with the proscriptive depictions of the domestic ideal that we find in many novels by their English counterparts). As in Russian men's novels, failed romantic unions and unhappy marriages were a central theme that pointed towards needed reforms of Russian society.

With novels as a crucial vehicle for social debate, characters often came to represent societal types. In his author's introduction, Lermontov is explicit that *A Hero of Our Time* is not a portrait of a single individual but 'a portrait composed of all the vices of our generation in the fullness of their development'.[28] Nikolai Dobroliubov's (1836–1861) article 'What Is Oblomovitis?' (*Chto takoe oblomovshchina?*, 1859) treats the unique hero of Goncharov's *Oblomov* (*Oblomov*, 1859) as a type and therefore representative of a broad social critique. Similarly, the initial reviewers' heated debates about the young nihilist Bazarov in Turgenev's *Fathers and Children* (*Ottsy i deti*, 1862) were about a generation, not an individual. Dmitrii Pisarev (1840–1868) announced that 'our whole younger generation with its aspirations and ideas can recognize itself in the characters of this novel'.[29] As Dobroliubov extrapolated from the individual to 'Oblomovitis', so Pisarev described the disease of 'Bazarovism'. Echoing Lermontov, he claimed it was 'a disease of our time'.[30] The identity struggles of individuals were often interpreted as issues of national self-definition. To depict a landowner is to comment on *the* landowner; Pushkin's Tatiana Larina becomes a representative of *the* Russian woman.

At the same time, however, Russian novels are also rightfully famous for their individualised psychology. Lermontov begins this process in *A Hero of Our Time* through a layered structure designed to bring the reader closer and

---

27 See Jane Costlow, 'Speaking the sorrow of women: Turgenev's "Neschastnaia" and Evgeniia Tur's "Antonina"', *Slavic Review* 50.2 (1991), 328–35.
28 Mikhail Lermontov, *A Hero of Our Time*, trans. Vladimir Nabokov and Dmitri Nabokov (Woodstock, New York: Ardis, 2002), p. 2.
29 Dmitrii Pisarev, 'Bazarov', in *Sochineniia*, vol. II, pp. 7–50, as printed in Ivan Turgenev, *Fathers and Children*, ed. and trans. Michael R. Katz, 2nd edn (New York: Norton, 2009), p. 193.
30 Pisarev, 'Bazarov', in Turgenev, *Fathers and Children*, p. 197.

closer to Pechorin, moving from a third-party recounting of his deeds, to the narrator's face-to-face encounter with him, and finally into Pechorin's own diaries where we gain unmediated access to his thoughts. Dostoevskii originally began writing *Crime and Punishment* in the first person but abandoned the draft and shifted to a third-person narration that relied on free indirect discourse, thus bringing us into the unsettled, feverish mind of Raskolnikov as he plots and commits murder. The psychology that interested Dostoevskii was that of a person pushed to the threshold, on the edge of breakdown: Ivan Karamazov talks to his devil as brain fever sets in; Prince Myshkin struggles to express his beliefs before falling into an epileptic fit (*The Idiot* (*Idiot*, 1874)); and Kirillov describes his world view before committing suicide (*Demons* (*Besy*, 1873)). Tolstoi, an equally gifted student of the psyche, took the opposite approach, finding psychological interest in the ordinary: the days when a character did *not* wish to murder his father or take an axe to an old woman. The contemporary critic Nikolai Chernyshevskii (1828–1889) praised Tolstoi for capturing the 'dialectics of the soul', tracing the subtle transition from one feeling to another.[31] Woolf claimed that 'after reading Tolstoy we always feel that we could sacrifice our skill in [comedy of manners] for something of the profound psychology and superb sincerity of the Russian writers'.[32]

This fascination with individual experience also affects the ideology of the Russian novel. Characters could stand for more than themselves, but they could also represent a particularity that undermined abstract, theoretical thinking. As Gary Saul Morson has argued:

> The novel is above all a genre that deals with the particulars of experience, and so it became a tool directed at the abstractions of ideological thinking. One may, in fact, identify a masterplot of an ideological novel: a hero proclaims a set of theory-driven beliefs with great energy and charisma; but in the course of the novel, events take place that reveal to the hero himself that reality is infinitely more complex than theories allow.[33]

Raskolnikov wishes to become a Napoleon and to step over moral boundaries, but after committing murder he realises that his theory of great men was

---

31 Nikolai Chernyshevskii, 'Detstvo i otrochestvo. Voennye rasskazy' [Childhood and boyhood. War stories], in S. P. Bychkov (ed.), *L. N. Tolstoi v russkoi kritike* [Tolstoy in Russian criticism] (Moscow: Gosudarstvennoe izdatel'stvo khudozhestvennoi literatury, 1960), p. 87.

32 Virginia Woolf, 'Tolstoy's "The Cossacks"', *Times Literary Supplement* 785 (1 Feb. 1917), 55.

33 Gary Saul Morson, 'Philosophy in the nineteenth-century novel', in Jones and Miller (eds.), *Cambridge Companion to the Classic Russian Novel*, p. 154.

flawed. Bazarov believes in science and the absolute power of reason but is shamefully overcome by his own emotional nature when he falls in love with Odintsova. In *War and Peace*, Prince Andrei Bolkonskii believes his greatest purpose is the quest for glory and his own 'Toulon' (the siege in which Napoleon first achieved fame), but as he lies near death on the battlefield and looks up at the sky, he understands a greater truth. The Russian hero is most heroic when forced to abandon his earlier ideas and is confounded by the infinite complexity of life.

Russian plots are dominated by existential striving, not tangible material goals like marriage, wealth, or stable family continuity. A typical plot line involves a weak man (of the type Turgenev labelled 'superfluous') encountering a morally superior woman, the possibility of their romantic union, a failure to commit, and the hero and heroine ending up apart. We see this first in *Eugene Onegin*, and then the pattern continues in Lermontov's 'Princess Mary' (in *A Hero of Our Time*); Turgenev's *Rudin* (*Rudin*, 1856), *A Nest of Gentlefolk* (*Dvorianskoe gnezdo*, 1859), and *Fathers and Children* (between Bazarov and Odintsova); and in many of the novels by Krestovskii (pseud.), Smirnova, and Tur. Rarely do the characters achieve matrimony and progeny, and even when they do, this does not guarantee happiness (Levin is still suicidal in *Anna Karenina*, and Olga in *Oblomov* is deeply depressed). The characters cannot be content with the typical markers of success in the European novel.

The greatest Russian Realists considered the spiritual an inseparable part of the material world. Their conception of Realism had a place for God in it. Biblical imagery plays a far greater role in the Russian novel than in those from western Europe, hinting at 'an eternal aspect beneath the illusion of immediate reality'.[34] Unlike the French Naturalists, who revelled in depicting the seedy underbelly of reality, the Russian Realists sought to portray human suffering with compassion and infused with an element of the divine. As de Vogüé beautifully expressed it, 'over and beyond known things which they describe exactly, they grant a secret attention to unknown things which they suspect'.[35]

Russia and the Russian Novel

The Russian novelistic tradition displayed its national character by literally making Russia and Russianness central to the texts. Pushkin's *Eugene Onegin* repeatedly references the development of the Russian literary language, with

34 Meyer, *How the Russians Read the French*, pp. 6–7.
35 De Vogüé, 'On Russian and French Realism', p. 336.

jokes about French words and the narrator's boast at his ability to translate Tatiana's love letter (written by her in French) into Russian. Belinskii called *Onegin* 'an encyclopedia of Russian life, and to the highest degree a national work', because of its depictions of all aspects of daily life in both the capital cities and on the rural gentry estate, including food, dress, dance, entertainment, music, language, folklore, family relations, and social etiquette.[36] With the perspective of one who had moved from the periphery of the empire to the metropole and observed Russia from within and without, Gogol was even more explicit about his national message. He closed *Dead Souls* with the now-famous image of Russia as a troika (a carriage drawn by three horses): 'Whither art thou soaring away to, then, Russia? Give me thy answer! But Russia gives none. With a wondrous ring does the jingle bell trill; the air, rent to shreds, thunders and turns to wind; all things on earth fly past, and eyeing it askance, all the other peoples and nations stand aside and give it the right of way.'[37] The culminating significance of Gogol's epic would seem to be the grandeur and unfathomability of Russia's flight.

Turgenev's first novel, *Rudin*, returned more pessimistically to this theme. The titular hero is a classic superfluous man, full of eloquence and passionate words but incapable of acting upon them. As one of his friends explains, 'Rudin's misfortune lies in the fact that he doesn't know Russia, and that's a grave misfortune indeed. Russia can get by without any of us, but none of us can get by without her.'[38] It is difficult to imagine an English or French character ever making the equivalent claim. The closing lines of *Rudin* evoke Gogol's troika. The humbled hero, having failed at everything, resignedly climbs into a carriage not headed for his desired destination: 'There was something helpless and pathetically submissive in his hunched-up figure ... And the troika trudged along at a slow trot, its small bells jangling irregularly.'[39] This is a darker take on Russia's potential, emphasising not the raw energy and exuberance of the Russian spirit but the Russian hero's failure to act with purpose.

Tolstoi's *War and Peace* is a true national epic, capturing for its readers the most heroic period in Russian history: the defeat of Napoleon's army in 1812. Tolstoi credits the victory to the spirit of the Russian army and the soldiers'

---

36 Vissarion Belinskii, *Stat'ia deviataia 'Evgenii Onegin'* [Ninth article 'Eugene Onegin'], in *Polnoe sobranie sochinenii* [Complete collected works], 13 vols. (Moscow: Izdatel'stvo Akademii nauk SSSR, 1953–9), vol. VII, p. 503.
37 Nikolai Gogol, *Dead Souls*, trans. Bernard Guilbert Guerney (New Haven: Yale University Press, 1996), p. 248.
38 Ivan Turgenev, *Rudin*, trans. Dora O'Brien (London: Alma Classics, 2012), p. 126.
39 Turgenev, *Rudin*, p. 131

innate patriotism. When Prince Andrei explains why they need a Russian leading the army, rather than a foreigner, he claims that in Smolensk the German field marshal 'could not understand' that fighting for Russian soil enflamed the troops' spirits, so that 'we beat back the French for two days in a row, and that that success increased our strength ten times'.[40] Kutuzov is an effective leader because he is a Russian and the troops all sense his shared love of the motherland. Tolstoi delights in the analogy of a national family with father Kutuzov; mother Russia (*matushka Rus'*); and their children, the suffering Russian people.

Goncharov's *The Precipice* (*Obryv*, 1869) also relies on the analogy of the Russian family. At the end of the novel, the hero, Raiskii, is in Rome, working on his art and surrounded by beauty, but still faithful to Russia: 'Behind him all the while three figures stood and called to him warmly: his [cousin] Vera, his [cousin] Marfen'ka, and his babushka. And behind them stood, drawing him to herself more strongly than they, still another figure, gigantic, another great "babushka" – Russia.'[41] In Dostoevskii's *The Brothers Karamazov*, when Dmitrii is put on trial for parricide, the lawyers on both sides invoke Russia as a claimant and participant. The prosecutor makes the Karamazovs representative of 'the Russian family' when he notes that 'certain basic, general elements of our modern-day educated society shine through, as it were, in the picture of this nice little family'.[42] Fedor Pavlovich 'is a father, and one of our modern-day fathers', he reminds the jurists, making the deceased a stand-in for all Russian fathers.[43] The defence attorney similarly raises the stakes, claiming to be heard by 'the whole of Russia' when he tells fathers to 'provoke not your children!'[44] Ultimately, it is not only Dmitrii on trial but the modern Russian family.

Morson argues that 'the Russian masterpieces, while surely the greatest novels, defy, rather than define, their genre'.[45] This was true at the time of their creation, but the Russians' self-conscious pushing of boundaries helped

40 Lev Tolstoi, *Polnoe sobranie sochinenii* [Complete collected works], 90 vols. (Moscow: Gosudarstvennoe izdatel'stvo khudozhestvennoi literatury, 1928–58), vol. XI, p. 207; English in Tolstoy, *War and Peace*, p. 772.
41 I. A. Goncharov, *Polnoe sobranie sochinenii i pisem v dvadtsati tomakh* [Complete collected works and letters in twenty volumes] (St Petersburg: Nauka, 1997–), vol. VII, p. 772.
42 Dostoevskii, *Polnoe sobranie sochinenii*, vol. XV, p. 125; English in Fyodor Dostoevsky, *The Brothers Karamazov: A Novel in Four Parts with Epilogue*, trans. Richard Pevear and Larissa Volokhonsky (London: Vintage Books, 2004), p. 695.
43 Dostoevskii, *Polnoe sobranie sochinenii*, vol. XV, p. 126; Dostoevsky, *Brothers Karamazov*, p. 696.
44 Dostoevskii, *Polnoe sobranie sochinenii*, vol. XV, p. 169; Dostoevsky, *Brothers Karamazov*, p. 744.
45 Morson, 'Philosophy in the nineteenth-century novel', p. 150.

redefine the genre. They loosened formal restrictions and expanded the psychological and philosophical scope, and thereby assured the novel's continuing stature into the twentieth century. With a new surge of interest in women writers and less canonical figures, more of the works that Russians thought would become classics are now being translated and reaching the reading public in the west. Through this process, our conception of the nineteenth-century tradition continues to evolve, while further reinforcing Woolf's claim that the Russians 'allowed human life in all its width and depth, with every shade of feeling and subtlety of thought, to flow into their pages'.

Further Reading

Freeborn, Richard, *The Rise of the Russian Novel: Studies in the Russian Novel from Eugene Onegin to War and Peace* (Cambridge: Cambridge University Press, 1973).

Jones, Malcolm, and Robin Feuer Miller (eds.), *The Cambridge Companion to the Classic Russian Novel* (Cambridge: Cambridge University Press, 1998).

Kahn, Andrew, 'The rise of the Russian novel and the problem of romance', in Jenny Mandler (ed.), *Remapping the Rise of the European Novel* (Oxford: Voltaire Foundation, 2007), pp. 185–98.

Todd, William Mills III, 'The ruse of the Russian novel', in Franco Moretti (ed.), *The Novel*, 2 vols. (Princeton: Princeton University Press, 2006), vol. I, *History, Geography, and Culture*, pp. 401–23.

3.6

The Short Story

LYUDMILA PARTS

'In a short story', Anton Chekhov (1860–1904) once wrote to a fellow writer, 'it is better not to say enough than to say too much'.[1] Between the two criteria – not enough and too much – lies the elusive nature of the short story, a genre which is often defined by what it is not. As Mary Louise Pratt has noted, comparisons with the novel feature regularly, and not always helpfully, in critical discussions of the short story. Alongside the novel, the short story seems 'incomplete': a fragment of text and a sample of life, dealing with a limited number of elements.[2] Yet the Formalists described it as a 'fundamental' form that preceded, and in many ways shaped, the emergence of the novel.[3]

Even the terminological uncertainty is telling. The contemporary term *rasskaz* was not widely accepted until the second half of the nineteenth century, when it supplanted eighteenth- and early nineteenth-century designations such as 'story' (*istoriia*), 'tale' (*povest'*), or 'anecdote' (*anekdot*). Notably, the English term 'short story' emphasises the length of the text, while the Russian *rasskaz* is linked to the verb 'to speak' and thus emphasises the text's relationship to the process of storytelling and to the oral tradition.

In this chapter, I argue that the brevity and inherent orality of the short story allowed for the introduction of new, often stigmatised subject matter and for experimentation with form and language. The short story indeed laid the groundwork for the novel, but not by providing shorter pieces to be assembled into a complex plot. Rather, its role was to work out innovative aesthetic and thematic models that the novel would later carry into the

---

1 Letter to I. Leontiev, 22 Jan. 1888, in A. P. Chekhov, *Sobranie sochinenii* [Collected works], 12 vols. (Moscow: Pravda, 1950), vol. XII, p. 71.
2 Mary Louise Pratt, 'The short story: The long and the short of it', *Poetics: International Review for the Theory of Literature* 10.2–3 (1981), 175–94.
3 Boris Eikhenbaum, 'O. Henry and the theory of the short story', trans. I. R. Titunik, in Charles E. May (ed.), *The New Short Story Theories* (Athens: Ohio University Press, 1994), p. 87.

cultural mainstream. For this reason, the short story often came to the fore during periods of literary and ideological change. The focus in this chapter will be on the period stretching from the end of the nineteenth century through the first decades of the twentieth century, but I will also situate those years within the evolution of the short story as a whole.

The Tale

By the end of the eighteenth century, Russian writers were searching for new literary structures that would advance developments in literary language while reflecting newly popular philosophical trends and changes in social life. The writer who implemented the most significant innovations in literary form and language was Nikolai Karamzin (1766–1826). Karamzin's 'Poor Liza' (*Bednaia Liza*, 1792), arguably Russian literature's first proper short story – or 'tale' (*povest'*), as it was called at the time (see Box 2.1) – condenses the familiar Sentimental plot about unhappy love while preserving not only its basic elements but also the principles of its world view (see Chapter 1.4). The story of a chaste peasant girl who falls in love with a well-meaning but weak-willed aristocrat progresses swiftly through all the expected stages: from courting to disenchantment and boredom, and ultimately, to abandonment and suicide. This swift progression shifts attention away from the moral lesson, thereby privileging the emotional over the social and focusing on the new hero, an ordinary person from the lower strata of society.[4] In Karamzin's hands, the Sentimental tale became a vehicle for literary language reform as well as an experiment in narrative voice: the true innovation of 'Poor Liza' is Karamzin's narrator, who is a character in his own right and is fond of metafictional commentary.

Aleksandr Pushkin (1799–1837), too, used the tale to develop new narrative modes. Each story in *The Tales of Belkin* (*Povesti Belkina*, 1830) is an experiment in genre: a Gothic tale, a Sentimental one, a Romantic adventure. Like Karamzin, Pushkin is interested in the figure of the narrator and in the process of storytelling. *The Tales of Belkin* opens with an elaborate and deliberately confusing delineation of the stories' provenance, thus emphasising the subjectivity of each and all narrators. In 'The Stationmaster' (*Stantsionnyi smotritel'*), a tribute to Karamzin's story, Pushkin rewrites the poor-girl plot: contrary to all expectations, his heroine, Dunia, seems happy

---

4 P. A. Orlov, *Russkaia sentimental'naia povest'* [The Russian sentimental tale] (Moscow: Izdatel'stvo Moskovskogo universiteta, 1979), p. 26.

with her choices. Beyond presenting a cautionary tale about relying too much on cautionary tales, Pushkin's dialogue with Karamzin situates his narrator at centre stage. This narrator tries to emulate the Karamzinian stance of heightened sensibilities but cannot remain elevated over the mundane. The narrator's relationship with both his material and the reader features among the key innovations that the tale brought to Russian literature.

The rise of the tale at the beginning of the nineteenth century heralded two major shifts in the cultural paradigm: from poetry to prose, and from elite circles of readers to a much larger and more dispersed readership, primarily via literary magazines and journals (see Chapters 2.3, 2.4). Among the popular writers of the 1820s and 1830s, Aleksandr Bestuzhev-Marlinskii (1797–1837) was hailed by Vissarion Belinskii (1811–1848; see Box 5.1), the most prominent critic of the time, as 'an instigator of the Russian tale', while Vladimir Odoevskii (1803–1869) and Mikhail Pogodin (1800–1875), not to mention Nikolai Gogol (1809–1852), wrote short tales so frequently that in 1835 Belinskii admitted that 'even the novel respectfully stepped aside and let the tale lead the way'.[5] Yet even as he acknowledged the tale's primacy, Belinskii saw little difference between the novel and the tale apart from their length. He was right: the tales of his time – namely, the Romantic, regional, and dialect tales with their focus on unusual settings and emotional states; the society tale and that of the superfluous man that critically assessed society for its shallowness and apathy; and the social tale in the style of the Natural School with its focus on the lives of the poor (see Chapter 1.5) – share with the novel a common set of thematic concerns and stylistic preferences.[6] Often, as in the case of Mikhail Lermontov's (1814–1841) novel *A Hero of Our Time* (*Geroi nashego vremeni*, 1840), shorter pieces could be arranged into a longer narrative by such framing devices as the hero's diaries, inserted narratives, and a complicated timeline.

As the tale developed and was recognised as an independent genre, it established its own characteristic set of themes, characters, and stylistic devices. Certain novelists used the short narratives to experiment with formal elements or introduce new character types. Ivan Turgenev's (1818–

---

5 Vissarion Belinskii, 'O russkoi povesti i povestiakh g. Gogolia' [On the Russian tale and the tales of Mr Gogol], in *Estetika i literaturnaia kritika* [Aesthetics and literary criticism], 2 vols. (Moscow: Gosudarstvennoe izdatel'stvo khudozhestvennoi literatury, 1959), vol. I, p. 130.
6 Viktor Terras, 'The Russian short story 1830–1850', in Charles A. Moser (ed.), *The Russian Short Story: A Critical History* (Boston: Twayne, 1986), pp. 1–5.

1883) cycle *Notes of a Hunter* (*Zapiski okhotnika*, 1852) affords its peasant characters an unprecedented degree of interiority (see Chapter 4.4). His 'First Love' (*Pervaia liubov'*, 1860) touches on such risqué topics as sex, domination, and the young hero's psychological trauma. Gogol's 'The Overcoat' (*Shinel'*, 1842) solidifies the archetype of Russian literature's most famous character, the 'little person' (see Chapter 4.3). Lev Tolstoi (1828–1910), in his early story 'Sebastopol in December' (*Sevastopol' v dekabre*, 1855), employs second-person narration, addressing the reader with turns of phrases such as 'you see' and 'you understand'. Fedor Dostoevskii (1821–1881) includes supernatural elements in 'Bobok' (*Bobok*, 1873). And the stories of Nikolai Leskov (1831–1895) are justly accredited with perfecting the narrative style of folksy, oral speech and naming it *skaz* (see Box 4.3). These, however, are the exceptions, since for the most part the Russian tales of the first half of the nineteenth century generally developed the familiar concerns of the Russian novel, with its focus on broad social issues, and did not invest in new types of character or formal experimentation. Once it did, the *tale* became the *short story* – a thoroughly modern genre.

Anton Chekhov and His Legacy

Towards the end of the nineteenth century, with the major novelists either dead or – in the case of Tolstoi – turning to short forms, the short story once again assumed its role as a genre of cultural transition. These were the early days of the Symbolist movement, with its focus on aesthetic experimentation (see Chapter 1.6), and this shift in literary paradigm in turn reflected a strong sense of political crisis. Following the political unrest of the 1860s and 1870s – when widespread social reforms generated civil unrest and terrorist movements, with subsequent government repressions and popular disillusionment – writers began to react against the utilitarian critics' demands for social engagement. The short story now permitted such writers as Gleb Uspenskii (1843–1902), Vladimir Korolenko (1853–1921), Fedor Sologub (1863–1927), Aleksandr Kuprin (1870–1938), and Aleksei Remizov (1877–1957) to depart from large-scale concepts of society, history, and social action – which had been the emphasis of the major novels of the nineteenth century – and to move towards notions of individuated conscience, subjectivity, and marginality. Like the liberal writers of previous generations, these writers of the 1880s and 1890s delved into the lives of the poor and the dispossessed. However, their attention was now drawn to extreme states of mind and body such as sickness, alcoholism, the terrors

of war, prostitution, and suicide. Moreover, they relocated their stories' dramatic development from the plot to the character's consciousness. In Vsevolod Garshin's (1855–1888) 'The Red Flower' (*Krasnyi tsvetok*, 1883), the clarity of the narrator's documentation of a madman's last days – in an asylum – defies the chaos of the hero's reasoning (see Chapter 4.9). Leonid Andreev's (1871–1919) 'The Story of the Seven Hanged' (*Rasskaz o semi poveshennykh*, 1908) examines the mental state of those awaiting execution.

The Russian Modernist short story, in a manner akin to its European counterpart, 'sought to articulate a more personal perception of human experience and to convey the hidden emanations of [people's] psyches'.[7] Herein lies a major difference between the short story and the novel: the novel, according to Frank O'Connor, is impossible 'without the concept of a normal society'.[8] Alberto Moravia distinguishes between the novel and the short story on the basis that ideology functions as bone structure. The novel possesses this ideological skeleton, 'however imprecise and contradictory it may be', and the short story does not.[9] The novel enters into a direct relationship with the dominant ideology of its time: it can be supportive of it, hostile to it, or take it for granted, but the ideological framework is always there; by contrast, the short story focuses predominantly on the individual's moral and emotional experience.

The author who finalised the shift to what we now recognise as the typical concerns of the modern short story is Anton Chekhov. Just as Pushkin's achievements in prose have been seen to influence the development of the short story throughout the nineteenth century, in the 1880s and 1890s Chekhov's stories gave the genre a new form; a new direction; and a new, unprecedented prestige.[10] Indeed, the twentieth-century Russian short story set the model for the genre to this day. From Katherine Mansfield to Raymond Carver, writers acknowledge their debt to Chekhov as a founding father of the modern short story, and its absolute master.

The well-documented unease provoked by Chekhov's poetics is an indication of how drastic this shift appeared at the time. To contemporary critics, Chekhov's stories seemed symptomatic not so much of new directions but of

7 Julian W. Connolly, 'The Russian short story 1880–1917', in Moser (ed.), *The Russian Short Story*, p. 135.
8 Frank O'Connor, 'The lonely voice', in Charles E. May (ed.), *Short Story Theories* (Athens: Ohio University Press, 1976), p. 86.
9 Alberto Moravia, 'The short story and the novel', in May (ed.), *Short Story Theories*, p. 149.
10 Charles A. Moser, 'Introduction: Pushkin and the Russian Short Story', in Moser (ed.), *The Russian Short Story*.

the decline, even destruction, of Russian literature.[11] His emphatically non-ideological stance, together with his objective, almost clinical point of view, earned him the title of a writer without principles and a 'killer of human hopes and illusions'.[12]

Chekhov's changes to the short form were subtle, but still significant enough to set the genre on new paths. His characters may share a world with the heroes of the Russian novel, but Chekhov's narrative stance was decisively different. He was often forced to explain his position to critics bewildered by what they perceived to be his inattention to the social problems of his time. It was those problems that the novel had usually addressed in depth. The critics, Chekhov insisted, 'confuse two concepts: answering the questions and formulating questions correctly. Only the latter is required of an artist.'[13] His poetics, therefore, were *heuristic* – he posed questions without expecting his characters to find answers, or even to realise the questions' importance. He was interested in how people come to know, or believe they have come to know, things about life and themselves.[14] His signature devices comprised the psychological close-up, laconicism, the absence of a discernible message, seemingly random details, and events that change nothing or trifles that change everything.[15] His central themes were human isolation, the impossibility of true communication and understanding, the passage of time, and the futility – if not absurdity – of approaching life with ready-made formulas.

Chekhov did not shy away from big issues but rather focused on how people approach complex and often unsolvable social problems. In a letter to his editor, he stated this explicitly: 'In my opinion, it is not the writer's job to solve such problems as God, pessimism, etc.; his job is merely to record who, under what conditions, said or thought what about God or pessimism.'[16] The story 'A Nervous Breakdown' (*Pripadok*, 1889) may seem to raise the problem of prostitution, but it is really about one man's thoughts about the problem. The law student Vassilev spends an evening at houses of vice with two friends who, unlike him, are not inclined to consider the social roots of,

11 Lyudmila Parts, *The Chekhovian Intertext: Dialogue with a Classic* (Columbus: Ohio State University Press, 2008), chap. 3.

12 Lev Shestov, *Chekhov and Other Essays* (Ann Arbor: University of Michigan Press, 1996), p. 4.

13 Letter to A. Suvorin, 27 Oct. 1888, in Chekhov, *Sobranie sochinenii*, vol. XII, p. 102.

14 Vladimir Kataev, *If We Could Only Know! An Interpretation of Chekhov* (Chicago: Ivan R. Dee, 2002).

15 Cathy Popkin, *The Pragmatics of Insignificance: Chekhov, Zoshchenko, Gogol* (Stanford: Stanford University Press, 1993).

16 Letter to A. Suvorin, 30 May 1888, in Chekhov, *Sobranie sochinenii*, vol. XII, p. 88.

and possible solutions to, prostitution. Vassilev does not find the answers either, but the story draws attention to his confrontation with his own bookish and rather naïve conceptions of vice. In 'Grief' (*Toska*, 1886), the world is an indifferent and lonely place where human connection is all but impossible. The coach driver Iona mourns the loss of his son but cannot find anyone who will listen to him talk about his grief. Iona's need to talk is so great that he finally describes his grief to his mare. Iona gets to tell his story, the mare listens, and Iona feels better.

Chekhov's focus on the individuated conscience determines the always subjective importance of the events in his characters' lives. In 'The Commotion' (*Perepolokh*, 1886), a governess's room is searched when the mistress's brooch goes missing. Not only is the young Mashenka's personal space violated, she also realises that her own social standing is no different from that of the servants in the house. She leaves her mistress's service, but there is no explanation as to why she feels she cannot remain in the house, where she is going, or what she expects to find there. An event that is unexceptional for most people becomes a life-changing moment of insight for one person. Mashenka's story is not about class inequality in general; rather, it is about a single moment in *her* life that has brought her to a painful but fundamental realisation. Similarly, in 'The Teacher of Literature' (*Uchitel' slovesnosti*, 1894), we leave the protagonist, Nikitin, at the moment of his painful realisation that his marriage, job, and life of philistine comfort no longer satisfy him. The last line reads: 'I must escape from here, I must escape today, or I shall go out of my mind!'[17] Overcoming his own illusions does not make Nikitin a rebel or a hero, and it certainly does not make him happy; yet, in Chekhov, self-awareness is of great value and understanding oneself is as much of a happy ending as one can hope for.

No happy endings, then. Indeed, endings, let alone happy ones, are a tricky thing in Chekhov, and in the post-Chekhov short story in general. Its disenfranchised hero and limited mode of knowing manifest themselves in a tendency towards plots that refuse to bracket the world within neatly defined parameters. This is typical of the modern story, which tends either to be open-ended or to offer an unsatisfactory ending that neither resolves the character's problem nor affirms the reader's sense of logic and order. Chekhov's stories and plays often end with characters leaving or dreaming of escape, and never with arrival. His last story, 'Betrothed' (*Nevesta*, 1903),

---

17 Anton Chekhov, *Later Short Stories 1888–1903*, trans. Constance Garnett (New York: The Modern Library, 1999), p. 283.

ends with the young heroine leaving her childhood home (not for the first time). Thus, 'full of life and high spirits [she] left the town – as she supposed for ever'.[18]

To those readers who have been conditioned by the great novelists of the nineteenth century to approach literature as moral philosophy, Chekhov's disinterest in moral lessons is striking. In his most famous story, 'The Lady with a Dog' (*Dama s sobachkoi*, 1899), Anna and Gurov are having an affair, lying to their spouses, and stealing moments alone together. And yet this remains one of the most lyrical love stories in world literature and has provided a master plot for many authors, including Joyce Carol Oates and William Bond, whose characters also stray into real love from what they thought would be a seaside summer romance. Chekhov leaves morality outside of the story by allowing only its protagonists to worry about human and divine judgement. The narrator provides no frame; and the reader is offered no narrative space for their own judgements. The story ends with Anna and Gurov talking about the future with very real and rare emotion, despite having found no solution to their predicament and, perhaps, not much happiness either: 'their love has changed them both'.[19] Perhaps this is enough.

After reading 'The Lady with a Dog', Maksim Gorkii (1868–1936) pronounced that Chekhov was 'killing realism'.[20] This statement is best understood – and given nuance – in the context of changing literary paradigms. Chekhov's writing was indeed a radical departure from the socially engaged Realist literature of the mid-nineteenth century, yet it remained too approachable to be described as Modernist. The Modernist method favoured experiments with form and style, while Chekhov perfected writing 'so simply about such simple things', as Gorkii put it.[21] The Modernist short story – though by no means simple, especially in its emphasis on language and form – continued nonetheless to build on Chekhov's discoveries in terms of both the short story's protagonist and events and its relationship with social concerns.

Ivan Bunin (1870–1953), the first Russian writer to win the Nobel Prize for Literature (1933), admired Chekhov but did not emulate his reserved style. Bunin's language is poetic in ways well-suited to the themes of memory, longing, and loss, which run through his works – from the elegiac sketches of

18 Chekhov, *Later Short Stories*, p. 628.   19 Chekhov, *Later Short Stories*, p. 584.
20 Maksim Gorky, *Selected Letters*, trans. Andrew Barratt and Barry P. Scherr (Oxford: Clarendon Press, 1997), p. 53.
21 Gorky, *Selected Letters*, p. 53.

the pre-revolutionary Russian countryside to the nostalgic backward glance of an émigré. Like Chekhov, Bunin never joined a literary movement, but his attention to form is typical of Modernist aesthetics: one of his best stories, 'Gentle Breath' (*Legkoe dykhanie*, 1916), is an exploration of the power of form. The events of the story, if reconstructed in proper sequence, are horrifying: a young girl, pretty and a little spoiled, is abused by a family friend and dies at the hands of another lover, in what is clearly an engineered suicide. However, the story's structure, its tone, and the way in which it hides the sordid details in the flow of lyric prose suppress the nature of the material, filling the story with a light and haunting lyricism.[22] The story 'Grammar of Love' (*Grammatika liubvi*, 1915) traces the protagonist's efforts to imbue the strange love story of his rural neighbour with mystery and poignancy. Of the various possible versions of the story (the woman may have died of natural causes or committed suicide; the man may have gone mad with grief or simply be a recluse), the protagonist, Ivlev, chooses to tell the story of a great, mysterious love. In his desire to fill the world with symbols in need of deciphering, Ivlev himself becomes an author, and a Modernist one at that. In Bunin's later stories, written in Paris in the 1930s, his émigré narrators similarly read the past as a poem about nostalgia and loss.

With language and mood moving to the foreground, the importance of other elements – most notably, plot development and psychological motivations – receded. The focus shifted to 'the primacy of "an experience" directly and emotionally created and encountered'.[23] The characters living through these experiences often belonged to a certain type; as O'Connor puts it, they are members of 'a submerged population group': 'outlawed figures wandering about the fringes of society'.[24] However, the 1917 revolution and subsequent civil war reconfigured the familiar criteria of marginality and belonging in society. In the 1920s and 1930s, literature's main concerns become trauma, violence, and the language of the new epoch.

The short story allowed for a swift reflection on the rapidly changing world while maintaining the focus on individual experiences of revolution and war. In Aleksei Nikolaevich Tolstoi's (1883–1945) 'Viper' (*Gadiuka*, 1928), a young woman is forced to transform from a pretty girl in a merchant family into a sexless revolutionary fighter in the civil war, and then into a clerk in the

---

22 Lev Vygotsky, 'Bunin's "Gentle Breath"', in *The Psychology of Art*, trans. Scripta Technica (Cambridge, MA: MIT Press, 1971).
23 Charles E. May, 'The nature of knowledge in short fiction', in May (ed.), *New Short Story Theories*, p. 133.
24 O'Connor, 'The lonely voice', pp. 86–7.

new Soviet bureaucracy. Each of these transformations almost kills her: the story opens with the description of a beautiful young body covered in scars. In Mikhail Bulgakov's (1891–1940) early story 'The Towel with a Cockerel' (*Polotentse s petukhom*), from the cycle *The Notes of a Young Doctor* (*Zapiski molodogo vracha*, 1926), a young woman loses her leg and barely recovers from severe blood loss. Her recovery could be read as a metaphor for the country, undergoing and surviving the bloody transformation to a new order.

The 1920s and 1930s were a time of short-story cycles. In a cycle, stories linked by a recurring character or setting might remain fully independent, but they might also form a near-novelistic unity. Read as a whole, the cycle modifies the reader's 'experience of each of its component parts'.[25] Edyta Bojanowska suggests that the cycle is better suited than the novel to 'representing the flux of contemporaneity' and, moreover, that the contemporary 'novel itself may be undergoing a "contamination" by the story cycle poetics' (see Chapter 3.9).[26] If the Russian short story frequently conveys a sense of instability and uncertainty, then the novel tends to be concerned with continuity and the enduring problems of society and family. Thus, Lermontov's *A Hero of Our Time* qualifies as a novel, despite containing within it several stories that were published individually, because it develops broad social concerns typical of a novel. By contrast, the cycles of Bulgakov, Isaak Babel (1894–1940), and Daniil Kharms (1905–1942) maintain each story's focus on the immediate, individuated experience, and the emphasis is on fragmentation rather than wholeness. Moreover, Modernist artists are characteristically averse to totalities and conventions and see their creative project as part of a broader social and artistic transformation. The sense of unity created by the cycle's recurring elements does not reach the totalising unity of the novel and is continuously undermined by these Modernists' sense of the world as fragmentary and fragile.

In Babel's cycle of short stories *Red Cavalry* (*Konarmiia*, 1923–6), the central themes are identity and violence. The protagonist is a journalist travelling with the Red Army: like the author, he is a Jew among Russians and Ukrainians, an educated man among illiterate peasants and Cossacks, a man at odds with his identity among people who are comfortably incapable of reflection. His desire to belong to this community of violent men violates his sense of self and precipitates an enduring identity crisis. The *Odesa Stories*

---

25 Forrest L. Ingram, *Representative Short Story Cycles of the Twentieth Century: Studies in a Literary Genre* (Boston: De Gruyter Mouton, 2012), p. 19.
26 Edyta M. Bojanowska, '*E pluribus unum*: Isaac Babel's *Red Cavalry* as a story cycle', *Russian Review* 59.3 (2000), 386–7.

cycle (*Odesskie rasskazy*, 1921–4) is an exuberant celebration of Odesa's mythology, language, and heroes. Benia Krik, the gangster king of Odesa, manu-
factures his own status and larger-than-life persona. In 'How Things Were
Done in Odesa' (*Kak eto delalos' v Odesse*), form and content clash in a manner
reminiscent of Bunin's 'Gentle Breath': the tale of a botched robbery and the
funeral of its unintended victim turns into a celebration of the spirit of
Odesa's Jewish underworld. In this world, the petty crook Benia snubs the
cliché of the passive Jewish underdog and, through rhetoric alone, reinvents
himself as the king of Odesa. 'Guy de Maupassant' (*Giui de Mopassan*), too, is
about the power of the word. Babel brings together several elements:
a sensual story by Maupassant; a starving writer-translator in revolutionary
St Petersburg; and a wealthy voluptuous woman. He then adds a sprinkle of
epigrammatic metaliterary comments ('No iron spike can pierce a human
heart as icily as a period in the right place') and the story becomes a recipe for
transforming dreary reality into high art.[27] The story also meditates on the
artist's frequently tragic lot. Here, as in Babel's other stories, the language is
overloaded with metaphor, making for slow reading that is both difficult and
immensely satisfying.

In Andrei Platonov's (1899–1951) stories, we witness the birth of the new
world and its new man, who requires a new language. This language is at
times childlike, often mixed with Soviet ideological clichés. The effect is such
that the new world and its people stand fresh and vulnerable. In 'Fro' (*Fro*,
1936), the eponymous heroine struggles to love her husband and her country
as a proper new Soviet woman. For Fro, the difficult present and the radiant
future promised by communist ideology clash not as abstract categories but
as physical, bodily states. When Fedor goes away to build socialism in distant
lands, Fro's pining for her husband is physical: she cannot learn, sleep, or take
care of her body. Her domain, now empty, comprises home, bed, and body,
whereas his has grown to accommodate machines and engineering. This
conflict between the mechanical (standing in for the state) and the body
(representing the individual) is not resolved: Fro is slow to learn Fedor's
language of serving humankind, and Fedor must repeatedly escape the
confines of Fro's love. Platonov's language is austere and deliberately
unpoetic. The poet Joseph Brodsky (1940–1996) commented that Platonov
'wrote in the language of [socialist] utopia, in the language of his era. ...
Unlike most of his contemporaries – Babel, Boris Pilniak, Iurii Olesha,

---

27 Isaac Babel, *The Complete Works of Isaac Babel*, ed. Nathalie Babel, trans. Peter
Constantine (New York, London: W. W. Norton, 2002), p. 681.

Evgenii Zamiatin, Bulgakov, Mikhail Zoshchenko, who engaged in stylistic self-indulgence, that is, each played his own games with language (which is, after all, a form of escapism).'[28]

Mikhail Zoshchenko (1894–1958) indeed played his own linguistic games, though it would be unfair to say he escaped the reality of his time. On the contrary, the heroes of his extremely short stories eagerly participate in the Soviet project by learning its rules and language and stumbling through them with comic but endearing confidence. Zoshchenko's signature *skaz* – language that imitates oral speech (see Box 4.3) – allows for a hilarious mixture of such disparate layers as bureaucratic language, political slogans, and musings on the usefulness of opera. Cultural policies of the 1920s aimed to educate the peasant and worker not only in communist ideology but also in the behaviours of a cultured person: good manners, personal hygiene, dressing properly, and basic competency in literature and the theatre (see Chapter 4.7).[29] A parody of the new Soviet person, Zoshchenko's hero showcases the failure of these policies. In 'The Classy Lady' (*Aristokratka*, 1923), an outing to the opera culminates in a scandal at the buffet, with the story's real dramatic tension arising from the number of cakes the lady grabs from the counter. Much like her behaviour, the lady's speech (and that of the male narrator) is far from classy; it may be peppered with 'cultured' words, but it remains crude and ungrammatical. In 'The Galosh' (*Galosha*, 1927), a man who wants to recover a galosh lost on a tram spends a week dealing with the new Soviet bureaucracy at the lost property office. By the time he gets all the papers signed, he has lost the other galosh. Still, he exclaims in wonder: 'In other places, would they really have spent so much time on my galosh? . . . that's how marvellously our official machinery works!'[30] Zoshchenko's heroes live in a world whose absurdity they intuit but cannot fully comprehend.

The gentle absurd of Zoshchenko's stories took new (and darker) form in the work of Kharms. Kharms's very short stories in *Happenings* (*Sluchai*, 1930s) mark the world's incomprehensibility by undermining all accepted connections: between elements of reality, between words and their referents, between human actions and their motivations. The result is a terrible freedom from logic, psychology, societal norms, and morals. In 'The Plummeting Old

---

28 Iosif Brodskii, 'Posleslovie k "Kotlovanu" A. Platonova' [Afterword to *The Foundation Pit* by A. Platonov], in *Sochineniia Iosifa Brodskogo* [The works of Joseph Brodsky], 7 vols. (St Petersburg: Pushkinskii fond, 1997–2001), vol. VII, p. 73.

29 Sheila Fitzpatrick, *The Cultural Front: Power and Culture in Revolutionary Russia* (Ithaca: Cornell University Press, 1992).

30 Mikhail Zoshchenko, 'The galosh', in *The Galosh and Other Stories*, trans. Jeremy Hicks (London: Angel Books, 2000), p. 126.

Women' (*Vyvalivaiushchiesia starukhi*, 1930s), Kharms uses his favourite technique of senseless repetition: one after another, old women fall out of a window and die. Their death is stripped of meaning by its representation as something inhuman and merely mechanical (Henri Bergson, in *Laughter*, notes that this overcoming of the human by the mechanical is an abiding source of comedy).[31] Traditional plot and structures also play no role, including, most notably, the ending: if Chekhov's endings do not offer resolutions, in Kharms, 'the failure to finish the story is elevated to the level of genre'.[32] Absences and disappearances are key to Kharms's plots. His famous red-haired man in 'Blue Notebook No. 10' (*Golubaia tetrad' No. 10*, 1937; see Box 1.4) is a man who has no hair, no back, no legs, and so forth; thus, the story lets the man dissolve into nothingness, while simultaneously posing the philosophical question of the essence of existence: what is a man without physical attributes? Kharms's black humour fits in with a world devoid of all emotion and meaning – in other words, an absurd world.

The characters of Iurii Olesha (1899–1960), too, struggle with assigning meaning to the physical world. In 'Liompa' (*Liompa*, 1928), a dying man senses that his grasp of reality is waning when he observes two young boys learning the names of objects and those same, once familiar names escape him. Olesha's own life is sadly symbolic of the fate of many early Soviet writers: after his initial success in the 1920s, he was unable to find a common language with Soviet ideology and wrote virtually nothing for the rest of his life. Like the dying man in 'Liompa', he allowed the names of things to escape him. The exuberance of early Soviet literature dissipated. A genre that had thrived during these decades of social and cultural transition receded from the foreground of Soviet culture. Under strict ideological demands, the short story and the short-story cycle gave way to the monumental novels of Socialist Realism (see Chapters 1.8, 3.9).

From Post-Stalin to Post-Soviet

After Stalin's death in 1953, the thematic and formal possibilities sanctioned by the literary establishment underwent a series of short-lived expansions, and writers once again turned towards a more nuanced engagement with

---

31 Henri Bergson, *Laughter: An Essay on the Meaning of the Comic* (London: Macmillan, 1911).

32 Jean-Philipp Jaccard, 'Daniil Kharms in the context of Russian and European literature of the absurd', in Neil Cornwell (ed.), *Daniil Kharms and the Poetics of the Absurd: Essays and Materials* (New York: St Martin's Press, 1991), p. 63.

their experience. Now, as earlier, the short story proved a natural home for marginalised characters and ideologically suspect topics that were not suitable for the Soviet novel. Stories by Vasilii Aksenov (1932–2009), Iurii Kazakov (1927–1982), Fazil Iskander (1929–2016), Sergei Dovlatov (1941–1990), and Andrei Bitov (1937–2018) pushed the boundaries of Socialist Realism, exploring themes that did not require the ideological skeleton of the novel. With true formal experiments no longer acceptable, even in the relative liberalism of the Thaw, the short story focused on the relationship between the state and the individual, especially the artist; notions of otherness and dispossession; and such fundamental binaries of Russian culture as city and village.

Misfits and the socially marginal are favourite characters for writers as dissimilar as Vasilii Shukshin (1929–1974), a beloved screen actor and director, and Andrei Siniavskii (1925–1997), who wrote under the pseudonym Abram Terts and was imprisoned as a dissident. Shukshin's favourite character is a village oddball (*chudik*): a man who is eccentric, silly, and impractical, but also endearing. Even as he makes life difficult for himself and his loved ones, the oddball's colourful eccentricity is such that one cannot help but wonder how much poorer the world would be without him. In 'Mille Pardons, Madam' (*Mil' pardon, madam*, 1967), the oddball Bronka Pupkov is often berated by his fellow villagers for his strange urge to tell visiting hunters a fabricated but spellbinding story about how he had been sent to assassinate Hitler and got close enough to fire – but missed. Just as Bronka cannot resist the allure of power granted to the storyteller, his listeners cannot resist the suspense, and so they yield to his pace and, most importantly, keep him supplied with food and vodka. During his hour of storytelling, Bronka is a god of his fictional universe and, like every artist, he is willing to suffer for the privilege: the village council even threatens prosecution for distorting history. In Siniavskii's 'Graphomaniacs' (*Grafomany*, 1959), the hero is charmed by the same dream of artistic privilege. A bad writer, he stubbornly refuses to give up the pursuit of fame, because, as his wife knows, he 'lacks the courage to be a mere mortal'.[33] In 'Pkhents' (*Pkhents*, 1957), the protagonist is an actual alien, a plant-like creature from another planet who is trying to adapt and survive; the story is an obvious metaphor of otherness. It is significant that Siniavskii, an ethnic Russian, chose for his pseudonym the name of a Jewish thief from Odesa's underworld folklore; his literary alter-ego Abram Terts

---

33 Abram Tertz, *Fantastic Stories*, trans. Ronald Hingley (Evanston, IL: Northwestern University Press, 1987), p. 201.

exemplifies the inherent marginality and subversive nature of all art and, especially, of the short story.

The rural setting held a particular appeal for writers of the 1950 and 1960s as a counterpart to the Soviet novel, whose preferred locales were the city and the factory. The Village Prose writers (*derevenshchiki*), as they came to be known, included Shukshin, Vladimir Soloukhin (1924–1997), Valentin Rasputin (1937–2015), Vasilii Belov (1932–2012), Iurii Nagibin (1920–1994), and Aleksandr Solzhenitsyn (1918–2008). They turned to the village in search of unspoilt nature, national tradition, and peasant soulfulness, often decrying the degradation of the old ways and relying on *skaz* to give voice to their (usually) elderly characters. Most writers, however, preferred urban settings and characters. Works by Valerii Popov (1939–), Anatolii Kurchatkin (1944–), Iurii Trifonov (1925–1981), and Iurii Kazakov (1927–1982) are especially interesting for their explicit return to the Chekhovian partiality towards personal experience, rather than large social issues; their precise simplicity of writing; and plots in which endings offer no resolution. Stories by Trifonov and Kazakov exemplify the genre's tendency to focus on moments and private experiences – '*a* moment of truth' rather than *the* moment of truth, in Nadine Gordimer's formula.[34]

Varlam Shalamov's (1907–1982) stories stand apart for taking on the subject of the Stalinist prison camps: the inmates are beyond marginal; their experience cannot be truly comprehended. Shalamov spent almost two decades in these camps, but the stories in his *Kolyma Tales* (*Kolymskie rasskazy*, comp. 1954–73) are not biographical as such. He called his artistic method 'new prose', a style which demands the 'resurrection of emotion' and requires unusual, new details of description to make the story believable – not as one believes facts but as one believes 'an open heart wound' (see Chapter 3.10).[35] The camp for Shalamov is a negative experience that neither teaches nor elevates; rather, it invalidates common humanistic and cultural notions. The stories were not published in the Soviet Union until well after Perestroika in the late 1980s. Shalamov thus entered the literary scene at the same time as late Soviet writers such as Vladimir Makanin (1937–2017), Viacheslav Petsukh (1946–2019), Andrei Bitov (1937–2018), Viktoriia Tokareva (1937–), Liudmila Petrushevskaia (1938–), Tatiana Tolstaia (1951–), Evgenii Popov (1946–), and Liudmila Ulitskaia (1943–).

In the 1980s, during Perestroika and Glasnost, collections of short stories grew increasingly popular as multiple anthologies were published, most notably of women's prose. Some critics credit the short story with helping

---

34 Nadine Gordimer, 'The flash of fireflies', in May (ed.), *New Short Story Theories*, p. 265.
35 Varlam Shalamov, 'O proze' [About prose], in *Sobranie sochinenii* [Collected works], 6 vols. (Moscow: Terra, 2004–5), vol. V, p. 152.

to undermine the grand metanarratives of Soviet ideology.[36] During this period, the short story's subject matter – an individuated and marginalised conscience – became its most distinguishing characteristic. Western feminist and queer scholars have frequently described the short story as the literary form best suited to writing by women and other marginalised groups. The short story as 'the outlaw form' or 'the other of fictional prose narrative' undermines a simple linear narrative of culture and challenges the established cultural constructs of norm and identity.[37] The protagonists of these stories are women, children, and the elderly – those who are strangers in their own time and place, that is, marginal people deprived of full voice and agency.

Petrushevskaia's stories encapsulate these concerns. Her narrators dispassionately detail women's lives in late- and post-Soviet Russia, including those topics previously deemed unacceptable for both aesthetic and political reasons: poverty, overcrowded apartments, alcoholism, abortions, abandonment of the elderly, sickness, and broken families. Motherhood in Petrushevskaia is associated with pain and fear. Her narrators are angry, unfeeling, and rely on gossip, leaving it to the reader to fill the emotional void. Petrushevskaia's stories display an almost exaggerated orality: they sound like snatches of overheard conversations, with no proper beginning or end, and demonstrate a glaring absence of any organising authorial presence. Ulitskaia's short stories, too, focus on the female universe of family anxieties, but often against the backdrop of larger historical concerns. Her characters live through the traumatic experiences of the twentieth century – war, the Holocaust, antisemitism – and survive exclusively with the support of family and the bonds of friendship.

The twenty-first-century Postmodernist short stories by authors such as Nina Sadur (1950–2023), Lev Rubinshtein (1947–2024), Vladimir Sorokin (1955–), Iurii Buida (1954–), Viktor Pelevin (1962–), Sergei Lukianenko (1968–), and Zakhar Prilepin (1975–) also privilege the marginal subject in a world of epistemological limits. Pelevin playfully pushes the unconventionality of the short story's protagonist to the limit. The story 'Nika' (*Nika*, 1992) is a rereading of Bunin's 'Gentle Breath', but its protagonist is a cat – a fact

---

36 M. Galina, 'Literatura nochnogo zreniia. Malaia proza kak razrushitel' mifologicheskoi sistemy' [Literature of the night vision. Short prose as destroyer of a mythological system], *Voprosy Literatury* 5 (1997), 4.

37 Ellen Burton Harrington, 'Scribbling women and the outlaw form of the short story', in Harrington (ed.), *Scribbling Women and the Short Story Form: Approaches by American and British Women Writers* (New York: Peter Lang, 2008), p. 1; Axel Nissen, 'The queer short story', in Per Winther, Jacob Lothe, and Hans H. Skei (eds.), *The Art of Brevity: Excursions in Short Story Fiction Theory and Analysis* (Columbia: University of South Carolina Press, 2004), p. 181.

which only becomes clear to the reader in the last line of the story. Yet this playful self-reflexivity only reinforces the genre's flexibility and vitality.

Brevity may not be the essential feature of the short-story genre, but over the course of the twentieth century it served to narrow the genre's focus and to facilitate experimentation with form and subject. Each generation of writers considered the short form to be reflective of the tempo of their lives: in 1835, Belinskii bemoaned life's constant rush and bustle as the reason we 'no longer have time for big, long books'; in 1926, a school textbook deemed the Chekhov story a sign of 'the age of electricity, express trains, and airplanes'; and in 2017, a journal editorial blamed video clips and laziness for 'our addiction to short narrative' and predicted a collection of short stories consisting only of emojis.[38] The shortening of the short story invites us to consider the genre's essence, just as Kharms considers the human essence in his story of the red-haired man who possesses no human attributes. I conclude with Linor Goralik's (1975–) mini prose, which is characterised by brevity taken to extremes and amplified orality. Goralik's mini stories comprise snatches of fictional conversations that range in length from a few sentences to a paragraph, such as this: 'little doggie runs, dirty-dirty, its ears rosy-rosy and see-through. And here I thought: *Devil knows, maybe I should have given birth back then.*'[39] Stripped of everything one expects in a literary work of any genre – plot, characterisation, narrative itself – they nevertheless 'work' in the way that only the short story can: by giving a voice to an individuated, often suffering or confused consciousness. Like all short stories, they are arresting instances of being and transient insights into personal truths.

Further Reading

Erlich, Victor (ed.), *Modernism and Revolution: Russian Literature in Transition* (Cambridge, MA: Harvard University Press, 1994).

Luker, Nicholas (ed.), *The Short Story in Russia, 1900–1917* (Nottingham: Astra, 1991).

Moser, Charles A. (ed.), *The Russian Short Story: A Critical History* (Boston: Twayne, 1986).

Nilsson, Nils Åke (ed.), *Studies in Twentieth Century Russian Prose* (Stockholm: Almqvist & Wiksell, 1982).

Parts, Lyudmila (ed.), *The Russian Twentieth Century Short Story: A Critical Companion* (Boston: Academic Studies Press, 2009).

38 Belinskii, 'O russkoi povesti', p. 130; Ia. A. Nazarenko, *Istoriia russkoi literatury XIX veka* [History of Russian literature of the nineteenth century] (Moscow: Gosizdat, 1926), p. 387; Aleksandr Snegirev, 'Ia liubliu' [I love], *Druzhba Narodov* 2 (2017), 5.

39 Linor Goralik, 'They talk', trans. Michail Iossel, in Michael Iossel and Jeff Parker (eds.), *Rasskazy: New Fiction from a New Russia* (New York: Tin House Books, 2009), p. 30.

Drama II

JULIE CURTIS

As a form, drama may be considered exclusively as written play-texts or also in its transformation into theatre. The latter process is shaped by the author's original conception of the performance, which can be faithfully reproduced – or may be radically altered – in the process of staging. The authorial concept, together with the nature of the theatrical space, the director's vision, the stage design, and the actors' interpretations, all shape the audience experience, whether passive or participatory. In different eras one or more of these elements have gained greater prominence in the journey from page to stage.

Any history of post-Enlightenment Russian drama differs from the history of other genres in the Russian canon by virtue of the fact that – for several different, lengthy periods of historical time – any chronological account which attempted to suggest linear evolution and successive influences would be almost meaningless. The imperial 'theatre monopoly' (see Chapter 3.4), which held sway in the nineteenth century from the 1820s until the 1880s, meant that the court operated a censorship system over repertory and ensured that several nineteenth-century plays now held to be canonical remained unpublished or unperformed – or both – for three or four decades after their completion.[1] This is true of Aleksandr Pushkin's (1799–1837) *Boris Godunov* (*Boris Godunov*, 1825); Mikhail Lermontov's (1814–1841) *Masquerade* (*Maskarad*, 1835); Ivan Turgenev's (1818–1883) *A Month in the Country* (*Mesiats v derevne*, 1850); and Aleksandr Sukhovo-Kobylin's (1817–1903) plays, including *The Death of Tarelkin* (*Smert' Tarelkina*, 1869). The relaxations and greater freedoms of the post-reform era from the 1860s until 1917 permitted groundbreaking theatrical productions of these and other classic plays, but Soviet-era censorship from 1917 on ensured that, once

---

1 See Murray Frame, *School for Citizens: Theatre and Civil Society in Imperial Russia* (New Haven: Yale University Press, 2006).

again, in the twentieth century many play-texts would remain long unread and unperformed. The easing of censorship restrictions during the post-Stalin Thaw again saw the publication and staging of many dramatic texts from much earlier decades, alongside the emergence of new voices among playwrights and new directorial visionaries in the theatre. But only in the post-Soviet era, dating from the 1990s, was the world of theatre fully opened to free creativity and to texts of a new kind of drama altogether.

It is not enough, then, in the Russian context to think of drama – the texts of plays – as a self-sufficient genre. We need instead to trace the development of two interlocking phenomena – the writing of play-texts and their staging by theatres – as the true history of drama in Russia. These phenomena do not always advance in step with each other, and their problematic pattern is largely determined by the dominant political pressures of the day. Theatre nevertheless remains one of the trickiest art forms to police, partly because its nature varies from performance to performance, but above all because an innocuous-looking text can pass censorship procedures but may then convey unanticipated messages in production, as drama is transformed into theatre. Thinking about form in this expanded sense, to encompass both texts and their staging, this chapter will trace the evolution of theatrical form in Russia through the twentieth century and into the early twenty-first. It will give particular weight to periods of formal innovation – the years 1900–1930, the 'directors' theatre' of the late Thaw period, and the innovations of theatre in the first decades of the twenty-first century.

The Turn of the Century

The imperial theatre monopoly of the nineteenth century tended to foster a theatre experience for its audiences which involved either didactic messages reflecting state ideology or else pleasurable entertainment offered by ballet, opera, and light comedies. Production values supported the celebrity performer above all. The abolition of the monopoly in 1882, largely with the intention of promoting Russian theatre over western fashions, led to the creation of a dozen or so new commercial theatres in both Moscow and St Petersburg by the end of the century.[2] The subsequent decades gave rise to some of the most innovative experiments in the global history of theatrical form. The most famous of these new

---

2 Murray Frame, '"Freedom of the theatres": The abolition of the Russian imperial theatre monopoly', *Slavonic and East European Review* 83.2 (2005), 256, 289.

enterprises was the creative partnership of Anton Chekhov (1860–1904) with the directors of the Moscow Art Theatre, Konstantin Stanislavskii (1863–1938) and Vladimir Nemirovich-Danchenko (1858–1943). Their stagings of Chekhov's four most famous plays between 1898 and 1904 represented a fundamental rethinking of the theatre experience: middle-class audiences were now to observe the painful absurdities and comical trivia of life in the sprawling households of the declining gentry from a position 'on the fourth wall', at once intimate and excluded from what was happening on stage. Stanislavskii relished the full recreation of physical realia on stage, ranging from samovar steam to birdsong, with great attention paid to lighting and sound effects (including silent pauses). Subtle ensemble performances took over from the histrionics of celebrity stars of previous decades, and dramatic climaxes were replaced by inconclusive endings. Audiences were drawn into the elusive atmosphere of these performances, the founders of the theatre being fascinated by the potential they saw in Chekhov, as in Henrik Ibsen, for 'realism honed to the point of symbolism'.[3]

The early years of the twentieth century then saw Symbolist theatre coming into its own. Turning away from social theatre, mimetic realism, and psychological characterisation, Silver Age writers such as Viacheslav Ivanov (1866–1949), Fedor Sologub (1863–1927), Nikolai Evreinov (1879–1953), Valerii Briusov (1873–1924), and Aleksandr Blok (1880–1921) drew inspiration from sources ranging from *commedia dell'arte* to western Symbolist playwrights such as Maurice Maeterlinck in order to create a drama of the spirit: mystical and often introspective. The multiple cultural, literary, and philosophical references in their play-texts required the audience to be highly educated, so this tended to become an exclusive theatre for the intelligentsia. Blok's lyrical drama *The Puppet Show* (*Balaganchik*, 1906), for example, takes the traditional lovers' triangle of Pierrot, Harlequin, and Columbine (recognisably based on Blok's own emotional entanglements) and confronts them with a group of mystics. Love and death are confused, tender poetry combines with the sardonic revelation of theatrical artifice, and irony struggles against portentousness. Directed by Vsevolod Meierkhold (1874–1940), in this production rhythmical, gestural composition prevailed over naturalistic acting.

---

3 Vl. I. Nemirovich-Danchenko, *Stat'i. Rechi. Besedy. Pis'ma* [Articles. Speeches. Conversations. Letters] (Moscow: Iskusstvo, 1952), pp. 119, 183, also p. 107. See also K. S. Stanislavskii, *Moia zhizn' v iskusstve* [My life in art], 8th edn (Moscow: Iskusstvo, 1948), pp. 294–5.

1917 and Beyond

In theatrical terms, the two key events of 1917 – the February Revolution, which deposed the tsar, and the October Revolution, which saw the Bolsheviks overthrow the moderate Provisional Government – were each marked by further important productions by Meierkhold. His lavish production of Lermontov's *Masquerade* premiered on 25 February, just days before the tsar's abdication. With an enormous cast, the production was based on thousands of design sketches, every detail being slightly exaggerated in size to suggest how the protagonists were oppressed by their surroundings. This opulence provoked much criticism, but *Masquerade* was actually performed more than five hundred times between 1917 and 1941.[4] Meierkhold's interpretation of Sukhovo-Kobylin's *Death of Tarelkin* premiered on 23 October 1917, two days before the October coup. The play offers a denunciation of corruption and brutality in the police and justice system in the 1850s and 1860s. Meierkhold had originally trained in the school of Stanislavskii at the Moscow Art Theatre. In their landmark 1898 production of Chekhov's *Seagull* (*Chaika*, comp. 1895), his performance of the role of the aspiring, experimental young writer Treplev alongside Stanislavskii's own characterisation of the older, successful Realist writer Trigorin had neatly prefigured the rift that would open up between their respective directorial visions for the theatre. This tension would shape many theatrical developments until the late 1920s and beyond, as Meierkhold constructed his vision of participatory experimental theatre in opposition, implicit and explicit, to Stanislavskii's exploration of private life.

Shortly after the October Revolution, Meierkhold was one of the very few artists to attend a meeting about the future of culture at the invitation of the Bolshevik leader Vladimir Lenin. He was subsequently invited to take charge of the theatre section, or TEO (*teatral'nyi otdel*), of the emerging government institution that would become the Soviet Commissariat of Enlightenment (Narkompros). The slogan that he adopted in 1920 for this enterprise was 'Theatrical October', proclaiming the necessity of radical change in the theatre, as in politics and society.

One other key figure at that meeting with the Bolsheviks late in 1917 was the Futurist poet Vladimir Maiakovskii (1893–1930). Building on earlier Futurist convictions and experiments, Maiakovskii flung himself wholeheartedly (initially, at least) into the Bolshevik cause, and thus it was that he and

---

4 Edward Braun, *The Theatre of Meyerhold: Revolution on the Modern Stage* (London: Eyre Methuen, 1979), pp. 140–3.

Meierkhold came to collaborate on the first truly 'Soviet' play, *Mystery-Bouffe* (*Misteriia-Buff*, 1918, 1921), written to celebrate the first anniversary in 1918 of the October Revolution and redrafted and topically updated for its 1921 revival. The play retells the events before and after the October Revolution as an allegory, drawing upon the image of the Flood for the cataclysm which forces representatives of different Russian classes to take refuge on an ark. Eventually the 'unclean' workers travel through heaven and hell (they are unimpressed) to reach the new promised land, an electrified Moscow which welcomes them with supplies and tools for the construction of the new socialist state. The sets and costumes for the short-lived 1918 production were designed by the Ukrainian-born Suprematist artist Kazimir Malevich (1879–1935). Like all good agitprop, the performance ends with the hymn 'The Internationale' (in Maiakovskii's variant), sung in a demonstrative collective gesture by the audience together with the cast.

As a theatrical undertaking, *Mystery-Bouffe* was intended to encapsulate all the ambitions of 'Theatrical October'. The preface to the 1921 version proclaims that the text has no fixed status and may be freely rewritten by all future performers. With the author's rights and his sacrosanct text deposed from their pedestals, the project also attacked the very format of traditional theatre. A thrust stage and the removal of both curtain and proscenium arch would foster greater audience involvement and political engagement. The implicit 'fourth wall' of Stanislavskii's productions was decisively rejected. At around this time, indeed, many shows left the space of the theatre behind entirely – see, for example, outdoor mass spectacles such as the re-enactment of *The Storming of the Winter Palace* (*Vziatie Zimnego dvortsa*, 1920), staged for the third anniversary of October 1917. The content of *Mystery-Bouffe*, entirely drafted in witty Maiakovskian verse to make it more memorable, was also unabashedly propagandistic, aimed at the new, uneducated working-class audiences who had been granted free admission to theatres after 1917. This approach was diametrically opposed to the nuanced psychological realism of Stanislavskii and the Moscow Art Theatre, a point which was announced aggressively in the 'unclean' proletarian worker's prologue:

> For other theatres [. . .]
> the stage
> is a keyhole. [. . .]
> You peep through and you can see –
> auntie Manias
> and uncle Vanias

getting up to hanky-panky on the sofa.
But we're not interested
in uncles and aunties, –
you can find plenty of aunties and uncles at home.
We will also show you true life,
but the theatre has transformed it into the most extraordinary spectacle.[5]

Meierkhold would go on to explore avant-garde techniques in many of his subsequent productions (or 'spectacles'), drawing upon traditions such as *commedia dell'arte* as well as developing his own methods, such as the training of actors through physical exercise routines ('biomechanics'), the acting stunts and tricks known as 'eccentrism', and his broader ambitions for the 'circusisation' of theatre. But it was in *Mystery-Bouffe* that he and Maiakovskii attempted to create the first truly 'revolutionary' play, in its aesthetics as in its politics.[6]

While certain members of the Bolshevik leadership welcomed the innovations offered in the party's name by Meierkhold and Maiakovskii, others were less enthusiastic – the literary and cultural tastes of Lenin and his close circle were in fact notoriously conservative. Meierkhold was replaced after only a few months in his role running TEO by Nadezhda Krupskaia, Lenin's wife. In theatrical terms, this suspicion of the avant-garde soon found expression in the new theatrical slogan enunciated by Anatolii Lunacharskii, the Commissar for Enlightenment, who as early as 1923 (after theatres had been reprivatised under the New Economic Policy (NEP)) proclaimed the need to return to the classics: 'Back to Ostrovskii!'[7] The debate about what should constitute truly Soviet culture and drama was one which would play out with much vituperation over the following years.

The New Economic Policy Era

The relative liberalism of the NEP era (1921–8/9) saw great heterogeneity in the theatre but also to some extent a stepping back from the aesthetic radicalism of the revolutionary and civil war years (1917–21). New voices

---

5 From the prologue to *Misteriia-buff* (1921 version), in V. V. Maiakovskii, *Sochineniia* [Works], 3 vols. (Moscow: Khudozhestvennaia literatura, 1965), vol. III, p. 376.
6 Braun, *Theatre of Meyerhold*, pp. 148–62. See also Konstantin Rudnitsky, *Russian and Soviet Theatre: Tradition and the Avant-Garde* (London: Thames and Hudson, 1988), pp. 62–5.
7 Sheila Fitzpatrick, *The Commissariat of Enlightenment: Soviet Organization of Education and the Arts under Lunacharsky* (Cambridge: Cambridge University Press, 1970), pp. 11–25, 139–61.

such as Nikolai Erdman (1900–1970) and Evgenii Shvarts (1896–1958) offered satirical accounts of the confusing paradoxes of the NEP era. Erdman's slapstick comedy *The Warrant* (*Mandat*, 1925) was staged by Meierkhold in 1925 and, despite arousing controversy among Marxist critics for its mocking depiction of the opportunism and hypocrisy of those who purported to be living according to Bolshevik precepts, ran without hindrance until the early 1930s. By 1931, Meierkhold and Stanislavskii were vying to stage Erdman's next play *The Suicide* (*Samoubiitsa*, 1928), though both attempts eventually foundered.[8] At the height of the NEP, Mikhail Bulgakov (1891–1940) was being lionised across Moscow for his playwriting talents, which by 1929 saw four different plays of his being rehearsed or staged in the capital's leading theatres. His runaway first success was the adaptation made of his novel *The White Guard* (*Belaia gvardiia*, 1925), an autobiographical work in which he depicted the travails of a cultivated, middle-class Russian family enduring the civil war upheavals in Kyiv during 1918–19. The premiere of the Moscow Art Theatre production in October 1926 – under the less provocative title *The Days of the Turbins* (*Dni Turbinykh*) – was one of the theatrical sensations of the day. The Art Theatre brought to it all its expertise in staging Realist drama (Anatolii Smelianskii has argued that they in fact 'Chekhovised' Bulgakov's playscript[9]) to recreate a sensitive psychological portrait of a class, and indeed a world, which by then was lost forever. The debates which raged around the future direction of Soviet drama took this 'reactionary' production as a touchstone for pro-communist attacks on the remnants of the pre-revolutionary tradition. And yet, peculiarly, Stalin himself seems to have loved the play and attended performances at the Moscow Art Theatre over a dozen times. Stalin and other members of the government took an intense interest in monitoring the arts during this period, discussing individual plays, directors, and productions at full politburo meetings throughout the 1920s. Nobody could accuse them of indifference to the importance of art.

However, Bulgakov showed himself to be far more than a post-Chekhovian playwright, and in works such as *The Crimson Island* (*Bagrovyi ostrov*, 1926–7), a play which parodied Maiakovskii's *Mystery-Bouffe* while denouncing oppressive theatrical censorship, he demonstrated that he too was capable of writing texts suited to an avant-garde aesthetic. He challenged Meierkhold and Maiakovskii's claim to a monopoly on writing 'for the

---

8 John Freedman, *Silence's Roar: The Life and Drama of Nikolai Erdman* (Oakville, ON: Mosaic, 1992), pp. 52–166.

9 Anatolii Smelianskii, *Bulgakov v Khudozhestvennom teatre* [Bulgakov in the Art Theatre], 2nd rev. edn (Moscow: Iskusstvo, 1989), pp. 67, 72–7, 84–6, 93.

people', pointing out that mass audiences were actually flocking to clown shows and light entertainment, rather than to the cerebral avant-gardism of the Maiakovskii/Meierkhold partnership.[10]

These squabbles would soon become redundant as the NEP era drew to a close with Stalin's consolidation of political power in the late 1920s. This process coincided with strong attacks by 'proletarian' cultural organisations on writers perceived as reactionary. The eventual consequences of such disputes were far from trivial, of course: we have only to think of the tragic fate of Meierkhold, who was arrested in June 1939 and subjected to protracted tortures before being shot in February 1940; his actress wife was also mysteriously murdered.

Socialist Realism

The literary disputes which had inaugurated the 1930s were resolved in 1934 with the first congress of the newly formed Union of Soviet Writers, an event at which Socialist Realism was promulgated as 'the official method of Soviet literature and criticism'.[11] In his article 'On Plays' (O p'esakh, 1933), Maksim Gorkii (1868–1936) had called for civic drama to be based on plausible character conflict and the Stanislavskian mode of psychological realism was once again extolled.[12] It is easy to disparage the products of Socialist Realism, but it is also important to acknowledge that for a large part of the twentieth century – from the mid-1930s until the mid-1980s and beyond – these constituted for the vast majority of the Soviet population the only available cultural fare. Those still old enough to remember it may shrug it off now, like an immature aberration of their youth, but the social and cultural impact of Socialist Realism was enormous in its day. This was perhaps particularly true in the embodied art form that is theatre.

As an example of Socialist Realist drama at its most successful and wholesome, we can take Nikolai Pogodin's (1900–1962) play The Kremlin Chimes (Kremlevskie kuranty), commissioned in 1939, first performed in 1940–1, and then significantly revised in 1955–6. The Kremlin Chimes was the second in a historical trilogy Pogodin wrote about Lenin, who died in 1924. The trilogy's

---

10 J. A. E. Curtis, 'A theatrical battle of wits: Bulgakov, Maiakovskii, and Meierkhol'd', Modern Language Review 108.3 (2013), 928–30.

11 This definition was adopted in the constitution (ustav) of the Union of Soviet Writers. See Katerina Clark's comprehensive account of Socialist Realism in The Soviet Novel: History as Ritual (Chicago, London: University of Chicago Press, 1981, 1985), chap. 1.

12 Laurence Senelick and Sergei Ostrovsky (eds.), The Soviet Theater: A Documentary History (New Haven: Yale University Press, 2014), p. 9.

purpose was to look back at the achievements of the Bolshevik leader in order to consolidate the foundational myths of the modern Soviet state. The focus of the work, set in 1920, is the plan that Lenin had for the electrification of the Soviet Union, a project he would be unable to launch without the help of anti-Bolshevik 'bourgeois specialists', such as the engineer Zabelin. At the same time, Lenin notes that the chimes on the Spasskii Tower of the Kremlin have fallen silent during the civil war, and he ensures that a clockmaker is found to repair them, so that this play too, like Maiakovskii's *Mystery-Bouffe*, concludes with a rousing rendition of 'The Internationale' from the clock tower.

The writing here exemplifies many of the tenets of Socialist Realism in its Stalin-era variant, and the fate of the play's productions reveals a great deal about the unfolding of cultural history during the Soviet period. Pogodin, a man of peasant origins from Ukraine's Donetsk region, depicts Lenin as a strong leader with an appealing personality: he is humane, wry, approachable, even sentimental, and of course he inspires Zabelin to take on the project of electrification. The propaganda message is uncomplicated, but it is packaged in a nuanced version of traditional psychological realism which made it very palatable to Soviet audiences: from 1940 to 1941 the play ran in over fifty theatres simultaneously.

One of the reasons for the success of *The Kremlin Chimes* was that it was one of the first times that Stalin had been portrayed on stage alongside Lenin: a production photograph from 1942 shows Lenin with his arm around Stalin's shoulders, as together they persuade Zabelin to join the cause. However, in the post-Stalin era, and after Khrushchev's 'secret speech' to the Twentieth Party Congress of the Communist Party in 1956, the play received a final, fundamental revision by Pogodin. It then ran successfully in theatres for several decades more (including the Moscow Art Theatre from 1956). A film was also made of it in 1970, and a 1977 edition of Pogodin's trilogy was given a print run of 200,000 copies. The crucial change that Pogodin introduced in the Thaw period was to simply excise the part of Stalin, transforming the play into an unequivocal tribute to Lenin's achievements alone. The play's complex fate across several decades precisely illustrates what Katerina Clark has brilliantly demonstrated: that the true nature of Socialist Realism is an ever-shifting entity, a notion which continually alters to suit the prevailing exigencies of the Communist Party agenda at any given moment in history.[13]

---

13 See Clark, *The Soviet Novel*.

The Thaw and the Brezhnev Era

The decades after Stalin's death in 1953 were marked by an alternation between moments of liberalisation from the harsher constraints of Socialist Realism and reaffirmations of dogmatic communist values and renewed suspicion of experimentation in theatrical genres and forms. These tentative zigzags in cultural policy would mark developments across all genres of literature for a further thirty years, right up until the mid-1980s. The publication by Vladimir Pomerantsev (1907–1971) of his landmark article in the journal *New World* (*Novyi mir*, 1925–) under the title 'On Sincerity in Literature' (*Ob iskrennosti v literature*, 1953) opened the way towards a new focus on the inner, emotional dilemmas of the individual and away from the rhetoric of public duty and heroic deeds which had characterised the heyday of Socialist Realism. In drama, somewhat lacklustre new voices emerged, such as those of Aleksei Arbuzov (1908–1986) and Aleksandr Vampilov (1937–1972), to mention just a couple of the artists who came to dominate playwriting during the Thaw period. Their plays stepped away from Socialist Realist norms by reverting (fairly cautiously) to the eternal themes of drama, such as family, love, ambition, and jealousy, but at the same time they were formally unadventurous, remaining close to the Chekhovian tradition of Realist drama. Nowadays their plays are largely forgotten. At the time, their emotional appeal helped to foster enthusiasm for theatre-going across a wide spectrum of society, especially among women, and from the 1960s to the 1980s a trip to the theatre constituted a smart night out for the nascent Soviet middle class. Theatres were firmly established as state institutions, funded from government budgets, and were slow to change; this was the period when many of the important theatres in Russia established semi-permanent companies of actors, with top stars reprising their most popular roles for their fans for years on end – sometimes even decades. 'Stagnation' was a term that could be applied to the theatre scene, just as it came to characterise the Brezhnev era as a whole.

Of course, the picture was far from uniform during these decades, and innovation was being pursued in various guises. Between 1979 and 1981, for example, the director Viacheslav Spesivtsev (1943–) devised an entirely novel form of theatre production, which took place on a moving suburban train. The subject matter of this show, called *The Train of My Memory* (*Pamiati moei poezd*, premiere 1979), was politically irreproachable – the life-story of Lenin's comrade Feliks Dzerzhinskii, notorious for setting up the Cheka (which ultimately became the KGB/FSB). The entire performance took place inside

the train carriage as it travelled away from Moscow's Kursk Station and back again. Use was made of the exterior spaces as well, so that when the train stopped on a bridge over the River Moskva, the blinds were raised for the audience to watch a woman in a shawl walking towards the edge, as if to throw herself off; and at the final destination, spectators watched from the platform as political conspirators trudged through the snow of an adjacent field to share their secret plans. Innovative theatre-making was here tolerated by the authorities because of the unproblematic political messaging of the content.

If the playwrights of the post-Stalin era were for the most part not particularly adventurous, either formally or thematically, the period became known above all as the age of 'directors' theatre', and significant formal developments took place at the level of production. Groundbreaking productions were directed by the likes of Oleg Efremov (1927–2000), a socially engaged post-Stanislavskian director who focused on the directness and simplicity of acting techniques; Georgii Tovstonogov (1915–1989), who saw himself as *auteur* of his productions of many Russian classics; Anatolii Efros (1925–1987), who refreshed the Stanislavskian concept of the ensemble; and Lev Dodin (1944–), known for lengthy adaptations of Russian prose texts in which the actor co-creates the production. New theatres were opened, including the hugely influential Sovremennik Theatre and the Taganka Theatre, whose productions sold out after Iurii Liubimov (1917–2014) was appointed artistic director in 1964.[14] Liubimov adapted novels such as Lermontov's *A Hero of Our Time* (*Geroi nashego vremeni*, 1840; premiere 1964) as well as creating visually stunning new productions of William Shakespeare's *Hamlet* (*Gamlet*, premiere 1977, starring the popular songwriter and poet Vladimir Vysotskii (1938–1980)), and Pushkin's *Boris Godunov* (premiere 1982). One of his most popular productions was an adaptation of the belatedly published satirical novel of the 1930s, Bulgakov's *The Master and Margarita* (*Master i Margarita*, premiere 1971). Liubimov's characteristic approach involved structuring the performance as a kind of 'montage of attractions' (borrowed from Sergei Eisenstein's (1898–1948) cinema concept), with a rapid succession of visual impressions giving the audience a series of shocks. He would select a specific metaphor or leitmotif design image for each production – a long plank for *Boris Godunov*, for example, which served multiple visual and symbolic functions in the staging to underpin the play's

---

14 See Birgit Beumers, *Yury Lyubimov at the Taganka Theatre, 1964–1994* (Abingdon: Routledge, 1997).

core preoccupation with the struggle for power (the production was swiftly banned in 1982, before the premiere could take place, and was first staged in 1988).[15] Liubimov was the epitome of the autocratic theatre director, to the extent that he would stand at the back of the auditorium during a performance holding blinking coloured flashlights, first to establish and then to control the rhythm of the dialogue for the actors on stage. He was exiled in 1984 after speaking out against theatrical censorship, but he returned to Moscow in 1988, during Gorbachev's era of Perestroika. Many of these directors of the post-Stalin era were in fact revisiting the innovations of the early twentieth century, whether by drawing upon the non-ideological productions staged by Stanislavskii or developing the techniques of spectacle explored by Meierkhold.

Glasnost

After Mikhail Gorbachev took power in 1985 and proclaimed his new policy of Glasnost, fundamental transformations began in Soviet theatre, as in other spheres of culture. The term *glasnost'* is not readily translatable, but being rooted in the Slavonic term for 'voice' it suggests a policy of voicing that which has not been uttered previously and of allowing new voices to be heard. In many respects this notion has provided the broad framework within which theatre has developed in Russia up to the present day.

Two plays written in 1988, at the height of Gorbachev's Glasnost and at a time when state restrictions on repertory choices had only just been removed, encapsulate some of the many new avenues that had now opened up. Mikhail Shatrov's (1932–2010) *Onward, Onward, Onward!* (*Dal'she, dal'she, dal'she*, 1988), like Pogodin's *Kremlin Chimes*, was one of a trilogy of plays the author wrote about Lenin – and like Pogodin, Shatrov's purpose was to celebrate the Bolshevik leader. Shatrov first started writing after Khrushchev's 'secret speech' of 1956 made it apparent just how vindictively Stalin had eliminated all those who had created the October Revolution alongside Lenin. Among those 'Old Bolsheviks' were members of Shatrov's immediate family. In an ingenious device, Shatrov brings all the participants in the events of October 1917 together in some sort of metaphysical realm, where with the benefit of hindsight they thrash out how it was that Lenin's vision became so distorted by Stalin. Shatrov made prompt use of newly released documents from Soviet archives, to the extent that Iurii Afanasev,

---

15 Beumers, *Lyubimov*, pp. 249–50.

director of the Institute for State Historical Archives, commented ruefully that Shatrov's project was 'a bitter reproach to historians, who should have been undertaking such tasks themselves'.[16] Shatrov's work was personally endorsed by Gorbachev himself, since the two men's political convictions were essentially aligned, and in this respect one could argue that *Onward, Onward, Onward!* is one of the very final works of Soviet Socialist Realism, in that it efficiently conveys the propaganda message the regime wished to communicate. The play was briefly very controversial, but its topicality soon evaporated and the work was altogether forgotten in the turmoil that followed upon the collapse of the entire Soviet state in 1991. Within just a few years, Shatrov had abandoned the theatre and set up as a businessman – but his use of documentary here to fulfil cathartic personal and political testimonial functions was to prefigure many twenty-first-century developments.

Another play written in 1988 is a miniature by Liudmila Petrushevskaia (1938–), who is perhaps the best known among an entire generation of women playwrights (including Nina Sadur (1950–2023)), Liudmila Razumovskaia (1946–), and Olga Mukhina (1970–), to name but a few) who burst upon the scene from the late 1980s onwards. Petrushevskaia is a contemporary of Vampilov's, but unlike him is a constant innovator. Her piece *The Isolation Ward* (*Izolirovannyi boks*, 1988) is not one of her best-known works, but it neatly encapsulates the ways in which her writing rethought the entire concept of drama, whereas Shatrov in the same year was still chewing over the remnants of the past in a format that continued to rely upon a conventional theatrical space and audience.

Petrushevskaia describes two women, A and B, who find themselves sharing an isolation ward because of their terminal diagnoses. It is not even clear that this work can be called a play, since its few pages are simply constituted by their somewhat disjointed dialogue, in which they gradually reveal their anxieties about the children they will be leaving behind. Caryl Emerson speaks of Petrushevskaia's universe being 'grim and unsentimental' and notes that in her finely wrought dialogues there is a 'rejection of . . . all hope for a spark or a leap of communication between human beings'.[17] These

---

16 Iurii Afanasev, interview in *Sovetskaia kul'tura* [Soviet culture] (21 March 1987), 3, quoted in Julian Graffy, 'The literary press', in Graffy and Geoffrey A. Hosking (eds.), *Culture and the Media in the USSR Today* (New York: St Martin's Press, 1989), p. 141, n. 29.

17 Caryl Emerson, *The Cambridge Introduction to Russian Literature* (Cambridge: Cambridge University Press, 2008), p. 233.

women's stories reflect the breakdown of Soviet family life, since they have clearly brought up their children alone; but neither suggests that the state has treated them badly in any way, and they have no political grievances. These are simply the voices of ordinary individuals, describing the universal small-scale worries which have shaped their lives, at a moment when they are confronting their own mortality. After the didacticism of Socialist Realism, straightforward Realism becomes all the more powerful. This is a Glasnost play, in that it allows us to listen to the voices of ordinary folk whom we don't usually hear; but it is also a 'post-dramatic' play, in Hans-Thies Lehmann's sense of a play which no longer rests on plot, intrigue, and dramatic action in order to seize the audience's attention, and which does not seem to require any kind of conventional theatre space for its performance.

The Putin Era

Vladimir Putin's accession to the presidency a coincides with the emergence of a powerful movement in Russian theatre which came to be known as 'New Drama'. It was largely fuelled by a Moscow ensemble called Teatr.doc, founded by Elena Gremina (1956–2018) and Mikhail Ugarov (1956–2018). To some extent taking inspiration from seminars conducted in Russia from the late 1990s on by British theatre makers from London's Royal Court, the key focus for Teatr.doc, as the name suggests, was to explore the dramatic potential of documents and verbatim texts. Teatr.doc's own productions, plus the annual Liubimovka Festival for new writing in Russian hosted in their premises, provided the driving force for New Drama. Their projects drew in many partners from the former Soviet republics, especially Ukraine and Belarus, as well as the flourishing theatre schools and studios in the Russian provinces, in cities such as Ekaterinburg and Togliatti. While state-sponsored theatres looked for commercial success and tolerated the con-straints put upon their work by government awards of funding, Teatr.doc and a number of other independent theatres across the country were devel-oping enthusiastic and youthful audiences seeking new voices and open to new forms.

New Drama is characterised by a number of features: above all a truthful-ness to the document and spoken word which, in an extension of the spirit of Glasnost, has enabled voices from underrepresented groups such as prisoners and migrants to be heard for the first time on stage. Not surprisingly, this means that the texts of New Drama have been saturated with socially or ethnically specific language, plus an unprecedented quantity of obscenity and

blasphemy. The initial stance of Teatr.doc was to adopt a 'zero position', in other words to allow both sides of a controversial debate to be heard without steering the audience into supporting one or the other. For example, in the aftermath of the devastating 2004 terrorist assault on a school in Beslan, which led to the deaths of more than 300 people (over half of them children), Ugarov created a show called *September.doc* (*Sentiabr'.doc*, premiere 2005) in which the actors spoke text taken directly from social media, reflecting a variety of pro-Russian and pro-Chechen comments on the events. Shocking and touching opinions were uttered on both sides. In 2010, however, Gremina wrote *An Hour and Eighteen Minutes* (*Chas 18*, premiere 2010), in which she described the appalling death in custody of the Odesa-born lawyer Sergei Magnitskii, accused in a grotesquely unjust charge of crimes for which the police authorities had themselves been responsible. To their corruption was added callous brutality, which led to Magnitskii's agonising death, deprived of appropriate medical treatment. This text, which combined documentary materials with some invented sections, marked Teatr.doc's move away from its apparently neutral stance on political issues.

After 2012, when Putin took up the position of president for a third term, the Russian state shifted sharply towards the right in the cultural and social spheres. A whole range of legislation and broader cultural guidelines have been published and enacted, which all weaponise culture as an instrument in the creation of an exceptionalist, renewed Russian state. Much influenced by the Russian Orthodox Church, these regulations or guidelines shaping the current Putin era include: the banning of obscenity from all print literature, theatre, or film; severe penalties for offence to religious feeling (see, for example, the two-year prison sentences meted out to the members of Pussy Riot, who in 2012 created a brief punk video in a church, in which they called for the Virgin Mary to get rid of Putin); a ban on 'the promotion of non-traditional family values' (a code phrase for non-heterosexual relationships) to anyone under eighteen, together with a reluctance to address gender identity and social problems such as addiction and domestic abuse; restrictions on public interpretations of historical figures and events (Stalin, the Terror, the Second World War, communism) which do not conform to official government positions; and penalties for publishing anything deemed offensive to the authorities or government figures – which becomes an effective way of stifling investigations into political scandals. In many respects, Putin (himself a former KGB officer) is currently presiding over a reinstatement of Soviet-style Socialist Realism in the sense of a monolithic and all-embracing cultural policy for the entire nation, in which communist

ideology has been deftly – and rather successfully – replaced by religion and nationalism.

In theatre, the era of New Drama has petered out, in part due to the premature deaths in the spring of 2018 of both Ugarov and Gremina. Independent theatre has continued to struggle on, however, even though the freedoms New Drama explored seem to be once again in jeopardy, especially after the events of 2022. Until recently, some of the more conventional theatres did occasionally perform some of the best-known, text-focused authors of the last twenty years, such as Ivan Vyrypaev (1974–), whose violent and beautiful *Oxygen* (*Kislorod*, 2003) is the most accomplished literary play-text of the twenty-first century. Witness and testimonial theatre continued to flourish – see, for example, Aleksandra Polivanova (1976–) and Mikhail Kaluzhskii's (1967–) play *The Second Act: Grandchildren* (*Vtoroi akt. Vnuki*, 2012), in which therapeutic results are achieved for descendants of those who perpetrated Stalin's Terror.[18] Meanwhile, experimental drama has relished the new opportunities offered by multimedia and social media resources and techniques to take theatre away from text, away from authorship, away from audience identity, and out of the theatre space, leaving sets, costumes, lighting, and make-up all behind. Performance and audience participation increasingly challenge individuals to live and act and speak for themselves, precisely at a time when the state has sought to exert increasing control over all aspects of people's lives and social identity.

Further Reading

Beumers, Birgit, *Yury Lyubimov at the Taganka Theatre, 1964–1994* (Abingdon: Routledge, 1997).

Beumers, Birgit, and Mark Lipovetsky, *Performing Violence: Literary and Theatrical Experiments of New Russian Drama* (Bristol: Intellect, 2009).

Braun, Edward, *The Theatre of Meyerhold: Revolution on the Modern Stage* (London: Eyre Methuen, 1979).

Curtis, J. A. E. (ed.), *New Drama in Russian: Performance, Politics and Protest in Russia, Ukraine and Belarus* (London: Bloomsbury Academic, 2020).

Flynn, Molly, *Witness Onstage: Documentary Theatre in Twenty-first-Century Russia* (Manchester: Manchester University Press, 2019).

Frame, Murray, *School for Citizens: Theatre and Civil Society in Imperial Russia* (New Haven: Yale University Press, 2006).

18 For more on this genre of drama, see Molly Flynn, *Witness Onstage: Documentary Theatre in Twenty-First-Century Russia* (Manchester: Manchester University Press, 2019).

Leach, Robert, and Victor Borovsky (eds.), *A History of Russian Theatre* (Cambridge: Cambridge University Press, 1999).

Listengarten, Julia, *Russian Tragifarce: Its Cultural and Political Roots* (London: Associated University Presses, 2000).

Rudnitsky, Konstantin, *Russian and Soviet Theatre: Tradition and the Avant-Garde* (London: Thames and Hudson, 1988).

Russell, Robert, and Andrew Barratt (eds.), *Russian Theatre in the Age of Modernism* (Basingstoke: Macmillan, 1990).

Segel, Harold B., *Twentieth-Century Russian Drama: From Gorky to the Present*, updated edn (Baltimore: Johns Hopkins University Press, 1993).

Senelick, Laurence, and Sergei Ostrovsky (eds.), *The Soviet Theater: A Documentary History* (New Haven: Yale University Press, 2014).

Smeliansky, Anatoly, *The Russian Theatre after Stalin* (Cambridge: Cambridge University Press, 1999).

Verse II

ISOBEL PALMER

This chapter's temporal focus is the final decade of the nineteenth century and the first few decades of the twentieth, when a new generation of poets and theorists sought to revive and reinvigorate poetic expression after a long half-century dominated by Realist prose. The discoveries of this extraordinary period of artistic experiment and invention would resonate through the century to follow. Russian Modernists were, like their European counterparts, eager to break with tradition; to invent new poetic forms capacious enough to contend with the rapidly changing social, political, and technological circumstances of those years; and to express the new experiences to which these gave rise. As the series of overlapping accounts offered here illustrate, however, Modernist innovation did not always involve the straightforward rejection of formal convention. On the contrary, Modernist poetry in Russia is characterised above all by creative engagement with the traditional structures of poetic form, the precise functioning and effects of which they sought to identify and describe. This interest in poetic form was inextricable from the mystical and utopian dreams harboured by many Russian poets, resulting in the idiosyncratic blend of the spiritual and the scientific that characterises Russian Modernism's relationship with form.

The structure of this chapter reflects this expansive conception of form, examining, in turn, Modernism's engagement with the metrical and strophic structures that constitute poetic form in the strictest sense; the sonic and visual form of poetic texts; and modes of poetic address and poetry's role in public discourse. These frames have been selected to demonstrate the manner in which, during the early decades of the twentieth century, poets and an emergent generation of literary theorists engaged not only in formal experimentation but also in debates about the nature of form as such. In the final section, I turn to consider the resonance of these experiments in verse of the later twentieth and twenty-first centuries.

Metrical Forms

From the moment of its emergence in the early 1890s, Russian Modernism was defined in large part by its efforts to test and expand the metrical repertoire of Russian verse. The pace of innovation was rapid, at times remarkably so, with new metrical forms and rhythmic variations often invented and assimilated within the space of a few months. Although many of these forms were borrowed from western European counterparts – as, for example, when the energetic young Symbolist Valerii Briusov (1873–1924) produced direct translations of French Modernist verse – all nonetheless represent a new stage in Russian prosody, when forms originally taken on loan from foreign traditions (syllabo-tonic metre, for instance – see Chapter 3.3) became fully assimilated into a distinctively Russian prosodic idiom.

The period was, moreover, one during which the study of verse became a serious discipline. Poets themselves were at the forefront of this movement, often theorising their own work even as they were writing it. The Symbolist poet Andrei Belyi (1880–1934), for example, was the first to articulate the distinction between metre (the ideal scheme of stressed syllables in a line) and rhythm (their actual pattern). His seminal work on statistical versification in *Symbolism* (*Simvolizm*, 1910) would directly inspire two groups of young scholars – the Moscow Linguistic Circle (*Moskovskii linvisticheskii kruzhok*, or MLC, and the Petersburg-based Society for the Study of Poetic Language (*Obshchestvo izucheniia poeticheskogo iazyka*, or OPOIAZ), both formed in 1916 – who went on to systematise and refine Belyi's efforts. The Formal method, as the work of these scholars would become known, moved away from inherited conventions for the description of poetry (the metrical foot, for example) and towards dynamic theories such as that developed by Iurii Tynianov (1894–1943) in *The Problem of Verse Language* (*Problema stikhotvornogo iazyka*, 1924), which sought to account for metre and rhythm within the broader framework of the verse line, the stanza, and the whole poem as well as in relation to verse semantics, sound patterning, and rhyme.

As in so many countries, Modernism in Russia first gained momentum in opposition to what had come before. This meant a rejection of nineteenth-century positivism and the prose fiction that was one of its main vehicles. Disturbed by the increasing mechanisation and atomisation of modern life under industrial capitalism, on the one hand, and oppressed by the stagnation of imperial Russia's society and politics, on the other, the mystically inclined Symbolist poets sought an escape through poetry, which they regarded as

one means by which to expand understanding beyond that made possible through ordinary language and to bridge the gap between empirical reality (*realia*, as they termed it) and a transcendent beyond (*realoria*). Modernism's challenge to Pushkinian conventions of metre and rhyme and the increasingly complex metrical repertoire that came to replace them may be viewed as a product of this shift, as poets returned to those structures that most starkly differentiated verse from prose and which most closely resembled music, held during this period to be the highest, most spiritual art form.

In tonic verse, common in Russian folk songs, each line contains a fixed number of stressed positions separated by a varying number of unstressed syllables. Such non-classical verse forms appear occasionally in the nineteenth-century work of poets such as Mikhail Lermontov (1814–1841), but the Symbolists Briusov and Zinaida Gippius (1869–1945) were the first to use them extensively in their poetry. It was Aleksandr Blok (1880–1921), however, who ensured their canonical status, and particularly that of the *dol'nik*, a type of tonic verse in which intervals between stressed positions may consist of either one or two syllables. In his breakthrough 1905 collection, *Poems about a Beautiful Lady* (*Stikhi o prekrasnoi dame*, comp. 1901–2), the *dol'nik* acquired a distinctive pattern that would remain common in poetry through to the end of the 1920s:

> Vkhozhú ia v tëmnye khrámy,
> Soversháiu bédnyi obriád.
> Tam zhdú ia Prekrásnoi Dámy
> V mertsán'i krásnykh lampád.

> (I enter dark temples,
> Perform a meagre rite.
> There I await the Beautiful Lady
> In the shimmering red lamps' light.)[1]

As with almost all examples of *dol'nik* verse in this collection, each line contains three stressed syllables, with intervals limited to one or two unstressed syllables. Despite the relative consistency of Blok's *dol'nik*, the distribution of stressed syllables remains unpredictable and stands in tension with the hypnotic regularity of the poem's undulating masculine (final syllable stressed) and feminine (penultimate syllable stressed) rhymes. The

---

1 A. A. Blok, *Polnoe sobranie sochinenii* [Complete works], 20 vols. (Moscow: Nauka, 1997–), vol. I, p. 128. Translation cited from Stuart H. Goldberg, 'Your mistress or mine? Briusov, Blok and the boundaries of poetic "propriety"', *Slavic and East European Journal* 60.4 (2016), 663.

poem's form thus induces in the reader something of the same sense of anticipation and uncertainty as is experienced by this hero, whose longing for the Beautiful Lady – the earthly incarnation, according to Symbolist philosophy, of the divine Sophia, or eternal wisdom – is both hopeful and tempered by the fear that, as another poem in the collection ends, 'You will change your countenance' (*Izménish' óblik tý*).[2]

This latter poem, which begins 'I anticipate you' (*Predchúvstvuiu tebiá*), is one of a number in this collection that use syllabo-tonic metres, together creating a backdrop against which the less familiar *dol'nik* could be more easily assimilated into the metrical canon.[3] Once established, Blok and poets of the next generation were able to experiment more widely with the *dol'nik* and other tonic metres, varying the number of stressed syllables and the length of each line. While Acmeists such as Anna Akhmatova (1889–1966) and Osip Mandelshtam (1891–1938) tempered the novelty of the *dol'nik* by combining it with their preferred classical metres, Futurists such as Vladimir Maiakovskii (1893–1930) sought yet more innovative metrical forms to approximate the changing rhythms of modern life and technology, including more complex, polymetrical verse, in which multiple metres are combined within one poem, or even a single line (see Chapters 1.6, 1.7). Boris Pasternak's (1890–1960) early work, which was heavily influenced by Futurism, provides some striking examples of this latter approach, particularly in the 1916 collection *Over the Barriers* (*Poverkh bar'erov*).

Blok's *The Twelve* (*Dvenadtsat'*, 1918) represents one culmination of these pre-revolutionary developments. Composed over a few short nights in January 1918, this long poem, or *poema*, depicts a group of twelve red guardsmen wandering through revolutionary Petrograd. The poem weaves the tumult and noise of this urban space into a complex metrical landscape where the rhythms typical of popular forms such as gypsy romances – 'cruel songs' (*zhestokie romansy*) – and military marches mingle with snatches of speech and political slogans. The use of repeated refrains – in part two, for instance, where the line *Ékh, ékh, béz krestá!* ('Yeah, yeah, without the cross!') occurs three times – recalls the folk *chastushka*, a type of crude street song that often comments on current events.[4] Such language appears in Blok's *poema* in

2 Blok, *Polnoe sobranie sochinenii*, vol. I, p. 60.
3 Mikhail Gasparov, 'Blok v istorii russkogo stikha' [Blok in the history of Russian verse], in *Izbrannye trudy* [Selected works], 3 vols. (Moscow: Iazyki russkoi kul'tury, 1997), vol. III, pp. 449–68.
4 Maria Carlson, 'Alexander Blok, Twelve: A poema in a new translation', KU ScholarWorks (2010), http://hdl.handle.net/1808/6598, accessed 1 April 2022. (All quotations of the poem and its translation are from this edition.)

often-incongruent combinations. At the end of part three, for example, a proletarian *chastushka* based on common tropes from Bolshevik rhetoric ends with a line taken from Orthodox prayer:

> Mý na góre vsém burzhúiam
> Mirovói pozhár razdúem,
> Mirovói pozhár v kroví –
> Góspodi, blagosloví!

> (To the grief of all bourgeois
> We'll fan a worldwide conflagration,
> A conflagration drenched in blood –
> Give us Your blessing, O Lord!)

This motley crowd of metrical forms and lexical spheres evokes the anarchic atmosphere of Russia's Lenten carnival as well as the tumult of the revolutionary street. Yet the poem itself is far from chaotic. Its diverse rhythms are carefully orchestrated and participate in the creation of meaning, as illustrated by its opening lines:

> Chërnyi vécher.
> Bélyi snég.
> Véter, véter!
> Na nogákh ne stoít chelovék.
> Véter, véter –
> Na vsëm bózh'em svéte!

> (Black night.
> White snow.
> The wind, the wind!
> Impossible to stay on your feet.
> The wind, the wind!
> Blowing across God's world!)

The first three lines of the poem appear to be in trochaic dimeter (lines of two metrical feet composed of a stressed syllable followed by an unstressed syllable). However, the insistent beat of these lines is interrupted as the fourth line slips – like the man it describes – into anapaests (unstressed, unstressed, stressed). A similar effect is felt in line 6, where the intrusion of the *dol'nik* buffets the line's stresses much like the wind; the tonic metre that results then persists through the rest of the first part. Combining scattered urban rhythms with bursts of classical metre and degraded echoes of previously cherished Symbolist images, Blok's poem identifies the rhythm of modern life not with the thrill and speed of new technologies but with the

cacophony produced as the harsh cadences of a new world order collide with the last stutters of a world now dying away.

The *poema* enjoyed a revival during the 1910s and 1920s.[5] Such poems frequently employed complex polymetrical constructions to combine intense lyric expression with the sweep of narrative. Marina Tsvetaeva's (1892–1941) *Poem of the Mountain* (*Poema gory*, 1924) and *Poem of the End* (*Poema kontsa*, 1924) are exemplary in this regard. Characteristically for the period, Tsvetaeva's passionate, frequently stylised poetry makes use of a daring range of prosodic devices, with intricate sound patterning, striking punctuation, and strophic inventiveness further complicating the dense metrical and rhythmic structure of her work. Composed while the poet was living in emigration in Prague, her 'poems of the end' make explicit one important function taken on by *The Twelve* and the Modernist *poema* more broadly, which sing out the old world even as they seek a means by which to confront the challenges of the new – whether the pain of enforced emigration, as in Tsvetaeva's work; the new order's hostility towards lyric expression, as in Maiakovskii's *About That* (*Pro eto*, 1924); or, as in Akhmatova's later *Poem without a Hero* (*Poema bez geroia*, comp. 1940–62), the Modernist generation's sense of loss and culpability before its age.

This is not to say such poems were purely retrospective. In *The Twelve*, the disparate episodes presented in each part are spliced together in a poetic precursor to montage techniques developed by filmmakers such as Dziga Vertov (1896–1954) and Sergei Eisenstein (1898–1948) in the 1920s. Later, this technique would be taken up by Mikhail Kuzmin (1872–1936), whose autobiographical cycle 'The Trout Breaks the Ice' (*Forel' razbivaet led*, 1929) draws heavily on the poetics of silent film, among other cultural sources. The cinematic credentials of Blok's poem are reinforced by the stark chiaroscuro of its setting ('Black night / White snow'), an effect that is emphasised by the striking, Cubistic illustrations produced by Iurii Annenkov (1889–1974) for the poem's first published edition. Such illustrations further complicate the poem's metrical structure, expanding its rhythms beyond the confines of the poem's text and the individual line. In this sense, metrical experimentation during the Modernist period had as much to do with poetry's visual plane as with its musical lineage; it is to this aspect of poetic form I now turn.

---

5 Robert Bird, 'Envoicing history: On the narrative poem in Russian Modernism', *Slavic and East European Journal* 51.1 (2007), 53–73.

Intermedial Forms

If Russian Modernists engaged intently with the verse line, they were no less attentive to the individual unit of poetic expression: the word. The word was no longer viewed primarily as the medium of thought but as an object in its own right.

For Symbolists, seeking to overcome the division between the word's sound and its deeper significance, this was an object imbued with mystical significance. Ordinary metaphor was transformed into the symbol, a trope that set the range of potential meanings attached to the word reverberating far beyond the bounds of its direct referent and promised to uncover language's 'living' origins and 'the parallelism of the phenomenal and the noumenal', in the words of Viacheslav Ivanov (1866–1949), poet and leading theoretician of the movement.[6]

Numerous literary groups emerged to challenge Symbolism in the early 1910s on precisely this basis. As Mandelshtam wrote in 'About the Nature of the Word' (*O prirode slova*), published in 1922:

> The rose is a likeness of the sun, the sun is a likeness of the rose, a dove – of a girl, and a girl – of a dove. Images are gutted like scarecrows and packed with foreign content. Instead of a symbolic forest, a taxidermist's shop [. . .] Nothing is real or authentic [. . .] Eternal winking. Not a single clear word; only hints and implications.[7]

Acmeism, Mandelshtam declared, would instead call a rose a rose. Founded in 1912, the Acmeist movement rejected the mystical vagueness of Symbolist poetics in favour of 'Apollonian' clarity. Nonetheless, their work demonstrates something of the same concern with the word's capacity to reach beyond itself and straddle multiple realms. In Mandelshtam's precise, classical verse, however, the poet acts not as theurge but as a craftsman, an architect whose task was to bridge the gap between language and the 'formidable density' of things;[8] as the speaker states in 'Notre Dame' (*Notre Dame*), a central poem in Mandelshtam's first collection, *Stone* (*Kamen'*, 1913): 'Fortress Notre Dame,

---

6 Viacheslav Ivanov, 'Zavety simvolizma' [Testaments of Symbolism], in *Sobranie sochinenii* [Collected works], ed. D. V. Ivanova and O. Deshart, 4 vols. (Brussels: Foyer Oriental Chrétien, 1971–87), vol. II (1974), p. 596.

7 Sidney Monas, 'Osip Mandelstam: About the nature of the word', *Arion: A Journal of Humanities and the Classics* 2 (1975), 519. Translation modified.

8 Osip Mandelshtam, 'Utro akmeizma' [The morning of Acmeism], in *Polnoe sobranie sochinenii i pisem* [Complete collected works and letters], 3 vols. (Moscow: Progress-Pleiada, 2010), vol. II, p. 22. Translation cited from Victor Erlich, 'Russian poets in search of a poetics', *Comparative Literature* 4.1 (Winter 1952), 64.

the more attentively / I studied your vast ribs and frame, / the more I kept repeating: one day I too / will craft beauty from cruel weight.'[9]

At the heart of Russian Futurist poetics, by contrast, was *zaum'*, an invented 'transrational' language that dispensed entirely with the ordinary names for things. Locating language at the intersection between sound, vision, and performance, the *zaumniki*, as its practitioners were known, took verbal roots and fragments from existing words and combined them to create entirely new ones. The resulting 'sound-speech' (*zvukorech'*) was programmatically indeterminate, intended not to convey semantic meaning but to provoke an immediate, emotional response. This topic was at the centre of contemporary debates in psychology.[10] One of the earliest examples of transrational poetry is 'Incantation by Laughter' (*Zakliatie smekhom*, 1908–9) by Velimir Khlebnikov (1885–1922), a poem composed entirely of neologisms created from the root of the Russian for 'laughter'. While many of these neologisms are created using recognisable Russian affixes, the specific meaning of each is less important than the sound of laughter that the poem reproduces. Khlebnikov's eclectic interests – which ranged from Slavic etymology and mythology to mathematics, numerology, the language of birds, and more – inform his remarkable body of work, which even at its most epic (as in the 1922 *Zangezi* (*Zangezi*), a self-proclaimed 'supersaga' (*sverkhpovest'*)) demonstrates a persistent fascination with the word and the morpheme not simply as units of meaning but as windows into new planes of perception and new worlds.

Zaum' had consequences not only for the sound of poetry but also for its visual form. This is illustrated by Aleksei Kruchenykh's (1886–1968) 'Dyr bul shchyl' (*Dyr bul shchyl*, 1913), the first poem written entirely in *zaum'*, and one that quickly became shorthand for the Futurist movement. Defying poetry's ordinary left justification and even the usual horizontal of the written line, the poem's words and letters sprawl across the page to seep into the abstract drawings alongside which they are printed; handwritten and stylised, they call attention as much to their own form as to the poem's apparent lack thereof (see Figure 3.8.1). This was, as the title of the Cubo-Futurists' 1912 manifesto declared, 'A Slap in the Face of Public Taste' (*Poshchechina obshchestvennomu vkusu*), designed to shock the reader's sensibilities and to shake them out of habitual modes of perception.

9 Osip Mandelstam, 'Poems', trans. Robert Chandler and Boris Dralyuk, *The White Review* (Sept. 2013), www.thewhitereview.org/poetry/poems/, accessed 16 Jan. 2023.
10 Irina Svetlikova, *Istoki russkogo formalizma. Traditsiia psikhologizma i formal'naia shkola* [The sources of Russian Formalism. The tradition of psychologism and the Formal School] (Moscow: Novoe literaturnoe obozrenie, 2005).

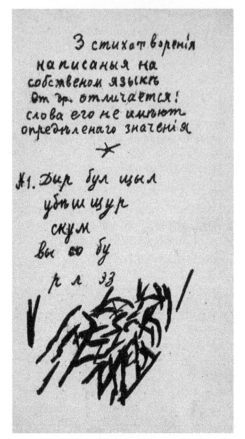

Figure 3.8.1 Aleksei Kruchenykh, 'Dyr bul shchyl', in *Pomada* (*Pomade*, 1913)

As the name implies, French Cubism was a major influence for the Cubo-Futurists, many of whom began their creative lives as visual artists. David Burliuk (1882–1967), the group's main funder and indefatigable promoter, met Maiakovskii while the two were students at the Moscow School of Art. Maiakovskii's early poetry makes extensive use of painterly devices such as *sdvig* (shift) and *faktura* (texture) in an effort to represent the new dynamism of urban life.[11] This is illustrated most vividly in 'But Could You?' (*A vy mogli by?*, 1913):

11 Juliette R. Stapanian, *Mayakovsky's Cubo-Futurist Vision* (Houston: Rice University Press, 1986).

A vý moglí by?
Ia srázu smázal kártu búdnia,
plesnúvshi krásku iz stakána;
ia pokazál na bliúde stúdnia
kosýe skúly okeána.
Na cheshué zhestiánoi rýby
prochël ia zóvy nóvykh gub.
A vý
noktiúrn sygrát'
moglí by
na fléite vodostóchnykh trúb?[12]

(**But Could You?**
I suddenly smeared the weekday map
splashing paint from a glass;
on a plate of aspic I revealed
the ocean's slanted cheeks.
On the scales of a tin fish
I read the summons of new lips.
But you
perform a nocturne
could you
on a drainpipe flute?)

The speaker appears to be a painter engaged in the composition of a Cubist still life in which frequent changes of scale and perspective draw apparently disparate objects and images into surprising configurations. Its variety of textures – smeared paint, jellied aspic, the tin fish – recall the collage technique frequently employed by Cubist visual artists, where scraps of newspaper and wallpaper pasted onto the canvas drew the viewer's attention as much to the material surface of the painting as to the painted scene. The poem does not just evoke this effect but reproduces it, through intricate sound patterning and the unexpected intermedial shift that comes with the speaker's turn to address the audience at the end. This is a still life *in verse*, we are reminded; the dynamism of the scene it depicts derives in no small part from its movement between visual, verbal, and vocal representation.

In *Tango with Cows* (*Tango s korovami*, 1914), Vasilii Kamenskii (1884–1961) pursued what he termed 'ferro-concrete' poetry, whereby the page was divided into angular quadrants reminiscent of Cubist painting, with words

12 Vladimir Maiakovskii, *Polnoe sobranie sochinenii* [Complete works], 13 vols. (Moscow: Gosudarstvennoe izdatel'stvo khudozhestvennoi literatury, 1955–61), vol. I, p. 40. Translation my own.

of different font types and sizes arranged in each; David and Nikolai (1890–1920) Burliuk contributed additional illustrations. This is a typical example of the handmade books that became a central part of avant-garde practice during this period. Indeed, the founding of Cubo-Futurism is typically dated to the publication of *Trap for Judges* (*Sadok sudei*, 1910), which, like *Tango*, was printed on old wallpaper and featured handwritten texts alongside lithographed prints. Made in collaboration with artists such as Mikhail Larionov (1881–1964), Natalia Goncharova (1861–1962), Kazimir Malevich (1879–1935), and Olga Rozanova (1886–1918), and drawing on diverse traditions such as popular *lubki* (satirical prints), Orthodox iconography, and street signage, these books challenged norms of (re)presentation, emphasising instead the materiality of the poetic text and seeking to establish more direct routes of communication by actively engaging the reader in the book as a tactile, and potentially transformative, experience. Such experiments continued into the 1920s and 1930s, when they became central to avant-garde efforts to bring a new Soviet subjectivity into being.

It was the apparent *lack* of form in such experiments that was most troubling to Futurism's many critics; 'the Cubo-Futurists are … turning poetry into nothing', as one writes in a 1913 review.[13] Yet much like the Symbolists before them, Futurist and even Acmeist artists did not so much dispense with traditional formal convention as test its limits, exaggerating the defining characteristics of poetic language – its boundary status between sense and sound or sight; the restraints imposed by the poetic line; the concentrated significance of the single stanza – in order to explore and exploit its specific capacities and power. Rejecting the Symbolist call to locate the deeper significance of words and their hidden meanings, 'Art as Device' (*Iskusstvo kak priem*, 1917) – a programmatic essay by the upstart young Formalist theorist Viktor Shklovskii (1893–1984) – instead argues for greater attentiveness to the verbal surface and formal structure of the text. The purpose of poetry, he and his contemporaries held, was not to transcend this world but to revitalise perception of it.

Performances

Modernist innovations in the sphere of poetry's sound and visual appearance were complemented and in some cases directly shaped by a simultaneous

---

13 Gerald Janecek, *Zaum: The Transrational Language of Russian Futurism* (San Diego: San Diego State University Press, 1996), p. 55.

surge of interest in poetry recitation, the theatre, and what scholars now identify as an early form of performance art.[14] While semi-public readings had long been a central feature of Russian literary life, these events acquired new significance as Modernist poets took to reading their own poetry aloud to audiences at public poetry evenings, a practice that Futurist poets transformed into boisterous poetic 'disputes', staged in large auditoriums or, occasionally, on street corners. Poetry began to absorb the intonations and lexicon of everyday, colloquial speech at an unprecedented rate. These circumstances rendered poetry a newly public genre oriented towards a mass audience, with consequences for the manner in which poetry was composed, consumed, and understood.

As public poetry readings and picture postcards made intimate encounters with the voices and faces of Modernist poets available to a mass audience, increasing importance was attached to poetic persona. While some attribute this to a neo-Romantic emphasis on the individual genius, Gregory Freidin identifies a more complex process whereby Russian poets sought to preserve the traditional authority of the poet-prophet in the face of an increasingly fragmented modern world through 'spell-binding' performances of their biographical work.[15] This practice also had a commercial aspect; Igor Severianin (1887–1941), leader of the so-called Ego-Futurists, enjoyed particular popularity and became a nationwide celebrity thanks to his 'poetry concerts' at which he half-read, half-sang original verse.

The Cubo-Futurists both disrupted this practice and took it to new extremes. Performing in one venue or another almost every day during some periods in 1913 and 1914 (including in far-flung provincial cities such as Kharkiv, Baku, and Tbilisi), Maiakovskii, David Burliuk, and their peers played with audience expectations of poetic authority by adopting larger-than-life personae; dressing in outlandish clothing; and mingling recitation of their avant-garde poetic experiments with lectures on art history, on the one hand, and deliberately shocking behaviour, on the other. Cubo-Futurist performance practice laid bare the mechanisms behind the Modernist poetic persona and sought to democratise the communicative situation upon which this persona relied by inviting (or inciting) audience participation to produce an effect.

14 RoseLee Goldberg, *Performance Art: From Futurism to the Present*, 3rd edn (London: Thames & Hudson, 2011).

15 Gregory Freidin, *A Coat of Many Colors: Osip Mandelstam and His Mythologies of Self-Presentation* (Berkeley: University of California Press, 1987), p. 7.

In the years following the revolution, poetry became an increasingly important medium for communicating revolutionary sentiment to the masses, though not without a concerted effort on the part of avant-garde poets to assert its usefulness. Maiakovskii designed eye-catching posters for the windows of the first Soviet news agency, the Russian Telegraph Agency (*Rossiiskoe telegrafnoe agenstvo*, or ROSTA), which combined caricatured sketches with catchy lines of rhymed verse throughout the civil war period to report on the latest events and to dramatise political slogans. Later, Maiakovskii would collaborate with the visual artist Aleksandr Rodchenko (1891–1956) as 'artist-constructors' to produce adverts for state products. In both cases, the utilitarian bent of pre-revolutionary Futurist poetry was made explicit; poetic language was to become a means of 'satisfying' concrete social and political 'needs', with poetry – as Maiakovskii declared in 1922 – just one among 'many areas of verbal formation (application form, article, telegram, poem, feuilleton, announcement, proclamation, advertisement, etc.)'.[16]

This is a striking statement for Maiakovskii – that 'Maiakomorphist', in Lev Trotskii's (1879–1940) memorable description – whose first published collection was entitled *I* (*Ia*, 1913), and whose best work stages a lyric baring of the poet's soul.[17] Yet, like many others in the years following the revolution, Maiakovskii was sincerely committed to devising a new, transformative mode for poetry that would emphasise not so much the poetic text as the audience's encounter with it. His collaboration with the painter El Lissitskii (1890–1941) on *For the Voice* (*Dlia golosa*, 1924) is a case in point. Inviting the reader to navigate its poems via a series of thumb-tabs and exploiting typography and layout to model the appropriate intonation, the book updated the popular pre-revolutionary series Reader-Declaimer (*Chtets-deklamator*, 1902–3) for the new Soviet age by rendering poetry a tactile and immersive experience, designed not just to entertain but to transform the Soviet reader's subjectivity; Maiakovskii's famous *lesenka* or stepladder line, designed to bring complex poetic forms to the masses, extended this experiment (see Box 1.3).

As poets sought to speak to new audiences, poetry became more receptive to the language of the street. Though pre-revolutionary poets such as Maiakovskii and Pasternak had made transformative use of an everyday idiom, the radical avant-garde programme of the Left Front of the Arts (*Levi front iskusstv*, LEF) now advocated for literature made from 'documents' of real life, which for poets meant colloquial language, criminal jargon, and Soviet neologisms. The rise of

16 Cited in Halina Stephan, *LEF and the Left Front of the Arts* (Munich: Verlag Otto Sanger, 1981), p. 92.
17 Leon Trotsky, *Literature and Revolution* (New York: Russell & Russell, 1957), p. 149.

proletarian poetry also had an effect on the poetic lexicon, as did the dialect and folksy intonations adopted by so-called peasant poets such as Sergei Esenin (1895–1925). In part due to this emphasis on colloquial speech, it was among poets of these latter groups that free verse – poetry without metre or rhyme – came to dominate in the 1920s, with many critics keen to emphasise the revolutionary credentials of such rhythmical freedom.

Eschewing official culture and the orator's podium, the members of OBERIU – the Union of Real Art (Ob"edinenie real'nogo iskusstva), formed in 1927 – preferred to host literary evenings at which they read their outlandish and daringly experimental poetry and staged absurdist performances. This approach was necessitated by the limited opportunities for publishing their work in the increasingly repressive political climate of the late 1920s and 1930s, but the group's 'literary hooliganism' – as official critics, accusing them of mocking Soviet reality, labelled their antics – and its penchant for ephemeral, often chaotic performances represent a serious effort to defend poetry and poetic form against the homogenising forces of official state culture. Driven by circumstance to make their living by writing poetry for children, these poets – including Daniil Kharms (1905–1942), Nikolai Oleinikov (1898–1937), and Aleksandr Vvedenskii (1904–1941) – frequently adopt a childlike voice in their poetry for adults, exploiting the scope this provided for syntactical and semantic deformations and alogical communication. Their work often plays on the resulting tension between the absurd or nonsensical and the rationality of regular metrical form and rhyme in what constitute profound explorations of the relationship between language and thought, poetry and meaning.

Despite these continued innovations, lyric poetry, the foremost genre of pre-revolutionary culture in the Russian Empire, was gradually eclipsed by narrative poetry and prose. The relative freedom enjoyed by poets during the years immediately following the revolution gave way in the 1930s to attacks on formalism and brutal suppression of the avant-garde. Even Maiakovskii, who had devoted himself almost entirely to political verse following the publication of About That in 1924, found himself under attack as organisations such as the Russian Association of Proletarian Writers (Rossiiskaia assotsiatsiia proletarskikh pisatelei, or RAPP) challenged their avant-garde counterparts, often in viciously strident and personal terms. His suicide in 1930 served as the tragic coda to a decade in which the lyric and poetic form, thrust into a public forum, became ideologically charged topics.[18]

18 Roman Jakobson, 'On a generation that squandered its poets', in Krystyna Pomorska and Stephen Rudy (eds.), Language in Literature (Cambridge, MA: Belknap Press of Harvard University Press, 1987), p. 274.

Modernist experimentation challenged the conventional limits of poetic form both on the page and beyond it. Whether expanding the metrical repertoire of Russian verse, examining its sonic and visual qualities, or exploring new points of view and public arenas, these experiments radically extended the purview of poetic form, which became one of the primary interfaces for the era's reconsideration and reconfiguration of the relations between art and life. The final part of this chapter will provide a brief overview of poetic developments in the decades since 1930.

Form after Modernism

With the adoption of Socialist Realism in 1934, poetry, like other art forms, came to be judged primarily on the basis of its intelligibility for the masses. With the exception of *dol'niki*, non-classical verse forms practically disappeared, as poets were exhorted to 'learn from the classics', a common refrain in debates about Soviet culture during this period.[19] While there was some room for experimentation in official literature, particularly during more liberal periods such as the Thaw, the characteristic variety of Modernist and avant-garde poetry quickly gave way to formal homogeneity and cliché; the ballad form, for example, felt to be particularly well suited to revolutionary subjects, became widespread. These decades also lacked the shared milieu that had been such an important incubator for Modernist and avant-garde poetic culture. Those poets who sought to distance themselves from official culture often worked in small, geographically dispersed groups. These circumstances led to the emergence of a number of distinctive poetic tendencies and laid the groundwork for the remarkable formal and stylistic variety of poetry since 1991.[20]

Perhaps the most famous late Soviet poet in the west is Joseph Brodsky (1940–1996), part of a group of young poets gathered around Akhmatova. His arrest and trial for 'parasitism' (*tuneiadstvo*) in 1964 marked the end of the so-called Thaw, the brief period of relative cultural freedom that had followed Stalin's death when poets such as Evgenii Evtushenko (1932–2017), Robert Rozhdestvenskii (1932–1994), and Andrei Voznesenskii (1933–2010)

---

19 See discussion in Michael S. Gorham, *Speaking in Soviet Tongues: Language Culture and the Politics of Voice in Revolutionary Russia* (DeKalb: Northern Illinois University Press, 2003), pp. 108–11.

20 Dmitrii Kuz'min, 'Russkaia poeziia v nachale XXI veka' [Russian poetry at the start of the twenty-first century] *Rets* 48 (Jan. 2008), 3–38, www.litkarta.ru/dossier/kuzmin-review/, accessed 16 Jan. 2023.

filled stadiums with crowds newly thirsty for poetry and the public display of sincerity it supplied. Voznesenskii's use of the three-stress *dol'nik* and complex polymetrical constructions as well as his inventive use of sound patterning, assonance, and internal rhyme recall Maiakovskii, as does the occasionally publicistic quality of his verse. Brodsky, by contrast, who read widely in English and American poetry during the eighteen months he spent in internal exile, rejected the political arena in favour of what in his 1987 Nobel Prize lecture he refers to as 'the privateness of the human condition'.[21] His work revived the Acmeist orientation towards world culture, and it followed these earlier poets in its combination of formal inventiveness with a classical sensibility. Brodsky's metrical repertoire is wide-ranging and includes both blank and tonic verse. Nonetheless, his insistence on preserving metrical structure and rhyme when translating his verse into English following his forced emigration in 1972 demonstrates the enormous importance he attached to the formal structures of Russian verse, while also illustrating vividly the new contexts with which he enriched his native tradition.

The return of formal experimentation in Thaw-era poetry was partly the result of a concerted effort on the part of literary officials to improve the quality of Soviet poetry.[22] The re-emergence of free verse during this period is characteristic. While free verse (in Russian, *verlibr*) had never come to dominate Russian prosody to the extent that it does in western European and Anglo-American traditions, almost all early twentieth-century poets produced at least one poem written in free verse – including, notably, those associated with the revolution and its aftermath, such as the proletarian poets. If free verse fell out of official favour by the 1930s, poets continued to produce such poetry through the decades leading up to and immediately following the Second World War. Indeed, officially sanctioned war poets such as Olga Berggolts (1910–1975), David Samoilov (1920–1990), Konstantin Simonov (1915–1979), and Evgenii Vinokurov (1925–1993) used free verse extensively, both in solemn verses about war and in realistic descriptions of life on the front. This demonstrates the flexibility of the form and the extent to which it has been assimilated by the Russian poetic tradition, in which free verse continues to play an increasingly prominent – though still not dominant – role.[23]

21 Joseph Brodsky, 'Nobel lecture', 8 Dec. 1987, www.nobelprize.org/prizes/literature/1987/brodsky/lecture/, accessed 16 Jan. 2023.

22 Emily Lygo, *Leningrad Poetry 1953–1975: The Thaw Generation* (Oxford: Peter Lang, 2010).

23 Iurii Orlitskii, 'Rannii russkii svobodnyi stikh' [Early Russian free verse], *Novoe literaturnoe obozrenie* [New literary review] 167 (2021).

Underground culture of the 1970s and 1980s saw two distinctive poetic cultures emerge in Russia's two capitals. Poets such as Elena Shvarts (1948–2010), Viktor Krivulin (1944–2001), and Sergei Stratanovskii (1944–) drew on the tradition of their native city, Leningrad, to explore the relationships between the present and past and the material and non-material or spiritual worlds in a neo-Modernist style that weaves concrete detail into complex intertextual dialogues. Centred in Moscow, Conceptualist poets such as Vsevolod Nekrasov (1934–2009), Lev Rubinshtein (1947–2024), and Dmitrii Prigov (1940–2007) focused instead on the gap between world and word. Rejecting the Thaw-era premise that the intimate speech of lyric verse was adaptable to the Soviet environment, Conceptual poetry took as its starting point the inevitable inauthenticity and non-freedom of all human expression, irrespective of its sociocultural context. This is the explicit subject of one of Nekrasov's best-known poems, dated 1964:

> svobóda ést'
> svobóda ést'
> svobóda ést'
> svobóda ést'
> svobóda ést'
> svobóda ést'
> svobóda ést' svobóda.
>
> (freedom is
> freedom is
> freedom is
> freedom is
> freedom is
> freedom is
> freedom is freedom.)[24]

Each line can be read either as a standalone statement ('there is freedom') or as running into the next to produce the tautological meaning made explicit in the final line. This syntactical ambivalence neatly expresses the contradictions of Soviet existence, where the liberation promised by official propaganda is negated by the lack of freedom to which the proliferation of linguistic cliché in a verbal environment saturated with ideological statements gives rise.

24 Translation cited from Gerald Janecek, *Everything Has Already Been Written: Moscow Conceptualist Poetry and Performance* (Evanston, IL: Northwestern University Press, 2018), p. 35.

While the poem reads as a comment upon the limitations placed upon expression in the Soviet Union, it also raises a question about the freedom or unfreedom of poetic speech more generally. Nekrasov's immediate predecessors were poets of what became known as the Lianozovo group, a loose collective of writers living in a suburb of Moscow called Lianozovo. Poets such as Evgenii Kropivnitskii (1893–1979), Genrikh Sapgir (1928–1999), and Igor Kholin (1920–1999) combined commonplace, often crude expressions and overheard statements with snippets of official discourse and concrete detail in their work, exploring the poetic patterns that emerged from the language and speech situations of everyday life and experimenting with new ways to organise verse. Nekrasov's poem, similarly, asserts its right to construct poetry from the language available, regardless of its 'poetic' credentials. At the same time, taking the regularity and repetition at the heart of poetic form to their logical extreme, the poem highlights the *lack* of freedom inherent in poetry as an art form.

In the 1970s and 1980s, Conceptualist poetry further exploited typographical and material possibilities, including unusual formats such as Rubinshtein's note-card poetry, in which, rather than segmented into lines and stanzas, snatches of language 'ready-mades' are organised on a series of catalogue cards such as those used in libraries. Conceptualist practice also built on its avant-garde heritage to subvert conventional poetic forms through performance, with the important difference that, whereas avant-garde experimentation evinced a total confidence in the power of the word to create new worlds, Conceptualism asserted precisely the opposite. Prigov in particular, who wrote over 35,000 poems, played with notions of authority and deconstructed poetic subjectivity through the adoption of multiple poetic personae, brought to life during charismatic readings or through reinterpretations of Russian classics that – like his mantric recitations of Aleksandr Pushkin's novel in verse, *Eugene Onegin* (*Evgenii Onegin*, 1825–32) – were both parodic and profound.[25]

Russian poetry, and poetry in Russian, since 1991 is too various to account for fully here; I can mention only a few of those whose work resonates with this chapter. One response to the Conceptualist project in contemporary Russian and Russophone poetry has been the emergence of a plain, prosaic style, as poets such as Kirill Medvedev (1975–) have turned to an almost documentary mode in an effort to recuperate authentic poetic expression (see

25 A version of this performance, recorded in February 2001, can be viewed online at 'Dmitry Prigov at Berkeley', Russian Writers at Berkeley, http://russianwriters.berke ley.edu/248-2/contents/dmitri-prigov/, accessed 23 Jan. 2020.

Chapter 1.10).[26] Others – such as those involved in the Laboratory of Poetic Actionism (see Chapter 1.10) – mingle Conceptualist and avant-garde practices, bringing their work out into the street in a radically democratic gesture aimed at 'de-alienating daily life by filling urban space with poetry': 'Poetry belongs to everyone, or it doesn't exist at all', as their slogan has it.[27] Still others have looked to narrative and epic poetry in their search for poetic forms capacious enough to grapple with history, both personal and national. In the diverse and distinctive work of poets such as Elena Fanailova (1962–), Maria Stepanova (1972–), Polina Barskova (1976–), or Galina Rymbu (1990–), these themes and others are explored in a poetic idiom that is both steeped in tradition and unmistakably modern, mingling classical and non-classical metrical forms with free verse, lyrical imagery with contemporary colloquialisms and the rhetoric of Putin-era propaganda. Reviving 'an archaic notion of poetry as speaking on behalf of multitudes', such poetry tests the limits of poetic self-expression to explore individual and social identity, both inherited and invented.[28]

Perhaps, as poet and critic Grigorii Dashevskii (1964–2013) contended in the midst of the 2011–13 anti-government protests, it is time for poetry to come out of the 'laboratory' of formal experimentation and into the public square – to leave behind the allusiveness of metrical and other forms of intertextual quotation in favour of free verse and the broader audience to which such poetry appeals.[29] Nonetheless, despite the distance that separates the current era from that of Modernism, the formal organisation of verse remains a powerful tool for contemporary poets seeking to bring their work into dialogue with a complex reality.

Further Reading

Boym, Svetlana, *Death in Quotation Marks: Cultural Myths of the Modern Poet* (Cambridge, MA: Harvard University Press, 1991).

Gronas, Mikhail, *Cognitive Poetics and Cultural Memory: Russian Literary Mnemonics* (New York: Routledge, 2011).

26 Ilya Kukulin, 'Documentalist strategies in contemporary Russian poetry', trans. Josephine von Zitzewitz, *Russian Review* 69.4 (2010), 585–614.

27 Laboratory of Poetry Actionism, https://poetryactionism.wordpress.com, accessed 23 Jan. 2020. Some of the same poets are involved in the literary journal *[Translit]*.

28 Irina Shevelenko, 'Introduction', in Maria Stepanova, *The Voice Over*, ed. Irina Shevelenko (New York: Columbia University Press, 2021), p. xlviii.

29 Grigorii Dashevskii, 'Kak chitat' sovremennuiu poeziu' [How to read contemporary poetry], Openspace.ru (10 Feb. 2012), http://os.colta.ru/literature/events/details/34 232, accessed 6 April 2022.

Janecek, Gerald, *The Look of Russian Literature: Avant-garde Visual Experiments, 1900–1930* (Princeton: Princeton University Press, 1984).

Kochulsky, Irene E., *The Revival of the Russian Literary Avantgarde: The Thaw Generation and Beyond* (Munich: Otto Sagner, 2001).

Markov, Vladimir, *Russian Futurism: A History* (Berkeley: University of California Press, 1968).

Pyman, Avril, *A History of Russian Symbolism* (Cambridge: Cambridge University Press, 1994).

Sandler, Stephanie (ed.), *Rereading Russian Poetry* (New Haven: Yale University Press, 1999).

Wachtel, Michael, *The Development of Russian Verse* (Cambridge: Cambridge University Press, 1998).

3.9

The Novel II

EVGENY DOBRENKO

In 1921, Evgenii Zamiatin (1884–1937), one of the most visionary Russian writers of the twentieth century, concluded his essay 'I Am Afraid' (*Ia boius'*) with a piercing admission: 'I am afraid that the only future possible for Russian literature is its past.'[1] This prophecy was hotly discussed at the time. Many dismissed Zamiatin's fears as unfounded: for them, the literature born of the Bolshevik Revolution was too innovative, searching, and daring. But people living in a revolutionary era tend to forget about longue durée history, which has its own specifics in Russia and the Soviet Union. As the politician Petr Stolypin is said to have aphoristically formulated it at the very beginning of the twentieth century, in Russia everything changes over ten years and nothing changes over two hundred years.

The popular perception of Russian history as cyclical, which drove Bolshevik revolutionaries to desperation, was realised in Russian culture itself.[2] However, this cyclicality was never an exercise in simple repetition; rather it constituted an attempt to replay the past in a modernised version, to rewrite the answers to the 'eternal questions' (see Chapter 3.5), to update the eternal themes – about human nature, good and evil, the ideal, about power and God, about the weakness of strength and the strength of weakness – for the present. In the literature-centric Russian culture of the nineteenth century, the novel had become one of the most advanced forms of national identity, of assembling and collecting social memory, and of expressing the collective imagination. Could the twentieth-century novel escape the cyclical tendencies of Russian history?

---

1 Yevgeny Zamyatin, *A Soviet Heretic: Essays*, ed. and trans. Mirra Ginsburg (Chicago: University of Chicago Press, 1970), p. 12.
2 See Vladimir Paperny, *Architecture in the Age of Stalin: Culture Two* (Cambridge: Cambridge University Press, 2011).

Two trends, two force fields, took shape in the history of the Russian novel from its origins in the nineteenth century. The first, the so-called harmonious tradition, is associated with Aleksandr Pushkin (1799–1837), Ivan Turgenev (1818–1883), Ivan Goncharov (1812–1891), and Lev Tolstoi (1828–1910), while the second, the 'disharmonious' one, brings to mind Nikolai Gogol (1809–1852), Nikolai Leskov (1831–1895), and Fedor Dostoevskii (1821–1881). According to this binary, the first is associated with the wholeness of the world, mental health, and rationalism. The second has to do with discontinuity, the unknowability of the world, perversity, and morbidness. The first tradition gravitated towards naturalism, realism, and epic narrative conventions, and the second towards a displacement of natural proportions, fantasy, and the grotesque. These two traditions took their definitive shape towards the end of the nineteenth century, and it was at this very moment that the Russian literary canon took on particular significance in an era of great political change.

Nineteenth-century literature in Russian – and the novel as its highest manifestation – came to be seen as the greatest expression of Russian national self-awareness. As a corollary, the profound crisis of political, social, and cultural life and the radical breakdown of Russian history that took place in the twentieth century produced a sense that any new instantiation of the novel could no longer engage in dialogue with the Russian classics. However, not only did that dialogue take place but it was much more profound than anticipated. Indeed, it can be argued that this dialogue both preserved Russian national consciousness through an era of powerful historical transformation and shaped the originality and formal innovations of the twentieth-century Russian novel.

The history of Russia since the beginning of the twentieth century has several milestones that divide it into distinctly different eras: 1917 (the Bolshevik Revolution), 1953 (the death of Stalin), and 1991 (the collapse of the Soviet Union). Accordingly, although in terms of formal innovation the centre of gravity of this chapter is naturally the age of the 'Modernist' novels that were produced in the first three decades of the twentieth century, the overall range will be greater. This examination of the twentieth-century novel is divided into four sections, showing how the novel emerged as an acutely sensitive form of reflection and a concentration of national identity in an era of unprecedented change. It is through the dialogue with its legacies – and in particular with the Tolstoian and Dostoevskian models – that the novel's evolution can be seen.

Transgression: The Modernist Novel

The early twentieth-century period known as the Silver Age saw artists across different forms and media negotiating a perceived loss of the wholeness, purity, and standards of beauty inherent in the so-called Golden Age of the nineteenth century. The exhaustion of the former paths of the novel seemed obvious to everyone, but only the Symbolists were ready to take on the challenge. They set out to renew the Russian novel, to combine the new Modernist aesthetic arriving from the west with the tradition of the Russian classic novel, and in so doing to give it a new life.

Artistic Modernism responded to a world in flux, in a condition of crisis and transformation: it viewed the world as torn, irrational, displaced, and deprived of its former wholeness. This is reflected in the forms, style, and poetics of the Modernist novel. From the 1890s, the main trend in the novel's development for several decades was linked to the traditions and practices of Gogol, Leskov, and Dostoevskii, who had pictured the world as dangerously displaced, unknowable, and threatening. Practically the first to herald the new aesthetic of the novel, providing exemplars of a new Symbolist novel, was Fedor Sologub (1863–1927).

Sologub's *Bad Dreams* (*Tiazhelye sny*, 1895) centres on a broken, wicked man who is simultaneously a dreamer who thinks instead of acting. He is mired in the mud of a small provincial town, the life of which manifests itself through a fog of his own bad dreams. In Sologub's next novel, *The Petty Demon* (*Melkii bes*, 1905), this troublesome, morbid dream becomes even more dense and impenetrable. The main character, the sinister sadist and teacher Peredonov, is a reincarnation of Dostoevskii's underground man. The underground world of Dostoevskii's 'little man', ridden with envy, spite, and extreme egotism, reveals itself here with new force, superimposed onto a plot involving the perverse sexual relations of the young characters. The text's many evil forces condense in the figure of Nedotykomka, a shapeless, half-fantasised incarnation of evil. Sologub's image of the devil had a literary genealogy: it came from Gogol's *Evenings on a Farm near Dikanka* (*Vechera na khutore bliz Dikan'ki*, 1831–2) and resettled in Dostoevskii's *The Brothers Karamazov* (*Brat'ia Karamazovy*, 1881) and 'Bobok' (*Bobok*, 1873) before finding its place in Sologub's decadent novels, which are permeated with decay, psychosis, altered consciousness, severe delirium, and morbidity.

This atmosphere of threatening irrational reality dissolved, one might say, into the very poetics and form of the Symbolist novel. An example of this is Aleksei Remizov's (1877–1957) *The Pond* (*Prud*, 1905), which is characterised by

fragmentary composition and an associative combination of disparate episodes. One can barely sense any plot development; in place of key events, fragmentary details fall apart like an image on an impressionist's canvas. The novel's language is stylised after folk speech, echoing the tradition of Leskov, the master of folk-tale style. At the level of its characters, the novel reproduces the world of Dostoevskii's strange, pained, broken people. The themes of the Antichrist and cyclicality never leave the novel, in which life itself is depicted as having lost all its meaning.

The apex of the Symbolist novel was Andrei Belyi's (1880–1934) *Petersburg* (*Peterburg*, 1913–14, 1922). In this novel, the image of the city – a small island of western rationalism in the east, shimmering, disappearing into darkness, doomed to destruction – goes straight back to the city of Gogol's so-called Petersburg tales (published between 1835 and 1842). But the novel's plot, with a secretive terrorist revolutionary organisation, provocateurs, murders, and confused relationships between parents and children, continues the world of the novels of Dostoevskii, who remained a central figure for those Russian religious thinkers of the early twentieth century (Vladimir Solovev (1853–1900), Nikolai Fedorov (1829–1903), Vasilii Rozanov (1856–1919), Lev Shestov (1866–1938), Sergei Bulgakov (1871–1944), Nikolai Berdiaev (1874–1948), Nikolai Losskii (1870–1965), and others) who exerted a definitive influence on the development of Russian literature in this period.

If Silver Age literature harked back to Dostoevskii explicitly and programmatically, then for early Soviet literature he became, for political reasons, a persona non grata. But despite the fact that his so-called reactionary philosophy was publicly repudiated, Dostoevskii's legacy continued to fuel the revolutionary-era Soviet novel. As Leonid Leonov (1899–1994) put it, 'The Dostoevskii school is more congenial to me than that of Tolstoi. . . . Tolstoi is a forest standing on a riverbank, but Dostoevskii is the reflection of this forest in the river, and therefore the reflection is always more profound, inscrutable, and mysterious; it goes a depth that we can never even reach.'[3] The Dostoevskian inheritance took many forms: fantasies of the grand inquisitor modernised and transplanted into contemporary mass society in Zamiatin's anti-utopia *We* (*My*, comp. 1920); the underground man immersed in Soviet everyday life and transformed into Kavalerov, the main character of Iurii Olesha's (1899–1960) novel *Envy* (*Zavist'*, 1927); or the themes of betrayal, apostasy, and provocation amid the intelligentsia protagonists in Maksim

---

3 *Vek Leonida Leonova. Problemy tvorchestva. Vospominaniia* [Leonid Leonov's century. Problems of creative work. Memoirs] (Moscow: IMLI RAN, 2001), p. 341.

Gorkii's (1868–1936) *The Life of Klim Samgin* (*Zhizn' Klima Samgina*, 1925–36). The novels of Mikhail Bulgakov (1891–1940), up to his major work *The Master and Margarita* (*Master i Margarita*, comp. 1928–40), were written in line with the Dostoevskian tradition: doubles and madmen, the devil in Moscow, fantastic transformations, and distortions of reality. Bulgakov drew on a genealogy that included not only Dostoevskii but a longer tradition that led from Gogol to his favourite writer, Mikhail Saltykov-Shchedrin (1826–1889). This tradition also fuelled the work of Andrei Platonov (1899–1951). The pathologically brooding characters in his novels *Chevengur* (*Chevengur*, 1929) and *The Foundation Pit* (*Kotlovan*, 1930) are passionate champions for a communist utopia which, before their eyes, is transforming into an anti-utopia. Soviet reality, with its collectivisation and industrialisation, is portrayed satirically. Platonov's characters live in a world of the absurd, and they play their part in creating that world.

In his work, Platonov used a wide range of artistic devices, mainly in the sphere of language: in the narrative and stylisation of characters' speech, and in narrative voice. Platonov's language was unique and distinctive, but he was not alone in seeking new linguistic forms to do justice to a changed reality. So-called ornamental prose – in which a prosaic narrative was subordinated to the laws of poetry and reality merged with myth – gave rise to vivid exemplars of the new type of novel. Here, language was exposed to the powerful influence of extraliterary elements advancing under the aegis of democratisation of style. One need only recall here the orality of the narrative voice (*skaz*) in Boris Pilniak's (1894–1938) *The Naked Year* (*Golyi god*, 1922) or the folkloric stylisation in Aleksandr Malyshkin's (1892–1938) *The Fall of Dair* (*Padenie Daira*, 1921) and Lidiia Seifullina's (1889–1954) 'Virineia' (*Virineia*, 1924).

Russian Modernism, which saw the world as split and discontinuous, full of contradictions and counterpoint, combined the democratic orality of *skaz* with devices of fragmentation and montage. This contributed to a flowering of the short story in the 1920s. Many of the most important short stories of the era, however, combined their Modernist montage of fragmented reality with a novelesque, or even epic, world view. This was the case, for example, in Isaak Babel's (1894–1940) *Odesa Stories* (*Odesskie rasskazy*, 1921–4) and his story cycle *Red Cavalry* (*Konarmiia*, 1923–6), as well as in the *Partisan Tales* (*Partizanskie povesti*, 1923) of Vsevolod Ivanov (1895–1963), and the cycles of short stories by Mikhail Zoshchenko (1894–1958). These cycles can be considered within the context of not only the short story (see Chapter 3.6) but also the Modernist novel. Their episodic structure reflected the breakdown

and loss of the wholeness of the world that resulted from the historical cataclysms of the early twentieth century. Under such conditions, the novel as a synthetic genre disintegrated.

In his visionary essay 'The End of the Novel' (*Konets romana*, 1922), the poet Osip Mandelshtam (1891–1938) predicted that, in the coming era, 'the fate of the novel will be nothing more than the story of the atomization of biography as a form of personal existence, even more than atomization: the catastrophic death of biography'. He posited that as a result of the historical convulsions of the age, people had been 'cast out of their own biographies like balls out of billiard pockets', and hence the death of the traditional novel was inevitable. After all, 'interest in psychological motivation . . . is torn out by the root and discredited by the coming powerlessness of psychological motives when faced by the real forces whose psychologically motivated reprisals are becoming more brutal by the hour. The very notion of action by an individual is being replaced by another, more socially meaningful one, the notion of adaptation.'[4]

Projected onto the history of the Russian novel, this sounds like a sentence within the Tolstoian tradition. But, as the Formalist critic Viktor Shklovskii (1893–1984) observed in formulating a key law of literary development in those same years, 'as literary schools change, the inheritance passes not from the father to the son, but from the uncle to the nephew'.[5] The history of the Russian novel in this period was to follow just such an indirect genealogy.

Regression: The Socialist Realist Novel

With the proclamation of Socialist Realism as the sole artistic method of Soviet literature in 1934 (see Chapter 1.8), the conditions of literary production changed radically, as did the very matrix of the Soviet novel. It had to become populist, accessible, educational, and party-minded. An exemplar for such literature was to be found in the 'proletarian' literature of the 1920s created by a new generation of non-professional writers sponsored by the Russian Association of Proletarian Writers (*Rossiiskaia assotsiatsiia proletarskikh pisatelei*, or RAPP). The predominant style of this literature was

---

4 Osip Mandel'shtam, 'Konets romana' [The end of the novel], in *Sobranie sochinenii v dvukh tomakh* [Collected works in two volumes] (Moscow: Khudozhestvennaia literatura, 1990), vol. II, pp. 203–4.

5 Viktor Shklovskii, *Gamburgskii schet: Stat'i – vospominaniia – esse (1914–1933)* [The Hamburg score: Articles – memoirs – essays (1914–1933)] (Moscow: Sovetskii pisatel', 1990), p. 121.

conventional and attractive to the mass reader; it was easily mastered by an author who had neither extensive education nor writerly habits. Narratives shared a basic master plot, consistently repeated across texts with only minor variations. The master plot made the Soviet educational process visible and supplied politically correct accents: it told the story of an emblematic hero and their journey to political consciousness, via labour and participation in the collective.[6] It relied on a Tolstoian psychologism that was meant to explain the motivations of its characters' behaviour to the reader.[7] Above all, proletarian literature was programmatically epigonic. Its banner proclaimed 'Learn from the Classics' – and the 'classics' here were, above all, the works of Tolstoi. The aspiration to create a 'Red Lev Tolstoi' was the main effort of the proletarian writers. The apparent integrity, monologism, and harmony of the Tolstoian world was in accordance with the world to be constructed by Socialist Realism – harmonised, perfected, and authoritatively explained.

The new Soviet Writers' Union, which had been established with a single 'artistic method', created the conditions for an expansion of the conventions of 1920s proletarian literature into all the literature being created in the Soviet Union. Its central genre was the novel, which was constructed on the core plot that had been developed in the 1920s – in, for example, Aleksandr Fadeev's (1901–1956) The Rout (Razgrom, 1927) or Aleksandr Serafimovich's (1863–1949) The Iron Flood (Zheleznyi potok, 1924). Its 'path to consciousness' master plot, which inscribed its heroes into a Stalinist 'great family', relied on stylistic conventions transferred to Soviet material from Tolstoi's novels.[8]

This meant the development of a psychologism that created the distinctive verisimilitude of Socialist Realist novels from the 1930s through to the 1950s. The evolution of the so-called industrial novel (the Socialist Realist master plot transposed into a factory setting), which first arose in the 1920s, typifies this. Whereas Fedor Gladkov's (1883–1958) Cement (Tsement, 1925) was notable for a mix of literary styles, the industrial novel in its heyday, which came during the early 1930s, was still stylistically eclectic but attempted to synthesise the devices of the avant-garde chronicle, the literature of fact, and a montage structure with the devices of traditional psychological writing – as in Valentin Kataev's (1897–1986) Time, Forward! (Vremia vpered!, 1932),

---

6 See Katerina Clark, The Soviet Novel: History as Ritual (Chicago: University of Chicago Press, 1985).
7 See Evgeny Dobrenko, The Making of the State Reader: Social and Aesthetic Contexts of the Reception of Soviet Literature (Stanford: Stanford University Press, 1997).
8 See Clark, The Soviet Novel.

Marietta Shaginian's (1888–1982) *Hydrocentral* (*Gidrotsentral'*, 1931), and others. However, the postwar industrial novel (e.g. the works of Vasilii Azhaev (1915–1968), Anna Karavaeva (1893–1979), and Vsevolod Kochetov (1912–1973)) relied completely upon the traditional conventions of psychological writing. In this respect, it is interesting to compare the industrial novel with the collective farm novel (a parallel genre in which action took place in the vast collective farms established during the first and second Five-Year Plans). As a genre, the collective farm novel was never influenced by any avant-garde tradition, and its form developed completely within the vein of Socialist Realist aesthetics. Therefore, from its origins – novels about collectivisation, such as Fedor Panferov's (1896–1960) *Bruski* (*Bruski*, 1928–37), or Mikhail Sholokhov's (1905–1984) *Virgin Soil Upturned* (*Podniataia tselina*, 1932–59) – right up through the flowering of the collective farm novel after the war (e.g. works by Galina Nikolaeva (1911–1965), Semen Babaevskii (1909–2000), and Grigorii Medynskii (1899–1984)), this genre was wholly built upon primitive psychologism of a quasi-Tolstoian model.

The second distinctive feature of the Soviet novel was its autobiographical quality, which created an essential effect of authenticity and was supposed to evoke the reader's trust. Here, too, the Soviet novel resorted to a Tolstoian tradition, as developed in his autobiographical trilogy of *Childhood* (*Detstvo*, 1852), *Boyhood* (*Otrochestvo*, 1854), and *Youth* (*Iunost'*, 1857), where he combined the Bildungsroman with new forms of psychological writing and with autobiographical features. This tradition was taken up by Gorkii in his own trilogy – *Childhood* (*Detstvo*, 1913–14), *In the World* (*V liudiakh*, 1916), and *My Universities* (*Moi universitety*, 1923) – and then by Aleksei Nikolaevich Tolstoi (1883–1945) in *Nikita's Childhood* (*Detstvo Nikity*, 1922). Here the principle of the authenticity of the author's experience was asserted. This vein found a continuation in Soviet literature in novels such as Dmitrii Furmanov's (1891–1926) *Chapaev* (*Chapaev*, 1923), Nikolai Ostrovskii's (1904–1936) *How the Steel Was Tempered* (*Kak zakalialas' stal'*, 1934), and Anton Makarenko's (1888–1939) *Pedagogical Poem* (*Pedagogicheskaia poema*, 1935), in which autobiographical features were subordinated to the Socialist Realist master plot and were called upon to flesh out an otherwise striking lack of authenticity. This emphasis on authenticity ran counter to the fundamental unreality of so-called Socialist Realism. In Soviet Socialist Realist literature, which relied heavily on fictive ideological tropes, the depiction of Soviet reality as it ought to be ceased to have even a superficial resemblance to reality. The autobiographical features of the Soviet novel served to fill up the space left by its loss of authenticity.

The third, and most significant, vector in the development of the Soviet novel was monumentalism. In 1924, long before the proclamation of Socialist Realism, Aleksei Tolstoi had theorised:

> As opposed to aestheticism, I would contrast a literature of monumental realism. . . . Its zeal is universal happiness, perfection. Its faith is the greatness of mankind. Its path leads directly to a higher aim: in passion, in the grandiose exertion to create a type of great man . . . We should not fear ponderous descriptions, nor excessive length, nor exhaustive characterizations: monumental realism![9]

Aleksei Tolstoi came to see Socialist Realism as the realisation of his 'monumental realism' – a hybrid of mythology and history. He brought this to fruition in the genre of the historical novel – such as *Peter I* (*Petr I*, 1929–34) – a genre which was to flourish in the 1930s through the 1950s. But the creation of a new history was a much more pressing issue for the Soviet regime. Socialist Realism created a new epic form, simultaneously trustworthy as history and attractive as myth, that aimed to imbue the Soviet order and the Soviet version of the past with historical legitimacy. The recipe for such a novel had been created in *War and Peace* (*Voina i mir*, 1868–9). Like Lev Tolstoi's novel, Soviet 'novel-epics' combined the idea of the individual family with the idea of the nation. Great historical events (revolution, collectivisation, war) formed the backdrop for the flow of life of a number of generations of several families. This genre acquired the name 'panoramic novel', and it was built upon an alternation of battle scenes with family scenes; it combined psychologism with lengthy generalised reflections from the author, obviously harking back to the genre model of *War and Peace*. Novels such as Sholokhov's *The Quiet Don* (*Tikhii Don*, 1928–40) and Konstantin Simonov's (1915–1979) *The Living and the Dead* (*Zhivye i mertvye*, 1959–71) were studied in universities and reprinted numerous times; not only did they enjoy an enormous popularity and garner screen adaptations but their authors, too, were rewarded with power and privileges.

It is clear, then, that the artistic devices that predominated in the Socialist Realist novel, borrowed in the main from Lev Tolstoi, were used as compensation: psychologism compensated for the lack of real personality in a society indoctrinated by total collectivism; the autobiographical element simulated the absent authenticity of personal experience, an authenticity that was

---

9 Aleksei Tolstoi, 'Zadachi literatury' [Tasks of literature], in *Iz istorii sovetskoi esteticheskoi mysli 1917–1932 godov* [From the history of Soviet aesthetic thought, 1917–1932] (Moscow: Iskusstvo, 1980), pp. 189–90.

dangerous owing to its unpredictability and resistance to surveillance; and the monumental, epic quality healed the historical ruptures of the twentieth century. But every time the artistic devices developed by the Russian classics were used in the Soviet novel, they were purged of their existential, social, humanist, and religious content, reduced to nothing more than something to carry out politically relevant, urgent functions. This aesthetic parasitism of the Socialist Realist novel demonstrated that the monopoly of a single trend from the multifaceted national tradition of the novel leads to not only a hypertrophying of the device but also its formalisation and depletion. Socialist Realism might be considered a sort of aesthetic utopia: it abrogated history by creating a novelistic aesthetic in which Modernism apparently had never existed.

Reinvention: The Realist Novel

The political liberalisation that came after Stalin's death in 1953 led to an abrupt expansion of the cultural field in which Soviet literature developed: the interpretative restrictions that had reduced all of Russian classic literature to an illustration of class struggle under tsarism were weakened; works of 1920s writers that had been repressed or forbidden during Stalin's time were returned to readers; works of émigré writers whose names were not even to be mentioned during the Stalin era began to be published; and international classics and contemporary foreign literature began to be published more actively.[10] All of this expanded the range of writing and destroyed the monopoly of Socialist Realism. Now the Soviet novel was able to draw from various sources. Despite this, the national tradition remained central to the force field of Soviet literature. It began, however, to be utilised in more versatile ways.

Taking first place in the remaking of Soviet prose in this period was the so-called minor novelistic genre – the short novel, or *povest'* (see Box 2.1). As opposed to the 'thick novel', in the *povest'* there are no secondary plot lines: the events unfold in a logical way in a localised time and space, and as a rule there are fewer characters than in a novel, a result of which being that the novel's usual distinction between primary and secondary characters is lacking. The dominance of the *povest'* reflected a shift from the artificial

---

10 See Maurice Friedberg, *Decade of Euphoria: Western Literature in Post-Stalin Russia, 1954–64* (Bloomington: Indiana University Press, 1977); Eleonory Gilburd, *To See Paris and Die: The Soviet Lives of Western Culture* (Cambridge, MA: Harvard University Press, 2018).

ideological synthesis of Socialist Realism to a realistic analysis of human motivations, behaviour, and feelings. It was only towards the end of the 1970s and in the early 1980s that the *povest'* yielded ground again to the novel: analysis gave way to synthesis. After his so-called Moscow cycle of shorter prose, for example, Iurii Trifonov (1925–1981) published the novels *The Old Man* (*Starik*, 1978) and *Time and Place* (*Vremia i mesto*, 1981). After his short novels of the war, Iurii Bondarev (1924–2020) created several major novels, including *The Shore* (*Bereg*, 1975). Viktor Astafev (1924–2001), after decades of writing short novels, came out with a novel late in life, *The Cursed and the Slain* (*Prokliaty i ubity*, 1990–4). The Russophone Kyrgyz author Chingiz Aitmatov (1928–2008) would follow the same path, producing *The Day Lasts More than a Hundred Years* (*I dol'she veka dlitsia den'*, 1980) near the end of his career. The novel became the genre that summed up one's creative work.

On the whole, the history of the Soviet novel demonstrates the triumph of genre over ideology. An example of such a victory is the phenomenon one might call the anti-Soviet Soviet novel, in which the genre canon established in Soviet literature in the 1930s through the 1950s – aiming for a combination of epic style, psychological writing, and the journalistic elements of Tolstoi's novels – is preserved, but with an anti-Soviet ideological message. Boris Pasternak (1890–1960), in writing *Doctor Zhivago* (*Doktor Zhivago*, pub. in Milan, 1957), demonstrated that the tradition of the Russian classic novel not only remained alive but also had an enormous potential for development and enrichment. On the one hand, *Doctor Zhivago* provided a broad picture of the uncensored history of Russia in the first half of the twentieth century, completely casting aside the Socialist Realist master plot; on the other, it contained a huge dose of melodrama and sentimentality in its descriptions of the characters' sufferings and the conventional literary twists and turns of the plot (improbable meetings and coincidences, miraculous omens, overheard conversations, guardian angels). Pasternak wanted to create a Christian novel that combined traditions from Charles Dickens, Dostoevskii, and Johann Wolfgang Goethe. But the novel does have elements of the Tolstoian epic in its interweaving of the families' lives and the historical cataclysms, as well as in the peculiarities of a poet's prose. It is also in fundamental dialogue with the Russian classics in its treatment of the eternal questions – life and death, Russian history, the intelligentsia and revolution, Christianity and Jewishness.

Vasilii Grossman (1905–1964) wrote *Life and Fate* (*Zhizn' i sud'ba*, 1959) as a continuation of his epic novel about the battle of Stalingrad, *For a Just Cause* (*Za pravoe delo*, 1952), originally titled *Stalingrad* (see Chapter 2.7). However,

the two books of this cycle, although they share a single complex of characters, plot lines, and stylistic conventions, are based on opposite political assumptions. The first novel, created in the Stalinist era, has a generally Soviet interpretation of the war, while the second is fraught with such potentially explosive content, not only anti-Stalinist but also anti-Soviet, that it caused one of the most extraordinary events in the history of Russian literature – the 'arrest' of the novel in 1961, when, after the manuscript was submitted to a literary journal for publication, a KGB raid seized the manuscript and all associated materials (even typewriter ribbons). Thus, the obvious orientation towards the conventions of the Tolstoian novel did not hinder the realisation of political premises directly opposed to the state's agenda. As Grossman had followed the Tolstoian compositional structure, Anatolii Rybakov (1911–1998) in his trilogy *Children of the Arbat* (*Deti Arbata*, 1982), *Fear* (*Strakh*, 1990), and *Dust and Ashes* (*Prakh i pepel*, 1994) followed the Tolstoian conventions of psychological analysis, creating extensive interior monologues for Stalin and his younger characters.

Neither Grossman nor Rybakov aspired to tear free from the force field of the Tolstoian novel. Indeed, it was so powerful that attempts to escape it, even on the part of such a major artist as Aleksandr Solzhenitsyn (1918–2008), ended up as merely modifications of the established genre model. In Solzhenitsyn's works, a combination of autobiographical, documentary, and journalistic elements (at different times and in varying constellations) created modifications to the novelistic genre. Initially writing short stories and the short novel *One Day in the Life of Ivan Denisovich* (*Odin den' Ivana Denisovicha*, comp. 1959, pub. 1962), Solzhenitsyn's aspirations to a more major genre were realised in the novels *First Circle* (*V kruge pervom*, comp. 1958, pub. in New York in 1968) and *Cancer Ward* (*Rakovyi korpus*, comp. 1966, pub. in Frankfurt in 1968). A strong autobiographical element lies at the heart of these works. Later, Solzhenitsyn shifted to a semi-documentary style, creating *The Gulag Archipelago* (*Arkhipelag GULAG*, comp. 1968, pub. in Paris, 1973). Finally, in *The Red Wheel* (*Krasnoe koleso*, 1970–91), he combined historical documentary with fiction based on autobiography – the main fictional character, Sania (Isaakii) Lazhenitsyn, is based on the author's father, Isaakii Semenovich Solzhenitsyn. Although Solzhenitsyn's particular combination of documentary, journalism, and autobiography differed significantly from the Tolstoian structure of an epic novel, where the familial and historical plots were in balance, Solzhenitsyn's leanings towards the Tolstoian epic model are apparent here: he created a new epic structure but he refused to call it a novel. *The Red Wheel* was, its subtitle proclaimed, 'a tale in measured periods of time'.

Abnegation: The Postmodernist Novel

The Formalist critic Iurii Tynianov (1894–1943) once asserted that 'every deformity, every "mistake," every "abnormality" of normative poetics is, potentially, a new constructive principle'.[11] In late Soviet *samizdat* and *tamizdat* (self-publishing and publishing outside the Soviet Union; see Chapter 2.9) and in nonconformist art, Soviet aesthetics were regarded as a mistake, an abnormality, and a deformity – as a dead end into which political utilitarianism had led. Soviet aesthetics were therefore subject to rejection either through reference to the original tradition or through re-aestheticisation of Soviet artistic experience itself.

Andrei Bitov (1937–2018) was a pioneer of such strategies. His novel *Pushkin House* (*Pushkinskii dom*, comp. 1964–71) is exemplary of meta-prose, in which the subject of reflection became classic literature itself, as well as Modernist and Soviet literature. Immersing the action in a museum, an oversaturated solution of culture, Bitov shows that 'any contact of contemporary consciousness with cultural tradition, even strictly literary contact, is fruitless for a consciousness poisoned by simulation, and is destructive to tradition itself'.[12]

Venedikt Erofeev (1939–1990) became a guide into the world of this consciousness with his *Moscow–Petushki* (*Moskva–Petushki*, 1969–70), which he called a *poema*, but which – like Gogol's *poema Dead Souls* (*Mertvye dushi*, 1842) – despite its fragmentary and poetic style, localisation of action and space, and limited temporal frames can be considered a novel owing to its dimension of aesthetic experimentation, its synthesis of irony and tragedy, its deep immersion into the world of the 'little man', and its revelation of national psychology. Demonstrating the collapse of the Soviet utopia, the Modernist project, the idea of progress, and rationality as a whole, Erofeev's text interweaves Old Testament reminiscences, the everyday language of the lowest social classes, and Soviet officialese, all undigested in the mass consciousness of Soviet ideological constructs and surfacing in the flickering consciousness of its hero, who is poisoned by alcohol and who lives in a state of persistent bingeing.

Working with Soviet discourse and its aesthetic products became a significant strategy of late- and post-Soviet underground art, in particular

---

11 Iurii Tynianov, 'Literaturnyi fakt' [The literary fact], in *Poetika. Istoriia literatury. Kino* [Poetics. History of literature. Cinema] (Moscow: Nauka, 1977), p. 263.

12 Mark Lipovetskii, *Russkii postmodernism* [Russian Postmodernism] (Ekaterinburg: Ural'skii gosudarstvennyi pedagogicheskii universitet, 1997), p. 138.

that of the Medical Hermeneutics (*Meditsinskaia germenevtika*) art group, whose leading exponents, the authors Sergei Anufriev (1964–) and Pavel Peppershtein (1966–), created the novel *The Mythogenic Love of Castes* (*Mifogennaia liubov' kast*, 1999–2002). Here art is dissolved into a fantasy made from the texts that shaped the consciousness of Soviet children. Through the narcotic haze of a mind altered by hallucinatory mushrooms, the novel presents the history of the 'Great Patriotic War' (Second World War) as a duality. It is both a real historical event and a Soviet myth. The novel overcomes this duality, blurring the division between history and myth and revealing their shared potency in the Soviet mass consciousness. It is an attempt to grapple with the powerful legacy of Soviet culture itself.

These texts form part of what can be called the Russian Postmodernist novel. Here, the specifics of Russian Postmodernism are important (see Chapter 1.9). Russian Postmodernism was a reaction not so much to Modernism as to Russia's own national tradition (including that of the novel). It became a method of overcoming literary convention and making a radical break with tradition. Conventional belles-lettres, which were perceived to embody the ideology and qualities rejected by Postmodernism (completeness, insularity, integrality), became a key arena for Postmodernist play in contemporary Russian literature. This can be seen particularly clearly in the novels of Vladimir Sorokin (1955–). Almost all of them – such as *The Norm* (*Norma*, 1983), *Marina's Thirtieth Love* (*Tridtsataia liubov' Mariny*, 1984), and *Four Stout Hearts* (*Serdtsa chetyrekh*, 1991) – feature an exquisitely stylised combination of the classic Russian novel, Socialist Realism, and Soviet officialese. Sorokin's texts are meta-novels, combining plausible reincarnations of classic writers with improbable transformations of language and the act of writing as well as naturalism with anti-utopia – as in, for example, *Blue Lard* (*Goluboe salo*, 1999) and *Telluria* (*Telluriia*, 2013).

Pastiche, ever-present quotation, the grotesque, and an ironic play with official Soviet discourse became the hallmarks of the so-called 'Sots Art' novel, wherein one can classify Dmitrii Prigov's (1940–2007) vividly grotesque novel *Live in Moscow* (*Zhivite v Moskve*, 2000), as well as Viktor Pelevin's (1962–) novels *Omon Ra* (*Omon Ra*, 1992), *Chapaev and Void* (*Chapaev i Pustota*, 1996), and *Generation 'P'* (*Generation 'P'*, 1999). In Pelevin's novels the most improbable events (be they the characters' simultaneous presence in different time periods or their association with ancient Egyptian and Indian gods) are always linked to a confluence of discursive streams, in the midst of which Soviet official discourse or myth is present. By being included in the endless play of meanings, not only does this discourse lose its monopoly,

its 'naturalness', and its homogeneity but it is also revealed as artificial, disjointed, and hollow.

Mikhail Shishkin (1961–) is another recognised master of contemporary discursive experimentation; his novels are constructed as a kaleidoscope of narrative strategies. For instance, the novel *Maidenhair (Venerin volos,* 2005) is constructed in different modalities: one moment in the form of an interrogation and the horrific stories about what happens to refugees, another in the form of a biography of the popular singer Izabella Iureva, and then in the genre of an autobiographical narrative. Plot lines become entangled and bizarrely interwoven, creating a complicated polyphonic narrative in which time and space are fantastically jumbled and events from the past surface in the present, providing answers to the existential questions raised in the past. *The Letter-Book (Pis'movnik,* 2010) is predicated as the correspondence between two lovers at the turn of the twentieth century. However, it becomes clear that the hero is writing letters from a remote, non-existent war, while the heroine is addressing her letters to a certain lover at the end of the century. Nonetheless, similar themes are interwoven in the letters.

Just as literary discourse is deconstructed and narrative devices are laid bare in Sorokin's and Shishkin's novels, so history is the target of Vladimir Sharov (1952–2018). History, after all, had been transformed into a true idée fixe in Russian literature of the nineteenth and, particularly, twentieth centuries.[13] As a narrative that had been used to legitimise ideology, it was a second crucial arena for Postmodernist play.[14] A professional historian, Sharov includes religious, theological, philosophical, political, and social teachings in his novels. He populates national myths with real historical figures, creating not so much parallel history as parallel reality. In *Rehearsals (Repetitsii,* 1992), 300 years of Russian history are presented as a performance directed by a Frenchman, adapted from a play about Russia as the 'promised land' written by the patriarch Nikon. In *Be as Children (Bud'te kak deti,* 2008), Vladimir Lenin organises a crusade of homeless children to the Holy Land in search of a bright future. In Sharov's later novels, he focused increasingly on personal and family biography and an autobiographical stratum. His authorial presence sometimes even became demonstrative when, as in *Return to Egypt (Vozvrashchenie v Egipet,* 2013), the narrator is indicated by his initials, V. Sh.

---

13 See Andrew Wachtel, *An Obsession with History: Russian Writers Confront the Past* (Stanford: Stanford University Press, 1993).
14 See Kevin Platt, *History in a Grotesque Key: Russian Literature and the Idea of Revolution* (Stanford: Stanford University Press, 1997).

The traditional reliance on biography, autobiography, and family history can be observed, then, in the contemporary Russian novel. But the contemporary genre does not so much reproduce as it desacralises and deconstructs the traditional conventions of the Russian (auto)biographical and family novel through the author's biography. This is certainly the case with Aleksandr Chudakov's (1938–2005) *A Gloom Is Cast upon the Ancient Steps* (*Lozhitsia mgla na starye stupeni*, 2000), which mixes a family saga with real autobiography, shifting narrative perspectives and subjects, and breaking chronological linearity. In the novels of Liudmila Ulitskaia (1943–), this is done through fictitious family histories that interweave the family's history with that of the country, following metaphors of waking and sleeping, interweaving physiological and esoteric elements. The trilogy of Dina Rubina (1952–), *People of the Air* (*Liudi vozdukha*, 2008–10) is also composed of mystical fable novels: in *Leonardo's Handwriting* (*Pocherk Leonardo*, 2008), the main female protagonist is a descendant of Wolf Messing, writes in the style of Leonardo da Vinci's script, and has a mystical connection to mirrors; in *The White Dove of Cordova* (*Belaia golubka Kordovy*, 2009), the main protagonist is a genius artist as well as a respected expert and adventurer, who also happens to possess an unbelievable talent for forging art; finally, *Petrushka's Syndrome* (*Sindrom Petrushki*, 2010) tells of a genius puppeteer who creates a puppet by means of which he generates a different reality. The protagonists of Rubina's novels are citizens of the world, 'people of the air' who possess the higher freedom without which creative work is impossible.

In a certain sense, this is a metaphor for the contemporary Russian novel, bent on disrupting the rut of national tradition from which it had, with varying degrees of success, been trying to dislodge itself for the whole of the twentieth century. Its flowering and diversity today thrive – by no means accidentally – on a programmatic break from national traditions. In turn, this liberation also coincides with the end of the cult of literature in Russia. The novel ceased to be the repository and domain of national identity. It became an arena for play, fantasy, imagination, modelling, and learning – a space of freedom. And just as Russian literature was reduced to its own size, becoming just literature, so the Russian novel became just a novel.

Further Reading

Brown, Deming, *The Last Years of Soviet Russian Literature: Prose Fiction 1975–1991* (Cambridge: Cambridge University Press, 1994).

Brown, Deming, *Soviet Russian Literature since Stalin* (Cambridge: Cambridge University Press, 1978).

Brown, Edward, *Russian Literature since the Revolution* (Cambridge, MA: Harvard University Press, 1982).

Clark, Katerina, *Soviet Novel: History as Ritual* (Chicago: University of Chicago Press, 1981).

Erlich, Victor, *Modernism and Revolution: Russian Literature in Transition* (Cambridge, MA: Harvard University Press, 1994).

Gillespie, David, *The Twentieth-Century Russian Novel: An Introduction* (Oxford: Berg, 1996).

Lipovetsky, Mark, *Russian Postmodernist Fiction: Dialogue with Chaos* (London: Routledge, 2015).

3.10

Self-Writing

EMILY VAN BUSKIRK

Memoir, autobiography, and other forms of self-writing have often been peripheral to the better-known literary genres described elsewhere in this section of the *New Cambridge History of Russian Literature*. These forms have tended to flourish when canonical fictional genres have been in flux. For example, as Lidiia Ginzburg (1902–1990) has shown, in the 1840s and 1850s Aleksandr Herzen (1812–1870) and other intellectuals analysed the outcome of the 1848 revolutions in memoirs and letters, at a point when the Russian socio-psychological novel had not yet fully developed.[1] When, after decades of dominance, the novel eventually reached a perceived crisis point in the 1920s, Russian prose writers turned to documentary prose for literary inspiration and renewal. Diary and memoir became vitally significant again in the 1950s and early 1960s, during Khrushchev's Thaw, as Soviet citizens challenged the officially sanctioned aesthetics of Socialist Realism in an effort to reveal the truth about the Stalinist Terror and camps. In the twentieth century and beyond, the boundaries of literature opened to such a degree that authors could routinely use life narratives to lend structure to their artistic works, whether quasi-memoir, diary-novel, or autofiction.

One reason to study documentary literature, according to Ginzburg, is its potential for innovation, for revealing 'those relations in life that have not yet been mediated by the plot inventions of artists'.[2] For instance, women's self-writing – not a subject of her scholarship – captures worlds of experience that were hardly represented in the largely male Russian novelistic tradition. (Ginzburg herself, who wrote in Russian and was born to Jewish parents in Odesa in 1902, was an author as well as a theorist of documentary prose, and her writings will anchor much of this chapter.) Ginzburg traces key elements

---

1 Lydia Ginzburg, *On Psychological Prose*, trans. Judson Rosengrant (Princeton: Princeton University Press, 1991), p. 197.
2 Ginzburg, *On Psychological Prose*, p. 21.

in the transition from Romanticism to Realism, ranging from analysis and self-examination in the Russian psychological novels of the nineteenth century (including the effort to interpret all phenomena philosophically) to the letters and human documents of the 1830s and 1840s written by members of an important intellectual circle – Mikhail Bakunin (1814–1876), Nikolai Stankevich (1813–1840), and Vissarion Belinskii (1811–1848; see Box 5.1). If one is interested in concepts of the self or the relationship of ideology and ethics to personality, the best place to look – Ginzburg's theories suggest – is what she calls 'in-between literature', the aesthetic structures of which mediate between those of everyday life and novels.

Autobiography is historically one of the most heterogeneous forms of literature.[3] It is also one of the most nationally idiosyncratic genres.[4] For instance, the act of laying bare one's private life is a defining aspect of the western tradition, but it is not at all dominant in the Russian one. Again following Ginzburg, what might be said to unite memoir, confession, and other forms of self-writing is their '*orientation toward authenticity* of which the reader never ceases to be aware, but which is far from always being the same thing as factual exactitude'.[5] In fact, 'unreliability' is the essence of the genre, because 'selection, judgment, and point of view come into play' with every aspect of the writing beyond the purely informative. Documentary writers draw generalisations from specific experiences, present their lives as reaffirming certain ideas, and create powerful symbols or metaphors; the memoirist uses imagination to fill in the gaps left by memory but cannot simply 'create the things and events that are most convenient to him'.[6]

This chapter presents various genres or forms under the umbrella of self-writing, four of them centrally: autobiography, memoir, diary, and documentary literature. Autobiography (a term now seen as privileging the western, masculine, autonomous subject[7]) has been defined by Philippe Lejeune as 'Retrospective prose narrative written by a real person concerning his own

---

3 Jane Gary Harris, 'Diversity of discourse: Autobiographical statements in theory and practice', in Harris (ed.), *Autobiographical Statements in Twentieth-Century Russian Literature* (Princeton: Princeton University Press, 1990), p. 3. See also Helga Schwalm, 'Autobiography', in Peter Hühn et al. (eds.), *The Living Handbook of Narratology* (Hamburg: Hamburg University, 2014), www.lhn.uni-hamburg.de/article/autobiog raphy, accessed 15 June 2021.

4 Catriona Kelly, 'The authorized version: The auto/biographies of Vera Panova', in M. Liljeström, A. Rosenholm, and I. Savkina (eds.), *Models of Self: Russian Women's Autobiographical Texts* (Helsinki: Kikimora, 2000), p. 68.

5 Ginzburg, *On Psychological Prose*, p. 6.   6 Ginzburg, *On Psychological Prose*, p. 7.

7 Sidonie Smith and Julia Watson, *Reading Autobiography: A Guide for Interpreting Life Narratives* (Minneapolis: University of Minnesota Press, 2001), p. 3.

existence, where the focus is his individual life, in particular the story of his personality.'[8] Like memoirs and diaries, autobiography is most often narrated in the first person and in prose. The act of narration splits an 'I now' from an 'I then', a narrating self from a narrated one. Memoir – in Russian, *vospominaniia* (reminiscences) or *memuary* (imported from the French) – places a spotlight jointly on oneself and one's milieu, with one's own story meant to shed light on a collective experience or moment in history. While autobiography often begins with childhood, memoir tends to select a particularly significant event in adulthood as its inception point. Memoir is a more common form in Russian literature than autobiography as such, which can in part be explained by the cultural value placed on the community over the individual. Diaries, as daily accounts, create a close temporal relationship between the writing and written subject and tend towards privacy and intimacy; they may not have an addressee.[9] The writer often becomes a regular reader of the diary entries that produce a record of a changing self, the act of reading thus becoming a constituent aspect of the writing process. Documentary prose, a term that has special resonance for the Russian tradition, especially in the postwar period, can refer to a genre that combines document and artistry and may encompass oral history, memoir, and semi-fiction.

Most of my examples are literary, chosen with an eye to highlighting the evolution of their forms and aesthetic devices. Some, however, play around at the boundaries of fiction and non-fiction. Their authors are writers by profession, usually members of the intelligentsia. The chapter's temporal focus lies in the period stretching from the end of the Second World War to the late Soviet period.

Stories of Russian Lives

Scholars frequently identify the auto-hagiography *Life of Archpriest Avvakum, Written by Himself* (*Zhitie protopopa Avvakuma, im samim napisan-noe*, comp. 1672–5) as the first example of Russian self-writing. Aspects of this narrative that became widespread in the tradition of self-writing (as well as in Russian literature more generally) include Avvakum Petrov's (1620–1682) writing from internal exile, his opposition to secular and ecclesiastical authority, and his chattiness and combination of stylistic registers.

---

8 Philippe Lejeune, 'The autobiographical pact', in Paul John Eakin (ed.), *On Autobiography*, trans. Katherine Leary (Minneapolis: University of Minnesota Press, 1989), p. 4.

9 See Irina Paperno, 'What can be done with diaries?', *Russian Review* 64.4 (2004), 561–73.

While seventeenth-century France was the birthplace of the modern memoir,[10] Russian memoirs as such started appearing in the eighteenth century in the wake of Peter I's (r. 1682–1725) Europeanising reforms (which brought secularisation, modernisation, and the establishment of a civil and military service along with a table of ranks).[11] Most of these works tended to focus on achievements for the state. Written for family and friends, some of them reached influential readers such as Petr Viazemskii (1792–1878) and Aleksandr Pushkin (1799–1837).[12]

An important shift in the purpose of the memoir was inaugurated by Aleksandr Radishchev (1749–1802), often called the first Russian *intelligent* (see Chapter 4.5). His *Life of Fedor Vasilevich Ushakov* (*Zhitie Fedora Vasil'evicha Ushakova*, 1789) shared many of the features of the gentry memoir that came before, including descriptions of social life, concerns with power relations, and references to patronage. What was new, as historian Barbara Walker has shown, was the treatment of group concerns and values, in part through the canonisation of certain figures (such as Radishchev's teacher and mentor, Ushakov) and the demonisation of others (a despotic, corrupt man named von Alten Bokum). Radishchev became the founder of the 'contemporaries' memoir – Walker's term for works that often carry 'such titles as "The Memoirs (*vospominaniia*) of Contemporaries (*sovremennikov*) about so-and-so", or "So-and-so in the Memoirs (*v vospominaniiakh*) of Contemporaries (*sovremennikov*)"' – which eventually became a mainstay of the Russian, and then Soviet, intelligentsia. Walker notes surges of popularity in the mid-nineteenth century, the 1920s, and finally the 1950s through the late Soviet period. The writing of such memoirs could bolster informal networks (as well as the reputations of certain members), which provided moral, intellectual, social, and economic support that was sorely needed in an often-hostile world.[13]

After Russia's victory in the Napoleonic Wars (1813), memoirs hastened to glorify national heroes and Russian history.[14] This is true even of the subversive memoir-travelogue by Nadezhda Durova (1783–1866; also known as Aleksandr Aleksandrov, see Chapter 2.6), *Notes of a Cavalry Maiden* (*Zapiski*

---

10 Ginzburg, *On Psychological Prose*, 6.

11 A. G. Tartakovskii, *Russkaia memuaristika XVIII–pervoi poloviny XIX veka* [Russian memoir from the eighteenth to the first half of the nineteenth century] (Moscow: Nauka, 1991), p. 7.

12 Beth Holmgren, introduction to Holmgren (ed.), *The Russian Memoir: History and Literature* (Evantson, IL: Northwestern University Press, 2003), pp. xvi–xvii.

13 Barbara Walker, 'On reading Soviet memoirs: A history of the "contemporaries" genre as an institution of Russian intelligentsia culture from the 1790s to the 1970s', *Russian Review* 59.3 (2000), 329, 335.

14 See Tartakovskii's thesis, discussed in Holmgren, introduction, p. xvii.

kavelerist-devitsy, published by Pushkin in *The Contemporary* (*Sovremennik*), 1836), in which the author tells of their adventures, disguised as a man, fighting Napoleon's armies as a member of the Russian cavalry. Durova breaks with gender norms but nevertheless writes as a devoted subject of Tsar Nicholas I (r. 1825–55). A much less plot-driven example of the memoir, which became important for twentieth- and twenty-first-century Russian authors, is Viazemskii's *Old Notebook* (*Staraia zapisnaia knizhka*, comp. 1813–77). As Ginzburg notes, Viazemskii makes a monumental, composite work out of a miniature form by juxtaposing various genres of self-writing: anecdote, memoiristic fragment, political or literary-critical argument, character sketch, aphorism.[15] Viazemskii himself (like Ginzburg and the Formalists) conceived of intermediary literature as paving the way for new artistic forms.[16]

The flexibility and openness of self-writing (including its greater accessibility to female authors) are not conducive to the formation of strong lines of literary tradition, the likes of which one finds in the Russian novel. Nevertheless, certain influential texts came to serve as models for authors in the latter half of the nineteenth century and beyond: Lev Tolstoi's (1828–1910) *Childhood* (*Detstvo*, 1852) – followed by *Boyhood* (*Otrochestvo*, 1854) and *Youth* (*Iunost'*, 1857) – and Herzen's *My Past and Thoughts* (*Byloe i dumy*, 1852–68).

Childhood, which marked Tolstoi's literary debut, is a fictionalised auto-biography in the form of a Bildungsroman. Tolstoi became a steady practitioner of moral self-examination and psychological analysis – not only in his diaries but also in his novels, which Ginzburg calls 'psychologically and ethically documentary'.[17] *Childhood* begins with the narrator's memory of waking up, just past his tenth birthday, to his German tutor swatting a fly just above his head. The scene is characteristically detailed in both its physical and emotional descriptions. Thinking the tutor especially 'nasty' and then regretting this judgement, the sensitive boy works himself up into hysterics.[18] The lie he invents to explain away his tears – a dream about his mother's death – is

---

15 Lidiia Ginzburg, introduction to Petr Viazemskii, *Staraia zapisnaia knizhka* [Old notebook], ed. Ginzburg (Leningrad: Izdatel'stvo pisatelei, 1929), pp. 42–3.

16 Lidiia Ginzburg, 'Viazemskii – literator' [Viazemskii – *literateur*], in B. Eikhenbaum and Iu. Tynianov (eds.), *Russkaia proza: Sbornik statei* [Russian prose: A collection of articles] (Leningrad: Academia, 1926) pp. 102–4, republished in L. Ia. Ginzburg, *Raboty dovoennogo vremeni* [Works of the prewar period], ed. Stanislav Savitskii (St Petersburg: Petropolis, 2007), p. 102.

17 Lidiia Ginzburg, *O psikhologicheskoi proze* [On psychological prose], 2nd edn (Leningrad: Khudozhestvennaia literatura, 1977), p. 300; English in Ginzburg, *On Psychological Prose*, p. 245 (the wording of Rosengrant's translation is different from mine).

18 Leo Tolstoy, *Childhood, Boyhood, Youth*, trans. Judson Rosengrant (London: Penguin Books, 2012), p. 5.

powerful enough to make him cry in earnest, and it comes true by the end of the narrative (throughout the work, artistic and social conventions lead the narrator into falsehoods, which he senses painfully). *Childhood* is not strictly speaking 'self-writing'. It is more accurately a pseudo-autobiography: a fictional narrator recalls his early years, which are based in part on Tolstoi's.[19] The majority of this tightly structured work takes place over just two days (Tolstoi's first quasi-fictional literary experiment was a failed record of the internal impressions of a single day).

Heavily influenced by Jean-Jacques Rousseau, *Childhood* was the first Russian depiction of a child's inner perspective, with its quick emotional reversals, endearing naïveté, and acute sensitivity. Tolstoi's model of a happy childhood (separating the sphere of the mother, on the idyllic country estate, from that of the father, in the artificial high society of Moscow) was so influential that subsequent autobiographers found themselves faced with a choice of explicitly accepting or rejecting it. Maksim Gorkii's (1868–1936) autobiographical trilogy – *Childhood* (*Detstvo*, 1913–14), *In the World* (*V liudiakh*, 1916), *My Universities* (*Moi universitety*, 1923) – is structurally indebted to Tolstoi. Lev Trotskii (1879–1940; see Box 5.3) polemicises with the model in *My Life* (*Moia zhizn'*, 1930): 'only a few have a happy childhood. The idealization of childhood originated in the old literature of the privileged.'[20]

Herzen's *My Past and Thoughts* (begun in the year of Tolstoi's *Childhood*) begins with the young author asking his Russian nurse, 'come tell me once more how the French came to Moscow', referring to events in the year of his birth, 1812. Herzen adds that 'Tales of the fire of Moscow, of the battle of Borodino, of the Berezina, of the taking of Paris were my cradle-songs, my nursery stories, my Iliad and my Odyssey.'[21] He goes on to represent his life as a reflection of larger historical forces. The memoir, published in eight parts, spans his childhood, imprisonment and exile, travels in Europe, and life in London. Herzen's philosophical reflections, essays, and analysis together create an amalgam of historiography and autobiography.[22] The overarching idea of a clash of the new and old worlds serves to unify the fragments, which thus tell the story of a young person's ideological development as

---

19 Andrew Wachtel, *The Battle for Childhood: Creation of a Russian Myth* (Stanford: Stanford University Press, 1990), p. 3.
20 Leon Trotsky, *My Life: An Attempt at Autobiography* (Mineola, New York: Dover Publications, Inc., 2007), p. 1.
21 Alexander Herzen, *My Past and Thoughts*, trans. Constance Garnett (Berkeley: University of California Press, 1982) pp. 3, 10.
22 Ginzburg, *On Psychological Prose*, p. 199.

a revolutionary committed to fighting autocracy (Herzen, writing from emigration, evaded censorship).[23] Herzen casts himself as a member of the intelligentsia, creating what Irina Paperno has argued is *the* definitive contemporaries memoir, which future generations, particularly Soviet intellectuals, would come to use as a model. Herzen adapted Hegelianism for a description of Russian life: instead of distinguishing only 'world-historic individuals' (on the level of Napoleon) as having a significant story to tell, he told of 'the reflection of history in someone who *accidentally* got in its way'.[24] In a radical remaking of Hegel's optimistic vision of progress, Herzen struggles in a world that is unjust, catastrophic, and violent.[25]

Following Herzen's example, radical women revolutionaries of the 1870s such as Vera Figner (1852–1942) wrote their personal memoirs as histories of revolution (*Memoirs of a Revolutionist* (*Zapechatlennyi trud*, 1921–2)). They inscribed their histories into the tradition of the male revolutionary, privileging the account of their commitment to the people over stories of gender discrimination. Aleksandra Kollontai (1872–1952), a Bolshevik revolutionary of a later generation, also focused her self-writing (*Autobiography of a Sexually Emancipated Communist Woman* (*Avtobiografiia seksual'no emansipirovannoi kommunistki*, 1926)) on public activities rather than personal life and censored sections treating her own feminist journalism and theories.[26] An alternative female autobiographic tradition, traced by Barbara Heldt, was created over time by Princess Ekaterina Dashkova (1743–1810), Nadezhda Durova, Nadezhda Sokhanskaia (1823–1884, whose autobiography centres in Kharkiv, Ukraine, which was then in the Russian Empire), Liubov Mendeleeva-Blok (1881–1939), Marina Tsvetaeva (1892–1941), and others. All of these authors treat family life, mothers, and daughters in a much more central way than male autobiographers. In Heldt's account, these authors react not only to life but also to both the fictional tradition of the heroine in Russian literature and the reigning movements of their respective times.[27]

23 Ginzburg, *On Psychological Prose*, p. 204.

24 Herzen, preface to part 5 of *My Past and Thoughts*, quoted in Ginzburg, *On Psychological Prose*, p. 203.

25 Irina Paperno, 'Personal accounts of the Soviet experience', *Kritika: Explorations in Russian and Eurasian History* 3.4 (2002), 586.

26 Beth Holmgren, 'For the good of the cause: Russian women's autobiography in the twentieth century', in Toby W. Clyman and Diana Greene (eds.), *Women Writers in Russian Literature* (Westport, CT: Praeger, 1994), pp. 129–30.

27 Barbara Heldt, *Terrible Perfection: Women and Russian Literature* (Bloomington: Indiana University Press, 1987).

Self-Writing after the Crisis of the Novel

The cataclysmic events of the First World War, the Bolshevik Revolution, and large-scale industrialisation and urbanisation threw into question all absolute values and previously accepted notions of the wholeness of self. Within literature, this spurred a 'crisis of the novel' as non-fictional forms moved from the periphery to the centre while many writers turned to innovative blends of fiction and autobiography (see Chapter 3.9). Autobiographical experiments of the Russian Silver Age, such as Vasilii Rozanov's (1856–1919) fragmentary trilogy – *Solitaria* (*Uedinennoe*, 1912), *Fallen Leaves: Basketful One* (*Opavshie list'ia: korob 1*, 1913), and *Basketful Two* (*Opavshie list'ia: korob 2*, 1915) – had already explored the atomised self and the idea of the end of literature: 'And I have a strange premonition that I am the *last writer*, after whom literature in general will cease . . . "The self" is terrible, disgusting, enormous and tragic with the final tragedy, because in my "self" the colossal millennia-old "self" of literature has somehow dialectically "dissolved and disappeared!"'[28]

Osip Mandelshtam (1891–1938) articulated 'the end of the novel' in an essay of the same name (*Konets romana*, 1922) as a result of the new 'epoch of powerful social movements and organized mass actions', the declining value of the 'individual in history', Einsteinian relativity, and a reality so over-powering as to cause biographies to disintegrate and psychological motiv-ation to lose relevance.[29] This sentiment had its counterparts in the unwinding of the distinct hero in the work of Tomas Musil, Virginia Woolf, James Joyce, Samuel Beckett, Andrei Belyi (1880–1934), and others, as well as in the submergence of narrative in memory and consciousness in Marcel Proust's *In Search of Lost Time*.

As a response to this crisis around the traditional novel, one finds at least four noteworthy strains of non-fiction in the 1920s. The first is the 'literature of fact' elaborated by the New LEF group – Osip Brik (1888–1945), Sergei Tretiakov (1892–1937), Nikolai Chuzhak (1876–1937), and Viktor Shklovskii (1893–1984) – which advocated for journalism and even the biography of a thing. This strain had close cousins in documentary cinema such as that of Dziga Vertov (1896–1954) with his camera-eye. The second (in some ways

---

28 Vasilii Rozanov, *Uedinennoe* [Solitaria], ed. A. N. Nikoliukina (Moscow: Politizdat, 1990), p. 206. Quoted and translated in Anna Lisa Crone, 'Rozanov and autobiography: The case of Vasily Vasilievich', in Harris (ed.), *Autobiographical Statements*, p. 51.

29 Osip Mandelstam, 'The end of the novel', in Jane Gary Harris (ed.), *Mandelstam: The Complete Critical Prose and Letters*, trans. Harris and Constance Link (Ann Arbor, MI: Ardis, 1979), pp. 198–201.

a subcategory) is prose by Formalist scholars, in particular Boris Eikhenbaum (1886–1959) with his *My Periodical* (*Moi vremennik*, 1929) and Shklovskii with his *A Sentimental Journey* (*Sentimental'noe puteshestvie*, 1923), *Zoo, or Letters Not about Love, or the New Heloise* (*Zoo, ili pis'ma ne o liubvi, ili tret'ia Eloiza*, 1923), and *Third Factory* (*Tret'ia fabrika*, 1926). The Formalists included theory and criticism within autobiographical literature, seeking to shift their readers' reception of other forms as a way out of the novel's impasse.[30] Like Herzen, they replaced the invented worlds of novels with a direct analysis of life experience.[31] The third strain is the quasi-autobiographical fictions of Modernist writers from Odesa, which was then part of the Russian Empire: Isaak Babel (1894–1940), Iurii Olesha (1899–1960), and Valentin Kataev (1897–1986) – Konstantin Paustovskii (1892–1968), who grew up in Kyiv, is also considered part of this group.[32] And the fourth is the experimental autobiographical prose by such poets as Vladimir Maiakovskii (1893–1930), Boris Pasternak (1890–1960), Tsvetaeva, and Mandelshtam, which often inhabits the child's perspective but also depicts personal life as a reflection of history (especially Mandelshtam's autobiography of his own childhood, *The Noise of Time* (*Shum vremeni*, 1925)).

In the 1930s, self-writing, including memoir and diaries, was self-censored and hidden away in desk drawers, so as not to be turned into incriminating evidence. Hypothetical or potential new definitions of the self and literary forms that would reflect reality were largely stymied by the doctrine of Socialist Realism and its hero, the 'new Soviet person'. Lidiia Chukovskaia (1907–1996), whose notes record interactions with Anna Akhmatova (1889–1966) during Stalin's purges, asks, 'could one even conceive of keeping a real diary in those days? The content of our conversations, whispers, guesses, silences of that time is scrupulously absent from these notes.'[33] Nevertheless, there were Soviet citizens who documented their daily lives, as part of their earnest self-work to become model subjects and their effort to 'ideologize' their lives in the model of Herzen.[34] Mikhail Zoshchenko's (1894–1958) literary autobiography *Before Sunrise* (*Pered voskhodom solntsa*, partially

---

30 Gary Saul Morson, *The Boundaries of Genre* (Evanston, IL: Northwestern University Press, 1981), pp. 51–8.
31 Ginzburg, *On Psychological Prose*, pp. 201, 208.
32 Rebecca Jane Stanton, *Isaak Babel and the Self-Invention of Odessan Modernism* (Evanston, IL: Northwestern University Press, 2012).
33 Lydia Chukovskaya, *The Akhmatova Journals: Volume 1; 1938–1941* (Evanston, IL: Northwestern University Press, 1994), p. 5.
34 Jochen Hellbeck, *Revolution on My Mind: Writing a Diary under Stalin* (Cambridge, MA: Harvard University Press, 2009), p. 11. On the 1920s, see also Igal Halfin, *From Darkness to Light: Class Consciousness and Salvation in Revolutionary Russia* (Pittsburgh: University of Pittsburgh Press, 2000).

published in 1943) can perhaps be seen in this context: he performs a Freudian analysis of mental illness on the way towards his supposed conversion into a Soviet new person. But significantly, he spends more time on the 'negative' part of his development than on the mechanics of his transformation.

Before we enter into the Soviet postwar period, a digression is in order on Vladimir Nabokov (1899–1977), who in emigration wrote what many have hailed as one of the greatest autobiographies in any language. Wishing to escape the role of a political writer with a vendetta against the land that had banished his family, Nabokov insists that his autobiography has no greater purpose than to follow 'thematic designs through one's own life' (see Chapter 4.10).[35] Having become famous for his novels, he was also writing to salvage for his life those figures he had written into fiction: 'the man in me revolts against the fictionist'.[36] Yet Nabokov (especially in the English edition) cannot refrain from including anti-Soviet rebukes, for example telling of how the street name of the family's house in St Petersburg/Leningrad was changed to 'Herzen', 'a famous liberal (whom this commemoration by a police state would hardly have gratified)'; Herzen was lionised by the Soviet state as an anti-tsarist revolutionary, despite the fact that his brand of democratic humanism was far from Bolshevism.[37] The author lists *My Past and Thoughts* as one of his father's favourite books. Nabokov gestures towards Hegel (in a pointedly personal, apolitical way) when presenting his life as a spiral or 'spiritualized circle' with a thetic (Russian), antithetic (European), and synthetic (American) period.[38]

Nabokov wrote the autobiography in English (with the exception of one chapter written first in French) and published it in parts (1940–51) before bringing it together as a single integrated work (*Conclusive Evidence*, 1951). He then translated it into Russian as *Other Shores* (*Drugie berega*, 1954 in the émigré press) and finally 're-Englished' the work as *Speak, Memory: An Autobiography Revisited* (1966), revising it in the process. The autobiography is a testament to what Nabokov calls an 'almost pathological keenness of the retrospective faculty'.[39] Presented in roughly chronological order with digressions on butterflies, chess, and family heraldry as well as sketches of family members and tutors, Nabokov's narratives convey a kind of timelessness. He navigates his past with

---

35 Vladimir Nabokov, *Speak, Memory* (New York: Quality Paperback Book Club, 1967), p. 27; Russian in Nabokov, *Drugie berega* [Other shores] (New York: Izdatel'stvo imeni Chekhova, 1954), p. 19.
36 Nabokov, *Speak, Memory*, p. 95; this sentence is not included in *Drugie berega*.
37 Nabokov, *Speak, Memory*, p. 18, photo caption; not included in *Drugie berega*.
38 Nabokov, *Speak, Memory*, p. 275; *Drugie berega*, p. 235.
39 Nabokov, *Speak, Memory*, p. 75; *Drugie berega*, p. 64.

the help of his 'magic carpet', mimicking the free migration of butterflies. The autobiography shows the influence of Tolstoi's *Childhood*, for example in the division of the world of the mother, with her connection to Russian spirituality, country estates, and mushroom-picking, from the sphere of the father, immersed in urban, political, Europeanised life. Fittingly, when Nabokov recalls learning of Tolstoi's death in 1910, his father reports in French, 'Tolstoy vient de mourir' ('Tolstoy just died'), whereas his mother reacts with a quintessentially Russian expression, 'Da chto ti' (something like 'good gracious').[40]

After the War and Camps

The Second World War and the release of prisoners from the Gulag after Stalin's death in 1953 lent enormous impetus to Russian memoir and documentary prose. As Varlam Shalamov (1907–1982) reflected in his essay 'On Prose' (*O proze*, 1965, pub. posthumously), 'People who have gone through war, revolution, and concentration camps have no time for the novel. . . . The enormous interest worldwide in the genre of memoir is a voice and sign of the times. . . . Today's reader engages only with documents.'[41] While Shalamov identifies 'the camp theme in its broad interpretation' as the single most important topic of his time, there are two additional defining topoi in memoirs of the Thaw: Stalin's Terror and the war. Psychological states of fear, unfreedom, extreme suffering (sometimes making heroes, more often only victims) unite them. Many authors also comment on the fate of the intelligentsia and its degree of responsibility for the horrors that followed the Bolshevik Revolution.

The city of Leningrad, under deadly siege between September 1941 and January 1944, was a historical disaster that spurred an incredible volume of self-writing. Party officials encouraged diaries, which they intended to use to compile a history of the blockade.[42] Women survived and remained in Leningrad in greater proportions than men, and their writings form the primary corpus of testimonies about the siege. The diaries of Vera Inber (1890–1972) – *Almost Three Years* (*Pochti tri goda*, 1946) – directly reflect on the heightened inspiration that many writers felt, even when facing

40 Nabokov, *Speak, Memory*, p. 207; *Drugie berega*, p. 189.
41 Varlam Shalamov, 'On prose', trans. Brian R. Johnson, in Mark Lipovetsky and Lisa Ryoko Wakamiya (eds.), *Late and Post-Soviet Russian Literature: A Reader*, book 2, *Thaw and Stagnation (1954–1986)* (Boston: Academic Studies Press, 2015), pp. 111–12, with minor change of Johnson's translation of 'man' to 'person' (for *chelovek*).
42 Alexis Peri, *The War Within: Diaries from the Siege of Leningrad* (Cambridge, MA: Harvard University Press, 2017), p. 13.

hunger and surrounded by death. Olga Freidenberg (1890–1955), a major classicist (and Boris Pasternak's cousin) wrote a quasi-ethnographic account of the blockade in her diary-memoir 'The Siege of a Human Being' (*Osada cheloveka*, partially pub. 1986, 1987), a central part of her autobiographical chronicle, *The Race of Life* (*Probeg zhizni*, as yet unpublished).[43] She describes the double tyranny of Hitler and Stalin as besieging everything, trapping 'the city, me, my body and psyche in a special ultra-imprisoned way of life'.[44]

After the Leningrad Affair (a purge of the city's political elite in 1949–53), the subject of the blockade long disappeared from print. In 1977, a censored edition of Ales Adamovich (1927–1994; a Belarusian writer who wrote in both Belarusian and Russian) and Daniil Granin's (1919–2017) *Book of the Blockade* (*Blokadnaia kniga*) came out, a work of documentary prose that combines interviews with survivors, diary excerpts, and editorial passages about the heroism of the *blokadniki*. Following this publication, Ginzburg was inspired to publish one of her own blockade narratives, which she began in 1942 and revised over the intervening decades: *Notes of a Blockade Person* (*Zapiski blokadnogo cheloveka*, 1984, in abbreviated form). Centring her narrative around a generalised representative of the intelligentsia, Ginzburg draws on Herzen's notion of the historic significance of individual suffering. She practises Tolstoian self-examination and dialogue analysis (seeing self-assertion at the root of every conversation) and refers in the work's finale to Proust (who demonstrated how to regain time by describing it). Ginzburg's writings are neither diary nor memoir. They rely on meticulous observation of others and of the self. She draws parallels between the Terror and the siege, and she documents the 'blockade person', for whom unfreedom 'penetrated into all aspects of himself, all the way up to the very minutest ones'.[45] She notes that the catastrophic experiences of the twentieth century have proven to her generation over and over, 'the ineradicable nature of social evil and the illusoriness of the individual consciousness'.[46]

43 Irina Paperno, '"Osada cheloveka": Blokadnye zapiski Ol'gi Freidenberg v antropologicheskoi perspektive' ['The siege of a human being': The blockade notes of Ol'ga Freidenberg in anthropological perspective], *Novoe literaturnoe obozrenie* [New literary review] 139 (2016), 184.

44 Paperno, '"Osada cheloveka"', 186, translation mine.

45 Lydia Ginzburg, 'Draft "theoretical section" of the manuscript "Otter's Day" (excerpts)', trans. Emily Van Buskirk, in Van Buskirk (ed.), *Notes from the Blockade*, trans. Alan Myers (London: Vintage, 2016), p. 128. Translation slightly adjusted.

46 Ginzburg, *Notes from the Blockade*, p. 123.

Olga Berggolts (1910–1975), whose siege poetry gave Leningraders hope and a sense of their collective identities, published a lyric memoir early in the Thaw. Her *Daytime Stars* (*Dnevnye zvezdy*, 1953–62) proceeds achronologically, treating the revolution, moments from the 1930s, and the blockade, but skipping over her numerous personal tragedies, arrest, and imprisonment during the Terror (about which she did write in her diaries). The author fretted about this ('How can I write about the subject of consciousness, and leave out the main thing – the last two or three years, i.e., prison?') and planned to connect prison and the blockade in a second volume (never written).[47]

Diary writing was widespread in the Thaw, when authors took up the project of reforming socialism in their own personal writings and investigations of Soviet life.[48] Because of the distortions and systematic destruction of evidence carried out by the Stalinist authorities, memoir recovered the authority which it had lost in the late nineteenth century.[49] Aleksandr Tvardovskii (1910–1971), the editor of the thick journal *New World* (*Novyi mir*, 1925–) (see Chapter 2.4), kept a diary in this era, both as a writer's notebook and as a record for posterity. One of his innovations at *New World* was a section called 'Diary of a Writer' (*Dnevnik pisatelia*, after Fedor Dostoevskii (1821–1881)), which featured essays, sketches, diaries, and documentary prose. He remarked that 'fiction is living out its days', while insisting that the 'development of a memoir-sketch genre' would mean that 'art would not vanish, as long as the truth was in place'.[50]

Ilia Erenburg's (1891–1967) *People. Years. Life* (*Liudi. Gody. Zhizn'*, published in *New World* 1960–3 and 1965) was one of the first texts to return to public discourse the names and stories of writers, artists, and political figures who had been arrested and killed in Stalin's Terror. Erenburg's memoirs are an example of the contemporaries genre, and, like other texts of the period, show the influence of Herzen. For reasons of both censorship and self-censorship,

---

47 Ol'ga Berggol'ts, *Vstrecha: Dnevnye zvezdy, pis'ma, dnevniki, zametki, plany* (Meeting: Daytime stars, letters, diaries, notes, plans) (Moscow: Russkaia kniga, 2000), pp. 316–17, 220, quoted in Katharine Hodgson, 'Foreword: Finding memory in the margins', in Olga Berggolts, *Daytime Stars*, trans. and ed. Lisa A. Kirschenbaum (Madison: University of Wisconsin Press), p. xx.

48 Anatoly Pinsky, 'The diaristic form and subjectivity under Khrushchev', *Slavic Review* 73.4 (2014), 805–27.

49 Holmgren, introduction, p. xiv.

50 Aleksandr Tvardovskii, diary entry from 28 Nov. 1963, quoted in Pinsky, 'Diaristic form', 812. Russian original available online through the project 'Prozhito: Dnevniki i vospominaniia' ['Lived': Diaries and reminiscences], https://prozhito.org/note/195445, accessed 23 Jan. 2023.

they leave out details not only about Erenburg's acquaintances but about his own methods of surviving the Stalin era. Another noteworthy memoir of the Thaw era is Shklovskii's *Once Upon a Time* (*Zhili byli*, 1964). Shklovskii, in his seventies, tries to write a revisionist life story, admitting obscurely to his guilt (whether for his anti-Bolshevik activities, Formalist criticism, or both is unclear). Meanwhile, he skips over important moments or narrates them incompletely, while also drawing attention to the flaws of memory and falsifications in the genre of memoir as a whole. Perhaps intentionally, he thus undermines the ideological correctness that seems, at first impression, to guide the narrative.

During the Thaw, writers sought to speak the truth about the camps and the Terror, whether in autobiographical fictions, documentary prose, or memoir. Evgeniia Ginzburg (1904–1977; no relation to Lidiia) created her two-part memoir, *Into the Whirlwind* and *Within the Whirlwind* (*Krutoi marsh-rut*, volumes I and II, pub. in Milan in 1967 and 1979, respectively), as a Bildungsroman, wherein a young communist, arrested during the Terror, gradually becomes conscious of the evils of Stalinism. She maintains her faith in the revolution and in Lenin, hoping for reform of the party and system.[51] Ginzburg signals the Terror as the theme of the memoir in the first line: 'The year 1937 began, to all intents and purposes, at the end of 1934 – to be exact, on the first of December' (a reference to the murder of Leningrad Party boss Sergei Kirov, which set off the purges). Like Herzen, she connects her personal fate to the national one; she quotes him, 'Everything is destroyed, the freedom of the world and my happiness.'[52] Holding onto a dogged optimism despite the tragedies that beset her, she demonstrates how Russian poetry (having been memorised) can become a tool of survival, the basis of an all-important human connection.

Evgeniia Ginzburg's account is more than a contemporaries memoir – she adopts a broadly humanist position. She could be said to follow the model of Dostoevskii, whose semi-fictional novel *Notes from the House of the Dead* (*Zapiski iz mertvogo doma*, 1862) – the first Russian prison camp narrative – draws sympathetic portraits of inmates from all classes. Women's narratives of the Terror showcase the female friendships that developed in extreme adversity; they succeed in rescuing women's lives and memories from oblivion. They also help initiate a post-Stalinist turn towards the

---

51 See, for example, Eugenia Ginzburg, *Within the Whirlwind*, trans. Ian Boland (San Diego: Harcourt Brace Jovanovich, 1979), p. 423.
52 Eugenia Ginzburg, *Journey into the Whirlwind*, trans. Paul Stevenson and Max Hayward (San Diego: Harcourt Brace Jovanovich, 1967), p. 94.

private realm.[53] Rather than just teach the lessons of revolutionaries à la Herzen, these authors speak of how to remain human.[54]

Memoirs of the Terror were written not only by camp survivors but also by the wives, widows, daughters, and mothers of those who were arrested, executed, or sent to the Gulag. In a society and literary tradition that remained patriarchal well into late Soviet times, women gained cultural power and significance in their role as preservers of unofficial texts left behind by male writers and of their memories of silenced authors.[55] Nadezhda Mandelshtam (1899–1980) came into authorship through her reminiscences of her husband Osip Mandelshtam's life and fate, focusing on the years leading up to his death in a transit camp. First published in New York, the two volumes *Hope against Hope* (*Vospominaniia*, 1970) and *Hope Abandoned* (*Vtoraia kniga*, 1972) are filled with lively anecdotes and gossip (a trademark of the contemporaries memoir), but they also at times employ narrative omniscience (a novelistic device). Nadezhda Mandelshtam offers up a critique of the intelligentsia and its complicity in the violent consequences of the revolution: 'It was, after all, these people of the twenties who demolished the old values and invented the formulas which even now come in so handy to justify the unprecedented experiment undertaken by our young State: you cannot make an omelet without breaking eggs.'[56] She posits her account (parts of which have been disputed by other memoirists) as authoritative while acknowledging the impossibility of true witness: 'We all became slightly unbalanced mentally ... What value can such people have as witnesses?'[57] She remains an optimist about the persistent, even innate, quality of good.[58]

Shalamov, whose *Kolyma Tales* (*Kolymskie rasskazy*, comp. 1954–73) depict life at the extremes more effectively than those of any other chronicler of the Gulag, wrote that the most important thing for a writer was to 'preserve the living soul'.[59] His Kolyma tales resemble short stories rather than memoirs, with their tight plots and (minimally drawn, quasi-fictional, sometimes autobiographical) characters (see Chapter 3.6). While writing with a mission

53 Holmgren, 'For the good', p. 132.
54 See, for example, Maria Ioffe, *Odna noch': Povest' o pravde* [One night: A tale about the truth] (New York: Khronika, 1978), p. 127, cited in Holmgren, 'For the good', p. 132.
55 Holmgren, 'For the good', p. 136.
56 Nadezhda Mandelstam, *Hope against Hope: A Memoir*, trans. Max Hayward (New York: Modern Library, 1999) p. 169.
57 Mandelstam, *Hope against Hope*, p. 89. See Charles Isenberg, 'The rhetoric of *Hope against Hope*', in Harris (ed.), *Autobiographical Statements*, pp. 193–206.
58 Mandelstam, *Hope against Hope*, p. 39.   59 Shalamov, 'On prose', p. 122.

to administer a 'slap in the face' to Stalinism,[60] Shalamov maintained that there is nothing positive to learn, that camp experiences are absolutely negative. He rejected the didacticism of Tolstoi and the psychological novel and tended to be suspicious of the intelligentsia's claims to being less susceptible to moral degradation in the camps. His stories shock the reader with the inhumanity of Kolyma, the reduction of the human to the animal. The effect is heightened by Shalamov's rejection of analysis; he claimed that 'analysis in [*The Kolyma Tales*] is in the very absence of analysis'.[61]

Analysis is key, however, in the works of Lidiia Ginzburg, who increased its proportion in response to the illogic of the misfortunes that befell her. Her largest book of prose published while she lived was *Person at a Writing Table* (*Chelovek za pis'mennym stolom*, 1989). Her analysis was not only psychological: she tried to look at what she called a person's 'relatively stable social function' (that is, their role as a bureaucrat, scholar, avant-gardist, publisher) and how it could interact in complicated ways with their personality (as a flatterer, organiser, charmer, careerist) to positive or negative effects, calling the unearthing of 'functions, mechanisms, structures' the 'methodology of the twentieth century'.[62] Ginzburg, like Herzen, tried to find typical aspects in her own fate, even though she was in some ways marginal to Soviet society (as a lesbian, a Jew, an intellectual of uncertain employment, and a desk-drawer writer). She wrote of a generalised version of herself, using the third-person masculine pronoun 'he'. Writing oneself as another is central to all autobiography, and to women's self-writing in particular, but here it reaches full rhetorical expression. Like Shalamov, Vasilii Grossman (1905–1964), and other postwar writers, Ginzburg thought literature should speak of '*how* ever to survive and endure without losing one's human image'.[63] Trying to escape what she saw as the chill of memoir time (that is, its distance from the time of writing), she gravitated towards the diary. Yet she also wanted to achieve the kind of retrospectivity that is possible in the memoir or, even better, the novel (whose fictions she rejected). Her solution was to write a 'diary in the form of a novel' – a quasi-definition of her genre which she simultaneously rejected as inadequate.[64]

60 Varlam Shalamov, 'O moei proze' [On my prose] (1971), Shalamov.ru, https://shalamov.ru/library/21/61.html, accessed 16 June 2021.
61 Shalamov, 'On prose', p. 123.
62 Lidiia Ginzburg, 'O satire i ob analize' [On satire and analysis], in *Zapisnye knizhki. Vospominaniia. Esse* [Notebooks. Reminiscences. Essays] (St Petersburg: Iskusstvo–SPb, 2002), pp. 251–9 (quotation on p. 254).
63 Ginzburg, *Zapisnye knizhki*, p. 198.   64 Ginzburg, *Zapisnye knizhki*, p. 142.

Writing for the desk drawer, as did Lidiia Ginzburg and many Soviet memoirists and diarists who hoped for eventual publication, gives rise to a poetics of unfinalisability. Ginzburg wrote of the need to test her texts not just on her close friends but on the general reader,[65] and also noticed her works acquiring 'literary predecessors' as they remained hidden for decades. This unfinalisability was felt also by Evgeniia Ginzburg, who writes, 'When in the twilight of your days you read through the unpublished part of the book still lying in your desk, you feel an irresistible need to change it again and again (to alter not the facts, of course, but the selection, treatment, and, above all, your judgments on them).' She expressed anxiety that these alterations would 'damage the work'.[66]

In the late Soviet period, memoirs and diaries were published en masse, as their authors sought to make public their personal stories as a documentary record of the end of the Soviet epoch.[67] Paperno, in her work on this corpus, has traced the Herzenian historicist self-consciousness in virtually all Soviet memoirists.[68] A non-Herzenian example bridging the late Soviet and early post-Soviet years might be the books of Svetlana Aleksievich (1948–; a Belarusian who writes in Russian), which she retrospectively framed as a five-book cycle, *Voices of Utopia* (*Golosa utopii*, 1985–2013). Aleksievich in some ways writes against the intelligentsia tradition – pointedly choosing the voices of the less bookish 'Sovoks' (a derogatory name for *Homo sovieticus*, with which she herself identifies) as more authentic. Trained as a journalist and mentored by Adamovich (co-author of the *Book of the Blockade* and other works of documentary prose), she writes about war, nuclear disaster, and the post-Soviet transition. She transforms dialogues and interviews into a polyphony of countless voices in a documentary prose that bridges history and creative literature.

Post-Soviet Experiments in Self-Writing

Scholar-writers of the post-Soviet period have often combined literature and analysis in fragmentary form. Andrei Zorin (1956–), reviewing the literary critic Mikhail Gasparov's (1935–2005) *Notes and Excerpts* (*Zapisi i vypiski*, 2001), discusses a trend towards the philological and the personal. Following the tradition of Lidiia Ginzburg and Petr Viazemskii, Gasparov uses a loose organisational principle for his notes, in this case the arbitrary order of the

---

65 Ginzburg, *Zapisnye knizhki*, p. 188.   66 Ginzburg, *Within the Whirlwind*, p. 417.
67 Irina Paperno, *Stories of the Soviet Experience: Memoirs, Diaries, Dreams* (Ithaca: Cornell University Press, 2009), pp. xi–xii.
68 Paperno, *Stories*, p. 10.

alphabet (though he disrupts alphabetical order).[69] Other works of self-writing by scholars include Mikhail Bezrodnyi's (1957–) *End Quote* (*Konets tsitaty*, 1996), Andrei Sergeev's (1933–1998) *Stamp Album* (*Al'bom dlia marok*, 1997), Aleksandr Zholkovskii's (1937–) *Illegible* (*NRZB*, 1991), and Petr Vail's (1949–2009) *Genius Loci* (*Genii mesta*, 1999).

A brilliant example of the personalisation of the philological, and also of a kind of collective authorship, is Mariia Stepanova's (1972–) autobiographical novel *In Memory of Memory* (*Pamiati pamiati*, 2018), which engages in dialogue with Roland Barthes, W. G. Sebald, Susan Sontag, Osip Mandelshtam, and Lidiia Ginzburg, with excursions on Siegfried Kracauer, Jacques Rancière, and Marianne Hirsch. Stepanova sets out to recover, using photographs, diaries, postcards, letters, and material objects, the history and memory of her family. It is a 'quite ordinary' family, she writes: 'mere lodgers in history's house' to the point where her grandparents' 'efforts in life were dedicated to remaining invisible'. Rescuing their lives 'from the shadows', her book turns out to be about 'the way memory works, and what memory wants from me'.[70]

Contemporary Russian self-writing flourishes today across diverse genres and media. There are self-published narratives on the internet and social media. There is a documentary turn in theatre as well as in poetry, especially that which is related to disaster, trauma, terrorism, and war. Ilya Kukulin has explicated this trend among male poets – Stanislav Lvovskii (1972–), Kirill Medvedev (1975–), Boris Khersonskii (1950–) – but one should also name women poets such as Lida Iusupova (1963–), and, in her siege poetry and prose, Polina Barskova (1976–).[71] With open literary borders, self-writing continues to expand, developing alongside new concepts of the self that have yet to reach full articulation. Post-Soviet subjects continue to reflect on history and its traumas in memoirs, documentary prose, and autofiction. The poet Oksana Vasiakina's (1989–) autofictional novel *Wound* (*Rana*, 2021) is highly acclaimed; one could also name works in this genre by Olga Breininger (1987–), Alla Gorbunova (1985–), and Evgenii Shtorn (1983–).

69 Andrei Zorin, 'Ot a do ia i obratno' [From A to Z and back], *Neprikosnovennyi zapas* [Untapped reserve] 3 (2000), Zhurnal'nyi zal [Hall of journals], https://magazines.go rky.media/nz/2000/3/ot-a-do-ya-i-obratno.html, accessed 14 June 2021.

70 Maria Stepanova, *In Memory of Memory: A Romance*, trans. Sasha Dugdale (New York: New Directions, 2021), pp. 27, 23, 21, 20.

71 Ilya Kukulin, 'Documentalist strategies in contemporary Russian poetry', *Russian Review* 69.4 (2010), 585–614. On Iusupova, see Josephine von Zitzewitz, '"The scar we know" shows how Lida Yusupova shaped Russian feminist poetry', *Words without Borders* (18 May 2021), www.wordswithoutborders.org/book-review/the-scar-we-kno w-shows-how-lida-yusupova-shaped-russian-feminist-poetry, accessed 14 June 2021.

Self-publishing on blogs and social media has created new possibilities for continuous self-presentation, confession, exposure, and dialogue, facilitating complex interfaces between the private and the public. It has yet to be seen what kinds of texts and understandings this will produce.

Further Reading

Engelstein, Laura, and Stephanie Sandler (eds.), *Self and Story in Russian History* (Ithaca: Cornell University Press, 2000).

Ginzburg, Lydia, *On Psychological Prose*, trans. Judson Rosengrant (Princeton: Princeton University Press, 1991).

Harris, Jane Gary, *Autobiographical Statements in Twentieth-Century Russian Literature* (Princeton: Princeton University Press, 1990).

Heldt, Barbara, *Terrible Perfection: Women and Russian Literature* (Bloomington: Indiana University Press, 1987).

Holmgren, Beth, *The Russian Memoir: History and Literature* (Evantson, IL: Northwestern University Press, 2003).

Paperno, Irina, *Stories of the Soviet Experience: Memoirs, Diaries, Dreams* (Ithaca: Cornell University Press, 2009).

Smith, Sidonie, and Julia Watson (eds.), *Reading Autobiography: A Guide for Interpreting Life Narratives* (Minneapolis: University of Minnesota Press, 2001).

Toker, Leona, *Return from the Archipelago: Narratives of Gulag Survivors* (Bloomington: Indiana University Press, 2000).

Wachtel, Andrew, *The Battle for Childhood: Creation of a Russian Myth* (Stanford: Stanford University Press, 1990).

Walker, Barbara, 'On reading Soviet memoirs: A history of the "contemporaries" genre as an institution of Russian intelligentsia culture from the 1790s to the 1970s', *Russian Review* 59.3 (2000), 327–52.

(Plat)forms after Genres

ELLEN RUTTEN

Multimedia writing and reading rank among the most exciting challenges for scholars of contemporary Russian literature. How should we define literary activity on the internet – the mechanism that today inevitably mediates all forms of literary production and dissemination (see Chapter 2.11)? How should we assess the forms of writing that circulate on Russophone digital platforms? Can a subtly written Facebook entry in verse by the poet Galina Rymbu (1990–) be considered literature? To what extent can the text-oriented tools of traditional literary studies help us make sense of Olia Lialina's (1971–) GIF-laden online stories? And how do understandings of literature as high-brow cultural practice help us unpack TikTok odes to Russian classics produced by teenagers?

The travels across media of online writings prompt us to rethink what literature is and how it works. These cross-medial writings do not appear out of nowhere, however. Just as elsewhere, in Russia writers have rarely stuck strictly to pen and paper to express themselves. Russian literature has long spilled over into social, cultural, and political life – in odes, for instance, in salon readings, or in such less genteel shapes as the performances of Russia's Futurists in the 1910s (think of Vladimir Maiakovskii (1893–1930), in bright-yellow blouse, radish as brooch, ranting in public against 'the filthy stigmas' of fine taste).[1] And Russia's leading literary tales have been recycled, revised, and illustrated in popular media ever since the seventeenth century, when the popular prints that we call *lubki* found their way to Russian marketplaces and private homes.

But between the late 1960s and today, Russophone professional and lay authors have been leaving the printed page and climbing onto other (later online) platforms, and pairing words with (moving) images with special

---

[1] Mark Steinberg, *The Russian Revolution, 1905–1921* (Oxford: Oxford University Press, 2017), p. 328.

fervour. In this chapter, I follow the forms that their activities have taken beyond the printed book in the past decades. I do so with particular attention to digital writing forms and digital platforms. And I do so in a survey that covers the mid-1990s to the early 2020s – I halt, in other words, at the moment when new restrictions to free speech took full flight in Russia and when the full-scale Russian war in Ukraine also upturned (online) literary life in many other respects.[2]

Just as, in the early twentieth century, Russian Formalists explored how linguistic and formal devices shaped literary language, so today experts in digital platform studies explore how different computational platforms define the creative writing that is produced on those platforms. They argue that to understand literary output that is produced in computational systems we should differentiate not between neatly monolithic 'online' and 'offline' spaces but between different online platforms and their distinct dynamics. With this suggestion in mind, in this chapter I do not draw such formal or generic distinctions as prose versus poetry or ballads versus free verse. Rather, I distinguish between literary production on websites as opposed to blogs or on Facebook as opposed to Instagram – that is, across various digital platforms. By way of prelude, I start this exploration with a peek into the emphatically multimedial literary field that unfolded in late Soviet Russia.

Little Coffins, Poor Looks: The Late Soviet and Perestroika Years

In the nonconformist literary scene that thrived in apartments and other non-institutional spaces in the late Soviet period, books were merely one of many material literary carriers (see Chapter 1.9). The Moscow Conceptualist poet and one-time librarian Lev Rubinshtein (1947–2024) read poems from library file cards; the poet and fiction author Genrikh Sapgir (1928–1999) wrote sonnets by hand on men's shirts; and the poet-artist Dmitrii Prigov (1940–2007) engaged in a whole range of visual, performative, and acoustic alternatives to traditional book publishing (see Chapter 3.8). Prigov glued hand-typed lyrical manifestoes onto walls and fences; he stapled and sealed them into unreadable closed-up paper packages, calling them 'little coffins' (*grobiki*); and he screamed verse recitations at performances, together with jazz musicians.

---

2 For a publication that inventories, in technologically innovative forms and formats, a broad range of writerly responses to this new phase in Russian literary history, I refer to the first volume (2022) of the open-access *Russian Oppositional Arts Review*, ed. Linor Goralik, http://roar-review.com, accessed 3 Feb. 2023.

Prigov and his nonconformist contemporaries started exploring substitutes for book publishing for pragmatic reasons: in the late Soviet era, their writings were simply not acceptable for formal publication. But with time, hand-typed, handwritten, spoken, or performed alternatives to published books also became fashionable in nonconformist literary circles as tokens of intellectual integrity (see Chapter 2.9).

The Perestroika years brought an end to the institutional repression that beckoned late Soviet nonconformists beyond book-print media. Material deficits did still hamper literary production – but even when writers had access to proper publishing facilities, some preserved an interest in the dowdy-looking multimedial alternatives to classic book publishing that had thrived in late Soviet underground circles. This interest resonates tangibly in the art book *Deep into Russia* (*V glub' Rossii*, 1994), for instance. The makers, artist Oleg Kulik (1961–) and writer Vladimir Sorokin (1955–), deconstruct Russian pastoral writing in short prose fragments and zoophilic photographs. The album's bad binding and overall gawky presentation – it includes black-and-white photographs of poor quality, and invitations for the book presentation were handwritten and included corny jokes – oozes chaotic friends-among-themselves amateurism. Its poor looks are deceptive, however: in making the album, Kulik and Sorokin consciously chose to imitate the look of hand-circulated documents of the late Soviet period, or, in their own words, 'to stick to the aesthetics of samizdat ... to the very end', together with a binder whom they praised for working 'on very shitty machines, with drunk hands'.[3]

The Rise of Russian Electronic Literature

Kulik and Sorokin's poorly glued photo album, Prigov's staged screams, and other cross-medial works by late Soviet writers all come to us, as literary historian Sabine Hänsgen puts it, in 'a form other than the Gutenberg-style book'.[4] These works prompt the following question: how does narrative, and literary writing in general, operate when expressed through letters *and* visuals, gestures, and sounds? As explained in this chapter's introduction, this question is not new. But in the late 1990s, it acquired added urgency across different world localities, Russia included. The rise of digital media

---

3 Oleg Kulik, 'Dialogi s Olegom Kulikom #7. Zhivotnoe. Brat'ia' [Dialogues with Oleg Kulik #7. Animal. Brothers], interview by Dmitrii Bavil'skii, *Topos* (23 Sept. 2002), www.topos.ru/article/530, accessed 3 Feb. 2023.
4 Sabine Hänsgen, 'Poetic performance: Script and voice', in Gerald Janecek (ed.), *Staging the Image: Dmitry Prigov as Artist and Writer* (Bloomington, IN: Slavica, 2018), p. 5.

then triggered an upsurge of hypertext storytelling, interactive narratives, and other literary practices that are hard to grasp in the language of text-oriented literary theorising. There seemed, in short, to be a need for new understandings of literary form.

Initially, what interested experts most in online writing was its perceived newness. Specialists unpacked 'What hypertexts can do that print narratives cannot',[5] for instance, and offered useful – if, at times, hardcore binary – definitions of 'cyberfiction', among other principally novel forms and genres. But with time, early attempts to unravel what-is-*new*-in-new-media-literature were increasingly criticised by scholars who said that digital media are never 'entirely new' but always 'the infolded effect of older media regimes'.[6] Their interventions fed a more nuanced understanding of electronic literature – as digital-culture specialist Scott Rettberg calls those 'new forms and genres of writings that exploit the capabilities of computers and networks' and that 'would not be possible without the contemporary digital context'.[7] Together with other experts, Rettberg has offered helpful historical contextualisations of the new literary forms that we see online, in analyses that combine insights from literary, visual, and media studies.

The same studies also help us to understand the specificity of Russian electronic writings, whose manifestations across different online platforms simultaneously build on and integrate local traditions and global communication technologies. In the remainder of this chapter, I look at Russian electronic writing through a threefold diachronic lens. First, I introduce early electronic writings from the mid- and late 1990s. Russian authors and artists then played a lead role in the production of 'net.art' – a term used for work by a loosely connected group of artists from different localities who, since the 1990s, have used GIFs, hyperlinks, code, and other digital technologies to create web-based writing and art. I then discuss influential examples of what literary scholars Varvara Smurova and Irina Kaspe call *okololiteraturnyi* (literally 'near-literary') writing – that is, the blend of literary and more practically oriented writing that we witness in weblogs by Russian writers in the 2000s and 2010s.[8] I conclude with a survey of 'social media literature' –

5 Jane Yellowlees Douglas, 'What hypertexts can do that print narratives cannot', *The Reader* 28.1 (1992).
6 Kiene Brillenburg Wurth, *Between Page and Screen: Remaking Literature through Cinema* (New York: Fordham University Press, 2012), p. 7.
7 Scott Rettberg, *Electronic Literature* (Oxford: Polity, 2018), cover text.
8 Irina Kaspe and Varvara Smurova, 'LiveJournal.com, russkaia versiia: Poplach' o nem, pokuda on zhivoi ...' [Livejournal.com, Russian version: Cry about it while it lasts ...], *Neprikosnovennyi zapas* [Untapped reserve] 4.24 (2011), Zhurnal'nyi zal [Hall of journals],

to use communication scholar Thomas Bronwen's catchphrase for literature created and read on such social media platforms as Facebook, its Russian equivalent Vkontakte, Instagram, and Twitter.[9]

Together, the writings considered here demonstrate that, in the digital age, neat demarcations of online versus offline literary production are unproductive. Media theorists have long warned against such sharp demarcations. 'Our lived reality', in the words of Nathan Jurgenson, 'is the result of the constant interpenetration of the online and offline'; just as elsewhere, in Russia 'the Web … comprises real people with real bodies, histories, and politics'[10] – and Russian writers today move back and forth between print and online media (see Chapter 2.11).

In the writings that I discuss in this chapter, this multimediality has an important corollary in genre and form. In the early 2000s, communication scientists explained that weblogs are hybrid formats that, rather than encompassing one fixed online genre, can fulfil a broad range of different narrative functions and genres simultaneously. Net.art stories, writer's blogs, and social-media literature similarly express and unite multiple conventional literary genres at the same time – but as we will see, they do operate within distinct platforms, each of which come with their own technologically rather than literarily driven conventions.

GIFs and Links: The 1990s

Experts typify early views on online writing, and hypertext writing in particular, in terms of utopian vistas and as new and emancipatory narrative modes. Both inside and outside Russia, the 1990s were a decade of enchantment with the audiovisual and networking opportunities that digital technologies offered. Among professional artists and writers, these opportunities spawned dreams about shared, collective knowledge and transnational solidarity.[11] With Soviet-era media manipulations fresh in their minds, however, Russophone media artists and writers also voiced scepticism. 'Pseudo-interactive' was what artist

---

https://magazines.gorky.media/nz/2002/4/livejournal-com-russkaya-versiya-poplac h-o-nem-poka-on-zhivoj.html, accessed 3 Feb. 2023.

9 Thomas Bronwen, *Literature and Social Media* (New York: Routledge, 2020), pp. 63, 89.

10 Nathan Jurgenson, 'The IRL fetish,' *New Inquiry* (28 June 2012), https://thenewinquiry .com/the-irl-fetish/, accessed 3 Feb. 2023.

11 On these dreams, see Vlad Strukov, 'Digital art: A sourcebook of ideas for conceptualizing new practices, networks and modes of self-expression,' in D. Gritsenko, M. Wijermars, and M. Kopotev (eds.), *The Palgrave Handbook of Digital Russia Studies* (Cham: Palgrave Macmillan, 2021), pp. 241–54.

Aleksei Shulgin (1963–) called online creative projects in 1997, in a widely cited essay titled 'Art, Power and Communication'. 'It seems', Shulgin explained, 'that manipulation is the only form of communication' that consumers of these projects know. 'They are happily following' the 'very few options' that their makers offer: 'press left or right button, jump or sit'.[12]

Shulgin is one of several writers, artists, and critics who, at the time, took a wary stance towards the collective and interactive ideals that early web adepts applauded so fiercely. This scepticism notwithstanding, however, we do witness an emphatically interactive (and technology-induced) shift in understanding of literary form at the time: as is clear in retrospect, many pioneers of Russian electronic literature offered readers the opportunity to make their way through textual or visual/audiovisual stories by choosing and clicking hyperlinks or GIFs. The Anglophone hypertext *My Boyfriend Came Back from the War* is perhaps the best-known Russian example of a scrollable story through which each reader clicks her own path. This narrative was created in 1996 by Olia Lialina, a Russian internet artist and curator who writes in English but is based in Moscow. Reader-viewers follow, in the words of cultural theorist Vlad Strukov, 'a Chekhov-style drama of misunderstanding' between a female protagonist and her boyfriend, who returns from a nameless war.[13] Their reunion is arduous: he proposes without success, she hints at having an affair. Rather than through linear narration, this plot unfolds on black web pages with white browser frames and clickable short HTML texts ('you don't trust me, i see'; 'you want me?'; 'TOMORROW') as well as in static and animated bitmap images (a window; a clock; a woman's face).[14] When readers click the texts and images, these split into smaller frames, and ultimately, the different narrative routes end in a collage of empty black frames. Amid the widespread euphoria about technology and communication, this ending, as specialists have demonstrated, paradoxically signals a contemporary 'breakdown in communication' and estrangement rather than dialogue.[15]

My Boyfriend Came Back from the War is one of many influential net. artworks, digital stories, and essays by Lialina; on her own site the artist helpfully (and wittily: the page opens with tiny GIFs of Lialina dancing, making music, hula hooping) clusters this oeuvre for viewers.[16] The

12 Alexei Shulgin, 'Art, power, and communication,' Nettime (7 Oct. 1996), www.net time.org/Lists-Archives/nettime-l-9610/msg00036.html, accessed 3 Feb. 2023.

13 Strukov, 'Digital art,' p. 246.

14 Olia Lialina, *My Boyfriend Came Back from the War* (1996), www.teleportacia.org/war/, accessed 3 Feb. 2023.

15 Strukov, 'Digital art,' p. 246.

16 Olia Lialina, website homepage, http://art.teleportacia.org/olia.html, accessed 3 Feb. 2023.

popularity of *My Boyfriend Came Back from the War* in particular is hard to overestimate. Other (web) artists repeatedly remixed the work, and in 2016, the Dutch hybrid-art space MU devoted an entire exhibition to it.[17] Part of this transnational appeal lies in the story's cinematic qualities; it has a strong filmic appeal and, at times, Lialina openly winks at early Soviet cinema. This filmic power is not coincidental: Lialina, who has worked as a film critic and curator, has called *My Boyfriend Came Back from the War* and her other early works attempts to put her 'filmic way of thinking in the net'.[18]

Not all pioneers of early Russian electronic literature chose to probe the multimedial affordances of the internet, however. Around the same time that *My Boyfriend Came Back from the War* appeared, other artists built experiments solely from words. A case in point is *Roman* (*Roman*, 1995), by the Estonian/ Russian writer and literary historian Roman Leibov (1963–). *Roman* is a hyper-novel and literary experiment that, just like Lialina's work, revolves around an open-ended love story. Like Lialina, Leibov invites readers to click in various ways through his story by following hyperlinks. But unlike *My Boyfriend Came Back from the War*, this love story consists of text-only, paragraph-length passages, in which the author's scholarly affinity with Russian prose classics resonates tangibly. Exemplary are the novel's first lines (which, according to an annotation below the text, Leibov had already written in 1987):

> A young man loved a girl and wrote her a love letter, but was afraid to send it via mail, so he went to her house at night to drop it in her mailbox. The mailbox was located on the ground floor, and one floor higher the same girl was standing and kissing another man. And the young man with the letter understood this only after dropping his letter in the mailbox. Then a problem emerged: what to do? He tried to pry out the letter without success.[19]

Rather than the world of cinema, what this tragicomic opening passage – formatted in black (and, for hyperlinks, blue) Times New Roman font on white web pages – evokes is the world of the print novel or short story.

If, however, Leibov revived literary tradition on some levels, he defied it on others. Rather than Cyrillic, he wrote his narrative in Roman letters: the title alludes to the author's first name; to relevant genre and plot conventions

---

17 For details, see 'Olia Lialina: 20 years of *My Boyfriend Came Back From The War*', MU, https://mu.nl/en/exhibitions/olia-lialina-20-years-of-my-boyfriend-came-back-from-t he-war, accessed 27 July 2021.
18 Olia Lialina, interview by Josephine Bosma, 5 Aug. 1997, www.nettime.org/Lists-Arc hives/nettime-l-9708/msg00009.html, accessed 3 Feb. 2023.
19 Roman Leibov, *Roman* (1995), https://kodu.ut.ee/~roman_l/hyperfiction/htroman .html, accessed 3 Feb. 2023 (my translation).

(the Russian word *roman* means both 'novel' and 'romance'); *and* to the Roman font in which Leibov wrote the text, as Cyrillic web encodings did not yet exist at the time. And rather than replicating the single-authorship model that dominates traditional literary production, Leibov used the possibilities of web-based writing to turn *Roman* into an exercise in collective authorship. He asked readers to share alternative versions of the story, which he then included in the work.[20] As a result, *Roman*'s reader today clicks her way through texts by 'M.', 'A. Kilobitov', and 'Majkl', among other co-authors. The project's lifespan was limited, however. As Henrike Schmidt formulates it, 'after a year of organic growth, the text became unreadable and Leibov stopped the experiment, which from the beginning was intended as a philological critique of hypertext theory' rather than a smooth head-to-tail read.[21]

Leibov's and Lialina's works are examples drawn from a long list of early electronic exercises in interactive fiction writing – a practice that has its roots in earlier literary experiments with interactivity and that today still flourishes in Russia and elsewhere. They are also mere samples from a much longer list of literary texts, libraries, contests, reviews, and journals that started to crowd the Russophone web from the mid-1990s onwards. The history of those initiatives is told both elsewhere in this volume (see Chapter 2.11) and in a swiftly growing body of scholarship that historically contextualises and theorises the 'RuLiNet', as the Russian literary internet is sometimes lovingly called. Here we leave that story for what it is, however, and we shift to a new phase in Russian electronic writing.

'Near-Literariness' and Blogs: The 2000s to mid-2010s

Lialina, Leibov, and other early RuLiNet pioneers wrote their work when online writing was a relatively idiosyncratic choice for a limited group of (often unapologetically geeky) writers. How different the situation looked by 2004, when the influential literary critic Dmitrii Kuzmin (1968–) became convinced that of the youngest literary generation, 'practically all authors'

---

20 For Leibov's instructions on how to read and co-author his hypernovel, see 'Kak pisat' ROMAN', https://kodu.ut.ee/~roman_l/hyperfiction/how_to_write.html#6, accessed 3 Feb. 2023.

21 Henrike Schmidt, 'From samizdat to New Sincerity: Digital literature on the Russian-language internet', in Gritsenko, Wijermars, and Kopotev (eds.), *Palgrave Handbook of Digital Russia Studies*, p. 264.

entered the professional scene 'via the Internet'.[22] Kuzmin referred to Russian authors in particular, but a similar move towards online literary production could be observed elsewhere.[23] Literary historian Marjorie Perloff predicted this situation as early as 1991, when she argued: 'There is today no landscape uncontaminated by sound bytes or computer blips, no mountain peak or lonely valley beyond the reach of the cellular phone and the micro-cassette player. Increasingly, then, the poet's arena is the electronic world.'[24] If Perloff was referring to a transnational literary transition, in Russia the shift to 'the electronic world' (or rather to multiple electronic platforms) in the 2000s also included a more local trend – Kaspe and Smurova's *okololiteraturnost'*. Kaspe and Smurova introduce this neologism, which roughly translates as 'near-literariness', in a blog survey where multiple professional authors' blogs pass in review. They argue that Russian blogger-writers tend to pitch their blogs as a literary 'safety zone'. Rather than being 'the centre of attention', in writer's blogs literary discourse is embedded in a mishmash of 'emphatic reactions, mundane advice, literary instructions, offers to help out, to bring some tangerines, to adjust the second paragraph, or to rearrange a few words'.[25]

To understand what 'near-literary' writing looks like, it is useful to zoom in on the blog writings of Dmitrii Vodennikov (1968–). Vodennikov is a poet who enjoys a solid status both among literary professionals and broader audiences. Writer and critic Miroslav Nemirov (1961–2016) has called the poet a literary 'pop star', whose live performances spawn a 'rock-concert'-like 'mass-induced ecstasy' among audiences.[26] Such idolisation is not unprecedented: literary stardom is formative to the reception of Fedor Dostoevskii (1821–1881), Ivan Turgenev (1818–1883), and other leading names in Russian literary history.[27] New, however, is the extent to which Vodennikov ponders and

22 Dmitrii Kuz'min, 'Istoriia i nekotorye etapy russkogo literaturnogo Interneta' [History and some stages of the Russian literary internet], *Radio Svoboda* (9 Aug. 2004), https://archive.svoboda.org/programs/sc/2004/sc.080904.asp, accessed 3 Feb. 2023.

23 Not coincidentally, a mere two years earlier the University of California, Los Angeles, had hosted the first international conference of the Electronic Literature Organization – still the leading organisation for the study of electronic literature. See Eric Dean Rasmussen, 'Electronic Literature Organization 2002: State of the arts symposium', ELMCIP, file:///Users/thomasvandalen/Downloads/mhttps://elmcip.net/node/900, accessed 3 Feb. 2023.

24 Marjorie Perloff, *Radical Artifice: Writing Poetry in the Age of Media* (Chicago: University of Chicago Press, 1991), p. xiii.

25 Kaspe and Smurova, 'LiveJournal.com'.

26 Miroslav Nemirov, 'Poet kak pop-zvezda' [The poet as pop star], *Vzgliad* (6 July 2005), https://vz.ru/culture/2005/7/6/1510.html, accessed 3 Feb. 2023.

27 Nemirov, 'Poet kak pop-zvezda'.

feeds his own fame – through multiple (online-)media performances and by publishing regularly in the news media, but also through poking fun in interviews (where the tall, slender, blond Vodennikov jokes, for instance, that 'my beauty is my curse'[28]) and through verses that simultaneously critique and amplify the poet's reputation as a beacon of a 'new' or 'post-postmodern' sincerity in Russian writing. 'Dozens of articles have been written about me', he wrote in 2001 in 'Men Can Also Fake an Orgasm' (*Muzhchiny tozhe mogut imitirovat' orgazm*) – a poem whose title squarely puts anxieties about sincerity on the agenda:

> 'Sense of an exalted cry'
> 'Stormy flower of an unconsolidated neomodernism'
> 'Word-subject in its polyphonic text'
> ... and even
> 'The new sincerity, the new sensitivity, the new word.'
> My God, on what have you wasted
> my invaluable life.[29]

In this passage Vodennikov sounds ambivalent about his public popularity – which, as said, he consistently fuels in practice. Indeed, from the early 2000s onwards, he stoked his public recognition yet more actively through his LiveJournal blog. Vodennikov used the diary-like set-up and the interactive and multimedial possibilities of this online platform for precisely the type of near-literary practices to which Smurova and Kaspe point. Between its launch in 2004 and the early 2010s, he utilised the blog to post a blend of new poetry, photographs, and reproductions of paintings; to pose questions ('what will you devour, er, sorry, eat on New Year's Eve?') and debate the answers with readers; and to promote upcoming shows and interviews.[30] In doing so, he further deepened the doubts about authorial identity that he had sown in verses and interviews. Vodennikov shared ambivalent views on authorial sincerity not only in concrete posts (by labelling one post, for example, '"the new sincerity" is dead, while I am still alive'[31]) but also in meta-comments about his blog. When I interviewed him in the late 2000s, he claimed to value

---

28 Dmitrii Vodennikov, 'Sredi novykh poetov ia samyi chitaemyi ...' [Among the new poets I am the most widely read ...], interview by Zakhar Prilepin, *APN Nizhnii Novgorod* (19 Nov. 2007), www.apn-nn.ru/pub_s/1484.html, accessed 3 Feb. 2023.

29 Dmitrii Vodennikov, *Muzhchiny tozhe mogut imitirovat' orgazm* [Men can also fake an orgasm] (Moscow: OGI, 2002).

30 For Vodennikov's Livejournal, see http://vodennikov.livejournal.com (2004–), accessed 3 Feb. 2023.

31 Dmitrii Vodennikov, 'novaia iskrennost' mertva, a ia eshche zhiv' [the new sincerity is dead but I am still alive], Livejournal (27 March 2007), https://vodennikov.livejournal.com/683336.html, accessed 3 Feb. 2023.

social seclusion too much to have instantly appreciated blogs *and* to see his blog as a means to embrace 'openheartedness'.[32]

The same near-literary writing that reigns in Vodennikov's blog dominates the weblogs of such popular Russian writers-with-blogs as Linor Goralik (1975–), Tatiana Tolstaia (1951–), and Svetlana Martynchik (1965–; known under her pen name Maks Frai).[33] Not coincidentally, the latter has praised her blog for permitting her to publish 'all kinds of obligatory crudshit that no one needs'.[34] But Vodennikov's posts also emblematise a second broader trend among professional Russian writer-bloggers between the 2000s and mid-2010s: that of 'subver[ting] ... the established view of authors of Russian literature and their sacrosanct status', as Gernot Howanitz puts it.[35] Rather than the distanced relationship between Writer (with intentional capital W) and reader that traditionally ruled Russian literary history, in Vodennikov's and other LiveJournal blogs we see a situation where, in Howanitz's words, '[r]eaders on the one side and authors on the other all sit at the computer and look at the same website using the same programmes and tools'; and where readers can 'post feedback for the authors in the comments section, which generally appears below the text', which 'evens out the status difference even further'.[36] This increasingly close relationship between online authors and their readers should not be confused with wholly unstratified, unlimited reciprocity: blogger-writers exert undeniable control over the exchange and many relinquish the comment function altogether. But as Vodennikov's posts demonstrate, blogging technologies do encourage previously unseen forms of medium-specific self-representation and reader–writer interconnection.

Social Media Literature: The 2010s to Today

If the 1990s was the era of cyber-utopianism, the 2010s and early 2020s are the age of web critique. Experts now frame social media platforms as hotbeds

---

32 Personal interview with the author, 14 May 2009.

33 For Goralik's most active blog, currently not in use, see http://snorapp.livejournal .com (2002–18); for Tolstaia's, see http://tanyant.livejournal.com (2007–18); and for Frai's, https://ru-maks-frei.livejournal.com/ (2009–12), all accessed 3 Feb. 2023.

34 Maks Frai, 'Maksimal'no svobodnyi russkii inorodnyi skazochnik' [A maximally free Russian foreign storyteller], *Zhivoi zhurnal slovami pisatelei* [Livejournal in writers' words] (2003), www.russ.ru/krug/20030627_mf.html (archival/dead link), accessed 3 Feb. 2023.

35 Gernot Howanitz, 'The life and death of the Russian blog,' *ZOiS Spotlight* 11 (2019), https://en.zois-berlin.de/publications/zois-spotlight/archiv-2019/the-life-and-deat h-of-the-russian-blog, accessed 3 Feb. 2023.

36 Howanitz, 'Life and death'.

of hyper-individualism and of commercial or downright neocolonial exploitation.

'Social media literature' – Bronwen's term for literature created and read on social media platforms – takes shape against the background of these concerns, and in Russia, as elsewhere, authors are well aware of the catch-22 that social media offers. As creative professionals, they inevitably capitalise on their private lives through these media. This is not to say that authors lose all control: the poet Vera Polozkova (1986–) actively cultivates a sense of her own celebrity by tagging readers, inviting reader responses, and otherwise encouraging collaborative co-creation with her audience (see Chapter 2.10).

Collaborative creativity is also formative to the social-media presence of arguably today's most acclaimed Russophone poet: Galina Rymbu. Via Facebook, Vkontakte, and Instagram, Rymbu shares a near-literary, multimedial mixture of brazenly theoretical, movingly lyrical, unabashedly self-promotional, and deeply personal written and visual/audiovisual posts.[37] Personal photos predominate on her Instagram account; on her Facebook and Vkontakte accounts, by contrast, the personal blends more systematically with the professional, commercial, and intellectual. But in each profile, the self-proclaimed queer feminist Rymbu is enough of an activist to keep the reins in her own hands.

On 20 July 2021, her birthday, Rymbu posted the poem 'I am looking for a Marcuse / book / urgently ...' (*ishchu Markuze / knigi / srochno*) on Facebook. '[W]e need different relations to theory', its lyrical 'I' claims:

> a different closeness
> the type of theory that is really a fairy tale
> that you can read to your son while travelling
> ... words that can care and befriend
> texts that marvel me
> ... where meaning and meaningless are one
> as brother and sister
> in one room[38]

The poem epitomises both Rymbu's poetics and her social-media presence: the author blends hardboiled theory and politics (calling philosopher Herbert Marcuse an ecofeminist, for instance) with family tropes ('your son', 'brother and sister'); favours fluid co-existences (of theories and tales, of meaning and

---

37 For her profiles on each, see: www.facebook.com/GalinaRymbu/, https://vk.com/id21009049, www.instagram.com/galinarymbu/, all accessed 3 Feb. 2023.

38 Galina Rymbu, 'ishchu Markuze ...' [I am looking for a Marcuse ...], Facebook (20 July 2021), www.facebook.com/GalinaRymbu, accessed 3 Feb. 2023.

meaninglessness, of brother and sister) over neat dichotomies; and couples lyric expression with practical inquiry and interaction with readers (the request for a Marcuse copy seems genuine, and in the comments, readers not only congratulate Rymbu on her birthday but also offer copies of the desired book).

If the poem exemplifies Rymbu's online writing, it also emblematises the broader 'constructive principle' that Mark Lipovetsky calls *feisbuchnost'* (Facebookness). 'A poem, shared on an author's page on Facebook', Lipovetsky argues, 'functions as a gesture, just like any other expression in that space. ... Not only does a poem published on Facebook doubtlessly find an audience, but, adjoining unpredictable contexts in each reader's friend-feed, it obtains a new (and in part political) sound, too.'[39] Reading Rymbu's poetry in print collections is indeed a more predictable practice than that of viewing her digitally shared verses, announcements, or family photos: online, readers can see the author's posts amid entries by those other users to whom they happen to link.

These features of near-literariness and *feisbuchnost'* make it hard to frame Rymbu's social media literature as literature per se. In this respect her online activities are not exclusive. Poet, non-fiction author, and journalist Mariia Stepanova (1972–) uses Facebook to post new verses and promotional links (as well as intimate family photos, but these Stepanova shares not as public entries but with her (roughly 1,700) Facebook friends only).[40] The same platform hosts similarly diverse content by Vodennikov, who, in 2009, exchanged an active LiveJournal presence for an equally active Facebook profile.[41] An even more motley blend of (video-)poetry, performances, announcements, diary-like entries, and quick jokes resonates in the vast social-media output of poet Roman Osminkin (1979–). By the summer of 2021, Osminkin hosted frequently updated Instagram, Facebook, and Twitter accounts as well as his own YouTube channel.[42] The online presence of these

39 Mark Lipovetsky, 'Mezhdu Prigovym i LEFom: Performativnaia poetika Romana Osminkina' [Between Prigov and LEF: The performative poetics of Roman Osminkin], *Novoe literaturnoe obozrenie* [New literary review] 3.145 (2017), www.nlo books.ru/magazines/novoe_literaturnoe_obozrenie/145_nlo_3_2017/article/12496/, accessed 3 Feb. 2023.

40 Maria Stepanova [Facebook profile] www.facebook.com/maria.stepanova.372, accessed 3 Feb. 2023.

41 Dmitry Vodennikov [Facebook profile] www.facebook.com/DmitryVodennikov. In 2009, Vodennikov also started a (much less active and since 2016 silent) Twitter account, https://twitter.com/vodennikov, accessed 27 July 2021.

42 See Roman Osminkin's social-media profiles: www.instagram.com/osminkinromanser geevitch/, www.facebook.com/profile.php?id=100000332535250, https://twitter.com/osyayoyo, https://www.youtube.com/user/osminkin, all accessed 3 Feb. 2023.

and other writers demonstrates how social-media platforms complicate 'divisions ... between material that is conceived of as existing outside or inside of a stable core literary artefact'. Rather than hardcore literary venues, these platforms are spaces 'where the literary can be celebrated, shared, reviewed, curated, marketed and sold' – although in the case of anti-capitalist poets like Rymbu or Osminkin, 'selling' is best understood in broad terms, as (non-commercial) public outreach.[43]

Conclusion

This chapter mapped activities by professional writers. Online, these activities deftly intersect with a spectrum of popular literary practices that, today, ranges from fanfiction writing (online narratives in which fans reuse and mix well-known fictive settings or characters) to literary trolling (the use of literary devices in inflammatory, digressive social-media discourse) to pleas for the joy of reading on the video-sharing app TikTok.[44]

Popular literary practices demonstrate how (online) multimedial literary practices defy classic takes on literary writing. 'Near-literariness', 'Facebookness', and 'social-media literature' are helpful conceptual tools to unpack the multimedial, platform-based, and – in some cases – emphatically collective and interactive life beyond the page that Russian writers and their works both live online. The same tools help us to grasp the extent to which online writing clashes with genre conventions. Online writings, as we saw, encompass various genres; they are hybrid, and they refute clear formal and genre-constricted boundaries. Even if we shun the insistence on radical newness that early critics of online writings embraced, it is hard to deny that electronic literature is, by default, a literature of platforms after genres.

Further Reading

Bronwen, Thomas, *Literature and Social Media* (New York: Routledge, 2020).
Hänsgen, Sabine, 'Poetic performance: Script and voice', in Gerald Janecek (ed.), *Staging the Image: Dmitry Prigov as Artist and Writer* (Bloomington, IN: Slavica, 2018), pp. 5–22.
Howanitz, Gernot, 'The life and death of the Russian blog', *ZOiS Spotlight* 11 (2019), https:// en.zois-berlin.de/publications/zois-spotlight/archiv-2019/the-life-and-death-of-the-rus sian-blog.

43 Bronwen, *Social Media Literature*, p. 6.
44 On fanfiction and trolling, see Natalia Samutina (ed.), 'Populiarnye literaturnye prak-tiki v Rossii' [Popular literary practices in Russia], special issue, *Russian Literature* 118 (2020).

Jurgenson, Nathan, 'The IRL fetish', *New Inquiry* (28 June 2012), https://thenewinquiry.com/the-irl-fetish/.

Perloff, Marjorie, *Radical Artifice: Writing Poetry in the Age of Media* (Chicago: University of Chicago Press, 1991).

Rettberg, Scott, *Electronic Literature* (Oxford: Polity, 2018).

Schmidt, Henrike, 'From samizdat to New Sincerity: Digital literature on the Russian-language internet', in Daria Gritsenko, Mariëlle Wijermars, and Mikhail Kopotev (eds.), *The Palgrave Handbook of Digital Russia Studies* (Cham: Palgrave Macmillan, 2021), pp. 255–75.

Shulgin, Alexei, 'Art, power, and communication', *Nettime* (7 Oct. 1996), www.nettime.org/Lists-Archives/nettime-l-9610/msg00036.html.

Strukov, Vlad, 'Digital art: A sourcebook of ideas for conceptualizing new practices, networks and modes of self-expression', in Gritsenko, Wijermars, and Kopotov (eds.), *Palgrave Handbook of Digital Russia Studies*, pp. 241–54.

Boxes 5
Critical Frames

Box 5.1   Critical Frames

Box 5.1   Vissarion Belinskii

Vissarion Belinskii (1811–1848) is the most famous and influential literary critic in the history of Russian literature. Despite regular attempts to demonstrate the destructive effect of his ideas, Belinskii's reputation has proved resilient. Yet the reasons why he remains such an influential figure can be hard to grasp.

Belinskii's assessments do not always coincide with subsequent views on the literary canon, yet his intuitions could be impressive. For instance, he declared the primacy of Nikolai Gogol in the Russian canon long before Gogol had produced *Inspector General* (*Revizor*, 1836), *Dead Souls* (*Mertvye dushi*, 1842), or 'The Overcoat' (*Shinel'*, 1842). Belinskii also admired the works of the young Mikhail Lermontov, who at the time had published very little. His review of *Inspector General* determined the main trend in the history of its interpretation, seeing it through a social lens. By contrast, his interpretation of Aleksandr Pushkin's *Eugene Onegin* (*Evgenii Onegin*, 1825–32) as a truthful representation of social life has had less traction, as has his interpretation of the behaviour of the novel's heroine, Tatiana Larina, which in his view reflects a debilitating fear of public opinion, an atrophy of the spirit paralysed by the morals of high society. Such judgements are rarely shared by subsequent readers.

In Soviet scholarship it was claimed that Belinskii created an independent aesthetic system. The claim is weak. Belinskii discussed aesthetic issues with great passion, but his views on art were an eclectic and unstable mix of contradictory western European theories. In his early years as a literary critic, Belinskii espoused the philosophical principles of Friedrich Schelling. Towards the end of the 1830s, he attempted to combine Schellingian philosophy and Hegelian aesthetics. This was the brief period known as his 'reconciliation with reality', when he also adopted pro-governmental political views. In the next phase of his ideological development, Belinskii tried again to combine barely compatible components by supplementing German aesthetics with the ideas of French Utopian Socialists.

Belinskii's distinctive significance lies instead in the fact that he showed to Russian readers how a critic could become a public figure and how the analysis and interpretation of a literary work could become a political act. Throughout his career Belinskii was an effective exponent of the new media – the 'thick journal' (see Chapter 2.4). As a professional man of letters, Belinskii was constantly in print, systematically promoting his key ideas. The influence of Belinskii's criticism on politics was acknowledged not only by other writers

but also by the authorities, who viewed such ideas as dangerous. In 1849 Fedor Dostoevskii and other members of the Petrashevskii circle were almost executed for reading aloud Belinskii's open letter to Gogol, written just before the critic's death in the previous year.

Although Belinskii was of gentry origin, his lifestyle and beliefs were closer to those of the *raznochintsy* (people whose social and/or professional standing set them outside Russia's rigidly defined class system) who would become more active figures in Russian literature during the 1860s. Ivan Turgenev dedicated his novel *Fathers and Children* (*Ottsy i deti*, 1862) to the memory of Belinskii. There, the main hero is also a nobleman who does not want to act like one. For Belinskii literature was, on the one hand, his sole source of income; his remarkable productivity is partly attributable to the need to sustain himself and his family. On the other hand, literature was for him – as it was to become for the subsequent Russian intelligentsia – the main source of ideas about society, the authorities, and reality more broadly.

Belinskii's aesthetic ideas were closely linked to his notion of the role of literature in society. His first major article, 'Literary Reveries' (*Literaturnye mechtaniia*, 1834), featured the paradoxical assertion: 'We have no literature'. The article was grounded in the Romantic conviction that writers must express the spirit of their times and of their nation, and it reflects Belinskii's frustration that in Russia neither writers nor readers were ready for such a role. By contrast, towards the end of his career Belinskii tended to appeal not to complex philosophical doctrines but to the taste of readers who, in his view, were primarily interested not in works of artistic genius but in truthful narratives about the lives of the population of the capital – above all lowly bureaucrats, poor workers, and other victims of the political order.

In Belinskii's critical essays across different periods, one can find contradictory statements about political, social, and literary issues. His reputation as a progressive thinker needs to be seen in the context of Russian imperialism (he detested the Ukrainian nationalism of Taras Shevchenko, for example). However, more significant for Russian literature than Belinskii's ideas was the figure of the critic himself: the critic trying to solve such issues with the help of literature and trying to help the public to understand them.

Kirill Zubkov
Translated by Katerina Pavlidi

Box 5.2   Critical Frames

Box 5.2   Viktor Shklovskii

Viktor Shklovskii (1893–1984) was a bold literary theorist and highly original writer whose early article-manifestos helped establish Russian Formalism. Provocateur and *enfant terrible*, Shklovskii is an unlikely poster child for the school of literary criticism whose representatives include Iurii Tynianov, Boris Eikhenbaum, Boris Tomashevskii, and Roman Jakobson. Nevertheless, by virtue of his radicalism, patterns of self-contradiction, and creative exuberance, he epitomises what it was to be an artist-intellectual of the generation that came of age during the years of revolution.

'Art as Device' (*Iskusstvo kak priem*, 1917), one of Shklovskii's first articles, remains his most influential – published in English and French translation in 1965, it had an impact on French Structuralism, for instance. Its central idea is that art de-automatises (increases, lengthens, deepens) our perception of the world around us, so that we see and feel things in strange, new ways. The signature artistic device through which this transformation comes about is *ostranenie* (Shklovskii's neologism, based on a Russian root of *strann-* for 'strange', with one 'n' lopped off), variously translated as enstrangement, estrangement, or defamiliarisation. *Ostranenie* becomes art's purpose ('what we call art exists in order to give back the sensation of life, in order to make us feel things, in order to make the stone stony', in Alexandra Berlina's 2017 translation) but also extends beyond the world of literature, with implications for our lives as moral beings. The strongest literary examples from 'Art as Device' hail from the writings of Lev Tolstoi, who employs this device to critique social conventions such as property ownership. At the same time, for Shklovskii, the capacity of devices to draw attention to themselves, to lay themselves bare, means that the artfulness of art trumps all content: 'Art is the means to live through the making of a thing; what has been made does not matter in art' (Berlina's translation). For Shklovskii in his early period, literary evolution is driven by the need for new forms and devices when the old ones have lost their capacity and defamiliarising power.

Among Shklovskii's many contributions to narratology is the distinction between *fabula* and *siuzhet*: *fabula* refers to the sequence of events of a story as they would happen chronologically in time, whereas *siuzhet* refers to the order in which a story is told. He also produced studies of particular artists and works, including Laurence Sterne's *Tristam Shandy* and Cervantes's *Don Quixote*; a biography of Tolstoi; and writings on contemporaries such as Vladimir Maiakovskii, Iurii Olesha, Isaak Babel, and the filmmaker Sergei Eisenstein.

Shklovskii is the author of wonderful autobiographical fictions, for which his own life provided excellent material. He had served in the First World War for the Provisional Government, as a right-wing Socialist Revolutionary, being twice wounded and awarded a medal for exceptional bravery. He took part in an anti-Bolshevik coup, because of which he fled the country via the Gulf of Finland to avoid arrest. While in temporary exile in Berlin, Shklovskii wrote *Zoo, or Letters Not about Love, or the New Heloise* (*Zoo, ili pis'ma ne o liubvi, ili tret'ia Eloiza*, 1923) and *A Sentimental Journey* (*Sentimental'noe puteshestvie*, 1923). When he returned to Russia, he settled in Moscow (rather than his home city of St Petersburg/Petrograd/Leningrad), where he joined the literary group the Left Front of the Arts (*Levyi front isskustv*, or LEF, 1923–5), together with Russian Futurists and Formalists, and then the New Left Front of Arts (*Novyi LEF*, 1927–9), which he left in 1928. LEF artists and theorists sought to maintain post-revolutionary relevance through the creation of a 'literature of fact', which would renew art by reconnecting to life and turning towards journalism and documentary. In this period Shklovskii wrote a third unconventional autobiography: *Third Factory* (*Tret'ia fabrika*, 1926). All of Shklovskii's creative works have Formalist theory and method woven into their compositional fabric, and all are playfully ironic while also being emotionally powerful (one could describe Shklovskii's scholarship this way, too). Shklovskii's student Lidiia Ginzburg famously said of *Zoo*: 'Do you think that Shklovskii actually used the formal method to write *Zoo*, the tenderest novel of our time?'

By 1930, the Formalists and their Institute for the History of Arts were shut down; literary scholars needed to employ Marxist-Leninist theory or go into other professions. Shklovskii issued a strange statement, 'Monument to Scientific Error' (*Pamiatnik nauchnoi oshibke*, 1930), recanting his views in an act Richard Sheldon aptly called 'ostensible surrender' or 'outward obedience undermined by defiance'. In the remaining decades of his long life, Shklovskii continued to write film scripts, criticism, theory, and memoir.

Emily Van Buskirk

Box 5.3 Critical Frames

Box 5.3 Lev Trotskii

Lev, or Leon, Trotskii (1879–1940) was a leading figure in the October Revolution, a commander of the Red Army during the civil war, and a key player in the government in the first half of the 1920s. He also played a decisive role in shaping Soviet ideology and culture. Often a dissenting voice in the party, Trotskii was seen as a threat by Joseph Stalin and his allies after Vladimir Lenin's death. He was removed from the politburo in 1925, then expelled from the Soviet Union in 1929. He eventually settled in Mexico, where he continued his activism throughout the 1930s, attracting international attention for his criticism of Stalin's Soviet Union and his articulation of an alternative model of communism. He was assassinated by a Soviet agent in 1940.

Trotskii was a major voice in the fierce debates about the role of literature in building socialism. His defining work was *Literature and Revolution* (*Literatura i revoliutsiia*, 1923), a collection of essays laying out his vision for socialist culture and assessing Soviet literature in its present form. While dismissive of openly counter-revolutionary literature, including religious or mystical writing, Trotskii took an open-minded approach towards the various literary groups that had come out in favour of the revolution. He refused to endorse any one single camp, finding something to praise – and much to criticise – in all of them. He admitted the talent of avant-garde writers such as Vladimir Maiakovskii and the Futurists but poured cold water on their claims of novelty and argued that they had not overcome their individualism. He recognised the ingenuity of Formalists such as Viktor Shklovskii but stated his fundamental disagreement with their approach to literature, which he saw as privileging aesthetic considerations without an understanding of the social and historical circumstances that had produced them.

Yet Trotskii was equally critical of the 'proletarian' movement that championed working-class writers and content: he saw a germ of talent in their work but believed that they lacked maturity and artistic technique. He rejected the term 'proletarian art', arguing that the proletariat could produce genuine art only once the class structures that made them a proletariat had been truly vanquished. Trotskii also wrote at length about the 'fellow travellers' (*poputchiki*): writers such as Sergei Esenin and Boris Pilniak, who in his view nominally supported the revolution and the communist ideal but lacked a true understanding of Marxism. While Trotskii nevertheless saw some value in their writing for the dialectical development of literature, the term was taken up eagerly by Soviet writers and brandished as a weapon against their ideological opponents.

Trotskii was an incisive – and often acerbic – critic of current trends in Soviet writing but sketched the contours of his own vision of socialist art in rather vague terms, insisting that the current priority must be a drive for mass literacy. He avoided providing a recipe for success in terms of genres, forms, or styles and did not privilege any of his contemporaries by naming them forerunners to socialist art. However, he did write at length about the merging of art and life: socialist art would be a kind of 'life-building' (*zhiznes-troitel'stvo*) – the division between art and industry would fall away and 'the forms of everyday life will acquire a dynamic theatricality'. Such ideas were not unique to Trotskii; attempts to achieve this fusion of art and life can be seen in many of the experiments of the 1920s. Trotskii argued against placing art directly under party control, but his suggestion that the party should play a supportive rather than a commanding role in art left room for ambiguity.

By the time of Trotskii's expulsion from the Soviet Union, the centralisation of art and literature was proceeding apace, and the directives of Socialist Realism in the 1930s put the party firmly in control. Trotskii, in exile, offered a powerful critique of Stalinism as a degeneration of the revolution. Socialist Realist art was, in his view, the product of a bureaucratic machine. In a *Partisan Review* essay 'Art and Politics' (1938), Trotskii lambasted the official art of the Soviet Union as based on 'lies and deceit', aimed only at 'exalt[ing] the "leader"' and 'fabricat[ing] an heroic myth'. Trotskii, who had established an international following, supported an alternative vision of revolutionary art, working closely with the Mexican artists Frida Kahlo and Diego Rivera as well as the French writer André Breton. In 1938, he and Breton co-wrote a 'Manifesto for a Revolutionary Art', published under the names of Breton and Rivera. Trotskii's death in 1940 put an end to these activities, but he has continued to inspire revolutionaries and artists for over a century.

Connor Doak

Box 5.4   Critical Frames

Box 5.4   Mikhail Bakhtin

Mikhail Bakhtin (1895–1975) has been read as fundamentally (indeed canonically) Marxist; as a correction to Formalism's detachment of text from social and historical context. Yet he has also been read as critical of Marxism, as an underground Christian mystic, and as proto-Poststructuralist. His understanding of language and society as fundamentally dialogic, as emerging from dialogue, has influenced countless thinkers on the left and the right of the political spectrum. He has been neglected, repressed, recovered, appropriated, translated and mistranslated, made ubiquitous, made meaningless, discovered, and neglected again. Authorship and intent alike have been disputed too many times to count, as if parody or proof of the (meta) narrative of his theoretical project.

Bakhtin emerged from a geographically, linguistically, and culturally diverse Russian Empire and then Soviet Union. Born in Orel in 1895, his wanderings and political and academic exiles took him from Vilnius (Lithuania) and Odesa (Ukraine) to the University of St Petersburg, then to Vitebsk (Belarus), Kazakhstan, and the Mordovian Pedagogical Institute in Saransk before he died in Moscow in 1975. He became an international brand, however, after his posthumous rediscovery – driven in no small part by the Postmodernist era's enthusiasm for a Soviet fellow traveller who espoused a philosophy of emergent pluralism as early as the 1920s. To Julia Kristeva and other critical theory stars of the 1970s and 1980s, Bakhtin was the Soviet Marxist philosopher of language who prefigured Poststructuralism. To younger generations of Marxists in the twenty-first century, Bakhtin remains a cornerstone of a leftist internationale to be guarded vigilantly from appropriations by the centre or right. For both, his central insight is that emancipatory language finds many ways of subverting the singular discourse of power.

Bakhtin's early seminal work, *Problems of Dostoevskii's Poetics* (*Problemy poetiki Dostoevskogo*, 1929; revised and extended 1963) arrives at an understanding of Fedor Dostoevskii's novels as 'dialogic' and therefore 'unfinaliseable': a rebuttal of and rebuke to western thought and cultural tendencies towards monologism. If the monologic world view imposes a voice of authority that reduces persons to things, dialogic discourse is social, intertextual, and emergent. With Lev Tolstoi in the role of monologic foil, Bakhtin reads Dostoevskii as the discoverer of the 'polyphonic' novel, with its plurality of unmerged voices and views. Dostoevskii's characters are not only many but open: evolving in response to one another, ever on the threshold of change, liminal.

The Dialogic Imagination is the English-language title given to a selection of essays that were written from 1934 to 1941 and first published in Russian in 1975 as *Problems of Literature and Aesthetics* (*Problemy literatury i estetiki*). The essays develop the concepts of 'dialogism' as a kind of discourse that resists monologisation and of 'heteroglossia' as the co-existence of many languages within any single one. They also propose a theory of genre. According to Bakhtin, the novel is unique in its ability to capture the diversity that other literary forms, such as the epic, all too often write out of the world. The concept of 'chronotope', or the time–space organisation of a literary text, further helps distinguish the novel form.

Bakhtin's dissertation *Rabelais and His World* (*Tvorchestvo Fransua Rable i narodnaia kul'tura srednevekov'ia i Renessansa*), written during the Second World War and rejected for the doctorate, was finally published in 1965. Turning to Rabelais's *Gargantua and Pantagruel* (c. 1532–64), Bakhtin imagines life and language in the Renaissance as a balance between language that is permitted and language that is suppressed, between official and folk practices. What he terms the 'carnivalesque' is that subversive and emancipatory mode of expression that bursts through the permitted language in the form of humour and chaos, that celebrates the profane and the (otherwise) impermissible.

The extant text of *Toward a Philosophy of the Act* (*K filosofii postupka*, comp. 1919–21, pub. 1986) consists of an introduction and first chapter dedicated to an exploration of the world experienced through 'performed acts', rather than imagined through abstract concepts in the Kantian tradition. *Speech Genres and Other Late Essays* (1986) is an English-language collection of essays first published together as *The Aesthetics of Verbal Creativity* (*Estetika slovesnogo tvorchestva*, 1979). It deals with, among other topics, the difference between living language and Saussurean linguistics; genres as existing well beyond literary texts; and an exploration of the open flow of dialogue, addressed to both an immediate interlocutor and an ever-future, ever-changing 'super-addressee' of posterity.

Marijeta Bozovic

Box 5.5   Critical Frames

Box 5.5   Iurii Lotman

The semiotician Iurii Lotman (1922–1993) was a pillar of the Moscow-Tartu school of cultural history, which was the USSR's main site for the reception of European Structuralism, and a unique phenomenon in Soviet humanities. Throughout his career, Lotman endeavoured to reconceptualise the humanities as a scientific discipline, occasionally bringing them into dialogue with the life sciences and cybernetics, and to practise cultural analysis across the disciplinary divides. He based his pioneering work on fresh interpretations of both the Russian classics and lesser-known authors, keeping the focus on the period stretching from the 1780s to the 1830s. Together, his research and teaching made the single most significant individual contribution to the field of Russian literary studies since the Formalists.

Despite having moved from Leningrad to Tartu in Estonia (because his Jewish origins meant that only a provincial university would employ him), Lotman became deeply integrated within Soviet academic and cultural institutions. Lotman chaired the Russian Studies department at the University of Tartu from 1960 and regularly prepared annotated editions of works by the authors he studied. He published works such as *Analysis of the Poetic Text: The Structure of Poetry (Analiz poeticheskogo teksta: Struktura stikha,* 1972) while also situating poetry within a broader semiotic process, as in his book *The Structure of the Artistic Text (Struktura khudozhestvennogo teksta,* 1970). In 1956 he founded the academic journal *Sign Systems Studies,* which was unequivocally transdisciplinary and widely read outside the socialist bloc. Beyond the specialist realm, Lotman popularised the study of literature and history through televised lectures on Russian aristocratic culture. It is thanks to his many disciples, friends, and interlocutors that his own work is now more widely edited, commented upon, and translated than that of some of the authors whom he studied, such as Nikolai Karamzin and Aleksandr Radishchev.

At the core of Lotman's approach to culture is a rather eclectic method combining textual analysis and historical reconstruction, on the one hand, and typologies and models borrowed from the natural sciences, structural anthropology, and linguistics, on the other. Like other scholars of his time, he worked chiefly within the bounds of the literary canon, but for him, as for the Formalists, well-known authors or canonised texts were more than just venerated monuments – they exemplified and crystallised a particular constellation of social and cultural codes or linguistic and poetic structures. Lotman regarded these codes and structures as socially and

historically situated, and he argued that they could be studied through both the writings and the personal 'gestures' of authors and historical figures who inscribed their lives into the networks of meanings available at a given time. Lotman's analysis of the Decembrist nobles who rose up against the tsar in 1825 thus expands the sphere of their cultural production beyond their political programmes and literary texts: they created, according to Lotman, a particular type of behaviour, or public persona, beginning with the way they talked. For Lotman, the theatricality that characterised this behaviour was an important feature of Russian noble culture in the imperial period. For a student of this culture, the task is thus to document public behaviour and interpret it within the framework of the cultural scripts that were available to people at the time. Together, these elements form an overall cultural text.

In keeping with his semiotic approach, Lotman applied the term 'text' to a variety of artistic media and actively uncovered layers of their meaning across literature, theatre, painting, cinema, and everyday life. While the literary text was arguably his main analytical unit, he believed that the researcher should not consider literature or, more generally, art as a closed system. Lotman's analyses therefore include historical documents such as laws or recorded interrogations and personal narratives of historical actors such as their private letters or memoirs. His commentaries (*Kommentarii*, 1980) to Aleksandr Pushkin's *Eugene Onegin* (*Evgenii Onegin*, 1825–32) provide perhaps the most famous example of this approach. Here, a masterpiece of nineteenth-century literature, well established within the Soviet canon, is clarified by the annotations of an erudite scholar who is able to navigate between the author's life (Lotman himself wrote a biography of Pushkin); references to classical and modern European literature that are often cited in their original languages; and the social codes, ideas, and material culture of the 1820s.

Shortly after Lotman's death, Mikhail Gasparov, another brilliant philologist, provocatively linked the former's method to Marxism (albeit a Marxism free of Marxist ideology). Others have drawn parallels between Lotman's writings and contemporaneous approaches to texts and culture such as Structuralism, New Historicism, or Clifford Geertz's interpretation of culture. The most striking feature of Lotman's writing is perhaps as follows: he was a historian and a theorist who conceived culture anew in an intellectual environment that was hostile towards fresh conceptualisations.

Alexei Evstratov

Boxes 6
Literature beyond Literature

Box 6.1 The Igor Myth

The *Tale of Igor's Campaign* (*Slovo o polku Igoreve*) is a literary text that has acquired emblematic significance far beyond literature, in discourses of cultural and national identity in both Russia and Ukraine. It is short, fewer than ten pages of modern printed text, yet its status is incalculable. Its subject is not, on the surface, a hugely consequential event: a failed foray against the steppe nomads in 1185 led by a minor prince of the Rus ruling family, Igor Sviatoslavich of Novgorod-Seversk. Yet in the lyrical imagination, the episode acquires almost cosmic resonance. In the densely metaphorical narrative, nature itself participates and responds. Rus princes and nomad chieftains are falcons and wild oxen, skies darken, lances sing, rivers are invoked as if people, and the fingers of a bard are falcons descending upon swans. The local events of Igor's campaign are woven into a fabric of allusions stretching into the remote dynastic and mythical past and across the territories of his extended kin. When the princely clan is disunited, nature itself is fractured. Igor Sviatoslavich is the contingent (anti-)hero, but the deeper subject is the Land of Rus itself.

A sixteenth-century manuscript of the Igor tale was discovered in the early 1790s in a monastery in Iaroslavl. A copy was made for Catherine II (r. 1762–96). In 1800 the text was published in print. Suddenly, as if out of nowhere, the empress's Slav subjects discovered that their Middle Ages, too, had produced a literary work of imaginative genius that could stand comparison with western European classics such as the *Chanson de Roland* or the *Niebelungenlied*. Then, in 1812, the manuscript perished in the fire of Moscow during Napoleon's invasion.

The circumstances of its discovery and subsequent disappearance in an age of pseudo-medieval forgeries across Europe have prompted a tradition of scepticism as to whether the Igor tale ever existed at all as a medieval text. Doubts about its authenticity have been articulated sporadically from the early nineteenth century to the twenty-first. Because of the cultural weight that the work has come to bear, such doubts have sometimes been treated as unpatriotic, irrespective of the merits of the argument. In fact, thanks in particular to detailed analyses of its underlying linguistic structure, the overwhelming scholarly consensus is that, although the received text may be corrupt in many ways, it derives from an authentic work of the late twelfth century.

Scepticism aside, the cultural resonances of the Igor tale are astonishingly diverse. Neither the brevity of the tale nor the absence of a surviving

Box 6.1   Literature beyond Literature

medieval manuscript text has hindered the proliferation of works dedicated to or inspired by it. It is textually and linguistically difficult. Many of its locutions are obscure. Hence it has allowed plenty of scope for interpretation and conjecture, for re-presentation in accessible Russian, for creative reimagining in words and across media. The scholarly bibliography is enormous, culminating in a five-volume encyclopedia of the Igor tale and a six-volume dictionary of its vocabulary. It has spawned prolific literary offspring in many forms and genres. The editors of the first edition labelled it a song. Verse translations began to appear as early as 1803. Half a dozen were published within a couple of decades, and versions have continued to be produced with remarkable frequency through to the twenty-first century. Well-known poets who have retold the Igor tale include Vasilii Zhukovskii (in 1819), Apollon Maikov (1868), Konstantin Balmont (1930), and Nikolai Zabolotskii (1946). One of its several English versions is by Vladimir Nabokov. Visual transpositions of the Igor tale have multiplied since the mid-nineteenth century in scores of illustrated editions and suites of engravings. Among the better-known illustrators of the Igor tale are the graphic artist Vladimir Favorskii and Mstislav Dobuzhinskii, a member of the World of Art (*Mir iskusstva*) group. Heroes of the Igor tale are set in stone and in bronze. Monumental sculptures of its protagonists, and even of its imagined author, have multiplied.

Perhaps the best-known reimagining of the Igor tale is Aleksandr Borodin's opera *Prince Igor*. Borodin worked on this opera from 1869, though it remained unfinished at his death in 1887. It was edited and supplemented for performance by Nikolai Rimskii-Korsakov and Aleksandr Glazunov and remains in the international repertoire to this day. Apart from the popularity of individual fragments of the opera such as the Polovtsian dances, echoes of Borodin's *Prince Igor* can be heard in such diverse contexts as an album by Pink Floyd and episodes of *The Simpsons*.

Simon Franklin

Box 6.2 Literature in Art

From Aleksandr Pushkin's sketches for his novel in verse *Eugene Onegin* (*Evgenii Onegin*, 1825–32) to Dmitrii Prigov's subversive 'stikhograms' (a visual poetry constructed from fragments of Soviet clichés) in the 1970s, from the 'perspectival vision' of Lev Tolstoi's narrative in *War and Peace* (*Voina i mir*, 1868–9) to the photographs in Sergei Tretiakov's avant-garde photojournalism of the 1920s, Russian writers of all stripes have drawn directly and indirectly on visual art in their writing and creative practice.

A particularly concentrated period of such cross-fertilisation was the Modernist era. In the first two decades of the twentieth century, the journal *World of Art* (*Mir iskusstva*, 1898–1904) regularly featured lush reproductions of modern visual art, both Russian and western European, alongside articles on art, literature, music, and theatre. Like many Modernist artists and critics, *World of Art* regarded the synthesis of the arts as its ultimate goal. Working simultaneously as graphic artists, book designers, set makers, writers, and critics, figures associated with the journal (known as *miriskussniki*), such as Aleksandr Benois and Konstantin Somov, sought to realise this aim in their stylised depictions of earlier epochs. Benois's evocative illustrations of night-time St Petersburg for Pushkin's narrative poem *The Bronze Horseman* (*Mednyi vsadnik*, 1833) are typical in this regard.

The images produced by the painter Mikhail Vrubel for Mikhail Lermontov's long narrative poem *The Demon* (*Demon*, 1839) are another notable example. These lyrical images eschew realist depiction in favour of suggestive evocations of mood and state of mind. For the Symbolist poet Aleksandr Blok, the brooding demon at the centre of paintings such as *The Demon Seated* (*Demon sidiashchii*, 1890) was not simply an illustration of Lermontov's poem but functioned, more urgently, as a self-portrait of the artist-theurge, divinely chosen to communicate spiritual truths through art. In the essay 'On the Current State of Russian Symbolism' (*O sovremennom sostoianii russkogo simvolizma*, 1910), written shortly after Vrubel's death, Blok drew on the deep blues and violets of this and other paintings by Vrubel to describe the suffering to which this artist-theurge was condemned.

The relationship between image and text could go beyond mere illustration, however. Elena Guro, for example, published books – *The Hurdy-Gurdy* (*Sharmanka*, 1909), *Autumn Dream* (*Osennii son*, 1912), and *Little Camels of the Sky* (*Nebesnye verbliuzhata*, 1914; published posthumously) – in which sketchy, suggestive drawings of the natural world work in dialogue with

Box 6.2 Literature beyond Literature

fragmentary texts to communicate her sense that the essence of things lay beyond that which could be represented by ordinary linguistic means. Many of the Futurist poets who burst onto the scene in the early 1910s were originally visual artists by training; Guro, for instance – who, until her death in 1913, was the only female member of the poetic group Hylea, later known as the Cubo-Futurists – exhibited paintings in major avant-garde exhibitions. But even those who were not originally visual artists kept company and collaborated with artists such as Natalia Goncharova, Mikhail Larionov, and others to produce artistic manifestos, put on exhibitions, stage plays, and more. These writers and visual artists shared a desire to examine and expand the technical and formal properties of their respective arts, and to explore the relation between the two. Paintings such as Kazimir Malevich's *Englishman in Moscow* (*Anglichanin v Moskve*, 1914) or *Woman at an Advertising Column* (*Dama u afishnogo stolba*, 1914) draw attention to the surface of the canvas and foreground the material existence of the verbal sign by layering fragments of signboards, advertisements, or newspaper clippings with abstract and recognisable shapes.

While the debt to French Cubism is clear, the combination of text and image in these paintings also shares something with the 'transrational' (*zaumnyi*) experiments of Aleksei Kruchenykh, Velimir Khlebnikov, Guro, and other of their Cubo-Futurist peers. Drawing attention to individual letters, morphemes, and words, *zaum'* and its strange sound combinations defamiliarise language and its relationship to meaning, rendering it physically material. Like Malevich's paintings, such texts are visible as objects *in* the world as well as representations *of* that world. This effect is intensified by the handwritten or lithographed form in which *zaum'* poems frequently appeared. In *Group of Three* (*Troe*, 1913), for example – a book of poetry by Kruchenykh, Khlebnikov, and Guro that was designed and illustrated by Malevich – words and letters are transformed into shapes in abstract compositions and poetry is printed alongside visual imagery. The line between written text and visual art, representation and its material means, is blurred.

Isobel Palmer

Box 6.3 Literature in Music

For most people outside of Russia, *Eugene Onegin* (*Evgenii Onegin*) is a Romantic opera by Petr Tchaikovskii – one of the twenty-five most performed operas in the world – not a novel in verse by Aleksandr Pushkin. Similarly, they would credit *Boris Godunov* (*Boris Godunov*) to the composer Modest Musorgskii, with little awareness of Pushkin's drama (or Nikolai Karamzin's history) on which the opera is based. Many great works of Russian literature have had a musical afterlife, one which can overshadow the original, especially for foreign audiences.

The close relationship between Russian literature and music goes back to the eighteenth century, with the creation of an art music tradition in Russia (supplementing folk and church music traditions). By the end of the century, poets were composing lyrics to fit the melodies of Russian folk songs, a genre known as 'Russian song' (*russkaia pesnia*). The French *romance* – simple poetry set for single voice – also made its way into Russia. Such sentimental parlour music became a staple in upper-class homes. Russian lyric poetry of the early nineteenth century was often turned into parlour song almost immediately, with more than seventy settings of Pushkin's poems completed during the poet's lifetime. Close ties between poetry and art song continued into the twentieth century. In the Soviet period, Dmitrii Shostakovich composed song cycles based on the poetry of Aleksandr Blok and Marina Tsvetaeva, while Sergei Prokofiev set the verse of poets ranging from Pushkin, to Konstantin Balmont, to Anna Akhmatova. Late-twentieth-century bards such as Vladimir Vysotskii blurred the musical-poetic boundary even further, writing songs whose lyrics were also published as poetry.

Musical adaptations of Russian literary classics for the stage have had an even greater reach, spanning many genres from classical opera, to ballet, to rock opera and musical. In opera – as in other genres – Pushkin is king, with close to 150 works based on his writings. Many of Russia's famous composers – Mikhail Glinka, Aleksandr Dargomyzhskii, César Cui, Musorgskii, Nikolai Rimskii-Korsakov, Tchaikovskii, Sergei Rakhmaninov – have operatised a wide range of Pushkin's writings, from mock-epic, to drama, to 'little tragedy' (all four have been set), *poema*, short story, novel in verse, and historical novel.

Pushkin is in good company on the opera stage, however. All of Lev Tolstoi's major novels – *War and Peace* (*Voina i mir*), *Anna Karenina* (*Anna Karenina*), and *Resurrection* (*Voskresenie*) – have been operatised. Tolstoi might seem like a less obvious choice for composers than the compact, lyrical

Box 6.3 Literature beyond Literature

Pushkin, but ingenious means were devised to reflect the texture and shape of Tolstoian prose, especially by Prokofiev and his wife, Mira Mendelson, in *War and Peace*. Fedor Dostoevskii's works – also less obviously operatic – have been masterfully adapted by Leoš Janáček in *From the House of the Dead* (based on *Notes from the House of the Dead* (*Zapiski iz mertvogo doma*)), and by Prokofiev in *The Gambler* (*Igrok*). Even the eccentric Nikolai Gogol has found his way to the opera stage through Musorgskii's (unfinished) *The Marriage* (*Zhenit'ba*), Shostakovich's *The Nose* (*Nos*), and Rodion Shchedrin's *Dead Souls* (*Mertvye dushi*).

While opera libretti and their source texts share the medium of words, balletic adaptations rely on the interaction of music and rhythmic movement to capture elements of plot, emotion, tone, character, and relationship. A surprisingly wide range of texts have been adapted in this medium, from obvious choices centred on a love plot like *Onegin* and *Anna Karenina*, to less obvious ones like Dostoevskii's *Crime and Punishment* (*Prestuplenie i nakazanie*) and Gogol's 'The Overcoat' (*Shinel'*). The contemporary ballet choreographer Boris Eifman has built much of his career on such adaptations, working with a diverse range of source texts, including Anton Chekhov's *The Seagull* (*Chaika*), Dostoevskii's *The Brothers Karamazov* (*Brat'ia Karamazovy*), and Akhmatova's *Requiem* (*Rekviem*).

Both inside and outside of Russia, the Russian classics remain popular source texts for classical ballet and opera as well as musicals, rock-operas, and musical parodies. Dave Malloy's 2012 *Natasha, Pierre, and the Great Comet of 1812* is representative of this wave, paring *War and Peace* down to one essential sequence of scenes that would be comprehensible to foreign audiences unfamiliar with the sprawling novel. In the same spirit, a Russian operetta of *Anna Karenina* advertises itself as 'a world classic in a single breath'. Many of these new works strive for relevance through more diverse casting, everyday language, and a pastiche of contemporary musical styles aimed at increased accessibility. Levente Gyöngyösi's 2017 'opera-musical' of Mikhail Bulgakov's *The Master and Margarita* (*Master i Margarita*) brings together symphonic orchestra and rock band to accompany rich visual spectacle: a rotating stage, dancers and acrobats, an airborne Christ, and Margarita flying on a broomstick.

Anna A. Berman

Box 6.4 Literature in Film

The tension between literature and film fascinated early Soviet filmmakers. Dziga Vertov spurned written screenplays in pursuit of a complete separation from the language of theatre and literature. Sergei Eisenstein, on the other hand, developed his montage theory in constant dialogue with classic Russian literature. In one essay, Eisenstein shows how Aleksandr Pushkin's *Poltava* (*Poltava*, 1829) intercuts lines that can be read as wide shots with others he sees as close-ups to produce a powerful effect. Montage, for Eisenstein, became a way to bring literariness to the screen.

In the postwar era, a new generation of filmmakers used literature to question the narrative and realist underpinnings of cinema. Marlen Khutsiev's *I Am Twenty* (*Mne dvadtsat' let*, 1965), for instance, features a public poetry reading, during which the camera lingers on the inspired expressions on the protagonists' faces. The scene does little to move the plot but becomes one of the film's emotional centres. In Georgii Daneliia's *I Walk around Moscow* (*Ia shagaiu po Moskve*, 1964), a central scene – added after censors objected to the film's general plotlessness – recites Anton Chekhov's maxim that if a gun appears in one act, it should go off in the next, while the film itself flies in the face of such dictates. Filmmakers of the era saw their work as more lyrical than narrative, perhaps none more so than Andrei Tarkovskii, who connected scenes and images through feeling and association, rather than cause and effect. One of his most personal films, *Mirror* (*Zerkalo*, 1975), interlaces vivid dreamlike vignettes with his own father's poetry read by the director offscreen. This emphasis on lyric over narrative can be understood as a subtle rejection of the dictates of Socialist Realism in film. At the end of the Soviet era, Kira Muratova connected the failure of realist aesthetics more broadly to the decay of Soviet society itself. Her bleak *Asthenic Syndrome* (*Asticheskii sindrom*, 1989) begins as three old women chant: 'In my childhood, in my early youth, I thought it was enough for everyone to read Lev Nikolaevich Tolstoi and everyone would understand absolutely everything. And everyone would become kind and intelligent.' The camera then turns to the main character wailing at her husband's grave and more scenes of existential distress.

Nevertheless, it has been precisely the Realist novel that has provided the most direct connection between literature and film. As Yuri Tsivian has argued, Realist literature broadly construed provided the source texts and narrative expectations for much of early cinema.

Box 6.4 Literature beyond Literature

In the Brezhnev era a resurgence of Realist adaptations, prominently featuring Tolstoi's work, effectively sacralised a national canon of classic literature. Aleksandr Zarkhi's *Anna Karenina* (1967), for instance, opens with a long shot of the novel's famous first line, complete with pre-revolutionary orthography and an illuminated dropped capital letter. By framing 'All happy families . . .' as visually analogous to scripture, this film literalises the reverent undertones implicit in many late Soviet adaptations of classical literature.

In the last Soviet decades, another mode of literary adaptation appeared, represented by some of Nikita Mikhalkov's early directorial work. Instead of presenting faithful, scene-by-scene screen versions of classic literature, such films crack open the finished literary text to freely develop its elements and recombine them with other sources. In the first post-Soviet decade, this tendency developed into more radical deconstructions of classic literature, made primarily for the festival circuit by a new generation of young directors, such as Valerii Todorovskii's *Katia Izmailova* (*Podmoskovnye vechera*, 1994, inspired by Nikolai Leskov's 'Lady Macbeth of Mtsensk'), Sergei Gazarov's *Inspector* (*Revizor*, 1996), and Iurii Grymov's *Mu-Mu* (*Mu-Mu*, 1998).

By the early 2000s, many literary adaptations had moved to the small screen where the mini-series format accommodated scrupulous reconstructions of big novels. Vladimir Bortko's *The Master and Margarita* (*Master i Margarita*, 2005) and Gleb Panfilov's *The First Circle* (*V kruge pervom*, 2006), for instance, at once sacralised their source texts, and – as Irina Kaspe has argued – flattened them, downplaying humour and turning sharply anti-Stalinist novels into nostalgia films meant for mass audiences. As the Putin era has progressed, many literary adaptations have taken on populist and nationalist overtones, paving the way for occupation and war. Perhaps best exemplified by Fedor Bondarchuk's brutal *Stalingrad* (*Stalingrad*, 2013), such films plunder the canon for stories and visions capable of fuelling today's militant ideology.

Despite its frequent co-optation by political power, the ongoing relationship between literature and film is an ever-developing mediation between the verbal and the visual, the lyrical and the narrative. Literature in film connects canons to new media, classics to new audiences, allowing for – indeed often forcing – the constant re-examination and reinvention of both artistic forms.

Bradley A. Gorski

Box 6.5 The Pushkin Myth

That Aleksandr Pushkin (1799–1837) is their greatest, most beloved poet has been to generations of Russian readers a matter of reality, not myth. Twenty-six Pushkin museums spread across the former Soviet Union, jubilees at predictable intervals (1899, 1937, 1949, 1987, 1999), major celebrations in 1880 (at the unveiling of a statue in Moscow) and 1921 (the inaugural annual Pushkin celebration), and scholarly conferences, as well as numerous films, novels, and popular biographies about the poet, have kept Pushkin front and centre in Russian cultural consciousness, giving him a prominence that no other writer can rival. In chronically book-starved Russia, massive publication projects, beginning with the expiration of Pushkin's copyright in 1887, have made him Russia's most published writer. Omnivorous scholarship, recorded in a shelf full of bibliographies, has exhaustively explored his life and works, including his ancestry, his acquaintances, his descendants, his love life, his day-to-day activities, his library, his politics, his religiosity, and his language. Scholarly commentaries have emphasised his roots in native traditions and in European literature, his libertinism and spirituality, his rebelliousness and loyalty to the empire – and not without convincing support from his writings. The many genres he practised, the wealth of unfinished drafts he left behind, and the allusiveness of his writing have made such support readily available.

At the same time, 'Pushkin' has become much more than the corpus of his writings or of critical scholarship, and it is here that mythmaking can lend narrative shape to demonstrable fact. The principal elements of this mythology involve its setting in what came to be known as the Golden Age of Russian poetry, Pushkin's tragic role in this setting, and the attribution to Pushkin of a founding role in Russian letters.

A young schoolboy with an exceptional gift for poetry, Pushkin reached his teens as Russia was undergoing an upsurge of confident expectation. The Russian army had chased Napoleon back to France and celebrated by quaffing Veuve Clicquot in Paris. Emperor Alexander I (r. 1801–25) hinted at giving Poland a constitution. Pushkin's social class – the educated, westernised nobility – could enjoy works by a pleiad of young poets and could dream not only of a prestigious national literature but of literature shaping a public sphere in which issues of national life could be openly debated. The Russian language was beginning to acquire the ability to capture emotional depth and, in its stylistic registers, the ability to come to grips with two centuries of cultural and political turbulence. But the

Box 6.5   Literature beyond Literature

minuscule part of the population capable of appreciating and supporting these changes – no more than one in five hundred – also felt the insufficiencies of Russian culture and the lack of a leading light. In Pushkin's words, 'Only a leader was missing; a leader was soon found.'

Pushkin wrote this about the Cossack rebel of the 1770s Emelian Pugachev, but in the realm of Russian letters it came to be said of Pushkin himself. By his mid-teens he had broken into print and was accepted by his fellow poets as potentially the most talented poet of the age. By the time he was twenty, he was acknowledged as such, and the compositions subsequently known as his southern poems made him the best-selling poet of the 1820s. By his thirties, however, Pushkin was considered by many past his prime. He wasn't, but many of his best poems, such as *The Bronze Horseman* (*Mednyi vsadnik*, 1833), were unknown to the public. Censorship, six years of exile, and hostile reviewers became the opening acts of a martyr's life, which culminated in his death in a duel at the age of thirty-seven. The themes of fate and foreboding which reverberate through Pushkin's works highlight this tragic plot in popular consciousness and make its conclusion the end of the Golden Age.

Pushkin may not have written the national epic which his friends and contemporary reviewers expected of him, but he answered the need for leadership in other ways, helping him to fill another mythic role, that of 'lawgiver' for Russian literature. Pushkin's carefree and irresponsible public behaviour masked, as the poet Vasilii Zhukovskii came to realise in posthumously organising Pushkin's papers, the effort that Pushkin invested in his verse: 'there is no line which wasn't several times crossed out'. In the Soviet period this dedicated artistry, together with the range of Pushkin's writings and his innovations in literary form (such as his verse novel *Eugene Onegin* (*Evgenii Onegin*, 1825–32), made him the forefather of modern Russian literature and the founder of the Russian literary language. But already for his contemporaries he had become 'Proteus' (Nikolai Gnedich), 'the sun of Russian poetry' (Vladimir Odoevskii), 'our everything' (Apollon Grigorev), and 'the national poet' (Nikolai Gogol).

William Mills Todd III

HISTORY 4

★

HEROES

The Saint

SERGEY IVANOV

A saint is somebody believed to be one. To become recognised as a Christian saint, one has to have died in the flesh. Theoretically, a saint does not have to have a biography at all: a saint is a citizen of the heavenly Jerusalem, and the church celebrates the date of the saint's death, not birth. Yet in practice, in order to be proclaimed a saint, one must have had one's earthly life written down. This paradox could have consequences for the form of a saint's *vita* (the written life). Sometimes the *vita* consisted entirely of posthumous miracles; in other cases, *vitae* were compiled from ready-made clichés long after their heroes' deaths: since eternal reality is immutable, a stereotype was regarded as a correct way to reflect it. Nevertheless, in many instances someone would gather the details of the future protagonist's life, miracles, sayings, and good deeds while the not-yet-saint still existed in the flesh. In some cases, such dossiers grew into authentically literary works.

In this chapter, we are interested in saints as literary characters – not as social figures or objects of popular devotion. The main part of the chapter deals with characters who have been recognised as saints by the church and who are thus the heroes of *vitae*. In the latter part of the chapter, we will also consider aspects of hagiographic representation that have migrated into post-medieval literature, though here the definition of sainthood (generally in a metaphorical sense) is more problematic.

The Medieval Saint

The saint is the main hero of medieval literature. The concept of sainthood was adopted into early Rus Christianity from Byzantium, and the textual repertoire of early Rus (conventionally, from the eleventh century to the Mongol invasions of the mid-thirteenth century) supplied templates and

traditions that were, in turn, adopted into Muscovite Christianity.[1] Among the books brought to the newly converted Rus were numerous hagiographic texts which had been translated from Greek into Slavonic in Moravia and Bulgaria. Hagiography served both liturgical and monastic purposes; it also served as private reading for medieval Slavs.[2] The repertoire of translated Slavic hagiography includes more than three hundred items.[3] Large numbers of Byzantine Lives of saints were translated as parts of complete collections, such as the *Menologia* – a set of abridged Lives arranged in calendar order. In Rus, the peculiar genre of *Prolog* emerged (see Chapter 3.1): a huge compilation of short *vitae* and admonitory stories, which became staple reading throughout the Middle Ages and was still being read until the late nineteenth century by peasants (predominantly Old Believers), merchants, and curious noblemen, including writers such as Lev Tolstoi (1828–1910) and Nikolai Leskov (1831–1895).

More than sixty extended Lives also appeared in manuscript form in Rus between the eleventh and fourteenth centuries, many of which were purposely chosen for translation. Especially intriguing is the great popularity of a specific group of rather long Lives of exotic Byzantine saints containing eschatological material and perhaps compiled in Constantinople during the tenth century: those of Saints Basil the Younger,[4] Andrew the Fool,[5] and Nephon of Constantia.[6] All were translated into Slavonic relatively soon after being composed in Greek and were copied many times. They seem both to reflect and to stimulate an interest in popular eschatology. In early Rus, and then in Muscovy, Andrew the Fool was for centuries perceived as the role model for local 'holy foolery' (see below).

1 Russian, Ukrainian, and Belarusian cultures all have roots in early Rus. On the relationship of early Rus (before the Mongol invasions of the mid-thirteenth century) to later Muscovy and Russia, see the editors' introduction to this volume; also Chapter 1.1.
2 For bibliography on hagiography, see Gerhard Podskalsky, *Theologische Literatur des Mittelalters in Bulgarien und Serbien (865–1459)* (Munich: Beck, 2000), pp. 271–2.
3 Klimentina Ivanova, *Bibliotheca hagiographica Balcano-Slavica* (Sofia: Akademichno Izdatel'stvo, 2008); O. V. Tvorogov, *Perevodnye Zhitiia v Russkoi knizhnosti XI–XV vekov. Katalog* [Translated Lives in Russian book culture of the eleventh to fifteenth centuries. A catalogue] (Moscow: Al'ians-Archeo, 2008).
4 Tatiana Pentkovskaia, Liudmila Shchegoleva, and Sergei Ivanov (eds.), *Zhitie Vasiliia Novogo v drevneishem slavianskom perevode. T. I. Issledovaniia. Teksty* [The Life of Basil the Younger in the earliest Slavonic translation. Vol. I. Studies. Texts] (Moscow: Iazyki slavianskikh kul'tur, 2018).
5 A. M. Moldovan (ed.), *Zhitie Andreia Iurodivogo v slavianskoi pis'mennosti* [The Life of Andrew the Fool in Slavonic letters] (Moscow: Azbukovnik, 2000).
6 A. V. Rystenko (ed.), *Materialy z istorii vizantiis'ko-slov'ians'koi literatury ta movy* [Materials from the history of Byzantino-Slavic literature and language] (Odesa: Tsentral'na naukova biblioteka, 1928).

The structure of the Rus and Muscovite corpus of hagiographic texts was, however, different from that of Byzantium. In the Russian tradition there were three local stylites (saints who lived on the top of columns), while in Byzantium there were at least double that number; there were just two Rus non-princely female saints recognised before the twentieth century, as opposed to more than twenty-five (not counting martyrs) in the Byzantine Empire; there was not a single transvestite saint from Rus, yet there were ten among the Greeks; and not a single holy harlot, in contrast to nine in Byzantine hagiography. While some paths of asceticism remained untrodden, others, on the contrary, gained much greater success among the East Slavs than in Byzantium. Thus, holy fools, prominent in early and mid-Byzantine sainthood, all but faded away, whereas in Rus their number was constantly increasing until the very end of the Muscovite period; there are dozens of them, and their cultural importance is incomparably greater than among the Greeks. Similarly, in Byzantium there was only one holy emperor, Constantine the Great (rare attempts to sanctify other rulers resulted in failure), whereas as many as fifty princes from Rus were eventually canonised.[7]

By far the most famous of the early Rus princely saints are Boris and Gleb – the sons of Prince Vladimir (Volodymyr) Sviatoslavich (d. 1015), the baptiser of Rus, whose own sainthood was eclipsed by that of his sons. Boris and Gleb are the earliest Rus saints in the proper sense of the word. Their cult originated in the eleventh century and remained prominent in Muscovy and beyond. Both young princes fell victim to a power struggle in 1015, and although their deaths were not caused by religious persecution, they were designated martyrs – or more precisely, passion-bearers (*strastoterptsy*) – in the eleventh- and twelfth-century texts dedicated to them. This term was a rendering of the Greek *athlophoros*, one of the epithets for martyrs. In Muscovy, by analogy with Boris and Gleb, another prince – the tsarevich Dmitrii Ivanovich of Uglich (d. 1591, aged eight), who was also supposed to have been killed for political reasons – was referred to by the same term. In the twentieth century, the Russian émigré thinker George Fedotov proclaimed that 'passion-bearing' was a specifically East Slav (in his undifferentiated terminology, 'Russian') kind of sainthood, which allegedly reflected the local perception of Christianity.[8] However, it has been shown that comparable phenomena can be found in many nascent European Christianities: in

7 George P. Fedotov, *The Russian Religious Mind*, vol. I, *Kievan Christianity: The Tenth to the Thirteenth Centuries* (Cambridge, MA: Harvard University Press, 2013), p. 51.
8 Fedotov, *Russian Religious Mind*, vol. I, pp. 94–110.

the Czech lands as well as in Scandinavia, the first saints were descendants of ruling dynasties assassinated for political reasons.

The popularity of Boris and Gleb must have looked scandalous to the Byzantines. One Greek metropolitan of Rus 'was in great fear, and in doubt'[9] concerning their sanctity, and another 'did not firmly believe in the saints'.[10]

The hagiographic works dedicated to Boris and Gleb can be read as true pieces of literature, sprinkled with affective details.[11] By contrast with early Christian martyrs, who rush towards their deaths with enthusiasm, the princely brothers, although they reject the idea of fighting or fleeing and humbly accept their fate, bemoan their earthly life in a humane manner. In spite of numerous biblical details and allusions, the narrative is anything but stereotyped and leaves an impression of vividness and simplicity.

The figure of the founder of a monastery is well attested in Byzantine hagiography. The early Rus *Life of Feodosii of the Caves* (*Zhitie Feodosiia Pecherskogo*), written by the monk Nestor within a few years of the saint's death in 1074,[12] perfectly fits the paradigm, yet this text is highly original and contains a lot of distinctive details. For example, the saint's mother is depicted as a woman with a domineering temper who tries to bend Feodosii to her will for many years, until she finally gives up. The main concern of the saint is the well-being of the monastery, and all of his miracles are performed to that effect. Another important trait of Feodosii is his deep involvement in the political life of Kyiv.[13] He is a practical man who, 'though simple and unlettered, was wiser than the philosophers'.[14]

Paterika are assemblages about holy men: short anecdotes, miracles, abridged Lives, etc., often focused on a particular place or region. The first original Rus paterikon (*paterik*) is from the Caves monastery in Kyiv.[15] The Kyivan *Paterik* features tales about a range of monks from the eleventh and twelfth centuries. Its collection of cameos presents a concentrated depiction of saintly passions and ardent asceticism. The holy fathers have to cope with two forms of distraction: on the one hand, from the secular world, which

---

9 Marvin Kantor (trans.), *Medieval Slavic Lives of Saints and Princes* (Ann Arbor: University of Michigan, 1983), p. 209.

10 Kantor, *Medieval Slavic Lives*, p. 215.

11 Paul Hollingsworth (trans.), *The Hagiography of Kievan Rus* (Cambridge, MA: Ukrainian Research Institute of Harvard University, 1992), pp. 3–32, 97–134.

12 Hollingsworth, *Hagiography of Kievan Rus*, pp. 33–96.

13 David Kirk Prestel, 'The search for the word: Echoes of the Apophthegma in the Kievan Caves Patericon', *Russian Review* 5.4 (1998), 568–82.

14 Hollingsworth, *Hagiography of Kievan Rus*, p. 36.

15 Muriel Heppel (trans.), *The 'Paterik' of the Kievan Caves Monastery* (Cambridge, MA: Harvard University Press, 1989).

constantly intrudes into the monastic life; on the other, from demons who incessantly attempt to deflect monks from the true path. A demon can easily disguise itself as a monk, as an angel, or even as Christ himself. An angel may paint an icon to help a monk fulfil an order, while demons can be coerced into dragging logs or grinding grain. The monastic elders are anything but meek: they stink, mock each other, and severely punish the lazy. Miracles are common and not necessarily pleasant: the righteous elder in charge of burying the dead can order dead monks to turn in their graves, change places, or even temporarily come back to life, if they are needed.

A saint is always a living anomaly, while the church is the embodiment of routine. The latter gradually figures out ways of dealing with the former, but not in all cases. The first conflict between the two in early Rus hagiography is found in the *Life of Avraamii of Smolensk* (*Zhitie Avraamiia Smolenskogo*, first quarter of the thirteenth century).[16] This saint is a doomsday preacher. He is a monk, but his sermons are directed towards the secular world. 'The devil instigated some of the priests and monks to oppose him and some towns-people to come out and upbraid him.'[17] The superior orders Avraamii to cease his teaching – the saint begins to wander around, preaching and living by alms. But his troubles grow: 'Some slandered Avraamii to the bishop, others maligned and insulted him, others called him heretic, others accused him of reading mysterious books and others of frequenting women . . . There was no one in the town who would not malign the blessed Avraamii.'[18] Avraamii is the first Rus saint who is an outcast, holy in spite of condemnation from all sides, church included.

Varlaam of Khutyn (d. late twelfth or early thirteenth century) is the first saint whose Life is a palimpsest of many layers. He lived in Novgorod, where he founded a monastery. Legends about Varlaam began circulating soon after his death, but hagiographers knew too little to compose an extensive *vita*. In one redaction after another, the text was augmented with new details, and it continued to evolve until the seventeenth century. As a result, different kinds of tales mentioning Varlaam as the main character (or his grave) exist in hundreds of copies.[19] This kind of textual history – not so unusual throughout

---

16 Hollingsworth, *Hagiography of Kievan Rus*, pp. lxix–lxxx, 135–63.
17 Hollingsworth, *Hagiography of Kievan Rus*, p. 142.
18 Hollingsworth, *Hagiography of Kievan Rus*, pp. 146–7.
19 L. A. Dmitriev, *Zhitiinye povesti russkogo severa kak pamiatniki literatury XIII–XVII vv.* [Hagiographic tales of the Russian north as works of literature] (Leningrad: Nauka, 1973), pp. 13–95, 271–81.

the age of devotion (see Chapter 1.1) – means that it is not possible to treat this saint as a single, unitary literary hero.

Prince Aleksandr Nevskii (1221–1263) became the first in a long list of saintly princes praised not for non-resistance – as Boris and Gleb – but, on the contrary, for their military and diplomatic triumphs.[20] The panegyric in his honour, which laid the foundation for his cult, has very little in common with traditional hagiography. It is closer to a military tale, like those in the chronicles, as it says nothing of his birth, childhood, or feats of asceticism. If Aleksandr is the symbol of glory, Prince Mikhail of Chernihiv serves as a symbol of martyrdom, having accepted death in 1246 in the Mongols' camp, to which he had gone voluntarily to expose the oppressors' false creed.

By far the most famous early Muscovite saint, whose Life is preserved in the greatest number of copies, is Sergii of Radonezh (1314–1392).[21] He founded a monastery that has since become the most important one in Russia, the Troitse-Sergieva Lavra to the northeast of Moscow. The hagiographer is an accomplished writer who puts together a classic *vita* combining vivid details with clichés and politics with humour. For example, the saint's childhood inability to learn his letters, which he overcomes suddenly thanks to a miracle, is a commonplace of hagiography, but in Sergii's case the story is told quite dramatically: as his brother and other pupils make rapid progress, Sergii is mocked and punished; feeling hurt, he prays tearfully until he meets a mysterious monk who 'injects' him with knowledge. The fact that our hero lived in a forest, surrounded by wild beasts, is common enough; what is unusual is that, while taming a bear, he 'trembled as any human would'.[22] The saint is said to treat all people equally and never to get irritable – but he castigates a servant who dares taste the food sent to him by a prince, lectures the Greek bishop who doubts his sanctity, and immediately leaves his monastery when he hears his brother's boast that it was he who had chosen the spot on which it was built. Although secluded from the world, Sergii is constantly conversing with church and secular authorities and even gives his blessing to Prince Dmitrii Ivanovich of Moscow (r. 1359–89) to go and fight the Tatars. He miraculously helps the prince in his victory over the Tatars in the battle of Kulikovo (1380).

20 Mari Isoaho, *The Image of Alexandr Nevskiy in Medieval Russia: Warrior and Saint* (Leiden: Brill, 2006).
21 David B. Miller, *Saint Sergius of Radonezh, His Trinity Monastery, and the Formation of the Russian Identity* (DeKalb: Northern Illinois University Press, 2010).
22 *Biblioteka literatury Drevnei Rusi* [Library of early Rus literature], 20 vols. (St Petersburg: Nauka, 1997–2020), vol. VI (1999), p. 300.

For dozens of founders of monasteries in the Russian north in the fifteenth to nineteenth centuries, or rather for their hagiographers, Sergii served as a role model. However, we should not ignore other types of holiness. Missionary saints are practically unheard of in Byzantium (if we exclude the Slavonic-language *vitae* of Cyril and Methodius), and they are also comparatively rare in Rus. The most famous such saint is Stefan of Perm (d. 1396), the apostle of the Komi people. Stefan's hagiographer, Epifanii Premudryi ('the Wise', d. c. 1420), is believed to have spent some time in Byzantium, and this Life is written in the highly ornate style known as 'word-weaving'.[23] Stefan creates an alphabet for the Komi language and settles among the 'barbarians', baptising and teaching. He does not rely on the military and administrative power of the state. Indeed, he even defends – as best he can – his flock from oppression by the Muscovite authorities.[24] His main traits are his angelic patience and constant preparedness for martyrdom.

The most colourful saint of this early period is Nikita of Pereiaslavl, who lived sometime between the twelfth and early fifteenth centuries.[25] Nikita starts out as a municipal judiciary official who takes bribes (in one version) or as a robber who commits crimes (in another), but then one day he buys some meat at the market; as his wife is preparing it, the pot emits an incessant flow of blood and foam. Eventually, Nikita's wife begins to see the boiling parts of a human body: 'sometimes a head, sometimes an arm, sometimes a foot'.[26] When Nikita hears about this, he leaves his home and goes to a monastery, where he confesses all his sins to the father superior but is barred from entering (the 'robber' version adds that the father superior is afraid Nikita has come to kill him). The repentant sinner then spends days in a pond, tormented by insects and snakes, before he is finally admitted to the monastery. There he puts iron chains on his body and digs a cave for himself (in one version) or constructs a pillar (in another). Finally, Nikita is assassinated by two former accomplices who rob him of his iron chains.

The final establishment of Muscovite autocracy was accompanied by the centralisation of sanctification. The process of canonisation was taken over

23 Faith C. M. Kitch, *The Literary Style of Epifanij Premudryj: 'Pletenije Sloves'* (Munich: Verlag Otto Sagner, 1976).
24 Sergei Ivanov, *'Pearls before Swine': Missionary Work in Byzantium* (Paris: Collège de France-CNRS, 2015), pp. 182–3.
25 M. A. Fedotova, 'Zhitie Nikity Stolpnika Pereiaslavskogo (rukopisnaia traditsiia Zhitiia)' [The Life of Nikita the Stylite of Pereiaslavl (the manuscript tradition of the Life)], in T. R. Rudi and S. A. Semiachko (eds.), *Russkaia agiografiia. Issledovaniia. Publikatsii. Polemika* [Russian hagiography. Studies. Publications. Debates] (St Petersburg: Dmitrii Bulanin, 2005), pp. 309–31.
26 Fedotova, 'Zhitie Nikity', p. 323.

by Moscow. Church councils of 1547 and 1549 proclaimed dozens of new saints (some for universal and some for local veneration) and excluded many others. The *Great Menaion for Reading* (see Chapter 3.1), the vast compilation of hagiographic material for every day of the year, was completed in the mid-sixteenth century under the auspices of Metropolitan Makarii (1481/2–1563).

In the sixteenth century, hagiography began to absorb – much more energetically than before – elements of folk tales, on the one hand, and of secular literature, on the other. The best example of both is 'The Tale of Petr and Fevroniia of Murom' (*Povest' o Petre i Fevronii Muromskikh*).[27] Its author, the monk Ermolai-Erazm, is also known for having composed several other works.[28] The most interesting character is Fevroniia, a common village girl and a witch. After she cures Prince Petr from scabs caused by a dragon, she demands that he promise to marry her. Upon recovery, the prince reneges on his promise and Fevroniia casts a spell on him. He gets the scabs back and this time has to marry her. The boyars, and especially their wives, feel humiliated by the low-born princess and urge the couple to leave Murom, but then the nobles immediately become involved in bloody strife and soon ask Petr and Fevroniia to return to power. Had these characters not been widely venerated as saints, we would never recognise them as such.

Another captivating story of a dubious saint is the Russian legend about Andrew of Crete. This Byzantine author of the eighth century composed the famous *Great Canon*, recited for several days during the liturgy of Lent. The hero of this epitome of ardent repentance confesses all possible sins, which at the end of the sixteenth century inspired a tale that had nothing to do with either the official *vita* of Andrew of Crete, widely known in Russia, or with Byzantine hagiography in general. This new sixteenth-century version of Andrew is an Orthodox Christian Oedipus: due to an ominous prophesy, he is abandoned by his parents immediately after birth; many years later, as a result of unforeseeable circumstances, he kills his father and marries his mother. This wandering plot is aggravated by blood-curdling details: baby Andrew is found by a nun and raised in a nunnery; when he grows up, he seduces all 300 nuns and, in the end, also the mother superior! When the sacrilege of his parricide and incest are revealed, Andrew asks different priests

---

27 R. P. Dmitrieva (ed.), *Povest' o Petre i Fevronii* [The tale of Petr and Fevroniia] (Leningrad: Nauka, 1979), pp. 147–208. This edition prints several redactions of the work.

28 Jack Haney, 'On the "Tale of Peter and Fevronia, wonderworkers of Murom"', *Canadian-American Slavic Studies* 13.1–2 (1979), 139–62; Ludmila A. Zebrina Pruner, 'The Hagiographic *genre* and the Vita of Peter and Fevroniia', unpublished PhD thesis, University of Pittsburgh (1983).

for absolution, but they refuse and so he kills them, one after another. Finally, a bishop, afraid for his own life, imposes a penance on Andrew: he must sit in a well three fathoms deep and half a fathom wide, covered by an iron lid, and must pray until the bottom of the well rises to ground level. Andrew spends thirty years in the well and this, according to the story, is how and when he composes his *Great Canon*. After he miraculously re-emerges from his well, the bishop absolves him of his sins. Moreover, when the bishop dies, Andrew becomes bishop himself.[29] This weirdest of legends became highly popular. It exists in six versions and has survived in more than fifty manuscript copies.

The topic of excessive repentance expiating the most abominable crimes obviously appealed to public sentiment in Rus. In the *Life of Varlaam of Keret* (*Zhitie Varlaama Keretskogo*, sixteenth century), a priest murders his wife whom he suspects of infidelity. To atone for his sin, he exhumes her body, puts it in his boat, and sails through the inhospitable icy waters of the White Sea for three years, until the corpse completely decomposes. Through this feat of asceticism, Varlaam acquires a miraculous ability of a quite specific kind: he chases away the worms that gnaw the wood of fishermen's boats. This is a sign of absolution.[30]

Whereas normally the Lives of the hierarchs of the church are not especially interesting from a literary point of view, the *vita* of the Metropolitan Filip is an exception:[31] the story of the confrontation between the despotic autocrat Ivan IV 'the Terrible' (r. 1533–84) and the staunch saint is depicted with mastery and passion. Though imbued with bookish borrowings, the text, written at the turn of the seventeenth century, seems to contain elements of eye-witness testimonies or is otherwise coloured by the author's vivid imagination. Step by step the tension builds: the metropolitan admonishes the tsar and begins to reproach him for his policies; the bishops who promised Filip their solidarity then backtrack because of their fear of the tsar; Ivan gradually loses patience, and his confidants denounce the metropolitan; Filip understands that his intransigence will cost him his life, but he does not give up; a special commission is sent to the monastery where he began his church career to look for compromising evidence against him; the commission find nothing, but

29 N. K. Gudzii, 'K legendam ob Iude predatele i Andree Kritskom' [On the legends of Judas the Traitor and of Andrew of Crete], *Russkii filologicheskii vestnik* [Russian philological messenger] 73.1 (1915), 32–4.
30 Mitrofan Badanin, *Prepodobnyi Varlaam Keretskii* [The venerable Varlaam Keretskii] (St Petersburg: Ladan, 2007).
31 I. A. Lobakova (ed.), *Zhitie mitropolita Filippa. Issledovanie i teksty* [The Life of Metropolitan Filip. Studies and texts] (St Petersburg: Dmitrii Bulanin, 2006).

nevertheless, with carrots and sticks, they compel monks to testify against Filip. Finally, in 1569:

> On Sunday, when Philip celebrated the Divine Liturgy, the tsar came to the church service. Saint Philip ... stood in his designated place, the tsar approached him three times and asked for a blessing, but the saint did not answer. And the boyars said: 'Holy eminence, Tsar Ivan Vasilevich demands that you bless him.' The blessed one said: 'O tsar! Outside the walls of the church Christian blood is shed innocently and people die in vain.' The tsar fell into a rage and said: 'Oh, Philip! Are you resisting our power?'[32]

The metropolitan is defrocked, beaten, and exiled to a provincial monastery, where he is soon strangled by a henchman of the tsar. Until his last breath he refuses to bless the tyrant.

By far the strangest type of Russian sainthood is 'holy foolery' (*iurodstvo*). This kind of sanctity has Byzantine roots, but it became prominent in Russia from the mid-fifteenth century and reached its peak in the sixteenth and seventeenth centuries. A holy fool is a pretend madman or hooligan who is reputed to be concealing his holiness in order to escape human veneration. While Byzantine holy fools conduct themselves provocatively by playing lechers and blasphemers, Russian *iurodivye* stand out for their ragged clothing, terrifying prophecies, and political audacity. Although such 'fools for Christ's sake' embody the spontaneous protest against the routinisation of Christianity, in the sixteenth century the church tended to welcome them into the fold. Only in the seventeenth century did it begin to push them out to the margins. Out of the motley crowd of canonised *iurodivye*, we choose only one: Vasilii the Blessed (see Chapter 4.9).[33] He lived as a beggar in Moscow in the house of a pious widow, walked around naked, committed various acts of debauchery at the market, threw stones at the houses of God-fearing citizens, and kissed the walls of sinners' houses. He predicted misfortunes, caused death, and told unpleasant truths to the formidable tsar Ivan IV. What's more, he smashed into pieces a miracle-working icon of the Virgin in the presence of a crowd of worshippers: he was the only one to see with his spiritual eyes that, under the painted surface, the devil was depicted.

Halfway between a *vita* and a secular biography is the *Life of Iulianiia Osorina* (*Zhitie Iulianii Osor'inoi*), written by her own son in the first half of the seventeenth century. The heroine is neither a nun nor a princess; she is

---

32 Lobakova (ed.), *Zhitie mitropolita Filippa*, p. 188, cf. p. 218.

33 Sergey Ivanov (trans.), 'Vasilii the Blessed', in Albrecht Berger and Sergey Ivanov (eds.), *Holy Fools and Divine Madmen: Sacred Insanity through Ages and Cultures* (Munich: Ars Una, 2018), pp. 274–94.

illiterate and neither attends church nor has a spiritual instructor; and she has a husband and gives birth to thirteen children. Iulianiia is extremely kind and charitable. During a plague she welcomes the sick and washes their sore-covered bodies; during a famine she gives away everything she has to save people from death, and the bread that she bakes from bark is sweeter than real bread. What turns this *vita* into a piece of literature is its numerous tiny details: 'she [an orphan brought up by her aunt] respected the aunt and her daughters and was obedient to them, but her inclination was to prayers and fasting. Because of this, she was cursed a lot by her aunt and derided by her cousins who said to her: "You are half-witted if you torment your flesh and ruin your beauty!"'[34] Even hagiographic clichés in this life are permeated with lively details: Iulianiia's passion for alms-giving is so great that she tricks her mother-in-law, pretending that she feels constant hunger and asking for additional food, which she in fact gives to the beggars; and after her husband refuses to let her take the veil, she demands that they have no sexual intercourse – he agrees and they then sleep in the same room but in different beds. The author himself intrudes into the narrative with personal observations, such as his note that 'Many times we saw that, while she was asleep, her fingers were still moving the prayer-beads.'[35]

A unique example of auto-hagiography is the *Life of Archpriest Avvakum, Written by Himself* (*Zhitie protopopa Avvakuma, im samim napisannoe*, comp. 1672–5) by Avvakum Petrov (1620–1682), the leader of the Old Believers in the seventeenth century.[36] On the one hand, Avvakum pictures himself as an authentic, conventional saint: he works miracles, chases demons, and staunchly endures persecutions and even torture. The only missing detail is his martyrly death, which he was, of course, unable to describe. On the other hand, the text is in some dimensions highly realistic, is sprinkled with humour, and shows the very strong personality of its author. Avvakum is passionate: he is full of tenderness towards his family and his comrades in their common struggle; he is imbued with hatred towards his enemies and betrayers; and he displays disdain towards the weak and conformist majority. The narrator is merciless towards himself: when he gets sexually aroused at the confessions of a girl, he burns his fingers in the flame of a candle (in

---

34 T. I. Rudi (ed.), *Zhitie Iulianii Lazarevskoi (Poves' ob Ul'ianii Osor'inoi)* [The Life of Iulianiia Lazarevskaia (The tale of Ulianiia Osorina)] (St Petersburg: Nauka, 1996), pp. 104, 122–3.
35 Rudi (ed.), *Zhitie Iulianii Lazarevskoi*, p. 110.
36 Archpriest Avvakum, *The Life Written by Himself*, trans. Kenneth N. Brostrom (New York: Columbia University Press, 2021).

imitation of the saints of old); and when he beats his wife in a fit of temper, he orders all his household to beat him. Yet he never abandons self-irony. Supernatural reality for Avvakum is something familiar and homely: an angel visits him in his prison, hands him a spoon, and treats him to very tasty cabbage soup; and demons constantly vex him by rearranging his kitchenware, etc. Avvakum's autobiography is a masterpiece of personal literature in which the traditions of old hagiography still survive (see Chapter 3.10).

The Post-medieval Saint

Peter I's (r. 1682–1725) revolution changed the saint's status completely. High society became radically secularised; the church was incorporated into the new, bureaucratic state. Hagiography ceased to be the common reading for all social strata. New canonisations stopped; new, completely secular literature appeared. In post-Petrine Russia, the very term 'saint' should be applied with caution. What is our criterion here for identifying secular literary characters as saints? Virtue, indiscriminate forgiveness, and meekness are not enough. The saint's way of seeing must transcend the visible world and should imply the existence of a higher reality, impenetrable for ordinary people. Some 'saints' of post-medieval literature were new representations of saints who figured in the medieval tradition, others were invented for new purposes.

In the nineteenth century, historical saints became characters of modern literature. Take, for example, the holy fool Nikolka the Iron Cap from Aleksandr Pushkin's (1799–1837) *Boris Godunov* (*Boris Godunov*, 1825).[37] The image is borrowed primarily from numerous legends about the *iurodivyi* Nikola Salos, who had allegedly saved the city of Pskov from the wrath of Ivan the Terrible in 1570. Yet there is a crucial difference between the two: an Old Russian *iurodivyi* sows terror – even the tsar is afraid of him; Nikolka, on the other hand, is a harmless and vulnerable simpleton – but still he is the only voice of truth: 'No prayers for the Herod-Tsar. Our Lady won't allow it.' The only free person, Pushkin intimates in his tragedy, is a fool. And he means himself when he quips in a letter, 'I couldn't possibly hide all my ears under the holy fool's cap. They stick out!'[38]

37 Alexandr Pushkin, *Boris Godunov and Other Dramatic Works*, trans. James Falen (Oxford: Oxford University Press, 2007), pp. 72–3.
38 A. S. Pushkin, *Polnoe sobranie sochnenii v shestnadtsati tomakh* [Complete works in sixteen volumes] (Moscow, Leningrad: Izdatel'stvo Akademii nauk SSSR, 1937–1959), vol. XIII (1937), pp. 239–40.

In the mid-nineteenth century, several of the canonical Russian writers became deeply interested in the figure of the saintly hero. At first it was the peasant. In 1854, Nikolai Nekrasov (1821–1878) wrote the poem 'Vlas' (*Vlas*),[39] where a great sinner sees hell in a vision and, in repentance, abandons his possessions, puts on iron fetters, and begins the wandering life of a beggar. Another even more paradoxical hero can be found in his long narrative poem *Who Can Be Happy in Russia?* (*Komu na Rusi zhit' khorosho?*, 1876). The robber and murderer Kudeiar is suddenly overcome with remorse, renames himself Pitirim, and secludes himself in a forest. An angel announces that his sins will be expiated if he manages to fell a large tree with only a knife. The anchorite toils at the tree for many years but makes little progress, until a rich landlord finds him and begins to boast of his crimes. In a fit of anger, Pitirim kills him with his knife – and the huge tree instantly falls by itself. So, for Nekrasov, sanctity is something acquired after a fall. His first attempt to create a 'revolutionary saint' was his poem 'In Memory of Dobroliubov' (*Pamiati Dobroliubova*, 1864). While enumerating the virtues of his hero, the poet suddenly mentions his bodily 'chastity', a virtue which is not typically required of a freedom fighter but which resembles the Christian paradigm.

The merging of these two paradigms is even more pronounced in the novel *What Is to Be Done?* (*Chto delat'?*, 1863), written by Nikolai Chernyshevskii (1828–1889) while in prison for sedition (see Chapter 4.7). Rakhmetov, a peripheral character in the novel,[40] is a fully fledged saint of the religion of revolution:[41] he cuts off all family ties, abstains from any sexual relations, trains his body by fasting and other privations, and, finally, tests his will by sleeping on a bed of nails.

Fedor Dostoevskii (1821–1881) was the writer who agonised over the problem of sainthood most intensely. His earliest saintly character is Prince Myshkin in *The Idiot* (*Idiot*, 1874). Lev Myshkin is a meek truth-teller, trusting and innocent (in all senses). His kindness and unbiased mind, his humility and compassion attract people, especially children, but lead also to unforeseen and tragic consequences. At the beginning of the novel, he recovers from his mental illness; at the end, he loses his mind completely.

39 N. A. Nekrasov, 'Vlas', in *Polnoe sobranie sochinenii* [Complete works], 15 vols. (Leningrad: Nauka, 1981–2000), vol. I (1981), pp. 152–4.
40 Nikolai G. Tchernuishevsky, *Vital Question; or, What Is to Be Done?*, trans. N. Haskell Dole and S. S. Skidelsky (New York: Thomas Y. Crowell, 1866), pp. 233–315.
41 Marcia A. Morris, *Saints and Revolutionaries: The Ascetic Hero in Russian Literature* (New York: SUNY Press, 1993), pp. 127–47.

The next stage in the development of Dostoevskian sainthood is Makar Dolgorukii in *The Adolescent* (*Podrostok*, 1876). Illiterate and unconnected to the church, he wanders across Russia and believes this to be his religious duty. His main trait is 'mirth of heart',[42] which he is ready to appreciate even in non-believers.

The most attention to sanctity is paid in the last of Dostoevskii's novels, *The Brothers Karamazov* (*Brat'ia Karamazovy*, 1881). There are two saints among its characters: the elder Zosima and Alesha, the youngest of the brothers. The former is a monk and a *starets*, a spiritual instructor. He does not teach dogma or about the church in general but wonders instead about man's vocation before God. His secularised approach causes indignation among the zealots, and they are jubilant when Zosima dies and his corpse putrefies, which is perceived as a sign of heavenly disfavour. Alesha, Zosima's novice, leaves the monastery and immerses himself in the atmosphere permeated with filth, passions, and unbelief embodied by his father, Fedor; his brother Mitia; and his brother Ivan, respectively. This blushing, sheepish, but firm youngster, who also attracts the love of children, embodies for the author Russia's bright future – but what this saintly future will be, Dostoevskii himself does not exactly know.

Of all nineteenth-century Russian writers, Nikolai Leskov was the one who wrote in ways that came closest to the traditional understanding of what sainthood is. In his novels, we meet a whole array of saintly characters: the priest Tuberozov in the novel *Cathedral Folk* (*Soboriane*, 1872) rebels in his sermons against shallow ritualism and refuses to repent even in the face of punishment; the missionary Kiriak defends his newly converted Yakut flock from state officials in the story 'At the Edge of the World' (*Na kraiu sveta*, 1875); the butler Pavlin sacrifices everything to make a poor orphan girl happy in *Pavlin* (*Pavlin*, 1874); and the dairy farmer Golovan takes care of people struck with the plague in the story 'The Death-Defying Golovan' (*Nesmertel'nyi Golovan*, 1880; see Chapter 4.4). At the same time, Leskov tried hard to breathe life into numerous traditional hagiographic legends, which he loved to retell in slightly modernised versions.

Lev Tolstoi's aversion to the mystical side of righteousness led him to create characters like Platon Karataev in *War and Peace* (*Voina i mir*, 1868) as a symbol of the naïve acceptance of life in all its manifestations. In 'Father Sergii' (*Otets Sergii*, 1898), Tolstoi exposes the self-complacency of traditional religious

---

42 Fyodor Dostoevsky, *The Adolescent*, trans. Richard Pevear and Larissa Volokhonsky (New York, London, and Toronto: Alfred A. Knopf, 2003), p. 268.

saintliness which attracts crowds of pilgrims. As Father Sergii understands in the end, the one who is truly righteous is Pashenka, the humble, self-effacing woman who fully commits herself to serving her family. In the last years of his life, Tolstoi wrote a series of stories featuring saints – 'Two Old Men' (*Dva starika*, 1885), 'Three Elders' (*Tri startsa*, 1885), and 'Palechek the Buffoon' (*Shut Palechek*, 1907) – and in each case, energetic, beneficent saintliness is shown against the backdrop of hollow, sanctimonious piety.

At the beginning of the twentieth century, a new saint – the descendant of Rakhmetov – appears in Russian literature: a selfless communist hero. The first in this line is Pavel Vlasov, the protagonist of Maksim Gorkii's (1868–1936) *Mother* (*Mat'*, 1906). Having discovered what he regards as the ultimate truth, Pavel renounces women and alcohol and holds in contempt personal freedom and family ties. Sacrifices are perceived as necessary by the creators of the new communist hagiography.

After the Bolshevik Revolution, such characters became very common in Soviet literature. All of them live for the happy future, which will come if their faith is ardent and their self-negation total. Yet the most glaring example here is Pavel Korchagin from Nikolai Ostrovskii's (1904–1936) autobiographical novel *How the Steel Was Tempered* (*Kak zakalialas' stal'*, 1934). His resemblance to a Christian ascetic is complete: he (the author as well as his hero) is struck with paralysis and, still alive, becomes the object of pious pilgrimage for great crowds of people, like a holy relic.

Many Soviet writers constructed their communist heroes in the Christian mould. Andrei Platonov (1899–1951) approached his task differently. In his *Chevengur* (*Chevengur*, 1929), he creates a surreal world in which nearly any character can be suspected of holiness. The peculiar mixture of love and hatred, self-denial, and rejection of the laws of nature makes the reader believe that in this enchanting atmosphere of fairy tale / nightmare anything is possible. His characters who declare the advent of communism in the small town of Chevengur are the saints of this apocalyptic universe. Platonov called this phenomenon 'living holiness'.[43] But utopia soon turned into anti-utopia, and in Platonov's next novel, *The Foundation Pit* (*Kotlovan*, 1930), the most saintly figures are a dying girl and a fanatical, class-conscious bear.

For centuries, Russian literature was, for Russians, not just belles-lettres.[44] Secular literature had a quasi-religious status, writers were perceived as

---

43 Andrei Platonov, *Chevengur*, trans. Anthony Olcott (Ann Arbor, MI: Ardis, 1978), p. 163.
44 Cf. Katerina Clark, *The Soviet Novel: History as Ritual* (Chicago: University of Chicago Press, 1985), pp. 47–50.

prophets,[45] and literary heroes as role models. The gradual disappearance of the saint from Russian literature during the last half-century is indicative of both literature and its perception.

Further Reading

Alissandratos, Julia, 'Hagiographical commonplaces and medieval prototypes in N. G. Chernyshevsky's *What Is to Be Done?*', *St Vladimir's Theological Quarterly* 26 (1982), 103–17.

Alissandratos, Julia, 'New approaches to the problem of identifying the genre of the *Life of Julijana Lazarevskaja*', *Cyrillomethodianum* 7 (1983), 235–44.

Alissandratos, Julia, 'Leo Tolstoy's "Father Sergius" and the Russian hagiographical tradition', *Cyrillomethodianum* 8–9 (1984–5), 149–63.

Alissandratos, Julia, 'A stylization of hagiographical composition in Nicolay Leskov's "Singlethought" (*Odnodum*)', *Slavic and East European Journal* 27 (1983), 416–32.

Arndt, Charles, 'Making saints out of soldiers: Nikolaj Leskov's "Kadetskii monastyr'" and hagiographization of the recent past', *Russian Literature* 90 (2017), 1–25.

Børtnes, Jostein, *Visions of Glory: Studies in Early Russian Hagiography*, trans. Jostein Børtnes and Paul L. Nielsen (Oslo: Solum Forlag, 1988).

Flath, Carol A., 'The Passion of Dmitrii Karamazov', *Slavic Review* 58 (1999), 584–99.

Harris, Adrienne M., 'The Lives and deaths of a Soviet saint in the post-Soviet period: The case of Zoia Kosmodem'ianskaia', *Canadian Slavonic Papers* 53 (2011), 273–304.

Kahla, Elina, *Life as Exploit: Representations of Twentieth-Century Saintly Women in Russia* (Helsinki: Kikimora Publications, 2007).

Kobets, Svitlana, 'The subtext of Christian asceticism in Aleksandr Solzhenitsyn's *One Day in the Life of Ivan Denisovich*', *Slavic and East European Journal* 42 (1998), 661–76.

Linner, Sven, *Starets Zosima in "The Brothers Karamazov": A Study in the Mimesis of Virtue* (Stockholm: Almqvist & Wiksell International, 1975).

Walsh, Harry H., and Paul Alessi, 'The "Apophthegmata patrum" and Tolstoy's "Father Sergius"', *Comparative Literature Studies* 19 (1982), 1–10.

Ziolkowski, Margaret, *Hagiography and Modern Russian Literature*. (Princeton: Princeton University Press, 1988).

---

45 Aleksandr M. Panchenko, 'Russkii poet, ili Mirskaia sviatost' kak religiozno-kul'turnaia problema' [The Russian poet, or secular sanctity as a religious-cultural question], in *Russkaia istoriia i kul'tura* [Russian history and culture] (St Petersburg: Iuna, 1999), pp. 359–73.

The Ruler

TATIANA SMOLIAROVA

Of all European literatures, the Russian literary canon has perhaps been the one most focused on the figure of the ruler. To some extent, early modern Russian literature originates from and revolves around this figure, the ruler being its main sponsor, addressee, object, and – at times – even its author. The crucial and immediate role played by the ruler in the literary process from the early eighteenth century for at least two centuries may be explained by two inextricably intertwined ideas: the tsar as the Lord's anointed,[1] and the tsar as the cornerstone of the entire edifice of the Russian Enlightenment.[2] By contrast with some European countries – especially France, where the ruler(s) and the Enlightenment were at odds with each other – in Russia the progress of the state and the progress of reason were seen and represented as two parts of the same process.[3]

Throughout eighteenth-century Russian literature, from Feofan Prokopovich (1681–1736) at the beginning of the century to Gavriil Derzhavin (1743–1816) at the end, the rulers themselves were represented as granting and administering cosmic harmony on earth. Their military victories, alliances, and peace treaties, as well as their well-being and passions, were not just objects of representation but themes for artistic and philosophical reflection. 'The progress of the state was perceived as the progress of reason and enlightenment – not the individual progress of a given society'.[4] In Russia, the ruler and the Enlightenment (with all its diverse manifestations in literature and the arts) went hand in hand until roughly the turn of the nineteenth century, when the state was, finally,

---

1 Boris Uspenskij and Viktor Zhivov, 'Tsar and God: Semiotic aspects of the sacralization of the monarch in Russia', in Marcus C. Levitt (ed.), 'Tsar and God' and Other Essays in Russian Cultural Semiotics (Boston: Academic Studies Press, 2012), pp. 1–112.
2 Victor Zhivov, 'The state myth in the era of Enlightenment and its destruction in late eighteenth-century Russia', in Levitt (ed.), 'Tsar and God' and Other Essays, pp. 239–58.
3 Zhivov, 'State myth', p. 242.   4 Zhivov, 'State myth', p. 242.

outflanked by culture. The poet, once the singer and admirer of the ruler and the state, then became their appraiser.

This chapter focuses mainly on the period from the mid-eighteenth to the early nineteenth centuries, starting with a brief 'prehistory' of the theme and concluding with a section on how the traditions were maintained or transformed in subsequent literature.

The figure of the ruler can be seen as an axis of sorts, connecting major stages of the literary tradition, such as mythology, fairy tale, and literature per se. Russian literary rulers include historical figures and fictional characters: the former are fictionalised and mythologised, the latter are relatively few. The textual culture of late medieval Muscovy incorporated images of rulers from the literature of early medieval Rus, in works such as the autobiographical *Instruction* (*Pouchenie*) by Prince Vladimir (Volodymyr) Monomakh (prince of Kyiv 1113–25), or the *Supplication* (*Molenie*) attributed to the perhaps fictional Daniil Zatochnik ('the Exile') in various versions from the early thirteenth century onwards. The chronicle tradition is devoted mainly to representations of rulers. Notable among quasi-fictional works from Muscovy itself is the macabre narrative *Tale of Drakula* (*Skazanie o Drakule*) of the late fifteenth century (see Chapter 1.1). The early historical rulers most subject to mythologisation were Ivan IV ('the Terrible', r. 1533–84), Peter I ('the Great', r. 1682–1725), and Catherine II (also 'the Great', r. 1762–96).[5] While Ivan and Peter are both associated with cruelty – boundless and senseless in the former, measured and expedient in the latter – Peter and Catherine share wisdom, tirelessness, and (at times) mercy as their archetypal features.

Early Panegyric: Peter I

The towering figure of Peter I was constructed in his lifetime and in the wake of his rule in the writings of Feofan Prokopovich, his personal ideologue and chief imperial theologian. Prokopovich was one of the wittiest and most learned people of his epoch, a gem in the scanty field of the barely nascent Russian literature. Given the overall scarcity of literary texts in the Petrine era, the emerging nation had to be shaped primarily by visual means, by an entire system of symbols and emblems (such was the title of the emblem book – *Symbola et emblemata* – commissioned by Peter in eight languages and

---

5 For a comparative analysis of the myths of Ivan and Peter, see Kevin M. F. Platt, *Terror and Greatness: Ivan and Peter as Russian Myths* (Ithaca: Cornell University Press, 2011).

printed in Amsterdam in 1705, which was the chief source of images to be put together in allegorical constructions).[6] In this somewhat logoclastic atmosphere, Prokopovich's texts were involved in shaping not only the figure of the ruler but verbal representation as such. His sermons and panegyrics (largely based on Roman panegyrics such as Pliny the Younger's *Panegyric of Trajan*) are full of passion and tenderness towards the ruler. For him, Peter was a true demiurge, the tsar creating a new country almost *ex nihilo*.[7] Peter was also a warrior, sharing the hardships of military campaigns with his subjects, soldiers, and mariners, and an avid and indefatigable student of sciences and skills in peacetime.

Throughout Prokopovich's texts, the first Russian emperor is presented as a composite character of the most important biblical and historical rulers. His 'Sermon on the Interment of Peter the Great' (*Slovo na pogrebenie Petra Velikogo*, 1725) is orchestrated by recurrent parallels to biblical and historical figures. Each paragraph opens with such a symbolic equation, very much in the spirit of the above-mentioned *Symbols and Emblems*:

> Russia, he was your Samson whom no one in the world expected would appear to you and at whom the whole world marveled when he did appear. . . . O Russia, he was your Japheth, who accomplished a deed unheard of in your history, the building and sailing of ships, a fleet new in the world but in no way inferior to the old . . . He was your Moses, O Russia! Are not his laws like a firm helmet of truth and like the unbreakable fetters of maleficence! . . . Russia, he was your Solomon, who had received his very great reason and wisdom from the Lord. . . . And he was, o Russian church, your David and Constantine . . . How great was his desire and seeking in him for greater learning among the clergy, a higher godliness among the people, and the greatest reform in every sphere of life.[8]

Feofan Prokopovich sees divine providence in the very fact that so many remarkable qualities were bestowed upon the youngest son of the previous tsar, Aleksei Mikhailovich (r. 1645–76), a youth who managed to outwit and defeat the many enemies and adversaries who surrounded him. Moreover, providence is construed as a constructive force: not only Peter's accession to

---

6 On the centrality of the visual in the eighteenth century, see Marcus C. Levitt, *The Visual Dominant in Eighteenth-Century Russia* (DeKalb: Northern Illinois University Press, 2011).

7 Lindsey Hughes, 'Secularization and westernization revisited: Art and architecture in seventeenth-century Russia', in Jarmo Kotilaine and Marshall Poe (eds.), *Modernizing Muscovy: Reform and Social Change in Seventeenth-Century Russia* (London: Routledge Curzon, 2005), p. 245.

8 Feofan Prokopovich, 'Sermon on the interment of Peter the Great', in Harold B. Segel (ed.), *The Literature of Eighteenth-Century Russia*, 2 vols. (New York: Dutton, 1967), vol. I, pp. 143–5.

the throne but also his every action as a ruler is directed and sanctified. For Prokopovich, a ruler like Peter is the best proof of God's blessing of the entire Russian nation. This construct, underlying all of his writings, seems to be rhetorical rather than theological: by these ornate, verbal, almost performative means, Feofan establishes and confirms Peter's right to the audacious renovation and rebuilding of an entire country.

It is in Prokopovich's universal and multifaceted portraits of the first Russian emperor that the future representation of Peter I as a virtual Renaissance man is rooted, as, for instance, in Aleksandr Pushkin's (1799–1837) 'Stanzas' (*Stansy*, 1826), addressed to Nicholas I (r. 1825–55) in the early days of his reign:

> The scholar's and the hero's role,
> The shipwright's, seaman's – were his own,
> For with his all-embracing soul
> He was the workman on the throne.[9]

The Classic Templates: From the First Odes to Pushkin

Literary genres in Russia can be defined and compared, inter alia, based on how they treat the figure of the ruler. Feofan Prokopovich's sermons and panegyrics paved the way for the solemn ode, a remarkably steady genre dating back to antiquity and continuing through the twentieth century. Since Pindar, celebratory odes have been addressed to rulers and have taken them as their main objects, the pinnacles of their composition. This is true for most European literatures. What fundamentally distinguishes the Russian situation is that for at least three decades – from the 1730s through the 1760s – the ode was basically the *only* active genre (see Chapter 3.3). It was the ode that served as the testing ground not just for state ideology but for emerging Russian versification. This accounts for the seamless interconnection between the histories of poetic forms and political ideas in Russia.

One of the main features of the transition from the panegyrics of the 1730s to the odes of the 1740s was the shift in emphasis from the ruler him- or herself to the state that he or she now embodied. The images of the state and the ruler that personified it became superimposed. In Russia this process was facilitated by the fact that during the entire odic period the throne was occupied almost exclusively by women, and that in the allegorical tradition

---

9 Alexander Pushkin, *Selected Lyric Poetry*, trans. James E. Falen (Evanston, IL: Northwestern University Press, 2009), p. 108.

lands and countries were always represented as female figures, regardless of their grammatical gender.

However, in order to demonstrate the ruler's might and versatility, the Russian ode had to combine male and female features, making the ruler almost an androgynous figure. The very first Russian Pindaric ode, 'The Solemn Ode on the Surrender of the City of Gdansk' (*Oda torzhestvennaia o sdache goroda Gdanska*, 1734), originally written in syllabic (and then rewritten in syllabo-tonic) verses, was composed by Vasilii Trediakovskii (1703–1768). An adaptation of Nicolas Boileau's (1636–1711) legendary 'Ode on the Taking of Namur' (1693), this ode adjusted the image of Louis, his virtues, and prowess to fit the image of the empress Anna Ioannovna (r. 1730–40):[10]

> What leader shines with wondrous helmet?
> Is it not Minerva hurling her spear?
> 'Tis evident that Heaven sent her,
> for in all respects she is a goddess;
> fearful is she even without her shield or aegis.
> 'Tis the Russian Empress Anna.[11]

The image of the empress combines not only conventionally male and female features but also brings together Europe and Asia, upon both of which she shines as a universal life-giving sun:

> Beautiful and favorable sun
> of the European and Asian sky!
> O Russian monarch!
> Many times blessed,
> because you are so dear to your subjects,
> because you rule them so benignly!
> Your name is already fearful to the world
> and the universe will not contain your glory.
> Wishing to be obedient to you,
> all of it marvels at the flower of beauty.[12]

In both Prokopovich's sermon and Trediakovskii's ode, a recurrent motif emerges – that of the ruler's glory being too great to be encompassed by the universe. Likewise, the ode itself is conceived as a three-dimensional structure, a kind of box, to be filled with a poetic account of the ruler's virtues and

---

10 See Gary Marker, 'The gender troubles of Feofan Prokopovich', *Canadian-American Slavic Studies* 54.1–3 (2020), 198–228.
11 Segel (ed.), *Literature of Eighteenth-Century Russia*, vol. I, p. 174.
12 Segel (ed.), *Literature of Eighteenth-Century Russia*, vol. I, p. 174.

deeds. Since this is a box, not a bottomless pit, it has its limits – in contrast with the virtues and deeds themselves, which overflow it.

Another crucial motif of the ode, dating back to its roots and bringing together Horatian and Pindaric modes, is that of the absolute dependence of this glory for longevity on the word of the singer, enhanced in Russian by the assonance of the words for 'glory' (*slava*) and 'word' (*slovo*). The Horatian understanding of the inextricable link between the eternal life of the state and the poet's immortality permeates the Russian odic consciousness.[13] These and other constituent motifs of the ode were adjusted and fine-tuned by Mikhail Lomonosov (1711–1765), a fisherman's son and a Renaissance man who was a true polymath (chemist, physicist, geologist, philologist, etc.) and, first and foremost, a poet. Despite Trediakovskii's early experiments with the ode, it was Lomonosov who earned the symbolic status of 'the Russian Pindar'. In the reign of Elizabeth (1741–62), Peter I's younger daughter, court life in general and the ode as its metonymy in particular settled down and acquired a regular rhythm, both political and poetic (see Chapter 3.3 on the metrical implications of the change of ruler).

Mythologically speaking, the odic ruler is a mixture of Mars, the Roman god of war, and Minerva, the goddess of wisdom, with all their multiple attributes. The military attributes of the ruler, relentlessly expanding his or her power, produce images of the Russian Empire's boundless space ('from ... to ...', derived from the German formula *von ... bis ...*). The complementary 'ethnographic' eulogy shows the ruler admired by the most diverse and remote subjects, represented as living at the extremities of the empire, still wearing animal skins and altogether violent, yet aspiring to enlightenment, as, for instance, in Lomonosov's ode addressed to Elizabeth in 1742:

> Your renown has captivated even those people
> Who wander among the beasts,
> Who graze with savage lions.
> They will rise up with us for your honour.

So, if in geographic space the ruler is an incarnation of Mars, accumulating new lands and territories, in the ethnographic space of the ode the ruler is an incarnation of Minerva, wisely charming and taming wild nations.[14] As mentioned above, one can barely distinguish between the body of the

---

13 Nadezhda Iu. Alekseeva, *Russkaia oda: Razvitie odicheskoi formy v XVII–XVIII vekakh* [The Russian ode: The development of odic form in the seventeenth and eighteenth centuries] (St Petersburg: Nauka, 2005).

14 Zhivov, 'State myth', pp. 249–51.

ruler and the body of the state, often represented as a huge female figure worked into the landscape. The best example of such an anthropomorphic landscape is to be found in Lomonosov's 'Ode on the Anniversary of the Empress Elizabeth's Ascent to the Throne' (*Oda na den' vosshestviia na prestol Imperatritsy Elizavety Petrovny*, 1748), in which we see Russia touching the clouds with her head, stretching her legs into the steppes, and resting her elbow on the Caucasus.

Lomonosov's major rival in the poetic field, the mordant critic of his odes' Baroque excesses, was Aleksandr Sumarokov (1717–1777). Though in practice Sumarokov's own odes were often close to the Lomonosovian archetype, they also contain some strikingly personal lines, imbued with tenderness, bitterness, and hope, as in an ode addressed to the future emperor Paul I (r. 1796–1801), then seventeen years old, on his name day, 29 June, in 1771:

> The planets and the earth are specks,
> And we, too, swirl about as dust.
> Empires are as mere scraps of clay.
> But what does he [Paul] think of the tsars
> That by this universe are raised to greatness?
> A tsar does not attain his status by the fact
> That he may choose to strike or to enslave,
> Or that all stand before his throne in fear,
> Or that he holds people in his power,
> And, if he wish, deprives them of their lives.[15]

The ideas expressed in these lines are also at the core of Sumarokov's plays. Building on Shakespeare and Corneille, Sumarokov develops his dramatic plots around coups d'état and spectacular royal violence. In *Hamlet* (*Gamlet*, 1748), a loose adaptation of Shakespeare's play provided with a happy ending and alluding to Elizabeth's own coup of 1741, the prince's path towards recapturing his father's throne by force emerges as the play's central theme. Similarly, *The False Dmitrii* (*Dmitrii Samozvanets*, 1770) stages the madness and fall of a tyrant, crushed by the temptations of absolute authority, and the successful coup d'état which destroys him, without questioning the principle of royal rule or the secretive politics of the court. The usurping tyrant and the benevolent ruler emerge in

---

15 A. P. Sumarokov, 'Oda gosudariu tsesarevichu Pavlu Petrovichu v den' ego tezoime- nitstva iiunia 29 chisla 1771 goda' [Ode to his highness the tsarevich Pavel Petrovich on his name day, 29 June 1771], in A. P. Sumarokov, *Izbrannye proizvedenia* [Selected works] (Leningrad: Sovetskii pisatel', 1957), p. 76.

Sumarokov's drama as two faces of sovereignty, often attributed to a single character.[16]

Each ode being a monument to a ruler (even a living one), the most frequent word used in connection with the ruler is *vozdvignut'* (to erect, raise up). The relationship between the poet and the ruler is described as vertical: the former looks up at the latter from below and exalts him or her even more with his poetic soaring. At the same time, the poet and the ruler are organically connected: in a sense, the poet is the ruler's substitute as a mediator between God and people. The poet's fame takes over the ruler's glory, using the very same formulae of geographic and ethnographic span. The first attempt to shift from the vertical to the horizontal plane takes place in Gavriil Derzhavin's poem 'On the Birth, in the North, of a Royal Scion' (*Na rozhdenie v severe porfirorodnogo otroka*, 1779) celebrating the birth (in 1777) of the future emperor Alexander I (r. 1801–25), son of Paul I and grandson of Catherine II. The tiny ruler-to-be is presented in the poem surrounded by fairies and genies, as if in an archetypal *les dons des fées* moment of a fairy tale à la Charles Perrault. In his characteristic manner, Derzhavin blends the serious occasion of the ode, its mischievous tone, and an essential message – godlike as he is, the ruler should first and foremost be a human on the throne:

> In a word, they blessed him, off'ring
> Every faculty and gift,
> And each pow'r brought to perfection
> Needful for a king of men;
> But the last, who wished to waken
> Virtue in the infant, said:
> May you govern well your passions,
> Hold the throne, yet be – a man![17]

This intertwining of the panegyric and playful is perfected in 'Felitsa' (*Felitsa*, 1782), Derzhavin's most famous ode, which played a pivotal role both in his own life and in the history of the genre. Opening with an almost liturgical apostrophe, 'O Princess, fair as a divinity' ('Bogopodobnaia tsarevna'), the ode first introduces the empress as a supreme, divine being, elevated above the vanity of the world and the human foibles of her subjects, and then drifts away from her godlike qualities to focus on her consummate humanness.[18] The

---

16 On Sumarokov's tragedies, see Kirill Ospovat, *Terror and Pity: Aleksandr Sumarokov and the Theater of Power in Elizabethan Russia* (Boston: Academic Studies Press, 2016).
17 G. R. Derzhavin, *Poetic Works: A Bilingual Album*, ed. Alexander Levitsky, Brown Slavic Contributions 12 (Providence, RI: Brown University, 2001), p. 144.
18 Derzhavin, *Poetic Works*, p. 27.

principal novelty of 'Felitsa' is the poet's exquisite transgression of the conventional distance between the ruler and her subjects; the poet speaks to her over the heads of her courtiers (from whose restless multitude she is starkly separated). Moreover, the poet dares to speak about himself, about his predilections and silly habits, *alongside* those of the ruler. This is even done syntactically, with subordinate clauses often replaced by compound ones; for example, following a list of Catherine's everyday pursuits, the poet continues: 'But I, not rising until noontime, / Drink coffee and enjoy a smoke; / I make vacations of my work days.'[19] The very continuity, or, rather, *contiguity* of the poet and the ruler completely alters the previous pattern of their relationship. At the same time, in this groundbreaking text Derzhavin returns to some features of the Peter described and admired in Feofan Prokopovich's sermon (first and foremost the eagerness to learn and work):

> Not following your *murzas'* custom,
> You often go about on foot,
> And only have the simplest dishes
> Permitted in your dining room.
> Not valuing your leisure hours,
> You read and write before a lectern,
> And grant a true felicity
> Unto all mortals by your writings.[20]

The playful rhetoric of 'Felitsa' is based on paradoxical, satirical eulogy.[21] The norm is presented as something incredible, extraordinary, unheard of:

> And 'tis a thing unheard of also,
> Though worthy just of you alone,
> That you permit the people boldly
> To know and think of everything
> Both in the open and the secret,
> And that you do prohibit no one
> To speak of you both true and false.[22]

In his biography of Derzhavin, published in 1931, the poet Vladislav Khodasevich (1886–1939) concluded that 'Felitsa' was, in effect, a destruction of the very genre that it purported to represent: 'The ode as such was not transformed, because the poem had ceased to be an ode; to such an extent

---

19 Derzhavin, *Poetic Works*, p. 29.   20 Derzhavin, *Poetic Works*, p. 28.
21 Iurii K. Shcheglov, 'Igrovaia retorika Felitsy' ['Felitsa's playful rhetoric'], in *Izbrannye trudy* [Selected works] (Moscow: Rossiiskii gosudarstvennyi gumanitarnyi universitet, 2013), pp. 168–88.
22 Derzhavin, *Poetic Works*, p. 133.

was the odic tradition of Russo-French classicism destroyed in it.'[23] Even if this statement is a little bit of a stretch as a whole, Derzhavin's mischievous ode – with its notable daring (the levelling of the author and the ruler) and its emphasis on *mercy* as the key feature of the ruler – does pave the way for what is perhaps the most important scene representing the ruler in all of Russian literature: the scene of the encounter between Catherine II and Masha (Maria Ivanovna) Mironova, the 'captain's daughter' of Pushkin's novel of the same name (*Kapitanskaia dochka*, 1836).

Masha is the daughter of the intrepid Captain Mironov, a commandant of a Siberian fortress who was killed during the rebellion of the Cossack Emelian Pugachev (1773–5). She has come a long way to meet the empress, seeking a pardon for her unfairly condemned beloved, Petr Grinev – yet she does not recognise Catherine in 'a lady with a lap dog' into whom she happens to run:

> Suddenly a little white dog of English breed barked and ran towards her. Maria Ivanovna was frightened and stopped. At the same moment she heard a pleasant woman's voice:
>
> 'Don't be afraid, she doesn't bite.'
>
> And Maria Ivanovna saw a lady sitting on a bench opposite the monument. Maria Ivanovna sat down at the other end of the bench. The lady looked at her intently; Maria Ivanovna, for her part, casting several sidelong glances, managed to examine her from head to foot. She was wearing a white morning dress, a nightcap, and a jacket. She seemed about forty. Her face, plump and red-cheeked, expressed dignity and calm, and her light-blue eyes and slight smile had an ineffable charm. The lady was first to break the silence.[24]

Not recognising the empress, Masha speaks to her quite freely – to the extent of crying, 'Oh, that's not true!', when the former says that the petition for Grinev would never be granted by the empress because 'he joined the impostor ... as an immoral and pernicious scoundrel'. This exclamation makes the empress 'flush all over', yet she does not reveal her true identity: she keeps pretending to be just someone 'received at court'. After listening to Grinev's true story, Catherine changes her mind and, summoning Masha to the palace several hours later, not only grants her petition but also, feeling

---

23 Vladislav Khodasevich, *Derzhavin: A Biography*, trans. Angela Brintlinger (Madison: University of Wisconsin Press, 2007), pp. 97–8.

24 Alexander Pushkin, *The Captain's Daughter*, in *Novels, Tales, Journeys: The Complete Prose of Alexander Pushkin*, trans. Richard Pevear and Larissa Volokhonsky (New York: Alfred A. Knopf, 2016), pp. 344–5.

'in debt to Captain Mironov's daughter', 'takes upon herself to see her established'.[25]

Meeting the empress, Masha Mironova faces personified history itself.[26] Such an encounter of a fictional character with a historical figure is at the very core of Pushkin's adaptation of Walter Scott's paradigm of historical writing, with his love for placing historical figures into fictional worlds. Likewise, Peter Grinev (the storyteller) meets Pugachev (the impostor) on various occasions and is 'pardoned' and saved by him at the decisive hour. Mercy and humanity are the two chief features of the ruler for Pushkin in the 1830s.[27] In granting mercy to the young protagonists of the novel, both 'rulers', the empress and the imposter, go well beyond their respective 'laws' and ignore the opinions of their respective 'courtiers'.

The same thing happens in Pushkin's poem *Angelo* (*Andzhelo*, 1833).[28] Based on the plot of Shakespeare's *Measure for Measure*, it, too, substitutes mercy for the ruler's justice. Angelo acknowledges that he has committed a crime and should be sentenced to death; yet at the last minute:

> Isabella
> Angelically petitioned for his soul,
> And even knelt before the Duke to plead,
> 'Have mercy, lord,' she said.
> 'Do not condemn
> This man for my sake. Ere he cast his eyes
> On me, he'd lived (as far as I can tell,
> And so I think) a just and honest life.
> Forgive him!'
> And the Duke forgave him.

25 Pushkin, *Captain's Daughter*, p. 346.
26 See A. K. Zholkovskii, 'Ochnye stavki s vlastitelem. Iz istorii odnoi pushkinskoi paradigmy' [Face-to-face encounters with the ruler. From the history of one Pushkinian paradigm], in *Ochnye stavki s vlastitelem. Stat'i o russkoi literature* [Face-to-face encounters with the ruler. Essays on Russian literature] (Moscow: Rossiiskii gosudarstvennyi gumanitarnyi universitet, 2011), pp. 115–38.
27 Iu. M. Lotman, 'Ideinaia struktura "Kapitanskoi Dochki"' [The ideological structure of 'The Captain's Daughter'], in Iu. K. Lotman, *Pushkin* (St Petersburg: Iskusstvo-SPb, 1995), pp. 212–27. See also N. Iu. Alekseeva, 'K voprosu o teme milosti v russkoi literature XVIII veka' [On the theme of mercy in Russian literature of the eighteenth century], in A. Kostin (ed.), *Von Wenigen (Ot nemnogikh)* [From the few] (St Petersburg: Izdatel'stvo Pushkinskogo doma, 2008), pp. 8–17.
28 See the annotated edition by Aleksandr Dolinin: *Aleksandr Pushkin, Andzhelo, kommentarii Aleksandra Dolinina* [Aleksandr Pushkin. Angelo. Commentary by Aleksandr Dolinin] (Moscow: Ruteniia, 2022).

In both *Angelo* and *The Captain's Daughter*, the mercy scene bears the essential meaning.

The foundational text of what would later be known as the 'St Petersburg text' of Russian literature is Pushkin's *The Bronze Horseman* (*Mednyi vsadnik*, 1833), with its famous subtitle 'a Petersburg tale'. It establishes the image of the ruler through his creation, the marvellous, incredible, paradoxical city of St Petersburg – the city that was not meant to be and yet emerged out of a swamp in spite of nature's resistance and only due to the supernatural will of Peter I (just one of the distant echoes of Feofan Prokopovich's rhetoric of uniqueness to be found in Pushkin's verse). The text of the poem moves from panegyric to paradox, from the opening ode to 'Peter's creation', shifting from the spatial (*von . . . bis . . .*) to the temporal panorama ('where before there was . . . now there is . . .'), and finally to the tragedy of madness at the end. Pushkin uses the odic mode in all the descriptions of the city and of the monument that dominates it – the equestrian statue of Peter I.

Yet the first of Pushkin's writings to be focused on the figure of the ruler was his drama *Boris Godunov* (*Boris Godunov*, 1825).[29] Pushkin's Boris is a curious, contradictory figure, a rapacious ruler with no right to the crown, who, the author implies, was prepared to pay for his power with the murder of a boy, Ivan IV's son Prince Dmitrii. Yet Pushkin also focuses on him as a tender father to his children and a thoughtful statesman. One of the most important reflections on the figure and destiny of the ruler in the play is uttered by Pimen, the chronicler. Addressing the young monk Grigorii, who would later proclaim himself to be the supposedly surviving prince Dmitrii, Pimen juxtaposes two 'great tsars', Ivan the Terrible (*groznyi*, here rendered as 'the Dread'), who is 'wearied by executions', and his son Tsar Fyodor (i.e. Feodor), whose meekness finally made Russia thrive – yet not for long:

> Ivan the Dread sought peace and consolation
> By living like a monk inside his court.
> His palace, full of vain and haughty men,
> Took on the aspect of a monastery;
> [. . .]
>   And here I saw the Tsar,
> Wearied by fits of rage, and executions –
> Right here – the brooding, silent, dread Iván.
> [. . .]
> And contemplate his son, Tsar Fyódor, too,

29 Alexander Pushkin, *Boris Godunov and Other Dramatic Works*, trans. James E. Falen (Oxford: Oxford University Press, 2007).

Who sat upon the throne and yearned in vain
To lead a silent hermit's humble life.
He made his private rooms a cell for prayer,
Where all the grievous burdens of his power
Would not disturb his shy and saintly soul.[30]

It is at this pivotal moment that Grigorii's idea of assuming the guise of Dmitrii takes shape.[31] For Sumarokov in *The False Dmitrii*, Dmitrii had been simply the embodiment of evil, since there could be nothing more terrifying than the idea of taking the place of the Lord's anointed on earth. For the writer and historian Nikolai Karamzin (1766–1826), Dmitrii was, first and foremost, providence's tool against Boris Godunov ('As if by the action of supernatural powers Dmitrii's shadow rose from the coffin').[32] Pushkin turns him into a kind of Romantic hero, who prefers a brief life full of events and passions – a life to be *remembered* forever (a version of Greek *kleos*) – to the long, calm, eventless existence of a monk.

Literary Rulers after Pushkin

Aleksei Konstantinovich Tolstoi (1817–1875) took up and adapted the theme in his dramatic trilogy *The Death of Ivan the Terrible* (*Smert' Ioanna Groznogo*, 1866), *Tsar Feodor Ioannovich* (*Tsar' Fedor Ioannovich*, 1868), and *Tsar Boris* (*Tsar' Boris*, 1870). Covering the period from 1584 to 1605, the plays of the trilogy each illustrate a particular kind of monarch and a particular philosophy of how to rule the state. Each ruler has a tragic flaw that brings on disaster. The central play, *Tsar Feodor Ioannovich*, is perhaps the most important. Tolstoi's Feodor is a figure of the utmost piety and humanity, a man whose deeply ingrained benevolence and humility are almost unimaginable in a Russian tsar. He wants to act virtuously and piously, seeks to establish harmony among his most intransigent subjects, and aspires to concord in the etymological sense of the word (from Latin *cum corde*, 'with the heart', 'in harmony').

---

30 Pushkin, *Boris Godunov*, pp. 22–3.
31 On the treatment of the prince-pretender, see Olga Maiorova, 'Tsarevich-samozvanets v sotsial'noi mifologii poreformennoi epokhi' [The tsarevich-pretender in the social mythology of post-reform Russia], *Rossia-Russia. Novaia Seriia: Kul'turnye praktiki v ideologicheskoi perspective* [Rossiia/Russia. New series: Cultural practices in ideological perspective] 3.11 (1999), 204–32.
32 Nikolai Karamzin, *Istoriia gosudarstva rossiiskogo* [History of the Russian state], 12 vols. (St Petersburg: Tipografia N. Grecha, 1818–29), vol. XI (1824), p. 124.

Pushkin's line, 'God came to love the meekness of this Tsar', is echoed in Tsar Feodor's words to Godunov, his brother-in-law, in Tolstoi's tragedy:

> You see, I know that I am not able to take the reins of government into my own hands. What manner of a Tsar am I? It is not difficult to deceive me and cheat me in all affairs. In one thing only I will not be deceived: when I must decide whether a thing is black or white – no, I will not be deceived then! This, brother-in-law, does not require wisdom but merely fairness.[33]

Whereas Ivan thought nothing of executing someone for the slightest offence, Feodor is made to pardon everyone and to take the blame upon himself. The major dramatic collisions of the tragedy unfold beyond its main character; the tsar is simply unwilling to partake in the struggle and would be happy to give up his inherited title. Still, he must rule, and abdication is something that he cannot do.

Besides tragedy, another notable strand in the depiction of rulers in the later nineteenth century was parody, and the principal representative of this strand in fiction is *The History of a Town* (*Istoriia odnogo goroda*, 1870) by Mikhail Saltykov-Shchedrin (1826–1889), with its ingenious use of conventional historiography for utterly burlesque purposes. The town of Glupov (meaning 'Stupidville') is utopia and dystopia in one. Shchedrin, once a state bureaucrat himself, creates its topsy-turvy world by turning inside out not only specific features of the Russian bureaucracy but also all the elements of the myth of the genesis of Russian state-building. It takes the form of a history of the city's mayors (*gradonachal'niki*), presented as grotesque parodies of Russia's rulers. Usually interpreted as a bitter satire of Russia's history, *The History of a Town* also satirises rulers in general: the rulers are not as bad and weak as their Russian prototypes alone but as any and every political order, in the author's view. Both the perverted and the 'civilised' worlds have no future.

The 1860s was a productive period for diverse representations of the ruler. In the writings of Lev Tolstoi (1828–1910), we find both a continuation and a reversal of Pushkin's idea of history: if one of Pushkin's major claims in *The Captain's Daughter* is that history is made not only by people such as Catherine II and Pugachev but also by the Masha Mironovas and Peter Grinevs of this world, Tolstoi takes this philosophy to its extremes – history is made and moved *only* by simple yet powerful people such as Captain Tushin or Platon Karataev, the two most humble and luminous characters in

---

33 Alexei Tolstoy, *Tsar Fyodor Ivanovitch: A Play in Five Acts*, trans. Jenny Covan (London: Brentano's, 1922), p. 55.

War and Peace (*Voina i mir*, 1868–9). In contrast with Pushkin, Tolstoi rarely brings his 'ordinary' fictional characters into direct exchanges with rulers. A significant exception is Nikolai Rostov's encounter with Alexander I in *War and Peace*. Rostov's almost ecstatic perception of the emperor ('his rapturous senses felt [Alexander's] approach [. . .] this sun moved ever closer, spreading rays of mild and majestic light')[34] is undermined by the latter's peremptoriness, in stark contrast to the 'ineffable charm' in Pushkin's depiction of Alexander's grandmother, Catherine.

Some thirty years later, Tolstoi wrote *Hadji Murat* (*Khadzhi-Murat*, 1904) – one of the most heartbreaking stories of Russian war in the Caucasus (see Chapter 4.8). Both the Russian emperor and the imam Shamil are represented here as cruel and paltry creatures. The portrait of Nicholas I in *Hadji Murat* is arguably the most odious depiction of a ruler in Russian literature. The chapter which contains it was censored from pre-revolutionary editions and was enthusiastically highlighted in Soviet times. The ruler's portrait is given on a specific date, 1 January 1852:

> Nicholas, in a black tunic without epaulettes, but with small shoulder straps, sat at the table, his enormous body tight-laced across the over-grown belly, and looked at the entering men with his immobile, lifeless gaze. His long, white face, with its enormous, receding brow emerging from the slicked-down hair at his temples, artfully joined to the wig that covered the bald patch, was especially cold and immobile that day. His eyes, always dull, looked duller than usual; his compressed lips under the twirled mustaches, and his fat cheeks, propped on his high collar, freshly shaved, with regular, sausage-shaped side-whiskers left on them, and his chin pressed into the collar, gave his face an expression of displeasure and even of wrath. The cause of this mood was fatigue.[35]

The relentlessly meticulous details combine to create a quintessential image of inflated nothingness and artificiality. The 'lifelessness' of Nicholas's gaze is repeated throughout the novel. The cause of the fatigue mentioned by Tolstoi was Nicholas's one-night stand with a young innocent girl, who told him how 'when still a child, she had fallen in love with him from his portraits, had idolized him'.[36] Comparing the petite girl with the 'imposing shoulders' of his permanent lover, Nelidova, and having some unpleasant

---

34 Leo Tolstoy, *War and Peace*, trans. Richard Pevear and Larissa Volokhonsky (New York: Alfred Knopf, 2007), p. 255.
35 Leo Tolstoy, *Hadji Murat*, in *'The Death of Ivan Ilyich' and Other Stories*, trans. Richard Pevear and Larissa Volokhonsky (New York: Alfred A. Knopf, 2009), p. 437.
36 Tolstoy, *Hadji Murat*, p. 443.

après-goût, he tries to stifle this feeling: 'he began thinking about something that always soothed him: about what a great man he was.'[37] Tolstoi is looking back at Nicholas I from the time of his great grandson, Nicholas II (r. 1894–1917) – in a sense, taking over Pushkin's perspective in the 'Stanzas' discussed earlier, yet reversing it by projecting the image of an ancestor onto that of the current ruler not in order to regain evanescent hope but rather to dispel remaining illusions.

Literary Rulers after the Revolution

Eclipsed by other lyric genres in the nineteenth century, the ode and the eulogistic mode come back in the 1920s, after the revolution. The year 1923 marks the bifurcation of the ode, a split between the genre's pragmatics and poetics. The former is associated, first and foremost, with Vladimir Maiakovskii's (1893–1930) poems (rarely designated as odes per se), celebrating anniversaries of the October Revolution; the latter is associated with Osip Mandelshtam's (1891–1938) deliberately obscure writings, permeated with allusions that reach back to Ovid and Pindar.

In the 1920s, the key text for the treatment of the leader (*vozhd'*), rather than the ruler as such, is Maiakovskii's poem *Vladimir Ilich Lenin* (*Vladimir Il'ich Lenin*), composed in the wake of Lenin's death in January 1924. It is in this poem – written in Maiakovskii's characteristic 'staircase' (*lesenka*) form (see Box 1.3) – that a new canon emerges, a new myth, and together with it the very language of representing a leader that would be taken up and developed by generations of Soviet poets. At the same time, this new mythology was deeply rooted in the old one:

> And smoothly
> > Into construction's docks
> Sailed
> > The colossal country of Soviets.
> Lenin
> > Himself
> > > Heaves timber and iron
> To patch up
> > The breaks and ruptures [. . .][38]

---

37 Tolstoy, *Hadji Murat*, p. 444.
38 Vladimir Mayakovsky, *Vladimir Ilyich Lenin*, trans. Dorian Rottenberg (Ripon: Smokestack Books, 2017), pp. 156–7.

The image of the docks and Lenin's readiness to fix 'the breaks and ruptures' with his own hands bring to mind not only the Horatian topos of the ship of state but also distant echoes of Peter I as he was represented from Feofan Prokopovich to Pushkin. Lenin is seen here through the image of Peter as a new Peter. Thus, the image of the great leader is associated with that of the great ruler. Of course, Lenin cannot be presented as the Lord's anointed, yet Maiakovskii manages to integrate this tradition in reverse:

> Your divinity's decease
> > Won't rouse
> > a mote of feeling.
> No!
> > Today
> > > Real pain
> > > > Chills every heart.
> We're burying
> > The earthliest of beings
> That ever came to play an earthly part.[39]

It is this poem that provided the entire Soviet era to come with rhetorical questions and ready-made formulae to talk about Lenin, such as the now proverbial 'the most humane of all us humans' (*samyi chelovechnyi chelovek*).[40]

Among those who were deeply influenced by Maiakovskii's rhetoric were Boris Pasternak (1890–1960) and Osip Mandelshtam. This is how Lenin appears towards the end of Pasternak's 'Sublime Malady' (*Vysokaia bolezn'*, 1923–8):

> If he appealed to proven facts,
> He knew that when he rinsed their mouths
> With the logic of his simple words,
> These became the pith of history.
> Not wheedling, courting, but at ease
> Before her face, always prepared
> To question, study, and to goad,
> He was her trusted confidant.
> In envy only of the ages,
> And jealous of their jealousy
> Alone, he ruled the tides of thought,
> And through that mastery – the State.[41]

---

39 Mayakovsky, *Vladimir Ilyich Lenin*, pp. 36–7.
40 Mayakovsky, *Vladimir Ilyich Lenin*, pp. 42–3.
41 Boris Pasternak, 'Sublime malady', in *Poems*, trans. Eugene M. Kayden (Ann Arbor: University of Michigan Press, 1959), p. 73.

The very wording here is odic – with strong stylistic echoes of Lomonosovian rhetorical devices.

In the summer of 1934, Joseph Stalin telephoned Pasternak to talk about Mandelshtam, who had been arrested in May. This phone call is among the most notorious instances of direct communication between poet and ruler and is another Walter-Scottian (or Hegelian) moment of an 'ordinary man' running into history itself. Pasternak was so dumbfounded that he could not even concentrate on defending Mandelshtam and famously suggested at the end that he and Stalin 'should meet at some point to talk about life and death'.[42] After a short silence, Stalin hung up.[43]

Unlike large numbers of the arrests of the 1930s, Mandelshtam was detained for a reason. In November 1933 he had written his Stalin epigram, famous for its first line: 'We live, not feeling the land beneath us' ('My zhivem, pod soboiu ne chuia strany'). In his lifetime, Mandelshtam oscillated between accepting the surrounding reality and rejecting it; 1933 was a period of rejection, at which point he wrote the epigram, with its terrifying image of the 'Kremlin highlander':

> Like worms his thick fingers are fat,
> His words like pound weights are correct,
> His cockroach moustache is full of laughter,
> His army boots shine, he is sought after[44]

Mandelshtam read this poem to over a dozen people. He was subsequently arrested but sentenced to only three years of internal exile, and he was later even allowed to join his wife in Voronezh. There, in Voronezh, the pendulum swung the other way, and Mandelshtam decided that he should now accept Soviet reality and be understood by everyone. Three years after the epigram, he wrote his 'Ode to Stalin' (*Oda Stalinu*, 1937):

> He is bending over a podium as if over a mountain
> Into the hillocks of heads. A debtor stronger than any claim.
> His mighty eyes are decisively kind,

42 L. M. Batkin, 'Son razuma. O sotsiokul'turnyh mashtabah lichnosti Stalina' [Reason's sleep. The sociocultural dimensions of Stalin's personality], in *Osmyslit' kul't Stalina* [Rethinking the cult of Stalin] (Moscow: Progress, 1989), p. 10.

43 See Irina Paperno, 'Sovetskii opyt, avtobiographicheskoe pis'mo i istoricheskoe soznanie: Ginzburg, Gertsen, Gegel'' [Soviet experience, the autobiographical letter, and historical consciousness: Ginzburg, Herzen, Hegel], *Novoe literaturnoe obozrenie* [New literary review] 68.4 (2004), 102–27.

44 Osip Mandelstam, 'Stalin's epigram', trans. Ian Probstein, in Charles Bernstein, 'Ian Probstein: Three translations of Osip Mandelstam's "Stalin's epigram"', *Jacket2* (11 Aug. 2014), https://jacket2.org/commentary/ian-probstein-mandelstam-stalin-epigram, accessed 1 Feb. 2023.

His thick eyebrow is glaring at somebody,
And I would like to mark with an arrow
The firmness of his mouth – the father of stubborn speeches;
His eyelid, sculpted, complicated and abrupt,
Projects, verily, out of a million frames.
He is – all sincerity, he is – all brass of fame.
And his farsighted hearing is intolerant to muffling.
His careworn little wrinkles are playfully stretching
To reach out to all who are ready for living and dying[45]

The images unfold in such a way that a new odic space is created: in the middle is the vertical, with a mountain turning into a hero; on the periphery is the horizontal, a square full of people, the mounds of human heads stretching off into the distance. The close-up of a hero on a rostrum with a crowd below may also refer to a famous pictorial representation of Lenin and to some newsreels of Stalin himself.[46]

Many scholars have been eager to see in this poem some traces of Aesopian language, some hints at a deeper content. Yet there are none. Mandelshtam's tragedy was his deep belief that Stalin had read his epigram and yet showed mercy to his humble subject – just like Peter I or Catherine II in the olden days. Just as Pushkin – addressing his 'Stanzas' to Nicholas I, who had just released him from exile – believed that he would enjoy the trust and confidence of the emperor and be allowed to speak his mind, so Mandelshtam hoped to be accepted. Had he himself accepted self-exile, maybe he would have survived.[47] As Mikhail Gasparov has shown in his analysis of the ode, Mandelshtam models his relationship with the ruler on Ovid's with Augustus. Like Ovid, Mandelshtam is exiled; like Ovid, he feels guilty; like Ovid, he dreams of being pardoned and of reuniting with his severe yet fair judge, the ruler, in their common cultural area.[48]

The story of the relationship of poets (and writers) and rulers, past and present, in the story of Russian culture may be continued further into the

45 Osip Mandelstam, 'Ode to Stalin', trans. Gregory Freidin, in Freidin, *A Coat of Many Colors: Osip Mandelstam and His Mythologies of Self-Presentation* (Berkeley: University of California Press, 2010), p. 258.

46 For a close reading of the ode and an overview of Mandelshtam's 'civic lyrics' of the mid-1930s, see Mikhail L. Gasparov, *O. Mandel'shtam. Grazhdanskaia lirika 1937 goda* [O. Mandelshtam. His civic lyrics of 1937] (Moscow: Rossiiskii gosudarstvennyi gumanitarnyi universitet, 1996).

47 Gleb Morev, *Osip Mandel'shtam. Fragmenty literaturnoi biographii. 1920–1930-e gody* [Osip Mandelshtam. Fragments of a literary biography. 1920s–1930s] (Moscow: Novoe izdatel'stvo, 2022).

48 Gasparov, *O. Mandel'shtam*, pp. 94–5.

twentieth and twenty-first centuries. It is, as we have seen, a process in which the figure of the ruler functions as a space into which broader ideas can be projected. Perhaps more than in other cultures, the poet and the ruler do not just sit side by side but play complementary roles in a larger structure, shaped by ideological frameworks. A specific mythology of power is created, is developed, and takes on a life of its own. The ruler is a fictitious figure that lets us construct the future, time, and ourselves as a community. To speak about the ruler in Russian literature is to speak about the nature of literature; to write about the ruler is to write about oneself.

Further Reading

Brandenberger, David, and Kevin Platt (eds.), *Epic Revisionism: Russian History and Literature as Stalinist Propaganda* (Madison: University of Wisconsin Press, 2006).

Maiorova, Olga, *From the Shadow of Empire: Defining the Russian Nation through Cultural Mythology, 1855 – 1870* (Madison: University of Wisconsin Press, 2010).

Pavlov, Andrei, and Maureen Perrie, *Ivan the Terrible* (London, New York: Routledge, 2013).

Plamper, Jan, *The Stalin Cult: A Study in the Alchemy of Power* (New Haven: Yale University Press, 2012).

Platt, Kevin M. F., *Terror and Greatness: Ivan and Peter as Russian Myths* (Ithaca: Cornell University Press, 2011).

Uspenskij, Boris, and Viktor Zhivov, 'Tsar and God: Semiotic aspects of the sacralization of the monarch in Russia', in Marcus C. Levitt (ed.), *'Tsar and God' and Other Essays in Russian Cultural Semiotics* (Boston: Academic Studies Press, 2012), pp. 1–112.

Wortman, Richard, *Scenarios of Power* (Princeton: Princeton University Press, 2006).

Zhivov, Victor, 'The State myth in the era of Enlightenment and its destruction in late eighteenth-century Russia', in Uspenskij and Zhivov, *'Tsar and God' and other Essays*, pp. 239–58.

4.3

The Lowly Civil Servant

CATHY POPKIN

Low-level civil servants were both an inescapable fact of Russian reality and a product of the Russian – and Russophone – literary imagination. The elaborate bureaucratic hierarchy that structured government service in St Petersburg also shaped the Petersburg text.

Peter I's (r. 1682–1725) rank-based system had been elaborated in the first decades of the eighteenth century as part of the emperor-tsar's creation of a new capital city. Peter complemented his hubristic act of civil engineering (constructing his city on a swamp) with a formidable array of social reforms, most pertinently his imperial table of ranks. The table established three parallel hierarchies for civil, court, and military service, respectively: the ranks and titles of each were arrayed in descending order, with the first class – chancellors, generals, and the like – at the top, down to the fourteenth class (registrars, foot soldiers) at the very bottom.

The best-known minor civil servants of literary provenance are nineteenth-century creatures, poor Petersburg clerks (often copy clerks) ripped from the bottom half of the bureaucratic hierarchy, for whom the pecking order was debilitating. Insignificant, impoverished, downtrodden, meek, a faceless cog in the bureaucratic machine, the lowly civil servant was cast as a victim of his rank, powerless and deserving of pity. So enduring has this narrative of victimhood proved that it's easy to forget that the table of ranks was conceived not to subjugate but to enable the enterprising to *rise* through the ranks by dint of education and good work (as opposed to birthright), acquiring thereby not merely a higher position but potentially even nobility status (personal nobility at the ninth class, hereditary nobility at the eighth). In this vehicle for advancement Peter sought to break the stranglehold of the landowning gentry, but the social mobility he envisioned for state employees was real. It also served to awaken desire and generate plot.

Tales of the poor civil servant (*bednyi chinovnik*) became popular in the 1820s, with such unremarkable, everyday characters edging out the more dramatic figures of Romanticism.[1] But only in the 1830s was the humble clerk embraced by high culture. Aleksandr Pushkin (1799–1837) himself wrote two *chinovnik* texts, the first a short story, 'The Stationmaster' (*Stantsionnyi smotritel'*, 1830), the second a narrative poem, *The Bronze Horseman* (*Mednyi vsadnik*, 1833). Nikolai Gogol's (1809–1852) entry into the sweepstakes, 'The Diary of a Madman' (*Zapiski sumasshedshego*), came out in 1835, together with 'Nevsky Prospect' (*Nevskii Prospekt*) and followed by 'The Nose' (*Nos*, 1836). Gogol's acknowledged masterpiece of the genre, 'The Overcoat' (*Shinel'*), appeared in 1842 to universal acclaim – and widespread imitation. Fedor Dostoevskii's (1821–1881) first novel, *Poor Folk* (*Bednye liudi*), was published in early 1846, followed by *The Double* (*Dvoinik*, 1846) soon afterward. These works and their clerks in their literary heyday (1830–50) will be the focus of this chapter.

The Back Story

What took this character so long to coalesce when Muscovy's network of government chancelleries had emerged in embryonic form during the fifteenth century; was formally incorporated by the mid-sixteenth; and by the seventeenth comprised 150 government bureaus with innumerable bureaucrats to administer them, an endless supply of records to keep, and armies of scribes (*pod"iachie*) to copy them? While less elaborate than Peter's, the Muscovite org chart, too, was unabashedly hierarchical and the copy clerks chronically underpaid.[2]

Whatever hardships they may have endured, the pre-Petrine clerks inspired no outpouring of sympathetic portraits. Not until the eighteenth century did they become regular subject matter, and then chiefly as the target of satirical essays: Aleksandr Sumarokov (1717–1777), whose concerns were linguistic and orthographic, described copy clerks with contempt, but not for being civil servants; virtually all nobles, Sumarokov included, were in state service themselves. Rather, he decried the copyists' butchery of the Russian language in such diatribes as 'On Copy Clerks' (*O kopiistakh*, 1759) and 'To

---

1 Aleksandr Tseitlin, *Povesti o bednom chinovnike Dostoevskogo (k istorii odnogo siuzheta)* [Dostoevskii's tales of the poor civil servant (on the history of a theme)] (Moscow: Armianskii literaturno-khudozhestvennyi kruzhok, 1923), pp. 3–5.

2 Peter Brown, 'Muscovite government bureaus', *Russian History* 10.3 (1983), 269–72, 282–3; Brown, 'The service land chancellery clerks of seventeenth-century Russia: Their regime, salaries, and economic survival', *Jahrbücher für Geschichte Osteuropas* [Yearbooks for the history of eastern Europe] 52.1 (2004), 33–45.

Clerks, Copyists, or Scribes, that is, To Anyone Who Writes Without Knowing What He's Writing' (*K pod"iachemu, pistsu ili pisariu, to est', k takomu cheloveku, kotoryi pishet, ne znaia togo, chto on pishet*, 1759) – all those inept scribblers who are destroying 'our beautiful language'.[3] Other eighteenth-century writers penned satirical verse exposing more venal forms of corruption; in Vasilii Maikov's (1728–1778) 'Thief and Copy Clerk' (*Vor i pod"iachii*, 1767) the two 'criminals' differ not only in that the thief prowls in the dark while the bribe-taking clerk steals shamelessly in the bright light of day, but in that the thief who robs a copy clerk is only stealing from a fellow criminal, whereas the bribe-taking clerk defrauds the innocent.

Even in the first two decades of the nineteenth century, the copy clerk was much maligned, remaining the stuff of satirical journals. Not until the 1820s do these impoverished civil servants acquire plots of their own, turning up in short prose, on stage, and in longer works of diverse style and genre.[4] What unified these early *chinovnik* texts (and distinguished them from the decade's popular society tales) was their tone: while the society tale cultivated a detached, urbane sensibility, the *chinovnik* story sought an affective response – pathos, especially with regard to the beaten-down protagonist.[5] Well established by the end of the 1820s, the lowly civil servant became the active ingredient in both 'high' literary reworkings and programmatic criticism in the decades to come.

The 1830s and 1840s, which brought the poor, victimised clerk into the literary mainstream, also introduced the intervening variable of Vissarion Belinskii (1811–1848), the influential literary critic whose authoritative readings set the stage for everyone else's (see Box 5.1). Belinskii built an entire platform on the era's *chinovnik* stories. Publishing his first major article in 1834, he bewailed the absence of a national literature, only to herald the birth of a magnificent new Russian literary tradition with the publication of Gogol's first Petersburg stories in 1835.[6] Belinskii's excitement, which only gained in intensity with Gogol's 'The Overcoat' in 1842, centred on a few things. First, there was his own unwavering commitment to social justice,

---

3 Marcus C. Levitt, 'The barbarians among us, or Sumarokov's views on orthography', in *Early Modern Russian Letters: Texts and Contexts* (Boston: Academic Studies Press, 2017), pp. 248, 255–6. Sumarokov's campaign against *pod"iachie* extended to his comedies and fables as well.

4 Tseitlin, *Povesti o bednom chinovnike*, p. 7.

5 Elizabeth C. Shepard, 'Pavlov's "Demon" and Gogol's "Overcoat"', *Slavic Review* 33.2 (1974), 292.

6 V. G. Belinskii, 'Literaturnye mechtaniia: Elegiia v proze' [Literary reveries: An elegy in prose], in *Polnoe sobranie sochinenii* [Complete collected works], 13 vols. (Moscow: Akademiia nauk SSSR, 1953–9), vol. I, pp. 23, 87, 101; Belinskii, 'O russkoi povesti i povestiakh g. Gogolia ("Mirgorod" i "Arabeski")' [On the Russian short story and Mr Gogol ('Mirgorod' and 'Arabesques')], in *Polnoe sobranie sochinenii*, vol. I, pp. 284–307.

which for Belinskii entailed an inextricable relationship between reality and fiction – in both directions. Literary texts were meant to depict social reality above all because the object was to affect it, to change things for the better: an 'affective' (emotional) response was essential to spark a visceral reaction to social ills. Second (in conjunction with the first), Belinskii championed the depiction of the character he dubbed the 'little person' (*malen'kii chelovek*),[7] the pitiable *chinovnik* found in abundance in the era's literary texts. Gogol's 'Overcoat', he felt, had initiated a new mode of writing about the poor and powerless, making the little person the protagonist of choice. Third, Belinskii celebrated what he saw as Gogol's realism, his true-to-life portrayals of lowly civil servants and the oppressive Petersburg bureaucracy that dehumanised them, treatments that had brought Russian literature into the age of 'naturalism'. The chief feature of Gogol's naturalism, Belinskii maintained, was his use of social types – characters easily recognisable from real life.[8]

But while these literary civil servants surely owed their existence to their real-world counterparts, the extent to which the former depict or resemble the latter is open to dispute. The more salient models for literary clerks were the literary clerks preceding them; these precursors served as the ground against which any new figure emerged, the deviations from the paradigm only confirming its resilience. Indeed, it is this dynamic recrafting of source texts and characters that made the little person such a big deal – and a long-lasting one. Conceptualised as a social type, the poor civil servant readily became a literary one, serving authors with varied agendas throughout the nineteenth century, handily surviving the dismantling of the table of ranks in 1917, and signifying his way into post-Soviet literary space.

Low Rank, High Profile: The Literary Heyday of the Poor *Chinovnik* (1830–1850)

Pushkin's 'The Stationmaster', the earliest of the tales of low-level civil servants to have made it into the canon, is hardly true to type: the stationmaster is no copy clerk, nor are his power struggles bureaucratic. Moreover, they take place somewhere 'out there' rather than in the bureaucratic capital. But Samson *is*

---

7 Belinskii, '"Gore ot uma". Komediia v chetyrekh deistviiakh, v stikhakh. Sochinenie A. S. Griboedova' [*Woe from Wit*. A comedy in four acts, in verse, by A. S. Griboedov], in *Polnoe sobranie sochinenii*, vol. III, p. 468. The Russian is unmarked for gender; *chelovek* means 'person'. The character in question, however, was male as a matter of course.
8 Belinskii, 'O russkoi povesti', pp. 287–93, 295–6; Belinskii, 'Mysli i zametki o russkoi literatury' [Thoughts and notes on Russian literature], in *Polnoe sobranie sochinenii*, vol. IX, pp. 432–6, 439–42.

a civil servant of the lowest rank (collegiate registrar, fourteenth class), and sympathy is amply elicited on his behalf. Not one to pass up an opportunity to take on his high-culture precursors, though, Pushkin endows his *chinovnik* with a lovely daughter of 'about fourteen' (her age re-emphasising her father's rank) who is seduced by an aristocratic traveller: in this storyline Pushkin invokes the master Sentimentalist plot of Nikolai Karamzin's (1766–1826) 'Poor Liza' (*Bednaia Liza*, 1792), in which the seduction and abandonment of an innocent peasant girl by a wealthy nobleman leads the unfortunate girl to drown herself in despair (see Chapter 1.4). Pushkin gives us instead a daughter whose romantic liaison is auspicious and whose future looks bright; the only abandoned victim is Samson. In replacing Karamzin's wronged peasant girl with a 'poor stationmaster' defined by his rank and victimhood, Pushkin invokes – and departs from – the Sentimentalist paradigm while explicitly embracing the powerless civil servant. Notably, too, in making the narrator of this little person story the worst bully of all, he puts his characteristic metaliterary spin on the popular *chinovnik*-as-victim tale.

Not until his monumental narrative poem *The Bronze Horseman* does Pushkin place a poor, insignificant clerk in St Petersburg, thereby laying the foundation for the Petersburg myth itself. Mythology notwithstanding, the poem's setting was grimly real: the Petersburg flood of 1824, which resulted in hundreds of casualties and incalculable damage. Yet this story of historical destruction is prefaced by a prologue of creation – that of the city itself, starring Peter I, its visionary founder (unnamed but unmistakable), framed as a larger-than-life being who contains the waters and commands the elements themselves (see Chapter 4.2).

These cosmic terms are limited to the prologue, but Peter's outsized presence dominates the poem – in the starkest contrast to the actual protagonist, a petty clerk named Evgenii who loses his beloved, his sanity, and finally his life when the waters prove stronger than the walls built to contain them. Having begun his work with a higher-profile protagonist, Pushkin ultimately opted for a low-ranking civil servant to foreground the difference in stature between Evgenii the little person and Peter the great one, who, thinking to rule the forces of nature, had engineered the urban landscape that ultimately destroys the poor clerk. Evgenii's poverty is real, his dreams modest, and his power to pursue them non-existent – again, in contrast to his omnipotent, plan-fulfilling counterpart. In the poem proper, the part of Peter is played by the city's famous Falconet statue, which portrays the emperor astride his horse, one arm extended in a gesture of mastery while his mount rears. Evgenii rides out the storm in the same square as 'Peter', clinging perilously to a sculpted

animal himself, sick with worry about his Parasha as the waters rise. The sculpted Peter, meanwhile, keeps his head averted indifferently.

Once the waters recede and Evgenii can reach the island where Parasha lives, he finds corpses everywhere and her little hut simply washed away. We understand from his maniacal laughter that, having been stripped of everything else, Evgenii has now lost his mind. He wanders for weeks, socially and existentially unmoored, until he stumbles upon the statue of Peter and, in a moment of implacable (if impotent) rage, shakes his fist at the 'royal effigy'. But then Evgenii panics, having seemed to see the rider turn his face towards him in anger and derision, and runs for his life, with the 'Bronze Colossus' galloping in pursuit throughout the night.[9] Pushkin leaves ambiguous the status of that chase, which has either a psychiatric explanation or a supernatural one.

While the compassion for Evgenii is unmistakable, the crux of the story remains his gesture of defiance. Insubordination raises its fist in so many respects here: when Peter dares to redefine the contours of God's creation; when the 'impudent waves' overleap the orderly contours laid down by the city's founder;[10] when the Decembrist revolt raises its collective fist against the tsar in 1825; and, crucially, in the poem's own (risky) allusions to that uprising. Hardly surprising that Pushkin's poem was suppressed and censored for its references to the historical insurrection. At every level, rebellion ends in madness or destruction.

Markedly less primordial, Gogol's *chinovnik* tales are sometimes regarded as iconic renderings of the nineteenth-century capital and its dehumanising bureaucracy – oddly, since 'The Overcoat' ends with its protagonist rising from the dead and 'The Diary of a Madman' is the work of a psychotic clerk. In 'Madman' (Gogol's only work written in the first person), the events as reported diverge starkly from bureaucratic norms: Poprishchin records the correspondence of dogs, cites non-existent dates, and eventually reports his own accession to the vacant throne of Spain. Despite the futility of Poprishchin's goals (proving that he is *not* a non-entity and winning the heart of the director's daughter), they are not irrational: he longs only to rise in the table of ranks. Alas, while Poprishchin enjoys personal nobility by virtue of his existing rank (ninth class), he will never advance to the eighth

9 A. S. Pushkin, *Polnoe sobranie sochinenii v shestnadtsati tomakh* [Complete works in sixteen volumes] (Leningrad: Izdatel'stvo Akademii nauk SSSR, 1937–59), vol. V (1948), p. 148; A. S. Pushkin, *The Bronze Horseman: A St Petersburg Story*, trans. John Dewey, available at www.tyutchev.org.uk/Download/Bronze%20Horseman.pdf, accessed 1 Feb. 2023, p. 17.

10 Pushkin, *Polnoe sobranie sochinenii*, vol. V, p. 143.

class and the *hereditary* nobility it confers – not that he's likely to produce descendants in any case.

And yet produce them he does: Poprishchin bequeaths his particular form of dissatisfaction ('Why am I just a Titular Councilor?? . . . Why precisely a *Titular* Councilor?'[11]) to just about every literary *chinovnik* to come. In this, Gogol permanently alters the table of ranks itself – at least its literary instantiation – reimagining the official hierarchy to convert his *own* poor clerks into titular councillors (ninth class), while they couldn't possibly have been that highly placed in reality.[12] Clearly from very early on in the development of the *chinovnik* tale, historical referent yields to fictional prototype. The rank of titular councillor is thus written indelibly into the script, along with the copy-clerk job and the lunatic idea of marrying the director's daughter – so much so that departures from these norms come to signify the most.

'The Overcoat' (1842) remains Gogol's most difficult text to characterise, for its story is occluded by its own discursive excesses (digressions, obfuscation, hyperbole, absurd logic). Never in doubt, however, is the poor clerk's rank – titular councillor (of course) – or, as the narrator puts it, eternal titular councillor, for like the madman Poprishchin, this clerk will never rise from the ninth class to the eighth. Even among copy clerks, Akakii Akakievich cuts a pathetic figure. Inseparable from his writing, defined exclusively by ink on paper, he takes pleasure in the alphabet itself. Declining the opportunity to alter a document, he retreats to the reproduction of words without meaningful content. Disinclined to diverge from the script(ure), Akakii Akakievich most resembles his namesake: the devout, long-suffering scribe St Akakios of Sinai.[13]

Akakii Akakievich's troubles begin when his threadbare overcoat can no longer hold a patch: his material needs assail his verbal counter-reality. Akakii's new longing for substance marks the awakening of desire as he exchanges his former (sensual?) deprivation for the palpable temptations proffered by his diabolical tailor. His existence grows fuller, almost 'as if he

---

11 N. V. Gogol', 'Zapiski sumasshedshego' [The diary of a madman], in *Polnoe sobranie sochinenii* [Complete collected works], 14 vols. (Moscow: Akademiia Nauk SSSR, 1937–52), vol. III, p. 206.

12 Irina Reyfman, *How Russia Learned to Write: Literature and the Imperial Table of Ranks* (Madison: University of Wisconsin Press, 2016), pp. 86, 109–15.

13 See F. C. Driessen, *Gogol as a Short Story Writer: A Study of His Technique of Composition*, trans. Ian F. Finlay (The Hague: Mouton, 1965), pp. 194, 229; and John Schillinger, '"The Overcoat" as a travesty of hagiography', *Slavic and East European Journal* 16.1 (1972), 36–41.

were married'.[14] When Akakii's beloved overcoat is stolen on its first night out, he turns for assistance to a 'Person of Consequence' (*znachitel'noe litso*), a general, whose verbal assault – 'How dare you?', 'Do you know with whom you are speaking?' – mortifies the defenceless clerk.[15] Akakii stumbles home blindly, takes to his bed, and dies in delirium.

But wait! There's more! Petersburg soon finds itself terrorised by a mysterious figure who snatches people's overcoats all across town. The phantom is recognised as the ghost of Akakii Akakievich, who only stops menacing the city once he locates the Person of Consequence himself and absconds with the latter's luxurious overcoat. St Akakios, too, had appeared to his tormenter as a ghost.

The debatable solidity of its protagonist notwithstanding, Belinskii praised the concreteness of the story's content, which provided 'the greatest instantiation . . . of the theme of the disadvantaged "little man" as the victim of an uncaring, rank- and power-crazy Russian official society'.[16] He also insisted that Gogol reproduced reality so faithfully that foreigners read his work to learn about conditions in Russia.[17] His depictions are not merely realistic, but *real*. Several questions are raised by this:

(1) Akakii unquestionably fits the bill as a disadvantaged little person – but to what extent is his tiny, circumscribed life the product of an oppressive environment? Akakii appears unperturbed by his social standing (unlike titular councillor Poprishchin, wholly obsessed with his rank). He delights in his work and serves with love, limited less by salary than by disinclination to pursue other diversions. Akakii's smallness is more characterological than occupational.

(2) Does the story of Akakii elicit the compassion for the little person that Belinskii credits Gogol with inspiring? Or is this *chinovnik* grotesquely dehumanised by the story's representation? The so-called humanitarian passage (about the cruelty of man to man) in Gogol's story is too over-the-top to accept at face value; the features of the narration that make the story comical (or annoying) consistently undercut the reader's feelings of

14 Gogol', 'Shinel'' [The overcoat], in *Polnoe sobranie sochinenii*, vol. III, p. 154.

15 Gogol', 'Shinel'', p. 167.

16 Gary Jahn, 'Lesson 7: The young Dostoevsky and the dawn of Realism', unpublished study notes, University of Minnesota website, http://lol-russ.umn.edu/hpgary/Rus s3421/lesson7.htm, section 'The dawn of Realism and V. G. Belinskii', accessed 11 July 2021.

17 Belinskii, 'Vzgliad na russkuiu literaturu 1846 goda' [A look at Russian literature of 1846], in *Polnoe sobranie sochinenii*, vol. X, pp. 15–17; Belinskii, 'Mysli i zametki', pp. 439–40.

compassion. Opinions are mixed on the extent to which Akakii inspires or even allows for empathic response.[18]

(3) What, then, of Belinskii's demand for true-to-life presentation and the capacity to change things for the better? To speak of 'realism' seems like a stretch, even before zombie Akakii turns up and the fantastic becomes a regular feature of the Petersburg *chinovnik* tales.[19] Nor, in his ludicrous extremity, does Akakii 'typify' anything (Belinskii's index of realistic representation since 1835). The Realist Gogol, it has been suggested, was an invention of Belinskii, Gogolian hyperbole and illogic rendering the critic's claim of true-to-life depiction tendentious.[20]

In this text predicated on verbal prodigality, Akakii Akakievich himself might best be characterised as a repetition of syllables – from his reiterative name to his rote reproduction of letters to his inchoate speech patterns; even in a chapter on 'heroes', it is difficult to describe him as a 'human subject'. From the perspective of the 1840s intelligentsia, though, the very depiction of a downtrodden man in a hostile environment bespoke a social conscience and an awareness of the hierarchical structures that consigned an insignificant *chinovnik* to poverty, anxiety, and misery. In this respect, 'The Overcoat' played a central part in the development of Russian Realism in its little person plot line.

Whether or not 'The Overcoat' had a salubrious effect on the social reality it depicts, it had a lasting impact on Russian literary culture. As a perpetual titular councillor, Akakii became a literary fixture along with his bureaucratic setting and a few recurrent motifs (the encounter with a Person of Consequence joins Poprishchin's unrequited love for the director's daughter) that animated *chinovnik* narratives for generations to come. Even Dostoevskii, who rewrote virtually every aspect of Gogol's tales, made his unfortunate clerks titular councillors too, departing thereby from the reality of rank, cleaving instead to Gogol's fictional tradition.[21]

---

18 See, for example, Victor Terras, *A History of Russian Literature* (New Haven: Yale University Press, 1991), p. 259; and Richard Peace, 'The nineteenth century: The Natural School and its aftermath, 1840–55', in Charles A. Moser (ed.), *Cambridge History of Russian Literature*, revised edn (Cambridge: Cambridge University Press, 1992), p. 198.

19 Nancy Workman calls this 'unrealism' in her dissertation, 'Unrealism: Bureaucratic absurdity in nineteenth-century Russian literature', unpublished PhD thesis, Columbia University (1998).

20 Andrew Kahn, Mark Lipovetsky, Irina Reyfman, and Stephanie Sandler, *A History of Russian Literature* (Oxford: Oxford University Press, 2018), p. 425.

21 Reyfman, *How Russia Learned*, pp. 86, 109–15, 150.

Between 1842 and 1850 alone, some 150 imitations of 'The Overcoat' appeared in print, though most of these contributed nothing new.[22] The foremost counterexample was published in 1846: *Poor Folk*, the first novel of the still undiscovered Fedor Dostoevskii, who handily remade Gogol's clerks and their coats to his own specifications. When Belinskii read Dostoevskii's manuscript about a destitute Petersburg copy clerk (a titular councillor, of course) living in intractable poverty behind a partition in his landlady's kitchen, he applauded the writer's evident commitment to the downtrodden and oppressed. Dostoevskii's depiction of the vulnerability of the urban poor provided in sharp detail the social consciousness Belinskii had celebrated (prematurely?) in Gogol's 'Overcoat'.[23] But Dostoevskii had a bone to pick with his predecessor, who, he felt, had made a caricature of Akakii Akakievich, thereby dehumanising his protagonist more than the bureaucracy had.

Dostoevskii's strategy was to provide access to the heart and mind – and the psychological complexity – of his impoverished *chinovnik* by casting him as one of the correspondents in an epistolary novel. In letters addressed to the young woman across the way, Makar Devushkin articulates his views on the life he leads, expressing his longing, anguish, and keen sense of shame, and thus revealing his human dignity, if also obscuring his more questionable sides. Moreover, insofar as Dostoevskii's little person has an addressee, he demonstrates his capacity to use his words to communicate with another human being, a far cry from Akakii's recopying for his eyes alone. In fact, Devushkin expresses above all his concern for the well-being of his correspondent, Varvara Alekseevna, who is vulnerable in the extreme and seems already to have been victimised by one sexual predator. Prevented by her fragile health from providing for herself, she is on the verge of going under. Only from *her* letters do we understand that, despite her repeated objections, Devushkin sends her gifts and all the money he can spare – plus much more that he can't. Meanwhile, he edges closer to ruin and life on the streets himself.

The epistolary novel was an anachronistic form by the time Dostoevskii wrote *Poor Folk*, but it served to motivate the author's access to the firsthand experience of the destitute themselves, thereby providing the basis for subtle psychological portraiture. Devushkin gives voice to insights about human behaviour that will animate characters created by the mature Dostoevskii, especially concerning the human response to poverty:

> I don't mind going about without an overcoat and without boots; I can stand anything, and put up with anything. . . . – but what will people say? . . . You

22 Tseitlin, *Povesti o bednom chinovnike*, pp. 7–8.   23 Peace, 'Nineteenth century', p. 219.

know it is for the sake of other people one wears an overcoat, yes, and boots too you put on, perhaps, on their account.[24]

But the clerk's discernment – or candour – has its limits, particularly regarding his own desires. Surely, as Carol Apollonio points out, Devushkin's readiness to camp out in a narrow slice of kitchen reflects his ability to watch Varvara's window from there. His thinly disguised voyeurism tracks with other predatory instincts that accompany the protective ones: his emotional interventions to dissuade Varvara from accepting employment as a governess or the proposal of a suitor *might* ensure her safety, but they certainly keep her dependent on him.[25] Devushkin's darker potential anticipates Dostoevskii's later work as well.

Most apparent in *Poor Folk*, though, is Dostoevskii's backward look at his immediate predecessor and the continuities that emphasise their differences. Whereas Akakii, lacking personal relationships, famously thinks of his garment-in-the-making as a 'partner in life',[26] Dostoevskii gives Devushkin a real-life significant other for whose sake he is prepared to do without an overcoat altogether – and who plans to make an overcoat for *him*. Varvara's most explicit intertextual role is to send Devushkin earlier works from the little person tradition. He adores Pushkin's 'Stationmaster' on the grounds that 'it was as if I had written it myself',[27] so true to life does he find it. 'The Overcoat', conversely, enrages him. Incensed by the fact that he both recognises himself in the depiction of Akakii and sees the portrait as vicious caricature, Devushkin faults Gogol's work for being, on the one hand, too close for comfort ('And here now all one's private and public life is being dragged into literature, it is all printed, read, laughed and gossiped about! Why, it will be impossible to show oneself in the street'), and on the other hand, 'untrue to life, for there cannot have been such a clerk'.[28]

Like Akakii, Devushkin is a copy clerk; but unlike his incoherent forebear, Devushkin wields his words in pursuit of style, making a stab at the poetic, falling at times into the language of Sentimentalism, but fluent in all manner of speech acts. When, despite Devushkin's affecting supplications, Varvara

24 F. M. Dostoevskii, *Bednye liudi* [Poor folk], in *Polnoe sobranie sochinenii v tridtsati tomakh* [Complete collected works in thirty volumes] (Leningrad: Izdatel'stvo Nauka, 1972–90), vol. I, p. 76; trans. Constance Garnett in Fyodor Dostoevsky, *'The Gambler' and Other Stories* (London: William Heinemann, 1914), p. 218.

25 Carol Apollonio, *Dostoevsky's Secrets: Reading against the Grain* (Evanston, IL: Northwestern University Press, 2009), pp. 14–26.

26 Gogol', 'Shinel'', p. 154.   27 Dostoevskii, *Bednye liudi*, p. 59; trans. Garnett, p. 186.

28 Dostoevskii, *Bednye liudi*, p. 63; trans. Garnett, p. 191.

departs with the odious Bykov, becoming as permanently unattainable as any director's daughter, her physical removal shakes him less than the impossibility of continuing their correspondence. 'To whom will I write letters?' he scrawls, tearfully, in the end. 'Ask yourself to whom is he going to write letters?'[29] Devushkin writes as if his life depends on it because it does. Without an addressee, Devushkin (who even wears boots for other people) will in effect be reduced to retracing attractive letters of the alphabet for himself and stringing together words without meaningful syntax.

While in *Poor Folk* Dostoevskii takes on Akakii and his 'Overcoat', his second novel, *The Double*, also published in 1846, goes to town with Gogol's 'Madman' – down to the hero's fixation on the director's daughter as the marker for ascent to higher rank and status, precisely what Dostoevskii's Goliadkin desperately desires. Unlike Poprishchin, however, whose delusions close rank around him to protect him from a reality that doesn't comport with his wishes, Goliadkin is divided against *himself*: he goes mad with ambition, 'all the while utterly despising ambition and even suffering from the fact that he has come to suffer from such nonsense as ambition'.[30] Eventually he decompensates completely, and Goliadkin Junior – a carbon copy of the copy clerk Goliadkin – makes his fatal appearance. Significantly, the novel never clarifies the ontological status of Goliadkin's evil twin; readers oscillate between the psychological explanation for Goliadkin Junior and the supernatural one. The subtitle – 'A Petersburg Poem' – suggests that, as in Pushkin's *Bronze Horseman*, this ambiguity will not be resolved.

As an evolving literary type rather than a stable form, then, the canonical little person was serially reimagined to serve the purposes of each successive author and work. Yet the writers who identified themselves with the Natural School (see Chapter 1.5), which had coalesced in 1842–3 in the wake of Belinskii's assessment of 'The Overcoat' as maximally true to life, made a more programmatic commitment to the *social* types identified by the critic. Nikolai Nekrasov's (1821–1878) almanac, *The Physiology of St Petersburg* (*Fiziologiia Peterburga*, 1845), with an introduction by Belinskii, was dedicated to the realistic depiction of the plight of clerks and other low-born Petersburg types. Only Nekrasov's poem 'The Clerk' (*Chinovnik*, 1844) exposed the Petersburg clerk as an opportunist and dissembler rather than the poor, helpless victim from *chinovnik* fiction. That portrayal, however, had more

29 Dostoevskii, *Bednye liudi*, p. 107; trans. Garnett, p. 243.
30 Dostoevskii, *Polnoe sobranie sochinenii*, vol. XVIII, p. 31, from his newspaper column 'Peterburgskaia letopis'' [Petersburg chronicle] for 15 June 1847.

to do with Nekrasov's aspirations as a satirist than with any departure from the shared commitment to the urban poor.

Afterlives: The Lasting Legacy

Nekrasov's satirical take on the low-ranking clerk was prescient: following the death of Nicholas I (r. 1825–55), Mikhail Saltykov-Shchedrin (1826–1889) began publishing his sardonic *Provincial Sketches* (*Gubernskie ocherki*, 1856), dedicated to exposing not the hardships but the wholesale dishonesty of civil servants at every level of the hierarchy, the table of ranks having institutionalised the implacable ambition that produced an all-encompassing system of bribery. Saltykov-Shchedrin's *Sketches* kicked off the era of the satirical exposé (*oblichitel'naia literatura*), opening up a public sphere for discussion of social issues, particularly in the inherently public arena of theatre. And while plays about bribe-taking bureaucrats were nothing new, in earlier works – like Gogol's *Inspector General* (*Revizor*, 1836) – bribery was simply a given, a premise rather than a problem, the context for comedy rather than the target of pointed critique.[31]

Interestingly, the plays that took on the intractable problem of corruption in the latter half of the 1850s all featured an *honest* clerk. In Aleksandr Ostrovskii's (1823–1886) *A Profitable Position* (*Dokhodnoe mesto*, 1856, premiere 1863), an educated young clerk with strong moral convictions resists every pressure to comply with the civil-service norm – till the bitter end, when he seems resigned to do as the Romans do, not because he is weak or has abandoned his principles, but because the system is such that 'it's essentially impossible and probably inadvisable *not* to accept bribes'.[32] In devising this resolution, Ostrovskii avoids reducing complexity to a facile opposition between honesty and dishonesty. The play's *chinovniki* who do take bribes are not villains; they participate because that's their culture – they've had no exposure to the western values that call it into question. Ostrovskii's play explores bureaucratic corruption as a confrontation between 'two incompatible cultures that inform the history and moral sensibility' of mid-century Russia.[33]

The late-century heir-apparent to the *chinovnik* drama, Anton Chekhov (1860–1904), engaged energetically with low-ranking clerks – but not, with

31 Kirill Zubkov and Andrei Fedotov (eds.), *Oblichiteli: Russkie p'esy o chinovnikakh 1850-kh godov* [Exposés: Russian plays about civil servants in the 1850s] (Moscow: Commonplace, 2019), pp. 8–12.
32 Zubkov and Fedotov (eds.), *Oblichiteli*, pp. 19, 21.
33 Zubkov and Fedotov (eds.), *Oblichiteli*, pp. 22–4.

rare exceptions, in his plays. Moreover, rather than reprising the corruption plots of the 1850s, he went back to the canonical little person character of the 1830s and 1840s – only he had no use for the insignificant clerk as long-suffering victim. 'The Death of a Government Clerk' (*Smert' chinovnika*, 1883), Chekhov's best-known send-up of the *chinovnik* tale (especially Gogol's 'Overcoat'), features a clerk who sneezes during a theatre performance, accidentally spraying the gentleman in front of him – not surprisingly, a Person of Consequence. The distraught clerk makes repeated efforts to apologise, and despite the general's reassurances (Don't mention it!), mention it he does, in increasingly intrusive scenarios. Finally, he so oppresses the general with explanations that the latter can only stamp his foot and shriek, 'Get out!!' The terror-stricken clerk backs away, stumbles home blindly (like the devastated Akakii), and 'without taking off his uniform, lay down on the couch and . . . died'.[34] Here, the aggressor is not the general but the clerk. Chekhov's little people are usually their own worst enemies. This one cannot rest until he gets his orders from the general and lays down his life in the new uniform he had donned for the occasion.

While the stakes have mounted in Andrei Belyi's (1880–1934) Symbolist novel *Petersburg* (*Peterburg*, 1913–14, 1922) – bombs, revolution, apocalypse, the void – the symbolic currency is familiar. As befits a novel named after Peter's city, again threatened with destruction, *Petersburg* re-enlists the cast of Pushkin's *Bronze Horseman*: the insignificant *chinovnik* Evgenii has become a vulnerable member of a terrorist cell, and the gigantic equestrian statue (Peter on his rearing steed) reprises its earlier role as fearsome aggressor. Belyi's *Petersburg* also reinscribes Gogol's bureaucratic epicentre, where a Person of Consequence heads up a department that will not be named, countless copy clerks reduplicate countless documents, and verbal scraps circulate as shadowy inhabitants. Yet it makes no pretence of realist portraiture of its disenfranchised poor – or its highly ranked officials. Nor do the expected oppositions hold up: Apollon Apollonovich, bureaucratic head of state, turns out to be a little person in every respect, on the scale of the 'tiny figure' of Dudkin the revolutionary.[35] 'Apollon Apollonovich also embodies simultaneously the high-ranking Person of Consequence and the lowly Akakii Akakievich. Tiny Dudkin finally assumes the most elevated

34 A. P. Chekhov, 'Smert' chinovnika' [The death of a government clerk], in *Polnoe sobranie sochinenii i pisem v tridtsati tomakh* [Complete collected works and letters in thirty volumes] (Moscow: Izdatel'stvo Nauka, 1974–83), vol. II, pp. 165–6.

35 Andrei Belyi, *Peterburg* [Petersburg], ed. L. K. Dolgopolov (Moscow: Izdatel'stvo Nauka, 1981), pp. 380–6.

position – as the metallic horseman, outstretched arm and all, astride the huge man he has murdered – and the avenging horseman heralds nothing short of apocalypse.

The nullification of the imperial table of ranks in 1917 didn't eliminate civil servants or make them any more honest. In Mikhail Bulgakov's (1891–1940) *Master and Margarita* (*Master i Margarita*, comp. 1928–40), bureaucrats, petty and otherwise, epitomise the greed of Stalinist Moscow in the 1930s, especially the hypocrisy and cowardice of the state literary and theatrical hierarchies. When the devil visits Moscow, speaking only the truth ('all secrets revealed'[36]), the corrupt civil servants are unmasked, their come-uppance taking uproariously funny forms. Suffering at the hands of the cowardly functionaries is the eponymous master, whose embedded novel about the historical events in Jerusalem at the time of Jesus corroborates the devil's truth. This Jerusalem strand focuses on decisions made by Pontius Pilate about the life and death of Jesus, that especially consequential little person, thereby exploring the ramifications of power and hierarchy at every level.

Bulgakov's novel was too volatile for publication in his lifetime. It waited over twenty-five years to appear, even in censored form (1966). Varlam Shalamov's (1907–1982) short story 'Handwriting' (*Pocherk*, 1964) had to be smuggled out of the Soviet Union to be published at all; it came out in the west in 1978 in Shalamov's *Kolyma Tales* (*Kolymskie rasskazy*, comp. 1954–73), a collection of accounts of his seventeen years in Stalinist concentration camps, presented with minimal affect and no self-dramatisation. The 'handwriting' sequence occurs in 1938, Kolyma's deadliest year, when the protagonist no longer notices that prisoners removed from the barracks every night never return. Summoned by the camp investigator and instructed to copy names, Krist requests no explanation and receives none. After weeks of this, the investigator asks Krist for his first name and patronymic and subsequently consigns one file to the fire. Only many years later does Krist understand that it had been his own. All those whose names he'd transcribed had been shot. Even the investigator was shot. Krist wasn't.

Copying saved Krist. Yet Krist was essentially signing death warrants, never thinking to warn those whose time was up. Then again, he had never peeked at the heading under the fold to see what the document was

---

36 M. A. Bulgakov, *Master i Margarita* [The Master and Margarita], in *Sobranie sochinenii* [Collected works], 10 vols. (Ann Arbor, MI: Ardis, 1989–90), vol. VIII, p. 109.

for.[37] Does it matter that he wasn't naming names but repeating them? Is he saved or condemned by this account? Significantly, Krist's handwriting was calligraphic, a thing of rare beauty. He is compared not to the copy clerk Akakii but to the protagonist of Aleksandr Kuprin's (1870–1938) story 'The Tsar's Scribe' (*Tsarskii pisar'*, 1918), whose extraordinary calligraphy is a dying art. What makes Krist's a lifesaving one?

A more recent exploration of the salvific potential of artful replication appears in *The Winter Queen* (*Azazel'*, 1998), the first volume of Boris Akunin's (1956–) popular Erast Fandorin detective series. As a post-Soviet look at pre-Soviet Russia (1876–1914) that makes it to Soviet times (1918) in the most recent volume, the series recapitulates a lot of literary and historical-political ground, and it does so in an instructive way. Fandorin begins his career in nineteenth-century Moscow as a collegiate registrar (fourteenth class), a clerk who copies (and recopies) his reports 'with all the flourishes and curlicues'[38] of the tsar's scribe and becomes the series' detective, revisiting – and reconfiguring – a bunch of now-familiar charac-ters and motifs. Fandorin is multilingual and an incorrigible clothes horse, the antithesis of the virtually mute Akakii in his threadbare 'dressing gown'.[39] Like all civil servants Fandorin works for the state, but as an official in the Criminal Investigation Division of the Moscow Police, he sits squarely on the investigator's side of Krist's table, thereby complicating the intelligentsia's customarily progressive profile – not to mention that of the anarchists evoked by the author's pseudonym (B. Akunin), a not very veiled reference to the nineteenth-century anarchist and revolutionary Mikhail Bakunin (1814–1876).[40]

The ideological havoc wreaked by this scrambling of oppositions contributes to the pleasure first of recognising the text's literary allusions and then of taking in their surprising new valence: here the table of ranks and secret police occupy the plus column.[41] Or, when *The Winter Queen* opens with a remix of the opening scene of *Master and Margarita* – fittingly, since the Azazel of the Russian title of Akunin's novel is one

37 Leona Toker, 'Testimony and doubt: Varlam Shalamov's "How It Began" and "Handwriting"', in Markku Lehtimäki, Simo Leisti, and Marja Rytkönen (eds.), *Real Stories, Imagined Realities: Fictionality and Non-Fictionality in Literary Constructs and Historical Contexts* (Tampere: Tampere University Press, 2007), pp. 51–68, also at Shalamov.ru (2007), https://shalamov.ru/en/research/121/, accessed 29 June 2021.
38 B. Akunin, *Azazel'* (Moscow: Zakharov, 1998), p. 15.   39 Gogol', 'Shinel'', pp. 147, 150.
40 Caryl Emerson, *The Cambridge Introduction to Russian Literature* (Cambridge: Cambridge University Press, 2008), pp. 97, 244–6. The author's real name is Grigorii Chkhartishvili.
41 Kahn et al., *History of Russian Literature*, p. 562; Emerson, *Cambridge Introduction*, p. 245.

of the devil's associates in Bulgakov's – we delight in recognising the original despite the all-new cast. Akunin's unabashed reliance on (and the sheer number of) such intelligentsia inside jokes foregrounds their function as memes: they operate by invoking exclusive cultural knowledge cleverly manipulated to change it up; the original must remain palpable for the creativity of the divergence to be appreciated, and the difference must be sufficient to avoid mere repetition that contributes nothing new (like the imitation 'Overcoats' that flooded the market in the 1840s). Admittedly all literary evolution proceeds by renegotiating the contours of the same-but-different. But in the case of Russian literature's ubiquitous clerk, the copyist's own verbatim reproduction of originals makes the potential for rote repetition explicit. Perhaps this accounts for the lasting fixation on copy clerks, when the lower civil-service ranks included equally wretched stationmasters, postmasters, schoolmasters, and more.

How are we to understand Russian literature's endless fascination with copying and recopying, not to mention its own inclination to follow suit by reaching for the same cast (Akakii, Evgenii, Poprishchin, Devushkin, Goliadkin) again and again? Is it a function of the canonical characters' superstar creators? Or the insistence by the nineteenth century's foremost literary critic that these characters were somehow 'typical'? Why redeploy the usual suspects for 200 years when they actually inhabited only two decades, especially given that, over the long haul, literary *chinovniki* have been more consistently the object of disdain than of pity? How has the poor, beleaguered little person become the default when he seems to have been an aberration? The how, one suspects, addresses the why. As a meme *avant-la-lettre*, Russian literature's copy clerk has been serially repurposed with both the *Witz* (ingenuity: the capacity to perceive similarity and draw associations among divergent things) and the *Scharfsinn* (acumen: the intellectual discernment that conduces to drawing distinctions) to keep both operations perceptible and each successive instantiation provocative enough to elicit the kind of delight that prompts people to forward ingenious memes.

Thus, even Akakii Akakievich, the copyist paralysed by the mere prospect of altering a word in an existing document, lives beguilingly on, less as an overcoat-snatching ghost than as an ongoing negotiation of sameness and difference, a medium for both cultural memory and artistic innovation.

Further Reading

Belinsky, Vissarion, *Selected Philosophical Works* (Moscow: Foreign Language Publishing House, 1956).

Frank, Joseph, *Dostoevsky: The Seeds of Revolt, 1821–1849* (Princeton: Princeton University Press, 1976).

Maguire, Muireann, 'The little man in the overcoat: Gogol and Krzhizhanovsky', in Katherine Bowers and Ani Kokobobo (eds.), *Russian Writers and the Fin de Siècle: The Twilight of Realism* (Cambridge: Cambridge University Press, 2015).

Marullo, Thomas Gaiton, 'Nekrasov's *činovniki*: A new look at Russia's "little men"', *Slavic and East European Journal* 21.4 (1977), 483–94.

Rosenshield, Gary, *Challenging the Bard: Dostoevsky and Pushkin, a Study of Literary Relationship* (Madison: University of Wisconsin Press, 2013).

Shore, Rima, *Scrivener Fiction: The Copyist and His Craft in Nineteenth-Century Fiction* (New York: Columbia University, 1989).

The Peasant

ALEXEY VDOVIN

The road along which I was carrying – and am still carrying – my writer's cross will soon end, I think ... [...] the end is nigh! ...

I was tired of the long journey ... [...] The road, heavy and dirty, wove ever more deeply into the thick, dark forest, and I was afraid to look back, afraid to think how I was walking persistently and stubbornly along the road, groping, stumbling into trees, tripping, and sinking into the dirt; and thinking only of how to leave, how to get out of the dark forest to freedom, to the open, to the light of day! ...

If you were to write about my journey along that road, you would need a whole book, to which you could give this one-word title: *Horror* ...[1]

So begins 'About Myself' (*Pro sebia*, 1916), a short story by Semen Podiachev (1836–1934), a popular peasant writer from the early twentieth century. Living in constant poverty, Podiachev tried to remain a writer while also supporting his family. Both ventures failed: Podiachev never became a writer of repute, his son died of starvation and illness, and Podiachev buried him. The narrator of 'About Myself' is a peasant tormented by terrible guilt at the repercussions of his own choice to write about his experiences.

Podiachev is not included in the Russian literary canon. Indeed, that canon contains almost no peasant authors. But peasant protagonists inhabit the pages of all modern Russian literature, from the first comedies and idylls of the mid-eighteenth century through to the works of Village Prose writers (*derevenshchiki*) who depicted modern village life in the 1960s and 1970s. The reasons for this are obvious. For the duration of almost the entire nineteenth

---

1 Semen Podiachev, 'Pro sebia' [About myself], in Aleksei Vdovin and Andrei Fedotov (eds.), *Seryi muzhik: Narodnaia zhizn' v rasskazakh zabytykh russkikh pisatelei XIX veka* [Grey muzhik: Popular life in the stories of forgotten Russian writers of the nineteenth century] (Moscow: Common Place, 2017), p. 104.

century, between 80 and 90 per cent of the country's population were serfs of various kinds: some owned by landowners, some by the court, and some by the state.[2] This silent majority created the material environment in which nobles – the nation's educated elite – created literary masterpieces, many of them about peasants.

How did the literature of the educated elite portray peasants and common people? This chapter will provide an account of the ways in which, over its long history, Russian literature sought to compensate for the structural social inequality of the peasant economy by creating genres and forms in which peasant men and women served as the protagonists. It will focus in particular on the period of the Great Reforms of the 1860s, and especially the years before and after the abolition of serfdom in 1861, which represented the apogee of this process, as literature both provoked and reflected the transformation of peasants from bonded subjects of a feudal system into free legal and economic entities. It will reveal how peasant-themed literature from the 1840s to 1860s was varied and encompassed a wide range of plots and issues, incorporating works by a range of lesser-known writers alongside works by canonical authors such as Ivan Turgenev (1818–1883), Lev Tolstoi (1828–1910), Nikolai Leskov (1831–1895), and Anton Chekhov (1860–1904).

Prototypes

Peasants populate canonical Russian literary texts as minor characters, but few of these are memorable. In this sense, their marginal position in the text reflects the very subjugation and lack of rights they faced in social reality. Their space within the narrative is often minimal: they appear in the roles of coachmen, chambermaids, footmen, domestic servants, valets, stewards, or as the nameless figures of farmers in the landscape.[3] They are assistants, helping the narrative to advance, or resourceful servants, in the vein of Cervantes's prototype, Sancho Panza. Key examples of such characters in eighteenth- and nineteenth-century literature include Aniuta in Aleksandr Radishchev's (1749–1802) *A Journey from St Petersburg to Moscow* (*Puteshestvie iz Peterburga v Moskvu*, 1790), Tatiana's nanny in Aleksandr Pushkin's (1799–1837) *Eugene Onegin* (*Evgenii Onegin*, 1825–32), Chichikov's footman Petrushka in

2 David Moon, *The Russian Peasantry 1600–1930: The World the Peasants Made* (London: Addison Wesley Longman, 1999), p. 2.

3 See Bruce Robbins, *The Servant's Hand: English Fiction from Below* (New York: Columbia University Press, 1986); John Barrell, *The Dark Side of the Landscape: The Rural Poor in English Painting 1730–1840* (Cambridge: Cambridge University Press, 1980).

Dead Souls (*Mertvye dushi*, 1842) by Nikolai Gogol (1809–1852), and Zakhar the valet in Ivan Goncharov's (1812–1891) *Oblomov* (*Oblomov*, 1859). These and dozens of other minor peasant men and women have in common their designation via a fixed character type.

Peasants, however, were the occasional heroes of Russian literature even in the eighteenth century. This was primarily in two genres: Aleksandr Sumarokov's (1717–1777) eclogues (pastoral poems) of the 1750s–1770s, and the comic operas of the 1770s. If eclogues were adaptations of French texts by Bernard de Fontenelle and bore no relation to the real, everyday life of Russian peasants,[4] then comic opera may be considered the genre which discovered the peasant theme as a subject for representation – and in which representatives of the lower social classes took the role of protagonist for the first time.[5] In 1779, for example, a sensational success awaited Aleksandr Ablesimov's (1742–1783) comic opera *The Miller Who Was a Wizard, a Cheat and a Matchmaker* (*Mel'nik-koldun, obmanshchik i svat*), in which a cunning miller arranges a wedding between Filimon, an affluent and free peasant, and Aniuta, a young woman of noble descent, thus overcoming the financial and class conflicts between their parents. Through its onstage representation of peasant wedding rituals, folk dances, everyday scenery, and popular speech, Ablesimov's *Miller* satisfied a demand which first appeared among educated audiences at the end of the eighteenth century for the 'Russian' and the 'folk'. It thus became one of the most common repertoire pieces in the history of Russian theatre (performed even in the 1950s in the Soviet Union) and established an influential tradition of the comic, yet at the same time verisimilar, portrayal of peasant life.

This and many other comic operas from the end of the eighteenth century bear witness to the fact that, even if a peasant was the protagonist, his role was limited by the strict rules of the genre. First comic opera, and then 'sentimental drama' – or melodrama – at the start of the nineteenth century (e.g. the popular play *Liza, or the Triumph of Gratitude* (*Liza, ili Torzhestvo blagodarnosti*, 1802), by Nikolai Ilin (1777–1823)), dictated a scenario to the author: the seduction of an innocent peasant woman by a young nobleman, outraged honour, or an attempt to move from one social class to another. As

---

4 See Joachim Klein, 'Pastoral'naia poeziia russkogo klassitsizma' [Pastoral poetry of Russian Classicism], in *Put' kul'turnogo importa: Trudy po russkoi literature XVIII veka* [The journey of cultural import: Research on Russian literature of the eighteenth century] (Moscow: Iazyki slavianskoi kul'tury, 2005), pp. 19–215.
5 Joachim Klein, *Russkaia literatura v XVIII veke* [Russian literature in the eighteenth century] (Moscow: Indrik, 2010), p. 269.

contemporary critics observed, comedies of this kind were aimed at the educated elite and ultimately reinforced the status quo, articulating class boundaries and social roles.[6]

In the late eighteenth and early nineteenth centuries, the cultures of Sentimentalism and early Romanticism engaged in new ways with the peasant theme (see Chapter 1.4). Depictions of the peasantry merged with the wider early modern period's influential myth of a lost paradise, recoverable in the bosom of nature, with an emphasis on peaceful rural life in opposition to the corrupt lifestyle of the growing towns. Friedrich Schiller provided a trenchant analysis of this myth in his treatise 'On Naïve and Sentimental Poetry' (1795). According to Schiller, the present urban age had developed a nostalgic 'sentimental' taste which, in its yearning for a lost golden age, was drawn to 'the customs of the country folk, and [of] the primitive world'.[7] The contemplation of those 'more naïve' than the observer gives him a particular kind of enjoyment, brought to fulfilment in the genres of the idyll and the pastoral.[8]

Schiller's ideas help us to understand the cultural, aesthetic, and generic framework within which works about peasants were created and read until the mid-nineteenth century. The year 1792 saw the appearance of the first literary prose text with a peasant protagonist who was not a serf. Nikolai Karamzin's (1766–1826) 'Poor Liza' (*Bednaia Liza*, 1792) established an influential generic and narrative model, which scholars term 'sentimental-pastoral'.[9] The pastoral nature of the story is in the text's frequent references to topoi such as shepherds and pastures as well as in the plot: while selling flowers in Moscow, a free peasant named Liza – who lives near the city with her mother – meets a nobleman named Erast who seduces her with promises of marriage and then suddenly disappears. One fine day, the lovelorn Liza encounters Erast in Moscow and learns that he is marrying an elderly, rich widow. Unable to bear the betrayal, Liza commits suicide. This denouement

---

6 See Andrey L. Zorin, 'Redkaia veshch': "Sandunovskii skandal" i russkii dvor vremen Frantsuzskoi revoliutsii' [A rare thing: The 'Sandunovskii scandal' and the Russian court at the time of the French Revolution], *Novoe literaturnoe obozrenie* [New literary review] 80 (2006), 91–110.

7 Friedrich Schiller, *'Naive and Sentimental Poetry' and 'On the Sublime': Two Essays*, trans. Julius A. Elias (New York: Frederick Ungar, 1966), p. 83; Russian translation in Schiller, *Sobranie sochinenii* [Collected works], 7 vols. (Moscow: Gosudarstvennoe izdatel'stvo khudozhestvennoi literatury, 1955–7), vol. VI, p. 385.

8 See Paul Alpers, *What Is Pastoral?* (Chicago: University of Chicago Press, 1996), pp. 28–37.

9 Anthony Cross, 'Raznovidnosti idillii v tvorchestve Karamzina' [Varieties of idyll in the works of Karamzin], *XVIII vek* [The eighteenth century] 8 (1969), 221; Klein, *Russkaia literatura v XVIII veke*, p. 387.

works to propagate the patriarchal social model of the time: the violated honour of the peasant girl deceived by a nobleman is not restored, and the sin which lies on her soul (Liza feels that she is a criminal) can only be expiated through suicide.[10] The class boundaries between nobles and peasants remain unshakeable, however much Erast might assure his lover to the contrary. All that remains for the narrator and the reader is to weep – and to revel in the well-written story (see Chapters 1.4, 3.6).

'Poor Liza' was a distinctly modern version of the pastoral idyll. Its pastoral retinue was placed in a specific everyday context and social framework, and the hero's state of mind is presented through introspection. Indeed, this text provides the first instance in Russian literature of what Dorrit Cohn describes as the 'transparent mind' technique.[11] Karamzin posits near-complete transparency in describing the heart and mind of his heroine. Access to her presents no epistemological or rhetorical problem, and there are no narratorial comments which acknowledge difficulty in conveying what is happening in the protagonist's mind. On the contrary, the narrator employs what Geoffrey Leech and Michael Short have called 'narrative reports of the thought act' to convey Liza's thoughts.[12] For example, when Erast allegedly goes to war, the narrator says: 'Oh! she thought, Why have I been abandoned in this wasteland? What keeps me from flying after dear Erast? I am not afraid of war; I am only afraid without my friend. I want to live with him, to die with him, or to save his precious life by my own death.'[13] Such instances point to the lack of any problematisation of the peasant world view or of its presentation in the narrative. This is unsurprising: an insistence on a shared human nature – independent of its connection with social estate or class – was a feature of Karamzin's ideology. The minds of the noble Erast and of the peasant Liza function according to shared stylistic rules; in this way the text avoids exoticising Liza's emotional and intellectual processes. Karamzin's narrative experiment proved to be a one-off, however. While the narrative would be replicated dozens of times, first in Sentimental fiction from 1800 to 1810 and later in prose about the common people from 1830 to 1860, no other

---

10 Colleen Lucey, *Love for Sale: Representing Prostitution in Imperial Russia* (Ithaca: Cornell University Press, 2021).

11 Dorrit Cohn, *Transparent Minds: Narrative Modes for Presenting Consciousness in Fiction* (Princeton: Princeton University Press, 1978); Victoria Somoff, *The Imperative of Reliability: Russian Prose on the Eve of the Novel, 1820s–1850s* (Evanston, IL: Northwestern University Press, 2015).

12 Geoffrey Leech and Michael Short, *Style in Fiction: A Linguistic Introduction to English Fictional Prose* (Harlow: Pearson Longman, 2001), pp. 270–6.

13 Harold B. Segel (ed.), *The Literature of Eighteenth Century Russia: A History and Anthology,* 2 vols. (New York: E. P. Dutton, 1967), vol. II, p. 90.

Russian prose work before 1840 came close to it in its use of transparency in portraying the peasant mind. Indeed, later texts would emphasise rather the impossibility of penetrating its dark recesses.

Realism and the Peasant Protagonist

The next substantive breakthrough in the portrayal of both free and enserfed peasants was made in the 1840s in the works of Dmitrii Grigorovich (1822–1899), with the novellas *The Village* (*Derevnia*, 1846) and *Anton Goremyka* (*Anton Goremyka*, 1847), and Turgenev, with the cycle *Notes of a Hunter* (*Zapiski okhotnika*, 1852), along with those of the poet Nikolai Nekrasov (1821–1878). As Mikhail Saltykov-Shchedrin (1826–1889) reminisced: 'I remember *The Village*, I remember *Anton Goremyka* ... It was the first fertile spring rain, the first kindly human tears, and from Grigorovich's swift hand the idea that peasants are people, both in Russian literature and in Russian society, struck firm root.'[14]

The innovations of Grigorovich and Turgenev lay in both content and form. From an ideological perspective, peasants began to be portrayed in two key ways: as the victims of violence by their landlords or families; and as the bearers of the best qualities of the Russian nation as a whole. There was a background to such an idealisation: in the 1830s, the categories of national character and nationality became dominant trends, both in aesthetics and in state ideology. Literary criticism gave preference to those images of peasants which satisfied the criterion of national character – for example, Turgenev's sketch 'Khor and Kalinych' (*Khor i Kalinych*, 1847) in *Notes of a Hunter*. Equally, state ideology encouraged the creation of works which organically combined the peasant theme with the ideal of autocracy: Mikhail Glinka's (1804–1857) opera *A Life for the Tsar* (*Zhizn' za tsaria*, 1836) pictured a serf named Ivan Susanin saving Mikhail, the future founder of the Romanov dynasty, from the Polish-Lithuanian troops in 1613.

With regard to form, Grigorovich, Turgenev, and Nekrasov not only made peasants their protagonists but also developed new methods of portraying the peasant psyche and way of life. Peasants had, of course, been protagonists before Grigorovich and Turgenev; however, almost none of these stories from the 1820s–1830s – for example, Glinka's *Luka and Maria* (*Luka da Mar'ia*, 1818) and Mikhail Pogodin's (1800–1875) *The Pauper* (*Nishchii*, 1826) – have found their

---

14 Mikhail Saltykov-Shchedrin, *Sobranie sochinenii v dvadtsati tomakh* [Collected works in twenty volumes] (Moscow: Khudozhestvennaia literatura, 1965–77), vol. XIII, p. 468.

way into the canon. They did, however, play an important role in the development of the genre known as 'stories from the life of peasants', which emerged at the start of the 1850s. These were unpretentious narratives, often constructed as a tragic story of disenfranchised life related by a soldier, peasant, or coachman to an educated narrator. Initially, elements of the older genres of idyll and pastoral hid behind the generic title 'stories from the life of peasants', especially if the text's setting was confined to the village or the boundaries of the family or commune. Over the course of the decade, however, as 1861 and the abolition of serfdom approached, critics and commentators demanded ever more insistently that writers reject the nostalgic, unproblematic portrayal of everyday peasant life and its idealisation.

Stories from the life of peasants can be characterised by the following four features: 'protagonicity', 'ethnographism', use of the 'peasant voice', and the portrayal of the 'peasant mind'. The first of these features, protagonicity, points to the fact that the protagonists were always peasants and that the narration concentrated on describing their familial or communal life, often in contact or conflict with that of the landed nobility. This prompted a series of popular narrative models: the marriage plot, the seduction plot, the violence plot (from within the family or from the landlord), and narratives of demonic temptation. Marriage plots were generally tragic: marriage between the lovers was forbidden, as in *The Sandpiper* (*Kulik*, 1841) by bilingual Ukrainian and Russian writer Evgenii Grebenka (Yevhen Hrebenka, 1812–1848) or Turgenev's 'Ermolai and the Miller's Wife' (*Ermolai i mel'nichikha*, 1847) and *Mumu* (*Mumu*, 1854). The seduction plot, with its prototype in Karamzin's 'Poor Liza', also examined the tragic consequences of love and/or sexual relations between a nobleman and a peasant woman, as in Aleksandr Herzen's (1812–1870) *The Thieving Magpie* (*Soroka-vorovka*, 1848) and Turgenev's 'The Meeting' (*Svidanie*, 1850). The violence plot first appeared in Russian prose in 1846 in Grigorovich's *The Village*, where Akulina's forced marriage is the source of all her catastrophes. The number of such narratives increased through the 1850s, reaching their peak on the eve of emancipation. Finally, the demonic temptation plot expressed the purported fragility of peasant religious faith and the susceptibility of peasants to demonic temptation. This focus on the ethical conflict of temptation would later provide the narrative momentum for Lev Tolstoi's drama of 1887, *The Power of Darkness* (*Vlast' t'my*).

The ethnographism of peasant literature was predetermined by the subject matter; in the era of Realism, it was possible to recount peasant life reliably only by including ethnographic material in the text: descriptions of everyday

life, realia, language, and folklore. Literary ethnographism in this period was an organic part of a wider ethnographic boom in the late 1840s when, under the aegis of the Russian Geographical Society (founded in 1845), a special academic discourse formed and the collection of ethnographic materials intensified. Writers strove to embrace as many distinct social groups of peasants and as much of the realia of their farm, trade, and home life as possible. Thus, Aleksei Pisemskii's (1821–1881) short story 'The Petersburger' (*Pitershchik*, 1852) shows the fate of Klementii, a peasant seasonal worker (i.e. a serf who works in St Petersburg and sends a quit-rent – a sum of money set by a serfholder – to his landlord). In Grigorovich's *Anton Goremyka*, we see a shockingly dismal picture of the destitution endured by Anton, whose last horse is seized. By contrast, Turgenev's 'Khor and Kalinych' depicts the strong and even prosperous peasant household of the quit-rent-paying Khor. At the same time, writers often emphasised peasant traditions and rituals: weddings, funerals, village gatherings, fortune-telling, sorcery, traditional healing, horse doctory, etc. Finally, many stories about peasants were saturated with Russian, Ukrainian, and other Slavonic folklore: folk songs, sayings, proverbs, and bywords were inserted into their texts, and heroes recount popular beliefs and legends. In Turgenev's *Notes of a Hunter*, for example, several tales are constructed on motifs from folk superstition and legends: 'Bezhin Meadow' (*Bezhin lug*, 1851), 'Kasian from the Beautiful Lands' (*Kas'ian s Krasivoi Mechi*, 1851), and 'Singers' (*Pevtsy*, 1850). In the second half of the nineteenth century, Leskov relied mostly on folkloric, apocryphal, and legendary material to create his peasant heroes in *The Enchanted Wanderer* (*Ocharovannyi strannik*, 1873), *The Death-Defying Golovan* (*Nesmertel'nyi Golovan*, 1880), and 'The Left-Hander' (*Levsha*, 1881).

An important element of literary ethnographism is the emphasis on the 'peasant voice'. In many tales, the narrator either gives the floor to the heroes to speak about themselves or imitates oral peasant speech in the form of *skaz* (see Box 4.3; Chapter 3.6). Peasant speech in Russian literature differed greatly from its real pronunciation, with all of the latter's specific linguistic and aural deviations from the conventional literary norm. While at the turn of the nineteenth century authors were afraid to portray 'incorrect' and 'dissonant' peasant dialect – which was often completely unintelligible to the educated reader – later authors such as Turgenev, Pisemskii, and Tolstoi ingeniously brought peasant speech into literary language. In *Notes of a Hunter*, Turgenev created individualised forms of peasants' and commoners' voices with aural and intonational diversity. As early as 'Khor and Kalinych', the narrator focuses attention on the oral

component of the two contrasting heroes' individuality: 'During my talks with Khor I heard for the first time the simple, intelligent speech of the Russian peasant.'[15] In 'Bezhin Lea', each of the boys' speech is individualised. In 'Kasian from the Beautiful Lands', the main hero's strangeness is formed through a description of his oral manner and the timbre of his voice: 'The strange little old man spoke with a very pronounced dwelling on each word. The sound of his voice also astonished me. Not only was there nothing decrepit about it but it was surprisingly sweet, youthful and almost feminine in its gentleness.'[16] In Tolstoi's *War and Peace* (*Voina i mir*, 1868–9), the celebrated speech form of Platon Karataev is in consonance with this Turgenevian characterisation: intelligible (not dialect), rhythmical, and saturated with numerous proverbs and bywords.

Finally, voice is also linked with the fourth feature of stories from the life of peasants: the portrayal of the 'peasant mind'. While for Karamzin the peasant mind and thought were implicitly transparent and available, in the second half of the nineteenth century Realist narrative conventions demanded that writers use a more complicated technique for communicating their heroes' inner lives. It would be impossible within the framework of Realist conventions to create a text without the requisite excursion into its hero's mind. However, in the case of the peasant protagonist, this was complex. Not only was the peasant mind unfamiliar to the elite writer but – according to the observations of critics, philosophers, and ethnographers of the time – peasants possessed less developed intellectual capacities than the educated classes and were almost incapable of introspection. One of the first to attempt to capture this alien quality of the peasant mind was Grigorovich in *The Village*. Unlike Karamzin, Grigorovich split his heroine's interiority into feelings and thoughts. Where her feelings are portrayed as open to being read and related by the narrator (conveyed through a description of her sufferings, fits of passion, and pain), her thoughts prove at best semi-transparent and mainly opaque. Akulina is presented as almost mute in the novella: the violence from the nobility towards serfs, and also from her family, hardens her and leads to her refusal to speak. Turgenev's renowned novella *Mumu* used this same technique of semi-transparency. At first it seems to emphasise the opacity of the peasant mind: the protagonist is the deaf-mute Gerasim, whose thoughts

---

15 Ivan Turgenev, *Polnoe sobranie sochinenii v tridtsati tomakh* [Collected works in thirty volumes] (Moscow: Nauka, 1979), vol. III, p. 17; English translation in I. Turgenev, *Sketches from a Hunter's Album*, trans. Richard Freeborn (St Ives: Penguin, 1990), p. 25.

16 Turgenev, *Polnoe sobranie sochinenii*, vol. III, p. 110; Turgenev, *Sketches*, pp. 125–6.

the narrator cannot penetrate because the hero cannot speak.[17] However, the narrator's ability to feel for Gerasim still remains (the verb 'felt' appears several times).

In sum, we can describe the golden age of depicting peasants in Russian literature (on the eve of the abolition of serfdom) through an apparent paradox: the formation of the peasant as a fully fledged hero/heroine and an entity in literature only became possible through an assertion of the opacity and incomprehensibility of his/her mind. This epistemological model of peasant opacity came into being in both public discourse (criticism, philosophy, literary sketches) and literary fiction towards the end of the 1840s. What caused such a surge of stories about peasants in Russia? It could be argued that these stories offered an answer to the two most important sociocultural and political contradictions of the era: serfdom and the rise of Russian nationalism as a specific ideology. But the correlation between social reality and literature was complex. After all, serfdom had existed in Russia before the 1840s, but the new literary genre formed only at the very start of the 1850s. This may be due partly to the influence of Realist prescriptions (the genre was genetically related to the Natural School; see Chapter 1.5) – or, to use the language of the era, of the positivist-philological paradigm. As Josephine Donovan has shown, during the first thirty to forty years of the nineteenth century a 'local colour' movement formed in Anglophone, French, German, Czech, Russian, and American literatures (and later in other European literatures, too), and one of its most important thematic niches was stories of the lives of peasants. Such stories appeared as a reaction to the urbanisation and unification of rural life, to the rise of nationalism, and to the consolidation of national states and their systems of governing their inhabitants.[18]

In this respect, works about peasants performed an important cultural function in Russian literature, creating stable images and narrative models which symbolically encoded the cultured elite's notion of the Russian national character. The peasant, cast as a domestic 'other', acted as a model for Russianness itself, providing stories of national identity and awakening feelings of patriotism. During the 1850s, peasants became an object of cultural consumption in hitherto unprecedented volumes by the elite of the Russian

---

17 See Somoff, *Imperative of Reliability*, pp. 111–38.
18 Josephine Donovan, *European Local-Color Literature: National Tales, Dorfgeschichten, Romans Champetres* (London: Continuum, 2010); see also Franco Moretti, *Graphs, Maps, Trees: Abstract Models for a Literary History* (New York: Verso, 2005), chap. 2.

Empire.[19] The peak of this consumption came in the most dramatic years of the mid-nineteenth century: the Crimean War – so traumatic for Russia – and the first years after the abolition of serfdom.

The peasant 'other' was an idealised image in the vast majority of works before the emancipation of the serfs. Such are the strange, enigmatic peasants in Turgenev's *Notes of a Hunter* (Khor and Kalinych, Kasian from 'Kasian from the Beautiful Lands', the half saint Lukeria from 'Living Relic' (*Zhivye moshchi*, 1874)); Tolstoi's strong handymen in *A Morning of a Landed Proprietor* (*Utro pomeshchika*, 1856); Gleb Savinov, the head of the family of fishermen in Grigorovich's novel *The Fishermen* (*Rybaki*, 1853); and many others. The idealisation of the peasant led to the appearance of a clichéd image in Russian literature of the peasant as truth-seeker and bearer of God, a voice of conscience for the main heroes who seek the meaning of life. Such, for example, are the many peasants in Tolstoi's prose: Platon Karataev exercises a decisive influence on the transformation of protagonist Pierre Bezukhov's mind in *War and Peace*; Platon Fokanych does so on Konstantin Levin in *Anna Karenina* (*Anna Karenina*, 1878); and Gerasim does so on Ivan Ilich in *The Death of Ivan Ilich* (*Smert' Ivana Il'icha*, 1886). Although Tolstoi later created entirely different, much more verisimilar figures of peasants in drama (for example, in *The Power of Darkness*), these earlier characters remain his emblematic peasant protagonists. Such figures are also the 'righteous ones' in Leskov's cycle of the same name from the late 1870s to early 1880s: the dull craftsman Left-Hander ('The Left-Hander'), Ivan Fliagin (*The Enchanted Wanderer*), and Golovan (*The Death-Defying Golovan*).

Only from the end of the 1850s did works begin to appear in Russian literature in which authors attempted to approach peasants impartially, rejecting old conventions. One of the first to try an entirely new anti-literary and anti-idyllic approach to the peasant theme was the bilingual Ukrainian-Russian woman writer Marko Vovchok (pseud. of Mariia Vilinska, 1833–1907). Her *Stories from the Folk Life of Russia* (*Rasskazy iz narodnogo russkogo byta*, 1859) depicted the tragic fates of peasant women in the Russian Empire, subject to unprecedented violence from both family and landlord. Vovchok's success was assured by her first collection, *Popular [Ukrainian] Stories* (*Narodni opovidannia*, 1858), which was published in St Petersburg in Ukrainian, then translated into Russian, and later became a classic of Ukrainian literature. The blurring of Ukrainian and Russian

19 An analogous process had run forty to fifty years earlier in British culture. See Jeremy Burchard, *Paradise Lost: Rural Idyll and Social Change in England since 1800* (London: I. B. Tauris, 2002), pp. 2–3.

identities in the formation of this text is indicative of a broader trend – it should be noted, however, that while Vovchok creates stereotypes of Ukrainian and Russian peasant types, she does present her Ukrainian protagonists as possessing greater mental freedom than their Russian equivalents, despite social constraints. Another line of new literature about peasants was connected with Nikolai Uspenskii (1837–1889), who in 1861 released a collection of short stories which were heralded by the radical critic Nikolai Chernyshevskii (1828–1889) as a new direction. The collection consists of twenty-four texts, a section of which are theatrical scenes. The majority of the texts have no plot, no characters, no ethnographism, no landscapes. They depict ordinary situations from daily peasant life: chance events and fragments of reality without beginning or end – as if alluding to the fact that nothing significant can happen in the life of a peasant. Thus, the short story 'Old Woman' (*Starukha*, 1857) presents an elderly woman who tells of how both her sons were conscripted into the army by the steward, with whom one of their wives then willingly lived as his lover. In the short story 'The Good Existence' (*Khoroshee zhit'e*, 1858), a publican tells of his happy life and extols the drunkenness of Russian peasants, who squander their last kopecks on drink in the tavern. Uspenskii's short sketches were very popular in Russia on the eve of the abolition of serfdom, but afterwards they quickly went out of date.

The Free Serf

The abolition of serfdom on 19 February 1861 is a symbolic boundary beyond which, in many ways, a different peasant literature begins. As the Marxist critic Petr Tkachev (1844–1886) remarked, as soon as peasants became independent economic and legal entities, this led to the appearance of new ways of representing them in literature.[20] In this sense, the 1860s and 1870s were a time of maximum diversity in the models used for depicting peasants and their various types. Central among them was the 'grey muzhik': an average, 'normal' peasant, often completely unremarkable and therefore particularly suited to illustrating the author's ideology. The diversity of types of peasants spawned yet another problem in their representation: the features of an

20 Petr N. Tkachev, 'Muzhik v salonakh sovremennoi belletristiki' [The *muzhik* in the salons of contemporary fiction], in Tkachev, *Izbrannye sochineniia na sotsial'no-politicheskie temy v chetyrekh tomakh* [Selected works on social and political topics in four volumes] (Moscow: Obshchestvo polikatorzhan i ssyl'no-poselentsev, 1932–4), vol. IV, p. 282. The article was serialised in the journal *Delo* (The cause) in 1879.

'authentic' peasant, so familiar from the prose of Turgenev and Grigorovich, became increasingly difficult to perceive and reproduce, since the boundaries between the classes began to erode after 1861, providing the subject for numerous post-reform era dramas.[21]

In this period, the genre of stories from the life of peasants lost its distinct contours, dissolving into a flow of texts about new subjects (free peasants, workers, the petty bourgeois) and giving way to novels which were increasingly being written about peasants. Peasant protagonists were normalised in Russian literature; hence scholars state that it is impossible to highlight any one model or pattern for the depiction of peasants in literature of the 1860s–1880s. It is more accurate to speak of competing images of peasants, of ways of rationalising and conceptualising them. The social, fictitious 'peasant' of literary and journalistic texts disintegrated into conflicting images of grey muzhiks, *kulaks* (prosperous peasants), paupers, and economic migrants, all of which reflected the ideologies of those who wrote them – the various parties of populists (*narodniki*) who went to the countryside to enlighten the people: Marxists, monarchists, and liberals. As before 1861, behind these literary images and types of peasants stood the educated elite's notions and fears about the past, present, and future of Russia.[22]

On the one hand, many authors continued to see peasants (whether ethnically Russian or ethnically Ukrainian) as the bearers of the best features of an idea of the 'Russian' character and to use them as a nostalgic image of bygone, pre-reform life. Examples of this include Tolstoi's short story 'Polikushka' (*Polikushka*, 1863) depicting the tragic suicide of the eponymous peasant; Leskov's 'The Life of a Peasant Martyress' (*Zhitie odnoi baby*, 1863), the touching story of an unsuccessful flight by two serf-lovers, and his novella *The Death-Defying Golovan*, the story of a righteous serf who buys his freedom, repeatedly saves the entire village from various misfortunes, and sacrifices his own life for others; and Turgenev's 'Living Relic', a hymn to the spiritual strength of a paralysed Russian peasant woman.

On the other hand, a whole generation of so-called *raznochintsy* (of non-noble origin) authors entered literature in the post-reform years and left memorable descriptions of contemporary peasant life which had nothing in

---

21 Kirill Iu. Zubkov and Anastassia S. Pernikova, 'Literaturnye premii, sotsial'nye granitsy i natsional'nyi teatr: Krest'ianin v russkoi dramaturgii epokhi Velikikh reform' [Literary prizes, social boundaries, and national theatre: Peasants in Russian drama in the era of the Great Reforms'], *Russian Literature* 119 (2021), 71–101.

22 Cathy Frierson, *Peasant Icons: Representations of Rural People in Late Nineteenth-Century Russia* (Oxford: Oxford University Press, 1993).

common with the idyll and which offered the readers a dismal picture of destitution, social insecurity, and inequality among Russian (Orthodox) and other ethnic groups of peasants. The most resonant authors of the 1860s to work in this movement were the essayists Aleksandr Levitov (1835–1877), Vasilii Sleptsov (1836–1878), Gleb Uspenskii (1843–1902), and particularly Fedor Reshetnikov (1841–1871). Reshetnikov's ethnographic sketch *The Podlipnayans* (*Podlipovtsy*, 1864) shook contemporaries through its shocking description of the dismal way of life in deserted Permian villages of the Urals (now the Perm Krai). Under the author's lens falls a forsaken village in the Urals, sparsely populated with semi-pagan Permians who barely speak Russian, avoid calling for the priest, and bury their dead without communion. Reshetnikov's narrator is not shy in emphasising that his heroes Pila and Sysoika are at a lower stage of development compared with Russians. This idea takes shape in the text through zoomorphic descriptions of the protagonists. Meanwhile, in a break with the tradition of Grigorovich and Turgenev, Reshetnikov makes the mind and thoughts of his heroes transparent; he even uses free indirect discourse and introspection to convey the heroes' innermost thoughts. The combination of free indirect discourse as the form of creating human subjectivity with the inhumane, wild thoughts of the heroes of *The Podlipnayans* creates a terrifying impression.

The mass migration of peasants after 1861 was the subject of Reshetnikov's experimental novel *Where Is Life Better?* (*Gde luchshe?*, 1868) about the hard lot of two households from the Urals who migrate from factory to factory, from town to town, in search of wages and a better life. The peculiarity of the novel, which staggered contemporaries, was that it lacked the customary protagonist. Instead, the first half of the novel consisted of a fragmentary description of the trajectories of many peasants. Thus, the figure of a spectral, collective subject took shape: the people who experience suffering and endure want.[23]

This model of a collective peasant subject was also a feature of the two most prominent novels of the 1870s: Pavel Zasodimskii's (1843–1912) *The Chronicles of the Village of Smurino* (*Khronika sela Smurina*, 1874) and Nikolai Zlatovratskii's (1845–1911) *Foundations: The Story of a Village* (*Ustoi: Istoriia odnoi derevni*, 1878–82). Today, these novels are considered to be at the extreme periphery of the Russian literary canon, whose front row is occupied by the novels of Tolstoi, Dostoevskii, Turgenev, and Goncharov. Unlike the experimental Reshetnikov,

---

23 See Helen Stuhr-Rommereim, 'The limits of Realism and the proletariat on the horizon: Fedor Reshetnikov's *Where Is It Better?*', *Russian Review* 80.1 (2021), 100–21.

Zasodimskii and Zlatovratskii reproduced the novelistic models of prose about nobles but made the life of a village the object of their narrative. Thus, *The Chronicles of the Village of Smurino* may be defined generically as a novel of social failure: a merchant named Kriazhev organises a mutual assistance office, a peasant co-operative, a school, and trade with the town in his native village but suffers a fiasco in confrontation with the local wealthy peasants (*kulaks*). The novel's romantic thread (the relationship between Kriazhev and Evgesha) is undeveloped and marginal relative to the protagonist's social projects. The novel notably emphasises the gap between the heroes' language, which approaches literary language, and the realistic language in which the inhabitants of Smurino actually express themselves and, perhaps, think. This language breaks through into the novel in quotations from a newspaper article by a *kulak* named Lisin, which constitutes a shocking mixture of bureaucratic expressions and biblical images. The most crucial among them – 'the mark of the Antichrist' (this was the novel's original title before the editor, Saltykov-Shchedrin, removed it) – points to the village inhabitants' archaic way of thinking.[24] The peasants live in captivity to rumours and conspiracy theorists' yarns about the end of the world, which will begin with the arrival of the railway, banks, and peasant co-operatives.

In the spectrum of literary commentary on how peasant life had changed after the emancipation, a special place belongs to Nikolai Nekrasov's verse epic *Who Can Be Happy in Russia?* (*Komu na Rusi zhit' khorosho?*, 1876), which relates the wanderings of seven temporarily obliged peasants (i.e. peasants paying off a redemption on the land to a landlord) through Russia, in search of someone gladdened by the reforms. Predictably, like the heroes of Reshetnikov's novel, Nekrasov's peasants do not find a single citizen who is satisfied with his position. Only Grisha Dobrosklonov, a hybrid democrat, socialist, and activist, emerges as contented with his own fate, allowing Nekrasov to bring his epopee to a conclusion. Against the backdrop of standardised peasant novels, short stories, and dramas, the uniqueness of Nekrasov's text is felt all the more keenly through its strange form – a mix of folkloric verse, song lyrics, and the traditions of high, civic poetry (see Box 2.5) – which made this poem a cult text of the Russian intelligentsia, who considered it to be the ideal expression of the people's thoughts and Nekrasov himself as their 'ventriloquist'.[25]

---

24 Pavel V. Zasodimskii, *Khronika sela Smurina* (Moscow: Gosudarstvennoe izdatel'stvo khudozhestvennoi literatury, 1959), p. 261.
25 See Alexander Ogden, 'Peasant listening, listening to peasants: Miscommunication and ventriloquism in Nekrasov's *Komu na Rusi zhit' khorosho*', *Russian Review* 72.4 (2013), 590–606.

The Twentieth-Century Peasant

By the end of the nineteenth century, Russian literature had normalised the peasant theme, and the peasant protagonist was no longer limited to particular genres or particular stylistic and rhetorical methods of writing. For example, in short stories by Chekhov such as 'Peasants' (*Muzhiki*, 1897) and 'In the Ravine' (*V ovrage*, 1899), the main peasant heroes are no longer marked as specifically 'other' and are depicted by the same formal means as other social groups. Nikolai, the protagonist of 'Peasants' who serves as a footman in a hotel in Moscow, becomes fatally ill and returns to his native village to die; but Chekhov no longer sees anything idyllic in the village way of life. This life – with its regular drunkenness and violence – is as poor and beggarly as that of urban workers and the petty bourgeoisie.[26] Several early short stories by Maksim Gorkii (1868–1936) were written with this same demythologising logic: the peasants in 'Chelkash' (*Chelkash*, 1895) and 'The Peasant' (*Muzhik*, 1900) appear as ambiguous, complicated characters endowed with both positive and negative characteristics and complicated internal dynamics.

All of the above-mentioned lines of tension converge in the works of Ivan Bunin (1870–1953), who in a few dozen short stories in the 1910s summed up the peasant theme's 150-year development. The most famous and canonical text on this theme was his novella *The Village* (*Derevnia*, 1910), in which the narrator uses the transparent mind technique to relate the fate of the Krasov brothers, two contemporary peasants. Tikhon has made his fortune and is now the new master of a landowner's former country estate, while the philosophising Kuzma is an unskilled worker, who has published a collection of his own poems. The brothers come together and try to start life afresh, but they undergo a complicated existential crisis which, prior to Bunin, it had not been customary to describe in relation to peasants.

Thanks to the remaining redemptive transactions (i.e. payments that peasants had to make in order to obtain land to farm) having been finalised in the 1890s, the number of literate peasants rose to 17 per cent (according to the 1897 census), the field of literature substantially broadened, and professional literary writers increasingly appeared from among the peasants: Sergei Semenov (1868–1922), Skitalets (Stepan Petrov, 1869–1941), Semen Podiachev (1836–1934), Grigorii Deev-Khomiakovskii (1888–1946), Sergei Esenin (1895–1925), and others. Many of them actually entered the market during the era of Modernism, when almost all of the various trends, from Symbolism to the

---

26 See Baktygul Aliev, 'Desacralizing the idyll: Chekhov's transformation of the pastoral', *Russian Review* 69.3 (2010), 463–76.

avant-garde, were engaged in constructing their own mythology of art (see Chapters 1.6, 1.7). Peasant protagonists (and stylised images of the village) frequently played an essential role in this. For example, in Andrei Belyi's (1880–1934) *The Silver Dove* (*Serebrianyi golub'*, 1909) a peasant carpenter named Kudeiarov and his wife, Matrena, represent a dark 'eastern' and 'Asiatic' social force, which contrasts with the civilised 'western' and 'European' heroes from the intelligentsia. In lyric poetry, outstanding new poets such as Esenin and Nikolai Kliuev (1884–1937) constructed their peasant voices from archaic, folkloric, and literary models, thereby satisfying the public's newly intensified demand for 'Russianness', which was constructed and reinvented anew.[27]

The already complicated position of various types of peasants in early twentieth-century Russia changed dramatically after the 1917 revolution and the civil war. Vladimir Lenin's policy of 'village reconstruction' was actually premised on village 'de-peasantisation' (the physical destruction of accustomed forms of farming and of private ownership of animals and the harvest); collectivisation (the creation of collective farms, or *kolkhozy*); and 'dekulakisation' (the oppression of the most affluent – and, in practice, all other – peasants). These events – tragic for peasants – were embodied in diametrically opposing styles in early Soviet literature of the 1920s–1930s. On the one hand, Modernist works about the village, such as Leonid Leonov's (1899–1994) *The Petushikhinskii Breakthrough* (*Petushikhinskii prolom*, 1923) and Andrei Platonov's (1899–1951) *For Future Use* (*Vprok*, 1931), appeared under the still relatively lax censorship of the 1920s. The former recounts the Soviet authorities' innovations in the village of Petushikha using an ornamental *skaz* style (see Box 4.3). In *For Future Use*, Platonov satirically depicted the formation of collective farms and was criticised personally by Joseph Stalin. On the other hand, works about collectivisation also sprang from the pens of writers loyal to the Soviet authorities, in which the authors adhered to the government's official account. Mikhail Sholokhov's (1905–1984) *Virgin Soil Upturned* (*Podniataia tselina*, 1932–59) thus optimistically narrates the successful creation of a collective farm on the Don.

Collectivisation, the Stalinist repressions, and the catastrophic devastation of the Second World War with its accompanying urbanisation led to the essential destruction of traditional peasant culture and the peasant way of life in the 1950s and 1960s. Consequently, in the second half of the twentieth

27 Alexander Ogden, 'The impossible peasant voice in Russian culture: Stylization and mimicry', *Slavic Review* 64.3 (2005), 517–37.

century, images of the peasantry came to connote an increasingly mythologised other life, a reservoir of symbols and motifs for anyone who did not agree with the communist path of village growth in the form of collective and state farms. An entire movement and group of authors conventionally termed Village Prose writers addressed these questions from 1955 until the very end of the 1970s (see Chapter 3.6). Their works thematised what Kathleen Parthé describes as 'the rural/urban split, criticism of government policy in the countryside, the revival of Russian national and religious sentiment, a search for national values, a concern for the environment, and a nostalgia generated by the loss of traditional rural life'.[28] All of these motifs are present in the most major works of authors who depicted contemporary village life in the 1970s and 1980s: Fedor Abramov's (1920–1983) *Brothers and Sisters* (*Brat'ia i sestry*, 1959), Aleksandr Solzhenitsyn's (1918–2008) *Matrena's Home* (*Matrenin dvor*, 1963), Vasilii Belov's (1932–2012) *Business as Usual* (*Privychnoe delo*, 1966), and Valentin Rasputin's (1937–2015) *Farewell to Matera* (*Proshchanie s Materoi*, 1976), among others.

With the last collective farms having disappeared by the mid-1990s and the transformation of those which had survived the crisis into regular farms, it is difficult to speak of the peasant as an extant entity and object of portrayal in post-Soviet Russia and literature. In any event, the notion of 'peasant' is no longer applicable to the inhabitants of modern Russian hamlets and villages. Thus the 'peasant' as a literary hero or heroine is a figure found principally in the nineteenth- and twentieth-century texts that have been our focus here. In broader cultural terms, the peasant protagonist was a figure in which national or ethnic identity (whether Russian, Ukrainian, or Belarusian) was elided – a product of the imperial cultural imagination.

Translated by Delphi Mayther

Further Reading

Glickman, R., 'An alternative view of the peasantry: The *raznochintsy* writers of the 1860s', *Slavic Review* 32.4 (1973), 693–704.

Herman, D., *Poverty of the Imagination: Nineteenth-Century Russian Literature about the Poor* (Evanston, IL: Northwestern University Press, 2001).

Herzberg, J., *Gegenarchive: Bäuerliche Autobiographik zwischen Zarenreich und Sowjetunion* [Counter-archives: Peasant autobiography between the tsarist empire and the Soviet Union] (Bielefeld: Transcript Verlag, 2014).

---

28 K. Parthé, *Russian Village Prose: The Radiant Past* (Princeton: Princeton University Press, 1992), p. 3.

Ivanits, L., *Dostoevsky and the Russian People* (Cambridge: Cambridge University Press, 2011).

Masing-Delic, I., 'Philosophy, myth and art in Turgenev's *Sketches from a Hunter's Album*', *Russian Review* 50.4 (1991), 437–50.

Ogden, A., 'Fashioning a folk identity: The "peasant-poet" tradition in Russia (Lomonsov, Kol'tsov, Kliuev)', *Intertexts* 5.1 (2001), 32–45.

Razuvalova, A., *Pisateli-'derevenshchiki': Literatura i konservativnaia ideologiia 1970-kh godov* ['Derevenshchik' authors: Literature and conservative ideology of the 1970s] (Moscow: Novoe literaturnoe obozrenie, 2015).

Vdovin, A. V., '"Nevedomyi mir": Russkaia i evropeickaia estetika i problema reprezentatsii krest'ian v literature serediny XIX veka' ['Unknown world': Russian and European aesthetics and the problem of representing peasants in mid-nineteenth century literature], *Novoe literaturnoe obozrenie* [New literary review] 146 (2016), 287–315.

Woodhouse J., 'A landlord's sketches? D. V. Grigorovic and peasant genre fiction', *Journal of European Studies* 16.4 (1986), 271–94.

Woodhouse J., 'Tales from another country: Fictional treatments of the Russian peasantry, 1847–1861', *Rural History* 2.2 (1991), 171–86.

Woodhouse J., 'Pisemsky's *Sketches from Peasant Life*: An attempt at a non-partisan reading', in Derek Offord (ed.), *The Golden Age of Russian Literature and Thought: Selected Papers from the Fourth World Congress for Soviet and East European Studies, Harrogate, 1990* (New York: St Martin's Press, 1992), pp. 84–102.

Zink, A., *Wie aus Bauern Russen wurden: Die Konstruktion des Volkes in der Literatur des Russischen Realismus 1860–1880* [How peasants became Russians: The construction of the folk in Russian Realist literature 1860–1880] (Zürich: Theologischer Verlag, 2009).

The *Intelligent*

KONSTANTINE KLIOUTCHKINE

The term 'intelligentsia', one of Russian culture's prominent contributions to the global vocabulary, has had a rich and complicated history since its appearance in the Russian press in the late 1860s. It purported to describe a particular kind of educated person as part of a group or a social class, yet it repeatedly failed to generate consensus as to the criteria by which that person or group could be defined. While journalists, critics, and scholars negotiated its ambivalent meanings, the term gradually grew in cultural prominence. In the process, literary representations of what the *intelligent* might be came to play a leading role in describing the experience of those intellectuals whom Russian culture expected to be distinct from ordinary educated people.

When the notion of the intelligentsia gained prominence in 1868 it highlighted the growing number of 'intellectual proletarians' – educated people who found themselves alienated from the state and from social institutions as well as from the means of production. By the turn of the 1880s, however, a broader, more ambivalent, and more lasting understanding had emerged: the *intelligent*, while continuing to feel alienated, now carried a moral responsibility to direct his or her intellectual distinction towards improving the overall social order – a responsibility that routinely entailed doubts regarding his or her capacity to live up to these high expectations. As fiction increasingly described the specifics of the *intelligent*'s moral commitments and existential insecurities, Russian culture evolved a discursive tradition that retroactively envisioned the intelligentsia as having been manifested by the country's writers in their literary texts, starting well before the appearance of the term 'intelligentsia' itself.

The meaning of the term 'intelligentsia' has been mobile, changing along with broad cultural shifts over time. Conceptual self-dissolution has been essential to that process. Even during the classical period, when the meaning of the term as referring to a 'progressively minded intellectual proletariat'

appeared relatively clear, it was haunted by unanswerable questions: what exactly did it mean to be progressive, which intellectuals were distinct, and in what sense were they proletarian? The uncertainty of the term continued to increase in later periods, and its ambivalence became a force that generated new debates.

From the broad cultural perspective of the late twentieth century and beyond, the notion of the intelligentsia developed through three distinct periods: its prehistory, from the late eighteenth to the middle of the nineteenth century; the 'classical' period, between 1860 and 1880; and the longue durée from the 1880s to the present day. Focusing on the literary representation of the *intelligent* primarily during the classical period, this chapter shows that the term has been applied to persons and literary characters who did not themselves know the term, to those who knew the term but would have been shocked to discover that they could be identified by it, and to those who intensely resisted that identification but could not escape it in the eyes of their contemporaries and their later readers. A theme that runs through the chapter is, thus, the profound ambivalence of the figure of the *intelligent* across the Russian cultural tradition.

Prehistory: 1770–1860

Histories of the intelligentsia as retrospectively conceived (that is, applying the concept to phenomena that pre-date the invention of the word itself) tend to go back to the reign of Catherine II (r. 1762–96) and the context of the development of a semi-independent press by the literary-satirical journals and their main publisher, Nikolai Novikov (1744–1818), at the turn of the 1770s. The leading champion of the future intelligentsia at that early time was Aleksandr Radishchev (1749–1802), whose travelogue *A Journey from St Petersburg to Moscow* (*Puteshestvie iz Peterburga v Moskvu*, 1790) – for which the author was persecuted by the government – describes extreme forms of social injustice and state incompetence.

In this retrospective view of the intelligentsia, the next stage is commonly represented by the leaders of the Decembrist uprising against Tsar Nicholas I (r. 1825–55) in 1825. However, the Decembrists – belonging to a noble military elite – could hardly be envisioned as socially alienated, and their literary achievements, though in some cases notable (the leading Decembrist, Kondratii Ryleev (1795–1826), was a poet, for example), fell short of achieving a lasting legacy. In contrast with historical figures, it was a literary character who emerged as an early *intelligent*: Aleksandr Chatskii, the protagonist of

Aleksandr Griboedov's (1795–1829) play *Woe from Wit* (*Gore ot uma*, comp. 1824), proclaims broad humanitarian ideals and vehemently attacks Moscow society for failing to live up to his moral standards. As he finds himself ostracised, the text raises a question about the cause of his failure: was it the product of his progressive views or of his lack of intelligence in seeking to change an obviously intransigent milieu?

Whereas Chatskii was an isolated figure, the next generation of proto-*intelligents* came to be envisioned as comprising the members of philosophical circles, especially those associated with the University of Moscow from the late 1820s to the 1840s (although, even as the university introduced these figures to each other, their socialisation and intellectual life transpired independently from that institution). The notion of independent circles (*kruzhki*) of institutionally alienated, like-minded intellectuals would gain lasting currency in later visions of the intelligentsia experience (see also Chapter 2.3).

The towering figures to emerge from that environment were Aleksandr Herzen (1812–1870) and Mikhail Bakunin (1814–1876), who enjoyed wide-ranging careers in European revolutionary movements between the 1840s and 1860s. Herzen proved especially influential in Russian culture on the strength of his memoirs, *My Past and Thoughts* (*Byloe i dumy*, 1852–68). This work articulates a combination of high spiritual ideals and a growing sense of their failure to sustain his life. Most importantly, Herzen figures that combination as central to the tragic fate of an intellectual in history. The intellectual cannot avoid being a victim of historical process: the wheel of history, incommensurate with any individual's ideals and efforts, invariably destroys his or her life. Herzen's emphasis on the tragic relation between history and the intellectual would later become formative to many Soviet intellectuals' understanding of their condition (see Chapter 3.10).

One of the leading fiction writers to describe the challenges facing a progressively minded intellectual in the 1840s and 1850s was Ivan Turgenev (1818–1883). Turgenev developed the tradition of Russian literary representations of the 'superfluous man' – a person out of joint with his social world. A series of protagonists in his novels *Rudin* (*Rudin*, 1856), *A Nest of Gentlefolk* (*Dvorianskoe gnezdo*, 1859), and *On the Eve* (*Nakanune*, 1860) express the progressive values of their time but lack the energy to pursue their ideals in practice. This character type is also a victim of history. His early life shaped by repressive state rule under Nicholas I, Turgenev's hero remains incapable of social action after the tsar's death in 1855. This type's historically conditioned failure is most painfully manifested in his private life. Even as Turgenev's superfluous men inspire admiration and experience love, they

prove incapable of forming romantic – let alone marital – relationships, fleeing commitment at the moment that requires action. An extreme version of this type found expression in the eponymous character of Ivan Goncharov's (1812–1891) novel *Oblomov* (*Oblomov*, 1859). This largely sympathetic but hilariously absurd figure spends the opening third of the novel unsuccessfully trying to get out of bed. By 1862, Turgenev was able to envision a new type of hero in his novel *Fathers and Children* (*Ottsy i deti*), which features a highly energetic and – pointedly – non-gentry intellectual, Bazarov. This character marks the development of a cultural figure that would become central to the classical version of the *intelligent*.

The 'Classical' Period: 1860–1880

The reason the period between 1860 and 1880 has been called 'classical' reflects the appearance of the term 'intelligentsia' itself and, moreover, the relatively consistent meaning that the latter term maintained in those decades. At the turn of 1868, several progressive journalists began to use the term as part of their shared vision of the new type of intellectual, whom they described as an educated person radically alienated from social institutions and the means of production. The intellectuals coming of age after 1860 appeared distinctive in lacking the economic resources that their predecessors had derived from their respective positions in the traditional social world as members of the gentry, clergy, merchantry, or state bureaucracy. Moreover, the intellectual skills of the young intelligentsia remained in little demand in the as yet underdeveloped economy. The self-realisation of these new intellectuals became bound up with their own efforts to effect social change. The first step in that direction had to involve learning from independent sources of knowledge, such as progressive journalists' writings about the principles of social science, including the Marxist vision of historical development.[1] Formal training in the country's educational institutions was viewed as insufficient and possibly even counterproductive insofar as schools and universities lagged behind the current scientific knowledge that was disseminated primarily by the progressive press. The classical intelligentsia emerged as part of a new contract between writers and readers in the developing Russian press that worked to cultivate audiences in the context of print capitalism. In contrast to the earlier view of progressive intellectuals

---

1 P. N. Tkachev, 'Podrastaiushchie sily' [Rising forces], *Delo* [The cause] 9 (1868), sect. 'Sovremennoe obozrenie' [Contemporary review], 1–28, esp. 3–8.

as solitary actors or as members of friendly circles, the classical intelligentsia were participants in an imagined community of educated people whose lives were organised by their shared engagement with the medium of print. The journalists who championed the term 'intelligentsia' belonged to the most culturally influential and economically successful institutions in that medium.

The year 1868 marked a new consolidation of Russian progressive discourse. Progressive journalism had come to dominate the country's press in the late 1850s when Alexander II (r. 1855–81) introduced sweeping liberal reforms, including – most notably – the emancipation of the serfs. By 1860, the broad cultural impulse towards progressive speech had coalesced in two journals, *The Contemporary* (*Sovremennik*, 1836–66) and *The Russian Word* (*Russkoe slovo*, 1859–66). In 1866, an assassination attempt by Dmitrii Karakozov against Alexander II provoked government reaction, forcing the closure of progressive publications. Within two years, however, both progressive journals had, in effect, re-emerged under new titles. In 1866 the editor of *The Russian Word* was installed at a new journal, *The Cause* (*Delo*, 1866–88), while in 1868 the former editor of *The Contemporary* took over the editorship of *Notes of the Fatherland* (*Otechestvennye zapiski*, 1839–84; see Chapter 2.4). It was at that moment that their essayists and commentators came to reassess the status of writers and readers by using the word 'intelligentsia'. In that effort, they formed a distinct understanding of who the intelligentsia were and of the discursive tradition that had produced them.

The values of the intelligentsia developed in opposition to those of earlier generations of progressive intellectuals. Whereas most of the figures mentioned in the above prehistory came from the gentry, the intelligentsia – regardless of the origins of its particular members – was culturally opposed to that social estate. In everyday life, that opposition included the rejection of earlier standards of polite comportment by way of cultivating crude manners and styles of dress. Ideologically, the intelligentsia rejected the earlier interest in philosophy and the arts in order to foreground the importance of the natural and social sciences, especially biology, physiology, sociology, and economics. Such scientific focus also involved the rejection of religious values, as part of the act of distancing themselves from the social estate of the clergy. The sciences informed the new intelligentsia ethics, which prescribed that a person rely on the utilitarian calculus of pleasure and pain to understand his or her experience and to work out rules of conduct. In particular, scientific calculations suggested that true happiness derived from a person's altruistic work to improve life for all. Accordingly, one was

expected to make an altruistic effort on behalf of social progress, with a view towards enjoying its rewards in the future.

These values had developed in the earlier discussions about readers and writers in the progressive press, which provided the conceptual genealogy for the descriptions of the intelligentsia in 1868 and beyond. The central types in that genealogy were the 'nihilists' of Turgenev's *Fathers and Children*, the 'new people' of Nikolai Chernyshevskii's (1828–1889) novel *What Is to Be Done? (Chto delat'?*, 1863), and the 'intellectual proletariat' of Dmitrii Pisarev's (1840–1868) criticism of the mid-1860s.

In *Fathers and Children*, Turgenev's Bazarov is a medical student who believes that the natural sciences will resolve the questions of human existence once scientific knowledge becomes sufficiently advanced. Working towards that knowledge, Bazarov occupies himself on a summer vacation by dissecting frogs, whose physiology, he thinks, will offer insight into the functioning of any living being. Away from his experiments, Bazarov ridicules his gentry associates for their attachment to art and literature, social conventions, and polite conversation. Furthermore, he shocks them by denying the values of human affection and love.

Whereas Bazarov's nihilism stops short of answers regarding social action beyond the cultivation of scientific knowledge, Chernyshevskii's *What Is to Be Done?* spells out those solutions for the 'new people' it describes, offering them an overall programme of personal life conducive to wholesale social change. Like Bazarov, Chernyshevskii's two leading male characters are medical students committed to the development, dissemination, and application of scientific knowledge. They rely on the ethics of rational egoism, which teaches them that happiness involves calculating how to constrain one's immediate desires in a way that generates longer-term individual and social rewards. The novel's main new person, however, is its heroine, Vera Pavlovna, who proves best able to translate the new world view into practical life. She does so by organising economically profitable women's communes which combine productive labour with mutual education and support. The novel also features, in the character of Rakhmetov, a hero of the future – a putative revolutionary whose ethics, the novel hints, lead him to radical agitation among the underprivileged masses. Ultimately, the novel provides a vision of communist utopia that should result from the new people's combined activities.

A leading critic to champion the nihilists and the new people was Dmitrii Pisarev, whose articles – including those on Turgenev's and Chernyshevskii's

characters – proved so influential that the new people's self-designation, *pisarevtsy*, was named after him and became nearly as common as the label 'nihilists'. Pisarev's influence derived from his ability to take the rhetoric of the new people to the extreme. As early as 1861, he called for the destruction of 'anything that could be destroyed' in order to test what remained and assess its value as the foundation for progress.[2] Developing the economic aspect of Chernyshevskii's vision, Pisarev described the new people as the 'intellectual proletariat'.[3] In 1864 he argued that the intellectual capital embodied in such persons was the leading force of social transformation.[4] Pisarev had not read Karl Marx, but his language provided a bridge to the Marxist discussions about the intelligentsia by later critics.

The language of the new people in the progressive journals of the 1860s looked back for inspiration to the work of Vissarion Belinskii (1811–1848; see Box 5.1) in the 1840s. Especially productive was Belinskii's conception of a new kind of public expression that would rely on the involvement of new types of writer and reader. His conception served as the basis for the organisation, in 1847, of *The Contemporary*, which became the paradigmatic progressive journal of the late 1850s. Belinskii rejected the aesthetic and social hierarchies of his day in order to foreground the 'ordinary readers and writers' whom he expected to join forces in a shared ideological effort. That effort emphasised the role of criticism, both aesthetic and social. Adopted by later progressive journalists, Belinskii's language became especially resonant in Nikolai Dobroliubov's (1836–1861) discussions of 'realist criticism' at the turn of the 1860s, and in Petr Lavrov's (1823–1900) descriptions of 'critically thinking persons' in 1868.[5]

The classical intelligentsia's emphasis on social criticism and the popularisation of science, along with its rejection of the arts, conditioned its members to fail in creating literary works of lasting value. The leading fiction writers of the period, including Ivan Turgenev, Fedor Dostoevskii (1821–1881), and Lev Tolstoi (1828–1910), engaged in often acrimonious opposition to the

2 D. I. Pisarev, 'Skholastika XIX veka' [Nineteenth-century scholastics], *Russkoe slovo* [The Russian word] 5.9 (1861), cited in Daniel Brower, *Training the Nihilists: Education and Radicalism in Tsarist Russia* (Ithaca: Cornell University Press, 1975), p. 15.

3 D. I. Pisarev, 'Nereshennyi vopros' [Unresolved question], *Russkoe slovo* 9, sect. 2 (1864), 1–44; 10, sect. 2, 1–58; 11, sect. 2, 1–64.

4 D. I. Pisarev, 'Tsvety nevinnogo iumora' [The flowers of harmless humour], *Russkoe slovo* 2, sect. 2 (1864), 41–2; D. I. Pisarev, 'Novyi tip' [The new type], *Russkoe slovo* 10 (1865).

5 N. A. Dobroliubov, 'Luch sveta v temnom tsarstve' [A ray of light in the kingdom of darkness], *Sovremennik* [The Contemporary] 10, sect. 3 (1860), 233–92; P. L. Lavrov, 'Istoricheskie pis'ma' [Notes on history], *Nedelia* [The Week] 1–47 (1868).

progressive press. The writers who would enter the future literary canon distinguished themselves with anti-nihilist, anti-progressive, or anti-intelligentsia novels. Of these, the more notable were Nikolai Leskov's (1831–1895) *No Way Out* (*Nekuda*, 1864), Goncharov's *The Precipice* (*Obryv*, 1869), and Dostoevskii's *Demons* (*Besy*, 1873).

The format of the thick journal, however, demanded that creative literature be a significant part of it (see Chapter 2.4), and progressive journals did publish an abundant amount of fiction that even at the time was broadly understood to be aesthetically second-rate. Indeed, the rejection of aesthetic standards was explicit in progressive fiction, and especially so in Chernyshevskii's *What Is to Be Done?* Among such fiction, a particularly prominent genre was the novel about progressive young people. The number of these novels peaked at the turn of the 1870s, shortly after critics had theorised the iteration of the new people as the intelligentsia.

These novels continuously reimagined the ordinary lives of those who adopted progressive ideological schemata. The master narrative of this genre introduced young men and women discussing the canonical progressive texts and followed them as they rejected the prevalent cultural conventions and pursued social engagement. They worked as teachers, doctors, and nurses among the lower classes, both in the capitals and in the provinces; helped to liberate women from oppressive social conditions; organised co-operatives; and participated in publishing enterprises to disseminate new knowledge. For all their aspirations, however, this master narrative led its characters to a dead end: the progressive novel was unable to imagine an ideologically appropriate future. Government censorship prevented descriptions of radical social change or revolutionary activity beyond rather vague hints. More importantly, the expectations of literary Realism demanded that the novel place its characters in existing social and economic circumstances if it were to envision their sustainable existence. Where Chernyshevskii's utopia offered fantasies of rapid economic success, and where Pisarev hoped for swift progress actuated by intellectual capital, the progressive novel had to describe its 'intellectual proletarians' as supporting themselves by ordinary intellectual careers in a slowly developing modern economy.

The challenges inherent in the progressive narrative found an early model in two tales by Nikolai Pomialovskii (1835–1863), a largely forgotten writer whose prose had been viewed as offering significant promise before he died of alcoholism at the age of twenty-eight in 1863. His tales *Bourgeois Happiness* (*Meshchanskoe schast'e*, 1861) and *Molotov* (*Molotov*, 1861) describe a non-gentry hero whose progressive values and personal energy make him capable of

social independence and romantic success. However, he is unable to envision a coherent life beyond a 'petit-bourgeois' marriage and professional work in government bureaucracy – ultimately, he commits to working as an archival clerk while supplementing his income by serving as a manager in the building in which he lives.

The master narrative of the progressive novel gained expression in the titles of the more prominent texts of the era. The life of the characters begins in the *Putrid Marshes* (*Gnilye bolota*, A. K. Sheller-Mikhailov (1838–1900), 1864) of traditional Russian life before the liberal reforms. Once social change is under way, the heroes engage in the struggle between *The Old and the New Russia* (*Staraia i novaia Rossiia*, D. K. Girs (1836–1886), 1868) and go through *Hard Times* (*Trudnoe vremia*, V. A. Sleptsov (1836–1878), 1865). Yet they move forward *Step by Step* (*Shag za shagom*, I. V. Omulevskii (1836–1883), 1870–1), improving themselves and trying to effect social change while also organising co-operative enterprises, as in *A Story of a Cooperative* (*Istoriia odnogo tovarishchestva*, N. F. Bazhin (1843–1908), 1869). These projects, however, lead to *No Exodus* (*Bez iskhoda*, K. M. Staniukovich (1843–1903), 1873), as the characters ultimately fail in their quest for transformation. Staniukovich described his heroes as democrats and populists, a label that corresponded to the populist movement gaining prominence in the mid-1870s. Educated young people sought to engage with the country's peasant population to stimulate social change by way of education, economic enterprise, propaganda, and even calls for insurrection. That movement sputtered out largely on account of the intelligentsia's failure to gain any understanding from among the broad populace, as the progressive novel itself commonly described.

Just one literary text deriving from the progressive tradition survived beyond its time. This was Ivan Turgenev's *Virgin Soil* (*Nov'* 1877), though this novel owed its status more to the name of its author than to critics' or readers' appreciation of its aesthetic qualities. Observing the populist developments of the 1870s mostly from abroad, Turgenev drew the material for his novel from progressive fiction, especially the aforementioned *Hard Times* and *No Exodus*, absorbing their plots and character types. The novel features a radical non-gentry university graduate, Aleksei Nezhdanov, who attempts to effect change by joining the populist movement in the countryside. Employed as a tutor to the daughter of a noble family in rural Russia, he educates her in progressive values and conducts radical propaganda among the local peasants. What distinguishes Nezhdanov is his resolve to act on his principles, in contrast to most of the novel's other progressive figures, who adopt the radical language and lifestyle merely as the current fashions of

bohemian life. Predictably, Nezhdanov's radical efforts gain no traction, where-upon he returns to St Petersburg, struggles with ill health, and ultimately commits suicide while still in his twenties. His progressive associates scatter, leaving only two characters to persevere into the new life. Nezhdanov's pupil at the noble estate, Marianna, inspired by him to the point of romantic infatuation, proceeds after his death to marry the only other viable progressive figure in the novel. That figure is Vasilii Solomin, whose views, however, lead him to a career as a manager in a factory that draws its workers from the destitute provincial peasantry. Marianna and Solomin are committed to grad-ualist philanthropic work among that proletarian population, even as they participate in the development of Russian capitalism.

The progressive novel's difficulty in imagining an inspiring life caused even sympathetic critics to recognise that fiction about the new people described how 'the mountain' of ideological aspirations produced 'the mouse' of banal existence.[6] Ultimately, the progressive novel suggested that, while progressive language became increasingly commonplace in the public sphere, the growing intelligentsia was constituted by ordinary educated people coming of age after the turn of the 1860s. It suggested that many new people experienced economic and social precarity, which manifested in various forms of self-destruction, including suicide and alcoholism. Most of these people, however, made peace with bourgeois life, and the viable characters of these novels increasingly pursued careers without a clear philanthropic aspect at their core, taking jobs as lawyers, bureaucratic executives, and factory managers.[7] Perhaps most alarmingly, the progressive novel expressed a mounting concern that progressive language had become so culturally ubiquitous that it ceased to work as a distinguishing feature of any truly progressive section within the educated public.

By the late 1870s, the relatively focused self-understanding of the classical intelligentsia had failed to produce a social effect or a meaningful narrative of long-term personal life. At that time, the classical understanding began to merge with two alternative meanings of the term 'intelligentsia', which had been far less culturally prominent. One meaning was very broad and described the educated strata of any society while raising a question about the relation between the elites and the common people. The other meaning of 'intelligentsia'

---

6 A. M. Skabichevskii, with reference to the novels of Sheller-Mikhailov, cited in D. N. Ovsianiko-Kulikovskii (ed.), *Istoriia russkoi literatury XIX v.* [A history of Russian literature of the nineteenth century], 10 vols. (Moscow: Mir, 1908–10), vol. IV, p. 137.

7 E.g. D. L. Mordovtsev, *Signs of the Time* (*Znameniia vremeni*, 1869); A. K. Sheller-Mikhailov, *The Fall* (*Padenie*, 1870); I. A. Kushchevskii, *Nikolai Negorev or a Prospering Russian* (*Nikolai Negorev ili blagopoluchnyi rossiianin*, 1871).

was being cultivated by opponents of the very notion itself, including Tolstoi and Dostoevskii, who used the term, respectively, to satirise the unfounded intellectual pretentions of the upper classes and to warn about the moral failure of those who distanced themselves from the common people and shared national values. The merging of these meanings of the term 'intelligentsia' made for a terminological ambivalence that would only grow with time. Within the Russian cultural context, this ambivalence would continue to combine the intelligentsia's self-reflective assumption of a higher moral calling in progressive historical development with a nagging sense of its own failure. It added to that a scepticism as to the moral implications of making a claim to intellectual distinction in the first place.

Before the diverse implications of this intelligentsia condition could play out, Pavel Annenkov (1813–1887) articulated a representative broad vision of the Russian intelligentsia in his memoir, *A Remarkable Decade: 1838–1848* (*Zamechatel'noe desiatiletie*, 1880). Remembering the intellectual circles of his youth (see Chapter 2.3), Annenkov, aware that the term 'intelligentsia' was anachronistic, used it to describe progressively minded intellectual elites as a long-ranging feature of Russian culture and society. Annenkov's interest was historicist and analytical: he was interested in intellectuals as members of different cultural formations at different periods in Russian history and in the inevitable contradictions that each historical period imposed on its intellectual elites. His conceptual approach emphasised the recognition that there was not one Russian intelligentsia but rather different intelligentsias in different periods, each with its own social status and functions, with its own relation to the state, its own engagement with the means of production, and its own set of cultural values. Thus, the very title of his memoir highlighted the intelligentsia of the 1840s as distinct from that of the 1860s and 1870s. Even as Annenkov's historicist view would remain relevant into the longue durée of Russian history, his usage of the term invited a less discriminating treatment of 'intelligentsia' as a word that purported to describe a continuous, coherent, and somehow uniform phenomenon distinctive of Russian life and its educated persons.

Post-history: 1880 Onwards

In the last two decades of the nineteenth century, references to the intelligentsia in literary and other texts became so routine that most educated people came to view themselves through this term. The challenges inherent in such routinisation appeared especially pronounced in the writings of

Anton Chekhov (1860–1904). Chekhov himself was celebrated as a representative intelligentsia figure on account of his humanitarian projects, the humanity of his art, and his status as a leading Russian writer. However, he treated the term with intense aversion, insisting – especially in his correspondence – that the aura of the intelligentsia's distinction concealed its moral failure, lack of true intelligence, and inability to engage in meaningful social action. His work repeatedly describes that pattern as organising his characters' lives. For instance, his play *Uncle Vania* (*Diadia Vania*, 1897) features a range of intelligentsia types: a self-important and vacuous professor of philology; Uncle Vania's mendacious mother, continuously reading what she views as progressive journalism; a provincial doctor disillusioned by his work and succumbing to alcoholism; and Uncle Vania and his niece, who selflessly toil to maintain their familial estate but fail to find meaning in this barely sustainable enterprise. One of the central features of Chekhov's art is the sense of the prison-house in the assumptions of the intelligentsia: his characters struggle in vain to find an alternative language by which to make sense of their experience.

In the years between the Russian revolutions of 1905 and 1917, Chekhov's insight into the intelligentsia was taken to an extreme in Andrei Belyi's (1880–1934) seminal novel *Petersburg* (*Peterburg*, 1913–14, 1922). Its hero, the radical intelligentsia figure Nikolai Ableukhov, is instructed by a terrorist organisation to set off a bomb in the house of his father, a high-ranking state bureaucrat. Even as the terrorist plot is clear, Belyi portrays the novel's radical characters as incapable of organising their lives in any coherent way, so much so that their experiences acquire a hallucinatory aspect verging on clinical insanity. Ultimately, it is the ticking-clock mechanism in the bomb that organises both their lives and the world of the novel. Tellingly, the bomb goes off by mistake and the terrorists fail to achieve their goal. In Belyi's novel, the assumptions of the radical intelligentsia work as a force that destroys the lives of its own subjects.

After the Bolshevik Revolution, in the context of radical historical developments, the question of the intelligentsia's relationship with the nation and its people gained new relevance. The social change that had been central to what the intelligentsia viewed as its historical goal took place, but it was unclear as to what the intelligentsia's status would be in the new world. Isaak Babel (1894–1940) explored this question in his stories, especially the cycle *Red Cavalry* (*Konarmiia*, 1923–6), which describes the confusion of an intellectual swept up in the violence of civil war as a military journalist. The discrepancy between historical demands and personal resources is manifested in what the

hero views as his representative act of obligatory violence: expected to prove his adherence to the cause of the revolution, he kills a goose and orders a peasant woman to cook it for his fellow soldiers.

Mikhail Bulgakov (1891–1940) treated the paradox and precariousness of the intelligentsia's new historical condition allegorically in his novella *Heart of a Dog* (*Sobach'e serdtse*, 1925). In it, Professor Preobrazhenskii, a doctor searching for the secret of rejuvenation, transplants human organs into a stray dog. The operation is successful beyond imagination as the dog transforms into a human being who adopts the habits of the post-revolutionary proletarian. This subject, however, turns against his master by trying to take over his apartment, denouncing him to the secret police, and eventually drawing a gun on him. The doctor sees no recourse but to reverse the operation, turning the proletarian back into a dog. Of course, Soviet history would show that the reversal was impossible and the pre-revolutionary intelligentsia would become victims of the regime that they had helped to create.

In the meantime, Soviet life was producing a new generation of educated people who looked to make sense of their status in the new world. Iurii Olesha's (1899–1960) novel *Envy* (*Zavist'*, 1927) addresses the condition of the new intellectual. According to the novel, the standard Soviet expectation was that every educated person should engage in the developing society by becoming an 'industrial man', working to increase its material wealth. That project, however, appeared absurd to those who wanted to transcend the banal material expectations that the novel satirises in the figure of Andrei Babichev, whose goal was to produce as much sausage for the populace as possible. The emphasis on material comforts could seem an ideological betrayal of the intelligentsia's high moral standards. However, the personal success of such conformist professionals could also become an object of envy for others. In its other protagonists, most specifically the young Ivan Kavalerov, the novel portrays educated men who failed to succeed in the new conditions as a new version of the socially superfluous person. In contrast to Turgenev's superfluous men of the 1850s, their new iteration had no cultural or intellectual distinction to offer: alienation and resentment became the dominant markers of educated misfits in the Soviet system.

The Stalinist purges and the Second World War caused extreme social dislocation and also curtailed the possibilities for public representations of the intelligentsia. However, two seminal intelligentsia texts were written by its reluctant members who survived the calamities of history. Anna Akhmatova (1889–1966), especially in her epic *Poem without a Hero* (*Poema bez geroia*, comp. 1940–62), and Boris Pasternak (1890–1960) in his novel *Doctor Zhivago* (*Doktor*

Zhivago, pub. in Milan, 1957) surveyed the history of their generation. Their respective approaches to the intelligentsia emphasised new aspects of this notion. Akhmatova's work highlighted the Russian pre-revolutionary intelligentsia's cultural achievement and aesthetic sensibilities as the sustaining forces in the survival of the group's remaining members. Pasternak, by contrast, focused on Christian spirituality as a source of redemption in the context of the inevitable compromises and eventual destruction that the intelligentsia had to endure.

The work of these two authors exemplifies how the understanding of the idea of the intelligentsia has proved historically malleable: their notions of the aesthetic and spiritual aspects of the intelligentsia experience would have been entirely alien to the proto-intelligentsia's irreligious world view and the classical intelligentsia's rejection of art. Such nuanced and sometimes invisible cultural differences between the generations of educated people in Russia became central to the work of Lidiia Ginzburg (1902–1990), who wrote between the 1920s and 1980s in a variety of genres: scholarly cultural history, diary, memoir, and experimental prose. Among the central themes of Ginzburg's writing is precisely the uneasy and usually confusing relationship between different generations of the educated elites, each of which could claim itself as the bearer of an ostensibly continuous intelligentsia tradition in Russian life. Ginzburg's historicist treatment of Russian intellectuals was inspired by Aleksandr Herzen's mid-nineteenth-century formative insights (see Chapter 3.10).

The postwar generation of the intelligentsia, emerging in the optimistic context of the liberalisation of the Thaw era, produced yet another vision of the social status and functions of intellectuals. At the turn of the 1960s, a range of young poets – including Evgenii Evtushenko (1932–2017), Andrei Voznesenskii (1933–2010), and Bella Akhmadulina (1937–2010) – became remarkably popular as they inspired the *intelligent* to adopt a newly romantic vision of using one's intellectual distinction to accelerate social change within the framework of Soviet socialism. At the same time as artists and especially poets became cult figures on account of their inspirational energy, the new Thaw culture emphasised scientific optimism, particularly in relation to technological development; the discovery of the country's natural resources; and, ultimately, the exploration of the universe. An especially popular version of this optimistic view was articulated in science fiction by the brothers Arkadii (1925–1991) and Boris (1933–2012) Strugatskii. Their intelligentsia heroes appealed to an increasingly prominent group of scientists, engineers, and diverse technical workers that flowed out of the expanding educational

institutions of the Soviet Union. The Strugatskiis' heroes of the 1960s speak to their audiences in a combination of charismatic humour and irony, on the one hand, and an apparently untroubled optimism about the technical intelligentsia's ability to bring about rapid social progress, on the other.

That period of optimism, however, proved short-lived. By the turn of the 1970s, hopes for change had yielded to a recognition that the intelligentsia, once again, had failed to translate their hopes into social reality and instead had become mired in the vicissitudes of bourgeois life as ordinary intellectual professionals under a regime that forced them into continuous social and moral compromise. Among the more prominent literary documents of this experience was Iurii Trifonov's (1925–1981) novella *The House on the Embankment* (*Dom na naberezhnoi*, 1976), which describes the ways in which the representatives of different intelligentsia generations from the 1920s to the 1960s, despite their best intentions, succumbed to mutual competition for the ordinary rewards of Soviet life, ranging from claims to cultural distinction to the acquisition of material rewards. Whereas Trifonov's novel works with a broad historical framework, Liudmila Petrushevskaia's (1938–) prose – including, for instance, her story 'Our Circle' (*Svoi krug*, 1988) – focuses its narrative on intimate life, while reviving the notion of the intelligentsia circles. Bordering on cynicism, Petrushevskaia describes the intimately related intelligentsia members as primarily engaged in continuous romantic and marital intrigue even as they assume that they share in the country's artistic achievements and intellectual tradition. One might wonder what is left of the notion of the intelligentsia in such late Soviet texts. The characters of these texts routinely view themselves as the intelligentsia but appear to have lost the sense of what the term might mean. Moreover, the word that might have promised an aura of distinction has come to sound like a hypocritical claim.

A question that needs addressing is why the notion of the intelligentsia emerged in Russia rather than in another country. One answer has to do with the broadly recognised logocentric aspect of Russian culture, in which literature has been the privileged conduit of life in the context of restrictions on direct political or social expression. However, I would suggest that we may want to understand this logocentrism as the Russian version of the development of print capitalism in the west. In a country as large as Russia, capitalism developed fastest in the technology of print, which required relatively little investment and was concentrated in the capital cities. The notion of the intelligentsia as the 'new people' emerged first as a phenomenon in the Russian press, which produced both writers and readers by explaining to variously educated people that their primary community was that of the

press itself as they found themselves alienated from the world outside of print. Accordingly, it was the press as a leading force of modern life in Russia that produced the *intelligent* as a figure whose distinction lay in a commitment to print-mediated information.

After the end of the Soviet Union, literary representations of the intelligentsia lost their cultural prominence, even as debates about the role of the intelligentsia have at times been heated in the country's journalism since then. One reason proposed for this development links it to a sense (erroneous, of course) of an 'end of history', especially in view of the aforementioned cultural tradition – from Herzen to Ginzburg – that treats the changes in the self-understanding of intellectuals as part of a historical process. It might be that the explanation as to why the notion of the intelligentsia has become less prominent in Russian culture involves the decline of the social status of literature in the country's life due to the development of new media technologies and the rapid growth of not only educated but diversely articulate audiences (see Chapters 2.11, 3.11). If Russian culture has emphasised its literary production as the country's unique cultural achievement, and if the status of the intelligentsia has been a central literary question, then the end of the history of the intelligentsia relates to the decreasing role of literature at the time when the culture of print is yielding to the culture of digital mediation. The bloggers, influencers, and ordinary authors in digital media, as well as the new cadres of intellectual technology professionals, are less likely to understand themselves through the notions of the intelligentsia that have been disseminated by Russian literature in print.

Further Reading

Berlin, Isaiah, *Russian Thinkers* (New York: Viking Press, 1978).

Brower, Daniel R., *Training the Nihilists: Education and Radicalism in Tsarist Russia* (Ithaca: Cornell University Press, 1975).

Confino, Michael, 'On intellectuals and intellectual traditions in eighteenth- and nineteenth-century Russia', in *Russia before the 'Radiant Future': Essays in Modern History, Culture, and Society* (New York: Berghahn Books, 2011), pp. 83–118.

Frede, Victoria, *Doubt, Atheism and the Nineteenth-Century Russian Intelligentsia* (Madison: University of Wisconsin Press, 2011).

Manchester, Laurie, *Holy Fathers, Secular Sons: Clergy, Intelligentsia and the Modern Self in Revolutionary Russia* (DeKalb: Northern Illinois University Press, 2011).

Nahirny, Vladimir C., *The Russian Intelligentsia: From Torment to Conviction* (New Brunswick, NJ: Transaction Books, 1983).

Pipes, Richard (ed.), *The Russian Intelligentsia* (New York: Columbia University Press, 1961).

4.6

The Russian Woman

ANNA A. BERMAN

To include 'the Russian woman' in a history of literary heroes might at first seem essentialising. Is it defensible to argue for a category of hero that can be applied to one half of the Russian population? What is meant by *the* Russian woman: was she a singular type in Russian literature? Does the term refer to an actual woman, or to woman as symbol? Sensitive to these questions, this chapter begins with the active quest of nineteenth-century authors to define the *idea* of the Russian woman and then explores how depictions of this type evolved as the social and political context shifted over time. This is not a discussion of 'great Russian heroines', but rather of one particular type that entered Russian literature with Tatiana Larina, the heroine of Aleksandr Pushkin's (1799–1837) novel in verse *Eugene Onegin* (*Evgenii Onegin*, 1825–32). Serving as an ideal for over half a century, Tatiana created a brand of Russian femininity defined by soulfulness, fidelity, self-sacrifice, and patient suffering that shared much in common with the ideal of all-enduring Mother Russia herself. Authors returned again and again to Tatiana's image, both using her as the model for their heroines and reflexively attempting to shape her legacy to match their own philosophies.[1]

Although Tatiana came to represent Russian womanhood, the ideal of the Russian woman did not remain static. The second half of the chapter turns to the subsequent development of her image from the mid- to late nineteenth century through the Soviet period and up to the present day. Woven into this discussion is an examination of female authors' approaches to the question of the Russian woman in relation to those of male authors. As early feminist critics have shown, in the Russian tradition 'most female characters in male-authored texts are not *only* women – they are both more

---

[1] Caryl Emerson, 'Tatiana', in Sonia Stephan (ed.), *A Plot of Her Own: The Female Protagonist in Russian Literature* (Evanston, IL: Northwestern University Press, 1995), pp. 6–20.

and less than women'.[2] Did heroines penned by women escape this double bind?

Tatiana and Her Legacy

Ensconced in the Russian countryside, Pushkin's Tatiana Larina is a quiet, bookish girl who prefers her dreamy inner life and rambles around her family's rural estate to the companionship of her lighthearted sister, caring mother, and their rustic social world. Her dreams are shaped by the Sentimental novels of Samuel Richardson, Jean-Jacques Rousseau, and Madame de Staël, so when the Byronic dandy Eugene Onegin settles at his neighbouring estate, Tatiana's vivid imagination quickly transforms him into a literary hero. New vistas open up before her. In a moment of great resolve and reckless daring, she writes to Onegin, confessing her love. He rejects her overture honourably but sternly. Then follows a period of rupture: an unfortunate duel between Onegin and the suitor of Tatiana's sister, in which the latter is killed; Onegin's departure; and the seasons during which he restlessly wanders abroad, while Tatiana is sent to Moscow to be married off. Several years later, the pair re-encounter each other in St Petersburg. Tatiana is now of high rank and social standing, and Onegin is instantly smitten with this new, imposing lady. Mirroring Tatiana's youthful confession, he writes to her, declaring his love. They meet, and Tatiana rejects him with words that would echo through the Russian canon: 'I love you (why should I dissemble?); / But I am now another's wife, / And I'll be faithful all my life.'[3]

Half a century after Pushkin penned these lines, Fedor Dostoevskii (1821–1881), in a speech about Pushkin, called Tatiana 'the apotheosis of Russian womanhood'.[4] What he found in her image can serve as a guide to the ideal of the Russian woman in nineteenth-century Russian literature. While her type was not the only one that Russian authors depicted – there were also emancipated women, society women, saintly mothers, fallen women, grotesque old hags, and many who defy easy characterisation – none of these was treated as *the* Russian woman.[5] For, indeed, the first thing Dostoevskii

---

2 Rosalind Marsh, 'An image of their own?: Feminism, revisionism and Russian culture', in Marsh (ed.), *Women and Russian Culture: Projections and Self-Perceptions* (New York: Berghahn Books, 1998), p. 10.

3 Alexander Pushkin, *Eugene Onegin: A Novel in Verse*, trans. James E. Falen (Oxford: Oxford University Press, 2009), p. 210.

4 Fyodor Dostoevsky, *A Writer's Diary: Volume 2, 1877–1881*, trans. Kenneth Lantz (Evanston, IL: Northwestern University Press), p. 1285.

5 Marsh provides a comprehensive exploration of these various types in 'An image of their own?'.

emphasised about Tatiana was her Russianness. He made her famous rejection of Onegin representative of national character, claiming: 'She said this specifically as a Russian woman', and again for emphasis, '"as a Russian woman" (and not a southern woman or some Frenchwoman).'[6] While Onegin is rootless, raised in the Europeanised atmosphere of St Petersburg, for Dostoevskii Tatiana 'stands solidly on her own native soil'.[7]

In making this claim, Dostoevskii had to overlook the ways in which Pushkin clearly modelled Tatiana on a European heroine and her own predilection for the western literature that shaped her world view. Yet Dostoevskii was right that Tatiana is also connected with her homeland, most famously in the lines: 'Tatyana (with a Russian duty / That held her heart, she knew not why) / Profoundly loved, in its cold beauty, / The Russian winter passing by.'[8] Pushkin also shows her to be deeply engaged with aspects of traditional Russian folk culture. She participates in fortune-telling, drinks tea from a samovar, listens to peasant singing, shares a warm bond with her peasant nanny, has a dream full of folkloric imagery, and wanders freely in the Russian woods. Although the poet's image of Tatiana evolved throughout the eight years of his work on the novel – reflecting western fads for native folklore – Pushkin helped initiate a pattern of Russian heroines symbolising Russia herself. In Ivan Turgenev's (1818–1883) *A Nest of Gentlefolk* (*Dvorianskoe gnezdo*, 1859), for example, Liza is a descendant of this Tatiana tradition. Like Tatiana, she lives in a quiet, provincial backwater and has her heart's peace destroyed by a disaffected intellectual from the city. She rivals Tatiana in her spiritual elevation. As Pushkin did with Tatiana, Turgenev highlights Liza's Russianness: 'It would never have occurred to Liza that she was a patriot; but she found Russian people to her liking; the Russian way of thinking delighted her.'[9]

Lev Tolstoi (1828–1910) would take this idea a step further in *War and Peace* (*Voina i mir*, 1868–9). In this massive epic, the lives of the heroes are paralleled by events on the national scale, with 'the attempted abduction of Natasha by the seductive but treacherous Anatole' mirroring 'the violation of Russia by the seductive but treacherous Napoleon', as Caryl Emerson has argued.[10] In one of Russian literature's most famous passages, Tolstoi makes explicit

---

6 Dostoevsky, *Writer's Diary: Volume 2*, p. 1287.
7 Dostoevsky, *Writer's Diary: Volume 2*, p. 1285.   8 Pushkin, *Eugene Onegin*, p. 110.
9 Ivan Turgenev, *Polnoe sobranie sochinenii i pisem v dvadtsati vos'mi tomakh* [Complete collected works and letters in twenty-eight volumes] (Moscow: Izdatel'stvo Akademii nauk SSSR, 1960–8), vol. VII, p. 234.
10 Caryl Emerson, 'Leo Tolstoy and the rights of music under Stalin', *Tolstoy Studies Journal* 14 (2002), 5.

Natasha Rostova's special link to her homeland, despite her having been raised in a noble household full of foreign influences. After a day of wolf hunting, she is at the rustic home of a neighbour, eating traditional Russian foods and listening to traditional folk music. When the coachman begins to play the balalaika, Natasha is enchanted: 'Just as the uncle's mushrooms, honey, and liqueurs seemed the best in the world to her, so this song, too, seemed to her at that moment the height of musical loveliness.'[11] Moved by the music, she throws off the kerchief she is wrapped in and jumps up to dance: 'Where, how, and when had this little countess, brought up by an émigré Frenchwoman, sucked this spirit in from the Russian air she breathed, where had she gotten these ways, which should have been long supplanted by the *pas de châle*? Yet that spirit and these ways were those very inimitable, unstudied Russian ones which the uncle expected of her.'[12] Natasha embodies Russianness.

For all these Russian heroines, their goodness comes naturally and not through the seeking and struggle faced by many male heroes. The peasant-dancing Natasha knows intuitively that her family must leave their precious belongings behind and fill their carts with wounded soldiers as they flee burning Moscow in 1812. It is a decisionless decision to help her brother Russians. As Rosalind Marsh has noted, 'The heroine frequently becomes a "non-cognating" symbol of the Russian soul.'[13] Indeed, the 'Russian woman' character type contributed to this myth of the 'Russian soul' that was propagated by authors and artists who wished to establish an ideal of Russians' unique meekness; spirituality; and patient, all-suffering nature. While Dostoevskii's Raskolnikov intellectualises his guilt after committing murder in *Crime and Punishment* (*Prestuplenie i nakazanie*, 1867), Sonia Marmeladova knows intuitively that he must 'accept suffering and redeem [himself] by it'. She tells him to 'Go now, this minute, stand in the crossroads, bow down, and first kiss the earth you've defiled, then bow to the whole world, on all four sides, and say aloud to everyone: "I have killed!"'[14] Her mixture of Christian ideas of sin and resurrection and notions of the import- ance of Mother Earth links Sonia with the dual faith (*dvoeverie*) of village Orthodoxy. Sonia is a classic Russian woman who sacrifices herself first for her family and then for Raskolnikov, whom she has come to love through her

---

11 Leo Tolstoy, *War and Peace*, trans. Richard Pevear and Larissa Volokhonsky (New York: Alfred A. Knopf, 2007), p. 511.
12 Tolstoy, *War and Peace*, p. 512.   13 Marsh, 'An image of their own?', p. 9.
14 Fyodor Dostoevsky, *Crime and Punishment*, trans. Richard Pevear and Larissa Volokhonsky (London: Vintage Books, 2007), p. 420.

infinite compassion for his suffering. This selfless compassion is a grave weight to carry.

Dostoevskii's wilful interpretation of Tatiana exemplifies this same kind of moral burden. For Dostoevskii, Tatiana showed that 'the Russian woman is bold. The Russian woman will boldly follow one in whom she believes, and she has proved that.' Sonia is ready to follow Raskolnikov to Siberia – just as after the failed Decembrist coup in 1825, the real-life Decembrist wives followed their husbands into Siberian exile with great courage and fortitude and contributed to the model of Russian womanhood for future writers. However, Tatiana is not only bold, but also deeply moral. For Dostoevskii, Tatiana rejects Onegin *whom she still loves* in order to stay with her husband because her betrayal would cause too much pain to this 'honorable man who loves her': 'betrayal would cast shame and disgrace upon him and would mean his death. And can one person found his happiness on the unhappiness of another?'[15] These words resemble the famous 'Rebellion' of Ivan Karamazov in Dostoevskii's final novel, *The Brothers Karamazov* (*Brat'ia Karamazovy*, 1881), which he was writing at the same time as the Pushkin speech. Ivan would not agree to build 'the edifice of human destiny with the object of making people happy in the finale, of giving them peace and rest at last' if to do so meant 'inevitably and unavoidably [to] torture just one tiny creature'.[16] Dostoevskii turns Tatiana into the mouthpiece of moral dilemmas illustrated in his own novels. Her rejection of Onegin, for him, represents the truth that 'Happiness is found not only in the pleasures of love, but also in the higher harmony of the spirit.'.[17]

This higher harmony was a central feature of the praises to Russian women that would be sung by poets, novelists, and other writers throughout the intervening half-century between Pushkin's Tatiana and Dostoevskii's characterisation of her. And indeed, many of these writers would return to the figure of Tatiana, reworking her image in the heroines of their own novels. In her debut novel, *A Mistake* (*Oshibka*, 1849), Evgeniia Tur (pen name for Elizaveta Vasilevna Salias de Tournemire, *née* Sukhovo-Kobylina, 1815–1892) essentially adapts Tatiana's experiences to her own time. Like Tatiana, Tur's heroine – Olga – lives with her mother and a younger, more gregarious sister. Like Tatiana, she is bookish and alone, even within her loving family: 'From her early youth there was in her not an inability to have fun, but a lack

---

15 Dostoevsky, *Writer's Diary: Volume 2*, p. 1287.
16 Fyodor Dostoevsky, *The Brothers Karamazov*, trans. Richard Pevear and Larissa Volokhonsky (London: Vintage Books, 2004), p. 245.
17 Dostoevsky, *Writer's Diary: Volume 2*, p. 1287.

of the elements to amuse her. Later she developed an indifference to everything that was outside of her inner life, to which she attached herself passionately.'[18] Like Tatiana, Olga has a deep, poetic soul and throws herself into reading. And like Tatiana (and many other Russian heroines), she is fated to love a weaker man who does not deserve her. Olga becomes engaged to her beloved, Aleksandr, but he does not live up to her spiritual depths and, over the course of the winter season, he is seduced away by a society coquette. Recognising that she has lost his heart, Olga releases him from their engagement and ends the novel alone – but still morally superior.

Turgenev was deeply influenced by Tur's writings (more than he liked to acknowledge), and he would undertake the same exercise of 'rewriting *Onegin*' in his own debut novel, *Rudin* (*Rudin*, 1856).[19] His Natalia also lives on a country estate with her mother. Thin and dark like Tatiana, 'Her emotions ran strong and deep, but only in secret.'[20] She regularly reads Pushkin. When the eponymous hero appears at their estate, Natalia's soul is inspired by his lofty idealism and eloquent speeches. The two ultimately acknowledge their love in a meeting in the garden (where Tatiana's most important rendezvous with Onegin also takes place). However, their words are overheard, Natalia's mother is informed, and she forbids the match. Natalia calls Rudin to a final meeting, informs him of her mother's words, and asks him what to do. The strong heroine is ready to sacrifice everything, but Rudin says, 'submit to fate'. Natalia is not Tatiana. Her ideal is crushed: 'I come to you for advice at a moment like this, and your first word is "submit"! Submit! So this is how you enact your theories about independence, about sacrifice, which . . .'[21] She cannot continue. Natalia perfectly embodies Barbara Heldt's central argument in her pioneering feminist study of the Russian canon: 'The "natural" perfection of the Russian heroine exemplified a standard not met by Russian society as a whole . . . It was, thus, a terrible perfection, frightening to men who could not match it in "manly" action and inhibiting to women who were supposed to incarnate it, or else.'[22] When his eloquence is put to the test and he is

---

18 Evgeniia Tur, *Povesti i rasskazy* [Tales and stories], 4 vols. (Moscow: Tipografiia Katkova, 1859), vol. II, p. 35.

19 For Tur's influence on Turgenev, see Jane T. Costlow, 'Speaking the sorrow of women: Turgenev's "Neschastnaia" and Evgeniia Tur's "Antonina"', *Slavic Review* 50.2 (1991), 328–35.

20 Ivan Sergeevich Turgenev, *Rudin*, in *The Essential Turgenev*, trans. Elizabeth Cheresh Allen (Evanston, IL: Northwestern University Press), p. 225.

21 Turgenev, *Rudin*, p. 264.

22 Barbara Heldt, *Terrible Perfection: Women and Russian Literature* (Bloomington: Indiana University Press, 1987), p. 5.

forced to action, Rudin cannot live up to Natalia. In his farewell letter, he tells her: 'in meeting you, I met an absolutely honest, upright soul for the first time in my life'.[23] And it was too much for him.

Shifting Ideals and the Woman Question

The position of women in Russian society – their education, economic opportunities, and roles in the family – was one of the central questions being debated in Russia in the mid- to late nineteenth century under the rubric of the 'woman question'. For most Russians up to this period, ideas about the traditional Russian family and the roles of husbands and wives were prescribed by works like the *Domostroi*, a sixteenth-century domestic manual about life in Old Muscovy. There, the author clearly outlines the role of a wife: 'Whatever her husband orders, she must accept with love; she must fulfill his every command.'[24] Children (even in noble households) were to be taught with the rod. Though it may be impossible to determine how closely people actually followed the *Domostroi*'s teachings, it remained a persistent source of ideology for centuries. When Russia's first code of laws was published in 1832, it followed the same patriarchal spirit, granting all power to husbands and fathers. But as debates about women's rights took off across Europe, and as Russia began preparing for the emancipation of its serfs at mid-century, the oppressed status of women burst upon the public discourse with a series of articles by the radical Mikhail Mikhailov (1829–1865) and others.

Literature both reflected and contributed to the debate as novelists set out to redefine the Russian woman within this new sociohistorical context. When an emancipated woman appeared as a secondary character, she was often caricatured and disparaged, like the dishevelled Kukshina in Turgenev's *Fathers and Children* (*Ottsy i deti*, 1862) or the arrogant, ignorant female student in Dostoevskii's *Demons* (*Besy*, 1873). But authors who made the Russian woman a central figure often had a more sympathetic take on this type, infusing her with Tatiana's qualities. Many critics credit Turgenev with creating a 'symbol of women's emancipation in Russia' in Elena Strakhova, the heroine of *On the Eve* (*Nakanune*, 1860), but Elena is also

---

23 Turgenev, *Rudin*, p. 275.
24 Carolyn Johnston Pouncy (ed. and trans.), *The 'Domostroi': Rules for Russian Households in the Time of Ivan the Terrible* (Ithaca: Cornell University Press, 1994), p. 124.

a model of spiritual purity and fidelity like Tatiana.[25] Raised in a stifling, patriarchal home with a tyrannical father who has totally cowed her mother, Elena rejects the suitor her parents have chosen for her and instead secretly marries a Bulgarian radical named Insarov. The couple goes abroad, where Insarov shortly dies of consumption. Instead of returning to Russia, however, Elena joins the Sisters of Mercy. Justifying the decision in her farewell letter to her parents, she asks: 'What is to be done in Russia?' – the implication being that at that time, the late 1850s, there is no role for her, or any civically or politically engaged woman, in her homeland.[26]

Joe Andrew claims that Nikolai Chernyshevskii's (1828–1889) *What Is to Be Done? (Chto delat'?,* 1863) 'is a direct riposte to this, in his view, defamatory rhetorical question'.[27] Chernyshevskii's novel, written while he was imprisoned in the Peter and Paul Fortress, became a bible for Russian radicals. Its heroine, Vera Pavlovna, was read not only as *the* Russian woman of the new age but also as a practical guide to liberation. She is a rejection of the dreamy, spiritual Tatiana model. Rather than highlighting Vera's uniqueness, Chernyshevskii instead emphasises the fact that she is an ordinary young woman and therefore an attainable model. Like Turgenev's Elena, she is raised in a stifling home with parents whose sole aim is to marry her off profitably. Rather than submit, Vera escapes from the 'cellar' through a fictitious marriage to her brother's tutor, the medical student Lopukhov. They set up life together with separate rooms and strict guidelines for co-operative living, yet marriage is not the focus of the novel, or of Vera's life. Instead, she devotes herself to meaningful work, establishing a sewing collective. When Vera falls in love with Lopukhov's best friend, Dr Kirsanov, Lopukhov frees her to remarry by faking his own suicide and leaving the country, only to return years later as the foreigner Beaumont. He too remarries, and the bigamous quartet set up house together in connected apartments.

Vera, meanwhile, continues to develop, contemplating the position of women in Russian society: 'Many paths of independent activity that haven't been closed to us by law are barred by social custom', she reflects. 'But of

---

25 Caroline de Maegd-Soëp, *The Emancipation of Women in Russian Literature and Society: A Contribution to the Knowledge of the Russian Society during the 1860's* (Ghent: Ghent State University, 1978), p. 236.
26 Turgenev, *Polnoe sobranie sochinenii i pisem,* vol. VIII, p. 165.
27 Joe Andrew, *Women in Russian Literature, 1780–1863* (Basingstoke: Palgrave Macmillan, 1988), p. 155.

those paths, I can embark on any one I choose, as long as I've resolved to endure the initial opposition of social convention.'[28] The path Vera chooses is to follow her husband and to become a doctor. Chernyshevskii also endows her with children, though he has little to say about how she balances professional and familial duties. In this utopian vision, the Russian woman can have it all: husband, children, career, social life (a balance modern women could only dream of). In that sense, the depiction of the emancipated woman in *Fictitious Marriage* (*Fiktivnyi brak*, 1876), by S. Dolgina (pen name for Sofia Mundt, 1848–?), is probably more honest. Marianna has married an honest widower in a fictitious marriage, but ultimately the (already married) couple fall in love. They finally admit to their emotions and shift into a more traditional marriage, but there is no mention of children. Instead, the final description of the couple is of their good deeds, with Marianna serving as helpmate to her husband. Following in the Tatiana tradition, Dolgina empha-sises Marianna's moral goodness, even in this more liberal context.

Tolstoi's *Anna Karenina* (*Anna Karenina*, 1878) also foregrounds the ques-tion of the options open to women in Russian society. In one of the novel's multiple plots, Tolstoi essentially returns to Tatiana's dilemma with his titular heroine and imagines what would have happened half a century later if she had made the opposite choice: to leave her husband for the man she loves. In another plot, Anna's sister-in-law, Dolly Oblonskaia, struggles to raise a growing brood of children with limited means and a philandering husband; and in a third, Dolly's sister Kitty mistakenly gives her heart to a brilliant aide-de-camp with no serious matrimonial intentions and must gain wisdom before she is ready to enter marriage and family life with the man who truly loves her. All these plots intertwine at a dinner party at the Oblonskiis' where the guests discuss the woman question directly. Significantly, it is only the men who speak until Dolly finally interjects at the end of the debate. Directly following this conversation, she pulls aside Anna's husband, Aleksei Karenin, to discuss his plans for divorcing his unfaithful wife, thus situating their exchange in the context of the earlier discussion. Begging him not to take this step, Dolly exclaims: 'No, it's terrible! She'll be no one's wife, she'll be ruined!'[29] Dolly can see no role for a woman outside of marriage; she embodies the faithful, all-suffering ideal – and yet her own existence does not appear all that ideal in Tolstoi's telling.

28 Nikolai Chernyshevsky, *What Is to Be Done?*, trans. Michael R. Katz (Ithaca: Cornell University Press, 1989), p. 347.
29 Leo Tolstoy, *Anna Karenina*, trans. Richard Pevear and Larissa Volokhonsky (New York: Penguin Books, 2000), p. 394.

Although the Karenins do not divorce, Anna ultimately leaves her husband and sets up a life with her lover and their illegitimate child. Outside the confines of society, she plays with Russia's rigid gender roles, taking up masculine activities like horseback riding and serious reading about architecture and agronomy as well as using contraception to reject what many believed was women's natural duty and calling. Yet despite her best attempts, Anna ultimately finds life in her undefined, non-legitimated relations with Vronskii, outside of society, too painful to bear. In this novel, Tolstoi ultimately reaffirms the place of the Russian woman in the home as faithful wife and mother through Kitty's plot line; by the time he wrote *Resurrection* (*Voskresenie*, 1899), however, even he would reject this traditional ideal.

Just as men discuss the woman question at the Oblonskiis' dinner party and men wrote the first articles about the woman question in the Russian press, most of the authors I have discussed thus far are male because the traditional view of the Russian woman has been shaped most influentially by men. Yet this may be due to processes of canonisation rather than to what had an impact at the time. The morally superior Russian heroine may have begun as a male ideal in works like Nikolai Karamzin's (1766–1826) 'Poor Liza' (*Bednaia Liza*, 1792) and Pushkin's *Eugene Onegin*, but over the course of the nineteenth century many women writers also contributed to the tradition of writing about spiritually elevated heroines whose weak lovers prove unworthy of them. Such a model is at the heart of *A Mistake* and *Antonina* (*Antonina*, 1851), by Evgeniia Tur; *Anna Mikhailovna* (*Anna Mikhailovna*, 1849) and *Ursa Major* (*Bol'shaia medveditsa*, 1871), by V. Krestovskii (pseudonym) (pen name for Nadezhda Khvoshchinskaia, 1821–1889); *Strength of Character* (*Sila kharaktera*, 1876), by Sofia Smirnova (1852–1921); and countless other works by once-prominent women writers. These authors showed greater sensitivity than male authors did to the constraints under which female characters laboured, their stifled position in the family, and their lack of economic opportunities. They also showed a greater awareness that seeking an escape from the paternal home through a marriage often left women equally – if not more – unfree. Even an escape to a life of work, which some of the heroines of Krestovskii (pseud.) manage, did not guarantee greater life fulfilment. This is not to claim a radical difference between men's and women's writing (an argument can be made for more commonality than difference), but rather to suggest that our picture of the Russian woman should be tempered by an awareness that not only men were attempting to shape her image. In women's works, however, she more often stood for

herself – a particular Russian woman – rather than representing an ideal of Russianness or a foil for the weak strivings of men.

One example of such a free-standing woman who offers an answer to Elena Strakhova's question 'What is to be done in Russia?' is the heroine of Krestovskii's *The Boarding School Girl* (*Pansionerka*, 1861). Like Elena and Chernyshevskii's Vera Pavlovna, Krestovskii's Lolenka escapes a marriage planned by her parents, but her escape lies not through another marriage (fictitious or otherwise) but through female independence. With the help of an aunt, she leaves her provincial home for St Petersburg, where she learns to support herself as an artist. Krestovskii, however, does not portray this escape as an unalloyed victory and even denied that the novel's ending was intended to be happy.[30] In the final conversation of the novel, Lolenka debates her choice with the hero, Veretitsyn. She defends her right to reject her family, while Veretitsyn defends his beloved, Sofia, who took the opposite path – marrying a landowner she did not love and remaining in the provinces to care for him and his family (classic Tatiana material). Likening Sofia to a martyr, he claims: 'She set out against vulgarity, egotism, the half educated, insults, cruelty … There's no higher deed in our age.'[31] Krestovskii herself does not take a side in this debate, leaving the ideal for the Russian woman an open question.

Other authors handled the issue with humour. Anton Chekhov's (1860–1904) 'The Darling' (*Dushechka*, 1899) offers a parody of the submissive woman who devotes herself completely to the man in her life (here a progression of men), forming her entire character around his interests and desires. Olenka has no existence of her own and goes from being a passionate devotee of the theatre with her first husband, to a logging aficionado with no time for the arts in a second relationship, to finally embracing the outlook of a schoolboy she has unofficially adopted, unaware that the poor child cannot bear her intrusive presence. In her play *The Woman Question* (*Zhenskii vopros*, 1907), Teffi (pseud. for Nadezhda Lokhvitskaia, 1872–1952) has the young feminist Katia fall asleep and dream of a world reversed, where women hold all the power while men tend to the home and contemplate the 'man question' and equal rights. A brash aunt (who has been promoted to the rank of general) drinks, tells stories about life in the regiment, and attributes the physical inferiority of men to the heaviness of their brains, while a female professor attempts some hanky-panky with the

30 See Karen Rosneck's introduction to Nadezhda Khvoshchinskaya, *The Boarding-School Girl*, trans. Rosneck (Evanston, IL: Northwestern University Press, 2000), p. xiii.
31 Khvoshchinskaya, *Boarding-School Girl*, p. 136.

defenceless male servant. In the dream, Katia's beloved, Andrei, tells her he will not marry her for the same reason she herself had used to reject him in reality: he cannot bear to be saddled with the housework after the wedding. Upon awaking and discovering with relief that it was all a dream, Katya is ready to embrace her female role, marry Andrei, and take on the household duties.

From the Russian to the Soviet Woman

With the upheaval of the Bolshevik Revolution and civil war, the world the Russian woman inhabited was remade, and she had to adapt to her new environment. The sprawling plot of Boris Pasternak's (1890–1960) *Doctor Zhivago* (*Doktor Zhivago*, pub. in Milan, 1957) spans the first half of the twentieth century, making its heroine, Lara, emblematic of the transition from Russian to Soviet womanhood. Like earlier models, Lara has a deep spiritual nature: 'She did not believe in ritual. But sometimes, to be able to bear life, she needed the accompaniment of an inner music ... That music was God's word of life, and it was to weep over it that she went to church.'[32] Early in life she questions why her fate 'is to see everything and take it all so much to heart'.[33] Living through seduction by her mother's powerful lover, world war, revolution, civil war, and regime change, Lara develops a practical, survival-oriented side that matches her spirituality in its strength. She fires a gun at an adversary, supports herself and a daughter while living in exile, and works as a nurse for the wounded. Lara has an affair with the titular Iurii Zhivago, but in the new context of the twentieth century and war this choice carries little of the baggage that it did for Anna Karenina. Despite much of her life being lived in the Soviet Union, Lara reads as the last great Russian woman – but one who carries within her seeds of the new type who would be born after 1917.

This new type – the Soviet woman – would be dedicated to the Soviet project (see Chapter 4.7). In the 1920s this often meant rejecting rather than embracing hearth and home: eating in communal kitchens and giving up children to be raised institutionally. The state took on many of the roles traditionally filled by the family, and the burdens of motherhood were 'lifted from women's shoulders', in the words of the Bolshevik feminist Aleksandra Kollontai (1872–1952).[34]

---

32 Boris Pasternak, *Doctor Zhivago*, trans. Max Hayward and Manya Harari (New York: Pantheon Books, 1991), p. 49.
33 Pasternak, *Doctor Zhivago*, p. 24.
34 A. Kollontai, *Trud zhenshchiny v evolutsii khoziaistva* [The labour of women in the evolution of the household], 2nd edn (Moscow: Gosizdat, 1928; first pub. 1923), p. 146.

When Gleb returns from the civil war at the start of Fedor Gladkov's (1883–1958) *Cement* (*Tsement*, 1925), he is shocked to find his wife, Dasha, calling him 'Comrade' and rejecting her former domestic duties. 'Do you want flowers on the window-sill, Gleb, and a bed overloaded with feather pillows?', she asks him. 'No, Gleb; I spent the winter in an unheated room (there's a fuel crisis, you know), and I eat dinner in the communal restaurant. You see, I'm a free Soviet citizen.'[35] In Socialist Realist novels of the 1930s and onwards, the bookish and dreamy Tatianas were replaced by robust *kolkhoz* (collective farm) workers, daring scientists, and brainy engineers who built on the legacy of their emancipated sisters Lolenka and Vera Pavlovna. Yet outside of officially sanctioned literature, authors like Mikhail Bulgakov (1891–1940) continued to play with the more traditional Russian woman type. In *The Master and Margarita* (*Master i Margarita*, comp. 1928–40, pub. 1966–7), Bulgakov showed how her character would be inverted by Soviet realities. Margarita is ready to 'boldly follow one in whom she believes', just like Turgenev's Natalia or Dostoevskii's Sonia Marmeladova. But in the novel's fantastical version of Moscow in the 1930s, this means not an adherence to dreamy idealism but allying herself with the devil and his gang in order to be reunited with her beloved Master.

State-sanctioned literature could not allow women such personally motivated plot lines that ignored the Soviet project. In her pioneering study of women in Soviet literature until 1964, Xenia Gasiorowska has identified four primary types, each associated with a different stratum of society: the peasant (who shifted from being the model housewife to the model kolkhoz worker); the proletarian (young working girls who became the heroines of industrial novels); the Amazon (women who participated in the civil war or the Second World War); and the female member of the intelligentsia (both useless former bourgeoisie or wives of the Soviet upper-crust and dedicated working professionals of the postwar era).[36] The details of each type shifted in accordance with changing ideology, but what remained consistent was the new sense of purpose provided by the Soviet mission. Part of this mission became motherhood, as the state pushed policies aimed at increasing the birth rate in order to provide more citizens for its workforce.

Even as the desire for domestic life was renormalised in Soviet fiction after the Second World War, the Soviet woman remained *more* than a wife and mother. She faced a double identity and thus double bind that has not been

35 Fyodor Vasilievich Gladkov, *Cement*, trans. A. S. Arthur and C. Ashleigh (Evanston, IL: Northwestern University Press, 1994), p. 28.
36 Xenia Gasiorowska, *Women in Soviet Fiction: 1917–1964* (Madison: University of Wisconsin Press, 1968).

resolved to this day: having gained the freedom and purpose of a man, she was still burdened with the requirements of being a woman, leaving her with 'a double set of duties, civic and domestic'.[37] Despite their talk of equality, Soviet heroes never did the housework. Natalia Baranskaia's (1908–2004) *A Week like Any Other* (*Nedelia kak nedelia*, 1969) captures this difficulty for the early Brezhnev era as it traces the struggles of an educated working woman and mother of two on an ordinary week, reshaping the poetic suffering and self-sacrifice of Pushkin's Tatiana in more quotidian, prosaic terms.

The ideal of the faithful, all-enduring woman survived in the Soviet era, articulated most famously by the poetic persona of Anna Akhmatova's (1889–1966) *Requiem* (*Rekviem*, comp. 1934–61). This cycle of poems is a lyrical lament that captures the suffering of the Russian people under the Stalinist purges. Akhmatova's only son was imprisoned for the third time in 1938, and she joined the hopeless, frozen queue of women who spent hour after hour, day after day standing outside the prison hoping for a glimpse or word of their loved ones on the other side of the walls. *Requiem*'s 'Instead of a Preface' captures a moment in the queue, when one of the women recognises the poetic persona and asks, 'Can you describe this?', to which the poetic persona answers, 'I can.'[38] The cycle gives voice to all Russian women and their patient suffering, transforming Akhmatova into Russia's 'keening muse', in the words of Joseph Brodsky (1940–1996).[39] *Requiem* emphasises the role of the mother, again asserting a parallel between the Russian woman and suffering Mother Russia.

In the late and post-Soviet eras, some authors inverted this dynamic, showing the damage wrought on the family by the Soviet system by writing about mothers who inflicted suffering on their offspring. Liudmila Petrushevskaia's (1938–) cruel mothers are of this mould in tales such as 'Our Circle' (*Svoi krug*, 1988) and her novel *The Time: Night* (*Vremia noch'*, comp. 1988–90, pub. 1992).[40] The latter's heroine, Anna Andrianovna, considers herself a 'mystical namesake' (*tezka* – literally one who shares a name) of Anna Akhmatova, yet despite her beliefs, she is *not* the devoted mother of

---

37 Gasiorowska, *Women in Soviet Fiction*, p. 11.
38 Anna Akhmatova, *Sochineniia v dvukh tomakh* [Works in two volumes] (Moscow: Izdatel'stvo 'Tsitadel'', 1996), vol. I, p. 196.
39 Joseph Brodsky, 'The keening muse', in *Less Than One: Selected Essays* (New York: Farrar Straus Giroux, 1986), pp. 34–52.
40 Rosalind Marsh, 'New mothers for a new era? Images of mothers and daughters in post-Soviet prose in historical and cultural perspective', *Modern Language Review* 107.4 (2012), 1208.

Requiem.[41] Even as she talks of her devotion to her children and grandson, she reveals herself to be a perversion of the sacrificial mother ideal, antagonising her family and ending the novel totally alone. It is hard to see traces of the nineteenth-century Russian woman type, save in the sense of suffering and struggle women like Anna face in their new, unrelentingly bleak world.

The quest to define the Russian woman continued into the Putin era with a return to the government-sanctioned glorification of motherhood and the domestic sphere (an attempt to combat declining birth rates). Tatiana's ideal spread beyond literature into many facets of Russian culture. City buses in St Petersburg in 2018 were decorated with scenes from *Eugene Onegin*: Tatiana seated at her writing table with the opening words of her letter to Onegin, 'I write to you, what more can I say', on one side of the doors and Onegin standing on the other side next to a quote from his rejection of her, 'Learn to have control over yourself.' In the 2010s and early 2020s, the ideal of the devoted and self-sacrificing woman has been at the heart of scores of formulaic melodramas on television channels such as Russia-1 and Telekanal domashnii (Home TV channel) and the YouTube channel 'SMOTRIM Russkie serialy' (WATCH Russian TV series). The loving, gentle heroine usually starts the show with a man who is weak and unworthy of her. She is forced into difficult straits (often left for another woman or abandoned when her lover fakes death to escape gambling debts or an embezzlement scandal), and through her fortitude and nurturing instinct (she typically works at a school or nursery, or as a nanny) she wins the heart of a deserving man and ends up in domestic bliss. Virtue and traditional women's roles are rewarded. In this way, the Russian woman is made to serve larger ideological aims: she reinforces a social structure in which women are again confined to the domestic sphere, valued for their fidelity and maternal instincts.

But this soft, feminine ideal has not been universal. Feminist writers and artists have pushed back, though their works are aimed less at defining a type than at analysing the conditions faced by women and critiquing women's place in Russian society. Russia's controversial 2021 entry in the popular Eurovision Song Contest – 'Russian Woman', by the Tajik-Russian singer Manizha (1991–) – is emblematic of this opposing tendency, which is also present in the writings on the feminist platform *F-Letter* (see Chapter 1.10).[42]

---

41 Liudmila Petrushevskaia, *Vremia noch'* [The time: night], in *Kak mnogo znaiut zhenshchiny: Povesti, rasskazy, skazki, p'esy* [What women know: Novellas, stories, tales, plays] (Moscow: AST, 2013), p. 619.

42 *F-Letter*, https://syg.ma/f-writing, accessed 3 March 2023.

Manizha emphasises the Russian woman's need for strength, just as Dostoevskii did in his Pushkin speech a century and a half earlier. The refrain (in English) includes the lyrics: 'Every Russian woman needs to know (ha, ha) / You're strong enough, you're gonna break the wall.'[43] The Russian woman retains her strength, yet Manizha's lyrics also point to the struggles real Russian women still face. The song criticises the incredible pressures women remain under – two centuries after Tatiana – to attain and maintain their 'terrible perfection'.

Further Reading

Andrew, Joe, *Women in Russian Literature, 1780–1863* (Basingstoke: Palgrave Macmillan, 1988).

Gasiorowska, Xenia, *Women in Soviet Fiction: 1917–1964* (Madison: University of Wisconsin Press, 1968).

Hasty, Olga, *Pushkin's Tatiana* (Madison: University of Wisconsin Press, 1999).

Heldt, Barbara, *Terrible Perfection: Women and Russian Literature* (Bloomington: Indiana University Press, 1987).

Hubbs, Joanna, *Mother Russia: The Feminine Myth in Russian Culture* (Bloomington: Indiana University Press, 1988).

Kelly, Catriona, *A History of Russian Women's Writing: 1820–1992* (Oxford: Clarendon Press, 1994).

Marsh, Rosalind (ed.), *Women and Russian Culture: Projections and Self-Perceptions* (New York: Berghahn Books, 1998).

Stephan, Sonia (ed.), *A Plot of Her Own: The Female Protagonist in Russian Literature* (Evanston, IL: Northwestern University Press, 1995).

---

43 Manizha (vocalist and lyricist), *'Russian Woman'*, by Manizha, Ori Avni, and Ori Kaplan (independently released, 2021).

4.7

The New Person

EMMA WIDDIS

In his 1914 poem 'We Grow out of Iron' (*My rastem iz zheleza*), the poet Aleksei Gastev (1882–1939) pictured himself becoming one with a vast hangar of metal girders above him. 'I have grown iron shoulders', he proclaimed: 'Into my veins runs new iron blood.'[1] The words of this poem were echoed in the lyrics of the popular 'Aviator's March' (*Aviamarsh*, 1923): 'Reason gave us steel wings / And a fiery motor in place of a heart.'[2] These texts shared a common vision: that the radically reformulated social and political world of revolutionary Russia needed – and would inevitably create – new human types. In the words of the Bolshevik leader Lev Trotskii (1879–1940; see Box 5.3), the human species was to 'enter a stage of radical transformation', both physical and mental: 'Man will become immeasurably stronger, more intelligent and subtle; his body will become more harmonious, his movements more rhythmic, his voice more musical.'[3] For Trotskii, this physical self-regulation would be enabled by (and would enable) mental discipline: an iron will.

The image of the 'new Soviet person' (*novyi sovetskii chelovek*) did not emerge *ex nihilo* from the ashes of the Bolshevik Revolution, however. It has a longer history: the search for an ideal model of human life, a vision of the human as perfectible via the application of rational principles to regulate body and mind. Literature provided a key space for this search. It could offer both a picture of, and a manual for, that ideal life. Vladimir Lenin located the

---

1 Aleksei Gastev, *Poeziia rabochego udara* [Poetry of the worker's blow] (Moscow: Khudozhestvennaia literatura, 1971), p. 19.

2 Pavel German (lyrics), 'Aviamarsh' [Aviators' march], music by Iulii Khait. Cited from sovmusic.ru, www.sovmusic.ru/text.php?fname=marshair, accessed 20 Feb. 2023 [my translation]. Valentin Antonov has dated the composition of the text to 1923. See V. Antonov, 'Dva marsha: Kto u kogo?' [Two marches: Who and whose?], vilavi.ru (2006), http://vilavi.ru/pes/aviamarsh/avir.shtml, accessed 3 Aug. 2022.

3 Leon Trotsky, *Literature and Revolution*, ed. W. Keach, trans. R. Strunsky (Chicago: Haymarket Books, 2005), p. 207.

prototype of the ideal Bolshevik revolutionary in the radical heroes of nineteenth-century literary texts and particularly in key novels of the 1860s. He even named an important revolutionary pamphlet *What Is to Be Done?* (*Chto delat'?*, 1902) in reference to the 1863 novel by Nikolai Chernyshevskii (1828–1889) of the same name (see Chapters 1.5, 4.5).

In this chapter, I will set out some of the key texts that shaped the 'new person' as a literary protagonist from the second half of the nineteenth century up to the figure of the ideal worker in Socialist Realist texts of the 1930s and beyond. The main temporal focus of this chapter, however, will fall in the decade following 1917. The fictional new person that emerged in the years following the revolution was not in fact a straightforward child of the radicals of the 1860s. Rather, this figure was a complex hybrid of those iron-willed proto-revolutionaries and at least one other archetype of Russian literature: the *malen'kii chelovek* (the 'little [implicitly ordinary] person', a victim of social and political structures; see Chapter 4.3). The revolution of 1917 promised the end of the era of the little person as a hero of Russian Realist fiction: the character would be reforged as the vanguard of the revolution, the new Soviet person. This was to be the age of the collective, of the ordinary-exceptional hero born from the proletariat and shaped by the Soviet world. In practice, however, this new literary protagonist took shape in a complex tension between competing imperatives: between exceptionalism and ordinariness, individual and collective; between ideals of spontaneous energy and iron discipline; between the emancipation of the body and control of the mind.

Pre-revolutionary Prototypes

In his influential novel *What Is to Be Done?*, subtitled *Stories about New People* (*Chto delat'? Rasskazy o novykh liudiakh*, 1863), Chernyshevskii, a self-proclaimed member of the radical political opposition, set out to picture a new model of domestic life: man and woman living equitably together, with equal rights. Through its three protagonists – a progressive love triangle of Vera Pavlovna and the two men who love her (Lopukhov and Kirsanov) – it presents an ideal of rational egoism: the constraint of personal desire for the longer-term goal of self-realisation on a higher plane. Lopukhov and Kirsanov are medical students; through their sponsorship of her learning and through the marriage of equality that she has with Lopukhov, which liberates her from her family home, Vera Pavlovna undergoes a path to political consciousness.

The true agent of transformation in *What Is to Be Done?*, however, is a fourth figure: Rakhmetov. He guides and influences the other protagonists' self-realisation. Rakhmetov (notably lacking even a first name) is often seen as a prototype for the new person in Russian literature. His biography is presented almost as a hagiography (see Chapter 4.1), set out from the main narrative of the novel. Ascetic and determined, Rakhmetov sacrifices his personal satisfaction for the sake of a greater social good. He renounces love and sex; he eats not for pleasure but for strength (only red meat, a 'boxer's diet'); he sleeps first on a 'strip of felt, not even folding it double' and later on a bed of nails.[4] Rakhmetov builds himself in mind and body, through a combination of learning, labour (work as a barge hauler), and physical self-regulation. When asked why he sleeps on that bed of nails, he makes his purpose clear: "'A trial,' he replied. 'It is necessary. . . . Now I know that I can do it.'"[5]

In schematic terms, it is common to distinguish between the 'superfluous' (*lishnie*) men who were the frequent protagonists of literature of the earlier part of the nineteenth century – including Aleksandr Pushkin's (1799–1837) eponymous Eugene Onegin (*Evgenii Onegin*, 1825–32), Pechorin in Mikhail Lermontov's (1814–1841) *A Hero of Our Time* (*Geroi nashego vremeni*, 1840), and the hero of Ivan Turgenev's (1818–1883) *The Diary of a Superfluous Man* (*Dnevnik lishnego cheloveka*, 1850) – and the 'new people', such as Rakhmetov, who belonged to the radical intelligentsia of the 1860s (see Chapter 4.5). The superfluous hero is one whose idealism and desire is matched by incapacity and leads to a sense of futility. The new person, by contrast, may still be superfluous in a Russian society that is not ready for their visions and dreams but is marked by an urgent determination to act. This evolution is visualised in the titular questions of Aleksandr Herzen's (1812–1870) *Who Is to Blame?* (*Kto vinovat?*, 1846) and, twenty years later, Chernyshevskii's more determined *What Is to Be Done?*: a move from diagnosis to cure.

The protagonists in two of Turgenev's novels, *Rudin* (*Rudin*, 1856) and *Fathers and Children* (*Ottsy i deti*, 1862), reflect the same trajectory; they also reveal the limits of radical possibility in this period of Russian history. In *Rudin*, Turgenev portrayed his eponymous protagonist as full of ideas but incapable of acting on them. By the 1860s, however, the conditions for self-realisation appeared to be different, and the case for change more urgent. In

---

4 Nikolai Chernyshevskii, *What Is to Be Done?*, trans. Michael R. Katz (Ithaca: Cornell University Press, 1989), p. 281.
5 Chernyshevskii, *What Is to Be Done?*, p. 288.

Fathers and Children, the young hero Bazarov is marked by his total rejection of social convention. The critic Dmitrii Pisarev (1840–1868), himself a political radical and editor of the journal *The Russian Word* (*Russkoe slovo*, 1859–66), described Bazarov as a representative of the younger generation and his 'illness' as an 'illness of our times'.[6] Bazarov's fate is not a happy one: his faith in science and reason as the sole bases of truth and value renders him unable to operate in the human world. His hyperrational consciousness was famously satirised and challenged by Fedor Dostoevskii (1821–1881) – notably, for instance, in his *Notes from Underground* (*Zapiski iz podpol'ia*, 1864) and *Demons* (*Besy*, 1873), in both of which a hyperrational ego imprisons the radical thinker in a spiral of self-defeating argument, devoid of meaning and spirituality.

The 1860s and 1870s were a period of hope and disillusion, as the initial optimism of the reforms of Alexander II (r. 1855–81) mutated into a sense that those reforms had not gone far enough. This gave rise to increasingly radical political formations. The tsar's assassination by the People's Will revolutionary group sparked a period of counter-reform under his son Alexander III (r. 1881–94). Yet the ideal of the new person did not disappear entirely in literary texts. In his novel *Mother* (*Mat'*, 1906), Maksim Gorkii (1868–1936) created the figure of Pavel Vlasov. Pavel is a factory worker, raised by his mother in a bleak settlement, his father an abusive drunk. Through books, Pavel and his young friends discover not just knowledge but political truth. They mount a political protest and are arrested, and Pavel is sent to prison. Gorkii restages the trope of radical self-formation and gives it more specific political and revolutionary urgency with his young proletarian hero.

In all three of these archetypal novels of the new person – *What Is to Be Done?*, *Fathers and Children*, and *Mother* – the role of the new person was above all to educate those around them. Rakhmetov plays a key role in the self-realisation of the novel's other main protagonists. In Gorkii's text, rather than Pavel himself, it is his eponymous mother, Pelageia, who forms the novel's emotional centre of gravity; through her exposure to the ideas and dreams of her son and his friends, she acquires political consciousness. Bazarov's pedagogical project is more flawed, but the charismatic impact of the protagonist is without question. Already, then, we see both the strengths and the limits of the new person as hero. These figures are plot motivators, but they are not the centre of gravity – emotional or ethical – in the texts. They function as

---

6 D. I. Pisarev, 'Bazarov', in *Literaturnaia kritika v trekh tomakh* [Literary criticism in three volumes] (Leningrad: Khudozhestvennaia literatura, 1981), vol. I, p. 236.

catalysts of human transformation, but in themselves they are not fully developed characters. Indeed, Chernyshevskii was explicit that Rakhmetov is not the novel's main protagonist. Rather, he is there to set the example of an extreme: to make clear to readers, as to the other protagonists, the heights of possible human attainment and self-sacrifice.

Bolshevik New People: Iron and Leather

After the revolution, the dream of creating entirely new models of human life seemed suddenly both urgent and possible. Artists and ideologues, writers and political leaders shared a rhetoric of transformation: a new and specific-ally Soviet person was to be created by the conditions of revolution and the structures of the new post-revolutionary world. The shape of this ideal human type, however, was not yet clear. Indeed, through the two decades following the revolution, the figure of the new Soviet person was a muddled coagulation of different revolutionary imperatives.

In one sense, Rakhmetov's exemplary lack of humanness was a starting point for this new human type: ascetic self-sacrifice, iron self-discipline, and the rational articulation of a vision of a new world. Lenin stated unambigu-ously: 'Almost every one of our prominent socialists of the sixties and seventies possessed no small share of the Rakhmetov spirit.'[7] At the centre of the Bolshevik revolutionary vision, as articulated by Lenin in the pamphlet *What Is to Be Done?*, was the harnessing of the innate revolutionary energy of the masses, to be achieved by the controlled and class-conscious action of Bolsheviks. This was described as a passage from 'spontaneity' (*stikhiinost'*) to 'consciousness' (*soznatel'nost'*).[8] Rakhmetov's model of self-creation became a prototype for this transformation in its conscious regulation of body and mind and its techniques of self-improvement.

During the difficult years of the civil war, early Bolshevik literary heroes were often characterised by force and willpower. In Aleksandr Serafimovich's (1863–1949) fierce civil war narrative *The Iron Flood* (*Zheleznyi potok*, 1924), an exemplary leader, Kozhuk (whose Ukrainian accent acts as evidence of his status as one of the people), transforms the disorderly rabble of an exhausted Red Army battalion into a fierce fighting force by imposing his iron will.

---

7 V. I. Lenin, 'G. V. Plekhanov. "N. G. Chernyshevskii". Vvedenie' [G. V. Plekhanov, 'N. G. Chernyshevskii'. Foreword], in *Polnoe sobranie sochinenii* [Complete works], 5th edn, 55 vols. (Moscow: Izdatel'stvo politicheskoi literatury, 1958–65), vol. XXIX, p. 542.
8 V. I. Lenin, *What Is to Be Done? Burning Questions of Our Movement*, in *Collected Works*, vol. 5: *May 1901–February 1902* (Moscow: Progress Publishers, 1977), pp. 373–87.

Kozhuk is a realised metaphor of the iron man: he has 'iron jaws', a 'broken-iron voice'.[9] Like his pre-revolutionary forebears, he lacks three-dimensional humanness: those iron jaws act as a synecdoche for him throughout the text, and they expand to create and maintain the iron discipline of his battalion. As with Rakhmetov, Kozukh's biography is inserted into the text as a compressed narrative of self-transformation. There is one crucial difference, however: Kozukh has emerged not from the elite but from poverty. His is a journey from illiterate shepherd, through self-taught literacy, to military heroism. He is an exemplary member of the new proletariat.

The image of Kozukh as a 'man of iron' points to metal as a central metaphor of Soviet culture: the ideal of a technological reforging of the human. There was a pre-revolutionary legacy to this image; Pavel Vlasov in Gorkii's *Mother*, for instance, had been described as an 'iron man'.[10] As we saw above, Gastev's poem 'We Grow out of Iron' brought this metaphor into vivid relief for the revolutionary age. It reflected a broader emphasis on human physical and mental transformation as enabled by technology and on the dissolution of the boundary between human and machine. As the poet Vladimir Maiakovskii (1893–1930) put it in his long poem '150 000 000' (1921), 'Our legs / are the lightening rails of trains.'[11] Metaphors of iron, and iron people, evolved and mutated during the 1920s and 1930s. They signalled both a rapprochement with technology and the machine, and the importance placed on willpower and self-discipline in the creation of the new person. Joseph Stalin's own pseudonymous name (replacing his Georgian birthname of Dzhugashvili) came from the Russian for steel (*stal'*). Standing over Lenin's body in 1924, he pronounced: 'We Communists are people of a special mould. We are made from a special material.'[12] Nikolai Ostrovskii's (1904–1936) novel of 1934 described the formation of its hero as exemplary communist through its title metaphor: *How the Steel Was Tempered* (*Kak zakalialas' stal'*).

In the first years after the revolution, however, the image of the new person was more complex. The consistent emphasis on willpower was often linked to a set of other potentially contradictory impulses. This complexity

9 A. S. Serafimovich, *Zheleznyi potok* [The iron flood], in *Zheleznyi potok. Rasskazy* [The iron flood. Stories] (Leningrad: Lenizdat, 1973), pp. 10, 133.

10 M. Gor'kii, *Mat'* [Mother], in *Sobranie sochinenii v tridtsati tomakh* [Collected works in thirty volumes] (Moscow: Gosudarstvenoe izdatel'stvo khudozhestvennoi literatury, 1949–55), vol. VII, p. 270.

11 Vladimir Maiakovskii, '150 000 000', in *Polnoe sobranie sochinenii* [Complete works], 13 vols. (Moscow: Khudozhestvennaia literatura, 1955–61), vol. II, p. 113.

12 J. Stalin, 'On the death of Lenin: A speech delivered at the second All-Union Congress of Soviets, January 26, 1924', in *Works*, vol. VI: 1924 (Moscow: OGIZ, Gosudarstvennoe izdatel'stvo politicheskoi literatury, 1947), p. 47.

was explicitly foregrounded in the 1922 novel of Boris Pilniak (1894–1938), *The Naked Year* (*Golyi god*), which created one of the most striking literary images of revolutionary people. Described as 'leather people in leather jackets (Bolsheviks!)', Pilniak's protagonists embody many of the characteristics of the new revolutionary hero. The 'leather people' are 'all the same size, each one a leather beauty, each one strong, with curls in ringlets under the peaked cap pushed back on his head; each had, more than anything else, willpower in his protruding cheekbones, in the lines around his mouth and in his lumbering movements – and daring. Of Russia's rough, crumbling national spirit (*narodnost'*) – the best slice.' The text continues: 'none of them has ever read Karl Marx'.[13]

Several elements of Pilniak's description bear further analysis: sameness (collectivity); physicality (strength); daring and vitality (*derzanie*); and the intriguing dyad of lack of education and national (peasant) spirit. In what follows, I will explore each of these qualities as linked to a set of thematic preoccupations, which reveal the multiple and contradictory elements that were at play in these early formulations of the new Soviet person.

The I and the We

Pilniak's leather people are 'all the same size', with nothing distinguishing them from one another. Here, however, the lack of fully formed human contours, which, in Rakhmetov and his peers, represented a failure, is reconfigured as a strength. The remaking of the human in post-revolutionary Russia was an overcoming of self: a dissolving of the individual into the Bolshevik collective. The psychologist Aron Zalkind (1886–1936) envisaged a psychological transformation in which collective feeling would replace 'individualistic narcissism'.[14] The new person would achieve self-realisation *within* the collective. Self-abnegation would give rise to self-fulfilment. This points to a key tension in the image of the new Soviet person. As Mark Steinberg notes, the project of self-transformation via willpower

---

13 B. Pil'niak, *Golyi god* [The naked year], in *Sobranie sochinenii v shesti tomakh* [Collected works in six volumes] (Moscow: Terra-Knizhnyi klub, 2003–4), vol. I, p. 44.

14 Aron Zalkind, 'Pionerskoe detskoe dvizhenie, kak forma kul'traboty sredi proletariata' [The Children's Pioneer Movement as a form of cultural education among the proletariat], *Vestnik truda* 3 (March 1924), 108; English translation in William G. Rosenberg (ed.), *Bolshevik Visions: First Phase of the Cultural Revolution in Russia*, 2nd edn, 2 vols. (Ann Arbor: Michigan University Press, 1990), vol. II, pp. 84–91.

had echoes of the Nietzschean *Übermensch* (superman).[15] As such it would appear contrary to the collectivist impulse. In *The Iron Flood*, for example, there is potential conflict between the exceptional self-realisation of Kozukh, a larger-than-life hero, and the collectivist imperative. Such a contradiction ran through early Soviet explorations of the new hero and became a fault line around which many of their most complex interrogations of the value of individuality took place. What stood to be lost with the realisation of the homogeneous collective subject?

With their lack of psychological complexity, Pilniak's leather people reflect a second principle of revolutionary rhetoric: that the social and political transformations brought about by the Bolsheviks would bring a parallel transformation of human bodies and minds. The leather people are liberated from individual feelings. As the text proclaims: 'You can't dampen them with the lemonade of psychology.'[16] In this respect, the text echoes a broader anti-psychologist impulse within early revolutionary culture. The complex and tormenting individual mind was a bourgeois disease. As the filmmaker Dziga Vertov (1896–1954) asserted: 'The psychological prevents man from being as precise as a stopwatch; it interferes with his desire for kinship with the machine.'[17]

This rhetoric was widespread. As noted above, Trotskii famously envisaged the revolution as enabling a newly harmonised human type, a regulation of the unpredictable impulses of body and mind. This regulation of the body was envisaged in two related but distinct ways. On the one hand, the exercise of willpower (the mind) must *tame* bodily impulse and channel energy productively. As Steinberg notes, for new Soviet people 'what the animal body values – the pleasures of food, reproduction, sexual satisfaction, security, domination over others – has little essential value'.[18] On the other hand, the potentially disruptive mind (psyche) itself would be regulated and constrained by the newly controlled body.

It is important to signal here that, in early Soviet culture, the product of bodily regulation was understood also as sensory fulfilment, enhanced vitality, and power. These dual impulses of regulation and emancipation were present in the many images of the human-machine in the culture of the

---

15 Mark D. Steinberg, *The Proletarian Imagination: Self, Modernity, and the Sacred in Russia, 1910–1925* (Ithaca: Cornell University Press, 2002), p. 113.
16 Pil'niak, *Golyi god*, p. 44.
17 Dziga Vertov, 'We: A version of a manifesto', in Richard Taylor and Ian Christie (eds.), *The Film Factory: Russian and Soviet Cinema in Documents 1896–1939* (London: Routledge, 1990), p. 69. Originally published in *Kinofot* 1 (25–31 Aug. 1922), 11–12.
18 Steinberg, *Proletarian Imagination*, p. 117.

period. Iurii Olesha's (1899–1960) novel *Envy* (*Zavist'*, 1927) presented an exemplary new person in Volodia Makarov, a self-proclaimed man-machine. Makarov is an outstanding sportsman of the new Soviet type – dedicated to the victory of the collective, rather than to individual acclaim. His regulation of bodily impulse enables his participation in the new world.

Alongside Makarov, however, *Envy* pictured a second, larger-than-life new person, whose contours raised more complex questions about bodily regulation. A generation older than Makarov, Andrei Babichev derives his status as a revolutionary new person from his participation in the civil war. A model of revolutionary self-formation, he is a leading force in the new Soviet world. His body, like Makarov's, is a perfectly functioning machine: the novel opens with a vivid glimpse ('Go, peristalsis, go!') of his highly efficient bowels.[19] Yet Babichev's body is characterised by surplus: its heightened efficiency shades into excess and corpulence. And this excess is mirrored in other elements of Babichev's characterisation: his appetite, his emotions, and his ego are all outsize. He lacks the self-discipline and self-abnegation that were key features of the ideal new person.

In Babichev, perhaps, Olesha took aim at the cult of self-realisation and its uncomfortable relationship with individualism. The character also signals, however, the ways in which human body *and* mind – emotion, imagination, appetite – resist disciplinary mechanisms. Humanness itself emerges as surplus in *Envy*. But it is in that surplus that the emotional and artistic weight of the text is to be found. In the figure of the young narrator, Ivan Kavalerov, and his richly distorting poetic visions, the novel offered a compelling reminder of the value of subjectivity and all that could be lost if the Soviet dream of the new person were to take shape.

Gender, Sex, and the New Person

Babichev's unruly corporeality visualised a key tension in Soviet images of the efficient and emancipated human-machine. The rhetoric of the healthy body had an inevitable flipside: a fear of the body and its uncontrollable impulses; and a related fear of the uncontrollable psyche. Eric Naiman suggests that, in literature of the 1920s, these fears were concentrated into a particular anxiety around the female body. Babichev is a curious hybrid of man and woman: while he has the groin of an antelope, his soft pectorals are

---

19 Iurii Olesha, 'Zavist'' [Envy], *Zavist', Tri tolstiaka, Ni dnia bez strochki* [Envy, Three fat men, No day without a line] (Moscow: Khudozhestvennaia literatura, 1989), p. 12.

like breasts. What was the gender, then, of the ideal Soviet person? We should recall that for many critics it was the female Vera Pavlovna who was the true heroine of Chernyshevskii's *What Is to Be Done?*. Similarly, the key political journey in Gorkii's *Mother* was that of Pelageia. According to the ideals of Soviet ideology, with its liberation from bourgeois patriarchy, the new Soviet person could surely be either male or female.

Overall, however, as Eliot Borenstein notes, for all its claims to gender neutrality the new person in the early Soviet period was a distinctly masculine image – even when explicitly claiming not to be.[20] In Fedor Gladkov's (1883–1958) *Cement* (*Tsement*, 1925), as in *What Is to Be Done?*, the female character Dasha follows a path to self-realisation through escape from traditional marriage. Yet Dasha's passage to consciousness and into the collective involves an overcoming of her own 'traditional' female desires. Similarly, Aleksandra Kollontai's (1872–1952) *Vasilisa Malygina* (*Vasilisa Malygina*, 1923) pictures an apparently exemplary new person in its eponymous heroine. At the end of the novel, Vasilisa liberates herself from the toxic bourgeois influence of her lover and heads into a collectivised future. Yet the creation of this new female prototype is only possible through an overcoming – even elimination – of the female body. Vasilisa is consistently described in terms that signal her body as unfeminine, and the text recounts the surmounting of desire by what Catriona Kelly calls Vasilisa's 'principled promiscuity'.[21]

More broadly, sexual desire was a threat to the new Soviet person, regardless of gender. It was one of a bundle of human impulses and drives that threatened the health of the social, collective body. The control of libidinous desire would enable its disruptive energy to be productively redirected into the collective labour project. Evgenii Zamiatin's (1884–1937) 1920 novel *We* (*My*; the novel was censored in the Soviet Union and first published in English in 1924) put the Bolshevik utopia's underlying project of sexual regulation into focus in a fictional 'One State'. There, the nameless inhabitants ('numbers') are given 'pink tickets' that control their right to sexual activity, aiming to satisfy need without releasing excess. The narrator D-503's erotic encounter with the unruly female I-330 triggers the undoing of his collectivist mindset, turning him into a political rebel.

20 Eliot Borenstein, *Men without Women: Masculinity and Revolution in Russian Fiction, 1917–1929* (Durham, NC: Duke University Press, 2001).

21 Catriona Kelly, 'The new Soviet man and woman', in Simon Dixon (ed.), *The Oxford Handbook of Modern Russian History*, online edn (Oxford: Oxford Academic, 16 Dec. 2013), https://doi.org/10.1093/oxfordhb/9780199236701.013.024, accessed 3 Aug. 2022.

Two Visions of Revolutionary Subjectivity:
Spontaneity and Consciousness

Another tension made visible in Pilniak's leather people is between two ideals of revolutionary transformation. Revolution could be seen as the victory of technology and reason, led by an urban proletariat. Or it could be an iconoclastic revolt, a surge of spontaneous energy from the 'uncivilised' Russian peasantry. Although Lenin had articulated the progression *from* spontaneity *to* consciousness as the essential trajectory of revolution, in practice both categories remained potent in early Soviet visions of revolutionary subjectivity. In *The Naked Year*, the revolution appears as an explosion of pre-Petrine Russia's innately populist spirit of rebellion and vigour. With their 'daring', and their Russian 'national spirit', Pilniak's leather people do not resemble mechanised men of iron. As the Marxist literary critic Aleksandr Voronskii (1884–1937) noted in 1922, 'Pilniak greeted the Revolution primarily not as a breakthrough into a steel-encased future, but in a rebellious spirit. He sought and found in it an animalist, prehistorical visage.'[22] Pilniak was not alone. The poet Aleksandr Blok (1880–1921) memorably conceptualised the Bolshevik Revolution as a peasant revolt in his poem *The Twelve* (*Dvenadtsat'*, 1918), and in his poem 'The Scythians' (*Skify*, 1918) it appears as a barbaric attack on the west carried out by untamed 'Scythian' horsemen galloping from Russia's distant east. In his essay 'The Collapse of Humanism' (*Krushenie gumanizma*, 1919), Blok pointed to the coming of the 'savage chorus' of the masses, the elemental energy of liberated, rebellious bodies.[23]

Such emphases on spontaneity and the power of instinctual rebellion complicated the contours of the new Soviet person, and of the Soviet body. In Pilniak's memorable words, in the short story 'Ivan and Maria' (*Ivan da Mar'ia*, 1922), 'the whole revolution smells of sexual organs'.[24] The relationship between energy and control (spontaneity and consciousness) was further complicated by the Soviet Union's imperial project and the melting pot of ethnicities that lay beneath the homogenising ideal of the new Soviet person (see Chapter 4.8). In *Sky-blue Sands* (*Golubye peski*, 1923) by Vsevolod Ivanov (1895–1963), Vasilii Zapus is a Bolshevik sent to organise agitation in the Kyrgyz steppe. He is charismatic and vital, and a hero in the revolutionary

---

22 Alexander Konstantinovich Voronsky, *Art as the Cognition of Life: Selected Writings 1911–1936*, ed. and trans. Philip Choate (Oak Park, MI: Mehring Books, 1998), p. 58.
23 Aleksandr Blok, 'Krushenie gumanizma' [The collapse of humanism], in *Sobranie sochinenii v 8 tomakh* [Collected works in 8 volumes], ed. V. Orlov (Moscow: Sovetskii pisatel', 1960–3), vol. VI, p. 113.
24 Pil'niak, 'Ivan da Mar'ia' [Ivan and Maria], in *Sobranie sochinenii*, p. 253.

mould, but it is notable that he lacks the element of conscious rationality that Lenin had articulated as essential for a Bolshevik leader. A similar polarity structured Isaak Babel's (1894–1940) cycle of short stories *Red Cavalry* (*Konarmiia*, 1923–6), a civil war narrative picturing the campaign of the eponymous Red Cavalry on the border with Poland, seen through the eyes of the Jewish intellectual writer Kirill Liutov. The Cossack horsemen in the cavalry, co-opted to fight for Bolshevik power, are powerful agents of the new world, marked by a physical vitality and energy that holds Liutov in thrall. He is torn between contradictory imperatives, mesmerised by the power of the new world – given seductive physical form in these uneducated cavalrymen – but also horrified by its violent reality. As Liutov struggles to reconcile conscience and consciousness with the embodied spontaneity of the revolutionary age, the text offers no resolved image of the Bolshevik new person.

Abstractions and Realities

Red Cavalry stages an encounter between the intellectual and the new world that reflects another key tension shaping the emergence of the fictional new Soviet person. Like Babel's cavalrymen, whose rudimentary grasp of Bolshevik ideology is underlined, none of the leather people in Pilniak's *The Naked Year* 'has ever read Karl Marx'. Members of the proletarian class, they are inheritors of the legacy of the little person as hero-protagonist in Russian literature (see Chapter 4.3). Now, however, it was the duty of such little people to lead the new world. In one sense, the proletarian origins of the Soviet new person were an essential guarantor of revolutionary credentials. In another, the anti-intellectualism of the leather people was to emerge as a fault line which made the vulnerabilities of the Soviet project visible.

The satirical novella *Heart of a Dog* (*Sobach'e serdtse*, 1925) by Mikhail Bulgakov (1891–1940) takes aim at the pseudo-scientific grounds that supported some of the most utopian projects for the remodelling of the human species – and their abstractions. Professor Preobrazhenskii transplants the testes and pituitary glands of a man into the body of a stray dog, Sharik. The result is the rapid growth of a quite literally new person: Sharikov. Sharikov, however – for all his excellent proletarian credentials – exhibits few of the qualities of the ideal new Soviet person. He speaks the vulgar new language of the regime, with its absurd combination of ideological aggressions and bureaucratic neologisms. He is driven by impulses and

unbridled appetites and has a total lack of culture and refinement. Bulgakov's novella is not a straightforward critique of Sharikov, however. Tracking Professor Preobrazhenskii's horrified response to the results of his experiment in creating a new human type, it offers a nuanced satire on the bourgeois-intellectual's instinctive distaste for the real-life forms of the proletarian hero.

Two other writers drew attention to a collision between the abstract ideal of the perfectly harmonised new human type and the stubbornly imperfect reality of actual Soviet bodies. The short stories of Mikhail Zoshchenko (1894–1958), published through the 1920s to enormous popular acclaim, showed the unruly corporeality and awkwardness of real human subjects struggling to adjust to a new world. Written in *skaz* (a first-person narrative which emulates oral speech; see Box 4.3), and thus allowing the new Soviet voice to emerge in all its unformed imperfection, Zoshchenko's tiny vignettes focus on bathrooms, on waterproof boots, on a person's attachment to their very own scrubbing brush. However, like Anton Chekhov (1860–1904) before him, Zoshchenko doesn't rail against the banalities of the everyday. He reveals them as a fundamental condition of humanness and as hindering (or making impossible) the emergence of that ideal new person.

Zoshchenko's relationship with the revolutionary project was a distant one, but the personal commitment of Andrei Platonov (1899–1951) to the socialist utopia was never in question. As Thomas Seifrid notes, Platonov was 'proletarian in origin as well as political orientation', and as Steinberg observes, his fiction was a bold attempt to envisage a new model of human life, embedded in the vitalist rhetoric of early revolutionary utopianism.[25] Yet Platonov also faced head-on the empty promises of the abstract ideological terms that were used to envisage new Soviet people and the new world. In *The Foundation Pit* (*Kotlovan*, 1930), the engineer Prushevskii dreams of building a 'proletarian home'. A true Bolshevik engineer-ideologue, he wants to transform the world – and the people in it – via the rational application of ideas and willpower. Like so many of the engineer-dreamers in Platonov's fiction, however, he runs up against the obdurate, embodied reality of human life and human needs. Failing to provide basic comfort, shelter, and sustenance for its inhabitants, the foundation pit of his utopian home becomes a space of suffering and death.

---

25 Thomas Seifrid, *A Companion to Andrei Platonov's 'The Foundation Pit'* (Boston: Academic Studies Press, 2009), p. 61; Steinberg, *Proletarian Imagination*, p. 120.

The Positive Soviet Hero

Through the long 1920s then, the search for an ideal form for the new Soviet person was complicated by a set of contradictory impulses and a sustained exploration of the horizons of human possibility. In one sense, the advent of Socialist Realism as the official form of Soviet literature in 1934 marked a resolution of some of those tensions. In Dmitrii Furmanov's (1891–1926) novel *Chapaev* (*Chapaev*, 1923) – made into a highly successful film by the brothers Georgii (1899–1946) and Sergei (1900–1959) Vasiliev in 1935, hailed as a model for Socialist Realist cinema – the protagonist, Chapaev (a real-life historical figure), is a heroic military leader, defined by his bravery, courage, and intuitive battlefield brilliance. But he lacks education and political consciousness. The novel's second protagonist, Klychkov (representing the author Furmanov himself), is a Bolshevik commissar and intellectual. The friendship between the two men brings about a dual transformation, where each man absorbs some of the other's positive qualities and the duelling imperatives of spontaneity and consciousness are brought into harmony.

Together, Chapaev and Klychkov add up to an ideal new person. And as Socialist Realism took shape in Soviet fiction during the 1930s, they fused to form the prototype of the typical positive socialist hero. Katerina Clark has identified the guiding 'master plot' of Socialist Realist narratives as tracing the passage from spontaneity to consciousness, via willpower and self-discipline, in indicative 'typical' heroes.[26] In the classic production novel, for instance, a young hero arrives in any given microcosm of Soviet society (factory, *kolkhoz*, provincial town, etc.) and concocts a scheme for solving the problems in that community (usually the non-fulfilment of state production targets). The hero mobilises the local people and, after a series of trials, the triumphant conclusion is the completion of the task and a celebration to mark this achievement. Thus, the production novel enacts a passage to consciousness for the Soviet hero, and his or her community, which is incorporated into the great Soviet socialist narrative.

With his or her narrative of self-realisation, the Socialist Realist positive hero inherited the legacy of Rakhmetov. A key difference, however, was that the self-realisation of the Soviet individual was made possible only by participation in the collective. The Socialist Realist hero-protagonist must be ideologically motivated, loyal to the party, and a curious combination of typical and exceptional. Ostrovskii's *How the Steel Was Tempered*, for example,

---

26 Katerina Clark, *The Soviet Novel: History as Ritual*, 3rd edn (Bloomington: Indiana University Press, 2000).

tracks Pavel Korchagin's passage to consciousness (his 'tempering') across his lifetime through political education, participation in the collective project, and the overcoming of personal and shared obstacles. Indeed, the trope of the trial or obstacle and its overcoming was an essential element in the ideal Soviet biography. In Boris Polevoi's (1908–1981) *Tale of a Real Man* (*Povest' o nastoiashchem cheloveke*, 1946), the hero-protagonist's passage to true heroism is made possible only *after* he loses both of his legs. The forced containment of potential bodily or emotional excess is what makes possible the self-realisation of the true Stalinist hero.[27]

In Socialist Realist production novels, then, the hybrid and complex figure of the new person solidified into the image of the positive hero. Increasingly coherent narrative plots and realist style reflected a newly assumed coherence in the Soviet self. The positive hero was marked by a lack of complex interior life but with a distinctly articulated set of moral attributes, which replaced the earlier emphasis on total physical and psychic transformation.

Later Soviet People

In the repeated biographies of positive heroes across Socialist Realist texts, Sovietness emerged as a moral framework. In 1961, the publication of the *Moral Code of the Builder of Communism* (*Moral'nyi kodeks stroitelia kommunizma*) fixed these qualities in official terms at a time when, six years after Nikita Khrushchev's historic speech denouncing the cult of Stalin, it might have appeared that their legacy was being thoroughly tested. Alongside collectivism and 'conscientious labour', the *Moral Code* listed 'honesty and truthfulness, moral purity, simplicity and modesty in personal life'.[28] It reflected – in real life – the qualities of the positive hero in literary texts, in a vision of a cohesive and integrated self.

In official Soviet literature, the model of the positive hero was maintained with considerable consistency. But it also provided a model against (and within) which alternative models of fictional subjectivity began to emerge. Following Vladimir Pomerantsev's (1907–1971) landmark call in 1953 for literature to exhibit 'sincerity', diverse writers engaged in a search for

27 Lilya Kaganovsky, *How the Soviet Man Was Unmade: Cultural Fantasy and Male Subjectivity under Stalin* (Pittsburgh: University of Pittsburgh Press, 2008).

28 'The moral code of the builders of communism, 1961' [Moral'nyi kodeks stroitelia kommunizma], trans. Deborah Field. *Seventeen Moments in Soviet History: An Online Archive of Primary Sources*, www.sovmusic.ru/text.php?fname=marshair, accessed 20 Feb. 2023.

a model of the literary protagonist as both individual *and* collective, and in which subjective experience could be reclaimed as part of a remodelled version of the Soviet hero.[29] Mikhail Sholokhov's (1905–1984) short story 'The Fate of a Man' (*Sud'ba cheloveka*, 1957) and Ilia Erenburg's (1891–1967) novel *The Thaw* (*Ottepel'*, 1954) are indicative examples of this complex and ultimately self-defeating project. In Andrei Bitov's (1937–2018) *Pushkin House* (*Pushkinskii dom*, comp. 1964–71) – a text which could not be published through official channels – the protagonist, Leva, is presented as a collage of contradictory characteristics. The novel is in conscious dialogue with its literary prototypes: Leva alludes directly to both Chernyshevskii's Rakhmetov and to Maraseev, the disabled hero of Polevoi's *Tale of a Real Man*, in ironic references to his own failures. In *Pushkin House* the iron discipline and willpower of the new person is transformed and distorted into the passivity of the Soviet intelligentsia. More significantly still, the self emerges not as 'typical' and not according to the Marxist materialist principle that people are products of their time. Rather, the self is complex, individual, imperfect, and in formation.

It was perhaps in late Soviet science fiction that the long history of the new (Soviet) person as literary protagonist came to its final and unheroic end, though its legacy continues to fuel post-Soviet literary production (see Chapter 1.9). The novel *Monday Begins on Saturday* (*Ponedel'nik nachinaet-sia v subbotu*, 1965), by the brothers Arkadii (1925–1991) and Boris (1933–2012) Strugatskii, locates much of its satire in the laboratory of Professor Vybegallo, whose project is to create the 'completely satisfied man' (an allusion to the Soviet dogma that communism could eliminate human needs and desires by the satisfaction of all basic requirements). And with its cybernetic reproductions of ideal human types, Vladimir Savchenko's (1933–2005) *Self-Discovery* (*Otkrytie sebia*, 1967) offers a similarly parodic undoing of the dreams of perfected humanity.

Making – and Unmaking – New Soviet Readers

The parodic impulse evident in late Soviet science fiction was amplified in the work of the so-called Conceptualist writers and visual artists – Dmitrii Prigov (1940–2007), Andrei Monastyrskii (1949–), Ilia Kabakov (1933–2023), and Erik Bulatov (1933–), among others – and has shaped the legacy of the new Soviet person as a literary protagonist, in particular since the collapse of the Soviet

---

29 Vladimir Pomerantsev, 'Ob iskrennosti v literature' [On sincerity in literature], *Novyi mir* [New world] 12 (Dec. 1953), 218–45.

Union in 1991. The Conceptualists faced the powerful legacy of the literary image of the new Soviet person head on. They recognised the impossibility of forming models of subjectivity *outside* the dominant frameworks of Soviet language and imagery. Sharing the deconstructive impulses of Postmodernism, their approach rather was to take those frameworks to an extreme, to render them absurd and to expose their discursive nature. In this way they took aim not only at the new Soviet person but at the language – and the literary system – that had created and sustained it.

Prigov's performance poems are particularly notable examples of this double aim. His cycle of poems *The Apotheosis of the Policeman* (*Apofeoz militsanera*, 1976–8), for instance, presents an ordinary Soviet policeman as a larger-than-life symbol of power and authority, straddling heaven and earth. Repeated in performance, with Prigov in uniform, the poems reveal the fundamental emptiness behind the Soviet language of power and authority. Two of the most influential novelists of late and post-Soviet Russia can be seen as heirs of the Conceptualists. Vladimir Sorokin's (1955–) short story 'The First Saturday Workday' (*Pervyi subbotnik*, 1984) is one of many works in which the author enacts a grotesque *reductio ad absurdum* of the rhetoric of Soviet self-improvement, as a young enthusiast's transition to Soviet manhood is marked by a monumental farting competition. Viktor Pelevin's (1962–) novel *Omon Ra* (*Omon Ra*, 1992) offers a parodic Soviet Bildungsroman of the eponymous character Omon (named by his policeman father after the acronym for a branch of the Soviet military police), who dreams of becoming a cosmonaut. The cult of heroic overcoming is parodied when Omon discovers that as a part of his training in the space academy he will have his legs amputated below the knee (like Maraseev in Polevoi's *Tale of a Real Man*).

In the works of the Conceptualists and their post-Soviet heirs, and in their strategies of repetition, desecration, and desacralisation, the new Soviet person is revealed to be nothing more than a simulacrum, formed by the slogans and images of Soviet propaganda. This unmasking co-exists, however, with a crucial acknowledgement of the power and influence of those narratives – and their enduring legacy. Indeed, as Prigov, Pelevin, and Sorokin recognised, the fictional protagonists in the texts discussed in this chapter were not the only new Soviet people that Soviet-era writers sought to construct – or the most important. In Evgeny Dobrenko's memorable words, 'One could define Soviet culture as a political and aesthetic project *radically focused on the recipient*.'[30]

---

30 Evgeny Dobrenko, *The Making of the State Reader: Social and Aesthetic Contexts of the Reception of Soviet Literature*, trans. Jesse M. Savage (Stanford: Stanford University Press, 1997), p. 2.

Readers themselves were the ultimate new Soviet people to be formed by the pedagogic texts in which the figure of the new person appeared. The task of post-Soviet Postmodernism (see Chapter 1.9) has been to deconstruct not only the image of the new Soviet person but also the very idea that literature can or should offer models of how to live.

The story of the new person in Russian and Soviet literature, then, is one which traces the emergence of a dream and follows its transformation into a coercive strategy. Certainly, in the full flowering of the narratives of the positive hero from the mid-1930s on, literary models of human behaviour aimed at education, regulation, and containment. Yet it is important to remember that, for all its eventual uniformity and even dogmatism, the initial utopian project of forming a new kind of ideal person was one which engaged a range of diverse thinkers and writers in an ambitious inquiry as to the limits of human possibility – and the shape of humanness itself.

Further Reading

Borenstein, Eliot, *Men without Women: Masculinity and Revolution in Russian Fiction, 1917–1929* (Durham, NC: Duke University Press, 2001).

Clark, Katerina, *The Soviet Novel: History as Ritual*, 3rd edn (Bloomington: Indiana University Press, 2000).

Dobrenko, Evgeny, *The Making of the State Reader: Social and Aesthetic Contexts of the Reception of Soviet Literature*, trans. Jesse M. Savage (Stanford: Stanford University Press, 1997).

Hellebust, Rolf, *Flesh to Metal: Soviet Literature and the Alchemy of Revolution* (Ithaca: Cornell University Press, 2002).

Kelly, Catriona, 'The new Soviet man and woman', in Simon Dixon (ed.), *The Oxford Handbook of Modern Russian History*, online edn (Oxford: Oxford Academic, 16 Dec. 2013), https://doi.org/10.1093/oxfordhb/9780199236701.013.024.

Mathewson, Rufus W., Jr, *The Positive Hero in Russian Literature*, 2nd edn (Evanston, IL: Northwestern University Press, 2000).

Naiman, Eric, *Sex in Public: The Incarnation of Early Soviet Ideology* (Princeton: Princeton University Press, 1997).

Paperno, Irina, *Chernyshevsky and the Age of Realism: A Study in the Semiotics of Behavior* (Stanford: Stanford University Press, 1988).

Soboleva, Maja, 'The concept of the "new Soviet man" and its short history', *Canadian-American Slavic Studies* 51.1 (2017), 64–85.

Steinberg, Mark D., *The Proletarian Imagination: Self, Modernity, and the Sacred in Russia, 1910–1925* (Ithaca: Cornell University Press, 2002).

4.8

The Non-Russian

MICHAEL KUNICHIKA

In 1913, the poet Velimir Khlebnikov (1885–1922) published an essay titled 'On Expanding the Boundaries of Russian Literature' (*O rasshirenii predelov russkoi slovesnosti*) in the journal *The Slav* (*Slavianin*). In it, he described the fates of the empire and literature as intertwined and observed the role that Russian literature could play in guiding the former. In his view, the literary canon suffered from 'artificial narrowness': it 'is hardly aware of the existence of the Jews. Nor is there any creation or achievement that might express the spirit of the continent and the soul of the conquered natives, as in Longfellow's "Hiawatha." An expanded model of Russian literature might serve instead to convey the breath of life from the conquered to the conqueror, Sviatogor and Ilya Muromets.' For Khlebnikov, representing a broader range of the population could even bring a measure of political stability: 'The mind of the land cannot only be Great Russian. It would be better if it were continental.'[1] Literature, in Khlebnikov's view, constructs an imperium of letters whose ultimate goal is political cohesion.

Scholars and writers have long meditated on ethnic difference in the Russian context: how literature should represent the Russian Empire's subject peoples; how those peoples have represented themselves; and what these representations have meant over time for Russian politics and culture. This chapter will broadly term these peoples the 'non-Russian', but their guises were many. What values was the figure of the non-Russian made to embody? How did these representations reflect the imperial situations of both Russia and later the Soviet Union? The coming pages consider how, in different ways and at different times, Russian writers – and writers writing in Russian – have answered these questions.

---

1 Velimir Khlebnikov, *Collected Works*, 3 vols. (Cambridge, MA: Harvard University Press, 1987), vol. III, p. 47.

To provide an account of non-Russian protagonists is no small challenge given the designation's history, broad geographic and ethnic application, and cultural function. It is also challenging because the concept of non-Russianness obtains its form and value within shifting frameworks and historical periods. The non-Russian literary protagonist thus embodies a set of continually changing cultural values. These values shift, moreover, as part of an interrogation of Russian national and/or imperial identity itself, reflecting qualities that a given writer thinks that Russia lacks or that another writer wishes Russia to embody. In this sense, the literary figuring of the non-Russian typifies what Hayden White has identified as a technique of 'self-definition by negation', which appears in cultural contexts 'when men were uncertain as to the precise quality of their sensed humanity'.[2] The technique not only can affirm a nation's (superior) humanity or civilisational status but can also call it into question.

Notably, the non-Russian can technically be from anywhere not Russia; he or she can even occasionally be an ethnic Russian who no longer seems adequately so. Though imperial situations might incline us to first identify the non-Russian as an imperial subject, the term 'non-Russian' can designate anyone: even a Russian ruler such as Catherine II ('the Great', r. 1762–96) or other Romanov tsars who were not ethnically Russian could fall into the category. My emphasis (and limit) in these pages will be on non-Russian figures whom Russian writers and thinkers mobilised in forcing a reckoning with Russia's own cultural and political status or ambition. These figures were often positively evaluated and served as the ethnic counterparts of the so-called positive hero of Russian letters.[3] The positive values with which the non-Russian protagonist was invested often rested upon concepts of freedom (as opposed to the constraints of civilisation), forms of 'authentic' life, proximity to nature, communal bonds, or distinctive and praiseworthy cultural traditions considered threatened by, resistant to, or preferrable to modernity and modernisation – and all the other processes typifying state planning brought about by imperial control, across a long historical range from Russification to collectivisation.

Throughout modern Russian letters, the figures who incarnate such values have a range of diverse heritages, both ethnic and religious, including Jewish,

---

2 Hayden White, 'The forms of wildness', in Edward J. Dudley and Maximillian E. Novak (eds.), *The Wild Man Within: An Image in Western Thought from the Renaissance to Romanticism* (Pittsburgh: University of Pittsburgh Press, 1973), pp. 151–2.

3 A classic statement on this figure is Rufus W. Mathewson, *The Positive Hero in Russian Literature* (Evanston, IL: Northwestern University Press, 1999).

Muslim, Chechen, Siberian, and Central Asian. They also include other prominent figures such as the Caucasian mountaineer or the Cossack. Each has been forced into service playing the non-Russian; each perhaps deserves their own chapter. These figures belong to corresponding geographies: the Caucasus mountains, which had long been the cynosure of Russian imperial conquest and one of several places where Russian writers first located the 'noble savage';[4] Central Asia, another major space of imperial conquest, from which nomads – conjured as fearsome and 'frightful hordes' (in particular the so-called Golden Horde that dominated Rus in the thirteenth and fourteenth centuries) – had emanated to subjugate Rus and at moments of cultural distress loom up as mythological spectres threatening to do so again;[5] and Siberia, another space bespeaking vastness, radical alienation, and exilic punishment.[6]

To understand how Russian writers encountered (and conjured) non-Russians while testing the very boundary and identity of Russia itself, we can track these representations from the Russian Romantic period, when many commonplaces associated with these figures were enshrined. Later writers belonging to other movements – from Realism to Modernism and Socialist Realism – grappled with the legacies of these images, often polemically, when crafting visions of the non-Russian. The focus of this chapter falls between 1890 and 1930, when this process of definition of self and other through the non-Russian protagonist reveals particular intensity. As a whole, however, the chapter shows a steady increase of non-Russian figures taking central roles in literary works and also sees individual characters moving from the ethnic peripheries into the centre of their respective artistic works. All the more striking is the increasing prominence of ethnically non-Russian writers who use the Russian language to claim their own narratives. Throughout the long history of their representation, the lives of non-Russians were made to serve as arenas in which different visions of culture and history, and an array of historical and political forces, were set into competition.

---

4 Susan Layton, *Russian Literature and Empire: Conquest of the Caucasus from Pushkin to Tolstoy* (Cambridge: Cambridge University Press, 1994); Harsha Ram, *The Imperial Sublime: A Russian Poetics of Empire* (Madison: University of Wisconsin Press, 2003).
5 See Willard Sunderland, *Taming the Wild Field: Colonization and Empire on the Russian Steppe* (Ithaca: Cornell University Press, 2004).
6 See Yuri Slezkine, *Arctic Mirrors: Russia and the Small Peoples of the North* (Ithaca: Cornell University Press, 1994).

Romantic Commonplaces

Literary historians frequently point towards Russia's Romantic period as establishing the essential and enduring parameters for the positive evaluation of non-Russian characters. Licensed by such thinkers as Jean-Jacques Rousseau and his influential critique of civilisation, Russian writers (like their European counterparts) began identifying local versions of the 'noble savage', who seemingly lived in harmony with nature, ignoring or disdaining the trappings of civilisation. These characters embodied the freedom and vitality of spirit which Russian writers, feeling themselves to be bereft of these values, admired even as they considered them in relation to imperial conquest.

While the genealogy and geography of non-Russians created in Romantic writing could be found throughout the empire, the Caucasus mountains were a charged locus. The south of the empire is usually considered the equivalent of what the east and Near East meant for European orientalism.[7] Works such as Aleksandr Pushkin's (1799–1837) 'The Prisoner of the Caucasus' (*Kavkazskii plennik*, 1822) and Mikhail Lermontov's (1814–1841) *A Hero of Our Time* (*Geroi nashego vremeni*, 1840) were essential in consolidating the myth of the Caucasus as a space of Romantic freedom and thus registering ambivalence towards Russia's imperial ambitions of subjugating the mountaineers. Lermontov's 'Bela' (*Bela*), the story which opens *A Hero of Our Time*, features one of the few female non-Russian protagonists, who is captured by the titular 'hero' of the novel as a whole, Pechorin; a romantic plot ensues between the two, with Bela's eventual death frequently seen as an allegory of imperial conquest. (Vladimir Nabokov (1899–1977) thought Bela indicated Lermontov's 'ineptitude' in crafting women characters and deemed her 'an Oriental beauty on the lid of a box of Turkish delight'.[8]) A similar framework shaped the lesser-known Aleksandr Bestuzhev-Marlinskii's (1797–1837) *Ammalat-Bek* (*Ammalat-Bek*, 1832), the eponymous hero of which is a Tartar Bey fighting against the Russians in the Caucasian Wars (1817–64). Ammalat-Bek served as a paradigmatic character for later writers who polemicised with the qualities-cum-clichés that Bestuzhev-Marlinskii would

---

7 See, for example, Layton, 'Nineteenth-century Russian mythologies of Caucasian savagery', in Daniel R. Brower and Edward J. Lazzerini (eds.), *Russia's Orient: Imperial Borderlands and Peoples, 1700–1917* (Bloomington: Indiana University Press, 1997), pp. 80–99; Monika Greenleaf, *Pushkin and Romantic Fashion: Fragment, Elegy, Orient, Irony* (Stanford: Stanford University Press, 1994); Ram, *Imperial Sublime*.

8 Vladimir Nabokov, translator's foreword to *Mikhail Lermontov, A Hero of Our Time*, trans. Vladimir Nabokov and Dmitry Nabokov (Woodstock, New York: Ardis, 2002), p. xviii.

enshrine in his descriptions, with their sultry, ornate orientalism. Notably, in all these texts, the Caucasian highlanders were not represented as Others, who were deemed illegible and unknowable,[9] but rather as figures whose motives and psyches were given some expression in the work. In this way, these works enabled imperial conquest not to be considered axiomatically good, even if most of them ultimately served to legitimise conquest.

While Pushkin both consolidated and created many of these paradigmatic figures, he himself is also an essential figure who demonstrates how the Russian/non-Russian binary was frequently on the verge of productive collapse. Pushkin's own genealogy, which combined Russian and African heritage, is a remarkable case in point.[10] Among the works in which the poet reflected upon his complex heritage, his unfinished *The Moor of Peter the Great (Arap Petra Velikogo*, 1837), whose central protagonist is the non-Russian Ibragim Gannibal, represents a key text in which the non-Russian is a positive type who defies facile (and hardly stable) binaries of self and other and unsettles categories of nationality and citizenship. As a French character says to Ibrahim, 'Russia is not your native land. I don't suppose you'll ever see your torrid birthplace again, but your long stay in France has made you equally alien to the climate and the way of life in semi-savage Russia.'[11] In the figure of Ibrahim, the non-Russian ends up embodying Russian civilisation and values, while the westernised Russian – as represented by other characters – ceases to be Russian.

The Moor typifies a pronounced tendency of Russian literary texts to assume the ability to articulate the perspectives of the non-Russian on Russia and thus provide an external view on Russian identity itself. In imagining not only European perspectives on Russia but also the views of those subject to the empire, Russian writers situate themselves within various polarities and related vantage points – those, for example, of the colonised and coloniser, or the benighted and the cultivated. For many Russian writers, the non-Russian protagonist functions as a vehicle enabling them to speak from both positions simultaneously. For this reason, attending to non-Russian protagonists allows

---

9 See Katya Hokanson, *Writing at Russia's Border* (Toronto: University of Toronto Press, 2008), esp. chapter 4.

10 For more, see the remarkable volume Catharine Theimer Nepomnyashchy, Nicole Svobodny, and Ludmilla A. Trigos (eds.), *Under the Sky of My Africa: Alexander Pushkin and Blackness* (Evanston, IL: Northwestern University Press, 2005).

11 Alexander Pushkin, *The Moor of Peter the Great*, in *Novels, Tales, Journeys: The Complete Prose of Alexander Pushkin*, trans. Richard Pevear and Larissa Volokhonsky (New York: Alfred A. Knopf, 2016), p. 8.

us to think through the aesthetics and politics of imperialism as they have been codified and challenged by Russian writers.

The Non-Russian, Realism, and Ethnography

In the second half of the nineteenth century, as the Realist mode became established as the literary mainstream (see Chapter 1.5), the shape of the non-Russian protagonist shifted. In this period, the encounter with the non-Russian was increasingly figured as part of a trope of exploration and a putative commitment to ethnographic accuracy. The trope of exploration operated in service of two related tasks: acquiring knowledge about territory and attempting to define both the self and the nation. As Susan Layton has observed (extending the work of Hans Rogger), this practice acquired heightened value in Russian culture since there was 'genuine perplexity about just what constituted distinctively Russian national character, [which] meant that two unknowns were operating at once, those of the Russian and of the myriad non-Russians in the mutual encounter with each other'.[12] Layton has elevated this kind of encounter to a 'practice of searching for the national self via encounters with some "other," non-Westernized sphere'.[13]

In the mid- to late nineteenth century, then, the writer emerged as a kind of ethnographer of others and of the self. For a writer taking up the task of narrating the life of a non-Russian, ethnography emerged as a mode to overcome the representational commonplaces the Romantics had enshrined. Lev Tolstoi (1828–1910), for example, in The Cossacks (Kazaki, 1863), extensively describes Cossack customs alongside the desire of the work's main character, the Russian nobleman Dmitrii Olenin, to join the Cossacks. Olenin's goal ultimately fails (thus reaffirming the boundary between Russian and non-Russian), but not before he has affirmed that his experience has rid him of 'all his trite and vulgar dreams of the Caucasus'. The narrator continues this repudiation of Romanticism: 'Here he had found nothing that resembled his dreams, or the descriptions of the Caucasus he had heard and read. "Here there are no burkas, Amalat-Beks, heroes or villains"'.[14] What's

---

12 Layton, 'Nineteenth-century Russian mythologies', pp. 80–1. Layton cites Hans Rogger, National Consciousness in Eighteenth-Century Russia (Cambridge, MA: Harvard University Press, 1980), p. 6.
13 Layton, 'Nineteenth-century Russian mythologies', p. 81.
14 Leo Tolstoy, The Cossacks and Other Stories, trans. David McDuff (New York: Penguin, 2006), p. 122.

notable here is the interweaving of different literary-historical moments, as though the text were reaching not just beyond the kind of Romantic heroes we saw earlier but beyond previously envisioned literary plots.

By devoting narratorial attention to the Cossack's sense of work, gender relations, and property, Tolstoi's ethnographically inflected work indicates its heightened commitment to realist representation:

> A Cossack, who considers it improper to speak affectionately or idly to his wife in front of strangers, involuntarily feels her superiority when he is alone with her, face to face. The whole of his house, the whole of his property, the whole of his economy has been acquired by her and is solely sustained by her efforts and care. Although he is firmly convinced that physical labour is shameful for a Cossack and is only proper for a Nogay labourer or a woman, he vaguely senses that everything he possesses and calls his own is the product of that labour.[15]

Such a passage demonstrates how the narrator's ethnographic eye in this text destabilises a variety of cultural hierarchies. Tolstoi writes from the perspective of the non-Russian not only to critique Russian life and values but also to challenge those of other non-Russians. Consider another passage: 'this small, Christian people, isolated in a corner of the earth, surrounded by semi-savage Mohameddan tribes and by soldiers, considers itself to be at a high stage of development and acknowledges only the Cossack as a human being'.[16] Through such characterisations, Tolstoi can establish various civilisational comparisons, typifying an ethnographic mode in which non-Russians can claim superiority over Russians and cultural hierarches can be subverted. These civilisational comparisons not only reveal how the categories of self and other, Russian and non-Russian, are central to claims of cultural superiority but also demonstrate how relative they are.

Tolstoi developed this approach further with *Hadji Murat* (*Khadzhi-Murat*, 1904), one of the most emblematic Russian literary texts featuring a non-Russian protagonist. The work's eponymous protagonist is an ethnic Avar rebel, whose perspective and motivations throughout the work – focusing on Russia's imperial campaigns in the Caucasus in the 1850s – are conveyed alongside various perspectives and narrative lines, which include other Caucasian resistors (most prominently Imam Shamil, who battled against Nicholas I (r. 1825–55)). In this way, the narrative allows one to see the non-Russian as possessing not only his or her own essential values but also distinctive and equally legitimate (or equally illegitimate and hubristic)

---

15 Tolstoy, *Cossacks*, p. 19.   16 Tolstoy, *Cossacks*, pp. 18–19.

perspectives on the world. While the work does look back to certain Romantic tropes of Caucasian mountaineers from Pushkin to Lermontov, it is also a study in how to think about the noble savage beyond the binary of Russian vs. non-Russian. It confers some agency (and hubristic blindness) onto Hadji Murat, while also seeing him as subject to a range of forces (not just Russian) which he tries to assert control over or adroitly manoeuvre to his own advantage. He fails. The text reminds us to appreciate the perspective of the other as that other tries to assert its own sense of the world.

One finds a similar literary-ethnographic unsettling of literary representation and the destabilising of civilisational comparisons in Anton Chekhov's (1860–1904) *Sakhalin Island* (*Ostrov Sakhalin*, 1895), which provides an account of the author's trip to a penal colony in the newly annexed territory of Sakhalin in 1890. As Cathy Popkin has noted, this work aims to 'establish a sense of tremendous distance and *difference* from the center of Russian culture'.[17] On the one hand, it seeks to classify the world along lines of ethnic difference; on the other, it offers an elaborate account of the interaction of Russian with non-Russian and of the alienation of one from the other. Chekhov's narrator, for example, focuses on such groups as the Giliaks and various 'minority peoples' (*malye narody*) of the north. He remarks:

> From the cured salmon fillets, which they eat as chasers to their vodka, to their conversations, one feels in all this something peculiar, non-Russian. While I sailed along the Amur, I had the feeling that I was not in Russia but somewhere else, Patagonia or Texas; not to speak of the original, non-Russian nature, it seemed to me the entire time that the way of Russian life was utterly foreign to native Amurs, that Pushkin and Gogol are incomprehensible here and thus unnecessary, that our history is boring, and that we, who have arrived from Russia, seem like foreigners.[18]

Sakhalin has been annexed by the Russian Empire, and yet geopolitical space does not map onto acculturated, Russified space, and so the encounter there is one of cultural estrangement. Sakhalin is also a space where one encounters the collapse of boundaries. As such, it is an intense microcosm of empire even as it confounds and confoundingly domesticates it: 'Catholics, Lutherans, and even Tatars and Jews, not infrequently live with Russians. In one cabin in Alexandrovsk I encountered a Russian woman in a large company of Kirgiz

17 Cathy Popkin, 'Chekhov as ethnographer: Epistemological crisis on Sakhalin Island', *Slavic Review* 51.1 (1992), 37.
18 Anton Chekhov, *Sakhalin Island*, trans. Brian Reeve (London: Oneworld Classics, 2007), p. 42.

and Caucasian men whom she was serving at table, and I recorded her as being the cohabitant of a Tatar, or as she called him, a Chechen.'[19] For a writer who sought to affirm distinctions and difference, miscegenation caused a kind of panic (and certainly descriptive allure) in Chekhov; races, here, intermingle all too closely and, moreover, proliferate in their hybridity. The boundary between the Russian and non-Russian collapses in the penal colony, which is a specific site in Russia's real and symbolic geography: it is a space where the imprisoned are sent to maintain one kind of political order only to have the order of ethnic distinction collapse as the prisoners interact with each other and with native peoples in the regions.

If writers adopted ethnographic tasks, explorers and ethnographers also produced representations of non-Russians that enjoyed broad appeal. We see this interest several decades later with the explorer-writer Vladimir Arsenev (1872–1930), for example, who published his account of expeditions to Siberia, undertaken between 1902 and 1907, as *Dersu Uzala* (*Dersu Uzala*, 1923). The titular character is a Siberian trapper who serves as a guide to Arsenev, who is himself bound up with the imperial project since he is both an ethnographer in service of the empire and part of a military exploratory group travelling throughout the Russian Far East. Arsenev undertakes extensive descriptions of Siberian natives, with a particular focus on the eponymous Dersu, whose vast understanding of the region, and thus of nature, contrasts with that of Arsenev himself. Notably, Dersu is no simpleton or primitive without a past or future. His eventual death – which is initiated by his contact with Arsenev – serves as a critique of the imperial project and a lament for the forms of life that civilisation and modernisation threaten.

Modernism and the Transvaluation of the Non-Russian

The various forces of modernisation, political upheaval, and revolutionary possibility combined to give heightened charge to the start of the twentieth century. Against a backdrop that seemed by turns revolutionary and apocalyptic, writers placed the binary of the Russian and non-Russian on the verge of aesthetically productive collapse. It was a distinctive feature of Russian Modernist texts (see Chapter 1.7) that they put on display the drama and polemical force of these battles around cultural identity. Their visions of

---

19 Chekhov, *Sakhalin*, p. 231.

collapsing binaries emerged alongside the fevered anxieties generated by the political events of the anti-colonial Boxer Rebellion (1899–1901) and the Russo-Japanese War (1904–5), which Modernist mythologisers saw as a kind of eternal return of the Asiatic hordes, threatening to launch Russia into upheaval once again.[20]

This was particularly the case when the non-Russian was figured as Asian, in particular Mongol-Tatar. Russian Modernist literature saw numerous writers grappling with the legacy of the subordination of Rus to the Mongol Empire as a matter of style, form, and cultural identity. It was a vogue for Modernist writers to announce their Tatar heritage. Nabokov, for example, writes: 'Genghis Khan, who is said to have fathered the first Nabok, a petty Tartar prince in the twelfth century who married a Russian damsel in an era of intensely artistic Russian culture'.[21] The protagonists of Andrei Belyi's (1880–1934) *Petersburg* (*Peterburg*, 1913–14, 1922) – a key text of Russian and European Modernism – are Apollon Apollonovich Ableukhov and Nikolai Appolonovich Ableukhov, whose family name harks back to the history of Rus-Tatar intermarriage. Heritage – and, in particular, mixed heritage – becomes a central theme of the work. Belyi introduces his character with a kind of fanciful patrimony:

> Apollon Apollonovich Ableukhov was of venerable stock: he had Adam as his ancestor. But that is not the main thing: it is more important that one member of this venerable stock was Shem, progenitor of the Semitic, Hessitic, and red-skinned peoples.
>
> Here let us make a transition to ancestors of an age not so remote. . . . in the reign of the Empress Anna Ioannovna, Mirza Ab-Lai, the great-great-grandfather of the senator, valiantly entered the Russian service, having received, upon Christian baptism, the name Andrei and the sobriquet Ukhov. For brevity's sake, Ab-Lai-Ukhov was later changed to Ableukhov, plain and simple.
>
> This was the great-great-grandfather who was the source of the stock.[22]

20 Michael Kunichika, *'Our Native Antiquity': Archaeology and Aesthetics in the Culture of Russian Modernism* (Boston: Academic Studies Press, 2015); Susanna Soojung Lim, *China and Japan in the Russian Imagination, 1685–1922: To the Ends of the Orient* (London: Routledge, 2013); Ram, *Imperial Sublime*.

21 V. Nabokov, *Strong Opinions* (New York: McGraw-Hill, 1973), p. 119, quoted in Andrey Bely, *Petersburg*, trans. Robert A. Maguire and John E. Malmstad (Bloomington: Indiana University Press, 1978), p. 299. For more on the 'fashionable' invocation of Mongol heritage among the Russian nobility, see Maguire and Malmstad's full note on the Kyrgyz-Kaisak horde, pp. 298–9.

22 Bely, *Petersburg*, p. 3.

This sense of mixed blood is not just playful, however; it slips in a sense of danger. The Asian element, which can be traced back to the senator's Mongol heritage as a descendant of Ab-Lai, always threatens to erupt:

> Nikolai Apollonovich remembered: he was an old Turanian who had been incarnated in the blood, in the flesh of the hereditary nobility, in order to carry out a secret mission: to shake everything to its very foundation. The Ancient Dragon was to feed on tainted blood, and to consume everything in flame. The ancient Orient had rained a hail of bombs on our age. And Nikolai Apollonovich was ... exploding, and on his face appeared a Mongol expression.[23]

In Nikolai's case, the combination of blood heredity and mythological transmigration transforms him into a force that is apocalyptic, revolutionary, and anarchic. One of the central themes of these lines – and of the novel as a whole – is the instability of the opposition between Russian and non-Russian and its constant re-emergence as an accursed dilemma of Russian culture. This emphasis on Russia's hybrid historical and cultural identity was typical of the reimagining of Russia's past in the first decades of the twentieth century. The Modernist turn to the past was hardly sui generis; it drew not only upon previous literary traditions but also on decades of art-historical, archaeological, and philological research demonstrating the vast interrelations of Russia with other cultures. The classification 'non-Russian' was a matter of degrees and far from stable, as 'Russian' came to encompass – in various hands – more and more inheritances and bloodlines.

Among the most crucial artistic statements in this vein was Aleksandr Blok's (1880–1921) proclamation in his poem 'The Scythians' (*Skify*, 1918): 'Yes, we are Scythians! Yes, we are Asians / With slanted and avaricious eyes!'[24] The poem, written on the heels of the 1917 revolution, marks an essential shift in how writers embraced the non-Russian, transforming a whole range of previous works (such as Belyi's *Petersburg*) where Russian poets and writers had expressed ambivalence towards the potential re-emergence of an Asiatic threat. In reaching back towards the Scythians as the poet's quintessential ancestor, Blok announces a historical mission – Russia is an Asiatic country that is destined to free the 'old world'. Blok's turn towards lyrical barbarism

---

23 Bely, *Petersburg*, p. 166.
24 Aleksandr Blok, *Dvenadtsat'*; *Skify* (St Petersburg: Tipografiia Nikolaevskoi voennoi akademii, 1918), p. 43, cited in Ram, *Imperial Sublime*, p. 231. For another analysis of Blok's 'The Scythians', see Carol Avins, 'The barbarian lyre: Challenging the West', in *Border Crossings: The West and Russian Identity in Soviet Literature; 1917–1934* (Berkeley: University of California Press, 1983), pp. 28–34.

typifies a whole generation of Russian Modernists, in particular those of Futurist tendencies, who valorised returning to a brute state in order to simultaneously escape the trappings of civilisation and advance the cause of socialist revolution.

Ethnicities and the Revolution

After 1917, the non-Russian protagonist came to the fore as a central player in the revolutionary drama unfolding on page, stage, and screen. As we saw above, such voices were certainly present before the revolution, but the post-revolutionary period was distinct in that, while looking back to the literary past in fashioning – often polemically – their central protagonists, writers also positioned a broader range of figures from ethnic nationalities as central to advancing a fresh, essential, and often ideological plot of liberation as the bearers of revolutionary consciousness.[25]

The revolution and ensuing civil war served as a frequent backdrop for the emergence of non-Russian protagonists. In the work of writers such as Khlebnikov, with whom we started this chapter, non-Russian revolutionary figures such as Kaveh the Blacksmith – central to the Persian epic *Shahnameh* (c. 900 CE) – re-emerged as celebrated mythological paradigms for revolutionary movements. Ivan Novokshonov's (1896–1943) *Heir of Genghis Kahn* (*Potomok Chingiskhana*), which the author worked on throughout the 1920s, served as the basis for Vsevolod Pudovkin's (1893–1953) celebrated 1928 film, tells the story of the Buriat-Mongol character Dorzhi, who rejects his training to become a lama, joins the partisans, and falls into the hands of the white army, who want him to become a puppet ruler of Mongolia on the premise that he is the great Khan's heir. Ultimately Dorzhi asserts his own independence from the roles others would have him play in order to take up the revolutionary cause and lead his people against their imperialist oppressors. Such roles might suggest that these non-Russians were not so much agents but rather decorative ethnic masks for a revolutionary ideology that had trouble grappling with ethnic or national particularity and tradition. Still, these figures demand attention because they disclose how writers navigated tensions that emerged when non-Russian ethnicities were made to embody historical roles straddling revolution and ethnic nationality and tradition, religion and secular modernisation, ethnic culture and economic class.

---

25 Yuri Slezkine, 'The USSR as communal apartment, or how a socialist state promoted ethnic particularism', *Slavic Review* 53.2 (1994), 414–52.

It is also important to note the complexity of the politics of representation in the post-revolutionary years. There was a call for Soviet society – and culture – to distinguish itself from 'western' imperialism and its associated cultural forms such as exoticism. This gave significant attention to the ideological implications of representing non-Russians. The very question of how to represent the other became central to the critical inquiry of a range of writers and critics in the 1920s.

Among the most stylistically and philosophically interesting works attempting to craft an alternative vision of the non-Russian protagonist is Andrei Platonov's (1899–1951) *Soul* (*Dzhan*, 1930). Set within the desolate wastes of Central Asia, the work is an outstanding demonstration of how Modernist form seems so frequently to have cut its teeth on ethnography, on encounters with otherness that add pressure to how to represent difference. *Soul* introduces its main protagonist from the outset in the following way: 'Into the courtyard of the Moscow Economic Institute entered the non-Russian person Nazar Chagataev.'[26] Chagataev, in fact, recapitulates the hybrid figures we have seen earlier: his father is 'Ivan Chagataev, a Russian soldier in the Khiva expeditionary force' and his mother, Gyulchatay, is Turkmen.[27] His hybridity gives him particular cachet with his mother's people, to whom he will eventually bring socialism:

> [Nazar] could not leave the nation on its own to die, because he himself, after being abandoned by his mother in the desert, had been taken care of by a shepherd and by Soviet power – and an unknown man, Stalin, had fed him and preserved him for life and development.[28]

The novel's plot, however, makes a notable shift when the character Aidym, a young girl, comes to the fore to help Chagataev advance the Dzhan nation's progress towards socialism.

Soviet texts centring on positive non-Russian characters typically made them navigate ethnicity and revolutionary ideology, and such plots are found within texts of a broad range of literary styles and forms. A major work in this regard is Isaak Babel's (1894–1940) *Red Cavalry* (*Konarmiia*, 1923–6), which provides a remarkable consideration of a non-Russian narrator, the Jewish figure Liutov, who is part of a company of Cossacks. As Carol Avins has observed, Babel's Liutov adopts various personae throughout the work, as both a secular Jew and a committed revolutionary, witnessing figures belonging to traditional

---

26 Andreii Platonovich Platonov, *Soul and Other Stories*, trans. Robert Chandler and Elizabeth Chandler (New York: New York Review Books, 2008), p. 131.
27 Platonov, *Soul*, p. 14. 28 Platonov, *Soul*, p. 67.

Jewish life being subjected to the staggering violence of the Cossacks.[29] The work starkly renders the contradictions of modern identity as readers become privy to the arduous and conflicted processes through which Liutov negotiates the traditions that constitute his identity and the forces of revolutionary violence that would annul them. In that capacity, he opens a question that was to face many ethnicities during the post-revolutionary period: what will become of their own traditions and ethnic identities after the revolution and in their commitment to it? How can one participate in the revolution and thus in modernity without abandoning tradition?

This predicament also informed Mikhail Sholokhov's (1905–1984) novel *The Quiet Don* (*Tikhii Don*, 1928–40), which presents a striking parallel with Babel's work since it takes the Don Cossacks as its central protagonists.[30] Among the most controversial and then celebrated works of the time, the novel is remarkable in focusing its entire perspective on a non-Russian group and showing an increasing awareness of the permeability of the category of 'non-Russian' through the complex identity of the Cossack. The plot follows the peregrination of a central character, the Don Cossack Grigorii Melekhov, who presents various ambiguities, which critics of the time thought made him a 'tragic hero'.[31] The novel reflects the consolidation of Socialist Realism as the primary mode of Soviet cultural production (see Chapter 1.8), albeit in a peculiar way, since despite the overriding realism of its structure and plot, the work nevertheless presents an ambiguous picture of allegiances to the revolution and Soviet government. Early in the work – which has been considered an epic novel, drawing frequent comparisons to Tolstoi's *War and Peace* (*Voina i mir*, 1868–9) as well as to the range of representations of Cossacks we've touched on above – Sholokhov has a group of Cossacks sitting and reading a work entitled *A Short History of the Don Cossacks*:

> they laboured through the book for three evenings, reading about the free life of the past, about Pugachev, Stenka Razin and Vasily Bulovin. Finally they came down to recent times. The unknown author poured scorn on the Cossacks' miserable existence, he jeered intelligently and powerfully at the authorities and the system, the Czar's government, and the Cossackry itself, which has hired itself out to the monarchs as their bodyguard.[32]

29 Carol J. Avins, 'Kinship and concealment in *Red Cavalry* and Babel's *1920s Diary*', *Slavic Review* 53.3 (1994), 694–710.
30 Mikhail Sholokhov, *And Quiet Flows the Don* (New York: Vintage Books, 1989).
31 For an overview of the critical response to Sholokhov's novel, see Richard Hallett, 'Criticism of "Tikhii Don" 1928–1940', *Slavonic and East European Review* 46.106 (1968), 60–74.
32 Sholokhov, *And Quiet Flows the Don*, p. 115.

Sholokhov shows how the Cossacks occupy an ambiguous status in Russian culture between the non-Russian and the Russian. Some are ethnically Russian, and they have, over time, espoused different religions. Most notably, over a long history of representation, Cossacks have navigated various relationships to the state. As a character says later in the text, expressing the Cossack nationalism for which Sholokhov's novel became known (and occasionally criticised):

> We shall restore the order destroyed by the Russian Czars and turn out all the foreigners. . . . The land is ours. It was awash with our fathers' blood and fertilized with their bones; but for four hundred years we have been in subjection to Russia, defending her interests and not thinking of ourselves. We have a way out to the sea. We shall have a strong fighting army, and neither the Ukraine nor even Russia will dare violate our independence. Life will be like a fairy-tale then![33]

Another vision of the non-Russian emerges here: that of nationalist movements that might be ethnically Russian yet nevertheless seek political separation and autonomy. The novel does not ultimately permit this vision to succeed – the Cossacks are crushed and Melekhov, broken from war and fate, cannot reconcile the multiple historical visions and contradictions he is made to navigate.

One way to think about these various works is to see them in relation to the image of the 'noble savage' or the simple folk with which we began this chapter. In the post-revolutionary period, these non-Russian figures were no longer able to serve as cultural alternatives, insofar as a return to nature became increasingly unavailable as an alternative in the post-revolutionary Soviet utopia. Instead, non-Russian literary protagonists in the early to mid-Soviet period reveal lives thrust into the course of history, changed by encroaching modernisation. In these new conditions, they must navigate questions of freedom and allegiance, and, if possible, they must reconcile their specific mode of life to the new time in which they find themselves.

Centring the Ethnic Other

In the late Soviet period, such non-Russian figures and their fates were increasingly able to occupy a central space in literary works and to be situated in relation to broader historical trajectories and forces. In this regard, the Kyrgyz writer Chingiz Aitmatov (1928–2008), who produced his major works

33 Sholokhov, *And Quiet Flows the Don*, p. 408.

in Russian, provides us with an instructive account. Writing in 1980, in the preface to his novel *The Day Lasts More than a Hundred Years* (*I dol'she veka dlitsia den'*, 1980), Aitmatov remarks:

> The main object of socialist realism, in my view, is to present the image of the working man. However, I am far from confining the meaning of 'hard worker' to one sort – the 'simple, natural person' who assiduously tills the land and tends the cattle. In the clash between the eternal and the present in life, a hard worker is interesting and important in so much as he is an individual in the dimension of his soul and in so far as he reflects the time in which he lives. So I have tried to put Burannyi Edigei in the centre of things – that is, in the centre of the problems that concern me.[34]

Aitmatov's focus is on the specific period in which he is writing, and the novel itself is written under the conditions of late Socialist Realism. Yet in this passage he gives us a unique statement on what it means for a literary work to promote a non-Russian protagonist to a central place. This centring recognises how non-Russian peoples have mediated, and occasionally even mastered, the various forces – historical, political, geopolitical – that transect their lives; or else it invites the reader to lament the protagonist's subjection to those forces and the losses this necessitates. This is no longer simply the technique of self-definition by negation with which we began this chapter, and which structured representations of the non-Russian protagonist over a long duration. Instead in Aitmatov's work, and in literary works emerging in the decades since, we find other forms of representation: non-Russian writers writing in Russian and fashioning new forms for the non-Russian protagonist.

In the late Soviet period and after the collapse of the Soviet Union in 1991, a remarkable range of non-Russian writers came to prominence. Their works testify to a remapping of literature in Russian that took shape in the final decades of the Soviet Union and in the post-Soviet period. In the work of writers from throughout the republics, we find a dynamic thinking about the nature of non-Russian identity. A notable late Soviet example is the Kazakh writer Olzhas Suleimenov (1936–), whose *AZ i IA: The Book of a Well-Intentioned Reader* (*AZ i IA: Kniga blagonamerennogo chitatelia*) appeared in 1975. Its title is a play on the Russian *Aziia*, or Asia, broken into the Church Slavonic first-person pronoun, *az*, and *ia*, the Russian pronoun for 'I', indicative of the linguistic and poetic play typifying this

---

34 Chinghiz Aitmatov, *The Day Lasts More than a Hundred Years*, trans. John French (Bloomington: Indiana University Press, 1988), p. xvii.

hybrid work of linguistic and philological exploration devoted to the study of the medieval text *The Tale of Igor's Campaign* (*Slovo o polku Igorove*; see Box 6.1). The book provoked broad debate due to its highlighting of the Turkic elements of the *Tale* and its consideration of Russian and Turkic identities and interrelations.[35] After the collapse of the Soviet Union in 1991, the urgency of this articulation of a non-Russian identity (and its complexity, given the interrelations of ethnicities and shifting cultural and political geographies) became still more clear. Iurii Buida (1954–), for example, considers the fractures of geography, history, and identity of the post-Soviet period in *The Prussian Bride* (*Prusskaia nevesta*, 1998), which undertakes a complex fashioning of identity in relation to the Russian and Prussian cultural histories in the city of Kaliningrad/Königsberg.

It is notable, however, that for all the particularities of recent literary developments, representations of the non-Russian in the post-Soviet period continue to emerge from histories of violence and upheaval, political and historical. What many of these post-Soviet works feature, like their literary predecessors, are meditations on the experiences and lives of non-Russian peoples that find themselves subject to the Russian state's geopolitical ambitions. Perhaps one way to think through the figure of the non-Russian that we see highlighted in the past three decades is to consider the return of the Caucasian plot, initiated by Romanticism. Again and again in this region, we see the entanglement between Russia's imperial ambition and post-Soviet geopolitics. Vladimir Makanin's (1937–2017) short story 'A Prisoner of the Caucasus' (*Kavkazskii plennik*, 1995), for example, takes up a literary plot initiated by Lermontov, Pushkin, and Tolstoi to think through the First Chechen War (1994–6). Another work, *I Am a Chechen!* (*Ia – chechenets!*, 2006) by German Sadulaev (1973–), testifies to the intricate nature of post-Soviet ethnic identity as it is formulated in the post-Soviet period: 'At the time we were taught that we belonged to one great nation called the Soviet People. And we believed it. . . . But now we're taught that we are Chechens. And this vast country has suddenly become foreign.'[36] This extraordinary text presents a portrait of fractured and reconstituted identities as they confront histories of violence in the very places where Russian identity and Russia's borders have been so frequently contested. Sadulaev presents a uniquely Chechen perspective on these histories, but

---

35 See Harsha Ram, 'Imagining Eurasia: The poetics and ideology of Olzhas Suleimenov's *AZ i IA*', *Slavic Review* 60.2 (2001), 289–311.
36 German Sadulaev, *I Am a Chechen!*, trans. Anna Gunin (London: Harvill Press, 2011), p. 31.

non-Russian characters have been a key presence in Russian letters for the past two centuries. Their fates testify to the irreconcilable differences and forces – of ethnic self, nationality, and history – to which they are subject.

Further Reading

Brower, Daniel R., and Edward J. Lazzerini (eds.), *Russia's Orient: Imperial Borderlands and Peoples, 1700–1917* (Bloomington: Indiana University Press, 1997).

Dudley, Edward J., and Maximillian E. Novak (eds.), *The Wild Man Within: An Image in Western Thought from the Renaissance to Romanticism* (Pittsburgh: University of Pittsburgh Press, 1973).

Hokanson, Katya, *Writing at Russia's Border* (Toronto: University of Toronto Press, 2008).

Layton, Susan, *Russian Literature and Empire: Conquest of the Caucasus from Pushkin to Tolstoy* (Cambridge: Cambridge University Press, 1994).

Mathewson, Rufus W., *The Positive Hero in Russian Literature* (Evanston, IL: Northwestern University Press, 1999).

Ram, Harsha, *The Imperial Sublime: A Russian Poetics of Empire* (Madison: University of Wisconsin Press, 2003).

Sunderland, Willard, *Taming the Wild Field: Colonization and Empire on the Russian Steppe* (Ithaca: Cornell University Press, 2004).

4.9

The Madman

REBECCA REICH

On 8 August 2012, the political activist and performance artist Mariia Alekhina (1988–) delivered a closing statement at her trial for 'hooliganism motivated by religious hatred'. Earlier that year, she and other members of the band Pussy Riot had mounted the altar of Moscow's Cathedral of Christ the Saviour and staged a 'punk prayer' protesting against Vladimir Putin's policies. Court-appointed psychiatrists had declared her responsible for her actions, but they had also diagnosed her with 'an emotionally unstable personality disorder', marked by what they described as a 'lack of regard for generally accepted norms and rules'.[1] In her statement, Alekhina quoted the words of a Soviet-era icon of protest. 'The authorities don't take into account the historical experience of the phenomenon of dissent', she said. 'As the dissident Bukovskii wrote in the 1970s, "How unfortunate is that country where simple honesty is perceived as heroism in the best of cases, and as a psychological disorder in the worst."'[2] Not only was Alekhina likening her pathologisation to the Soviet-era practice of confining dissidents to psychiatric hospitals, she was also echoing the dissidents' own tactic of using the literary tradition to recast their 'madness' as sanity. 'Let these fools consider us psychos – or rather the other way around, let these psychos consider us fools', Vladimir Bukovskii (1942–2019) himself had written in 1978. 'We recalled all those books about madmen: Chekhov, Gogol, Akutagawa, and of course *The Good Soldier Švejk*. We laughed our heads off at the doctors and

---

1 'Tekst prigovora uchastnitsam gruppy Pussy Riot' [Text of the verdict on the members of the Pussy Riot group], *Bol'shoi gorod* [Big city] (21 Aug. 2012), www.bg.ru/stories/11662/, accessed 23 Aug. 2012.

2 Elena Kostiuchenko, '"Tak nazyvaemyi protsess" – poslednee slovo Nadezhdy Tolokonnikovoi, Marii Alekhinoi i Ekateriny Samutsevich' ['A so-called trial' – the closing statements of Nadezhda Tolokonnikova, Mariia Alekhina and Ekaterina Samutsevich], *Novaia gazeta* [New newspaper] (9 Aug. 2012), https://novayagazeta.ru/articles/2012/08/09/50935-171-tak-nazyvaemyy-protsess-187/, accessed 14 Jan. 2023.

ourselves.'[3] Rather than reject the label of 'madman', dissidents such as Bukovskii and, later, Alekhina have sought to redefine it. Literary texts have provided them with a discourse of madness to counter the diagnostic authority of the state.

Among its many vibrant traditions, Russian literature boasts a genealogy of madman-heroes whose deviant behaviour reveals as much about changes in Russian society as it does about the characters themselves. The figure of the madman has been invoked in a variety of social, cultural, and political contexts from the medieval period to the present day. This chapter investigates the origins of the tradition before focusing in more detail on the period between Joseph Stalin's death in 1953 and the Soviet Union's collapse in 1991, when state-sponsored punitive psychiatry heightened the currency of representations of madness. In particular, it identifies four strains of literary madness that experienced a marked resurgence in the post-Stalin period: the divine madman, exemplified by the holy fool who tests society's virtue and speaks truth to power; the creative madman, whose irrational behaviour stems from poetic inspiration and the generative power of the word; the rational madman, who follows a logical system to pathological extremes or inverts that paradigm by determinedly revolting against reason; and the political madman, whose sanity is often pathologised by a society that itself has lost its mind. These paradigms of madness constructed an intertextual web of allusions and character types that have been embodied and amended over time. Here they are grouped under the general heading 'heroes' even though the ambiguity of madness means that features of the madman have frequently appeared in characters who might also be described as 'anti-heroes'. Madmen-heroes have indeed varied across Russian history, yet together they have invoked and reinforced the authority of the tradition as a whole.

Paradigms of Madness

The literary figure of the madman did not emerge in a historical vacuum. During the medieval and early modern periods, mental illness was widely ascribed divine properties, but the arrival of Enlightenment ideas in the eighteenth century recast it in scientific terms. The nineteenth century saw the founding of Russia's first asylums and the professionalisation of

---

3 Vladimir Bukovskii, *I vozvrashchaetsia veter . . .: Avtobiografiia* [And the wind returns . . .: Autobiography] (Moscow: Zakharov, 2007), p. 185.

psychiatry through the establishment of journals, universities, and regionally administered care. At the turn of the twentieth century, anxieties about crime, sexuality, and mob violence seized the popular imagination. Some psychiatrists addressed these concerns through theories of social contagion and degeneration, while others offered psychoanalytic explanations of the workings of the unconscious. In the first decades of Soviet rule, psychiatrists searched for a theoretical model of the mind that would accord with Marxist-Leninist ideology. Proponents of 'mental hygiene' linked mental illness to social circumstances, which, if revolutionised, might restore society's health. Such ideas were superseded by a biological school that attributed mental disorders to failures of the nervous system itself. The ascension of the prominent psychiatrist Andrei Snezhnevskii in the late Stalin period cemented a turn within the discipline to the scientific classification of diseases and the development of physical and psychopharmacological methods of treatment. These treatment methods staked a claim to diagnostic authority that would eventually serve to support the pathologisation of dissidents after Stalin's death.[4]

It was against this historical backdrop that Russian literature produced the pantheon of madmen on which post-Stalinist writers would subsequently draw. Chief among these heroes was the divine madman, most recognisable from medieval and early modern texts as the holy fool whose apparent madness was a form of self-abasement that provoked scorn and derision, thus prompting society to respond in ways that revealed its true nature (see Chapter 4.1). The *vitae* of the fifteenth- and sixteenth-century holy fools Basil the Blessed and Ioann of Moscow thus describe their heroes wandering the streets half-naked and questioning the virtue of none less than the tsar. If early autocrats tolerated holy fools as a check on power, modern rulers sought to remove such checks by desacralising the tradition. The divinity of the figure came into question as holy fools were subjected to the secular disciplinary tools of prosecution and hospitalisation. It was left to Russia's

---

4 On the history of Russian psychiatry and psychology, see Daniel Beer, *Renovating Russia: The Human Sciences and the Fate of Liberal Modernity, 1880–1930* (Ithaca: Cornell University Press, 2008); Sidney Bloch and Peter Reddaway, *Psychiatric Terror: How Soviet Psychiatry Is Used to Suppress Dissent* (New York: Basic Books, 1977); Julie Vail Brown, 'The professionalization of Russian psychiatry: 1857–1911', unpublished PhD thesis, University of Pennsylvania (1981); Alexander Etkind, *Eros of the Impossible: The History of Psychoanalysis in Russia* (Boulder, CO: Westview Press, 1997); David Joravsky, *Russian Psychology: A Critical History* (Oxford: Blackwell, 1989); Benjamin Zajicek, 'Scientific psychiatry in Stalin's Soviet Union: The politics of modern medicine and the struggle to define "Pavlovian" psychiatry, 1939–1953', unpublished PhD thesis, University of Chicago (2009).

literary writers to resurrect the divine associations of holy foolishness. In Aleksandr Pushkin's (1799–1837) drama *Boris Godunov* (*Boris Godunov*, 1825), a holy fool confronts the tsar on Red Square, accusing him publicly of the crime that torments him privately and refusing to grant him absolution. Eight years later, in his narrative poem *The Bronze Horseman* (*Mednyi vsadnik*, 1833), Pushkin produced a secular counterpart in the civil servant Evgenii, who loses his mind as a storm floods St Petersburg. Circling the titular monument to Peter I (r. 1682–1725), the 'madman' raises his fist at the tsar before lurching through the streets, the statue in pursuit. Whereas holy foolishness had been associated with feigning in medieval texts, Pushkin combines its visionary implications with the prospect of actual insanity.[5]

The growth of psychiatric knowledge in the late nineteenth century cast further doubt on holy fools' responsibility for their actions. In Fedor Dostoevskii's (1821–1881) novel *The Idiot* (*Idiot*, 1874), Prince Myshkin's revelations are brought on by epileptic fits. Elsewhere, Dostoevskii used the trope of holy foolishness to stage a fraught debate between scientific and spiritual world views.[6] The blessedness of the holy fools Maria Lebiadkina in *Demons* (*Besy*, 1873) and Stinking Lizaveta in *The Brothers Karamazov* (*Brat'ia Karamazovy*, 1881) signals the shortcomings of reason, while the antics of Semen Iakovlevich, also in *Demons*, parody a societal fashion for adulating holy fools. Elements of the paradigm may also be seen in Lev Tolstoi's (1828–1910) story 'The Diary of a Madman' (*Zapiski sumasshedshego*, 1883), where insanity stands in for spiritual revelation, and in the work of Vasilii Rozanov (1856–1919), which combines elements of sanctity and profanity. Although these features figured less prominently in literature of the first half of the Soviet period, they would re-emerge in force after Stalin's death.

As the divine madman became a fixture of modern literature, so, too, did the creative madman. Rooted in classical notions of the insanity of inspiration, this paradigmatic hero arose in the early nineteenth century when Romantic writers began to link irrationality with creativity and the reinvention of reality through words. In Pushkin's verse 'God grant that I not lose my mind . . .' (*Ne dai mne bog soiti s uma . . .*, 1833), the poet first imagines madness as a space of freedom: 'I would sing out in fiery delirium, / I would abandon myself to a daze / Of discordant, strange reveries.' But before long, a more terrifying picture takes hold: the poet envisions himself locked in

---

5 Gary Rosenshield, *Pushkin and the Genres of Madness: The Masterpieces of 1833* (Madison: University of Wisconsin Press, 2003), pp. 116–17.

6 Harriet Murav, *Holy Foolishness: Dostoevsky's Novels and the Poetics of Cultural Critique* (Stanford: Stanford University Press, 1992).

a madhouse that echoes with 'the shouts of my comrades, / And the abuse of the night wardens, / And shrieking, and the clanking of chains.'[7] Nikolai Gogol's (1809–1852) story 'The Diary of a Madman' (*Zapiski sumasshedshego*, 1835) recasts this vision in a parodic vein, as the claustrophobia of insanity becomes a function of the alternative reality that the diarist, Poprishchin, generates through words – a deflation of the association between madness and creativity which Dostoevskii revisits in his novel *The Double* (*Dvoinik*, 1846).[8]

Vsevolod Garshin (1855–1888) offers more critical distance through the third-person narration of his story 'The Red Flower' (*Krasnyi tsvetok*, 1883). When the madman-hero happens upon his 'great thought', he reports that he can now live 'outside of space, everywhere or nowhere, however you like'.[9] Yet the sense of liberation that he reports is undercut by his death within the confines of an asylum. This kind of dichotomy between creativity and insanity remains unresolved in Anton Chekhov's (1860–1904) story 'The Black Monk' (*Chernyi monakh*, 1893), in which a scholar abandons himself to visions of a monk who convinces him of his genius. Later brought to his senses, the former madman protests: 'I was losing my mind, I had delusions of grandeur, but the result was that I was cheerful, vigorous, and even happy, I was interesting and original. Now I've become more sober and sedate, and the result is that I'm like everyone else: I'm a mediocrity, and it bores me to live . . .'[10] A more unambiguously positive vision of the link between creativity and irrationality inspired the poetry that Aleksei Kruchenykh (1886–1968) and Velimir Khlebnikov (1885–1922) produced in the 1910s: a universal language of *zaum'* that aimed to convey a meaning 'beyond sense'. Other Modernist writers, such as Andrei Belyi (1880–1934) and Aleksandr Blok (1880–1921), renewed the legacy of Romanticism through the notion of *zhiznetvorchestvo*, or 'life-creation', which described how art might be treated as reality and reality as art. In the 1920s, the displays of eccentric behaviour by the Absurdist writer Daniil Kharms (1905–1942) presaged the kind of performance art that would feature centrally in representations of madness of the late and post-Soviet periods. The Stalin period, with its artistic doctrine of Socialist Realism and its aim to reinvent reality itself, would also become

---

7 A. S. Pushkin, 'Ne dai mne bog soiti s uma . . .' [God grant that I not lose my mind . . .], in *Polnoe sobranie sochinenii* [Complete collected works], 17 vols. (Leningrad: Akademiia nauk SSSR, 1937–59), vol. III, pp. 322–3.

8 Rosenshield, *Pushkin and the Genres of Madness*, pp. 25–6, 191–2.

9 V. M. Garshin, 'Krasnyi tsvetok' [The red flower], in *Sochineniia* [Works] (Moscow: Gosudarstvennoe izdatel'stvo khudozhestvennoi literatury, 1960), p. 199.

10 A. P. Chekhov, 'Chernyi monakh' [The black monk], in *Sochineniia v chetyrekh tomakh* [Works in four volumes] (Moscow: Pravda, 1984), vol. II, p. 374.

fodder for pathologisation by subsequent writers who presented it as a collective form of creative madness.

Where the creative madman offered an imaginative antithesis to the Enlightenment cult of reason, the rational madman embodied reason spun out of control. Here it is the pull of science, and not art, that leads to insanity as the protagonist either revolts against rationality or follows their own logic to illogical extremes. The hero of Dostoevskii's novella *Notes from Underground* (*Zapiski iz podpol'ia*, 1864) would rather cast himself as a madman than subordinate himself to the cult of reason, yet his revolt against rationality is itself a product of obsessive reasoning. In *Crime and Punishment* (*Prestuplenie i nakazanie*, 1867), by contrast, Raskolnikov believes he is acting rationally when he kills a pawnbroker, based on the theory that he is an extraordinary man destined to contribute to humanity. That the act turns out to have been driven by mundane circumstance may, however, reveal him to be an ordinary man deluded by his own theory. Raskolnikov's unhinged hyperrationality is echoed in *Demons* by that of Kirillov, whose dogged assertion of free will leads him to the conclusion that he must kill himself.

Inverting the rational madman paradigm was the literary hero who revolted against reason, whether consciously or unconsciously. In Zinaida Gippius's (1869–1945) story 'The Madwoman' (*Sumasshedshaia*, 1903), the landowner Ivan Vasilevich cannot understand why his wife would reject his enlightened world view and declare herself mad. After she checks herself into a psychiatric hospital, he continues to cede authority to science: 'I'm a medical ignoramus. The doctors know best.'[11] Ivan Vasilevich's inability to recognise the limitations of reason reveals him to be the genuinely deluded character. Other turn-of-the-century works suggest that people are propelled by urges that the rational mind cannot control. After witnessing the rape of his sweetheart, the hero of Leonid Andreev's (1871–1919) story 'The Abyss' (*Bezdna*, 1902) throws himself on her prostrate body: 'Nemovetskii had been left behind somewhere, and the one here now was pawing the hot body with passionate cruelty and speaking with a madman's cunning sneer.'[12] Reason cannot tame the instincts that lurk within. Yet those same instincts offer hope of salvation from the reason-bound dystopia of Evgenii Zamiatin's (1884–1937) novel *We* (*My*, comp. 1920) as the exposure of the hero, D-503, to ancient ways of life spurs dreams that he takes

11 Z. N. Gippius, 'Sumasshedshaia' [The madwoman], in *Sochineniia* [Works] (Leningrad: Khudozhestvennaia literatura, 1991), p. 481.
12 L. N. Andreev, 'Bezdna' [The abyss], in *Sobranie sochinenii* [Collected works], 6 vols. (Moscow: Khudozhestvennaia literatura, 1990–6), vol. I, pp. 366–7.

for mental illness until he realises that 'everyone must go mad! It's imperative that everyone goes mad, and as soon as possible!'[13]

Representations of rational madness hinge on a paradox. On the one hand, they depict insanity as the point where reason collapses or goes too far. On the other hand, it is precisely by mapping out that point that they reassert the boundaries of sanity. The political madman inhabits a similarly ambiguous space between mental illness and mental health. In response to a state or society that seeks to diagnose deviations from its norms, the political madman redefines those deviations as evidence of sanity within a world gone mad. Works that feature political madmen frequently validate their capacity for *inakomyslie*, or 'thinking differently', by asserting literature's own authority to define and assign the label of madness. In Aleksandr Griboedov's (1795– 1829) verse comedy *Woe from Wit* (*Gore ot uma*, comp. 1824), the hero, Chatskii, uses the literary technique of irony to discredit his pathologisation. 'All as one, you branded me a madman', he tells his tormenters. 'You are right: only he who walks through fire could spend a single day with you and breathe the same air without losing his reason.'[14] By ironically adopting the pathological label thrust upon him, Chatskii uses it to suggest that it is in fact society that has lost its mind.

In life, as well as on the page, thinking differently precipitated pathologisation. In 1836, the philosopher Petr Chaadaev (1794–1856) wrote that Russia's development lagged behind that of the west and he was declared insane and confined to house arrest as a result. His case left an imprint on subsequent depictions of hospitalisation, most notably Chekhov's story 'Ward No. 6' (*Palata No. 6*, 1892). The physician Ragin is pathologised for visiting the patient Gromov, whom he praises as the clear-thinking exception to a deluded society. 'If only you knew, my friend, how sick I am of the general madness, worthlessness, dullness, and with what joy I talk with you each time!' Ragin says.[15] The price of diagnosing society's ills becomes clear at the story's end, when the doctor himself is confined to the psychiatric ward. Mikhail Bulgakov's (1891–1940) novel *The Master and Margarita* (*Master i Margarita*, comp. 1928–40) sets similarly high stakes in a meeting between the poet Ivan Bezdomnyi and the Master, a novelist, that takes place within a psychiatric hospital. The Master embraces his diagnosis and urges Bezdomnyi to do the same: 'Both you and I are madmen, what's the point

---

13 Evgenii Zamiatin, *My* [We], in *Sobranie sochinenii v piati tomakh* [Collected works in five volumes] (Moscow: Russkaia kniga, 2003–11), vol. II, p. 317.

14 A. S. Griboedov, *Gore ot uma* [Woe from wit] (Moscow: AST, 2016), p. 139.

15 Chekhov, 'Palata No. 6' [Ward no. 6], in *Sochineniia v chetyrekh tomakh*, vol. II, p. 313.

in denying it!' he says. 'Don't you see, [the devil] shocked you and you went off the rails, as you clearly had the constitution for it. But the story you're telling me undoubtedly took place in reality. It's just that it's so out of the ordinary that naturally even Stravinskii, a psychiatrist of genius, did not believe you.'[16] In the Stalin-era Moscow of Bulgakov's novel, literature becomes the surest means of detecting the madness that grips society.

Madness in the Post-Stalin Period

Stalin's death in 1953 prompted the resurgence of the madman-hero as Soviet society reassessed its traumatic history of mass arrest, incarceration, and execution as well as of the 'cult of personality' of Stalin himself. In his 'secret speech' at the Twentieth Party Congress in 1956, Nikita Khrushchev denounced his predecessor's crimes and affirmed the state's commitment to a new era of rationality, legality, and enlightened modernity. Yet over the ensuing decades, and particularly after Leonid Brezhnev came to power in 1964, many writers and intellectuals became convinced that reforms had failed and society had not broken with its Stalinist past. Some writers challenged the hegemony of Marxism-Leninism by embracing irrationality in their literary works. Others invoked the genealogy of madmen-heroes to allege the continued irrationality of society and the state. Reports of punitive hospitalisation circulated through *samizdat* – an unsanctioned network of hand-produced texts (see Chapter 2.9) – lending particular currency to literary works that deployed what Shoshana Felman has called the self-negating 'rhetoric of madness'. According to Felman, texts that stake a purposeful claim to insanity in fact achieve the opposite effect of asserting their authors' responsibility for their actions.[17] This rhetoric pertained especially to depictions of the political madman, yet in deploying that model, writers of the late Soviet period also incorporated aspects of that madman's divine, creative, and rational counterparts. Texts that centred on mental illness raised the possibility that the madness they depicted might become a reality – and, indeed, their heroes often revelled in such madness. Yet in deploying self-conscious devices such as irony and parody, they also asserted the hero's self-awareness and frequently reversed the diagnostic gaze. The madman-hero came to function as an

16 Mikhail Bulgakov, *Master i Margarita* [The Master and Margarita] (St Petersburg: Azbuka, 2011), p. 247.
17 Shoshana Felman, *Writing and Madness (Literature/Philosophy/Psychoanalysis)*, trans. Martha Noel Evans, Shoshana Felman, and Brian Massumi (Palo Alto, CA: Stanford University Press, 2003), p. 252.

epistemological compass for charting the line between normality and abnormality in a society unmoored from its bearings.

Andrei Siniavskii (1925–1997) was among the first post-Stalinist writers to transform the madman-hero into a means of reflecting the irrationality of society and the state. Central to his unsanctioned works is a preoccupation with extreme psychological states and a stylistic orientation towards what he called Fantastic Realism: the depiction of life through a highly aestheticised lens that serves to restore awareness of the contours of reality. For Siniavskii, who published his unsanctioned works abroad under the pseudonym Abram Terts, it was precisely this line between art and life that Socialist Realism had pathologically blurred. The rational madness of Lenin's theories and the creative madness of their implementation by Stalin unite in the figure of Leonid Tikhomirov, the hero of his novella *Liubimov* (*Liubimov*, 1962–3). A bicycle repairman who uses mind control to seize power in his town, Tikhomirov reads Marxist theory as proof that 'consciousness must also be able to change and produce some sort of material result'. What begins as a form of rational madness soon gives way to creative madness, however: 'Never had Tikhomirov commanded such power to rule the masses and to charge them with untold reserves of energy. Only his own thoughts were beyond his control, and the smallest thoughtlet, the slightest mental tic, whatever nonsense popped into his head was at once brought to life by those around him.'[18] The town becomes a mad projection of Tikhomirov's creative vision.

Madness acts as a framework for self-analysis in Joseph Brodsky's (1940–1996) narrative poem *Gorbunov and Gorchakov* (*Gorbunov i Gorchakov*, 1965–8). Set in a psychiatric hospital, the poem is voiced nearly entirely by the two title characters, who combine to form a single persona. Gorchakov, with his prosaic rhetoric and materialism, embodies rationality and the state-sanctioned dictum that 'existence determines consciousness'. Gorbunov, by contrast, maintains that consciousness can reshape existence through words. The psychiatrists enlist Gorchakov in silencing Gorbunov. Yet Gorchakov's pleas for Gorbunov to resume speaking assert the need for a balance between consciousness and existence. In the poem's final lines, Gorchakov imagines that the silenced Gorbunov has transformed the hospital corridor into an open seascape where his imagination can roam free. But Gorchakov,

18 Abram Terts, *Liubimov*, in *Sobranie sochinenii v dvukh tomakh* [Collected works in two volumes] (Moscow: SP 'Start', 1992), vol. I, pp. 34, 104. On *Liubimov* and Siniavskii more generally, see Rebecca Reich, *State of Madness: Psychiatry, Literature and Dissent after Stalin* (DeKalb: Northern Illinois University Press, 2018), chap. 4.

confined by the hospital's walls, is unable to join Gorbunov's maritime wanderings, and so the poem ends with an ellipsis that indicates his own silencing as well.[19] Consciousness and existence must maintain their balance if the poetic persona is to speak.

By the end of the 1960s, readers of samizdat were receiving reports of a disturbing means of political repression: the psychiatric diagnosis and hospitalisation of dissidents. Among the most prolific writers on this topic were Vladimir Bukovskii, Viktor Fainberg (1931–2023), Semen Gluzman (1946–), Natalia Gorbanevskaia (1936–2013), Petro Grigorenko (1907–1987), Roi (1925–) and Zhores (1925–2018) Medvedev, Viktor Nekipelov (1928–1989), Aleksandr Podrabinek (1953–), Valerii Tarsis (1906–1983), and Aleksandr Volpin (1924–2016). Their writings on punitive psychiatry came in the form of not only imaginative texts, but also documentary ones: essays, memoirs, pamphlets, and unofficial psychiatric reports. Yet even in these less overtly literary genres, the madman-hero came to the fore. Bukovskii and Gluzman's 'Manual on Psychiatry for Differently Thinking People' (*Posobie po psikhiatrii dlia inakomysliashchikh*, 1974) begins with an epigraph that features Chaadaev and Pushkin:

PUSHKIN: You're a madman yourself!

CHAADAEV: Why am I a madman?

PUSHKIN: You understand equality but live in servitude.

CHAADAEV (thoughtfully): Then you are right: I am a madman.[20]

Adapted from Andrei Platonov's (1899–1951) play *The Lycée Pupil* (*Uchenik litseia*, 1950), the epigraph presents Chaadaev as the original political madman: the sane exception to a society that has irrationally enslaved itself. The fact that it is a young Pushkin who prompts Chaadaev towards this realisation identifies literature itself as the source of the political madman's claim to authority.

---

19 Iosif Brodskii, 'Gorbunov i Gorchakov' [Gorbunov and Gorchakov], in *Stikhotvoreniia i poemy* [Verses and poems], ed. Lev Losev, Novaia biblioteka poeta [New poets library], 2 vols. (St Petersburg: Vita Nova, 2011), vol. I, p. 246. On *Gorbunov and Gorchakov* and Brodsky more generally, see Reich, *State of Madness*, chap. 3.

20 V. Bukovskii and S. Gluzman, 'Posobie po psikhiatrii dlia inakomysliashchikh' [Manual on psychiatry for differently thinking people], *Khronika zashchity prav v SSSR* [Chronicle of human rights in the USSR] 13 (Jan.–Feb. 1975), 36. On dissident writings about madness and psychiatric hospitalisation, see Reich, *State of Madness*, chap. 2.

The literary tradition of the political madman takes centre stage in Tarsis's novel *Ward No. 7* (*Palata No. 7*, 1966), based on the dissident author's psychiatric confinement. At one point, the writer-protagonist Valentin Almazov challenges his party-line psychiatrist by redefining their respective roles: 'So if you don't want to make a scene, let's agree on our terms. I'm a prisoner, and you're my jailer. There will be no talk of medicine, health, next of kin. No medicines, no examinations. Are we clear?'[21] Another, more sympathetic physician offers his own diagnosis of the pathologies of society: Stalinist repressions have produced deep-seated traumas that psychiatry is powerless to treat. In place of this discredited psychiatry, Tarsis presents a series of literary narratives of heroes who combine what initially appears to be creative or rational madness with determined action that affirms their sanity. Almazov's insistence on using words to reinvent reality thus becomes a means of political resistance. His fellow patient Tolia, by contrast, roots his dissidence in a rational critique of the state that drives him to attempt suicide. As is suggested through repeated references to Chekhov's 'Ward No. 6', literature establishes the dissident's sanity in the face of diagnosis.

In Venedikt Erofeev's (1939–1990) alcohol-drenched prose poem *Moscow–Petushki* (*Moskva–Petushki*, 1969–70), a commuter train moving from one station to the next becomes the liminal setting for the narrator's own vacillation among various types of madman-hero. Venichka, who shares Erofeev's name as well as many of his biographical details, pursues the sacred through the profane in ways that recall the divine madman, yet he also resembles a creative madman in his propensity for reinventing reality through words. That the realities he invents often follow Marxist-Leninist logic serves to parody the rational madness of official discourse. Yet the text ultimately brackets this rhetoric of madness by signalling its authorial persona's own critical distance. 'That's exactly what Johann von Goethe did, the old fool', Venichka explains. 'You think he didn't want to drink? Of course he did. So instead of kicking the bucket himself, he made all of his characters drink in his place.' Alcoholism becomes an experiment in madness that, when foisted on the hero Venichka, enables the authorial persona of Erofeev himself to pull back from that psychological brink. Goethe, Venichka continues, 'was himself on the verge of committing suicide, so in order to rid himself of the temptation he made Werther do it instead of himself'.[22] Erofeev conflates alcoholism with madness still more explicitly in the play

---

21 Valerii Tarsis, *Palata No. 7* [Ward no. 7] (Frankfurt am Main: Posev, 1966), p. 62.
22 Venedikt Erofeev, *Moskva–Petushki* [Moscow–Petushki], in *Sobranie sochinenii* [Collected works], 2 vols. (Moscow: Vagrius, 2007), vol. I, p. 92.

Walpurgis Night, or The Steps of the Commander (Val'purgieva noch', ili Shagi komandora, 1985), which is set in a psychiatric hospital. Like Venichka, the alcoholic hero Gurevich shares much in common with Erofeev. But there are also key differences that signal the authorial persona's awareness that Gurevich is not in fact saving his fellow patients, as he believes, but rather condemning them to alcohol poisoning and death.[23]

Like Brodsky's 'Gorbunov and Gorchakov', Sasha Sokolov's (1943–) novel *A School for Fools (Shkola dlia durakov,* 1973) unfolds as a stream-of-consciousness dialogue between two halves of a single self: a teenage boy in a school for the disabled. Nymphaea's rational voice welcomes the medical interventions of the psychiatrist Dr Zauze, while his creative voice revels in its use of language to bend the conventional rules of space and time: 'Neither you nor I, nor any of our acquaintances, is in any condition to explain what we have in mind when we talk about time, conjugate the verb *to be,* and divide life into yesterday, today and tomorrow, as if these words mean something different from each other.'[24] Reason bows to a poetic language that is free to shape reality according to its own logic. Yet as Oliver Ready has noted, the novel's apparent praise for madness is undermined by the spectre of actual disability. That Sokolov never resolves this tension transforms *A School for Fools* into a critique of the metaphorical uses of madness throughout Russian literature.[25]

Insanity also figured prominently in the guitar poetry of the Soviet bards, whose folk-inspired melodies frequently voice the madman's perspective. Aleksandr Galich's (1918–1977) 'The Right to a Holiday, or a Ballad about How I Visited my Brother, Who Was Being Treated in the Psychiatric Hospital at Belye Stolby' *(Pravo na otdykh* ..., 1965) narrates the poet's transformation into a patient when he swaps places with his hospitalised brother. Vladimir Vysotskii (1938–1980) casts himself as a madman in songs such as 'Case History II' *(Istoriia bolezni II,* 1975), where he challenges a psychiatrist's motives by pointing to the spectre of punitive psychiatry: 'What will it be, a diagnosis? / Or will I be handed down a sentence?'[26] Nor

23 On *Walpurgis Night* and Erofeev more generally, see Reich, *State of Madness,* chap. 5.
24 Sasha Sokolov, *Shkola dlia durakov; Mezhdu sobakoi i volkom; Palisandriia; Esse* [A school for fools; Between dog and wolf; Palisandriia; Essays] (St Petersburg: Azbuka, 2011), p. 23.
25 Oliver Ready, *Persisting in Folly: Russian Writers in Search of Wisdom, 1963–2013* (Oxford: Peter Lang, 2017), pp. 184, 214.
26 Vladimir Vysotskii, 'Istoriia bolezni II: Nikakoi oshibki' [Case history II: No error here], in *Sobranie sochinenii v chetyrekh tomakh* [Collected works in four volumes] (Moscow: Vremia, 2008), vol. II, p. 217.

did the madman-hero pass by the Soviet Union's nascent rock-music scene, from Akvarium's incantation of 'I'm a schizo' in their song of the same name (*Ia – shizo*, 1973), to Aleksandr Bashlachev's (1960–1988) sarcastic expression of gratitude to his doctors in 'Ward No. 6' (*Palata No. 6*, 1983) and the band Alisa's jaunty paeans to madness in 'The Madhouse' (*Sumasshedshii dom*) and 'Open Day' (*Den' otkrytykh dverei*) from the 1980s.

Whereas the bards looked for ways to suggest a sincere and unmediated relationship between singer and listener, members of the Moscow Conceptualist movement of the 1970s and early 1980s exposed the critical role of language in conceptualising sanity and insanity. Dmitrii Prigov's (1940–2007) short piece 'A Description of Objects' (*Opisanie predmetov*, 1979) adopts the hyperrational voice of a Soviet ideologue in such a way as to expose the irrationality of Marxist-Leninist discourse. Yet Prigov also assumed the persona of the creative madman in wild performances of his prose and poetry that echoed the performance art of the Soviet avant-garde. Similar concerns surface in the art and prose of Ilia Kabakov (1933–2023). In his book *The Mental Institution, or Institute of Creative Research* (*Sumasshedshii dom, ili institut kreativnykh issledovanii*, 1991), describing an installation of the same name, Kabakov offers a quadrilingual prospectus of a psychiatric clinic that attributes insanity to 'an extremely strong, creative impulse, which was suppressed or changed by different problems in the patient's life'. The cure lies in the 'extraction of creativity from its primal, undefined phase, to reveal and give form to the tendency which is embedded in it'.[27] Kabakov inverts the paradigm of creative madness to present it as genius that has been stopped in its tracks; it is by allowing patients to realise their potential that the clinic restores them to health.

Writers of the late Soviet period sometimes blurred the line between rational and creative madness by transforming the rejection of reason into a mode of underground 'life-creation'. In the 1960s, the writer Iurii Mamleev (1931–2015) played host to a literary circle known for deviant behaviours that resembled those he also depicted in his prose.[28] Such behaviours become markers of sanity in the story 'The Madmen of the Future' (*Dushevnobol'nye budushchego*, 1960s), which is set 500 years ahead in time. The hero, Gorrilov, is hospitalised by a panel of psychiatrists precisely because he shows zero

27 I. Kabakov, *Sumasshedshii dom, ili institut kreativnykh issledovanii: Installiatsiia* [The mental institution, or the institute of creative research: Installation] (Malmo: Rooseum, 1991), pp. 9, 35–6.
28 Oliver Ready, '"Questions to which reason has no answer": Iurii Mamleev's irrationalism in European context', in Olga Tabachnikova (ed.), *Facets of Russian Irrationalism between Art and Life: Mystery inside Enigma* (Leiden: Brill Rodopi, 2016), pp. 500–1.

propensity towards compulsive creativity, delirium, or violence. On his way to the hospital, Gorrilov observes streets strewn with drug addicts in the throes of erotic fantasies and citizens with poetic expressions distorting their faces. 'What a misfortune it is to be normal', he thinks of himself.[29] The only patient deemed more 'normal' than he – and therefore more mentally ill in this context – is kept in solitary confinement for insisting that two times two is four. Today's norm becomes tomorrow's abnormality in a world controlled by Dostoevskian 'underground men' who are free to insist that two times two makes five. In Viktor Erofeev's (1947–) story 'Life with an Idiot' (*Zhizn' s idiotom*, 1980), however, reason is rejected in the present day. Sentenced by the state to live with a madman, the writer-narrator handpicks a candidate who he believes will fulfil his literary ideal of the holy fool. Yet there is little that is elevating about Vova, the patient he takes into his home: he wrecks the apartment; rapes the wife of the narrator; and embarks on a sexual relationship with the narrator that culminates in their joint murder of the wife. The narrator is hospitalised only to be made madman-companion to another citizen, whom he presumably will torment in similar ways.

Though the madman-hero figured most prominently among male writers of the late Soviet period, several female writers developed alternative models. One feature of these texts is their subversive take on the literary tradition's fetishisation of mental illness or disability. Tatiana Tolstaia (1951–) deflates the myth of creative madness in her story 'Night' (*Noch'*, 1987) by adopting the perspective of a disabled man whose belief that he is destined to become a writer results in little more than his repetition of a single word. Turning the tables on divine madness in her novella *The South* (*Iug*, 1992), Nina Sadur (1950–2023) concludes with the protagonist, Olia, joining two pilgrims on their way to Mount Athos. Olia is reborn as the holy fool Mariia, yet her sanctity is belied by the cruelty she has shown throughout the novella. Much like the certificate of insanity that a chance acquaintance advises her to obtain, Olia's apparently divine madness lacks the genuinely redemptive power of the holy fool.

Diagnoses fly thick and fast in Liudmila Petrushevskaia's (1938–) novel *The Time: Night* (*Vremia noch'*, comp. 1988–90, pub. 1992). Cash-strapped Anna claims to be a selfless matriarch to her convict son, her serially pregnant daughter, and her grandson. But she also imagines herself a poet in the likeness of Anna Akhmatova (1889–1966). In her own poetic cycle *Requiem*

---

29 Iurii Mamleev, 'Dushevnobol'nye budushchego' [The madmen of the future], in *Izbrannoe* [Favorites] (Moscow: 'Terra'– 'Terra', 1993), p. 371.

(*Rekviem*, comp. 1934–62), Akhmatova had used the image of madness to describe her grief at her son's arrest:

> Already madness has half-covered
> My soul with its wing,
> And gives it fiery wine to drink,
> And beckons it to the black valley.[30]

In keeping with Felman's 'rhetoric of madness', Akhmatova professes insanity only to deny it through the cogency of her self-pathologisation. Yet in Petrushevskaia's novel there is no self-reckoning as Anna pathologises her daughter Alena instead: 'It's a typical psychosis. Heredity will always tell.' By 'heredity', Anna is suggesting that Alena acquired her alleged insanity not from herself but from her grandmother (Anna's mother), and as evidence she misquotes several lines from *Requiem*: 'mother in the nuthouse, son in prison, say a prayer for me, as the genius poet wrote'.[31] The literary lineage of Akhmatova's madwoman provides Anna with the words she needs to convince herself that she is responsible for her actions.

Afterlives of Madness

Writers of the late Soviet period took a paradoxical approach to the question of where, and whether, to draw a line between sanity and insanity. On the one hand, they challenged that opposition by using their works to explore the nuances and ambiguities of madness. On the other hand, they invoked a literary tradition of heroes whose claim to madness implied a binary point of contrast. The normative character of official Soviet culture rendered the opposition between sanity and insanity a potent means of passing judgement on society. Yet the collapse of the regime in 1991 lessened the force of that opposition. Post-Soviet writers have continued to deploy madness as a means of both reassessing the past and making sense of the exhilarations and dislocations that came in its wake. But with less sense of a binding norm against which abnormality could be defined, the figure of the madman-hero lost some of its valence.

30 Anna Akhmatova, *Rekviem* [Requiem], in *Maloe sobranie sochinenii* [Brief collected works] (St Petersburg: Azbuka, 2016), p. 338
31 Liudmila Petrushevskaia, *Vremia noch'. Roman* [The time: night. A novel], in *Zhizn' eto teatr* [Life is a theatre] (St Petersburg: Amfora, 2006), p. 336. Akhmatova's original verse reads 'Husband in the grave, son in prison, / Say a prayer for me'. Akhmatova, *Rekviem*, p. 331.

The 1990s saw the appearance of several novels in which the madman became a prism for re-examining the relationships between past and present, individual and society. Vladimir Sharov's (1952–2018) *Before and During* (*Do i vo vremia*, 1993) begins with the writer Alesha checking himself into a psychiatric hospital to treat a head injury. As if compensating for his memory loss, Alesha decides to narrate the life histories of his fellow inmates and of people outside the hospital. Fact and fiction combine to present the madhouse as a space for reimagining the past and escaping the boundaries of self. By contrast, Viktor Pelevin's (1962–) *Chapaev and Void* (*Chapaev i Pustota*, 1996) portrays creative madness as a solipsistic retreat from present-day society. Pelevin divides his storyline between the hero Petr Pustota's competing realities: the first as a psychiatric patient in 1990s Moscow and the second as a decadent poet during the civil war. These timeframes overlap as the novel progresses, with language and imagery moving back and forth to suggest the constructed nature of both realities. Life becomes the canvas for an unhinged creativity that ultimately communicates only with itself.

The relationship between creativity and insanity also comes to the fore in post-Soviet depictions of divine madness. Whereas in *Moscow–Petushki* Venedikt Erofeev had linked his hero Venichka's verbal brilliance to his rebellion against the traditionally masculine realm of reason, the female holy fool of Svetlana Vasilenko's (1956–) 'Little Fool' (*Durochka*, 1998) is so thoroughly identified with her emotions and her body that she proves unable to speak.[32] When the director of a Stalin-era orphanage dismisses the mute Ganna as an animal, the girl's guardian objects that her silence preserves her 'immortal soul'.[33] Instead, Ganna expresses her creative powers by performing miracle cures and, in a time-defying leap to Khrushchev's nuclear age, birthing a giant red sun that may save humanity. By contrast with Vasilenko's work, where the madwoman's body becomes a source of power, Liudmila Ulitskaia's (1943–) play *Seven Saints from the Village of Briukho* (*Semero sviatykh iz derevni Briukho*, 2001) disrupts any association between insanity and the female body's creative capacities. The character Mania presents as a female holy fool, but when Bolsheviks strip her corpse of its clothing, it is revealed as belonging to a man.

---

32 On the gendered nature of the holy fool trope, see Helena Goscilo, 'Madwomen without attics: The crazy creatrix and the procreative iurodivaia', in Angela Brintlinger and Ilya Vinitsky (eds.), *Madness and the Mad in Russian Culture* (Toronto: University of Toronto Press, 2007), p. 232.

33 Svetlana Vasilenko, 'Durochka' [Little fool], *Novyi mir* [New world] 11 (November 1998), 13.

Rather than distance themselves from medical labels through irony or redefinition, as often happened in the late Soviet period, contemporary writers have displayed a greater readiness to inhabit them as experiences to be investigated firsthand. In the 2000s, as Ready has argued, representations of the madman shifted towards a focus on mental and physical disability.[34] Ruben David Gonsales Galego's (1968–) memoir *White on Black* (*Beloe na chernom*, 2002) accordingly chronicles the gap between the Soviet Union's rhetoric of equal rights and actual mistreatment of disabled citizens. Born with cerebral palsy, Galego grew up immersed in Socialist Realist novels about heroes who had overcome adversity, yet in the memoir he describes finding few avenues for following in their footsteps. Told that disabled children are euthanised in America, he responds bitterly: 'I don't want to be fed for free; I'll never find a useful profession. I want the injection, the fatal injection. I want to go to America.'[35] Documentary forms such as Galego's memoir lay claim to capturing the visceral experience of marginalisation where imaginative forms such as the novel are shown to fail.

Yet even as representations of disability came to the fore in the early Putin era, the madman-hero found a new home in politically motivated performance art. As the Pussy Riot member Nadezhda Tolokonnikova (1989–) said during the band's 2012 trial, 'We were seeking real sincerity and simplicity, and we found them in the holy foolishness of the punk performance.'[36] Whereas literary works tend to foreground their own utterances, performance art shines a spotlight on its audience's response. For Pussy Riot, this audience included not just the worshippers present in the Cathedral of Christ the Saviour when they recorded their 'punk prayer', but also the online audience that watched them later on. The literary tradition of the holy fool thus enabled Tolokonnikova to frame the trial as the response of a society that had been provoked into revealing its true nature. The performance artist Petr Pavlenskii (1984–) made similar use of an audience's response when, in 2014, he climbed the wall of Moscow's Serbskii Institute for Forensic Psychiatry – which in the Soviet years had become synonymous with psychiatric abuse – and cut off part of his ear. Within minutes he was removed from the wall and taken inside for evaluation. The response of the institute appeared to confirm Pavlenskii's implication that

34 Ready, *Persisting in Folly*, pp. 369–74, 386–7.
35 Ruben David Gonsales Gal'ego, *Beloe na chernom* [White on black] (St Petersburg: Limbus Press, 2009), p. 55.
36 Kostiuchenko, '"Tak nazyvaemyi protsess"'. See also Ready, *Persisting in Folly*, pp. 384–5.

psychiatric abuse was ongoing, while also asserting the performer's power to direct the drama of diagnosis. By prompting his own evaluation, Pavlenskii suggested that it is not the psychiatrist but the artist who determines what madness means. Armed with the force of the literary tradition, the madman storms the hospital.

Further Reading

Brintlinger, Angela, and Ilya Vinitsky (eds.), *Madness and the Mad in Russian Culture* (Toronto: University of Toronto Press, 2007).

Ivanov, Sergey A., *Holy Fools in Byzantium and Beyond*, trans. Simon Franklin (Oxford: Oxford University Press, 2006).

Murav, Harriet, *Holy Foolishness: Dostoevsky's Novels and the Poetics of Cultural Critique* (Stanford: Stanford University Press, 1992).

Ready, Oliver, *Persisting in Folly: Russian Writers in Search of Wisdom, 1963–2013* (Oxford: Peter Lang, 2017).

Reich, Rebecca, *State of Madness: Psychiatry, Literature, and Dissent after Stalin* (DeKalb: Northern Illinois University Press, 2018).

Rosenshield, Gary, *Pushkin and the Genres of Madness: The Masterpieces of 1833* (Madison: University of Wisconsin Press, 2003).

Sirotkina, Irina, *Diagnosing Literary Genius: A Cultural History of Psychiatry in Russia, 1880–1930* (Baltimore: Johns Hopkins University Press, 2002).

White, Frederick H., *Degeneration, Decadence and Disease in the Russian Fin de Siècle: Neurasthenia in the Life and Work of Leonid Andreev* (Manchester: Manchester University Press, 2014).

4.10

The Émigré

LISA RYOKO WAKAMIYA

In 1849, one year after leaving Russia, the writer and philosopher Aleksandr Herzen (1812–1870) wrote about his voluntary exile in *From the Other Shore* (*S togo berega*), a book of essays inspired by the French revolution of 1848. It is 'free speech that keeps me here', he wrote from Paris. 'For its sake I am willing to sacrifice everything.'[1] Herzen understood that to agitate for political reform he needed to write from abroad, where his self-published almanac *The Polar Star* (*Poliarnaia zvezda*, 1855–69) and newspaper *The Bell* (*Kolokol*, 1857–67) could be printed uncensored and smuggled into Russia. For Herzen, emigration was part of a nexus of activity – founding an émigré press; providing financial assistance to political émigrés; demanding the abolition of serfdom; writing memoirs, fiction, and philosophical essays – that realised the call of the individual to social action.

Literature about Russians abroad includes memoirs and other non-fiction narratives of exile and emigration, often by writers who, like Herzen, wrote from firsthand experience. It also includes fiction by writers who may or may not have emigrated themselves. Emigration is at once a biographical fact and a literary phenomenon; this has led to conflicting approaches to its interpretation. As lived experience and historical reality, emigration provides context for literature written abroad. Together with other biographical and historical events, emigration is part of the fabric of the émigré writer's work and contributes to its shape and meaning. Herzen embraced the link between the writer's life and history, proclaiming that 'Emigration is the first symptom of the approaching revolution.'[2] Other émigré writers, however, asserted the right to produce autonomous art, independent of the political, historical, or biographical context in which it was written. Vladimir Nabokov

---

1 Alexander Herzen, *From the Other Shore*, in *Selected Philosophical Works* (Moscow: Foreign Languages Publishing House, 1956), p. 341.
2 Herzen, *From the Other Shore*, p. 346.

(1899–1977), for instance, claimed that it was wholly irrelevant that his novel *Invitation to a Beheading (Priglashenie na kazn', 1936)* was written in Berlin 'some fifteen years after escaping from the Bolshevist regime, and just before the Nazi regime reached its full volume of welcome'.[3] He called the novel a 'violin in a void'[4] – a work of transcendent ahistoricity.

Both approaches are relevant for understanding Russian émigré literature from the perspective of the present. Herzen has been described as the pioneer of *tamizdat*, the Cold War-era term for literature printed abroad, and even as a potential source of inspiration for members of the opposition movements in Vladimir Putin's Russia.[5] At the same time, Nabokov's English-language works – *Lolita* (1955), *Pnin* (1957), and *Speak, Memory: An Autobiography Revisited* (1966), among others – have long been part of the Anglophone literary canon for their refractions of the linguistic, geographic, and temporal displacement of the émigré in America. The philosopher Mikhail Bakhtin (1895–1975; see Box 5.4) has argued that works of literature have a 'posthumous life' in which 'they are enriched with new meanings, new significance' through encounters with a reader or another text at a remove 'in time, in space, in culture'.[6] Enabling this process are the protagonists found in works of émigré literature – archetypal figures who resonate across generations, minimally disguised authorial alter egos, and migrants who elicit an unexpected jolt of recognition – all created in their historical moment, yet open to new meanings beyond their time and émigré milieu.

This chapter begins by identifying archetypes of the émigré 'hero' that populated Russian literature produced in emigration from 1917 through the mid-twentieth century. The chapter's temporal centre of gravity is the mid-1970s to the present, a period when works shaped by exile and emigration – as a creative impulse, historical phenomenon, or lived experience – were produced by writers who left Russia as well as by those who stayed behind. A concluding section reflects on current developments in Russian émigré writing as a wave of writers, catalysed by Russia's February 2022 invasion of

---

3 Vladimir Nabokov, *Invitation to a Beheading* (New York: Vintage, 1989), p. 5.
4 Nabokov, *Invitation to a Beheading*, p. 7.
5 Boris Paramonov and Aleksandr Genis, 'Chitaia Gertsena v Amerike. K 200-letiiu pisatelia' [Reading Herzen in America. In commemoration of the writer's bicentennial], *Radio Svoboda* (2 April 2012), www.svoboda.org/a/24535478.html, accessed 26 Jan. 2023; Alexander Yanov, 'What can the New Decemberists learn from Alexander Herzen?', *Institute of Modern Russia* (15 May 2012), https://imrussia.org/en/nation/238-what-an-the-new-decembrists-learn-from-alexander-herzen, accessed 26 Jan. 2023.
6 Mikhail Bakhtin, 'Response to a question from the *Novy mir* editorial staff', in *Speech Genres and Other Late Essays*, ed. and trans. Vern McGee (Austin: University of Texas Press, 1986), pp. 4, 7.

Ukraine, takes up the task of writing abroad. In shifting the focus from exiled writers and dissidents – the traditional 'heroes' of Russian literary history – to the narrators and protagonists who dramatise the experience of relocating to another country, this chapter foregrounds the discursive structures that organise émigré writing. Zinovy Zinik (1945–), who left Moscow for Jerusalem in 1975 and settled in London in 1977, proposes that the binaries of past and present, here and there, form a repressive and limiting set of doubles that the creative writer must learn to negotiate.[7] Many of the works discussed in this chapter adopt these binaries to associate the past, tradition, and Russian émigré literature itself with dominant values, underlining the ways in which binary impulses accommodate imperial ideology through their presentation of purportedly universal structural oppositions. Other works discussed here challenge the implications of binary formations by metatextually addressing their creative and ideological untenability and embedding Russian émigré literature within multilingual, transnational literatures of Modernism and migration.

Any consideration of Russian émigré writing must begin with a definition of its parameters. As 'Russian' may refer to both a writer's nationality and language, defining Russian émigré literature involves confronting questions of inclusion and exclusion. Belarusian, Ukrainian, Central Asian, and other non-Russian writers also write in Russian about the experience of emigration, and a study that focuses on Russophone writing by Russian writers risks the exclusion or the appropriation of their works. Russian is the first language of expression for many non-Russian writers. For them, especially in the pre-revolutionary and Soviet periods, crossing borders between lands where Russian was, or had been decreed, the official language was not conventionally regarded as emigration, and their writing was not considered émigré literature but subsumed into the Russian canon. For bilingual non-Russian writers who adopt the Russian language for their creative work, writing in Russian has reduced their opportunities to write or publish in their indigenous languages (see Chapter 4.8). A focus on Russophone writing also marginalises works about emigration by multilingual writers for whom Russian is only one possible language of expression (see Nabokov, Irène Némirovsky (1903–1942), Zinaida Shakhovskaia (1906–2001), Vasily Yanovsky (1906–1989)) and excludes diaspora writers who write about emigration exclusively in languages other than Russian. Among the latter may be counted Lena

---

7 Zinovii Zinik, 'Emigratsiia kak literaturnyi priem' [Emigration as literary device], in *Emigratsiia kak literaturnyi priem* [Emigration as literary device] (Moscow: Novoe literaturnoe obozrenie, 2011), pp. 20–1.

Gorelik (1981–), Olga Grjasnowa (1984–), and Wladimir Kaminer (1967–), who write in German; Andrei Makine (1957–), who writes in French; and Boris Zaidman (1963–), who was born in the former Soviet city of Kishinev (now Chișinău, the capital of the Republic of Moldova), has lived in Israel since 1975, and writes in Hebrew. This group includes a sizeable cohort of Anglophone writers born in the 1970s in the Soviet Union and raised in North America, David Bezmozgis (1973–), Gary Shteyngart (1972–), and Lara Vapnyar (1975–) among them. For these writers, writing about the Russian émigré experience in English was critical for their debut stories and novels, as the themes and conventions of immigrant fiction in North America reflected their own metafictional positioning as literary newcomers. In excluding non-Russophone immigrant writing and literature by non-Russian, Russophone émigré writers, this chapter presents only a partial portrait of the émigré protagonist. More comprehensive surveys, such as those identified in the list of Further Reading, expand the linguistic and spatial dimensions of the émigré hero through consideration of works by multilingual and transnational writers, while maintaining a balance between individual writers' creative and linguistic identities and the complexities of their literature, born between two or more cultures and rendered in one or more languages.

Archetypes of Emigration

The history of Russian émigré literature in the twentieth century began after the mass migration that followed the October Revolution of 1917. Among those who settled abroad were a generation of writers who had established careers in Russia before emigrating, including Ivan Bunin (1870–1953), who would receive the Nobel Prize for Literature in 1933, Georgii Adamovich (1892–1971), Mark Aldanov (1886–1957), Zinaida Gippius (1869–1945), Vladislav Khodasevich (1886–1939), Dmitrii Merezhkovskii (1865–1941), Aleksei Remizov (1877–1957), Ivan Shmelev (1873–1953), Teffi (pseud. of Nadezhda Lokhvitskaia, 1872–1952), and Boris Zaitsev (1881–1972). A younger generation of writers would make their names abroad, among them Nina Berberova (1901–1993), Gaito Gazdanov (1903–1971), Boris Poplavskii (1903–1935), and Vladimir Nabokov.

While it is difficult to generalise about this diverse group, the experience of emigration led writers from the older generation to take it upon themselves to sustain the classical literary tradition and safeguard it from the radical formal and ideological changes that had begun to characterise Soviet literature. For many, this entailed exploring the relationship between the private and

social self in semi-autobiographical coming-of-age narratives set in pre-revolutionary Russia. Bunin's *The Life of Arsenev* (*Zhizn' Arsen'eva*, 1927–39) exemplifies the genre; other models include Shmelev's *The Summer of the Lord* (*Leto Gospodne*, 1933–48) and Aleksandr Kuprin's (1870–1938) *The Junkers* (*Iunkera*, 1933). Bunin's few émigré protagonists represent older versions of his young heroes, no longer discovering the world and themselves as if they were the first to do so but hardened by age and experience. The three stories in the collection *Dark Avenues* (*Temnye allei*, 1946) that are set in France ('In Paris' (*V Parizhe*); 'Cold Autumn' (*Kholodnaia osen'*); and 'Vengeance' (*Mest'*) depict romance ruptured by death or abandonment, with only the memory of past love or faint hopes for a future relationship sustaining their broken émigré protagonists. Meanwhile, the satirical writer Teffi's story 'Ke Fer?' (*Ke fer?*, 1920) renders the French 'Que faire?', ironically echoing the title of Nikolai Chernyshevskii's (1828–1889) *What Is to Be Done?* (*Chto delat'?*, 1863), the influential paean to utilitarianism (see Chapters 4.5, 4.7), to pose the very question that Russian émigrés asked themselves as they tried to adapt to new lives. As Teffi's émigrés seek to glamorise their surroundings and pasts, the author positions herself as an observer of human weakness, caricaturing their efforts at self-reinvention while sympathising with the sense of emptiness from which they emerge.

Bunin and Teffi's younger contemporaries wrote almost exclusively about non-Russians and émigrés. For them, the émigré was more than a nostalgic echo of the past they had left behind, and they distinguished themselves from their predecessors by engaging with French Modernism and exploring new ways to represent a fragmented or unstable subjectivity. Nina Berberova's *The Accompanist* (*Akkompaniatorsha*, 1934) and *The Book of Happiness* (*Kniga o schast'e*, 1938) rewrite the gendered tropes of memory found in earlier émigré writing, which focused almost exclusively on male experience. *The Accompanist* centres on the power imbalance between two women: Maria Nikolaevna Travina is a soprano whose ambition and talent launch her charmed career from St Petersburg to Paris and eventually the United States; Sonechka, her young accompanist, despite living and working with Travina on her path to success, finds herself abandoned and destitute in a rented room in Paris. Their two fates have been described as iterations of Berberova's own émigré experience.[8] *The Book of Happiness* is similarly autobiographical, drawing on the difficulties that emerged in Berberova's relationship with the poet Vladislav Khodasevich

---

8 Nadya L. Peterson, 'The private "I" in the works of Nina Berberova', *Slavic Review* 60.3 (2001), 507.

following their move to Berlin and her need to independently find affirmation in her life and art. In *Night Roads* (*Nochnye dorogi*, 1941), Gaito Gazdanov adopts the perspective of an émigré taxi driver to depict a mobile subject in 'a world that was born and died again each day, in which, naturally, there was no concept of beginning or end, nor any idea of meaning or direction'.[9] Existential questions similarly structure Gazdanov's *The Spectre of Alexander Wolf* (*Prizrak Aleksandra Vol'fa*, 1947–8). Its young narrator lives in Paris, haunted by his memory of shooting a man in Russia during the civil war and standing over the dying man's body. By chance he comes across an autobiographical story by Alexander Wolf, in which Wolf describes being shot by a young man during the war. Believing Wolf to be the man he thought he killed, the narrator begins a search for answers about his past while living abroad. For both Berberova and Gazdanov, whose fiction drew on their own experiences, the émigré comes into being through relationships with the world and with others. Where Berberova sees opportunities and challenges as her protagonists navigate inequitable interpersonal relationships, Gazdanov reveals the disintegration of the self amid social encounters that produce neither self-knowledge nor understanding of others.

Vladimir Nabokov's metafictional stories about failed artists engage the reader in recognising the myopic cruelty of their simulacral worlds.[10] In his view, the experience of writing abroad led writers towards analogic thinking based on subjectively perceived similarities between people, experiences, and places. The writerly act of generalising from these imprecise analogies presented an aesthetic problem with ethical implications. In Nabokov's first novel, *Mary* (*Mashen'ka*, 1926), the writer-protagonist reimagines details of his past – by now a familiar trope of émigré prose – while exposing the risks of creating a private world that integrates others only to the degree that they serve his imagined ideal. His self-serving escape from the double world of his émigré social reality and his imagination has devastating consequences for others. Martin Edelweiss, the émigré protagonist of *Glory* (*Podvig*, 1932), is by Nabokov's own admission a self-portrait, but 'much more naïve than I ever was'.[11] This naïveté leads Martin to seek out idealised destinations that exist solely in his imagination. His narcissistic pursuit of these imaginary worlds concludes with a clandestine

---

9 Gaito Gazdanov, *Night Roads*, trans. Justin Doherty (Evanston, IL: Northwestern University Press, 2009), p. 198.

10 Vladislav Khodasevich, 'On Sirin', trans. Michael H. Walker, ed. Simon Karlinsky and Robert P. Hughes, *TriQuarterly* 17 (Winter 1970), 96–101.

11 Vladimir Nabokov, *Glory*, trans. Dmitri Nabokov in collaboration with the author (New York: Vintage, 1991), p. xi.

attempt to cross into the Soviet Union from Latvia and, finally, with his disappearance. *The Eye* (*Sogliadatai*, 1930) doubles the émigré protagonist following his suicide: he becomes at once the first-person narrator of the story and the failed artist Smurov whom the narratorial I/eye observes. For Nabokov, the solipsism that produces an imagined world is not a sustained act of creativity but a form of madness, a false perceptiveness masquerading as artistry that lacks accuracy and conscience.

Nabokov's two programmatic works, *The Gift* (*Dar*, 1938) and *Invitation to a Beheading*, feature protagonists who develop an aesthetic conscience that confronts the solipsism portrayed in the above-mentioned novels. Fedor Godunov-Cherdyntsev, the young narrator-protagonist of *The Gift*, fails at his first creative efforts when he projects too much of himself into his biography of his deceased father. After working through the influence of Aleksandr Pushkin (1799–1837) and Nikolai Gogol (1809–1852) and rejecting Chernyshevskii, he turns to writing with newfound respect for the autonomy of others, an understanding of his literary genealogy, and genuine feelings of pity and love.[12] *The Gift* is the last work Nabokov wrote in Russian; it appeared in the leading Paris émigré literary journal *Contemporary Notes* (*Sovremennye zapiski*, 1920–40), which ceased publication two years later. As a metafictional meditation on a disappearing literary milieu, *The Gift*'s true heroine, according to its author, is Russian literature itself.[13] In *Invitation to a Beheading*, the artist-protagonist Cincinnatus C. forces himself to conform to the banal conventions of a world that appears to be a stage set occupied by actors or automatons rather than a place for living, thinking beings. As he learns to assert his individuality and reject this false world, it collapses around him. The Modernist aesthetics and sociopolitical dimensions of the novel align it with other fictional works concerned with authoritarianism, the world as simulacrum, interwar alienation, and the constraints of fiction itself.[14]

The experience of emigration to Berlin, Paris, and other cultural capitals promoted prescriptive attitudes towards the preservation of the past among the earlier generation of writers, while the younger generation embarked on a search for new identities in the present. In their works, memory is not

---

12 Julian W. Connolly, 'The major Russian novels', in Connolly (ed.), *The Cambridge Companion to Nabokov* (Cambridge: Cambridge University Press, 2005), pp. 143, 146, 149.
13 Vladimir Nabokov, foreword to *The Gift* (New York: Vintage, 1991), p. ii.
14 Nabokov claimed that émigré critics had identified the influence of Kafka's *The Trial* on *Invitation to a Beheading*, an influence he denied; see V. Nabokov, foreword to *Invitation to a Beheading* (New York: Vintage, 1989), p. 6.

a shared idyll but an individual and unreliable domain that becomes increasingly at odds with present experience. The variation among their depictions of émigré protagonists suggests that philosophical considerations of what constituted the self were as important to the development of their work as lived experience.

Exiles and Émigrés of the Late Soviet Period

The figure of the émigré re-emerges later in the twentieth century in the work of writers who emigrated or were exiled from Soviet Russia from the mid-1970s through the early 1980s. This generation produced two Nobel laureates, the novelist-historian Aleksandr Solzhenitsyn (1918–2008) and the poet-essayist Joseph Brodsky (1940–1996), each of whom epitomised an archetype of the émigré writer – the dissident and the cosmopolitan aesthete – that harmonised with his respective creative principles.[15] After Solzhenitsyn's forced exile, western audiences tended to associate Soviet émigré writers with political dissidence, but most of his contemporaries – Vasilii Aksenov (1933–2009), Iuz Aleshkovskii (1929–2022), Sergei Dovlatov (1941–1990), Anatolii Gladilin (1935–2018), Eduard Limonov (1943–2020), Andrei Siniavskii (1925–1997, pseud. Abram Terts), Sasha Sokolov (1943–), Vladimir Voinovich (1932–2018), and Zinovy Zinik among them – saw themselves primarily as fiction writers. Arguing for the right of the author – and of Russian émigré literature – to exist outside politics, many of them refused to discuss the theme of emigration, proposing that to do so would allow sociopolitical events, rather than aesthetic principles, to organise their work. Like the previous generation's émigrés who disavowed the historical and political contexts in which they were writing, some affiliated their creative work with the past while others forged new identities and aesthetics abroad. Solzhenitsyn himself did not write about the Russian emigration while living in exile in the United States from 1976 to 1994, dedicating those years primarily to *The Red Wheel* (*Krasnoe koleso*, 1970–91) – a multivolume epic about the causes and consequences of the October Revolution – and his memoir *The Little Grain Fell between Two Millstones* (*Ugodilo zernyshko promezh dvukh zhernovov*, 1998–2003).

15 The second wave of emigration, which emerged with the displacement of Russians after the Second World War, has been described as 'an emigration of individuals' rather than a mass movement; see Tatiana Fesenko, cited in John Glad, *Russia Abroad* (Tenafly, NJ: Hermitage, 1999), p. 347. This is likely a consequence of the second wave consisting primarily of scholars and academics and its relatively few fiction writers experiencing difficulty establishing themselves in first-wave publishing venues. Glad, *Russia Abroad*, pp. 247–8.

Brodsky positioned his experience of exile between literary autonomy and tradition, advocating for the former while upholding the proscriptive restraints of the latter. In his 1988 essay 'The Condition We Call Exile', he acknowledges that 'The current interest in the literature of exiles has to do, of course, with the rise of tyrannies.'[16] He urges writers to accept exile as a metaphysical condition, rather than remain 'forever at the receiving end of things', and correspondingly warns that exile accelerates the writer's tendency towards retrospection, isolation, and conservatism.[17] 'To keep yourself from getting closed and shelved', he advises, 'you've got to tell your reader . . . something qualitatively novel – about his world and himself'. Brodsky proposes that autonomy is the 'qualitatively novel stuff we may tell that reader about'.[18] The poet Olga Sedakova (1949–) has noted that Brodsky's autonomy was a 'rare independence'.[19] Yet when Brodsky states that through exile the writer 'gets closer to the seat of the ideals that inspired him all along',[20] he refers to the writer's pedigree, hinting at his own affinities with Roman antiquity, the Baroque, and the classical Russian literary tradition while elsewhere claiming that Central European and Ukrainian literature are traditions that cannot legitimise the poet's claims to world culture.[21] If we accept Lev Loseff's (1937–2009) assertion that '[b]etween Brodsky in life and Brodsky in verse there is very little difference',[22] the persona of the exiled poet that Brodsky presents becomes paradoxical, at once guided by principles of individual autonomy and the restriction of which literary cultures can grant such autonomy.

Brodsky's contemporaries – prose writers who wrote fiction about life in emigration – would also maintain the debatable position that their work was not informed by politics. Some emphasised the continuities between their Soviet and émigré literary personae in quasi-autobiographical writings, while others disavowed the paradigms that informed their early émigré writing as they transitioned to new priorities. In a 2017 conversation with Boris Akunin

---

16 Joseph Brodsky, 'The condition we call exile', in *On Grief and Reason* (New York: Farrar, Straus, Giroux, 1995), p. 28.
17 Brodsky, 'Condition we call exile', p. 26.   18 Brodsky, 'Condition we call exile', p. 31.
19 Olga Sedakova, 'A rare independence', in Valentina Polukhina (ed.), *Brodsky through the Eyes of His Contemporaries* (Boston: Academic Studies Press, 2008), p. 279.
20 Brodsky, 'Condition we call exile', p. 24.
21 See Mark Lipovetsky, 'Russian (non-)answers to (post-)colonial questions', *Zeitschrift für Slavische Philologie* 72.1 (2016), 33; and Olga Bertelsen, 'Joseph Brodsky's imperial consciousness', *Scripta Historica* (Instytut Historii Akademii Pomorskiej w Słupsku) 21 (2015), 263–9.
22 Lev Loseff, *Joseph Brodsky: A Literary Life* (New Haven: Yale University Press, 2011), p. 140.

(pseud. of Grigorii Chkhartishvili, 1956–), Zinik cited an observation by Vladislav Khodasevich about early twentieth-century émigrés and argued that it was equally applicable to émigrés of the second half of the century: 'there is not going to be Russian literature in immigration and exile because Russian writers don't want to regard themselves as émigré writers, that is, they don't want to write about their present'. Naming Sergei Dovlatov, Eduard Limonov, and Igor Pomerantsev (1948–), Zinik observed that 'there were only a few of us who started to write about the present life abroad'.[23] Zinik claims that his own early protagonists, appearing in texts written in Russian 'from a Moscow point of view', 'make excuses for their departure, for their actions in the past . . . for their present happiness'.[24] These narratives of self-reproach give way to later works of fiction and non-fiction – written as often in English as in Russian and 'from a London point of view' – that range from autobiographical stories and memoirs (*At Home Abroad* (*U sebia za granitsei*, 2007), *Letters from the Third Shore* (*Pis'ma tret'ego berega*, 2008), *History Thieves* (2010)) to experimental novels (*Sounds Familiar* (2016), *The Orgone Box* (*Iashchik orgona*, 2017)) and a study of Sabbatai Zevi, the Sephardic rabbi from Smyrna who converted to Islam in 1666 (*A Yarmulke under the Turban* (*Ermolka pod turbanom*, 2018)). In this transition, in which he moved from writing in one literary language to switching between two, Zinik increasingly presented himself as neither an émigré writer nor Russian nor British but something in-between.

Most writers who wrote fiction about émigré life did so in quasi-autobiographical forms. Somewhere between a writer of fiction and creative non-fiction, Sergei Dovlatov 'mix[ed] truth and invention' to document his life events 'by artistic means'. He claimed that his greatest pride was to observe 'friends and relatives try to add footnotes to my stories, to elaborate on certain facts as they recollect them – which means they take my inventions for the real thing'.[25] His camp narrative *The Zone* (*Zona*, 1982) alternates between letters Dovlatov ostensibly wrote to his publisher, Igor Efimov, from February to June 1982 as he prepared his book for publication in

23 Boris Akunin and Zinovy Zinik in conversation with Anne McElvoy, 'Russian art and exile. Part of breaking free: A century of Russian culture', *BBC Sounds* (13 Nov. 2017), quoted passage at 32:50, www.bbc.co.uk/sounds/play/p05mx6kv, accessed 25 Jan. 2023.
24 Zinik, 'Emigratsiia kak literaturnyi priem', p. 18. Zinik distinguishes between his early work written from a 'Moscow point of view' and later work written from a 'London point of view' in '. . . Potomu chto ia – vrun' [Because I am a liar], interview by Igor' Pomerantsev, *Radio Svoboda* (18 Dec. 2019), www.svoboda.org/a/30334293.html, accessed 25 Jan. 2023.
25 Jane Bobko, 'Interview with Sergei Dovlatov', *Threepenny Review* 20 (Winter 1985), 17.

New York, and stories first about, then by, the author's alter ego Boris Alikhanov, who like Dovlatov himself served as a prison camp guard from 1962 to 1965. As Alikhanov shifts from protagonist to narrator, his 'I' overlaps with that of Dovlatov's letters. In Dovlatov's words, 'the author and the hero gradually merge into a single documentary person and that person is the writer'.[26] As they converge, Dovlatov recognises other equivalences, such as those between the guards and prisoners in the camp, who 'were very similar to each other, and even interchangeable'.[27] In place of Nabokov's double world, Dovlatov's émigré writer-protagonist unites past and present, prisoner and prison sentry, author and narrator, truth and invention to create a comprehensive self-portrait that extends across all his work.

Vasilii Aksenov cultivated an émigré literary persona that accorded with his earlier, pre-emigration work. *In Search of Melancholy Baby* (*V poiskakh grustnogo bebi*, 1987), a memoir interspersed with fictional passages about a Muscovite living in the United States, mirrors the narrative structure and urbane self-image that Aksenov introduced in his Soviet-era travelogue *Around the Clock Non-Stop* (*Kruglye sutki non-stop*, 1978). The quasi-autobiographical narrator in both works is simultaneously a misunderstood outsider and a worldly traveller, and the narrative persona Aksenov cultivated as a Soviet writer to address individual priorities easily transitions into that of an émigré in the United States, where 'all come from somewhere else'.[28] Aksenov gave up this literary persona when his Russian citizenship was reinstated in 1990. As he eventually began to divide his time between Washington, DC and Moscow, then Moscow and Biarritz, he created a new diasporic literary identity belonging to multiple homelands. In *The New Sweet Style* (*Novyi sladostnyi stil'*, 1997), Soviet theatre director Aleksandr Korbach is exiled to the United States, where he is welcomed by distant relatives. Korbach later returns to Moscow on 19 August 1991 and joins the protests against the communist coup. From Moscow he travels to Tel Aviv, where the remains of an early ancestor were discovered during an archaeological dig. At home everywhere, the diasporic artist and his narrative homecomings signal the end of Aksenov's literary and biographical emigration.

---

26 Dovlatov's description of his use of this device in a work in progress called 'Five corners' is applicable here. S. Dovlatov, Letter to Igor' Efimov (20 Feb. 1982), in *Epistoliarnyi roman. S Igorem Efimovym* [An epistolary novel. With Igor Efimov] (Moscow: Zakharov, 2001), p. 163.

27 Sergei Dovlatov, *The Zone*, trans. Anne Frydman (Richmond: Alma Classics, 2011), p. 49.

28 Vassily Aksyonov, *In Search of Melancholy Baby*, trans. Michael Henry Heim and Antonina W. Bouis (New York: Random House, 1987), p. 36.

Eduard Limonov's multiple fictional memoirs establish their émigré subject through excess and earnestness, chronicling his development over the sixteen years he lived in New York and Paris. His debut novel, *It's Me, Eddie* (*Eto ia – Edichka*, 1979), introduces Edichka – a picaro and dandy thoroughly disenchanted with émigré life in New York. In Russia he was a poet; here, he is 'scum'.[29] Edichka is unemployed, on welfare, and contemptuous of everyone, save for those who live on the fringes of society like him. He attends classes in English as a second language, interacts with disenfranchised fellow émigrés, and has casual sexual encounters with men and women. On a good day, proud of his knowledge of the city, he confidently walks its streets, taking pleasure in displaying his body in tight shirts and 'high heels without fail'.[30] On bad days, he indulges the depths of his loneliness and hatred. His final invective-filled declamation – 'Fuck you, cocksucking bastards! You can all go straight to hell!'[31] – is a provocation directed towards the literati as much as it is towards bourgeois Americans and the reader. Limonov's subsequent fictional memoirs similarly document the life of the writer in emigration to monumentalise him for posterity and are characterised by their sustained lack of irony and of claims to authenticity. He ultimately disavowed this émigré persona when he returned to Russia in 1994 and established himself as leader of the National Bolshevik Party.

As the above examples demonstrate, some writers opted to stay abroad, while others adapted their lives and work to the end of emigration as an ancillary outcome of the end of Soviet rule. A few of the latter – Aksenov, Limonov, Solzhenitsyn, and Voinovich, among others – returned to a reformed Russia in the 1990s. The moving targets of Voinovich's political satire reflect changes in how emigration figured in the popular and literary imagination from the late 1980s into the 1990s. Émigré writers' inflated sense of self-importance informed Voinovich's *Moscow 2042* (*Moskva 2042*, 1986), in which Sim Simych Karnavalov, a thinly veiled caricature of Solzhenitsyn, is revived from suspended animation to become 'Emperor and Autocrat of All the Russias'.[32] In his novel *A Displaced Person* (*Peremeshchennoe litso*, 2007), Voinovich pilloried post-Soviet Russia's social and economic reforms by narrating the return to Russia of the simple hero of his classic novel *The Life and Extraordinary Adventures of Private Ivan Chonkin* (*Zhizn' i neobychainye*

29 Eduard Limonov, *It's Me, Eddie*, trans. S. L. Campbell (New York: Random House, 1983), p. 5.
30 Limonov, *It's Me, Eddie*, p. 214.   31 Limonov, *It's Me, Eddie*, p. 264.
32 Vladimir Voinovich, *Moscow 2042*, trans. Richard Lourie (San Diego: Harcourt Brace Jovanovich, 1987), p. 406.

prikliucheniia soldata Ivana Chonkina, comp. 1963–9). Now a successful American farmer, Chonkin is more effectively reformed than his homeland.

Emigration and Post-Soviet Russian Writing

The post-Soviet period is characterised by voluntary emigration rather than forced exile, and emigration has taken on varied meanings for contemporary authors, among them recent émigrés and those who have continued to work in Russia. In the 2000s, political developments – including, but not limited to, the imprisonment of the oligarch Mikhail Khodorkovskii on false charges, Putin's election to a third presidential term, the rise of popular opposition movements, and the annexation of Crimea and invasion of Ukraine – led to increased engagement among some writers. In this climate, writers have variously described how the conditions in which they live relate to those in which they write. Tatiana Tolstaia (1951–), who lived in the United States from 1990 to 1999 and currently lives in Russia, explores her ambivalence towards emigration in her autobiographically inflected collection *Aetherial Worlds* (*Legkie miry*, 2014), which returns émigré narrators and travellers to a state of wandering between the timeworn binaries of then and now, here and there. The title story's émigré narrator buys a ramshackle house with the intent to restore it, but the construction is never finished. Her inability, or unwillingness, to create a permanent home abroad emblematises the unsettled voice of the collection. Russia-based writers of genre fiction have presented creative variations on the social phenomenon of emigration as economic opportunity or political safe haven. Roman Arbitman's (1962–2020) political thriller and roman-à-clef *Ministry of Justice* (*Ministerstvo spravedlivosti*, 2020) goes so far as to envision successful liberal reforms in Russia, with Justice Department agents scouring the globe to arrest ultra-conservative members of Putin's state apparatus who have gone into hiding abroad and Khodorkovskii, the oligarch turned émigré-philanthropist, returning to Russia to serve as the director of a historical museum. At the other end of the political spectrum, Viacheslav Rybakov's (1954–) paranoid fantasy *At Another's Feast* (*Na chuzhom piru*, 2000) imagines a manufactured brain drain as Russian scientists are lured to the United States; those patriots who refuse to emigrate are killed by the CIA.

Boris Akunin, the best-selling author of detective novels and historical fiction who left Moscow following the annexation of Crimea in 2014 and who divides his time between France, England, and Spain, has compared his situation to that of Russian writers in Europe in the nineteenth century in

that he was not forced into exile but chose to emigrate. 'In 2014, something changed', he said. Seeing on Moscow's streets the orange and black St George ribbons 'that have become the symbol of aggressive patriotism, my mind refused to function . . . I felt I couldn't write and work there any longer.'[33] In a conversation with Akunin about the difficulty of living in today's Russia, Mikhail Shishkin (1961–), who emigrated to Switzerland in 1998, observed that over the past century of Russia's history, 'the most active and educated part of the population was consistently eliminated by its own state or emigrated'.[34] The novel *Maidenhair* (*Venerin volos*, 2005) draws from Shishkin's own experience as an interpreter for the Swiss immigration authorities, interviewing Russian speakers seeking political asylum. Its protagonist, 'the Interpreter', determines human fates while sitting in his institutional office. The asylum seekers' stories appear alongside the biography of a Soviet singer, letters the interpreter writes to his son, and historical and literary excursuses, intertwining the stories people create about themselves with stories inherited from others. Here, as in several of his short stories, Shishkin's émigré protagonists are writers, translators, storytellers. They are also bureaucrats and, like the interpreter in *Maidenhair*, must learn new ethical coordinates that distinguish between 'honourable' and 'correct' decisions. The language they leave behind is distinct from the one they create anew when they move abroad. As the narrator of the story 'In a Boat Scratched on a Wall' (*V lodke, natsarapannoi na stene*, 2008) observes, 'Words create realities and decide destinies.'[35] In creating a new language, Shishkin's protagonists integrate themselves and others into the world of stories around them while imagining a place for these stories in the future.

Aleksandra Petrova (1964–) lived in Jerusalem from 1993 to 1998 and currently resides in Rome. Like Shishkin, she identifies emigration as one of many possible paths by which human stories become integrated into the broader history of global migration. Petrova's *Appendix* (*Appendiks*, 2016) weaves together the stories of eight migrant protagonists, all of whom have found themselves in Rome. The narrator Olga links her memory of the childhood operation that removed her vestigial organ to the childhood

33 Akunin and Zinik with McElvoy, 'Russian art and exile', at 16:25.
34 Boris Akunin and Mikhail Shishkin, '"Chtob on provalilsia, visantiiskii orel s dvumia golovami". Boris Akunin i Mikhail Shishkin sporiat o tom, obrechena li Rossiia' ['So that [the nation] would come apart, a Byzantine eagle with two heads'. Boris Akunin and Mikhail Shishkin debate whether Russia is doomed], *Afisha* (29 July 2013), https://daily.afisha.ru/archive/gorod/archive/akounin-vs-shishkin/, accessed 25 Jan. 2023.
35 Mikhail Shishkin, 'In a boat scratched on a wall', trans. Marian Schwartz, in *Calligraphy Lesson: The Collected Stories* (Dallas: Deep Vellum, 2015), p. 167.

losses experienced by the other protagonists. Petrova intertwines the protagonists' personal histories of loss with contemporary and ancient narratives of migration and overlaps allusions to the tales of Aeneas's wanderings with references to recent crises that have brought waves of refugees to Italy. She dedicates *Appendix* to 'all who disappeared in the waters of the Mediterranean Sea and in the waters of oblivion', proposing that, taken together, the individual stories of outcasts and immigrants constitute a new founding myth for the city of Rome.[36]

While Shishkin and Petrova see Russian émigré literature as one of many world literary traditions that contribute to shared narratives of human experience, Liudmila Ulitskaia (1943–) historically contextualises emigration within the dominant narratives that shaped Soviet life. She most frequently portrays emigration as a path taken by intellectuals who upheld admirable values but were not always able to transform those ideals into meaningful action.[37] In *The Funeral Party* (*Veselye pokhorony*, 1997), Alik, an émigré artist and intellectual, is terminally ill. His impending death in New York and the protest against the August 1991 coup taking place in Moscow prefigure the end of emigration as an institution of progressive values and ethical integrity. Nevertheless, his relationship with his daughter hints that these values may have a future in a younger, Anglophone generation. Voicing the sentiment that it was more ethical for intellectuals to remain in the Soviet Union than it was to leave,[38] *The Big Green Tent* (*Zelenyi shater*, 2010) features a dissident poet who refuses to emigrate and kills himself when forced to collaborate with the KGB. The complex attitude Ulitskaia evinces towards emigration reflects her concerns about the perseverance of dissidence and a culture of ethics in the wake of state practices that for decades have silenced intellectuals or facilitated their departure. These concerns have taken on new dimensions following Ulitskaia's own emigration, and that of many other Russian writers, after Russia's invasion of Ukraine in February 2022.

36 Aleksandra Petrova, Dedication to *Appendiks* [Appendix] (Moscow: Novoe literaturnoe obozrenie, 2016), [5].
37 Elizabeth A. Skomp and Benjamin M. Sutcliffe, *Ludmila Ulitskaya and the Art of Tolerance* (Madison: University of Wisconsin Press, 2015), pp. 104–5, 123.
38 Zinik also expresses this view in Akunin and Zinik with McElvoy, 'Russian art and exile', starting at 32:20.

Conclusion

The exodus of writers from Russia that began soon after Russia declared war on Ukraine has intensified efforts to re-evaluate the association between literary emigration and the writer as a voice of moral authority. Ulitskaia previously contributed to this re-evaluation in her novels through her portrayals of Soviet-era émigré 'heroes' as isolated idealists, pitiable for their ineffectiveness. After February 2022, however, she was to confront these associations herself when she was criticised by a Ukrainian audience member at a public event in Berlin for expressing hopes that Russia's war in Ukraine would remain 'minor' and comparing the hurried conditions in which she left her Moscow apartment to the homelessness experienced by Ukrainians whose residences have been destroyed by bombing.[39]

In an essay recounting her arrival in Sri Lanka after her decision to emigrate, the writer Anna Starobinets (1978–) associates staying in Russia with silence or being silenced. 'The only thing I can do well is string words together in Russian', she professes. 'Perhaps I'll be more useful like this for toppling the regime, than if I shut my mouth or went to prison.'[40] For Starobinets, a binary relation correlates silence with state power and emigration and writing with 'toppling the regime'.

Statements such as Ulitskaia's and Starobinets's reflect their self-positioning within a cultural paradigm in which the act of emigration itself constitutes a loss that demands equal, if not greater, attention than the losses the Russian state inflicts on others, even during war. This paradigm of loss legitimates the émigré writer's work, perpetuating the need to carry on writing Russian literature in emigration and positioning literature by Russian authors as a discourse of moral integrity. Ulitskaia's public statement in Berlin and Starobinets's orientalising claim that the 'jungles of Sri Lanka symbolize my homelessness' marginalise others to foreground the Russian writer's centrality in this paradigm.[41] Only when a newly imagined émigré

---

39 Liudmila Ulitskaia, 'Liudmila Ulitskaia: O bezumii Putina, voine i emigratsii' [Liudmila Ulitskaia: On Putin's madness, the war and emigration], My Russian Rights (YouTube channel), 22 March 2022, www.youtube.com/watch?v=axo9TI3bfhA, accessed 25 Jan. 2023. The sold-out event took place on 18 March 2022 at PANDA platforma, a non-profit cultural centre in Berlin. All funds raised by the event were donated to organisations providing humanitarian aid in Ukraine or supporting Ukrainian refugees in Berlin.

40 Anna Starobinets, 'Statement by Anna Starobinets about the war in Ukraine' (original in Russian on Facebook, 11 March 2022), trans. Muireann Maguire. A copy of the statement can be found on the website of Katherine E. Young, a translator of Starobinets: https://katherine-young-poet.com/anna-starobinets/, accessed 25 Jan. 2023.

41 Starobinets, 'Statement'.

hero breaks out of this dynamic will postwar Russian émigré writing speak to a broader readership.

The émigré scholar Gleb Struve (1898–1985) feared that Russian émigré literature would disappear with the dispersal of its writers across Europe, Asia, and the United States, particularly if they adopted the languages of their new countries of residence.[42] This has not come to pass; there is no single essence of Russian émigré writing that circulates and then becomes globalised, homogenised, and eventually obsolete. Recent fiction that addresses the experience of emigration spans national and linguistic boundaries, draws from biography, global literatures, sociopolitical phenomena, even visions of alternate reality. For some writers, émigré literature has internalised a self-perpetuating and isolated view of itself. Yet the émigré protagonist will endure as a social and literary figure with continued waves of emigration and adaptation to new contexts, languages, and global situations. As long as writers explore the émigré condition in their art by integrating their stories into everyday global socialities and politics and by metabolising human experience through the words of others, émigré literature will discover new facets of experience that define the émigré's place in a changing world.

Further Reading

Beaujour, Elizabeth Klosty, *Alien Tongues: Bilingual Russian Writers of the First Emigration* (Ithaca: Cornell University Press, 1989).

Caffee, Naomi Beth, 'Russophonia: Towards a transnational conception of Russian-language literature', unpublished PhD thesis, University of California, Los Angeles (2013).

Glad, John, *Conversations in Exile* (Durham, NC: Duke University Press, 1993).

Matich, Olga, with Michael Heim, *The Third Wave: Russian Literature in Emigration* (Ann Arbor, MI: Ardis, 1984).

Platt, Kevin (ed.), *Global Russian Cultures* (Madison: University of Wisconsin Press, 2020).

Raeff, Marc, *Russia Abroad: A Cultural History of the Russian Emigration, 1919–1939* (Oxford: Oxford University Press, 1990).

Rubins, Maria (ed.), *Redefining Russian Literary Diaspora, 1920–2020* (London: UCL Press, 2021).

Slobin, Greta, *Russians Abroad: Literary and Cultural Politics of Diaspora (1919–1939)*, ed. Katerina Clark, Nancy Condee, Dan Slobin, and Mark Slobin (Boston: Academic Studies Press, 2013).

Wanner, Adrian, *Out of Russia: Fictions of a New Translingual Diaspora* (Evanston, IL: Northwestern University Press, 2011).

---

42 Gleb Struve, 'The aesthetic function in Russian literature', *Slavic Review* 21.3 (1962), 425–6.

Index

Entries for authors have been arranged with titles of works preceding subheadings of other types. Themed subheadings reflect the four-history structure of this volume (i.e. movements, mechanisms, forms, and heroes), with narrower terms selected from the chapter topics within each history (e.g. 'novel form' or 'censorship'). Broader subheadings (e.g. 'forms') indicate mentions across many chapters in a history, with 'other' preceding the history name (e.g. 'other forms') if there are also chapter-level subheadings within the entry (e.g. 'novel form'). Numerical titles are filed as if spelled out (e.g. '41° (group)' is under 'F').

Nicholas I, Emperor
censorship, 297, 335, 348
civil servant figures, 731
drama, 532
intelligentsia, depictions of, 757, 758
Realism, 98
as ruler, depictions of, 702, 713–14
satire, 215
Nicholas II, Emperor, 714
Nietzsche, Friedrich, 115, 324, 795
Nikita of Pereiaslavl, Saint, 689
Nikitin, Afanasii, 454
Nikitin, Viktor, 284
Nikitina, Evdoksiia, 272
Nikola Salos/Nikolka the Iron Cap, 694
Nikolaeva, Galina
Harvest, The (Zhatva), 154
Nikolev, Nikolai, 263
Nikon, Patriarch, 37, 43
Nikonova, Ry (Anna Tarshis), 175
NKVD (People's Commissariat for Internal
Affairs), 272, 348, 364
Nobel Prize, 384, 560, 602, 849
non-Russians, depictions of
introduction, 806–8
late and post-Soviet eras, 820–3
Modernism, 814–17, 818
Realism, 811–14
Romanticism, 809–11, 822
Soviet era, 817–20
Northern Bee, The (Severnaia pchela) (journal),
92, 286
Northern Post, The (Severnaia pochta)
(journal), 381
Notes of the Fatherland (Otechestvennye zapiski)
(journal), 91, 93, 95, 281, 288–90, 302, 303,
308, 760
novel form
Classicism, age of, 65–6
collective farm novels, 154, 614
contemporary movements, 187
family novels, 156
genres, mixing of, 541–4
historical-revolutionary novels, 156, 615
industrial novels, 155, 613–14
intelligentsia, depictions of, 761–5
internet, mechanism of, 649–50
introduction, 537–9, 607–8
Modernism, 609–12
other mechanisms, 294, 355, 389
Postmodernism, 176–80, 619–22
povest', 213
Realism, 90, 96–7, 99–103, 549, 616–18, 676

Russian tradition, 539–41, 545–51, 608
self-writing forms, 612, 614, 615, 618, 621–2,
628, 631–4, 662
and short-story form, 555–7, 562–3, 566,
611–12, 618
Socialist Realism, 153–6, 612–16
thick journals, mechanism of, 278–84, 285,
538, 546
verse forms, 541–2, 611
Novel-Newspaper (Roman-gazeta) (journal), 311
Novgorod epic cycle, 488
Novikov, Nikolai
*Attempt at an Historical Dictionary of Russian
Writers, An (Opyt istoricheskogo slovaria
o rossiiskikh pisateliakh)*, 295
Drone, The (Truten') (journal), 64–5
Classicism, age of, 64–5
court, 254
intelligentsia, depictions of, 757
publisher, 295, 304
Novokshonov, Ivan
*Heir of Genghis Kahn (Potomok
Chingiskhana)*, 817
Nuvel, Valter, 326

O'Hara, Frank, 145
OBERIU (*Ob"edinenie real'nogo iskusstva*,
Union of Real Art), 128, 271, 375, 600
Obolduev, Georgii, 222
October (Oktiabr') (group), 140
October (Oktiabr') (journal), 385
odes
Classicism, age of, 56, 62, 63, 67–8
panegyric odes, 56, 62, 253–4, 706, 710
rulers, depictions of, 702–8, 710, 714, 716–17
solemn odes, 56, 253–4, 504, 506, 507–8,
510, 702
syllabo-tonic verse, 505–9
voice, 356
war, 444
Odoevskii, Vladimir, 74, 78, 80, 267, 302,
555, 679
Okhapkin, Oleg, 381
Okudzhava, Bulat, 363–4, 366–7
Oleinikov, Nikolai, 600
Olesha, Iurii
Envy (Zavist'), 128, 610, 768, 796
'Liompa', 565
Three Fat Men (Tri tolstiaka), 219
forms, 216, 219, 565, 610
hero types, 768, 796
Modernism, 128, 143
omniscient narrators, 90, 459–60